I0458879

COMPILATION OF SELECTED
SURFACE TRANSPORTATION LAWS
VOLUME 1 :
HIGHWAY, TRANSIT, AND HIGHWAY SAFETY LAWS

As amended through the 118th Congress.

Prepared By M. TWINCHEK

2025

Forward

T his Compilation of Selected United States Surface Transportation Laws is a resource for those interested in U.S. surface transportation policy including the construction and improvement of highways and transit facilities, freight transportation, commercial transportation vehicle operations, and the implementation of safety and research programs. This volume includes title 23 United States Code relating to highways; further statutes continue in volume 2.

The materials included comes from publicly available, open source information, prepared for the public by the Office of the Legislative Counsel of the U.S. House of Representatives and the Office of the Law Revision Counsel.

Items listed as a Statute Compilation do not appear in the U.S. Code or that have been classified to a title of the U.S. Code that has not been enacted into positive law. Each Statute Compilation incorporates the amendments made to the underlying statute since it was originally enacted and are current as of the date noted.

This compilation is not an official document and should not be cited as evidence of any law. The official version of Federal law is found in the United States Statutes at Large and in the U.S. Code, the legal effect of which is established in sections 112 and 204, respectively, of title 1, United States Code.

A special thanks is extended to the Office of Law Revision Counsel and the House Office of the Legislative Counsel for providing the U.S. Code and statute compilations; and to the Government Publications Office for hosting and making these available for use to the public. An additional thank you is offered to the staff of the House and Senate Committees who were gracious in responding to inquiries and providing background information on the legislation included. Questions and comments may be directed to:

M. Twinchek
Email: mtwinchek@outlook.com

i

Contents

Selected Provisions of
Title 23 U.S.C.– Highways

CHAPTER 1
FEDERAL-AID HIGHWAYS

TITLE 23—HIGHWAYS

This title was enacted by Pub. L. 85–767, §1, Aug. 27, 1958, 72 Stat. 885

[1] *So in original. Does not conform to chapter heading.*

CHAPTER 1—FEDERAL-AID HIGHWAYS

§101. DEFINITIONS AND DECLARATION OF POLICY

(a) DEFINITIONS.—In this title, the following definitions apply:

(1) APPORTIONMENT.—The term "apportionment" includes unexpended apportionments made under prior authorization laws.

(2) ASSET MANAGEMENT.—The term "asset management" means a strategic and systematic process of operating, maintaining, and improving physical assets, with a focus on both engineering and economic analysis based upon quality information, to identify a structured sequence of maintenance, preservation, repair, rehabilitation, and replacement actions that will achieve and sustain a desired state of good repair over the lifecycle of the assets at minimum practicable cost.

(3) CARPOOL PROJECT.—The term "carpool project" means any project to encourage the use of carpools and vanpools, including provision of carpooling opportunities to the elderly and individuals with disabilities, systems for locating potential riders and informing them of carpool opportunities, acquiring vehicles for carpool use, designating existing highway lanes as preferential carpool highway lanes, providing related traffic control devices, designating existing facilities for use for preferential parking for carpools, and real-time ridesharing projects, such as projects where drivers, using an electronic transfer of funds, recover costs directly

associated with the trip provided through the use of location technology to quantify those direct costs, subject to the condition that the cost recovered does not exceed the cost of the trip provided.

(4) CONSTRUCTION.—The term "construction" means the supervising, inspecting, actual building, and incurrence of all costs incidental to the construction or reconstruction of a highway or any project eligible for assistance under this title, including bond costs and other costs relating to the issuance in accordance with section 122 of bonds or other debt financing instruments and costs incurred by the State in performing Federal-aid project related audits that directly benefit the Federal-aid highway program. Such term includes—

(A) preliminary engineering, engineering, and design-related services directly relating to the construction of a highway project, including engineering, design, project development and management, construction project management and inspection, surveying, assessing resilience, mapping (including the establishment of temporary and permanent geodetic control in accordance with specifications of the National Oceanic and Atmospheric Administration), and architectural-related services;

(B) reconstruction, resurfacing, restoration, rehabilitation, and preservation;

(C) acquisition of rights-of-way;

(D) relocation assistance, acquisition of replacement housing sites, and acquisition and rehabilitation, relocation, and construction of replacement housing;

(E) elimination of hazards of railway-highway grade crossings;

(F) elimination of roadside hazards;

(G) improvements that directly facilitate and control traffic flow, such as grade separation of intersections, widening of lanes, channelization of traffic, traffic control systems, and passenger loading and unloading areas;

(H) improvements that reduce the number of wildlife-vehicle collisions, such as wildlife crossing structures; and

(I) capital improvements that directly facilitate an effective vehicle weight enforcement program, such as scales (fixed and portable), scale pits, scale installation, and scale houses.

(5) COUNTY.—The term "county" includes corresponding units of government under any other name in States that do not have county organizations and, in those States in which the county government does not have jurisdiction over highways, any local government unit vested with jurisdiction over local highways.

(6) FEDERAL-AID HIGHWAY.—The term "Federal-aid highway" means a public highway eligible for assistance under this chapter other than a highway functionally classified as a local road or rural minor collector.

(7) FEDERAL LANDS ACCESS TRANSPORTATION FACILITY.—The term "Federal Lands access transportation facility" means a public highway, road, bridge, trail, or transit system that is located on, is adjacent to, or provides access to Federal lands for which title or maintenance responsibility is vested in a State, county, town, township, tribal, municipal, or local government.

(8) FEDERAL LANDS TRANSPORTATION FACILITY.—The term "Federal lands transportation facility" means a public highway, road, bridge, trail, or transit system

that is located on, is adjacent to, or provides access to Federal lands for which title and maintenance responsibility is vested in the Federal Government, and that appears on the national Federal lands transportation facility inventory described in section 203(c).

(9) FOREST DEVELOPMENT ROADS AND TRAILS.—The term "forest development roads and trails" means forest roads and trails under the jurisdiction of the Forest Service.

(10) FOREST ROAD OR TRAIL.—The term "forest road or trail" means a road or trail wholly or partly within, or adjacent to, and serving the National Forest System that is necessary for the protection, administration, and utilization of the National Forest System and the use and development of its resources.

(11) HIGHWAY.—The term "highway" includes—

(A) a road, street, and parkway;

(B) a right-of-way, bridge, railroad-highway crossing, tunnel, drainage structure including public roads on dams, sign, guardrail, and protective structure, in connection with a highway; and

(C) a portion of any interstate or international bridge or tunnel and the approaches thereto, the cost of which is assumed by a State transportation department, including such facilities as may be required by the United States Customs and Immigration Services in connection with the operation of an international bridge or tunnel.

(12) INTERSTATE SYSTEM.—The term "Interstate System" means the Dwight D. Eisenhower National System of Interstate and Defense Highways described in section 103(c).

(13) MAINTENANCE.—The term "maintenance" means the preservation of the entire highway, including surface, shoulders, roadsides, structures, and such traffic-control devices as are necessary for safe and efficient utilization of the highway.

(14) MAINTENANCE AREA.—The term "maintenance area" means an area that was designated as an air quality nonattainment area, but was later redesignated by the Administrator of the Environmental Protection Agency as an air quality attainment area, under section 107(d) of the Clean Air Act (42 U.S.C. 7407(d)).

(15) NATIONAL HIGHWAY FREIGHT NETWORK.—The term "National Highway Freight Network" means the National Highway Freight Network established under section 167.

(16) NATIONAL HIGHWAY SYSTEM.—The term "National Highway System" means the Federal-aid highway system described in section 103(b).

(17) NATURAL INFRASTRUCTURE.—The term "natural infrastructure" means infrastructure that uses, restores, or emulates natural ecological processes and—

(A) is created through the action of natural physical, geological, biological, and chemical processes over time;

(B) is created by human design, engineering, and construction to emulate or act in concert with natural processes; or

(C) involves the use of plants, soils, and other natural features, including through the creation, restoration, or preservation of vegetated areas using materials appropriate to the region to manage stormwater and runoff, to attenuate flooding and storm surges, and for other related purposes.

(18) OPERATING COSTS FOR TRAFFIC MONITORING, MANAGEMENT, AND CONTROL.—The term "operating costs for traffic monitoring, management, and control" includes labor costs, administrative costs, costs of utilities and rent, and other costs associated with the continuous operation of traffic control, such as integrated traffic control systems, incident management programs, and traffic control centers.

(19) OPERATIONAL IMPROVEMENT.—The term "operational improvement"—

(A) means (i) a capital improvement for installation of traffic surveillance and control equipment, computerized signal systems, motorist information systems, integrated traffic control systems, incident management programs, and transportation demand management facilities, strategies, and programs, and (ii) such other capital improvements to public roads as the Secretary may designate, by regulation; and

(B) does not include resurfacing, restoring, or rehabilitating improvements, construction of additional lanes, interchanges, and grade separations, and construction of a new facility on a new location.

(20) PROJECT.—The term "project" means any undertaking eligible for assistance under this title.

(21) PROJECT AGREEMENT.—The term "project agreement" means the formal instrument to be executed by the Secretary and the recipient as required by section 106.

(22) PUBLIC AUTHORITY.—The term "public authority" means a Federal, State, county, town, or township, Indian tribe, municipal or other local government or instrumentality with authority to finance, build, operate, or maintain toll or toll-free facilities.

(23) PUBLIC ROAD.—The term "public road" means any road or street under the jurisdiction of and maintained by a public authority and open to public travel.

(24) RESILIENCE.—The term "resilience", with respect to a project, means a project with the ability to anticipate, prepare for, or adapt to conditions or withstand, respond to, or recover rapidly from disruptions, including the ability—

(A)(i) to resist hazards or withstand impacts from weather events and natural disasters; or

(ii) to reduce the magnitude or duration of impacts of a disruptive weather event or natural disaster on a project; and

(B) to have the absorptive capacity, adaptive capacity, and recoverability to decrease project vulnerability to weather events or other natural disasters.

(25) RURAL AREAS.—The term "rural areas" means all areas of a State not included in urban areas.

(26) SAFETY IMPROVEMENT PROJECT.—The term "safety improvement project" means a strategy, activity, or project on a public road that is consistent with the State strategic highway safety plan and corrects or improves a roadway feature that constitutes a hazard to road users or addresses a highway safety problem.

(27) SECRETARY.—The term "Secretary" means Secretary of Transportation.

(28) STATE.—The term "State" means any of the 50 States, the District of Columbia, or Puerto Rico.

(29) STATE FUNDS.—The term "State funds" includes funds raised under the authority of the State or any political or other subdivision thereof, and made available for expenditure under the direct control of the State transportation department.

(30) STATE STRATEGIC HIGHWAY SAFETY PLAN.—The term "State strategic highway safety plan" has the same meaning given such term in section 148(a).

(31) STATE TRANSPORTATION DEPARTMENT.—The term "State transportation department" means that department, commission, board, or official of any State charged by its laws with the responsibility for highway construction.

(32) TRANSPORTATION SYSTEMS MANAGEMENT AND OPERATIONS.—

(A) IN GENERAL.—The term "transportation systems management and operations" means integrated strategies to optimize the performance of existing infrastructure through—

(i) the implementation of multimodal and intermodal, cross-jurisdictional systems, services, and projects designed to preserve capacity and improve security, safety, and reliability of the transportation system; and

(ii) the consideration of incorporating natural infrastructure.

(B) INCLUSIONS.—The term "transportation systems management and operations" includes—

(i) actions such as traffic detection and surveillance, corridor management, freeway management, arterial management, active transportation and demand management, work zone management, emergency management, traveler information services, congestion pricing, parking management, automated enforcement, traffic control, commercial vehicle operations, freight management, and coordination of highway, rail, transit, bicycle, and pedestrian operations; and

(ii) coordination of the implementation of regional transportation system management and operations investments (such as traffic incident management, traveler information services, emergency management, roadway weather management, intelligent transportation systems, communication networks, and information sharing systems) requiring agreements, integration, and interoperability to achieve targeted system performance, reliability, safety, and customer service levels.

(33) TRIBAL TRANSPORTATION FACILITY.—The term "tribal transportation facility" means a public highway, road, bridge, trail, or transit system that is located on or provides access to tribal land and appears on the national tribal transportation facility inventory described in section 202(b)(1).

(34) TRUCK STOP ELECTRIFICATION SYSTEM.—The term "truck stop electrification system" means a system that delivers heat, air conditioning, electricity, or communications to a heavy-duty vehicle.

(35) URBAN AREA.—The term "urban area" means an urbanized area or, in the case of an urbanized area encompassing more than one State, that part of the urbanized area in each such State, or urban place as designated by the Bureau of the Census having a population of 5,000 or more and not within any urbanized area, within boundaries to be fixed by responsible State and local officials in cooperation with each other, subject to approval by the Secretary. Such boundaries shall encompass, at

a minimum, the entire urban place designated by the Bureau of the Census, except in the case of cities in the State of Maine and in the State of New Hampshire.

(36) URBANIZED AREA.—The term "urbanized area" means an area with a population of 50,000 or more designated by the Bureau of the Census, within boundaries to be fixed by responsible State and local officials in cooperation with each other, subject to approval by the Secretary. Such boundaries shall encompass, at a minimum, the entire urbanized area within a State as designated by the Bureau of the Census.

(b) DECLARATION OF POLICY.—

(1) ACCELERATION OF CONSTRUCTION OF FEDERAL-AID HIGHWAY SYSTEMS.—Congress declares that it is in the national interest to accelerate the construction of Federal-aid highway systems, including the Dwight D. Eisenhower National System of Interstate and Defense Highways, because many of the highways (or portions of the highways) are inadequate to meet the needs of local and interstate commerce for the national and civil defense.

(2) COMPLETION OF INTERSTATE SYSTEM.—Congress declares that the prompt and early completion of the Dwight D. Eisenhower National System of Interstate and Defense Highways (referred to in this section as the "Interstate System"), so named because of its primary importance to the national defense, is essential to the national interest. It is the intent of Congress that the Interstate System be completed as nearly as practicable over the period of availability of the forty years' appropriations authorized for the purpose of expediting its construction, reconstruction, or improvement, inclusive of necessary tunnels and bridges, through the fiscal year ending September 30, 1996, under section 108(b) of the Federal-Aid Highway Act of 1956 (70 Stat. 374), and that the entire system in all States be brought to simultaneous completion. Insofar as possible in consonance with this objective, existing highways located on an interstate route shall be used to the extent that such use is practicable, suitable, and feasible, it being the intent that local needs, to the extent practicable, suitable, and feasible, shall be given equal consideration with the needs of interstate commerce.

(3) TRANSPORTATION NEEDS OF 21ST CENTURY.—Congress declares that—

(A) it is in the national interest to preserve and enhance the surface transportation system to meet the needs of the United States for the 21st Century;

(B) the current urban and long distance personal travel and freight movement demands have surpassed the original forecasts and travel demand patterns are expected to continue to change;

(C) continued planning for and investment in surface transportation is critical to ensure the surface transportation system adequately meets the changing travel demands of the future;

(D) among the foremost needs that the surface transportation system must meet to provide for a strong and vigorous national economy are safe, efficient, resilient, and reliable—

(i) national and interregional personal mobility (including personal mobility in rural and urban areas) and reduced congestion;

(ii) flow of interstate and international commerce and freight transportation;

13

and

(iii) travel movements essential for national security;

(E) special emphasis should be devoted to providing safe and efficient access for the type and size of commercial and military vehicles that access designated National Highway System intermodal freight terminals;

(F) the connection between land use and infrastructure is significant;

(G) transportation should play a significant role in promoting economic growth, improving the environment, and sustaining the quality of life; and

(H) the Secretary should take appropriate actions to preserve and enhance the Interstate System to meet the needs of the 21st Century.

(4) EXPEDITED PROJECT DELIVERY.—

(A) IN GENERAL.—Congress declares that it is in the national interest to expedite the delivery of surface transportation projects by substantially reducing the average length of the environmental review process.

(B) POLICY OF THE UNITED STATES.—Accordingly, it is the policy of the United States that—

(i) the Secretary shall have the lead role among Federal agencies in carrying out the environmental review process for surface transportation projects;

(ii) each Federal agency shall cooperate with the Secretary to expedite the environmental review process for surface transportation projects;

(iii) project sponsors shall not be prohibited from carrying out preconstruction project development activities concurrently with the environmental review process;

(iv) programmatic approaches shall be used to reduce the need for project-by-project reviews and decisions by Federal agencies; and

(v) the Secretary shall identify opportunities for project sponsors to assume responsibilities of the Secretary where such responsibilities can be assumed in a manner that protects public health, the environment, and public participation.

(c) It is the sense of Congress that under existing law no part of any sums authorized to be appropriated for expenditure upon any Federal-aid highway which has been apportioned pursuant to the provisions of this title shall be impounded or withheld from obligation, for purposes and projects as provided in this title, by any officer or employee in the executive branch of the Federal Government, except such specific sums as may be determined by the Secretary of the Treasury, after consultation with the Secretary of Transportation, are necessary to be withheld from obligation for specific periods of time to assure that sufficient amounts will be available in the Highway Trust Fund to defray the expenditures which will be required to be made from such fund.

(d) No funds authorized to be appropriated from the Highway Trust Fund shall be expended by or on behalf of any Federal department, agency, or instrumentality other than the Federal Highway Administration unless funds for such expenditure are identified and included as a line item in an appropriation Act and are to meet obligations of the United States heretofore or hereafter incurred under this title attributable to the construction of Federal-aid highways or highway planning, research, or development, or as otherwise specifically authorized to be appropriated from the Highway Trust Fund by Federal-aid highway legislation.

(e) It is the national policy that to the maximum extent possible the procedures to be utilized by the Secretary and all other affected heads of Federal departments, agencies, and instrumentalities for carrying out this title and any other provision of law relating to the Federal highway programs shall encourage the substantial minimization of paperwork and interagency decision procedures and the best use of available manpower and funds so as to prevent needless duplication and unnecessary delays at all levels of government.

(Pub. L. 85–767, Aug. 27, 1958, 72 Stat. 885; Pub. L. 86–70, §21(e)(1), June 25, 1959, 73 Stat. 146; Pub. L. 86–624, §17(a), July 12, 1960, 74 Stat. 415; Pub. L. 87–866, §6(a), Oct. 23, 1962, 76 Stat. 1147; Pub. L. 88–423, §3, Aug. 13, 1964, 78 Stat. 397; Pub. L. 89–574, §4(a), Sept. 13, 1966, 80 Stat. 767; Pub. L. 90–495, §§4(a), 8, 15, Aug. 23, 1968, 82 Stat. 816, 819, 822; Pub. L. 91–605, title I, §§104(a), 106(a), 107, 117(d), 130, 141, Dec. 31, 1970, 84 Stat. 1714, 1716, 1718, 1724, 1732, 1737; Pub. L. 93–87, title I, §§105, 106(a), 107, 108, 152(1), Aug. 13, 1973, 87 Stat. 253–255, 276; Pub. L. 93–643, §102(b), Jan. 4, 1975, 88 Stat. 2281; Pub. L. 94–280, title I, §§107(a), 108, May 5, 1976, 90 Stat. 430, 431; Pub. L. 95–599, title I, §106, Nov. 6, 1978, 92 Stat. 2693; Pub. L. 97–424, title I, §§126(c), 159, Jan. 6, 1983, 96 Stat. 2115, 2135; Pub. L. 100–17, title I, §§102(b)(3), 108, 109, 133(b)(2), (3), Apr. 2, 1987, 101 Stat. 135, 146, 171; Pub. L. 101–427, Oct. 15, 1990, 104 Stat. 927; Pub. L. 102–240, title I, §§1001(g), 1005, 1006(g)(1), 1007(c), Dec. 18, 1991, 105 Stat. 1916, 1922, 1927, 1931; Pub. L. 104–59, title III, §§301(b), 311(b), Nov. 28, 1995, 109 Stat. 578, 583; Pub. L. 105–178, title I, §1201, June 9, 1998, 112 Stat. 164; Pub. L. 109–59, title I, §§1122, 1909(a), Aug. 10, 2005, 119 Stat. 1196, 1470; Pub. L. 110–244, title I, §101(h), June 6, 2008, 122 Stat. 1574; Pub. L. 112–141, div. A, title I, §§1103, 1301(c), 1501, July 6, 2012, 126 Stat. 419, 528, 560; Pub. L. 114–94, div. A, title I, §1103, Dec. 4, 2015, 129 Stat. 1328; Pub. L. 117–58, div. A, title I, §§11103, 11123(a), 11525(a), Nov. 15, 2021, 135 Stat. 453, 499, 607.)

§102. PROGRAM EFFICIENCIES

(a) ACCESS OF MOTORCYCLES.—No State or political subdivision of a State may enact or enforce a law that applies only to motorcycles and the principal purpose of which is to restrict the access of motorcycles to any highway or portion of a highway for which Federal-aid highway funds have been utilized for planning, design, construction, or maintenance.

(b) SAVINGS PROVISION.—Nothing in this section shall affect the authority of a State or political subdivision of a State to regulate motorcycles for safety.

(Pub. L. 85–767, Aug. 27, 1958, 72 Stat. 887; Pub. L. 102–240, title I, §1016(a), Dec. 18, 1991, 105 Stat. 1945; Pub. L. 105–178, title I, §§1206, 1209, 1212(a)(2)(A)(i), 1304, June 9, 1998, 112 Stat. 185, 186, 193, 227; Pub. L. 109–59, title I, §1121(b)(1), Aug. 10, 2005, 119 Stat. 1195; Pub. L. 112–141, div. A, title I, §1502, July 6, 2012, 126 Stat. 561; Pub. L. 117–58, div. A, title I, §11310(a), Nov. 15, 2021, 135 Stat. 536.)

§103. NATIONAL HIGHWAY SYSTEM

(a) IN GENERAL.—For the purposes of this title, the Federal-aid system is the National Highway System, which includes the Interstate System.

(b) NATIONAL HIGHWAY SYSTEM.—

(1) DESCRIPTION.—The National Highway System consists of the highway routes and connections to transportation facilities that shall—

(A) serve major population centers, international border crossings, ports, airports, public transportation facilities, and other intermodal transportation facilities and other major travel destinations;

(B) meet national defense requirements; and

(C) serve interstate and interregional travel and commerce.

(2) COMPONENTS.—The National Highway System described in paragraph (1) consists of the following:

(A) The National Highway System depicted on the map submitted by the Secretary of Transportation to Congress with the report entitled "Pulling Together: The National Highway System and its Connections to Major Intermodal Terminals" and dated May 24, 1996, and modifications approved by the Secretary before the date of enactment of the MAP–21.

(B) Other urban and rural principal arterial routes, and border crossings on those routes, that were not included on the National Highway System before the date of enactment of the MAP–21.

(C) Other connector highways (including toll facilities) that were not included in the National Highway System before the date of enactment of the MAP–21 but that provide motor vehicle access between arterial routes on the National Highway System and a major intermodal transportation facility.

(D) A strategic highway network that—

(i) consists of a network of highways that are important to the United States strategic defense policy, that provide defense access, continuity, and emergency capabilities for the movement of personnel, materials, and equipment in both peacetime and wartime, and that were not included on the National Highway System before the date of enactment of the MAP–21;

(ii) may include highways on or off the Interstate System; and

(iii) shall be designated by the Secretary, in consultation with appropriate Federal agencies and the States.

(E) Major strategic highway network connectors that—

(i) consist of highways that provide motor vehicle access between major military installations and highways that are part of the strategic highway network but were not included on the National Highway System before the date of enactment of the MAP–21; and

(ii) shall be designated by the Secretary, in consultation with appropriate Federal agencies and the States.

(3) MODIFICATIONS TO NHS.—

(A) IN GENERAL.—The Secretary may make any modification to the National Highway System, including any modification consisting of a connector to a major intermodal terminal or the withdrawal of a road from that system, that is proposed by a State if the Secretary determines that the modification—

(i) meets the criteria established for the National Highway System under this title after the date of enactment of the MAP–21; and

(ii)(I) enhances the national transportation characteristics of the National Highway System; or

(II) in the case of the withdrawal of a road, is reasonable and appropriate.

(B) COOPERATION.—

(i) IN GENERAL.—In proposing a modification under this paragraph, a State shall cooperate with local and regional officials.

(ii) URBANIZED AREAS.—In an urbanized area, the local officials shall act through the metropolitan planning organization designated for the area under section 134.

(c) INTERSTATE SYSTEM.—

(1) DESCRIPTION.—

(A) IN GENERAL.—The Dwight D. Eisenhower National System of Interstate and Defense Highways within the United States (including the District of Columbia and Puerto Rico) consists of highways designed, located, and selected in accordance with this paragraph.

(B) DESIGN.—

(i) IN GENERAL.—Except as provided in clause (ii), highways on the Interstate System shall be designed in accordance with the standards of section 109(b).

(ii) EXCEPTION.—Highways on the Interstate System in Alaska and Puerto Rico shall be designed in accordance with such geometric and construction standards as are adequate for current and probable future traffic demands and the needs of the locality of the highway.

(C) LOCATION.—Highways on the Interstate System shall be located so as—

(i) to connect by routes, as direct as practicable, the principal metropolitan areas, cities, and industrial centers;

(ii) to serve the national defense; and

(iii) to the maximum extent practicable, to connect at suitable border points with routes of continental importance in Canada and Mexico.

(D) SELECTION OF ROUTES.—To the maximum extent practicable, each route of the Interstate System shall be selected by joint action of the State transportation departments of the State in which the route is located and the adjoining States, in cooperation with local and regional officials, and subject to the approval of the Secretary.

(2) MAXIMUM MILEAGE.—The mileage of highways on the Interstate System shall not exceed 43,000 miles, exclusive of designations under paragraph (4).

(3) MODIFICATIONS.—The Secretary may approve or require modifications to the Interstate System in a manner consistent with the policies and procedures established under this subsection.

(4) INTERSTATE SYSTEM DESIGNATIONS.—

(A) ADDITIONS.—If the Secretary determines that a highway on the National Highway System meets all standards of a highway on the Interstate System and that the highway is a logical addition or connection to the Interstate System, the Secretary may, upon the affirmative recommendation of the State or States in which the highway is located, designate the highway as a route on the Interstate System.

(B) DESIGNATIONS AS FUTURE INTERSTATE SYSTEM ROUTES.—

(i) IN GENERAL.—Subject to clauses (ii) through (vi), if the Secretary determines that a highway on the National Highway System would be a logical addition or connection to the Interstate System and would qualify for designation as a route on the Interstate System under subparagraph (A) if the highway met all standards of a highway on the Interstate System, the Secretary may, upon the affirmative recommendation of the State or States in which the highway is located, designate the highway as a future Interstate System route.

(ii) WRITTEN AGREEMENT.—A designation under clause (i) shall be made only upon the written agreement of each State described in that clause that the highway will be constructed to meet all standards of a highway on the Interstate System by not later than the date that is 25 years after the date of the agreement.

(iii) FAILURE TO COMPLETE CONSTRUCTION.—If a State described in clause (i) has not substantially completed the construction of a highway designated under this subparagraph by the date specified in clause (ii), the Secretary shall remove the designation of the highway as a future Interstate System route.

(iv) EFFECT OF REMOVAL.—Removal of the designation of a highway under clause (iii) shall not preclude the Secretary from designating the highway as a route on the Interstate System under subparagraph (A) or under any other provision of law providing for addition to the Interstate System.

(v) RETROACTIVE EFFECT.—An agreement described in clause (ii) that is entered into before August 10, 2005, shall be deemed to include the 25-year time limitation described in that clause, regardless of any earlier construction completion date in the agreement.

(vi) REFERENCES.—No law, rule, regulation, map, document, or other record of the United States, or of any State or political subdivision of a State, shall refer to any highway designated as a future Interstate System route under this subparagraph, and no such highway shall be signed or marked, as a highway on the Interstate System, until such time as the highway—

(I) is constructed to the geometric and construction standards for the Interstate System; and

(II) has been designated as a route on the Interstate System.

(C) FINANCIAL RESPONSIBILITY.—Except as provided in this title, the designation of a highway under this paragraph shall create no additional Federal financial responsibility with respect to the highway.

(5) EXEMPTION OF INTERSTATE SYSTEM.—

(A) IN GENERAL.—Except as provided in subparagraph (B), the Interstate System shall not be considered to be a historic site under section 303 of title 49 or section 138 of this title, regardless of whether the Interstate System or portions or elements of the Interstate System are listed on, or eligible for listing on, the National Register of Historic Places.

(B) INDIVIDUAL ELEMENTS.—Subject to subparagraph (C)—

(i) the Secretary shall determine, through the administrative process established for exempting the Interstate System from section 306108 of title 54, those individual elements of the Interstate System that possess national or exceptional historic significance (such as a historic bridge or a highly significant engineering feature); and

(ii) those elements shall be considered to be historic sites under section 303 of title 49 or section 138 of this title, as applicable.

(C) CONSTRUCTION, MAINTENANCE, RESTORATION, AND REHABILITATION ACTIVITIES.—Subparagraph (B) does not prohibit a State from carrying out construction, maintenance, preservation, restoration, or rehabilitation activities for a portion of the Interstate System referred to in subparagraph (B) upon compliance with section 303 of title 49 or section 138 of this title, as applicable, and section

306108 of title 54.

(Pub. L. 85–767, Aug. 27, 1958, 72 Stat. 887; Pub. L. 86–70, §21(d)(1), June 25, 1959, 73 Stat. 145; Pub. L. 86–624, §17(b), (c), July 12, 1960, 74 Stat. 415; Pub. L. 87–866, §8(a), Oct. 23, 1962, 76 Stat. 1147; Pub. L. 90–238, Jan. 2, 1968, 81 Stat. 772; Pub. L. 90–495, §§14, 21, Aug. 23, 1968, 82 Stat. 822, 826; Pub. L. 91–605, title I, §§106(b), 124, Dec. 31, 1970, 84 Stat. 1716, 1729; Pub. L. 93–87, title I, §§109(a), 110(a), (b), 137, 148(a)–(c), (e), Aug. 13, 1973, 87 Stat. 255, 256, 268, 274; Pub. L. 93–643, §125, Jan. 4, 1975, 88 Stat. 2290; Pub. L. 94–280, title I, §§109, 110, 111(a), May 5, 1976, 90 Stat. 431, 433; Pub. L. 95–599, title I, §107(a), (b), (f)(1), Nov. 6, 1978, 92 Stat. 2694, 2695; Pub. L. 96–106, §§1, 2(a), (c), Nov. 9, 1979, 93 Stat. 796; Pub. L. 96–144, §2, Dec. 13, 1979, 93 Stat. 1084; Pub. L. 97–424, title I, §§107(a)–(c)(1), (d), (e), 108(f), Jan. 6, 1983, 96 Stat. 2101–2104; Pub. L. 100–17, title I, §103(b), (f)(1), Apr. 2, 1987, 101 Stat. 136, 141; Pub. L. 102–240, title I, §§1006(a), (b), (d), 1011, title III, §3003(b), Dec. 18, 1991, 105 Stat. 1923, 1925, 1935, 2088; Pub. L. 103–272, §5(f)(1), July 5, 1994, 108 Stat. 1374; Pub. L. 103–429, §§3(1), 7(a)(4)(B), Oct. 31, 1994, 108 Stat. 4377, 4389; Pub. L. 104–59, title I, §101, title III, §301(a), Nov. 28, 1995, 109 Stat. 569, 578; Pub. L. 104–287, §2, Oct. 11, 1996, 110 Stat. 3388; Pub. L. 105–178, title I, §1106(b), June 9, 1998, 112 Stat. 131; Pub. L. 109–59, title I, §§1106, 1118(b)(1), title VI, §§6006(a)(1), 6007, Aug. 10, 2005, 119 Stat. 1166, 1181, 1872, 1873; Pub. L. 112–141, div. A, title I, §1104(a), July 6, 2012, 126 Stat. 422; Pub. L. 113–287, §5(f)(1), Dec. 19, 2014, 128 Stat. 3268; Pub. L. 114–94, div. A, title I, §1122(e), Dec. 4, 2015, 129 Stat. 1369.)

§104. APPORTIONMENT

(a) ADMINISTRATIVE EXPENSES.—

(1) IN GENERAL.—There is authorized to be appropriated from the Highway Trust Fund (other than the Mass Transit Account) to be made available to the Secretary for administrative expenses of the Federal Highway Administration—

(A) $490,964,697 for fiscal year 2022;

(B) $500,783,991 for fiscal year 2023;

(C) $510,799,671 for fiscal year 2024;

(D) $521,015,664 for fiscal year 2025; and

(E) $531,435,977 for fiscal year 2026.

(2) PURPOSES.—The amounts authorized to be appropriated by this subsection shall be used—

(A) to administer the provisions of law to be funded from appropriations for the Federal-aid highway program and programs authorized under chapter 2;

(B) to make transfers of such sums as the Secretary determines to be appropriate to the Appalachian Regional Commission for administrative activities associated with the Appalachian development highway system; and

(C) to reimburse, as appropriate, the Office of Inspector General of the Department of Transportation for the conduct of annual audits of financial statements in accordance with section 3521 of title 31.

(3) AVAILABILITY.—The amounts made available under paragraph (1) shall remain available until expended.

(b) DIVISION AMONG PROGRAMS OF STATE'S SHARE OF BASE APPORTIONMENT.—The Secretary shall distribute the amount of the base apportionment apportioned to a State for a fiscal year under subsection (c) among the national highway performance program, the surface transportation block grant program, the highway safety improvement program, the congestion mitigation and air quality improvement program, the national highway freight program, the carbon reduction program under section 175, to carry out subsection (c) of the PROTECT program under section 176, and to carry out section 134 as follows:

(1) NATIONAL HIGHWAY PERFORMANCE PROGRAM.—For the national highway performance program, 59.0771195921461 percent of the amount remaining after distributing amounts under paragraphs (4), (5), and (6).

(2) SURFACE TRANSPORTATION BLOCK GRANT PROGRAM.—For the surface transportation block grant program, 28.7402203421251 percent of the amount remaining after distributing amounts under paragraphs (4), (5), and (6).

(3) HIGHWAY SAFETY IMPROVEMENT PROGRAM.—For the highway safety improvement program, 6.70605141316253 percent of the amount remaining after distributing amounts under paragraphs (4), (5), and (6).

(4) CONGESTION MITIGATION AND AIR QUALITY IMPROVEMENT PROGRAM.—

(A) IN GENERAL.—For the congestion mitigation and air quality improvement program, an amount determined for the State under subparagraphs (B) and (C).

(B) TOTAL AMOUNT.—The total amount for the congestion mitigation and air quality improvement program for all States shall be—

(i) $2,536,490,803 for fiscal year 2022;

(ii) $2,587,220,620 for fiscal year 2023;

(iii) $2,638,965,032 for fiscal year 2024;

(iv) $2,691,744,332 for fiscal year 2025; and

(v) $2,745,579,213 for fiscal year 2026.

(C) STATE SHARE.—For each fiscal year, the Secretary shall distribute among the States the total amount for the congestion mitigation and air quality improvement program under subparagraph (B) so that each State receives an amount equal to the proportion that—

(i) the amount apportioned to the State for the congestion mitigation and air quality improvement program for fiscal year 2020; bears to

(ii) the total amount of funds apportioned to all States for that program for fiscal year 2020.

(5) NATIONAL HIGHWAY FREIGHT PROGRAM.—

(A) IN GENERAL.—For the national highway freight program under section 167, the Secretary shall set aside from the base apportionment determined for a State under subsection (c) an amount determined for the State under subparagraphs (B) and (C).

(B) TOTAL AMOUNT.—The total amount set aside for the national highway freight program for all States shall be—

(i) $1,373,932,519 for fiscal year 2022;

(ii) $1,401,411,169 for fiscal year 2023;

(iii) $1,429,439,392 for fiscal year 2024;

(iv) $1,458,028,180 for fiscal year 2025; and

(v) $1,487,188,740 for fiscal year 2026.

(C) STATE SHARE.—For each fiscal year, the Secretary shall distribute among the States the total set-aside amount for the national highway freight program under subparagraph (B) so that each State receives the amount equal to the proportion that—

(i) the total base apportionment determined for the State under subsection (c);

bears to

(ii) the total base apportionments for all States under subsection (c).

(6) METROPOLITAN PLANNING.—

(A) IN GENERAL.—To carry out section 134, an amount determined for the State under subparagraphs (B) and (C).

(B) TOTAL AMOUNT.—The total amount for metropolitan planning for all States shall be—

(i) $438,121,139 for fiscal year 2022;

(ii) $446,883,562 for fiscal year 2023;

(iii) $455,821,233 for fiscal year 2024;

(iv) $464,937,657 for fiscal year 2025; and

(v) $474,236,409 for fiscal year 2026.

(C) STATE SHARE.—For each fiscal year, the Secretary shall distribute among the States the total amount to carry out section 134 under subparagraph (B) so that each State receives an amount equal to the proportion that—

(i) the amount apportioned to the State to carry out section 134 for fiscal year 2020; bears to

(ii) the total amount of funds apportioned to all States to carry out section 134 for fiscal year 2020.

(7) CARBON REDUCTION PROGRAM.—For the carbon reduction program under section 175, 2.56266964565637 percent of the amount remaining after distributing amounts under paragraphs (4), (5), and (6).

(8) PROTECT FORMULA PROGRAM.—To carry out subsection (c) of the PROTECT program under section 176, 2.91393900690991 percent of the amount remaining after distributing amounts under paragraphs (4), (5), and (6).

(c) CALCULATION OF AMOUNTS.—

(1) STATE SHARE.—For fiscal year 2022 and each fiscal year thereafter, the amount for each State shall be determined as follows:

(A) INITIAL AMOUNTS.—The initial amounts for each State shall be determined by multiplying—

(i) the base apportionment; by

(ii) the share for each State, which shall be equal to the proportion that—

(I) the amount of apportionments that the State received for fiscal year 2021; bears to

(II) the amount of those apportionments received by all States for that fiscal year.

(B) GUARANTEED AMOUNTS.—The initial amounts resulting from the calculation under subparagraph (A) shall be adjusted to ensure that each State receives an aggregate apportionment that is—

(i) equal to at least 95 percent of the estimated tax payments paid into the Highway Trust Fund (other than the Mass Transit Account) in the most recent fiscal year for which data are available that are—

(I) attributable to highway users in the State; and

(II) associated with taxes in effect on July 1, 2019, and only up to the rate those taxes were in effect on that date;

(ii) at least 2 percent greater than the apportionment that the State received for fiscal year 2021; and

(iii) at least 1 percent greater than the apportionment that the State received for the previous fiscal year.

(2) STATE APPORTIONMENT.—On October 1 of fiscal year 2022 and each fiscal year thereafter, the Secretary shall apportion the sums authorized to be appropriated for expenditure on the national highway performance program under section 119, the surface transportation block grant program under section 133, the highway safety improvement program under section 148, the congestion mitigation and air quality improvement program under section 149, the national highway freight program under section 167, the carbon reduction program under section 175, to carry out subsection (c) of the PROTECT program under section 176, and to carry out section 134 in accordance with paragraph (1).

(d) METROPOLITAN PLANNING.—

(1) USE OF AMOUNTS.—

(A) USE.—

(i) IN GENERAL.—Except as provided in clause (ii), the amounts apportioned to a State under subsection (b)(6) shall be made available by the State to the metropolitan planning organizations responsible for carrying out section 134 in the State.

(ii) STATES RECEIVING MINIMUM APPORTIONMENT.—A State that received the minimum apportionment for use in carrying out section 134 for fiscal year 2009 may, subject to the approval of the Secretary, use the funds apportioned under subsection (b)(6) to fund transportation planning outside of urbanized areas.

(B) UNUSED FUNDS.—Any funds that are not used to carry out section 134 may be made available by a metropolitan planning organization to the State to fund activities under section 135.

(2) DISTRIBUTION OF AMOUNTS WITHIN STATES.—

(A) IN GENERAL.—The distribution within any State of the planning funds made available to organizations under paragraph (1) shall be in accordance with a formula that—

(i) is developed by each State and approved by the Secretary; and

(ii) takes into consideration, at a minimum, population, status of planning, attainment of air quality standards, metropolitan area transportation needs, and other factors necessary to provide for an appropriate distribution of funds to carry out section 134 and other applicable requirements of Federal law.

(B) REIMBURSEMENT.—Not later than 15 business days after the date of receipt by a State of a request for reimbursement of expenditures made by a metropolitan planning organization for carrying out section 134, the State shall reimburse, from amounts distributed under this paragraph to the metropolitan planning organization by the State, the metropolitan planning organization for those expenditures.

(3) DETERMINATION OF POPULATION FIGURES.—For the purpose of determining population figures under this subsection, the Secretary shall use the latest available data from the decennial census conducted under section 141(a) of title 13, United States Code.

(e) CERTIFICATION OF APPORTIONMENTS.—

(1) IN GENERAL.—The Secretary shall—

(A) on October 1 of each fiscal year, certify to each of the State transportation departments the amount that has been apportioned to the State under this section for the fiscal year; and

(B) to permit the States to develop adequate plans for the use of amounts apportioned under this section, advise each State of the amount that will be apportioned to the State under this section for a fiscal year not later than 90 days before the beginning of the fiscal year for which the sums to be apportioned are authorized.

(2) NOTICE TO STATES.—If the Secretary has not made an apportionment under this section for a fiscal year beginning after September 30, 1998, by not later than the date that is the twenty-first day of that fiscal year, the Secretary shall submit, by not later than that date, to the Committee on Transportation and Infrastructure of the House of Representatives and the Committee on Environment and Public Works of the Senate, a written statement of the reason for not making the apportionment in a timely manner.

(3) APPORTIONMENT CALCULATIONS.—

(A) IN GENERAL.—The calculation of official apportionments of funds to the States under this title is a primary responsibility of the Department and shall be carried out only by employees (and not contractors) of the Department.

(B) PROHIBITION ON USE OF FUNDS TO HIRE CONTRACTORS.—None of the funds made available under this title shall be used to hire contractors to calculate the apportionments of funds to States.

(f) TRANSFER OF HIGHWAY AND TRANSIT FUNDS.—

(1) TRANSFER OF HIGHWAY FUNDS FOR TRANSIT PROJECTS.—

(A) IN GENERAL.—Subject to subparagraph (B), amounts made available for transit projects or transportation planning under this title may be transferred to and administered by the Secretary in accordance with chapter 53 of title 49.

(B) NON-FEDERAL SHARE.—The provisions of this title relating to the non-Federal share shall apply to the amounts transferred under subparagraph (A).

(2) TRANSFER OF TRANSIT FUNDS FOR HIGHWAY PROJECTS.—

(A) IN GENERAL.—Subject to subparagraph (B), amounts made available for highway projects or transportation planning under chapter 53 of title 49 may be transferred to and administered by the Secretary in accordance with this title.

(B) NON-FEDERAL SHARE.—The provisions of chapter 53 of title 49 relating to the non-Federal share shall apply to amounts transferred under subparagraph (A).

(3) TRANSFER OF FUNDS AMONG STATES OR TO AN OPERATING ADMINISTRATION OF THE DEPARTMENT OF TRANSPORTATION.—

(A) IN GENERAL.—Subject to subparagraph (B), the Secretary may, at the request of a State, transfer amounts apportioned or allocated under this title to the State to another State, or to an operating administration of the Department of Transportation, for the purpose of funding 1 or more projects that are eligible for assistance with amounts so apportioned or allocated.

(B) APPORTIONMENT.—The transfer shall have no effect on any apportionment of amounts to a State under this section.

(C) FUNDS SUBALLOCATED TO URBANIZED AREAS.—Amounts that are apportioned or allocated to a State under subsection (b)(3) (as in effect on the day before the date of enactment of the MAP–21) or subsection (b)(2) and attributed to an urbanized area of a State with a population of more than 200,000 individuals under section 133(d) may be transferred under this paragraph only if the metropolitan planning organization designated for the area concurs, in writing, with the transfer request.

(4) TRANSFER OF OBLIGATION AUTHORITY.—Obligation authority for amounts transferred under this subsection shall be transferred in the same manner and amount as the amounts for the projects that are transferred under this section.

(g) HIGHWAY TRUST FUND TRANSPARENCY AND ACCOUNTABILITY REPORTS.—

(1) COMPILATION OF DATA.—Not later than 180 days after the date of enactment of the FAST Act, the Secretary shall compile data in accordance with this subsection on the use of Federal-aid highway funds made available under this title.

(2) REQUIREMENTS.—The Secretary shall ensure that the reports required under this subsection are made available in a user-friendly manner on the public Internet website of the Department of Transportation and can be searched and downloaded by users of the website.

(3) CONTENTS OF REPORTS.—

(A) APPORTIONED AND ALLOCATED PROGRAMS.—On a semiannual basis, the Secretary shall make available a report on funding apportioned and allocated to the States under this title that describes—

(i) the amount of funding obligated by each State, year-to-date, for the current fiscal year;

(ii) the amount of funds remaining available for obligation by each State;

(iii) changes in the obligated, unexpended balance for each State, year-to-date, during the current fiscal year, including the obligated, unexpended balance at the end of the preceding fiscal year and current fiscal year expenditures;

(iv) the amount and program category of unobligated funding, year-to-date, available for expenditure at the discretion of the Secretary;

(v) the rates of obligation on and off the National Highway System, year-to-date, for the current fiscal year of funds apportioned, allocated, or set aside under this section, according to—

(I) program;

(II) funding category or subcategory;

(III) type of improvement;

(IV) State; and

(V) sub-State geographical area, including urbanized and rural areas, on the basis of the population of each such area; and

(vi) the amount of funds transferred by each State, year-to-date, for the current fiscal year between programs under section 126.

(B) PROJECT DATA.—On an annual basis, the Secretary shall make available a report that provides, for any project funded under this title (excluding projects for which funds are transferred to agencies other than the Federal Highway

Administration) with an estimated total cost as of the start of construction greater than $25,000,000, and to the maximum extent practicable, other projects funded under this title, project data describing—

(i) the specific location of the project;

(ii) the total cost of the project;

(iii) the amount of Federal funding obligated for the project;

(iv) the program or programs from which Federal funds have been obligated for the project;

(v) the type of improvement being made, such as categorizing the project as—

(I) a road reconstruction project;

(II) a new road construction project;

(III) a new bridge construction project;

(IV) a bridge rehabilitation project; or

(V) a bridge replacement project;

(vi) the ownership of the highway or bridge;

(vii) whether the project is located in an area of the State with a population of—

(I) less than 5,000 individuals;

(II) 5,000 or more individuals but less than 50,000 individuals;

(III) 50,000 or more individuals but less than 200,000 individuals; or

(IV) 200,000 or more individuals; and

(viii) available information on the estimated cost of the project as of the start of project construction, or the revised cost estimate based on a description of revisions to the scope of work or other factors affecting project cost other than cost overruns.

(h) BASE APPORTIONMENT DEFINED.—In this section, the term "base apportionment" means the combined amount authorized for appropriation for the national highway performance program under section 119, the surface transportation block grant program under section 133, the highway safety improvement program under section 148, the congestion mitigation and air quality improvement program under section 149, the national highway freight program under section 167, the carbon reduction program under section 175, to carry out subsection (c) of the PROTECT program under section 176, and to carry out section 134.

(Pub. L. 85–767, Aug. 27, 1958, 72 Stat. 889; Pub. L. 86–70, §21(e)(2), June 25, 1959, 73 Stat. 146; Pub. L. 86–657, §8(g), July 14, 1960, 74 Stat. 525; Pub. L. 87–866, §10(a), Oct. 23, 1962, 76 Stat. 1148; Pub. L. 88–157, §§2, 3, Oct. 24, 1963, 77 Stat. 276; Pub. L. 88–423, §4(a), Aug. 13, 1964, 78 Stat. 397; Pub. L. 89–574, §4(b), Sept. 13, 1966, 80 Stat. 767; Pub. L. 90–495, §4(b), Aug. 23, 1968, 82 Stat. 816; Pub. L. 91–605, title I, §§104(b), 106(c), Dec. 31, 1970, 84 Stat. 1714, 1717; Pub. L. 93–87, title I, §§106(b), 111(a), 112, title II, §227, Aug. 13, 1973, 87 Stat. 254, 256, 257, 292; Pub. L. 94–280, title I, §§106(b), 107(b), 112(a)–(g), 113(a), title II, §206, May 5, 1976, 90 Stat. 429, 430, 433–435, 453; Pub. L. 95–599, title I, §§108–110, 116(b), Nov. 6, 1978, 92 Stat. 2695, 2696, 2699; Pub. L. 97–134, §§4(c), 5, Dec. 29, 1981, 95 Stat. 1700; Pub. L. 100–17, title I, §§102(b)(1), (2), 114(e)(1), Apr. 2, 1987, 101 Stat. 135, 153; Pub. L. 100–202, §101(l) [title III, §347(a)], Dec. 22, 1987, 101 Stat. 1329–358, 1329–388; Pub. L. 101–516, title III, §333 (part), Nov. 5, 1990, 104 Stat. 2184; Pub. L. 102–143, title III, §333(c), Oct. 28, 1991, 105 Stat. 947; Pub. L. 102–240, title I, §§1001(c)–(e), 1003(e), 1006(e), (f), 1007(b), 1008(b), 1009(d), 1010, 1024(b), (c)(2), 1028(g), Dec. 18, 1991, 105 Stat. 1915, 1916, 1926, 1930, 1932, 1934, 1962, 1968; Pub. L. 104–59, title III, §§302, 319(a)(2), 337(f), title IV, §410, Nov. 28, 1995, 109 Stat.

[§105. Repealed. Pub. L. 117–58, div. A, title I,
§11501(a), Nov. 15, 2021, 135 Stat. 578]

CHAPTER 1—FEDERAL-AID HIGHWAYS

578, 589, 603, 633; Pub. L. 105–130, §§4(a)(3), 5(b), Dec. 1, 1997, 111 Stat. 2556; Pub. L. 105–178, title I, §§1103(a)–(k), (o), 1212(a)(2)(A), June 9, 1998, 112 Stat. 118–125, 193; Pub. L. 105–206, title IX, §9002(c)(3), July 22, 1998, 112 Stat. 835; Pub. L. 106–159, title I, §101(b), Dec. 9, 1999, 113 Stat. 1751; Pub. L. 108–178, §4(d), Dec. 15, 2003, 117 Stat. 2641; Pub. L. 109–59, title I, §§1103, 1107–1109(a), 1118(b)(2), 1401(a)(3)(A), (b), Aug. 10, 2005, 119 Stat. 1161, 1166–1168, 1181, 1225; Pub. L. 110–244, title I, §101(i), (m)(3)(A), June 6, 2008, 122 Stat. 1574, 1576; Pub. L. 112–141, div. A, title I, §§1105(a), 1519(c)(3), July 6, 2012, 126 Stat. 427, 575; Pub. L. 114–94, div. A, title I, §§1104(a)–(e)(1), 1402(a), 1446(d)(5)(A), Dec. 4, 2015, 129 Stat. 1329–1332, 1405, 1438; Pub. L. 117–58, div. A, title I, §§11104, 11525(b), Nov. 15, 2021, 135 Stat. 454, 607.)

[§105. Repealed. Pub. L. 117–58, div. A, title I, §11501(a), Nov. 15, 2021, 135 Stat. 578]

Section, added Pub. L. 114–94, div. A, title I, §1403(a), Dec. 4, 2015, 129 Stat. 1407, related to availability of additional amounts of contract authority based on additional deposits into the Highway Trust Fund.

A prior section 105, Pub. L. 85–767, Aug. 27, 1958, 72 Stat. 891; Pub. L. 86–624, §17(b), July 12, 1960, 74 Stat. 415; Pub. L. 89–564, title II, §206, Sept. 9, 1966, 80 Stat. 736; Pub. L. 91–605, title I, §§106(d), 132, Dec. 31, 1970, 84 Stat. 1717, 1732; Pub. L. 93–87, title I, §109(b), Aug. 13, 1973, 87 Stat. 255; Pub. L. 95–599, title I, §§111, 112, Nov. 6, 1978, 92 Stat. 2696; Pub. L. 97–424, title I, §109(a), Jan. 6, 1983, 96 Stat. 2104; Pub. L. 102–240, title I, §1105(g)(7), Dec. 18, 1991, 105 Stat. 2036; Pub. L. 105–178, title I, §1104(a), (c), June 9, 1998, 112 Stat. 127; Pub. L. 105–206, title IX, §9002(d), July 22, 1998, 112 Stat. 835; Pub. L. 109–59, title I, §1104(a), Aug. 10, 2005, 119 Stat. 1163; Pub. L. 110–244, title I, §101(m)(3)(B), June 6, 2008, 122 Stat. 1576, related to the equity bonus program, prior to repeal by Pub. L. 112–141, div. A, title I, §1519(b)(1)(A), July 6, 2012, 126 Stat. 575, effective Oct. 1, 2012.

§106. Project approval and oversight

(a) In General.—

(1) Submission of plans, specifications, and estimates.—Except as otherwise provided in this section, each State transportation department shall submit to the Secretary for approval such plans, specifications, and estimates for each proposed project as the Secretary may require.

(2) Project agreement.—The Secretary shall act on the plans, specifications, and estimates as soon as practicable after the date of their submission and shall enter into a formal project agreement with the State transportation department recipient formalizing the conditions of the project approval.

(3) Contractual obligation.—The execution of the project agreement shall be deemed a contractual obligation of the Federal Government for the payment of the Federal share of the cost of the project.

(4) Guidance.—In taking action under this subsection, the Secretary shall be guided by section 109.

(b) Project Agreement.—

(1) Provision of state funds.—The project agreement shall make provision for State funds required to pay the State's non-Federal share of the cost of construction of the project (including payments made pursuant to a long-term concession agreement, such as availability payments) and to pay for maintenance of the project after

completion of construction.

(2) REPRESENTATIONS OF STATE.—If a part of the project is to be constructed at the expense of, or in cooperation with, political subdivisions of the State, the Secretary may rely on representations made by the State transportation department with respect to the arrangements or agreements made by the State transportation department and appropriate local officials for ensuring that the non-Federal contribution will be provided under paragraph (1).

(c) ASSUMPTION BY STATES OF RESPONSIBILITIES OF THE SECRETARY.—

(1) NHS PROJECTS.—For projects under this title that are on the National Highway System, including projects on the Interstate System, the State may assume the responsibilities of the Secretary under this title for design, plans, specifications, estimates, contract awards, and inspections with respect to the projects unless the Secretary determines that the assumption is not appropriate.

(2) NON NHS PROJECTS. For projects under this title that are not on the National Highway System, the State shall assume the responsibilities of the Secretary under this title for design, plans, specifications, estimates, contract awards, and inspection of projects, unless the State determines that such assumption is not appropriate.

(3) AGREEMENT.—The Secretary and the State shall enter into an agreement relating to the extent to which the State assumes the responsibilities of the Secretary under this subsection.

(4) LIMITATION ON INTERSTATE PROJECTS.—

(A) IN GENERAL.—The Secretary shall not assign any responsibilities to a State for projects the Secretary determines to be in a high risk category, as defined under subparagraph (B).

(B) HIGH RISK CATEGORIES.—The Secretary may define the high risk categories under this subparagraph on a national basis, a State-by-State basis, or a national and State-by-State basis, as determined to be appropriate by the Secretary.

(d) RESPONSIBILITIES OF THE SECRETARY.—Nothing in this section, section 133, or section 149 shall affect or discharge any responsibility or obligation of the Secretary under—

(1) section 113 or 114; or

(2) any Federal law other than this title (including section 5333 of title 49).

(e) VALUE ENGINEERING ANALYSIS.—

(1) DEFINITION OF VALUE ENGINEERING ANALYSIS.—

(A) IN GENERAL.—In this subsection, the term "value engineering analysis" means a systematic process of review and analysis of a project, during the planning and design phases, by a multidisciplinary team of persons not involved in the project, that is conducted to provide recommendations such as those described in subparagraph (B) for—

(i) providing the needed functions safely, reliably, and at the lowest overall lifecycle cost;

(ii) improving the value and quality of the project; and

(iii) reducing the time to complete the project.

(B) INCLUSIONS.—The recommendations referred to in subparagraph (A) include, with respect to a project—

(i) combining or eliminating otherwise inefficient use of costly parts of the original proposed design for the project; and

(ii) completely redesigning the project using different technologies, materials, or methods so as to accomplish the original purpose of the project.

(2) ANALYSIS.—The State shall provide a value engineering analysis for—

(A) each project on the National Highway System receiving Federal assistance with an estimated total cost of $50,000,000 or more;

(B) a bridge project on the National Highway System receiving Federal assistance with an estimated total cost of $40,000,000 or more; and

(C) any other project the Secretary determines to be appropriate.

(3) MAJOR PROJECTS.—The Secretary may require more than 1 analysis described in paragraph (2) for a major project described in subsection (h).

(4) REQUIREMENTS.—

(A) VALUE ENGINEERING PROGRAM.—The State shall develop and carry out a value engineering program that—

(i) establishes and documents value engineering program policies and procedures;

(ii) ensures that the required value engineering analysis is conducted before completing the final design of a project;

(iii) ensures that the value engineering analysis that is conducted, and the recommendations developed and implemented for each project, are documented in a final value engineering report; and

(iv) monitors, evaluates, and annually submits to the Secretary a report that describes the results of the value analyses that are conducted and the recommendations implemented for each of the projects described in paragraph (2) that are completed in the State.

(B) BRIDGE PROJECTS.—The value engineering analysis for a bridge project under paragraph (2) shall—

(i) include bridge superstructure and substructure requirements based on construction material; and

(ii) be evaluated by the State—

(I) on engineering and economic bases, taking into consideration acceptable designs for bridges; and

(II) using an analysis of lifecycle costs and duration of project construction.

(5) DESIGN-BUILD PROJECTS.—A requirement to provide a value engineering analysis under this subsection shall not apply to a project delivered using the design-build method of construction.

(f) LIFE-CYCLE COST ANALYSIS.—

(1) USE OF LIFE-CYCLE COST ANALYSIS.—The Secretary shall develop recommendations for the States to conduct life-cycle cost analyses. The recommendations shall be based on the principles contained in section 2 of Executive Order No. 12893 and shall be developed in consultation with the American Association of State Highway and Transportation Officials. The Secretary shall not require a State to conduct a life-cycle cost analysis for any project as a result of the recommendations required under this subsection.

(2) Life-cycle cost analysis defined.—In this subsection, the term "life-cycle cost analysis" means a process for evaluating the total economic worth of a usable project segment by analyzing initial costs and discounted future costs, such as maintenance, user costs, reconstruction, rehabilitation, restoring, and resurfacing costs, over the life of the project segment.

(g) Oversight Program.—

(1) Establishment.—

(A) In general.—The Secretary shall establish an oversight program to monitor the effective and efficient use of funds authorized to carry out this title.

(B) Minimum requirement.—At a minimum, the program shall be responsive to all areas relating to financial integrity and project delivery.

(2) Financial integrity.—

(A) Financial management systems.—The Secretary shall perform annual reviews that address elements of the State transportation departments' financial management systems that affect projects approved under subsection (a).

(B) Project costs.—The Secretary shall develop minimum standards for estimating project costs and shall periodically evaluate the practices of States for estimating project costs, awarding contracts, and reducing project costs.

(3) Project delivery.—

(A) In general.—The Secretary shall perform reviews that address elements of the project delivery system of a State, which elements include one or more activities that are involved in the life cycle of a project from conception to completion of the project.

(B) Frequency.—

(i) In general.—Except as provided in clauses (ii) and (iii), the Secretary shall carry out a review under subparagraph (A) not less frequently than once every 2 years.

(ii) Consultation with state.—The Secretary, after consultation with a State, may make a determination to carry out a review under subparagraph (A) for that State less frequently than provided under clause (i).

(iii) Cause.—If the Secretary determines that there is a specific reason to require a review more frequently than provided under clause (i) with respect to a State, the Secretary may carry out a review more frequently than provided under that clause.

(4) Responsibility of the states.—

(A) In general.—The States shall be responsible for determining that subrecipients of Federal funds under this title have—

(i) adequate project delivery systems for projects approved under this section; and

(ii) sufficient accounting controls to properly manage such Federal funds.

(B) Periodic review.—The Secretary shall periodically review the monitoring of subrecipients by the States.

(5) Specific oversight responsibilities.—

(A) Effect of section.—Nothing in this section shall affect or discharge any oversight responsibility of the Secretary specifically provided for under this title or other Federal law.

(B) APPALACHIAN DEVELOPMENT HIGHWAYS.—The Secretary shall retain full oversight responsibilities for the design and construction of all Appalachian development highways under section 14501 of title 40.

(h) MAJOR PROJECTS.—

(1) IN GENERAL.—Notwithstanding any other provision of this section, a recipient of Federal financial assistance for a project under this title with an estimated total cost of $500,000,000 or more, and recipients for such other projects as may be identified by the Secretary, shall submit to the Secretary for each project—

(A) a project management plan; and

(B) an annual financial plan, including a phasing plan when applicable.

(2) PROJECT MANAGEMENT PLAN.—A project management plan shall document—

(A) the procedures and processes that are in effect to provide timely information to the project decisionmakers to effectively manage the scope, costs, schedules, and quality of, and the Federal requirements applicable to, the project; and

(B) the role of the agency leadership and management team in the delivery of the project.

(3) FINANCIAL PLAN.—A financial plan—

(A) shall be based on detailed estimates of the cost to complete the project;

(B) shall provide for the annual submission of updates to the Secretary that are based on reasonable assumptions, as determined by the Secretary, of future increases in the cost to complete the project;

(C) may include a phasing plan that identifies fundable incremental improvements or phases that will address the purpose and the need of the project in the short term in the event there are insufficient financial resources to complete the entire project. If a phasing plan is adopted for a project pursuant to this section, the project shall be deemed to satisfy the fiscal constraint requirements in the statewide and metropolitan planning requirements in sections 134 and 135;

(D) for a project in which the project sponsor intends to carry out the project through a public-private partnership agreement, shall include a detailed value for money analysis or similar comparative analysis for the project; and

(E) shall assess the appropriateness of a public-private partnership to deliver the project.

(i) OTHER PROJECTS.—A recipient of Federal financial assistance for a project under this title with an estimated total cost of $100,000,000 or more that is not covered by subsection (h) shall prepare an annual financial plan. Annual financial plans prepared under this subsection shall be made available to the Secretary for review upon the request of the Secretary.

(j) USE OF ADVANCED MODELING TECHNOLOGIES.—

(1) DEFINITION OF ADVANCED MODELING TECHNOLOGY.—In this subsection, the term "advanced modeling technology" means an available or developing technology, including 3-dimensional digital modeling, that can—

(A) accelerate and improve the environmental review process;

(B) increase effective public participation;

(C) enhance the detail and accuracy of project designs;

(D) increase safety;

(E) accelerate construction, and reduce construction costs; or

(F) otherwise expedite project delivery with respect to transportation projects that receive Federal funding.

(2) PROGRAM.—With respect to transportation projects that receive Federal funding, the Secretary shall encourage the use of advanced modeling technologies during environmental, planning, financial management, design, simulation, and construction processes of the projects.

(3) ACTIVITIES.—In carrying out paragraph (2), the Secretary shall—

(A) compile information relating to advanced modeling technologies, including industry best practices with respect to the use of the technologies;

(B) disseminate to States information relating to advanced modeling technologies, including industry best practices with respect to the use of the technologies; and

(C) promote the use of advanced modeling technologies.

(4) COMPREHENSIVE PLAN.—The Secretary shall develop and publish on the public website of the Department of Transportation a detailed and comprehensive plan for the implementation of paragraph (2).

(Pub. L. 85–767, Aug. 27, 1958, 72 Stat. 892; Pub. L. 88–157, §7(a), Oct. 24, 1963, 77 Stat. 278; Pub. L. 91–605, title I, §§106(e), 142, Dec. 31, 1970, 84 Stat. 1717, 1737; Pub. L. 94–280, title I, §114, May 5, 1976, 90 Stat. 436; Pub. L. 100–17, title I, §133(b)(4), Apr. 2, 1987, 101 Stat. 171; Pub. L. 102–240, title I, §§1016(b), 1018(a), Dec. 18, 1991, 105 Stat. 1945, 1948; Pub. L. 104–59, title III, §303, Nov. 28, 1995, 109 Stat. 578; Pub. L. 105–178, title I, §1305(a)–(c), June 9, 1998, 112 Stat. 227–229; Pub. L. 109–59, title I, §1904(a), Aug. 10, 2005, 119 Stat. 1465; Pub. L. 112–141, div. A, title I, §1503(a), July 6, 2012, 126 Stat. 561; Pub. L. 114–94, div. A, title II, §2002(b), Dec. 4, 2015, 129 Stat. 1446; Pub. L. 117–58, div. A, title I, §§11307(f), 11508(d)(1), Nov. 15, 2021, 135 Stat. 534, 587.)

§107. ACQUISITION OF RIGHTS-OF-WAY—INTERSTATE SYSTEM

(a) In any case in which the Secretary is requested by a State to acquire lands or interests in lands (including within the term "interests in lands", the control of access thereto from adjoining lands) required by such State for right-of-way or other purposes in connection with the prosecution of any project for the construction, reconstruction, or improvement of any section of the Interstate System, the Secretary is authorized, in the name of the United States and prior to the approval of title by the Attorney General, to acquire, enter upon, and take possession of such lands or interests in lands by purchase, donation, condemnation, or otherwise in accordance with the laws of the United States (including sections 3114 to 3116 and 3118 of title 40), if—

(1) the Secretary has determined either that the State is unable to acquire necessary lands or interests in lands, or is unable to acquire such lands or interests in lands with sufficient promptness; and

(2) the State has agreed with the Secretary to pay, at such time as may be specified by the Secretary an amount equal to 10 per centum of the costs incurred by the Secretary, in acquiring such lands or interests in lands, or such lesser percentage which represents the State's pro rata share of project costs as determined in accordance with subsection (c) [1] of section 120 of this title.

The authority granted by this section shall also apply to lands and interests in lands received as grants of land from the United States and owned or held by railroads or other corporations.

(b) The costs incurred by the Secretary in acquiring any such lands or interests in lands may include the cost of examination and abstract of title, certificate of title, advertising, and any fees incidental to such acquisition. All costs incurred by the Secretary in connection with the acquisition of any such lands or interests in lands shall be paid from the funds for construction, reconstruction, or improvement of the Interstate System apportioned to the State upon the request of which such lands or interests in lands are acquired, and any sums paid to the Secretary by such State as its share of the costs of acquisition of such lands or interests in lands shall be deposited in the Treasury to the credit of the appropriation for Federal-aid highways and shall be credited to the amount apportioned to such State as its apportionment of funds for construction, reconstruction, or improvement of the Interstate System, or shall be deducted from other moneys due the State for reimbursement from funds authorized to be appropriated under section 108(b) of the Federal-Aid Highway Act of 1956.

(c) The Secretary is further authorized and directed by proper deed, executed in the name of the United States, to convey any such lands or interests in lands acquired in any State under the provisions of this section, except the outside five feet of any such right-of-way in any State which does not provide control of access, to the State transportation department of such State or such political subdivision thereof as its laws may provide, upon such terms and conditions as to such lands or interests in lands as may be agreed upon by the Secretary and the State transportation department or political subdivisions to which the conveyance is to be made. Whenever the State makes provision for control of access satisfactory to the Secretary, the outside five feet then shall be conveyed to the State by the Secretary, as herein provided.

(d) Whenever rights-of-way, including control of access, on the Interstate System are required over lands or interests in lands owned by the United States, the Secretary may make such arrangements with the agency having jurisdiction over such lands as may be necessary to give the State or other person constructing the projects on such lands adequate rights-of-way and control of access thereto from adjoining lands, and any such agency is directed to cooperate with the Secretary in this connection.

(Pub. L. 85–767, Aug. 27, 1958, 72 Stat. 892; Pub. L. 105–178, title I, §1212(a)(2)(A)(i), June 9, 1998, 112 Stat. 193; Pub. L. 109–284, §3(1), Sept. 27, 2006, 120 Stat. 1211.)

    [1] *See References in Text note below.*

§108. ADVANCE ACQUISITION OF REAL PROPERTY

(a) IN GENERAL.—

(1) AVAILABILITY OF FUNDS.—For the purpose of facilitating the timely and economical acquisition of real property interests for a transportation improvement eligible for funding under this title, the Secretary, upon the request of a State, may make available, for the acquisition of real property interests, such funds apportioned to the State as may be expended on the transportation improvement, under such rules and regulations as the Secretary may issue.

(2) CONSTRUCTION.—The agreement between the Secretary and the State for the reimbursement of the cost of the real property interests shall provide for the actual

construction of the transportation improvement within a period not to exceed 20 years following the fiscal year for which the request is made, unless the Secretary determines that a longer period is reasonable.

(b) Federal participation in the cost of real property interests acquired under subsection (a) of this section shall not exceed the Federal pro rata share applicable to the class of funds from which Federal reimbursement is made.

(c) STATE-FUNDED EARLY ACQUISITION OF REAL PROPERTY INTERESTS.—

(1) IN GENERAL.—A State may carry out, at the expense of the State, acquisitions of interests in real property for a project before completion of the review process required for the project under the National Environmental Policy Act of 1969 (42 U.S.C. 4321 et seq.) without affecting subsequent approvals required for the project by the State or any Federal agency.

(2) ELIGIBILITY FOR REIMBURSEMENT.—Subject to paragraph (3), funds apportioned to a State under this title may be used to participate in the payment of—

(A) costs incurred by the State for acquisition of real property interests, acquired in advance of any Federal approval or authorization, if the real property interests are subsequently incorporated into a project eligible for surface transportation block grant program funds; and

(B) costs incurred by the State for the acquisition of land necessary to preserve environmental and scenic values.

(3) TERMS AND CONDITIONS.—The Federal share payable of the costs described in paragraph (2) shall be eligible for reimbursement out of funds apportioned to a State under this title when the real property interests acquired are incorporated into a project eligible for surface transportation block grant program funds, if the State demonstrates to the Secretary and the Secretary finds that—

(A) any land acquired, and relocation assistance provided, complied with the Uniform Relocation Assistance and Real Property Acquisition Policies Act of 1970;

(B) the requirements of title VI of the Civil Rights Act of 1964 have been complied with;

(C) the State has a mandatory comprehensive and coordinated land use, environment, and transportation planning process under State law and the acquisition is certified by the Governor as consistent with the State plans before the acquisition;

(D) the acquisition is determined in advance by the Governor to be consistent with the State transportation planning process pursuant to section 135 of this title;

(E) the alternative for which the real property interest is acquired is selected by the State pursuant to regulations to be issued by the Secretary which provide for the consideration of the environmental impacts of various alternatives;

(F) before the time that the cost incurred by a State is approved for Federal participation, environmental compliance pursuant to the National Environmental Policy Act of 1969 (42 U.S.C. 4321 et seq.) has been completed for the project for which the real property interest was acquired by the State, and the acquisition has been approved by the Secretary under this title, and in compliance with section 303 of title 49, section 7 of the Endangered Species Act, and all other applicable environmental laws shall be identified by the Secretary in regulations; and

(G) before the time that the cost incurred by a State is approved for Federal participation, the Secretary has determined that the property acquired in advance of Federal approval or authorization did not influence the environmental assessment of the project, the decision relative to the need to construct the project, or the selection of the project design or location.

(d) FEDERALLY FUNDED EARLY ACQUISITION OF REAL PROPERTY INTERESTS.—

(1) DEFINITION OF ACQUISITION OF A REAL PROPERTY INTEREST.—In this subsection, the term "acquisition of a real property interest" includes the acquisition of—

(A) any interest in land;

(B) a contractual right to acquire any interest in land; or

(C) any other similar action to acquire or preserve rights-of-way for a transportation facility.

(2) AUTHORIZATION.—The Secretary may authorize the use of funds apportioned to a State under this title for the acquisition of a real property interest by a State.

(3) STATE CERTIFICATION.—A State requesting Federal funding for an acquisition of a real property interest shall certify in writing, with concurrence by the Secretary, that—

(A) the State has authority to acquire the real property interest under State law; and

(B) the acquisition of the real property interest—

(i) is for a transportation purpose;

(ii) will not cause any significant adverse environmental impact;

(iii) will not limit the choice of reasonable alternatives for the project or otherwise influence the decision of the Secretary on any approval required for the project;

(iv) does not prevent the lead agency from making an impartial decision as to whether to accept an alternative that is being considered in the environmental review process;

(v) is consistent with the State transportation planning process under section 135;

(vi) complies with other applicable Federal laws (including regulations);

(vii) will be acquired through negotiation, without the threat of condemnation; and

(viii) will not result in a reduction or elimination of benefits or assistance to a displaced person required by the Uniform Relocation Assistance and Real Property Acquisition Policies Act of 1970 (42 U.S.C. 4601 et seq.) and title VI of the Civil Rights Act of 1964 (42 U.S.C. 2000d et seq.).

(4) ENVIRONMENTAL COMPLIANCE.—

(A) IN GENERAL.—Before authorizing Federal funding for an acquisition of a real property interest, the Secretary shall complete the review process under the National Environmental Policy Act of 1969 (42 U.S.C. 4321 et seq.) with respect to the acquisition of the real property interest.

(B) INDEPENDENT UTILITY.—The acquisition of a real property interest—

(i) shall be treated as having independent utility for purposes of the review process under the National Environmental Policy Act of 1969 (42 U.S.C. 4321 et seq.); and

(ii) shall not limit consideration of alternatives for future transportation improvements with respect to the real property interest.

(5) PROGRAMMING.—

(A) IN GENERAL.—The acquisition of a real property interest for which Federal funding is requested shall be included as a project in an applicable transportation improvement program under sections 134 and 135 and sections 5303 and 5304 of title 49.

(B) ACQUISITION PROJECT.—The acquisition project may consist of the acquisition of a specific parcel, a portion of a transportation corridor, or an entire transportation corridor.

(6) DEVELOPMENT.—Real property interests acquired under this subsection may not be developed in anticipation of a project until all required environmental reviews for the project have been completed.

(7) REIMBURSEMENT.—If Federal-aid reimbursement is made for real property interests acquired early under this section and the real property interests are not subsequently incorporated into a project eligible for surface transportation funds within the time allowed by subsection (a)(2), the Secretary shall offset the amount reimbursed against funds apportioned to the State.

(8) OTHER REQUIREMENTS AND CONDITIONS.—

(A) APPLICABLE LAW.—The acquisition of a real property interest shall be carried out in compliance with all requirements applicable to the acquisition of real property interests for federally funded transportation projects.

(B) ADDITIONAL CONDITIONS.—The Secretary may establish such other conditions or restrictions on acquisitions under this subsection as the Secretary determines to be appropriate.

(Pub. L. 85–767, Aug. 27, 1958, 72 Stat. 893; Pub. L. 86–35, §1, May 29, 1959, 73 Stat. 62; Pub. L. 90–495, §7(a), (b), Aug. 23, 1968, 82 Stat. 818; Pub. L. 93–87, title I, §113, Aug. 13, 1973, 87 Stat. 257; Pub. L. 94–280, title I, §115, May 5, 1976, 90 Stat. 436; Pub. L. 102–240, title I, §1017(a), (b), Dec. 18, 1991, 105 Stat. 1947; Pub. L. 102–388, title III, §346, Oct. 6, 1992, 106 Stat. 1553; Pub. L. 103–429, §3(2), Oct. 31, 1994, 108 Stat. 4377; Pub. L. 105–178, title I, §§1211(e)(1), 1301(a), June 9, 1998, 112 Stat. 188, 225; Pub. L. 112–141, div. A, title I, §1302, July 6, 2012, 126 Stat. 528; Pub. L. 114–94, div. A, title I, §1109(c)(5), Dec. 4, 2015, 129 Stat. 1343; Pub. L. 117–58, div. A, title I, §11525(c), Nov. 15, 2021, 135 Stat. 607.)

§109. STANDARDS

(a) IN GENERAL.—The Secretary shall ensure that the plans and specifications for each proposed highway project under this chapter provide for a facility that will—

(1) adequately serve the existing and planned future traffic of the highway in a manner that is conducive to safety, durability, and economy of maintenance; and

(2) be designed and constructed in accordance with criteria best suited to accomplish the objectives described in paragraph (1) and to conform to the particular needs of each locality.

(b) The geometric and construction standards to be adopted for the Interstate System shall be those approved by the Secretary in cooperation with the State transportation departments. Such standards, as applied to each actual construction project, shall be adequate to enable such project to accommodate the types and volumes of traffic anticipated for such project for the twenty-year period commencing on the date of approval by the Secretary, under section 106 of this title, of the plans, specifications, and estimates for actual construction of such project. Such standards shall in all cases provide for at least four lanes of traffic. The right-of-way width of the Interstate System shall be adequate to permit construction of projects on the Interstate System to such standards. The Secretary shall apply such standards uniformly throughout all the States.

(c) DESIGN CRITERIA FOR NATIONAL HIGHWAY SYSTEM.—

(1) IN GENERAL.—A design for new construction, reconstruction, resurfacing (except for maintenance resurfacing), restoration, or rehabilitation of a highway on the National Highway System (other than a highway also on the Interstate System) shall consider, in addition to the criteria described in subsection (a)—

(A) the constructed and natural environment of the area;

(B) the environmental, scenic, aesthetic, historic, community, and preservation impacts of the activity;

(C) cost savings by utilizing flexibility that exists in current design guidance and regulations; and

(D) access for other modes of transportation.

(2) DEVELOPMENT OF CRITERIA.—The Secretary, in cooperation with State transportation departments, may develop criteria to implement paragraph (1). In developing criteria under this paragraph, the Secretary shall consider—

(A) the results of the committee process of the American Association of State Highway and Transportation Officials as used in adopting and publishing "A Policy on Geometric Design of Highways and Streets", including comments submitted by interested parties as part of such process;

(B) the publication entitled "Flexibility in Highway Design" of the Federal Highway Administration;

(C) "Eight Characteristics of Process to Yield Excellence and the Seven Qualities of Excellence in Transportation Design" developed by the conference held during 1998 entitled "Thinking Beyond the Pavement National Workshop on Integrating Highway Development with Communities and the Environment while Maintaining Safety and Performance";

(D) the publication entitled "Highway Safety Manual" of the American Association of State Highway and Transportation Officials;

(E) the publication entitled "Urban Street Design Guide" of the National Association of City Transportation Officials;

(F) the publication of the Federal Highway Administration entitled "Wildlife Crossing Structure Handbook: Design and Evaluation in North America" and dated March 2011; and

(G) any other material that the Secretary determines to be appropriate.

(d) MANUAL ON UNIFORM TRAFFIC CONTROL DEVICES.—

(1) IN GENERAL.—On any highway project in which Federal funds hereafter participate, or on any such project constructed since December 20, 1944, the location, form and character of informational, regulatory and warning signs, curb and pavement or other markings, and traffic signals installed or placed by any public

authority or other agency, shall be subject to the approval of the State transportation department with the concurrence of the Secretary, who is directed to concur only in such installations as will promote the safety, inclusion, and mobility of all users and efficient utilization of the highways.

(2) UPDATES.—Not later than 18 months after the date of enactment of the Surface Transportation Reauthorization Act of 2021 and not less frequently than every 4 years thereafter, the Secretary shall update the Manual on Uniform Traffic Control Devices.

(e) INSTALLATION OF SAFETY DEVICES.—

(1) HIGHWAY AND RAILROAD GRADE CROSSINGS AND DRAWBRIDGES.—No funds shall be approved for expenditure on any Federal-aid highway, or highway affected under chapter 2 of this title, unless proper safety protective devices complying with safety standards determined by the Secretary at that time as being adequate shall be installed or be in operation at any highway and railroad grade crossing or drawbridge on that portion of the highway with respect to which such expenditures are to be made.

(2) TEMPORARY TRAFFIC CONTROL DEVICES.—No funds shall be approved for expenditure on any Federal-aid highway, or highway affected under chapter 2, unless proper temporary traffic control devices to improve safety in work zones will be installed and maintained during construction, utility, and maintenance operations on that portion of the highway with respect to which such expenditures are to be made. Installation and maintenance of the devices shall be in accordance with the Manual on Uniform Traffic Control Devices.

(f) The Secretary shall not, as a condition precedent to his approval under section 106 of this title, require any State to acquire title to, or control of, any marginal land along the proposed highway in addition to that reasonably necessary for road surfaces, median strips, bikeways, pedestrian walkways, gutters, ditches, and side slopes, and of sufficient width to provide service roads for adjacent property to permit safe access at controlled locations in order to expedite traffic, promote safety, and minimize roadside parking.

(g) Not later than January 30, 1971, the Secretary shall issue guidelines for minimizing possible soil erosion from highway construction. Such guidelines shall apply to all proposed projects with respect to which plans, specifications, and estimates are approved by the Secretary after the issuance of such guidelines.

(h) Not later than July 1, 1972, the Secretary, after consultation with appropriate Federal and State officials, shall submit to Congress, and not later than 90 days after such submission, promulgate guidelines designed to assure that possible adverse economic, social, and environmental effects relating to any proposed project on any Federal-aid system have been fully considered in developing such project, and that the final decisions on the project are made in the best overall public interest, taking into consideration the need for fast, safe and efficient transportation, public services, and the costs of eliminating or minimizing such adverse effects and the following:

(1) air, noise, and water pollution;

(2) destruction or disruption of man-made and natural resources, aesthetic values, community cohesion and the availability of public facilities and services;

(3) adverse employment effects, and tax and property value losses;

(4) injurious displacement of people, businesses and farms; and

(5) disruption of desirable community and regional growth.

Such guidelines shall apply to all proposed projects with respect to which plans, specifications, and estimates are approved by the Secretary after the issuance of such guidelines.

(i) The Secretary, after consultation with appropriate Federal, State, and local officials, shall develop and promulgate standards for highway noise levels compatible with different land uses and after July 1, 1972, shall not approve plans and specifications for any proposed project on any Federal-aid system for which location approval has not yet been secured unless he determines that such plans and specifications include adequate measures to implement the appropriate noise level standards. The Secretary, after consultation with the Administrator of the Environmental Protection Agency and appropriate Federal, State, and local officials, may promulgate standards for the control of highway noise levels for highways on any Federal-aid system for which project approval has been secured prior to July 1, 1972. The Secretary may approve any project on a Federal-aid system to which noise-level standards are made applicable under the preceding sentence for the purpose of carrying out such standards. Such project may include, but is not limited to, the acquisition of additional rights-of-way, the construction of physical barriers, and landscaping. Sums apportioned for the Federal-aid system on which such project will be located shall be available to finance the Federal share of such project. Such project shall be deemed a highway project for all purposes of this title.

(j) The Secretary, after consultation with the Administrator of the Environmental Protection Agency, shall develop and promulgate guidelines to assure that highways constructed pursuant to this title are consistent with any approved plan for—

(1) the implementation of a national ambient air quality standard for each pollutant for which an area is designated as a nonattainment area under section 107(d) of the Clean Air Act (42 U.S.C. 7407(d)); or

(2) the maintenance of a national ambient air quality standard in an area that was designated as a nonattainment area but that was later redesignated by the Administrator as an attainment area for the standard and that is required to develop a maintenance plan under section 175A of the Clean Air Act (42 U.S.C. 7505a).

(k) The Secretary shall not approve any project involving approaches to a bridge under this title, if such project and bridge will significantly affect the traffic volume and the highway system of a contiguous State without first taking into full consideration the views of that State.

(l)(1) In determining whether any right-of-way on any Federal-aid highway should be used for accommodating any utility facility, the Secretary shall—

(A) first ascertain the effect such use will have on highway and traffic safety, since in no case shall any use be authorized or otherwise permitted, under this or any other provision of law, which would adversely affect safety;

(B) evaluate the direct and indirect environmental and economic effects of any loss of productive agricultural land or any impairment of the productivity of any agricultural land which would result from the disapproval of the use of such right-of-way for the accommodation of such utility facility; and

(C) consider such environmental and economic effects together with any interference with or impairment of the use of the highway in such right-of-way which would result from the use of such right-of-way for the accommodation of such utility facility.

(2) For the purpose of this subsection—

(A) the term "utility facility" means any privately, publicly, or cooperatively owned line, facility, or system for producing, transmitting, or distributing communications, power, electricity, light, heat, gas, oil, crude products, water, steam, waste, storm water not connected with highway drainage, or any other similar commodity, including any fire or police signal system or street lighting system, which directly or indirectly serves the public; and

(B) the term "right-of-way" means any real property, or interest therein, acquired, dedicated, or reserved for the construction, operation, and maintenance of a highway.

(m) PROTECTION OF NONMOTORIZED TRANSPORTATION TRAFFIC.—The Secretary shall not approve any project or take any regulatory action under this title that will result in the severance of an existing major route or have significant adverse impact on the safety for nonmotorized transportation traffic and light motorcycles, unless such project or regulatory action provides for a reasonable alternate route or such a route exists.

(n) It is the intent of Congress that any project for resurfacing, restoring, or rehabilitating any highway, other than a highway access to which is fully controlled, in which Federal funds participate shall be constructed in accordance with standards to preserve and extend the service life of highways and enhance highway safety.

(o) COMPLIANCE WITH STATE LAWS FOR NON-NHS PROJECTS.—

(A) [1] IN GENERAL.—Projects (other than highway projects on the National Highway System) shall be designed, constructed, operated, and maintained in accordance with State laws, regulations, directives, safety standards, design standards, and construction standards.

(B) [1] LOCAL JURISDICTIONS.—Notwithstanding subparagraph (A), a local jurisdiction may use a roadway design guide recognized by the Federal Highway Administration and adopted by the local jurisdiction that is different from the roadway design guide used by the State in which the local jurisdiction is located for the design of projects on all roadways under the ownership of the local jurisdiction (other than a highway on the National Highway System) for which the local jurisdiction is the project sponsor, provided that the design complies with all other applicable Federal laws.

(p) SCENIC AND HISTORIC VALUES.—Notwithstanding subsections (b) and (c), the Secretary may approve a project for the National Highway System if the project is designed to—

(1) allow for the preservation of environmental, scenic, or historic values;

(2) ensure safe use of the facility; and

(3) comply with subsection (a).

(q) PHASE CONSTRUCTION.—Safety considerations for a project under this title may be met by phase construction consistent with the operative safety management system established in accordance with a statewide transportation improvement program approved by the Secretary.

(r) PAVEMENT MARKINGS.—The Secretary shall not approve any pavement markings project that includes the use of glass beads containing more than 200 parts per million of arsenic or lead, as determined in accordance with Environmental Protection Agency

[§110. Repealed. Pub. L. 112–141, div. A, title I, §1519(b)(1)(A), July 6, 2012, 126 Stat. 575]

CHAPTER 1—FEDERAL-AID HIGHWAYS

testing methods 3052, 6010B, or 6010C.

(s) ELECTRIC VEHICLE CHARGING STATIONS.—

(1) STANDARDS.—Electric vehicle charging infrastructure installed using funds provided under this title shall provide, at a minimum—

(A) non-proprietary charging connectors that meet applicable industry safety standards; and

(B) open access to payment methods that are available to all members of the public to ensure secure, convenient, and equal access to the electric vehicle charging infrastructure that shall not be limited by membership to a particular payment provider.

(2) TREATMENT OF PROJECTS.—Notwithstanding any other provision of law, a project to install electric vehicle charging infrastructure using funds provided under this title shall be treated as if the project is located on a Federal-aid highway.

(Pub. L. 85–767, Aug. 27, 1958, 72 Stat. 894; Pub. L. 88–157, §4, Oct. 24, 1963, 77 Stat. 277; Pub. L. 89–574, §§5(a), 14, Sept. 13, 1966, 80 Stat. 767, 771; Pub. L. 91–605, title I, §136(a), (b), Dec. 31, 1970, 84 Stat. 1734; Pub. L. 93–87, title I, §§114, 152(2), 156, Aug. 13, 1973, 87 Stat. 257, 276, 277; Pub. L. 95–599, title I, §§113, 116(d), 141(f), (g), Nov. 6, 1978, 92 Stat. 2696, 2699, 2711; Pub. L. 96–106, §3, Nov. 9, 1979, 93 Stat. 797; Pub. L. 97–424, title I, §110(a), Jan. 6, 1983, 96 Stat. 2105; Pub. L. 102–240, title I, §1016(c)–(f)(1), Dec. 18, 1991, 105 Stat. 1946; Pub. L. 104–59, title III, §§304, 305(a), Nov. 28, 1995, 109 Stat. 579, 580; Pub. L. 105–178, title I, §§1202(c), 1212(a)(2)(A), 1306, June 9, 1998, 112 Stat. 169, 193, 229; Pub. L. 109–59, title I, §1110(a), (c), title VI, §6008, Aug. 10, 2005, 119 Stat. 1170, 1171, 1874; Pub. L. 112–141, div. A, title I, §§1504, 1519(c)(3), formerly §1519(c)(4), July 6, 2012, 126 Stat. 564, 575, renumbered §1519(c)(3), Pub. L. 114–94, div. A, title I, §1446(d)(5)(B), Dec. 4, 2015, 129 Stat. 1438; Pub. L. 114–94, div. A, title I, §1404(a), Dec. 4, 2015, 129 Stat. 1409; Pub. L. 117–58, div. A, title I, §§11123(d), 11129, Nov. 15, 2021, 135 Stat. 506, 508.)

[1] *Designations so in original.*

[§110. REPEALED. PUB. L. 112–141, DIV. A, TITLE I, §1519(B)(1)(A), JULY 6, 2012, 126 STAT. 575]

Section, added and amended Pub. L. 105–178, title I, §1105(a), (c), June 9, 1998, 112 Stat. 130; Pub. L. 105–206, title IX, §9002(e), July 22, 1998, 112 Stat. 835; Pub. L. 106–113, div. B, §1000(a)(5) [title III, §304], Nov. 29, 1999, 113 Stat. 1536, 1501A–306; Pub. L. 106–159, title I, §102(a)(2), Dec. 9, 1999, 113 Stat. 1752; Pub. L. 109–59, title I, §1105(a)–(e), Aug. 10, 2005, 119 Stat. 1165, 1166, related to revenue aligned budget authority.

Another section 110 was renumbered section 126 of this title.

A prior section 110, Pub. L. 85–767, Aug. 27, 1958, 72 Stat. 894, related to project agreements, prior to repeal by Pub. L. 105–178, title I, §1105(a), June 9, 1998, 112 Stat. 130.

§111. AGREEMENTS RELATING TO USE OF AND ACCESS TO RIGHTS-OF-WAY—INTERSTATE SYSTEM

(a) IN GENERAL.—All agreements between the Secretary and the State transportation department for the construction of projects on the Interstate System shall contain a clause providing that the State will not add any points of access to, or exit from, the project in addition to those approved by the Secretary in the plans for such project, without the prior approval of the Secretary. Such agreements shall also contain a clause providing that the State will not permit automotive service stations or other commercial establishments for serving motor vehicle users to be constructed or located on the rights-of-way of the Interstate System and will not change the boundary of any right-of-way on the Interstate System to accommodate construction of, or afford access to, an automotive service station or other commercial establishment. Such agreements may, however, authorize a State or political subdivision thereof to use or permit the use of the airspace above and below the established grade line of the highway pavement for such purposes as will not impair the full use and safety of the highway, as will not require or permit vehicular access to such space directly from such established grade line of the highway, or otherwise interfere in any way with the free flow of traffic on the Interstate System. Nothing in this section, or in any agreement entered into under this section, shall require the discontinuance, obstruction, or removal of any establishment for serving motor vehicle users on any highway which has been, or is hereafter, designated as a highway or route on the Interstate System (1) if such establishment (A) was in existence before January 1, 1960, (B) is owned by a State, and (C) is operated through concessionaries or otherwise, and (2) if all access to, and exits from, such establishment conform to the standards established for such a highway under this title.

(b) REST AREAS.—

(1) IN GENERAL.—Notwithstanding subsection (a), the Secretary shall permit a State to acquire, construct, operate, and maintain a rest area along a highway on the Interstate System in such State.

(2) LIMITED ACTIVITIES.—The Secretary shall permit limited commercial activities within a rest area under paragraph (1), if the activities are available only to customers using the rest area and are limited to—

(A) commercial advertising and media displays if such advertising and displays are—

(i) exhibited solely within any facility constructed in the rest area; and

(ii) not legible from the main traveled way;

(B) items designed to promote tourism in the State, limited to books, DVDs, and other media;

(C) tickets for events or attractions in the State of a historical or tourism-related nature;

(D) travel-related information, including maps, travel booklets, and hotel coupon booklets; and

(E) lottery machines, provided that the priority afforded to blind vendors under subsection (c) applies to this subparagraph.

(3) PRIVATE OPERATORS.—A State may permit a private party to operate such commercial activities.

(4) LIMITATION ON USE OF REVENUES.—A State shall use any revenues received from the commercial activities in a rest area under this section to cover the costs of acquiring, constructing, operating, and maintaining rest areas in the State.

(c) VENDING MACHINES.—Notwithstanding subsection (a), any State may permit the placement of vending machines in rest and recreation areas, and in safety rest areas, constructed or located on rights-of-way of the Interstate System in such State. Such vending machines may only dispense such food, drink, and other articles as the

State transportation department determines are appropriate and desirable. Such vending machines may only be operated by the State. In permitting the placement of vending machines, the State shall give priority to vending machines which are operated through the State licensing agency designated pursuant to section 2(a)(5) of the Act of June 20, 1936, commonly known as the "Randolph-Sheppard Act" (20 U.S.C. 107a(a)(5)). The costs of installation, operation, and maintenance of vending machines shall not be eligible for Federal assistance under this title.

(d) MOTORIST CALL BOXES.—

(1) IN GENERAL.—Notwithstanding subsection (a), a State may permit the placement of motorist call boxes on rights-of-way of the National Highway System. Such motorist call boxes may include the identification and sponsorship logos of such call boxes.

(2) SPONSORSHIP LOGOS.—

(A) APPROVAL BY STATE AND LOCAL AGENCIES.—All call box installations displaying sponsorship logos under this subsection shall be approved by the highway agencies having jurisdiction of the highway on which they are located.

(B) SIZE ON BOX.—A sponsorship logo may be placed on the call box in a dimension not to exceed the size of the call box or a total dimension in excess of 12 inches by 18 inches.

(C) SIZE ON IDENTIFICATION SIGN.—Sponsorship logos in a dimension not to exceed 12 inches by 30 inches may be displayed on a call box identification sign affixed to the call box post.

(D) SPACING OF SIGNS.—Sponsorship logos affixed to an identification sign on a call box post may be located on the rights-of-way at intervals not more frequently than 1 per every 5 miles.

(E) DISTRIBUTION THROUGHOUT STATE.—Within a State, at least 20 percent of the call boxes displaying sponsorship logos shall be located on highways outside of urbanized areas with a population greater than 50,000.

(3) NONSAFETY HAZARDS.—The call boxes and their location, posts, foundations, and mountings shall be consistent with requirements of the Manual on Uniform Traffic Control Devices or any requirements deemed necessary by the Secretary to assure that the call boxes shall not be a safety hazard to motorists.

(e) JUSTIFICATION REPORTS.—If the Secretary requests or requires a justification report for a project that would add a point of access to, or exit from, the Interstate System (including new or modified freeway-to-crossroad interchanges inside a transportation management area), the Secretary may permit a State transportation department to approve the report.

(Pub. L. 85–767, Aug. 27, 1958, 72 Stat. 895; Pub. L. 87–61, title I, §104(a), June 29, 1961, 75 Stat. 122; Pub. L. 95–599, title I, §114, Nov. 6, 1978, 92 Stat. 2697; Pub. L. 100–17, title I, §110(a), Apr. 2, 1987, 101 Stat. 146; Pub. L. 104–59, title III, §306, Nov. 28, 1995, 109 Stat. 580; Pub. L. 105–178, title I, §1212(a)(2)(A)(i), June 9, 1998, 112 Stat. 193; Pub. L. 109–59, title I, §1412, Aug. 10, 2005, 119 Stat. 1234; Pub. L. 110–244, title I, §104, June 6, 2008, 122 Stat. 1578; Pub. L. 112–141, div. A, title I, §§1505, 1539(a), July 6, 2012, 126 Stat. 564, 587; Pub. L. 114–94, div. A, title I, §1405, Dec. 4, 2015, 129 Stat. 1410.)

§112. Letting of contracts

(a) In all cases where the construction is to be performed by the State transportation department or under its supervision, a request for submission of bids shall be made by advertisement unless some other method is approved by the Secretary. The Secretary shall require such plans and specifications and such methods of bidding as shall be effective in securing competition.

(b) Bidding Requirements.—

(1) In general.—Subject to paragraphs (2) and (3), construction of each project, subject to the provisions of subsection (a) of this section, shall be performed by contract awarded by competitive bidding, unless the State transportation department demonstrates, to the satisfaction of the Secretary, that some other method is more cost effective or that an emergency exists. Contracts for the construction of each project shall be awarded only on the basis of the lowest responsive bid submitted by a bidder meeting established criteria of responsibility. No requirement or obligation shall be imposed as a condition precedent to the award of a contract to such bidder for a project, or to the Secretary's concurrence in the award of a contract to such bidder, unless such requirement or obligation is otherwise lawful and is specifically set forth in the advertised specifications.

(2) Contracting for engineering and design services.—

(A) General rule.—Subject to paragraph (3), each contract for program management, construction management, feasibility studies, preliminary engineering, design, engineering, surveying, mapping, or architectural related services with respect to a project subject to the provisions of subsection (a) of this section shall be awarded in the same manner as a contract for architectural and engineering services is negotiated under chapter 11 of title 40.

(B) Performance and audits.—Any contract or subcontract awarded in accordance with subparagraph (A), whether funded in whole or in part with Federal-aid highway funds, shall be performed and audited in compliance with cost principles contained in the Federal Acquisition Regulations of part 31 of title 48, Code of Federal Regulations.

(C) Indirect cost rates.—Instead of performing its own audits, a recipient of funds under a contract or subcontract awarded in accordance with subparagraph (A) shall accept indirect cost rates established in accordance with the Federal Acquisition Regulations for 1-year applicable accounting periods by a cognizant Federal or State government agency, if such rates are not currently under dispute.

(D) Application of rates.—Once a firm's indirect cost rates are accepted under this paragraph, the recipient of the funds shall apply such rates for the purposes of contract estimation, negotiation, administration, reporting, and contract payment and shall not be limited by administrative or de facto ceilings of any kind.

(E) Prenotification; confidentiality of data.—A recipient of funds requesting or using the cost and rate data described in subparagraph (D) shall notify any affected firm before such request or use. Such data shall be confidential and shall not be accessible or provided, in whole or in part, to another firm or to any government agency which is not part of the group of agencies sharing cost data under this paragraph, except by written permission of the audited firm. If prohibited by law, such cost and rate data shall not be disclosed under any circumstances.

(F) EXCLUSION.—Subparagraphs (B), (C), (D) and (E) herein shall not apply to the States of West Virginia or Minnesota.

(3) DESIGN-BUILD CONTRACTING.—

(A) IN GENERAL.—A State transportation department or local transportation agency may award a design-build contract for a qualified project described in subparagraph (C) using any procurement process permitted by applicable State and local law.

(B) LIMITATION ON FINAL DESIGN.—Final design under a design-build contract referred to in subparagraph (A) shall not commence before compliance with section 102 of the National Environmental Policy Act of 1969 (42 U.S.C. 4332).

(C) QUALIFIED PROJECTS.—A qualified project referred to in subparagraph (A) is a project under this chapter (including intermodal projects) for which the Secretary has approved the use of design-build contracting under criteria specified in regulations issued by the Secretary.

(D) REGULATORY PROCESS.—Not later than 90 days after the date of enactment of the SAFETEA–LU, the Secretary shall issue revised regulations under section 1307(c) of the Transportation Equity Act for 21st Century (23 U.S.C. 112 note; 112 Stat. 230) that—

(i) do not preclude a State transportation department or local transportation agency, prior to compliance with section 102 of the National Environmental Policy Act of 1969 (42 U.S.C. 4332), from—

(I) issuing requests for proposals;

(II) proceeding with awards of design-build contracts; or

(III) issuing notices to proceed with preliminary design work under design-build contracts;

(ii) require that the State transportation department or local transportation agency receive concurrence from the Secretary before carrying out an activity under clause (i); and

(iii) preclude the design-build contractor from proceeding with final design or construction of any permanent improvement prior to completion of the process under such section 102.

(E) DESIGN-BUILD CONTRACT DEFINED.—In this paragraph, the term "design-build contract" means an agreement that provides for design and construction of a project by a contractor, regardless of whether the agreement is in the form of a design-build contract, a franchise agreement, or any other form of contract approved by the Secretary.

(4) METHOD OF CONTRACTING.—

(A) IN GENERAL.—

(i) 2-PHASE CONTRACT.—A contracting agency may award a 2-phase contract to a construction manager or general contractor for preconstruction and construction services.

(ii) PRECONSTRUCTION SERVICES PHASE.—In the preconstruction services phase of a contract under this paragraph, the contractor shall provide the contracting agency with advice for scheduling, work sequencing, cost engineering, constructability, cost estimating, and risk identification.

(iii) AGREEMENT.—Prior to the start of the construction services phase, the contracting agency and the contractor may agree to a price and other factors specified in regulation for the construction of the project or a portion of the project.

(iv) CONSTRUCTION PHASE.—If an agreement is reached under clause (iii), the contractor shall be responsible for the construction of the project or portion of the project at the negotiated price and in compliance with the other factors specified in the agreement.

(B) SELECTION.—A contract shall be awarded to a contractor under this paragraph using a competitive selection process based on qualifications, experience, best value, or any other combination of factors considered appropriate by the contracting agency.

(C) TIMING.—

(i) RELATIONSHIP TO NEPA PROCESS.—Prior to the completion of the environmental review process required under section 102 of the National Environmental Policy Act of 1969 (42 U.S.C. 4332), a contracting agency may—

(I) issue requests for proposals;

(II) proceed with the award of a contract for preconstruction services under subparagraph (A)(ii); and

(III) issue notices to proceed with a preliminary design and any work related to preliminary design, to the extent that those actions do not limit any reasonable range of alternatives.

(ii) CONSTRUCTION SERVICES PHASE.—A contracting agency shall not proceed with the award of the construction services phase of a contract under subparagraph (A)(iv) and shall not proceed, or permit any consultant or contractor to proceed, with final design or construction until completion of the environmental review process required under section 102 of the National Environmental Policy Act of 1969 (42 U.S.C. 4332).

(iii) APPROVAL REQUIREMENT.—Prior to authorizing construction activities, the Secretary shall approve—

(I) the price estimate of the contracting agency for the entire project; and

(II) any price agreement with the general contractor for the project or a portion of the project.

(iv) DESIGN ACTIVITIES.—

(I) IN GENERAL.—A contracting agency may proceed, at the expense of the contracting agency, with design activities at any level of detail for a project before completion of the review process required for the project under the National Environmental Policy Act of 1969 (42 U.S.C. 4321 et seq.) without affecting subsequent approvals required for the project.

(II) REIMBURSEMENT.—Design activities carried out under subclause (I) shall be eligible for Federal reimbursement as a project expense in accordance with the requirements under section 109(r).

(v) TERMINATION PROVISION.—The Secretary shall require a contract to include an appropriate termination provision in the event that a no-build alternative is selected.

(c) The Secretary shall require as a condition precedent to his approval of each contract awarded by competitive bidding pursuant to subsection (b) of this section, and subject to the provisions of this section, a sworn statement, executed by, or on behalf of, the person, firm, association, or corporation to whom such contract is to be awarded, certifying that such person, firm, association, or corporation has not, either directly or indirectly, entered into any agreement, participated in any collusion, or otherwise taken any action in restraint of free competitive bidding in connection with such contract.

(d) No contract awarded by competitive bidding pursuant to subsection (b) of this section, and subject to the provisions of this section, shall be entered into by any State transportation department or local subdivision of the State without compliance with the provisions of this section, and without the prior concurrence of the Secretary in the award thereof.

(e) STANDARDIZED CONTRACT CLAUSE CONCERNING SITE CONDITIONS.—

(1) GENERAL RULE.—The Secretary shall issue regulations establishing and requiring, for inclusion in each contract entered into with respect to any project approved under section 106 of this title a contract clause, developed in accordance with guidelines established by the Secretary, which equitably addresses each of the following:

(A) Site conditions.

(B) Suspensions of work ordered by the State (other than a suspension of work caused by the fault of the contractor or by weather).

(C) Material changes in the scope of work specified in the contract.

The guidelines established by the Secretary shall not require arbitration.

(2) LIMITATION ON APPLICABILITY.—

(A) STATE LAW.—Paragraph (1) shall apply in a State except to the extent that such State adopts or has adopted by statute a formal procedure for the development of a contract clause described in paragraph (1) or adopts or has adopted a statute which does not permit inclusion of such a contract clause.

(B) DESIGN-BUILD CONTRACTS.—Paragraph (1) shall not apply to any design-build contract approved under subsection (b)(3).

(f) SELECTION PROCESS.—A State may procure, under a single contract, the services of a consultant to prepare any environmental impact assessments or analyses required for a project, including environmental impact statements, as well as subsequent engineering and design work on the project if the State conducts a review that assesses the objectivity of the environmental assessment, environmental analysis, or environmental impact statement prior to its submission to the Secretary.

(g) TEMPORARY TRAFFIC CONTROL DEVICES.—

(1) ISSUANCE OF REGULATIONS.—The Secretary, after consultation with appropriate Federal and State officials, shall issue regulations establishing the conditions for the appropriate use of, and expenditure of funds for, uniformed law enforcement officers, positive protective measures between workers and motorized traffic, and installation and maintenance of temporary traffic control devices during construction, utility, and maintenance operations.

(2) EFFECTS OF REGULATIONS.—Based on regulations issued under paragraph (1), a State shall—

(A) develop separate pay items for the use of uniformed law enforcement officers, positive protective measures between workers and motorized traffic, and installation and maintenance of temporary traffic control devices during construction, utility, and maintenance operations; and

(B) incorporate such pay items into contract provisions to be included in each contract entered into by the State with respect to a highway project to ensure compliance with section 109(e)(2).

(3) LIMITATION.—Nothing in the regulations shall prohibit a State from implementing standards that are more stringent than those required under the regulations.

(4) POSITIVE PROTECTIVE MEASURES DEFINED.—In this subsection, the term "positive protective measures" means temporary traffic barriers, crash cushions, and other strategies to avoid traffic accidents in work zones, including full road closures.

(Pub. L. 85–767, Aug. 27, 1958, 72 Stat. 895; Pub. L. 90–495, §22(c), Aug. 23, 1968, 82 Stat. 827; Pub. L. 96–470, title I, §112(b)(1), Oct. 19, 1980, 94 Stat. 2239; Pub. L. 97–424, title I, §112, Jan. 6, 1983, 96 Stat. 2106; Pub. L. 100–17, title I, §111, Apr. 2, 1987, 101 Stat. 147; Pub. L. 104–59, title III, §307(a), Nov. 28, 1995, 109 Stat. 581; Pub. L. 105–178, title I, §§1205, 1212(a)(2)(A)(i), 1307(a), (b), June 9, 1998, 112 Stat. 184, 193, 229, 230; Pub. L. 107–217, §3(e)(1), Aug. 21, 2002, 116 Stat. 1299; Pub. L. 109–59, title I, §§1110(b), 1503, Aug. 10, 2005, 119 Stat. 1170, 1238; Pub. L. 109–115, div. A, title I, §174, Nov. 30, 2005, 119 Stat. 2426; Pub. L. 112–141, div. A, title I, §1303(a), July 6, 2012, 126 Stat. 531; Pub. L. 117–58, div. A, title I, §11525(d), Nov. 15, 2021, 135 Stat. 607.)

§113. PREVAILING RATE OF WAGE

(a) The Secretary shall take such action as may be necessary to insure that all laborers and mechanics employed by contractors or subcontractors on the construction work performed on highway projects on the Federal-aid highways authorized under the highway laws providing for the expenditure of Federal funds upon Federal-aid highways, shall be paid wages at rates not less than those prevailing on the same type of work on similar construction in the immediate locality as determined by the Secretary of Labor in accordance with sections 3141–3144, 3146, and 3147 of title 40.

(b) In carrying out the duties of subsection (a) of this section, the Secretary of Labor shall consult with the highway department of the State in which a project on any Federal-aid highway is to be performed. After giving due regard to the information thus obtained, he shall make a predetermination of the minimum wages to be paid laborers and mechanics in accordance with the provisions of subsection (a) of this section which shall be set out in each project advertisement for bids and in each bid proposal form and shall be made a part of the contract covering the project.

(c) The provisions of the section shall not be applicable to employment pursuant to apprenticeship and skill training programs which have been certified by the Secretary of Transportation as promoting equal employment opportunity in connection with Federal-aid highway construction programs.

(Pub. L. 85–767, Aug. 27, 1958, 72 Stat. 895; Pub. L. 90–495, §12(a), Aug. 23, 1968, 82 Stat. 821; Pub. L. 97–424, title I, §149, Jan. 6, 1983, 96 Stat. 2131; Pub. L. 100–17, title I, §133(b)(5), Apr. 2, 1987, 101 Stat. 171; Pub. L. 102–240, title I, §1006(g)(2), Dec. 18, 1991, 105 Stat. 1927; Pub. L. 107–217, §3(e)(2), Aug. 21, 2002, 116 Stat. 1299; Pub. L. 112–141, div. A, title I, §1104(c)(2), July 6, 2012, 126

Stat. 427.)

§114. Construction

(a) Construction Work In General.—The construction of any Federal-aid highway or a portion of a Federal-aid highway shall be undertaken by the respective State transportation departments or under their direct supervision. The Secretary shall have the right to conduct such inspections and take such corrective action as the Secretary determines to be appropriate. The construction work and labor in each State shall be performed under the direct supervision of the State transportation department and in accordance with the laws of that State and applicable Federal laws. Construction may be begun as soon as funds are available for expenditure pursuant to subsection (a) of section 118 of this title. After July 1, 1973, the State transportation department shall not erect on any project where actual construction is in progress and visible to highway users any informational signs other than official traffic control devices conforming with standards developed by the Secretary of Transportation.

(b) Convict Labor and Convict Produced Materials.—

(1) Limitation on convict labor.—Convict labor shall not be used in construction of Federal-aid highways or portions of Federal-aid highways unless the labor is performed by convicts who are on parole, supervised release, or probation.

(2) Limitation on convict produced materials.—Materials produced after July 1, 1991, by convict labor may only be used in such construction—

(A) if such materials are produced by convicts who are on parole, supervised release, or probation from a prison; or

(B) if such materials are produced by convicts in a qualified prison facility and the amount of such materials produced in such facility for use in such construction during any 12-month period does not exceed the amount of such materials produced in such facility for use in such construction during the 12-month period ending July 1, 1987.

(3) Qualified prison facility defined.—As used in this subsection, "qualified prison facility" means any prison facility in which convicts, during the 12-month period ending July 1, 1987, produced materials for use in construction of highways or portions of highways located on a Federal-aid system in existence during that period.

(c) Construction Work in Alaska.—

(1) In general.—The Secretary shall ensure that a worker who is employed on a remote project for the construction of a highway or portion of a highway located on a Federal-aid system in the State of Alaska and who is not a domiciled resident of the locality shall receive meals and lodging.

(2) Lodging.—The lodging under paragraph (1) shall be in accordance with section 1910.142 of title 29, Code of Federal Regulations (relating to temporary labor camp requirements).

(3) Per diem.—

(A) In general.—Contractors are encouraged to use commercial facilities and lodges on remote projects, however, when such facilities are not available, per diem in lieu of room and lodging may be paid on remote Federal highway projects at a basic rate of $75.00 per day or part of a day the worker is employed on the project. Where the contractor provides or furnishes room and lodging or pays a per diem, the cost of the amount shall not be considered a part of wages and shall be excluded from the calculation of wages.

(B) SECRETARY OF LABOR.—Such per diem rate shall be adopted by the Secretary of Labor for all applicable remote Federal highway projects in Alaska.

(C) EXCEPTION.—Per diem shall not be allowed on any of the following remote projects for the construction of a highway or portion of a highway located on a Federal-aid system:

(i) West of Livengood on the Elliot Highway.

(ii) Mile 0 on the Dalton Highway to the North Slope of Alaska; north of Mile 20 on the Taylor Highway.

(iii) East of Chicken on the Top of the World Highway and south of Tetlin Junction to the Alaska Canadian border.

(4) DEFINITIONS.—In this subsection, the following definitions apply:

(A) REMOTE.—The term "remote", as used with respect to a project, means that the project is 65 road miles or more from the international airport in Fairbanks, Anchorage, or Juneau, Alaska, as the case may be, or is inaccessible by road in a 2-wheel drive vehicle.

(B) RESIDENT.—The term "resident", as used with respect to a project, means a person living within 65 road miles of the midpoint of the project for at least 12 consecutive months prior to the award of the project.

(d) VETERANS EMPLOYMENT.—

(1) IN GENERAL.—Subject to paragraph (2), a recipient of Federal financial assistance under this chapter shall, to the extent practicable, encourage contractors working on a highway project funded using the assistance to make a best faith effort in the hiring or referral of laborers on any project for the construction of a highway to veterans (as defined in section 2108 of title 5) who have the requisite skills and abilities to perform the construction work required under the contract.

(2) ADMINISTRATION.—This subsection shall not—

(A) apply to projects subject to section 140(d); or

(B) be administered or enforced in any manner that would require an employer to give a preference to any veteran over any equally qualified applicant who is a member of any racial or ethnic minority, a female, or any equally qualified former employee.

(Pub. L. 85–767, Aug. 27, 1958, 72 Stat. 896; Pub. L. 86–657, §8(f), July 14, 1960, 74 Stat. 525; Pub. L. 93–87, title I, §115, Aug. 13, 1973, 87 Stat. 258; Pub. L. 97–424, title I, §148, Jan. 6, 1983, 96 Stat. 2131; Pub. L. 98–473, title II, §226, Oct. 12, 1984, 98 Stat. 2030; Pub. L. 100–17, title I, §112(a), (b)(1), Apr. 2, 1987, 101 Stat. 148; Pub. L. 102–240, title I, §1019, Dec. 18, 1991, 105 Stat. 1948; Pub. L. 105–178, title I, §1212(a)(2)(A), June 9, 1998, 112 Stat. 193; Pub. L. 109–59, title I, §§1409(d), 1904(b), Aug. 10, 2005, 119 Stat. 1232, 1467; Pub. L. 112–141, div. A, title I, §1506, July 6, 2012, 126 Stat. 564.)

§115. ADVANCE CONSTRUCTION

(a) IN GENERAL.—The Secretary may authorize a State to proceed with a project authorized under this title—

(1) without the use of Federal funds; and

(2) in accordance with all procedures and requirements applicable to the project other than those procedures and requirements that limit the State to implementation

of a project—

(A) with the aid of Federal funds previously apportioned or allocated to the State; or

(B) with obligation authority previously allocated to the State.

(b) OBLIGATION OF FEDERAL SHARE.—The Secretary, on the request of a State and execution of a project agreement, may obligate all or a portion of the Federal share of a project authorized to proceed under this section from any category of funds for which the project is eligible.

(c) INCLUSION IN TRANSPORTATION IMPROVEMENT PROGRAM.—The Secretary may approve an application for a project under this section only if the project is included in the transportation improvement program of the State developed under section 135(g).

(Pub. L. 85–767, Aug. 27, 1958, 72 Stat. 896; Pub. L. 90–495, §25(a), (b), Aug. 23, 1968, 82 Stat. 828, 829; Pub. L. 93–643, §111, Jan. 4, 1975, 88 Stat. 2285; Pub. L. 96–106, §4, Nov. 9, 1979, 93 Stat. 797; Pub. L. 97–424, title I, §113, Jan. 6, 1983, 96 Stat. 2106; Pub. L. 100–17, title I, §113(a)–(d)(1), Apr. 2, 1987, 101 Stat. 149, 150; Pub. L. 102–302, §103, June 22, 1992, 106 Stat. 252; Pub. L. 104–59, title III, §308, Nov. 28, 1995, 109 Stat. 582; Pub. L. 105–178, title I, §§1103(l)(3)(A), 1106(c)(1)(A), 1226(a), title V, §5119(d), June 9, 1998, 112 Stat. 126, 136, 452; Pub. L. 105–206, title IX, §9003(a), July 22, 1998, 112 Stat. 837; Pub. L. 109–59, title I, §1501(a), Aug. 10, 2005, 119 Stat. 1235; Pub. L. 110–244, title I, §101(j), June 6, 2008, 122 Stat. 1574; Pub. L. 117–58, div. A, title I, §11525(e), Nov. 15, 2021, 135 Stat. 607.)

§116. MAINTENANCE

(a) DEFINITIONS.—In this section, the following definitions apply:

(1) PREVENTIVE MAINTENANCE.—The term "preventive maintenance" includes pavement preservation programs and activities.

(2) PAVEMENT PRESERVATION PROGRAMS AND ACTIVITIES.—The term "pavement preservation programs and activities" means programs and activities employing a network level, long-term strategy that enhances pavement performance by using an integrated, cost-effective set of practices that extend pavement life, improve safety, and meet road user expectations.

(b) It shall be the duty of the State transportation department or other direct recipient to maintain, or cause to be maintained, any project constructed under the provisions of this chapter or constructed under the provisions of prior Acts.

(c) AGREEMENT.—In any State in which the State transportation department or other direct recipient is without legal authority to maintain a project described in subsection (b), the transportation department or direct recipient shall enter into a formal agreement with the appropriate officials of the county or municipality in which the project is located to provide for the maintenance of the project.

(d) If at any time the Secretary shall find that any project constructed under the provisions of this chapter, or constructed under the provisions of prior Acts, is not being properly maintained, he shall call such fact to the attention of the State transportation department or other direct recipient. If, within ninety days after receipt of such notice, such project has not been put in proper condition of maintenance, the Secretary shall withhold approval of further projects of all types in the State highway district, municipality, county, other political or administrative subdivision of the State, or the entire State in which such project is located, whichever the Secretary deems most appropriate, until such project shall have been put in proper condition of maintenance.

(e) PREVENTIVE MAINTENANCE.—A preventive maintenance activity shall be eligible for Federal assistance under this title if the State demonstrates to the satisfaction of the Secretary that the activity is a cost-effective means of extending the useful life of a Federal-aid highway.

(Pub. L. 85–767, Aug. 27, 1958, 72 Stat. 896; Pub. L. 86–70, §21(d)(2), (e)(3), June 25, 1959, 73 Stat. 145, 146; Pub. L. 90–495, §26, Aug. 23, 1968, 82 Stat. 829; Pub. L. 95–599, title I, §124(d), Nov. 6, 1978, 92 Stat. 2705; Pub. L. 97–424, title I, §114, Jan. 6, 1983, 96 Stat. 2107; Pub. L. 100–17, title I, §125(b)(2), Apr. 2, 1987, 101 Stat. 167; Pub. L. 104–59, title III, §309, Nov. 28, 1995, 109 Stat. 582; Pub. L. 105–178, title I, §1212(a)(2)(A)(i), June 9, 1998, 112 Stat. 193; Pub. L. 109–59, title I, §1111(b)(1), Aug. 10, 2005, 119 Stat. 1171; Pub. L. 112–141, div. A, title I, §1507, July 6, 2012, 126 Stat. 565.)

§117. NATIONALLY SIGNIFICANT MULTIMODAL FREIGHT AND HIGHWAY PROJECTS

(a) ESTABLISHMENT.—

(1) IN GENERAL.—There is established a nationally significant freight and highway projects program to provide financial assistance for projects of national or regional significance.

(2) GOALS.—The goals of the program shall be to—

(A) improve the safety, efficiency, and reliability of the movement of freight and people in and across rural and urban areas;

(B) generate national or regional economic benefits and an increase in the global economic competitiveness of the United States;

(C) reduce highway or freight congestion and bottlenecks;

(D) improve connectivity between modes of freight transportation;

(E) enhance the resiliency of critical highway or freight infrastructure and help protect the environment;

(F) improve roadways vital to national energy security, including highways that support movement of energy equipment; and

(G) address the impact of population growth on the movement of people and freight.

(b) GRANT AUTHORITY.—

(1) IN GENERAL.—In carrying out the program established in subsection (a), the Secretary may make grants, on a competitive basis, in accordance with this section.

(2) GRANT AMOUNT.—Except as otherwise provided, each grant made under this section shall be in an amount that is at least $25,000,000.

(3) GRANT ADMINISTRATION.—The Secretary may—

(A) retain not more than a total of 2 percent of the funds made available to carry out this section for the National Surface Transportation and Innovative Finance Bureau to review applications for grants under this section; and

(B) transfer portions of the funds retained under subparagraph (A) to the relevant Administrators to fund the award and oversight of grants provided under this section.

(c) ELIGIBLE APPLICANTS.—

(1) IN GENERAL.—The Secretary may make a grant under this section to the following:

(A) A State or a group of States.

(B) A metropolitan planning organization that serves an urbanized area (as defined by the Bureau of the Census) with a population of more than 200,000 individuals.

(C) A unit of local government or a group of local governments.

(D) A political subdivision of a State or local government.

(E) A special purpose district or public authority with a transportation function, including a port authority.

(F) A Federal land management agency that applies jointly with a State or group of States.

(G) A tribal government or a consortium of tribal governments.

(H) A multistate corridor organization.

(I) A multistate or multijurisdictional group of entities described in this paragraph.

(2) APPLICATIONS.—To be eligible for a grant under this section, an entity specified in paragraph (1) shall submit to the Secretary an application in such form, at such time, and containing such information as the Secretary determines is appropriate.

(d) ELIGIBLE PROJECTS.—

(1) IN GENERAL.—Except as provided in subsection (e), the Secretary may make a grant under this section only for a project that—

(A) is—

(i) a highway freight project carried out on the National Highway Freight Network established under section 167;

(ii) a highway or bridge project carried out on the National Highway System, including—

(I) a project to add capacity to the Interstate System to improve mobility; or

(II) a project in a national scenic area;

(iii) a freight project that is—

(I) a freight intermodal or freight rail project; or

(II) within the boundaries of a public or private freight rail, water (including ports), or intermodal facility and that is a surface transportation infrastructure project necessary to facilitate direct intermodal interchange, transfer, or access into or out of the facility;

(iv) a railway-highway grade crossing or grade separation project;

(v) a wildlife crossing project;

(vi) a surface transportation infrastructure project that—

(I) is located within the boundaries of or functionally connected to an international border crossing area in the United States;

(II) improves a transportation facility owned by a Federal, State, or local government entity; and

(III) increases throughput efficiency of the border crossing described in subclause (I), including—

(aa) a project to add lanes;

(bb) a project to add technology; and

(cc) other surface transportation improvements;

(vii) a project for a marine highway corridor designated by the Secretary under section 55601(c) of title 46 (including an inland waterway corridor), if the Secretary determines that the project—

(I) is functionally connected to the National Highway Freight Network; and

(II) is likely to reduce on-road mobile source emissions; or

(viii) a highway, bridge, or freight project carried out on the National Multimodal Freight Network established under section 70103 of title 49; and

(B) has eligible project costs that are reasonably anticipated to equal or exceed the lesser of—

(i) $100,000,000; or

(ii) in the case of a project—

(I) located in 1 State, 30 percent of the amount apportioned under this chapter to the State in the most recently completed fiscal year; or

(II) located in more than 1 State, 50 percent of the amount apportioned under this chapter to the participating State with the largest apportionment under this chapter in the most recently completed fiscal year.

(2) LIMITATION.—

(A) IN GENERAL.—Not more than 30 percent of the amounts made available for grants under this section for each of fiscal years 2022 through 2026 may be used to make grants for projects described in paragraph (1)(A)(iii) and such a project may only receive a grant under this section if—

(i) the project will make a significant improvement to freight movements on the National Highway Freight Network; and

(ii) the Federal share of the project funds only elements of the project that provide public benefits.

(B) EXCLUSIONS.—The limitation under subparagraph (A)—

(i) shall not apply to a railway-highway grade crossing or grade separation project; and

(ii) with respect to a multimodal project, shall apply only to the non-highway portion or portions of the project.

(e) SMALL PROJECTS.—

(1) IN GENERAL.—The Secretary shall reserve not less than 15 percent of the amounts made available for grants under this section each fiscal year to make grants for projects described in subsection (d)(1)(A) that do not satisfy the minimum threshold under subsection (d)(1)(B).

(2) GRANT AMOUNT.—Each grant made under this subsection shall be in an amount that is at least $5,000,000.

(3) PROJECT SELECTION CONSIDERATIONS.—In addition to other applicable requirements, in making grants under this subsection the Secretary shall consider—

(A) the cost effectiveness of the proposed project;

(B) the effect of the proposed project on mobility in the State and region in which the project is carried out; and

(C) the effect of the proposed project on safety on freight corridors with significant hazards, such as high winds, heavy snowfall, flooding, rockslides, mudslides, wildfire, wildlife crossing onto the roadway, or steep grades.

(4) REQUIREMENT.—Of the amounts reserved under paragraph (1), not less than 30

percent shall be used for projects in rural areas (as defined in subsection (i)(3)).

(f) ELIGIBLE PROJECT COSTS.—Grant amounts received for a project under this section may be used for—

(1) development phase activities, including planning, feasibility analysis, revenue forecasting, environmental review, preliminary engineering and design work, and other preconstruction activities; and

(2) construction, reconstruction, rehabilitation, acquisition of real property (including land related to the project and improvements to the land), environmental mitigation (including a project to replace or rehabilitate a culvert, or to reduce stormwater runoff for the purpose of improving habitat for aquatic species), construction contingencies, acquisition of equipment, and operational improvements directly related to improving system performance.

(g) PROJECT REQUIREMENTS.—The Secretary may select a project described under this section (other than subsection (e)) for funding under this section only if the Secretary determines that—

(1) the project will generate national or regional economic, mobility, or safety benefits;

(2) the project will be cost effective;

(3) the project will contribute to the accomplishment of 1 or more of the national goals described under section 150 of this title;

(4) the project is based on the results of preliminary engineering;

(5) with respect to related non-Federal financial commitments—

(A) 1 or more stable and dependable sources of funding and financing are available to construct, maintain, and operate the project; and

(B) contingency amounts are available to cover unanticipated cost increases;

(6) the project cannot be easily and efficiently completed without other Federal funding or financial assistance available to the project sponsor; and

(7) the project is reasonably expected to begin construction not later than 18 months after the date of obligation of funds for the project.

(h) ADDITIONAL CONSIDERATIONS.—In making a grant under this section, the Secretary shall consider—

(1) utilization of nontraditional financing, innovative design and construction techniques, or innovative technologies;

(2) utilization of non-Federal contributions;

(3) contributions to geographic diversity among grant recipients, including the need for a balance between the needs of rural and urban communities;

(4) enhancement of freight resilience to natural hazards or disasters, including high winds, heavy snowfall, flooding, rockslides, mudslides, wildfire, wildlife crossing onto the roadway, or steep grades;

(5) whether the project will improve the shared transportation corridor of a multistate corridor organization, if applicable; and

(6) prioritizing projects located in States in which neither the State nor an eligible entity in that State has been awarded a grant under this section.

(i) RURAL AREAS.—

(1) IN GENERAL.—The Secretary shall reserve not less than 25 percent of the

amounts made available for grants under this section, including the amounts made available under subsection (e), each fiscal year to make grants for projects located in rural areas.

(2) EXCESS FUNDING.—In any fiscal year in which qualified applications for grants under this subsection will not allow for the amount reserved under paragraph (1) to be fully utilized, the Secretary shall use the unutilized amounts to make grants under subsection (e).

(3) RURAL AREA DEFINED.—In this subsection, the term "rural area" means an area that is outside an urbanized area with a population of over 200,000.

(j) FEDERAL ASSISTANCE.—

(1) FEDERAL SHARE.—

(A) IN GENERAL.—Except as provided in subparagraph (B) or for a grant under subsection (q), the Federal share of the cost of a project assisted with a grant under this section may not exceed 60 percent.

(B) SMALL PROJECTS.—In the case of a project described in subsection (e)(1), the Federal share of the cost of the project shall be 80 percent.

(2) MAXIMUM FEDERAL INVOLVEMENT.—Except for grants under subsection (q), Federal assistance other than a grant under this section may be used to satisfy the non-Federal share of the cost of a project for which such a grant is made, except that—

(A) for a State with a population density of not more than 80 persons per square mile of land area, based on the 2010 census, the maximum share of the total Federal assistance provided for a project receiving a grant under this section shall be the applicable share under section 120(b); and

(B) for a State not described in subparagraph (A), the total Federal assistance provided for a project receiving a grant under this section may not exceed 80 percent of the total project cost.

(3) FEDERAL LAND MANAGEMENT AGENCIES.—Notwithstanding any other provision of law, any Federal funds other than those made available under this title or title 49 may be used to pay the non-Federal share of the cost of a project carried out under this section by a Federal land management agency, as described under subsection (c)(1)(F).

(k) EFFICIENT USE OF NON-FEDERAL FUNDS.—

(1) IN GENERAL.—Notwithstanding any other provision of law and subject to approval by the Secretary under paragraph (2)(B), in the case of any grant for a project under this section, during the period beginning on the date on which the grant recipient is selected and ending on the date on which the grant agreement is signed—

(A) the grant recipient may obligate and expend non-Federal funds with respect to the project for which the grant is provided; and

(B) any non-Federal funds obligated or expended in accordance with subparagraph (A) shall be credited toward the non-Federal cost share for the project for which the grant is provided.

(2) REQUIREMENTS.—

(A) APPLICATION.—In order to obligate and expend non-Federal funds under paragraph (1), the grant recipient shall submit to the Secretary a request to obligate and expend non-Federal funds under that paragraph, including—

(i) a description of the activities the grant recipient intends to fund;

(ii) a justification for advancing the activities described in clause (i), including an assessment of the effects to the project scope, schedule, and budget if the request is not approved; and

(iii) the level of risk of the activities described in clause (i).

(B) Approval.—The Secretary shall approve or disapprove each request submitted under subparagraph (A).

(C) Compliance with applicable requirements.—Any non-Federal funds obligated or expended under paragraph (1) shall comply with all applicable requirements, including any requirements included in the grant agreement.

(3) Effect.—The obligation or expenditure of any non-Federal funds in accordance with this subsection shall not—

(A) affect the signing of a grant agreement or other applicable grant procedures with respect to the applicable grant;

(B) create an obligation on the part of the Federal Government to repay any non-Federal funds if the grant agreement is not signed; or

(C) affect the ability of the recipient of the grant to obligate or expend non-Federal funds to meet the non-Federal cost share for the project for which the grant is provided after the period described in paragraph (1).

(l) Treatment of Freight Projects.—Notwithstanding any other provision of law, a freight project carried out under this section shall be treated as if the project is located on a Federal-aid highway.

(m) TIFIA Program.—At the request of an eligible applicant under this section, the Secretary may use amounts awarded to the entity to pay subsidy and administrative costs necessary to provide the entity Federal credit assistance under chapter 6 with respect to the project for which the grant was awarded.

(n) Congressional Notification.—

(1) In general.—Not later than 60 days before the date on which a grant is provided for a project under this section, the Secretary shall submit to the Committees on Commerce, Science, and Transportation and Environment and Public Works of the Senate and the Committee on Transportation and Infrastructure of the House of Representatives a report describing the proposed grant, including—

(A) an evaluation and justification for the applicable project; and

(B) a description of the amount of the proposed grant award.

(2) Congressional disapproval.—The Secretary may not make a grant or any other obligation or commitment to fund a project under this section if a joint resolution is enacted disapproving funding for the project before the last day of the 60-day period described in paragraph (1).

(o) Applicant Notification.—

(1) In general.—Not later than 60 days after the date on which a grant recipient for a project under this section is selected, the Secretary shall provide to each eligible applicant not selected for that grant a written notification that the eligible applicant was not selected.

(2) Inclusion.—A written notification under paragraph (1) shall include an offer for a written or telephonic debrief by the Secretary that will provide—

(A) detail on the evaluation of the application of the eligible applicant; and

(B) an explanation of and guidance on the reasons the application was not selected for a grant under this section.

(3) RESPONSE.—

(A) IN GENERAL.—Not later than 30 days after the eligible applicant receives a written notification under paragraph (1), if the eligible applicant opts to receive a debrief described in paragraph (2), the eligible applicant shall notify the Secretary that the eligible applicant is requesting a debrief.

(B) DEBRIEF.—If the eligible applicant submits a request for a debrief under subparagraph (A), the Secretary shall provide the debrief by not later than 60 days after the date on which the Secretary receives the request for a debrief.

(p) REPORTS.—

(1) ANNUAL REPORT.—

(A) IN GENERAL.—Notwithstanding any other provision of law, not later than 30 days after the date on which the Secretary selects a project for funding under this section, the Secretary shall submit to the Committee on Environment and Public Works of the Senate and the Committee on Transportation and Infrastructure of the House of Representatives a report that describes the reasons for selecting the project, based on any criteria established by the Secretary in accordance with this section.

(B) INCLUSIONS.—The report submitted under subparagraph (A) shall specify each criterion established by the Secretary that the project meets.

(C) AVAILABILITY.—The Secretary shall make available on the website of the Department of Transportation the report submitted under subparagraph (A).

(D) APPLICABILITY.—This paragraph applies to all projects described in subparagraph (A) that the Secretary selects on or after October 1, 2021.

(2) COMPTROLLER GENERAL.—

(A) ASSESSMENT.—The Comptroller General of the United States shall conduct an assessment of the establishment, solicitation, selection, and justification process with respect to the funding of projects under this section.

(B) REPORT.—Not later than 1 year after the date of enactment of the Surface Transportation Reauthorization Act of 2021 and annually thereafter, the Comptroller General of the United States shall submit to the Committee on Environment and Public Works of the Senate and the Committee on Transportation and Infrastructure of the House of Representatives a report that describes, for each project selected to receive funding under this section—

(i) the process by which each project was selected;

(ii) the factors that went into the selection of each project; and

(iii) the justification for the selection of each project based on any criteria established by the Secretary in accordance with this section.

(3) INSPECTOR GENERAL.—Not later than 1 year after the date of enactment of the Surface Transportation Reauthorization Act of 2021 and annually thereafter, the Inspector General of the Department of Transportation shall—

(A) conduct an assessment of the establishment, solicitation, selection, and justification process with respect to the funding of projects under this section; and

(B) submit to the Committee on Environment and Public Works of the Senate and the Committee on Transportation and Infrastructure of the House of Representatives a final report that describes the findings of the Inspector General of the Department of Transportation with respect to the assessment conducted under subparagraph (A).

(q) STATE INCENTIVES PILOT PROGRAM.—

(1) ESTABLISHMENT.—There is established a pilot program to award grants to eligible applicants for projects eligible for grants under this section (referred to in this subsection as the "pilot program").

(2) PRIORITY.—In awarding grants under the pilot program, the Secretary shall give priority to an application that offers a greater non-Federal share of the cost of a project relative to other applications under the pilot program.

(3) FEDERAL SHARE.—

(A) IN GENERAL.—Notwithstanding any other provision of law, the Federal share of the cost of a project assisted with a grant under the pilot program may not exceed 50 percent.

(B) NO FEDERAL INVOLVEMENT.—

(i) IN GENERAL.—For grants awarded under the pilot program, except as provided in clause (ii), an eligible applicant may not use Federal assistance to satisfy the non-Federal share of the cost under subparagraph (A).

(ii) EXCEPTION.—An eligible applicant may use funds from a secured loan (as defined in section 601(a)) to satisfy the non-Federal share of the cost under subparagraph (A) if the loan is repayable from non-Federal funds.

(4) RESERVATION.—

(A) IN GENERAL.—Of the amounts made available to provide grants under this section, the Secretary shall reserve for each fiscal year $150,000,000 to provide grants under the pilot program.

(B) UNUTILIZED AMOUNTS.—In any fiscal year during which applications under this subsection are insufficient to effect an award or allocation of the entire amount reserved under subparagraph (A), the Secretary shall use the unutilized amounts to provide other grants under this section.

(5) SET-ASIDES.—

(A) SMALL PROJECTS.—

(i) IN GENERAL.—Of the amounts reserved under paragraph (4)(A), the Secretary shall reserve for each fiscal year not less than 10 percent for projects eligible for a grant under subsection (e).

(ii) REQUIREMENT.—For a grant awarded from the amount reserved under clause (i)—

(I) the requirements of subsection (e) shall apply; and

(II) the requirements of subsection (g) shall not apply.

(B) RURAL PROJECTS.—

(i) IN GENERAL.—Of the amounts reserved under paragraph (4)(A), the Secretary shall reserve for each fiscal year not less than 25 percent for projects eligible for a grant under subsection (i).

(ii) REQUIREMENT.—For a grant awarded from the amount reserved under clause (i), the requirements of subsection (i) shall apply.

(6) REPORT TO CONGRESS.—Not later than 2 years after the date of enactment of this subsection, the Secretary shall submit to the Committee on Environment and Public Works and the Committee on Commerce, Science, and Transportation of the Senate and the Committee on Transportation and Infrastructure of the House of Representatives a report that describes the administration of the pilot program, including—

(A) the number, types, and locations of eligible applicants that have applied for grants under the pilot program;

(B) the number, types, and locations of grant recipients under the pilot program;

(C) an assessment of whether implementation of the pilot program has incentivized eligible applicants to offer a greater non-Federal share for grants under the pilot program; and

(D) any recommendations for modifications to the pilot program.

(r) MULTISTATE CORRIDOR ORGANIZATION DEFINED.—For purposes of this section, the term "multistate corridor organization" means an organization of a group of States developed through cooperative agreements, coalitions, or other arrangements to promote regional cooperation, planning, and shared project implementation for programs and projects to improve transportation system management and operations for a shared transportation corridor.

(s) ADDITIONAL AUTHORIZATION OF APPROPRIATIONS.—In addition to amounts made available from the Highway Trust Fund, there are authorized to be appropriated to carry out this section, to remain available for a period of 3 fiscal years following the fiscal year for which the amounts are appropriated—

(1) $1,000,000,000 for fiscal year 2022;

(2) $1,100,000,000 for fiscal year 2023;

(3) $1,200,000,000 for fiscal year 2024;

(4) $1,300,000,000 for fiscal year 2025; and

(5) $1,400,000,000 for fiscal year 2026.

(Added Pub. L. 114–94, div. A, title I, §1105(a), Dec. 4, 2015, 129 Stat. 1332; amended Pub. L. 116–159, div. B, title I, §1102, Oct. 1, 2020, 134 Stat. 726; Pub. L. 117–58, div. A, title I, §11110(a), Nov. 15, 2021, 135 Stat. 468.)

§118. AVAILABILITY OF FUNDS

(a) DATE AVAILABLE FOR OBLIGATION.—Except as otherwise specifically provided, authorizations from the Highway Trust Fund (other than the Mass Transit Account) to carry out this title shall be available for obligation on the date of their apportionment or allocation or on October 1 of the fiscal year for which they are authorized, whichever occurs first.

(b) PERIOD OF AVAILABILITY.—Except as otherwise specifically provided, funds apportioned or allocated pursuant to this title in a State shall remain available for obligation in that State for a period of 3 years after the last day of the fiscal year for which the funds are authorized. Any amounts so apportioned or allocated that remain unobligated at the end of that period shall lapse.

(c) OBLIGATION AND RELEASE OF FUNDS.—

(1) IN GENERAL.—Funds apportioned or allocated to a State for a purpose for any

fiscal year shall be considered to be obligated if a sum equal to the total of the funds apportioned or allocated to the State for that purpose for that fiscal year and previous fiscal years is obligated.

(2) RELEASED FUNDS.—Any funds released by the final payment for a project, or by modifying the project agreement for a project, shall be—

(A) credited to the same class of funds previously apportioned or allocated to the State for the project; and

(B) immediately available for obligation.

(3) NET OBLIGATIONS.—Notwithstanding any other provision of law (including a regulation), obligations recorded against funds made available under this subsection shall be recorded and reported as net obligations.

(d) Funds made available to the State of Alaska and the Commonwealth of Puerto Rico under this title may be expended for construction of access and development roads that will serve resource development, recreational, residential, commercial, industrial, or other like purposes.

(Pub. L. 85–767, Aug. 27, 1958, 72 Stat. 897; Pub. L. 89–574, §7(a), Sept. 13, 1966, 80 Stat. 768; Pub. L. 94–280, title I, §117(a), May 5, 1976, 90 Stat. 436; Pub. L. 95–599, title I, §115(a), Nov. 6, 1978, 92 Stat. 2697; Pub. L. 96–106, §5(a), Nov. 9, 1979, 93 Stat. 797; Pub. L. 97–424, title I, §115, Jan. 6, 1983, 96 Stat. 2107; Pub. L. 100–17, title I, §§114(a)–(c), (e)(2)–(4), 115, Apr. 2, 1987, 101 Stat. 150–153; Pub. L. 102–240, title I, §1020, Dec. 18, 1991, 105 Stat. 1948; Pub. L. 102–388, title IV, §409, Oct. 6, 1992, 106 Stat. 1565; Pub. L. 105–178, title I, §§1106(c)(1)(B), 1107(b), 1226(b), June 9, 1998, 112 Stat. 136, 137; Pub. L. 105–206, title IX, §9003(a), July 22, 1998, 112 Stat. 837; Pub. L. 109–59, title I, §§1111(a), 1501(b), Aug. 10, 2005, 119 Stat. 1171, 1235; Pub. L. 112–141, div. A, title I, §1519(b)(1)(B), (c)(4), formerly (c)(5), July 6, 2012, 126 Stat. 575, renumbered §1519(c)(4), Pub. L. 114–94, div. A, title I, §1446(d)(5)(B), Dec. 4, 2015, 129 Stat. 1438.)

§119. NATIONAL HIGHWAY PERFORMANCE PROGRAM

(a) ESTABLISHMENT.—The Secretary shall establish and implement a national highway performance program under this section.

(b) PURPOSES.—The purposes of the national highway performance program shall be—

(1) to provide support for the condition and performance of the National Highway System;

(2) to provide support for the construction of new facilities on the National Highway System;

(3) to ensure that investments of Federal-aid funds in highway construction are directed to support progress toward the achievement of performance targets established in an asset management plan of a State for the National Highway System; and

(4) to provide support for activities to increase the resiliency of the National Highway System to mitigate the cost of damages from sea level rise, extreme weather events, flooding, wildfires, or other natural disasters.

(c) ELIGIBLE FACILITIES.—Except as provided in subsection (d), to be eligible for funding apportioned under section 104(b)(1) to carry out this section, a facility shall be located on the National Highway System, as defined in section 103.

(d) ELIGIBLE PROJECTS.—Funds apportioned to a State to carry out the national highway performance program may be obligated only for a project on an eligible facility that is—

(1)(A) a project or part of a program of projects supporting progress toward the achievement of national performance goals for improving infrastructure condition, safety, congestion reduction, system reliability, or freight movement on the National Highway System; and

(B) consistent with sections 134 and 135; and

(2) for 1 or more of the following purposes:

(A) Construction, reconstruction, resurfacing, restoration, rehabilitation, preservation, or operational improvement of segments of the National Highway System.

(B) Construction, replacement (including replacement with fill material), rehabilitation, preservation, and protection (including scour countermeasures, seismic retrofits, impact protection measures, security countermeasures, and protection against extreme events) of bridges on the National Highway System.

(C) Construction, replacement (including replacement with fill material), rehabilitation, preservation, and protection (including impact protection measures, security countermeasures, and protection against extreme events) of tunnels on the National Highway System.

(D) Inspection and evaluation, as described in section 144, of bridges and tunnels on the National Highway System, and inspection and evaluation of other highway infrastructure assets on the National Highway System, including signs and sign structures, earth retaining walls, and drainage structures.

(E) Training of bridge and tunnel inspectors, as described in section 144.

(F) Construction, rehabilitation, or replacement of existing ferry boats and ferry boat facilities, including approaches, that connect road segments of the National Highway System.

(G) Construction, reconstruction, resurfacing, restoration, rehabilitation, and preservation of, and operational improvements for, a Federal-aid highway not on the National Highway System, and construction of a transit project eligible for assistance under chapter 53 of title 49, if—

(i) the highway project or transit project is in the same corridor as, and in proximity to, a fully access-controlled highway designated as a part of the National Highway System;

(ii) the construction or improvements will reduce delays or produce travel time savings on the fully access-controlled highway described in clause (i) and improve regional traffic flow; and

(iii) the construction or improvements are more cost-effective, as determined by benefit-cost analysis, than an improvement to the fully access-controlled highway described in clause (i).

(H) Bicycle transportation and pedestrian walkways in accordance with section 217.

(I) Highway safety improvements for segments of the National Highway System.

(J) Capital and operating costs for traffic and traveler information monitoring, management, and control facilities and programs.

(K) Development and implementation of a State asset management plan for the National Highway System in accordance with this section, including data collection, maintenance, and integration and the cost associated with obtaining, updating, and licensing software and equipment required for risk-based asset management and performance-based management.

(L) Infrastructure-based intelligent transportation systems capital improvements, including the installation of vehicle-to-infrastructure communication equipment.

(M) Environmental restoration and pollution abatement in accordance with section 328.

(N) Control of noxious weeds and aquatic noxious weeds and establishment of native species in accordance with section 329.

(O) Environmental mitigation efforts related to projects funded under this section, as described in subsection (g).

(P) Construction of publicly owned intracity or intercity bus terminals servicing the National Highway System.

(Q) Undergrounding public utility infrastructure carried out in conjunction with a project otherwise eligible under this section.

(R) Resiliency improvements on the National Highway System, including protective features described in subsection (k)(2).

(S) Implement activities to protect segments of the National Highway System from cybersecurity threats.

(e) STATE PERFORMANCE MANAGEMENT.—

(1) IN GENERAL.—A State shall develop a risk-based asset management plan for the National Highway System to improve or preserve the condition of the assets and the performance of the system.

(2) PERFORMANCE DRIVEN PLAN.—A State asset management plan shall include strategies leading to a program of projects that would make progress toward achievement of the State targets for asset condition and performance of the National Highway System in accordance with section 150(d) and supporting the progress toward the achievement of the national goals identified in section 150(b).

(3) SCOPE.—In developing a risk-based asset management plan, the Secretary shall encourage States to include all infrastructure assets within the right-of-way corridor in such plan.

(4) PLAN CONTENTS.—A State asset management plan shall, at a minimum, be in a form that the Secretary determines to be appropriate and include—

(A) a summary listing of the pavement and bridge assets on the National Highway System in the State, including a description of the condition of those assets;

(B) asset management objectives and measures;

(C) performance gap identification;

(D) lifecycle cost and risk management analyses, both of which shall take into consideration extreme weather and resilience;

(E) a financial plan; and

(F) investment strategies.

(5) REQUIREMENT FOR PLAN.—

(A) IN GENERAL.—Notwithstanding section 120, each fiscal year, if the Secretary determines that a State has not developed and implemented a State asset management plan consistent with this section, the Federal share payable on account of any project or activity for which funds are obligated by the State in that fiscal year under this section shall be 65 percent.

(B) DETERMINATION.—The Secretary shall make the determination under subparagraph (A) for a fiscal year not later than the day before the beginning of such fiscal year.

(6) CERTIFICATION OF PLAN DEVELOPMENT PROCESS.—

(A) IN GENERAL.—Not later than 90 days after the date on which a State submits a request for approval of the process used by the State to develop the State asset management plan for the National Highway System, the Secretary shall—

(i) review the process; and

(ii)(I) certify that the process meets the requirements established by the Secretary; or

(II) deny certification and specify actions necessary for the State to take to correct deficiencies in the State process.

(B) RECERTIFICATION.—Not less frequently than once every 4 years, the Secretary shall review and recertify that the process used by a State to develop and maintain the State asset management plan for the National Highway System meets the requirements for the process, as established by the Secretary.

(C) OPPORTUNITY TO CURE.—If the Secretary denies certification under subparagraph (A), the Secretary shall provide the State with—

(i) not less than 90 days to cure the deficiencies of the plan, during which time period all penalties and other legal impacts of a denial of certification shall be stayed; and

(ii) a written statement of the specific actions the Secretary determines to be necessary for the State to cure the plan.

(7) PERFORMANCE ACHIEVEMENT.—A State that does not achieve or make significant progress toward achieving the targets of the State for performance measures described in section 150(d) for the National Highway System shall include as part of the performance target report under section 150(e) a description of the actions the State will undertake to achieve the targets.

(8) PROCESS.—Not later than 18 months after the date of enactment of the MAP–21, the Secretary shall, by regulation and in consultation with State departments of transportation, establish the process to develop the State asset management plan described in paragraph (1).

(f) INTERSTATE SYSTEM AND NHS BRIDGE CONDITIONS.—

(1) CONDITION OF INTERSTATE SYSTEM.—

(A) PENALTY.—If a State reports that the condition of the Interstate System, excluding bridges on the Interstate System, has fallen below the minimum condition level established by the Secretary under section 150(c)(3), the State shall be required, during the following fiscal year—

(i) to obligate, from the amounts apportioned to the State under section 104(b)(1), an amount that is not less than the amount of funds apportioned to the State for fiscal year 2009 under the Interstate maintenance program for the purposes described in this section (as in effect on the day before the date of enactment of the MAP–21), except that for each year after fiscal year 2013, the amount required to be obligated under this clause shall be increased by 2 percent over the amount required to be obligated in the previous fiscal year; and

(ii) to transfer, from the amounts apportioned to the State under section 104(b)(2) (other than amounts suballocated to metropolitan areas and other areas of the State under section 133(d)) to the apportionment of the State under section 104(b)(1), an amount equal to 10 percent of the amount of funds apportioned to the State for fiscal year 2009 under the Interstate maintenance program for the purposes described in this section (as in effect on the day before the date of enactment of the MAP–21).

(B) RESTORATION.—The obligation requirement for the Interstate System in a State required by subparagraph (A) for a fiscal year shall remain in effect for each subsequent fiscal year until such time as the condition of the Interstate System in the State exceeds the minimum condition level established by the Secretary.

(2) CONDITION OF NHS BRIDGES.—

(A) PENALTY.—If the Secretary determines that, for the 3-year-period preceding the date of the determination, more than 10 percent of the total deck area of bridges in the State on the National Highway System is located on bridges that have been classified as in poor condition, an amount equal to 50 percent of funds apportioned to such State for fiscal year 2009 to carry out section 144 (as in effect the day before enactment of MAP–21) shall be set aside from amounts apportioned to a State for a fiscal year under section 104(b)(1) only for eligible projects on bridges on the National Highway System.

(B) RESTORATION.—The set-aside requirement for bridges on the National Highway System in a State under subparagraph (A) for a fiscal year shall remain in effect for each subsequent fiscal year until such time as less than 10 percent of the total deck area of bridges in the State on the National Highway System is located on bridges that have been classified as in poor condition, as determined by the Secretary.

(g) ENVIRONMENTAL MITIGATION.—

(1) ELIGIBLE ACTIVITIES.—In accordance with all applicable Federal law (including regulations), environmental mitigation efforts referred to in subsection (d)(2)(O) include participation in natural habitat and wetlands mitigation efforts relating to projects funded under this title, which may include—

(A) participation in mitigation banking or other third-party mitigation arrangements, such as—

(i) the purchase of credits from commercial mitigation banks;

(ii) the establishment and management of agency-sponsored mitigation banks; and

(iii) the purchase of credits or establishment of in-lieu fee mitigation programs;

(B) contributions to statewide and regional efforts to conserve, restore, enhance, and create natural habitats and wetlands; and

(C) the development of statewide and regional environmental protection plans, including natural habitat and wetland conservation and restoration plans.

(2) INCLUSION OF OTHER ACTIVITIES.—The banks, efforts, and plans described in paragraph (1) include any such banks, efforts, and plans developed in accordance with applicable law (including regulations).

(3) TERMS AND CONDITIONS.—The following terms and conditions apply to natural habitat and wetlands mitigation efforts under this subsection:

(A) Contributions to the mitigation effort may—

(i) take place concurrent with, or in advance of, commitment of funding under this title to a project or projects; and

(ii) occur in advance of project construction only if the efforts are consistent with all applicable requirements of Federal law (including regulations) and State transportation planning processes.

(B) Credits from any agency-sponsored mitigation bank that are attributable to funding under this section may be used only for projects funded under this title, unless the agency pays to the Secretary an amount equal to the Federal funds attributable to the mitigation bank credits the agency uses for purposes other than mitigation of a project funded under this title.

(4) PREFERENCE.—At the discretion of the project sponsor, preference shall be given, to the maximum extent practicable, to mitigating an environmental impact through the use of a mitigation bank, in-lieu fee, or other third-party mitigation arrangement, if the use of credits from the mitigation bank or in-lieu fee, or the other third-party mitigation arrangement for the project, is approved by the applicable Federal agency.

(h) TIFIA PROGRAM.—Upon Secretarial approval of credit assistance under chapter 6, the Secretary, at the request of a State, may allow the State to use funds apportioned under section 104(b)(1) to pay subsidy and administrative costs necessary to provide an eligible entity Federal credit assistance under chapter 6 with respect to a project eligible for assistance under this section.

(i) ADDITIONAL FUNDING ELIGIBILITY FOR CERTAIN BRIDGES.—

(1) IN GENERAL.—Funds apportioned to a State to carry out the national highway performance program may be obligated for a project for the reconstruction, resurfacing, restoration, rehabilitation, or preservation of a bridge not on the National Highway System, if the bridge is on a Federal-aid highway.

(2) LIMITATION.—A State required to make obligations under subsection (f) shall ensure such requirements are satisfied in order to use the flexibility under paragraph (1).

(j) CRITICAL INFRASTRUCTURE.—

(1) CRITICAL INFRASTRUCTURE DEFINED.—In this subsection, the term "critical infrastructure" means those facilities the incapacity or failure of which would have a debilitating impact on national or regional economic security, national or regional energy security, national or regional public health or safety, or any combination of those matters.

(2) CONSIDERATION.—The asset management plan of a State may include consideration of critical infrastructure from among those facilities in the State that are

eligible under subsection (c).

(3) RISK REDUCTION.—A State may use funds apportioned under this section for projects intended to reduce the risk of failure of critical infrastructure in the State.

(k) PROTECTIVE FEATURES.—

(1) IN GENERAL.—A State may use not more than 15 percent of the funds apportioned to the State under section 104(b)(1) for each fiscal year for 1 or more protective features on a Federal-aid highway or bridge not on the National Highway System, if the protective feature is designed to mitigate the risk of recurring damage or the cost of future repairs from extreme weather events, flooding, or other natural disasters.

(2) PROTECTIVE FEATURES DESCRIBED.—A protective feature referred to in paragraph (1) includes—

(A) raising roadway grades;

(B) relocating roadways in a base floodplain to higher ground above projected flood elevation levels or away from slide prone areas;

(C) stabilizing slide areas;

(D) stabilizing slopes;

(E) lengthening or raising bridges to increase waterway openings;

(F) increasing the size or number of drainage structures;

(G) replacing culverts with bridges or upsizing culverts;

(H) installing seismic retrofits on bridges;

(I) adding scour protection at bridges, installing riprap, or adding other scour, stream stability, coastal, or other hydraulic countermeasures, including spur dikes; and

(J) the use of natural infrastructure to mitigate the risk of recurring damage or the cost of future repair from extreme weather events, flooding, or other natural disasters.

(3) SAVINGS PROVISION.—Nothing in this subsection limits the ability of a State to carry out a project otherwise eligible under subsection (d) using funds apportioned under section 104(b)(1).

(Added Pub. L. 95–599, title I, §116(a), Nov. 6, 1978, 92 Stat. 2698; amended Pub. L. 96–106, §18, Nov. 9, 1979, 93 Stat. 799; Pub. L. 97–134, §§6, 7, Dec. 29, 1981, 95 Stat. 1701; Pub. L. 97–424, title I, §116(a)(1), (2), (b), (c), Jan. 6, 1983, 96 Stat. 2109; Pub. L. 98–229, §8(b), Mar. 9, 1984, 98 Stat. 56; Pub. L. 99–190, §101(e) [title III, §327], Dec. 19, 1985, 99 Stat. 1267, 1289; Pub. L. 100–17, title I, §116(a)–(c)(1), Apr. 2, 1987, 101 Stat. 154, 155; Pub. L. 100–202, §101(l) [title III, §347(b)], Dec. 22, 1987, 101 Stat. 1329–358, 1329–388; Pub. L. 102–240, title I, §1009(a), (b), (e)(1), (3)–(5), Dec. 18, 1991, 105 Stat. 1933, 1934; Pub. L. 105–178, title I, §1107(a), (d), June 9, 1998, 112 Stat. 137; Pub. L. 105–206, title IX, §9002(f), July 22, 1998, 112 Stat. 836; Pub. L. 112–141, div. A, title I, §1106(a), July 6, 2012, 126 Stat. 432; Pub. L. 114–94, div. A, title I, §§1106, 1406(a), 1407(a), 1446(a)(1), Dec. 4, 2015, 129 Stat. 1337, 1410, 1437; Pub. L. 116–94, div. H, title I, §129A, Dec. 20, 2019, 133 Stat. 2953; Pub. L. 117–58, div. A, title I, §§11105, 11524(a), Nov. 15, 2021, 135 Stat. 457, 606.)

§120. FEDERAL SHARE PAYABLE

(a) INTERSTATE SYSTEM PROJECTS.—

(1) IN GENERAL.—Except as otherwise provided in this chapter, the Federal share payable on account of any project on the Interstate System (including a project to add high occupancy vehicle lanes and a project to add auxiliary lanes but excluding

a project to add any other lanes) shall be 90 percent of the total cost thereof, plus a percentage of the remaining 10 percent of such cost in any State containing unappropriated and unreserved public lands and nontaxable Indian lands, individual and tribal, exceeding 5 percent of the total area of all lands therein, equal to the percentage that the area of such lands in such State is of its total area; except that such Federal share payable on any project in any State shall not exceed 95 percent of the total cost of such project.

(2) STATE-DETERMINED LOWER FEDERAL SHARE.—In the case of any project subject to paragraph (1), a State may determine a lower Federal share than the Federal share determined under such paragraph.

(b) OTHER PROJECTS.—Except as otherwise provided in this title, the Federal share payable on account of any project or activity carried out under this title (other than a project subject to subsection (a)) shall be—

(1) 80 percent of the cost thereof, except that in the case of any State containing nontaxable Indian lands, individual and tribal, and public domain lands (both reserved and unreserved) exclusive of national forests and national parks and monuments, exceeding 5 percent of the total area of all lands therein, the Federal share, for purposes of this chapter, shall be increased by a percentage of the remaining cost equal to the percentage that the area of all such lands in such State, is of its total area; or

(2) 80 percent of the cost thereof, except that in the case of any State containing nontaxable Indian lands, individual and tribal, public domain lands (both reserved and unreserved), national forests, and national parks and monuments, the Federal share, for purposes of this chapter, shall be increased by a percentage of the remaining cost equal to the percentage that the area of all such lands in such State is of its total area; except that the Federal share payable on any project in a State shall not exceed 95 percent of the total cost of any such project. In any case where a State elects to have the Federal share provided in paragraph (2) of this subsection, the State must enter into an agreement with the Secretary covering a period of not less than 1 year, requiring such State to use solely for purposes eligible for assistance under this title (other than paying its share of projects approved under this title) during the period covered by such agreement the difference between the State's share as provided in paragraph (2) and what its share would be if it elected to pay the share provided in paragraph (1) for all projects subject to such agreement. In the case of any project subject to this subsection, a State may determine a lower Federal share than the Federal share determined under the preceding sentences of this subsection.

(c) INCREASED FEDERAL SHARE.—

(1) CERTAIN SAFETY PROJECTS.—The Federal share payable on account of any project for traffic control signalization, maintaining minimum levels of retroreflectivity of highway signs or pavement markings, traffic circles (also known as "roundabouts"), safety rest areas, pavement marking, shoulder and centerline rumble strips and stripes, commuter carpooling and vanpooling, rail-highway crossing closure, or installation of traffic signs, traffic lights, guardrails, impact attenuators, concrete barrier endtreatments, breakaway utility poles, vehicle-to-infrastructure communication equipment, or priority control systems for emergency

vehicles or transit vehicles at signalized intersections may amount to 100 percent of the cost of construction of such projects; except that not more than 10 percent of all sums apportioned for all the Federal-aid programs for any fiscal year in accordance with section 104 of this title shall be used under this subsection. In this subsection, the term "safety rest area" means an area where motor vehicle operators can park their vehicles and rest, where food, fuel, and lodging services are not available, and that is located on a segment of highway with respect to which the Secretary determines there is a shortage of public and private areas at which motor vehicle operators can park their vehicles and rest.

(2) CMAQ PROJECTS.—The Federal share payable on account of a project or program carried out under section 149 with funds obligated in fiscal year 2008 or 2009, or both, shall be not less than 80 percent and, at the discretion of the State, may be up to 100 percent of the cost thereof.

(3) INNOVATIVE PROJECT DELIVERY.—

(A) IN GENERAL.—Except as provided in subparagraph (C), the Federal share payable on account of a project, program, or activity carried out with funds apportioned under paragraph (1), (2), (5)(D), or (6) of section 104(b) may, at the discretion of the State, be up to 100 percent for any such project, program, or activity that the Secretary determines—

(i) contains innovative project delivery methods that improve work zone safety for motorists or workers and the quality of the facility;

(ii) contains innovative technologies, engineering or design approaches, manufacturing processes, financing, or contracting or project delivery methods that improve the quality of, extend the service life of, or decrease the long-term costs of maintaining highways and bridges;

(iii) accelerates project delivery while complying with other applicable Federal laws (including regulations) and not causing any significant adverse environmental impact; or

(iv) reduces congestion related to highway construction.

(B) EXAMPLES.—Projects, programs, and activities described in subparagraph (A) may include the use of—

(i) prefabricated bridge elements and systems and other technologies to reduce bridge construction time;

(ii) innovative construction equipment, materials, or techniques, including the use of in-place recycling technology and digital 3-dimensional modeling technologies;

(iii) innovative contracting methods, including the design-build and the construction manager-general contractor contracting methods and alternative bidding;

(iv) intelligent compaction equipment;

(v) innovative pavement materials that have a demonstrated life cycle of 75 or more years, are manufactured with reduced greenhouse gas emissions, and reduce construction-related congestion by rapidly curing;

(vi) contractual provisions that provide safety contingency funds to incorporate safety enhancements to work zones prior to or during roadway construction activities; or

(vii) contractual provisions that offer a contractor an incentive payment for early completion of the project, program, or activity, subject to the condition that the incentives are accounted for in the financial plan of the project, when applicable.

(C) LIMITATIONS.—

(i) IN GENERAL.—In each fiscal year, a State may use the authority under subparagraph (A) for up to 10 percent of the combined apportionments of the State under paragraphs (1), (2), (5)(D), and (6) of section 104(b).

(ii) FEDERAL SHARE INCREASE.—The Federal share payable on account of a project, program, or activity described in subparagraph (A) may be increased by up to 5 percent of the total project cost.

(4) POOLED FUNDING.—Notwithstanding any other provision of law, the Secretary may waive the non-Federal share of the cost of a project or activity under section 502(b)(6) that is carried out with amounts apportioned under section 104(b)(2) after considering appropriate factors, including whether—

(A) decreasing or eliminating the non-Federal share would best serve the interests of the Federal-aid highway program; and

(B) the project or activity addresses national or regional high priority research, development, and technology transfer problems in a manner that would benefit multiple States or metropolitan planning organizations.

(d) The Secretary may rely on a statement from the Secretary of the Interior as to the area of the lands referred to in subsections (a) and (b) of this section. The Secretary of the Interior is authorized and directed to provide such statement annually.

(e) EMERGENCY RELIEF.—The Federal share payable for any repair or reconstruction provided for by funds made available under section 125 for any project on a Federal-aid highway, including the Interstate System, shall not exceed the Federal share payable on a project on the system as provided in subsections (a) and (b), except that—

(1) the Federal share payable for eligible emergency repairs to minimize damage, protect facilities, or restore essential traffic accomplished within 270 days after the actual occurrence of the natural disaster or catastrophic failure may amount to 100 percent of the cost of the repairs;

(2) the Federal share payable for any repair or reconstruction of Federal land transportation facilities, other Federally owned roads that are open to public travel, and tribal transportation facilities may amount to 100 percent of the cost of the repair or reconstruction;

(3) the Secretary shall extend the time period in paragraph (1) taking into consideration any delay in the ability of the State to access damaged facilities to evaluate damage and the cost of repair; and

(4) the Federal share payable for eligible repairs to restore damaged facilities to predisaster condition may amount to 90 percent of the cost of the repairs if the eligible expenses incurred by the State due to natural disasters or catastrophic failures in a Federal fiscal year exceeds the annual apportionment of the State under section 104 for the fiscal year in which the disasters or failures occurred.

(f) The Secretary is authorized to cooperate with the State transportation departments and with the Department of the Interior in the construction of Federal-aid highways within Indian reservations and national parks and monuments under the jurisdiction of the Department of the Interior and to pay the amount assumed therefor from the funds apportioned in accordance with section 104 of this title to the State wherein the reservations and national parks and monuments are located.

(g) Notwithstanding any other provision of this section or of this title, the Federal share payable on account of any project under this title in the Virgin Islands, Guam, American Samoa, or the Commonwealth of the Northern Mariana Islands shall be 100 per centum of the total cost of the project.

(h) INCREASED NON-FEDERAL SHARE.—Notwithstanding any other provision of this title and subject to such criteria as the Secretary may establish, a State may contribute an amount in excess of the non-Federal share of a project under this title so as to decrease the Federal share payable on such project.

(i) CREDIT FOR NON-FEDERAL SHARE.—

(1) ELIGIBILITY.—

(A) IN GENERAL.—A State may use as a credit toward the non-Federal share requirement for any funds made available to carry out this title (other than the emergency relief program authorized by section 125) or chapter 53 of title 49 toll revenues that are generated and used by public, quasi-public, and private agencies to build, improve, or maintain highways, bridges, or tunnels that serve the public purpose of interstate commerce.

(B) SPECIAL RULE FOR USE OF FEDERAL FUNDS.—If the public, quasi-public, or private agency has built, improved, or maintained the facility using Federal funds, the credit under this paragraph shall be reduced by a percentage equal to the percentage of the total cost of building, improving, or maintaining the facility that was derived from Federal funds.

(C) FEDERAL FUNDS DEFINED.—In this paragraph, the term "Federal funds" does not include loans of Federal funds or other financial assistance that must be repaid to the Government.

(2) MAINTENANCE OF EFFORT.—

(A) IN GENERAL.—The credit for any non-Federal share provided under this subsection shall not reduce nor replace State funds required to match Federal funds for any program under this title.

(B) CONDITION ON RECEIPT OF CREDIT.—To receive a credit under paragraph (1) for a fiscal year, a State shall enter into such agreement as the Secretary may require to ensure that the State will maintain its non-Federal transportation capital expenditures in such fiscal year at or above the average level of such expenditures for the preceding 3 fiscal years; except that if, for any 1 of the preceding 3 fiscal years, the non-Federal transportation capital expenditures of the State were at a level that was greater than 130 percent of the average level of such expenditures for the other 2 of the preceding 3 fiscal years, the agreement shall ensure that the State will maintain its non-Federal transportation capital expenditures in the fiscal year of the credit at or above the average level of such expenditures for the other 2 fiscal years.

(C) TRANSPORTATION CAPITAL EXPENDITURES DEFINED.—In subparagraph (B), the term "non-Federal transportation capital expenditures" includes any payments made by the State for issuance of transportation-related bonds.

(3) TREATMENT.—

(A) LIMITATION ON LIABILITY.—Use of a credit for a non-Federal share under this subsection that is received from a public, quasi-public, or private agency—

(i) shall not expose the agency to additional liability, additional regulation, or additional administrative oversight; and

(ii) shall not subject the agency to any additional Federal design standards or laws (including regulations) as a result of providing the non-Federal share other than those to which the agency is already subject.

(B) CHARTERED MULTISTATE AGENCIES.—When a credit that is received from a chartered multistate agency is applied to a non-Federal share under this subsection, such credit shall be applied equally to all charter States.

(j) USE OF FEDERAL AGENCY FUNDS.—Notwithstanding any other provision of law, any Federal funds other than those made available under this title and title 49 may be used to pay the non-Federal share of the cost of any transportation project that is within, adjacent to, or provides access to Federal land, the Federal share of which is funded under this title or chapter 53 of title 49.

(k) USE OF FEDERAL LAND AND TRIBAL TRANSPORTATION FUNDS.—Notwithstanding any other provision of law, the funds authorized to be appropriated to carry out the tribal transportation program under section 202 and the Federal lands transportation program under section 203 may be used to pay the non-Federal share of the cost of any project that is funded under this title or chapter 53 of title 49 and that provides access to or within Federal or tribal land.

(l) FEDERAL SHARE FLEXIBILITY PILOT PROGRAM.—

(1) ESTABLISHMENT.—Not later than 180 days after the date of enactment of the Surface Transportation Reauthorization Act of 2021, the Secretary shall establish a pilot program (referred to in this subsection as the "pilot program") to give States additional flexibility with respect to the Federal requirements under this section.

(2) PROGRAM.—

(A) IN GENERAL.—Notwithstanding any other provision of law, a State participating in the pilot program (referred to in this subsection as a "participating State") may determine the Federal share on a project, multiple-project, or program basis for projects under any of the following:

(i) The national highway performance program under section 119.

(ii) The surface transportation block grant program under section 133.

(iii) The highway safety improvement program under section 148.

(iv) The congestion mitigation and air quality improvement program under section 149.

(v) The national highway freight program under section 167.

(vi) The carbon reduction program under section 175.

(vii) Subsection (c) of the PROTECT program under section 176.

(B) REQUIREMENTS.—

(i) MAXIMUM FEDERAL SHARE.—Subject to clause (iii), the Federal share of the cost of an individual project carried out under a program described in subparagraph (A) by a participating State and to which the participating State is applying the Federal share requirements under the pilot program may be up to 100 percent.

(ii) MINIMUM FEDERAL SHARE.—No individual project carried out under a program described in subparagraph (A) by a participating State and to which the participating State is applying the Federal share requirements under the pilot program shall have a Federal share of 0 percent.

(iii) DETERMINATION.—The average annual Federal share of the total cost of all projects authorized under a program described in subparagraph (A) to which a participating State is applying the Federal share requirements under the pilot program shall be not more than the average of the maximum Federal share of those projects if those projects were not carried out under the pilot program.

(C) SELECTION.—

(i) APPLICATION.—A State seeking to be a participating State shall—

(I) submit to the Secretary an application in such form, at such time, and containing such information as the Secretary may require; and

(II) have in place adequate financial controls to allow the State to determine the average annual Federal share requirements under the pilot program.

(ii) REQUIREMENT.—For each of fiscal years 2022 through 2026, the Secretary shall select not more than 10 States to be participating States.

(Pub. L. 85–767, Aug. 27, 1958, 72 Stat. 898; Pub. L. 86–70, §21(d)(4), (e)(4), June 25, 1959, 73 Stat. 145, 146; Pub. L. 86–342, title I, §107(b), Sept. 21, 1959, 73 Stat. 613; Pub. L. 86–657, §3, July 14, 1960, 74 Stat. 522; Pub. L. 88–658, Oct. 13, 1964, 78 Stat. 1090; Pub. L. 89–574, §9(a), Sept. 13, 1966, 80 Stat. 769; Pub. L. 90–495, §§27(b), 34, Aug. 23, 1968, 82 Stat. 829, 835; Pub. L. 91–605, title I, §§106(f), 108(a), 109(b), 128, Dec. 31, 1970, 84 Stat. 1718, 1719, 1731; Pub. L. 95–599, title I, §§117, 129(a)–(c), (i), Nov. 6, 1978, 92 Stat. 2699, 2707, 2708; Pub. L. 97–424, title I, §§109(b), 117, 123(a), 153(f), 156(c), Jan. 6, 1983, 96 Stat. 2105, 2109, 2113, 2133, 2134; Pub. L. 98–78, title III, §318, Aug. 15, 1983, 97 Stat. 473; Pub. L. 100–17, title I, §117(a)–(c)(1), (d), (e), Apr. 2, 1987, 101 Stat. 155, 156; Pub. L. 102–240, title I, §§1021(a), (b), 1022(a), Dec. 18, 1991, 105 Stat. 1950, 1951; Pub. L. 104–59, title III, §310(a), Nov. 28, 1995, 109 Stat. 582; Pub. L. 104–205, title III, §353(a), Sept. 30, 1996, 110 Stat. 2980; Pub. L. 105–178, title I, §§1111(a)–(c), 1113(a), (c), formerly (d), 1115(a), (f)(1), 1212(a)(2)(A)(ii), June 9, 1998, 112 Stat. 145, 151, 152, 154, 193; Pub. L. 105–206, title IX, §§9002(i), 9006(a)(2), July 22, 1998, 112 Stat. 836, 848; Pub. L. 109–59, title I, §§1111(b)(2), 1116(c), 1119(a), 1905, 1947, Aug. 10, 2005, 119 Stat. 1171, 1177, 1181, 1467, 1513; Pub. L. 110–140, title XI, §1131, Dec. 19, 2007, 121 Stat. 1763; Pub. L. 112–141, div. A, title I, §§1304(b), 1508, July 6, 2012, 126 Stat. 532, 565; Pub. L. 114–94, div. A, title I, §§1104(e)(2), 1408, Dec. 4, 2015, 129 Stat. 1332, 1410; Pub. L. 117–58, div. A, title I, §11107, Nov. 15, 2021, 135 Stat. 459.)

§121. PAYMENT TO STATES FOR CONSTRUCTION

(a) IN GENERAL.—The Secretary, from time to time as the work progresses, may make payments to a State for costs of construction incurred by the State on a project (including payments made pursuant to a long-term concession agreement, such as availability payments). Such payments may also be made for the value of the materials—

(1) that have been stockpiled in the vicinity of the construction in conformity to plans and specifications for the projects; and

(2) that are not in the vicinity of the construction if the Secretary determines that because of required fabrication at an off-site location the material cannot be stockpiled in such vicinity.

§122. Payments to States for bond and other
debt instrument financing
CHAPTER 1—FEDERAL-AID HIGHWAYS

(b) PROJECT AGREEMENT.—No payment shall be made under this chapter except for a project covered by a project agreement. After completion of the project in accordance with the project agreement, a State shall be entitled to payment out of the appropriate sums apportioned or allocated to the State of the unpaid balance of the Federal share payable for such project.

(c) Such payments shall be made to such official or officials or depository as may be designated by the State transportation department and authorized under the laws of the State to receive public funds of the State.

(Pub. L. 85–767, Aug. 27, 1958, 72 Stat. 899; Pub. L. 88–157, §7(b), Oct. 24, 1963, 77 Stat. 278; Pub. L. 93–87, title I, §117, Aug. 13, 1973, 87 Stat. 259; Pub. L. 94–280, title I, §118(a), May 5, 1976, 90 Stat. 437; Pub. L. 100–17, title I, §133(b)(6), Apr. 2, 1987, 101 Stat. 171; Pub. L. 102–240, title I, §1018(b), Dec. 18, 1991, 105 Stat. 1948; Pub. L. 105–178, title I, §§1212(a)(2)(A)(i), 1302, June 9, 1998, 112 Stat. 193, 226; Pub. L. 114–94, div. A, title II, §2002(a), Dec. 4, 2015, 129 Stat. 1446.)

§122. PAYMENTS TO STATES FOR BOND AND OTHER DEBT INSTRUMENT FINANCING

(a) DEFINITION OF ELIGIBLE DEBT FINANCING INSTRUMENT.—In this section, the term "eligible debt financing instrument" means a bond or other debt financing instrument, including a note, certificate, mortgage, or lease agreement, issued by a State or political subdivision of a State or a public authority, the proceeds of which are used for an eligible project under this title.

(b) FEDERAL REIMBURSEMENT.—Subject to subsections (c) and (d), the Secretary may reimburse a State for expenses and costs incurred by the State or a political subdivision of the State and reimburse a public authority for expenses and costs incurred by the public authority for—

(1) interest payments under an eligible debt financing instrument;

(2) the retirement of principal of an eligible debt financing instrument;

(3) the cost of the issuance of an eligible debt financing instrument;

(4) the cost of insurance for an eligible debt financing instrument; and

(5) any other cost incidental to the sale of an eligible debt financing instrument (as determined by the Secretary).

(c) CONDITIONS ON PAYMENT.—The Secretary may reimburse a State or public authority under subsection (b) with respect to a project funded by an eligible debt financing instrument after the State or public authority has complied with this title with respect to the project to the extent and in the manner that would be required if payment were to be made under section 121.

(d) FEDERAL SHARE.—The Federal share of the cost of a project payable under this section shall not exceed the Federal share of the cost of the project as determined under section 120.

(e) STATUTORY CONSTRUCTION.—Notwithstanding any other provision of law, the eligibility of an eligible debt financing instrument for reimbursement under subsection (b) shall not—

(1) constitute a commitment, guarantee, or obligation on the part of the United States to provide for payment of principal or interest on the eligible debt financing instrument; or

(2) create any right of a third party against the United States for payment under the eligible debt financing instrument.

(Pub. L. 85–767, Aug. 27, 1958, 72 Stat. 900; Pub. L. 95–599, title I, §115(b), Nov. 6, 1978, 92 Stat. 2698; Pub. L. 97–424, title I, §107(f), Jan. 6, 1983, 96 Stat. 2103; Pub. L. 100–17, title I, §133(b)(7), Apr. 2, 1987, 101 Stat. 171; Pub. L. 104–59, title III, §311(a), Nov. 28, 1995, 109 Stat. 583.)

§123. RELOCATION OF UTILITY FACILITIES

(a) DEFINITIONS.—In this section:

(1) COST OF RELOCATION.—The term "cost of relocation" includes the entire amount paid by a utility properly attributable to the relocation of a utility facility, minus any increase in the value of the new facility and any salvage value derived from the old facility.

(2) EARLY UTILITY RELOCATION PROJECT.—The term "early utility relocation project" means utility relocation activities identified by the State for performance before completion of the environmental review process for the transportation project.

(3) ENVIRONMENTAL REVIEW PROCESS.—The term "environmental review process" has the meaning given the term in section 139(a).

(4) TRANSPORTATION PROJECT.—The term "transportation project" means a project.

(5) UTILITY FACILITY.—The term "utility facility" means any privately, publicly, or cooperatively owned line, facility, or system for producing, transmitting, or distributing communications, power, electricity, light, heat, gas, oil, crude products, water, steam, waste, stormwater not connected with highway drainage, or any other similar commodity, including any fire or police signal system or street lighting system, that directly or indirectly serves the public.

(6) UTILITY RELOCATION ACTIVITY.—The term "utility relocation activity" means an activity necessary for the relocation of a utility facility, including preliminary and final design, surveys, real property acquisition, materials acquisition, and construction.

(b) REIMBURSEMENT TO STATES.—

(1) IN GENERAL.—If a State pays for the cost of relocation of a utility facility necessitated by the construction of a transportation project, Federal funds may be used to reimburse the State for the cost of relocation in the same proportion as Federal funds are expended on the transportation project.

(2) LIMITATION.—Federal funds shall not be used to reimburse a State under this section if the payment to the utility—

(A) violates the law of the State; or

(B) violates a legal contract between the utility and the State.

(3) REQUIREMENT.—A reimbursement under paragraph (1) shall be made only if the State demonstrates to the satisfaction of the Secretary that the State paid the cost of the utility relocation activity from funds of the State with respect to transportation projects for which Federal funds are obligated subsequent to April 16, 1958, for work, including utility relocation activities.

(4) REIMBURSEMENT ELIGIBILITY FOR EARLY RELOCATION PRIOR TO TRANSPORTATION PROJECT ENVIRONMENTAL REVIEW PROCESS.—

(A) IN GENERAL.—In addition to the requirements under paragraphs (1) through (3), a State may carry out, at the expense of the State, an early utility relocation project for a transportation project before completion of the environmental review process for the transportation project.

(B) REQUIREMENTS FOR REIMBURSEMENT.—Funds apportioned to a State under this title may be used to pay the costs incurred by the State for an early utility relocation project only if the State demonstrates to the Secretary, and the Secretary finds that—

(i) the early utility relocation project is necessary to accommodate a transportation project;

(ii) the State provides adequate documentation to the Secretary of eligible costs incurred by the State for the early utility relocation project;

(iii) before the commencement of the utility relocation activities, an environmental review process was completed for the early utility relocation project that resulted in a finding that the early utility relocation project—

(I) would not result in significant adverse environmental impacts; and

(II) would comply with other applicable Federal environmental requirements;

(iv) the early utility relocation project did not influence—

(I) the environmental review process for the transportation project;

(II) the decision relating to the need to construct the transportation project; or

(III) the selection of the transportation project design or location;

(v) the early utility relocation project complies with all applicable provisions of law, including regulations issued pursuant to this title;

(vi) the early utility relocation project follows applicable financial procedures and requirements, including documentation of eligible costs and the requirements under section 109(l), but not including requirements applicable to authorization and obligation of Federal funds;

(vii) the transportation project for which the early utility relocation project was necessitated was included in the applicable transportation improvement program under section 134 or 135;

(viii) before the cost incurred by a State is approved for Federal participation, environmental compliance pursuant to the National Environmental Policy Act of 1969 (42 U.S.C. 4321 et seq.) has been completed for the transportation project for which the early utility relocation project was necessitated; and

(ix) the transportation project that necessitated the utility relocation activity is approved for construction.

(C) SAVINGS PROVISION.—Nothing in this paragraph affects other eligibility requirements or authorities for Federal participation in payment of costs incurred for utility relocation activities.

(c) APPLICABILITY OF OTHER PROVISIONS.—Nothing in this section affects the applicability of other requirements that would otherwise apply to an early utility relocation project, including any applicable requirements under—

(1) section 138;

(2) the Uniform Relocation Assistance and Real Property Acquisition Policies Act of 1970 (42 U.S.C. 4601 et seq.), including regulations under part 24 of title 49, Code of Federal Regulations (or successor regulations);

(3) title VI of the Civil Rights Act of 1964 (42 U.S.C. 2000d et seq.); or

(4) an environmental review process.

(Pub. L. 85–767, Aug. 27, 1958, 72 Stat. 900; Pub. L. 100–17, title I, §133(b)(8), Apr. 2, 1987, 101 Stat. 171; Pub. L. 112–141, div. A, title I, §1104(c)(3), July 6, 2012, 126 Stat. 427; Pub. L. 117–58, div. A, title I, §11315, Nov. 15, 2021, 135 Stat. 540.)

§124. BRIDGE INVESTMENT PROGRAM

(a) DEFINITIONS.—In this section:

(1) ELIGIBLE PROJECT.—

(A) IN GENERAL.—The term "eligible project" means a project to replace, rehabilitate, preserve, or protect 1 or more bridges on the National Bridge Inventory under section 144(b).

(B) INCLUSIONS.—The term "eligible project" includes—

(i) a bundle of projects described in subparagraph (A), regardless of whether the bundle of projects meets the requirements of section 144(j)(5); and

(ii) a project to replace or rehabilitate culverts for the purpose of improving flood control and improved habitat connectivity for aquatic species.

(2) LARGE PROJECT.—The term "large project" means an eligible project with total eligible project costs of greater than $100,000,000.

(3) PROGRAM.—The term "program" means the bridge investment program established by subsection (b)(1).

(b) ESTABLISHMENT OF BRIDGE INVESTMENT PROGRAM.—

(1) IN GENERAL.—There is established a bridge investment program to provide financial assistance for eligible projects under this section.

(2) GOALS.—The goals of the program shall be—

(A) to improve the safety, efficiency, and reliability of the movement of people and freight over bridges;

(B) to improve the condition of bridges in the United States by reducing—

(i) the number of bridges—

(I) in poor condition; or

(II) in fair condition and at risk of falling into poor condition within the next 3 years;

(ii) the total person miles traveled over bridges—

(I) in poor condition; or

(II) in fair condition and at risk of falling into poor condition within the next 3 years;

(iii) the number of bridges that—

(I) do not meet current geometric design standards; or

(II) cannot meet the load and traffic requirements typical of the regional transportation network; and

(iv) the total person miles traveled over bridges that—

(I) do not meet current geometric design standards; or

(II) cannot meet the load and traffic requirements typical of the regional transportation network; and

(C) to provide financial assistance that leverages and encourages non-Federal contributions from sponsors and stakeholders involved in the planning, design, and construction of eligible projects.

(c) GRANT AUTHORITY.—

(1) IN GENERAL.—In carrying out the program, the Secretary may award grants, on a competitive basis, in accordance with this section.

(2) GRANT AMOUNTS.—Except as otherwise provided, a grant under the program shall be—

(A) in the case of a large project, in an amount that is—

(i) adequate to fully fund the project (in combination with other financial resources identified in the application); and

(ii) not less than $50,000,000; and

(B) in the case of any other eligible project, in an amount that is—

(i) adequate to fully fund the project (in combination with other financial resources identified in the application); and

(ii) not less than $2,500,000.

(3) MAXIMUM AMOUNT.—Except as otherwise provided, for an eligible project receiving assistance under the program, the amount of assistance provided by the Secretary under this section, as a share of eligible project costs, shall be—

(A) in the case of a large project, not more than 50 percent; and

(B) in the case of any other eligible project, not more than 80 percent.

(4) FEDERAL SHARE.—

(A) MAXIMUM FEDERAL INVOLVEMENT.—Federal assistance other than a grant under the program may be used to satisfy the non-Federal share of the cost of a project for which a grant is made, except that the total Federal assistance provided for a project receiving a grant under the program may not exceed the Federal share for the project under section 120.

(B) OFF-SYSTEM BRIDGES.—In the case of an eligible project for an off-system bridge (as defined in section 133(f)(1))—

(i) Federal assistance other than a grant under the program may be used to satisfy the non-Federal share of the cost of a project; and

(ii) notwithstanding subparagraph (A), the total Federal assistance provided for the project shall not exceed 90 percent of the total eligible project costs.

(C) FEDERAL LAND MANAGEMENT AGENCIES AND TRIBAL GOVERNMENTS.—Notwithstanding any other provision of law, Federal funds other than Federal funds made available under this section may be used to pay the remaining share of the cost of a project under the program by a Federal land management agency or a Tribal government or consortium of Tribal governments.

(5) CONSIDERATIONS.—

(A) IN GENERAL.—In awarding grants under the program, the Secretary shall consider—

(i) in the case of a large project, the ratings assigned under subsection (g)(5)(A);

(ii) in the case of an eligible project other than a large project, the quality rating assigned under subsection (f)(3)(A)(ii);

(iii) the average daily person and freight throughput supported by the eligible project;

(iv) the number and percentage of bridges within the same State as the eligible project that are in poor condition;

(v) the extent to which the eligible project demonstrates cost savings by bundling multiple bridge projects;

(vi) in the case of an eligible project of a Federal land management agency, the extent to which the grant would reduce a Federal liability or Federal infrastructure maintenance backlog;

(vii) geographic diversity among grant recipients, including the need for a balance between the needs of rural and urban communities; and

(viii) the extent to which a bridge that would be assisted with a grant—

(I) is, without that assistance—

(aa) at risk of falling into or remaining in poor condition; or

(bb) in fair condition and at risk of falling into poor condition within the next 3 years;

(II) does not meet current geometric design standards based on—

(aa) the current use of the bridge; or

(bb) load and traffic requirements typical of the regional corridor or local network in which the bridge is located; or

(III) does not meet current seismic design standards.

(B) REQUIREMENT.—The Secretary shall—

(i) give priority to an application for an eligible project that is located within a State for which—

(I) 2 or more applications for eligible projects within the State were submitted for the current fiscal year and an average of 2 or more applications for eligible projects within the State were submitted in prior fiscal years of the program; and

(II) fewer than 2 grants have been awarded for eligible projects within the State under the program;

(ii) during the period of fiscal years 2022 through 2026, for each State described in clause (i), select—

(I) not fewer than 1 large project that the Secretary determines is justified under the evaluation under subsection (g)(4); or

(II) 2 eligible projects that are not large projects that the Secretary determines are justified under the evaluation under subsection (f)(3); and

(iii) not be required to award a grant for an eligible project that the Secretary does not determine is justified under an evaluation under subsection (f)(3) or (g)(4).

(6) CULVERT LIMITATION.—Not more than 5 percent of the amounts made available for each fiscal year for grants under the program may be used for eligible projects that consist solely of culvert replacement or rehabilitation.

(d) ELIGIBLE ENTITY.—The Secretary may make a grant under the program to any of the following:

(1) A State or a group of States.

(2) A metropolitan planning organization that serves an urbanized area (as designated by the Bureau of the Census) with a population of over 200,000.

(3) A unit of local government or a group of local governments.

(4) A political subdivision of a State or local government.

(5) A special purpose district or public authority with a transportation function.

(6) A Federal land management agency.

(7) A Tribal government or a consortium of Tribal governments.

(8) A multistate or multijurisdictional group of entities described in paragraphs (1) through (7).

(e) ELIGIBLE PROJECT REQUIREMENTS.—The Secretary may make a grant under the program only to an eligible entity for an eligible project that—

(1) in the case of a large project, the Secretary recommends for funding in the annual report on funding recommendations under subsection (g)(6), except as provided in subsection (g)(1)(B);

(2) is reasonably expected to begin construction not later than 18 months after the date on which funds are obligated for the project; and

(3) is based on the results of preliminary engineering.

(f) COMPETITIVE PROCESS AND EVALUATION OF ELIGIBLE PROJECTS OTHER THAN LARGE PROJECTS.—

(1) COMPETITIVE PROCESS.—

(A) IN GENERAL.—The Secretary shall—

(i) for the first fiscal year for which funds are made available for obligation under the program, not later than 60 days after the date on which the template under subparagraph (B)(i) is developed, and in subsequent fiscal years, not later than 60 days after the date on which amounts are made available for obligation under the program, solicit grant applications for eligible projects other than large projects; and

(ii) not later than 120 days after the date on which the solicitation under clause (i) expires, conduct evaluations under paragraph (3).

(B) REQUIREMENTS.—In carrying out subparagraph (A), the Secretary shall—

(i) develop a template for applicants to use to summarize project needs and benefits, including benefits described in paragraph (3)(B)(i); and

(ii) enable applicants to use data from the National Bridge Inventory under section 144(b) to populate templates described in clause (i), as applicable.

(2) APPLICATIONS.—An eligible entity shall submit to the Secretary an application at such time, in such manner, and containing such information as the Secretary may require.

(3) EVALUATION.—

(A) IN GENERAL.—Prior to providing a grant under this subsection, the Secretary shall—

(i) conduct an evaluation of each eligible project for which an application is received under this subsection; and

(ii) assign a quality rating to the eligible project on the basis of the evaluation under clause (i).

(B) REQUIREMENTS.—In carrying out an evaluation under subparagraph (A), the Secretary shall—

(i) consider information on project benefits submitted by the applicant using the template developed under paragraph (1)(B)(i), including whether the project will generate, as determined by the Secretary—

(I) costs avoided by the prevention of closure or reduced use of the bridge to be improved by the project;

(II) in the case of a bundle of projects, benefits from executing the projects as a bundle compared to as individual projects;

(III) safety benefits, including the reduction of accidents and related costs;

(IV) person and freight mobility benefits, including congestion reduction and reliability improvements;

(V) national or regional economic benefits;

(VI) benefits from long-term resiliency to extreme weather events, flooding, or other natural disasters;

(VII) benefits from protection (as described in section 133(b)(10)), including improving seismic or scour protection;

(VIII) environmental benefits, including wildlife connectivity;

(IX) benefits to nonvehicular and public transportation users;

(X) benefits of using—

(aa) innovative design and construction techniques; or

(bb) innovative technologies; or

(XI) reductions in maintenance costs, including, in the case of a federally-owned bridge, cost savings to the Federal budget; and

(ii) consider whether and the extent to which the benefits, including the benefits described in clause (i), are more likely than not to outweigh the total project costs.

(g) COMPETITIVE PROCESS, EVALUATION, AND ANNUAL REPORT FOR LARGE PROJECTS.—

(1) IN GENERAL.—

(A) APPLICATIONS.—The Secretary shall establish an annual date by which an eligible entity submitting an application for a large project shall submit to the Secretary such information as the Secretary may require, including information described in paragraph (2), in order for a large project to be considered for a recommendation by the Secretary for funding in the next annual report under paragraph (6).

(B) FIRST FISCAL YEAR.—Notwithstanding subparagraph (A), for the first fiscal year for which funds are made available for obligation for grants under the program, the Secretary may establish a date by which an eligible entity submitting an application for a large project shall submit to the Secretary such information as the Secretary may require, including information described in paragraph (2), in order for a large project to be considered for immediate execution of a grant agreement.

(2) INFORMATION REQUIRED.—The information referred to in paragraph (1) includes—

(A) all necessary information required for the Secretary to evaluate the large project; and

(B) information sufficient for the Secretary to determine that—

(i) the large project meets the applicable requirements under this section; and

(ii) there is a reasonable likelihood that the large project will continue to meet the requirements under this section.

(3) DETERMINATION; NOTICE.—On making a determination that information submitted to the Secretary under paragraph (1) is sufficient, the Secretary shall provide a written notice of that determination to—

(A) the eligible entity that submitted the application;

(B) the Committee on Environment and Public Works of the Senate; and

(C) the Committee on Transportation and Infrastructure of the House of Representatives.

(4) EVALUATION.—The Secretary may recommend a large project for funding in the annual report under paragraph (6), or, in the case of the first fiscal year for which funds are made available for obligation for grants under the program, immediately execute a grant agreement for a large project, only if the Secretary evaluates the proposed project and determines that the project is justified because the project—

(A) addresses a need to improve the condition of the bridge, as determined by the Secretary, consistent with the goals of the program under subsection (b)(2);

(B) will generate, as determined by the Secretary—

(i) costs avoided by the prevention of closure or reduced use of the bridge to be improved by the project;

(ii) in the case of a bundle of projects, benefits from executing the projects as a bundle compared to as individual projects;

(iii) safety benefits, including the reduction of accidents and related costs;

(iv) person and freight mobility benefits, including congestion reduction and reliability improvements;

(v) national or regional economic benefits;

(vi) benefits from long-term resiliency to extreme weather events, flooding, or other natural disasters;

(vii) benefits from protection (as described in section 133(b)(10)), including improving seismic or scour protection;

(viii) environmental benefits, including wildlife connectivity;

(ix) benefits to nonvehicular and public transportation users;

(x) benefits of using—

(I) innovative design and construction techniques; or

(II) innovative technologies; or

(xi) reductions in maintenance costs, including, in the case of a federally-owned bridge, cost savings to the Federal budget;

(C) is cost effective based on an analysis of whether the benefits and avoided costs described in subparagraph (B) are expected to outweigh the project costs;

(D) is supported by other Federal or non-Federal financial commitments or revenues adequate to fund ongoing maintenance and preservation; and

(E) is consistent with the objectives of an applicable asset management plan of the project sponsor, including a State asset management plan under section 119(e) in the case of a project on the National Highway System that is sponsored by a State.

(5) RATINGS.—

(A) IN GENERAL.—The Secretary shall develop a methodology to evaluate and rate a large project on a 5-point scale (the points of which include "high", "medium-high", "medium", "medium-low", and "low") for each of—
    (i) paragraph (4)(B);
    (ii) paragraph (4)(C); and
    (iii) paragraph (4)(D).
(B) REQUIREMENT.—To be considered justified and receive a recommendation for funding in the annual report under paragraph (6), a project shall receive a rating of not less than "medium" for each rating required under subparagraph (A).
(C) INTERIM METHODOLOGY.—In the first fiscal year for which funds are made available for obligation for grants under the program, the Secretary may establish an interim methodology to evaluate and rate a large project for each of—
    (i) paragraph (4)(B);
    (ii) paragraph (4)(C); and
    (iii) paragraph (4)(D).
(6) ANNUAL REPORT ON FUNDING RECOMMENDATIONS FOR LARGE PROJECTS.—
(A) IN GENERAL.—Not later than the first Monday in February of each year, the Secretary shall submit to the Committees on Transportation and Infrastructure and Appropriations of the House of Representatives and the Committees on Environment and Public Works and Appropriations of the Senate a report that includes—
    (i) a list of large projects that have requested a recommendation for funding under a new grant agreement from funds anticipated to be available to carry out this subsection in the next fiscal year;
    (ii) the evaluation under paragraph (4) and ratings under paragraph (5) for each project referred to in clause (i);
    (iii) the grant amounts that the Secretary recommends providing to large projects in the next fiscal year, including—
        (I) scheduled payments under previously signed multiyear grant agreements under subsection (j);
        (II) payments for new grant agreements, including single-year grant agreements and multiyear grant agreements; and
        (III) a description of how amounts anticipated to be available for the program from the Highway Trust Fund for that fiscal year will be distributed; and
    (iv) for each project for which the Secretary recommends a new multiyear grant agreement under subsection (j), the proposed payout schedule for the project.
(B) LIMITATIONS.—
    (i) IN GENERAL.—The Secretary shall not recommend in an annual report under this paragraph a new multiyear grant agreement provided from funds from the Highway Trust Fund unless the Secretary determines that the project can be completed using funds that are anticipated to be available from the Highway Trust Fund in future fiscal years.
    (ii) GENERAL FUND PROJECTS.—The Secretary—

(I) may recommend for funding in an annual report under this paragraph a large project using funds from the general fund of the Treasury; but

(II) shall not execute a grant agreement for that project unless—

(aa) funds other than from the Highway Trust Fund have been made available for the project; and

(bb) the Secretary determines that the project can be completed using funds other than from the Highway Trust Fund that are anticipated to be available in future fiscal years.

(C) CONSIDERATIONS.—In selecting projects to recommend for funding in the annual report under this paragraph, or, in the case of the first fiscal year for which funds are made available for obligation for grants under the program, projects for immediate execution of a grant agreement, the Secretary shall—

(i) consider the amount of funds available in future fiscal years for multiyear grant agreements as described in subparagraph (B); and

(ii) assume the availability of funds in future fiscal years for multiyear grant agreements that extend beyond the period of authorization based on the amount made available for large projects under the program in the last fiscal year of the period of authorization.

(D) PROJECT DIVERSITY.—In selecting projects to recommend for funding in the annual report under this paragraph, the Secretary shall ensure diversity among projects recommended based on—

(i) the amount of the grant requested; and

(ii) grants for an eligible project for 1 bridge compared to an eligible project that is a bundle of projects.

(h) ELIGIBLE PROJECT COSTS.—A grant received for an eligible project under the program may be used for—

(1) development phase activities, including planning, feasibility analysis, revenue forecasting, environmental review, preliminary engineering and design work, and other preconstruction activities;

(2) construction, reconstruction, rehabilitation, acquisition of real property (including land related to the project and improvements to the land), environmental mitigation, construction contingencies, acquisition of equipment, and operational improvements directly related to improving system performance; and

(3) expenses related to the protection (as described in section 133(b)(10)) of a bridge, including seismic or scour protection.

(i) TIFIA PROGRAM.—On the request of an eligible entity carrying out an eligible project, the Secretary may use amounts awarded to the entity to pay subsidy and administrative costs necessary to provide to the entity Federal credit assistance under chapter 6 with respect to the eligible project for which the grant was awarded.

(j) MULTIYEAR GRANT AGREEMENTS FOR LARGE PROJECTS.—

(1) IN GENERAL.—A large project that receives a grant under the program in an amount of not less than $100,000,000 may be carried out through a multiyear grant agreement in accordance with this subsection.

(2) REQUIREMENTS.—A multiyear grant agreement for a large project described in paragraph (1) shall—

(A) establish the terms of participation by the Federal Government in the project;

(B) establish the maximum amount of Federal financial assistance for the project in accordance with paragraphs (3) and (4) of subsection (c);

(C) establish a payout schedule for the project that provides for disbursement of the full grant amount by not later than 4 fiscal years after the fiscal year in which the initial amount is provided;

(D) determine the period of time for completing the project, even if that period extends beyond the period of an authorization; and

(E) attempt to improve timely and efficient management of the project, consistent with all applicable Federal laws (including regulations).

(3) SPECIAL FINANCIAL RULES.—

(A) IN GENERAL.—A multiyear grant agreement under this subsection—

(i) shall obligate an amount of available budget authority specified in law; and

(ii) may include a commitment, contingent on amounts to be specified in law in advance for commitments under this paragraph, to obligate an additional amount from future available budget authority specified in law.

(B) STATEMENT OF CONTINGENT COMMITMENT.—The agreement shall state that the contingent commitment is not an obligation of the Federal Government.

(C) INTEREST AND OTHER FINANCING COSTS.—

(i) IN GENERAL.—Interest and other financing costs of carrying out a part of the project within a reasonable time shall be considered a cost of carrying out the project under a multiyear grant agreement, except that eligible costs may not be more than the cost of the most favorable financing terms reasonably available for the project at the time of borrowing.

(ii) CERTIFICATION.—The applicant shall certify to the Secretary that the applicant has shown reasonable diligence in seeking the most favorable financing terms.

(4) ADVANCE PAYMENT.—Notwithstanding any other provision of law, an eligible entity carrying out a large project under a multiyear grant agreement—

(A) may use funds made available to the eligible entity under this title for eligible project costs of the large project until the amount specified in the multiyear grant agreement for the project for that fiscal year becomes available for obligation; and

(B) if the eligible entity uses funds as described in subparagraph (A), the funds used shall be reimbursed from the amount made available under the multiyear grant agreement for the project.

(k) UNDERTAKING PARTS OF PROJECTS IN ADVANCE UNDER LETTERS OF NO PREJUDICE.—

(1) IN GENERAL.—The Secretary may pay to an applicant all eligible project costs under the program, including costs for an activity for an eligible project incurred prior to the date on which the project receives funding under the program if—

(A) before the applicant carries out the activity, the Secretary approves through a letter to the applicant the activity in the same manner as the Secretary approves other activities as eligible under the program;

(B) a record of decision, a finding of no significant impact, or a categorical exclusion under the National Environmental Policy Act of 1969 (42 U.S.C. 4321 et seq.) has been issued for the eligible project; and

(C) the activity is carried out without Federal assistance and in accordance with all applicable procedures and requirements.

(2) INTEREST AND OTHER FINANCING COSTS.—

(A) IN GENERAL.—For purposes of paragraph (1), the cost of carrying out an activity for an eligible project includes the amount of interest and other financing costs, including any interest earned and payable on bonds, to the extent interest and other financing costs are expended in carrying out the activity for the eligible project, except that interest and other financing costs may not be more than the cost of the most favorable financing terms reasonably available for the eligible project at the time of borrowing.

(B) CERTIFICATION.—The applicant shall certify to the Secretary that the applicant has shown reasonable diligence in seeking the most favorable financing terms under subparagraph (A).

(3) NO OBLIGATION OR INFLUENCE ON RECOMMENDATIONS.—An approval by the Secretary under paragraph (1)(A) shall not—

(A) constitute an obligation of the Federal Government; or

(B) alter or influence any evaluation under subsection (f)(3)(A)(i) or (g)(4) or any recommendation by the Secretary for funding under the program.

(l) FEDERALLY-OWNED BRIDGES.—

(1) DIVESTITURE CONSIDERATION.—In the case of a bridge owned by a Federal land management agency for which that agency applies for a grant under the program, the agency—

(A) shall consider options to divest the bridge to a State or local entity after completion of the project; and

(B) may apply jointly with the State or local entity to which the bridge may be divested.

(2) TREATMENT.—Notwithstanding any other provision of law, section 129 shall apply to a bridge that was previously owned by a Federal land management agency and has been transferred to a non-Federal entity under paragraph (1) in the same manner as if the bridge was never federally owned.

(m) TREATMENT OF PROJECTS.—Notwithstanding any other provision of law, a project assisted under this section shall be treated as a project on a Federal-aid highway under this chapter.

(n) CONGRESSIONAL NOTIFICATION.—Not later than 30 days before making a grant for an eligible project under the program, the Secretary shall submit to the Committee on Transportation and Infrastructure of the House of Representatives and the Committee on Environment and Public Works of the Senate a written notification of the proposed grant that includes—

(1) an evaluation and justification for the eligible project; and

(2) the amount of the proposed grant.

(o) REPORTS.—

(1) ANNUAL REPORT.—Not later than August 1 of each fiscal year, the Secretary shall make available on the website of the Department of Transportation an annual

report that lists each eligible project for which a grant has been provided under the program during the fiscal year.

(2) GAO ASSESSMENT AND REPORT.—Not later than 3 years after the date of enactment of the Surface Transportation Reauthorization Act of 2021, the Comptroller General of the United States shall—

(A) conduct an assessment of the administrative establishment, solicitation, selection, and justification process with respect to the funding of grants under the program; and

(B) submit to the Committee on Transportation and Infrastructure of the House of Representatives and the Committee on Environment and Public Works of the Senate a report that describes—

(i) the adequacy and fairness of the process under which each eligible project that received a grant under the program was selected; and

(ii) the justification and criteria used for the selection of each eligible project.

(p) LIMITATION.—

(1) LARGE PROJECTS.—Of the amounts made available out of the Highway Trust Fund (other than the Mass Transit Account) to carry out this section for each of fiscal years 2022 through 2026, not less than 50 percent, in aggregate, shall be used for large projects.

(2) UNUTILIZED AMOUNTS.—If, in fiscal year 2026, the Secretary determines that grants under the program will not allow for the requirement under paragraph (1) to be met, the Secretary shall use the unutilized amounts to make other grants under the program during that fiscal year.

(q) TRIBAL TRANSPORTATION FACILITY BRIDGE SET ASIDE.—

(1) IN GENERAL.—Of the amounts made available from the Highway Trust Fund (other than the Mass Transit Account) for a fiscal year to carry out this section, the Secretary shall use, to carry out section 202(d)—

(A) $16,000,000 for fiscal year 2022;

(B) $18,000,000 for fiscal year 2023;

(C) $20,000,000 for fiscal year 2024;

(D) $22,000,000 for fiscal year 2025; and

(E) $24,000,000 for fiscal year 2026.

(2) TREATMENT.—For purposes of section 201, funds made available for section 202(d) under paragraph (1) shall be considered to be part of the tribal transportation program.

(Added Pub. L. 117–58, div. A, title I, §11118(a), Nov. 15, 2021, 135 Stat. 484.)

§125. EMERGENCY RELIEF

(a) IN GENERAL.—Subject to this section and section 120, an emergency fund is authorized for expenditure by the Secretary for the repair or reconstruction of highways, roads, and trails, in any area of the United States, including Indian reservations, that the Secretary finds have suffered serious damage as a result of—

(1) a natural disaster over a wide area, such as by a flood, hurricane, tidal wave, earthquake, severe storm, wildfire, or landslide; or

(2) catastrophic failure from any external cause.

(b) RESTRICTION ON ELIGIBILITY.—Funds under this section shall not be used for the repair or reconstruction of a bridge that has been permanently closed to all vehicular traffic by the State or responsible local official because of imminent danger of collapse due to a structural deficiency or physical deterioration.

(c) FUNDING.—

(1) IN GENERAL.—Subject to the limitations described in paragraph (2), there are authorized to be appropriated from the Highway Trust Fund (other than the Mass Transit Account) such sums as are necessary to establish the fund authorized by this section and to replenish that fund on an annual basis.

(2) LIMITATIONS.—The limitations referred to in paragraph (1) are that—

(A) not more than $100,000,000 is authorized to be obligated in any 1 fiscal year commencing after September 30, 1980, to carry out this section, except that, if for any fiscal year the total of all obligations under this section is less than the amount authorized to be obligated for the fiscal year, the unobligated balance of that amount shall—

(i) remain available until expended; and

(ii) be in addition to amounts otherwise available to carry out this section for each year; and

(B)(i) pending such appropriation or replenishment, the Secretary may obligate from any funds appropriated at any time for obligation in accordance with this title, including existing Federal-aid appropriations, such sums as are necessary for the immediate prosecution of the work herein authorized; and

(ii) funds obligated under this subparagraph shall be reimbursed from the appropriation or replenishment.

(d) ELIGIBILITY.—

(1) IN GENERAL.—The Secretary may expend funds from the emergency fund authorized by this section only for the repair or reconstruction of highways on Federal-aid highways in accordance with this chapter, except that—

(A) no funds shall be so expended unless an emergency has been declared by the Governor of the State with concurrence by the Secretary, unless the President has declared the emergency to be a major disaster for the purposes of the Robert T. Stafford Disaster Relief and Emergency Assistance Act (42 U.S.C. 5121 et seq.) for which concurrence of the Secretary is not required; and

(B) the Secretary has received an application from the State transportation department that includes a comprehensive list of all eligible project sites and repair costs by not later than 2 years after the natural disaster or catastrophic failure.

(2) COST LIMITATION.—

(A) DEFINITION OF COMPARABLE FACILITY.—In this paragraph, the term "comparable facility" means a facility that—

(i) meets the current geometric and construction standards required for the types and volume of traffic that the facility will carry over its design life; and

(ii) incorporates economically justifiable improvements that will mitigate the risk of recurring damage from extreme weather, flooding, and other natural disasters.

(B) LIMITATION.—The total cost of a project funded under this section may not exceed the cost of repair or reconstruction of a comparable facility.

(3) PROTECTIVE FEATURES.—

(A) IN GENERAL.—The cost of an improvement that is part of a project under this section shall be an eligible expense under this section if the improvement is a protective feature that will mitigate the risk of recurring damage or the cost of future repair from extreme weather, flooding, and other natural disasters.

(B) PROTECTIVE FEATURES DESCRIBED.—A protective feature referred to in subparagraph (A) includes—

(i) raising roadway grades;

(ii) relocating roadways in a floodplain to higher ground above projected flood elevation levels or away from slide prone areas;

(iii) stabilizing slide areas;

(iv) stabilizing slopes;

(v) lengthening or raising bridges to increase waterway openings;

(vi) increasing the size or number of drainage structures;

(vii) replacing culverts with bridges or upsizing culverts;

(viii) installing seismic retrofits on bridges;

(ix) adding scour protection at bridges, installing riprap, or adding other scour, stream stability, coastal, or other hydraulic countermeasures, including spur dikes; and

(x) the use of natural infrastructure to mitigate the risk of recurring damage or the cost of future repair from extreme weather, flooding, and other natural disasters.

(4) DEBRIS REMOVAL.—The costs of debris removal shall be an eligible expense under this section only for—

(A) an event not declared a major disaster or emergency by the President under the Robert T. Stafford Disaster Relief and Emergency Assistance Act (42 U.S.C. 5121 et seq.);

(B) an event declared a major disaster or emergency by the President under that Act if the debris removal is not eligible for assistance under section 403, 407, or 502 of that Act (42 U.S.C. 5170b, 5173, 5192); or

(C) projects eligible for assistance under this section located on tribal transportation facilities, Federal lands transportation facilities, or other federally owned roads that are open to public travel (as defined in subsection (e)(1)).

(5) SUBSTITUTE TRAFFIC.—Notwithstanding any other provision of this section, actual and necessary costs of maintenance and operation of ferryboats or additional transit service providing temporary substitute highway traffic service, less the amount of fares charged for comparable service, may be expended from the emergency fund authorized by this section for Federal-aid highways.

(e) TRIBAL TRANSPORTATION FACILITIES, FEDERAL LANDS TRANSPORTATION FACILITIES, AND PUBLIC ROADS ON FEDERAL LANDS.—

(1) DEFINITIONS.—In this subsection, the following definitions apply:

(A) OPEN TO PUBLIC TRAVEL.—The term "open to public travel" means, with respect to a road, that, except during scheduled periods, extreme weather conditions, or emergencies, the road—

(i) is maintained;

(ii) is open to the general public; and

(iii) can accommodate travel by a standard passenger vehicle, without restrictive gates or prohibitive signs or regulations, other than for general traffic control or restrictions based on size, weight, or class of registration.

(B) STANDARD PASSENGER VEHICLE.—The term "standard passenger vehicle" means a vehicle with 6 inches of clearance from the lowest point of the frame, body, suspension, or differential to the ground.

(2) EXPENDITURE OF FUNDS.—Notwithstanding subsection (d)(1), the Secretary may expend funds from the emergency fund authorized by this section, independently or in cooperation with any other branch of the Federal Government, a State agency, a tribal government, an organization, or a person, for the repair or reconstruction of tribal transportation facilities, Federal lands transportation facilities, and other federally owned roads that are open to public travel, whether or not those facilities are Federal-aid highways.

(3) REIMBURSEMENT.—

(A) IN GENERAL.—The Secretary may reimburse Federal and State agencies (including political subdivisions) for expenditures made for projects determined eligible under this section, including expenditures for emergency repairs made before a determination of eligibility.

(B) TRANSFERS.—With respect to reimbursements described in subparagraph (A)—

(i) those reimbursements to Federal agencies and Indian tribal governments shall be transferred to the account from which the expenditure was made, or to a similar account that remains available for obligation; and

(ii) the budget authority associated with the expenditure shall be restored to the agency from which the authority was derived and shall be available for obligation until the end of the fiscal year following the year in which the transfer occurs.

(f) TREATMENT OF TERRITORIES.—For purposes of this section, the Virgin Islands, Guam, American Samoa, and the Commonwealth of the Northern Mariana Islands shall be considered to be States and parts of the United States, and the chief executive officer of each such territory shall be considered to be a Governor of a State.

(g) PROTECTING PUBLIC SAFETY AND MAINTAINING ROADWAYS.—The Secretary may use not more than 5 percent of amounts from the emergency fund authorized by this section to carry out projects that the Secretary determines are necessary to protect the public safety or to maintain or protect roadways that are included within the scope of an emergency declaration by the Governor of the State or by the President, in accordance with this section, and the Governor deems to be an ongoing concern in order to maintain vehicular traffic on the roadway.

(Pub. L. 85–767, Aug. 27, 1958, 72 Stat. 901; Pub. L. 86–342, title I, §107(a), Sept. 21, 1959, 73 Stat. 612; Pub. L. 89–574, §9(b), (c), Sept. 13, 1966, 80 Stat. 769; Pub. L. 90–495, §27(a), Aug. 23, 1968, 82 Stat. 829; Pub. L. 91–605, title I, §109(a), Dec. 31, 1970, 84 Stat. 1718; Pub. L. 92–361, Aug. 3, 1972, 86 Stat. 503; Pub. L. 94–280, title I, §119, May 5, 1976, 90 Stat. 437; Pub. L. 95–599, title I, §119, Nov. 6, 1978, 92 Stat. 2700; Pub. L. 96–106, §19, Nov. 9, 1979, 93 Stat. 799; Pub. L. 97–424, title I, §153(a), (c), (d), (h), Jan. 6, 1983, 96 Stat. 2132, 2133; Pub. L. 99–190, §101(e) [title III, §334], Dec. 19, 1985,

99 Stat. 1267, 1290; Pub. L. 99–272, title IV, §4103, Apr. 7, 1986, 100 Stat. 114; Pub. L. 100–17, title I, §§118(a)(1), (b)(1), (2), 133(b)(9), Apr. 2, 1987, 101 Stat. 156, 171; Pub. L. 100–707, §109(k), Nov. 23, 1988, 102 Stat. 4709; Pub. L. 102–240, title I, §1022(b), Dec. 18, 1991, 105 Stat. 1951; Pub. L. 102–302, §101, June 22, 1992, 106 Stat. 252; Pub. L. 105–178, title I, §§1113(b), 1212(a)(2)(A)(i), June 9, 1998, 112 Stat. 151, 193; Pub. L. 112–141, div. A, title I, §1107, July 6, 2012, 126 Stat. 437; Pub. L. 114–94, div. A, title I, §1107, Dec. 4, 2015, 129 Stat. 1337; Pub. L. 116–94, div. H, title I, §127, Dec. 20, 2019, 133 Stat. 2953; Pub. L. 117–58, div. A, title I, §11106, Nov. 15, 2021, 135 Stat. 458.)

§126. TRANSFERABILITY OF FEDERAL-AID HIGHWAY FUNDS

(a) IN GENERAL.—Notwithstanding any other provision of law, subject to subsection (b), a State may transfer from an apportionment under section 104(b) not to exceed 50 percent of the amount apportioned for the fiscal year to any other apportionment of the State under that section.

(b) APPLICATION TO CERTAIN SET-ASIDES.—

(1) IN GENERAL.—Funds that are subject to sections 104(d) and 133(d)(1)(A) shall not be transferred under this section.

(2) FUNDS TRANSFERRED BY STATES.—Funds transferred by a State under this section of the funding set aside for a State under section 133(h) for a fiscal year—

(A) may only come from the portion of those funds that are available for obligation in any area of the State under section 133(h); and

(B) may only be transferred if the Secretary certifies that the State—

(i) held a competition in compliance with the guidance issued to carry out section 133(h) and provided sufficient time for applicants to apply;

(ii) offered to each eligible entity, and provided on request of an eligible entity, technical assistance; and

(iii) demonstrates that there were not sufficiently suitable applications from eligible entities to use the funds to be transferred.

(Added Pub. L. 105–178, title I, §1310(a), June 9, 1998, 112 Stat. 234, §110; renumbered §126, Pub. L. 106–159, title I, §102(a)(1), Dec. 9, 1999, 113 Stat. 1752; amended Pub. L. 109–59, title I, §1401(a)(3)(B), Aug. 10, 2005, 119 Stat. 1225; Pub. L. 112–141, div. A, title I, §1509(a), July 6, 2012, 126 Stat. 567; Pub. L. 114–94, div. A, title I, §§1109(c)(1), 1446(a)(2), Dec. 4, 2015, 129 Stat. 1343, 1437; Pub. L. 117–58, div. A, title I, §11109(b)(2), Nov. 15, 2021, 135 Stat. 468.)

§127. VEHICLE WEIGHT LIMITATIONS—INTERSTATE SYSTEM

(a) IN GENERAL.—

(1) The Secretary shall withhold 50 percent of the apportionment of a State under section 104(b)(1) in any fiscal year in which the State does not permit the use of The Dwight D. Eisenhower System of Interstate and Defense Highways within its boundaries by vehicles with a weight of twenty thousand pounds carried on any one axle, including enforcement tolerances, or with a tandem axle weight of thirty-four thousand pounds, including enforcement tolerances, or a gross weight of at least eighty thousand pounds for vehicle combinations of five axles or more.

(2) However, the maximum gross weight to be allowed by any State for vehicles using The Dwight D. Eisenhower System of Interstate and Defense Highways shall be twenty thousand pounds carried on one axle, including enforcement tolerances, and a tandem axle weight of thirty-four thousand pounds, including enforcement tolerances and with an overall maximum gross weight, including enforcement tolerances, on a group of two or more consecutive axles produced by application of the following

formula:

$$W=500 \left(\frac{LN}{N-1} +12N+36 \right)$$

where W equals overall gross weight on any group of two or more consecutive axles to the nearest five hundred pounds, L equals distance in feet between the extreme of any group of two or more consecutive axles, and N equals number of axles in group under consideration, except that two consecutive sets of tandem axles may carry a gross load of thirty-four thousand pounds each providing the overall distance between the first and last axles of such consecutive sets of tandem axles (1) is thirty-six feet or more, or (2) in the case of a motor vehicle hauling any tank trailer, dump trailer, or ocean transport container before September 1, 1989, is 30 feet or more: *Provided*, That such overall gross weight may not exceed eighty thousand pounds, including all enforcement tolerances, except for vehicles using Interstate Route 29 between Sioux City, Iowa, and the border between Iowa and South Dakota or vehicles using Interstate Route 129 between Sioux City, Iowa, and the border between Iowa and Nebraska, and except for those vehicles and loads which cannot be easily dismantled or divided and which have been issued special permits in accordance with applicable State laws, or the corresponding maximum weights permitted for vehicles using the public highways of such State under laws or regulations established by appropriate State authority in effect on July 1, 1956, except in the case of the overall gross weight of any group of two or more consecutive axles on any vehicle (other than a vehicle comprised of a motor vehicle hauling any tank trailer, dump trailer, or ocean transport container on or after September 1, 1989), on the date of enactment of the Federal-Aid Highway Amendments of 1974, whichever is the greater.

(3) Any amount which is withheld from apportionment to any State pursuant to the foregoing provisions shall lapse if not released and obligated within the availability period specified in section 118(b).

(4) This section shall not be construed to deny apportionment to any State allowing the operation within such State of any vehicles or combinations thereof, other than vehicles or combinations subject to subsection (d) of this section, which the State determines could be lawfully operated within such State on July 1, 1956, except in the case of the overall gross weight of any group of two or more consecutive axles, on the date of enactment of the Federal-Aid Highway Amendments of 1974.

(5) With respect to the State of Hawaii, laws or regulations in effect on February 1, 1960, shall be applicable for the purposes of this section in lieu of those in effect on July 1, 1956.

(6) With respect to the State of Colorado, vehicles designed to carry 2 or more precast concrete panels shall be considered a nondivisible load.

(7) With respect to the State of Michigan, laws or regulations in effect on May 1, 1982, shall be applicable for the purposes of this subsection.

(8) With respect to the State of Maryland, laws and regulations in effect on June 1,

1993, shall be applicable for the purposes of this subsection.

(9) The State of Louisiana may allow, by special permit, the operation of vehicles with a gross vehicle weight of up to 100,000 pounds for the hauling of sugarcane during the harvest season, not to exceed 100 days annually.

(10) With respect to Interstate Routes 89, 93, and 95 in the State of New Hampshire—

(A) State laws (including regulations) concerning vehicle weight limitations that were in effect on January 1, 1987, and are applicable to State highways other than the Interstate System, shall be applicable in lieu of the requirements of this subsection; and

(B) effective June 30, 2016, a combination of truck-tractor and dump trailer equipped with 6 axles or more with a gross weight of up to 99,000 pounds shall be permitted if the distances between the extreme axles, excluding the steering axle, is 28 feet or more.

(11)(A) With respect to all portions of the Interstate Highway System in the State of Maine, laws (including regulations) of that State concerning vehicle weight limitations applicable to other State highways shall be applicable in lieu of the requirements under this subsection.

(B) With respect to all portions of the Interstate Highway System in the State of Vermont, laws (including regulations) of that State concerning vehicle weight limitations applicable to other State highways shall be applicable in lieu of the requirements under this subsection.

(12) HEAVY DUTY VEHICLES.—

(A) IN GENERAL.—Subject to subparagraphs (B) and (C), in order to promote reduction of fuel use and emissions because of engine idling, the maximum gross vehicle weight limit and the axle weight limit for any heavy-duty vehicle equipped with an idle reduction technology shall be increased by a quantity necessary to compensate for the additional weight of the idle reduction system.

(B) MAXIMUM WEIGHT INCREASE.—The weight increase under subparagraph (A) shall be not greater than 550 pounds.

(C) PROOF.—On request by a regulatory agency or law enforcement agency, the vehicle operator shall provide proof (through demonstration or certification) that—

(i) the idle reduction technology is fully functional at all times; and

(ii) the 550-pound gross weight increase is not used for any purpose other than the use of idle reduction technology described in subparagraph (A).

(13) MILK PRODUCTS.—A vehicle carrying fluid milk products shall be considered a load that cannot be easily dismantled or divided.

(b) REASONABLE ACCESS.—No State may enact or enforce any law denying reasonable access to motor vehicles subject to this title to and from the Interstate Highway System to terminals and facilities for food, fuel, repairs, and rest.

(c) OCEAN TRANSPORT CONTAINER DEFINED.—For purposes of this section, the term "ocean transport container" has the meaning given the term "freight container" by the International Standards Organization in Series 1, Freight Containers, 3rd Edition (reference number IS0668–1979(E)) as in effect on the date of the enactment of this subsection.

(d) LONGER COMBINATION VEHICLES.—

(1) PROHIBITION.—

(A) GENERAL CONTINUATION RULE.—A longer combination vehicle may continue to operate only if the longer combination vehicle configuration type was authorized by State officials pursuant to State statute or regulation conforming to this section and in actual lawful operation on a regular or periodic basis (including seasonal operations) on or before June 1, 1991, or pursuant to section 335 of the Department of Transportation and Related Agencies Appropriations Act, 1991 (104 Stat. 2186).

(B) APPLICABILITY OF STATE LAWS AND REGULATIONS.—All such operations shall continue to be subject to, at the minimum, all State statutes, regulations, limitations and conditions, including, but not limited to, routing-specific and configuration-specific designations and all other restrictions, in force on June 1, 1991; except that subject to such regulations as may be issued by the Secretary pursuant to paragraph (5) of this subsection, the State may make minor adjustments of a temporary and emergency nature to route designations and vehicle operating restrictions in effect on June 1, 1991, for specific safety purposes and road construction.

(C) WYOMING.—In addition to those vehicles allowed under subparagraph (A), the State of Wyoming may allow the operation of additional vehicle configurations not in actual operation on June 1, 1991, but authorized by State law not later than November 3, 1992, if such vehicle configurations comply with the single axle, tandem axle, and bridge formula limits set forth in subsection (a) and do not exceed 117,000 pounds gross vehicle weight.

(D) OHIO.—In addition to vehicles which the State of Ohio may continue to allow to be operated under subparagraph (A), such State may allow longer combination vehicles with 3 cargo carrying units of 28½ feet each (not including the truck tractor) not in actual operation on June 1, 1991, to be operated within its boundaries on the 1-mile segment of Ohio State Route 7 which begins at and is south of exit 16 of the Ohio Turnpike.

(E) ALASKA.—In addition to vehicles which the State of Alaska may continue to allow to be operated under subparagraph (A), such State may allow the operation of longer combination vehicles which were not in actual operation on June 1, 1991, but which were in actual operation prior to July 5, 1991.

(F) IOWA.—In addition to vehicles that the State of Iowa may continue to allow to be operated under subparagraph (A), the State may allow longer combination vehicles that were not in actual operation on June 1, 1991, to be operated on Interstate Route 29 between Sioux City, Iowa, and the border between Iowa and South Dakota or Interstate Route 129 between Sioux City, Iowa, and the border between Iowa and Nebraska.

(2) ADDITIONAL STATE RESTRICTIONS.—

(A) IN GENERAL.—Nothing in this subsection shall prevent any State from further restricting in any manner or prohibiting the operation of longer combination vehicles otherwise authorized under this subsection; except that such restrictions or prohibitions shall be consistent with the requirements of sections 31111–31114 of title 49.

(B) Minor adjustments.—Any State further restricting or prohibiting the operations of longer combination vehicles or making minor adjustments of a temporary and emergency nature as may be allowed pursuant to regulations issued by the Secretary pursuant to paragraph (5) of this subsection, shall, within 30 days, advise the Secretary of such action, and the Secretary shall publish a notice of such action in the Federal Register.

(3) Publication of list.—

(A) Submission to secretary.—Within 60 days of the date of the enactment of this subsection, each State (i) shall submit to the Secretary for publication in the Federal Register a complete list of (I) all operations of longer combination vehicles being conducted as of June 1, 1991, pursuant to State statutes and regulations; (II) all limitations and conditions, including, but not limited to, routing-specific and configuration-specific designations and all other restrictions, governing the operation of longer combination vehicles otherwise prohibited under this subsection; and (III) such statutes, regulations, limitations, and conditions; and (ii) shall submit to the Secretary copies of such statutes, regulations, limitations, and conditions.

(B) Interim list.—Not later than 90 days after the date of the enactment of this subsection, the Secretary shall publish an interim list in the Federal Register, consisting of all information submitted pursuant to subparagraph (A). The Secretary shall review for accuracy all information submitted by the States pursuant to subparagraph (A) and shall solicit and consider public comment on the accuracy of all such information.

(C) Limitation.—No statute or regulation shall be included on the list submitted by a State or published by the Secretary merely on the grounds that it authorized, or could have authorized, by permit or otherwise, the operation of longer combination vehicles, not in actual operation on a regular or periodic basis on or before June 1, 1991.

(D) Final list.—Except as modified pursuant to paragraph (1)(C) of this subsection, the list shall be published as final in the Federal Register not later than 180 days after the date of the enactment of this subsection. In publishing the final list, the Secretary shall make any revisions necessary to correct inaccuracies identified under subparagraph (B). After publication of the final list, longer combination vehicles may not operate on the Interstate System except as provided in the list.

(E) Review and correction procedure.—The Secretary, on his or her own motion or upon a request by any person (including a State), shall review the list issued by the Secretary pursuant to subparagraph (D). If the Secretary determines there is cause to believe that a mistake was made in the accuracy of the final list, the Secretary shall commence a proceeding to determine whether the list published pursuant to subparagraph (D) should be corrected. If the Secretary determines that there is a mistake in the accuracy of the list the Secretary shall correct the publication under subparagraph (D) to reflect the determination of the Secretary.

(4) Longer combination vehicle defined.—For purposes of this section, the term "longer combination vehicle" means any combination of a truck tractor and 2 or

more trailers or semitrailers which operates on the Interstate System at a gross vehicle weight greater than 80,000 pounds.

(5) REGULATIONS REGARDING MINOR ADJUSTMENTS.—Not later than 180 days after the date of the enactment of this subsection, the Secretary shall issue regulations establishing criteria for the States to follow in making minor adjustments under paragraph (1)(B).

(e) OPERATION OF CERTAIN SPECIALIZED HAULING VEHICLES ON INTERSTATE ROUTE 68.—The single axle, tandem axle, and bridge formula limits set forth in subsection (a) shall not apply to the operation on Interstate Route 68 in Garrett and Allegany Counties, Maryland, of any specialized vehicle equipped with a steering axle and a tridem axle and used for hauling coal, logs, and pulpwood if such vehicle is of a type of vehicle as was operating in such counties on United States Route 40 or 48 for such purpose on August 1, 1991.

(f) OPERATION OF CERTAIN SPECIALIZED HAULING VEHICLES ON CERTAIN WISCONSIN HIGHWAYS.—If the 104-mile portion of Wisconsin State Route 78 and United States Route 51 between Interstate Route 94 near Portage, Wisconsin, and Wisconsin State Route 29 south of Wausau, Wisconsin, is designated as part of the Interstate System under section 103(c)(4)(A), the single axle weight, tandem axle weight, gross vehicle weight, and bridge formula limits set forth in subsection (a) shall not apply to the 104-mile portion with respect to the operation of any vehicle that could legally operate on the 104-mile portion before the date of the enactment of this subsection.

(g) OPERATION OF CERTAIN SPECIALIZED HAULING VEHICLES ON CERTAIN PENNSYLVANIA HIGHWAYS.—If the segment of United States Route 220 between Bedford and Bald Eagle, Pennsylvania, is designated as part of the Interstate System, the single axle weight, tandem axle weight, gross vehicle weight, and bridge formula limits set forth in subsection (a) shall not apply to that segment with respect to the operation of any vehicle which could have legally operated on that segment before the date of the enactment of this subsection.

(h) WAIVER FOR A ROUTE IN STATE OF MAINE DURING PERIODS OF NATIONAL EMERGENCY.—

(1) IN GENERAL.—Notwithstanding any other provision of this section, the Secretary, in consultation with the Secretary of Defense, may waive or limit the application of any vehicle weight limit established under this section with respect to the portion of Interstate Route 95 in the State of Maine between Augusta and Bangor for the purpose of making bulk shipments of jet fuel to the Air National Guard Base at Bangor International Airport during a period of national emergency in order to respond to the effects of the national emergency.

(2) APPLICABILITY.—Emergency limits established under paragraph (1) shall preempt any inconsistent State vehicle weight limits.

(i) SPECIAL PERMITS DURING PERIODS OF NATIONAL EMERGENCY.—

(1) IN GENERAL.—Notwithstanding any other provision of this section, a State may issue special permits during an emergency to overweight vehicles and loads that can easily be dismantled or divided if—

(A) the President has declared the emergency to be a major disaster under the Robert T. Stafford Disaster Relief and Emergency Assistance Act (42 U.S.C. 5121 et seq.);

(B) the permits are issued in accordance with State law; and

(C) the permits are issued exclusively to vehicles and loads that are delivering relief supplies.

(2) EXPIRATION.—A permit issued under paragraph (1) shall expire not later than 120 days after the date of the declaration of emergency under subparagraph (A) of that paragraph.

(j) OPERATION OF VEHICLES ON CERTAIN OTHER WISCONSIN HIGHWAYS.—If any segment of the United States Route 41 corridor, as described in section 1105(c)(57) of the Intermodal Surface Transportation Efficiency Act of 1991, is designated as a route on the Interstate System, a vehicle that could operate legally on that segment before the date of such designation may continue to operate on that segment, without regard to any requirement under subsection (a).

(k) OPERATION OF VEHICLES ON CERTAIN MISSISSIPPI HIGHWAYS.—If any segment of United States Route 78 in Mississippi from mile marker 0 to mile marker 113 is designated as part of the Interstate System, no limit established under this section may apply to that segment with respect to the operation of any vehicle that could have legally operated on that segment before such designation.

(l) OPERATION OF VEHICLES ON CERTAIN KENTUCKY HIGHWAYS.—

(1) IN GENERAL.—If any segment of highway described in paragraph (2) is designated as a route on the Interstate System, a vehicle that could operate legally on that segment before the date of such designation may continue to operate on that segment, without regard to any requirement under subsection (a).

(2) DESCRIPTION OF HIGHWAY SEGMENTS.—The highway segments referred to in paragraph (1) are as follows:

(A) Interstate Route 69 in Kentucky (formerly the Wendell H. Ford (Western Kentucky) Parkway) from the Interstate Route 24 Interchange, near Eddyville, to the Edward T. Breathitt (Pennyrile) Parkway Interchange.

(B) The Edward T. Breathitt (Pennyrile) Parkway (to be designated as Interstate Route 69) in Kentucky from the Wendell H. Ford (Western Kentucky) Parkway Interchange to near milepost 77, and on new alignment to an interchange on the Audubon Parkway, if the segment is designated as part of the Interstate System.

(3) ADDITIONAL HIGHWAY SEGMENTS.—

(A) IN GENERAL.—If any segment of highway described in clauses (i) through (v) is designated as a route of the Interstate System, a vehicle that could operate legally on that segment before the date of such designation may continue to operate on that segment, without regard to any requirement under subsection (a), except that such vehicle shall not exceed a gross vehicle weight of 120,000 pounds. The highway segments referred to in this paragraph are as follows:

(i) The William H. Natcher Parkway (to be designated as a spur of Interstate Route 65) from Interstate Route 65 in Bowling Green, Kentucky, to United States Route 60 in Owensboro, Kentucky.

(ii) The Julian M. Carroll (Purchase) Parkway (to be designated as Interstate Route 69) in Kentucky from the Tennessee state line to the interchange with Interstate Route 24, near Calvert City.

(iii) The Wendell H. Ford (Western Kentucky) Parkway (to be designated as a spur of Interstate Route 69) from the interchange with the William H. Natcher Parkway in Ohio County, Kentucky, west to the interchange of the Western Kentucky Parkway with the Edward T. Breathitt (Pennyrile) Parkway.

(iv) The Edward T. Breathitt (Pennyrile) Parkway (to be designated as a spur of Interstate Route 69) from Interstate 24, north to Interstate 69.

(v) The Louie B. Nunn Cumberland Expressway (to be designated as a spur of Interstate Route 65) from the interchange with Interstate Route 65 in Barren County, Kentucky, east to the interchange with United States Highway 27 in Somerset, Kentucky.

(B) NONDIVISIBLE LOAD OR VEHICLE.—Nothing in this paragraph shall prohibit the State from issuing a permit for a nondivisible load or vehicle with a gross vehicle weight that exceeds 120,000 pounds.

(m) COVERED HEAVY-DUTY TOW AND RECOVERY VEHICLES.—

(1) IN GENERAL.—The vehicle weight limitations set forth in this section do not apply to a covered heavy-duty tow and recovery vehicle.

(2) COVERED HEAVY-DUTY TOW AND RECOVERY VEHICLE DEFINED.—In this subsection, the term "covered heavy-duty tow and recovery vehicle" means a vehicle that—

(A) is transporting a disabled vehicle from the place where the vehicle became disabled to the nearest appropriate repair facility; and

(B) has a gross vehicle weight that is equal to or exceeds the gross vehicle weight of the disabled vehicle being transported.

(n) OPERATION OF VEHICLES ON CERTAIN HIGHWAYS IN THE STATE OF TEXAS.—If any segment in the State of Texas of United States Route 59, United States Route 77, United States Route 281, United States Route 84, Texas State Highway 44, or another roadway is designated as Interstate Route 69, a vehicle that could operate legally on that segment before the date of the designation may continue to operate on that segment, without regard to any requirement under this section.

(o) CERTAIN LOGGING VEHICLES IN THE STATE OF WISCONSIN.—

(1) IN GENERAL.—The Secretary shall waive, with respect to a covered logging vehicle, the application of any vehicle weight limit established under this section.

(2) COVERED LOGGING VEHICLE DEFINED.—In this subsection, the term "covered logging vehicle" means a vehicle that—

(A) is transporting raw or unfinished forest products, including logs, pulpwood, biomass, or wood chips;

(B) has a gross vehicle weight of not more than 98,000 pounds;

(C) has not less than 6 axles; and

(D) is operating on a segment of Interstate Route 39 in the State of Wisconsin from mile marker 175.8 to mile marker 189.

(p) OPERATION OF CERTAIN SPECIALIZED VEHICLES ON CERTAIN HIGHWAYS IN THE STATE OF ARKANSAS.—If any segment of United States Route 63 between the exits for highways 14 and 75 in the State of Arkansas is designated as part of the Interstate System, the single axle weight, tandem axle weight, gross vehicle weight, and bridge formula limits under subsection (a) and the width limitation under section 31113(a) of title 49 shall not apply to that segment with respect to the operation of any vehicle that could operate legally on that segment before the date of the designation.

(q) CERTAIN LOGGING VEHICLES IN THE STATE OF MINNESOTA.—

(1) IN GENERAL.—The Secretary shall waive, with respect to a covered logging vehicle, the application of any vehicle weight limit established under this section.

(2) COVERED LOGGING VEHICLE DEFINED.—In this subsection, the term "covered logging vehicle" means a vehicle that—

(A) is transporting raw or unfinished forest products, including logs, pulpwood, biomass, or wood chips;

(B) has a gross vehicle weight of not more than 99,000 pounds;

(C) has not less than 6 axles; and

(D) is operating on a segment of Interstate Route 35 in the State of Minnesota from mile marker 235.4 to mile marker 259.552.

(r) EMERGENCY VEHICLES.—

(1) IN GENERAL.—Notwithstanding subsection (a), a State shall not enforce against an emergency vehicle a vehicle weight limit (up to a maximum gross vehicle weight of 86,000 pounds) of less than—

(A) 24,000 pounds on a single steering axle;

(B) 33,500 pounds on a single drive axle;

(C) 62,000 pounds on a tandem axle; or

(D) 52,000 pounds on a tandem rear drive steer axle.

(2) EMERGENCY VEHICLE DEFINED.—In this subsection, the term "emergency vehicle" means a vehicle designed to be used under emergency conditions—

(A) to transport personnel and equipment; and

(B) to support the suppression of fires and mitigation of other hazardous situations.

(s) NATURAL GAS AND ELECTRIC BATTERY VEHICLES.—A vehicle, if operated by an engine fueled primarily by natural gas or powered primarily by means of electric battery power, may exceed the weight limit on the power unit by up to 2,000 pounds (up to a maximum gross vehicle weight of 82,000 pounds) under this section.

(t) VEHICLES IN IDAHO.—A vehicle limited or prohibited under this section from operating on a segment of the Interstate System in the State of Idaho may operate on such a segment if such vehicle–

(1) has a gross vehicle weight of 129,000 pounds or less;

(2) other than gross vehicle weight, complies with the single axle, tandem axle, and bridge formula limits set forth in subsection (a); and

(3) is authorized to operate on such segment under Idaho State law.

(u) VEHICLES IN NORTH DAKOTA.—A vehicle limited or prohibited under this section from operating on a segment of the Interstate System in the State of North Dakota may operate on such a segment if such vehicle—

(1) has a gross vehicle weight of 129,000 pounds or less;

(2) other than gross vehicle weight, complies with the single axle, tandem axle, and bridge formula limits set forth in subsection (a); and

(3) is authorized to operate on such segment under North Dakota State law.

(v) OPERATION OF VEHICLES ON CERTAIN NORTH CAROLINA HIGHWAYS.—If any segment in the State of North Carolina of United States Route 17, United States Route 29, United States Route 52, United States Route 64, United States Route 70, United States Route 74, United States Route 117, United States Route 220, United States Route 264, or United States Route 421 is designated as a route on the Interstate System, a vehicle that could operate legally on that segment before the date of such designation may continue to operate on that segment, without regard to any requirement under subsection (a).

(w) OPERATION OF VEHICLES ON CERTAIN OKLAHOMA HIGHWAYS.—If any segment of the highway referred to in paragraph (96) of section 1105(c) of the Intermodal Surface Transportation Efficiency Act of 1991 (Public Law 102–240; 105 Stat. 2032) is designated as a route on the Interstate System, a vehicle that could operate legally on that segment before the date of such designation may continue to operate on that segment, without any regard to any requirement under this section.

(x) CERTAIN AGRICULTURAL VEHICLES IN THE STATE OF MISSISSIPPI.—

(1) IN GENERAL.—The State of Mississippi may allow, by special permit, the operation of a covered agricultural vehicle on the Interstate System in the State of Mississippi if such vehicle does not exceed—

(A) a gross vehicle weight of 88,000 pounds; and

(B) 110 percent of the maximum weight on any axle or axle group described in subsection (a)(2), including any enforcement tolerance.

(2) COVERED AGRICULTURAL VEHICLE DEFINED.—In this subsection, the term "covered agricultural vehicle" means a vehicle that is transporting unprocessed agricultural crops used for food, feed or fiber, or raw or unfinished forest products, including logs, pulpwood, biomass or wood chips.

(y) OPERATION OF CERTAIN VEHICLES IN WEST VIRGINIA.—

(1) IN GENERAL.—The State of West Virginia may allow, by special permit, the operation of a vehicle that is transporting materials and equipment on the Interstate System in the State of West Virginia if such vehicle does not exceed 110 percent of the maximum weight on any axle or axle group described in subsection (a)(2), including any enforcement tolerance, provided the remaining gross vehicle weight requirements of subsection (a) are met.

(2) DEFINITION.—In this subsection, the term "materials and equipment" means materials and equipment that are used on a project eligible under this chapter.

(Pub. L. 85–767, Aug. 27, 1958, 72 Stat. 902; Pub. L. 86–624, §17(e), July 12, 1960, 74 Stat. 416; Pub. L. 93–643, §106, Jan. 4, 1975, 88 Stat. 2283; Pub. L. 94–280, title I, §120, May 5, 1976, 90 Stat. 438; Pub. L. 97–424, title I, §133, formerly §133(a), Jan. 6, 1983, 96 Stat. 2123, renumbered §133, Pub. L. 100–17, title I, §133(a)(3), Apr. 2, 1987, 101 Stat. 170; Pub. L. 100–17, title I, §119, Apr. 2, 1987, 101 Stat. 157; Pub. L. 100–202, §101(l) [title III, §347(c)], Dec. 22, 1987, 101 Stat. 1329–358, 1329–388; Pub. L. 101–427, Oct. 15, 1990, 104 Stat. 927; Pub. L. 102–240, title I, §1023(a), (b), (d), Dec. 18, 1991, 105 Stat. 1951, 1952, 1954; Pub. L. 103–331, title III, §332, Sept. 30, 1994, 108 Stat. 2493; Pub. L. 103–429, §3(3), Oct. 31, 1994, 108 Stat. 4377; Pub. L. 104–59, title III, §312(a)(1), (2), (b), Nov. 28, 1995, 109 Stat. 584; Pub. L. 104–88, title IV, §§404, 405(a)(1), Dec. 29, 1995, 109 Stat. 956; Pub. L. 105–178, title I, §§1106(c)(2)(B), 1212(d)(1), June 9, 1998, 112 Stat. 136, 194; Pub. L. 107–107, div. A, title X, §1064, Dec. 28, 2001, 115 Stat. 1233; Pub. L. 108–447, div. J, title I, §121, Dec. 8, 2004, 118 Stat. 3347; Pub. L. 109–58, title VII, §756(c), Aug. 8, 2005, 119 Stat. 832; Pub. L. 109–59, title I, §1111(b)(3), Aug. 10, 2005, 119 Stat. 1171; Pub. L. 111–117, div. A, title I, §194(a), (c), (d), (f), Dec. 16, 2009, 123 Stat. 3072, 3073; Pub. L. 112–55, div. C, title I, §125, Nov. 18, 2011, 125 Stat. 655; Pub. L.

112–141, div. A, title I, §§1404(a), 1510, 1511, July 6, 2012, 126 Stat. 557, 567; Pub. L. 113–235, div. K, title I, §125, Dec. 16, 2014, 128 Stat. 2709; Pub. L. 114–94, div. A, title I, §§1409, 1410, 1446(a)(3), Dec. 4, 2015, 129 Stat. 1411, 1437; Pub. L. 114–113, div. L, title I, §124, Dec. 18, 2015, 129 Stat. 2847; Pub. L. 115–141, div. L, title I, §§127, 129A, Mar. 23, 2018, 132 Stat. 988; Pub. L. 116–6, div. G, title IV, §§421, 422, Feb. 15, 2019, 133 Stat. 474; Pub. L. 116–94, div. H, title IV, §425(a), Dec. 20, 2019, 133 Stat. 3018; Pub. L. 117–58, div. A, title I, §11515, Nov. 15, 2021, 135 Stat. 599; Pub. L. 118–42, div. F, title IV, §425, Mar. 9, 2024, 138 Stat. 395.)

§128. Public hearings

(a) Any State transportation department which submits plans for a Federal-aid highway project involving the by passing of or, going through any city, town, or village, either incorporated or unincorporated, shall certify to the Secretary that it has had public hearings, or has afforded the opportunity for such hearings, and has considered the economic and social effects of such a location, its impact on the environment, and its consistency with the goals and objectives of such urban planning as has been promulgated by the community. Any State transportation department which submits plans for an Interstate System project shall certify to the Secretary that it has had public hearings at a convenient location, or has afforded the opportunity for such hearings for the purpose of enabling persons in rural areas through or contiguous to whose property the highway will pass to express any objections they may have to the proposed locations of such highway. Such certification shall be accompanied by a report which indicates the consideration given to the economic, social, environmental and other effects of the plan or highway location or design and various alternatives which were raised during the hearing or which were otherwise considered.

(b) When hearings have been held under subsection (a), the State transportation department shall submit a copy of the transcript of said hearings to the Secretary, together with the certification and report.

(Pub. L. 85–767, Aug. 27, 1958, 72 Stat. 902; Pub. L. 90–495, §24, Aug. 23, 1968, 82 Stat. 828; Pub. L. 91–605, title I, §135, Dec. 31, 1970, 84 Stat. 1734; Pub. L. 105–178, title I, §1212(a)(2)(A)(i), June 9, 1998, 112 Stat. 193.)

§129. Toll roads, bridges, tunnels, and ferries

(a) Basic Program.—

(1) Authorization for federal participation.—Subject to the provisions of this section, Federal participation shall be permitted on the same basis and in the same manner as construction of toll-free highways is permitted under this chapter in the—

(A) initial construction of a toll highway, bridge, or tunnel or approach to the highway, bridge, or tunnel;

(B) initial construction of 1 or more lanes or other improvements that increase capacity of a highway, bridge, or tunnel (other than a highway on the Interstate System) and conversion of that highway, bridge, or tunnel to a tolled facility, if the number of toll-free lanes, excluding auxiliary lanes, after the construction is not less than the number of toll-free lanes, excluding auxiliary lanes, before the construction;

(C) initial construction of 1 or more lanes or other improvements that increase the capacity of a highway, bridge, or tunnel on the Interstate System and conversion of that highway, bridge, or tunnel to a tolled facility, if the number of toll-free non-HOV lanes, excluding auxiliary lanes, after such construction is not less than the number of toll-free non-HOV lanes, excluding auxiliary lanes, before such construction;

(D) reconstruction, resurfacing, restoration, rehabilitation, or replacement of a toll highway, bridge, or tunnel or approach to the highway, bridge, or tunnel;

(E) reconstruction or replacement of a toll-free bridge or tunnel and conversion of the bridge or tunnel to a toll facility;

(F) reconstruction of a toll-free Federal-aid highway (other than a highway on the Interstate System) and conversion of the highway to a toll facility;

(G) reconstruction, restoration, or rehabilitation of a highway on the Interstate System if the number of toll-free non-HOV lanes, excluding auxiliary lanes, after reconstruction, restoration, or rehabilitation is not less than the number of toll-free non-HOV lanes, excluding auxiliary lanes, before reconstruction, restoration, or rehabilitation;

(H) conversion of a high occupancy vehicle lane on a highway, bridge, or tunnel to a toll facility; and

(I) preliminary studies to determine the feasibility of a toll facility for which Federal participation is authorized under this paragraph.

(2) OWNERSHIP.—Each highway, bridge, tunnel, or approach to the highway, bridge, or tunnel constructed under this subsection shall—

(A) be publicly owned; or

(B) be privately owned if the public authority with jurisdiction over the highway, bridge, tunnel, or approach has entered into a contract with 1 or more private persons to design, finance, construct, and operate the facility and the public authority will be responsible for complying with all applicable requirements of this title with respect to the facility.

(3) LIMITATIONS ON USE OF REVENUES.—

(A) IN GENERAL.—A public authority with jurisdiction over a toll facility shall ensure that all toll revenues received from operation of the toll facility are used only for—

(i) debt service with respect to the projects on or for which the tolls are authorized, including funding of reasonable reserves and debt service on refinancing;

(ii) a reasonable return on investment of any private person financing the project, as determined by the State or interstate compact of States concerned;

(iii) any costs necessary for the improvement and proper operation and maintenance of the toll facility, including reconstruction, resurfacing, restoration, and rehabilitation;

(iv) if the toll facility is subject to a public-private partnership agreement, payments that the party holding the right to toll revenues owes to the other party under the public-private partnership agreement; and

(v) if the public authority certifies annually that the tolled facility is being adequately maintained, any other purpose for which Federal funds may be obligated by a State under this title.

(B) ANNUAL AUDIT.—

(i) IN GENERAL.—A public authority with jurisdiction over a toll facility shall conduct or have an independent auditor conduct an annual audit of toll facility records to verify adequate maintenance and compliance with subparagraph (A), and report the results of the audits, together with the results of the audit under paragraph (9)(C), to the Secretary.

(ii) RECORDS.—On reasonable notice, the public authority shall make all records of the public authority pertaining to the toll facility available for audit by the Secretary.

(C) NONCOMPLIANCE.—If the Secretary concludes that a public authority has not complied with the limitations on the use of revenues described in subparagraph (A), the Secretary may require the public authority to discontinue collecting tolls until an agreement with the Secretary is reached to achieve compliance with the limitation on the use of revenues described in subparagraph (A).

(4) SPECIAL RULE FOR FUNDING.—

(A) IN GENERAL.—In the case of a toll facility under the jurisdiction of a public authority of a State (other than the State transportation department), on request of the State transportation department and subject to such terms and conditions as the department and public authority may agree, the Secretary, working through the State department of transportation, shall reimburse the public authority for the Federal share of the costs of construction of the project carried out on the toll facility under this subsection in the same manner and to the same extent as the department would be reimbursed if the project was being carried out by the department.

(B) SOURCE.—The reimbursement of funds under this paragraph shall be from sums apportioned to the State under this chapter and available for obligations on projects on the Federal-aid highways in the State on which the project is being carried out.

(5) LIMITATION ON FEDERAL SHARE.—The Federal share payable for a project described in paragraph (1) shall be a percentage determined by the State, but not to exceed 80 percent.

(6) MODIFICATIONS.—If a public authority (including a State transportation department) with jurisdiction over a toll facility subject to an agreement under this section or section 119(e), as in effect on the day before the effective date of title I of the Intermodal Surface Transportation Efficiency Act of 1991 (105 Stat. 1915), requests modification of the agreement, the Secretary shall modify the agreement to allow the continuation of tolls in accordance with paragraph (3) without repayment of Federal funds.

(7) LOANS.—

(A) IN GENERAL.—

(i) LOANS.—Using amounts made available under this title, a State may loan to a public or private entity constructing or proposing to construct under this section a toll facility or non-toll facility with a dedicated revenue source an amount equal to all or part of the Federal share of the cost of the project if the project has a revenue source specifically dedicated to the project.

(ii) DEDICATED REVENUE SOURCES.—Dedicated revenue sources for non-toll facilities include excise taxes, sales taxes, motor vehicle use fees, tax on real property, tax increment financing, and such other dedicated revenue sources as the Secretary determines appropriate.

(B) COMPLIANCE WITH FEDERAL LAWS.—As a condition of receiving a loan under this paragraph, the public or private entity that receives the loan shall ensure that the project will be carried out in accordance with this title and any other applicable Federal law, including any applicable provision of a Federal environmental law.

(C) SUBORDINATION OF DEBT.—The amount of any loan received for a project under this paragraph may be subordinated to any other debt financing for the project.

(D) OBLIGATION OF FUNDS LOANED.—Funds loaned under this paragraph may only be obligated for projects under this paragraph.

(E) REPAYMENT.—The repayment of a loan made under this paragraph shall commence not later than 5 years after date on which the facility that is the subject of the loan is open to traffic.

(F) TERM OF LOAN.—The term of a loan made under this paragraph shall not exceed 30 years from the date on which the loan funds are obligated.

(G) INTEREST.—A loan made under this paragraph shall bear interest at or below market interest rates, as determined by the State, to make the project that is the subject of the loan feasible.

(H) REUSE OF FUNDS.—Amounts repaid to a State from a loan made under this paragraph may be obligated—

(i) for any purpose for which the loan funds were available under this title; and

(ii) for the purchase of insurance or for use as a capital reserve for other forms of credit enhancement for project debt in order to improve credit market access or to lower interest rates for projects eligible for assistance under this title.

(I) GUIDELINES.—The Secretary shall establish procedures and guidelines for making loans under this paragraph.

(8) STATE LAW PERMITTING TOLLING.—If a State does not have a highway, bridge, or tunnel toll facility as of the date of enactment of the MAP–21, before commencing any activity authorized under this section, the State shall have in effect a law that permits tolling on a highway, bridge, or tunnel.

(9) EQUAL ACCESS FOR OVER-THE-ROAD BUSES.—

(A) IN GENERAL.—An over-the-road bus that serves the public shall be provided access to a toll facility under the same rates, terms, and conditions as public transportation vehicles.

(B) REPORTS.—

(i) IN GENERAL.—Not later than 90 days after the date of enactment of this subparagraph, a public authority that operates a toll facility shall report to the Secretary any rates, terms, or conditions for access to the toll facility by public transportation vehicles that differ from the rates, terms, or conditions applicable to over-the-road buses.

(ii) UPDATES.—A public authority that operates a toll facility shall report to the Secretary any change to the rates, terms, or conditions for access to the toll facility by public transportation vehicles that differ from the rates, terms, or conditions applicable to over-the-road buses by not later than 30 days after the date on which the change takes effect.

(iii) PUBLICATION.—The Secretary shall publish information reported to the Secretary under clauses (i) and (ii) on a publicly accessible internet website.

(C) ANNUAL AUDIT.—

(i) IN GENERAL.—A public authority (as defined in section 101(a)) with jurisdiction over a toll facility shall—

(I) conduct or have an independent auditor conduct an annual audit of toll facility records to verify compliance with this paragraph; and

(II) report the results of the audit, together with the results of the audit under paragraph (3)(B), to the Secretary.

(ii) RECORDS.—After providing reasonable notice, a public authority described in clause (i) shall make all records of the public authority pertaining to the toll facility available for audit by the Secretary.

(iii) NONCOMPLIANCE.—If the Secretary determines that a public authority described in clause (i) has not complied with this paragraph, the Secretary may require the public authority to discontinue collecting tolls until an agreement with the Secretary is reached to achieve compliance.

(10) HIGH OCCUPANCY VEHICLE USE OF CERTAIN TOLL FACILITIES.—Notwithstanding section 102(a), in the case of a toll facility that is on the Interstate System and that is constructed or converted after the date of enactment of the Surface Transportation Reauthorization Act of 2021, the public authority with jurisdiction over the toll facility shall allow high occupancy vehicles, transit, and paratransit vehicles to use the facility at a discount rate or without charge, unless the public authority, in consultation with the Secretary, determines that the number of those vehicles using the facility reduces the travel time reliability of the facility.

(11) DEFINITIONS.—In this subsection, the following definitions apply:

(A) HIGH OCCUPANCY VEHICLE; HOV.—The term "high occupancy vehicle" or "HOV" means a vehicle with not fewer than 2 occupants.

(B) INITIAL CONSTRUCTION.—

(i) IN GENERAL.—The term "initial construction" means the construction of a highway, bridge, tunnel, or other facility at any time before it is open to traffic.

(ii) EXCLUSIONS.—The term "initial construction" does not include any improvement to a highway, bridge, tunnel, or other facility after it is open to traffic.

(C) OVER-THE-ROAD BUS.—The term "over-the-road bus" has the meaning given the term in section 301 of the Americans with Disabilities Act of 1990 (42 U.S.C. 12181).

(D) PUBLIC AUTHORITY.—The term "public authority" means a State, interstate compact of States, or public entity designated by a State.

(E) TOLL FACILITY.—The term "toll facility" means a toll highway, bridge, or tunnel or approach to the highway, bridge, or tunnel constructed under this subsection.

(b) Notwithstanding the provisions of section 301 of this title, the Secretary may permit Federal participation under this title in the construction of a project constituting an approach to a ferry, whether toll or free, the route of which is a public road and has not been designated as a route on the Interstate System. Such ferry may be either publicly or privately owned and operated, but the operating authority and the amount of fares charged for passage shall be under the control of a State agency or official, and all revenues derived from publicly owned or operated ferries shall be applied to payment of the cost of construction or acquisition thereof, including debt service, and to actual and necessary costs of operation, maintenance, repair, and replacement.

(c) Notwithstanding section 301 of this title, the Secretary may permit Federal participation under this title in the construction of ferry boats and ferry terminal facilities (including ferry maintenance facilities), whether toll or free, and the procurement of transit vehicles used exclusively as an integral part of an intermodal ferry trip, subject to the following conditions:

(1) It is not feasible to build a bridge, tunnel, combination thereof, or other normal highway structure in lieu of the use of such ferry.

(2) The operation of the ferry shall be on a route classified as a public road within the State and which has not been designated as a route on the Interstate System or on a public transit ferry eligible under chapter 53 of title 49. Projects under this subsection may be eligible for both ferry boats carrying cars and passengers and ferry boats carrying passengers only.

(3)(A) The ferry boat or ferry terminal facility shall be publicly owned or operated or majority publicly owned if the Secretary determines with respect to a majority publicly owned ferry or ferry terminal facility that such ferry boat or ferry terminal facility provides substantial public benefits.

(B) Any Federal participation shall not involve the construction or purchase, for private ownership, of a ferry boat, ferry terminal facility, or other eligible project under this section.

(4) The operating authority and the amount of fares charged for passage on such ferry shall be under the control of the State or other public entity, and all revenues derived therefrom shall be applied to actual and necessary costs of operation, maintenance, repair, debt service, negotiated management fees, and, in the case of a privately operated toll ferry, for a reasonable rate of return.

(5) Such ferry may be operated only within the State (including the islands which comprise the State of Hawaii and the islands which comprise any territory of the United States) or between adjoining States or between a point in a State and a point in the Dominion of Canada. Except with respect to operations between the islands which comprise the State of Hawaii, operations between the islands which comprise any territory of the United States, operations between a point in a State and a point in the Dominion of Canada, and operations between any two points in Alaska and between Alaska and Washington, including stops at appropriate points in the Dominion of Canada, no part of such ferry operation shall be in any foreign or international waters.

(6) The ferry service shall be maintained in accordance with section 116.

(7)(A) No ferry boat or ferry terminal with Federal participation under this title may be sold, leased, or otherwise disposed of, except in accordance with part 200 of title 2, Code of Federal Regulations.

(B) The Federal share of any proceeds from a disposition referred to in subparagraph (A) shall be used for eligible purposes under this title.

(d) CONGESTION RELIEF PROGRAM.—

(1) DEFINITIONS.—In this subsection:

(A) ELIGIBLE ENTITY.—The term "eligible entity" means any of the following:

(i) A State, for the purpose of carrying out a project in an urbanized area with a population of more than 1,000,000.

(ii) A metropolitan planning organization, city, or municipality, for the purpose of carrying out a project in an urbanized area with a population of more than 1,000,000.

(B) INTEGRATED CONGESTION MANAGEMENT SYSTEM.—The term "integrated congestion management system" means a system for the integration of management and operations of a regional transportation system that includes, at a minimum, traffic incident management, work zone management, traffic signal timing, managed lanes, real-time traveler information, and active traffic management, in order to maximize the capacity of all facilities and modes across the applicable region.

(C) PROGRAM.—The term "program" means the congestion relief program established under paragraph (2).

(2) ESTABLISHMENT.—The Secretary shall establish a congestion relief program to provide discretionary grants to eligible entities to advance innovative, integrated, and multimodal solutions to congestion relief in the most congested metropolitan areas of the United States.

(3) PROGRAM GOALS.—The goals of the program are to reduce highway congestion, reduce economic and environmental costs associated with that congestion, including transportation emissions, and optimize existing highway capacity and usage of highway and transit systems through—

(A) improving intermodal integration with highways, highway operations, and highway performance;

(B) reducing or shifting highway users to off-peak travel times or to nonhighway travel modes during peak travel times; and

(C) pricing of, or based on, as applicable—

(i) parking;

(ii) use of roadways, including in designated geographic zones; or

(iii) congestion.

(4) ELIGIBLE PROJECTS.—Funds from a grant under the program may be used for a project or an integrated collection of projects, including planning, design, implementation, and construction activities, to achieve the program goals under paragraph (3), including—

(A) deployment and operation of an integrated congestion management system;

(B) deployment and operation of a system that implements or enforces high occupancy vehicle toll lanes, cordon pricing, parking pricing, or congestion pricing;

(C) deployment and operation of mobility services, including establishing account-based financial systems, commuter buses, commuter vans, express operations, paratransit, and on-demand microtransit; and

(D) incentive programs that encourage travelers to carpool, use nonhighway travel modes during peak period, or travel during nonpeak periods.

(5) APPLICATION; SELECTION.—

(A) APPLICATION.—To be eligible to receive a grant under the program, an eligible entity shall submit to the Secretary an application at such time, in such manner, and containing such information as the Secretary may require.

(B) PRIORITY.—In providing grants under the program, the Secretary shall give priority to projects in urbanized areas that are experiencing a high degree of recurrent congestion.

(C) FEDERAL SHARE.—The Federal share of the cost of a project carried out with a grant under the program shall not exceed 80 percent of the total project cost.

(D) MINIMUM AWARD.—A grant provided under the program shall be not less than $10,000,000.

(6) USE OF TOLLING.—

(A) IN GENERAL.—Notwithstanding subsection (a)(1) and section 301 and subject to subparagraphs (B) and (C), the Secretary shall allow the use of tolls on the Interstate System as part of a project carried out with a grant under the program.

(B) REQUIREMENTS.—The Secretary may only approve the use of tolls under subparagraph (A) if—

(i) the eligible entity has authority under State, and if applicable, local, law to assess the applicable toll;

(ii) the maximum toll rate for any vehicle class is not greater than the product obtained by multiplying—

(I) the toll rate for any other vehicle class; and

(II) 5;

(iii) the toll rates are not charged or varied on the basis of State residency;

(iv) the Secretary determines that the use of tolls will enable the eligible entity to achieve the program goals under paragraph (3) without a significant impact to safety or mobility within the urbanized area in which the project is located; and

(v) the use of toll revenues complies with subsection (a)(3).

(C) LIMITATION.—The Secretary may not approve the use of tolls on the Interstate System under the program in more than 10 urbanized areas.

(7) FINANCIAL EFFECTS ON LOW-INCOME DRIVERS.—A project under the program—

(A) shall include, if appropriate, an analysis of the potential effects of the project on low-income drivers; and

(B) may include mitigation measures to deal with any potential adverse financial effects on low-income drivers.

(Pub. L. 85–767, Aug. 27, 1958, 72 Stat. 902; Pub. L. 86–657, §§5, 8(a), July 14, 1960, 74 Stat. 523, 524; Pub. L. 90–495, §28, Aug. 23, 1968, 82 Stat. 829; Pub. L. 91–605, title I, §§133, 139, Dec. 31, 1970, 84 Stat. 1732, 1736; Pub. L. 92–434, §7, Sept. 26, 1972, 86 Stat. 732; Pub. L. 93–87, title I, §§118, 132, 139, Aug. 13, 1973, 87 Stat. 259, 267, 270; Pub. L. 93–643, §108, Jan. 4, 1975, 88 Stat. 2284; Pub. L. 94–280, title I, §121, May 5, 1976, 90 Stat. 438; Pub. L. 95–599, title I, §120, Nov. 6, 1978, 92 Stat. 2700; Pub. L. 100–17, title I, §120(a), (b), Apr. 2, 1987, 101 Stat. 157, 158; Pub. L. 100–202, §101(l) [title III, §347(d)], Dec. 22, 1987, 101 Stat. 1329–358, 1329–388; Pub. L. 100–457, title III, §§326, 335, Sept. 30, 1988, 102 Stat. 2150, 2153; Pub. L. 102–240, title I, §1012(a), (c), Dec. 18, 1991,

105 Stat. 1936, 1938; Pub. L. 102–388, title IV, §410, Oct. 6, 1992, 106 Stat. 1565; Pub. L. 104–59, title III, §313(a)–(c), Nov. 28, 1995, 109 Stat. 585, 586; Pub. L. 105–178, title I, §§1106(c)(1)(C), 1207(a), 1211(f), formerly 1211(g), June 9, 1998, 112 Stat. 136, 185, 189; Pub. L. 105–206, title IX, §9003(d)(5), July 22, 1998, 112 Stat. 840; Pub. L. 109–59, title I, §1801(f), Aug. 10, 2005, 119 Stat. 1456; Pub. L. 112–141, div. A, title I, §1512(a), July 6, 2012, 126 Stat. 567; Pub. L. 114–94, div. A, title I, §§1112(c), 1411(a), Dec. 4, 2015, 129 Stat. 1346, 1412; Pub. L. 117–58, div. A, title I, §§11117(a), 11404, 11523, Nov. 15, 2021, 135 Stat. 483, 558, 605.)

§130. RAILWAY-HIGHWAY CROSSINGS

(a) Subject to section 120 and subsection (b) of this section, the entire cost of construction of projects for the elimination of hazards of railway-highway crossings, including the separation or protection of grades at crossings, the reconstruction of existing railroad grade crossing structures, the relocation of highways to eliminate grade crossings, and projects at grade crossings to eliminate hazards posed by blocked grade crossings due to idling trains, may be paid from sums apportioned in accordance with section 104 of this title. In any case when the elimination of the hazards of a railway-highway crossing can be effected by the relocation of a portion of a railway at a cost estimated by the Secretary to be less than the cost of such elimination by one of the methods mentioned in the first sentence of this section, then the entire cost of such relocation project, subject to section 120 and subsection (b) of this section, may be paid from sums apportioned in accordance with section 104 of this title.

(b) The Secretary may classify the various types of projects involved in the elimination of hazards of railway-highway crossings, and may set for each such classification a percentage of the costs of construction which shall be deemed to represent the net benefit to the railroad or railroads for the purpose of determining the railroad's share of the cost of construction. The percentage so determined shall in no case exceed 10 per centum. The Secretary shall determine the appropriate classification of each project.

(c) Any railroad involved in a project for the elimination of hazards of railway-highway crossings paid for in whole or in part from sums made available for expenditure under this title, or prior Acts, shall be liable to the United States for the net benefit to the railroad determined under the classification of such project made pursuant to subsection (b) of this section. Such liability to the United States may be discharged by direct payment to the State transportation department of the State in which the project is located, in which case such payment shall be credited to the cost of the project. Such payment may consist in whole or in part of materials and labor furnished by the railroad in connection with the construction of such project. If any such railroad fails to discharge such liability within a six-month period after completion of the project, it shall be liable to the United States for its share of the cost, and the Secretary shall request the Attorney General to institute proceedings against such railroad for the recovery of the amount for which it is liable under this subsection. The Attorney General is authorized to bring such proceedings on behalf of the United States, in the appropriate district court of the United States, and the United States shall be entitled in such proceedings to recover such sums as it is considered and adjudged by the court that such railroad is liable for in the premises. Any amounts recovered by the United States under this subsection shall be credited to miscellaneous receipts.

(d) SURVEY AND SCHEDULE OF PROJECTS.—Each State shall conduct and systematically maintain a survey of all highways to identify those railroad crossings which may require separation, relocation, or protective devices, and establish and implement a schedule of projects for this purpose. At a minimum, such a schedule shall provide signs for all railway-highway crossings.

(e) FUNDS FOR RAILWAY-HIGHWAY GRADE CROSSINGS.—

(1) IN GENERAL.—

(A) SET ASIDE.—Before making an apportionment under section 104(b)(3) for a fiscal year, the Secretary shall set aside, from amounts made available to carry out the highway safety improvement program under section 148 for such fiscal year, for the elimination of hazards, the installation of protective devices at railway-highway crossings, the replacement of functionally obsolete warning devices, and as described in subparagraph (B), not less than $245,000,000 for each of fiscal years 2022 through 2026.

(B) REDUCING TRESPASSING FATALITIES AND INJURIES.—A State may use funds set aside under subparagraph (A) for projects to reduce pedestrian fatalities and injuries from trespassing at grade crossings.

(C) OBLIGATION AVAILABILITY.—Sums set aside each fiscal year under subparagraph (A) shall be available for obligation in the same manner as funds apportioned under section 104(b)(1).

(2) SPECIAL RULE.—If a State demonstrates to the satisfaction of the Secretary that the State has met all its needs for installation of protective devices at railway-highway crossings, the State may use funds made available by this section for other highway safety improvement program purposes.

(f) APPORTIONMENT.—

(1) FORMULA.—Fifty percent of the funds set aside to carry out this section pursuant to subsection (e)(1) shall be apportioned to the States in accordance with the formula set forth in section 104(b)(3)(A) as in effect on the day before the date of enactment of the MAP–21, and 50 percent of such funds shall be apportioned to the States in the ratio that total public railway-highway crossings in each State bears to the total of such crossings in all States.

(2) MINIMUM APPORTIONMENT.—Notwithstanding paragraph (1), each State shall receive a minimum of one-half of 1 percent of the funds apportioned under paragraph (1).

(3) FEDERAL SHARE.—The Federal share payable on account of any project financed with funds set aside to carry out this section shall be 100 percent of the cost thereof.

(g) ANNUAL REPORT.—

(1) IN GENERAL.—Not later than August 31 of each year, each State shall submit a report to the Administrator of the Federal Highway Administration that describes—

(A) the progress being made to implement the railway-highway crossings program authorized under this section; and

(B) the effectiveness of the improvements made as a result of such implementation.

(2) CONTENTS.—Each report submitted pursuant to paragraph (1) shall contain an assessment of—

(A) the costs of the various treatments employed by the State to implement the railway-highway crossings program; and

(B) the effectiveness of such treatments, as measured by the accident experience at the locations that received such treatments.

(3) COORDINATION.—Not later than 30 days after the Federal Highway Administration's acceptance of each report submitted pursuant to paragraph (1), the Administrator of the Federal Highway Administration shall make such report available to the Administrator of the Federal Railroad Administration.

(h) USE OF FUNDS FOR MATCHING.—Funds authorized to be appropriated to carry out this section may be used to provide a local government with funds to be used on a matching basis when State funds are available which may only be spent when the local government produces matching funds for the improvement of railway-highway crossings.

(i) INCENTIVE PAYMENTS FOR AT-GRADE CROSSING CLOSURES.—

(1) IN GENERAL.—Notwithstanding any other provision of this section and subject to paragraphs (2) and (3), a State may, from sums available to the State under this section, make incentive payments to local governments in the State upon the permanent closure by such governments of public at-grade railway-highway crossings under the jurisdiction of such governments.

(2) INCENTIVE PAYMENTS BY RAILROADS.—A State may not make an incentive payment under paragraph (1) to a local government with respect to the closure of a crossing unless the railroad owning the tracks on which the crossing is located makes an incentive payment to the government with respect to the closure.

(3) AMOUNT OF STATE PAYMENT.—The amount of the incentive payment payable to a local government by a State under paragraph (1) with respect to a crossing may not exceed the lesser of—

(A) the amount of the incentive payment paid to the government with respect to the crossing by the railroad concerned under paragraph (2); or

(B) $100,000.

(4) USE OF STATE PAYMENTS.—A local government receiving an incentive payment from a State under paragraph (1) shall use the amount of the incentive payment for transportation safety improvements.

(j) BICYCLE SAFETY.—In carrying out projects under this section, a State shall take into account bicycle safety.

(k) EXPENDITURE OF FUNDS.—Not more than 8 percent of funds apportioned to a State to carry out this section may be used by the State for compilation and analysis of data in support of activities carried out under subsection (g).

(l) NATIONAL CROSSING INVENTORY.—

(1) INITIAL REPORTING OF CROSSING INFORMATION.—Not later than 1 year after the date of enactment of the Rail Safety Improvement Act of 2008 or within 6 months of a new crossing becoming operational, whichever occurs later, each State shall report to the Secretary of Transportation current information, including information about warning devices and signage, as specified by the Secretary, concerning each previously unreported public crossing located within its borders.

(2) PERIODIC UPDATING OF CROSSING INFORMATION.—On a periodic basis beginning not later than 2 years after the date of enactment of the Rail Safety Improvement

Act of 2008 and on or before September 30 of every year thereafter, or as otherwise specified by the Secretary, each State shall report to the Secretary current information, including information about warning devices and signage, as specified by the Secretary, concerning each public crossing located within its borders.

(Pub. L. 85–767, Aug. 27, 1958, 72 Stat. 903; Pub. L. 100–17, title I, §121(a), Apr. 2, 1987, 101 Stat. 159; Pub. L. 104–59, title III, §325(a), Nov. 28, 1995, 109 Stat. 591; Pub. L. 104–205, title III, §353(b), Sept. 30, 1996, 110 Stat. 2980; Pub. L. 105–178, title I, §§1111(d), 1202(d), 1212(a)(2)(A)(i), June 9, 1998, 112 Stat. 146, 170, 193; Pub. L. 109–59, title I, §1401(c), formerly §1401(d), Aug. 10, 2005, 119 Stat. 1226, renumbered §1401(c), Pub. L. 110–244, title I, §101(s)(1), June 6, 2008, 122 Stat. 1577; Pub. L. 110–244, title I, §101(l), June 6, 2008, 122 Stat. 1575; Pub. L. 110–432, div. A, title II, §204(c), Oct. 16, 2008, 122 Stat. 4871; Pub. L. 112–141, div. A, title I, §1519(c)(5), formerly §1519(c)(6), July 6, 2012, 126 Stat. 575, renumbered §1519(c)(5), Pub. L. 114–94, div. A, title I, §1446(d)(5)(B), Dec. 4, 2015, 129 Stat. 1438; Pub. L. 114–94, div. A, title I, §§1108, 1412, Dec. 4, 2015, 129 Stat. 1416; Pub. L. 117–58, div. A, title I, §§11108(a)–(d), 11525(f), div. B, title II, §22403(c), Nov. 15, 2021, 135 Stat. 461, 607, 736.)

§131. CONTROL OF OUTDOOR ADVERTISING

(a) The Congress hereby finds and declares that the erection and maintenance of outdoor advertising signs, displays, and devices in areas adjacent to the Interstate System and the primary system should be controlled in order to protect the public investment in such highways, to promote the safety and recreational value of public travel, and to preserve natural beauty.

(b) Federal-aid highway funds apportioned on or after January 1, 1968, to any State which the Secretary determines has not made provision for effective control of the erection and maintenance along the Interstate System and the primary system of outdoor advertising signs, displays, and devices which are within six hundred and sixty feet of the nearest edge of the right-of-way and visible from the main traveled way of the system, and Federal-aid highway funds apportioned on or after January 1, 1975, or after the expiration of the next regular session of the State legislature, whichever is later, to any State which the Secretary determines has not made provision for effective control of the erection and maintenance along the Interstate System and the primary system of those additional outdoor advertising signs, displays, and devices which are more than six hundred and sixty feet off the nearest edge of the right-of-way, located outside of urban areas, visible from the main traveled way of the system, and erected with the purpose of their message being read from such main traveled way, shall be reduced by amounts equal to 10 per centum of the amounts which would otherwise be apportioned to such State under section 104 of this title, until such time as such State shall provide for such effective control. Any amount which is withheld from apportionment to any State hereunder shall be reapportioned to the other States. Whenever he determines it to be in the public interest, the Secretary may suspend, for such periods as he deems necessary, the application of this subsection to a State.

(c) Effective control means that such signs, displays, or devices after January 1, 1968, if located within six hundred and sixty feet of the right-of-way and, on or after July 1, 1975, or after the expiration of the next regular session of the State legislature, whichever is later, if located beyond six hundred and sixty feet of the right-of-way located outside of urban areas, visible from the main traveled way of the system, and erected with the purpose of their message being read from such main traveled way, shall, pursuant to this section, be limited to (1) directional and official signs and notices, which signs and notices shall include, but not be limited to, signs and notices pertaining to natural wonders, scenic and historical attractions, which are required or authorized by law, which shall conform to national standards hereby authorized to be promulgated by the Secretary hereunder, which standards shall contain provisions concerning lighting, size, number, and spacing of signs, and such other requirements as may be appropriate to implement this section, (2) signs, displays, and devices advertising the sale or lease of property upon which they are located, (3) signs, displays, and devices, including those which may be changed at reasonable intervals by electronic process or by remote control, advertising activities conducted on the property on which they are located, (4) signs lawfully in existence on October 22, 1965, determined by the State, subject to the approval of the Secretary, to be landmark signs, including signs on farm structures or natural surfaces, or historic or artistic significance the preservation of which would be consistent with the purposes of this section, and (5) signs, displays, and devices advertising the distribution by nonprofit organizations of free coffee to individuals traveling on the Interstate System or the primary system. For the purposes of this subsection, the term "free coffee" shall include coffee for which a donation may be made, but is not required.

(d) In order to promote the reasonable, orderly and effective display of outdoor advertising while remaining consistent with the purposes of this section, signs, displays, and devices whose size, lighting and spacing, consistent with customary use is to be determined by agreement between the several States and the Secretary, may be erected and maintained within six hundred and sixty feet of the nearest edge of the right-of-way within areas adjacent to the Interstate and primary systems which are zoned industrial or commercial under authority of State law, or in unzoned commercial or industrial areas as may be determined by agreement between the several States and the Secretary. The States shall have full authority under their own zoning laws to zone areas for commercial or industrial purposes, and the actions of the States in this regard will be accepted for the purposes of this Act. Whenever a bona fide State, county, or local zoning authority has made a determination of customary use, such determination will be accepted in lieu of controls by agreement in the zoned commercial and industrial areas within the geographical jurisdiction of such authority. Nothing in this subsection shall apply to signs, displays, and devices referred to in clauses (2) and (3) of subsection (c) of this section.

(e) Any sign, display, or device lawfully in existence along the Interstate System or the Federal-aid primary system on September 1, 1965, which does not conform to this section shall not be required to be removed until July 1, 1970. Any other sign, display, or device lawfully erected which does not conform to this section shall not be required to be removed until the end of the fifth year after it becomes nonconforming.

(f) The Secretary shall, in consultation with the States, provide within the rights-of-way for areas at appropriate distances from interchanges on the Interstate System, on which signs, displays, and devices giving specific information in the interest of the traveling public may be erected and maintained. The Secretary may also, in consultation with the States, provide within the rights-of-way of the primary system for areas in which signs, displays, and devices giving specific information in the interest of the traveling public may be erected and maintained. Such signs shall conform to national standards to be promulgated by the Secretary.

(g) Just compensation shall be paid upon the removal of any outdoor advertising sign, display, or device lawfully erected under State law and not permitted under subsection (c) of this section, whether or not removed pursuant to or because of this section. The Federal share of such compensation shall be 75 per centum. Such compensation shall be paid for the following:

(A) The taking from the owner of such sign, display, or device of all right, title, leasehold, and interest in such sign, display, or device; and

(B) The taking from the owner of the real property on which the sign, display, or device is located, of the right to erect and maintain such signs, displays, and devices thereon.

(h) All public lands or reservations of the United States which are adjacent to any portion of the Interstate System and the primary system shall be controlled in accordance with the provisions of this section and the national standards promulgated by the Secretary.

(i) In order to provide information in the specific interest of the traveling public, the State transportation departments are authorized to maintain maps and to permit information directories and advertising pamphlets to be made available at safety rest areas. Subject to the approval of the Secretary, a State may also establish information centers at safety rest areas and other travel information systems within the rights-of-way for the purpose of informing the public of places of interest within the State and providing such other information as a State may consider desirable. The Federal share of the cost of establishing such an information center or travel information system shall be that which is provided in section 120 for a highway project on that Federal-aid system to be served by such center or system. A State may permit the installation of signs that acknowledge the sponsorship of rest areas within such rest areas or along the main traveled way of the system, provided that such signs shall not affect the safe and efficient utilization of the Interstate System and the primary system. The Secretary shall establish criteria for the installation of such signs on the main traveled way, including criteria pertaining to the placement of rest area sponsorship acknowledgment signs in relation to the placement of advance guide signs for rest areas.

(j) Any State transportation department which has, under this section as in effect on June 30, 1965, entered into an agreement with the Secretary to control the erection and maintenance of outdoor advertising signs, displays, and devices in areas adjacent to the Interstate System shall be entitled to receive the bonus payments as set forth in the agreement, but no such State transportation department shall be entitled to such payments unless the State maintains the control required under such agreement: *Provided,* That permission by a State to erect and maintain information displays which may be changed at reasonable intervals by electronic process or remote control and which provide public service information or advertise activities conducted on the property on which they are located shall not be considered a breach of such agreement or the control required thereunder. Such payments shall be paid only from appropriations made to carry out this section. The provisions of this subsection shall not be construed to exempt any State from controlling outdoor advertising as otherwise provided in this section.

(k) Subject to compliance with subsection (g) of this section for the payment of just compensation, nothing in this section shall prohibit a State from establishing standards imposing stricter limitations with respect to signs, displays, and devices on the Federal-aid highway systems than those established under this section.

(l) Not less than sixty days before making a final determination to withhold funds from a State under subsection (b) of this section, or to do so under subsection (b) of section 136, or with respect to failing to agree as to the size, lighting, and spacing of signs, displays, and devices or as to unzoned commercial or industrial areas in which signs, displays, and devices may be erected and maintained under subsection (d) of this section, or with respect to failure to approve under subsection (g) of section 136, the Secretary shall give written notice to the State of his proposed determination and a statement of the reasons therefor, and during such period shall give the State an opportunity for a hearing on such determination. Following such hearing the Secretary shall issue a written order setting forth his final determination and shall furnish a copy of such order to the State. Within forty-five days of receipt of such order, the State may appeal such order to any United States district court for such State, and upon the filing of such appeal such order shall be stayed until final judgment has been entered on such appeal. Summons may be served at any place in the United States. The court shall have jurisdiction to affirm the determination of the Secretary or to set it aside, in whole or in part. The judgment of the court shall be subject to review by the United States court of appeals for the circuit in which the State is located and to the Supreme Court of the United States upon certiorari or certification as provided in title 28, United States Code, section 1254. If any part of an apportionment to a State is withheld by the Secretary under subsection (b) of this section or subsection (b) of section 136, the amount so withheld shall not be reapportioned to the other States as long as a suit brought by such State under this subsection is pending. Such amount shall remain available for apportionment in accordance with the final judgment and this subsection. Funds withheld from apportionment and subsequently apportioned or reapportioned under this section shall be available for expenditure for three full fiscal years after the date of such apportionment or reapportionment as the case may be.

(m) There is authorized to be appropriated to carry out the provisions of this section, out of any money in the Treasury not otherwise appropriated, not to exceed $20,000,000 for the fiscal year ending June 30, 1966, not to exceed $20,000,000 for the fiscal year ending June 30, 1967, not to exceed $2,000,000 for the fiscal year ending June 30, 1970, not to exceed $27,000,000 for the fiscal year ending June 30, 1971, not to exceed $20,500,000 for the fiscal year ending June 30, 1972, and not to exceed $50,000,000 for the fiscal year ending June 30, 1973. The provisions of this chapter relating to the obligation, period of availability and expenditure of Federal-aid primary highway funds shall apply to the funds authorized to be appropriated to carry out this section after June 30, 1967. A State may use any funds apportioned to it under section 104 of this title for removal of any sign, display, or device lawfully erected which does not conform to this section.

(n) No sign, display, or device shall be required to be removed under this section if the Federal share of the just compensation to be paid upon removal of such sign, display, or device is not available to make such payment. Funds apportioned to a State under section 104 of this title shall not be treated for purposes of the preceding sentence as being available to the State for making such a payment except to the extent that the State, in its discretion, expends such funds for such a payment.

(o) The Secretary may approve the request of a State to permit retention in specific areas defined by such State of directional signs, displays, and devices lawfully erected under State law in force at the time of their erection which do not conform to the requirements of subsection (c), where such signs, displays, and devices are in existence on the date of enactment of this subsection and where the State demonstrates that such signs, displays, and devices (1) provide directional information about goods and services in the interest of the traveling public, and (2) are such that removal would work a substantial economic hardship in such defined area.

(p) In the case of any sign, display, or device required to be removed under this section prior to the date of enactment of the Federal-Aid Highway Act of 1974, which sign, display, or device was after its removal lawfully relocated and which as a result of the amendments made to this section by such Act is required to be removed, the United States shall pay 100 per centum of the just compensation for such removal (including all relocation costs).

(q)(1) During the implementation of State laws enacted to comply with this section, the Secretary shall encourage and assist the States to develop sign controls and programs which will assure that necessary directional information about facilities providing goods and services in the interest of the traveling public will continue to be available to motorists. To this end the Secretary shall restudy and revise as appropriate existing standards for directional signs authorized under subsections 131(c)(1) and 131(f) to develop signs which are functional and esthetically compatible with their surroundings. He shall employ the resources of other Federal departments and agencies, including the National Endowment for the Arts, and employ maximum participation of private industry in the development of standards and systems of signs developed for those purposes.

(2) Among other things the Secretary shall encourage States to adopt programs to assure that removal of signs providing necessary directional information, which also were providing directional information on June 1, 1972, about facilities in the interest of the traveling public, be deferred until all other nonconforming signs are removed.

(r) REMOVAL OF ILLEGAL SIGNS.—

(1) BY OWNERS.—Any sign, display, or device along the Interstate System or the Federal-aid primary system which was not lawfully erected, shall be removed by the owner of such sign, display, or device not later than the 90th day following the effective date of this subsection.

(2) BY STATES.—If any owner does not remove a sign, display, or device in accordance with paragraph (1), the State within the borders of which the sign, display, or device is located shall remove the sign, display, or device. The owner of the removed sign, display, or device shall be liable to the State for the costs of such removal. Effective control under this section includes compliance with the first sentence of this paragraph.

(s) SCENIC BYWAY PROHIBITION.—If a State has a scenic byway program, the State may not allow the erection along any highway on the Interstate System or Federal-aid primary system which before, on, or after the effective date of this subsection, is designated as a scenic byway under such program of any sign, display, or device which is not in conformance with subsection (c) of this section. Control of any sign, display, or device on such a highway shall be in accordance with this section. In designating a scenic byway for purposes of this section and section 1047 of the Intermodal Surface Transportation Efficiency Act of 1991, a State may exclude from such designation any segment of a highway that is inconsistent with the State's criteria for designating State scenic byways. Nothing in the preceding sentence shall preclude a State from signing any such excluded segment, including such segment on a map, or carrying out similar activities, solely for purposes of system continuity.

(t) PRIMARY SYSTEM DEFINED.—For purposes of this section, the terms "primary system" and "Federal-aid primary system" mean the Federal-aid primary system in existence on June 1, 1991, and any highway which is not on such system but which is on the National Highway System.

(Pub. L. 85–767, Aug. 27, 1958, 72 Stat. 904; Pub. L. 86–342, title I, §106, Sept. 21, 1959, 73 Stat. 612; Pub. L. 87–61, title I, §106, June 29, 1961, 75 Stat. 123; Pub. L. 88–157, §5, Oct. 24, 1963, 77 Stat. 277; Pub. L. 89–285, title I, §101, Oct. 22, 1965, 79 Stat. 1028; Pub. L. 89–574, §8(a), Sept. 13, 1966, 80 Stat. 768; Pub. L. 90–495, §6(a)–(d), Aug. 23, 1968, 82 Stat. 817; Pub. L. 91–605, title I, §122(a), Dec. 31, 1970, 84 Stat. 1726; Pub. L. 93–643, §109, Jan. 4, 1975, 88 Stat. 2284; Pub. L. 94–280, title I, §122, May 5, 1976, 90 Stat. 438; Pub. L. 95–599, title I, §§121, 122, Nov. 6, 1978, 92 Stat. 2700, 2701; Pub. L. 96–106, §6, Nov. 9, 1979, 93 Stat. 797; Pub. L. 102–240, title I, §1046(a)–(c), Dec. 18, 1991, 105 Stat. 1995, 1996; Pub. L. 102–302, §104, June 22, 1992, 106 Stat. 253; Pub. L. 104–59, title III, §314, Nov. 28, 1995, 109 Stat. 586; Pub. L. 105–178, title I, §1212(a)(2)(A), June 9, 1998, 112 Stat. 193; Pub. L. 112–141, div. A, title I, §§1519(c)(6), formerly 1519(c)(7), 1539(b), July 6, 2012, 126 Stat. 576, 587, renumbered §1519(c)(6), Pub. L. 114–94, div. A, title I, §1446(d)(5)(B), Dec. 4, 2015, 129 Stat. 1438.)

§132. PAYMENTS ON FEDERAL-AID PROJECTS UNDERTAKEN BY A FEDERAL AGENCY

(a) IN GENERAL.—In a case in which a proposed Federal-aid project is to be undertaken by a Federal agency in accordance with an agreement between a State and the Federal agency, the State may—

(1) direct the Secretary to transfer the funds for the Federal share of the project directly to the Federal agency; or

(2) make such deposit with, or payment to, the Federal agency as is required to meet the obligation of the State under the agreement for the work undertaken or to be undertaken by the Federal agency.

(b) REIMBURSEMENT.—On execution with a State of a project agreement described in subsection (a), the Secretary may reimburse the State, using any available funds, for the estimated Federal share under this title of the obligation of the State deposited or paid under subsection (a)(2).

(c) RECOVERY AND CREDITING OF FUNDS.—Any sums reimbursed to the State under this section which may be in excess of the Federal pro rata share under the provisions of this title of the State's share of the cost as set forth in the approved final voucher submitted by the State shall be recovered and credited to the same class of funds from which the Federal payment under this section was made.

(Added Pub. L. 86–657, §4(a), July 14, 1960, 74 Stat. 522; amended Pub. L. 109–59, title I, §1119(b), Aug. 10, 2005, 119 Stat. 1182.)

§133. SURFACE TRANSPORTATION BLOCK GRANT PROGRAM

(a) ESTABLISHMENT.—The Secretary shall establish a surface transportation block grant program in accordance with this section to provide flexible funding to address State and local transportation needs.

(b) ELIGIBLE PROJECTS.—Funds apportioned to a State under section 104(b)(2) for the surface transportation block grant program may be obligated for the following:

(1) Construction of—

(A) highways, bridges, tunnels, including designated routes of the Appalachian development highway system and local access roads under section 14501 of title 40;

(B) ferry boats and terminal facilities—

(i) that are eligible for funding under section 129(c); or

(ii) that are privately or majority-privately owned, but that the Secretary determines provide a substantial public transportation benefit or otherwise meet the foremost needs of the surface transportation system described in section 101(b)(3)(D);

(C) transit capital projects eligible for assistance under chapter 53 of title 49;

(D) infrastructure-based intelligent transportation systems capital improvements, including the installation of vehicle-to-infrastructure communication equipment;

(E) truck parking facilities eligible for funding under section 1401 of MAP–21 (23 U.S.C. 137 note);

(F) border infrastructure projects eligible for funding under section 1303 of SAFETEA–LU (23 U.S.C. 101 note); and

(G) wildlife crossing structures.

(2) Operational improvements and capital and operating costs for traffic monitoring, management, and control facilities and programs.

(3) Environmental measures eligible under sections 119(g), 148(a)(4)(B)(xvii), 328, and 329 and transportation control measures listed in section 108(f)(1)(A) (other than clause (xvi) of that section) of the Clean Air Act (42 U.S.C. 7408(f)(1)(A)).

(5) [1] Highway and transit safety infrastructure improvements and programs, including projects eligible under section 130 and installation of safety barriers and nets on bridges.

(6) Fringe and corridor parking facilities and programs in accordance with section 137 and carpool projects in accordance with section 146.

(7) Recreational trails projects eligible for funding under section 206 including the maintenance and restoration of existing recreational trails,,[2] pedestrian and bicycle projects in accordance with section 217 (including modifications to comply with accessibility requirements under the Americans with Disabilities Act of 1990 (42 U.S.C. 12101 et seq.)), and the safe routes to school program under section 208.

(8) Planning, design, or construction of boulevards and other roadways largely in the right-of-way of former Interstate System routes or other divided highways.

(9) Development and implementation of a State asset management plan for the National Highway System and a performance-based management program for other public roads.

(10) Protection (including painting, scour countermeasures, seismic retrofits, impact protection measures, security countermeasures, and protection against extreme events) for bridges (including approaches to bridges and other elevated structures) and tunnels on public roads, and inspection and evaluation of bridges and tunnels and other highway assets.

(11) Surface transportation planning programs, highway and transit research and development and technology transfer programs, and workforce development, training, and education under chapter 5 of this title.

(12) Surface transportation infrastructure modifications to facilitate direct intermodal interchange, transfer, and access into and out of a port terminal.

(13) Projects and strategies designed to support congestion pricing, including electronic toll collection and travel demand management strategies and programs.

(14) Projects and strategies designed to reduce the number of wildlife-vehicle collisions, including project-related planning, design, construction, monitoring, and preventative maintenance.

(15) The installation of electric vehicle charging infrastructure and vehicle-to-grid infrastructure.

(16) The installation and deployment of current and emerging intelligent transportation technologies, including the ability of vehicles to communicate with infrastructure, buildings, and other road users.

(17) Planning and construction of projects that facilitate intermodal connections between emerging transportation technologies, such as magnetic levitation and hyperloop.

(18) Protective features, including natural infrastructure, to enhance the resilience of a transportation facility otherwise eligible for assistance under this section.

(19) Measures to protect a transportation facility otherwise eligible for assistance under this section from cybersecurity threats.

(20) At the request of a State, and upon Secretarial approval of credit assistance under chapter 6, subsidy and administrative costs necessary to provide an eligible entity Federal credit assistance under chapter 6 with respect to a project eligible for assistance under this section.

(21) The creation and operation by a State of an office to assist in the design, implementation, and oversight, including conducting value for money analyses or similar comparative analyses, of public-private partnerships eligible to receive funding under this title and chapter 53 of title 49, and the payment of a stipend to unsuccessful private bidders to offset their proposal development costs, if necessary to encourage robust competition in public-private partnership procurements.

(22) Any type of project eligible under this section as in effect on the day before the date of enactment of the FAST Act, including projects described under section 101(a)(29) as in effect on such day.

(23) Rural barge landing, dock, and waterfront infrastructure projects in accordance with subsection (j).

(24) Projects to enhance travel and tourism.

(c) LOCATION OF PROJECTS.—A surface transportation block grant project may not be undertaken on a road functionally classified as a local road or a rural minor collector unless the road was on a Federal-aid highway system on January 1, 1991, except—

(1) for a bridge or tunnel project (other than the construction of a new bridge or tunnel at a new location);

(2) for a project described in paragraphs (5) through (15) and paragraph (23) of subsection (b);

(3) for a project described in section 101(a)(29), as in effect on the day before the date of enactment of the FAST Act;

(4) for a bridge project for the replacement of a low water crossing (as defined by the Secretary) with a bridge; and

(5) as approved by the Secretary.

(d) ALLOCATIONS OF APPORTIONED FUNDS TO AREAS BASED ON POPULATION.—

(1) CALCULATION.—Of the funds apportioned to a State under section 104(b)(2) (after the set aside of funds under subsection (h))—

(A) 55 percent for each of fiscal years 2022 through 2026 shall be obligated under this section, in proportion to their relative shares of the population of the State—

(i) in urbanized areas of the State with an urbanized area population of over 200,000;

(ii) in urbanized areas of the State with an urbanized area population of not less than 50,000 and not more than 200,000;

(iii) in urban areas of the State with a population not less than 5,000 and not more than 49,999; and

(iv) in other areas of the State with a population less than 5,000; and

(B) the remainder may be obligated in any area of the State.

(2) METROPOLITAN AREAS.—Funds attributed to an urbanized area under paragraph (1)(A)(i) may be obligated in the metropolitan area established under section 134 that encompasses the urbanized area.

(3) LOCAL CONSULTATION.—

(A) CONSULTATION WITH METROPOLITAN PLANNING ORGANIZATIONS.—For purposes of clause (ii) of paragraph (1)(A), a State shall—

(i) establish a process to consult with all metropolitan planning organizations in the State that represent an urbanized area described in that clause; and

(ii) describe how funds allocated for areas described in that clause will be allocated equitably among the applicable urbanized areas during the period of fiscal years 2022 through 2026.

(B) CONSULTATION WITH REGIONAL TRANSPORTATION PLANNING ORGANIZATIONS.—For purposes of clauses (iii) and (iv) of paragraph (1)(A), before obligating funding attributed to an area with a population less than 50,000, a State shall consult with the regional transportation planning organizations that represent the area, if any.

(4) DISTRIBUTION AMONG URBANIZED AREAS OF OVER 200,000 POPULATION.—

(A) IN GENERAL.—Except as provided in subparagraph (B), the amount of funds that a State is required to obligate under paragraph (1)(A)(i) shall be obligated in urbanized areas described in paragraph (1)(A)(i) based on the relative population of the areas.

(B) OTHER FACTORS.—The State may obligate the funds described in subparagraph (A) based on other factors if the State and the relevant metropolitan planning organizations jointly apply to the Secretary for the permission to base the obligation on other factors and the Secretary grants the request.

(5) APPLICABILITY OF PLANNING REQUIREMENTS.—Programming and expenditure of funds for projects under this section shall be consistent with sections 134 and 135.

(e) OBLIGATION AUTHORITY.—

(1) IN GENERAL.—A State that is required to obligate in an urbanized area with an urbanized area population of over 200,000 individuals under subsection (d) funds apportioned to the State under section 104(b)(2) shall make available during the period of fiscal years 2022 through 2026 an amount of obligation authority distributed to the State for Federal-aid highways and highway safety construction programs for use in the area that is equal to the amount obtained by multiplying—

(A) the aggregate amount of funds that the State is required to obligate in the area under subsection (d) during the period; and

(B) the ratio that—

(i) the aggregate amount of obligation authority distributed to the State for Federal-aid highways and highway safety construction programs during the period; bears to

(ii) the total of the sums apportioned to the State for Federal-aid highways and highway safety construction programs (excluding sums not subject to an obligation limitation) during the period.

(2) JOINT RESPONSIBILITY.—Each State, each affected metropolitan planning organization, and the Secretary shall jointly ensure compliance with paragraph (1).

(f) BRIDGES NOT ON FEDERAL-AID HIGHWAYS.—

(1) DEFINITION OF OFF-SYSTEM BRIDGE.—In this subsection, the term "off-system bridge" means a highway bridge or low water crossing (as defined by the Secretary) located on a public road, other than a bridge or low water crossing (as defined by the Secretary) on a Federal-aid highway.

(2) SPECIAL RULE.—

(A) SET-ASIDE.—Of the amounts apportioned to a State for fiscal year 2013 and each fiscal year thereafter under this section, the State shall obligate for activities described in paragraphs (1)(A) and (10) of subsection (b) for off-system bridges, projects and activities described in subsection (b)(1)(A) for the replacement of low water crossings with bridges, and projects and activities described in subsection (b)(10) for low water crossings (as defined by the Secretary), an amount that is not less than 20 percent of the amount of funds apportioned to the State for the highway bridge program for fiscal year 2009, except that amounts allocated under subsection (d) shall not be obligated to carry out this subsection.

(B) REDUCTION OF EXPENDITURES.—The Secretary, after consultation with State and local officials, may reduce the requirement for expenditures for off-system bridges under subparagraph (A) with respect to the State if the Secretary determines that the State has inadequate needs to justify the expenditure.

(3) CREDIT FOR BRIDGES NOT ON FEDERAL-AID HIGHWAYS.—Notwithstanding any other provision of law, with respect to any project not on a Federal-aid highway for

the replacement of a bridge, rehabilitation of a bridge, or replacement of a low water crossing (as defined by the Secretary) with a bridge that is wholly funded from State and local sources, is eligible for Federal funds under this section, is noncontroversial, is certified by the State to have been carried out in accordance with all standards applicable to such projects under this section, and is determined by the Secretary upon completion to be no longer a deficient bridge or, in the case of a replacement of a low water crossing with a bridge, is determined by the Secretary on completion to have improved the safety of the location—

    (A) any amount expended after the date of enactment of this subsection from State and local sources for the project in excess of 20 percent of the cost of construction of the project may be credited to the non-Federal share of the cost of other bridge projects in the State that are eligible for Federal funds under this section; and

    (B) that crediting shall be conducted in accordance with procedures established by the Secretary.

(g) SPECIAL RULE FOR AREAS OF LESS THAN 50,000 POPULATION.—

    (1) IN GENERAL.—Notwithstanding subsection (c), and except as provided in paragraph (2), up to 15 percent of the amounts required to be obligated by a State under clauses (iii) and (iv) of subsection (d)(1)(A) for each fiscal year may be obligated on—

    (A) roads functionally classified as rural minor collectors or local roads; or

    (B) on critical rural freight corridors designated under section 167(e).

    (2) SUSPENSION.—The Secretary may suspend the application of paragraph (1) with respect to a State if the Secretary determines that the authority provided under paragraph (1) is being used excessively by the State.

(h) STP SET-ASIDE.—

    (1) IN GENERAL.—Of the funds apportioned to a State under section 104(b)(2) for fiscal year 2022 and each fiscal year thereafter—

    (A) the Secretary shall set aside an amount equal to 10 percent to carry out this subsection; and

    (B) the State's share of that total is determined by multiplying the amount under subparagraph (A) by the ratio that—

    (i) the amount apportioned to the State for the transportation enhancements program for fiscal year 2009 under section 133(d)(2), as in effect on the day before the date of enactment of MAP–21; bears to

    (ii) the total amount of funds apportioned to all States for the transportation enhancements program for fiscal year 2009.

    (2) ALLOCATION WITHIN A STATE.—

    (A) IN GENERAL.—Except as provided in subparagraph (B), funds set aside for a State under paragraph (1) shall be obligated within that State in the manner described in subsection (d), except that, for purposes of this paragraph (after funds are made available under paragraph (5))—

    (i) for fiscal year 2022 and each fiscal year thereafter, the percentage referred to in paragraph (1)(A) of that subsection shall be deemed to be 59 percent; and

    (ii) paragraph (3) of subsection (d) shall not apply.

(B) LOCAL CONTROL.—A State may allocate up to 100 percent of the funds referred to in subparagraph (A)(i) if—

(i) the State submits to the Secretary a plan that describes—

(I) how funds will be allocated to counties, metropolitan planning organizations, regional transportation planning organizations as described in section 135(m), or local governments;

(II) how the entities described in subclause (I) will carry out a competitive process to select projects for funding and report selected projects to the State;

(III) the legal, financial, and technical capacity of the entities described in subclause (I);

(IV) how input was gathered from the entities described in subclause (I) to ensure those entities will be able to comply with the requirements of this subsection; and

(V) how the State will comply with paragraph (8); and

(ii) the Secretary approves the plan submitted under clause (i).

(3) ELIGIBLE PROJECTS.—Funds set aside under this subsection may be obligated for—

(A) projects or activities described in section 101(a)(29) or 213, as those provisions were in effect on the day before the date of enactment of the FAST Act (Public Law 114–94; 129 Stat. 1312);

(B) projects and activities under the safe routes to school program under section 208; and

(C) activities in furtherance of a vulnerable road user safety assessment (as defined in section 148(a)).

(4) ACCESS TO FUNDS.—

(A) ELIGIBLE ENTITY DEFINED.—In this paragraph, the term "eligible entity" means—

(i) a local government;

(ii) a regional transportation authority;

(iii) a transit agency;

(iv) a natural resource or public land agency;

(v) a school district, local education agency, or school;

(vi) a tribal government;

(vii) a metropolitan planning organization that serves an urbanized area with a population of 200,000 or fewer;

(viii) a nonprofit entity;

(ix) any other local or regional governmental entity with responsibility for or oversight of transportation or recreational trails (other than a metropolitan planning organization that serves an urbanized area with a population of over 200,000 or a State agency) that the State determines to be eligible, consistent with the goals of this subsection; and

(x) a State, at the request of an entity described in clauses (i) through (ix).

(B) COMPETITIVE PROCESS.—A State or metropolitan planning organization required to obligate funds in accordance with paragraph (2) shall develop a competitive process to allow eligible entities to submit projects for funding that

122

achieve the objectives of this subsection.

(C) SELECTION.—A metropolitan planning organization for an area described in subsection (d)(1)(A)(i) shall select projects under the competitive process described in subparagraph (B) in consultation with the relevant State.

(D) PRIORITIZATION.—The competitive process described in subparagraph (B) shall include prioritization of project location and impact in high-need areas as defined by the State, such as low-income, transit-dependent, rural, or other areas.

(5) CONTINUATION OF CERTAIN RECREATIONAL TRAILS PROJECTS.—For each fiscal year, a State shall—

(A) obligate an amount of funds set aside under this subsection equal to the amount of the funds apportioned to the State for fiscal year 2009 under section 104(h)(2), as in effect on the day before the date of enactment of MAP–21, for projects relating to recreational trails under section 206;

(B) return 1 percent of those funds to the Secretary for the administration of that program; and

(C) comply with the provisions of the administration of the recreational trails program under section 206, including the use of apportioned funds described in subsection (d)(3)(A) of that section.

(6) STATE FLEXIBILITY.—

(A) RECREATIONAL TRAILS.—A State may opt out of the recreational trails program under paragraph (5) if the Governor of the State notifies the Secretary not later than 30 days prior to apportionments being made for any fiscal year.

(B) LARGE URBANIZED AREAS.—A metropolitan planning area may use not to exceed 50 percent of the funds set aside under this subsection for an urbanized area described in subsection (d)(1)(A)(i) for any purpose eligible under subsection (b).

(C) IMPROVING ACCESSIBILITY AND EFFICIENCY.—

(i) IN GENERAL.—A State may use an amount equal to not more than 5 percent of the funds set aside for the State under this subsection, after allocating funds in accordance with paragraph (2)(A), to improve the ability of applicants to access funding for projects under this subsection in an efficient and expeditious manner by providing—

(I) to applicants for projects under this subsection application assistance, technical assistance, and assistance in reducing the period of time between the selection of the project and the obligation of funds for the project; and

(II) funding for 1 or more full-time State employee positions to administer this subsection.

(ii) USE OF FUNDS.—Amounts used under clause (i) may be expended—

(I) directly by the State; or

(II) through contracts with State agencies, private entities, or nonprofit entities.

(7) FEDERAL SHARE.—

(A) REQUIRED AGGREGATE NON-FEDERAL SHARE.—The average annual non-Federal share of the total cost of all projects for which funds are obligated under this subsection in a State for a fiscal year shall be not less than the average non-Federal share of the cost of the projects that would otherwise apply.

(B) FLEXIBLE FINANCING.—Subject to subparagraph (A), notwithstanding section 120—

(i) funds made available to carry out section 148 may be credited toward the non-Federal share of the costs of a project under this subsection if the project—

(I) is an eligible project described in section 148(e)(1); and

(II) is consistent with the State strategic highway safety plan (as defined in section 148(a));

(ii) the non-Federal share for a project under this subsection may be calculated on a project, multiple-project, or program basis; and

(iii) the Federal share of the cost of an individual project in this section may be up to 100 percent.

(C) REQUIREMENT.—Subparagraph (B) shall only apply to a State if the State has adequate financial controls, as certified by the Secretary, to account for the average annual non-Federal share under this paragraph.

(8) ANNUAL REPORTS.—

(A) IN GENERAL.—Each State or metropolitan planning organization responsible for carrying out the requirements of this subsection shall submit to the Secretary an annual report that includes—

(i) the number of project applications received for each fiscal year, including—

(I) the aggregate cost of the projects for which applications are received; and

(II) the types of projects to be carried out, expressed as percentages of the total apportionment of the State under this subsection; and

(ii) a list of each project selected for funding for each fiscal year, including, for each project—

(I) the fiscal year during which the project was selected;

(II) the fiscal year in which the project is anticipated to be funded;

(III) the recipient;

(IV) the location, including the congressional district;

(V) the type;

(VI) the cost; and

(VII) a brief description.

(B) PUBLIC AVAILABILITY.—The Secretary shall make available to the public, in a user-friendly format on the Web site of the Department of Transportation, a copy of each annual report submitted under subparagraph (A).

(i) TREATMENT OF PROJECTS.—Notwithstanding any other provision of law, projects funded under this section (excluding those carried out under subsection (h)(5)) shall be treated as projects on a Federal-aid highway under this chapter.

(j) RURAL BARGE LANDING, DOCK, AND WATERFRONT INFRASTRUCTURE PROJECTS.—

(1) IN GENERAL.—A State may use not more than 5 percent of the funds apportioned to the State under section 104(b)(2) for eligible rural barge landing, dock, and waterfront infrastructure projects described in paragraph (2).

(2) ELIGIBLE PROJECTS.—An eligible rural barge landing, dock, or waterfront infrastructure project referred to in paragraph (1) is a project for the planning,

designing, engineering, or construction of a barge landing, dock, or other waterfront infrastructure in a rural community or a Native village (as defined in section 3 of the Alaska Native Claims Settlement Act (43 U.S.C. 1602)) that is off the road system.

(k) PROJECTS IN RURAL AREAS.—

(1) SET ASIDE.—Notwithstanding subsection (c), in addition to the activities described in subsections (b) and (g), of the amounts apportioned to a State for each fiscal year to carry out this section, not more than 15 percent may be—

(A) used on eligible projects under subsection (b) or maintenance activities on roads functionally classified as rural minor collectors or local roads, ice roads, or seasonal roads; or

(B) transferred to—

(i) the Appalachian Highway System Program under 14501 [3] of title 40; or

(ii) the Denali access system program under section 309 of the Denali Commission Act of 1998 (42 U.S.C. 3121 note; Public Law 105–277).

(2) SAVINGS CLAUSE.—Amounts allocated under subsection (d) shall not be used to carry out this subsection, except at the request of the applicable metropolitan planning organization.

(Added Pub. L. 102–240, title I, §1007(a)(1), Dec. 18, 1991, 105 Stat. 1927; amended Pub. L. 103–429, §3(4), Oct. 31, 1994, 108 Stat. 4377; Pub. L. 104–59, title III, §§315, 316, Nov. 28, 1995, 109 Stat. 586, 587; Pub. L. 105–178, title I, §§1108(a)–(e), 1212(a)(2)(A)(i), June 9, 1998, 112 Stat. 138–140, 193; Pub. L. 109–59, title I, §1113(a)–(b)(2), (c)–(e), title VI, §6006(a)(2), Aug. 10, 2005, 119 Stat. 1171, 1172, 1872; Pub. L. 112–141, div. A, title I, §§1108, 1519(c)(7), formerly §1519(c)(8), July 6, 2012, 126 Stat. 440, 576, renumbered §1519(c)(7), Pub. L. 114–94, div. A, title I, §1446(d)(5)(B), Dec. 4, 2015, 129 Stat. 1438; Pub. L. 114–94, div. A, title I, §§1109(b), 1407(b), 1446(d)(5)(C), Dec. 4, 2015, 129 Stat. 1338, 1410, 1438; Pub. L. 117–58, div. A, title I, §§11109(a), (b)(1), 11508(d)(2), Nov. 15, 2021, 135 Stat. 461, 465, 588.)

[1] So in original. There is no par. (4).

[2] So in original.

[3] So in original. Probably should be preceded by "section".

§134. METROPOLITAN TRANSPORTATION PLANNING

(a) POLICY.—It is in the national interest—

(1) to encourage and promote the safe and efficient management, operation, and development of surface transportation systems that will serve the mobility needs of people and freight, foster economic growth and development within and between States and urbanized areas better connect housing and employment,,[1] and take into consideration resiliency needs while minimizing transportation-related fuel consumption and air pollution through metropolitan and statewide transportation planning processes identified in this chapter; and

(2) to encourage the continued improvement and evolution of the metropolitan and statewide transportation planning processes by metropolitan planning organizations, State departments of transportation, and public transit operators as guided by the planning factors identified in subsection (h) and section 135(d).

(b) DEFINITIONS.—In this section and section 135, the following definitions apply:

(1) METROPOLITAN PLANNING AREA.—The term "metropolitan planning area" means the geographic area determined by agreement between the metropolitan planning organization for the area and the Governor under subsection (e).

(2) METROPOLITAN PLANNING ORGANIZATION.—The term "metropolitan planning organization" means the policy board of an organization established as a result of the designation process under subsection (d).

(3) NONMETROPOLITAN AREA.—The term "nonmetropolitan area" means a geographic area outside designated metropolitan planning areas.

(4) NONMETROPOLITAN LOCAL OFFICIAL.—The term "nonmetropolitan local official" means elected and appointed officials of general purpose local government in a nonmetropolitan area with responsibility for transportation.

(5) REGIONAL TRANSPORTATION PLANNING ORGANIZATION.—The term "regional transportation planning organization" means a policy board of an organization established as the result of a designation under section 135(m).

(6) TIP.—The term "TIP" means a transportation improvement program developed by a metropolitan planning organization under subsection (j).

(7) URBANIZED AREA.—The term "urbanized area" means a geographic area with a population of 50,000 or more, as determined by the Bureau of the Census.

(c) GENERAL REQUIREMENTS.—

(1) DEVELOPMENT OF LONG-RANGE PLANS AND TIPS.—To accomplish the objectives in subsection (a), metropolitan planning organizations designated under subsection (d), in cooperation with the State and public transportation operators, shall develop long-range transportation plans and transportation improvement programs through a performance-driven, outcome-based approach to planning for metropolitan areas of the State.

(2) CONTENTS.—The plans and TIPs for each metropolitan area shall provide for the development and integrated management and operation of transportation systems and facilities (including accessible pedestrian walkways, bicycle transportation facilities, and intermodal facilities that support intercity transportation, including intercity buses and intercity bus facilities and commuter vanpool providers) that will function as an intermodal transportation system for the metropolitan planning area and as an integral part of an intermodal transportation system for the State and the United States.

(3) PROCESS OF DEVELOPMENT.—The process for developing the plans and TIPs shall provide for consideration of all modes of transportation and shall be continuing, cooperative, and comprehensive to the degree appropriate, based on the complexity of the transportation problems to be addressed.

(d) DESIGNATION OF METROPOLITAN PLANNING ORGANIZATIONS.—

(1) IN GENERAL.—To carry out the transportation planning process required by this section, a metropolitan planning organization shall be designated for each urbanized area with a population of more than 50,000 individuals—

(A) by agreement between the Governor and units of general purpose local government that together represent at least 75 percent of the affected population (including the largest incorporated city (based on population) as determined by the Bureau of the Census); or

(B) in accordance with procedures established by applicable State or local law.

(2) STRUCTURE.—Not later than 2 years after the date of enactment of MAP-21, each metropolitan planning organization that serves an area designated as a transportation management area shall consist of—

(A) local elected officials;

(B) officials of public agencies that administer or operate major modes of transportation in the metropolitan area, including representation by providers of public transportation; and

(C) appropriate State officials.

(3) REPRESENTATION.—

(A) IN GENERAL.—Designation or selection of officials or representatives under paragraph (2) shall be determined by the metropolitan planning organization according to the bylaws or enabling statute of the organization.

(B) PUBLIC TRANSPORTATION REPRESENTATIVE.—Subject to the bylaws or enabling statute of the metropolitan planning organization, a representative of a provider of public transportation may also serve as a representative of a local municipality.

(C) POWERS OF CERTAIN OFFICIALS.—An official described in paragraph (2)(B) shall have responsibilities, actions, duties, voting rights, and any other authority commensurate with other officials described in paragraph (2).

(D) CONSIDERATIONS.—In designating officials or representatives under paragraph (2) for the first time, subject to the bylaws or enabling statute of the metropolitan planning organization, the metropolitan planning organization shall consider the equitable and proportional representation of the population of the metropolitan planning area.

(4) LIMITATION ON STATUTORY CONSTRUCTION.—Nothing in this subsection shall be construed to interfere with the authority, under any State law in effect on December 18, 1991, of a public agency with multimodal transportation responsibilities—

(A) to develop the plans and TIPs for adoption by a metropolitan planning organization; and

(B) to develop long-range capital plans, coordinate transit services and projects, and carry out other activities pursuant to State law.

(5) CONTINUING DESIGNATION.—A designation of a metropolitan planning organization under this subsection or any other provision of law shall remain in effect until the metropolitan planning organization is redesignated under paragraph (6).

(6) REDESIGNATION PROCEDURES.—

(A) IN GENERAL.—A metropolitan planning organization may be redesignated by agreement between the Governor and units of general purpose local government that together represent at least 75 percent of the existing planning area population (including the largest incorporated city (based on population) as determined by the Bureau of the Census) as appropriate to carry out this section.

(B) RESTRUCTURING.—A metropolitan planning organization may be restructured to meet the requirements of paragraph (2) without undertaking a redesignation.

(7) DESIGNATION OF MORE THAN 1 METROPOLITAN PLANNING

ORGANIZATION.—More than 1 metropolitan planning organization may be designated within an existing urbanized area (as defined by the Bureau of the Census) only if the Governor and the existing metropolitan planning organization determine that the size and complexity of the area make designation of more than 1 metropolitan planning organization for the area appropriate.

(e) METROPOLITAN PLANNING AREA BOUNDARIES.—

(1) IN GENERAL.—For the purposes of this section, the boundaries of a metropolitan planning area shall be determined by agreement between the metropolitan planning organization and the Governor.

(2) INCLUDED AREA.—Each metropolitan planning area—

(A) shall encompass at least the existing urbanized area and the contiguous area expected to become urbanized within a 20-year forecast period for the transportation plan; and

(B) may encompass the entire metropolitan statistical area or consolidated metropolitan statistical area, as defined by the Bureau of the Census.

(3) IDENTIFICATION OF NEW URBANIZED AREAS WITHIN EXISTING PLANNING AREA BOUNDARIES.—The designation by the Bureau of the Census of new urbanized areas within an existing metropolitan planning area shall not require the redesignation of the existing metropolitan planning organization.

(4) EXISTING METROPOLITAN PLANNING AREAS IN NONATTAINMENT.—

(A) IN GENERAL.—Notwithstanding paragraph (2), except as provided in subparagraph (B), in the case of an urbanized area designated as a nonattainment area for ozone or carbon monoxide under the Clean Air Act (42 U.S.C. 7401 et seq.) as of the date of enactment of the SAFETEA–LU, the boundaries of the metropolitan planning area in existence as of such date of enactment shall be retained.

(B) EXCEPTION.—The boundaries described in subparagraph (A) may be adjusted by agreement of the Governor and affected metropolitan planning organizations in the manner described in subsection (d)(6).

(5) NEW METROPOLITAN PLANNING AREAS IN NONATTAINMENT.—In the case of an urbanized area designated after the date of enactment of the SAFETEA–LU, as a nonattainment area for ozone or carbon monoxide, the boundaries of the metropolitan planning area—

(A) shall be established in the manner described in subsection (d)(1);

(B) shall encompass the areas described in paragraph (2)(A);

(C) may encompass the areas described in paragraph (2)(B); and

(D) may address any nonattainment area identified under the Clean Air Act (42 U.S.C. 7401 et seq.) for ozone or carbon monoxide.

(f) COORDINATION IN MULTISTATE AREAS.—

(1) IN GENERAL.—The Secretary shall encourage each Governor with responsibility for a portion of a multistate metropolitan area and the appropriate metropolitan planning organizations to provide coordinated transportation planning for the entire metropolitan area.

(2) INTERSTATE COMPACTS.—The consent of Congress is granted to any 2 or more States—

(A) to enter into agreements or compacts, not in conflict with any law of the United States, for cooperative efforts and mutual assistance in support of activities authorized under this section as the activities pertain to interstate areas and localities within the States; and

(B) to establish such agencies, joint or otherwise, as the States may determine desirable for making the agreements and compacts effective.

(3) RESERVATION OF RIGHTS.—The right to alter, amend, or repeal interstate compacts entered into under this subsection is expressly reserved.

(g) MPO CONSULTATION IN PLAN AND TIP COORDINATION.—

(1) NONATTAINMENT AREAS.—If more than 1 metropolitan planning organization has authority within an urbanized area (as defined by the Bureau of the Census) or an area which is designated as a nonattainment area for ozone or carbon monoxide under the Clean Air Act (42 U.S.C. 7401 et seq.), each metropolitan planning organization shall consult with the other metropolitan planning organizations designated for such area and the State in the coordination of plans and TIPs required by this section.

(2) TRANSPORTATION IMPROVEMENTS LOCATED IN MULTIPLE MPOS.—If a transportation improvement, funded from the Highway Trust Fund or authorized under chapter 53 of title 49, is located within the boundaries of more than 1 metropolitan planning area, the metropolitan planning organizations shall coordinate plans and TIPs regarding the transportation improvement.

(3) RELATIONSHIP WITH OTHER PLANNING OFFICIALS.—

(A) IN GENERAL.—The Secretary shall encourage each metropolitan planning organization to consult with officials responsible for other types of planning activities that are affected by transportation in the area (including State and local planned growth, economic development, housing, tourism, natural disaster risk reduction, environmental protection, airport operations, and freight movements) or to coordinate its planning process, to the maximum extent practicable, with such planning activities.

(B) REQUIREMENTS.—Under the metropolitan planning process, transportation plans and TIPs shall be developed with due consideration of other related planning activities within the metropolitan area, and the process shall provide for the design and delivery of transportation services within the metropolitan area that are provided by—

(i) recipients of assistance under chapter 53 of title 49;

(ii) governmental agencies and nonprofit organizations (including representatives of the agencies and organizations) that receive Federal assistance from a source other than the Department of Transportation to provide nonemergency transportation services; and

(iii) recipients of assistance under section 204.

(4) COORDINATION BETWEEN MPOS.—If more than 1 metropolitan planning organization is designated within an urbanized area (as defined by the Bureau of the Census) under subsection (d)(7), the metropolitan planning organizations designated within the area shall ensure, to the maximum extent practicable, the consistency of any data used in the planning process, including information used in forecasting travel demand.

(5) SAVINGS CLAUSE.—Nothing in this subsection requires metropolitan planning organizations designated within a single urbanized area to jointly develop planning documents, including a unified long-range transportation plan or unified TIP.

(h) SCOPE OF PLANNING PROCESS.—

(1) IN GENERAL.—The metropolitan planning process for a metropolitan planning area under this section shall provide for consideration of projects and strategies that will—

(A) support the economic vitality of the metropolitan area, especially by enabling global competitiveness, productivity, and efficiency;

(B) increase the safety of the transportation system for motorized and nonmotorized users;

(C) increase the security of the transportation system for motorized and nonmotorized users;

(D) increase the accessibility and mobility of people and for freight;

(E) protect and enhance the environment, promote energy conservation, improve the quality of life, and promote consistency between transportation improvements and State and local planned growth, housing, and economic development patterns;

(F) enhance the integration and connectivity of the transportation system, across and between modes, for people and freight;

(G) promote efficient system management and operation;

(H) emphasize the preservation of the existing transportation system;

(I) improve the resiliency and reliability of the transportation system and reduce or mitigate stormwater impacts of surface transportation; and

(J) enhance travel and tourism.

(2) PERFORMANCE-BASED APPROACH.—

(A) IN GENERAL.—The metropolitan transportation planning process shall provide for the establishment and use of a performance-based approach to transportation decisionmaking to support the national goals described in section 150(b) of this title and the general purposes described in section 5301 of title 49.

(B) PERFORMANCE TARGETS.—

(i) SURFACE TRANSPORTATION PERFORMANCE TARGETS.—

(I) IN GENERAL.—Each metropolitan planning organization shall establish performance targets that address the performance measures described in section 150(c), where applicable, to use in tracking progress towards attainment of critical outcomes for the region of the metropolitan planning organization.

(II) COORDINATION.—Selection of performance targets by a metropolitan planning organization shall be coordinated with the relevant State to ensure consistency, to the maximum extent practicable.

(ii) PUBLIC TRANSPORTATION PERFORMANCE TARGETS.—Selection of performance targets by a metropolitan planning organization shall be coordinated, to the maximum extent practicable, with providers of public transportation to ensure consistency with sections 5326(c) and 5329(d) of title 49.

(C) TIMING.—Each metropolitan planning organization shall establish the performance targets under subparagraph (B) not later than 180 days after the date on which the relevant State or provider of public transportation establishes the performance targets.

(D) INTEGRATION OF OTHER PERFORMANCE-BASED PLANS.—A metropolitan planning organization shall integrate in the metropolitan transportation planning process, directly or by reference, the goals, objectives, performance measures, and targets described in other State transportation plans and transportation processes, as well as any plans developed under chapter 53 of title 49 by providers of public transportation, required as part of a performance-based program.

(3) FAILURE TO CONSIDER FACTORS.—The failure to consider any factor specified in paragraphs (1) and (2) shall not be reviewable by any court under this title or chapter 53 of title 49, subchapter II of chapter 5 of title 5, or chapter 7 of title 5 in any matter affecting a transportation plan, a TIP, a project or strategy, or the certification of a planning process.

(i) DEVELOPMENT OF TRANSPORTATION PLAN.—

(1) REQUIREMENTS.—

(A) IN GENERAL.—Each metropolitan planning organization shall prepare and update a transportation plan for its metropolitan planning area in accordance with the requirements of this subsection.

(B) FREQUENCY.—

(i) IN GENERAL.—The metropolitan planning organization shall prepare and update such plan every 4 years (or more frequently, if the metropolitan planning organization elects to update more frequently) in the case of each of the following:

(I) Any area designated as nonattainment, as defined in section 107(d) of the Clean Air Act (42 U.S.C. 7407(d)).

(II) Any area that was nonattainment and subsequently designated to attainment in accordance with section 107(d)(3) of that Act (42 U.S.C. 7407(d)(3)) and that is subject to a maintenance plan under section 175A of that Act (42 U.S.C. 7505a).

(ii) OTHER AREAS.—In the case of any other area required to have a transportation plan in accordance with the requirements of this subsection, the metropolitan planning organization shall prepare and update such plan every 5 years unless the metropolitan planning organization elects to update more frequently.

(2) TRANSPORTATION PLAN.—A transportation plan under this section shall be in a form that the Secretary determines to be appropriate and shall contain, at a minimum, the following:

(A) IDENTIFICATION OF TRANSPORTATION FACILITIES.—

(i) IN GENERAL.—An identification of transportation facilities (including major roadways, public transportation facilities, intercity bus facilities, multimodal and intermodal facilities, nonmotorized transportation facilities, and intermodal connectors) that should function as an integrated metropolitan transportation system, giving emphasis to those facilities that serve important national and regional transportation functions.

(ii) FACTORS.—In formulating the transportation plan, the metropolitan planning organization shall consider factors described in subsection (h) as the factors relate to a 20-year forecast period.

(B) PERFORMANCE MEASURES AND TARGETS.—A description of the performance measures and performance targets used in assessing the performance of the transportation system in accordance with subsection (h)(2).

(C) SYSTEM PERFORMANCE REPORT.—A system performance report and subsequent updates evaluating the condition and performance of the transportation system with respect to the performance targets described in subsection (h)(2), including—

(i) progress achieved by the metropolitan planning organization in meeting the performance targets in comparison with system performance recorded in previous reports; and

(ii) for metropolitan planning organizations that voluntarily elect to develop multiple scenarios, an analysis of how the preferred scenario has improved the conditions and performance of the transportation system and how changes in local policies and investments have impacted the costs necessary to achieve the identified performance targets.

(D) MITIGATION ACTIVITIES.—

(i) IN GENERAL.—A long-range transportation plan shall include a discussion of types of potential environmental mitigation activities and potential areas to carry out these activities, including activities that may have the greatest potential to restore and maintain the environmental functions affected by the plan.

(ii) CONSULTATION.—The discussion shall be developed in consultation with Federal, State, and tribal wildlife, land management, and regulatory agencies.

(E) FINANCIAL PLAN.—

(i) IN GENERAL.—A financial plan that—

(I) demonstrates how the adopted transportation plan can be implemented;

(II) indicates resources from public and private sources that are reasonably expected to be made available to carry out the plan; and

(III) recommends any additional financing strategies for needed projects and programs.

(ii) INCLUSIONS.—The financial plan may include, for illustrative purposes, additional projects that would be included in the adopted transportation plan if reasonable additional resources beyond those identified in the financial plan were available.

(iii) COOPERATIVE DEVELOPMENT.—For the purpose of developing the transportation plan, the metropolitan planning organization, transit operator, and State shall cooperatively develop estimates of funds that will be available to support plan implementation.

(F) OPERATIONAL AND MANAGEMENT STRATEGIES.—Operational and management strategies to improve the performance of existing transportation facilities to relieve vehicular congestion and maximize the safety and mobility of people and goods.

(G) CAPITAL INVESTMENT AND OTHER STRATEGIES.—Capital investment and other strategies to preserve the existing and projected future metropolitan transportation infrastructure, provide for multimodal capacity increases based on regional priorities and needs, and reduce the vulnerability of the existing transportation infrastructure to natural disasters.

(H) TRANSPORTATION AND TRANSIT ENHANCEMENT ACTIVITIES.—Proposed transportation and transit enhancement activities including consideration of the role that intercity buses may play in reducing congestion, pollution, and energy consumption in a cost-effective manner and strategies and investments that preserve and enhance intercity bus systems, including systems that are privately owned and operated.

(3) COORDINATION WITH CLEAN AIR ACT AGENCIES.—In metropolitan areas that are in nonattainment for ozone or carbon monoxide under the Clean Air Act (42 U.S.C. 7401 et seq.), the metropolitan planning organization shall coordinate the development of a transportation plan with the process for development of the transportation control measures of the State implementation plan required by that Act.

(4) OPTIONAL SCENARIO DEVELOPMENT.—

(A) IN GENERAL.—A metropolitan planning organization may, while fitting the needs and complexity of its community, voluntarily elect to develop multiple scenarios for consideration as part of the development of the metropolitan transportation plan, in accordance with subparagraph (B).

(B) RECOMMENDED COMPONENTS.—A metropolitan planning organization that chooses to develop multiple scenarios under subparagraph (A) shall be encouraged to consider—

(i) potential regional investment strategies for the planning horizon;

(ii) assumed distribution of population and employment;

(iii) assumed distribution of population and housing;

(iv) a scenario that, to the maximum extent practicable, maintains baseline conditions for the performance measures identified in subsection (h)(2);

(v) a scenario that improves the baseline conditions for as many of the performance measures identified in subsection (h)(2) as possible;

(vi) revenue constrained scenarios based on the total revenues expected to be available over the forecast period of the plan; and

(vii) estimated costs and potential revenues available to support each scenario.

(C) METRICS.—In addition to the performance measures identified in section 150(c), metropolitan planning organizations may evaluate scenarios developed under this paragraph using locally-developed measures.

(5) CONSULTATION.—

(A) IN GENERAL.—In each metropolitan area, the metropolitan planning organization shall consult, as appropriate, with State and local agencies responsible for land use management, natural resources, environmental protection, conservation, and historic preservation concerning the development of a long-range transportation plan.

(B) ISSUES.—The consultation shall involve, as appropriate—

(i) comparison of transportation plans with State conservation plans or maps, if available; or

(ii) comparison of transportation plans to inventories of natural or historic resources, if available.

(6) PARTICIPATION BY INTERESTED PARTIES.—

(A) IN GENERAL.—Each metropolitan planning organization shall provide citizens, affected public agencies, representatives of public transportation employees, public ports, freight shippers, providers of freight transportation services, private providers of transportation (including intercity bus operators, employer-based commuting programs, such as a carpool program, vanpool program, transit benefit program, parking cash-out program, shuttle program, or telework program), representatives of users of public transportation, representatives of users of pedestrian walkways and bicycle transportation facilities, representatives of the disabled, affordable housing organizations, and other interested parties with a reasonable opportunity to comment on the transportation plan.

(B) CONTENTS OF PARTICIPATION PLAN.—A participation plan—

(i) shall be developed in consultation with all interested parties; and

(ii) shall provide that all interested parties have reasonable opportunities to comment on the contents of the transportation plan.

(C) METHODS.—In carrying out subparagraph (A), the metropolitan planning organization shall, to the maximum extent practicable—

(i) hold any public meetings at convenient and accessible locations and times;

(ii) employ visualization techniques to describe plans; and

(iii) make public information available in electronically accessible format and means, such as the World Wide Web, as appropriate to afford reasonable opportunity for consideration of public information under subparagraph (A).

(D) USE OF TECHNOLOGY.—A metropolitan planning organization may use social media and other web-based tools—

(i) to further encourage public participation; and

(ii) to solicit public feedback during the transportation planning process.

(7) PUBLICATION.—A transportation plan involving Federal participation shall be published or otherwise made readily available by the metropolitan planning organization for public review, including (to the maximum extent practicable) in electronically accessible formats and means, such as the World Wide Web, approved by the metropolitan planning organization and submitted for information purposes to the Governor at such times and in such manner as the Secretary shall establish.

(8) SELECTION OF PROJECTS FROM ILLUSTRATIVE LIST.—Notwithstanding paragraph (2)(E), a State or metropolitan planning organization shall not be required to select any project from the illustrative list of additional projects included in the financial plan under paragraph (2)(E).

(j) METROPOLITAN TIP.—

(1) DEVELOPMENT.—

(A) IN GENERAL.—In cooperation with the State and any affected public transportation operator, the metropolitan planning organization designated for a metropolitan area shall develop a TIP for the metropolitan planning area that—

(i) contains projects consistent with the current metropolitan transportation plan;

(ii) reflects the investment priorities established in the current metropolitan transportation plan; and

(iii) once implemented, is designed to make progress toward achieving the performance targets established under subsection (h)(2).

(B) OPPORTUNITY FOR COMMENT.—In developing the TIP, the metropolitan planning organization, in cooperation with the State and any affected public transportation operator, shall provide an opportunity for participation by interested parties in the development of the program, in accordance with subsection (i)(5).

(C) FUNDING ESTIMATES.—For the purpose of developing the TIP, the metropolitan planning organization, public transportation agency, and State shall cooperatively develop estimates of funds that are reasonably expected to be available to support program implementation.

(D) UPDATING AND APPROVAL.—The TIP shall be—

(i) updated at least once every 4 years; and

(ii) approved by the metropolitan planning organization and the Governor.

(2) CONTENTS.—

(A) PRIORITY LIST.—The TIP shall include a priority list of proposed Federally supported projects and strategies to be carried out within each 4-year period after the initial adoption of the TIP.

(B) FINANCIAL PLAN.—The TIP shall include a financial plan that—

(i) demonstrates how the TIP can be implemented;

(ii) indicates resources from public and private sources that are reasonably expected to be available to carry out the program;

(iii) identifies innovative financing techniques to finance projects, programs, and strategies; and

(iv) may include, for illustrative purposes, additional projects that would be included in the approved TIP if reasonable additional resources beyond those identified in the financial plan were available.

(C) DESCRIPTIONS.—Each project in the TIP shall include sufficient descriptive material (such as type of work, termini, length, and other similar factors) to identify the project or phase of the project.

(D) PERFORMANCE TARGET ACHIEVEMENT.—The transportation improvement program shall include, to the maximum extent practicable, a description of the anticipated effect of the transportation improvement program toward achieving the performance targets established in the metropolitan transportation plan, linking investment priorities to those performance targets.

(3) INCLUDED PROJECTS.—

(A) PROJECTS UNDER THIS TITLE AND CHAPTER 53 OF TITLE 49.—A TIP developed under this subsection for a metropolitan area shall include the projects within the area that are proposed for funding under chapter 1 of this title and chapter 53 of title 49.

(B) PROJECTS UNDER CHAPTER 2.—

(i) REGIONALLY SIGNIFICANT PROJECTS.—Regionally significant projects proposed for funding under chapter 2 shall be identified individually in the transportation improvement program.

(ii) OTHER PROJECTS.—Projects proposed for funding under chapter 2 that are not determined to be regionally significant shall be grouped in 1 line item or identified individually in the transportation improvement program.

(C) CONSISTENCY WITH LONG-RANGE TRANSPORTATION PLAN.—Each project shall be consistent with the long-range transportation plan developed under subsection (i) for the area.

(D) REQUIREMENT OF ANTICIPATED FULL FUNDING.—The program shall include a project, or an identified phase of a project, only if full funding can reasonably be anticipated to be available for the project or the identified phase within the time period contemplated for completion of the project or the identified phase.

(4) NOTICE AND COMMENT.—Before approving a TIP, a metropolitan planning organization, in cooperation with the State and any affected public transportation operator, shall provide an opportunity for participation by interested parties in the development of the program, in accordance with subsection (i)(5).

(5) SELECTION OF PROJECTS.—

(A) IN GENERAL.—Except as otherwise provided in subsection (k)(4) and in addition to the TIP development required under paragraph (1), the selection of Federally funded projects in metropolitan areas shall be carried out, from the approved TIP—

(i) by—

(I) in the case of projects under this title, the State; and

(II) in the case of projects under chapter 53 of title 49, the designated recipients of public transportation funding; and

(ii) in cooperation with the metropolitan planning organization.

(B) MODIFICATIONS TO PROJECT PRIORITY.—Notwithstanding any other provision of law, action by the Secretary shall not be required to advance a project included in the approved TIP in place of another project in the program.

(6) SELECTION OF PROJECTS FROM ILLUSTRATIVE LIST.—

(A) NO REQUIRED SELECTION.—Notwithstanding paragraph (2)(B)(iv), a State or metropolitan planning organization shall not be required to select any project from the illustrative list of additional projects included in the financial plan under paragraph (2)(B)(iv).

(B) REQUIRED ACTION BY THE SECRETARY.—Action by the Secretary shall be required for a State or metropolitan planning organization to select any project from the illustrative list of additional projects included in the financial plan under paragraph (2)(B)(iv) for inclusion in an approved TIP.

(7) PUBLICATION.—

(A) PUBLICATION OF TIPS.—A TIP involving Federal participation shall be published or otherwise made readily available by the metropolitan planning organization for public review.

(B) PUBLICATION OF ANNUAL LISTINGS OF PROJECTS.—

(i) IN GENERAL.—An annual listing of projects, including investments in pedestrian walkways and bicycle transportation facilities, for which Federal funds have been obligated in the preceding year shall be published or otherwise made available by the cooperative effort of the State, transit operator, and metropolitan planning organization for public review.

(ii) REQUIREMENT.—The listing shall be consistent with the categories identified in the TIP.

(k) TRANSPORTATION MANAGEMENT AREAS.—

(1) IDENTIFICATION AND DESIGNATION.—

(A) REQUIRED IDENTIFICATION.—The Secretary shall identify as a transportation management area each urbanized area (as defined by the Bureau of the Census) with a population of over 200,000 individuals.

(B) DESIGNATIONS ON REQUEST.—The Secretary shall designate any additional area as a transportation management area on the request of the Governor and the metropolitan planning organization designated for the area.

(2) TRANSPORTATION PLANS.—In a transportation management area, transportation plans shall be based on a continuing and comprehensive transportation planning process carried out by the metropolitan planning organization in cooperation with the State and public transportation operators.

(3) CONGESTION MANAGEMENT PROCESS.—

(A) IN GENERAL.—Within a metropolitan planning area serving a transportation management area, the transportation planning process under this section shall address congestion management through a process that provides for effective management and operation, based on a cooperatively developed and implemented metropolitan-wide strategy, of new and existing transportation facilities eligible for funding under this title and chapter 53 of title 49 through the use of travel demand reduction (including intercity bus operators, employer-based commuting programs such as a carpool program, vanpool program, transit benefit program, parking cash-out program, shuttle program, or telework program), job access projects, and operational management strategies.

(B) SCHEDULE.—The Secretary shall establish an appropriate phase-in schedule for compliance with the requirements of this section but no sooner than 1 year after the identification of a transportation management area.

(C) CONGESTION MANAGEMENT PLAN.—A metropolitan planning organization serving a transportation management area may develop a plan that includes projects and strategies that will be considered in the TIP of such metropolitan planning organization. Such plan shall—

(i) develop regional goals to reduce vehicle miles traveled during peak commuting hours and improve transportation connections between areas with high job concentration and areas with high concentrations of low-income households;

(ii) identify existing public transportation services, employer-based commuter programs, and other existing transportation services that support access to jobs in the region; and

(iii) identify proposed projects and programs to reduce congestion and increase job access opportunities.

(D) PARTICIPATION.—In developing the plan under subparagraph (C), a metropolitan planning organization shall consult with employers, private and nonprofit providers of public transportation, transportation management organizations, and organizations that provide job access reverse commute projects or job-related services to low-income individuals.

(4) HOUSING COORDINATION PROCESS.—

(A) IN GENERAL.—Within a metropolitan planning area serving a transportation management area, the transportation planning process under this section may address the integration of housing, transportation, and economic development strategies through a process that provides for effective integration, based on a cooperatively developed and implemented strategy, of new and existing transportation facilities eligible for funding under this title and chapter 53 of title 49.

(B) COORDINATION IN INTEGRATED PLANNING PROCESS.—In carrying out the process described in subparagraph (A), a metropolitan planning organization may—

(i) consult with—

(I) State and local entities responsible for land use, economic development, housing, management of road networks, or public transportation; and

(II) other appropriate public or private entities; and

(ii) coordinate, to the extent practicable, with applicable State and local entities to align the goals of the process with the goals of any comprehensive housing affordability strategies established within the metropolitan planning area pursuant to section 105 of the Cranston-Gonzalez National Affordable Housing Act (42 U.S.C. 12705) and plans developed under section 5A of the United States Housing Act of 1937 (42 U.S.C. 1437c–1).

(C) HOUSING COORDINATION PLAN.—

(i) IN GENERAL.—A metropolitan planning organization serving a transportation management area may develop a housing coordination plan that includes projects and strategies that may be considered in the metropolitan transportation plan of the metropolitan planning organization.

(ii) CONTENTS.—A plan described in clause (i) may—

(I) develop regional goals for the integration of housing, transportation, and economic development strategies to—

(aa) better connect housing and employment while mitigating commuting times;

(bb) align transportation improvements with housing needs, such as housing supply shortages, and proposed housing development;

(cc) align planning for housing and transportation to address needs in relationship to household incomes within the metropolitan planning area;

(dd) expand housing and economic development within the catchment areas of existing transportation facilities and public transportation services when appropriate, including higher-density development, as locally determined;

(ee) manage effects of growth of vehicle miles traveled experienced in the metropolitan planning area related to housing development and economic development;

(ff) increase share of households with sufficient and affordable access to the transportation networks of the metropolitan planning area;

(II) identify the location of existing and planned housing and employment, and transportation options that connect housing and employment; and

(III) include a comparison of transportation plans to land use management plans, including zoning plans, that may affect road use, public transportation ridership, and housing development.

(5) SELECTION OF PROJECTS.—

(A) IN GENERAL.—All Federally funded projects carried out within the boundaries of a metropolitan planning area serving a transportation management area under this title (excluding projects carried out on the National Highway System) or under chapter 53 of title 49 shall be selected for implementation from the approved TIP by the metropolitan planning organization designated for the area in consultation with the State and any affected public transportation operator.

(B) NATIONAL HIGHWAY SYSTEM PROJECTS.—Projects carried out within the boundaries of a metropolitan planning area serving a transportation management area on the National Highway System shall be selected for implementation from the approved TIP by the State in cooperation with the metropolitan planning organization designated for the area.

(6) CERTIFICATION.—

(A) IN GENERAL.—The Secretary shall—

(i) ensure that the metropolitan planning process of a metropolitan planning organization serving a transportation management area is being carried out in accordance with applicable provisions of Federal law; and

(ii) subject to subparagraph (B), certify, not less often than once every 4 years, that the requirements of this paragraph are met with respect to the metropolitan planning process.

(B) REQUIREMENTS FOR CERTIFICATION.—The Secretary may make the certification under subparagraph (A) if—

(i) the transportation planning process complies with the requirements of this section and other applicable requirements of Federal law; and

(ii) there is a TIP for the metropolitan planning area that has been approved by the metropolitan planning organization and the Governor.

(C) EFFECT OF FAILURE TO CERTIFY.—

(i) WITHHOLDING OF PROJECT FUNDS.—If a metropolitan planning process of a metropolitan planning organization serving a transportation management area is not certified, the Secretary may withhold up to 20 percent of the funds attributable to the metropolitan planning area of the metropolitan planning organization for projects funded under this title and chapter 53 of title 49.

(ii) RESTORATION OF WITHHELD FUNDS.—The withheld funds shall be restored to the metropolitan planning area at such time as the metropolitan planning process is certified by the Secretary.

(D) REVIEW OF CERTIFICATION.—In making certification determinations under this paragraph, the Secretary shall provide for public involvement appropriate to the metropolitan area under review.

(l) REPORT ON PERFORMANCE-BASED PLANNING PROCESSES.—

(1) IN GENERAL.—The Secretary shall submit to Congress a report on the effectiveness of the performance-based planning processes of metropolitan planning organizations under this section, taking into consideration the requirements of this subsection.

(2) REPORT.—Not later than 5 years after the date of enactment of the MAP–21, the Secretary shall submit to Congress a report evaluating—

(A) the overall effectiveness of performance-based planning as a tool for guiding transportation investments;

(B) the effectiveness of the performance-based planning process of each metropolitan planning organization under this section;

(C) the extent to which metropolitan planning organizations have achieved, or are currently making substantial progress toward achieving, the performance targets specified under this section and whether metropolitan planning organizations are developing meaningful performance targets; and

(D) the technical capacity of metropolitan planning organizations that operate within a metropolitan planning area with a population of 200,000 or less and their ability to carry out the requirements of this section.

(3) PUBLICATION.—The report under paragraph (2) shall be published or otherwise made available in electronically accessible formats and means, including on the Internet.

(m) ABBREVIATED PLANS FOR CERTAIN AREAS.—

(1) IN GENERAL.—Subject to paragraph (2), in the case of a metropolitan area not designated as a transportation management area under this section, the Secretary may provide for the development of an abbreviated transportation plan and TIP for the metropolitan planning area that the Secretary determines is appropriate to achieve the purposes of this section, taking into account the complexity of transportation problems in the area.

(2) NONATTAINMENT AREAS.—The Secretary may not permit abbreviated plans or TIPs for a metropolitan area that is in nonattainment for ozone or carbon monoxide under the Clean Air Act (42 U.S.C. 7401 et seq.).

(n) ADDITIONAL REQUIREMENTS FOR CERTAIN NONATTAINMENT AREAS.—

(1) IN GENERAL.—Notwithstanding any other provisions of this title or chapter 53 of title 49, for transportation management areas classified as nonattainment for ozone or carbon monoxide pursuant to the Clean Air Act (42 U.S.C. 7401 et seq.), Federal funds may not be advanced in such area for any highway project that will result in a significant increase in the carrying capacity for single-occupant vehicles unless the project is addressed through a congestion management process.

(2) APPLICABILITY.—This subsection applies to a nonattainment area within the metropolitan planning area boundaries determined under subsection (e).

(o) LIMITATION ON STATUTORY CONSTRUCTION.—Nothing in this section shall be construed to confer on a metropolitan planning organization the authority to impose legal requirements on any transportation facility, provider, or project not eligible under this title or chapter 53 of title 49.

(p) FUNDING.—Funds apportioned under section 104(b)(6) or section 5305(g) of title 49 shall be available to carry out this section.

(q) CONTINUATION OF CURRENT REVIEW PRACTICE.—Since plans and TIPs described in this section are subject to a reasonable opportunity for public comment, since individual projects included in plans and TIPs are subject to review under the National Environmental Policy Act of 1969 (42 U.S.C. 4321 et seq.), and since decisions by the Secretary concerning plans and TIPs described in this section have not been reviewed under that Act as of January 1, 1997, any decision by the Secretary concerning a plan or TIP described in this section shall not be considered to be a Federal action subject to review under that Act.

(r) BI-STATE METROPOLITAN PLANNING ORGANIZATION.—

(1) DEFINITION OF BI-STATE MPO REGION.—In this subsection, the term "Bi-State MPO Region" has the meaning given the term "region" in subsection (a) of Article II of the Lake Tahoe Regional Planning Compact (Public Law 96–551; 94 Stat. 3234).

(2) TREATMENT.—For the purpose of this title, the Bi-State MPO Region shall be treated as—

(A) a metropolitan planning organization;

(B) a transportation management area under subsection (k); and

(C) an urbanized area, which is comprised of a population of 145,000 in the State of California and a population of 65,000 in the State of Nevada.

(3) SUBALLOCATED FUNDING.—

(A) PLANNING.—In determining the amounts under subparagraph (A) of section 133(d)(1) that shall be obligated for a fiscal year in the States of California and Nevada under clauses (i), (ii), and (iii) of that subparagraph, the Secretary shall, for each of those States—

(i) calculate the population under each of those clauses;

(ii) decrease the amount under section 133(d)(1)(A)(iii) by the population specified in paragraph (2) of this subsection for the Bi-State MPO Region in that State; and

(iii) increase the amount under section 133(d)(1)(A)(i) by the population specified in paragraph (2) of this subsection for the Bi-State MPO Region in that State.

(B) STBGP SET ASIDE.—In determining the amounts under paragraph (2) of section 133(h) that shall be obligated for a fiscal year in the States of California and Nevada, the Secretary shall, for the purpose of that subsection, calculate the populations for each of those States in a manner consistent with subparagraph (A).

(Added Pub. L. 87–866, §9(a), Oct. 23, 1962, 76 Stat. 1148; amended Pub. L. 91–605, title I, §143, Dec. 31, 1970, 84 Stat. 1737; Pub. L. 95–599, title I, §169, Nov. 6, 1978, 92 Stat. 2723; Pub. L. 102–240, title I, §1024(a), Dec. 18, 1991, 105 Stat. 1955; Pub. L. 102–388, title V, §502(b), Oct. 6, 1992, 106 Stat. 1566; Pub. L. 103–429, §3(5), Oct. 31, 1994, 108 Stat. 4377; Pub. L. 104–59, title III, §317, Nov. 28, 1995, 109 Stat. 588; Pub. L. 105–178, title I, §1203(a)–(m), (o), June 9, 1998, 112 Stat. 170–179; Pub. L. 105–206, title IX, §9003(c), July 22, 1998, 112 Stat. 839; Pub. L. 109–59, title VI, §6001(a), Aug. 10, 2005, 119 Stat. 1839; Pub. L. 110–244, title I, §101(n), June 6, 2008, 122 Stat. 1576; Pub. L. 112–141, div. A, title I, §1201(a), July 6, 2012, 126 Stat. 500; Pub. L. 114–94, div. A, title I, §1201, Dec. 4, 2015, 129 Stat. 1371; Pub. L. 117–58, div. A, title I, §11201(a), (d), Nov. 15, 2021, 135 Stat. 516, 517.)

---

[1] So in original. Probably should be "urbanized areas, better connect housing and employment,".

§135. STATEWIDE AND NONMETROPOLITAN TRANSPORTATION PLANNING

(a) GENERAL REQUIREMENTS.—

(1) DEVELOPMENT OF PLANS AND PROGRAMS.—Subject to section 134, to accomplish the objectives stated in section 134(a), each State shall develop a statewide transportation plan and a statewide transportation improvement program for all areas of the State.

(2) CONTENTS.—The statewide transportation plan and the transportation improvement program developed for each State shall provide for the development and integrated management and operation of transportation systems and facilities (including accessible pedestrian walkways, bicycle transportation facilities, and intermodal facilities that support intercity transportation, including intercity buses and intercity bus facilities and commuter van pool providers) that will function as an intermodal transportation system for the State and an integral part of an intermodal transportation system for the United States.

(3) PROCESS OF DEVELOPMENT.—The process for developing the statewide plan and the transportation improvement program shall provide for consideration of all modes of transportation and the policies stated in section 134(a) and shall be continuing, cooperative, and comprehensive to the degree appropriate, based on the complexity of the transportation problems to be addressed.

(b) COORDINATION WITH METROPOLITAN PLANNING; STATE IMPLEMENTATION PLAN.—A State shall—

(1) coordinate planning carried out under this section with the transportation planning activities carried out under section 134 for metropolitan areas of the State and with statewide trade and economic development planning activities and related multistate planning efforts; and

(2) develop the transportation portion of the State implementation plan as required by the Clean Air Act (42 U.S.C. 7401 et seq.).

(c) INTERSTATE AGREEMENTS.—

(1) IN GENERAL.—Two or more States may enter into agreements or compacts, not in conflict with any law of the United States, for cooperative efforts and mutual assistance in support of activities authorized under this section related to interstate areas and localities in the States and establishing authorities the States consider desirable for making the agreements and compacts effective.

(2) RESERVATION OF RIGHTS.—The right to alter, amend, or repeal interstate compacts entered into under this subsection is expressly reserved.

(d) SCOPE OF PLANNING PROCESS.—

(1) IN GENERAL.—Each State shall carry out a statewide transportation planning process that provides for consideration and implementation of projects, strategies, and services that will—

(A) support the economic vitality of the United States, the States, nonmetropolitan areas, and metropolitan areas, especially by enabling global competitiveness, productivity, and efficiency;

(B) increase the safety of the transportation system for motorized and nonmotorized users;

(C) increase the security of the transportation system for motorized and nonmotorized users;

(D) increase the accessibility and mobility of people and freight;

(E) protect and enhance the environment, promote energy conservation, improve the quality of life, and promote consistency between transportation improvements and State and local planned growth and economic development patterns;

(F) enhance the integration and connectivity of the transportation system, across and between modes throughout the State, for people and freight;

(G) promote efficient system management and operation;

(H) emphasize the preservation of the existing transportation system;

(I) improve the resiliency and reliability of the transportation system and reduce or mitigate stormwater impacts of surface transportation; and

(J) enhance travel and tourism.

(2) PERFORMANCE-BASED APPROACH.—

(A) IN GENERAL.—The statewide transportation planning process shall provide for the establishment and use of a performance-based approach to transportation decisionmaking to support the national goals described in section 150(b) of this title and the general purposes described in section 5301 of title 49.

(B) PERFORMANCE TARGETS.—

(i) SURFACE TRANSPORTATION PERFORMANCE TARGETS.—

(I) IN GENERAL.—Each State shall establish performance targets that address the performance measures described in section 150(c), where applicable, to use in tracking progress towards attainment of critical outcomes for the State.

(II) COORDINATION.—Selection of performance targets by a State shall be coordinated with the relevant metropolitan planning organizations to ensure consistency, to the maximum extent practicable.

(ii) PUBLIC TRANSPORTATION PERFORMANCE TARGETS.—In areas not represented by a metropolitan planning organization, selection of performance targets by a State shall be coordinated, to the maximum extent practicable, with providers of public transportation to ensure consistency with sections 5326(c) and 5329(d) of title 49.

(C) INTEGRATION OF OTHER PERFORMANCE-BASED PLANS.—A State shall integrate into the statewide transportation planning process, directly or by reference, the goals, objectives, performance measures, and targets described in this paragraph, in other State transportation plans and transportation processes, as well as any plans developed pursuant to chapter 53 of title 49 by providers of public transportation in areas not represented by a metropolitan planning organization required as part of a performance-based program.

(D) USE OF PERFORMANCE MEASURES AND TARGETS.—The performance measures and targets established under this paragraph shall be considered by a State when developing policies, programs, and investment priorities reflected in the statewide transportation plan and statewide transportation improvement program.

(3) FAILURE TO CONSIDER FACTORS.—The failure to take into consideration the factors specified in paragraphs (1) and (2) shall not be subject to review by any court under this title, chapter 53 of title 49, subchapter II of chapter 5 of title 5, or

chapter 7 of title 5 in any matter affecting a statewide transportation plan, a statewide transportation improvement program, a project or strategy, or the certification of a planning process.

(e) ADDITIONAL REQUIREMENTS.—In carrying out planning under this section, each State shall, at a minimum—

(1) with respect to nonmetropolitan areas, cooperate with affected local officials with responsibility for transportation or, if applicable, through regional transportation planning organizations described in subsection (m);

(2) consider the concerns of Indian tribal governments and Federal land management agencies that have jurisdiction over land within the boundaries of the State; and

(3) consider coordination of transportation plans, the transportation improvement program, and planning activities with related planning activities being carried out outside of metropolitan planning areas and between States.

(f) LONG-RANGE STATEWIDE TRANSPORTATION PLAN.—

(1) DEVELOPMENT.—Each State shall develop a long-range statewide transportation plan, with a minimum 20-year forecast period for all areas of the State, that provides for the development and implementation of the intermodal transportation system of the State.

(2) CONSULTATION WITH GOVERNMENTS.—

(A) METROPOLITAN AREAS.—The statewide transportation plan shall be developed for each metropolitan area in the State in cooperation with the metropolitan planning organization designated for the metropolitan area under section 134.

(B) NONMETROPOLITAN AREAS.—

(i) IN GENERAL.—With respect to nonmetropolitan areas, the statewide transportation plan shall be developed in cooperation with affected nonmetropolitan officials with responsibility for transportation or, if applicable, through regional transportation planning organizations described in subsection (m).

(ii) ROLE OF SECRETARY.—The Secretary shall not review or approve the consultation process in each State.

(C) INDIAN TRIBAL AREAS.—With respect to each area of the State under the jurisdiction of an Indian tribal government, the statewide transportation plan shall be developed in consultation with the tribal government and the Secretary of the Interior.

(D) CONSULTATION, COMPARISON, AND CONSIDERATION.—

(i) IN GENERAL.—The long-range transportation plan shall be developed, as appropriate, in consultation with State, tribal, and local agencies responsible for land use management, natural resources, environmental protection, conservation, and historic preservation.

(ii) COMPARISON AND CONSIDERATION.—Consultation under clause (i) shall involve comparison of transportation plans to State and tribal conservation plans or maps, if available, and comparison of transportation plans to inventories of natural or historic resources, if available.

(3) PARTICIPATION BY INTERESTED PARTIES.—

(A) IN GENERAL.—In developing the statewide transportation plan, the State shall provide to—

(i) nonmetropolitan local elected officials or, if applicable, through regional transportation planning organizations described in subsection (m), an opportunity to participate in accordance with subparagraph (B)(i); and

(ii) citizens, affected public agencies, representatives of public transportation employees, public ports, freight shippers, private providers of transportation (including intercity bus operators, employer-based commuting programs, such as a carpool program, vanpool program, transit benefit program, parking cash-out program, shuttle program, or telework program), representatives of users of public transportation, representatives of users of pedestrian walkways and bicycle transportation facilities, representatives of the disabled, providers of freight transportation services, and other interested parties a reasonable opportunity to comment on the proposed plan.

(B) METHODS.—In carrying out subparagraph (A), the State shall, to the maximum extent practicable—

(i) develop and document a consultative process to carry out subparagraph (A)(i) that is separate and discrete from the public involvement process developed under clause (ii);

(ii) hold any public meetings at convenient and accessible locations and times;

(iii) employ visualization techniques to describe plans; and

(iv) make public information available in electronically accessible format and means, such as the World Wide Web, as appropriate to afford reasonable opportunity for consideration of public information under subparagraph (A).

(C) USE OF TECHNOLOGY.—A State may use social media and other web-based tools—

(i) to further encourage public participation; and

(ii) to solicit public feedback during the transportation planning process.

(4) MITIGATION ACTIVITIES.—

(A) IN GENERAL.—A long-range transportation plan shall include a discussion of potential environmental mitigation activities and potential areas to carry out these activities, including activities that may have the greatest potential to restore and maintain the environmental functions affected by the plan.

(B) CONSULTATION.—The discussion shall be developed in consultation with Federal, State, and tribal wildlife, land management, and regulatory agencies.

(5) FINANCIAL PLAN.—The statewide transportation plan may include—

(A) a financial plan that—

(i) demonstrates how the adopted statewide transportation plan can be implemented;

(ii) indicates resources from public and private sources that are reasonably expected to be made available to carry out the plan; and

(iii) recommends any additional financing strategies for needed projects and programs; and

(B) for illustrative purposes, additional projects that would be included in the adopted statewide transportation plan if reasonable additional resources beyond those identified in the financial plan were available.

(6) SELECTION OF PROJECTS FROM ILLUSTRATIVE LIST.—A State shall not be required to select any project from the illustrative list of additional projects included in the financial plan described in paragraph (5).

(7) PERFORMANCE-BASED APPROACH.—The statewide transportation plan shall include—

(A) a description of the performance measures and performance targets used in assessing the performance of the transportation system in accordance with subsection (d)(2); and

(B) a system performance report and subsequent updates evaluating the condition and performance of the transportation system with respect to the performance targets described in subsection (d)(2), including progress achieved by the metropolitan planning organization in meeting the performance targets in comparison with system performance recorded in previous reports;

(8) EXISTING SYSTEM.—The statewide transportation plan should include capital, operations and management strategies, investments, procedures, and other measures to ensure the preservation and most efficient use of the existing transportation system, including consideration of the role that intercity buses may play in reducing congestion, pollution, and energy consumption in a cost-effective manner and strategies and investments that preserve and enhance intercity bus systems, including systems that are privately owned and operated.

(9) PUBLICATION OF LONG-RANGE TRANSPORTATION PLANS.—Each long-range transportation plan prepared by a State shall be published or otherwise made available, including (to the maximum extent practicable) in electronically accessible formats and means, such as the World Wide Web.

(g) STATEWIDE TRANSPORTATION IMPROVEMENT PROGRAM.—

(1) DEVELOPMENT.—

(A) IN GENERAL.—Each State shall develop a statewide transportation improvement program for all areas of the State.

(B) DURATION AND UPDATING OF PROGRAM.—Each program developed under subparagraph (A) shall cover a period of 4 years and shall be updated every 4 years or more frequently if the Governor of the State elects to update more frequently.

(2) CONSULTATION WITH GOVERNMENTS.—

(A) METROPOLITAN AREAS.—With respect to each metropolitan area in the State, the program shall be developed in cooperation with the metropolitan planning organization designated for the metropolitan area under section 134.

(B) NONMETROPOLITAN AREAS.—

(i) IN GENERAL.—With respect to each nonmetropolitan area in the State, the program shall be developed in consultation with affected nonmetropolitan local officials with responsibility for transportation or, if applicable, through regional transportation planning organizations described in subsection (m).

(ii) ROLE OF SECRETARY.—The Secretary shall not review or approve the specific consultation process in the State.

(C) INDIAN TRIBAL AREAS.—With respect to each area of the State under the jurisdiction of an Indian tribal government, the program shall be developed in consultation with the tribal government and the Secretary of the Interior.

(3) PARTICIPATION BY INTERESTED PARTIES.—In developing the program, the State shall provide citizens, affected public agencies, representatives of public transportation employees, public ports, freight shippers, private providers of transportation (including intercity bus operators), providers of freight transportation services, representatives of users of public transportation, representatives of users of pedestrian walkways and bicycle transportation facilities, representatives of the disabled, and other interested parties with a reasonable opportunity to comment on the proposed program.

(4) PERFORMANCE TARGET ACHIEVEMENT.—A statewide transportation improvement program shall include, to the maximum extent practicable, a discussion of the anticipated effect of the statewide transportation improvement program toward achieving the performance targets established in the statewide transportation plan, linking investment priorities to those performance targets.

(5) INCLUDED PROJECTS.—

(A) IN GENERAL.—A transportation improvement program developed under this subsection for a State shall include Federally supported surface transportation expenditures within the boundaries of the State.

(B) LISTING OF PROJECTS.—

(i) IN GENERAL.—An annual listing of projects for which funds have been obligated for the preceding year in each metropolitan planning area shall be published or otherwise made available by the cooperative effort of the State, transit operator, and the metropolitan planning organization for public review.

(ii) FUNDING CATEGORIES.—The listing described in clause (i) shall be consistent with the funding categories identified in each metropolitan transportation improvement program.

(C) PROJECTS UNDER CHAPTER 2.—

(i) REGIONALLY SIGNIFICANT PROJECTS.—Regionally significant projects proposed for funding under chapter 2 shall be identified individually in the transportation improvement program.

(ii) OTHER PROJECTS.—Projects proposed for funding under chapter 2 that are not determined to be regionally significant shall be grouped in 1 line item or identified individually in the transportation improvement program.

(D) CONSISTENCY WITH STATEWIDE TRANSPORTATION PLAN.—Each project shall be—

(i) consistent with the statewide transportation plan developed under this section for the State;

(ii) identical to the project or phase of the project as described in an approved metropolitan transportation plan; and

(iii) in conformance with the applicable State air quality implementation plan developed under the Clean Air Act (42 U.S.C. 7401 et seq.), if the project is carried out in an area designated as a nonattainment area for ozone, particulate matter, or carbon monoxide under part D of title I of that Act (42 U.S.C. 7501 et seq.).

(E) Requirement of anticipated full funding.—The transportation improvement program shall include a project, or an identified phase of a project, only if full funding can reasonably be anticipated to be available for the project within the time period contemplated for completion of the project.

(F) Financial plan.—

(i) In general.—The transportation improvement program may include a financial plan that demonstrates how the approved transportation improvement program can be implemented, indicates resources from public and private sources that are reasonably expected to be made available to carry out the transportation improvement program, and recommends any additional financing strategies for needed projects and programs.

(ii) Additional projects.—The financial plan may include, for illustrative purposes, additional projects that would be included in the adopted transportation plan if reasonable additional resources beyond those identified in the financial plan were available.

(G) Selection of projects from illustrative list.—

(i) No required selection.—Notwithstanding subparagraph (F), a State shall not be required to select any project from the illustrative list of additional projects included in the financial plan under subparagraph (F).

(ii) Required action by the secretary.—Action by the Secretary shall be required for a State to select any project from the illustrative list of additional projects included in the financial plan under subparagraph (F) for inclusion in an approved transportation improvement program.

(H) Priorities.—The transportation improvement program shall reflect the priorities for programming and expenditures of funds, including transportation enhancement activities, required by this title and chapter 53 of title 49.

(6) Project selection for areas of less than 50,000 population.—

(A) In general.—Projects carried out in areas with populations of less than 50,000 individuals shall be selected, from the approved transportation improvement program (excluding projects carried out on the National Highway System and projects carried out under the bridge program or the Interstate maintenance program under this title or under sections 5310 and 5311 of title 49), by the State in cooperation with the affected nonmetropolitan local officials with responsibility for transportation or, if applicable, through regional transportation planning organizations described in subsection (m).

(B) Other projects.—Projects carried out in areas with populations of less than 50,000 individuals on the National Highway System or under the bridge program or the Interstate maintenance program under this title or under sections 5310 and 5311 of title 49 shall be selected, from the approved statewide transportation improvement program, by the State in consultation with the affected nonmetropolitan local officials with responsibility for transportation.

(7) Transportation improvement program approval.—Every 4 years, a transportation improvement program developed under this subsection shall be reviewed and approved by the Secretary if based on a current planning finding.

(8) Planning finding.—A finding shall be made by the Secretary at least every 4

years that the transportation planning process through which statewide transportation plans and programs are developed is consistent with this section and section 134.

(9) MODIFICATIONS TO PROJECT PRIORITY.—Notwithstanding any other provision of law, action by the Secretary shall not be required to advance a project included in the approved transportation improvement program in place of another project in the program.

(h) PERFORMANCE-BASED PLANNING PROCESSES EVALUATION.—

(1) IN GENERAL.—The Secretary shall establish criteria to evaluate the effectiveness of the performance-based planning processes of States, taking into consideration the following:

(A) The extent to which the State is making progress toward achieving, the performance targets described in subsection (d)(2), taking into account whether the State developed appropriate performance targets.

(B) The extent to which the State has made transportation investments that are efficient and cost-effective.

(C) The extent to which the State—

(i) has developed an investment process that relies on public input and awareness to ensure that investments are transparent and accountable; and

(ii) provides reports allowing the public to access the information being collected in a format that allows the public to meaningfully assess the performance of the State.

(2) REPORT.—

(A) IN GENERAL.—Not later than 5 years after the date of enactment of the MAP–21, the Secretary shall submit to Congress a report evaluating—

(i) the overall effectiveness of performance-based planning as a tool for guiding transportation investments; and

(ii) the effectiveness of the performance-based planning process of each State.

(B) PUBLICATION.—The report under subparagraph (A) shall be published or otherwise made available in electronically accessible formats and means, including on the Internet.

(i) FUNDING.—Funds apportioned under section 104(b)(6) and set aside under section 5305(g) of title 49 shall be available to carry out this section.

(j) TREATMENT OF CERTAIN STATE LAWS AS CONGESTION MANAGEMENT PROCESSES.—For purposes of this section and section 134, and sections 5303 and 5304 of title 49, State laws, rules, or regulations pertaining to congestion management systems or programs may constitute the congestion management process under this section and section 134, and sections 5303 and 5304 of title 49, if the Secretary finds that the State laws, rules, or regulations are consistent with, and fulfill the intent of, the purposes of this section and section 134 and sections 5303 and 5304 of title 49, as appropriate.

(k) CONTINUATION OF CURRENT REVIEW PRACTICE.—Since the statewide transportation plan and the transportation improvement program described in this section are subject to a reasonable opportunity for public comment, since individual projects included in the statewide transportation plans and the transportation improvement program are subject to review under the National Environmental Policy

Act of 1969 (42 U.S.C. 4321 et seq.), and since decisions by the Secretary concerning statewide transportation plans or the transportation improvement program described in this section have not been reviewed under that Act as of January 1, 1997, any decision by the Secretary concerning a metropolitan or statewide transportation plan or the transportation improvement program described in this section shall not be considered to be a Federal action subject to review under the National Environmental Policy Act of 1969 (42 U.S.C. 4321 et seq.).

(l) SCHEDULE FOR IMPLEMENTATION.—The Secretary shall issue guidance on a schedule for implementation of the changes made by this section, taking into consideration the established planning update cycle for States. The Secretary shall not require a State to deviate from its established planning update cycle to implement changes made by this section. States shall reflect changes made to their transportation plan or transportation improvement program updates not later than 2 years after the date of issuance of guidance by the Secretary under this subsection.

(m) DESIGNATION OF REGIONAL TRANSPORTATION PLANNING ORGANIZATIONS.—

(1) IN GENERAL.—To carry out the transportation planning process required by this section, a State may establish and designate regional transportation planning organizations to enhance the planning, coordination, and implementation of statewide strategic long-range transportation plans and transportation improvement programs, with an emphasis on addressing the needs of nonmetropolitan areas of the State.

(2) STRUCTURE.—A regional transportation planning organization shall be established as a multijurisdictional organization of nonmetropolitan local officials or their designees who volunteer for such organization and representatives of local transportation systems who volunteer for such organization.

(3) REQUIREMENTS.—A regional transportation planning organization shall establish, at a minimum—

(A) a policy committee, the majority of which shall consist of nonmetropolitan local officials, or their designees, and, as appropriate, additional representatives from the State, private business, transportation service providers, economic development practitioners, and the public in the region; and

(B) a fiscal and administrative agent, such as an existing regional planning and development organization, to provide professional planning, management, and administrative support.

(4) DUTIES.—The duties of a regional transportation planning organization shall include—

(A) developing and maintaining, in cooperation with the State, regional long-range multimodal transportation plans;

(B) developing a regional transportation improvement program for consideration by the State;

(C) fostering the coordination of local planning, land use, and economic development plans with State, regional, and local transportation plans and programs;

(D) providing technical assistance to local officials;

(E) participating in national, multistate, and State policy and planning development processes to ensure the regional and local input of nonmetropolitan areas;

(F) providing a forum for public participation in the statewide and regional transportation planning processes;

(G) considering and sharing plans and programs with neighboring regional transportation planning organizations, metropolitan planning organizations, and, where appropriate, tribal organizations; and

(H) conducting other duties, as necessary, to support and enhance the statewide planning process under subsection (d).

(5) STATES WITHOUT REGIONAL TRANSPORTATION PLANNING ORGANIZATIONS.—If a State chooses not to establish or designate a regional transportation planning organization, the State shall consult with affected nonmetropolitan local officials to determine projects that may be of regional significance.

(Added Pub. L. 90–495, §10(a), Aug. 23, 1968, 82 Stat. 820; amended Pub. L. 91–605, title I, §§106(g), 125, Dec. 31, 1970, 84 Stat. 1718, 1729; Pub. L. 93–87, title I, §119, Aug. 13, 1973, 87 Stat. 259; Pub. L. 94–280, title I, §123(a), May 5, 1976, 90 Stat. 439; Pub. L. 102–240, title I, §1025(a), Dec. 18, 1991, 105 Stat. 1962; Pub. L. 103–429, §3(6), Oct. 31, 1994, 108 Stat. 4378; Pub. L. 105–178, title I, §1204(a)–(h), June 9, 1998, 112 Stat. 180–184; Pub. L. 109–59, title VI, §6001(a), Aug. 10, 2005, 119 Stat. 1851; Pub. L. 112–141, div. A, title I, §1202(a), July 6, 2012, 126 Stat. 514; Pub. L. 114–94, div. A, title I, §§1104(e)(3), 1202, Dec. 4, 2015, 129 Stat. 1332, 1374; Pub. L. 117–58, div. A, title I, §§11201(b), (c), 11525(g), Nov. 15, 2021, 135 Stat. 517, 607.)

§136. CONTROL OF JUNKYARDS

(a) The Congress hereby finds and declares that the establishment and use and maintenance of junkyards in areas adjacent to the Interstate System and the primary system should be controlled in order to protect the public investment in such highways, to promote the safety and recreational value of public travel, and to preserve natural beauty.

(b) Federal-aid highway funds apportioned on or after January 1, 1968, to any State which the Secretary determines has not made provision for effective control of the establishment and maintenance along the Interstate System and the primary system of outdoor junkyards, which are within one thousand feet of the nearest edge of the right-of-way and visible from the main traveled way of the system, shall be reduced by amounts equal to 7 percent of the amounts which would otherwise be apportioned to such State under paragraphs (1) through (6) of section 104(b), until such time as such State shall provide for such effective control. Any amount which is withheld from apportionment to any State hereunder shall be reapportioned to the other States. Whenever he determines it to be in the public interest, the Secretary may suspend, for such periods as he deems necessary, the application of this subsection to a State.

(c) Effective control means that by January 1, 1968, such junkyards shall be screened by natural objects, plantings, fences, or other appropriate means so as not to be visible from the main traveled way of the system, or shall be removed from sight.

(d) The term "junk" shall mean old or scrap copper, brass, rope, rags, batteries, paper, trash, rubber debris, waste, or junked, dismantled, or wrecked automobiles, or parts thereof, iron, steel, and other old or scrap ferrous or nonferrous material.

(e) The term "automobile graveyard" shall mean any establishment or place of business which is maintained, used, or operated for storing, keeping, buying, or selling wrecked, scrapped, ruined, or dismantled motor vehicles or motor vehicle parts.

(f) The term "junkyard" shall mean an establishment or place of business which is maintained, operated, or used for storing, keeping, buying, or selling junk, or for the maintenance or operation of an automobile graveyard, and the term shall include garbage dumps and sanitary fills.

(g) Notwithstanding any provision of this section, junkyards, auto graveyards, and scrap metal processing facilities may be operated within areas adjacent to the Interstate System and the primary system which are within one thousand feet of the nearest edge of the right-of-way and which are zoned industrial under authority of State law, or which are not zoned under authority of State law, but are used for industrial activities, as determined by the several States subject to approval by the Secretary.

(h) Notwithstanding any provision of this section, any junkyard in existence on the date of enactment of this section which does not conform to the requirements of this section and which the Secretary finds as a practical matter cannot be screened, shall not be required to be removed until July 1, 1970.

(i) The Federal share of landscaping and screening costs under this section shall be 75 per centum.

(j) Just compensation shall be paid the owner for the relocation, removal, or disposal of junkyards lawfully established under State law. The Federal share of such compensation shall be 75 per centum.

(k) All public lands or reservations of the United States which are adjacent to any portion of the interstate and primary systems shall be effectively controlled in accordance with the provisions of this section.

(l) Nothing in this section shall prohibit a State from establishing standards imposing stricter limitations with respect to outdoor junkyards on the Federal-aid highway systems than those established under this section.

(m) There is authorized to be appropriated to carry out this section, out of any money in the Treasury not otherwise appropriated, not to exceed $20,000,000 for the fiscal year ending June 30, 1966, not to exceed $20,000,000 for the fiscal year ending June 30, 1967, not to exceed $3,000,000 for the fiscal year ending June 30, 1970, not to exceed $3,000,000 for the fiscal year ending June 30, 1971, not to exceed $3,000,000 for the fiscal year ending June 30, 1972, and not to exceed $5,000,000 for the fiscal year ending June 30, 1973. The provisions of this chapter relating to the obligation, period of availability, and expenditure of Federal-aid primary highway funds shall apply to the funds authorized to be appropriated to carry out this section after June 30, 1967.

(n) DEFINITIONS.—For purposes of this section, the terms "primary system" and "Federal-aid primary system" mean any highway that is on the National Highway System, which includes the Interstate Highway System.

(Added Pub. L. 89–285, title II, §201, Oct. 22, 1965, 79 Stat. 1030; amended Pub. L. 89–574, §8(a), Sept. 13, 1966, 80 Stat. 768; Pub. L. 90–495, §6(e), Aug. 23, 1968, 82 Stat. 818; Pub. L. 91–605, title I, §122(b), Dec. 31, 1970, 84 Stat. 1726; Pub. L. 93–643, §110, Jan. 4, 1975, 88 Stat. 2285; Pub. L. 112–141, div. A, title I, §1404(b), July 6, 2012, 126 Stat. 557; Pub. L. 114–94, div. A, title I, §1104(e)(4), Dec. 4, 2015, 129 Stat. 1332.)

§137. FRINGE AND CORRIDOR PARKING FACILITIES

(a) The Secretary may approve as a project on a Federal-aid highway the acquisition of land adjacent to the right-of-way outside a central business district, as defined by the

Secretary, and the construction of publicly owned parking facilities thereon or within such right-of-way, including the use of the air space above and below the established grade line of the highway pavement, to serve an urban area of fifty thousand population or more. Such parking facility shall be located and designed in conjunction with existing or planned public transportation facilities. In the event fees are charged for the use of any such facility, the rate thereof shall not be in excess of that required for maintenance and operation (including compensation to any person for operating such facility).

(b) The Secretary shall not approve any project under this section until—

(1) he has determined that the State, or the political subdivision thereof, where such project is to be located, or any agency or instrumentality of such State or political subdivision, has the authority and capability of constructing, maintaining, and operating the facility;

(2) he has entered into an agreement governing the financing, maintenance, and operation of the parking facility with such State, political subdivision, agency, or instrumentality, including necessary requirements to insure that adequate public transportation services will be available to persons using such facility; and

(3) he has approved design standards for constructing such facility developed in cooperation with the State transportation department.

(c) The term "parking facilities" for purposes of this section shall include access roads, buildings, structures, equipment, improvements, and interests in lands.

(d) Nothing in this section, or in any rule or regulation issued under this section, or in any agreement required by this section, shall prohibit (1) any State, political subdivision, or agency or instrumentality thereof, from contracting with any person to operate any parking facility constructed under this section, or (2) any such person from so operating such facility.

(e) The Secretary shall not approve any project under this section unless he determines that it is based on a continuing comprehensive transportation planning process carried on in accordance with section 134 of this title.

(f)(1) The Secretary may approve for Federal financial assistance from funds apportioned under section 104(b)(1), projects for designating existing facilities, or for acquisition of rights of way or construction of new facilities, including the addition of electric vehicle charging stations or natural gas vehicle refueling stations, for use as preferential parking for carpools, provided that such facilities (A) are located outside of a central business district and within an interstate highway corridor, and (B) have as their primary purpose the reduction of vehicular traffic on the interstate highway.

(2) Nothing in this subsection, or in any rule or regulation issued under this subsection, or in any agreement required by this subsection, shall prohibit (A) any State, political subdivision, or agency or instrumentality thereof, from contracting with any person to operate any parking facility designated or constructed under this subsection, or (B) any such person from so operating such facility. Any fees charged for the use of any such facility in connection with the purpose of this subsection shall not be in excess of the amount required for operation and maintenance, including compensation to any person for operating the facility.

(3) For the purposes of this subsection, the terms "facilities" and "parking facilities" are synonymous and shall have the same meaning given "parking facilities" in

subsection (c) of this section.

(g) FUNDING.—The addition of electric vehicle charging stations or natural gas vehicle refueling stations to new or previously funded parking facilities shall be eligible for funding under this section.

(Added Pub. L. 89–574, §8(c)(1), Sept. 13, 1966, 80 Stat. 768; amended Pub. L. 91–605, title I, §134(a), Dec. 31, 1970, 84 Stat. 1733; Pub. L. 97–424, title I, §118, Jan. 6, 1983, 96 Stat. 2110; Pub. L. 105–178, title I, §§1103(l)(3)(B), 1212(a)(2)(A)(i), June 9, 1998, 112 Stat. 126, 193; Pub. L. 109–59, title I, §1921, Aug. 10, 2005, 119 Stat. 1480; Pub. L. 112–141, div. A, title I, §1513(a), July 6, 2012, 126 Stat. 572.)

§138. PRESERVATION OF PARKLANDS

(a) DECLARATION OF POLICY.—

(1) IN GENERAL.—It is the national policy that special effort should be made to preserve the natural beauty of the countryside and public park and recreation lands, wildlife and waterfowl refuges, and historic sites.

(2) COOPERATION AND CONSULTATION.—

(A) IN GENERAL.—The Secretary shall cooperate and consult with the Secretaries of the Interior, Housing and Urban Development, and Agriculture, and with the States in developing transportation plans and programs that include measures to maintain or enhance the natural beauty of the lands traversed.

(B) TIMELINE FOR APPROVALS.—

(i) IN GENERAL.—The Secretary shall—

(I) provide an evaluation under this section to the Secretaries described in subparagraph (A); and

(II) provide a period of 30 days for receipt of comments.

(ii) ASSUMED ACCEPTANCE.—If the Secretary does not receive comments by 15 days after the deadline under clause (i)(II), the Secretary shall assume a lack of objection and proceed with the action.

(C) EFFECT.—Nothing in subparagraph (B) affects—

(i) the requirements under—

(I) subsections (b) through (f); or

(II) the consultation process under section 306108 of title 54; or

(ii) programmatic section 4(f) evaluations, as described in regulations issued by the Secretary.

(3) REQUIREMENT.—After the effective date of the Federal-Aid Highway Act of 1968, the Secretary shall not approve any program or project (other than any project for a Federal lands transportation facility) which requires the use of any publicly owned land from a public park, recreation area, or wildlife and waterfowl refuge of national, State, or local significance as determined by the Federal, State, or local officials having jurisdiction thereof, or any land from an historic site of national, State, or local significance as so determined by such officials unless—

(A) there is no feasible and prudent alternative to the use of the land; and

(B) the program includes all possible planning to minimize harm to such park, recreational area, wildlife and waterfowl refuge, or historic site resulting from such use.

(4) STUDIES.—In carrying out the national policy declared in this section the Secretary, in cooperation with the Secretary of the Interior and appropriate State and

local officials, is authorized to conduct studies as to the most feasible Federal-aid routes for the movement of motor vehicular traffic through or around national parks so as to best serve the needs of the traveling public while preserving the natural beauty of these areas.

(b) De Minimis Impacts.—

(1) Requirements.—

(A) Requirements for historic sites.—The requirements of this section shall be considered to be satisfied with respect to an area described in paragraph (2) if the Secretary determines, in accordance with this subsection, that a transportation program or project will have a de minimis impact on the area.

(B) Requirements for parks, recreation areas, and wildlife or waterfowl refuges.—The requirements of subsection (a)(1) shall be considered to be satisfied with respect to an area described in paragraph (3) if the Secretary determines, in accordance with this subsection, that a transportation program or project will have a de minimis impact on the area. The requirements of subsection (a)(2) with respect to an area described in paragraph (3) shall not include an alternatives analysis.

(C) Criteria.—In making any determination under this subsection, the Secretary shall consider to be part of a transportation program or project any avoidance, minimization, mitigation, or enhancement measures that are required to be implemented as a condition of approval of the transportation program or project.

(2) Historic sites.—With respect to historic sites, the Secretary may make a finding of de minimis impact only if—

(A) the Secretary has determined, in accordance with the consultation process required under section 306108 of title 54, that—

(i) the transportation program or project will have no adverse effect on the historic site; or

(ii) there will be no historic properties affected by the transportation program or project;

(B) the finding of the Secretary has received written concurrence from the applicable State historic preservation officer or tribal historic preservation officer (and from the Advisory Council on Historic Preservation if the Council is participating in the consultation process); and

(C) the finding of the Secretary has been developed in consultation with parties consulting as part of the process referred to in subparagraph (A).

(3) Parks, recreation areas, and wildlife or waterfowl refuges.—With respect to parks, recreation areas, or wildlife or waterfowl refuges, the Secretary may make a finding of de minimis impact only if—

(A) the Secretary has determined, after public notice and opportunity for public review and comment, that the transportation program or project will not adversely affect the activities, features, and attributes of the park, recreation area, or wildlife or waterfowl refuge eligible for protection under this section; and

(B) the finding of the Secretary has received concurrence from the officials with jurisdiction over the park, recreation area, or wildlife or waterfowl refuge.

(c) Satisfaction of Requirements for Certain Historic Sites.—

(1) In general.—The Secretary shall—

(A) align, to the maximum extent practicable, with the requirements of the National Environmental Policy Act of 1969 (42 U.S.C. 4321 et seq.) and section 306108 of title 54, including implementing regulations; and

(B) not later than 90 days after the date of enactment of this subsection, coordinate with the Secretary of the Interior and the Executive Director of the Advisory Council on Historic Preservation (referred to in this subsection as the "Council") to establish procedures to satisfy the requirements described in subparagraph (A) (including regulations).

(2) AVOIDANCE ALTERNATIVE ANALYSIS.—

(A) IN GENERAL.—If, in an analysis required under the National Environmental Policy Act of 1969 (42 U.S.C. 4321 et seq.), the Secretary determines that there is no feasible or prudent alternative to avoid use of a historic site, the Secretary may—

(i) include the determination of the Secretary in the analysis required under that Act;

(ii) provide a notice of the determination to—

(I) each applicable State historic preservation officer and tribal historic preservation officer;

(II) the Council, if the Council is participating in the consultation process under section 306108 of title 54; and

(III) the Secretary of the Interior; and

(iii) request from the applicable preservation officer, the Council, and the Secretary of the Interior a concurrence that the determination is sufficient to satisfy subsection (a)(1).

(B) CONCURRENCE.—If the applicable preservation officer, the Council, and the Secretary of the Interior each provide a concurrence requested under subparagraph (A)(iii), no further analysis under subsection (a)(1) shall be required.

(C) PUBLICATION.—A notice of a determination, together with each relevant concurrence to that determination, under subparagraph (A) shall—

(i) be included in the record of decision or finding of no significant impact of the Secretary; and

(ii) be posted on an appropriate Federal website by not later than 3 days after the date of receipt by the Secretary of all concurrences requested under subparagraph (A)(iii).

(3) ALIGNING HISTORICAL REVIEWS.—

(A) IN GENERAL.—If the Secretary, the applicable preservation officer, the Council, and the Secretary of the Interior concur that no feasible and prudent alternative exists as described in paragraph (2), the Secretary may provide to the applicable preservation officer, the Council, and the Secretary of the Interior notice of the intent of the Secretary to satisfy subsection (a)(2) through the consultation requirements of section 306108 of title 54.

(B) SATISFACTION OF CONDITIONS.—To satisfy subsection (a)(2), each individual described in paragraph (2)(A)(ii) shall concur in the treatment of the applicable historic site described in the memorandum of agreement or programmatic agreement developed under section 306108 of title 54.

(d) REFERENCES TO PAST TRANSPORTATION ENVIRONMENTAL AUTHORITIES.—
(1) SECTION 4(F) REQUIREMENTS.—The requirements of this section are commonly referred to as section 4(f) requirements (see section 4(f) of the Department of Transportation Act (Public Law 89–670; 80 Stat. 934) as in effect before the repeal of that section).

(2) SECTION 106 REQUIREMENTS.—The requirements of section 306108 of title 54 are commonly referred to as section 106 requirements (see section 106 of the National Historic Preservation Act of 1966 (Public Law 89–665; 80 Stat. 917) as in effect before the repeal of that section).

(e) BRIDGE EXEMPTION FROM CONSIDERATION.—A common post-1945 concrete or steel bridge or culvert (as described in 77 Fed. Reg. 68790) that is exempt from individual review under section 306108 of title 54 shall be exempt from consideration under this section.

(f) RAIL AND TRANSIT.—

(1) IN GENERAL.—Improvements to, or the maintenance, rehabilitation, or operation of, railroad or rail transit lines or elements thereof that are in use or were historically used for the transportation of goods or passengers shall not be considered a use of a historic site under subsection (a), regardless of whether the railroad or rail transit line or element thereof is listed on, or eligible for listing on, the National Register of Historic Places.

(2) EXCEPTIONS.—

(A) IN GENERAL.—Paragraph (1) shall not apply to—
(i) stations; or
(ii) bridges or tunnels located on—
(I) railroad lines that have been abandoned; or
(II) transit lines that are not in use.

(B) CLARIFICATION WITH RESPECT TO CERTAIN BRIDGES AND TUNNELS.—The bridges and tunnels referred to in subparagraph (A)(ii) do not include bridges or tunnels located on railroad or transit lines—
(i) over which service has been discontinued; or
(ii) that have been railbanked or otherwise reserved for the transportation of goods or passengers.

(Added Pub. L. 89–574, §15(a), Sept. 13, 1966, 80 Stat. 771; amended Pub. L. 90–495, §18(a), Aug. 23, 1968, 82 Stat. 823; Pub. L. 94–280, title I, §124, May 5, 1976, 90 Stat. 440; Pub. L. 100–17, title I, §133(b)(10), Apr. 2, 1987, 101 Stat. 171; Pub. L. 109–59, title VI, §6009(a)(1), Aug. 10, 2005, 119 Stat. 1874; Pub. L. 112–141, div. A, title I, §1119(c)(2), July 6, 2012, 126 Stat. 492; Pub. L. 113–287, §5(f)(2), Dec. 19, 2014, 128 Stat. 3268; Pub. L. 114–94, div. A, title I, §§1301(a), 1302(a), 1303(a), title XI, §11502(a), Dec. 4, 2015, 129 Stat. 1375, 1377, 1378, 1690; Pub. L. 117–58, div. A, title I, §11316, Nov. 15, 2021, 135 Stat. 543.)

§139. EFFICIENT ENVIRONMENTAL REVIEWS FOR PROJECT DECISIONMAKING AND ONE FEDERAL DECISION

(a) DEFINITIONS.—In this section, the following definitions apply:

(1) AGENCY.—The term "agency" means any agency, department, or other unit of Federal, State, local, or Indian tribal government.

(2) AUTHORIZATION.—The term "authorization" means any environmental license,

permit, approval, finding, or other administrative decision related to the environmental review process that is required under Federal law to site, construct, or reconstruct a project.

(3) ENVIRONMENTAL DOCUMENT.—The term "environmental document" includes an environmental assessment, finding of no significant impact, notice of intent, environmental impact statement, or record of decision under the National Environmental Policy Act of 1969 (42 U.S.C. 4321 et seq.).

(4) ENVIRONMENTAL IMPACT STATEMENT.—The term "environmental impact statement" means the detailed statement of environmental impacts required to be prepared under the National Environmental Policy Act of 1969 (42 U.S.C. 4321 et seq.).

(5) ENVIRONMENTAL REVIEW PROCESS.—

(A) IN GENERAL.—The term "environmental review process" means the process for preparing for a project an environmental impact statement, environmental assessment, categorical exclusion, or other document prepared under the National Environmental Policy Act of 1969 (42 U.S.C. 4321 et seq.).

(B) INCLUSIONS.—The term "environmental review process" includes the process and schedule, including a timetable for and completion of any environmental permit, approval, review, or study required for a project under any Federal law other than the National Environmental Policy Act of 1969 (42 U.S.C. 4321 et seq.).

(6) LEAD AGENCY.—The term "lead agency" means the Department of Transportation and, if applicable, any State or local governmental entity serving as a joint lead agency pursuant to this section.

(7) MAJOR PROJECT.—

(A) IN GENERAL.—The term "major project" means a project for which—

(i) multiple permits, approvals, reviews, or studies are required under a Federal law other than the National Environmental Policy Act of 1969 (42 U.S.C. 4321 et seq.);

(ii) the project sponsor has identified the reasonable availability of funds sufficient to complete the project;

(iii) the project is not a covered project (as defined in section 41001 of the FAST Act (42 U.S.C. 4370m)); and

(iv)(I) the head of the lead agency has determined that an environmental impact statement is required; or

(II) the head of the lead agency has determined that an environmental assessment is required, and the project sponsor requests that the project be treated as a major project.

(B) CLARIFICATION.—In this section, the term "major project" does not have the same meaning as the term "major project" as described in section 106(h).

(8) MULTIMODAL PROJECT.—The term "multimodal project" means a project that requires the approval of more than 1 Department of Transportation operating administration or secretarial office.

(9) PROJECT.—

(A) IN GENERAL.—The term "project" means any highway project, public transportation capital project, or multimodal project that, if implemented as proposed by the project sponsor, would require approval by any operating administration or secretarial office within the Department of Transportation.

(B) CONSIDERATIONS.—In determining whether a project is a project under subparagraph (A), the Secretary shall take into account, if known, any sources of Federal funding or financing identified by the project sponsor, including any discretionary grant, loan, and loan guarantee programs administered by the Department of Transportation.

(10) PROJECT SPONSOR.—The term "project sponsor" means the agency or other entity, including any private or public-private entity, that seeks approval of the Secretary for a project.

(11) STATE TRANSPORTATION DEPARTMENT.—The term "State transportation department" means any statewide agency of a State with responsibility for one or more modes of transportation.

(b) APPLICABILITY.—

(1) IN GENERAL.—The project development procedures in this section are applicable to all projects, including major projects, for which an environmental impact statement is prepared under the National Environmental Policy Act (42 U.S.C. 4321 et seq.) of 1969 and may be applied, as requested by a project sponsor and to the extent determined appropriate by the Secretary, to other projects for which an environmental document is prepared pursuant to such Act.

(2) FLEXIBILITY.—Any authorities granted in this section may be exercised, and any requirements established under this section may be satisfied, for a project, class of projects, or program of projects.

(3) PROGRAMMATIC COMPLIANCE.—

(A) IN GENERAL.—The Secretary shall allow for the use of programmatic approaches to conduct environmental reviews that—

(i) eliminate repetitive discussions of the same issues;

(ii) focus on the actual issues ripe for analyses at each level of review; and

(iii) are consistent with—

(I) the National Environmental Policy Act of 1969 (42 U.S.C. 4321 et seq.); and

(II) other applicable laws.

(B) REQUIREMENTS.—In carrying out subparagraph (A), the Secretary shall ensure that programmatic reviews—

(i) promote transparency, including the transparency of—

(I) the analyses and data used in the environmental reviews;

(II) the treatment of any deferred issues raised by agencies or the public; and

(III) the temporal and spatial scales to be used to analyze issues under subclauses (I) and (II);

(ii) use accurate and timely information, including through establishment of—

(I) criteria for determining the general duration of the usefulness of the review; and

(II) a timeline for updating an out-of-date review;

(iii) describe—

(I) the relationship between any programmatic analysis and future tiered analysis; and

(II) the role of the public in the creation of future tiered analysis;

(iv) are available to other relevant Federal and State agencies, Indian tribes, and the public; and

(v) provide notice and public comment opportunities consistent with applicable requirements.

(c) LEAD AGENCIES.—

(1) FEDERAL LEAD AGENCY.—

(A) IN GENERAL.—The Department of Transportation, or an operating administration thereof designated by the Secretary, shall be the Federal lead agency in the environmental review process for a project.

(B) MODAL ADMINISTRATION.—If the project requires approval from more than 1 modal administration within the Department, the Secretary may designate a single modal administration to serve as the Federal lead agency for the Department in the environmental review process for the project.

(2) JOINT LEAD AGENCIES.—Nothing in this section precludes another agency from being a joint lead agency in accordance with regulations under the National Environmental Policy Act of 1969 (42 U.S.C. 4321 et seq.).

(3) PROJECT SPONSOR AS JOINT LEAD AGENCY.—Any project sponsor that is a State or local governmental entity receiving funds under this title or chapter 53 of title 49 for the project shall serve as a joint lead agency with the Department for purposes of preparing any environmental document under the National Environmental Policy Act of 1969 (42 U.S.C. 4321 et seq.) and may prepare any such environmental document required in support of any action or approval by the Secretary if the Federal lead agency furnishes guidance in such preparation and independently evaluates such document and the document is approved and adopted by the Secretary prior to the Secretary taking any subsequent action or making any approval based on such document, whether or not the Secretary's action or approval results in Federal funding.

(4) ENSURING COMPLIANCE.—The Secretary shall ensure that the project sponsor complies with all design and mitigation commitments made jointly by the Secretary and the project sponsor in any environmental document prepared by the project sponsor in accordance with this subsection and that such document is appropriately supplemented if project changes become necessary.

(5) ADOPTION AND USE OF DOCUMENTS.—Any environmental document prepared in accordance with this subsection may be adopted or used by any Federal agency making any approval to the same extent that such Federal agency could adopt or use a document prepared by another Federal agency.

(6) ROLES AND RESPONSIBILITY OF LEAD AGENCY.—With respect to the environmental review process for any project, the lead agency shall have authority and responsibility—

(A) to take such actions as are necessary and proper, within the authority of the lead agency, to facilitate the expeditious resolution of the environmental review process for the project;

(B) to prepare or ensure that any required environmental impact statement or other document required to be completed under the National Environmental Policy Act of 1969 (42 U.S.C. 4321 et seq.) is completed in accordance with this section and applicable Federal law;

(C) to consider and respond to comments received from participating agencies on matters within the special expertise or jurisdiction of those agencies; and

(D) to calculate annually the average time taken by the lead agency to complete all environmental documents for each project during the previous fiscal year.

(7) PROCESS IMPROVEMENTS FOR PROJECTS.—

(A) IN GENERAL.—The Secretary shall review—

(i) existing practices, procedures, rules, regulations, and applicable laws to identify impediments to meeting the requirements applicable to projects under this section; and

(ii) best practices, programmatic agreements, and potential changes to internal departmental procedures that would facilitate an efficient environmental review process for projects.

(B) CONSULTATION.—In conducting the review under subparagraph (A), the Secretary shall consult, as appropriate, with the heads of other Federal agencies that participate in the environmental review process.

(C) REPORT.—Not later than 2 years after the date of enactment of the Surface Transportation Reauthorization Act of 2021, the Secretary shall submit to the Committee on Environment and Public Works of the Senate and the Committee on Transportation and Infrastructure of the House of Representatives a report that includes—

(i) the results of the review under subparagraph (A); and

(ii) an analysis of whether additional funding would help the Secretary meet the requirements applicable to projects under this section.

(d) PARTICIPATING AGENCIES.—

(1) IN GENERAL.—The lead agency shall be responsible for inviting and designating participating agencies in accordance with this subsection.

(2) INVITATION.—Not later than 45 days after the date of publication of a notice of intent to prepare an environmental impact statement or the initiation of an environmental assessment, the lead agency shall identify any other Federal and non-Federal agencies that may have an interest in the project, and shall invite such agencies to become participating agencies in the environmental review process for the project. The invitation shall set a deadline for responses to be submitted. The deadline may be extended by the lead agency for good cause.

(3) FEDERAL PARTICIPATING AGENCIES.—Any Federal agency that is invited by the lead agency to participate in the environmental review process for a project shall be designated as a participating agency by the lead agency unless the invited agency informs the lead agency, in writing, by the deadline specified in the invitation that the invited agency—

(A) has no jurisdiction or authority with respect to the project;

(B) has no expertise or information relevant to the project; and

(C) does not intend to submit comments on the project.

(4) EFFECT OF DESIGNATION.—

(A) REQUIREMENT.—A participating agency shall comply with the requirements of this section.

(B) IMPLICATION.—Designation as a participating agency under this subsection shall not imply that the participating agency—

(i) supports a proposed project; or

(ii) has any jurisdiction over, or special expertise with respect to evaluation of, the project.

(5) COOPERATING AGENCY.—A participating agency may also be designated by a lead agency as a "cooperating agency" under the regulations contained in part 1500 of title 40, Code of Federal Regulations.

(6) DESIGNATIONS FOR CATEGORIES OF PROJECTS.—The Secretary may exercise the authorities granted under this subsection for a project, class of projects, or program of projects.

(7) CONCURRENT REVIEWS.—Each participating agency and cooperating agency shall—

(A) carry out the obligations of that agency under other applicable law concurrently, and in conjunction, with the review required under the National Environmental Policy Act of 1969 (42 U.S.C. 4321 et seq.), unless doing so would impair the ability of the Federal agency to conduct needed analysis or otherwise carry out those obligations; and

(B) formulate and implement administrative, policy, and procedural mechanisms to enable the agency to ensure completion of the environmental review process in a timely, coordinated, and environmentally responsible manner.

(8) SINGLE ENVIRONMENTAL DOCUMENT.—

(A) IN GENERAL.—Except as inconsistent with paragraph (7) and except as provided in subparagraph (D), to the maximum extent practicable and consistent with Federal law, all Federal authorizations and reviews for a project shall rely on a single environmental document for each kind of environmental document prepared under the National Environmental Policy Act of 1969 (42 U.S.C. 4321 et seq.) under the leadership of the lead agency.

(B) USE OF DOCUMENT.—

(i) IN GENERAL.—To the maximum extent practicable, the lead agency shall develop environmental documents sufficient to satisfy the requirements for any Federal approval or other Federal action required for the project, including authorizations by other Federal agencies.

(ii) COOPERATION OF PARTICIPATING AGENCIES.—Other participating agencies shall cooperate with the lead agency and provide timely information to help the lead agency carry out this subparagraph.

(C) TREATMENT AS PARTICIPATING AND COOPERATING AGENCIES.—A Federal agency required to make an approval or take an action for a project, as described in subparagraph (B), shall work with the lead agency for the project to ensure that the agency making the approval or taking the action is treated as being both a participating and cooperating agency for the project.

(D) EXCEPTIONS.—The lead agency may waive the application of subparagraph (A) with respect to a project if—

(i) the project sponsor requests that agencies issue separate environmental documents;

(ii) the obligations of a cooperating agency or participating agency under the National Environmental Policy Act of 1969 (42 U.S.C. 4321 et seq.) have already been satisfied with respect to the project; or

(iii) the lead agency determines that reliance on a single environmental document (as described in subparagraph (A)) would not facilitate timely completion of the environmental review process for the project.

(9) PARTICIPATING AGENCY RESPONSIBILITIES.—An agency participating in the environmental review process under this section shall—

(A) provide comments, responses, studies, or methodologies on those areas within the special expertise or jurisdiction of the agency; and

(B) use the process to address any environmental issues of concern to the agency.

(10) TIMELY AUTHORIZATIONS FOR MAJOR PROJECTS.—

(A) DEADLINE.—Except as provided in subparagraph (C), all authorization decisions necessary for the construction of a major project shall be completed by not later than 90 days after the date of the issuance of a record of decision for the major project.

(B) DETAIL.—The final environmental impact statement for a major project shall include an adequate level of detail to inform decisions necessary for the role of the participating agencies and cooperating agencies in the environmental review process.

(C) EXTENSION OF DEADLINE.—The head of the lead agency may extend the deadline under subparagraph (A) if—

(i) Federal law prohibits the lead agency or another agency from issuing an approval or permit within the period described in that subparagraph;

(ii) the project sponsor requests that the permit or approval follow a different timeline; or

(iii) an extension would facilitate completion of the environmental review and authorization process of the major project.

(e) PROJECT INITIATION.—

(1) IN GENERAL.—The project sponsor shall notify the Secretary of the type of work, termini, length and general location of the proposed project (including any additional information that the project sponsor considers to be important to initiate the process for the proposed project), together with a statement of any Federal approvals anticipated to be necessary for the proposed project, for the purpose of informing the Secretary that the environmental review process should be initiated.

(2) SUBMISSION OF DOCUMENTS.—The project sponsor may satisfy the requirement under paragraph (1) by submitting to the Secretary any relevant documents containing the information described in that paragraph, including a draft notice for publication in the Federal Register announcing the preparation of an environmental review for the project.

(3) REVIEW OF APPLICATION.—Not later than 45 days after the date on which the

Secretary receives notification under paragraph (1), the Secretary shall provide to the project sponsor a written response that, as applicable—

(A) describes the determination of the Secretary—

(i) to initiate the environmental review process, including a timeline and an expected date for the publication in the Federal Register of the relevant notice of intent; or

(ii) to decline the application, including an explanation of the reasons for that decision; or

(B) requests additional information, and provides to the project sponsor an accounting regarding what documentation is necessary to initiate the environmental review process.

(4) REQUEST TO DESIGNATE A LEAD AGENCY.—

(A) IN GENERAL.—Any project sponsor may submit to the Secretary a request to designate the operating administration or secretarial office within the Department of Transportation with the expertise on the proposed project to serve as the Federal lead agency for the project.

(B) SECRETARIAL ACTION.—

(i) IN GENERAL.—If the Secretary receives a request under subparagraph (A), the Secretary shall respond to the request not later than 45 days after the date of receipt.

(ii) REQUIREMENTS.—The response under clause (i) shall—

(I) approve the request;

(II) deny the request, with an explanation of the reasons for the denial; or

(III) require the submission of additional information.

(iii) ADDITIONAL INFORMATION.—If additional information is submitted in accordance with clause (ii)(III), the Secretary shall respond to the submission not later than 45 days after the date of receipt.

(5) ENVIRONMENTAL CHECKLIST.—

(A) DEVELOPMENT.—The lead agency for a project, in consultation with participating agencies, shall develop, as appropriate, a checklist to help project sponsors identify potential natural, cultural, and historic resources in the area of the project.

(B) PURPOSE.—The purposes of the checklist are—

(i) to identify agencies and organizations that can provide information about natural, cultural, and historic resources;

(ii) to develop the information needed to determine the range of alternatives; and

(iii) to improve interagency collaboration to help expedite the permitting process for the lead agency and participating agencies.

(f) PURPOSE AND NEED; ALTERNATIVES ANALYSIS.—

(1) PARTICIPATION.—As early as practicable during the environmental review process, the lead agency shall provide an opportunity for involvement by participating agencies and the public in defining the purpose and need for a project.

(2) DEFINITION.—Following participation under paragraph (1), the lead agency shall define the project's purpose and need for purposes of any document which the

lead agency is responsible for preparing for the project.

(3) OBJECTIVES.—The statement of purpose and need shall include a clear statement of the objectives that the proposed action is intended to achieve, which may include—

(A) achieving a transportation objective identified in an applicable statewide or metropolitan transportation plan;

(B) supporting land use, economic development, or growth objectives established in applicable Federal, State, local, or tribal plans; and

(C) serving national defense, national security, or other national objectives, as established in Federal laws, plans, or policies.

(4) ALTERNATIVES ANALYSIS.—

(A) PARTICIPATION.—

(i) In general.—As early as practicable during the environmental review process, the lead agency shall provide an opportunity for involvement by participating agencies and the public in determining the range of alternatives to be considered for a project.

(ii) COMMENTS OF PARTICIPATING AGENCIES.—To the maximum extent practicable and consistent with applicable law, each participating agency receiving an opportunity for involvement under clause (i) shall limit the comments of the agency to subject matter areas within the special expertise or jurisdiction of the agency.

(iii) EFFECT OF NONPARTICIPATION.—A participating agency that declines to participate in the development of the purpose and need and range of alternatives for a project shall be required to comply with the schedule developed under subsection (g)(1)(B).

(B) RANGE OF ALTERNATIVES.—

(i) DETERMINATION.—Following participation under subparagraph (A), the lead agency shall determine the range of alternatives for consideration in any document which the lead agency is responsible for preparing for the project.

(ii) USE.—To the maximum extent practicable and consistent with Federal law, the range of alternatives determined for a project under clause (i) shall be used for all Federal environmental reviews and permit processes required for the project unless the alternatives must be modified—

(I) to address significant new information or circumstances, and the lead agency and participating agencies agree that the alternatives must be modified to address the new information or circumstances; or

(II) for the lead agency or a participating agency to fulfill the responsibilities of the agency under the National Environmental Policy Act of 1969 (42 U.S.C. 4321 et seq.) in a timely manner.

(C) METHODOLOGIES.—The lead agency also shall determine, in collaboration with participating agencies at appropriate times during the study process, the methodologies to be used and the level of detail required in the analysis of each alternative for a project.

(D) PREFERRED ALTERNATIVE.—At the discretion of the lead agency, the preferred alternative for a project, after being identified, may be developed to a higher level of detail than other alternatives in order to facilitate the development of mitigation measures or concurrent compliance with other applicable laws if the lead agency determines that the development of such higher level of detail will not prevent the lead agency from making an impartial decision as to whether to accept another alternative which is being considered in the environmental review process.

(E) REDUCTION OF DUPLICATION.—

(i) IN GENERAL.—In carrying out this paragraph, the lead agency shall reduce duplication, to the maximum extent practicable, between—

(I) the evaluation of alternatives under the National Environmental Policy Act of 1969 (42 U.S.C. 4321 et seq.); and

(II) the evaluation of alternatives in the metropolitan transportation planning process under section 134 or an environmental review process carried out under State law (referred to in this subparagraph as a "State environmental review process").

(ii) CONSIDERATION OF ALTERNATIVES.—The lead agency may eliminate from detailed consideration an alternative proposed in an environmental impact statement regarding a project if, as determined by the lead agency—

(I) the alternative was considered in a metropolitan planning process or a State environmental review process by a metropolitan planning organization or a State or local transportation agency, as applicable;

(II) the lead agency provided guidance to the metropolitan planning organization or State or local transportation agency, as applicable, regarding analysis of alternatives in the metropolitan planning process or State environmental review process, including guidance on the requirements of the National Environmental Policy Act of 1969 (42 U.S.C. 4321 et seq.) and any other Federal law necessary for approval of the project;

(III) the applicable metropolitan planning process or State environmental review process included an opportunity for public review and comment;

(IV) the applicable metropolitan planning organization or State or local transportation agency rejected the alternative after considering public comments;

(V) the Federal lead agency independently reviewed the alternative evaluation approved by the applicable metropolitan planning organization or State or local transportation agency; and

(VI) the Federal lead agency determined—

(aa) in consultation with Federal participating or cooperating agencies, that the alternative to be eliminated from consideration is not necessary for compliance with the National Environmental Policy Act of 1969 (42 U.S.C. 4321 et seq.); or

(bb) with the concurrence of Federal agencies with jurisdiction over a permit or approval required for a project, that the alternative to be eliminated from consideration is not necessary for any permit or approval under any other Federal law.

(g) COORDINATION AND SCHEDULING.—

(1) COORDINATION PLAN.—

(A) IN GENERAL.—Not later than 90 days after the date of publication of a notice of intent to prepare an environmental impact statement or the initiation of an environmental assessment, the lead agency shall establish a plan for coordinating public and agency participation in and comment on the environmental review process for a project or category of projects. The coordination plan may be incorporated into a memorandum of understanding.

(B) SCHEDULE.—

(i) IN GENERAL.—The lead agency shall establish as part of such coordination plan, after consultation with and the concurrence of each participating agency for the project and with the State in which the project is located (and, if the State is not the project sponsor, with the project sponsor), a schedule for completion of the environmental review process for the project.

(ii) FACTORS FOR CONSIDERATION.—In establishing the schedule, the lead agency shall consider factors such as—

(I) the responsibilities of participating agencies under applicable laws;

(II) resources available to the cooperating agencies;

(III) overall size and complexity of the project;

(IV) the overall time required by an agency to conduct an environmental review and make decisions under applicable Federal law relating to a project (including the issuance or denial of a permit or license) and the cost of the project; and

(V) the sensitivity of the natural and historic resources that could be affected by the project.

(iii) MAJOR PROJECT SCHEDULE.—To the maximum extent practicable and consistent with applicable Federal law, in the case of a major project, the lead agency shall develop, in concurrence with the project sponsor, a schedule for the major project that is consistent with an agency average of not more than 2 years for the completion of the environmental review process for major projects, as measured from, as applicable—

(I) the date of publication of a notice of intent to prepare an environmental impact statement to the record of decision; or

(II) the date on which the head of the lead agency determines that an environmental assessment is required to a finding of no significant impact.

(C) CONSISTENCY WITH OTHER TIME PERIODS.—A schedule under subparagraph (B) shall be consistent with any other relevant time periods established under Federal law.

(D) MODIFICATION.—

(i) IN GENERAL.—Except as provided in clause (ii), the lead agency may lengthen or shorten a schedule established under subparagraph (B) for good cause.

(ii) EXCEPTIONS.—

(I) MAJOR PROJECTS.—In the case of a major project, the lead agency may lengthen a schedule under clause (i) for a cooperating Federal agency by not more than 1 year after the latest deadline established for the major project by the lead agency.

(II) SHORTENED SCHEDULES.—The lead agency may not shorten a schedule under clause (i) if doing so would impair the ability of a cooperating Federal agency to conduct necessary analyses or otherwise carry out relevant obligations of the Federal agency for the project.

(E) FAILURE TO MEET DEADLINE.—If a cooperating Federal agency fails to meet a deadline established under subparagraph (D)(ii)(I)—

(i) the cooperating Federal agency shall submit to the Secretary a report that describes the reasons why the deadline was not met; and

(ii) the Secretary shall—

(I) transmit to the Committee on Environment and Public Works of the Senate and the Committee on Transportation and Infrastructure of the House of Representatives a copy of the report under clause (i); and

(II) make the report under clause (i) publicly available on the internet.

(F) DISSEMINATION.—A copy of a schedule under subparagraph (B), and of any modifications to the schedule, shall be—

(i) provided to all participating agencies and to the State transportation department of the State in which the project is located (and, if the State is not the project sponsor, to the project sponsor); and

(ii) made available to the public.

(2) COMMENT DEADLINES.—The lead agency shall establish the following deadlines for comment during the environmental review process for a project:

(A) For comments by agencies and the public on a draft environmental impact statement, a period of not more than 60 days after publication in the Federal Register of notice of the date of public availability of such document, unless—

(i) a different deadline is established by agreement of the lead agency, the project sponsor, and all participating agencies; or

(ii) the deadline is extended by the lead agency for good cause.

(B) For all other comment periods established by the lead agency for agency or public comments in the environmental review process, a period of no more than 30 days from availability of the materials on which comment is requested, unless—

(i) a different deadline is established by agreement of the lead agency, the project sponsor, and all participating agencies; or

(ii) the deadline is extended by the lead agency for good cause.

(3) DEADLINES FOR DECISIONS UNDER OTHER LAWS.—In any case in which a decision under any Federal law relating to a project (including the issuance or denial of a permit or license) is required to be made by the later of the date that is 180 days after the date on which the Secretary made all final decisions of the lead agency with respect to the project, or 180 days after the date on which an application was submitted for the permit or license, the Secretary shall submit to the Committee on Environment and Public Works of the Senate and the Committee on Transportation and Infrastructure of the House of Representatives and publish on the Internet—

(A) as soon as practicable after the 180-day period, an initial notice of the failure of the Federal agency to make the decision; and

(B) every 60 days thereafter until such date as all decisions of the Federal agency relating to the project have been made by the Federal agency, an additional notice that describes the number of decisions of the Federal agency that remain outstanding as of the date of the additional notice.

(4) INVOLVEMENT OF THE PUBLIC.—Nothing in this subsection shall reduce any time period provided for public comment in the environmental review process under existing Federal law, including a regulation.

(h) ISSUE IDENTIFICATION AND RESOLUTION.—

(1) COOPERATION.—The lead agency and the participating agencies shall work cooperatively in accordance with this section to identify and resolve issues that could delay completion of the environmental review process or could result in denial of any approvals required for the project under applicable laws.

(2) LEAD AGENCY RESPONSIBILITIES.—The lead agency shall make information available to the participating agencies as early as practicable in the environmental review process regarding the environmental and socioeconomic resources located within the project area and the general locations of the alternatives under consideration. Such information may be based on existing data sources, including geographic information systems mapping.

(3) PARTICIPATING AGENCY RESPONSIBILITIES.—Based on information received from the lead agency, participating agencies shall identify, as early as practicable, any issues of concern regarding the project's potential environmental or socioeconomic impacts. In this paragraph, issues of concern include any issues that could substantially delay or prevent an agency from granting a permit or other approval that is needed for the project.

(4) ISSUE RESOLUTION.—Any issue resolved by the lead agency with the concurrence of participating agencies may not be reconsidered unless significant new information or circumstances arise.

(5) INTERIM DECISION ON ACHIEVING ACCELERATED DECISIONMAKING.—

(A) IN GENERAL.—Not later than 30 days after the close of the public comment period on a draft environmental impact statement, the Secretary may convene a meeting with the project sponsor, lead agency, resource agencies, and any relevant State agencies to ensure that all parties are on schedule to meet deadlines for decisions to be made regarding the project.

(B) DEADLINES.—The deadlines referred to in subparagraph (A) shall be those established under subsection (g), or any other deadlines established by the lead agency, in consultation with the project sponsor and other relevant agencies.

(C) FAILURE TO ASSURE.—If the relevant agencies cannot provide reasonable assurances that the deadlines described in subparagraph (B) will be met, the Secretary may initiate the issue resolution and referral process described under paragraph (6) before the completion of the record of decision.

(6) ACCELERATED ISSUE RESOLUTION AND REFERRAL.—

(A) AGENCY ISSUE RESOLUTION MEETING.—

(i) IN GENERAL.—A Federal agency of jurisdiction, project sponsor, or the Governor of a State in which a project is located may request an issue resolution meeting to be conducted by the lead agency.

(ii) ACTION BY LEAD AGENCY.—The lead agency shall convene an issue resolution meeting under clause (i) with the relevant participating agencies and the project sponsor, including the Governor only if the meeting was requested by the Governor, to resolve issues that could—

(I) delay completion of the environmental review process; or

(II) result in denial of any approvals required for the project under applicable laws.

(iii) DATE.—A meeting requested under this subparagraph shall be held by not later than 21 days after the date of receipt of the request for the meeting, unless the lead agency determines that there is good cause to extend the time for the meeting.

(iv) NOTIFICATION.—On receipt of a request for a meeting under this subparagraph, the lead agency shall notify all relevant participating agencies of the request, including the issue to be resolved, and the date for the meeting.

(v) DISPUTES.—If a relevant participating agency with jurisdiction over an approval required for a project under applicable law determines that the relevant information necessary to resolve the issue has not been obtained and could not have been obtained within a reasonable time, but the lead agency disagrees, the resolution of the dispute shall be forwarded to the heads of the relevant agencies for resolution.

(vi) CONVENTION BY LEAD AGENCY.—A lead agency may convene an issue resolution meeting under this subsection at any time without the request of the Federal agency of jurisdiction, project sponsor, or the Governor of a State.

(B) ELEVATION OF ISSUE RESOLUTION.—

(i) IN GENERAL.—If issue resolution is not achieved by not later than 30 days after the date of a relevant meeting under subparagraph (A), the Secretary shall notify the lead agency, the heads of the relevant participating agencies, and the project sponsor (including the Governor only if the initial issue resolution meeting request came from the Governor) that an issue resolution meeting will be convened.

(ii) REQUIREMENTS.—The Secretary shall identify the issues to be addressed at the meeting and convene the meeting not later than 30 days after the date of issuance of the notice.

(C) REFERRAL OF ISSUE RESOLUTION.—

(i) REFERRAL TO COUNCIL ON ENVIRONMENTAL QUALITY.—

(I) IN GENERAL.—If resolution is not achieved by not later than 30 days after the date of an issue resolution meeting under subparagraph (B), the Secretary shall refer the matter to the Council on Environmental Quality.

(II) MEETING.—Not later than 30 days after the date of receipt of a referral from the Secretary under subclause (I), the Council on Environmental Quality shall hold an issue resolution meeting with the lead agency, the heads of relevant participating agencies, and the project sponsor (including the Governor only if an initial request for an issue resolution meeting came from the Governor).

(ii) REFERRAL TO THE PRESIDENT.—If a resolution is not achieved by not later than 30 days after the date of the meeting convened by the Council on Environmental Quality under clause (i)(II), the Secretary shall refer the matter directly to the President.

(7) FINANCIAL PENALTY PROVISIONS.—

(A) IN GENERAL.—A Federal agency of jurisdiction over an approval required for a project under applicable laws shall complete any required approval on an expeditious basis using the shortest existing applicable process.

(B) FAILURE TO DECIDE.—

(i) IN GENERAL.—If an agency described in subparagraph (A) fails to render a decision under any Federal law relating to a project that requires the preparation of an environmental impact statement or environmental assessment, including the issuance or denial of a permit, license, or other approval by the date described in clause (ii), an amount of funding equal to the amounts specified in subclause (I) or (II) shall be rescinded from the applicable office of the head of the agency, or equivalent office to which the authority for rendering the decision has been delegated by law by not later than 1 day after the applicable date under clause (ii), and once each week thereafter until a final decision is rendered, subject to subparagraph (C)—

(I) $20,000 for any project for which an annual financial plan is required under subsection (h) or (i) of section 106; or

(II) $10,000 for any other project requiring preparation of an environmental assessment or environmental impact statement.

(ii) DESCRIPTION OF DATE.—The date referred to in clause (i) is—

(I) the date that is 30 days after the date for rendering a decision as described in the project schedule established pursuant to subsection (g)(1)(B);

(II) if no schedule exists, the later of—

(aa) the date that is 180 days after the date on which an application for the permit, license, or approval is complete; and

(bb) the date that is 180 days after the date on which the Federal lead agency issues a decision on the project under the National Environmental Policy Act of 1969 (42 U.S.C. 4321 et seq.); or

(III) a modified date in accordance with subsection (g)(1)(D).

(C) LIMITATIONS.—

(i) IN GENERAL.—No rescission of funds under subparagraph (B) relating to an individual project shall exceed, in any fiscal year, an amount equal to 2.5 percent of the funds made available for the applicable agency office.

(ii) FAILURE TO DECIDE.—The total amount rescinded in a fiscal year as a result of a failure by an agency to make a decision by an applicable deadline shall not exceed an amount equal to 7 percent of the funds made available for the applicable agency office for that fiscal year.

(D) NO FAULT OF AGENCY.—A rescission of funds under this paragraph shall not be made if the lead agency for the project certifies that—

(i) the agency has not received necessary information or approvals from another entity, such as the project sponsor, in a manner that affects the ability of the agency to meet any requirements under State, local, or Federal law; or

(ii) significant new information or circumstances, including a major modification to an aspect of the project, requires additional analysis for the agency to make a decision on the project application.

(E) LIMITATION.—The Federal agency with jurisdiction for the decision from which funds are rescinded pursuant to this paragraph shall not reprogram funds to the office of the head of the agency, or equivalent office, to reimburse that office for the loss of the funds.

(F) AUDITS.—In any fiscal year in which any funds are rescinded from a Federal agency pursuant to this paragraph, the Inspector General of that agency shall—

(i) conduct an audit to assess compliance with the requirements of this paragraph; and

(ii) not later than 120 days after the end of the fiscal year during which the rescission occurred, submit to the Committee on Environment and Public Works of the Senate and the Committee on Transportation and Infrastructure of the House of Representatives a report describing the reasons why the transfers were levied, including allocations of resources.

(G) EFFECT OF PARAGRAPH.—Nothing in this paragraph affects or limits the application of, or obligation to comply with, any Federal, State, local, or tribal law.

(8) EXPEDIENT DECISIONS AND REVIEWS.—To ensure that Federal environmental decisions and reviews are expeditiously made—

(A) adequate resources made available under this title shall be devoted to ensuring that applicable environmental reviews under the National Environmental Policy Act of 1969 (42 U.S.C. 4321 et seq.) are completed on an expeditious basis and that the shortest existing applicable process under that Act is implemented; and

(B) the President shall submit to the Committee on Transportation and Infrastructure of the House of Representatives and the Committee on Environment and Public Works of the Senate, not less frequently than once every 120 days after the date of enactment of the MAP–21, a report on the status and progress of the following projects and activities funded under this title with respect to compliance with applicable requirements under the National Environmental Policy Act of 1969 (42 U.S.C. 4321 et seq.):

(i) Projects and activities required to prepare an annual financial plan under section 106(i).

(ii) A sample of not less than 5 percent of the projects requiring preparation of an environmental impact statement or environmental assessment in each State.

(i) PERFORMANCE MEASUREMENT.—The Secretary shall establish a program to measure and report on progress toward improving and expediting the planning and environmental review process.

(j) ASSISTANCE TO AFFECTED STATE AND FEDERAL AGENCIES.—

(1) IN GENERAL.—

(A) AUTHORITY TO PROVIDE FUNDS.—The Secretary may allow a public entity receiving financial assistance from the Department of Transportation under this title or chapter 53 of title 49 to provide funds to Federal agencies (including the Department), State agencies, and Indian tribes participating in the environmental review process for the project or program.

(B) USE OF FUNDS.—Funds referred to in subparagraph (A) may be provided only to support activities that directly and meaningfully contribute to expediting and improving permitting and review processes, including planning, approval, and consultation processes for the project or program.

(2) ACTIVITIES ELIGIBLE FOR FUNDING.—Activities for which funds may be provided under paragraph (1) include transportation planning activities that precede the initiation of the environmental review process, activities directly related to the environmental review process, dedicated staffing, training of agency personnel, information gathering and mapping, and development of programmatic agreements.

(3) USE OF FEDERAL LANDS HIGHWAY FUNDS.—The Secretary may also use funds made available under section 204 [1] for a project for the purposes specified in this subsection with respect to the environmental review process for the project.

(4) AMOUNTS.—Requests under paragraph (1) may be approved only for the additional amounts that the Secretary determines are necessary for the Federal agencies, State agencies, or Indian tribes participating in the environmental review process to meet the time limits for environmental review.

(5) CONDITION.—A request under paragraph (1) to expedite time limits for environmental review may be approved only if such time limits are less than the customary time necessary for such review.

(6) AGREEMENT.—Prior to providing funds approved by the Secretary for dedicated staffing at an affected agency under paragraphs (1) and (2), the affected agency and the requesting public entity shall enter into an agreement that establishes the projects and priorities to be addressed by the use of the funds.

(k) JUDICIAL REVIEW AND SAVINGS CLAUSE.—

(1) JUDICIAL REVIEW.—Except as set forth under subsection (l), nothing in this section shall affect the reviewability of any final Federal agency action in a court of the United States or in the court of any State.

(2) SAVINGS CLAUSE.—Nothing in this section shall be construed as superseding, amending, or modifying the National Environmental Policy Act of 1969 (42 U.S.C. 4321 et seq.) or any other Federal environmental statute or affect the responsibility of any Federal officer to comply with or enforce any such statute.

(3) LIMITATIONS.—Nothing in this section shall preempt or interfere with—

(A) any practice of seeking, considering, or responding to public comment; or

(B) any power, jurisdiction, responsibility, or authority that a Federal, State, or local government agency, metropolitan planning organization, Indian tribe, or project sponsor has with respect to carrying out a project or any other provisions of law applicable to projects, plans, or programs.

(l) LIMITATIONS ON CLAIMS.—

(1) IN GENERAL.—Notwithstanding any other provision of law, a claim arising under Federal law seeking judicial review of a permit, license, or approval issued by a Federal agency for a highway or public transportation capital project shall be barred unless it is filed within 150 days after publication of a notice in the Federal Register announcing that the permit, license, or approval is final pursuant to the law under which the agency action is taken, unless a shorter time is specified in the Federal law pursuant to which judicial review is allowed. Nothing in this subsection shall create a right to judicial review or place any limit on filing a claim that a person has violated the terms of a permit, license, or approval.

(2) NEW INFORMATION.—The Secretary shall consider new information received

after the close of a comment period if the information satisfies the requirements for a supplemental environmental impact statement under section 771.130 of title 23, Code of Federal Regulations. The preparation of a supplemental environmental impact statement when required shall be considered a separate final agency action and the deadline for filing a claim for judicial review of such action shall be 150 days after the date of publication of a notice in the Federal Register announcing such action.

(m) ENHANCED TECHNICAL ASSISTANCE AND ACCELERATED PROJECT COMPLETION.—

(1) DEFINITION OF COVERED PROJECT.—In this subsection, the term "covered project" means a project—

(A) that has an ongoing environmental impact statement under the National Environmental Policy Act of 1969 (42 U.S.C. 4321 et seq.); and

(B) for which at least 2 years, beginning on the date on which a notice of intent is issued, have elapsed without the issuance of a record of decision.

(2) TECHNICAL ASSISTANCE.—At the request of a project sponsor or the Governor of a State in which a project is located, the Secretary shall provide additional technical assistance to resolve for a covered project any outstanding issues and project delay, including by—

(A) providing additional staff, training, and expertise;

(B) facilitating interagency coordination;

(C) promoting more efficient collaboration; and

(D) supplying specialized onsite assistance.

(3) SCOPE OF WORK.—

(A) IN GENERAL.—In providing technical assistance for a covered project under this subsection, the Secretary shall establish a scope of work that describes the actions that the Secretary will take to resolve the outstanding issues and project delays, including establishing a schedule under subparagraph (B).

(B) SCHEDULE.—

(i) IN GENERAL.—The Secretary shall establish and meet a schedule for the completion of any permit, approval, review, or study, required for the covered project by the date that is not later than 4 years after the date on which a notice of intent for the covered project is issued.

(ii) INCLUSIONS.—The schedule under clause (i) shall—

(I) comply with all applicable laws;

(II) require the concurrence of the Council on Environmental Quality and each participating agency for the project with the State in which the project is located or the project sponsor, as applicable; and

(III) reflect any new information that becomes available and any changes in circumstances that may result in new significant impacts that could affect the timeline for completion of any permit, approval, review, or study required for the covered project.

(4) CONSULTATION.—In providing technical assistance for a covered project under this subsection, the Secretary shall consult, if appropriate, with resource and participating agencies on all methods available to resolve the outstanding issues and project delays for a covered project as expeditiously as possible.

(5) ENFORCEMENT.—

(A) IN GENERAL.—All provisions of this section shall apply to this subsection, including the financial penalty provisions under subsection (h)(6).

(B) RESTRICTION.—If the Secretary enforces this subsection under subsection (h)(6), the Secretary may use a date included in a schedule under paragraph (3)(B) that is created pursuant to and is in compliance with this subsection in lieu of the dates under subsection (h)(6)(B)(ii).

(n) ACCELERATED DECISIONMAKING IN ENVIRONMENTAL REVIEWS.—

(1) IN GENERAL.—In preparing a final environmental impact statement under the National Environmental Policy Act of 1969 (42 U.S.C. 4321 et seq.), if the lead agency modifies the statement in response to comments that are minor and are confined to factual corrections or explanations of why the comments do not warrant additional agency response, the lead agency may write on errata sheets attached to the statement instead of rewriting the draft statement, subject to the condition that the errata sheets

(A) cite the sources, authorities, and reasons that support the position of the agency; and

(B) if appropriate, indicate the circumstances that would trigger agency reappraisal or further response.

(2) SINGLE DOCUMENT.—To the maximum extent practicable, the lead agency shall expeditiously develop a single document that consists of a final environmental impact statement and a record of decision, unless—

(A) the final environmental impact statement makes substantial changes to the proposed action that are relevant to environmental or safety concerns; or

(B) there is a significant new circumstance or information relevant to environmental concerns that bears on the proposed action or the impacts of the proposed action.

(3) LENGTH OF ENVIRONMENTAL DOCUMENT.—

(A) IN GENERAL.—Notwithstanding any other provision of law and except as provided in subparagraph (B), to the maximum extent practicable, the text of the items described in paragraphs (4) through (6) of section 1502.10(a) of title 40, Code of Federal Regulations (or successor regulations), of an environmental impact statement for a project shall be 200 pages or fewer.

(B) EXEMPTION.—An environmental impact statement for a project may exceed 200 pages, if the lead agency establishes a new page limit for the environmental impact statement for that project.

(o) IMPROVING TRANSPARENCY IN ENVIRONMENTAL REVIEWS.—

(1) IN GENERAL.—Not later than 18 months after the date of enactment of this subsection, the Secretary shall—

(A) use the searchable Internet website maintained under section 41003(b) of the FAST Act—

(i) to make publicly available the status and progress of projects requiring an environmental assessment or an environmental impact statement with respect to compliance with applicable requirements of the National Environmental Policy Act of 1969 (42 U.S.C. 4321 et seq.) and any other Federal, State, or local approval required for those projects; and

(ii) to make publicly available the names of participating agencies not participating in the development of a project purpose and need and range of alternatives under subsection (f); and

(B) issue reporting standards to meet the requirements of subparagraph (A).

(2) FEDERAL, STATE, AND LOCAL AGENCY PARTICIPATION.—

(A) FEDERAL AGENCIES.—A Federal agency participating in the environmental review or permitting process for a project shall provide to the Secretary information regarding the status and progress of the approval of the project for publication on the Internet website referred to in paragraph (1)(A), consistent with the standards established under paragraph (1)(B).

(B) STATE AND LOCAL AGENCIES.—The Secretary shall encourage State and local agencies participating in the environmental review permitting process for a project to provide information regarding the status and progress of the approval of the project for publication on the Internet website referred to in paragraph (1)(A).

(3) STATES WITH DELEGATED AUTHORITY.—A State with delegated authority for responsibilities under the National Environmental Policy Act of 1969 (42 U.S.C. 4321 et seq.) pursuant to section 327 shall be responsible for supplying to the Secretary project development and compliance status for all applicable projects.

(p) ACCOUNTABILITY AND REPORTING FOR MAJOR PROJECTS.—

(1) IN GENERAL.—The Secretary shall establish a performance accountability system to track each major project.

(2) REQUIREMENTS.—The performance accountability system under paragraph (1) shall, for each major project, track, at a minimum—

(A) the environmental review process for the major project, including the project schedule;

(B) whether the lead agency, cooperating agencies, and participating agencies are meeting the schedule established for the environmental review process; and

(C) the time taken to complete the environmental review process.

(q) DEVELOPMENT OF CATEGORICAL EXCLUSIONS.—

(1) IN GENERAL.—Not later than 60 days after the date of enactment of this subsection, and every 4 years thereafter, the Secretary shall—

(A) in consultation with the agencies described in paragraph (2), identify the categorical exclusions described in section 771.117 of title 23, Code of Federal Regulations (or successor regulations), that would accelerate delivery of a project if those categorical exclusions were available to those agencies;

(B) collect existing documentation and substantiating information on the categorical exclusions described in subparagraph (A); and

(C) provide to each agency described in paragraph (2)—

(i) a list of the categorical exclusions identified under subparagraph (A); and

(ii) the documentation and substantiating information under subparagraph (B).

(2) AGENCIES DESCRIBED.—The agencies referred to in paragraph (1) are—

(A) the Department of the Interior;

(B) the Department of the Army;

(C) the Department of Commerce;

(D) the Department of Agriculture;

(E) the Department of Energy;

(F) the Department of Defense; and

(G) any other Federal agency that has participated in an environmental review process for a project, as determined by the Secretary.

(3) ADOPTION OF CATEGORICAL EXCLUSIONS.—

(A) IN GENERAL.—Not later than 1 year after the date on which the Secretary provides a list under paragraph (1)(C), an agency described in paragraph (2) shall publish a notice of proposed rulemaking to propose any categorical exclusions from the list applicable to the agency, subject to the condition that the categorical exclusion identified under paragraph (1)(A) meets the criteria for a categorical exclusion under section 1508.1 of title 40, Code of Federal Regulations (or successor regulations).

(B) PUBLIC COMMENT.—In a notice of proposed rulemaking under subparagraph (A), the applicable agency may solicit comments on whether any of the proposed new categorical exclusions meet the criteria for a categorical exclusion under section 1508.1 of title 40, Code of Federal Regulations (or successor regulations).

(Added Pub. L. 109–59, title VI, §6002(a), Aug. 10, 2005, 119 Stat. 1857; amended Pub. L. 112–141, div. A, title I, §§1305–1309, July 6, 2012, 126 Stat. 533–539; Pub. L. 114–94, div. A, title I, §1304(a)–(j)(1), Dec. 4, 2015, 129 Stat. 1378–1385; Pub. L. 117–58, div. A, title I, §§11301(a), 11525(h), Nov. 15, 2021, 135 Stat. 525, 607.)

[1] *See References in Text note below.*

§140. NONDISCRIMINATION

(a) Prior to approving any programs for projects as provided for in section 135, the Secretary shall require assurances from any State desiring to avail itself of the benefits of this chapter that employment in connection with proposed projects will be provided without regard to race, color, creed, national origin, or sex. The Secretary shall require that each State shall include in the advertised specifications, notification of the specific equal employment opportunity responsibilities of the successful bidder. In approving programs for projects on any of the Federal-aid systems, the Secretary, if necessary to ensure equal employment opportunity, shall require certification by any State desiring to avail itself of the benefits of this chapter that there are in existence and available on a regional, statewide, or local basis, apprenticeship, skill improvement or other upgrading programs, registered with the Department of Labor or the appropriate State agency, if any, which provide equal opportunity for training and employment without regard to race, color, creed, national origin, or sex. In implementing such programs, a State may reserve training positions for persons who receive welfare assistance from such State; except that the implementation of any such program shall not cause current employees to be displaced or current positions to be supplanted or preclude workers that are participating in an apprenticeship, skill improvement, or other upgrading program registered with the Department of Labor or the appropriate State agency from being referred to, or hired on, projects funded under this title without regard to the length of time of their participation in such program. The Secretary shall periodically obtain from the Secretary of Labor and the respective State transportation departments information which will enable the Secretary to judge compliance with the requirements of this section and the Secretary of Labor shall render to the Secretary such assistance and information as the Secretary of Transportation shall deem necessary to carry out the equal employment opportunity program required hereunder.

(b) The Secretary, in cooperation with any other department or agency of the Government, State agency, authority, association, institution, Indian tribal government, corporation (profit or nonprofit), or any other organization or person, is authorized to develop, conduct, and administer surface transportation and technology training, including skill improvement programs, and to develop and fund summer transportation institutes. From administrative funds made available under section 104(a), the Secretary shall deduct such sums as necessary, not to exceed $10,000,000 per fiscal year, for the administration of this subsection. Such sums so deducted shall remain available until expended. The provisions of section 6101(b) to (d) of title 41 shall not be applicable to contracts and agreements made under the authority herein granted to the Secretary. Notwithstanding any other provision of law, not to exceed ½ of 1 percent of funds apportioned to a State for the surface transportation block grant program under section 104(b) may be available to carry out this subsection upon request of the State transportation department to the Secretary.

(c) The Secretary, in cooperation with any other department or agency of the Government, State agency, authority, association, institution, Indian tribal government, corporation (profit or nonprofit), or any other organization or person, is authorized to develop, conduct, and administer training programs and assistance programs in connection with any program under this title in order that minority businesses may achieve proficiency to compete, on an equal basis, for contracts and subcontracts. From administrative funds made available under section 104(a), the Secretary shall deduct such sums as necessary, not to exceed $10,000,000 per fiscal year, for the administration of this subsection. The provisions of section 6101(b) to (d) of title 41 shall not be applicable to contracts and agreements made under the authority herein granted to the Secretary notwithstanding the provisions of section 3106 of title 41.

(d) INDIAN EMPLOYMENT.—Consistent with section 703(i) of the Civil Rights Act of 1964 (42 U.S.C. 2000e–2(i)), nothing in this section shall preclude the preferential employment of Indians living on or near a reservation on projects and contracts on Indian reservation roads. States may implement a preference for employment of Indians on projects carried out under this title near Indian reservations. The Secretary shall cooperate with Indian tribal governments and the States to implement this subsection.

(Added Pub. L. 90–495, §22(a), Aug. 23, 1968, 82 Stat. 826; amended Pub. L. 91–605, title I, §110, Dec. 31, 1970, 84 Stat. 1719; Pub. L. 93–87, title I, §120, Aug. 13, 1973, 87 Stat. 259; Pub. L. 94–280, title I, §126, May 5, 1976, 90 Stat. 440; Pub. L. 97–424, title I, §119, Jan. 6, 1983, 96 Stat. 2110; Pub. L. 100–17, title I, §122, Apr. 2, 1987, 101 Stat. 160; Pub. L. 102–240, title I, §1026, Dec. 18, 1991, 105 Stat. 1965; Pub. L. 102–388, title IV, §412, Oct. 6, 1992, 106 Stat. 1565; Pub. L. 105–178, title I, §§1208, 1212(a)(2)(A), June 9, 1998, 112 Stat. 186, 193; Pub. L. 109–59, title I, §1922, Aug. 10, 2005, 119 Stat. 1481; Pub. L. 111–350, §5(e)(1), Jan. 4, 2011, 124 Stat. 3847; Pub. L. 112–141, div. A, title I, §1109, July 6, 2012, 126 Stat. 444; Pub. L. 114–94, div. A, title I, §§1109(c)(5), 1446(d)(1), Dec. 4, 2015, 129 Stat. 1343, 1438; Pub. L. 117–58, div. A, title I, §11525(i), Nov. 15, 2021, 135 Stat. 607.)

§141. ENFORCEMENT OF REQUIREMENTS

(a) Each State shall certify to the Secretary before January 1 of each year that it is enforcing all State laws respecting maximum vehicle size and weights permitted on the Federal-aid primary system, the Federal-aid urban system, and the Federal-aid secondary system, including the Interstate System in accordance with section 127 of this title. Each State shall also certify that it is enforcing and complying with the provisions of section 127(d) of this title and section 31112 of title 49.

(b)(1) Each State shall submit to the Secretary such information as the Secretary shall, by regulation, require as necessary, in his opinion, to verify the certification of such State under subsection (b) of this section.

(2) If a State fails to certify as required by subsection (b) of this section or if the Secretary determines that a State is not adequately enforcing all State laws respecting such maximum vehicle size and weights, notwithstanding such a certification, then Federal-aid highway funds apportioned to such State for such fiscal year shall be reduced by amounts equal to 7 percent of the amount which would otherwise be apportioned to such State under paragraphs (1) through (6) of section 104(b).

(3) If within one year from the date that the apportionment for any State is reduced in accordance with paragraph (2) of this subsection the Secretary determines that such State is enforcing all State laws respecting maximum size and weights, the apportionment of such State shall be increased by an amount equal to such reduction. If the Secretary does not make such a determination within such one-year period, the amounts so withheld shall be reapportioned to all other eligible States.

(c) The Secretary shall reduce the State's apportionment of Federal-aid highway funds under section 104(b)(1) in an amount up to 8 percent of the amount to be apportioned in any fiscal year beginning after September 30, 1984, during which heavy vehicles, subject to the use tax imposed by section 4481 of the Internal Revenue Code of 1986, may be lawfully registered in the State without having presented proof of payment, in such form as may be prescribed by the Secretary of the Treasury, of the use tax imposed by section 4481 of such Code. Amounts withheld from apportionment to a State under this subsection shall be apportioned to the other States pursuant to the formulas of section 104(b)(1) and shall be available in the same manner and to the same extent as other Interstate funds apportioned at the same time to other States.

(Added Pub. L. 93–643, §107(a), Jan. 4, 1975, 88 Stat. 2284; amended Pub. L. 95–599, title I, §123(d), Nov. 6, 1978, 92 Stat. 2702; Pub. L. 97–424, title I, §143, Jan. 6, 1983, 96 Stat. 2129; Pub. L. 99–514, §2, Oct. 22, 1986, 100 Stat. 2095; Pub. L. 102–240, title I, §1023(c), Dec. 18, 1991, 105 Stat. 1954; Pub. L. 103–429, §3(7), Oct. 31, 1994, 108 Stat. 4378; Pub. L. 104–59, title II, §205(d)(1)(A), Nov. 28, 1995, 109 Stat. 577; Pub. L. 105–178, title I, §1103(l)(3)(C), June 9, 1998, 112 Stat. 126; Pub. L. 112–141, div. A, title I, §1404(c), (d), July 6, 2012, 126 Stat. 558; Pub. L. 114–94, div. A, title I, §1104(e)(5), Dec. 4, 2015, 129 Stat. 1332.)

§142. Public transportation

(a)(1) To encourage the development, improvement, and use of public mass transportation systems operating buses on Federal-aid highways for the transportation of passengers, so as to increase the traffic capacity of the Federal-aid highways for the movement of persons, the Secretary may approve as a project on any Federal-aid highway the construction of exclusive or preferential high occupancy vehicle lanes, highway traffic control devices, bus passenger loading areas and facilities (including shelters), and fringe and transportation corridor parking facilities, which may include electric vehicle charging stations or natural gas vehicle refueling stations, to serve high occupancy vehicle and public mass transportation passengers, and sums apportioned under section 104(b) of this title shall be available to finance the cost of projects under this paragraph. If fees are charged for the use of any parking facility constructed under this section, the rate thereof shall not be in excess of that required for maintenance and operation of the facility and the cost of providing shuttle service to and from the facility (including compensation to any person for operating the facility and for providing such shuttle service).

(2) In addition to the projects under paragraph (1), the Secretary may approve payment from sums apportioned under section 104(b)(2) for carrying out any capital transit project eligible for assistance under chapter 53 of title 49, capital improvement to provide access and coordination between intercity and rural bus service, and construction of facilities to provide connections between highway transportation and other modes of transportation.

(3) BUS CORRIDORS.—In addition to the projects described in paragraphs (1) and (2), the Secretary may approve payment from sums apportioned under paragraph (2) or (7) of section 104(b) for carrying out a capital project for the construction of a bus rapid transit corridor or dedicated bus lanes, including the construction or installation of—

(A) traffic signaling and prioritization systems;

(B) redesigned intersections that are necessary for the establishment of a bus rapid transit corridor;

(C) on-street stations;

(D) fare collection systems;

(E) information and wayfinding systems; and

(F) depots.

(b) Sums apportioned in accordance with section 104(b)(1) shall be available to finance the Federal share of projects for exclusive or preferential high occupancy vehicle, truck, and emergency vehicle routes or lanes. Routes constructed under this subsection shall not be subject to the third sentence of section 109(b) of this title.

(c) ACCOMMODATION OF OTHER MODES OF TRANSPORTATION.—The Secretary may approve as a project on any Federal-aid highway for payment from sums apportioned under section 104(b) modifications to existing highways eligible under the program that is the source of the funds on such highway necessary to accommodate other modes of transportation if such modifications will not adversely affect automotive safety.

(d) METROPOLITAN PLANNING.—Any project carried out under this section in an urbanized area shall be subject to the metropolitan planning requirements of section 134.

(e)(1) For all purposes of this title, a project authorized by subsection (a)(1) of this section shall be deemed to be a highway project.

(2) Projects authorized by subsection (a)(2) shall be subject to, and governed in accordance with, all provisions of this title applicable to projects on the surface transportation block grant program, except to the extent determined inconsistent by the Secretary.

(3) The Federal share payable on account of projects authorized by subsection (a) of this section shall be that provided in section 120 of this title.

(f) AVAILABILITY OF RIGHTS-OF-WAY.—In any case where sufficient land or air space exists within the publicly acquired rights-of-way of any highway, constructed in whole or in part with Federal-aid highway funds, to accommodate needed passenger, commuter, or high speed rail, magnetic levitation systems, and highway and nonhighway public mass transit facilities, the Secretary shall authorize a State to make such lands, air space, and rights-of-way available with or without charge to a publicly or privately owned authority or company or any other person for such purposes if such accommodation will not adversely affect automotive safety.

(g) The provision of assistance under subsection (a)(2) shall not be construed as bringing within the application of chapter 15 of title 5, United States Code, any non-supervisory employee of an urban mass transportation system (or of any other agency or entity performing related functions) to whom such chapter is otherwise inapplicable.

(h) Funds available for expenditure to carry out the purposes of subsection (a)(2) of this section shall be supplementary to and not in substitution for funds authorized and available for obligation pursuant to chapter 53 of title 49.

(Added Pub. L. 91–605, title I, §111(a), Dec. 31, 1970, 84 Stat. 1719; amended Pub. L. 93–87, title I, §121(a), Aug. 13, 1973, 87 Stat. 259; Pub. L. 94–280, title I, §127, May 5, 1976, 90 Stat. 440; Pub. L. 97–424, title I, §120, Jan. 6, 1983, 96 Stat. 2111; Pub. L. 102–240, title I, §1027(a)–(e), title III, §3003(b), Dec. 18, 1991, 105 Stat. 1966, 2088; Pub. L. 103–272, §5(f)(2), July 5, 1994, 108 Stat. 1374; Pub. L. 103–429, §7(a)(4)(C), Oct. 31, 1994, 108 Stat. 4389; Pub. L. 105–178, title I, §1103(l)(3)(D), (4), June 9, 1998, 112 Stat. 126; Pub. L. 112–141, div. A, title I, §§1513(b), 1519(c)(8), formerly §1519(c)(9), July 6, 2012, 126 Stat. 572, 576, renumbered §1519(c)(8), Pub. L. 114–94, div. A, title I, §1446(d)(5)(B), Dec. 4, 2015, 129 Stat. 1438; Pub. L. 114–94, div. A, title I, §§1109(c)(5), 1446(d)(5)(D), Dec. 4, 2015, 129 Stat. 1343, 1438; Pub. L. 117–58, div. A, title I, §11130, Nov. 15, 2021, 135 Stat. 509.)

§143. HIGHWAY USE TAX EVASION PROJECTS

(a) STATE DEFINED.—In this section, the term "State" means the 50 States and the District of Columbia.

(b) PROJECTS.—

(1) IN GENERAL.—The Secretary shall carry out highway use tax evasion projects in accordance with this subsection.

(2) FUNDING.—

(A) IN GENERAL.—From administrative funds made available under section 104(a), the Secretary may deduct such sums as are necessary, not to exceed $4,000,000 for each of fiscal years 2022 through 2026, to carry out this section.

(B) ALLOCATION OF FUNDS.—Funds made available to carry out this section may be allocated to the Internal Revenue Service and the States at the discretion of the Secretary, except that of funds so made available for each fiscal year, $2,000,000 shall be available only to carry out intergovernmental enforcement efforts, including research and training.

(3) CONDITIONS ON FUNDS ALLOCATED TO INTERNAL REVENUE SERVICE.—Except as otherwise provided in this section, the Secretary shall not impose any condition on the use of funds allocated to the Internal Revenue Service under this subsection.

(4) LIMITATION ON USE OF FUNDS.—Funds made available to carry out this section shall be used only—

(A) to expand efforts to enhance motor fuel tax enforcement;

(B) to fund additional Internal Revenue Service staff, but only to carry out functions described in this paragraph;

(C) to supplement motor fuel tax examinations and criminal investigations;

(D) to develop automated data processing tools to monitor motor fuel production and sales;

(E) to evaluate and implement registration and reporting requirements for motor fuel taxpayers;

(F) to reimburse State expenses that supplement existing fuel tax compliance efforts;

(G) to analyze and implement programs to reduce tax evasion associated with other highway use taxes;

(H) to support efforts between States and Indian tribes to address issues relating to State motor fuel taxes; and

(I) to analyze and implement programs to reduce tax evasion associated with foreign imported fuel.

(5) MAINTENANCE OF EFFORT.—The Secretary may not make an allocation to a State under this subsection for a fiscal year unless the State certifies that the aggregate expenditure of funds of the State, exclusive of Federal funds, for motor fuel tax enforcement activities will be maintained at a level that does not fall below the average level of such expenditure for the preceding 2 fiscal years of the State.

(6) FEDERAL SHARE.—The Federal share of the cost of a project carried out under this subsection shall be 100 percent.

(7) PERIOD OF AVAILABILITY.—Funds authorized to carry out this section shall remain available for obligation for a period of 3 years after the last day of the fiscal year for which the funds are authorized.

(8) USE OF SURFACE TRANSPORTATION BLOCK GRANT PROGRAM FUNDING.—In addition to funds made available to carry out this section, a State may expend up to ¼ of 1 percent of the funds apportioned to the State for a fiscal year under section 104(b)(2) on initiatives to halt the evasion of payment of motor fuel taxes.

(9) REPORTS.—The Commissioner of the Internal Revenue Service and each State shall submit to the Secretary, the Committee on Transportation and Infrastructure of the House of Representatives, and the Committee on Environment and Public Works of the Senate an annual report that describes the projects, examinations, and criminal investigations funded by and carried out under this section. Such report shall specify the estimated annual yield from such projects, examinations, and criminal investigations.

(c) EXCISE TAX FUEL REPORTING.—

(1) IN GENERAL.—Not later than 90 days after the date of enactment of the SAFETEA–LU, the Secretary shall enter into a memorandum of understanding with the Commissioner of the Internal Revenue Service for the purposes of—

(A) the additional development of capabilities needed to support new reporting requirements and databases established under such Act and the American Jobs Creation Act of 2004 (Public Law 108–357), and such other reporting requirements and database development as may be determined by the Secretary, in consultation with the Commissioner of the Internal Revenue Service, to be useful in the enforcement of fuel excise taxes, including provisions recommended by the Fuel Tax Enforcement Advisory Committee,

(B) the completion of requirements needed for the electronic reporting of fuel transactions from carriers and terminal operators,

(C) the operation and maintenance of an excise summary terminal activity reporting system and other systems used to provide strategic analyses of domestic and foreign motor fuel distribution trends and patterns,

(D) the collection, analysis, and sharing of information on fuel distribution and compliance or noncompliance with fuel taxes, and

(E) the development, completion, operation, and maintenance of an electronic claims filing system and database and an electronic database of heavy vehicle highway use payments.

(2) ELEMENTS OF MEMORANDUM OF UNDERSTANDING.—The memorandum of understanding shall provide that—

(A) the Internal Revenue Service shall develop and maintain any system under paragraph (1) through contracts,

(B) any system under paragraph (1) shall be under the control of the Internal Revenue Service, and

(C) any system under paragraph (1) shall be made available for use by appropriate State and Federal revenue, tax, and law enforcement authorities, subject to section 6103 of the Internal Revenue Code of 1986.

(3) FUNDING.—Of the amounts made available to carry out this section for each fiscal year, the Secretary shall make available to the Internal Revenue Service such funds as may be necessary to complete, operate, and maintain the systems under paragraph (1) in accordance with this subsection.

(4) REPORTS.—Not later than September 30 of each year, the Commissioner of the Internal Revenue Service shall provide reports to the Secretary on the status of the Internal Revenue Service projects funded under this subsection.

(Added Pub. L. 91–605, title I, §127(a), Dec. 31, 1970, 84 Stat. 1729; amended Pub. L. 93–87, title I, §122, Aug. 13, 1973, 87 Stat. 261; Pub. L. 105–178, title I, §1114(a), (c), June 9, 1998, 112 Stat. 152; Pub. L. 105–206, title IX, §9002(h), July 22, 1998, 112 Stat. 836; Pub. L. 109–59, title I, §1115(a), (b), Aug. 10, 2005, 119 Stat. 1175, 1176; Pub. L. 112–141, div. A, title I, §1110, July 6, 2012, 126 Stat. 444; Pub. L. 114–94, div. A, title I, §1110, Dec. 4, 2015, 129 Stat. 1344; Pub. L. 117–58, div. A, title I, §11120, Nov. 15, 2021, 135 Stat. 497.)

§144. NATIONAL BRIDGE AND TUNNEL INVENTORY AND INSPECTION STANDARDS

(a) FINDINGS AND DECLARATIONS.—

(1) FINDINGS.—Congress finds that—

(A) the condition of the bridges of the United States has improved since the date of enactment of the Transportation Equity Act for the 21st Century (Public Law 105–178; 112 Stat. 107), yet continued improvement to bridge conditions is essential to protect the safety of the traveling public and allow for the efficient movement of people and goods on which the economy of the United States relies; and

(B) the systematic preventative maintenance of bridges, and replacement and rehabilitation of deficient bridges, should be undertaken through an overall asset management approach to transportation investment.

(2) DECLARATIONS.—Congress declares that it is in the vital interest of the United States—

(A) to inventory, inspect, and improve the condition of the highway bridges and tunnels of the United States;

(B) to use a data-driven, risk-based approach and cost-effective strategy for systematic preventative maintenance, replacement, and rehabilitation of highway bridges and tunnels to ensure safety, resilience, and extended service life;

(C) to use performance-based bridge management systems to assist States in making timely investments;

(D) to ensure accountability and link performance outcomes to investment decisions;

(E) to ensure connectivity and access for residents of rural areas of the United States through strategic investments in National Highway System bridges and bridges on all public roads; and

(F) to ensure adequate passage of aquatic and terrestrial species, where appropriate.

(b) NATIONAL BRIDGE AND TUNNEL INVENTORIES.—The Secretary, in consultation with the States and Federal agencies with jurisdiction over highway bridges and tunnels, shall—

(1) inventory all highway bridges on public roads, on and off Federal-aid highways, including tribally owned and Federally owned bridges, that are bridges over waterways, other topographical barriers, other highways, and railroads;

(2) inventory all tunnels on public roads, on and off Federal-aid highways, including tribally owned and Federally owned tunnels;

(3) classify the bridges according to serviceability, safety, and essentiality for public use, including the potential impacts to emergency evacuation routes and to regional and national freight and passenger mobility if the serviceability of the bridge is restricted or diminished;

(4) based on that classification, assign each a risk-based priority for systematic preventative maintenance, replacement, or rehabilitation;

(5) determine the cost of replacing each bridge classified as in poor condition identified under this subsection with a comparable facility or the cost of rehabilitating the bridge; and

(6) determine if the replacement or rehabilitation of bridges and tunnels should include measures to enable safe and unimpeded movement for terrestrial and aquatic species.

(c) GENERAL BRIDGE AUTHORITY.—

(1) IN GENERAL.—Except as provided in paragraph (2) and notwithstanding any other provision of law, the General Bridge Act of 1946 (33 U.S.C. 525 et seq.) shall apply to bridges authorized to be replaced, in whole or in part, by this title.

(2) EXCEPTION.—Section 502(b) of the General Bridge Act of 1946 (33 U.S.C. 525(b)) and section 9 of the Act of March 3, 1899 (33 U.S.C. 401), shall not apply to any bridge constructed, reconstructed, rehabilitated, or replaced with assistance under this title, if the bridge is over waters that—

(A) are not used and are not susceptible to use in the natural condition of the water or by reasonable improvement as a means to transport interstate or foreign commerce; and

(B) are—

(i) not tidal; or

(ii) if tidal, used only by recreational boating, fishing, and other small vessels that are less than 21 feet in length.

(d) INVENTORY UPDATES AND REPORTS.—

(1) IN GENERAL.—The Secretary shall—

(A) annually revise the inventories authorized by subsection (b); and

(B) submit to the Committee on Transportation and Infrastructure of the House of Representatives and the Committee on Environment and Public Works of the Senate a report on the inventories.

(2) INSPECTION REPORT.—Not later than 2 years after the date of enactment of the MAP–21, each State and appropriate Federal agency shall report element level data to the Secretary, as each bridge is inspected pursuant to this section, for all highway bridges on the National Highway System.

(3) GUIDANCE.—The Secretary shall provide guidance to States and Federal agencies for implementation of this subsection, while respecting the existing inspection schedule of each State.

(4) BRIDGES NOT ON NATIONAL HIGHWAY SYSTEM.—The Secretary shall—

(A) conduct a study on the benefits, cost-effectiveness, and feasibility of requiring element-level data collection for bridges not on the National Highway System; and

(B) submit to the Committee on Transportation and Infrastructure of the House of Representatives and the Committee on Environment and Public Works of the Senate a report on the results of the study.

(e) BRIDGES WITHOUT TAXING POWERS.—

(1) IN GENERAL.—Notwithstanding any other provision of law, any bridge that is owned and operated by an agency that does not have taxing powers and whose functions include operating a federally assisted public transit system subsidized by toll revenues shall be eligible for assistance under this title, but the amount of such assistance shall in no event exceed the cumulative amount which such agency has expended for capital and operating costs to subsidize such transit system.

(2) INSUFFICIENT ASSETS.—Before authorizing an expenditure of funds under this subsection, the Secretary shall determine that the applicant agency has insufficient reserves, surpluses, and projected revenues (over and above those required for bridge and transit capital and operating costs) to fund the bridge project or activity eligible for assistance under this title.

(3) CREDITING OF NON-FEDERAL FUNDS.—Any non-Federal funds expended for the seismic retrofit of the bridge may be credited toward the non-Federal share required as a condition of receipt of any Federal funds for seismic retrofit of the bridge made available after the date of the expenditure.

(f) REPLACEMENT OF DESTROYED BRIDGES AND FERRY BOAT SERVICE.—

(1) IN GENERAL.—Notwithstanding any other provision of law, a State may use the funds apportioned under section 104(b)(2) to construct any bridge that replaces—

(A) any low water crossing (regardless of the length of the low water crossing);

(B) any bridge that was destroyed prior to January 1, 1965;

(C) any ferry that was in existence on January 1, 1984; or

(D) any road bridge that is rendered obsolete as a result of a Corps of Engineers flood control or channelization project and is not rebuilt with funds from the Corps of Engineers.

(2) FEDERAL SHARE.—The Federal share payable on any bridge construction carried out under paragraph (1) shall be 80 percent of the cost of the construction.

(g) HISTORIC BRIDGES.—

(1) DEFINITION OF HISTORIC BRIDGE.—In this subsection, the term "historic bridge" means any bridge that is listed on, or eligible for listing on, the National Register of Historic Places.

(2) COORDINATION.—The Secretary shall, in cooperation with the States, encourage the retention, rehabilitation, adaptive reuse, and future study of historic bridges.

(3) STATE INVENTORY.—The Secretary shall require each State to complete an inventory of all bridges on and off Federal-aid highways to determine the historic significance of the bridges.

(4) ELIGIBILITY.—

(A) IN GENERAL.—Subject to subparagraph (B), reasonable costs associated with actions to preserve, or reduce the impact of a project under this chapter on, the historic integrity of a historic bridge shall be eligible as reimbursable project costs under section 133 if the load capacity and safety features of the historic bridge are adequate to serve the intended use for the life of the historic bridge.

(B) BRIDGES NOT USED FOR VEHICLE TRAFFIC.—In the case of a historic bridge that is no longer used for motorized vehicular traffic, the costs eligible as reimbursable project costs pursuant to this chapter shall not exceed the estimated cost of demolition of the historic bridge.

(5) PRESERVATION.—Any State that proposes to demolish a historic bridge for a replacement project with funds made available to carry out this section shall first make the historic bridge available for donation to a State, locality, or responsible private entity if the State, locality, or responsible entity enters into an agreement—

(A) to maintain the bridge and the features that give the historic bridge its historic significance; and

(B) to assume all future legal and financial responsibility for the historic bridge, which may include an agreement to hold the State transportation department harmless in any liability action.

(6) COSTS INCURRED.—

(A) IN GENERAL.—Costs incurred by the State to preserve a historic bridge (including funds made available to the State, locality, or private entity to enable it to accept the bridge) shall be eligible as reimbursable project costs under this chapter in an amount not to exceed the cost of demolition.

(B) ADDITIONAL FUNDING.—Any bridge preserved pursuant to this paragraph shall not be eligible for any other funds authorized pursuant to this title.

(h) NATIONAL BRIDGE AND TUNNEL INSPECTION STANDARDS.—

(1) REQUIREMENT.—

(A) IN GENERAL.—The Secretary shall establish and maintain inspection standards for the proper inspection and evaluation of all highway bridges and tunnels for safety and serviceability.

(B) UNIFORMITY.—The standards under this subsection shall be designed to ensure uniformity of the inspections and evaluations.

(2) MINIMUM REQUIREMENTS OF INSPECTION STANDARDS.—The standards established under paragraph (1) shall, at a minimum—

(A) specify, in detail, the method by which the inspections shall be carried out by the States, Federal agencies, and tribal governments;

(B) establish the maximum time period between inspections;

(C) establish the qualifications for those charged with carrying out the inspections;

(D) require each State, Federal agency, and tribal government to maintain and make available to the Secretary on request—

(i) written reports on the results of highway bridge and tunnel inspections and notations of any action taken pursuant to the findings of the inspections; and

(ii) current inventory data for all highway bridges and tunnels reflecting the findings of the most recent highway bridge and tunnel inspections conducted; and

(E) establish a procedure for national certification of highway bridge inspectors and tunnel inspectors.

(3) STATE COMPLIANCE WITH INSPECTION STANDARDS.—The Secretary shall, at a minimum—

(A) establish, in consultation with the States, Federal agencies, and interested and knowledgeable private organizations and individuals, procedures to conduct reviews of State compliance with—

(i) the standards established under this subsection; and

(ii) the calculation or reevaluation of bridge load ratings; and

(B) establish, in consultation with the States, Federal agencies, and interested and knowledgeable private organizations and individuals, procedures for States to follow in reporting to the Secretary—

(i) critical findings relating to structural or safety-related deficiencies of highway bridges and tunnels; and

(ii) monitoring activities and corrective actions taken in response to a critical finding described in clause (i).

(4) REVIEWS OF STATE COMPLIANCE.—

(A) IN GENERAL.—The Secretary shall annually review State compliance with the standards established under this section.

(B) NONCOMPLIANCE.—If an annual review in accordance with subparagraph (A) identifies noncompliance by a State, the Secretary shall—

(i) issue a report detailing the issues of the noncompliance by December 31 of the calendar year in which the review was made; and

(ii) provide the State an opportunity to address the noncompliance by—

(I) developing a corrective action plan to remedy the noncompliance; or

(II) resolving the issues of noncompliance not later than 45 days after the date of notification.

(5) PENALTY FOR NONCOMPLIANCE.—

(A) IN GENERAL.—If a State fails to satisfy the requirements of paragraph (4)(B) by August 1 of the calendar year following the year of a finding of noncompliance, the Secretary shall, on October 1 of that year, and each year thereafter as may be necessary, require the State to dedicate funds apportioned to the State under sections 119 and 133 after the date of enactment of the MAP–21 to correct the noncompliance with the minimum inspection standards established under this subsection.

(B) AMOUNT.—The amount of the funds to be directed to correcting noncompliance in accordance with subparagraph (A) shall—

(i) be determined by the State based on an analysis of the actions needed to address the noncompliance; and

(ii) require approval by the Secretary.

(6) UPDATE OF STANDARDS.—Not later than 3 years after the date of enactment of the MAP–21, the Secretary shall update inspection standards to cover—

(A) the methodology, training, and qualifications for inspectors; and

(B) the frequency of inspection.

(7) RISK-BASED APPROACH.—In carrying out the revisions required by paragraph (6), the Secretary shall consider a risk-based approach to determining the frequency of bridge inspections.

(i) TRAINING PROGRAM FOR BRIDGE AND TUNNEL INSPECTORS.—

(1) IN GENERAL.—The Secretary, in cooperation with the State transportation departments, shall maintain a program designed to train appropriate personnel to carry out highway bridge and tunnel inspections.

(2) REVISIONS.—The training program shall be revised from time to time to take into account new and improved techniques.

(3) REQUIREMENT.—The first revision under paragraph (2) after the date of enactment of the Surface Transportation Reauthorization Act of 2021 shall include techniques to assess passage of aquatic and terrestrial species and habitat restoration potential.

(j) BUNDLING OF BRIDGE PROJECTS.—

(1) PURPOSE.—The purpose of this subsection is to save costs and time by encouraging States to bundle multiple bridge projects as 1 project.

(2) ELIGIBLE ENTITY DEFINED.—In this subsection, the term "eligible entity" means an entity eligible to carry out a bridge project under section 119 or 133.

(3) BUNDLING OF BRIDGE PROJECTS.—An eligible entity may bundle 2 or more similar bridge projects that are—

(A) eligible projects under section 119 or 133;

(B) included as a bundled project in a transportation improvement program under section 134(j) or a statewide transportation improvement program under section 135, as applicable; and

(C) awarded to a single contractor or consultant pursuant to a contract for engineering and design or construction between the contractor and an eligible entity.

(4) ITEMIZATION.—Notwithstanding any other provision of law (including regulations), a bundling of bridge projects under this subsection may be listed as—

    (A) 1 project for purposes of sections 134 and 135; and

    (B) a single project.

    (5) FINANCIAL CHARACTERISTICS.—Projects bundled under this subsection shall have the same financial characteristics, including—

    (A) the same funding category or subcategory; and

    (B) the same Federal share.

  (k) AVAILABILITY OF FUNDS.—In carrying out this section—

    (1) the Secretary may use funds made available to the Secretary under sections 104(a) and 503;

    (2) a State may use amounts apportioned to the State under section 104(b)(1) and 104(b)(2);

    (3) an Indian tribe may use funds made available to the Indian tribe under section 202; and

    (4) a Federal agency may use funds made available to the agency under section 503.

(Added Pub. L. 91–605, title II, §204(a), Dec. 31, 1970, 84 Stat. 1741; amended Pub. L. 93–87, title II, §204, Aug. 13, 1973, 87 Stat. 284; Pub. L. 93–643, §113, Jan. 4, 1975, 88 Stat. 2286; Pub. L. 95–599, title I, §124(a), Nov. 6, 1978, 92 Stat. 2702; Pub. L. 96–106, §§7, 8(a), Nov. 9, 1979, 93 Stat. 797; Pub. L. 97–327, §5(c), Oct. 15, 1982, 96 Stat. 1612; Pub. L. 97–424, title I, §§121(a), 122(a), Jan. 6, 1983, 96 Stat. 2111, 2112; Pub. L. 100–17, title I, §§123(a)–(d)(1), (3), (e), (f)(2), 128, 133(b)(11), Apr. 2, 1987, 101 Stat. 161–163, 167, 172; Pub. L. 102–240, title I, §1028(a)–(f), Dec. 18, 1991, 105 Stat. 1967, 1968; Pub. L. 103–220, §1, Mar. 17, 1994, 108 Stat. 100; Pub. L. 104–59, title III, §§318, 325(b), Nov. 28, 1995, 109 Stat. 588, 592; Pub. L. 105–178, title I, §§1109, 1115(f)(3); June 9, 1998, 112 Stat. 141; Pub. L. 105–206, title IX, §9002(i), July 22, 1998, 112 Stat. 836; Pub. L. 108–88, §2(b)(5), Sept. 30, 2003, 117 Stat. 1111; Pub. L. 108–202, §2(b)(3), Feb. 29, 2004, 118 Stat. 478; Pub. L. 108–224, §2(b)(2), Apr. 30, 2004, 118 Stat. 627; Pub. L. 108–263, §2(b)(2), June 30, 2004, 118 Stat. 698; Pub. L. 108–280, §2(b)(2), July 30, 2004, 118 Stat. 876; Pub. L. 108–310, §2(b)(5), Sept. 30, 2004, 118 Stat. 1145; Pub. L. 109–14, §2(b)(3), May 31, 2005, 119 Stat. 324; Pub. L. 109–20, §2(b)(2), July 1, 2005, 119 Stat. 346; Pub. L. 109–35, §2(b)(2), July 20, 2005, 119 Stat. 379; Pub. L. 109–37, §2(b)(2), July 22, 2005, 119 Stat. 394; Pub. L. 109–40, §2(b)(2), July 28, 2005, 119 Stat. 410; Pub. L. 109–59, title I, §1114, Aug. 10, 2005, 119 Stat. 1172; Pub. L. 110–244, title I, §101(m)(1), June 6, 2008, 122 Stat. 1575; Pub. L. 112–141, div. A, title I, §1111(a), July 6, 2012, 126 Stat. 445; Pub. L. 114–94, div. A, title I, §1111, Dec. 4, 2015, 129 Stat. 1344; Pub. L. 117–58, div. A, title I, §§11123(e), 11310(b), 11524(b), Nov. 15, 2021, 135 Stat. 506, 536, 606.)

§145. FEDERAL-STATE RELATIONSHIP

  (a) PROTECTION OF STATE SOVEREIGNTY.—The authorization of the appropriation of Federal funds or their availability for expenditure under this chapter shall in no way infringe on the sovereign rights of the States to determine which projects shall be federally financed. The provisions of this chapter provide for a federally assisted State program.

  (b) PURPOSE OF PROJECTS.—The projects described in section 1702 of the SAFETEA–LU, section 1602 of the Transportation Equity Act for the 21st Century, sections 1103 through 1108 of the Intermodal Surface Transportation Efficiency Act of 1991 (105 Stat. 2027 et seq.), and section 149(a) of the Surface Transportation and Uniform Relocation Assistance Act of 1987 (101 Stat. 181 et seq.) are intended to establish eligibility for Federal-aid highway funds made available for such projects by section 1101(a)(16) of the SAFETEA–LU, section 1101(a)(13) of the Transportation

Equity Act for the 21st Century, sections 1103 through 1108 of the Intermodal Surface Transportation Efficiency Act of 1991, and subsections (b), (c), and (d) of section 149 of the Surface Transportation and Uniform Relocation Assistance Act of 1987, respectively, and are not intended to define the scope or limits of Federal action in a manner inconsistent with subsection (a).

(Added Pub. L. 93–87, title I, §123(a), Aug. 13, 1973, 87 Stat. 261; amended Pub. L. 105–178, title I, §1601(b), June 9, 1998, 112 Stat. 256; Pub. L. 109–59, title I, §1701(e), Aug. 10, 2005, 119 Stat. 1256; Pub. L. 112–141, div. A, title I, §1519(c)(9), formerly §1519(c)(10), July 6, 2012, 126 Stat. 576, renumbered §1519(c)(9), Pub. L. 114–94, div. A, title I, §1446(d)(5)(B), Dec. 4, 2015, 129 Stat. 1438.)

§146. Carpool and Vanpool Projects

(a) In order to conserve fuel, decrease traffic congestion during rush hours, improve air quality, and enhance the use of existing highways and parking facilities, the Secretary may approve for Federal financial assistance from funds apportioned under section 104(b)(2) of this title, projects designed to encourage the use of carpools and vanpools. (As used hereafter in this section, the term "carpool" includes a vanpool.) Such a project may include, but is not limited to, such measures as providing carpooling opportunities to the elderly and handicapped, systems for locating potential riders and informing them of convenient carpool opportunities, acquiring vehicles appropriate for carpool use, designating existing highway lanes as preferential carpool highway lanes, providing related traffic control devices, and designating existing facilities for use as preferential parking for carpools.

(b) A project authorized by this section shall be subject to and carried out in accordance with all provisions of this title, except those provisions which the Secretary determines are inconsistent with this section.

(Added Pub. L. 95–599, title I, §126(a), Nov. 6, 1978, 92 Stat. 2705; amended Pub. L. 105–178, title I, §1103(l)(1), June 9, 1998, 112 Stat. 125; Pub. L. 112–141, div. A, title I, §1105(b), July 6, 2012, 126 Stat. 432.)

§147. Construction of Ferry Boats and Ferry Terminal Facilities

(a) Program.—The Secretary shall carry out a program for construction of ferry boats and ferry terminal facilities in accordance with section 129(c).

(b) Federal Share.—The Federal share of the cost of construction of ferry boats, ferry terminals, and ferry maintenance facilities under this section shall be 80 percent.

(c) Distribution of Funds.—Of the amounts made available to ferry systems and public entities responsible for developing ferries under this section for a fiscal year, 100 percent shall be allocated in accordance with the formula set forth in subsection (d).

(d) Formula.—Of the amounts allocated under subsection (c)—

    (1) 35 percent shall be allocated among eligible entities in the proportion that—

        (A) the number of ferry passengers, including passengers in vehicles, carried by each ferry system in the most recent calendar year for which data is available; bears to

        (B) the number of ferry passengers, including passengers in vehicles, carried by all ferry systems in the most recent calendar year for which data is available;

    (2) 35 percent shall be allocated among eligible entities in the proportion that—

        (A) the number of vehicles carried by each ferry system in the most recent calendar year for which data is available; bears to

(B) the number of vehicles carried by all ferry systems in the most recent calendar year for which data is available; and

(3) 30 percent shall be allocated among eligible entities in the proportion that—

(A) the total route nautical miles serviced by each ferry system in the most recent calendar year for which data is available; bears to

(B) the total route nautical miles serviced by all ferry systems in the most recent calendar year for which data is available.

(e) REDISTRIBUTION OF UNOBLIGATED AMOUNTS.—The Secretary shall—

(1) withdraw amounts allocated to an eligible entity under subsection (c) that remain unobligated by the end of the third fiscal year following the fiscal year for which the amounts were allocated; and

(2) in the subsequent fiscal year, redistribute the amounts referred to in paragraph (1) in accordance with the formula under subsection (d) among eligible entities for which no amounts were withdrawn under paragraph (1).

(f) MINIMUM AMOUNT.—Notwithstanding subsection (c), a State with an eligible entity that meets the requirements of this section shall receive not less than $100,000 under this section for a fiscal year.

(g) IMPLEMENTATION.—

(1) DATA COLLECTION.—

(A) NATIONAL FERRY DATABASE.—Amounts made available for a fiscal year under this section shall be allocated using the most recent data available, as collected and imputed in accordance with the national ferry database established under section 1801(e) of SAFETEA–LU (23 U.S.C. 129 note).

(B) ELIGIBILITY FOR FUNDING.—To be eligible to receive funds under subsection (c), data shall have been submitted in the most recent collection of data for the national ferry database under section 1801(e) of SAFETEA–LU (23 U.S.C. 129 note) for at least 1 ferry service within the State.

(2) ADJUSTMENTS.—On review of the data submitted under paragraph (1)(B), the Secretary may make adjustments to the data as the Secretary determines necessary to correct misreported or inconsistent data.

(h) AUTHORIZATION OF APPROPRIATIONS.—There are authorized to be appropriated out of the Highway Trust Fund (other than the Mass Transit Account) to carry out this section—

(1) $110,000,000 for fiscal year 2022;

(2) $112,000,000 for fiscal year 2023;

(3) $114,000,000 for fiscal year 2024;

(4) $116,000,000 for fiscal year 2025; and

(5) $118,000,000 for fiscal year 2026.

(i) PERIOD OF AVAILABILITY.—Notwithstanding section 118(b), funds made available to carry out this section shall remain available until expended.

(j) APPLICABILITY.—All provisions of this chapter that are applicable to the National Highway System, other than provisions relating to apportionment formula and Federal share, shall apply to funds made available to carry out this section, except as determined by the Secretary to be inconsistent with this section.

(k) ADDITIONAL USES.—Notwithstanding any other provision of law, in addition to other uses of funds under this section, an eligible entity may use amounts made available under this section to pay the operating costs of the eligible entity.

(Added Pub. L. 93–87, title I, §126(a), Aug. 13, 1973, 87 Stat. 263; amended Pub. L. 94–280, title I, §130, May 5, 1976, 90 Stat. 440; Pub. L. 105–178, title I, §1212(a)(2)(A)(i), June 9, 1998, 112 Stat. 193; Pub. L. 109–59, title I, §1801(a), Aug. 10, 2005, 119 Stat. 1455; Pub. L. 112–141, div. A, title I, §1121(a), July 6, 2012, 126 Stat. 493; Pub. L. 114–94, div. A, title I, §1112(a), Dec. 4, 2015, 129 Stat. 1345; Pub. L. 117–58, div. A, title I, §11121, div. G, title XI, §71103(g)(1), Nov. 15, 2021, 135 Stat. 497, 1326.)

§148. HIGHWAY SAFETY IMPROVEMENT PROGRAM

(a) DEFINITIONS.—In this section, the following definitions apply:

(1) HIGH RISK RURAL ROAD.—The term "high risk rural road" means any roadway functionally classified as a rural major or minor collector or a rural local road with significant safety risks, as defined by a State in accordance with an updated State strategic highway safety plan.

(2) HIGHWAY BASEMAP.—The term "highway basemap" means a representation of all public roads that can be used to geolocate attribute data on a roadway.

(3) HIGHWAY SAFETY IMPROVEMENT PROGRAM.—The term "highway safety improvement program" means projects, activities, plans, and reports carried out under this section.

(4) HIGHWAY SAFETY IMPROVEMENT PROJECT.—

(A) IN GENERAL.—The term "highway safety improvement project" means strategies, activities, and projects on a public road that are consistent with a State strategic highway safety plan and—

(i) correct or improve a hazardous road location or feature; or

(ii) address a highway safety problem.

(B) INCLUSIONS.—The term "highway safety improvement project" only includes a project for 1 or more of the following:

(i) An intersection safety improvement that provides for the safety of all road users, as appropriate, including a multimodal roundabout.

(ii) Pavement and shoulder widening (including addition of a passing lane to remedy an unsafe condition).

(iii) Installation of rumble strips or another warning device, if the rumble strips or other warning devices do not adversely affect the safety or mobility of bicyclists and pedestrians, including persons with disabilities.

(iv) Installation of a skid-resistant surface at an intersection or other location with a high frequency of crashes.

(v) An improvement for pedestrian or bicyclist safety or safety of persons with disabilities.

(vi) Construction and improvement of a railway-highway grade crossing safety feature, including installation of protective devices or a grade separation project.

(vii) The conduct of a model traffic enforcement activity at a railway-highway crossing.

(viii) Construction or installation of features, measures, and road designs to calm traffic and reduce vehicle speeds.

(ix) Elimination of a roadside hazard.

(x) Installation, replacement, and other improvement of highway signage and pavement markings, or a project to maintain minimum levels of retroreflectivity, that addresses a highway safety problem consistent with a State strategic highway safety plan.

(xi) Installation of a priority control system for emergency vehicles at signalized intersections.

(xii) Installation of a traffic control or other warning device at a location with high crash potential.

(xiii) Transportation safety planning.

(xiv) Collection, analysis, and improvement of safety data.

(xv) Planning integrated interoperable emergency communications equipment, operational activities, or traffic enforcement activities (including police assistance) relating to work zone safety.

(xvi) Installation of guardrails, barriers (including barriers between construction work zones and traffic lanes for the safety of road users and workers), and crash attenuators.

(xvii) The addition or retrofitting of structures or other measures to eliminate or reduce crashes involving vehicles and wildlife.

(xviii) Installation of yellow-green signs and signals at pedestrian and bicycle crossings and in school zones.

(xix) Construction and operational improvements on high risk rural roads.

(xx) Geometric improvements to a road for safety purposes that improve safety.

(xxi) A road safety audit.

(xxii) Roadway safety infrastructure improvements consistent with the recommendations included in the publication of the Federal Highway Administration entitled "Highway Design Handbook for Older Drivers and Pedestrians" (FHWA–RD–01–103), dated May 2001 or as subsequently revised and updated.

(xxiii) Truck parking facilities eligible for funding under section 1401 of the MAP–21.

(xxiv) Systemic safety improvements.

(xxv) Installation of vehicle-to-infrastructure communication equipment.

(xxvi) Installation or upgrades of traffic control devices for pedestrians and bicyclists, including pedestrian hybrid beacons and the addition of bicycle movement phases to traffic signals.

(xxvii) Roadway improvements that provide separation between pedestrians and motor vehicles or between bicyclists and motor vehicles, including medians, pedestrian crossing islands, protected bike lanes, and protected intersection features.

(xxviii) A pedestrian security feature designed to slow or stop a motor vehicle.

(xxix) A physical infrastructure safety project not described in clauses (i) through (xxviii).

(5) MODEL INVENTORY OF ROADWAY ELEMENTS.—The term "model inventory of roadway elements" means the listing and standardized coding by the Federal Highway Administration of roadway and traffic data elements critical to safety management, analysis, and decisionmaking.

(6) PROJECT TO MAINTAIN MINIMUM LEVELS OF RETROREFLECTIVITY.—The term "project to maintain minimum levels of retroreflectivity" means a project that is designed to maintain a highway sign or pavement marking retroreflectivity at or above the minimum levels prescribed in Federal or State regulations.

(7) ROAD SAFETY AUDIT.—The term "road safety audit" means a formal safety performance examination of an existing or future road or intersection by an independent multidisciplinary audit team.

(8) ROAD USERS.—The term "road user" means a motorist, passenger, public transportation operator or user, truck driver, bicyclist, motorcyclist, or pedestrian, including a person with disabilities.

(9) SAFE SYSTEM APPROACH.—The term "safe system approach" means a roadway design—

    (A) that emphasizes minimizing the risk of injury or fatality to road users; and

    (B) that—

        (i) takes into consideration the possibility and likelihood of human error;

        (ii) accommodates human injury tolerance by taking into consideration likely accident types, resulting impact forces, and the ability of the human body to withstand impact forces; and

        (iii) takes into consideration vulnerable road users.

(10) SAFETY DATA.—

    (A) IN GENERAL.—The term "safety data" means crash, roadway, and traffic data on a public road.

    (B) INCLUSION.—The term "safety data" includes, in the case of a railway-highway grade crossing, the characteristics of highway and train traffic, licensing, and vehicle data.

(11) SPECIFIED SAFETY PROJECT.—

    (A) IN GENERAL.—The term "specified safety project" means a project carried out for the purpose of safety under any other section of this title that is consistent with the State strategic highway safety plan.

    (B) INCLUSION.—The term "specified safety project" includes a project that—

        (i) promotes public awareness and informs the public regarding highway safety matters (including safety for motorcyclists, bicyclists, pedestrians, individuals with disabilities, and other road users);

        (ii) facilitates enforcement of traffic safety laws;

        (iii) provides infrastructure and infrastructure-related equipment to support emergency services;

        (iv) conducts safety-related research to evaluate experimental safety countermeasures or equipment; or

        (v) supports safe routes to school noninfrastructure-related activities described in section 208(g)(2).

(12) STATE HIGHWAY SAFETY IMPROVEMENT PROGRAM.—The term "State highway

safety improvement program" means a program of highway safety improvement projects, activities, plans and reports carried out as part of the Statewide transportation improvement program under section 135(g).

(13) STATE STRATEGIC HIGHWAY SAFETY PLAN.—The term "State strategic highway safety plan" means a comprehensive plan, based on safety data, developed by a State transportation department that—

(A) is developed after consultation with—

(i) a highway safety representative of the Governor of the State;

(ii) regional transportation planning organizations and metropolitan planning organizations, if any;

(iii) representatives of major modes of transportation;

(iv) State and local traffic enforcement officials;

(v) a highway-rail grade crossing safety representative of the Governor of the State;

(vi) representatives conducting a motor carrier safety program under section 31102, 31106, or 31309 of title 49;

(vii) motor vehicle administration agencies;

(viii) county transportation officials;

(ix) State representatives of nonmotorized users; and

(x) other major Federal, State, tribal, and local safety stakeholders;

(B) analyzes and makes effective use of State, regional, local, or tribal safety data;

(C) addresses engineering, management, operation, education, enforcement, and emergency services elements (including integrated, interoperable emergency communications) of highway safety as key factors in evaluating highway projects;

(D) considers safety needs of, and high-fatality segments of, all public roads, including non-State-owned public roads and roads on tribal land;

(E) considers the results of State, regional, or local transportation and highway safety planning processes;

(F) describes a program of strategies to reduce or eliminate safety hazards;

(G) includes a vulnerable road user safety assessment;

(H) is approved by the Governor of the State or a responsible State agency;

(I) is consistent with section 135(g); and

(J) is updated and submitted to the Secretary for approval as required under subsection (d)(2).

(14) SYSTEMIC SAFETY IMPROVEMENT.—The term "systemic safety improvement" means an improvement that is widely implemented based on high-risk roadway features that are correlated with particular crash types, rather than crash frequency.

(15) VULNERABLE ROAD USER.—The term "vulnerable road user" means a nonmotorist—

(A) with a fatality analysis reporting system person attribute code that is included in the definition of the term "number of non-motorized fatalities" in section 490.205 of title 23, Code of Federal Regulations (or successor regulations); or

(B) described in the term "number of non-motorized serious injuries" in that section.

(16) VULNERABLE ROAD USER SAFETY ASSESSMENT.—The term "vulnerable road user safety assessment" means an assessment of the safety performance of the State with respect to vulnerable road users and the plan of the State to improve the safety of vulnerable road users as described in subsection (l).

(b) PROGRAM.—

(1) IN GENERAL.—The Secretary shall carry out a highway safety improvement program.

(2) PURPOSE.—The purpose of the highway safety improvement program shall be to achieve a significant reduction in traffic fatalities and serious injuries on all public roads, including non-State-owned public roads and roads on tribal land.

(c) ELIGIBILITY.—

(1) IN GENERAL.—To obligate funds apportioned under section 104(b)(3) to carry out this section, a State shall have in effect a State highway safety improvement program under which the State—

(A) develops, implements, and updates a State strategic highway safety plan that identifies and analyzes highway safety problems and opportunities as provided in subsections (a)(13) and (d);

(B) produces a program of projects or strategies to reduce identified safety problems; and

(C) evaluates the strategic highway safety plan on a regularly recurring basis in accordance with subsection (d)(1) to ensure the accuracy of the data and priority of proposed strategies.

(2) IDENTIFICATION AND ANALYSIS OF HIGHWAY SAFETY PROBLEMS AND OPPORTUNITIES.—As part of the State highway safety improvement program, a State shall—

(A) have in place a safety data system with the ability to perform safety problem identification and countermeasure analysis—

(i) to improve the timeliness, accuracy, completeness, uniformity, integration, and accessibility of the safety data on all public roads, including non-State-owned public roads and roads on tribal land in the State;

(ii) to evaluate the effectiveness of data improvement efforts;

(iii) to link State data systems, including traffic records, with other data systems within the State;

(iv) to improve the compatibility and interoperability of safety data with other State transportation-related data systems and the compatibility and interoperability of State safety data systems with data systems of other States and national data systems;

(v) to enhance the ability of the Secretary to observe and analyze national trends in crash occurrences, rates, outcomes, and circumstances; and

(vi) to improve the collection of data on nonmotorized crashes and to differentiate the safety data for vulnerable road users, including bicyclists, motorcyclists, and pedestrians, from other road users;

(B) based on the analysis required by subparagraph (A)—

(i) identify hazardous locations, sections, and elements (including roadside obstacles, railway-highway crossing needs, and unmarked or poorly marked roads) that constitute a danger to motorists, vulnerable road users (including motorcyclists, bicyclists, pedestrians), and other highway users;

(ii) using such criteria as the State determines to be appropriate, establish the relative severity of those locations, in terms of crashes (including crash rates), fatalities, serious injuries, traffic volume levels, and other relevant data;

(iii) identify the number of fatalities and serious injuries on all public roads by location in the State;

(iv) identify highway safety improvement projects on the basis of crash experience, crash potential, crash rate, or other data-supported means; and

(v) consider which projects maximize opportunities to advance safety;

(C) adopt strategic and performance-based goals that—

(i) address traffic safety, including behavioral and infrastructure problems and opportunities on all public roads;

(ii) focus resources on areas of greatest need; and

(iii) are coordinated with other State highway safety programs;

(D) advance the capabilities of the State for safety data collection, analysis, and integration in a manner that—

(i) complements the State highway safety program under chapter 4 and the commercial vehicle safety plan under section 31102 of title 49;

(ii) includes all public roads, including public non-State-owned roads and roads on tribal land;

(iii) identifies hazardous locations, sections, and elements on all public roads that constitute a danger to motorists (including motorcyclists), bicyclists, pedestrians, persons with disabilities, and other highway users;

(iv) includes a means of identifying the relative severity of hazardous locations described in clause (iii) in terms of crashes (including crash rate), serious injuries, fatalities, and traffic volume levels;

(v) improves the ability of the State to identify the number of fatalities and serious injuries on all public roads in the State with a breakdown by functional classification and ownership in the State; and

(vi) improves the ability of the State to differentiate the fatalities and serious injuries of vulnerable road users, including bicyclists, motorcyclists, and pedestrians, from other road users;

(E)(i) determine priorities for the correction of hazardous road locations, sections, and elements (including railway-highway crossing improvements), as identified through safety data analysis;

(ii) identify opportunities for preventing the development of such hazardous conditions; and

(iii) establish and implement a schedule of highway safety improvement projects for hazard correction and hazard prevention; and

(F)(i) establish an evaluation process to analyze and assess results achieved by highway safety improvement projects carried out in accordance with procedures and criteria established by this section; and

(ii) use the information obtained under clause (i) in setting priorities for highway safety improvement projects.

(d) UPDATES TO STRATEGIC HIGHWAY SAFETY PLANS.—

(1) ESTABLISHMENT OF REQUIREMENTS.—

(A) IN GENERAL.—Not later than 1 year after the date of enactment of the MAP–21, the Secretary shall establish requirements for regularly recurring State updates of strategic highway safety plans.

(B) CONTENTS OF UPDATED STRATEGIC HIGHWAY SAFETY PLANS.—In establishing requirements under this subsection, the Secretary shall ensure that States take into consideration, with respect to updated strategic highway safety plans—

(i) the findings of road safety audits;

(ii) the locations of fatalities and serious injuries;

(iii) the locations that do not have an empirical history of fatalities and serious injuries, but possess risk factors for potential crashes;

(iv) rural roads, including all public roads, commensurate with fatality data;

(v) motor vehicle crashes that include fatalities or serious injuries to pedestrians and bicyclists;

(vi) the cost-effectiveness of improvements;

(vii) improvements to rail-highway grade crossings; and

(viii) safety on all public roads, including non-State-owned public roads and roads on tribal land.

(2) APPROVAL OF UPDATED STRATEGIC HIGHWAY SAFETY PLANS.—

(A) IN GENERAL.—Each State shall—

(i) update the strategic highway safety plans of the State in accordance with the requirements established by the Secretary under this subsection; and

(ii) submit the updated plans to the Secretary, along with a detailed description of the process used to update the plan.

(B) REQUIREMENTS FOR APPROVAL.—The Secretary shall not approve the process for an updated strategic highway safety plan unless—

(i) the updated strategic highway safety plan is consistent with the requirements of this subsection and subsection (a)(13); and

(ii) the process used is consistent with the requirements of this subsection.

(3) PENALTY FOR FAILURE TO HAVE AN APPROVED UPDATED STRATEGIC HIGHWAY SAFETY PLAN.—If a State does not have an updated strategic highway safety plan with a process approved by the Secretary by August 1 of the fiscal year beginning after the date of establishment of the requirements under paragraph (1), the State shall not be eligible to receive any additional limitation pursuant to the redistribution of the limitation on obligations for Federal-aid highway and highway safety construction programs that occurs after August 1 for each succeeding fiscal year until the fiscal year during which the plan is approved.

(e) ELIGIBLE PROJECTS.—

(1) IN GENERAL.—Funds apportioned to the State under section 104(b)(3) may be obligated to carry out—

(A) any highway safety improvement project on any public road or publicly owned bicycle or pedestrian pathway or trail;

(B) as provided in subsection (g); or

(C) any project to maintain minimum levels of retroreflectivity with respect to a public road, without regard to whether the project is included in an applicable State strategic highway safety plan.

(2) USE OF OTHER FUNDING FOR SAFETY.—

(A) EFFECT OF SECTION.—Nothing in this section prohibits the use of funds made available under other provisions of this title for highway safety improvement projects.

(B) USE OF OTHER FUNDS.—States are encouraged to address the full scope of the safety needs and opportunities of the States by using funds made available under other provisions of this title (except a provision that specifically prohibits that use).

(3) FLEXIBLE FUNDING FOR SPECIFIED SAFETY PROJECTS.—

(A) IN GENERAL.—To advance the implementation of a State strategic highway safety plan, a State may use not more than 10 percent of the amounts apportioned to the State under section 104(b)(3) for a fiscal year to carry out specified safety projects.

(B) RULE OF CONSTRUCTION.—Nothing in this paragraph requires a State to revise any State process, plan, or program in effect on the date of enactment of this paragraph.

(C) EFFECT OF PARAGRAPH.—

(i) REQUIREMENTS.—A project carried out under this paragraph shall be subject to all requirements under this section that apply to a highway safety improvement project.

(ii) OTHER APPORTIONED PROGRAMS.—Nothing in this paragraph prohibits the use of funds made available under other provisions of this title for a specified safety project that is a noninfrastructure project.

(f) DATA IMPROVEMENT.—

(1) DEFINITION OF DATA IMPROVEMENT ACTIVITIES.—In this subsection, the following definitions apply:

(A) IN GENERAL.—The term "data improvement activities" means a project or activity to further the capacity of a State to make more informed and effective safety infrastructure investment decisions.

(B) INCLUSIONS.—The term "data improvement activities" includes a project or activity—

(i) to create, update, or enhance a highway basemap of all public roads in a State;

(ii) to collect safety data, including data identified as part of the model inventory for roadway elements, for creation of or use on a highway basemap of all public roads in a State;

(iii) to store and maintain safety data in an electronic manner;

(iv) to develop analytical processes for safety data elements;

(v) to acquire and implement roadway safety analysis tools; and

(vi) to support the collection, maintenance, and sharing of safety data on all public roads and related systems associated with the analytical usage of that data.

(2) MODEL INVENTORY OF ROADWAY ELEMENTS.—The Secretary shall—

(A) establish a subset of the model inventory of roadway elements that are useful for the inventory of roadway safety; and

(B) ensure that States adopt and use the subset to improve data collection.

(g) SPECIAL RULES.—

(1) HIGH-RISK RURAL ROAD SAFETY.—If the fatality rate on rural roads in a State increases over the most recent 2-year period for which data are available, that State shall be required to obligate in the next fiscal year for projects on high risk rural roads an amount equal to at least 200 percent of the amount of funds the State received for fiscal year 2009 for high risk rural roads under subsection (f) of this section, as in effect on the day before the date of enactment of the MAP–21.

(2) OLDER DRIVERS.—If traffic fatalities and serious injuries per capita for drivers and pedestrians over the age of 65 in a State increases during the most recent 2-year period for which data are available, that State shall be required to include, in the subsequent Strategic Highway Safety Plan of the State, strategies to address the increases in those rates, taking into account the recommendations included in the publication of the Federal Highway Administration entitled "Highway Design Handbook for Older Drivers and Pedestrians" (FHWA–RD–01–103), and dated May 2001, or as subsequently revised and updated.

(3) VULNERABLE ROAD USER SAFETY.—If the total annual fatalities of vulnerable road users in a State represents not less than 15 percent of the total annual crash fatalities in the State, that State shall be required to obligate not less than 15 percent of the amounts apportioned to the State under section 104(b)(3) for the following fiscal year for highway safety improvement projects to address the safety of vulnerable road users.

(h) REPORTS.—

(1) IN GENERAL.—A State shall submit to the Secretary a report that—

(A) describes progress being made to implement highway safety improvement projects under this section;

(B) assesses the effectiveness of those improvements; and

(C) describes the extent to which the improvements funded under this section have contributed to reducing—

(i) the number and rate of fatalities on all public roads with, to the maximum extent practicable, a breakdown by functional classification and ownership in the State;

(ii) the number and rate of serious injuries on all public roads with, to the maximum extent practicable, a breakdown by functional classification and ownership in the State; and

(iii) the occurrences of fatalities and serious injuries at railway-highway crossings.

(2) CONTENTS; SCHEDULE.—The Secretary shall establish the content and schedule for the submission of the report under paragraph (1).

(3) TRANSPARENCY.—The Secretary shall make strategic highway safety plans submitted under subsection (d) and reports submitted under this subsection available to the public through—

(A) the website of the Department; and

(B) such other means as the Secretary determines to be appropriate.

(4) DISCOVERY AND ADMISSION INTO EVIDENCE OF CERTAIN REPORTS, SURVEYS, AND INFORMATION.—Notwithstanding any other provision of law, reports, surveys, schedules, lists, or data compiled or collected for any purpose relating to this section, shall not be subject to discovery or admitted into evidence in a Federal or State court proceeding or considered for other purposes in any action for damages arising from any occurrence at a location identified or addressed in the reports, surveys, schedules, lists, or other data.

(i) STATE PERFORMANCE TARGETS.—If the Secretary determines that a State has not met or made significant progress toward meeting the safety performance targets of the State established under section 150(d), the State shall—

(1) use obligation authority equal to the apportionment of the State for the prior year under section 104(b)(3) only for highway safety improvement projects under this section until the Secretary determines that the State has met or made significant progress toward meeting the safety performance targets of the State; and

(2) submit annually to the Secretary, until the Secretary determines that the State has met or made significant progress toward meeting the safety performance targets of the State, an implementation plan that—

(A) identifies roadway features that constitute a hazard to road users;

(B) identifies highway safety improvement projects on the basis of crash experience, crash potential, or other data-supported means;

(C) describes how highway safety improvement program funds will be allocated, including projects, activities, and strategies to be implemented;

(D) describes how the proposed projects, activities, and strategies funded under the State highway safety improvement program will allow the State to make progress toward achieving the safety performance targets of the State; and

(E) describes the actions the State will undertake to meet the safety performance targets of the State.

(j) FEDERAL SHARE OF HIGHWAY SAFETY IMPROVEMENT PROJECTS.—Except as provided in sections 120 and 130, the Federal share of the cost of a highway safety improvement project carried out with funds apportioned to a State under section 104(b)(3) shall be 90 percent.

(k) DATA COLLECTION ON UNPAVED PUBLIC ROADS.—

(1) IN GENERAL.—A State may elect not to collect fundamental data elements for the model inventory of roadway elements on public roads that are gravel roads or otherwise unpaved if—

(A) the State does not use funds provided to carry out this section for a project on any such roads until the State completes a collection of the required model inventory of roadway elements for the applicable road segment; and

(B) the State demonstrates that the State consulted with affected Indian tribes before ceasing to collect data with respect to such roads that are included in the National Tribal Transportation Facility Inventory under section 202(b)(1) of this title.

(2) RULE OF CONSTRUCTION.—Nothing in this subsection may be construed to allow a State to cease data collection related to serious injuries or fatalities.

(l) VULNERABLE ROAD USER SAFETY ASSESSMENT.—

(1) IN GENERAL.—Not later than 2 years after the date of enactment of this subsection, each State shall complete a vulnerable road user safety assessment.

(2) CONTENTS.—A vulnerable road user safety assessment under paragraph (1) shall include—

(A) a quantitative analysis of vulnerable road user fatalities and serious injuries that—

(i) includes data such as location, roadway functional classification, design speed, speed limit, and time of day;

(ii) considers the demographics of the locations of fatalities and serious injuries, including race, ethnicity, income, and age; and

(iii) based on the data, identifies areas as "high-risk" to vulnerable road users; and

(B) a program of projects or strategies to reduce safety risks to vulnerable road users in areas identified as high-risk under subparagraph (A)(iii).

(3) USE OF DATA.—In carrying out a vulnerable road user safety assessment under paragraph (1), a State shall use data from the most recent 5-year period for which data is available.

(4) REQUIREMENTS.—In carrying out a vulnerable road user safety assessment under paragraph (1), a State shall—

(A) take into consideration a safe system approach; and

(B) consult with local governments, metropolitan planning organizations, and regional transportation planning organizations that represent a high-risk area identified under paragraph (2)(A)(iii).

(5) UPDATE.—A State shall update the vulnerable road user safety assessment of the State in accordance with the updates required to the State strategic highway safety plan under subsection (d).

(6) REQUIREMENT FOR TRANSPORTATION SYSTEM ACCESS.—The program of projects developed under paragraph (2)(B) may not degrade transportation system access for vulnerable road users.

(7) GUIDANCE.—

(A) IN GENERAL.—Not later than 1 year after the date of enactment of this subsection, the Secretary shall develop guidance for States to carry out this subsection.

(B) CONSULTATION.—In developing the guidance under this paragraph, the Secretary shall consult with the States and relevant safety stakeholders.

(Added Pub. L. 93–87, title I, §129(b), Aug. 13, 1973, 87 Stat. 265; amended Pub. L. 95–599, title I, §§125, 129(d), Nov. 6, 1978, 92 Stat. 2705, 2707; Pub. L. 109–59, title I, §1401(a)(1), Aug. 10, 2005, 119 Stat. 1219; Pub. L. 112–141, div. A, title I, §1112(a), July 6, 2012, 126 Stat. 450; Pub. L. 114–94, div. A, title I, §§1113(a), 1406(b), Dec. 4, 2015, 129 Stat. 1347, 1410; Pub. L. 117–58, div. A, title I, §§11111(a), 11525(j), Nov. 15, 2021, 135 Stat. 475, 607.)

§149. CONGESTION MITIGATION AND AIR QUALITY IMPROVEMENT PROGRAM

(a) ESTABLISHMENT.—The Secretary shall establish and implement a congestion mitigation and air quality improvement program in accordance with this section.

(b) ELIGIBLE PROJECTS.—Except as provided in subsections (d) and (m)(1)(B)(ii), a State may obligate funds apportioned to it under section 104(b)(4) for the congestion mitigation and air quality improvement program only for a transportation project or program if the project or program is for an area in the State that is or was designated as a nonattainment area for ozone, carbon monoxide, or particulate matter under section 107(d) of the Clean Air Act (42 U.S.C. 7407(d)) and classified pursuant to section 181(a), 186(a), 188(a), or 188(b) of the Clean Air Act (42 U.S.C. 7511(a), 7512(a), 7513(a), or 7513(b)) or is or was designated as a nonattainment area under such section 107(d) after December 31, 1997, or is required to prepare, and file with the Administrator of the Environmental Protection Agency, maintenance plans under the Clean Air Act (42 U.S.C. 7401 et seq.) and—

(1)(A)(i) if the Secretary, after consultation with the Administrator determines, on the basis of information published by the Environmental Protection Agency pursuant to section 108(f)(1)(A) of the Clean Air Act (other than clause (xvi)) that the project or program is likely to contribute to—

(I) the attainment of a national ambient air quality standard in the designated nonattainment area; or

(II) the maintenance of a national ambient air quality standard in a maintenance area; and

(ii) a high level of effectiveness in reducing air pollution, in cases of projects or programs where sufficient information is available in the database established pursuant to subsection (h) to determine the relative effectiveness of such projects or programs; or,

(B) in any case in which such information is not available, if the Secretary, after such consultation, determines that the project or program is part of a program, method, or strategy described in such section 108(f)(1)(A);

(2) if the project or program is included in a State implementation plan that has been approved pursuant to the Clean Air Act and the project will have air quality benefits;

(3) the Secretary, after consultation with the Administrator of the Environmental Protection Agency, determines that the project or program is likely to contribute to the attainment or maintenance of a national ambient air quality standard, whether through reductions in vehicle miles traveled, fuel consumption, or through other factors;

(4) to establish or operate a traffic monitoring, management, and control facility or program, including advanced truck stop electrification systems, if the Secretary, after consultation with the Administrator of the Environmental Protection Agency, determines that the facility or program is likely to contribute to the attainment or maintenance in the area of a national ambient air quality standard;

(5) if the program or project improves traffic flow, including projects to improve signalization, construct high occupancy vehicle lanes, improve intersections, add turning lanes, improve transportation systems management and operations that mitigate congestion and improve air quality, and implement intelligent transportation system strategies and such other projects that are eligible for assistance under this section on the day before the date of enactment of this paragraph, including programs or projects to improve incident and emergency response or improve mobility, such as through real-time traffic, transit, and multimodal traveler information;

(6) if the project or program involves the purchase of integrated, interoperable

emergency communications equipment;

(7) if the project or program shifts traffic demand to nonpeak hours or other transportation modes, increases vehicle occupancy rates, or otherwise reduces demand for roads through such means as telecommuting, ridesharing, carsharing, shared micromobility (including bikesharing and shared scooter systems), alternative work hours, and pricing;

(8) if the project or program is for—

(A) the purchase of diesel replacements or retrofits that are—

(i) verified technologies (as defined in section 791 of the Energy Policy Act of 2005 (42 U.S.C. 16131)) for motor vehicles (as defined in section 216 of the Clean Air Act (42 U.S.C. 7550)); or

(ii) verified technologies (as defined in section 791 of the Energy Policy Act of 2005 (42 U.S.C. 16131)) for non-road vehicles and non-road engines (as defined in section 216 of the Clean Air Act (42 U.S.C. 7550)) that are used in construction projects or port-related freight operations that are—

(I) located in nonattainment or maintenance areas for ozone, PM_{10}, or $PM_{2.5}$ (as defined under the Clean Air Act (42 U.S.C. 7401 et seq.)); and

(II) funded, in whole or in part, under this title or chapter 53 of title 49;

(B) the conduct of outreach activities that are designed to provide information and technical assistance to the owners and operators of diesel equipment and vehicles regarding the purchase and installation of diesel replacements or retrofits; or

(C) the purchase of medium- or heavy-duty zero emission vehicles and related charging equipment;

(9) if the project or program is for the installation of vehicle-to-infrastructure communication equipment;

(10) if the project is for the modernization or rehabilitation of a lock and dam that—

(A) is functionally connected to the Federal-aid highway system; and

(B) the Secretary determines is likely to contribute to the attainment or maintenance of a national ambient air quality standard; or

(11) if the project is on a marine highway corridor, connector, or crossing designated by the Secretary under section 55601(c) of title 46 (including an inland waterway corridor, connector, or crossing) that—

(A) is functionally connected to the Federal-aid highway system; and

(B) the Secretary determines is likely to contribute to the attainment or maintenance of a national ambient air quality standard.

(c) SPECIAL RULES.—

(1) PROJECTS FOR PM–10 NONATTAINMENT AREAS.—A State may obligate funds apportioned to the State under section 104(b)(4) for a project or program for an area that is nonattainment for ozone or carbon monoxide, or both, and for PM–10 resulting from transportation activities, without regard to any limitation of the Department of Transportation relating to the type of ambient air quality standard such project or program addresses.

(2) ELECTRIC VEHICLE AND NATURAL GAS VEHICLE INFRASTRUCTURE.—A State may obligate funds apportioned under section 104(b)(4) for a project or program to

establish electric vehicle charging stations or natural gas vehicle refueling stations for the use of battery powered or natural gas fueled trucks or other motor vehicles at any location in the State (giving priority to corridors designated under section 151) except that such stations may not be established or supported where commercial establishments serving motor vehicle users are prohibited by section 111 of title 23, United States Code.

(3) HOV FACILITIES.—No funds may be provided under this section for a project which will result in the construction of new capacity available to single occupant vehicles unless the project consists of a high occupancy vehicle facility available to single occupant vehicles only at other than peak travel times.

(4) LOCKS AND DAMS; MARINE HIGHWAYS.—For each fiscal year, a State may not obligate more than 10 percent of the funds apportioned to the State under section 104(b)(4) for projects described in paragraphs (10) and (11) of subsection (b).

(d) STATES FLEXIBILITY.—

(1) STATES WITHOUT A NONATTAINMENT AREA.—If a State does not have, and never has had, a nonattainment area designated under the Clean Air Act (42 U.S.C. 7401 et seq.), the State may use funds apportioned to the State under section 104(b)(4) for any project in the State that—

(A) would otherwise be eligible under subsection (b) as if the project were carried out in a nonattainment or maintenance area; or

(B) is eligible under the surface transportation block grant program under section 133.

(2) STATES WITH A NONATTAINMENT AREA.—

(A) IN GENERAL.—If a State has a nonattainment area or maintenance area and received funds in fiscal year 2009 under section 104(b)(2)(D), as in effect on the day before the date of enactment of the MAP–21, above the amount of funds that the State would have received based on the nonattainment and maintenance area population of the State under subparagraphs (B) and (C) of section 104(b)(2), as in effect on the day before the date of enactment of the MAP–21, the State may use for any project that would otherwise be eligible under subsection (b) if the project were carried out in a nonattainment or maintenance area or is eligible under the surface transportation block grant program under section 133 an amount of funds apportioned to such State under section 104(b)(4) that is equal to the product obtained by multiplying—

(i) the amount apportioned to such State under section 104(b)(4) (excluding the amount of funds reserved under subsection (k)(1)); by

(ii) the ratio calculated under subparagraph (B).

(B) RATIO.—For purposes of this paragraph, the ratio shall be calculated as the proportion that—

(i) the amount for fiscal year 2009 such State was permitted by section 149(c)(2), as in effect on the day before the date of enactment of the MAP–21, to obligate in any area of the State for projects eligible under section 133, as in effect on the day before the date of enactment of the MAP–21; bears to

(ii) the total apportionment to such State for fiscal year 2009 under section 104(b)(2), as in effect on the day before the date of enactment of the MAP–21.

(3) CHANGES IN DESIGNATION.—If a new nonattainment area is designated or a previously designated nonattainment area is redesignated as an attainment area in a State under the Clean Air Act (42 U.S.C. 7401 et seq.), the Secretary shall modify, in a manner consistent with the approach that was in effect on the day before the date of enactment of MAP–21, the amount such State is permitted to obligate in any area of the State for projects eligible under section 133.

(e) APPLICABILITY OF PLANNING REQUIREMENTS.—Programming and expenditure of funds for projects under this section shall be consistent with the requirements of sections 134 and 135 of this title.

(f) PARTNERSHIPS WITH NONGOVERNMENTAL ENTITIES.—

(1) IN GENERAL.—Notwithstanding any other provision of this title and in accordance with this subsection, a metropolitan planning organization, State transportation department, or other project sponsor may enter into an agreement with any public, private, or nonprofit entity to cooperatively implement any project carried out under this section.

(2) FORMS OF PARTICIPATION BY ENTITIES.—Participation by an entity under paragraph (1) may consist of—

(A) ownership or operation of any land, facility, vehicle, or other physical asset associated with the project;

(B) cost sharing of any project expense;

(C) carrying out of administration, construction management, project management, project operation, or any other management or operational duty associated with the project; and

(D) any other form of participation approved by the Secretary.

(3) ALLOCATION TO ENTITIES.—A State may allocate funds apportioned under section 104(b)(4) to an entity described in paragraph (1).

(4) ALTERNATIVE FUEL PROJECTS.—In the case of a project that will provide for the use of alternative fuels by privately owned vehicles or vehicle fleets, activities eligible for funding under this subsection—

(A) may include the costs of vehicle refueling infrastructure, including infrastructure that would support the development, production, and use of emerging technologies that reduce emissions of air pollutants from motor vehicles and nonroad vehicles and nonroad engines used in construction projects or port-related freight operations, and other capital investments associated with the project;

(B) shall include only the incremental cost of an alternative fueled vehicle, as compared to a conventionally fueled vehicle, that would otherwise be borne by a private party; and

(C) shall apply other governmental financial purchase contributions in the calculation of net incremental cost.

(5) PROHIBITION ON FEDERAL PARTICIPATION WITH RESPECT TO REQUIRED ACTIVITIES.—A Federal participation payment under this subsection may not be made to an entity to fund an obligation imposed under the Clean Air Act (42 U.S.C. 7401 et seq.) or any other Federal law.

(g) COST-EFFECTIVE EMISSION REDUCTION GUIDANCE.—

(1) DEFINITIONS.—In this subsection, the following definitions apply:

(A) ADMINISTRATOR.—The term "Administrator" means the Administrator of the Environmental Protection Agency.

(B) DIESEL REPLACEMENT OR RETROFIT.—The term "diesel replacement or retrofit" means a replacement or retrofit, repowering, rebuilding, after treatment, or other technology, as determined by the Administrator.

(2) EMISSION REDUCTION GUIDANCE.—The Administrator, in consultation with the Secretary, shall publish a list of diesel replacement or retrofit technologies and supporting technical information for—

(A) diesel emission reduction technologies certified or verified by the Administrator, the California Air Resources Board, or any other entity recognized by the Administrator for the same purpose;

(B) diesel emission reduction technologies identified by the Administrator as having an application and approvable test plan for verification by the Administrator or the California Air Resources Board that is submitted not later than 18 months of the date of enactment of this subsection;

(C) available information regarding the emission reduction effectiveness and cost effectiveness of technologies identified in this paragraph, taking into consideration air quality and health effects.

(3) PRIORITY CONSIDERATION.—States and metropolitan planning organizations shall give priority in areas designated as nonattainment or maintenance for PM2.5 under the Clean Air Act (42 U.S.C. 7401 et seq.) in distributing funds received for congestion mitigation and air quality projects and programs from apportionments under section 104(b)(4) to projects that are proven to reduce PM2.5, including diesel replacements or retrofits.

(4) NO EFFECT ON AUTHORITY OR RESTRICTIONS.—Nothing in this subsection modifies or otherwise affects any authority or restriction established under the Clean Air Act (42 U.S.C. 7401 et seq.) or any other law (other than provisions of this title relating to congestion mitigation and air quality).

(h) INTERAGENCY CONSULTATION.—The Secretary shall encourage States and metropolitan planning organizations to consult with State and local air quality agencies in nonattainment and maintenance areas on the estimated emission reductions from proposed congestion mitigation and air quality improvement programs and projects.

(i) EVALUATION AND ASSESSMENT OF PROJECTS.—

(1) DATABASE.—

(A) IN GENERAL.—Using appropriate assessments of projects funded under the congestion mitigation and air quality program and results from other research, the Secretary shall maintain and disseminate a cumulative database describing the impacts of the projects, including specific information about each project, such as the project name, location, sponsor, cost, and, to the extent already measured by the project sponsor, cost-effectiveness, based on reductions in congestion and emissions.

(B) AVAILABILITY.—The database shall be published or otherwise made readily available by the Secretary in electronically accessible format and means, such as the Internet, for public review.

(2) COST EFFECTIVENESS.—

(A) IN GENERAL.—The Secretary, in consultation with the Administrator of the Environmental Protection Agency, shall evaluate projects on a periodic basis and develop a table or other similar medium that illustrates the cost-effectiveness of a range of project types eligible for funding under this section as to how the projects mitigate congestion and improve air quality.

(B) CONTENTS.—The table described in subparagraph (A) shall show measures of cost-effectiveness, such as dollars per ton of emissions reduced, and assess those measures over a variety of timeframes to capture impacts on the planning timeframes outlined in section 134.

(C) USE OF TABLE.—States and metropolitan planning organizations shall consider the information in the table when selecting projects or developing performance plans under subsection (l).

(j) OPTIONAL PROGRAMMATIC ELIGIBILITY.—

(1) IN GENERAL.—At the discretion of a metropolitan planning organization, a technical assessment of a selected program of projects may be conducted through modeling or other means to demonstrate the emissions reduction projection required under this section.

(2) APPLICABILITY.—If an assessment described in paragraph (1) successfully demonstrates an emissions reduction, all projects included in such assessment shall be eligible for obligation under this section without further demonstration of emissions reduction of individual projects included in such assessment.

(k) PRIORITY FOR USE OF FUNDS IN PM2.5 AREAS.—

(1) IN GENERAL.—For any State that has a nonattainment or maintenance area for fine particulate matter, an amount equal to 25 percent of the funds apportioned to each State under section 104(b)(4) for a nonattainment or maintenance area that are based all or in part on the weighted population of such area in fine particulate matter nonattainment shall be obligated to projects that—

(A) reduce such fine particulate matter emissions in such area, including diesel replacements or retrofits; and

(B) to the extent practicable, prioritize benefits to disadvantaged communities or low-income populations living in, or immediately adjacent to, such area.

(2) CONSTRUCTION EQUIPMENT AND VEHICLES.—In order to meet the requirements of paragraph (1), a State or metropolitan planning organization may elect to obligate funds to install diesel emission control technology on nonroad diesel equipment or on-road diesel equipment that is operated on a highway construction project within a PM2.5 nonattainment or maintenance area.

(3) PM2.5 NONATTAINMENT AND MAINTENANCE IN LOW POPULATION DENSITY STATES.—

(A) EXCEPTION.—In any State with a population density of 80 or fewer persons per square mile of land area, based on the most recent decennial census, the requirements under subsection (g)(3) and paragraphs (1) and (2) of this subsection shall not apply to a nonattainment or maintenance area in the State if—

(i) the nonattainment or maintenance area does not have projects that are part of the emissions analysis of a metropolitan transportation plan or transportation improvement program; and

(ii) regional motor vehicle emissions are an insignificant contributor to the air quality problem for PM2.5 in the nonattainment or maintenance area.

(B) CALCULATION.—If subparagraph (A) applies to a nonattainment or maintenance area in a State, the percentage of the PM2.5 set-aside under paragraph (1) shall be reduced for that State proportionately based on the weighted population of the area in fine particulate matter nonattainment.

(4) PORT-RELATED EQUIPMENT AND VEHICLES.—To meet the requirements under paragraph (1), a State or metropolitan planning organization may elect to obligate funds to the most cost-effective projects to reduce emissions from port-related landside nonroad or on-road equipment that is operated within the boundaries of a PM2.5 nonattainment or maintenance area.

(l) PERFORMANCE PLAN.—

(1) IN GENERAL.—Each metropolitan planning organization serving a transportation management area (as defined in section 134) with a population over 1,000,000 people representing a nonattainment or maintenance area shall develop a performance plan that—

(A) includes an area baseline level for traffic congestion and on-road mobile source emissions for which the area is in nonattainment or maintenance;

(B) describes progress made in achieving the air quality and traffic congestion performance targets described in section 150(d); and

(C) includes a description of projects identified for funding under this section and how such projects will contribute to achieving emission and traffic congestion reduction targets.

(2) UPDATED PLANS.—Performance plans shall be updated biennially and include a separate report that assesses the progress of the program of projects under the previous plan in achieving the air quality and traffic congestion targets of the previous plan.

(3) ASSISTANCE TO METROPOLITAN PLANNING ORGANIZATIONS.—

(A) IN GENERAL.—On the request of a metropolitan planning organization, the Secretary may assist the metropolitan planning organization tracking progress made in minority or low-income populations as part of a performance plan under this subsection.

(B) SAVINGS PROVISION.—Nothing in this paragraph provides the Secretary the authority—

(i) to change the performance measures under section 150(c)(5) or the performance targets established under section 134(h)(2) or 150(d); or

(ii) to establish any other Federal requirement.

(m) OPERATING ASSISTANCE.—

(1) IN GENERAL.—A State may obligate funds apportioned under section 104(b)(4) in an area of the State that is otherwise eligible for obligations of such funds for operating costs—

(A) under chapter 53 of title 49; or

(B) on—

(i) a system for which CMAQ funding was eligible, made available, obligated, or expended in fiscal year 2012; or

(ii) a State-supported Amtrak route with a valid cost-sharing agreement under section 209 of the Passenger Rail Investment and Improvement Act of 2008 (49 U.S.C. 24101 note; Public Law 110–432) and no current nonattainment areas under subsection (d).

(2) No TIME LIMITATION.—Operating assistance provided under paragraph (1) shall have no imposed time limitation if the operating assistance is for—

(A) a route described in subparagraph (B) of that paragraph; or

(B) a transit system that is located in—

(i) a non-urbanized area; or

(ii) an urbanized area with a population of 200,000 or fewer.

(Added Pub. L. 93–87, title I, §142(a), Aug. 13, 1973, 87 Stat. 272; amended Pub. L. 102–240, title I, §1008(a), Dec. 18, 1991, 105 Stat. 1932; Pub. L. 102–388, title III, §380, Oct. 6, 1992, 106 Stat. 1562; Pub. L. 104–59, title III, §319(a)(1), (b), Nov. 28, 1995, 109 Stat. 588, 589; Pub. L. 104–88, title IV, §405(a)(2), (b), Dec. 29, 1995, 109 Stat. 956, 957; Pub. L. 105–178, title I, §1110(a)–(d)(1), June 9, 1998, 112 Stat. 142, 143; Pub. L. 109–59, title I, §1808(a)–(f), Aug. 10, 2005, 119 Stat. 1461–1463; Pub. L. 112–141, div. A, title I, §1113(a), (b), July 6, 2012, 126 Stat. 460; Pub. L. 113–76, div. L, title I, §125, Jan. 17, 2014, 128 Stat. 587; Pub. L. 114–94, div. A, title I, §§1109(c)(5), 1114, Dec. 4, 2015, 129 Stat. 1343, 1348; Pub. L. 115–141, div. L, title IV, §421, Mar. 23, 2018, 132 Stat. 1045; Pub. L. 117–58, div. A, title I, §11115, Nov. 15, 2021, 135 Stat. 480.)

§150. NATIONAL GOALS AND PERFORMANCE MANAGEMENT MEASURES

(a) DECLARATION OF POLICY.—Performance management will transform the Federal-aid highway program and provide a means to the most efficient investment of Federal transportation funds by refocusing on national transportation goals, increasing the accountability and transparency of the Federal-aid highway program, and improving project decisionmaking through performance-based planning and programming.

(b) NATIONAL GOALS.—It is in the interest of the United States to focus the Federal-aid highway program on the following national goals:

(1) SAFETY.—To achieve a significant reduction in traffic fatalities and serious injuries on all public roads.

(2) INFRASTRUCTURE CONDITION.—To maintain the highway infrastructure asset system in a state of good repair.

(3) CONGESTION REDUCTION.—To achieve a significant reduction in congestion on the National Highway System.

(4) SYSTEM RELIABILITY.—To improve the efficiency of the surface transportation system.

(5) FREIGHT MOVEMENT AND ECONOMIC VITALITY.—To improve the National Highway Freight Network, strengthen the ability of rural communities to access national and international trade markets, and support regional economic development.

(6) ENVIRONMENTAL SUSTAINABILITY.—To enhance the performance of the transportation system while protecting and enhancing the natural environment.

(7) REDUCED PROJECT DELIVERY DELAYS.—To reduce project costs, promote jobs and the economy, and expedite the movement of people and goods by accelerating project completion through eliminating delays in the project development and delivery process, including reducing regulatory burdens and improving agencies' work practices.

(c) ESTABLISHMENT OF PERFORMANCE MEASURES.—

(1) IN GENERAL.—Not later than 18 months after the date of enactment of the MAP–21, the Secretary, in consultation with State departments of transportation, metropolitan planning organizations, and other stakeholders, shall promulgate a rulemaking that establishes performance measures and standards.

(2) ADMINISTRATION.—In carrying out paragraph (1), the Secretary shall—

(A) provide States, metropolitan planning organizations, and other stakeholders not less than 90 days to comment on any regulation proposed by the Secretary under that paragraph;

(B) take into consideration any comments relating to a proposed regulation received during that comment period; and

(C) limit performance measures only to those described in this subsection.

(3) NATIONAL HIGHWAY PERFORMANCE PROGRAM.—

(A) IN GENERAL.—Subject to subparagraph (B), for the purpose of carrying out section 119, the Secretary shall establish

(i) minimum standards for States to use in developing and operating bridge and pavement management systems;

(ii) measures for States to use to assess—

(I) the condition of pavements on the Interstate system;

(II) the condition of pavements on the National Highway System (excluding the Interstate);

(III) the condition of bridges on the National Highway System;

(IV) the performance of the Interstate System; and

(V) the performance of the National Highway System (excluding the Interstate System);

(iii) minimum levels for the condition of pavement on the Interstate System, only for the purposes of carrying out section 119(f)(1); and

(iv) the data elements that are necessary to collect and maintain standardized data to carry out a performance-based approach.

(B) REGIONS.—In establishing minimum condition levels under subparagraph (A)(iii), if the Secretary determines that various geographic regions of the United States experience disparate factors contributing to the condition of pavement on the Interstate System in those regions, the Secretary may establish different minimum levels for each region.

(4) HIGHWAY SAFETY IMPROVEMENT PROGRAM.—For the purpose of carrying out section 148, the Secretary shall establish measures for States to use to assess—

(A) serious injuries and fatalities per vehicle mile traveled; and

(B) the number of serious injuries and fatalities.

(5) CONGESTION MITIGATION AND AIR QUALITY PROGRAM.—For the purpose of carrying out section 149, the Secretary shall establish measures for States to use to assess—

(A) traffic congestion; and

(B) on-road mobile source emissions.

(6) NATIONAL FREIGHT MOVEMENT.—The Secretary shall establish measures for States to use to assess freight movement on the Interstate System.

(d) ESTABLISHMENT OF PERFORMANCE TARGETS.—

(1) IN GENERAL.—Not later than 1 year after the Secretary has promulgated the final rulemaking under subsection (c), each State shall set performance targets that reflect the measures identified in paragraphs (3), (4), (5), and (6) of subsection (c).

(2) DIFFERENT APPROACHES FOR URBAN AND RURAL AREAS.—In the development and implementation of any performance target, a State may, as appropriate, provide for different performance targets for urbanized and rural areas.

(e) REPORTING ON PERFORMANCE TARGETS.—Not later than 4 years after the date of enactment of the MAP–21 and biennially thereafter, a State shall submit to the Secretary a report that describes—

(1) the condition and performance of the National Highway System in the State;

(2) the effectiveness of the investment strategy document in the State asset management plan for the National Highway System;

(3) progress in achieving performance targets identified under subsection (d); and

(4) the ways in which the State is addressing congestion at freight bottlenecks, including those identified in the national freight strategic plan, within the State.

(Added Pub. L. 112–141, div. A, title I, §1203(a), July 6, 2012, 126 Stat. 524, amended Pub. L. 114–94, div. A, title I, §1446(a)(4)–(6), (d)(2)(A), Dec. 4, 2015, 129 Stat. 1437, 1438.)

§151. NATIONAL ELECTRIC VEHICLE CHARGING AND HYDROGEN, PROPANE, AND NATURAL GAS FUELING CORRIDORS

(a) IN GENERAL.—The Secretary shall periodically designate national electric vehicle charging and hydrogen, propane, and natural gas fueling corridors that identify the near- and long-term need for, and location of, electric vehicle charging infrastructure, hydrogen fueling infrastructure, propane fueling infrastructure, and natural gas fueling infrastructure at strategic locations along major national highways to support changes in the transportation sector that help achieve a reduction in greenhouse gas emissions and improve the mobility of passenger and commercial vehicles that employ electric, hydrogen fuel cell, propane, and natural gas fueling technologies across the United States.

(b) DESIGNATION OF CORRIDORS.—In designating the corridors under subsection (a), the Secretary shall—

(1) solicit nominations from State and local officials for facilities to be included in the corridors;

(2) incorporate existing electric vehicle charging, hydrogen fueling, propane fueling, and natural gas fueling corridors previously designated by the Federal Highway Administration or designated by a State or group of States; and

(3) consider the demand for, and location of, existing electric vehicle charging stations, hydrogen fueling stations, propane fueling stations, and natural gas fueling infrastructure.

(c) STAKEHOLDERS.—In designating corridors under subsection (a), the Secretary shall involve, on a voluntary basis, stakeholders that include—

(1) the heads of other Federal agencies;

(2) State and local officials;

(3) representatives of—

(A) energy utilities;

(B) the electric, fuel cell electric, propane, and natural gas vehicle industries;

(C) the freight and shipping industry;

(D) clean technology firms;

(E) the hospitality industry;

(F) the restaurant industry;

(G) highway rest stop vendors; and

(H) industrial gas and hydrogen manufacturers; and

(4) such other stakeholders as the Secretary determines to be necessary.

(d) REDESIGNATION.—

(1) INITIAL REDESIGNATION.—Not later than 180 days after the date of enactment of the Surface Transportation Reauthorization Act of 2021, the Secretary shall update and redesignate the corridors under subsection (a).

(2) SUBSEQUENT REDESIGNATION.—The Secretary shall establish a recurring process to regularly update and redesignate the corridors under subsection (a).

(e) REPORT.—During designation and redesignation of the corridors under this section, the Secretary shall issue a report that—

(1) identifies electric vehicle charging infrastructure, hydrogen fueling infrastructure, propane fueling infrastructure, and natural gas fueling infrastructure and standardization needs for electricity providers, industrial gas providers, natural gas providers, infrastructure providers, vehicle manufacturers, electricity purchasers, and natural gas purchasers;

(2) describes efforts, including through funds awarded through the grant program under subsection (f), that will aid efforts to achieve strategic deployment of electric vehicle charging infrastructure, hydrogen fueling infrastructure, propane fueling infrastructure, and natural gas fueling infrastructure in those corridors; and

(3) summarizes best practices and provides guidance, developed through consultation with the Secretary of Energy, for project development of electric vehicle charging infrastructure, hydrogen fueling infrastructure, propane fueling infrastructure and natural gas fueling infrastructure at the State, Tribal, and local level to allow for the predictable deployment of that infrastructure.

(f) GRANT PROGRAM.—

(1) DEFINITION OF PRIVATE ENTITY.—In this subsection, the term "private entity" means a corporation, partnership, company, or nonprofit organization.

(2) ESTABLISHMENT.—Not later than 1 year after the date of enactment of the Surface Transportation Reauthorization Act of 2021, the Secretary shall establish a grant program to award grants to eligible entities to carry out the activities described in paragraph (6).

(3) ELIGIBLE ENTITIES.—An entity eligible to receive a grant under this subsection is—

(A) a State or political subdivision of a State;

(B) a metropolitan planning organization;

(C) a unit of local government;

(D) a special purpose district or public authority with a transportation function, including a port authority;

(E) an Indian tribe (as defined in section 4 of the Indian Self-Determination and Education Assistance Act (25 U.S.C. 5304));

(F) a territory of the United States;

(G) an authority, agency, or instrumentality of, or an entity owned by, 1 or more entities described in subparagraphs (A) through (F); or

(H) a group of entities described in subparagraphs (A) through (G).

(4) APPLICATIONS.—To be eligible to receive a grant under this subsection, an eligible entity shall submit to the Secretary an application at such time, in such manner, and containing such information as the Secretary shall require, including—

(A) a description of how the eligible entity has considered—

(i) public accessibility of charging or fueling infrastructure proposed to be funded with a grant under this subsection, including—

(I) charging or fueling connector types and publicly available information on real-time availability; and

(II) payment methods to ensure secure, convenient, fair, and equal access;

(ii) collaborative engagement with stakeholders (including automobile manufacturers, utilities, infrastructure providers, technology providers, electric charging, hydrogen, propane, and natural gas fuel providers, metropolitan planning organizations, States, Indian tribes, and units of local governments, fleet owners, fleet managers, fuel station owners and operators, labor organizations, infrastructure construction and component parts suppliers, and multi-State and regional entities)—

(I) to foster enhanced, coordinated, public-private or private investment in electric vehicle charging infrastructure, hydrogen fueling infrastructure, propane fueling infrastructure, or natural gas fueling infrastructure;

(II) to expand deployment of electric vehicle charging infrastructure, hydrogen fueling infrastructure, propane fueling infrastructure, or natural gas fueling infrastructure;

(III) to protect personal privacy and ensure cybersecurity; and

(IV) to ensure that a properly trained workforce is available to construct and install electric vehicle charging infrastructure, hydrogen fueling infrastructure, propane fueling infrastructure, or natural gas fueling infrastructure;

(iii) the location of the station or fueling site, such as consideration of—

(I) the availability of onsite amenities for vehicle operators, such as restrooms or food facilities;

(II) access in compliance with the Americans with Disabilities Act of 1990 (42 U.S.C. 12101 et seq.);

(III) height and fueling capacity requirements for facilities that charge or refuel large vehicles, such as semi-trailer trucks; and

(IV) appropriate distribution to avoid redundancy and fill charging or fueling gaps;

(iv) infrastructure installation that can be responsive to technology advancements, such as accommodating autonomous vehicles, vehicle-to-grid technology, and future charging methods; and

(v) the long-term operation and maintenance of the electric vehicle charging infrastructure, hydrogen fueling infrastructure, propane fueling infrastructure, or natural gas fueling infrastructure, to avoid stranded assets and protect the investment of public funds in that infrastructure; and

(B) an assessment of the estimated emissions that will be reduced through the use of electric vehicle charging infrastructure, hydrogen fueling infrastructure, propane fueling infrastructure, or natural gas fueling infrastructure, which shall be conducted using the Alternative Fuel Life-Cycle Environmental and Economic Transportation (AFLEET) tool developed by Argonne National Laboratory (or a successor tool).

(5) CONSIDERATIONS.—In selecting eligible entities to receive a grant under this subsection, the Secretary shall—

(A) consider the extent to which the application of the eligible entity would—

(i) improve alternative fueling corridor networks by—

(I) converting corridor-pending corridors to corridor-ready corridors; or

(II) in the case of corridor-ready corridors, providing redundancy—

(aa) to meet excess demand for charging or fueling infrastructure; or

(bb) to reduce congestion at existing charging or fueling infrastructure in high-traffic locations;

(ii) meet current or anticipated market demands for charging or fueling infrastructure;

(iii) enable or accelerate the construction of charging or fueling infrastructure that would be unlikely to be completed without Federal assistance;

(iv) support a long-term competitive market for electric vehicle charging infrastructure, hydrogen fueling infrastructure, propane fueling infrastructure, or natural gas fueling infrastructure that does not significantly impair existing electric vehicle charging infrastructure, hydrogen fueling infrastructure, propane fueling infrastructure, or natural gas fueling infrastructure providers;

(v) provide access to electric vehicle charging infrastructure, hydrogen fueling infrastructure, propane fueling infrastructure, or natural gas fueling infrastructure in areas with a current or forecasted need; and

(vi) deploy electric vehicle charging infrastructure, hydrogen fueling infrastructure, propane fueling infrastructure, or natural gas fueling infrastructure for medium- and heavy-duty vehicles (including along the National Highway Freight Network established under section 167(c)) and in proximity to intermodal transfer stations;

(B) ensure, to the maximum extent practicable, geographic diversity among grant recipients to ensure that electric vehicle charging infrastructure, hydrogen fueling infrastructure, propane fueling infrastructure, or natural gas fueling infrastructure is available throughout the United States;

(C) consider whether the private entity that the eligible entity contracts with under paragraph (6)—

(i) submits to the Secretary the most recent year of audited financial statements; and

(ii) has experience in installing and operating electric vehicle charging infrastructure, hydrogen fueling infrastructure, propane fueling infrastructure, or natural gas fueling infrastructure; and

(D) consider whether, to the maximum extent practicable, the eligible entity and the private entity that the eligible entity contracts with under paragraph (6) enter into an agreement—

(i) to operate and maintain publicly available electric vehicle charging infrastructure, hydrogen fueling infrastructure, propane fueling infrastructure, or natural gas infrastructure; and

(ii) that provides a remedy and an opportunity to cure if the requirements described in clause (i) are not met.

(6) USE OF FUNDS.—

(A) IN GENERAL.—An eligible entity receiving a grant under this subsection shall only use the funds in accordance with this paragraph to contract with a private entity for acquisition and installation of publicly accessible electric vehicle charging infrastructure, hydrogen fueling infrastructure, propane fueling infrastructure, or natural gas fueling infrastructure that is directly related to the charging or fueling of a vehicle.

(B) LOCATION OF INFRASTRUCTURE.—Any publicly accessible electric vehicle charging infrastructure, hydrogen fueling infrastructure, propane fueling infrastructure, or natural gas fueling infrastructure acquired and installed with a grant under this subsection shall be located along an alternative fuel corridor designated under this section, on the condition that any affected Indian tribes are consulted before the designation.

(C) OPERATING ASSISTANCE.—

(i) IN GENERAL.—Subject to clauses (ii) and (iii), an eligible entity that receives a grant under this subsection may use a portion of the funds to provide to a private entity operating assistance for the first 5 years of operations after the installation of publicly available electric vehicle charging infrastructure, hydrogen fueling infrastructure, propane fueling infrastructure, or natural gas fueling infrastructure while the facility transitions to independent system operations.

(ii) INCLUSIONS.—Operating assistance under this subparagraph shall be limited to costs allocable to operating and maintaining the electric vehicle charging infrastructure, hydrogen fueling infrastructure, propane fueling infrastructure, or natural gas fueling infrastructure and service.

(iii) LIMITATION.—Operating assistance under this subparagraph may not exceed the amount of a contract under subparagraph (A) to acquire and install publicly accessible electric vehicle charging infrastructure, hydrogen fueling infrastructure, propane fueling infrastructure, or natural gas fueling infrastructure.

(D) TRAFFIC CONTROL DEVICES.—

(i) IN GENERAL.—Subject to this paragraph, an eligible entity that receives a grant under this subsection may use a portion of the funds to acquire and install traffic control devices located in the right-of-way to provide directional information to publicly accessible electric vehicle charging infrastructure, hydrogen fueling infrastructure, propane fueling infrastructure, or natural gas fueling infrastructure acquired, installed, or operated with the grant.

(ii) APPLICABILITY.—Clause (i) shall apply only to an eligible entity that—
(I) receives a grant under this subsection; and
(II) is using that grant for the acquisition and installation of publicly accessible electric vehicle charging infrastructure, hydrogen fueling infrastructure, propane fueling infrastructure, or natural gas fueling infrastructure.

(iii) LIMITATION ON AMOUNT.—The amount of funds used to acquire and install traffic control devices under clause (i) may not exceed the amount of a contract under subparagraph (A) to acquire and install publicly accessible charging or fueling infrastructure.

(iv) NO NEW AUTHORITY CREATED.—Nothing in this subparagraph authorizes an eligible entity that receives a grant under this subsection to acquire and install traffic control devices if the entity is not otherwise authorized to do so.

(E) REVENUE.—
(i) IN GENERAL.—An eligible entity receiving a grant under this subsection and a private entity referred to in subparagraph (A) may enter into a cost-sharing agreement under which the private entity submits to the eligible entity a portion of the revenue from the electric vehicle charging infrastructure, hydrogen fueling infrastructure, propane fueling infrastructure, or natural gas fueling infrastructure.

(ii) USES OF REVENUE.—An eligible entity that receives revenue from a cost-sharing agreement under clause (i) may only use that revenue for a project that is eligible under this title.

(7) CERTAIN FUELS.—The use of grants for propane fueling infrastructure under this subsection shall be limited to infrastructure for medium- and heavy-duty vehicles.

(8) COMMUNITY GRANTS.—
(A) IN GENERAL.—Notwithstanding paragraphs (4), (5), and (6), the Secretary shall reserve 50 percent of the amounts made available each fiscal year to carry out this section to provide grants to eligible entities in accordance with this paragraph.

(B) APPLICATIONS.—To be eligible to receive a grant under this paragraph, an eligible entity shall submit to the Secretary an application at such time, in such manner, and containing such information as the Secretary may require.

(C) ELIGIBLE ENTITIES.—An entity eligible to receive a grant under this paragraph is—
(i) an entity described in paragraph (3); and
(ii) a State or local authority with ownership of publicly accessible transportation facilities.

(D) ELIGIBLE PROJECTS.—The Secretary may provide a grant under this paragraph for a project that is expected to reduce greenhouse gas emissions and to expand or fill gaps in access to publicly accessible electric vehicle charging infrastructure, hydrogen fueling infrastructure, propane fueling infrastructure, or natural gas fueling infrastructure, including—
(i) development phase activities, including planning, feasibility analysis, revenue forecasting, environmental review, preliminary engineering and design work, and other preconstruction activities; and

(ii) the acquisition and installation of electric vehicle charging infrastructure, hydrogen fueling infrastructure, propane fueling infrastructure, or natural gas fueling infrastructure that is directly related to the charging or fueling of a vehicle, including any related construction or reconstruction and the acquisition of real property directly related to the project, such as locations described in subparagraph (E), to expand access to electric vehicle charging infrastructure, hydrogen fueling infrastructure, propane fueling infrastructure, or natural gas fueling infrastructure.

(E) PROJECT LOCATIONS.—A project receiving a grant under this paragraph may be located on any public road or in other publicly accessible locations, such as parking facilities at public buildings, public schools, and public parks, or in publicly accessible parking facilities owned or managed by a private entity.

(F) PRIORITY.—In providing grants under this paragraph, the Secretary shall give priority to projects that expand access to electric vehicle charging infrastructure, hydrogen fueling infrastructure, propane fueling infrastructure, or natural gas fueling infrastructure within—

(i) rural areas;

(ii) low- and moderate-income neighborhoods; and

(iii) communities with a low ratio of private parking spaces to households or a high ratio of multiunit dwellings to single family homes, as determined by the Secretary.

(G) ADDITIONAL CONSIDERATIONS.—In providing grants under this paragraph, the Secretary shall consider the extent to which the project—

(i) contributes to geographic diversity among eligible entities, including achieving a balance between urban and rural communities; and

(ii) meets current or anticipated market demands for charging or fueling infrastructure, including faster charging speeds with high-powered capabilities necessary to minimize the time to charge or refuel current and anticipated vehicles.

(H) PARTNERING WITH PRIVATE ENTITIES.—An eligible entity that receives a grant under this paragraph may use the grant funds to contract with a private entity for the acquisition, construction, installation, maintenance, or operation of electric vehicle charging infrastructure, hydrogen fueling infrastructure, propane fueling infrastructure, or natural gas fueling infrastructure that is directly related to the charging or fueling of a vehicle.

(I) MAXIMUM GRANT AMOUNT.—The amount of a grant under this paragraph shall not be more than $15,000,000.

(J) TECHNICAL ASSISTANCE.—Of the amounts reserved under subparagraph (A), the Secretary may use not more than 1 percent to provide technical assistance to eligible entities.

(K) ADDITIONAL ACTIVITIES.—The recipient of a grant under this paragraph may use not more than 5 percent of the grant funds on educational and community engagement activities to develop and implement education programs through partnerships with schools, community organizations, and vehicle dealerships to support the use of zero-emission vehicles and associated infrastructure.

(9) REQUIREMENTS.—

(A) PROJECT TREATMENT.—Notwithstanding any other provision of law, any project funded by a grant under this subsection shall be treated as a project on a Federal-aid highway under this chapter.

(B) SIGNS.—Any traffic control device or on-premises sign acquired, installed, or operated with a grant under this subsection shall comply with—

(i) the Manual on Uniform Traffic Control Devices, if located in the right-of-way; and

(ii) other provisions of Federal, State, and local law, as applicable.

(10) FEDERAL SHARE.—

(A) IN GENERAL.—The Federal share of the cost of a project carried out with a grant under this subsection shall not exceed 80 percent of the total project cost.

(B) RESPONSIBILITY OF PRIVATE ENTITY.—As a condition of contracting with an eligible entity under paragraph (6) or (8), a private entity shall agree to pay the share of the cost of a project carried out with a grant under this subsection that is not paid by the Federal Government under subparagraph (A).

(11) REPORT.—Not later than 3 years after the date of enactment of this subsection, the Secretary shall submit to the Committee on Environment and Public Works of the Senate and the Committee on Transportation and Infrastructure of the House of Representatives and make publicly available a report on the progress and implementation of this subsection.

(Added Pub. L. 114–94, div. A, title I, §1413(a), Dec. 4, 2015, 129 Stat. 1417; amended Pub. L. 117–58, div. A, title I, §11401(b), Nov. 15, 2021, 135 Stat. 546.)

§152. HAZARD ELIMINATION PROGRAM

(a) IN GENERAL.—

(1) PROGRAM.—Each State shall conduct and systematically maintain an engineering survey of all public roads to identify hazardous locations, sections, and elements, including roadside obstacles and unmarked or poorly marked roads, which may constitute a danger to motorists, bicyclists, and pedestrians, assign priorities for the correction of such locations, sections, and elements, and establish and implement a schedule of projects for their improvement.

(2) HAZARDS.—In carrying out paragraph (1), a State may, at its discretion—

(A) identify, through a survey, hazards to motorists, bicyclists, pedestrians, and users of highway facilities; and

(B) develop and implement projects and programs to address the hazards.

(b) The Secretary may approve as a project under this section any safety improvement project, including a project described in subsection (a).

(c) Funds authorized to carry out this section shall be available for expenditure on—

(1) any public road;

(2) any public surface transportation facility or any publicly owned bicycle or pedestrian pathway or trail; or

(3) any traffic calming measure.

(d) The Federal share payable on account of any project under this section shall be 90 percent of the cost thereof.

(e) Funds authorized to be appropriated to carry out this section shall be available for obligation in the same manner and to the same extent as if such funds were apportioned under section 104(b), except that the Secretary is authorized to waive provisions he deems inconsistent with the purposes of this section.

(f) Each State shall establish an evaluation process approved by the Secretary, to analyze and assess results achieved by safety improvement projects carried out in accordance with procedures and criteria established by this section. Such evaluation process shall develop cost-benefit data for various types of corrections and treatments which shall be used in setting priorities for safety improvement projects.

(g) Each State shall report to the Secretary of Transportation not later than December 30 of each year, on the progress being made to implement safety improvement projects for hazard elimination and the effectiveness of such improvements. Each State report shall contain an assessment of the cost of, and safety benefits derived from, the various means and methods used to mitigate or eliminate hazards and the previous and subsequent accident experience at these locations. The Secretary of Transportation shall submit a report to the Committee on Environment and Public Works of the Senate and the Committee on Transportation and Infrastructure of the House of Representatives not later than April 1 of each year on the progress being made by the States in implementing the hazard elimination program (including but not limited to any projects for pavement marking). The report shall include, but not be limited to, the number of projects undertaken, their distribution by cost range, road system, means and methods used, and the previous and subsequent accident experience at improved locations. In addition, the Secretary's report shall analyze and evaluate each State program, identify any State found not to be in compliance with the schedule of improvements required by subsection (a) and include recommendations for future implementation of the hazard elimination program.

(h) For the purposes of this section the term "State" shall have the meaning given it in section 401 of this title.

(Added Pub. L. 93–87, title II, §209(a), Aug. 13, 1973, 87 Stat. 286; amended Pub. L. 94–280, title I, §131, May 5, 1976, 90 Stat. 441; Pub. L. 95–599, title I, §168(a), Nov. 6, 1978, 92 Stat. 2722; Pub. L. 96–106, §10(b), Nov. 9, 1979, 93 Stat. 798; Pub. L. 97–375, title II, §210(b), Dec. 21, 1982, 96 Stat. 1826; Pub. L. 97–424, title I, §125, Jan. 6, 1983, 96 Stat. 2113; Pub. L. 100–17, title I, §133(b)(12), Apr. 2, 1987, 101 Stat. 172; Pub. L. 104–59, title III, §325(c), Nov. 28, 1995, 109 Stat. 592; Pub. L. 105–178, title I, §1401, June 9, 1998, 112 Stat. 235.)

§153. USE OF SAFETY BELTS AND MOTORCYCLE HELMETS

(a) AUTHORITY TO MAKE GRANTS.—The Secretary may make grants to a State in a fiscal year in accordance with this section if the State has in effect in such fiscal year—

(1) a law which makes unlawful throughout the State the operation of a motorcycle if any individual on the motorcycle is not wearing a motorcycle helmet; and

(2) a law which makes unlawful throughout the State the operation of a passenger vehicle whenever an individual in a front seat of the vehicle (other than a child who is secured in a child restraint system) does not have a safety belt properly fastened about the individual's body.

(b) USE OF GRANTS.—A grant made to a State under this section shall be used to adopt and implement a traffic safety program to carry out the following purposes:

(1) EDUCATION.—To educate the public about motorcycle and passenger vehicle

safety and motorcycle helmet, safety belt, and child restraint system use and to involve public health education agencies and other related agencies in these efforts.

(2) TRAINING.—To train law enforcement officers in the enforcement of State laws described in subsection (a).

(3) MONITORING.—To monitor the rate of compliance with State laws described in subsection (a).

(4) ENFORCEMENT.—To enforce State laws described in subsection (a).

(c) MAINTENANCE OF EFFORT.—A grant may not be made to a State under this section in any fiscal year unless the State enters into such agreements with the Secretary as the Secretary may require to ensure that the State will maintain its aggregate expenditures from all other sources for any traffic safety program described in subsection (b) at or above the average level of such expenditures in the State's 2 fiscal years preceding the date of the enactment of this section.

(d) FEDERAL SHARE.—A State may not receive a grant under this section in more than 3 fiscal years. The Federal share payable for a grant under this section shall not exceed—

(1) in the first fiscal year the State receives a grant, 75 percent of the cost of implementing in such fiscal year a traffic safety program described in subsection (b);

(2) in the second fiscal year the State receives a grant, 50 percent of the cost of implementing in such fiscal year such traffic safety program; and

(3) in the third fiscal year the State receives a grant, 25 percent of the cost of implementing in such fiscal year such traffic safety program.

(e) MAXIMUM AGGREGATE AMOUNT OF GRANTS.—The aggregate amount of grants made to a State under this section shall not exceed 90 percent of the amount apportioned to such State for fiscal year 1990 under section 402.

(f) ELIGIBILITY FOR GRANTS.—

(1) GENERAL RULE.—A State is eligible in a fiscal year for a grant under this section only if the State enters into such agreements with the Secretary as the Secretary may require to ensure that the State implements in such fiscal year a traffic safety program described in subsection (b).

(2) SECOND-YEAR GRANTS.—A State is eligible for a grant under this section in a fiscal year succeeding the first fiscal year in which a State receives a grant under this section only if the State in the preceding fiscal year—

(A) had in effect at all times a State law described in subsection (a)(1) and achieved a rate of compliance with such law of not less than 75 percent; and

(B) had in effect at all times a State law described in subsection (a)(2) and achieved a rate of compliance with such law of not less than 50 percent.

(3) THIRD-YEAR GRANTS.—A State is eligible for a grant under this section in a fiscal year succeeding the second fiscal year in which a State receives a grant under this section only if the State in the preceding fiscal year—

(A) had in effect at all times a State law described in subsection (a)(1) and achieved a rate of compliance with such law of not less than 85 percent; and

(B) had in effect at all times a State law described in subsection (a)(2) and achieved a rate of compliance with such law of not less than 70 percent.

(g) MEASUREMENTS OF RATES OF COMPLIANCE.—For the purposes of subsections (f)(2) and (f)(3), a State shall measure compliance with State laws described in subsection (a) using methods which conform to guidelines issued by the Secretary ensuring that such measurements are accurate and representative.

(h) PENALTY.—

(1) PRIOR TO FISCAL YEAR 2012.—If, at any time in a fiscal year beginning after September 30, 1994, and before October 1, 2011, a State does not have in effect a law described in subsection (a)(2), the Secretary shall transfer 3 percent of the funds apportioned to the State for the succeeding fiscal year under each of subsections (b)(1), (b)(2), and (b)(3) of section 104 [1] of this title to the apportionment of the State under section 402 of this title.

(2) FISCAL YEAR 2012 AND THEREAFTER.—If, at any time in a fiscal year beginning after September 30, 2011, a State does not have in effect a law described in subsection (a)(2), the Secretary shall transfer an amount equal to 2 percent of the funds apportioned to the State for the succeeding fiscal year under each of paragraphs (1), (2), and (4) of section 104(b) to the apportionment of the State under section 402.

(3) FEDERAL SHARE.—The Federal share of the cost of any project carried out under section 402 with funds transferred to the apportionment of section 402 shall be 100 percent.

(4) TRANSFER OF OBLIGATION AUTHORITY.—If the Secretary transfers under this subsection any funds to the apportionment of a State under section 402 for a fiscal year, the Secretary shall allocate an amount of obligation authority distributed for such fiscal year to the State for Federal-aid highways and highway safety construction programs for carrying out only projects under section 402 which is determined by multiplying—

(A) the amount of funds transferred to the apportionment of section 402 of the State under section 402 for such fiscal year; by

(B) the ratio of the amount of obligation authority distributed for such fiscal year to the State for Federal-aid highways and highway safety construction programs to the total of the sums apportioned to the State for Federal-aid highways and highway safety construction (excluding sums not subject to any obligation limitation) for such fiscal year.

(5) LIMITATION ON APPLICABILITY OF HIGHWAY SAFETY OBLIGATIONS.—Notwithstanding any other provision of law, no limitation on the total of obligations for highway safety programs carried out by the Federal Highway Administration under section 402 shall apply to funds transferred under this subsection to the apportionment of section 402.

(i) DEFINITIONS.—For the purposes of this section, the following definitions apply:

(1) MOTORCYCLE.—The term "motorcycle" means a motor vehicle which is designed to travel on not more than 3 wheels in contact with the surface.

(2) MOTOR VEHICLE.—The term "motor vehicle" has the meaning such term has under section 154 [1] of this title.

(3) PASSENGER VEHICLE.—The term "passenger vehicle" means a motor vehicle which is designed for transporting 10 individuals or less, including the driver, except that such term does not include a vehicle which is constructed on a truck chassis, a motorcycle, a trailer, or any motor vehicle which is not required on the date of

the enactment of this section under a Federal motor vehicle safety standard to be equipped with a belt system.

(4) SAFETY BELT.—The term "safety belt" means—

(A) with respect to open-body passenger vehicles, including convertibles, an occupant restraint system consisting of a lap belt or a lap belt and a detachable shoulder belt; and

(B) with respect to other passenger vehicles, an occupant restraint system consisting of integrated lap shoulder belts.

(j) AUTHORIZATION OF APPROPRIATIONS.—There is authorized to be appropriated out of the Highway Trust Fund (other than the Mass Transit Account) to carry out this section $17,000,000 for fiscal year 1992. From sums made available to carry out section 402 of this title, the Secretary shall make available $17,000,000 for fiscal year 1992 and $24,000,000 for each of fiscal years 1993 and 1994 to carry out this section.

(k) APPLICABILITY OF CHAPTER 1 PROVISIONS.—All provisions of this chapter that are applicable to National Highway System funds, other than provisions relating to the apportionment formula and provisions limiting the expenditures of such funds to Federal-aid systems, shall apply to funds authorized to be appropriated to carry out this section, except as determined by the Secretary to be inconsistent with this section and except that sums authorized by this section shall remain available until expended.

(Added Pub. L. 102–240, title I, §1031(a)(1), Dec. 18, 1991, 105 Stat. 1970; amended Pub. L. 104–59, title II, §205(e), Nov. 28, 1995, 109 Stat. 577; Pub. L. 112–141, div. A, title I, §1404(e), July 6, 2012, 126 Stat. 558; Pub. L. 114–94, div. A, title I, §1446(a)(7), Dec. 4, 2015, 129 Stat. 1437.)

[1] See References in Text note below.

§154. OPEN CONTAINER REQUIREMENTS

(a) DEFINITIONS.—In this section, the following definitions apply:

(1) ALCOHOLIC BEVERAGE.—The term "alcoholic beverage" has the meaning given the term in section 158(c).

(2) MOTOR VEHICLE.—The term "motor vehicle" means a vehicle driven or drawn by mechanical power and manufactured primarily for use on public highways, but does not include a vehicle operated exclusively on a rail or rails.

(3) OPEN ALCOHOLIC BEVERAGE CONTAINER.—The term "open alcoholic beverage container" means any bottle, can, or other receptacle—

(A) that contains any amount of alcoholic beverage; and

(B)(i) that is open or has a broken seal; or

(ii) the contents of which are partially removed.

(4) PASSENGER AREA.—The term "passenger area" shall have the meaning given the term by the Secretary by regulation.

(b) OPEN CONTAINER LAWS.—

(1) IN GENERAL.—For the purposes of this section, each State shall have in effect a law that prohibits the possession of any open alcoholic beverage container, or the consumption of any alcoholic beverage, in the passenger area of any motor vehicle (including possession or consumption by the driver of the vehicle) located on a public highway, or the right-of-way of a public highway, in the State.

(2) MOTOR VEHICLES DESIGNED TO TRANSPORT MANY PASSENGERS.—For the

purposes of this section, if a State has in effect a law that makes unlawful the possession of any open alcoholic beverage container by the driver (but not by a passenger)—

(A) in the passenger area of a motor vehicle designed, maintained, or used primarily for the transportation of persons for compensation; or

(B) in the living quarters of a house coach or house trailer,

the State shall be deemed to have in effect a law described in this subsection with respect to such a motor vehicle for each fiscal year during which the law is in effect.

(c) TRANSFER OF FUNDS.—

(1) FISCAL YEARS 2001 AND 2002.—On October 1, 2000, and October 1, 2001, if a State has not enacted or is not enforcing an open container law described in subsection (b), the Secretary shall transfer an amount equal to 1½ percent of the funds apportioned to the State on that date under each of paragraphs (1), (2), and (4) of section 104(b) to the apportionment of the State under section 402—

(A) to be used for impaired driving countermeasures; or

(B) to be directed to State and local law enforcement agencies for enforcement of laws prohibiting driving while intoxicated or driving under the influence and other related laws (including regulations), including the purchase of equipment, the training of officers, and the use of additional personnel for specific impaired driving countermeasures, dedicated to enforcement of the laws (including regulations).

(2) FISCAL YEAR 2022 AND THEREAFTER.—

(A) RESERVATION OF FUNDS.—

(i) IN GENERAL.—On October 1, 2021, and each October 1 thereafter, in the case of a State described in clause (ii), the Secretary shall reserve an amount equal to 2.5 percent of the funds to be apportioned to the State on that date under each of paragraphs (1) and (2) of section 104(b) until the State certifies to the Secretary the means by which the State will use those reserved funds in accordance with subparagraphs (A) and (B) of paragraph (1), and paragraph (3).

(ii) STATES DESCRIBED.—A State referred to in clause (i) is a State—

(I) that has not enacted or is not enforcing an open container law described in subsection (b); and

(II) for which the Secretary determined for the prior fiscal year that the State had not enacted or was not enforcing an open container law described in subsection (b).

(B) TRANSFER OF FUNDS.—As soon as practicable after the date of receipt of a certification from a State under subparagraph (A)(i), the Secretary shall—

(i) transfer the reserved funds identified by the State for use as described in subparagraphs (A) and (B) of paragraph (1) to the apportionment of the State under section 402; and

(ii) release the reserved funds identified by the State as described in paragraph (3).

(3) USE FOR HIGHWAY SAFETY IMPROVEMENT PROGRAM.—

(A) IN GENERAL.—A State may elect to use all or a portion of the funds reserved under paragraph (2) for activities eligible under section 148.

[§155. Repealed. Pub. L. 112–141, div. A, title I, §1519(b)(1)(A), July 6, 2012, 126 Stat. 575]

CHAPTER 1—FEDERAL-AID HIGHWAYS

(B) STATE DEPARTMENTS OF TRANSPORTATION.—If the State makes an election under subparagraph (A), the funds shall be transferred to the department of transportation of the State, which shall be responsible for the administration of the funds.

(4) FEDERAL SHARE.—The Federal share of the cost of a project carried out with funds transferred under paragraph (1) or (2), or used under paragraph (3), shall be 100 percent.

(5) DERIVATION OF AMOUNT TO BE TRANSFERRED.—The amount to be transferred or released under paragraph (2) may be derived from the following:

(A) The apportionment of the State under section 104(b)(1).

(B) The apportionment of the State under section 104(b)(2).

(6) TRANSFER OF OBLIGATION AUTHORITY.—

(A) IN GENERAL.—If the Secretary transfers under this subsection any funds to the apportionment of a State under section 402 for a fiscal year, the Secretary shall transfer an amount, determined under subparagraph (B), of obligation authority distributed for the fiscal year to the State for Federal-aid highways and highway safety construction programs for carrying out projects under section 402.

(B) AMOUNT.—The amount of obligation authority referred to in subparagraph (A) shall be determined by multiplying—

(i) the amount of funds transferred under subparagraph (A) to the apportionment of the State under section 402 for the fiscal year, by

(ii) the ratio that—

(I) the amount of obligation authority distributed for the fiscal year to the State for Federal-aid highways and highway safety construction programs, bears to

(II) the total of the sums apportioned to the State for Federal-aid highways and highway safety construction programs (excluding sums not subject to any obligation limitation) for the fiscal year.

(7) LIMITATION ON APPLICABILITY OF OBLIGATION LIMITATION.—Notwithstanding any other provision of law, no limitation on the total of obligations for highway safety programs under section 402 shall apply to funds transferred under this subsection to the apportionment of a State under such section.

(Added Pub. L. 105–178, title I, §1405(a), as added Pub. L. 105–206, title IX, §9005(a), July 22, 1998, 112 Stat. 843; amended Pub. L. 109–59, title I, §1401(a)(3)(C), Aug. 10, 2005, 119 Stat. 1225; Pub. L. 112–141, div. A, title I, §1402, July 6, 2012, 126 Stat. 556; Pub. L. 114–94, div. A, title I, §1446(a)(8), Dec. 4, 2015, 129 Stat. 1437; Pub. L. 117–58, div. A, title I, §11131(a), div. B, title IV, §24106(a), Nov. 15, 2021, 135 Stat. 509, 806.)

[§155. REPEALED. PUB. L. 112–141, DIV. A, TITLE I, §1519(B)(1)(A), JULY 6, 2012, 126 STAT. 575]

Section, added Pub. L. 93–643, §115(a), Jan. 4, 1975, 88 Stat. 2287; amended Pub. L. 95–599, title I, §129(e), Nov. 6, 1978, 92 Stat. 2708, related to access highways to public recreation areas on certain lakes.

§156. PROCEEDS FROM THE SALE OR LEASE OF REAL PROPERTY

(a) MINIMUM CHARGE.—Subject to section 142(f), a State shall charge, at a minimum, fair market value for the sale, use, lease, or lease renewal (other than for utility use and occupancy or for a transportation project eligible for assistance under this title) of real property acquired with Federal assistance made available from the Highway Trust Fund (other than the Mass Transit Account).

(b) EXCEPTIONS.—The Secretary may grant an exception to the requirement of subsection (a) for a social, environmental, or economic purpose.

(c) USE OF FEDERAL SHARE OF INCOME.—The Federal share of net income from the revenues obtained by a State under subsection (a) shall be used by the State for projects eligible under this title.

(Added Pub. L. 100–17, title I, §126(a), Apr. 2, 1987, 101 Stat. 167; amended Pub. L. 102–240, title I, §1027(f), Dec. 18, 1991, 105 Stat. 1967; Pub. L. 105–178, title I, §1303(a), June 9, 1998, 112 Stat. 227.)

§157. NATIONAL ENVIRONMENTAL POLICY ACT OF 1969 REPORTING PROGRAM

(a) DEFINITIONS.—In this section:

(1) CATEGORICAL EXCLUSION.—The term "categorical exclusion" has the meaning given the term in section 771.117(c) of title 23, Code of Federal Regulations (or a successor regulation).

(2) DOCUMENTED CATEGORICAL EXCLUSION.—The term "documented categorical exclusion" has the meaning given the term in section 771.117(d) of title 23, Code of Federal Regulations (or a successor regulation).

(3) ENVIRONMENTAL ASSESSMENT.—The term "environmental assessment" has the meaning given the term in section 1508.1 of title 40, Code of Federal Regulations (or a successor regulation).

(4) ENVIRONMENTAL IMPACT STATEMENT.—The term "environmental impact statement" means a detailed statement required under section 102(2)(C) of the National Environmental Policy Act of 1969 (42 U.S.C. 4332(2)(C)).

(5) FEDERAL AGENCY.—The term "Federal agency" includes a State that has assumed responsibility under section 327.

(6) NEPA PROCESS.—The term "NEPA process" means the entirety of the development and documentation of the analysis required under the National Environmental Policy Act of 1969 (42 U.S.C. 4321 et seq.), including the assessment and analysis of any impacts, alternatives, and mitigation of a proposed action, and any interagency participation and public involvement required to be carried out before the Secretary undertakes a proposed action.

(7) PROPOSED ACTION.—The term "proposed action" means an action (within the meaning of the National Environmental Policy Act of 1969 (42 U.S.C. 4321 et seq.)) under this title that the Secretary proposes to carry out.

(8) REPORTING PERIOD.—The term "reporting period" means the fiscal year prior to the fiscal year in which a report is issued under subsection (b).

(9) SECRETARY.—The term "Secretary" includes the governor or head of an applicable State agency of a State that has assumed responsibility under section 327.

(b) REPORT ON NEPA DATA.—

(1) IN GENERAL.—The Secretary shall carry out a process to track, and annually submit to the Committee on Environment and Public Works of the Senate and the Committee on Transportation and Infrastructure of the House of Representatives a report containing, the information described in paragraph (3).

(2) TIME TO COMPLETE.—For purposes of paragraph (3), the NEPA process—

(A) for an environmental impact statement—

(i) begins on the date on which the Notice of Intent is published in the Federal Register; and

(ii) ends on the date on which the Secretary issues a record of decision, including, if necessary, a revised record of decision; and

(B) for an environmental assessment—

(i) begins on the date on which the Secretary makes a determination to prepare an environmental assessment; and

(ii) ends on the date on which the Secretary issues a finding of no significant impact or determines that preparation of an environmental impact statement is necessary.

(3) INFORMATION DESCRIBED.—The information referred to in paragraph (1) is, with respect to the Department of Transportation—

(A) the number of proposed actions for which a categorical exclusion was issued during the reporting period;

(B) the number of proposed actions for which a documented categorical exclusion was issued by the Department of Transportation during the reporting period;

(C) the number of proposed actions pending on the date on which the report is submitted for which the issuance of a documented categorical exclusion by the Department of Transportation is pending;

(D) the number of proposed actions for which an environmental assessment was issued by the Department of Transportation during the reporting period;

(E) the length of time the Department of Transportation took to complete each environmental assessment described in subparagraph (D);

(F) the number of proposed actions pending on the date on which the report is submitted for which an environmental assessment is being drafted by the Department of Transportation;

(G) the number of proposed actions for which an environmental impact statement was completed by the Department of Transportation during the reporting period;

(H) the length of time that the Department of Transportation took to complete each environmental impact statement described in subparagraph (G);

(I) the number of proposed actions pending on the date on which the report is submitted for which an environmental impact statement is being drafted; and

(J) for the proposed actions reported under subparagraphs (F) and (I), the percentage of those proposed actions for which—

(i) funding has been identified; and

(ii) all other Federal, State, and local activities that are required to allow the proposed action to proceed are completed.

(Added Pub. L. 117–58, div. A, title I, §11312(a), Nov. 15, 2021, 135 Stat. 538.)

§158. NATIONAL MINIMUM DRINKING AGE

(a) WITHHOLDING OF FUNDS FOR NONCOMPLIANCE.—

(1) IN GENERAL.—

(A) FISCAL YEARS BEFORE 2012.—The Secretary shall withhold 10 per centum of the amount required to be apportioned to any State under each of sections 104(b)(1), 104(b)(3), and 104(b)(4) [1] of this title on the first day of each fiscal year after the second fiscal year beginning after September 30, 1985, in which the purchase or public possession in such State of any alcoholic beverage by a person who is less than twenty-one years of age is lawful.

(B) FISCAL YEAR 2012 AND THEREAFTER.—For fiscal year 2012 and each fiscal year thereafter, the amount to be withheld under this section shall be an amount equal to 8 percent of the amount apportioned to the noncompliant State, as described in subparagraph (A), under paragraphs (1) and (2) of section 104(b).

(2) STATE GRANDFATHER LAW AS COMPLYING.—If, before the later of (A) October 1, 1986, or (B) the tenth day following the last day of the first session the legislature of a State convenes after the date of the enactment of this paragraph, such State has in effect a law which makes unlawful the purchase and public possession in such State of any alcoholic beverage by a person who is less than 21 years of age (other than any person who is 18 years of age or older on the day preceding the effective date of such law and at such time could lawfully purchase or publicly possess any alcoholic beverage in such State), such State shall be deemed to be in compliance with paragraph (1) in each fiscal year in which such law is in effect.

(b) EFFECT OF WITHHOLDING OF FUNDS.—No funds withheld under this section from apportionment to any State after September 30, 1988, shall be available for apportionment to that State.

(c) ALCOHOLIC BEVERAGE DEFINED.—As used in this section, the term "alcoholic beverage" means—

(1) beer as defined in section 5052(a) of the Internal Revenue Code of 1986,

(2) wine of not less than one-half of 1 per centum of alcohol by volume, or

(3) distilled spirits as defined in section 5002(a)(8) of such Code.

(Added Pub. L. 98–363, §6(a), July 17, 1984, 98 Stat. 437; amended Pub. L. 99–272, title IV, §4104, Apr. 7, 1986, 100 Stat. 114; Pub. L. 99–514, §2, Oct. 22, 1986, 100 Stat. 2095; Pub. L. 105–178, title I, §1103(l)(2), June 9, 1998, 112 Stat. 125; Pub. L. 112–141, div. A, title I, §1404(f), July 6, 2012, 126 Stat. 558.)

[1] See References in Text note below.

§159. REVOCATION OR SUSPENSION OF DRIVERS' LICENSES OF INDIVIDUALS CONVICTED OF DRUG OFFENSES

(a) WITHHOLDING OF APPORTIONMENTS FOR NONCOMPLIANCE.—

(1) BEGINNING IN FISCAL YEAR 1996.—The Secretary shall withhold 10 percent of the amount required to be apportioned to any State under each of paragraphs (1), (3), and (5) (as in effect on the day before the date of enactment of the Transportation Equity Act for the 21st Century) of section 104(b) on the first day of each fiscal year which begins after the fourth calendar year following the effective date of this section if the State does not meet the requirements of paragraph (3) on the first day of such fiscal year.

(2) FISCAL YEAR 2012 AND THEREAFTER.—The Secretary shall withhold an amount

equal to 8 percent of the amount required to be apportioned to any State under each of paragraphs (1) and (2) of section 104(b) on the first day of each fiscal year beginning after September 30, 2011, if the State fails to meet the requirements of paragraph (3) on the first day of the fiscal year.

(3) REQUIREMENTS.—A State meets the requirements of this paragraph if—

(A) the State has enacted and is enforcing a law that requires in all circumstances, or requires in the absence of compelling circumstances warranting an exception—

(i) the revocation, or suspension for at least 6 months, of the driver's license of any individual who is convicted, after the enactment of such law, of—

(I) any violation of the Controlled Substances Act, or

(II) any drug offense; and

(ii) a delay in the issuance or reinstatement of a driver's license to such an individual for at least 6 months after the individual applies for the issuance or reinstatement of a driver's license if the individual does not have a driver's license, or the driver's license of the individual is suspended, at the time the individual is so convicted; or

(B) the Governor of the State—

(i) submits to the Secretary no earlier than the adjournment sine die of the first regularly scheduled session of the State's legislature which begins after the effective date of this section a written certification stating that the Governor is opposed to the enactment or enforcement in the State of a law described in subparagraph (A), relating to the revocation, suspension, issuance, or reinstatement of drivers' licenses to convicted drug offenders; and

(ii) submits to the Secretary a written certification that the legislature (including both Houses where applicable) has adopted a resolution expressing its opposition to a law described in clause (i).

(b) EFFECT OF NONCOMPLIANCE.—No funds withheld under this section from apportionments to any State shall be available for apportionment to that State.

(c) DEFINITIONS.—For purposes of this section—

(1) DRIVER'S LICENSE.—The term "driver's license" means a license issued by a State to any individual that authorizes the individual to operate a motor vehicle on highways.

(2) DRUG OFFENSE.—The term "drug offense" means any criminal offense which proscribes—

(A) the possession, distribution, manufacture, cultivation, sale, transfer, or the attempt or conspiracy to possess, distribute, manufacture, cultivate, sell, or transfer any substance the possession of which is prohibited under the Controlled Substances Act; or

(B) the operation of a motor vehicle under the influence of such a substance.

(3) CONVICTED.—The term "convicted" includes adjudicated under juvenile proceedings.

(Added Pub. L. 102–143, title III, §333(a), Oct. 28, 1991, 105 Stat. 944; amended Pub. L. 102–388, title III, §327(a), Oct. 6, 1992, 106 Stat. 1547; Pub. L. 105–178, title I, §1103(l)(3)(E), June 9, 1998, 112 Stat. 126; Pub. L. 112–141, div. A, title I, §1404(g), July 6, 2012, 126 Stat. 558.)

[§160. Repealed. Pub. L. 112–141, div. A, title I, §1519(b)(1)(A), July 6, 2012, 126 Stat. 575]

Section, added Pub. L. 102–240, title I, §1014(a), Dec. 18, 1991, 105 Stat. 1941, related to reimbursement for segments of the Interstate System constructed without Federal assistance.

§161. Operation of motor vehicles by intoxicated minors

(a) Withholding of Apportionments for Noncompliance.—

(1) Prior to fiscal year 2012.—The Secretary shall withhold 10 percent (including any amounts withheld under paragraph (1)) of the amount required to be apportioned to any State under each of paragraphs (1), (3), and (4) of section 104(b) [1] on October 1, 1999, and on October 1 of each fiscal year thereafter through fiscal year 2011, if the State does not meet the requirement of paragraph (3) on that date.

(2) Fiscal year 2012 and thereafter.—The Secretary shall withhold an amount equal to 8 percent of the amount required to be apportioned to any State under each of paragraphs (1) and (2) of section 104(b) on October 1, 2011, and on October 1 of each fiscal year thereafter, if the State does not meet the requirement of paragraph (3) on that date.

(3) Requirement.—A State meets the requirement of this paragraph if the State has enacted and is enforcing a law that considers an individual under the age of 21 who has a blood alcohol concentration of 0.02 percent or greater while operating a motor vehicle in the State to be driving while intoxicated or driving under the influence of alcohol.

(b) Period of Availability; Effect of Compliance and Noncompliance.—

(1) Period of availability of withheld funds.—

(A) Funds withheld on or before September 30, 2000.—Any funds withheld under subsection (a) from apportionment to any State on or before September 30, 2000, shall remain available until the end of the third fiscal year following the fiscal year for which the funds are authorized to be appropriated.

(B) Funds withheld after September 30, 2000.—No funds withheld under this section from apportionment to any State after September 30, 2000, shall be available for apportionment to the State.

(2) Apportionment of withheld funds after compliance.—If, before the last day of the period for which funds withheld under subsection (a) from apportionment are to remain available for apportionment to a State under paragraph (1), the State meets the requirement of subsection (a)(3), the Secretary shall, on the first day on which the State meets the requirement, apportion to the State the funds withheld under subsection (a) that remain available for apportionment to the State.

(3) Period of availability of subsequently apportioned funds.—Any funds apportioned pursuant to paragraph (2) shall remain available for expenditure until the end of the third fiscal year following the fiscal year in which the funds are so apportioned. Sums not obligated at the end of that period shall lapse.

(4) Effect of noncompliance.—If, at the end of the period for which funds withheld under subsection (a) from apportionment are available for apportionment to a State under paragraph (1), the State does not meet the requirement of subsection

(a)(3), the funds shall lapse.

(Added Pub. L. 104–59, title III, §320(a), Nov. 28, 1995, 109 Stat. 589; amended Pub. L. 105–178, title I, §1103(l)(3)(F), June 9, 1998, 112 Stat. 126; Pub. L. 112–141, div. A, title I, §1404(h), July 6, 2012, 126 Stat. 559.)

[1] See References in Text note below.

§162. NATIONAL SCENIC BYWAYS PROGRAM

(a) DESIGNATION OF ROADS.—

(1) IN GENERAL.—The Secretary shall carry out a national scenic byways program that recognizes roads having outstanding scenic, historic, cultural, natural, recreational, and archaeological qualities by designating the roads as—

(A) National Scenic Byways;

(B) All-American Roads; or

(C) America's Byways.

(2) CRITERIA.—The Secretary shall designate roads to be recognized under the national scenic byways program in accordance with criteria developed by the Secretary.

(3) NOMINATION.—

(A) IN GENERAL.—To be considered for a designation, a road must be nominated by a State, an Indian tribe, or a Federal land management agency and must first be designated as a State scenic byway, an Indian tribe scenic byway, or, in the case of a road on Federal land, as a Federal land management agency byway.

(B) NOMINATION BY INDIAN TRIBES.—An Indian tribe may nominate a road as a National Scenic Byway, an All-American Road, or one of America's Byways under paragraph (1) only if a Federal land management agency (other than the Bureau of Indian Affairs), a State, or a political subdivision of a State does not have—

(i) jurisdiction over the road; or

(ii) responsibility for managing the road.

(C) SAFETY.—An Indian tribe shall maintain the safety and quality of roads nominated by the Indian tribe under subparagraph (A).

(4) RECIPROCAL NOTIFICATION.—States, Indian tribes, and Federal land management agencies shall notify each other regarding nominations made under this subsection for roads that—

(A) are within the jurisdictional boundary of the State, Federal land management agency, or Indian tribe; or

(B) directly connect to roads for which the State, Federal land management agency, or Indian tribe is responsible.

(b) GRANTS AND TECHNICAL ASSISTANCE.—

(1) IN GENERAL.—The Secretary shall make grants and provide technical assistance to States and Indian tribes to—

(A) implement projects on highways designated as—

(i) National Scenic Byways;

(ii) All-American Roads;

(iii) America's Byways;

(iv) State scenic byways; or

(v) Indian tribe scenic byways; and

(B) plan, design, and develop a State or Indian tribe scenic byway program.

(2) PRIORITIES.—In making grants, the Secretary shall give priority to—

(A) each eligible project that is associated with a highway that has been designated as a National Scenic Byway, All-American Road, or 1 of America's Byways and that is consistent with the corridor management plan for the byway;

(B) each eligible project along a State or Indian tribe scenic byway that is consistent with the corridor management plan for the byway, or is intended to foster the development of such a plan, and is carried out to make the byway eligible for designation as—

(i) a National Scenic Byway;

(ii) an All-American Road; or

(iii) 1 of America's Byways; and

(C) each eligible project that is associated with the development of a State or Indian tribe scenic byway program.

(c) ELIGIBLE PROJECTS.—The following are projects that are eligible for Federal assistance under this section:

(1) An activity related to the planning, design, or development of a State or Indian tribe scenic byway program.

(2) Development and implementation of a corridor management plan to maintain the scenic, historical, recreational, cultural, natural, and archaeological characteristics of a byway corridor while providing for accommodation of increased tourism and development of related amenities.

(3) Safety improvements to a State scenic byway, Indian tribe scenic byway, National Scenic Byway, All-American Road, or one of America's Byways to the extent that the improvements are necessary to accommodate increased traffic and changes in the types of vehicles using the highway as a result of the designation as a State scenic byway, Indian tribe scenic byway, National Scenic Byway, All-American Road, or one of America's Byways.

(4) Construction along a scenic byway of a facility for pedestrians and bicyclists, rest area, turnout, highway shoulder improvement, overlook, or interpretive facility.

(5) An improvement to a scenic byway that will enhance access to an area for the purpose of recreation, including water-related recreation.

(6) Protection of scenic, historical, recreational, cultural, natural, and archaeological resources in an area adjacent to a scenic byway.

(7) Development and provision of tourist information to the public, including interpretive information about a scenic byway.

(8) Development and implementation of a scenic byway marketing program.

(d) LIMITATION.—The Secretary shall not make a grant under this section for any project that would not protect the scenic, historical, recreational, cultural, natural, and archaeological integrity of a highway and adjacent areas.

(e) SAVINGS CLAUSE.—The Secretary shall not withhold any grant or impose any requirement on a State or Indian tribe as a condition of providing a grant or technical assistance for any scenic byway unless the requirement is consistent with the authority provided in this chapter.

(f) FEDERAL SHARE.—The Federal share of the cost of carrying out a project under this section shall be 80 percent, except that, in the case of any scenic byway project along a public road that provides access to or within Federal or Indian land, a Federal land management agency may use funds authorized for use by the agency as the non-Federal share.

(Added Pub. L. 105–178, title I, §1219(a), June 9, 1998, 112 Stat. 219; amended Pub. L. 109–59, title I, §1802, Aug. 10, 2005, 119 Stat. 1456; Pub. L. 110–244, title I, §101(o), June 6, 2008, 122 Stat. 1576.)

§163. SAFETY INCENTIVES TO PREVENT OPERATION OF MOTOR VEHICLES BY INTOXICATED PERSONS

(a) GENERAL AUTHORITY.—The Secretary shall make a grant, in accordance with this section, to any State that has enacted and is enforcing a law that provides that any person with a blood alcohol concentration of 0.08 percent or greater while operating a motor vehicle in the State shall be deemed to have committed a per se offense of driving while intoxicated (or an equivalent per se offense).

(b) GRANTS.—For each fiscal year, funds authorized to carry out this section shall be apportioned to each State that has enacted and is enforcing a law meeting the requirements of subsection (a) in an amount determined by multiplying—

(1) the amount authorized to carry out this section for the fiscal year; by

(2) the ratio that the amount of funds apportioned to each such State under section 402 for such fiscal year bears to the total amount of funds apportioned to all such States under section 402 for such fiscal year.

(c) USE OF GRANTS.—A State may obligate funds apportioned under subsection (b) for any project eligible for assistance under this title.

(d) FEDERAL SHARE.—The Federal share of the cost of a project funded under this section shall be 100 percent.

(e) PENALTY.—

(1) FISCAL YEARS 2007 THROUGH 2011.—On October 1, 2006, and October 1 of each fiscal year thereafter through fiscal year 2011, if a State has not enacted or is not enforcing a law described in subsection (a), the Secretary shall withhold an amount equal to 8 percent of the amounts to be apportioned to the State on that date under each of paragraphs (1), (3), and (4) of section 104(b).[1]

(2) FISCAL YEAR 2012 AND THEREAFTER.—On October 1, 2011, and October 1 of each fiscal year thereafter, if a State has not enacted or is not enforcing a law described in subsection (a), the Secretary shall withhold an amount equal to 6 percent of the amounts to be apportioned to the State on that date under each of paragraphs (1) and (2) of section 104(b).

(3) FAILURE TO COMPLY.—If, within 4 years from the date that an apportionment for a State is withheld in accordance with this subsection, the Secretary determines that the State has enacted and is enforcing a law described in subsection (a), the apportionment of the State shall be increased by an amount equal to the amount withheld. If, at the end of such 4-year period, any State has not enacted or is not enforcing a law described in subsection (a) any amounts so withheld from such State shall lapse.

(f) AUTHORIZATION OF APPROPRIATIONS.—

(1) In general.—There are authorized to be appropriated out of the Highway Trust Fund (other than the Mass Transit Account) to carry out this section $55,000,000 for fiscal year 1998, $65,000,000 for fiscal year 1999, $80,000,000 for fiscal year 2000, $90,000,000 for fiscal year 2001, $100,000,000 for fiscal year 2002, $110,000,000 for fiscal year 2003, $110,000,000 for fiscal year 2004, and $110,000,000 for fiscal year 2005 $91,315,068 for the period of October 1, 2004, through July 30, 2005.[2]

(2) Availability of funds.—Notwithstanding section 118(b), the funds authorized by this subsection shall remain available until expended.

(Added Pub. L. 105–178, title I, §1404(a), June 9, 1998, 112 Stat. 240; amended Pub. L. 108–88, §6(a)(2), Sept. 30, 2003, 117 Stat. 1119; Pub. L. 108–202, §6(b), Feb. 29, 2004, 118 Stat. 483; Pub. L. 108–224, §5(b), Apr. 30, 2004, 118 Stat. 632; Pub. L. 108–263, §5(b), June 30, 2004, 118 Stat. 703; Pub. L. 108–280, §5(b), July 30, 2004, 118 Stat. 881; Pub. L. 108–310, §6(a)(2), Sept. 30, 2004, 118 Stat. 1152; Pub. L. 109–14, §5(a)(2), May 31, 2005, 119 Stat. 329; Pub. L. 109–20, §5(a)(2), July 1, 2005, 119 Stat. 351; Pub. L. 109–35, §5(a)(2), July 20, 2005, 119 Stat. 384; Pub. L. 109–37, §5(a)(2), July 22, 2005, 119 Stat. 399; Pub. L. 109–40, §5(a)(2), July 28, 2005, 119 Stat. 416; Pub. L. 109–59, title I, §1407(a), (b), Aug. 10, 2005, 119 Stat. 1231; Pub. L. 112–141, div. A, title I, §1404(i), July 6, 2012, 126 Stat. 559; Pub. L. 114–94, div. A, title I, §1446(a)(9), Dec. 4, 2015, 129 Stat. 1437.)

[1] See References in Text note below.

[2] So in original. The words "$91,315,068 for the period of October 1, 2004, through July 30, 2005" probably should not appear.

§164. Minimum penalties for repeat offenders for driving while intoxicated or driving under the influence

(a) Definitions.—In this section, the following definitions apply:

(1) 24-7 sobriety program.—The term "24-7 sobriety program" has the meaning given the term in section 405(d)(7)(A).

(2) Alcohol concentration.—The term "alcohol concentration" means grams of alcohol per 100 milliliters of blood or grams of alcohol per 210 liters of breath.

(3) Driving while intoxicated; driving under the influence.—The terms "driving while intoxicated" and "driving under the influence" mean driving or being in actual physical control of a motor vehicle while having an alcohol concentration above the permitted limit as established by each State.

(4) Motor vehicle.—The term "motor vehicle" means a vehicle driven or drawn by mechanical power and manufactured primarily for use on public highways, but does not include a vehicle operated solely on a rail line or a commercial vehicle.

(5) Repeat intoxicated driver law.—The term "repeat intoxicated driver law" means a State law or combination of laws or programs that provides, as a minimum penalty, that an individual convicted of a second or subsequent offense for driving while intoxicated or driving under the influence after a previous conviction for that offense shall—

(A) receive, for a period of not less than 1 year—

(i) a suspension of all driving privileges;

(ii) a restriction on driving privileges that limits the individual to operating only motor vehicles with an ignition interlock device installed, unless a special exception applies;

(iii) a restriction on driving privileges that limits the individual to operating motor vehicles only if participating in, and complying with, a 24-7 sobriety program; or

(iv) any combination of clauses (i) through (iii);

(B) receive an assessment of the individual's degree of abuse of alcohol and treatment as appropriate; and

(C) receive—

(i) in the case of the second offense—

(I) an assignment of not less than 30 days of community service; or

(II) not less than 5 days of imprisonment (unless the State certifies that the general practice is that such an individual will be incarcerated); and

(ii) in the case of the third or subsequent offense—

(I) an assignment of not less than 60 days of community service; or

(II) not less than 10 days of imprisonment (unless the State certifies that the general practice is that such an individual will receive 10 days of incarceration).

(6) SPECIAL EXCEPTION.—The term "special exception" means an exception under a State alcohol-ignition interlock law for the following circumstances:

(A) The individual is required to operate an employer's motor vehicle in the course and scope of employment and the business entity that owns the vehicle is not owned or controlled by the individual.

(B) The individual is certified by a medical doctor as being unable to provide a deep lung breath sample for analysis by an ignition interlock device.

(b) TRANSFER OF FUNDS.—

(1) FISCAL YEARS 2001 AND 2002.—On October 1, 2000, and October 1, 2001, if a State has not enacted or is not enforcing a repeat intoxicated driver law, the Secretary shall transfer an amount equal to 1½ percent of the funds apportioned to the State on that date under each of paragraphs (1), (3), and (4) of section 104(b) [1] to the apportionment of the State under section 402—

(A) to be used for alcohol- or multiple substance-impaired driving countermeasures; or

(B) to be directed to State and local law enforcement agencies for enforcement of laws prohibiting driving while intoxicated, driving while multiple substance-impaired, or driving under the influence and other related laws (including regulations), including the purchase of equipment, the training of officers, and the use of additional personnel for specific alcohol- or multiple substance-impaired driving countermeasures, dedicated to enforcement of the laws (including regulations).

(2) FISCAL YEAR 2022 AND THEREAFTER.—

(A) RESERVATION OF FUNDS.—

(i) IN GENERAL.—On October 1, 2021, and each October 1 thereafter, in the case of a State described in clause (ii), the Secretary shall reserve an amount equal to 2.5 percent of the funds to be apportioned to the State on that date under each of paragraphs (1) and (2) of section 104(b) until the State certifies to the Secretary the means by which the State will use those reserved funds in accordance with subparagraphs (A) and (B) of paragraph (1), and paragraph (3).

(ii) STATES DESCRIBED.—A State referred to in clause (i) is a State—

(I) that has not enacted or is not enforcing a repeat intoxicated driver law; and

(II) for which the Secretary determined for the prior fiscal year that the State had not enacted or was not enforcing a repeat intoxicated driver law.

(B) TRANSFER OF FUNDS.—As soon as practicable after the date of receipt of a certification from a State under subparagraph (A)(i), the Secretary shall—

(i) transfer the reserved funds identified by the State for use as described in subparagraphs (A) and (B) of paragraph (1) to the apportionment of the State under section 402; and

(ii) release the reserved funds identified by the State as described in paragraph (3).

(3) USE FOR HIGHWAY SAFETY IMPROVEMENT PROGRAM.—

(A) IN GENERAL.—A State may elect to use all or a portion of the funds reserved under paragraph (2) for activities eligible under section 148.

(B) STATE DEPARTMENTS OF TRANSPORTATION.—If the State makes an election under subparagraph (A), the funds shall be transferred to the department of transportation of the State, which shall be responsible for the administration of the funds.

(4) FEDERAL SHARE.—The Federal share of the cost of a project carried out with funds transferred under paragraph (1) or (2), or used under paragraph (3), shall be 100 percent.

(5) DERIVATION OF AMOUNT TO BE TRANSFERRED.—The amount to be transferred or released under paragraph (2) may be derived from the following:

(A) The apportionment of the State under section 104(b)(1).

(B) The apportionment of the State under section 104(b)(2).

(6) TRANSFER OF OBLIGATION AUTHORITY.—

(A) IN GENERAL.—If the Secretary transfers under this subsection any funds to the apportionment of a State under section 402 for a fiscal year, the Secretary shall transfer an amount, determined under subparagraph (B), of obligation authority distributed for the fiscal year to the State for Federal-aid highways and highway safety construction programs for carrying out projects under section 402.

(B) AMOUNT.—The amount of obligation authority referred to in subparagraph (A) shall be determined by multiplying—

(i) the amount of funds transferred under subparagraph (A) to the apportionment of the State under section 402 for the fiscal year, by

(ii) the ratio that—

(I) the amount of obligation authority distributed for the fiscal year to the State for Federal-aid highways and highway safety construction programs, bears to

(II) the total of the sums apportioned to the State for Federal-aid highways and highway safety construction programs (excluding sums not subject to any obligation limitation) for the fiscal year.

(7) LIMITATION ON APPLICABILITY OF OBLIGATION LIMITATION.—Notwithstanding

any other provision of law, no limitation on the total of obligations for highway safety programs under section 402 shall apply to funds transferred under this subsection to the apportionment of a State under such section.

(Added Pub. L. 105–178, title I, §1406(a), as added Pub. L. 105–206, title IX, §9005(a), July 22, 1998, 112 Stat. 845; amended Pub. L. 109–59, title I, §1401(a)(3)(C), Aug. 10, 2005, 119 Stat. 1225; Pub. L. 110–244, title I, §115, June 6, 2008, 122 Stat. 1606; Pub. L. 112–141, div. A, title I, §1403, July 6, 2012, 126 Stat. 556; Pub. L. 114–94, div. A, title I, §§1414, 1446(a)(10), Dec. 4, 2015, 129 Stat. 1420, 1437; Pub. L. 117–58, div. A, title I, §11131(b), div. B, title IV, §24107, Nov. 15, 2021, 135 Stat. 510, 807.)

---

1 See References in Text note below.

§165. TERRITORIAL AND PUERTO RICO HIGHWAY PROGRAM

(a) DIVISION OF FUNDS.—Of funds made available in a fiscal year for the territorial and Puerto Rico highway program—

(1) for the Puerto Rico highway program under subsection (b)—
(A) $173,010,000 shall be for fiscal year 2022;
(B) $176,960,000 shall be for fiscal year 2023;
(C) $180,120,000 shall be for fiscal year 2024;
(D) $183,675,000 shall be for fiscal year 2025; and
(E) $187,230,000 shall be for fiscal year 2026; and

(2) for the territorial highway program under subsection (c)—
(A) $45,990,000 shall be for fiscal year 2022;
(B) $47,040,000 shall be for fiscal year 2023;
(C) $47,880,000 shall be for fiscal year 2024;
(D) $48,825,000 shall be for fiscal year 2025; and
(E) $49,770,000 shall be for fiscal year 2026.

(b) PUERTO RICO HIGHWAY PROGRAM.—

(1) IN GENERAL.—The Secretary shall allocate funds made available to carry out this subsection to the Commonwealth of Puerto Rico to carry out a highway program in the Commonwealth.

(2) TREATMENT OF FUNDS.—Amounts made available to carry out this subsection for a fiscal year shall be administered as follows:

(A) APPORTIONMENT.—

(i) IN GENERAL.—For the purpose of imposing any penalty under this title or title 49, the amounts shall be treated as being apportioned to Puerto Rico under sections 104(b) and 144 (as in effect for fiscal year 1997) for each program funded under those sections in an amount determined by multiplying—

(I) the aggregate of the amounts for the fiscal year; by

(II) the proportion that—

(aa) the amount of funds apportioned to Puerto Rico for each such program for fiscal year 1997; bears to

(bb) the total amount of funds apportioned to Puerto Rico for all such programs for fiscal year 1997.

(ii) EXCEPTION.—Funds identified under clause (i) as having been apportioned for the national highway system, the surface transportation block grant program, and the Interstate maintenance program shall be deemed to have been apportioned 50 percent for the national highway performance program and 50 percent for the surface transportation program for purposes of imposing such penalties.

(B) PENALTY.—The amounts treated as being apportioned to Puerto Rico under each section referred to in subparagraph (A) shall be deemed to be required to be apportioned to Puerto Rico under that section for purposes of the imposition of any penalty under this title or title 49.

(C) ELIGIBLE USES OF FUNDS.—Of amounts allocated to Puerto Rico for the Puerto Rico Highway Program for a fiscal year—

(i) at least 50 percent shall be available only for purposes eligible under section 119;

(ii) at least 25 percent shall be available only for purposes eligible under section 148; and

(iii) any remaining funds may be obligated for activities eligible under chapter 1 and preventative maintenance on the National Highway System.

(3) EFFECT ON APPORTIONMENTS.—Except as otherwise specifically provided, Puerto Rico shall not be eligible to receive funds apportioned to States under this title.

(c) TERRITORIAL HIGHWAY PROGRAM.—

(1) TERRITORY DEFINED.—In this subsection, the term "territory" means any of the following territories of the United States:

(A) American Samoa.

(B) The Commonwealth of the Northern Mariana Islands.

(C) Guam.

(D) The United States Virgin Islands.

(2) PROGRAM.—

(A) IN GENERAL.—Recognizing the mutual benefits that will accrue to the territories and the United States from the improvement of highways in the territories, the Secretary may carry out a program to assist each government of a territory in the construction and improvement of a system of arterial and collector highways, and necessary inter-island connectors, that is—

(i) designated by the Governor or chief executive officer of each territory; and

(ii) approved by the Secretary.

(B) FEDERAL SHARE.—The Federal share of Federal financial assistance provided to territories under this subsection shall be in accordance with section 120(g).

(3) TECHNICAL ASSISTANCE.—

(A) IN GENERAL.—To continue a long-range highway development program, the Secretary may provide technical assistance to the governments of the territories to enable the territories, on a continuing basis—

(i) to engage in highway planning;

(ii) to conduct environmental evaluations;

(iii) to administer right-of-way acquisition and relocation assistance programs; and

(iv) to design, construct, operate, and maintain a system of arterial and collector highways, including necessary inter-island connectors.

(B) FORM AND TERMS OF ASSISTANCE.—Technical assistance provided under subparagraph (A), and the terms for the sharing of information among territories receiving the technical assistance, shall be included in the agreement required by paragraph (5).

(4) NONAPPLICABILITY OF CERTAIN PROVISIONS.—

(A) IN GENERAL.—Except to the extent that provisions of this chapter are determined by the Secretary to be inconsistent with the needs of the territories and the intent of this subsection, this chapter (other than provisions of this chapter relating to the apportionment and allocation of funds) shall apply to funds made available under this subsection.

(B) APPLICABLE PROVISIONS.—The agreement required by paragraph (5) for each territory shall identify the sections of this chapter that are applicable to that territory and the extent of the applicability of those sections.

(5) AGREEMENT.—

(A) IN GENERAL. Except as provided in subparagraph (D), none of the funds made available under this subsection shall be available for obligation or expenditure with respect to any territory until the chief executive officer of the territory has entered into an agreement (including an agreement entered into under section 215 as in effect on the day before the enactment of this section) with the Secretary providing that the government of the territory shall—

(i) implement the program in accordance with applicable provisions of this chapter and paragraph (4);

(ii) design and construct a system of arterial and collector highways, including necessary inter-island connectors, in accordance with standards that are—

(I) appropriate for each territory; and

(II) approved by the Secretary;

(iii) provide for the maintenance of facilities constructed or operated under this subsection in a condition to adequately serve the needs of present and future traffic; and

(iv) implement standards for traffic operations and uniform traffic control devices that are approved by the Secretary.

(B) TECHNICAL ASSISTANCE.—The agreement required by subparagraph (A) shall—

(i) specify the kind of technical assistance to be provided under the program;

(ii) include appropriate provisions regarding information sharing among the territories; and

(iii) delineate the oversight role and responsibilities of the territories and the Secretary.

(C) REVIEW AND REVISION OF AGREEMENT.—The agreement entered into under subparagraph (A) shall be reevaluated and, as necessary, revised, at least every 2 years.

(D) EXISTING AGREEMENTS.—With respect to an agreement under this subsection or an agreement entered into under section 215 of this title as in effect on the day before the date of enactment of this subsection—

(i) the agreement shall continue in force until replaced by an agreement entered into in accordance with subparagraph (A); and

(ii) amounts made available under this subsection under the existing agreement shall be available for obligation or expenditure so long as the agreement, or the existing agreement entered into under subparagraph (A), is in effect.

(6) ELIGIBLE USES OF FUNDS.—

(A) IN GENERAL.—Funds made available under this subsection may be used only for the following projects and activities carried out in a territory:

(i) Eligible surface transportation block grant program projects described in section 133(b).

(ii) Cost-effective, preventive maintenance consistent with section 116(e).

(iii) Ferry boats, terminal facilities, and approaches, in accordance with subsections (b) and (c) of section 129.

(iv) Engineering and economic surveys and investigations for the planning, and the financing, of future highway programs.

(v) Studies of the economy, safety, and convenience of highway use.

(vi) The regulation and equitable taxation of highway use.

(vii) Such research and development as are necessary in connection with the planning, design, and maintenance of the highway system.

(B) PROHIBITION ON USE OF FUNDS FOR ROUTINE MAINTENANCE.—None of the funds made available under this subsection shall be obligated or expended for routine maintenance.

(7) LOCATION OF PROJECTS.—Territorial highway program projects (other than those described in paragraphs (1), (2), (3), and (5) of section 133(c) and section 133(b)(13)) may not be undertaken on roads functionally classified as local.

(Added Pub. L. 109–59, title I, §1120(a), Aug. 10, 2005, 119 Stat. 1191; amended Pub. L. 112–141, div. A, title I, §1114(a), July 6, 2012, 126 Stat. 464; Pub. L. 114–94, div. A, title I, §§1109(c)(5), 1115, 1446(a)(11), Dec. 4, 2015, 129 Stat. 1343, 1349, 1438; Pub. L. 117–58, div. A, title I, §11126, Nov. 15, 2021, 135 Stat. 506.)

§166. HOV FACILITIES

(a) IN GENERAL.—

(1) AUTHORITY OF PUBLIC AUTHORITIES.—A public authority that has jurisdiction over the operation of a HOV facility shall establish the occupancy requirements of vehicles operating on the facility.

(2) OCCUPANCY REQUIREMENT.—Except as otherwise provided by this section, no fewer than two occupants per vehicle may be required for use of a HOV facility.

(b) EXCEPTIONS.—

(1) IN GENERAL.—Notwithstanding the occupancy requirement of subsection (a)(2), the exceptions in paragraphs (2) through (5) shall apply with respect to a public authority operating a HOV facility.

(2) MOTORCYCLES AND BICYCLES.—

(A) IN GENERAL.—Subject to subparagraph (B), the public authority shall allow motorcycles and bicycles to use the HOV facility.

(B) SAFETY EXCEPTION.—

(i) IN GENERAL.—A public authority may restrict use of the HOV facility by motorcycles or bicycles (or both) if the authority certifies to the Secretary that

such use would create a safety hazard and the Secretary accepts the certification.
(ii) ACCEPTANCE OF CERTIFICATION.—The Secretary may accept a certification under this subparagraph only after the Secretary publishes notice of the certification in the Federal Register and provides an opportunity for public comment.

(3) PUBLIC TRANSPORTATION VEHICLES.—The public authority may allow public transportation vehicles to use the HOV facility if the authority—

(A) establishes requirements for clearly identifying the vehicles;

(B) establishes procedures for enforcing the restrictions on the use of the facility by the vehicles; and

(C) provides equal access under the same rates, terms, and conditions for all public transportation vehicles and over-the-road buses serving the public.

(4) HIGH OCCUPANCY TOLL VEHICLES.—The public authority may allow vehicles not otherwise exempt pursuant to this subsection to use the HOV facility if the operators of the vehicles pay a toll charged by the authority for use of the facility and the authority—

(A) establishes a program that addresses how motorists can enroll and participate in the toll program;

(B) develops, manages, and maintains a system that will automatically collect the toll; and

(C) establishes policies and procedures to—

(i) manage the demand to use the facility by varying the toll amount that is charged;

(ii) enforce violations of use of the facility; and

(iii) ensure that over-the-road buses serving the public are provided access to the facility under the same rates, terms, and conditions as public transportation buses.

(5) LOW EMISSION AND ENERGY-EFFICIENT VEHICLES.—

(A) SPECIAL RULE.—Before September 30, 2025, if a public authority establishes procedures for enforcing the restrictions on the use of a HOV facility by vehicles described in clauses (i) and (ii), the public authority may allow the use of the HOV facility by—

(i) alternative fuel vehicles; and

(ii) any motor vehicle described in section 30D(d)(1) of the Internal Revenue Code of 1986.

(B) OTHER LOW EMISSION AND ENERGY-EFFICIENT VEHICLES.—Before September 30, 2019, the public authority may allow vehicles certified as low emission and energy-efficient vehicles under subsection (e), and labeled in accordance with subsection (e), to use the HOV facility if the operators of the vehicles pay a toll charged by the authority for use of the facility and the authority—

(i) establishes a program that addresses the selection of vehicles under this paragraph; and

(ii) establishes procedures for enforcing the restrictions on the use of the facility by the vehicles.

(C) AMOUNT OF TOLLS.—Under this paragraph, a public authority may charge no toll or may charge a toll that is less than or equal to tolls charged under paragraph (4).

(6) BLOOD TRANSPORT VEHICLES.—The public authority may allow blood transport vehicles that are transporting blood between a collection point and a hospital or storage center to use the HOV facility if the public authority establishes requirements for clearly identifying such vehicles.

(c) REQUIREMENTS APPLICABLE TO TOLLS.—

(1) IN GENERAL.—Notwithstanding section 301, tolls may be charged under paragraphs (4) and (5) of subsection (b), subject to the requirements of section 129.

(2) TOLL REVENUE.—Toll revenue collected under this section is subject to the requirements of section 129(a)(3).

(d) HOV FACILITY MANAGEMENT, OPERATION, MONITORING, AND ENFORCEMENT.—

(1) IN GENERAL.—A public authority that allows vehicles to use a HOV facility under paragraph (4) or (5) of subsection (b) shall submit to the Secretary a report demonstrating that the facility is not already degraded, and that the presence of the vehicles will not cause the facility to become degraded, and certify to the Secretary that the authority will carry out the following responsibilities with respect to the facility:

(A) Establishing, managing, and supporting a performance monitoring, evaluation, and reporting program for the facility that provides for continuous monitoring, assessment, and reporting on the impacts that the vehicles may have on the operation of the facility and adjacent highways and submitting to the Secretary annual reports of those impacts.

(B) Establishing, managing, and supporting an enforcement program that ensures that the facility is being operated in accordance with the requirements of this section.

(C) Limiting or discontinuing the use of the facility by the vehicles whenever the operation of the facility is degraded.

(D) MAINTENANCE OF OPERATING PERFORMANCE.—

(i) SUBMISSION OF PLAN.—Not later than 180 days after the date on which a facility is degraded under paragraph (2), the public authority with jurisdiction over the facility shall submit to the Secretary for approval a plan that details the actions the public authority will take to make significant progress toward bringing the facility into compliance with the minimum average operating speed performance standard through changes to the operation of the facility, including—

(I) increasing the occupancy requirement for HOV lanes;

(II) varying the toll charged to vehicles allowed under subsection (b) to reduce demand;

(III) discontinuing allowing non-HOV vehicles to use HOV lanes under subsection (b); or

(IV) increasing the available capacity of the HOV facility.

(ii) NOTICE OF APPROVAL OR DISAPPROVAL.—Not later than 60 days after the date of receipt of a plan under clause (i), the Secretary shall provide to the public authority a written notice indicating whether the Secretary has approved or disapproved the plan based on a determination of whether the implementation of the plan will make significant progress toward bringing the HOV facility into compliance with the minimum average operating speed performance standard.

(iii) ANNUAL PROGRESS UPDATES.—Until the date on which the Secretary determines that the public authority has brought the HOV facility into compliance with this subsection, the public authority shall submit annual updates that describe—

(I) the actions taken to bring the HOV facility into compliance; and

(II) the progress made by those actions.

(E) COMPLIANCE.—If the public authority fails to bring a facility into compliance under subparagraph (D), the Secretary shall subject the public authority to appropriate program sanctions under section 1.36 of title 23, Code of Federal Regulations (or successor regulations), until the performance is no longer degraded.

(F) WAIVER.—

(i) IN GENERAL.—Upon the request of a public authority, the Secretary may waive the compliance requirements of subparagraph (E), if the Secretary determines that—

(I) the waiver is in the best interest of the traveling public;

(II) the public authority is meeting the conditions under subparagraph (D); and

(III) the public authority has made a good faith effort to improve the performance of the facility.

(ii) CONDITION.—The Secretary may require, as a condition of providing a waiver under this subparagraph, that a public authority take additional actions, as determined by the Secretary, to maximize the operating speed performance of the facility, even if such performance is below the level set under paragraph (2).

(2) DEGRADED FACILITY.—

(A) DEFINITION OF MINIMUM AVERAGE OPERATING SPEED.—In this paragraph, the term "minimum average operating speed" means—

(i) 45 miles per hour, in the case of a HOV facility with a speed limit of 50 miles per hour or greater; and

(ii) not more than 10 miles per hour below the speed limit, in the case of a HOV facility with a speed limit of less than 50 miles per hour.

(B) STANDARD FOR DETERMINING DEGRADED FACILITY.—For purposes of paragraph (1), the operation of a HOV facility shall be considered to be degraded if vehicles operating on the facility are failing to maintain a minimum average operating speed 90 percent of the time over a consecutive 180-day period during morning or evening weekday peak hour periods (or both).

(C) MANAGEMENT OF LOW EMISSION AND ENERGY-EFFICIENT VEHICLES.—In managing the use of HOV lanes by low emission and energy-efficient vehicles that do not meet applicable occupancy requirements, a public authority may increase the percentages described in subsection (f)(3)(B)(i).

(e) CERTIFICATION OF LOW EMISSION AND ENERGY-EFFICIENT VEHICLES.—Not later than 180 days after the date of enactment of this section, the Administrator of the

Environmental Protection Agency shall—

(1) issue a final rule establishing requirements for certification of vehicles as low emission and energy-efficient vehicles for purposes of this section and requirements for the labeling of the vehicles; and

(2) establish guidelines and procedures for making the vehicle comparisons and performance calculations described in subsection (f)(3)(B), in accordance with section 32908(b) of title 49.

(f) DEFINITIONS.—In this section, the following definitions apply:

(1) ALTERNATIVE FUEL VEHICLE.—The term "alternative fuel vehicle" means a vehicle that is solely operating on—

(A) methanol, denatured ethanol, or other alcohols;

(B) a mixture containing at least 85 percent of methanol, denatured ethanol, and other alcohols by volume with gasoline or other fuels;

(C) natural gas;

(D) liquefied petroleum gas;

(E) hydrogen;

(F) coal derived liquid fuels;

(G) fuels (except alcohol) derived from biological materials;

(H) electricity (including electricity from solar energy); or

(I) any other fuel that the Secretary prescribes by regulation that is not substantially petroleum and that would yield substantial energy security and environmental benefits, including fuels regulated under section 490 of title 10, Code of Federal Regulations (or successor regulations).

(2) HOV FACILITY.—The term "HOV facility" means a high occupancy vehicle facility.

(3) LOW EMISSION AND ENERGY-EFFICIENT VEHICLE.—The term "low emission and energy-efficient vehicle" means a vehicle that—

(A) has been certified by the Administrator as meeting the Tier II emission level established in regulations prescribed by the Administrator under section 202(i) of the Clean Air Act (42 U.S.C. 7521(i)) for that make and model year vehicle; and

(B)(i) is certified by the Administrator of the Environmental Protection Agency, in consultation with the manufacturer, to have achieved not less than a 50-percent increase in city fuel economy or not less than a 25-percent increase in combined city-highway fuel economy (or such greater percentage of city or city-highway fuel economy as may be determined by a State under subsection (d)(2)(C)) relative to a comparable vehicle that is an internal combustion gasoline fueled vehicle (other than a vehicle that has propulsion energy from onboard hybrid sources); or

(ii) is an alternative fuel vehicle.

(4) OVER-THE-ROAD BUS.—The term "over-the-road bus" has the meaning given the term in section 301 of the Americans with Disabilities Act of 1990 (42 U.S.C. 12181).

(5) PUBLIC AUTHORITY.—The term "public authority" as used with respect to a HOV facility, means a State, interstate compact of States, public entity designated by a State, or local government having jurisdiction over the operation of the facility.

(6) PUBLIC TRANSPORTATION VEHICLE.—The term "public transportation vehicle" means a vehicle that—

(A) provides designated public transportation (as defined in section 221 of the Americans with Disabilities Act of 1990 (42 U.S.C. 12141) or provides public school transportation (to and from public or private primary, secondary, or tertiary schools); and

(B)(i) is owned or operated by a public entity;

(ii) is operated under a contract with a public entity; or

(iii) is operated pursuant to a license by the Secretary or a public authority to provide motorbus or school vehicle transportation services to the public.

(g) CONSULTATION OF MPO.—If a HOV facility charging tolls under paragraph (4) or (5) of subsection (b) is on the Interstate System and located in a metropolitan planning area established in accordance with section 134, the public authority shall consult with the metropolitan planning organization for the area concerning the placement and amount of tolls on the facility.

(Added Pub. L. 109–59, title I, §1121(a), Aug. 10, 2005, 119 Stat. 1192; amended Pub. L. 110–244, title I, §101(p), June 6, 2008, 122 Stat. 1576; Pub. L. 112–141, div. A, title I, §1514, July 6, 2012, 126 Stat. 572; Pub. L. 114–94, div. A, title I, §1411(b), Dec. 4, 2015, 129 Stat. 1413; Pub. L. 117–58, div. A, title I, §§11525(k), 11527, Nov. 15, 2021, 135 Stat. 607, 610.)

§167. NATIONAL HIGHWAY FREIGHT PROGRAM

(a) IN GENERAL.—

(1) POLICY.—It is the policy of the United States to improve the condition and performance of the National Highway Freight Network established under this section to ensure that the Network provides the foundation for the United States to compete in the global economy and achieve the goals described in subsection (b).

(2) ESTABLISHMENT.—In support of the goals described in subsection (b), the Administrator of the Federal Highway Administration shall establish a national highway freight program in accordance with this section to improve the efficient movement of freight on the National Highway Freight Network.

(b) GOALS.—The goals of the national highway freight program are—

(1) to invest in infrastructure improvements and to implement operational improvements on the highways of the United States that—

(A) strengthen the contribution of the National Highway Freight Network to the economic competitiveness of the United States;

(B) reduce congestion and bottlenecks on the National Highway Freight Network;

(C) reduce the cost of freight transportation;

(D) improve the year-round reliability of freight transportation; and

(E) increase productivity, particularly for domestic industries and businesses that create high-value jobs;

(2) to improve the safety, security, efficiency, and resiliency of freight transportation in rural and urban areas;

(3) to improve the state of good repair of the National Highway Freight Network;

(4) to use innovation and advanced technology to improve the safety, efficiency, and reliability of the National Highway Freight Network;

(5) to improve the efficiency and productivity of the National Highway Freight Network;

(6) to improve the flexibility of States to support multi-State corridor planning and the creation of multi-State organizations to increase the ability of States to address highway freight connectivity; and

(7) to reduce the environmental impacts of freight movement on the National Highway Freight Network.

(c) ESTABLISHMENT OF NATIONAL HIGHWAY FREIGHT NETWORK.—

(1) IN GENERAL.—The Administrator shall establish a National Highway Freight Network in accordance with this section to strategically direct Federal resources and policies toward improved performance of the Network.

(2) NETWORK COMPONENTS.—The National Highway Freight Network shall consist of—

(A) the primary highway freight system, as designated under subsection (d);

(B) critical rural freight corridors established under subsection (e);

(C) critical urban freight corridors established under subsection (f); and

(D) the portions of the Interstate System not designated as part of the primary highway freight system.

(d) DESIGNATION AND REDESIGNATION OF THE PRIMARY HIGHWAY FREIGHT SYSTEM.—

(1) INITIAL DESIGNATION OF PRIMARY HIGHWAY FREIGHT SYSTEM.—The initial designation of the primary highway freight system shall be the 41,518-mile network identified during the designation process for the primary freight network under section 167(d) of this title, as in effect on the day before the date of enactment of the FAST Act.

(2) REDESIGNATION OF PRIMARY HIGHWAY FREIGHT SYSTEM.—

(A) IN GENERAL.—Beginning 5 years after the date of enactment of the FAST Act, and every 5 years thereafter, using the designation factors described in subparagraph (E), the Administrator shall redesignate the primary highway freight system.

(B) REDESIGNATION MILEAGE.—Each redesignation may increase the mileage on the primary highway freight system by not more than 3 percent of the total mileage of the system.

(C) USE OF MEASURABLE DATA.—In redesignating the primary highway freight system, to the maximum extent practicable, the Administrator shall use measurable data to assess the significance of goods movement, including consideration of points of origin, destinations, and linking components of the United States global and domestic supply chains.

(D) INPUT.—In redesignating the primary highway freight system, the Administrator shall provide an opportunity for State freight advisory committees, as applicable, to submit additional miles for consideration.

(E) FACTORS FOR REDESIGNATION.—In redesignating the primary highway freight system, the Administrator shall consider—

(i) changes in the origins and destinations of freight movement in, to, and from the United States;

(ii) changes in the percentage of annual daily truck traffic in the annual average daily traffic on principal arterials;

(iii) changes in the location of key facilities;

(iv) land and water ports of entry;

(v) access to energy exploration, development, installation, or production areas;

(vi) access to other freight intermodal facilities, including rail, air, water, and pipelines facilities;

(vii) the total freight tonnage and value moved via highways;

(viii) significant freight bottlenecks, as identified by the Administrator;

(ix) the significance of goods movement on principal arterials, including consideration of global and domestic supply chains;

(x) critical emerging freight corridors and critical commerce corridors; and

(xi) network connectivity.

(e) CRITICAL RURAL FREIGHT CORRIDORS.—

(1) IN GENERAL.—A State may designate a public road within the borders of the State as a critical rural freight corridor if the public road is not in an urbanized area and—

(A) is a rural principal arterial roadway and has a minimum of 25 percent of the annual average daily traffic of the road measured in passenger vehicle equivalent units from trucks (Federal Highway Administration vehicle class 8 to 13);

(B) provides access to energy exploration, development, installation, or production areas;

(C) connects the primary highway freight system, a roadway described in subparagraph (A) or (B), or the Interstate System to facilities that handle more than—

(i) 50,000 20-foot equivalent units per year; or

(ii) 500,000 tons per year of bulk commodities;

(D) provides access to—

(i) a grain elevator;

(ii) an agricultural facility;

(iii) a mining facility;

(iv) a forestry facility; or

(v) an intermodal facility;

(E) connects to an international port of entry;

(F) provides access to significant air, rail, water, or other freight facilities in the State; or

(G) is, in the determination of the State, vital to improving the efficient movement of freight of importance to the economy of the State.

(2) LIMITATION.—A State may designate as critical rural freight corridors a maximum of 300 miles of highway or 20 percent of the primary highway freight system mileage in the State, whichever is greater.

(3) RURAL STATES.—Notwithstanding paragraph (2), a State with a population per square mile of area that is less than the national average, based on the 2010 census, may designate as critical rural freight corridors a maximum of 600 miles of highway or 25 percent of the primary highway freight system mileage in the State, whichever is greater.

(f) CRITICAL URBAN FREIGHT CORRIDORS.—

(1) URBANIZED AREA WITH POPULATION OF 500,000 OR MORE.—In an urbanized area with a population of 500,000 or more individuals, the representative metropolitan planning organization, in consultation with the State, may designate a public road within the borders of that area of the State as a critical urban freight corridor.

(2) URBANIZED AREA WITH A POPULATION LESS THAN 500,000.—In an urbanized area with a population of less than 500,000 individuals, the State, in consultation with the representative metropolitan planning organization, may designate a public road within the borders of that area of the State as a critical urban freight corridor.

(3) REQUIREMENTS FOR DESIGNATION.—A designation may be made under paragraph (1) or (2) if the public road—

    (A) is in an urbanized area, regardless of population; and

    (B)(i) connects an intermodal facility to—

        (I) the primary highway freight system;

        (II) the Interstate System; or

        (III) an intermodal freight facility;

    (ii) is located within a corridor of a route on the primary highway freight system and provides an alternative highway option important to goods movement;

    (iii) serves a major freight generator, logistic center, or manufacturing and warehouse industrial land; or

    (iv) is important to the movement of freight within the region, as determined by the metropolitan planning organization or the State.

(4) LIMITATION.—For each State, a maximum of 150 miles of highway or 10 percent of the primary highway freight system mileage in the State, whichever is greater, may be designated as a critical urban freight corridor under paragraphs (1) and (2).

(g) DESIGNATION AND CERTIFICATION.—

(1) DESIGNATION.—States and metropolitan planning organizations may designate corridors under subsections (e) and (f) and submit the designated corridors to the Administrator on a rolling basis.

(2) CERTIFICATION.—Each State or metropolitan planning organization that designates a corridor under subsection (e) or (f) shall certify to the Administrator that the designated corridor meets the requirements of the applicable subsection.

(h) USE OF APPORTIONED FUNDS.—

(1) IN GENERAL.—A State shall obligate funds apportioned to the State under section 104(b)(5) to improve the movement of freight on the National Highway Freight Network.

(2) FORMULA.—The Administrator shall calculate for each State the proportion that—

    (A) the total mileage in the State designated as part of the primary highway freight system; bears to

    (B) the total mileage of the primary highway freight system in all States.

(3) USE OF FUNDS.—

    (A) STATES WITH HIGH PRIMARY HIGHWAY FREIGHT SYSTEM MILEAGE.—If the proportion of a State under paragraph (2) is greater than or equal to 2 percent, the State may obligate funds apportioned to the State under section 104(b)(5) for projects on—

(i) the primary highway freight system;

(ii) critical rural freight corridors; and

(iii) critical urban freight corridors.

(B) STATES WITH LOW PRIMARY HIGHWAY FREIGHT SYSTEM MILEAGE.—If the proportion of a State under paragraph (2) is less than 2 percent, the State may obligate funds apportioned to the State under section 104(b)(5) for projects on any component of the National Highway Freight Network.

(4) FREIGHT PLANNING.—Notwithstanding any other provision of law, effective beginning 2 years after the date of enactment of the FAST Act, a State may not obligate funds apportioned to the State under section 104(b)(5) unless the State has developed a freight plan in accordance with section 70202 of title 49, except that the multimodal component of the plan may be incomplete before an obligation may be made under this section.

(5) ELIGIBILITY.—

(A) IN GENERAL.—Except as provided in this subsection, for a project to be eligible for funding under this section the project shall—

(i) contribute to the efficient movement of freight on the National Highway Freight Network; and

(ii) be identified in a freight investment plan included in a freight plan of the State that is in effect.

(B) OTHER PROJECTS.—For each fiscal year, a State may obligate not more than 30 percent of the total apportionment of the State under section 104(b)(5) for freight intermodal or freight rail projects, including projects—

(i) within the boundaries of public or private freight rail or water facilities (including ports);

(ii) that provide surface transportation infrastructure necessary to facilitate direct intermodal interchange, transfer, and access into or out of the facility;

(iii) for the modernization or rehabilitation of a lock and dam, if the Secretary determines that the project—

(I) is functionally connected to the National Highway Freight Network; and

(II) is likely to reduce on-road mobile source emissions; and

(iv) on a marine highway corridor, connector, or crossing designated by the Secretary under section 55601(c) of title 46 (including an inland waterway corridor, connector, or crossing), if the Secretary determines that the project—

(I) is functionally connected to the National Highway Freight Network; and

(II) is likely to reduce on-road mobile source emissions.

(C) ELIGIBLE PROJECTS.—Funds apportioned to the State under section 104(b)(5) for the national highway freight program may be obligated to carry out 1 or more of the following:

(i) Development phase activities, including planning, feasibility analysis, revenue forecasting, environmental review, preliminary engineering and design work, and other preconstruction activities.

(ii) Construction, reconstruction, rehabilitation, acquisition of real property (including land relating to the project and improvements to land), construction contingencies, acquisition of equipment, and operational improvements directly relating to improving system performance.

(iii) Intelligent transportation systems and other technology to improve the flow of freight, including intelligent freight transportation systems.

(iv) Efforts to reduce the environmental impacts of freight movement.

(v) Environmental and community mitigation for freight movement.

(vi) Railway-highway grade separation.

(vii) Geometric improvements to interchanges and ramps.

(viii) Truck-only lanes.

(ix) Climbing and runaway truck lanes.

(x) Adding or widening of shoulders.

(xi) Truck parking facilities eligible for funding under section 1401 of MAP–21 (23 U.S.C. 137 note).

(xii) Real-time traffic, truck parking, roadway condition, and multimodal transportation information systems.

(xiii) Electronic screening and credentialing systems for vehicles, including weigh-in-motion truck inspection technologies.

(xiv) Traffic signal optimization, including synchronized and adaptive signals.

(xv) Work zone management and information systems.

(xvi) Highway ramp metering.

(xvii) Electronic cargo and border security technologies that improve truck freight movement.

(xviii) Intelligent transportation systems that would increase truck freight efficiencies inside the boundaries of intermodal facilities.

(xix) Additional road capacity to address highway freight bottlenecks.

(xx) Physical separation of passenger vehicles from commercial motor freight.

(xxi) Enhancement of the resiliency of critical highway infrastructure, including highway infrastructure that supports national energy security, to improve the flow of freight.

(xxii) A highway or bridge project, other than a project described in clauses (i) through (xxi), to improve the flow of freight on the National Highway Freight Network.

(xxiii) Any other surface transportation project to improve the flow of freight into and out of a facility described in subparagraph (B).

(6) OTHER ELIGIBLE COSTS.—In addition to the eligible projects identified in paragraph (5), a State may use funds apportioned under section 104(b)(5) for—

(A) carrying out diesel retrofit or alternative fuel projects under section 149 for class 8 vehicles; and

(B) the necessary costs of—

(i) conducting analyses and data collection related to the national highway freight program;

(ii) developing and updating performance targets to carry out this section; and

(iii) reporting to the Administrator to comply with the freight performance target under section 150.

(7) APPLICABILITY OF PLANNING REQUIREMENTS.—Programming and expenditure

of funds for projects under this section shall be consistent with the requirements of sections 134 and 135.

(i) STATE PERFORMANCE TARGETS.—If the Administrator determines that a State has not met or made significant progress toward meeting the performance targets related to freight movement of the State established under section 150(d) by the date that is 2 years after the date of the establishment of the performance targets, the State shall include in the next report submitted under section 150(e) a description of the actions the State will undertake to achieve the targets, including—

(1) an identification of significant freight system trends, needs, and issues within the State;

(2) a description of the freight policies and strategies that will guide the freight-related transportation investments of the State;

(3) an inventory of freight bottlenecks within the State and a description of the ways in which the State is allocating national highway freight program funds to improve those bottlenecks; and

(4) a description of the actions the State will undertake to meet the performance targets of the State.

(j) INTELLIGENT FREIGHT TRANSPORTATION SYSTEM.—

(1) DEFINITION OF INTELLIGENT FREIGHT TRANSPORTATION SYSTEM.—In this section, the term "intelligent freight transportation system" means—

(A) innovative or intelligent technological transportation systems, infrastructure, or facilities, including elevated freight transportation facilities—

(i) in proximity to, or within, an existing right of way on a Federal-aid highway; or

(ii) that connect land ports-of entry [1] to existing Federal-aid highways; or

(B) communications or information processing systems that improve the efficiency, security, or safety of freight movements on the Federal-aid highway system, including to improve the conveyance of freight on dedicated intelligent freight lanes.

(2) OPERATING STANDARDS.—The Administrator shall determine whether there is a need for establishing operating standards for intelligent freight transportation systems.

(k) TREATMENT OF FREIGHT PROJECTS.—Notwithstanding any other provision of law, a freight project carried out under this section shall be treated as if the project were on a Federal-aid highway.

(Added Pub. L. 112–141, div. A, title I, §1115(a), July 6, 2012, 126 Stat. 468; amended Pub. L. 114–94, div. A, title I, §1116(a), Dec. 4, 2015, 129 Stat. 1349; Pub. L. 117–58, div. A, title I, §11114, title III, §13006(f), Nov. 15, 2021, 135 Stat. 479, 639.)

[1] *So in original.*

§168. INTEGRATION OF PLANNING AND ENVIRONMENTAL REVIEW

(a) DEFINITIONS.—In this section, the following definitions apply:

(1) ENVIRONMENTAL REVIEW PROCESS.—The term "environmental review process" has the meaning given the term in section 139(a).

(2) LEAD AGENCY.—The term "lead agency" has the meaning given the term in section 139(a).

(3) PLANNING PRODUCT.—The term "planning product" means a decision, analysis, study, or other documented information that is the result of an evaluation or decisionmaking process carried out by a metropolitan planning organization or a State, as appropriate, during metropolitan or statewide transportation planning under section 134 or 135, respectively.

(4) PROJECT.—The term "project" has the meaning given the term in section 139(a).

(5) PROJECT SPONSOR.—The term "project sponsor" has the meaning given the term in section 139(a).

(6) RELEVANT AGENCY.—The term "relevant agency" means the agency with authority under subparagraph (A) or (B) of subsection (b)(1).

(b) ADOPTION OR INCORPORATION BY REFERENCE OF PLANNING PRODUCTS FOR USE IN NEPA PROCEEDINGS.—

(1) IN GENERAL.—Subject to subsection (d) and to the maximum extent practicable and appropriate, the following agencies may adopt or incorporate by reference and use a planning product in proceedings relating to any class of action in the environmental review process of the project:

(A) The lead agency for a project, with respect to an environmental impact statement, environmental assessment, categorical exclusion, or other document prepared under the National Environmental Policy Act of 1969 (42 U.S.C. 4321 et seq.).

(B) The cooperating agency with responsibility under Federal law, with respect to the process for and completion of any environmental permit, approval, review, or study required for a project under any Federal law other than the National Environmental Policy Act of 1969 (42 U.S.C. 4321 et seq.), if consistent with that law.

(2) IDENTIFICATION.—If the relevant agency makes a determination to adopt or incorporate by reference and use a planning product, the relevant agency shall identify the agencies that participated in the development of the planning products.

(3) ADOPTION OR INCORPORATION BY REFERENCE OF PLANNING PRODUCTS.—The relevant agency may—

(A) adopt or incorporate by reference an entire planning product under paragraph (1); or

(B) select portions of a planning project under paragraph (1) for adoption or incorporation by reference.

(4) TIMING.—A determination under paragraph (1) with respect to the adoption or incorporation by reference of a planning product may—

(A) be made at the time the relevant agencies decide the appropriate scope of environmental review for the project; or

(B) occur later in the environmental review process, as appropriate.

(c) APPLICABILITY.—

(1) PLANNING DECISIONS.—The relevant agency in the environmental review process may adopt or incorporate by reference decisions from a planning product, including—

(A) whether tolling, private financial assistance, or other special financial measures are necessary to implement the project;

(B) a decision with respect to general travel corridor or modal choice, including a decision to implement corridor or subarea study recommendations to advance different modal solutions as separate projects with independent utility;

(C) the purpose and the need for the proposed action;

(D) preliminary screening of alternatives and elimination of unreasonable alternatives;

(E) a basic description of the environmental setting;

(F) a decision with respect to methodologies for analysis; and

(G) an identification of programmatic level mitigation for potential impacts of a project, including a programmatic mitigation plan developed in accordance with section 169, that the relevant agency determines are more effectively addressed on a national or regional scale, including—

(i) measures to avoid, minimize, and mitigate impacts at a national or regional scale of proposed transportation investments on environmental resources, including regional ecosystem and water resources; and

(ii) potential mitigation activities, locations, and investments.

(2) PLANNING ANALYSES.—The relevant agency in the environmental review process may adopt or incorporate by reference analyses from a planning product, including—

(A) travel demands;

(B) regional development and growth;

(C) local land use, growth management, and development;

(D) population and employment;

(E) natural and built environmental conditions;

(F) environmental resources and environmentally sensitive areas;

(G) potential environmental effects, including the identification of resources of concern and potential direct, indirect, and cumulative effects on those resources; and

(H) mitigation needs for a proposed project, or for programmatic level mitigation, for potential effects that the lead agency determines are most effectively addressed at a regional or national program level.

(d) CONDITIONS.—The relevant agency in the environmental review process may adopt or incorporate by reference a planning product under this section if the relevant agency determines, with the concurrence of the lead agency and, if the planning product is necessary for a cooperating agency to issue a permit, review, or approval for the project, with the concurrence of the cooperating agency, that the following conditions have been met:

(1) The planning product was developed through a planning process conducted pursuant to applicable Federal law.

(2) The planning product was developed in consultation with appropriate Federal and State resource agencies and Indian tribes.

(3) The planning process included broad multidisciplinary consideration of systems-level or corridor-wide transportation needs and potential effects, including

effects on the human and natural environment.

(4) The planning process included public notice that the planning products produced in the planning process may be adopted during a subsequent environmental review process in accordance with this section.

(5) During the environmental review process, the relevant agency has—

(A) made the planning documents available for public review and comment by members of the general public and Federal, State, local, and tribal governments that may have an interest in the proposed project;

(B) provided notice of the intention of the relevant agency to adopt or incorporate by reference the planning product; and

(C) considered any resulting comments.

(6) There is no significant new information or new circumstance that has a reasonable likelihood of affecting the continued validity or appropriateness of the planning product.

(7) The planning product has a rational basis and is based on reliable and reasonably current data and reasonable and scientifically acceptable methodologies.

(8) The planning product is documented in sufficient detail to support the decision or the results of the analysis and to meet requirements for use of the information in the environmental review process.

(9) The planning product is appropriate for adoption or incorporation by reference and use in the environmental review process for the project and is incorporated in accordance with, and is sufficient to meet the requirements of, the National Environmental Policy Act of 1969 (42 U.S.C. 4321 et seq.) and section 1502.21 of title 40, Code of Federal Regulations (as in effect on the date of enactment of the FAST Act).

(10) The planning product was approved within the 5-year period ending on the date on which the information is adopted or incorporated by reference.

(e) Effect of Adoption or Incorporation by Reference.—Any planning product adopted or incorporated by reference by the relevant agency in accordance with this section may be—

(1) incorporated directly into an environmental review process document or other environmental document; and

(2) relied on and used by other Federal agencies in carrying out reviews of the project.

(f) Rules of Construction.—

(1) In general.—This section does not make the environmental review process applicable to the transportation planning process conducted under this title and chapter 53 of title 49.

(2) Transportation planning activities.—Initiation of the environmental review process as a part of, or concurrently with, transportation planning activities does not subject transportation plans and programs to the environmental review process.

(3) Planning products.—This section does not affect the use of planning products in the environmental review process pursuant to other authorities under any other provision of law or restrict the initiation of the environmental review process during planning.

(Added Pub. L. 112–141, div. A, title I, §1310(a), July 6, 2012, 126 Stat. 540; amended Pub. L. 114–94, div. A, title I, §1305, Dec. 4, 2015, 129 Stat. 1386.)

§169. DEVELOPMENT OF PROGRAMMATIC MITIGATION PLANS

(a) IN GENERAL.—As part of the statewide or metropolitan transportation planning process, a State or metropolitan planning organization may develop 1 or more programmatic mitigation plans to address the potential environmental impacts of future transportation projects.

(b) SCOPE.—

(1) SCALE.—A programmatic mitigation plan may be developed on a regional, ecosystem, watershed, or statewide scale.

(2) RESOURCES.—The plan may encompass multiple environmental resources within a defined geographic area or may focus on a specific resource, such as aquatic resources, parkland, or wildlife habitat.

(3) PROJECT IMPACTS.—The plan may address impacts from all projects in a defined geographic area or may focus on a specific type of project.

(4) CONSULTATION.—The scope of the plan shall be determined by the State or metropolitan planning organization, as appropriate, in consultation with the agency or agencies with jurisdiction over the resources being addressed in the mitigation plan.

(c) CONTENTS.—A programmatic mitigation plan may include—

(1) an assessment of the condition of environmental resources in the geographic area covered by the plan, including an assessment of recent trends and any potential threats to those resources;

(2) an assessment of potential opportunities to improve the overall quality of environmental resources in the geographic area covered by the plan, through strategic mitigation for impacts of transportation projects;

(3) standard measures for mitigating certain types of impacts;

(4) parameters for determining appropriate mitigation for certain types of impacts, such as mitigation ratios or criteria for determining appropriate mitigation sites;

(5) adaptive management procedures, such as protocols that involve monitoring predicted impacts over time and adjusting mitigation measures in response to information gathered through the monitoring; and

(6) acknowledgment of specific statutory or regulatory requirements that must be satisfied when determining appropriate mitigation for certain types of resources.

(d) PROCESS.—Before adopting a programmatic mitigation plan, a State or metropolitan planning organization shall—

(1) consult with each agency with jurisdiction over the environmental resources considered in the programmatic mitigation plan;

(2) make a draft of the plan available for review and comment by applicable environmental resource agencies and the public;

(3) consider any comments received from such agencies and the public on the draft plan; and

(4) address such comments in the final plan.

(e) INTEGRATION WITH OTHER PLANS.—A programmatic mitigation plan may be integrated with other plans, including watershed plans, ecosystem plans, species recovery plans, growth management plans, and land use plans.

(f) CONSIDERATION IN PROJECT DEVELOPMENT AND PERMITTING.—If a programmatic mitigation plan has been developed pursuant to this section, any Federal agency responsible for environmental reviews, permits, or approvals for a transportation project shall give substantial weight to the recommendations in a programmatic mitigation plan when carrying out the responsibilities under the National Environmental Policy Act of 1969 (42 U.S.C. 4321 et seq.) or other Federal environmental law.

(g) PRESERVATION OF EXISTING AUTHORITIES.—Nothing in this section limits the use of programmatic approaches to reviews under the National Environmental Policy Act of 1969 (42 U.S.C. 4321 et seq.).

(Added Pub. L. 112–141, div. A, title I, §1311(a), July 6, 2012, 126 Stat. 543; amended Pub. L. 114–94, div. A, title I, §1306, Dec. 4, 2015, 129 Stat. 1389.)

§170. FUNDING FLEXIBILITY FOR TRANSPORTATION EMERGENCIES

(a) IN GENERAL.—Notwithstanding any other provision of law, a State may use up to 100 percent of any covered funds of the State to repair or replace a transportation facility that has suffered serious damage as a result of a natural disaster or catastrophic failure from an external cause.

(b) DECLARATION OF EMERGENCY.—Funds may be used under this section only for a disaster or emergency declared by the President pursuant to the Robert T. Stafford Disaster Relief and Emergency Assistance Act (42 U.S.C. 5121 et seq.).

(c) REPAYMENT.—Funds used under subsection (a) shall be repaid to the program from which the funds were taken in the event that such repairs or replacement are subsequently covered by a supplemental appropriation of funds.

(d) DEFINITIONS.—In this section, the following definitions apply:

(1) COVERED FUNDS.—The term "covered funds" means any amounts apportioned to a State under section 104(b), other than amounts suballocated to metropolitan areas and other areas of the State under section 133(d), but including any such amounts required to be set aside for a purpose other than the repair or replacement of a transportation facility under this section.

(2) TRANSPORTATION FACILITY.—The term "transportation facility" means any facility eligible for assistance under section 125.

(Added Pub. L. 112–141, div. A, title I, §1515(a), July 6, 2012, 126 Stat. 573.)

§171. WILDLIFE CROSSINGS PILOT PROGRAM

(a) FINDING.—Congress finds that greater adoption of wildlife-vehicle collision safety countermeasures is in the public interest because—

(1) according to the report of the Federal Highway Administration entitled "Wildlife-Vehicle Collision Reduction Study", there are more than 1,000,000 wildlife-vehicle collisions every year;

(2) wildlife-vehicle collisions—

(A) present a danger to—

(i) human safety; and

(ii) wildlife survival; and

(B) represent a persistent concern that results in tens of thousands of serious injuries and hundreds of fatalities on the roadways of the United States; and

(3) the total annual cost associated with wildlife-vehicle collisions has been

estimated to be $8,388,000,000; and

(4) wildlife-vehicle collisions are a major threat to the survival of species, including birds, reptiles, mammals, and amphibians.

(b) ESTABLISHMENT.—The Secretary shall establish a competitive wildlife crossings pilot program (referred to in this section as the "pilot program") to provide grants for projects that seek to achieve—

(1) a reduction in the number of wildlife-vehicle collisions; and

(2) in carrying out the purpose described in paragraph (1), improved habitat connectivity for terrestrial and aquatic species.

(c) ELIGIBLE ENTITIES.—An entity eligible to apply for a grant under the pilot program is—

(1) a State highway agency, or an equivalent of that agency;

(2) a metropolitan planning organization (as defined in section 134(b));

(3) a unit of local government;

(4) a regional transportation authority;

(5) a special purpose district or public authority with a transportation function, including a port authority;

(6) an Indian tribe (as defined in section 207(m)(1)), including a Native village and a Native Corporation (as those terms are defined in section 3 of the Alaska Native Claims Settlement Act (43 U.S.C. 1602));

(7) a Federal land management agency; or

(8) a group of any of the entities described in paragraphs (1) through (7).

(d) APPLICATIONS.—

(1) IN GENERAL.—To be eligible to receive a grant under the pilot program, an eligible entity shall submit to the Secretary an application at such time, in such manner, and containing such information as the Secretary may require.

(2) REQUIREMENT.—If an application under paragraph (1) is submitted by an eligible entity other than an eligible entity described in paragraph (1) or (7) of subsection (c), the application shall include documentation that the State highway agency, or an equivalent of that agency, of the State in which the eligible entity is located was consulted during the development of the application.

(3) GUIDANCE.—To enhance consideration of current and reliable data, eligible entities may obtain guidance from an agency in the State with jurisdiction over fish and wildlife.

(e) CONSIDERATIONS.—In selecting grant recipients under the pilot program, the Secretary shall take into consideration the following:

(1) Primarily, the extent to which the proposed project of an eligible entity is likely to protect motorists and wildlife by reducing the number of wildlife-vehicle collisions and improve habitat connectivity for terrestrial and aquatic species.

(2) Secondarily, the extent to which the proposed project of an eligible entity is likely to accomplish the following:

(A) Leveraging Federal investment by encouraging non-Federal contributions to the project, including projects from public-private partnerships.

(B) Supporting local economic development and improvement of visitation opportunities.

(C) Incorporation of innovative technologies, including advanced design techniques and other strategies to enhance efficiency and effectiveness in reducing wildlife-vehicle collisions and improving habitat connectivity for terrestrial and aquatic species.

(D) Provision of educational and outreach opportunities.

(E) Monitoring and research to evaluate, compare effectiveness of, and identify best practices in, selected projects.

(F) Any other criteria relevant to reducing the number of wildlife-vehicle collisions and improving habitat connectivity for terrestrial and aquatic species, as the Secretary determines to be appropriate, subject to the condition that the implementation of the pilot program shall not be delayed in the absence of action by the Secretary to identify additional criteria under this subparagraph.

(f) USE OF FUNDS.—

(1) IN GENERAL.—The Secretary shall ensure that a grant received under the pilot program is used for a project to reduce wildlife-vehicle collisions.

(2) GRANT ADMINISTRATION.—

(A) IN GENERAL.—A grant received under the pilot program shall be administered by—

(i) in the case of a grant to a Federal land management agency or an Indian tribe (as defined in section 207(m)(1), including a Native village and a Native Corporation (as those terms are defined in section 3 of the Alaska Native Claims Settlement Act (43 U.S.C. 1602))), the Federal Highway Administration, through an agreement; and

(ii) in the case of a grant to an eligible entity other than an eligible entity described in clause (i), the State highway agency, or an equivalent of that agency, for the State in which the project is to be carried out.

(B) PARTNERSHIPS.—

(i) IN GENERAL.—A grant received under the pilot program may be used to provide funds to eligible partners of the project for which the grant was received described in clause (ii), in accordance with the terms of the project agreement.

(ii) ELIGIBLE PARTNERS DESCRIBED.—The eligible partners referred to in clause (i) include—

(I) a metropolitan planning organization (as defined in section 134(b));

(II) a unit of local government;

(III) a regional transportation authority;

(IV) a special purpose district or public authority with a transportation function, including a port authority;

(V) an Indian tribe (as defined in section 207(m)(1)), including a Native village and a Native Corporation (as those terms are defined in section 3 of the Alaska Native Claims Settlement Act (43 U.S.C. 1602));

(VI) a Federal land management agency;

(VII) a foundation, nongovernmental organization, or institution of higher education;

(VIII) a Federal, Tribal, regional, or State government entity; and

(IX) a group of any of the entities described in subclauses (I) through (VIII).

(3) COMPLIANCE.—An eligible entity that receives a grant under the pilot program and enters into a partnership described in paragraph (2) shall establish measures to verify that an eligible partner that receives funds from the grant complies with the conditions of the pilot program in using those funds.

(g) REQUIREMENT.—The Secretary shall ensure that not less than 60 percent of the amounts made available for grants under the pilot program each fiscal year are for projects located in rural areas.

(h) ANNUAL REPORT TO CONGRESS.—

(1) IN GENERAL.—Not later than December 31 of each calendar year, the Secretary shall submit to Congress, and make publicly available, a report describing the activities under the pilot program for the fiscal year that ends during that calendar year.

(2) CONTENTS.—The report under paragraph (1) shall include—

(A) a detailed description of the activities carried out under the pilot program,

(B) an evaluation of the effectiveness of the pilot program in meeting the purposes described in subsection (b); and

(C) policy recommendations to improve the effectiveness of the pilot program.

(i) TREATMENT OF PROJECTS.—Notwithstanding any other provision of law, a project assisted under this section shall be treated as a project on a Federal-aid highway under this chapter.

(Added Pub. L. 117–58, div. A, title I, §11123(b)(1), Nov. 15, 2021, 135 Stat. 499.)

§172. WILDLIFE-VEHICLE COLLISION REDUCTION AND HABITAT CONNECTIVITY IMPROVEMENT

(a) STUDY.—

(1) IN GENERAL.—The Secretary shall conduct a study (referred to in this subsection as the "study") of the state, as of the date of the study, of the practice of methods to reduce collisions between motorists and wildlife (referred to in this section as "wildlife-vehicle collisions").

(2) CONTENTS.—

(A) AREAS OF STUDY.—The study shall—

(i) update and expand on, as appropriate—

(I) the report entitled "Wildlife Vehicle Collision Reduction Study: 2008 Report to Congress"; and

(II) the document entitled "Wildlife Vehicle Collision Reduction Study: Best Practices Manual" and dated October 2008; and

(ii) include—

(I) an assessment, as of the date of the study, of—

(aa) the causes of wildlife-vehicle collisions;

(bb) the impact of wildlife-vehicle collisions on motorists and wildlife; and

(cc) the impacts of roads and traffic on habitat connectivity for terrestrial and aquatic species; and

(II) solutions and best practices for—

(aa) reducing wildlife-vehicle collisions; and

(bb) improving habitat connectivity for terrestrial and aquatic species.

(B) Methods.—In carrying out the study, the Secretary shall—

(i) conduct a thorough review of research and data relating to—

(I) wildlife-vehicle collisions; and

(II) habitat fragmentation that results from transportation infrastructure;

(ii) survey current practices of the Department of Transportation and State departments of transportation to reduce wildlife-vehicle collisions; and

(iii) consult with—

(I) appropriate experts in the field of wildlife-vehicle collisions; and

(II) appropriate experts on the effects of roads and traffic on habitat connectivity for terrestrial and aquatic species.

(3) Report.—

(A) In general.—Not later than 18 months after the date of enactment of the Surface Transportation Reauthorization Act of 2021, the Secretary shall submit to Congress a report on the results of the study.

(B) Contents.—The report under subparagraph (A) shall include—

(i) a description of—

(I) the causes of wildlife-vehicle collisions;

(II) the impacts of wildlife-vehicle collisions; and

(III) the impacts of roads and traffic on—

(aa) species listed as threatened species or endangered species under the Endangered Species Act of 1973 (16 U.S.C. 1531 et seq.);

(bb) species identified by States as species of greatest conservation need;

(cc) species identified in State wildlife plans; and

(dd) medium and small terrestrial and aquatic species;

(ii) an economic evaluation of the costs and benefits of installing highway infrastructure and other measures to mitigate damage to terrestrial and aquatic species, including the effect on jobs, property values, and economic growth to society, adjacent communities, and landowners;

(iii) recommendations for preventing wildlife-vehicle collisions, including recommended best practices, funding resources, or other recommendations for addressing wildlife-vehicle collisions; and

(iv) guidance, developed in consultation with Federal land management agencies and State departments of transportation, State fish and wildlife agencies, and Tribal governments that agree to participate, for developing, for each State that agrees to participate, a voluntary joint statewide transportation and wildlife action plan—

(I) to address wildlife-vehicle collisions; and

(II) to improve habitat connectivity for terrestrial and aquatic species.

(b) Workforce Development and Technical Training.—

(1) In general.—Not later than 3 years after the date of enactment of the Surface Transportation Reauthorization Act of 2021, the Secretary shall, based on the study conducted under subsection (a), develop a series of in-person and online workforce development and technical training courses—

(A) to reduce wildlife-vehicle collisions; and

(B) to improve habitat connectivity for terrestrial and aquatic species.

(2) AVAILABILITY.—The Secretary shall—

(A) make the series of courses developed under paragraph (1) available for transportation and fish and wildlife professionals; and

(B) update the series of courses not less frequently than once every 2 years.

(c) STANDARDIZATION OF WILDLIFE COLLISION AND CARCASS DATA.—

(1) STANDARDIZED METHODOLOGY.—

(A) IN GENERAL.—The Secretary, acting through the Administrator of the Federal Highway Administration (referred to in this subsection as the "Secretary"), shall develop a quality standardized methodology for collecting and reporting spatially accurate wildlife collision and carcass data for the National Highway System, considering the practicability of the methodology with respect to technology and cost.

(B) METHODOLOGY.—In developing the standardized methodology under subparagraph (A), the Secretary shall—

(i) survey existing methodologies and sources of data collection, including the Fatality Analysis Reporting System, the General Estimates System of the National Automotive Sampling System, and the Highway Safety Information System; and

(ii) to the extent practicable, identify and correct limitations of those existing methodologies and sources of data collection.

(C) CONSULTATION.—In developing the standardized methodology under subparagraph (A), the Secretary shall consult with—

(i) the Secretary of the Interior;

(ii) the Secretary of Agriculture, acting through the Chief of the Forest Service;

(iii) Tribal, State, and local transportation and wildlife authorities;

(iv) metropolitan planning organizations (as defined in section 134(b));

(v) members of the American Association of State Highway Transportation Officials;

(vi) members of the Association of Fish and Wildlife Agencies;

(vii) experts in the field of wildlife-vehicle collisions;

(viii) nongovernmental organizations; and

(ix) other interested stakeholders, as appropriate.

(2) STANDARDIZED NATIONAL DATA SYSTEM WITH VOLUNTARY TEMPLATE IMPLEMENTATION.—The Secretary shall—

(A) develop a template for State implementation of a standardized national wildlife collision and carcass data system for the National Highway System that is based on the standardized methodology developed under paragraph (1); and

(B) encourage the voluntary implementation of the template developed under subparagraph (A).

(3) REPORTS.—

(A) METHODOLOGY.—The Secretary shall submit to Congress a report describing the standardized methodology developed under paragraph (1) not later than the later of—

(i) the date that is 18 months after the date of enactment of the Surface Transportation Reauthorization Act of 2021; and

(ii) the date that is 180 days after the date on which the Secretary completes the development of the standardized methodology.

(B) IMPLEMENTATION.—Not later than 4 years after the date of enactment of the Surface Transportation Reauthorization Act of 2021, the Secretary shall submit to Congress a report describing—

(i) the status of the voluntary implementation of the standardized methodology developed under paragraph (1) and the template developed under paragraph (2)(A);

(ii) whether the implementation of the standardized methodology developed under paragraph (1) and the template developed under paragraph (2)(A) has impacted efforts by States, units of local government, and other entities—

(I) to reduce the number of wildlife-vehicle collisions; and

(II) to improve habitat connectivity;

(iii) the degree of the impact described in clause (ii); and

(iv) the recommendations of the Secretary, including recommendations for further study aimed at reducing motorist collisions involving wildlife and improving habitat connectivity for terrestrial and aquatic species on the National Highway System, if any.

(d) NATIONAL THRESHOLD GUIDANCE.—The Secretary shall—

(1) establish guidance, to be carried out by States on a voluntary basis, that contains a threshold for determining whether a highway shall be evaluated for potential mitigation measures to reduce wildlife-vehicle collisions and increase habitat connectivity for terrestrial and aquatic species, taking into consideration—

(A) the number of wildlife-vehicle collisions on the highway that pose a human safety risk;

(B) highway-related mortality and the effects of traffic on the highway on—

(i) species listed as endangered species or threatened species under the Endangered Species Act of 1973 (16 U.S.C. 1531 et seq.);

(ii) species identified by a State as species of greatest conservation need;

(iii) species identified in State wildlife plans; and

(iv) medium and small terrestrial and aquatic species; and

(C) habitat connectivity values for terrestrial and aquatic species and the barrier effect of the highway on the movements and migrations of those species.

(Added Pub. L. 117–58, div. A, title I, §11123(c)(1), Nov. 15, 2021, 135 Stat. 502.)

§173. RURAL SURFACE TRANSPORTATION GRANT PROGRAM

(a) DEFINITIONS.—In this section:

(1) PROGRAM.—The term "program" means the program established under subsection (b)(1).

(2) RURAL AREA.—The term "rural area" means an area that is outside an urbanized area with a population of over 200,000.

(b) ESTABLISHMENT.—

(1) IN GENERAL.—The Secretary shall establish a rural surface transportation grant

program to provide grants, on a competitive basis, to eligible entities to improve and expand the surface transportation infrastructure in rural areas.

(2) GOALS.—The goals of the program shall be—

(A) to increase connectivity;

(B) to improve the safety and reliability of the movement of people and freight; and

(C) to generate regional economic growth and improve quality of life.

(3) GRANT ADMINISTRATION.—The Secretary may—

(A) retain not more than a total of 2 percent of the funds made available to carry out the program and to review applications for grants under the program; and

(B) transfer portions of the funds retained under subparagraph (A) to the relevant Administrators to fund the award and oversight of grants provided under the program.

(c) ELIGIBLE ENTITIES.—The Secretary may make a grant under the program to—

(1) a State;

(2) a regional transportation planning organization;

(3) a unit of local government;

(4) a Tribal government or a consortium of Tribal governments; and

(5) a multijurisdictional group of entities described in paragraphs (1) through (4).

(d) APPLICATIONS.—To be eligible to receive a grant under the program, an eligible entity shall submit to the Secretary an application in such form, at such time, and containing such information as the Secretary may require.

(e) ELIGIBLE PROJECTS.—

(1) IN GENERAL.—Except as provided in paragraph (2), the Secretary may make a grant under the program only for a project that is—

(A) a highway, bridge, or tunnel project eligible under section 119(d);

(B) a highway, bridge, or tunnel project eligible under section 133(b);

(C) a project eligible under section 202(a);

(D) a highway freight project eligible under section 167(h)(5);

(E) a highway safety improvement project, including a project to improve a high risk rural road (as those terms are defined in section 148(a));

(F) a project on a publicly-owned highway or bridge that provides or increases access to an agricultural, commercial, energy, or intermodal facility that supports the economy of a rural area; or

(G) a project to develop, establish, or maintain an integrated mobility management system, a transportation demand management system, or on-demand mobility services.

(2) BUNDLING OF ELIGIBLE PROJECTS.—

(A) IN GENERAL.—An eligible entity may bundle 2 or more similar eligible projects under the program that are—

(i) included as a bundled project in a statewide transportation improvement program under section 135; and

(ii) awarded to a single contractor or consultant pursuant to a contract for engineering and design or construction between the contractor and the eligible entity.

(B) ITEMIZATION.—Notwithstanding any other provision of law (including regulations), a bundling of eligible projects under this paragraph may be considered to be a single project, including for purposes of section 135.

(f) ELIGIBLE PROJECT COSTS.—An eligible entity may use funds from a grant under the program for—

(1) development phase activities, including planning, feasibility analysis, revenue forecasting, environmental review, preliminary engineering and design work, and other preconstruction activities; and

(2) construction, reconstruction, rehabilitation, acquisition of real property (including land related to the project and improvements to the land), environmental mitigation, construction contingencies, acquisition of equipment, and operational improvements.

(g) PROJECT REQUIREMENTS.—The Secretary may provide a grant under the program to an eligible project only if the Secretary determines that the project—

(1) will generate regional economic, mobility, or safety benefits;

(2) will be cost effective;

(3) will contribute to the accomplishment of 1 or more of the national goals under section 150;

(4) is based on the results of preliminary engineering; and

(5) is reasonably expected to begin construction not later than 18 months after the date of obligation of funds for the project.

(h) ADDITIONAL CONSIDERATIONS.—In providing grants under the program, the Secretary shall consider the extent to which an eligible project will—

(1) improve the state of good repair of existing highway, bridge, and tunnel facilities;

(2) increase the capacity or connectivity of the surface transportation system and improve mobility for residents of rural areas;

(3) address economic development and job creation challenges, including energy sector job losses in energy communities as identified in the report released in April 2021 by the interagency working group established by section 218 of Executive Order 14008 (86 Fed. Reg. 7628 (February 1, 2021));

(4) enhance recreational and tourism opportunities by providing access to Federal land, national parks, national forests, national recreation areas, national wildlife refuges, wilderness areas, or State parks;

(5) contribute to geographic diversity among grant recipients;

(6) utilize innovative project delivery approaches or incorporate transportation technologies;

(7) coordinate with projects to address broadband infrastructure needs; or

(8) improve access to emergency care, essential services, healthcare providers, or drug and alcohol treatment and rehabilitation resources.

(i) GRANT AMOUNT.—Except as provided in subsection (k)(1), a grant under the program shall be in an amount that is not less than $25,000,000.

(j) FEDERAL SHARE.—

(1) IN GENERAL.—Except as provided in paragraph (2), the Federal share of the cost of a project carried out with a grant under the program may not exceed 80 percent.

(2) FEDERAL SHARE FOR CERTAIN PROJECTS.—The Federal share of the cost of an eligible project that furthers the completion of a designated segment of the Appalachian Development Highway System under section 14501 of title 40, or addresses a surface transportation infrastructure need identified for the Denali access system program under section 309 of the Denali Commission Act of 1998 (42 U.S.C. 3121 note; Public Law 105–277) shall be up to 100 percent, as determined by the State.

(3) USE OF OTHER FEDERAL ASSISTANCE.—Federal assistance other than a grant under the program may be used to satisfy the non-Federal share of the cost of a project carried out with a grant under the program.

(k) SET ASIDES.—

(1) SMALL PROJECTS.—The Secretary shall use not more than 10 percent of the amounts made available for the program for each fiscal year to provide grants for eligible projects in an amount that is less than $25,000,000.

(2) APPALACHIAN DEVELOPMENT HIGHWAY SYSTEM.—The Secretary shall reserve 25 percent of the amounts made available for the program for each fiscal year for eligible projects that further the completion of designated routes of the Appalachian Development Highway System under section 14501 of title 40.

(3) RURAL ROADWAY LANE DEPARTURES.—The Secretary shall reserve 15 percent of the amounts made available for the program for each fiscal year to provide grants for eligible projects located in States that have rural roadway fatalities as a result of lane departures that are greater than the average of rural roadway fatalities as a result of lane departures in the United States, based on the latest available data from the Secretary.

(4) EXCESS FUNDING.—In any fiscal year in which qualified applications for grants under this subsection do not allow for the amounts reserved under paragraphs (1), (2), or (3) to be fully utilized, the Secretary shall use the unutilized amounts to make other grants under the program.

(l) CONGRESSIONAL REVIEW.—

(1) NOTIFICATION.—Not less than 60 days before providing a grant under the program, the Secretary shall submit to the Committee on Environment and Public Works of the Senate and the Committee on Transportation and Infrastructure of the House of Representatives—

(A) a list of all applications determined to be eligible for a grant by the Secretary;

(B) each application proposed to be selected for a grant, including a justification for the selection; and

(C) proposed grant amounts.

(2) COMMITTEE REVIEW.—Before the last day of the 60-day period described in paragraph (1), each Committee described in paragraph (1) shall review the list of proposed projects submitted by the Secretary.

(3) CONGRESSIONAL DISAPPROVAL.—The Secretary may not make a grant or any other obligation or commitment to fund a project under the program if a joint resolution is enacted disapproving funding for the project before the last day of the 60-day period described in paragraph (1).

(m) TRANSPARENCY.—

(1) IN GENERAL.—Not later than 30 days after providing a grant for a project under the program, the Secretary shall provide to all applicants, and publish on the website of the Department of Transportation, the information described in subsection (l)(1).

(2) BRIEFING.—The Secretary shall provide, on the request of an eligible entity, the opportunity to receive a briefing to explain any reasons the eligible entity was not selected to receive a grant under the program.

(n) REPORTS.—

(1) ANNUAL REPORT.—The Secretary shall make available on the website of the Department of Transportation at the end of each fiscal year an annual report that lists each project for which a grant has been provided under the program during that fiscal year.

(2) COMPTROLLER GENERAL.—

(A) ASSESSMENT.—The Comptroller General of the United States shall conduct an assessment of the administrative establishment, solicitation, selection, and justification process with respect to the awarding of grants under the program for each fiscal year.

(B) REPORT.—Each fiscal year, the Comptroller General shall submit to the Committee on Environment and Public Works of the Senate and the Committee on Transportation and Infrastructure of the House of Representatives a report that describes, for the fiscal year—

(i) the adequacy and fairness of the process by which each project was selected, if applicable; and

(ii) the justification and criteria used for the selection of each project, if applicable.

(o) TREATMENT OF PROJECTS.—Notwithstanding any other provision of law, a project assisted under this section shall be treated as a project on a Federal-aid highway under this chapter.

(Added Pub. L. 117–58, div. A, title I, §11132(a), Nov. 15, 2021, 135 Stat. 510.)

§174. STATE HUMAN CAPITAL PLANS

(a) IN GENERAL.—Not later than 18 months after the date of enactment of this section, the Secretary shall encourage each State to develop a voluntary plan, to be known as a "human capital plan", that provides for the immediate and long-term personnel and workforce needs of the State with respect to the capacity of the State to deliver transportation and public infrastructure eligible under this title.

(b) PLAN CONTENTS.—

(1) IN GENERAL.—A human capital plan developed by a State under subsection (a) shall, to the maximum extent practicable, take into consideration—

(A) significant transportation workforce trends, needs, issues, and challenges with respect to the State;

(B) the human capital policies, strategies, and performance measures that will guide the transportation-related workforce investment decisions of the State;

(C) coordination with educational institutions, industry, organized labor, workforce boards, and other agencies or organizations to address the human capital transportation needs of the State;

(D) a workforce planning strategy that identifies current and future human capital needs, including the knowledge, skills, and abilities needed to recruit and retain skilled workers in the transportation industry;

(E) a human capital management strategy that is aligned with the transportation mission, goals, and organizational objectives of the State;

(F) an implementation system for workforce goals focused on addressing continuity of leadership and knowledge sharing across the State;

(G) an implementation system that addresses workforce competency gaps, particularly in mission-critical occupations;

(H) in the case of public-private partnerships or other alternative project delivery methods to carry out the transportation program of the State, a description of workforce needs—

(i) to ensure that the transportation mission, goals, and organizational objectives of the State are fully carried out; and

(ii) to ensure that procurement methods provide the best public value;

(I) a system for analyzing and evaluating the performance of the State department of transportation with respect to all aspects of human capital management policies, programs, and activities; and

(J) the manner in which the plan will improve the ability of the State to meet the national policy in support of performance management established under section 150.

(2) PLANNING PERIOD.—If a State develops a human capital plan under subsection (a), the plan shall address a 5-year forecast period.

(c) PLAN UPDATES.—If a State develops a human capital plan under subsection (a), the State shall update the plan not less frequently than once every 5 years.

(d) RELATIONSHIP TO LONG-RANGE PLAN.—

(1) IN GENERAL.—Subject to paragraph (2), a human capital plan developed by a State under subsection (a) may be developed separately from, or incorporated into, the long-range statewide transportation plan required under section 135.

(2) EFFECT OF SECTION.—Nothing in this section requires a State, or authorizes the Secretary to require a State, to incorporate a human capital plan into the long-range statewide transportation plan required under section 135.

(e) PUBLIC AVAILABILITY.—Each State that develops a human capital plan under subsection (a) shall make a copy of the plan available to the public in a user-friendly format on the website of the State department of transportation.

(f) SAVINGS PROVISION.—Nothing in this section prevents a State from carrying out transportation workforce planning—

(1) not described in this section; or

(2) not in accordance with this section.

(Added Pub. L. 117–58, div. A, title I, §11203(a), Nov. 15, 2021, 135 Stat. 519.)

§175. CARBON REDUCTION PROGRAM

(a) DEFINITIONS.—In this section:

(1) METROPOLITAN PLANNING ORGANIZATION; URBANIZED AREA.—The terms "metropolitan planning organization" and "urbanized area" have the meaning given

those terms in section 134(b).

(2) TRANSPORTATION EMISSIONS.—The term "transportation emissions" means carbon dioxide emissions from on-road highway sources of those emissions within a State.

(3) TRANSPORTATION MANAGEMENT AREA.—The term "transportation management area" means a transportation management area identified or designated by the Secretary under section 134(k)(1).

(b) ESTABLISHMENT.—The Secretary shall establish a carbon reduction program to reduce transportation emissions.

(c) ELIGIBLE PROJECTS.—

(1) IN GENERAL.—Subject to paragraph (2), funds apportioned to a State under section 104(b)(7) may be obligated for projects to support the reduction of transportation emissions, including—

(A) a project described in section 149(b)(4) to establish or operate a traffic monitoring, management, and control facility or program, including advanced truck stop electrification systems;

(B) a public transportation project that is eligible for assistance under section 142;

(C) a project described in section 101(a)(29) (as in effect on the day before the date of enactment of the FAST Act (Public Law 114–94; 129 Stat. 1312)), including the construction, planning, and design of on-road and off-road trail facilities for pedestrians, bicyclists, and other nonmotorized forms of transportation;

(D) a project described in section 503(c)(4)(E) for advanced transportation and congestion management technologies;

(E) a project for the deployment of infrastructure-based intelligent transportation systems capital improvements and the installation of vehicle-to-infrastructure communications equipment, including retrofitting dedicated short-range communications (DSRC) technology deployed as part of an existing pilot program to cellular vehicle-to-everything (C–V2X) technology;

(F) a project to replace street lighting and traffic control devices with energy-efficient alternatives;

(G) the development of a carbon reduction strategy in accordance with subsection (d);

(H) a project or strategy that is designed to support congestion pricing, shifting transportation demand to nonpeak hours or other transportation modes, increasing vehicle occupancy rates, or otherwise reducing demand for roads, including electronic toll collection, and travel demand management strategies and programs;

(I) efforts to reduce the environmental and community impacts of freight movement;

(J) a project to support deployment of alternative fuel vehicles, including—

(i) the acquisition, installation, or operation of publicly accessible electric vehicle charging infrastructure or hydrogen, natural gas, or propane vehicle fueling infrastructure; and

(ii) the purchase or lease of zero-emission construction equipment and vehicles, including the acquisition, construction, or leasing of required supporting facilities;

(K) a project described in section 149(b)(8) for a diesel engine retrofit;

(L) a project described in section 149(b)(5) that does not result in the construction of new capacity; and

(M) a project that reduces transportation emissions at port facilities, including through the advancement of port electrification.

(2) FLEXIBILITY.—In addition to the eligible projects under paragraph (1), a State may use funds apportioned under section 104(b)(7) for a project eligible under section 133(b) if the Secretary certifies that the State has demonstrated a reduction in transportation emissions—

(A) as estimated on a per capita basis; and

(B) as estimated on a per unit of economic output basis.

(d) CARBON REDUCTION STRATEGY.

(1) IN GENERAL.—Not later than 2 years after the date of enactment of the Surface Transportation Reauthorization Act of 2021, a State, in consultation with any metropolitan planning organization designated within the State, shall develop a carbon reduction strategy in accordance with this subsection.

(2) REQUIREMENTS.—The carbon reduction strategy of a State developed under paragraph (1) shall—

(A) support efforts to reduce transportation emissions;

(B) identify projects and strategies to reduce transportation emissions, which may include projects and strategies for safe, reliable, and cost-effective options—

(i) to reduce traffic congestion by facilitating the use of alternatives to single-occupant vehicle trips, including public transportation facilities, pedestrian facilities, bicycle facilities, and shared or pooled vehicle trips within the State or an area served by the applicable metropolitan planning organization, if any;

(ii) to facilitate the use of vehicles or modes of travel that result in lower transportation emissions per person-mile traveled as compared to existing vehicles and modes; and

(iii) to facilitate approaches to the construction of transportation assets that result in lower transportation emissions as compared to existing approaches;

(C) support the reduction of transportation emissions of the State;

(D) at the discretion of the State, quantify the total carbon emissions from the production, transport, and use of materials used in the construction of transportation facilities within the State; and

(E) be appropriate to the population density and context of the State, including any metropolitan planning organization designated within the State.

(3) UPDATES.—The carbon reduction strategy of a State developed under paragraph (1) shall be updated not less frequently than once every 4 years.

(4) REVIEW.—Not later than 90 days after the date on which a State submits a request for the approval of a carbon reduction strategy developed by the State under paragraph (1), the Secretary shall—

(A) review the process used to develop the carbon reduction strategy; and

(B)(i) certify that the carbon reduction strategy meets the requirements of paragraph (2); or

(ii) deny certification of the carbon reduction strategy and specify the actions necessary for the State to take to correct the deficiencies in the process of the State in developing the carbon reduction strategy.

(5) TECHNICAL ASSISTANCE.—At the request of a State, the Secretary shall provide technical assistance in the development of the carbon reduction strategy under paragraph (1).

(e) SUBALLOCATION.—

(1) IN GENERAL.—For each fiscal year, of the funds apportioned to the State under section 104(b)(7)—

(A) 65 percent shall be obligated, in proportion to their relative shares of the population of the State—

(i) in urbanized areas of the State with an urbanized area population of more than 200,000;

(ii) in urbanized areas of the State with an urbanized population of not less than 50,000 and not more than 200,000;

(iii) in urban areas of the State with a population of not less than 5,000 and not more than 49,999; and

(iv) in other areas of the State with a population of less than 5,000; and

(B) the remainder may be obligated in any area of the State.

(2) METROPOLITAN AREAS.—Funds attributed to an urbanized area under paragraph (1)(A)(i) may be obligated in the metropolitan area established under section 134 that encompasses the urbanized area.

(3) DISTRIBUTION AMONG URBANIZED AREAS OF OVER 50,000 POPULATION.—

(A) IN GENERAL.—Except as provided in subparagraph (B), the amounts that a State is required to obligate under clauses (i) and (ii) of paragraph (1)(A) shall be obligated in urbanized areas described in those clauses based on the relative population of the areas.

(B) OTHER FACTORS.—The State may obligate the funds described in subparagraph (A) based on other factors if—

(i) the State and the relevant metropolitan planning organizations jointly apply to the Secretary for the permission to base the obligation on other factors; and

(ii) the Secretary grants the request.

(4) COORDINATION IN URBANIZED AREAS.—Before obligating funds for an eligible project under subsection (c) in an urbanized area that is not a transportation management area, a State shall coordinate with any metropolitan planning organization that represents the urbanized area prior to determining which activities should be carried out under the project.

(5) CONSULTATION IN RURAL AREAS.—Before obligating funds for an eligible project under subsection (c) in a rural area, a State shall consult with any regional transportation planning organization or metropolitan planning organization that represents the rural area prior to determining which activities should be carried out under the project.

(6) OBLIGATION AUTHORITY.—

(A) IN GENERAL.—A State that is required to obligate in an urbanized area with an urbanized area population of 50,000 or more under this subsection funds apportioned to the State under section 104(b)(7) shall make available during the period of fiscal years 2022 through 2026 an amount of obligation authority distributed to the State for Federal-aid highways and highway safety construction programs for use in the area that is equal to the amount obtained by multiplying—

(i) the aggregate amount of funds that the State is required to obligate in the area under this subsection during the period; and

(ii) the ratio that—

(I) the aggregate amount of obligation authority distributed to the State for Federal-aid highways and highway safety construction programs during the period; bears to

(II) the total of the sums apportioned to the State for Federal-aid highways and highway safety construction programs (excluding sums not subject to an obligation limitation) during the period.

(B) Joint responsibility.—Each State, each affected metropolitan planning organization, and the Secretary shall jointly ensure compliance with subparagraph (A).

(f) Federal Share.—The Federal share of the cost of a project carried out using funds apportioned to a State under section 104(b)(7) shall be determined in accordance with section 120.

(g) Treatment of Projects.—Notwithstanding any other provision of law, a project assisted under this section shall be treated as a project on a Federal-aid highway under this chapter.

(Added Pub. L. 117–58, div. A, title I, §11403(a), Nov. 15, 2021, 135 Stat. 555.)

§176. Promoting Resilient Operations for Transformative, Efficient, and Cost-saving Transportation (PROTECT) program

(a) Definitions.—In this section:

(1) Emergency event.—The term "emergency event" means a natural disaster or catastrophic failure resulting in—

(A) an emergency declared by the Governor of the State in which the disaster or failure occurred; or

(B) an emergency or disaster declared by the President.

(2) Evacuation route.—The term "evacuation route" means a transportation route or system that—

(A) is owned, operated, or maintained by a Federal, State, Tribal, or local government;

(B) is used—

(i) to transport the public away from emergency events; or

(ii) to transport emergency responders and recovery resources; and

(C) is designated by the eligible entity with jurisdiction over the area in which the route is located for the purposes described in subparagraph (B).

(3) Program.—The term "program" means the program established under subsection (b)(1).

(4) Resilience improvement.—The term "resilience improvement" means the

use of materials or structural or nonstructural techniques, including natural infrastructure—

(A) that allow a project—

(i) to better anticipate, prepare for, and adapt to changing conditions and to withstand and respond to disruptions; and

(ii) to be better able to continue to serve the primary function of the project during and after weather events and natural disasters for the expected life of the project; or

(B) that—

(i) reduce the magnitude and duration of impacts of current and future weather events and natural disasters to a project; or

(ii) have the absorptive capacity, adaptive capacity, and recoverability to decrease project vulnerability to current and future weather events or natural disasters.

(b) ESTABLISHMENT.—

(1) IN GENERAL.—The Secretary shall establish a program, to be known as the "Promoting Resilient Operations for Transformative, Efficient, and Cost-saving Transportation program" or the "PROTECT program".

(2) PURPOSE.—The purpose of the program is to provide grants for resilience improvements through—

(A) formula funding distributed to States to carry out subsection (c);

(B) competitive planning grants to enable communities to assess vulnerabilities to current and future weather events and natural disasters and changing conditions, including sea level rise, and plan transportation improvements and emergency response strategies to address those vulnerabilities; and

(C) competitive resilience improvement grants to protect—

(i) surface transportation assets by making the assets more resilient to current and future weather events and natural disasters, such as severe storms, flooding, drought, levee and dam failures, wildfire, rockslides, mudslides, sea level rise, extreme weather, including extreme temperature, and earthquakes;

(ii) communities through resilience improvements and strategies that allow for the continued operation or rapid recovery of surface transportation systems that—

(I) serve critical local, regional, and national needs, including evacuation routes; and

(II) provide access or service to hospitals and other medical or emergency service facilities, major employers, critical manufacturing centers, ports and intermodal facilities, utilities, and Federal facilities;

(iii) coastal infrastructure, such as a tide gate to protect highways, that is at long-term risk to sea level rise; and

(iv) natural infrastructure that protects and enhances surface transportation assets while improving ecosystem conditions, including culverts that ensure adequate flows in rivers and estuarine systems.

(c) ELIGIBLE ACTIVITIES FOR APPORTIONED FUNDING.—

(1) IN GENERAL.—Except as provided in paragraph (2), funds apportioned to the

State under section 104(b)(8) shall be obligated for activities eligible under subparagraph (A), (B), or (C) of subsection (d)(4).

(2) PLANNING SET-ASIDE.—Of the funds apportioned to a State under section 104(b)(8) for each fiscal year, not less than 2 percent shall be for activities described in subsection (d)(3).

(3) REQUIREMENTS.—

(A) PROJECTS IN CERTAIN AREAS.—If a project under this subsection is carried out, in whole or in part, within a base floodplain, the State shall—

(i) identify the base floodplain in which the project is to be located and disclose that information to the Secretary; and

(ii) indicate to the Secretary whether the State plans to implement 1 or more components of the risk mitigation plan under section 322 of the Robert T. Stafford Disaster Relief and Emergency Assistance Act (42 U.S.C. 5165) with respect to the area.

(B) ELIGIBILITIES.—A State shall use funds apportioned to the State under section 104(b)(8) for—

(i) a highway project eligible for assistance under this title;

(ii) a public transportation facility or service eligible for assistance under chapter 53 of title 49; or

(iii) a port facility, including a facility that—

(I) connects a port to other modes of transportation;

(II) improves the efficiency of evacuations and disaster relief; or

(III) aids transportation.

(C) SYSTEM RESILIENCE.—A project carried out by a State with funds apportioned to the State under section 104(b)(8) may include the use of natural infrastructure or the construction or modification of storm surge, flood protection, or aquatic ecosystem restoration elements that are functionally connected to a transportation improvement, such as—

(i) increasing marsh health and total area adjacent to a highway right-of-way to promote additional flood storage;

(ii) upgrades to and installation of culverts designed to withstand 100-year flood events;

(iii) upgrades to and installation of tide gates to protect highways;

(iv) upgrades to and installation of flood gates to protect tunnel entrances; and

(v) improving functionality and resiliency of stormwater controls, including inventory inspections, upgrades to, and preservation of best management practices to protect surface transportation infrastructure.

(D) FEDERAL COST SHARE.—

(i) IN GENERAL.—Except as provided in subsection (e)(1), the Federal share of the cost of a project carried out using funds apportioned to the State under section 104(b)(8) shall not exceed 80 percent of the total project cost.

(ii) NON-FEDERAL SHARE.—A State may use Federal funds other than Federal funds apportioned to the State under section 104(b)(8) to meet the non-Federal cost share requirement for a project under this subsection.

(E) ELIGIBLE PROJECT COSTS.—

(i) IN GENERAL.—Except as provided in clause (ii), eligible project costs for activities carried out by a State with funds apportioned to the State under section 104(b)(8) may include the costs of—

(I) development phase activities, including planning, feasibility analysis, revenue forecasting, environmental review, preliminary engineering and design work, and other preconstruction activities; and

(II) construction, reconstruction, rehabilitation, and acquisition of real property (including land related to the project and improvements to land), environmental mitigation, construction contingencies, acquisition of equipment directly related to improving system performance, and operational improvements.

(ii) ELIGIBLE PLANNING COSTS.—In the case of a planning activity described in subsection (d)(3) that is carried out by a State with funds apportioned to the State under section 104(b)(8), eligible costs may include development phase activities, including planning, feasibility analysis, revenue forecasting, environmental review, preliminary engineering and design work, other preconstruction activities, and other activities consistent with carrying out the purposes of subsection (d)(3).

(F) LIMITATIONS.—A State—

(i) may use not more than 40 percent of the amounts apportioned to the State under section 104(b)(8) for the construction of new capacity; and

(ii) may use not more than 10 percent of the amounts apportioned to the State under section 104(b)(8) for activities described in subparagraph (E)(i)(I).

(d) COMPETITIVE AWARDS.—

(1) IN GENERAL.—In addition to funds apportioned to States under section 104(b)(8) to carry out activities under subsection (c), the Secretary shall provide grants on a competitive basis under this subsection to eligible entities described in paragraph (2).

(2) ELIGIBLE ENTITIES.—Except as provided in paragraph (4)(C), the Secretary may make a grant under this subsection to any of the following:

(A) A State or political subdivision of a State.

(B) A metropolitan planning organization.

(C) A unit of local government.

(D) A special purpose district or public authority with a transportation function, including a port authority.

(E) An Indian tribe (as defined in section 207(m)(1)).

(F) A Federal land management agency that applies jointly with a State or group of States.

(G) A multi-State or multijurisdictional group of entities described in subparagraphs (A) through (F).

(3) PLANNING GRANTS.—Using funds made available under this subsection, the Secretary shall provide planning grants to eligible entities for the purpose of—

(A) in the case of a State or metropolitan planning organization, developing a resilience improvement plan under subsection (e)(2);

(B) resilience planning, predesign, design, or the development of data tools to simulate transportation disruption scenarios, including vulnerability assessments;

(C) technical capacity building by the eligible entity to facilitate the ability of the eligible entity to assess the vulnerabilities of the surface transportation assets and community response strategies of the eligible entity under current conditions and a range of potential future conditions; or

(D) evacuation planning and preparation.

(4) RESILIENCE GRANTS.—

(A) RESILIENCE IMPROVEMENT GRANTS.—

(i) IN GENERAL.—Using funds made available under this subsection, the Secretary shall provide resilience improvement grants to eligible entities to carry out 1 or more eligible activities under clause (ii).

(ii) ELIGIBLE ACTIVITIES.—

(I) IN GENERAL.—An eligible entity may use a resilience improvement grant under this subparagraph for 1 or more construction activities to improve the ability of an existing surface transportation asset to withstand 1 or more elements of a weather event or natural disaster, or to increase the resilience of surface transportation infrastructure from the impacts of changing conditions, such as sea level rise, flooding, wildfires, extreme weather events, and other natural disasters.

(II) INCLUSIONS.—An activity eligible to be carried out under this subparagraph includes—

(aa) resurfacing, restoration, rehabilitation, reconstruction, replacement, improvement, or realignment of an existing surface transportation facility eligible for assistance under this title;

(bb) the incorporation of natural infrastructure;

(cc) the upgrade of an existing surface transportation facility to meet or exceed a design standard adopted by the Federal Highway Administration;

(dd) the installation of mitigation measures that prevent the intrusion of floodwaters into surface transportation systems;

(ee) strengthening systems that remove rainwater from surface transportation facilities;

(ff) upgrades to and installation of structural stormwater controls;

(gg) a resilience project that addresses identified vulnerabilities described in the resilience improvement plan of the eligible entity, if applicable;

(hh) relocating roadways in a base floodplain to higher ground above projected flood elevation levels, or away from slide prone areas;

(ii) stabilizing slide areas or slopes;

(jj) installing riprap;

(kk) lengthening or raising bridges to increase waterway openings, including to respond to extreme weather;

(ll) increasing the size or number of drainage structures;

(mm) installing seismic retrofits on bridges;

(nn) adding scour protection at bridges;

(oo) adding scour, stream stability, coastal, and other hydraulic countermeasures, including spur dikes;

(pp) vegetation management practices in transportation rights-of-way to improve roadway safety, prevent against invasive species, facilitate wildfire control, and provide erosion control; and

(qq) any other protective features, including natural infrastructure, as determined by the Secretary.

(iii) PRIORITY.—The Secretary shall prioritize a resilience improvement grant to an eligible entity if—

(I) the Secretary determines—

(aa) the benefits of the eligible activity proposed to be carried out by the eligible entity exceed the costs of the activity; and

(bb) there is a need to address the vulnerabilities of surface transportation assets of the eligible entity with a high risk of, and impacts associated with, failure due to the impacts of weather events, natural disasters, or changing conditions, such as sea level rise, wildfires, and increased flood risk; or

(II) the eligible activity proposed to be carried out by the eligible entity is included in the applicable resilience improvement plan under subsection (e)(2).

(B) COMMUNITY RESILIENCE AND EVACUATION ROUTE GRANTS.—

(i) IN GENERAL.—Using funds made available under this subsection, the Secretary shall provide community resilience and evacuation route grants to eligible entities to carry out 1 or more eligible activities under clause (ii).

(ii) ELIGIBLE ACTIVITIES.—An eligible entity may use a community resilience and evacuation route grant under this subparagraph for 1 or more projects that strengthen and protect evacuation routes that are essential for providing and supporting evacuations caused by emergency events, including a project that—

(I) is an eligible activity under subparagraph (A)(ii), if that eligible activity will improve an evacuation route;

(II) ensures the ability of the evacuation route to provide safe passage during an evacuation and reduces the risk of damage to evacuation routes as a result of future emergency events, including restoring or replacing existing evacuation routes that are in poor condition or not designed to meet the anticipated demand during an emergency event, and including steps to protect routes from mud, rock, or other debris slides;

(III) if the eligible entity notifies the Secretary that existing evacuation routes are not sufficient to adequately facilitate evacuations, including the transportation of emergency responders and recovery resources, expands the capacity of evacuation routes to swiftly and safely accommodate evacuations, including installation of—

(aa) communications and intelligent transportation system equipment and infrastructure;

(bb) counterflow measures; or

(cc) shoulders;

(IV) is for the construction of new or redundant evacuation routes, if the eligible entity notifies the Secretary that existing evacuation routes are not sufficient to adequately facilitate evacuations, including the transportation of emergency responders and recovery resources;

(V) is for the acquisition of evacuation route or traffic incident management equipment or signage; or

(VI) will ensure access or service to critical destinations, including hospitals and other medical or emergency service facilities, major employers, critical manufacturing centers, ports and intermodal facilities, utilities, and Federal facilities.

(iii) PRIORITY.—The Secretary shall prioritize community resilience and evacuation route grants under this subparagraph for eligible activities that are cost-effective, as determined by the Secretary, taking into account—

(I) current and future vulnerabilities to an evacuation route due to future occurrence or recurrence of emergency events that are likely to occur in the geographic area in which the evacuation route is located, and

(II) projected changes in development patterns, demographics, and extreme weather events based on the best available evidence and analysis.

(iv) CONSULTATION.—In providing grants for community resilience and evacuation routes under this subparagraph, the Secretary may consult with the Administrator of the Federal Emergency Management Agency, who may provide technical assistance to the Secretary and to eligible entities.

(C) AT-RISK COASTAL INFRASTRUCTURE GRANTS.—

(i) DEFINITION OF ELIGIBLE ENTITY.—In this subparagraph, the term "eligible entity" means any of the following:

(I) A State (including the United States Virgin Islands, Guam, American Samoa, and the Commonwealth of the Northern Mariana Islands) in, or bordering on, the Atlantic, Pacific, or Arctic Ocean, the Gulf of Mexico, Long Island Sound, or 1 or more of the Great Lakes.

(II) A political subdivision of a State described in subclause (I).

(III) A metropolitan planning organization in a State described in subclause (I).

(IV) A unit of local government in a State described in subclause (I).

(V) A special purpose district or public authority with a transportation function, including a port authority, in a State described in subclause (I).

(VI) An Indian tribe in a State described in subclause (I).

(VII) A Federal land management agency that applies jointly with a State or group of States described in subclause (I).

(VIII) A multi-State or multijurisdictional group of entities described in subclauses (I) through (VII).

(ii) GRANTS.—Using funds made available under this subsection, the Secretary shall provide at-risk coastal infrastructure grants to eligible entities to carry out 1 or more eligible activities under clause (iii).

(iii) ELIGIBLE ACTIVITIES.—An eligible entity may use an at-risk coastal infrastructure grant under this subparagraph for strengthening, stabilizing, hardening, elevating, relocating, or otherwise enhancing the resilience of highway and non-rail infrastructure, including bridges, roads, pedestrian walkways, and bicycle lanes, and associated infrastructure, such as culverts and tide gates to protect highways, that are subject to, or face increased long-term future risks of, a weather event, a natural disaster, or changing conditions, including coastal flooding, coastal erosion, wave action, storm surge, or sea level rise, in order to improve transportation and public safety and to reduce costs by avoiding larger future maintenance or rebuilding costs.

(iv) CRITERIA.—The Secretary shall provide at-risk coastal infrastructure grants under this subparagraph for a project—

(I) that addresses the risks from a current or future weather event or natural disaster, including coastal flooding, coastal erosion, wave action, storm surge, or sea level change; and

(II) that reduces long-term infrastructure costs by avoiding larger future maintenance or rebuilding costs.

(v) COASTAL BENEFITS.—In addition to the criteria under clause (iv), for the purpose of providing at-risk coastal infrastructure grants under this subparagraph, the Secretary shall evaluate the extent to which a project will provide—

(I) access to coastal homes, businesses, communities, and other critical infrastructure, including access by first responders and other emergency personnel; or

(II) access to a designated evacuation route.

(5) GRANT REQUIREMENTS.—

(A) SOLICITATIONS FOR GRANTS.—In providing grants under this subsection, the Secretary shall conduct a transparent and competitive national solicitation process to select eligible projects to receive grants under paragraph (3) and subparagraphs (A), (B), and (C) of paragraph (4).

(B) APPLICATIONS.—

(i) IN GENERAL.—To be eligible to receive a grant under paragraph (3) or subparagraph (A), (B), or (C) of paragraph (4), an eligible entity shall submit to the Secretary an application in such form, at such time, and containing such information as the Secretary determines to be necessary.

(ii) PROJECTS IN CERTAIN AREAS.—If a project is proposed to be carried out by the eligible entity, in whole or in part, within a base floodplain, the eligible entity shall—

(I) as part of the application, identify the floodplain in which the project is to be located and disclose that information to the Secretary; and

(II) indicate in the application whether, if selected, the eligible entity will implement 1 or more components of the risk mitigation plan under section 322 of the Robert T. Stafford Disaster Relief and Emergency Assistance Act (42 U.S.C. 5165) with respect to the area.

(C) ELIGIBILITIES.—The Secretary may make a grant under paragraph (3) or subparagraph (A), (B), or (C) of paragraph (4) only for—

(i) a highway project eligible for assistance under this title;

(ii) a public transportation facility or service eligible for assistance under chapter 53 of title 49;

(iii) a facility or service for intercity rail passenger transportation (as defined in section 24102 of title 49); or

(iv) a port facility, including a facility that—

(I) connects a port to other modes of transportation;

(II) improves the efficiency of evacuations and disaster relief; or

(III) aids transportation.

(D) SYSTEM RESILIENCE.—A project for which a grant is provided under paragraph (3) or subparagraph (A), (B), or (C) of paragraph (4) may include the use of natural infrastructure or the construction or modification of storm surge, flood protection, or aquatic ecosystem restoration elements that the Secretary determines are functionally connected to a transportation improvement, such as—

(i) increasing marsh health and total area adjacent to a highway right-of-way to promote additional flood storage;

(ii) upgrades to and installing of culverts designed to withstand 100-year flood events;

(iii) upgrades to and installation of tide gates to protect highways; and

(iv) upgrades to and installation of flood gates to protect tunnel entrances.

(E) FEDERAL COST SHARE.—

(i) PLANNING GRANT.—The Federal share of the cost of a planning activity carried out using a planning grant under paragraph (3) shall be 100 percent.

(ii) RESILIENCE GRANTS.—

(I) IN GENERAL.—Except as provided in subclause (II) and subsection (e)(1), the Federal share of the cost of a project carried out using a grant under subparagraph (A), (B), or (C) of paragraph (4) shall not exceed 80 percent of the total project cost.

(II) TRIBAL PROJECTS.—On the determination of the Secretary, the Federal share of the cost of a project carried out using a grant under subparagraph (A), (B), or (C) of paragraph (4) by an Indian tribe (as defined in section 207(m)(1)) may be up to 100 percent.

(iii) NON-FEDERAL SHARE.—The eligible entity may use Federal funds other than Federal funds provided under this subsection to meet the non-Federal cost share requirement for a project carried out with a grant under this subsection.

(F) ELIGIBLE PROJECT COSTS.—

(i) RESILIENCE GRANT PROJECTS.—Eligible project costs for activities funded with a grant under subparagraph (A), (B), or (C) of paragraph (4) may include the costs of—

(I) development phase activities, including planning, feasibility analysis, revenue forecasting, environmental review, preliminary engineering and design work, and other preconstruction activities; and

(II) construction, reconstruction, rehabilitation, and acquisition of real property (including land related to the project and improvements to land), environmental mitigation, construction contingencies, acquisition of equipment directly related to improving system performance, and operational improvements.

(ii) PLANNING GRANTS.—Eligible project costs for activities funded with a grant under paragraph (3) may include the costs of development phase activities, including planning, feasibility analysis, revenue forecasting, environmental review, preliminary engineering and design work, other preconstruction activities, and other activities consistent with carrying out the purposes of that paragraph.

(G) LIMITATIONS.—

(i) IN GENERAL.—An eligible entity that receives a grant under subparagraph (A), (B), or (C) of paragraph (4)—

(I) may use not more than 40 percent of the amount of the grant for the construction of new capacity; and

(II) may use not more than 10 percent of the amount of the grant for activities described in subparagraph (F)(i)(I).

(ii) LIMIT ON CERTAIN ACTIVITIES.—For each fiscal year, not more than 25 percent of the total amount provided under this subsection may be used for projects described in subparagraph (C)(iii).

(H) DISTRIBUTION OF GRANTS.—

(i) IN GENERAL.—Subject to the availability of funds, an eligible entity may request and the Secretary may distribute funds for a grant under this subsection on a multiyear basis, as the Secretary determines to be necessary.

(ii) RURAL SET-ASIDE.—Of the amounts made available to carry out this subsection for each fiscal year, the Secretary shall use not less than 25 percent for grants for projects located in areas that are outside an urbanized area with a population of over 200,000.

(iii) TRIBAL SET-ASIDE.—Of the amounts made available to carry out this subsection for each fiscal year, the Secretary shall use not less than 2 percent for grants to Indian tribes (as defined in section 207(m)(1)).

(iv) REALLOCATION.—For any fiscal year, if the Secretary determines that the amount described in clause (ii) or (iii) will not be fully utilized for the grant described in that clause, the Secretary may reallocate the unutilized funds to provide grants to other eligible entities under this subsection.

(6) CONSULTATION.—In carrying out this subsection, the Secretary shall—

(A) consult with the Assistant Secretary of the Army for Civil Works, the Administrator of the Environmental Protection Agency, the Secretary of the Interior, and the Secretary of Commerce; and

(B) solicit technical support from the Administrator of the Federal Emergency Management Agency.

(7) GRANT ADMINISTRATION.—The Secretary may—

(A) retain not more than a total of 5 percent of the funds made available to carry out this subsection and to review applications for grants under this subsection; and

(B) transfer portions of the funds retained under subparagraph (A) to the relevant Administrators to fund the award and oversight of grants provided under this subsection.

(e) RESILIENCE IMPROVEMENT PLAN AND LOWER NON-FEDERAL SHARE.—

(1) FEDERAL SHARE REDUCTIONS.—

(A) IN GENERAL.—A State that receives funds apportioned to the State under section 104(b)(8) or an eligible entity that receives a grant under subsection (d) shall have the non-Federal share of a project carried out with the funds or grant, as applicable, reduced by an amount described in subparagraph (B) if the State or eligible entity meets the applicable requirements under that subparagraph.

(B) AMOUNT OF REDUCTIONS.—

(i) RESILIENCE IMPROVEMENT PLAN.—Subject to clause (iii), the amount of the non-Federal share of the costs of a project carried out with funds apportioned to a State under section 104(b)(8) or a grant under subsection (d) shall be reduced by 7 percentage points if—

(I) in the case of a State or an eligible entity that is a State or a metropolitan planning organization, the State or eligible entity has—

(aa) developed a resilience improvement plan in accordance with this subsection; and

(bb) prioritized the project on that resilience improvement plan; and

(II) in the case of an eligible entity not described in subclause (I), the eligible entity is located in a State or an area served by a metropolitan planning organization that has—

(aa) developed a resilience improvement plan in accordance with this subsection; and

(bb) prioritized the project on that resilience improvement plan.

(ii) INCORPORATION OF RESILIENCE IMPROVEMENT PLAN IN OTHER PLANNING.—Subject to clause (iii), the amount of the non-Federal share of the cost of a project carried out with funds under subsection (c) or a grant under subsection (d) shall be reduced by 3 percentage points if—

(I) in the case of a State or an eligible entity that is a State or a metropolitan planning organization, the resilience improvement plan developed in accordance with this subsection has been incorporated into the metropolitan transportation plan under section 134 or the long-range statewide transportation plan under section 135, as applicable; and

(II) in the case of an eligible entity not described in subclause (I), the eligible entity is located in a State or an area served by a metropolitan planning organization that incorporated a resilience improvement plan into the metropolitan transportation plan under section 134 or the long-range statewide transportation plan under section 135, as applicable.

(iii) LIMITATIONS.—

(I) MAXIMUM REDUCTION.—A State or eligible entity may not receive a reduction under this paragraph of more than 10 percentage points for any single project carried out with funds under subsection (c) or a grant under subsection (d).

(II) NO NEGATIVE NON-FEDERAL SHARE.—A reduction under this paragraph shall not reduce the non-Federal share of the costs of a project carried out with funds under subsection (c) or a grant under subsection (d) to an amount that is less than zero.

(2) PLAN CONTENTS.—A resilience improvement plan referred to in paragraph (1)—

(A) shall be for the immediate and long-range planning activities and investments of the State or metropolitan planning organization with respect to resilience of the surface transportation system within the boundaries of the State or metropolitan planning organization, as applicable;

(B) shall demonstrate a systemic approach to surface transportation system resilience and be consistent with and complementary of the State and local mitigation plans required under section 322 of the Robert T. Stafford Disaster Relief and Emergency Assistance Act (42 U.S.C. 5165);

(C) shall include a risk-based assessment of vulnerabilities of transportation assets and systems to current and future weather events and natural disasters, such as severe storms, flooding, drought, levee and dam failures, wildfire, rockslides, mudslides, sea level rise, extreme weather, including extreme temperatures, and earthquakes;

(D) may—

(i) designate evacuation routes and strategies, including multimodal facilities, designated with consideration for individuals without access to personal vehicles;

(ii) plan for response to anticipated emergencies, including plans for the mobility of—

(I) emergency response personnel and equipment; and

(II) access to emergency services, including for vulnerable or disadvantaged populations;

(iii) describe the resilience improvement policies, including strategies, land-use and zoning changes, investments in natural infrastructure, or performance measures that will inform the transportation investment decisions of the State or metropolitan planning organization with the goal of increasing resilience;

(iv) include an investment plan that—

(I) includes a list of priority projects; and

(II) describes how funds apportioned to the State under section 104(b)(8) or provided by a grant under the program would be invested and matched, which shall not be subject to fiscal constraint requirements; and

(v) use science and data and indicate the source of data and methodologies; and

(E) shall, as appropriate—

(i) include a description of how the plan will improve the ability of the State or metropolitan planning organization—

(I) to respond promptly to the impacts of weather events and natural disasters; and

(II) to be prepared for changing conditions, such as sea level rise and increased flood risk;

(ii) describe the codes, standards, and regulatory framework, if any, adopted and enforced to ensure resilience improvements within the impacted area of proposed projects included in the resilience improvement plan;

(iii) consider the benefits of combining hard surface transportation assets, and natural infrastructure, through coordinated efforts by the Federal Government and the States;

(iv) assess the resilience of other community assets, including buildings and housing, emergency management assets, and energy, water, and communication infrastructure;

(v) use a long-term planning period; and

(vi) include such other information as the State or metropolitan planning organization considers appropriate.

(3) NO NEW PLANNING REQUIREMENTS.—Nothing in this section requires a metropolitan planning organization or a State to develop a resilience improvement plan or to include a resilience improvement plan under the metropolitan transportation plan under section 134 or the long-range statewide transportation plan under section 135, as applicable, of the metropolitan planning organization or State.

(f) MONITORING.—

(1) IN GENERAL.—Not later than 18 months after the date of enactment of this section, the Secretary shall—

(A) establish, for the purpose of evaluating the effectiveness and impacts of projects carried out with a grant under subsection (d)—

(i) subject to paragraph (2), transportation and any other metrics as the Secretary determines to be necessary; and

(ii) procedures for monitoring and evaluating projects based on those metrics; and

(B) select a representative sample of projects to evaluate based on the metrics and procedures established under subparagraph (A).

(2) NOTICE.—Before adopting any metrics described in paragraph (1), the Secretary shall—

(A) publish the proposed metrics in the Federal Register; and

(B) provide to the public an opportunity for comment on the proposed metrics.

(g) REPORTS.—

(1) REPORTS FROM ELIGIBLE ENTITIES.—Not later than 1 year after the date on which a project carried out with a grant under subsection (d) is completed, the eligible entity that carried out the project shall submit to the Secretary a report on the results of the project and the use of the funds awarded.

(2) REPORTS TO CONGRESS.—

(A) ANNUAL REPORTS.—The Secretary shall submit to the Committee on Environment and Public Works of the Senate and the Committee on Transportation and Infrastructure of the House of Representatives, and publish on the website of the Department of Transportation, an annual report that describes the implementation of the program during the preceding calendar year, including—

(i) each project for which a grant was provided under subsection (d);

(ii) information relating to project applications received;

(iii) the manner in which the consultation requirements were implemented under subsection (d);

(iv) recommendations to improve the administration of subsection (d), including whether assistance from additional or fewer agencies to carry out the program is appropriate;

(v) the period required to disburse grant funds to eligible entities based on applicable Federal coordination requirements; and

(vi) a list of facilities that repeatedly require repair or reconstruction due to emergency events.

(B) FINAL REPORT.—Not later than 5 years after the date of enactment of the Surface Transportation Reauthorization Act of 2021, the Secretary shall submit to Congress a report that includes the results of the reports submitted under subparagraph (A).

(h) TREATMENT OF PROJECTS.—Notwithstanding any other provision of law, a project assisted under this section shall be treated as a project on a Federal-aid highway under this chapter.

(Added Pub. L. 117–58, div. A, title I, §11405(a), Nov. 15, 2021, 135 Stat. 561.)

§177. NEIGHBORHOOD ACCESS AND EQUITY GRANT PROGRAM

(a) IN GENERAL.—In addition to amounts otherwise available, there is appropriated for fiscal year 2022, out of any money in the Treasury not otherwise appropriated, $1,893,000,000, to remain available until September 30, 2026, to the Administrator of the Federal Highway Administration for competitive grants to eligible entities described in subsection (b)—

(1) to improve walkability, safety, and affordable transportation access through projects that are context-sensitive—

(A) to remove, remediate, or reuse a facility described in subsection (c)(1);

(B) to replace a facility described in subsection (c)(1) with a facility that is at-grade or lower speed;

(C) to retrofit or cap a facility described in subsection (c)(1);

(D) to build or improve complete streets, multiuse trails, regional greenways, or active transportation networks and spines; or

(E) to provide affordable access to essential destinations, public spaces, or transportation links and hubs;

(2) to mitigate or remediate negative impacts on the human or natural environment resulting from a facility described in subsection (c)(2) in a disadvantaged or underserved community through—

(A) noise barriers to reduce impacts resulting from a facility described in subsection (c)(2);

(B) technologies, infrastructure, and activities to reduce surface transportation-related greenhouse gas emissions and other air pollution;

(C) natural infrastructure, pervious, permeable, or porous pavement, or protective features to reduce or manage stormwater run-off resulting from a facility described in subsection (c)(2);

(D) infrastructure and natural features to reduce or mitigate urban heat island hot spots in the transportation right-of-way or on surface transportation facilities; or

(E) safety improvements for vulnerable road users; and

(3) for planning and capacity building activities in disadvantaged or underserved communities to—

(A) identify, monitor, or assess local and ambient air quality, emissions of transportation greenhouse gases, hot spot areas of extreme heat or elevated air pollution, gaps in tree canopy coverage, or flood prone transportation infrastructure;

(B) assess transportation equity or pollution impacts and develop local anti-displacement policies and community benefit agreements;

(C) conduct predevelopment activities for projects eligible under this subsection;

(D) expand public participation in transportation planning by individuals and organizations in disadvantaged or underserved communities; or

(E) administer or obtain technical assistance related to activities described in this subsection.

(b) ELIGIBLE ENTITIES DESCRIBED.—An eligible entity referred to in subsection (a) is—

(1) a State;

(2) a unit of local government;

(3) a political subdivision of a State;

(4) an entity described in section 207(m)(1)(E);

(5) a territory of the United States;

(6) a special purpose district or public authority with a transportation function;

(7) a metropolitan planning organization (as defined in section 134(b)(2)); or

(8) with respect to a grant described in subsection (a)(3), in addition to an eligible entity described in paragraphs (1) through (7), a nonprofit organization or institution of higher education that has entered into a partnership with an eligible entity described in paragraphs (1) through (7).

(c) FACILITY DESCRIBED.—A facility referred to in subsection (a) is—

(1) a surface transportation facility for which high speeds, grade separation, or other design factors create an obstacle to connectivity within a community; or

(2) a surface transportation facility which is a source of air pollution, noise, stormwater, or other burden to a disadvantaged or underserved community.

(d) INVESTMENT IN ECONOMICALLY DISADVANTAGED COMMUNITIES.—

(1) IN GENERAL.—In addition to amounts otherwise available, there is appropriated for fiscal year 2022, out of any money in the Treasury not otherwise appropriated, $1,262,000,000, to remain available until September 30, 2026, to the Administrator of the Federal Highway Administration to provide grants for projects in communities described in paragraph (2) for the same purposes and administered in the same manner as described in subsection (a).

(2) COMMUNITIES DESCRIBED.—A community referred to in paragraph (1) is a community that—

(A) is economically disadvantaged, underserved, or located in an area of persistent poverty;

(B) has entered or will enter into a community benefits agreement with representatives of the community;

(C) has an anti-displacement policy, a community land trust, or a community advisory board in effect; or

(D) has demonstrated a plan for employing local residents in the area impacted by the activity or project proposed under this section.

(e) ADMINISTRATION.—

(1) IN GENERAL.—A project carried out under subsection (a) or (d) shall be treated as a project on a Federal-aid highway.

(2) COMPLIANCE WITH EXISTING REQUIREMENTS.—Funds made available for a grant under this section and administered by or through a State department of transportation shall be expended in compliance with the U.S. Department of Transportation's Disadvantaged Business Enterprise Program.

(f) COST SHARE.—The Federal share of the cost of an activity carried out using a grant awarded under this section shall be not more than 80 percent, except that the Federal share of the cost of a project in a disadvantaged or underserved community may be up to 100 percent.

(g) TECHNICAL ASSISTANCE.—In addition to amounts otherwise available, there is appropriated for fiscal year 2022, out of any money in the Treasury not otherwise appropriated, $50,000,000, to remain available until September 30, 2026, to the Administrator of the Federal Highway Administration for—

(1) guidance, technical assistance, templates, training, or tools to facilitate efficient and effective contracting, design, and project delivery by units of local government;

(2) subgrants to units of local government to build capacity of such units of local government to assume responsibilities to deliver surface transportation projects; and

(3) operations and administration of the Federal Highway Administration.

(h) LIMITATIONS.—Amounts made available under this section shall not—

(1) be subject to any restriction or limitation on the total amount of funds available for implementation or execution of programs authorized for Federal-aid highways; and

(2) be used for a project for additional through travel lanes for single-occupant passenger vehicles.

(Added Pub. L. 117–169, title VI, §60501(a), Aug. 16, 2022, 136 Stat. 2080.)

§178. ENVIRONMENTAL REVIEW IMPLEMENTATION FUNDS

(a) ESTABLISHMENT.—In addition to amounts otherwise available, for fiscal year 2022, there is appropriated to the Administrator, out of any money in the Treasury not otherwise appropriated, $100,000,000, to remain available until September 30, 2026, for the purpose of facilitating the development and review of documents for the environmental review process for proposed projects through—

(1) the provision of guidance, technical assistance, templates, training, or tools to facilitate an efficient and effective environmental review process for surface transportation projects and any administrative expenses of the Federal Highway Administration to conduct activities described in this section; and

(2) providing funds made available under this subsection to eligible entities—

(A) to build capacity of such eligible entities to conduct environmental review processes;

(B) to facilitate the environmental review process for proposed projects by—

(i) defining the scope or study areas;

(ii) identifying impacts, mitigation measures, and reasonable alternatives;

(iii) preparing planning and environmental studies and other documents prior to and during the environmental review process, for potential use in the environmental review process in accordance with applicable statutes and regulations;

(iv) conducting public engagement activities; and

(v) carrying out permitting or other activities, as the Administrator determines to be appropriate, to support the timely completion of an environmental review process required for a proposed project; and

(C) for administrative expenses of the eligible entity to conduct any of the activities described in subparagraphs (A) and (B).

(b) COST SHARE.—

(1) IN GENERAL.—The Federal share of the cost of an activity carried out under this section by an eligible entity shall be not more than 80 percent.

(2) SOURCE OF FUNDS.—The non-Federal share of the cost of an activity carried out under this section by an eligible entity may be satisfied using funds made available to the eligible entity under any other Federal, State, or local grant program.

(c) DEFINITIONS.—In this section:

(1) ADMINISTRATOR.—The term "Administrator" means the Administrator of the Federal Highway Administration.

(2) ELIGIBLE ENTITY.—The term "eligible entity" means—

(A) a State;

(B) a unit of local government;

(C) a political subdivision of a State;

(D) a territory of the United States;

(E) an entity described in section 207(m)(1)(E);

(F) a recipient of funds under section 203; or

(G) a metropolitan planning organization (as defined in section 134(b)(2)).

(3) ENVIRONMENTAL REVIEW PROCESS.—The term "environmental review process" has the meaning given the term in section 139(a)(5).

(4) PROPOSED PROJECT.—The term "proposed project" means a surface transportation project for which an environmental review process is required.

(Added Pub. L. 117–169, title VI, §60505(a), Aug. 16, 2022, 136 Stat. 2083.)

§179. LOW-CARBON TRANSPORTATION MATERIALS GRANTS

(a) FEDERAL HIGHWAY ADMINISTRATION APPROPRIATION.—In addition to amounts otherwise available, there is appropriated for fiscal year 2022, out of any money in the Treasury not otherwise appropriated, $2,000,000,000, to remain available until September 30, 2026, to the Administrator to reimburse or provide incentives to eligible recipients for the use, in projects, of construction materials and products that have substantially lower levels of embodied greenhouse gas emissions associated with all relevant stages of production, use, and disposal as compared to estimated industry averages of similar materials or products, as determined by the Administrator of the Environmental Protection Agency, and for the operations and administration of the Federal Highway Administration to carry out this section.

(b) REIMBURSEMENT OF INCREMENTAL COSTS; INCENTIVES.—

(1) IN GENERAL.—The Administrator shall, subject to the availability of funds,

either reimburse or provide incentives to eligible recipients that use low-embodied carbon construction materials and products on a project funded under this title.

(2) REIMBURSEMENT AND INCENTIVE AMOUNTS.—

(A) INCREMENTAL AMOUNT.—The amount of reimbursement under paragraph (1) shall be equal to the incrementally higher cost of using such materials relative to the cost of using traditional materials, as determined by the eligible recipient and verified by the Administrator.

(B) INCENTIVE AMOUNT.—The amount of an incentive under paragraph (1) shall be equal to 2 percent of the cost of using low-embodied carbon construction materials and products on a project funded under this title.

(3) FEDERAL SHARE.—If a reimbursement or incentive is provided under paragraph (1), the total Federal share payable for the project for which the reimbursement or incentive is provided shall be up to 100 percent.

(4) LIMITATIONS.—

(A) IN GENERAL.—The Administrator shall only provide a reimbursement or incentive under paragraph (1) for a project on a—

(i) Federal-aid highway;

(ii) tribal transportation facility;

(iii) Federal lands transportation facility; or

(iv) Federal lands access transportation facility.

(B) OTHER RESTRICTIONS.—Amounts made available under this section shall not be subject to any restriction or limitation on the total amount of funds available for implementation or execution of programs authorized for Federal-aid highways.

(C) SINGLE OCCUPANT PASSENGER VEHICLES.—Funds made available under this section shall not be used for projects that result in additional through travel lanes for single occupant passenger vehicles.

(5) MATERIALS IDENTIFICATION.—The Administrator shall review the low-embodied carbon construction materials and products identified by the Administrator of the Environmental Protection Agency and shall identify low-embodied carbon construction materials and products—

(A) appropriate for use in projects eligible under this title; and

(B) eligible for reimbursement or incentives under this section.

(c) DEFINITIONS.—In this section:

(1) ADMINISTRATOR.—The term "Administrator" means the Administrator of the Federal Highway Administration.

(2) ELIGIBLE RECIPIENT.—The term "eligible recipient" means—

(A) a State;

(B) a unit of local government;

(C) a political subdivision of a State;

(D) a territory of the United States;

(E) an entity described in section 207(m)(1)(E);

(F) a recipient of funds under section 203;

(G) a metropolitan planning organization (as defined in section 134(b)(2)); or

(H) a special purpose district or public authority with a transportation function.

(3) GREENHOUSE GAS.—The term "greenhouse gas" means the air pollutants carbon

dioxide, hydrofluorocarbons, methane, nitrous oxide, perfluorocarbons, and sulfur hexafluoride.

(Added Pub. L. 117–169, title VI, §60506(a), Aug. 16, 2022, 136 Stat. 2085.)

[§§181 TO 190. RENUMBERED §§601 TO 610]

CHAPTER 2
OTHER HIGHWAYS

CHAPTER 2—OTHER HIGHWAYS

§201. FEDERAL LANDS AND TRIBAL TRANSPORTATION PROGRAMS

(a) PURPOSE.—Recognizing the need for all public Federal and tribal transportation facilities to be treated under uniform policies similar to the policies that apply to Federal-aid highways and other public transportation facilities, the Secretary of Transportation, in collaboration with the Secretaries of the appropriate Federal land management agencies, shall coordinate a uniform policy for all public Federal and tribal transportation facilities that shall apply to Federal lands transportation facilities, tribal transportation facilities, and Federal lands access transportation facilities.

(b) AVAILABILITY OF FUNDS.—

(1) AVAILABILITY.—Funds authorized for the tribal transportation program, the Federal lands transportation program, and the Federal lands access program shall be available for contract upon apportionment, or on October 1 of the fiscal year for which the funds were authorized if no apportionment is required.

(2) AMOUNT REMAINING.—Any amount remaining unexpended for a period of 3 years after the close of the fiscal year for which the funds were authorized shall lapse.

(3) OBLIGATIONS.—The Secretary of the department responsible for the administration of funds under this subsection may incur obligations, approve projects, and enter into contracts under such authorizations, which shall be considered to be contractual obligations of the United States for the payment of the cost thereof, the funds of which shall be considered to have been expended when obligated.

(4) EXPENDITURE.—

(A) IN GENERAL.—Any funds authorized for any fiscal year after the date of enactment of this section under the Federal lands transportation program, the Federal lands access program, and the tribal transportation program shall be considered to have been expended if a sum equal to the total of the sums authorized for the fiscal year and previous fiscal years have been obligated.

(B) CREDITED FUNDS.—Any funds described in subparagraph (A) that are released by payment of final voucher or modification of project authorizations shall be—

(i) credited to the balance of unobligated authorizations; and

(ii) immediately available for expenditure.

(5) APPLICABILITY.—This section shall not apply to funds authorized before the date of enactment of this paragraph.

(6) CONTRACTUAL OBLIGATION.—

(A) IN GENERAL.—Notwithstanding any other provision of law (including regulations), the authorization by the Secretary, or the Secretary of the appropriate Federal land management agency if the agency is the contracting office, of engineering and related work for the development, design, and acquisition associated with a construction project, whether performed by contract or agreement authorized by law, or the approval by the Secretary of plans, specifications, and estimates for construction of a project, shall be considered to constitute a contractual obligation of the Federal Government to pay the total eligible cost of—

(i) any project funded under this title; and

(ii) any project funded pursuant to agreements authorized by this title or any other title.

(B) EFFECT.—Nothing in this paragraph—

(i) affects the application of the Federal share associated with the project being undertaken under this section; or

(ii) modifies the point of obligation associated with Federal salaries and expenses.

(7) FEDERAL SHARE.—

(A) TRIBAL AND FEDERAL LANDS TRANSPORTATION PROGRAM.—The Federal share of the cost of a project carried out under the Federal lands transportation program or the tribal transportation program shall be 100 percent.

(B) FEDERAL LANDS ACCESS PROGRAM.—The Federal share of the cost of a project carried out under the Federal lands access program shall be be [1] up to 100 percent.

(c) TRANSPORTATION PLANNING.—

(1) TRANSPORTATION PLANNING PROCEDURES.—In consultation with the Secretary of each appropriate Federal land management agency, the Secretary shall implement transportation planning procedures for Federal lands and tribal transportation facilities that are consistent with the planning processes required under sections 134 and 135.

(2) APPROVAL OF TRANSPORTATION IMPROVEMENT PROGRAM.—The transportation improvement program developed as a part of the transportation planning process under this section shall be approved by the Secretary.

(3) INCLUSION IN OTHER PLANS.—Each regionally significant tribal transportation program, Federal lands transportation program, and Federal lands access program project shall be—

(A) developed in cooperation with State and metropolitan planning organizations; and

(B) included in appropriate tribal transportation program plans, Federal lands transportation program plans, Federal lands access program plans, State and metropolitan plans, and transportation improvement programs.

(4) INCLUSION IN STATE PROGRAMS.—The approved tribal transportation program, Federal lands transportation program, and Federal lands access program transportation improvement programs shall be included in appropriate State and metropolitan planning organization plans and programs without further action on the transportation improvement program.

(5) ASSET MANAGEMENT.—The Secretary and the Secretary of each appropriate Federal land management agency shall, to the extent appropriate, implement safety, bridge, pavement, and congestion management systems for facilities funded under the tribal transportation program and the Federal lands transportation program in support of asset management.

(6) DATA COLLECTION.—

(A) DATA COLLECTION.—

(i) IN GENERAL.—The Secretaries of the appropriate Federal land management agencies shall collect and report data necessary to implement the Federal lands transportation program, the Federal lands access program, and the tribal transportation program.

(ii) REQUIREMENT.—Data collected to implement the tribal transportation program shall be in accordance with the Indian Self-Determination and Education Assistance Act (25 U.S.C. 5301 et seq.).

(iii) INCLUSIONS.—Data collected under this paragraph includes—

(I) inventory and condition information on Federal lands transportation facilities and tribal transportation facilities; and

(II) bridge inspection and inventory information on any Federal bridge open to the public.

(B) STANDARDS.—The Secretary, in coordination with the Secretaries of the appropriate Federal land management agencies, shall define the collection and reporting data standards.

(C) TRIBAL DATA COLLECTION.—In addition to the data to be collected under subparagraph (A), not later than 90 days after the last day of each fiscal year, any entity carrying out a project under the tribal transportation program under section 202 shall submit to the Secretary and the Secretary of the Interior, based on obligations and expenditures under the tribal transportation program during the preceding fiscal year, the following data:

(i) The names of projects and activities carried out by the entity under the tribal transportation program during the preceding fiscal year.

(ii) A description of the projects and activities identified under clause (i).

(iii) The current status of the projects and activities identified under clause (i).

(iv) An estimate of the number of jobs created and the number of jobs retained by the projects and activities identified under clause (i).

(7) COOPERATIVE RESEARCH AND TECHNOLOGY DEPLOYMENT.—The Secretary may conduct cooperative research and technology deployment in coordination with Federal land management agencies, as determined appropriate by the Secretary.

(8) FUNDING.—

(A) IN GENERAL.—To carry out the activities described in this subsection for

Federal lands transportation facilities, Federal lands access transportation facilities, and other federally owned roads open to public travel (as that term is defined in section 125(e)), the Secretary shall for each fiscal year combine and use not greater than 20 percent of the funds authorized for programs under sections 203 and 204.

(B) OTHER ACTIVITIES.—In addition to the activities described in subparagraph (A), funds described under that subparagraph may be used for—

(i) bridge inspections on any federally owned bridge even if that bridge is not included on the inventory described under section 203; and

(ii) transportation planning activities carried out by Federal land management agencies eligible for funding under this chapter.

(d) REIMBURSABLE AGREEMENTS.—In carrying out work under reimbursable agreements with any State, local, or tribal government under this title, the Secretary—

(1) may, without regard to any other provision of law (including regulations), record obligations against accounts receivable from the entity; and

(2) shall credit amounts received from the entity to the appropriate account, which shall occur not later than 90 days after the date of the original request by the Secretary for payment.

(e) TRANSFERS.—

(1) IN GENERAL.—To enable the efficient use of funds made available for the Federal lands transportation program and the Federal lands access program, the funds may be transferred by the Secretary within and between each program with the concurrence of, as appropriate—

(A) the Secretary;

(B) the affected Secretaries of the respective Federal land management agencies;

(C) State departments of transportation; and

(D) local government agencies.

(2) CREDIT.—The funds described in paragraph (1) shall be credited back to the loaning entity with funds that are currently available for obligation at the time of the credit.

(f) ALTERNATIVE CONTRACTING METHODS.—

(1) IN GENERAL.—Notwithstanding any other provision of law (including the Federal Acquisition Regulation), a contracting method available to a State under this title may be used by the Secretary, on behalf of—

(A) a Federal land management agency, in using any funds pursuant to section 203, 204, or 308;

(B) a Federal land management agency, in using any funds pursuant to section 1535 of title 31 for any of the eligible uses described in sections 203(a)(1) and 204(a)(1) and paragraphs (1) and (2) of section 308(a); or

(C) a Tribal government, in using funds pursuant to section 202(b)(7)(D).

(2) METHODS DESCRIBED.—The contracting methods referred to in paragraph (1) shall include, at a minimum—

(A) project bundling;

(B) bridge bundling;

(C) design-build contracting;

(D) 2-phase contracting;

(E) long-term concession agreements; and

(F) any method tested, or that could be tested, under an experimental program relating to contracting methods carried out by the Secretary.

(3) EFFECT.—Nothing in this subsection—

(A) affects the application of the Federal share for the project carried out with a contracting method under this subsection; or

(B) modifies the point of obligation of Federal salaries and expenses.

(Added Pub. L. 112–141, div. A, title I, §1119(a), July 6, 2012, 126 Stat. 473; amended Pub. L. 114–94, div. A, title I, §§1117(a), 1120, Dec. 4, 2015, 129 Stat. 1356, 1358; Pub. L. 117–58, div. A, title I, §§11113(a), 11305(a), 11525(l), Nov. 15, 2021, 135 Stat. 479, 531, 607.)

¹ *So in original.*

§202. TRIBAL TRANSPORTATION PROGRAM

(a) USE OF FUNDS.—

(1) IN GENERAL.—Funds made available under the tribal transportation program shall be used by the Secretary of Transportation and the Secretary of the Interior to pay the costs of—

(A)(i) transportation planning, research, maintenance, engineering, rehabilitation, restoration, construction, and reconstruction of tribal transportation facilities;

(ii) adjacent vehicular parking areas;

(iii) interpretive signage;

(iv) acquisition of necessary scenic easements and scenic or historic sites;

(v) provisions for pedestrians and bicycles;

(vi) environmental mitigation in or adjacent to tribal land—

(I) to improve public safety and reduce vehicle-caused wildlife mortality while maintaining habitat connectivity; and

(II) to mitigate the damage to wildlife, aquatic organism passage, habitat, and ecosystem connectivity, including the costs of constructing, maintaining, replacing, or removing culverts and bridges, as appropriate;

(vii) construction and reconstruction of roadside rest areas, including sanitary and water facilities; and

(viii) other appropriate public road facilities as determined by the Secretary;

(B) operation and maintenance of transit programs and facilities that are located on, or provide access to, tribal land, or are administered by a tribal government; and

(C) any transportation project eligible for assistance under this title that is located within, or that provides access to, tribal land, or is associated with a tribal government.

(2) CONTRACT.—In connection with an activity described in paragraph (1), the Secretary and the Secretary of the Interior may enter into a contract or other appropriate agreement with respect to the activity with—

(A) a State (including a political subdivision of a State); or

(B) an Indian tribe.

(3) INDIAN LABOR.—Indian labor may be employed, in accordance with such rules

and regulations as may be promulgated by the Secretary of the Interior, to carry out any construction or other activity described in paragraph (1).

(4) FEDERAL EMPLOYMENT.—No maximum limitation on Federal employment shall be applicable to the construction or improvement of tribal transportation facilities.

(5) FUNDS FOR CONSTRUCTION AND IMPROVEMENT.—All funds made available for the construction and improvement of tribal transportation facilities shall be administered in conformity with regulations and agreements jointly approved by the Secretary and the Secretary of the Interior.

(6) ADMINISTRATIVE EXPENSES.—Of the funds authorized to be appropriated for the tribal transportation program, not more than 5 percent may be used by the Secretary or the Secretary of the Interior for program management and oversight and project-related administrative expenses.

(7) TRIBAL TECHNICAL ASSISTANCE CENTERS.—The Secretary of the Interior may reserve amounts from administrative funds of the Bureau of Indian Affairs that are associated with the tribal transportation program to fund tribal technical assistance centers under section 504(b).

(8) MAINTENANCE.—

(A) USE OF FUNDS.—Notwithstanding any other provision of this title, of the amount of funds allocated to an Indian tribe from the tribal transportation program, for the purpose of maintenance (excluding road sealing, which shall not be subject to any limitation), the Secretary shall not use an amount more than the greater of—

(i) an amount equal to 25 percent; or

(ii) $500,000.

(B) RESPONSIBILITY OF BUREAU OF INDIAN AFFAIRS AND SECRETARY OF THE INTERIOR.—

(i) BUREAU OF INDIAN AFFAIRS.—The Bureau of Indian Affairs shall retain primary responsibility, including annual funding request responsibility, for Bureau of Indian Affairs road maintenance programs on Indian reservations.

(ii) SECRETARY OF THE INTERIOR.—The Secretary of the Interior shall ensure that funding made available under this subsection for maintenance of tribal transportation facilities for each fiscal year is supplementary to, and not in lieu of, any obligation of funds by the Bureau of Indian Affairs for road maintenance programs on Indian reservations.

(C) TRIBAL-STATE ROAD MAINTENANCE AGREEMENTS.—

(i) IN GENERAL.—An Indian tribe and a State may enter into a road maintenance agreement under which an Indian tribe shall assume the responsibility of the State for—

(I) tribal transportation facilities; and

(II) roads providing access to tribal transportation facilities.

(ii) REQUIREMENTS.—Agreements entered into under clause (i) shall—

(I) be negotiated between the State and the Indian tribe; and

(II) not require the approval of the Secretary.

(9) COOPERATION.—

(A) IN GENERAL.—The cooperation of States, counties, or other local subdivisions may be accepted in construction and improvement.

(B) FUNDS RECEIVED.—Any funds received from a State, county, or local subdivision shall be credited to appropriations available for the tribal transportation program.

(10) COMPETITIVE BIDDING.—

(A) CONSTRUCTION.—

(i) IN GENERAL.—Subject to clause (ii) and subparagraph (B), construction of each project shall be performed by contract awarded by competitive bidding.

(ii) EXCEPTION.—Clause (i) shall not apply if the Secretary or the Secretary of the Interior affirmatively finds that, under the circumstances relating to the project, a different method is in the public interest.

(B) APPLICABILITY.—Notwithstanding subparagraph (A), section 23 of the Act of June 25, 1910 (25 U.S.C. 47) and section 7(b) of the Indian Self-Determination and Education Assistance Act (25 U.S.C. 5307(b)) shall apply to all funds administered by the Secretary of the Interior that are appropriated for the construction and improvement of tribal transportation facilities.

(b) FUNDS DISTRIBUTION.—

(1) NATIONAL TRIBAL TRANSPORTATION FACILITY INVENTORY.—

(A) IN GENERAL.—The Secretary of the Interior, in cooperation with the Secretary, shall maintain a comprehensive national inventory of tribal transportation facilities that are eligible for assistance under the tribal transportation program.

(B) TRANSPORTATION FACILITIES INCLUDED IN THE INVENTORY.—For purposes of identifying the tribal transportation system and determining the relative transportation needs among Indian tribes, the Secretary shall include, at a minimum, transportation facilities that are eligible for assistance under the tribal transportation program that an Indian tribe has requested, including facilities that—

(i) were included in the Bureau of Indian Affairs system inventory prior to October 1, 2004;

(ii) are owned by an Indian tribal government;

(iii) are owned by the Bureau of Indian Affairs;

(iv) were constructed or reconstructed with funds from the Highway Trust Fund under the Indian reservation roads program since 1983;

(v) are public roads or bridges within the exterior boundary of Indian reservations, Alaska Native villages, and other recognized Indian communities (including communities in former Indian reservations in the State of Oklahoma) in which the majority of residents are American Indians or Alaska Natives;

(vi) are public roads within or providing access to an Indian reservation or Indian trust land or restricted Indian land that is not subject to fee title alienation without the approval of the Federal Government, or Indian or Alaska Native villages, groups, or communities in which Indians and Alaska Natives reside, whom the Secretary of the Interior has determined are eligible for services generally available to Indians under Federal laws specifically applicable to Indians; or

(vii) are primary access routes proposed by tribal governments, including roads between villages, roads to landfills, roads to drinking water sources, roads to natural resources identified for economic development, and roads that provide access to intermodal terminals, such as airports, harbors, or boat landings.

(C) LIMITATION ON PRIMARY ACCESS ROUTES.—For purposes of this paragraph, a proposed primary access route is the shortest practicable route connecting 2 points of the proposed route.

(D) ADDITIONAL FACILITIES.—Nothing in this paragraph precludes the Secretary from including additional transportation facilities that are eligible for funding under the tribal transportation program in the inventory used for the national funding allocation if such additional facilities are included in the inventory in a uniform and consistent manner nationally.

(E) BRIDGES.—All bridges in the inventory shall be recorded in the national bridge inventory administered by the Secretary under section 144.

(2) REGULATIONS.—Notwithstanding sections 563(a) and 565(a) of title 5, the Secretary of the Interior shall maintain any regulations governing the tribal transportation program.

(3) BASIS FOR FUNDING FORMULA.—

(A) BASIS.—

(i) IN GENERAL.—After making the set asides authorized under subparagraph (C) and subsections (a)(6), (c), (d), and (e) on October 1 of each fiscal year, the Secretary shall distribute the remainder authorized to be appropriated for the tribal transportation program under this section among Indian tribes as follows:

(I) For fiscal year 2013—

(aa) for each Indian tribe, 80 percent of the total relative need distribution factor and population adjustment factor for the fiscal year 2011 funding amount made available to that Indian tribe; and

(bb) the remainder using tribal shares as described in subparagraphs (B) and (C).

(II) For fiscal year 2014—

(aa) for each Indian tribe, 60 percent of the total relative need distribution factor and population adjustment factor for the fiscal year 2011 funding amount made available to that Indian tribe; and

(bb) the remainder using tribal shares as described in subparagraphs (B) and (C).

(III) For fiscal year 2015—

(aa) for each Indian tribe, 40 percent of the total relative need distribution factor and population adjustment factor for the fiscal year 2011 funding amount made available to that Indian tribe; and

(bb) the remainder using tribal shares as described in subparagraphs (B) and (C).

(IV) For fiscal year 2016 and thereafter—

(aa) for each Indian tribe, 20 percent of the total relative need distribution factor and population adjustment factor for the fiscal year 2011 funding amount made available to that Indian tribe; and

(bb) the remainder using tribal shares as described in subparagraphs (B) and (C).

(ii) TRIBAL HIGH PRIORITY PROJECTS.—The High Priority Projects program as included in the Tribal Transportation Allocation Methodology of part 170 of title 25, Code of Federal Regulations (as in effect on the date of enactment of the MAP–21), shall not continue in effect.

(B) TRIBAL SHARES.—Tribal shares under this program shall be determined using the national tribal transportation facility inventory as calculated for fiscal year 2012, and the most recent data on American Indian and Alaska Native population within each Indian tribe's American Indian/Alaska Native Reservation or Statistical Area, as computed under the Native American Housing Assistance and Self-Determination Act of 1996 (25 U.S.C. 4101 et seq.), in the following manner:

(i) 27 percent in the ratio that the total eligible road mileage in each tribe bears to the total eligible road mileage of all American Indians and Alaskan Natives. For the purposes of this calculation, eligible road mileage shall be computed based on the inventory described in paragraph (1), using only facilities included in the inventory described in clause (i), (ii), or (iii) of paragraph (1)(B).

(ii) 39 percent in the ratio that the total population in each tribe bears to the total population of all American Indians and Alaskan Natives.

(iii) 34 percent shall be divided equally among each Bureau of Indian Affairs region. Within each region, such share of funds shall be distributed to each Indian tribe in the ratio that the average total relative need distribution factors and population adjustment factors from fiscal years 2005 through 2011 for a tribe bears to the average total of relative need distribution factors and population adjustment factors for fiscal years 2005 through 2011 in that region.

(C) TRIBAL SUPPLEMENTAL FUNDING.—

(i) TRIBAL SUPPLEMENTAL FUNDING AMOUNT.—Of funds made available for each fiscal year for the tribal transportation program, the Secretary shall set aside the following amount for a tribal supplemental program:

(I) If the amount made available for the tribal transportation program is less than or equal to $275,000,000, 30 percent of such amount.

(II) If the amount made available for the tribal transportation program exceeds $275,000,000—

(aa) $82,500,000; plus

(bb) 12.5 percent of the amount made available for the tribal transportation program in excess of $275,000,000.

(ii) TRIBAL SUPPLEMENTAL ALLOCATION.—The Secretary shall distribute tribal supplemental funds as follows:

(I) DISTRIBUTION AMONG REGIONS.—Of the amounts set aside under clause (i), the Secretary shall distribute to each region of the Bureau of Indian Affairs a share of tribal supplemental funds in proportion to the regional total of tribal shares based on the cumulative tribal shares of all Indian tribes within such region under subparagraph (B).

(II) DISTRIBUTION WITHIN A REGION.—Of the amount that a region receives under subclause (I), the Secretary shall distribute tribal supplemental funding among Indian tribes within such region as follows:

(aa) TRIBAL SUPPLEMENTAL AMOUNTS.—The Secretary shall determine—

(AA) which such Indian tribes would be entitled under subparagraph (A) to receive in a fiscal year less funding than they would receive in fiscal year 2011 pursuant to the relative need distribution factor and population adjustment factor, as described in subpart C of part 170 of title 25, Code of Federal Regulations (as in effect on the date of enactment of the MAP–21); and

(BB) the combined amount that such Indian tribes would be entitled to receive in fiscal year 2011 pursuant to such relative need distribution factor and population adjustment factor in excess of the amount that they would be entitled to receive in the fiscal year under subparagraph (B).

(bb) COMBINED AMOUNT.—Subject to subclause (III), the Secretary shall distribute to each Indian tribe that meets the criteria described in item (aa)(AA) a share of funding under this subparagraph in proportion to the share of the combined amount determined under item (aa)(BB) attributable to such Indian tribe.

(III) CEILING.—An Indian tribe may not receive under subclause (II) and based on its tribal share under subparagraph (A) a combined amount that exceeds the amount that such Indian tribe would be entitled to receive in fiscal year 2011 pursuant to the relative need distribution factor and population adjustment factor, as described in subpart C of part 170 of title 25, Code of Federal Regulations (as in effect on the date of enactment of the MAP–21).

(IV) OTHER AMOUNTS.—If the amount made available for a region under subclause (I) exceeds the amount distributed among Indian tribes within that region under subclause (II), the Secretary shall distribute the remainder of such region's funding under such subclause among all Indian tribes in that region in proportion to the combined amount that each such Indian tribe received under subparagraph (A) and subclauses (I), (II), and (III).

(4) TRANSFERRED FUNDS.—

(A) IN GENERAL.—Not later than 30 days after the date on which funds are made available to the Secretary of the Interior under this paragraph, the funds shall be distributed to, and made available for immediate use by, eligible Indian tribes, in accordance with the formula for distribution of funds under the tribal transportation program.

(B) USE OF FUNDS.—Notwithstanding any other provision of this section, funds made available to Indian tribes for tribal transportation facilities shall be expended on projects identified in a transportation improvement program approved by the Secretary.

(5) HEALTH AND SAFETY ASSURANCES.—Notwithstanding any other provision of law, an Indian tribal government may approve plans, specifications, and estimates and commence road and bridge construction with funds made available from the tribal transportation program through a contract or agreement under the Indian Self-Determination and Education Assistance Act (25 U.S.C. 5301 et seq.), if the Indian tribal government—

(A) provides assurances in the contract or agreement that the construction will meet or exceed applicable health and safety standards;

(B) obtains the advance review of the plans and specifications from a State-licensed civil engineer that has certified that the plans and specifications meet or exceed the applicable health and safety standards; and

(C) provides a copy of the certification under subparagraph (A) to the Deputy Assistant Secretary for Tribal Government Affairs, Department of Transportation, or the Assistant Secretary for Indian Affairs, Department of the Interior, as appropriate.

(6) Contracts and agreements with Indian tribes.—

(A) In general.—Notwithstanding any other provision of law or any interagency agreement, program guideline, manual, or policy directive, all funds made available through the Secretary of the Interior under this chapter and section 125(e) for tribal transportation facilities to pay for the costs of programs, services, functions, and activities, or portions of programs, services, functions, or activities, that are specifically or functionally related to the cost of planning, research, engineering, and construction of any tribal transportation facility shall be made available, upon request of the Indian tribal government, to the Indian tribal government for contracts and agreements for such planning, research, engineering, and construction in accordance with [1] Indian Self-Determination and Education Assistance Act (25 U.S.C. 5301 et seq.).

(B) Exclusion of agency participation.—All funds, including contract support costs, for programs, functions, services, or activities, or portions of programs, services, functions, or activities, including supportive administrative functions that are otherwise contractible to which subparagraph (A) applies, shall be paid in accordance with subparagraph (A), without regard to the organizational level at which the Department of the Interior has previously carried out such programs, functions, services, or activities.

(7) Contracts and agreements with Indian tribes.—

(A) In general.—Notwithstanding any other provision of law or any interagency agreement, program guideline, manual, or policy directive, all funds made available to an Indian tribal government under this chapter for a tribal transportation facility program or project shall be made available, on the request of the Indian tribal government, to the Indian tribal government for use in carrying out, in accordance with the Indian Self-Determination and Education Assistance Act (25 U.S.C. 5301 et seq.), contracts and agreements for the planning, research, design, engineering, construction, and maintenance relating to the program or project.

(B) Exclusion of agency participation.—In accordance with subparagraph (A), all funds, including contract support costs, for a program or project to which subparagraph (A) applies shall be paid to the Indian tribal government without regard to the organizational level at which the Department of the Interior has previously carried out, or the Department of Transportation has previously carried out under the tribal transportation program, the programs, functions, services, or activities involved.

(C) Consortia.—Two or more Indian tribes that are otherwise eligible to participate in a program or project to which this chapter applies may form a consortium to be considered as a single Indian tribe for the purpose of participating in the project under this section.

(D) SECRETARY AS SIGNATORY.—Notwithstanding any other provision of law, the Secretary is authorized to enter into a funding agreement with an Indian tribal government to carry out a tribal transportation facility program or project under subparagraph (A) that is located on an Indian reservation or provides access to the reservation or a community of the Indian tribe.

(E) FUNDING.—The amount an Indian tribal government receives for a program or project under subparagraph (A) shall equal the sum of the funding that the Indian tribal government would otherwise receive for the program or project in accordance with the funding formula established under this subsection and such additional amounts as the Secretary determines equal the amounts that would have been withheld for the costs of the Bureau of Indian Affairs for administration of the program or project.

(F) ELIGIBILITY.—

(i) IN GENERAL.—Subject to clause (ii) and the approval of the Secretary, funds may be made available under subparagraph (A) to an Indian tribal government for a program or project in a fiscal year only if the Indian tribal government requesting such funds demonstrates to the satisfaction of the Secretary financial stability and financial management capability during the 3 fiscal years immediately preceding the fiscal year for which the request is being made.

(ii) CONSIDERATIONS.—An Indian tribal government that had no uncorrected significant and material audit exceptions in the required annual audit of the contracts or self-governance funding agreements made by the Indian tribe with any Federal agency under the Indian Self-Determination and Education Assistance Act (25 U.S.C. 5301 et seq.) during the 3-fiscal year period referred in clause (i) shall be conclusive evidence of the financial stability and financial management capability of the Indian tribe for purposes of clause (i).

(G) ASSUMPTION OF FUNCTIONS AND DUTIES.—An Indian tribal government receiving funding under subparagraph (A) for a program or project shall assume all functions and duties that the Secretary of the Interior would have performed with respect to a program or project under this chapter, other than those functions and duties that inherently cannot be legally transferred under the Indian Self-Determination and Education Assistance Act (25 U.S.C. 5301 et seq.).

(H) POWERS.—An Indian tribal government receiving funding under subparagraph (A) for a program or project shall have all powers that the Secretary of the Interior would have exercised in administering the funds transferred to the Indian tribal government for such program or project under this section if the funds had not been transferred, except to the extent that such powers are powers that inherently cannot be legally transferred under the Indian Self-Determination and Education Assistance Act (25 U.S.C. 5301 et seq.).

(I) DISPUTE RESOLUTION.—In the event of a disagreement between the Secretary or the Secretary of the Interior and an Indian tribe over whether a particular function, duty, or power may be lawfully transferred to the Indian tribe under the Indian Self-Determination and Education Assistance Act (25 U.S.C. 5301 et seq.), the Indian tribe shall have the right to pursue all alternative dispute resolution and appeal procedures authorized by that Act, including regulations issued to carry out the Act.

(J) TERMINATION OF CONTRACT OR AGREEMENT.—On the date of the termination of a contract or agreement under this section by an Indian tribal government, the Secretary shall transfer all funds that would have been allocated to the Indian tribal government under the contract or agreement to the Secretary of the Interior to provide continued transportation services in accordance with applicable law.

(c) PLANNING.—

(1) IN GENERAL.—For each fiscal year, not more than 2 percent of the funds made available for the tribal transportation program shall be allocated among Indian tribal governments that apply for transportation planning pursuant to the Indian Self-Determination and Education Assistance Act (25 U.S.C. 5301 et seq.).

(2) REQUIREMENT.—An Indian tribal government, in cooperation with the Secretary of the Interior and, as appropriate, with a State, local government, or metropolitan planning organization, shall carry out a transportation planning process in accordance with section 201(c).

(3) SELECTION AND APPROVAL OF PROJECTS.—A project funded under this section shall be—

(A) selected by the Indian tribal government from the transportation improvement program; and

(B) subject to the approval of the Secretary of the Interior and the Secretary.

(d) TRIBAL TRANSPORTATION FACILITY BRIDGES.—

(1) NATIONWIDE PRIORITY PROGRAM.—The Secretary shall maintain a nationwide priority program for improving bridges eligible for the tribal transportation program classified as in poor condition, having low load capacity, or needing geometric improvements.

(2) USE OF FUNDS.—Funds made available to carry out this subsection shall be used—

(A) to carry out any planning, design, engineering, preconstruction, construction, and inspection of new or replacement tribal transportation facility bridges;

(B) to replace, rehabilitate, seismically retrofit, paint, apply calcium magnesium acetate, sodium acetate/formate, or other environmentally acceptable, minimally corrosive anti-icing and deicing composition; or

(C) to implement any countermeasure for tribal transportation facility bridges classified as in poor condition, having a low load capacity, or needing geometric improvements, including multiple-pipe culverts.

(3) ELIGIBLE BRIDGES.—To be eligible to receive funding under this subsection, a bridge described in paragraph (1) shall—

(A) have an opening of not less than 20 feet;

(B) be classified as a tribal transportation facility; and

(C) be classified as in poor condition, having a low load capacity, or needing geometric improvements.

(4) APPROVAL REQUIREMENT.—The Secretary may make funds available under this subsection for preliminary engineering, construction, and construction engineering

activities after approval of required documentation and verification of eligibility in accordance with this title.

(e) SAFETY.—

(1) FUNDING.—Before making any distribution under subsection (b), the Secretary shall set aside not more than 4 percent of the funds made available under the tribal transportation program for each fiscal year to be allocated based on an identification and analysis of highway safety issues and opportunities on tribal land, as determined by the Secretary, on application of the Indian tribal governments for eligible projects described in section 148(a)(4).

(2) PROJECT SELECTION.—An Indian tribal government, in cooperation with the Secretary of the Interior and, as appropriate, with a State, local government, or metropolitan planning organization, shall select projects from the transportation improvement program, subject to the approval of the Secretary and the Secretary of the Interior.

(f) FEDERAL-AID ELIGIBLE PROJECTS.—Before approving as a project on a tribal transportation facility any project eligible for funds apportioned under section 104 in a State, the Secretary shall, for projects on tribal transportation facilities, determine that the obligation of funds for the project is supplementary to and not in lieu of the obligation of a fair and equitable share of funds apportioned to the State under section 104.

(Added Pub. L. 112–141, div. A, title I, §1119(a), July 6, 2012, 126 Stat. 476; amended Pub. L. 114–94, div. A, title I, §§1118, 1446(a)(12), Dec. 4, 2015, 129 Stat. 1358, 1438; Pub. L. 117–58, div. A, title I, §§11524(c), 11525(m), title IV, §§14004, 14008(d), Nov. 15, 2021, 135 Stat. 606, 608, 648, 651.)

1 So in original. Probably should be followed by "the".

§203. FEDERAL LANDS TRANSPORTATION PROGRAM

(a) USE OF FUNDS.—

(1) IN GENERAL.—Funds made available under the Federal lands transportation program shall be used by the Secretary of Transportation and the Secretary of the appropriate Federal land management agency to pay the costs of—

(A) program administration, transportation planning, research, preventive maintenance, engineering, rehabilitation, restoration, construction, and reconstruction of Federal lands transportation facilities, and—

(i) adjacent vehicular parking areas;

(ii) acquisition of necessary scenic easements and scenic or historic sites;

(iii) provision for pedestrians and bicycles;

(iv) environmental mitigation in or adjacent to Federal land open to the public—

(I) to improve public safety and reduce vehicle-caused wildlife mortality while maintaining habitat connectivity; and

(II) to mitigate the damage to wildlife, aquatic organism passage, habitat, and ecosystem connectivity, including the costs of constructing, maintaining, replacing, or removing culverts and bridges, as appropriate;

(v) construction and reconstruction of roadside rest areas, including sanitary and water facilities;

(vi) congestion mitigation; and

(vii) other appropriate public road facilities, as determined by the Secretary;

(B) capital, operations, and maintenance of transit facilities;

(C) any transportation project eligible for assistance under this title that is on a public road within or adjacent to, or that provides access to, Federal lands open to the public; and

(D) not more $20,000,000 [1] of the amounts made available per fiscal year to carry out this section for activities eligible under subparagraph (A)(iv)(I).

(2) CONTRACT.—In connection with an activity described in paragraph (1), the Secretary and the Secretary of the appropriate Federal land management agency may enter into a contract or other appropriate agreement with respect to the activity with—

(A) a State (including a political subdivision of a State); or

(B) an Indian tribe.

(3) ADMINISTRATION.—All appropriations for the construction and improvement of Federal lands transportation facilities shall be administered in conformity with regulations and agreements jointly approved by the Secretary and the Secretary of the appropriate Federal land managing agency.

(4) COOPERATION.—

(A) IN GENERAL.—The cooperation of States, counties, or other local subdivisions may be accepted in construction and improvement.

(B) FUNDS RECEIVED.—Any funds received from a State, county, or local subdivision shall be credited to appropriations available for the class of Federal lands transportation facilities to which the funds were contributed.

(5) COMPETITIVE BIDDING.—

(A) IN GENERAL.—Subject to subparagraph (B), construction of each project shall be performed by contract awarded by competitive bidding.

(B) EXCEPTION.—Subparagraph (A) shall not apply if the Secretary or the Secretary of the appropriate Federal land management agency affirmatively finds that, under the circumstances relating to the project, a different method is in the public interest.

(6) NATIVE PLANT MATERIALS.—In carrying out an activity described in paragraph (1), the entity carrying out the activity shall consider, to the maximum extent practicable—

(A) the use of locally adapted native plant materials; and

(B) designs that minimize runoff and heat generation.

(b) AGENCY PROGRAM DISTRIBUTIONS.—

(1) IN GENERAL.—On October 1, 2011, and on October 1 of each fiscal year thereafter, the Secretary shall allocate the sums authorized to be appropriated for the fiscal year for the Federal lands transportation program on the basis of applications of need, as determined by the Secretary—

(A) in consultation with the Secretaries of the applicable Federal land management agencies; and

(B) in coordination with the transportation plans required under section 201 of the respective transportation systems of—

(i) the National Park Service;

(ii) the Forest Service;

(iii) the United States Fish and Wildlife Service;

(iv) the Corps of Engineers;

(v) the Bureau of Land Management;

(vi) the Bureau of Reclamation; and

(vii) independent Federal agencies with natural resource and land management responsibilities.

(2) APPLICATIONS.—

(A) REQUIREMENTS.—Each application submitted by a Federal land management agency shall include proposed programs at various potential funding levels, as defined by the Secretary following collaborative discussions with applicable Federal land management agencies.

(B) CONSIDERATION BY SECRETARY.—In evaluating an application submitted under subparagraph (A), the Secretary shall consider the extent to which the programs support performance management, including—

(i) the transportation goals of—

(I) a state of good repair of transportation facilities;

(II) a reduction of bridge deficiencies; and

(III) an improvement of safety;

(ii) high-use Federal recreational sites or Federal economic generators; and

(iii) the resource and asset management goals of the Secretary of the respective Federal land management agency.

(C) PERMISSIVE CONTENTS.—Applications may include proposed programs the duration of which extend over a multiple-year period to support long-term transportation planning and resource management initiatives.

(c) NATIONAL FEDERAL LANDS TRANSPORTATION FACILITY INVENTORY.—

(1) IN GENERAL.—The Secretaries of the appropriate Federal land management agencies, in cooperation with the Secretary, shall maintain a comprehensive national inventory of public Federal lands transportation facilities.

(2) TRANSPORTATION FACILITIES INCLUDED IN THE INVENTORIES.—To identify the Federal lands transportation system and determine the relative transportation needs among Federal land management agencies, the inventories shall include, at a minimum, facilities that—

(A) provide access to high-use Federal recreation sites or Federal economic generators, as determined by the Secretary in coordination with the respective Secretaries of the appropriate Federal land management agencies; and

(B) are owned by 1 of the following agencies:

(i) The National Park Service.

(ii) The Forest Service.

(iii) The United States Fish and Wildlife Service.

(iv) The Bureau of Land Management.

(v) The Corps of Engineers.

(vi) The Bureau of Reclamation.

(3) AVAILABILITY.—The inventories shall be made available to the Secretary.

(4) UPDATES.—The Secretaries of the appropriate Federal land management

agencies shall update the inventories of the appropriate Federal land management agencies, as determined by the Secretary after collaborative discussions with the Secretaries of the appropriate Federal land management agencies.

(5) REVIEW.—A decision to add or remove a facility from the inventory shall not be considered a Federal action for purposes of review under the National Environmental Policy Act of 1969 (42 U.S.C. 4321 et seq.).

(d) BICYCLE SAFETY.—The Secretary of the appropriate Federal land management agency shall prohibit the use of bicycles on each federally owned road that has a speed limit of 30 miles per hour or greater and an adjacent paved path for use by bicycles within 100 yards of the road unless the Secretary determines that the bicycle level of service on that roadway is rated B or higher.

(e) EFFICIENT IMPLEMENTATION OF NEPA.—

(1) DEFINITIONS.—In this subsection:

(A) ENVIRONMENTAL DOCUMENT. The term "environmental document" means an environmental impact statement, environmental assessment, categorical exclusion, or other document prepared under the National Environmental Policy Act of 1969 (42 U.S.C. 4321 et seq.).

(B) PROJECT.—The term "project" means a highway project, public transportation capital project, or multimodal project that—

(i) receives funds under this title; and

(ii) is authorized under this section or section 204.

(C) PROJECT SPONSOR.—The term "project sponsor" means the Federal land management agency that seeks or receives funds under this title for a project.

(2) ENVIRONMENTAL REVIEW TO BE COMPLETED BY FEDERAL HIGHWAY ADMINISTRATION.—The Federal Highway Administration may prepare an environmental document pursuant to the implementing procedures of the Federal Highway Administration to comply with the requirements of the National Environmental Policy Act of 1969 (42 U.S.C. 4321 et seq.) if—

(A) requested by a project sponsor; and

(B) all areas of analysis required by the project sponsor can be addressed.

(3) FEDERAL LAND MANAGEMENT AGENCIES ADOPTION OF EXISTING ENVIRONMENTAL REVIEW DOCUMENTS.—

(A) IN GENERAL.—To the maximum extent practicable, if the Federal Highway Administration prepares an environmental document pursuant to paragraph (2), that environmental document shall address all areas of analysis required by a Federal land management agency.

(B) INDEPENDENT EVALUATION.—Notwithstanding any other provision of law, a Federal land management agency shall not be required to conduct an independent evaluation to determine the adequacy of an environmental document prepared by the Federal Highway Administration pursuant to paragraph (2).

(C) USE OF SAME DOCUMENT.—In authorizing or implementing a project, a Federal land management agency may use an environmental document previously prepared by the Federal Highway Administration for a project addressing the same or substantially the same action to the same extent that the Federal land management agency could adopt or use a document previously prepared by another

Federal agency.

(4) APPLICATION BY FEDERAL LAND MANAGEMENT AGENCIES OF CATEGORICAL EXCLUSIONS ESTABLISHED BY FEDERAL HIGHWAY ADMINISTRATION.—In carrying out requirements under the National Environmental Policy Act of 1969 (42 U.S.C. 4321 et seq.) for a project, the project sponsor may use categorical exclusions designated under that Act in the implementing regulations of the Federal Highway Administration, subject to the conditions that—

 (A) the project sponsor makes a determination, in consultation with the Federal Highway Administration, that the categorical exclusion applies to the project;

 (B) the project satisfies the conditions for a categorical exclusion under the National Environmental Policy Act of 1969 (42 U.S.C. 4321 et seq.); and

 (C) the use of the categorical exclusion does not otherwise conflict with the implementing regulations of the project sponsor, except any list of the project sponsor that designates categorical exclusions.

(5) MITIGATION COMMITMENTS.—The Secretary shall assist the Federal land management agency with all design and mitigation commitments made jointly by the Secretary and the project sponsor in any environmental document prepared by the Secretary in accordance with this subsection.

(Added Pub. L. 112–141, div. A, title I, §1119(a), July 6, 2012, 126 Stat. 486; amended Pub. L. 114–94, div. A, title I, §1119, Dec. 4, 2015, 129 Stat. 1358; Pub. L. 117–58, div. A, title I, §§11112, 11311, Nov. 15, 2021, 135 Stat. 479, 536.)

 [1] *So in original.*

§204. FEDERAL LANDS ACCESS PROGRAM

(a) USE OF FUNDS.—

(1) IN GENERAL.—Funds made available under the Federal lands access program shall be used by the Secretary of Transportation and the Secretary of the appropriate Federal land management agency to pay the cost of—

 (A) transportation planning, research, engineering, preventive maintenance, rehabilitation, restoration, context-sensitive solutions, construction, and reconstruction of Federal lands access transportation facilities located on or adjacent to, or that provide access to, Federal land, and—

  (i) adjacent vehicular parking areas, including interpretive panels in or adjacent to those areas;

  (ii) acquisition of necessary scenic easements and scenic or historic sites;

  (iii) provisions for pedestrians and bicycles;

  (iv) environmental mitigation in or adjacent to Federal land to improve public safety and reduce vehicle-caused wildlife mortality while maintaining habitat connectivity;

  (v) construction and reconstruction of roadside rest areas, including sanitary and water facilities;

  (vi) contextual wayfinding markers;

  (vii) landscaping;

  (viii) cooperative mitigation of visual blight, including screening or removal; and

(ix) other appropriate public road facilities, as determined by the Secretary;

(B) operation and maintenance of transit facilities; and

(C) any transportation project eligible for assistance under this title that is within or adjacent to, or that provides access to, Federal land.

(2) CONTRACT.—In connection with an activity described in paragraph (1), the Secretary and the Secretary of the appropriate Federal land management agency may enter into a contract or other appropriate agreement with respect to the activity with—

(A) a State (including a political subdivision of a State); or

(B) an Indian tribe.

(3) ADMINISTRATION.—All appropriations for the construction and improvement of Federal lands access transportation facilities shall be administered in conformity with regulations and agreements approved by the Secretary.

(4) COOPERATION.—

(A) IN GENERAL.—The cooperation of States, counties, or other local subdivisions may be accepted in construction and improvement.

(B) FUNDS RECEIVED.—Any funds received from a State, county, or local subdivision for a Federal lands access transportation facility project shall be credited to appropriations available under the Federal lands access program.

(5) COMPETITIVE BIDDING.—

(A) IN GENERAL.—Subject to subparagraph (B), construction of each project shall be performed by contract awarded by competitive bidding.

(B) EXCEPTION.—Subparagraph (A) shall not apply if the Secretary or the Secretary of the appropriate Federal land management agency affirmatively finds that, under the circumstances relating to the project, a different method is in the public interest.

(6) NATIVE PLANT MATERIALS.—In carrying out an activity described in paragraph (1), the Secretary shall ensure that the entity carrying out the activity considers, to the maximum extent practicable—

(A) the use of locally adapted native plant materials; and

(B) designs that minimize runoff and heat generation.

(b) PROGRAM DISTRIBUTIONS.—

(1) IN GENERAL.—Funding made available to carry out the Federal lands access program shall be allocated among those States that have Federal land, in accordance with the following formula:

(A) 80 percent of the available funding for use in those States that contain at least 1 ½ percent of the total public land in the United States managed by the agencies described in paragraph (2), to be distributed as follows:

(i) 30 percent in the ratio that—

(I) recreational visitation within each such State; bears to

(II) the recreational visitation within all such States.

(ii) 5 percent in the ratio that—

(I) the Federal land area within each such State; bears to

(II) the Federal land area in all such States.

(iii) 55 percent in the ratio that—

(I) the Federal public road miles within each such State; bears to

(II) the Federal public road miles in all such States.

(iv) 10 percent in the ratio that—

(I) the number of Federal public bridges within each such State; bears to

(II) the number of Federal public bridges in all such States.

(B) 20 percent of the available funding for use in those States that do not contain at least 1 ½ percent of the total public land in the United States managed by the agencies described in paragraph (2), to be distributed as follows:

(i) 30 percent in the ratio that—

(I) recreational visitation within each such State; bears to

(II) the recreational visitation within all such States.

(ii) 5 percent in the ratio that—

(I) the Federal land area within each such State; bears to

(II) the Federal land area in all such States.

(iii) 55 percent in the ratio that—

(I) the Federal public road miles within each such State; bears to

(II) the Federal public road miles in all such States.

(iv) 10 percent in the ratio that—

(I) the number of Federal public bridges within each such State; bears to

(II) the number of Federal public bridges in all such States.

(2) DATA SOURCE.—Data necessary to distribute funding under paragraph (1) shall be provided by the following Federal land management agencies:

(A) The National Park Service.

(B) The Forest Service.

(C) The United States Fish and Wildlife Service.

(D) The Bureau of Land Management.

(E) The Corps of Engineers.

(c) PROGRAMMING DECISIONS COMMITTEE.—

(1) IN GENERAL.—Programming decisions shall be made within each State by a committee comprised of—

(A) a representative of the Federal Highway Administration;

(B) a representative of the State Department of Transportation; and

(C) a representative of any appropriate political subdivision of the State.

(2) CONSULTATION REQUIREMENT.—The committee described in paragraph (1) shall cooperate with each applicable Federal agency in each State before any joint discussion or final programming decision.

(3) PROJECT PREFERENCE.—In making a programming decision under paragraph (1), the committee shall give preference to projects that provide access to, are adjacent to, or are located within high-use Federal recreation sites or Federal economic generators, as identified by the Secretaries of the appropriate Federal land management agencies.

(Added Pub. L. 112–141, div. A, title I, §1119(a), July 6, 2012, 126 Stat. 489; amended Pub. L. 117–58, div. A, title I, §11113(b), Nov. 15, 2021, 135 Stat. 479.)

§205. FOREST DEVELOPMENT ROADS AND TRAILS

(a) Funds available for forest development roads and trails shall be used by the Secretary of Agriculture to pay for the costs of construction and maintenance thereof, including roads and trails on experimental and other areas under Forest Service administration. In connection therewith, the Secretary of Agriculture may enter into contracts with a State or civil subdivision thereof, and issue such regulations as he deems advisable.

(b) Cooperation of States, counties, or other local subdivisions may be accepted but shall not be required by the Secretary of Agriculture.

(c) Construction estimated to cost $50,000 or more per mile or $50,000 or more per project for projects with a length of less than one mile, exclusive of bridges and engineering, shall be advertised and let to contract. If such estimated cost is less than $50,000 per mile or $50,000 per project for projects with a length of less than one mile or if, after proper advertising, no acceptable bid is received or the bids are deemed excessive, the work may be done by the Secretary of Agriculture on his own account.

(d) Funds available for forest development roads and trails shall be available for adjacent vehicular parking areas, which may include electric vehicle charging stations or natural gas vehicle refueling stations, and for sanitary, water, and fire control facilities.

(Pub. L. 85–767, Aug. 27, 1958, 72 Stat. 907; Pub. L. 86–657, §8(c), July 14, 1960, 74 Stat. 524; Pub. L. 88–423, §4(d), Aug. 13, 1964, 78 Stat. 398; Pub. L. 90–495, §9, Aug. 23, 1968, 82 Stat. 820; Pub. L. 102–240, title I, §1032(c), Dec. 18, 1991, 105 Stat. 1975; Pub. L. 112–141, div. A, title I, §1513(c), July 6, 2012, 126 Stat. 572.)

§206. RECREATIONAL TRAILS PROGRAM

(a) DEFINITIONS.—In this section, the following definitions apply:

(1) MOTORIZED RECREATION.—The term "motorized recreation" means off-road recreation using any motor-powered vehicle, except for a motorized wheelchair.

(2) RECREATIONAL TRAIL.—The term "recreational trail" means a thoroughfare or track across land or snow, used for recreational purposes such as—

(A) pedestrian activities, including wheelchair use;

(B) skating or skateboarding;

(C) equestrian activities, including carriage driving;

(D) nonmotorized snow trail activities, including skiing;

(E) bicycling or use of other human-powered vehicles;

(F) aquatic or water activities; and

(G) motorized vehicular activities, including all-terrain vehicle riding, motorcycling, snowmobiling, use of off-road light trucks, or use of other off-road motorized vehicles.

(b) PROGRAM.—In accordance with this section, the Secretary, in consultation with the Secretary of the Interior and the Secretary of Agriculture, shall carry out a program to provide and maintain recreational trails.

(c) STATE RESPONSIBILITIES.—To be eligible for apportionments under this section—

(1) the Governor of the State shall designate the State agency or agencies that will be responsible for administering apportionments made to the State under this section; and

(2) the State shall establish a State recreational trail advisory committee that represents both motorized and nonmotorized recreational trail users, which shall meet not less often than once per fiscal year.

(d) USE OF APPORTIONED FUNDS.—

(1) IN GENERAL.—Funds apportioned to a State to carry out this section shall be obligated for recreational trails and related projects that—

(A) have been planned and developed under the laws, policies, and administrative procedures of the State; and

(B) are identified in, or further a specific goal of, a recreational trail plan, or a statewide comprehensive outdoor recreation plan required by chapter 2003 of title 54, that is in effect.

(2) PERMISSIBLE USES.—Permissible uses of funds apportioned to a State for a fiscal year to carry out this section include—

(A) maintenance and restoration of existing recreational trails;

(B) development and rehabilitation of trailside and trailhead facilities and trail linkages for recreational trails;

(C) purchase and lease of recreational trail construction and maintenance equipment;

(D) construction of new recreational trails, except that, in the case of new recreational trails crossing Federal lands, construction of the trails shall be—

(i) permissible under other law;

(ii) necessary and recommended by a statewide comprehensive outdoor recreation plan that is required by chapter 2003 of title 54 and that is in effect;

(iii) approved by the administering agency of the State designated under subsection (c)(1); and

(iv) approved by each Federal agency having jurisdiction over the affected lands under such terms and conditions as the head of the Federal agency determines to be appropriate, except that the approval shall be contingent on compliance by the Federal agency with all applicable laws, including the National Environmental Policy Act of 1969 (42 U.S.C. 4321 et seq.), the Forest and Rangeland Renewable Resources Planning Act of 1974 (16 U.S.C. 1600 et seq.), and the Federal Land Policy and Management Act of 1976 (43 U.S.C. 1701 et seq.);

(E) acquisition of easements and fee simple title to property for recreational trails or recreational trail corridors;

(F) assessment of trail conditions for accessibility and maintenance;

(G) development and dissemination of publications and operation of educational programs to promote safety and environmental protection, (as those objectives relate to one or more of the uses of recreational trails, supporting non-law enforcement trail safety and trail use monitoring patrol programs, and providing trail-related training), but in an amount not to exceed 5 percent of the apportionment made to the State for the fiscal year; and

(H) payment of costs to the State incurred in administering the program, but in an amount not to exceed 7 percent of the apportionment made to the State for the fiscal year.

(3) USE OF APPORTIONMENTS.—

(A) IN GENERAL.—Except as provided in subparagraphs (B) and (C), of the apportionments made to a State for a fiscal year to carry out this section—

(i) 40 percent shall be used for recreational trail or related projects that facilitate diverse recreational trail use within a recreational trail corridor, trailside, or trailhead, regardless of whether the project is for diverse motorized use, for diverse nonmotorized use, or to accommodate both motorized and nonmotorized recreational trail use;

(ii) 30 percent shall be used for uses relating to motorized recreation; and

(iii) 30 percent shall be used for uses relating to nonmotorized recreation.

(B) SMALL STATE EXCLUSION.—Any State with a total land area of less than 3,500,000 acres shall be exempt from the requirements of clauses (ii) and (iii) of subparagraph (A).

(C) STATE ADMINISTRATIVE COSTS.—State administrative costs eligible for funding under paragraph (2)(H) shall be exempt from the requirements of subparagraph (A).

(4) GRANTS.—

(A) IN GENERAL.—A State may use funds apportioned to the State to carry out this section to make grants to private organizations, municipal, county, State, and Federal Government entities, and other government entities as approved by the State after considering guidance from the State recreational trail advisory committee established under subsection (c)(2), for uses consistent with this section.

(B) COMPLIANCE.—A State that makes grants under subparagraph (A) shall establish measures to verify that recipients of the grants comply with the conditions of the program for the use of grant funds.

(e) ENVIRONMENTAL BENEFIT OR MITIGATION.—To the extent practicable and consistent with the other requirements of this section, a State should give consideration to project proposals that provide for the redesign, reconstruction, nonroutine maintenance, or relocation of recreational trails to benefit the natural environment or to mitigate and minimize the impact to the natural environment.

(f) FEDERAL SHARE.—

(1) IN GENERAL.—Subject to the other provisions of this subsection, the Federal share of the cost of a project and the Federal share of the administrative costs of a State under this section shall be determined in accordance with section 120(b).

(2) FEDERAL AGENCY PROJECT SPONSOR.—Notwithstanding any other provision of law, a Federal agency that sponsors a project under this section may contribute additional Federal funds toward the cost of a project, except that—

(A) the share attributable to the Secretary of Transportation may not exceed the amount determined in accordance with section 120(b) for the cost of a project under this section; and

(B) the share attributable to the Secretary and the Federal agency sponsoring the project may not exceed 95 percent of the cost of a project under this section.

(3) USE OF FUNDS FROM FEDERAL PROGRAMS TO PROVIDE NON-FEDERAL SHARE.—Notwithstanding any other provision of law, the non-Federal share of the cost of the project may include amounts made available by the Federal Government under any Federal program that are—

(A) expended in accordance with the requirements of the Federal program relating to activities funded and populations served; and

(B) expended on a project that is eligible for assistance under this section.

(4) USE OF RECREATIONAL TRAILS PROGRAM FUNDS TO MATCH OTHER FEDERAL PROGRAM FUNDS.—Notwithstanding any other provision of law, funds made available under this section may be used toward the non-Federal matching share for other Federal program funds that are—

(A) expended in accordance with the requirements of the Federal program relating to activities funded and populations served; and

(B) expended on a project that is eligible for assistance under this section.

(5) PROGRAMMATIC NON-FEDERAL SHARE.—A State may allow adjustments to the non-Federal share of an individual project for a fiscal year under this section if the Federal share of the cost of all projects carried out by the State under the program (excluding projects funded under paragraph (2) or (3)) using funds apportioned to the State for the fiscal year does not exceed the Federal share as determined in accordance with section 120(b).

(g) USES NOT PERMITTED.—A State may not obligate funds apportioned to carry out this section for—

(1) condemnation of any kind of interest in property;

(2) construction of any recreational trail on National Forest System land for any motorized use unless—

(A) the land has been designated for uses other than wilderness by an approved forest land and resource management plan or has been released to uses other than wilderness by an Act of Congress; and

(B) the construction is otherwise consistent with the management direction in the approved forest land and resource management plan;

(3) construction of any recreational trail on Bureau of Land Management land for any motorized use unless the land—

(A) has been designated for uses other than wilderness by an approved Bureau of Land Management resource management plan or has been released to uses other than wilderness by an Act of Congress; and

(B) the construction is otherwise consistent with the management direction in the approved management plan; or

(4) upgrading, expanding, or otherwise facilitating motorized use or access to recreational trails predominantly used by nonmotorized recreational trail users and on which, as of May 1, 1991, motorized use was prohibited or had not occurred.

(h) PROJECT ADMINISTRATION.—

(1) CREDIT FOR DONATIONS OF FUNDS, MATERIALS, SERVICES, OR NEW RIGHT-OF-WAY.—

(A) IN GENERAL.—Nothing in this title or other law shall prevent a project sponsor from offering to donate funds, materials, services, or a new right-of-way for the purposes of a project eligible for assistance under this section. Any funds, or the fair market value of any materials, services, or new right-of-way, may be donated by any project sponsor and shall be credited to the non-Federal share in accordance with subsection (f).

(B) FEDERAL PROJECT SPONSORS.—Any funds or the fair market value of any materials or services may be provided by a Federal project sponsor and shall be credited to the Federal agency's share in accordance with subsection (f).

(C) Planning and environmental assessment costs incurred prior to project approval.—The Secretary may allow preapproval planning and environmental compliance costs to be credited toward the non-Federal share of the cost of a project described in subsection (d)(2) (other than subparagraph (H)) in accordance with subsection (f), limited to costs incurred less than 18 months prior to project approval.

(2) Recreational purpose.—A project funded under this section is intended to enhance recreational opportunity and is not subject to section 138 of this title or section 303 of title 49.

(3) Continuing recreational use.—At the option of each State, funds apportioned to the State to carry out this section may be treated as Land and Water Conservation Fund apportionments for the purposes of section 200305(f)(3) of title 54.

(4) Cooperation by private persons.—

(A) Written assurances.—As a condition of making available apportionments for work on recreational trails that would affect privately owned land, a State shall obtain written assurances that the owner of the land will cooperate with the State and participate as necessary in the activities to be conducted.

(B) Public access.—Any use of the apportionments to a State to carry out this section on privately owned land must be accompanied by an easement or other legally binding agreement that ensures public access to the recreational trail improvements funded by the apportionments.

(i) Contract Authority.—Funds authorized to carry out this section shall be available for obligation in the same manner as if the funds were apportioned under chapter 1, except that the Federal share of the cost of a project under this section shall be determined in accordance with this section.

(j) Use of Other Apportioned Funds.—Funds apportioned to a State under section 104(b) that are obligated for a recreational trail or a related project shall be administered as if the funds were made available to carry out this section.

(Added Pub. L. 105–178, title I, §1112(a), June 9, 1998, 112 Stat. 146; amended Pub. L. 109–59, title I, §1109(b)–(e), Aug. 10, 2005, 119 Stat. 1168–1170; Pub. L. 110–244, title I, §101(q), June 6, 2008, 122 Stat. 1576; Pub. L. 113–287, §5(f)(3), Dec. 19, 2014, 128 Stat. 3268; Pub. L. 117–58, div. A, title I, §§11134, 11525(n), Nov. 15, 2021, 135 Stat. 515, 608.)

§207. Tribal transportation self-governance program

(a) Establishment.—Subject to the requirements of this section, the Secretary shall establish and carry out a program to be known as the tribal transportation self-governance program. The Secretary may delegate responsibilities for administration of the program as the Secretary determines appropriate.

(b) Eligibility.—

(1) In general.—Subject to paragraphs (2) and (3), an Indian tribe shall be eligible to participate in the program if the Indian tribe requests participation in the program by resolution or other official action by the governing body of the Indian tribe, and demonstrates, for the preceding 3 fiscal years, financial stability and financial management capability, and transportation program management capability.

(2) Criteria for determining financial stability and financial management

CAPACITY.—For the purposes of paragraph (1), evidence that, during the preceding 3 fiscal years, an Indian tribe had no uncorrected significant and material audit exceptions in the required annual audit of the Indian tribe's self-determination contracts or self-governance funding agreements with any Federal agency shall be conclusive evidence of the required financial stability and financial management capability.

(3) CRITERIA FOR DETERMINING TRANSPORTATION PROGRAM MANAGEMENT CAPABILITY.—The Secretary shall require an Indian tribe to demonstrate transportation program management capability, including the capability to manage and complete projects eligible under this title and projects eligible under chapter 53 of title 49, to gain eligibility for the program.

(c) COMPACTS.—

(1) COMPACT REQUIRED.—Upon the request of an eligible Indian tribe, and subject to the requirements of this section, the Secretary shall negotiate and enter into a written compact with the Indian tribe for the purpose of providing for the participation of the Indian tribe in the program.

(2) CONTENTS.—A compact entered into under paragraph (1) shall set forth the general terms of the government-to-government relationship between the Indian tribe and the United States under the program and other terms that will continue to apply in future fiscal years.

(3) AMENDMENTS.—A compact entered into with an Indian tribe under paragraph (1) may be amended only by mutual agreement of the Indian tribe and the Secretary.

(d) ANNUAL FUNDING AGREEMENTS.—

(1) FUNDING AGREEMENT REQUIRED.—After entering into a compact with an Indian tribe under subsection (c), the Secretary shall negotiate and enter into a written annual funding agreement with the Indian tribe.

(2) CONTENTS.—

(A) IN GENERAL.—

(i) FORMULA FUNDING AND DISCRETIONARY GRANTS.—A funding agreement entered into with an Indian tribe shall authorize the Indian tribe, as determined by the Indian tribe, to plan, conduct, consolidate, administer, and receive full tribal share funding, tribal transit formula funding, and funding to tribes from discretionary and competitive grants administered by the Department for all programs, services, functions, and activities (or portions thereof) that are made available to Indian tribes to carry out tribal transportation programs and programs, services, functions, and activities (or portions thereof) administered by the Secretary that are otherwise available to Indian tribes.

(ii) TRANSFERS OF STATE FUNDS.—

(I) INCLUSION OF TRANSFERRED FUNDS IN FUNDING AGREEMENT.—A funding agreement entered into with an Indian tribe shall include Federal-aid funds apportioned to a State under chapter 1 if the State elects to provide a portion of such funds to the Indian tribe for a project eligible under section 202(a). The provisions of this section shall be in addition to the methods for making funding contributions described in section 202(a)(9). Nothing in this section shall diminish the authority of the Secretary to provide funds to an Indian tribe under section 202(a)(9).

(II) METHOD FOR TRANSFERS.—If a State elects to provide funds described in subclause (I) to an Indian tribe—

(aa) the transfer may occur in accordance with section 202(a)(9); or

(bb) the State shall transfer the funds back to the Secretary and the Secretary shall transfer the funds to the Indian tribe in accordance with this section.

(III) RESPONSIBILITY FOR TRANSFERRED FUNDS.—Notwithstanding any other provision of law, if a State provides funds described in subclause (I) to an Indian tribe—

(aa) the State shall not be responsible for constructing or maintaining a project carried out using the funds or for administering or supervising the project or funds during the applicable statute of limitations period related to the construction of the project; and

(bb) the Indian tribe shall be responsible for constructing and maintaining a project carried out using the funds and for administering and supervising the project and funds in accordance with this section during the applicable statute of limitations period related to the construction of the project.

(B) ADMINISTRATION OF TRIBAL SHARES.—The tribal shares referred to in subparagraph (A) shall be provided without regard to the agency or office of the Department within which the program, service, function, or activity (or portion thereof) is performed.

(C) FLEXIBLE AND INNOVATIVE FINANCING.—

(i) IN GENERAL.—A funding agreement entered into with an Indian tribe under paragraph (1) shall include provisions pertaining to flexible and innovative financing if agreed upon by the parties.

(ii) TERMS AND CONDITIONS.—

(I) AUTHORITY TO ISSUE REGULATIONS.—The Secretary may issue regulations to establish the terms and conditions relating to the flexible and innovative financing provisions referred to in clause (i).

(II) TERMS AND CONDITIONS IN ABSENCE OF REGULATIONS.—If the Secretary does not issue regulations under subclause (I), the terms and conditions relating to the flexible and innovative financing provisions referred to in clause (i) shall be consistent with—

(aa) agreements entered into by the Department under—

(AA) section 202(b)(7); and

(BB) section 202(d)(5), as in effect before the date of enactment of MAP–21 (Public Law 112–141); or

(bb) regulations of the Department of the Interior relating to flexible financing contained in part 170 of title 25, Code of Federal Regulations, as in effect on the date of enactment of the FAST Act.

(3) TERMS.—A funding agreement shall set forth—

(A) terms that generally identify the programs, services, functions, and activities (or portions thereof) to be performed or administered by the Indian tribe; and

319

(B) for items identified in subparagraph (A)—

(i) the general budget category assigned;

(ii) the funds to be provided, including those funds to be provided on a recurring basis;

(iii) the time and method of transfer of the funds;

(iv) the responsibilities of the Secretary and the Indian tribe; and

(v) any other provision agreed to by the Indian tribe and the Secretary.

(4) SUBSEQUENT FUNDING AGREEMENTS.—

(A) APPLICABILITY OF EXISTING AGREEMENT.—Absent notification from an Indian tribe that the Indian tribe is withdrawing from or retroceding the operation of 1 or more programs, services, functions, or activities (or portions thereof) identified in a funding agreement, or unless otherwise agreed to by the parties, each funding agreement shall remain in full force and effect until a subsequent funding agreement is executed.

(B) EFFECTIVE DATE OF SUBSEQUENT AGREEMENT.—The terms of the subsequent funding agreement shall be retroactive to the end of the term of the preceding funding agreement.

(5) CONSENT OF INDIAN TRIBE REQUIRED.—The Secretary shall not revise, amend, or require additional terms in a new or subsequent funding agreement without the consent of the Indian tribe that is subject to the agreement unless such terms are required by Federal law.

(e) GENERAL PROVISIONS.—

(1) REDESIGN AND CONSOLIDATION.—

(A) IN GENERAL.—An Indian tribe, in any manner that the Indian tribe considers to be in the best interest of the Indian community being served, may—

(i) redesign or consolidate programs, services, functions, and activities (or portions thereof) included in a funding agreement; and

(ii) reallocate or redirect funds for such programs, services, functions, and activities (or portions thereof), if the funds are—

(I) expended on projects identified in a transportation improvement program approved by the Secretary; and

(II) used in accordance with the requirements in—

(aa) appropriations Acts;

(bb) this title and chapter 53 of title 49; and

(cc) any other applicable law.

(B) EXCEPTION.—Notwithstanding subparagraph (A), if, pursuant to subsection (d), an Indian tribe receives a discretionary or competitive grant from the Secretary or receives State apportioned funds, the Indian tribe shall use the funds for the purpose for which the funds were originally authorized.

(2) RETROCESSION.—

(A) IN GENERAL.—

(i) AUTHORITY OF INDIAN TRIBES.—An Indian tribe may retrocede (fully or partially) to the Secretary programs, services, functions, or activities (or portions thereof) included in a compact or funding agreement.

(ii) REASSUMPTION OF REMAINING FUNDS.—Following a retrocession described in clause (i), the Secretary may—

(I) reassume the remaining funding associated with the retroceded programs, functions, services, and activities (or portions thereof) included in the applicable compact or funding agreement;

(II) out of such remaining funds, transfer funds associated with Department of Interior programs, services, functions, or activities (or portions thereof) to the Secretary of the Interior to carry out transportation services provided by the Secretary of the Interior; and

(III) distribute funds not transferred under subclause (II) in accordance with applicable law.

(iii) CORRECTION OF PROGRAMS.—If the Secretary makes a finding under subsection (f)(2)(B) and no funds are available under subsection (f)(2)(A)(ii), the Secretary shall not be required to provide additional funds to complete or correct any programs, functions, services, or activities (or portions thereof).

(B) EFFECTIVE DATE.—Unless the Indian tribe rescinds a request for retrocession, the retrocession shall become effective within the timeframe specified by the parties in the compact or funding agreement. In the absence of such a specification, the retrocession shall become effective on—

(i) the earlier of—

(I) 1 year after the date of submission of the request; or

(II) the date on which the funding agreement expires; or

(ii) such date as may be mutually agreed upon by the parties and, with respect to Department of the Interior programs, functions, services, and activities (or portions thereof), the Secretary of the Interior.

(f) PROVISIONS RELATING TO SECRETARY.—

(1) DECISIONMAKER.—A decision that relates to an appeal of the rejection of a final offer by the Department shall be made either—

(A) by an official of the Department who holds a position at a higher organizational level within the Department than the level of the departmental agency in which the decision that is the subject of the appeal was made; or

(B) by an administrative judge.

(2) TERMINATION OF COMPACT OR FUNDING AGREEMENT.—

(A) AUTHORITY TO TERMINATE.—

(i) PROVISION TO BE INCLUDED IN COMPACT OR FUNDING AGREEMENT.—A compact or funding agreement shall include a provision authorizing the Secretary, if the Secretary makes a finding described in subparagraph (B), to—

(I) terminate the compact or funding agreement (or a portion thereof); and

(II) reassume the remaining funding associated with the reassumed programs, functions, services, and activities included in the compact or funding agreement.

(ii) TRANSFERS OF FUNDS.—Out of any funds reassumed under clause (i)(II), the Secretary may transfer the funds associated with Department of the Interior programs, functions, services, and activities (or portions thereof) to the Secretary of the Interior to provide continued transportation services in accordance with applicable law.

(B) Findings resulting in termination.—The finding referred to in subparagraph (A) is a specific finding of—

(i) imminent jeopardy to a trust asset, natural resources, or public health and safety that is caused by an act or omission of the Indian tribe and that arises out of a failure to carry out the compact or funding agreement, as determined by the Secretary; or

(ii) gross mismanagement with respect to funds or programs transferred to the Indian tribe under the compact or funding agreement, as determined by the Secretary in consultation with the Inspector General of the Department, as appropriate.

(C) Prohibition.—The Secretary shall not terminate a compact or funding agreement (or portion thereof) unless—

(i) the Secretary has first provided written notice and a hearing on the record to the Indian tribe that is subject to the compact or funding agreement; and

(ii) the Indian tribe has not taken corrective action to remedy the mismanagement of funds or programs or the imminent jeopardy to a trust asset, natural resource, or public health and safety.

(D) Exception.—

(i) In general.—Notwithstanding subparagraph (C), the Secretary, upon written notification to an Indian tribe that is subject to a compact or funding agreement, may immediately terminate the compact or funding agreement (or portion thereof) if—

(I) the Secretary makes a finding of imminent substantial and irreparable jeopardy to a trust asset, natural resource, or public health and safety; and

(II) the jeopardy arises out of a failure to carry out the compact or funding agreement.

(ii) Hearings.—If the Secretary terminates a compact or funding agreement (or portion thereof) under clause (i), the Secretary shall provide the Indian tribe subject to the compact or agreement with a hearing on the record not later than 10 days after the date of such termination.

(E) Burden of proof.—In any hearing or appeal involving a decision to terminate a compact or funding agreement (or portion thereof) under this paragraph, the Secretary shall have the burden of proof in demonstrating by clear and convincing evidence the validity of the grounds for the termination.

(g) Cost Principles.—In administering funds received under this section, an Indian tribe shall apply cost principles under the applicable Office of Management and Budget circular, except as modified by section 106 of the Indian Self-Determination and Education Assistance Act (25 U.S.C. 5325), other provisions of law, or by any exemptions to applicable Office of Management and Budget circulars subsequently granted by the Office of Management and Budget. No other audit or accounting standards shall be required by the Secretary. Any claim by the Federal Government against the Indian tribe relating to funds received under a funding agreement based on any audit conducted pursuant to this subsection shall be subject to the provisions of section 106(f) of that Act (25 U.S.C. 5325(f)).

(h) Transfer of Funds.—The Secretary shall provide funds to an Indian tribe under a funding agreement in an amount equal to—

(1) the sum of the funding that the Indian tribe would otherwise receive for the program, function, service, or activity in accordance with a funding formula or other allocation method established under this title or chapter 53 of title 49; and

(2) such additional amounts as the Secretary determines equal the amounts that would have been withheld for the costs of the Bureau of Indian Affairs for administration of the program or project.

(i) CONSTRUCTION PROGRAMS.—

(1) STANDARDS.—Construction projects carried out under programs administered by an Indian tribe with funds transferred to the Indian tribe pursuant to a funding agreement entered into under this section shall be constructed pursuant to the construction program standards set forth in applicable regulations or as specifically approved by the Secretary (or the Secretary's designee).

(2) MONITORING.—Construction programs shall be monitored by the Secretary in accordance with applicable regulations.

(j) FACILITATION.—

(1) SECRETARIAL INTERPRETATION.—Except as otherwise provided by law, the Secretary shall interpret all Federal laws, Executive orders, and regulations in a manner that will facilitate—

(A) the inclusion of programs, services, functions, and activities (or portions thereof) and funds associated therewith, in compacts and funding agreements; and

(B) the implementation of the compacts and funding agreements.

(2) REGULATION WAIVER.—

(A) IN GENERAL.—An Indian tribe may submit to the Secretary a written request to waive application of a regulation promulgated under this section with respect to a compact or funding agreement. The request shall identify the regulation sought to be waived and the basis for the request.

(B) APPROVALS AND DENIALS.—

(i) IN GENERAL.—Not later than 90 days after the date of receipt of a written request under subparagraph (A), the Secretary shall approve or deny the request in writing.

(ii) REVIEW.—The Secretary shall review any application by an Indian tribe for a waiver bearing in mind increasing opportunities for using flexible policy approaches at the Indian tribal level.

(iii) DEEMED APPROVAL.—If the Secretary does not approve or deny a request submitted under subparagraph (A) on or before the last day of the 90-day period referred to in clause (i), the request shall be deemed approved.

(iv) DENIALS.—If the application for a waiver is not granted, the agency shall provide the applicant with the reasons for the denial as part of the written response required in clause (i).

(v) FINALITY OF DECISIONS.—A decision by the Secretary under this subparagraph shall be final for the Department.

(k) DISCLAIMERS.—

(1) EXISTING AUTHORITY.—Notwithstanding any other provision of law, upon the election of an Indian tribe, the Secretary shall—

(A) maintain current tribal transportation program funding agreements and program agreements; or

(B) enter into new agreements under the authority of section 202(b)(7).

(2) LIMITATION ON STATUTORY CONSTRUCTION.—Nothing in this section may be construed to impair or diminish the authority of the Secretary under section 202(b)(7).

(l) APPLICABILITY OF INDIAN SELF-DETERMINATION AND EDUCATION ASSISTANCE ACT.—Except to the extent in conflict with this section (as determined by the Secretary), the following provisions of the Indian Self-Determination and Education Assistance Act shall apply to compact and funding agreements (except that any reference to the Secretary of the Interior or the Secretary of Health and Human Services in such provisions shall be treated as a reference to the Secretary of Transportation):

(1) Subsections (a), (b), (d), (g), and (h) of section 506 of such Act (25 U.S.C. 5386), relating to general provisions.

(2) Subsections (b) through (e) and (g) of section 507 of such Act (25 U.S.C. 5387), relating to provisions relating to the Secretary of Health and Human Services.

(3) Subsections (a), (b), (d), (e), (g), (h), (i), and (k) of section 508 of such Act (25 U.S.C. 5388), relating to transfer of funds.

(4) Section 510 of such Act (25 U.S.C. 5390), relating to Federal procurement laws and regulations.

(5) Section 511 of such Act (25 U.S.C. 5391), relating to civil actions.

(6) Subsections (a)(1), (a)(2), and (c) through (f) of section 512 of such Act (25 U.S.C. 5392), relating to facilitation, except that subsection (c)(1) of that section shall be applied by substituting "transportation facilities and other facilities" for "school buildings, hospitals, and other facilities".

(7) Subsections (a) and (b) of section 515 of such Act (25 U.S.C. 5395), relating to disclaimers.

(8) Subsections (a) and (b) of section 516 of such Act (25 U.S.C. 5396), relating to application of title I provisions.

(9) Section 518 of such Act (25 U.S.C. 5398), relating to appeals.

(m) DEFINITIONS.—

(1) IN GENERAL.—In this section, the following definitions apply (except as otherwise expressly provided):

(A) COMPACT.—The term "compact" means a compact between the Secretary and an Indian tribe entered into under subsection (c).

(B) DEPARTMENT.—The term "Department" means the Department of Transportation.

(C) ELIGIBLE INDIAN TRIBE.—The term "eligible Indian tribe" means an Indian tribe that is eligible to participate in the program, as determined under subsection (b).

(D) FUNDING AGREEMENT.—The term "funding agreement" means a funding agreement between the Secretary and an Indian tribe entered into under subsection (d).

(E) INDIAN TRIBE.—The term "Indian tribe" means any Indian or Alaska Native tribe, band, nation, pueblo, village, or community that is recognized as eligible for the special programs and services provided by the United States to Indians because of their status as Indians. In any case in which an Indian tribe has authorized another Indian tribe, an intertribal consortium, or a tribal organization to plan for or carry out programs, services, functions, or activities (or portions thereof) on its behalf under this section, the authorized Indian tribe, intertribal consortium, or tribal organization shall have the rights and responsibilities of the authorizing Indian tribe (except as otherwise provided in the authorizing resolution or in this title). In such event, the term "Indian tribe" as used in this section shall include such other authorized Indian tribe, intertribal consortium, or tribal organization.

(F) PROGRAM.—The term "program" means the tribal transportation self-governance program established under this section.

(G) SECRETARY.—The term "Secretary" means the Secretary of Transportation.

(H) TRANSPORTATION PROGRAMS.—The term "transportation programs" means all programs administered or financed by the Department under this title and chapter 53 of title 49.

(2) APPLICABILITY OF OTHER DEFINITIONS.—In this section, the definitions set forth in sections 4 and 501 of the Indian Self-Determination and Education Assistance Act (25 U.S.C. 5304; 5381) apply, except as otherwise expressly provided in this section.

(n) REGULATIONS.—

(1) IN GENERAL.—

(A) PROMULGATION.—Not later than 90 days after the date of enactment of the FAST Act, the Secretary shall initiate procedures under subchapter III of chapter 5 of title 5 to negotiate and promulgate such regulations as are necessary to carry out this section.

(B) PUBLICATION OF PROPOSED REGULATIONS.—Proposed regulations to implement this section shall be published in the Federal Register by the Secretary not later than 42 months after such date of enactment.

(C) EXPIRATION OF AUTHORITY.—The authority to promulgate regulations under subparagraph (A) shall expire 48 months after such date of enactment.

(D) EXTENSION OF DEADLINES.—A deadline set forth in subparagraph (B) or (C) may be extended up to 180 days if the negotiated rulemaking committee referred to in paragraph (2) concludes that the committee cannot meet the deadline and the Secretary so notifies the appropriate committees of Congress.

(2) COMMITTEE.—

(A) IN GENERAL.—A negotiated rulemaking committee established pursuant to section 565 of title 5 to carry out this subsection shall have as its members only Federal and tribal government representatives, a majority of whom shall be nominated by and be representatives of Indian tribes with funding agreements under this title.

(B) REQUIREMENTS.—The committee shall confer with, and accommodate participation by, representatives of Indian tribes, inter-tribal consortia, tribal organizations, and individual tribal members.

(C) ADAPTATION OF PROCEDURES.—The Secretary shall adapt the negotiated rulemaking procedures to the unique context of self-governance and the government-to-government relationship between the United States and Indian tribes.

(3) EFFECT.—The lack of promulgated regulations shall not limit the effect of this section.

(4) EFFECT OF CIRCULARS, POLICIES, MANUALS, GUIDANCE, AND RULES.—Unless expressly agreed to by the participating Indian tribe in the compact or funding agreement, the participating Indian tribe shall not be subject to any agency circular, policy, manual, guidance, or rule adopted by the Department, except regulations promulgated under this section.

(Added Pub. L. 114–94, div. A, title I, §1121(a), Dec. 4, 2015, 129 Stat. 1359; amended Pub. L. 115–235, §1, Aug. 14, 2018, 132 Stat. 2443; Pub. L. 117–58, div. A, title I, §11525(o), Nov. 15, 2021, 135 Stat. 608.)

§208. SAFE ROUTES TO SCHOOL

(a) DEFINITIONS.—In this section:

(1) IN THE VICINITY OF SCHOOLS.—The term "in the vicinity of schools", with respect to a school, means the approximately 2-mile area within bicycling and walking distance of the school.

(2) PRIMARY, MIDDLE, AND HIGH SCHOOLS.—The term "primary, middle, and high schools" means schools providing education from kindergarten through 12th grade.

(b) ESTABLISHMENT.—Subject to the requirements of this section, the Secretary shall establish and carry out a safe routes to school program for the benefit of children in primary, middle, and high schools.

(c) PURPOSES.—The purposes of the program established under subsection (b) shall be—

(1) to enable and encourage children, including those with disabilities, to walk and bicycle to school;

(2) to make bicycling and walking to school a safer and more appealing transportation alternative, thereby encouraging a healthy and active lifestyle from an early age; and

(3) to facilitate the planning, development, and implementation of projects and activities that will improve safety and reduce traffic, fuel consumption, and air pollution in the vicinity of schools.

(d) APPORTIONMENT OF FUNDS.—

(1) IN GENERAL.—Subject to paragraphs (2), (3), and (4), amounts made available to carry out this section for a fiscal year shall be apportioned among the States so that each State receives the amount equal to the proportion that—

(A) the total student enrollment in primary, middle, and high schools in each State; bears to

(B) the total student enrollment in primary, middle, and high schools in all States.

(2) MINIMUM APPORTIONMENT.—No State shall receive an apportionment under this section for a fiscal year of less than $1,000,000.

(3) SET-ASIDE FOR ADMINISTRATIVE EXPENSES.—Before apportioning under this subsection amounts made available to carry out this section for a fiscal year, the Secretary shall set aside not more than $3,000,000 of those amounts for the administrative expenses of the Secretary in carrying out this section.

(4) DETERMINATION OF STUDENT ENROLLMENTS.—Determinations under this subsection relating to student enrollments shall be made by the Secretary.

(e) ADMINISTRATION OF AMOUNTS.—Amounts apportioned to a State under this section shall be administered by the State department of transportation.

(f) ELIGIBLE RECIPIENTS.—Amounts apportioned to a State under this section shall be used by the State to provide financial assistance to State, local, Tribal, and regional agencies, including nonprofit organizations, that demonstrate an ability to meet the requirements of this section.

(g) ELIGIBLE PROJECTS AND ACTIVITIES.—

(1) INFRASTRUCTURE-RELATED PROJECTS.—

(A) IN GENERAL.—Amounts apportioned to a State under this section may be used for the planning, design, and construction of infrastructure-related projects that will substantially improve the ability of students to walk and bicycle to school, including sidewalk improvements, traffic calming and speed reduction improvements, pedestrian and bicycle crossing improvements, on-street bicycle facilities, off-street bicycle and pedestrian facilities, secure bicycle parking facilities, and traffic diversion improvements in the vicinity of schools.

(B) LOCATION OF PROJECTS.—Infrastructure-related projects under subparagraph (A) may be carried out on any public road or any bicycle or pedestrian pathway or trail in the vicinity of schools.

(2) NONINFRASTRUCTURE-RELATED ACTIVITIES.—

(A) IN GENERAL.—In addition to projects described in paragraph (1), amounts apportioned to a State under this section may be used for noninfrastructure-related activities to encourage walking and bicycling to school, including public awareness campaigns and outreach to press and community leaders, traffic education and enforcement in the vicinity of schools, student sessions on bicycle and pedestrian safety, health, and environment, and funding for training, volunteers, and managers of safe routes to school programs.

(B) ALLOCATION.—Not less than 10 percent and not more than 30 percent of the amount apportioned to a State under this section for a fiscal year shall be used for noninfrastructure-related activities under this paragraph.

(3) SAFE ROUTES TO SCHOOL COORDINATOR.—Each State shall use a sufficient amount of the apportionment of the State for each fiscal year to fund a full-time position of coordinator of the safe routes to school program of the State.

(h) CLEARINGHOUSE.—

(1) IN GENERAL.—The Secretary shall make grants to a national nonprofit organization engaged in promoting safe routes to schools—

(A) to operate a national safe routes to school clearinghouse;

(B) to develop information and educational programs on safe routes to school; and

(C) to provide technical assistance and disseminate techniques and strategies used for successful safe routes to school programs.

(2) FUNDING.—The Secretary shall carry out this subsection using amounts set aside for administrative expenses under subsection (d)(3).

(i) TREATMENT OF PROJECTS.—Notwithstanding any other provision of law, a project assisted under this section shall be treated as a project on a Federal-aid highway under chapter 1.

[§209. Repealed. Pub. L. 97–424, title I, §126(d), Jan. 6, 1983, 96 Stat. 2115]

CHAPTER 2—OTHER HIGHWAYS

(Added Pub. L. 117–58, div. A, title I, §11119(a), Nov. 15, 2021, 135 Stat. 495.)

[§209. REPEALED. PUB. L. 97–424, TITLE I, §126(D), JAN. 6, 1983, 96 STAT. 2115]

Section, Pub. L. 85–767, Aug. 27, 1958, 72 Stat. 908; Pub. L. 88–423, §4(b), Aug. 13, 1964, 78 Stat. 397, provided for use of funds for construction and maintenance of public lands highways, cooperation with State agencies, the application of section 112 of this title to public lands highways, and for use of such funds for adjacent ancillary facilities and services.

§210. DEFENSE ACCESS ROADS

(a) AUTHORIZATION.—

(1) IN GENERAL.—When defense access roads are certified to the Secretary as important to the national defense by the Secretary of Defense or such other official as the President may designate, the Secretary is authorized, out of the funds appropriated for defense access roads, to provide for—

(A) the construction and maintenance of defense access roads (including bridges, tubes, tunnels, and culverts or other hydraulic appurtenances on those roads) to—

(i) military reservations;

(ii) defense industry sites;

(iii) air or sea ports that are necessary for or are planned to be used for the deployment or sustainment of members of the Armed Forces, equipment, or supplies; or

(iv) sources of raw materials;

(B) the reconstruction or enhancement of, or improvements to, those roads to ensure the continued effective use of the roads, regardless of current or projected increases in mean tides, recurrent flooding, or other weather-related conditions or natural disasters; and

(C) replacing existing highways and highway connections that are shut off from general public use by necessary closures, closures due to mean sea level fluctuation and flooding, or restrictions at—

(i) military reservations;

(ii) air or sea ports that are necessary for or are planned to be used for the deployment or sustainment of members of the Armed Forces, equipment, or supplies; or

(iii) defense industry sites.

(2) If it is determined that an action of the Department of Defense will cause a significant transportation impact to access to a military reservation, the Secretary of Defense shall conduct a transportation needs assessment to assess the magnitude of the improvement required to address the impact. The Secretary of Defense, in consultation with the Secretary of Transportation, shall determine the magnitude of the required improvements without regard to the extent to which traffic generated by the reservation is greater than other traffic in the vicinity of the reservation.

(b) Funds appropriated for the purposes of this section shall be available, without regard to apportionment among the several States, for paying all or any part of the cost of construction, reconstruction, resurfacing, restoration, rehabilitation, and preservation of, or enhancements to, defense access roads.

(c) Funds appropriated for defense maneuvers and exercises, may be used by the Secretary in areas certified to the Secretary by the Secretary of Defense as maneuver areas for such activities for construction, maintenance, reconstruction, enhancement, improvement, and repair as may be necessary to keep the highways in those areas, which have been or may be used for training of the Armed Forces, in suitable condition for—
(1) that training; and
(2) repairing the damage to those highways caused by—
(A) weather-related events, increases in mean high tide levels, recurrent flooding, or natural disasters; or
(B) the operations of men and equipment in such training.

(d) Whenever any project for the construction of a circumferential highway around a city or of a radial intracity route thereto submitted by any State is certified by the Secretary of Defense, or such other official as the President may designate, as being important for civilian or military defense, such project may be constructed out of the funds heretofore or hereafter authorized to be appropriated for defense access roads.

(e) If the Secretary shall determine that the State transportation department of any State is unable to obtain possession and the right to enter upon and use the required rights-of-way, lands, or interest in lands, improved or unimproved, required for any project authorized by this section with sufficient promptness, the Secretary is authorized to acquire, enter upon, take possession thereof, and expend funds for projects thereon, prior to approval of title by the Attorney General, in the name of the United States, such rights-of-way, lands, or interest in lands as may be required in such State for such projects by purchase, donation, condemnation, or otherwise in accordance with the laws of the United States (including sections 3114 to 3116 and 3118 of title 40). The cost incurred by the Secretary in acquiring any such rights-of-way, lands, or interest in lands may include the cost of examination and abstract of title, certificate of title, advertising, and any fees incidental to such acquisition; and shall be payable out of the funds available for paying the cost or the Federal share of the cost of the project for which such rights-of-way, lands, or interests in lands are acquired. The Secretary is further authorized and directed by proper deed executed in the name of the United States to convey any lands or interests in lands acquired in any State under the provisions of prior Acts or of this section to the State transportation department of such State or to such political subdivision thereof as its laws may provide, upon such terms and conditions as may be agreed upon by the Secretary and the State transportation department, or political subdivisions to which the conveyance is to be made.

(f) The provisions of section 112 of this title are applicable to defense access roads.

(g) If the Secretary shall determine that it is necessary for the expeditious completion of any defense access road project the Secretary may advance to any State out of funds appropriated for defense access roads transferred and available to the Department of Transportation the Federal share of the cost of construction thereof to enable the State transportation department to make prompt payments for acquisition of rights-of-way, and for the construction as it progresses. The sums so advanced shall be deposited in a special fund by the State official authorized by State law to receive such funds, to be disbursed solely upon vouchers approved by the State transportation department for rights-of-way which have been or are being acquired and for construction and other

[§211. Repealed. Pub. L. 100–17, title I, §133(e)(1), Apr. 2, 1987, 101 Stat. 173]

CHAPTER 2—OTHER HIGHWAYS

activities actually performed under this section. Upon determination by the Secretary that funds advanced to any State under the provisions of this subsection are no longer required, the amount of the advance which is determined to be in excess of requirements for the project shall be repaid upon demand by the Secretary, and such repayments shall be returned to the credit of the appropriation from which the funds were advanced.

(h) Funds appropriated for the purposes of this section shall be available to pay the cost of repairing damage caused to highways by the operation of vehicles and equipment in the construction of classified military installations and facilities for ballistic missiles if the Secretary shall determine that the State transportation department of any State is, or has been, unable to prevent such damage by restrictions upon the use of such highways without interference with, or delay in, the completion of a contract for the construction of such military reservations or installations. This subsection shall apply notwithstanding any provision of contract holding a party thereto responsible for such damage, if the Secretary of Defense or his designee shall determine, in fact, that construction estimates and the bid of such party did not include allowance for repairing such damage. This subsection shall apply to damage caused by construction work commenced prior to June 1, 1961, and still in progress on that date and construction work which is commenced or for which a contract is awarded on or after June 1, 1961.

(i) REPAIR OF CERTAIN DAMAGES AND INFRASTRUCTURE.—The funds appropriated to carry out this section may be used to pay the cost of repairing damage caused, or any infrastructure to mitigate a risk posed, to a defense access road by recurrent or projected recurrent flooding, sea level fluctuation, a natural disaster, or any other current or projected change in applicable environmental conditions, if the Secretary determines that continued access to a military installation, defense industry site, air or sea port necessary for or planned to be used for the deployment or sustainment of members of the Armed Forces, equipment, or supplies, or to a source of raw materials, has been or is projected to be impacted by those events or conditions.

(Pub. L. 85–767, Aug. 27, 1958, 72 Stat. 908; Pub. L. 86–657, §8(d), July 14, 1960, 74 Stat. 524; Pub. L. 87–61, title I, §105, June 29, 1961, 75 Stat. 123; Pub. L. 97–424, title I, §155, Jan. 6, 1983, 96 Stat. 2134; Pub. L. 100–17, title I, §133(b)(15), Apr. 2, 1987, 101 Stat. 172; Pub. L. 105–178, title I, §1212(a)(2)(A)(i), June 9, 1998, 112 Stat. 193; Pub. L. 109–284, §3(2), Sept. 27, 2006, 120 Stat. 1211; Pub. L. 110–417, div. B, title XXVIII, §2814(a), Oct. 14, 2008, 122 Stat. 4728; Pub. L. 112–81, div. B, title XXVIII, §2816(a), Dec. 31, 2011, 125 Stat. 1689; Pub. L. 112–141, div. A, title I, §1516, July 6, 2012, 126 Stat. 574; Pub. L. 115–232, div. B, title XXVIII, §2865, Aug. 13, 2018, 132 Stat. 2285; Pub. L. 116–92, div. B, title XXVIII, §2808, Dec. 20, 2019, 133 Stat. 1885.)

[§211. REPEALED. PUB. L. 100–17, TITLE I, §133(E)(1), APR. 2, 1987, 101 STAT. 173]

Section, Pub. L. 85–767, Aug. 27, 1958, 72 Stat. 909, related to timber access road hearings.

[§212. REPEALED. PUB. L. 112–141, DIV. A, TITLE I, §1519(B)(1)(A), JULY 6, 2012, 126 STAT. 575]

Section, Pub. L. 85–767, Aug. 27, 1958, 72 Stat. 909, related to the Inter-American Highway.

[**§213. Repealed. Pub. L. 114–94, div. A, title I, §1109(c)(2), Dec. 4, 2015, 129 Stat. 1343]**

Section, added Pub. L. 112–141, div. A, title I, §1122(a), July 6, 2012, 126 Stat. 494, related to transportation alternatives.

A prior section 213, Pub. L. 85–767, Aug. 27, 1958, 72 Stat. 911, related to construction of Rama Road in Republic of Nicaragua, prior to repeal by Pub. L. 100–17, title I, §133(e)(1), Apr. 2, 1987, 101 Stat. 173.

[**§214. Repealed. Pub. L. 112–141, div. A, title I, §1119(b), July 6, 2012, 126 Stat. 491]**

Section, added Pub. L. 87–866, §6(b), Oct. 23, 1962, 76 Stat. 1147; amended Pub. L. 97–424, title I, §126(d), Jan. 6, 1983, 96 Stat. 2115, related to public lands development roads and trails.

[**§215. Repealed. Pub. L. 112–141, div. A, title I, §1114(b)(2)(A), July 6, 2012, 126 Stat. 468]**

Section, added Pub. L. 109–59, title I, §1118(a), Aug. 10, 2005, 119 Stat. 1179, related to territorial highway program.

A prior section 215, added Pub. L. 91–605, title I, §112(a), Dec. 31, 1970, 84 Stat. 1720; amended Pub. L. 95–599, title I, §129(f), Nov. 6, 1978, 92 Stat. 2708; Pub. L. 96–106, §9, Nov. 9, 1979, 93 Stat. 798; Pub. L. 100–17, title I, §133(b)(16), Apr. 2, 1987, 101 Stat. 172, related to territorial highway program, prior to repeal by Pub. L. 109–59, title I, §1118(a), Aug. 10, 2005, 119 Stat. 1179.

[**§216. Repealed. Pub. L. 112–141, div. A, title I, §1519(b)(1)(A), July 6, 2012, 126 Stat. 575]**

Section, added Pub. L. 91–605, title I, §113(a), Dec. 31, 1970, 84 Stat. 1721, related to the Darien Gap Highway.

§217. Bicycle transportation and pedestrian walkways

(a) Use of STP and Congestion Mitigation Program Funds.—Subject to project approval by the Secretary, a State may obligate funds apportioned to it under sections 104(b)(2) and 104(b)(4) of this title for construction of pedestrian walkways and bicycle and shared micromobility transportation facilities and for carrying out nonconstruction projects related to safe access for bicyclists and pedestrians.

(b) Use of National Highway Performance Program Funds.—Subject to project approval by the Secretary, a State may obligate funds apportioned to it under section 104(b)(1) of this title for construction of pedestrian walkways and bicycle transportation facilities on land adjacent to any highway on the National Highway System.

(c) Use of Federal Lands Highway Funds.—Funds authorized for forest highways, forest development roads and trails, public lands development roads and trails, park roads, parkways, Indian reservation roads, and public lands highways shall be available, at the discretion of the department charged with the administration of such funds, for the construction of pedestrian walkways and bicycle transportation facilities.

(d) State Bicycle and Pedestrian Coordinators.—Each State receiving an apportionment under sections 104(b)(2) and 104(b)(4) of this title shall use such amount of the apportionment as may be necessary to fund in the State department of transportation up to 2 positions of bicycle and pedestrian coordinator for promoting and facilitating the increased use of nonmotorized modes of transportation, including developing facilities for the use of pedestrians and bicyclists and public education, promotional, and safety programs for using such facilities.

(e) BRIDGES.—In any case where a highway bridge deck being replaced or rehabilitated with Federal financial participation is located on a highway on which pedestrians or bicyclists are permitted to operate at each end of such bridge, and the Secretary determines that the safe accommodation of pedestrians or bicyclists can be provided at reasonable cost as part of such replacement or rehabilitation, then such bridge shall be so replaced or rehabilitated as to provide such safe accommodations.

(f) FEDERAL SHARE.—For all purposes of this title, construction of a pedestrian walkway or a bicycle or shared micromobility transportation facility shall be deemed to be a highway project and the Federal share payable on account of such construction shall be determined in accordance with section 120(b).

(g) PLANNING AND DESIGN.—

(1) IN GENERAL.—Bicyclists and pedestrians shall be given due consideration in the comprehensive transportation plans developed by each metropolitan planning organization and State in accordance with sections 134 and 135, respectively. Bicycle transportation facilities and pedestrian walkways shall be considered, where appropriate, in conjunction with all new construction and reconstruction of transportation facilities, except where bicycle and pedestrian use are not permitted.

(2) SAFETY CONSIDERATIONS.—Transportation plans and projects shall provide due consideration for safety and contiguous routes for bicyclists and pedestrians. Safety considerations shall include the installation, where appropriate, and maintenance of audible traffic signals and audible signs at street crossings.

(h) USE OF MOTORIZED VEHICLES.—Motorized vehicles may not be permitted on trails and pedestrian walkways under this section, except for—

(1) maintenance purposes;

(2) when snow conditions and State or local regulations permit, snowmobiles;

(3) motorized wheelchairs;

(4) when State or local regulations permit, electric bicycles; and

(5) such other circumstances as the Secretary deems appropriate.

(i) TRANSPORTATION PURPOSE.—No bicycle project may be carried out under this section unless the Secretary has determined that such bicycle project will be principally for transportation, rather than recreation, purposes.

(j) DEFINITIONS.—In this section, the following definitions apply:

(1) BICYCLE TRANSPORTATION FACILITY.—The term "bicycle transportation facility" means a new or improved lane, path, or shoulder for use by bicyclists and a traffic control device, shelter, or parking facility for bicycles.

(2) ELECTRIC BICYCLE.—

(A) IN GENERAL.—The term "electric bicycle" means a bicycle—

(i) equipped with fully operable pedals, a saddle or seat for the rider, and an electric motor of less than 750 watts;

(ii) that can safely share a bicycle transportation facility with other users of such facility; and

(iii) that is a class 1 electric bicycle, class 2 electric bicycle, or class 3 electric bicycle.

(B) CLASSES OF ELECTRIC BICYCLES.—

(i) CLASS 1 ELECTRIC BICYCLE.—For purposes of subparagraph (A)(iii), the term "class 1 electric bicycle" means an electric bicycle, other than a class 3 electric bicycle, equipped with a motor that—

(I) provides assistance only when the rider is pedaling; and

(II) ceases to provide assistance when the speed of the bicycle reaches or exceeds 20 miles per hour.

(ii) CLASS 2 ELECTRIC BICYCLE.—For purposes of subparagraph (A)(iii), the term "class 2 electric bicycle" means an electric bicycle equipped with a motor that—

(I) may be used exclusively to propel the bicycle; and

(II) is not capable of providing assistance when the speed of the bicycle reaches or exceeds 20 miles per hour.

(iii) CLASS 3 ELECTRIC BICYCLE.—For purposes of subparagraph (A)(iii), the term "class 3 electric bicycle" means an electric bicycle equipped with a motor that—

(I) provides assistance only when the rider is pedaling; and

(II) ceases to provide assistance when the speed of the bicycle reaches or exceeds 28 miles per hour.

(3) PEDESTRIAN.—The term "pedestrian" means any person traveling by foot and any mobility-impaired person using a wheelchair.

(4) WHEELCHAIR.—The term "wheelchair" means a mobility aid, usable indoors, and designed for and used by individuals with mobility impairments, whether operated manually or motorized.

(Added Pub. L. 93–87, title I, §124(a), Aug. 13, 1973, 87 Stat. 262; amended Pub. L. 94–280, title I, §134, May 5, 1976, 90 Stat. 441; Pub. L. 95–599, title I, §141(h), Nov. 6, 1978, 92 Stat. 2712; Pub. L. 97–424, title I, §126A, formerly §126, Jan. 6, 1983, 96 Stat. 2116, renumbered §126A, Pub. L. 100–17, title I, §133(a)(2), Apr. 2, 1987, 101 Stat. 170; Pub. L. 100–17, title I, §127, Apr. 2, 1987, 101 Stat. 167; Pub. L. 102–240, title I, §1033, Dec. 18, 1991, 105 Stat. 1975; Pub. L. 104–59, title III, §310(b), Nov. 28, 1995, 109 Stat. 582; Pub. L. 105–178, title I, §1202(a), June 9, 1998, 112 Stat. 168; Pub. L. 109–59, title I, §1954, Aug. 10, 2005, 119 Stat. 1515; Pub. L. 112–141, div. A, title I, §1104(c)(4), July 6, 2012, 126 Stat. 427; Pub. L. 114–94, div. A, title I, §1446(a)(13), Dec. 4, 2015, 129 Stat. 1438; Pub. L. 117–58, div. A, title I, §§11133, 11525(p), Nov. 15, 2021, 135 Stat. 514, 608.)

§218. ALASKA HIGHWAY

(a) Recognizing the benefits that will accrue to the State of Alaska and to the United States from the reconstruction of the Alaska Highway from the Alaskan border at Beaver Creek, Yukon Territory, to Haines Junction in Canada and the Haines Cutoff Highway from Haines Junction in Canada to Haines, Alaska, the Secretary may provide for the necessary reconstruction of the highway using funds awarded through an applicable competitive grant program, if the highway meets all applicable eligibility requirements for the program, except for the specific requirements established by the agreement for the Alaska Highway Project between the Government of the United States and the Government of Canada. In addition to the funds described in the previous sentence, notwithstanding any other provision of law and on agreement with the State

[§219. Repealed. Pub. L. 100–17, title I,
§133(e)(1), Apr. 2, 1987, 101 Stat. 173]

CHAPTER 2—OTHER HIGHWAYS

of Alaska, the Secretary is authorized to expend on such highway or the Alaska Marine Highway System any Federal-aid highway funds apportioned to the State of Alaska under this title at a Federal share of 100 per centum. No expenditures shall be made for the construction of the portion of such highways that are in Canada unless an agreement is in place between the Government of Canada and the Government of the United States (including an agreement in existence on the date of enactment of the Surface Transportation Reauthorization Act of 2021) that provides, in part, that the Canadian Government—

(1) will provide, without participation of funds authorized under this title, all necessary right-of-way for the reconstruction of such highways;

(2) will not impose any highway toll, or permit any such toll to be charged for the use of such highways by vehicles or persons;

(3) will not levy or assess, directly or indirectly, any fee, tax, or other charge for the use of such highways by vehicles or persons from the United States that does not apply equally to vehicles or persons of Canada;

(4) will continue to grant reciprocal recognition of vehicle registration and driver's licenses in accordance with agreements between the United States and Canada; and

(5) will maintain such highways after their completion in proper condition adequately to serve the needs of present and future traffic.

(b) The survey and construction work undertaken in Canada pursuant to this section shall be under the general supervision of the Secretary.

(c) For purposes of this section, the term "Alaska Marine Highway System" includes all existing or planned transportation facilities and equipment in Alaska, including the lease, purchase, operation, repair, or construction of vessels, terminals, docks, floats, ramps, staging areas, parking lots, bridges and approaches thereto, and necessary roads.

(d) Notwithstanding any other provision of law, a project assisted under this section in the State of Alaska shall be treated as a project on a Federal-aid highway under chapter 1.

(Added Pub. L. 93–87, title I, §127(a)(1), Aug. 13, 1973, 87 Stat. 264; amended Pub. L. 94–147, Dec. 12, 1975, 89 Stat. 803; Pub. L. 97–424, title I, §158, Jan. 6, 1983, 96 Stat. 2135; Pub. L. 105–277, div. A, §101(g) [title III, §316], Oct. 21, 1998, 112 Stat. 2681–439, 2681–468; Pub. L. 108–7, div. I, title III, §327, Feb. 20, 2003, 117 Stat. 413; Pub. L. 109–59, title IV, §4409, Aug. 10, 2005, 119 Stat. 1778; Pub. L. 112–141, div. A, title I, §1519(c)(10), formerly §1519(c)(11), July 6, 2012, 126 Stat. 576, renumbered §1519(c)(10), Pub. L. 114–94, div. A, title I, §1446(d)(5)(B), Dec. 4, 2015, 129 Stat. 1438; Pub. L. 117–58, div. A, title I, §11116, div. G, title XI, §71103(g)(2), Nov. 15, 2021, 135 Stat. 482, 1326.)

[§219. REPEALED. PUB. L. 100–17, TITLE I, §133(E)(1), APR. 2, 1987, 101 STAT. 173]

Section, added Pub. L. 93–643, §122(a), Jan. 4, 1975, 88 Stat. 2289; amended Pub. L. 94–280, title I, §135(a), May 5, 1976, 90 Stat. 441; Pub. L. 95–599, title I, §168(d), Nov. 6, 1978, 92 Stat. 2723; Pub. L. 96–106, §10(a), Nov. 9, 1979, 93 Stat. 798, related to projects for safer off-system roads.

CHAPTER 3
GENERAL PROVISIONS

CHAPTER 3—GENERAL PROVISIONS

§301. Freedom from tolls

Except as provided in section 129 of this title with respect to certain toll bridges and toll tunnels, all highways constructed under the provisions of this title shall be free from tolls of all kinds.

(Pub. L. 85–767, Aug. 27, 1958, 72 Stat. 912.)

§302. State transportation department

(a) Any State desiring to avail itself of the provisions of this title shall have a State transportation department which shall have adequate powers, and be suitably equipped and organized to discharge to the satisfaction of the Secretary the duties required by this title. In meeting the provisions of this subsection, a State may engage, to the extent necessary or desirable, the services of private engineering firms.

(b) EFFECT OF COMPLIANCE.—Compliance with subsection (a) shall have no effect on the eligibility of costs.

(Pub. L. 85–767, Aug. 27, 1958, 72 Stat. 912; Pub. L. 89–574, §11, Sept. 13, 1966, 80 Stat. 770; Pub. L. 105–178, title I, §1212(a)(1), (2)(A)(i), (B)(ii), June 9, 1998, 112 Stat. 193.)

[§303. Repealed. Pub. L. 112–141, div. A, title I, §1519(b)(1)(A), July 6, 2012, 126 Stat. 575]

Section, added Pub. L. 102–240, title I, §1034(a), Dec. 18, 1991, 105 Stat. 1977; amended Pub. L. 103–429, §3(8), (9), Oct. 31, 1994, 108 Stat. 4378; Pub. L. 104–59, title II, §205(a), Nov. 28, 1995, 109 Stat. 576, related to management systems.

A prior section 303, Pub. L. 85–767, Aug. 27, 1958, 72 Stat. 912; Pub. L. 87–392, §1, Oct. 4, 1961, 75 Stat. 822; Pub. L. 88–426, title III, §305(24), Aug. 14, 1964, 78 Stat. 425; Pub. L. 91–605, title I, §114(a), Dec. 31, 1970, 84 Stat. 1722; Pub. L. 93–87, title I, §152(4), Aug. 13, 1973, 87 Stat. 276, provided for administrative organization of the Federal Highway Administration, prior to repeal by Pub. L. 97–449, §7(b), Jan. 12, 1983, 96 Stat. 2445. See section 104 of Title 49, Transportation.

§304. Participation by small business enterprises

It is declared to be in the national interest to encourage and develop the actual and potential capacity of small business and to utilize this important segment of our economy to the fullest practicable extent in construction of Federal-aid highways, including the Interstate System. In order to carry out that intent and encourage full and free competition, the Secretary should assist, insofar as feasible, small business enterprises in obtaining contracts in connection with the prosecution of the highway program.

(Pub. L. 85–767, Aug. 27, 1958, 72 Stat. 913; Pub. L. 112–141, div. A, title I, §1104(c)(5), July 6, 2012, 126 Stat. 427.)

§305. Archeological and paleontological salvage

Funds authorized to be appropriated to carry out this title to the extent approved as necessary by the highway department of any State, may be used for archeological and paleontological salvage in that State in compliance with the Act entitled "An Act for the preservation of American antiquities", approved June 8, 1906 (34 Stat. 225), and State laws where applicable,

(Pub. L. 85–767, Aug. 27, 1958, 72 Stat. 913; Pub. L. 86–657, §8(e), July 14, 1960, 74 Stat. 525.)

§306. Mapping

(a) In General.—In carrying out the provisions of this title, the Secretary shall, wherever practicable, authorize the use of photogrammetric methods in mapping, and the utilization of commercial enterprise for such services.

(b) Guidance.—The Secretary shall issue guidance to encourage States to utilize, to the maximum extent practicable, private sector sources for surveying and mapping services for projects under this title. In carrying out this subsection, the Secretary shall recommend appropriate roles for State government and private mapping and surveying activities, including—

(1) preparation of standards and specifications;

(2) research in surveying and mapping instrumentation and procedures and

[§307. Repealed. Pub. L. 105–178, title V, §5119(b), June 9, 1998, 112 Stat. 452]

CHAPTER 3—GENERAL PROVISIONS

technology transfer to the private sector;

(3) providing technical guidance, coordination, and administration of State surveying and mapping activities; and

(4) recommending methods for increasing the use by the States of private sector sources for surveying and mapping activities.

(c) IMPLEMENTATION.—The Secretary shall develop a process for the oversight and monitoring, on an annual basis, of the compliance of each State with the guidance issued under subsection (b).

(Pub. L. 85–767, Aug. 27, 1958, 72 Stat. 913; Pub. L. 104–59, title III, §321, Nov. 28, 1995, 109 Stat. 590; Pub. L. 112–141, div. A, title I, §1517(a), July 6, 2012, 126 Stat. 574.)

[§307. REPEALED. PUB. L. 105–178, TITLE V, §5119(B), JUNE 9, 1998, 112 STAT. 452]

Section, Pub. L. 85–767, Aug. 27, 1958, 72 Stat. 913; Pub. L. 87–866, §11, Oct. 23, 1962, 76 Stat. 1148; Pub. L. 88–157, §6, Oct. 24, 1963, 77 Stat. 277; Pub. L. 89–564, title I, §103, Sept. 9, 1966, 80 Stat. 735; Pub. L. 91–605, title I, §§115(c), 126, 136(c), Dec. 31, 1970, 84 Stat. 1723, 1729, 1735; Pub. L. 93–87, title I, §151, Aug. 13, 1973, 87 Stat. 276; Pub. L. 96–470, title I, §112(b)(2), Oct. 19, 1980, 94 Stat. 2239; Pub. L. 97–424, title I, §§156(a), (b), (d), 160(a), Jan. 6, 1983, 96 Stat. 2134, 2135; Pub. L. 100–17, title I, §§128, 129, 133(b)(17), Apr. 2, 1987, 101 Stat. 167, 169, 172; Pub. L. 102–240, title VI, §§6001, 6005, Dec. 18, 1991, 105 Stat. 2162, 2170; Pub. L. 103–429, §3(10), Oct. 31, 1994, 108 Stat. 4378; Pub. L. 104–59, title III, §325(d), Nov. 28, 1995, 109 Stat. 592, related to research and planning.

§308. COOPERATION WITH FEDERAL AND STATE AGENCIES AND FOREIGN COUNTRIES

(a) AUTHORIZED ACTIVITIES.—

(1) IN GENERAL.—The Secretary may perform, by contract or otherwise, authorized engineering or other services in connection with the survey, construction, maintenance, or improvement of highways for other Federal agencies, cooperating foreign countries, and State cooperating agencies.

(2) INCLUSIONS.—Services authorized under paragraph (1) may include activities authorized under section 214 of the Uniform Relocation Assistance and Real Property Acquisition Policies Act of 1970.

(3) REIMBURSEMENT.—Reimbursement for services carried out under this subsection (including depreciation on engineering and road-building equipment) shall be credited to the applicable appropriation.

(4) ALTERNATIVE CONTRACTING METHODS.—

(A) IN GENERAL.—Notwithstanding any other provision of law (including the Federal Acquisition Regulation), in performing services under paragraph (1), the Secretary may use any contracting method available to a State under this title.

(B) METHODS DESCRIBED.—The contracting methods referred to in subparagraph (A) shall include, at a minimum—

(i) project bundling;

(ii) bridge bundling;

(iii) design-build contracting;

(iv) 2-phase contracting;

(v) long-term concession agreements; and

(vi) any method tested, or that could be tested, under an experimental program relating to contracting methods carried out by the Secretary.

(b) Appropriations for the work of the Federal Highway Administration shall be available for expenses of warehouse maintenance and the procurement, care, and handling of supplies, materials, and equipment for distribution to projects under the supervision of the Federal Highway Administration, or for sale or distribution to other Government agencies, cooperating foreign countries, and State cooperating agencies, and the cost of such supplies and materials or the value of such equipment, including the cost of transportation and handling, may be reimbursed to current applicable appropriations.

(Pub. L. 85–767, Aug. 27, 1958, 72 Stat. 914; Pub. L. 93–87, title I, §152(5), Aug. 13, 1973, 87 Stat. 276; Pub. L. 112–141, div. A, title I, §1521(f), July 6, 2012, 126 Stat. 579; Pub. L. 117–58, div. A, title I, §11305(b), Nov. 15, 2021, 135 Stat. 532.)

[§309. Repealed. Pub. L. 112–141, div. A, title I, §1519(b)(1)(A), July 6, 2012, 126 Stat. 575]

Section, Pub. L. 85–767, Aug. 27, 1958, 72 Stat. 914; Pub. L. 93–87, title I, §152(5), Aug. 13, 1973, 87 Stat. 276, related to cooperation with other American Republics.

§310. Civil defense

In order to assure that adequate consideration is given to civil defense aspects in the planning and construction of highways constructed or reconstructed with the aid of Federal funds, the Secretary of Transportation is authorized and directed to consult, from time to time, with the Federal Civil Defense Administrator relative to the civil defense aspects of highways so constructed or reconstructed.

(Pub. L. 85–767, Aug. 27, 1958, 72 Stat. 914; Pub. L. 93–87, title I, §152(3), Aug. 13, 1973, 87 Stat. 276.)

§311. Highway improvements strategically important to the national defense

Funds made available under subsection (a) of section 104 of this title may be used to pay the entire engineering costs of the surveys, plans, specifications, estimates, and supervision of construction of projects for such urgent improvements of highways strategically important from the standpoint of the national defense as may be undertaken on the order of the Secretary and as the result of request of the Secretary of Defense or such other official as the President may designate. With the consent of a State, funds made available under subsection (b) of section 104 of this title may be used to the extent deemed necessary and advisable by the Secretary to carry out the provisions of this section.

(Pub. L. 85–767, Aug. 27, 1958, 72 Stat. 915.)

§312. Detail of Army, Navy, and Air Force officers

The Secretary of Defense, upon request of the Secretary, is authorized to make temporary details to the Federal Highway Administration of officers of the Army, the Navy, and the Air Force, without additional compensation, for technical advice and for consultation regarding highway needs for the national defense. Travel and subsistence expenses of officers so detailed shall be paid from appropriations available to the Department of Transportation on the same basis as authorized by law and by regulations of the Department of Defense for such officers.

(Pub. L. 85–767, Aug. 27, 1958, 72 Stat. 915; Pub. L. 93–87, title I, §152(5), (6), Aug. 13, 1973, 87 Stat. 276.)

§313. BUY AMERICA

(a) Notwithstanding any other provision of law, the Secretary of Transportation shall not obligate any funds authorized to be appropriated to carry out the Surface Transportation Assistance Act of 1982 (96 Stat. 2097) or this title and administered by the Department of Transportation, unless steel, iron, and manufactured products used in such project are produced in the United States.

(b) The provisions of subsection (a) of this section shall not apply where the Secretary finds—

(1) that their application would be inconsistent with the public interest;

(2) that such materials and products are not produced in the United States in sufficient and reasonably available quantities and of a satisfactory quality; or

(3) that inclusion of domestic material will increase the cost of the overall project contract by more than 25 percent.

(c) For purposes of this section, in calculating components' costs, labor costs involved in final assembly shall not be included in the calculation.

(d) The Secretary of Transportation shall not impose any limitation or condition on assistance provided under the Surface Transportation Assistance Act of 1982 (96 Stat. 2097) or this title that restricts any State from imposing more stringent requirements than this section on the use of articles, materials, and supplies mined, produced, or manufactured in foreign countries in projects carried out with such assistance or restricts any recipient of such assistance from complying with such State imposed requirements.

(e) INTENTIONAL VIOLATIONS.—If it has been determined by a court or Federal agency that any person intentionally—

(1) affixed a label bearing a "Made in America" inscription, or any inscription with the same meaning, to any product used in projects to which this section applies, sold in or shipped to the United States that was not made in the United States; or

(2) represented that any product used in projects to which this section applies, sold in or shipped to the United States that was not produced in the United States, was produced in the United States;

that person shall be ineligible to receive any contract or subcontract made with funds authorized under the Intermodal Surface Transportation Efficiency Act of 1991 pursuant to the debarment, suspension, and ineligibility procedures in subpart 9.4 of chapter 1 of title 48, Code of Federal Regulations.

(f) LIMITATION ON APPLICABILITY OF WAIVERS TO PRODUCTS PRODUCED IN CERTAIN FOREIGN COUNTRIES.—If the Secretary, in consultation with the United States Trade Representative, determines that—

(1) a foreign country is a party to an agreement with the United States and pursuant to that agreement the head of an agency of the United States has waived the requirements of this section, and

(2) the foreign country has violated the terms of the agreement by discriminating against products covered by this section that are produced in the United States and are covered by the agreement,

the provisions of subsection (b) shall not apply to products produced in that foreign country.

(g) WAIVERS.—

(1) IN GENERAL.—Not less than 15 days before issuing a waiver under this section, the Secretary shall provide to the public—

(A) notice of the proposed waiver;

(B) an opportunity for comment on the proposed waiver; and

(C) the reasons for the proposed waiver.

(2) REPORT.—Not less frequently than annually, the Secretary shall submit to the Committee on Environment and Public Works of the Senate and the Committee on Transportation and Infrastructure of the House of Representatives a report on the waivers provided under this section.

(h) APPLICATION TO HIGHWAY PROGRAMS.—The requirements under this section shall apply to all contracts eligible for assistance under this chapter for a project carried out within the scope of the applicable finding, determination, or decision under the National Environmental Policy Act of 1969 (42 U.S.C. 4321 et seq.), regardless of the funding source of such contracts, if at least 1 contract for the project is funded with amounts made available to carry out this title.

(Added and amended Pub. L. 109–59, title I, §1903(a), (c), Aug. 10, 2005, 119 Stat. 1464, 1465; Pub. L. 112–141, div. A, title I, §1518, July 6, 2012, 126 Stat. 574; Pub. L. 117–58, div. A, title I, §11513, Nov. 15, 2021, 135 Stat. 595.)

§314. RELIEF OF EMPLOYEES IN HAZARDOUS WORK

The Secretary is authorized in an emergency to use appropriations to the Department of Transportation for carrying out the provisions of this title for medical supplies, services, and other assistance necessary for the immediate relief of employees of the Federal Highway Administration engaged in hazardous work.

(Pub. L. 85–767, Aug. 27, 1958, 72 Stat. 915; Pub. L. 93–87, title I, §152(5), (6), Aug. 13, 1973, 87 Stat. 276.)

§315. RULES, REGULATIONS, AND RECOMMENDATIONS

Except as provided in sections 202(a)(5), 203(a)(3), and 205(a) of this title, the Secretary is authorized to prescribe and promulgate all needful rules and regulations for the carrying out of the provisions of this title. The Secretary may make such recommendations to the Congress and State transportation departments as he deems necessary for preserving and protecting the highways and insuring the safety of traffic thereon.

(Pub. L. 85–767, Aug. 27, 1958, 72 Stat. 915; Pub. L. 100–17, title I, §133(b)(18), Apr. 2, 1987, 101 Stat. 172; Pub. L. 105–178, title I, §1212(a)(2)(A)(ii), June 9, 1998, 112 Stat. 193; Pub. L. 112–141, div. A, title I, §1119(c)(3), July 6, 2012, 126 Stat. 492.)

§316. CONSENT BY UNITED STATES TO CONVEYANCE OF PROPERTY

For the purposes of this title the consent of the United States is given to any railroad or canal company to convey to the State transportation department of any State, or its nominee, any part of its right-of-way or other property in that State acquired by grant from the United States.

(Pub. L. 85–767, Aug. 27, 1958, 72 Stat. 915; Pub. L. 105–178, title I, §1212(a)(2)(A)(i), June 9, 1998, 112 Stat. 193.)

§317. APPROPRIATION FOR HIGHWAY PURPOSES OF LANDS OR INTERESTS IN LANDS OWNED BY THE UNITED STATES

(a) If the Secretary determines that any part of the lands or interests in lands owned by the United States is reasonably necessary for the right-of-way of any highway, or as a source of materials for the construction or maintenance of any such highway adjacent to such lands or interests in lands, the Secretary shall file with the Secretary of the Department supervising the administration of such lands or interests in lands a map showing the portion of such lands or interests in lands which it is desired to appropriate.

(b) If within a period of four months after such filing, the Secretary of such Department shall not have certified to the Secretary that the proposed appropriation of such land or material is contrary to the public interest or inconsistent with the purposes for which such land or materials have been reserved, or shall have agreed to the appropriation and transfer under conditions which he deems necessary for the adequate protection and utilization of the reserve, then such land and materials may be appropriated and transferred to the State transportation department, or its nominee, for such purposes and subject to the conditions so specified.

(c) If at any time the need for any such lands or materials for such purposes shall no longer exist, notice of the fact shall be given by the State transportation department to the Secretary and such lands or materials shall immediately revert to the control of the Secretary of the Department from which they had been appropriated.

(d) The provisions of this section shall apply only to projects constructed on a Federal-aid highway or under the provisions of chapter 2 of this title.

(Pub. L. 85–767, Aug. 27, 1958, 72 Stat. 916; Pub. L. 105–178, title I, §1212(a)(2)(A)(i), June 9, 1998, 112 Stat. 193; Pub. L. 112–141, div. A, title I, §1104(c)(6), July 6, 2012, 126 Stat. 427.)

§318. HIGHWAY RELOCATION DUE TO AIRPORT

Federal highway funds shall not be used for the reconstruction or relocation of any highway giving access to an airport constructed or extended after December 20, 1944, or for the reconstruction or relocation of any highway which has been or may be closed or the usefulness of which has been may be impaired by the location or construction of any airport constructed or extended after December 20, 1944, unless, prior to such construction or extension, as the case may be, the State transportation department and the Secretary have concurred with the officials in charge of the airport that the location of such airport or extension thereof and the consequent reconstruction or relocation of the highway are in the public interest.

(Pub. L. 85–767, Aug. 27, 1958, 72 Stat. 916; Pub. L. 105–178, title I, §1212(a)(2)(A)(i), June 9, 1998, 112 Stat. 193.)

§319. LANDSCAPING AND SCENIC ENHANCEMENT

(a) LANDSCAPE AND ROADSIDE DEVELOPMENT.—The Secretary may approve as a part of the construction of Federal-aid highways the costs of landscape and roadside development, including acquisition and development of publicly owned and controlled rest and recreation areas and sanitary and other facilities reasonably necessary to accommodate the traveling public, and for acquisition of interests in and improvement of strips of land necessary for the restoration, preservation, and enhancement of scenic beauty (including the enhancement of habitat and forage for pollinators) adjacent to such highways.

(b) PLANTING OF WILDFLOWERS.—

(1) GENERAL RULE.—The Secretary shall require the planting of native wildflower seeds or seedlings, or both, as part of any landscaping project under this section. At least ¼ of 1 percent of the funds expended for such landscaping project shall be used for such plantings.

(2) WAIVER.—The requirements of this subsection may be waived by the Secretary if a State certifies that native wildflowers or seedlings cannot be grown satisfactorily or planting areas are limited or otherwise used for agricultural purposes.

(3) GIFTS.—Nothing in this subsection shall be construed to prohibit the acceptance of native wildflower seeds or seedlings donated by civic organizations or other organizations and individuals to be used in landscaping projects.

(c) ENCOURAGEMENT OF POLLINATOR HABITAT AND FORAGE DEVELOPMENT AND PROTECTION ON TRANSPORTATION RIGHTS-OF-WAY.—In carrying out any program administered by the Secretary under this title, the Secretary shall, in conjunction with willing States, as appropriate—

(1) encourage integrated vegetation management practices on roadsides and other transportation rights-of-way, including reduced mowing; and

(2) encourage the development of habitat and forage for Monarch butterflies, other native pollinators, and honey bees through plantings of native forbs and grasses, including noninvasive, native milkweed species that can serve as migratory way stations for butterflies and facilitate migrations of other pollinators.

(Pub. L. 85–767, Aug. 27, 1958, 72 Stat. 916; Pub. L. 89–285, title III, §301(a), Oct. 22, 1965, 79 Stat. 1032; Pub. L. 89–574, §8(b), Sept. 13, 1966, 80 Stat. 768; Pub. L. 90–495, §6(f), Aug. 23, 1968, 82 Stat. 818; Pub. L. 94–280, title I, §136(a), May 5, 1976, 90 Stat. 442; Pub. L. 100–17, title I, §130, Apr. 2, 1987, 101 Stat. 169; Pub. L. 114–94, div. A, title I, §1415(a), Dec. 4, 2015, 129 Stat. 1421.)

§320. BRIDGES ON FEDERAL DAMS

(a) Each executive department, independent establishment, office, board, bureau, commission, authority, administration, corporation wholly owned or controlled by the United States, or other agency of the Government of the United States, hereinafter collectively and individually referred to as "agency", which on or after July 29, 1946, has jurisdiction over and custody of any dam constructed or to be constructed and owned by or for the United States, is authorized, with any funds available to it, to design and construct any such dam in such manner that it will constitute and serve as a suitable and adequate foundation to support a public highway bridge upon and across such dam, and to design and construct upon the foundation thus provided a public highway bridge upon and across such dam. The highway department of the State in which such dam shall be located, jointly with the Secretary, shall first determine and certify to such agency that such bridge is economically desirable and needed as a link in the State or Federal-aid highway systems, and shall request such agency to design and construct such dam so that it will serve as a suitable and adequate foundation for a public highway bridge and to design and construct such public highway bridge upon and across such dam, and shall agree to reimburse such agency pursuant to subsection (d) of this section for any additional costs which it may be required to incur because of the design and construction of such dam so that it will serve as a foundation for a public highway bridge and for expenditures which it may find it necessary to make in designing and constructing such public highway bridge upon and across such dam. In no case shall the design and construction of a bridge upon and across such dam be undertaken hereunder except by the agency having jurisdiction over and custody of the dam, acting directly or through contractors employed by it, and after such agency shall determine that it will be structurally feasible and will not interfere with the proper functioning and operation of the dam.

(b) Construction of any bridge upon and across any dam pursuant to this section shall not be commenced unless and until the State in which such bridge is to be located, or the appropriate subdivision of such State, shall enter into an agreement with such agency and with the Secretary to construct, or cause to be constructed, with or without the aid of Federal funds, the approach roads necessary to connect such bridge with existing public highways and to maintain, or cause to be maintained, such approach roads from and after their completion. Such agreement may also provide for the design and construction of such bridge upon and across the dam by such agency of the United States and for reimbursing such agency the costs incurred by it in the design and construction of the bridge as provided in subsection (d) of this section. Any such agency is hereby authorized to convey to the State, or to the appropriate subdivision thereof, without costs, such easements and rights-of-way in its custody or over lands of the United States in its custody and control as may be necessary, convenient, or proper for the location, construction, and maintenance of the approach roads referred to in this section including such roadside parks or recreational areas of limited size as may be deemed necessary for the accommodation of the traveling public. Any bridge constructed pursuant to this section upon and across a dam in the custody and jurisdiction of any agency of the United States, including such portion thereof, if any, as may extend beyond the physical limits of the dam, shall constitute and remain a part of said dam and be maintained by the agency. Any such agency may enter into any such contracts and agreements with the State or its subdivisions respecting public use of any bridge so located and constructed as may be deemed appropriate, but no such bridge shall be closed to public use by the agency except in cases of emergency or when deemed necessary in the interest of national security.

(c) All costs and expenses incurred and expenditures made by any agency in the exercise of the powers and authority conferred by this section (but not including any costs, expenses, or expenditures which would have been required in any event to satisfy a legal road or bridge relocation obligation or to meet operating or other agency needs) shall be recorded and kept separate and apart from the other costs, expenses, and expenditures of such agency, and no portion thereof shall be charged or allocated to flood control, navigation, irrigation, fertilizer production, the national defense, the development of power, or other program, purpose, or function of such agency.

(d) Not to exceed $65,000,000 of any money heretofore or hereafter appropriated for expenditure in accordance with the provisions of this title or prior Acts shall be available for expenditure by the Secretary in accordance with the provisions of this section, as an emergency fund, to reimburse any agency for any additional costs or expenditures which it may be required to incur because of the design and construction of any such dam so that it will constitute and serve as a foundation for a public highway bridge upon and across such dam and to reimburse any such agency for any costs, expenses, or expenditures which it may be required to make in designing and constructing any such bridge upon and across a dam in accordance with the provisions of this section, except such costs, expenses, or expenditures as would have been required of such agency in any event to satisfy a legal obligation to relocate a highway or bridge or to meet operating or other agency needs, and there is authorized to be appropriated any sum or sums necessary to reimburse the funds so expended by the Secretary from time to time under the authority of this section. Of each bridge constructed upon and across a dam under the provisions of this section, there may be financed wholly with Federal funds that portion thereof which is located within the physical limits of the masonry structure, or structures, of the dam, and the Secretary shall in his sole discretion determine what additional portion of the bridge, if any, may be so financed, such determination to be final and conclusive. The remainder of the bridge, and any necessary related approach roads, shall be financed by the State or its appropriate subdivision with or without the aid of Federal funds; but said portion of the bridge so financed by the State or its subdivisions, including such portion thereof, if any, as may extend beyond the physical limits of the dam, shall nevertheless be designed and constructed solely by the agency having custody and jurisdiction of the dam as provided in subsection (a) of this section.

(e) In making, reviewing, or approving the design of any bridge or approach structure to be constructed under this section, the agency shall, in matters relating to roadway design, loadings, clearances and widths, and traffic safeguards, give full consideration to and be guided by the standards and advice of the Secretary.

(f) The authority conferred by this section shall be in addition to and not in limitation of authority conferred upon any agency by any other law, and nothing in this section contained shall affect or be deemed to relate to any bridge, approach structure, or highway constructed or to be constructed by any such agency in furtherance of its lawful purposes and requirements or to satisfy a legal obligation incurred independently of this section.

(Pub. L. 85–767, Aug. 27, 1958, 72 Stat. 917; Pub. L. 86–342, title I, §108, Sept. 21, 1959, 73 Stat. 613; Pub. L. 88–423, §4(c), Aug. 13, 1964, 78 Stat. 398; Pub. L. 91–605, title I, §116(a), Dec. 31, 1970, 84 Stat. 1724; Pub. L. 93–87, title I, §128(a), Aug. 13, 1973, 87 Stat. 265; Pub. L. 93–643, §123(a), Jan. 4, 1975, 88 Stat. 2290; Pub. L. 94–280, title I, §137(a), May 5, 1976, 90 Stat. 443; Pub. L. 95–599, title I, §128(a), Nov. 6, 1978, 92 Stat. 2707.)

§321. SIGNS IDENTIFYING FUNDING SOURCES

If a State has a practice of erecting on projects under actual construction without Federal-aid highway assistance signs which indicate the source or sources of any funds used to carry out such projects, such State shall erect on all projects under actual construction with any funds made available out of the Highway Trust Fund (other than the Mass Transit Account) signs which are visible to highway users and which indicate each governmental source of funds being used to carry out such federally assisted projects and the amount of funds being made available by each such source.

(Added Pub. L. 109–59, title I, §1901(a), Aug. 10, 2005, 119 Stat. 1464.)

§322. MAGNETIC LEVITATION TRANSPORTATION TECHNOLOGY DEPLOYMENT PROGRAM

(a) DEFINITIONS.—In this section, the following definitions apply:

(1) ELIGIBLE PROJECT COSTS.—The term "eligible project costs"—

(A) means the capital cost of the fixed guideway infrastructure of a MAGLEV project, including land, piers, guideways, propulsion equipment and other components attached to guideways, power distribution facilities (including substations), control and communications facilities, access roads, and storage, repair, and maintenance facilities, but not including costs incurred for a new station; and

(B) includes the costs of preconstruction planning activities.

(2) FULL PROJECT COSTS.—The term "full project costs" means the total capital costs of a MAGLEV project, including eligible project costs and the costs of stations, vehicles, and equipment.

(3) MAGLEV.—The term "MAGLEV" means transportation systems employing magnetic levitation that would be capable of safe use by the public at a speed in excess of 240 miles per hour.

(4) PARTNERSHIP POTENTIAL.—The term "partnership potential" has the meaning given the term in the commercial feasibility study of high-speed ground transportation conducted under section 1036 of the Intermodal Surface Transportation Efficiency Act of 1991 (105 Stat. 1978).

(b) FINANCIAL ASSISTANCE.—

(1) IN GENERAL.—The Secretary shall make available financial assistance to pay the Federal share of full project costs of eligible projects selected under this section. Financial assistance made available under this section and projects assisted with the assistance shall be subject to section 5333(a) of title 49, United States Code.

(2) FEDERAL SHARE.—The Federal share of full project costs under paragraph (1) shall be not more than 2/3.

(3) USE OF ASSISTANCE.—Financial assistance provided under paragraph (1) shall be used only to pay eligible project costs of projects selected under this section.

(c) SOLICITATION OF APPLICATIONS FOR ASSISTANCE.—Not later than 180 days after the date of enactment of this subsection, the Secretary shall solicit applications from States, or authorities designated by 1 or more States, for financial assistance authorized by subsection (b) for planning, design, and construction of eligible MAGLEV projects.

(d) PROJECT ELIGIBILITY.—To be eligible to receive financial assistance under subsection (b), a project shall—

(1) involve a segment or segments of a high-speed ground transportation corridor that exhibit partnership potential;

(2) require an amount of Federal funds for project financing that will not exceed the sum of—

(A) the amounts made available under subsection (h)(1); and

(B) the amounts made available by States under subsection (h)(3);

(3) result in an operating transportation facility that provides a revenue producing service;

(4) be undertaken through a public and private partnership, with at least 1/3 of full project costs paid using non-Federal funds;

(5) satisfy applicable statewide and metropolitan planning requirements;

(6) be approved by the Secretary based on an application submitted to the Secretary by a State or authority designated by 1 or more States;

(7) to the extent that non-United States MAGLEV technology is used within the United States, be carried out as a technology transfer project; and

(8) be carried out using materials at least 70 percent of which are manufactured in the United States.

(e) PROJECT SELECTION CRITERIA.—Prior to soliciting applications, the Secretary shall establish criteria for selecting which eligible projects under subsection (d) will receive financial assistance under subsection (b). The criteria shall include the extent to which—

(1) a project is nationally significant, including the extent to which the project will demonstrate the feasibility of deployment of MAGLEV technology throughout the United States;

(2) timely implementation of the project will reduce congestion in other modes of transportation and reduce the need for additional highway or airport construction;

(3) States, regions, and localities financially contribute to the project;

(4) implementation of the project will create new jobs in traditional and emerging industries;

(5) the project will augment MAGLEV networks identified as having partnership potential;

(6) financial assistance would foster public and private partnerships for infrastructure development and attract private debt or equity investment;

(7) financial assistance would foster the timely implementation of a project; and

(8) life-cycle costs in design and engineering are considered and enhanced.

(f) PROJECT SELECTION.—

(1) PRECONSTRUCTION PLANNING ACTIVITIES.—Not later than 90 days after a deadline established by the Secretary for the receipt of applications, the Secretary shall evaluate the eligible projects in accordance with the selection criteria and select 1 or more eligible projects to receive financial assistance for preconstruction planning activities, including—

(A) preparation of such feasibility studies, major investment studies, and environmental impact statements and assessments as are required under State law;

(B) pricing of the final design, engineering, and construction activities proposed to be assisted under paragraph (2); and

(C) such other activities as are necessary to provide the Secretary with sufficient information to evaluate whether a project should receive financial assistance for final design, engineering, and construction activities under paragraph (2).

(2) FINAL DESIGN, ENGINEERING, AND CONSTRUCTION ACTIVITIES.—After completion of preconstruction planning activities for all projects assisted under paragraph (1), the Secretary shall select 1 of the projects to receive financial assistance for final design, engineering, and construction activities.

(g) JOINT VENTURES.—A project undertaken by a joint venture of United States and non-United States persons (including a project involving the deployment of non-United States MAGLEV technology in the United States) shall be eligible for financial assistance under this section if the project is eligible under subsection (d) and selected under subsection (f).

(h) FUNDING.—

(1) IN GENERAL.—

(A) CONTRACT AUTHORITY; AUTHORIZATION OF APPROPRIATIONS.—

(i) IN GENERAL.—There is authorized to be appropriated from the Highway Trust Fund (other than the Mass Transit Account) to carry out this section $15,000,000 for fiscal year 1999, $20,000,000 for fiscal year 2000, and $25,000,000 for fiscal year 2001.

(ii) CONTRACT AUTHORITY.—Funds authorized by this subparagraph shall be available for obligation in the same manner as if the funds were apportioned under chapter 1, except that—

(I) the Federal share of the cost of a project carried out under this section shall be determined in accordance with subsection (b), and

(II) the availability of the funds shall be determined in accordance with paragraph (2).

(B) NONCONTRACT AUTHORITY AUTHORIZATION OF APPROPRIATIONS.—

(i) IN GENERAL.—There are authorized to be appropriated from the Highway Trust Fund (other than the Mass Transit Account) to carry out this section (other than subsection (i)) $200,000,000 for each of fiscal years 2000 and 2001, $250,000,000 for fiscal year 2002, and $300,000,000 for fiscal year 2003.

(ii) AVAILABILITY.—Notwithstanding section 118(a), funds made available under clause (i) shall not be available in advance of an annual appropriation.

(2) AVAILABILITY OF FUNDS.—Funds made available under paragraph (1) shall remain available until expended.

(3) OTHER FEDERAL FUNDS.—Notwithstanding any other provision of law, funds made available to a State to carry out the surface transportation block grant program under section 133 and the congestion mitigation and air quality improvement program under section 149 may be used by the State to pay a portion of the full project costs of an eligible project selected under this section, without requirement for non-Federal funds.

(4) OTHER ASSISTANCE.—Notwithstanding any other provision of law, an eligible project selected under this section shall be eligible for other forms of financial assistance provided under this title and the Transportation Equity Act for the 21st Century, including loans, loan guarantees, and lines of credit.

(i) LOW-SPEED PROJECT.—

(1) IN GENERAL.—Notwithstanding any other provision of this section, of the funds made available by subsection (h)(1)(A) to carry out this section, $5,000,000 shall be made available to the Secretary to make grants for the research and development of low-speed superconductivity magnetic levitation technology for public transportation purposes in urban areas to demonstrate energy efficiency, congestion mitigation, and safety benefits.

(2) NONCONTRACT AUTHORITY AUTHORIZATION OF APPROPRIATIONS.—

(A) IN GENERAL.—There are authorized to be appropriated from the Highway Trust Fund (other than the Mass Transit Account) to carry out this subsection such sums as are necessary for each of fiscal years 2000 through 2003.

(B) AVAILABILITY.—Notwithstanding section 118(a), funds made available under subparagraph (A)—

(i) shall not be available in advance of an annual appropriation; and

(ii) shall remain available until expended.

(Added and amended Pub. L. 105–178, title I, §1218(a), (c), June 9, 1998, 112 Stat. 216; Pub. L. 105–206, title IX, §9003(i), July 22, 1998, 112 Stat. 841; Pub. L. 114–94, div. A, title I, §1109(c)(3), Dec. 4, 2015, 129 Stat. 1343.)

§323. DONATIONS AND CREDITS

(a) DONATIONS OF PROPERTY BEING ACQUIRED.—Nothing in this title, or in any other provision of law, shall be construed to prevent a person whose real property is being acquired in connection with a project under this title, after he has been fully informed of his right to receive just compensation for the acquisition of his property, from making a gift or donation of such property, or any part thereof, or of any of the compensation paid therefor, to a Federal agency, a State or a State agency, or a political subdivision of a State, as said person shall determine.

(b) CREDIT FOR ACQUIRED LANDS.—

(1) IN GENERAL.—Notwithstanding any other provision of this title, the State share of the cost of a project with respect to which Federal assistance is provided from the Highway Trust Fund (other than the Mass Transit Account) may be credited in an amount equal to the fair market value of any land that—

(A) is lawfully obtained by the State or a unit of local government in the State;

(B) is incorporated into the project;

(C) is not land described in section 138; and

(D) the Secretary determines will not influence the environmental assessment of the project, including—

(i) the decision as to the need to construct the project;

(ii) the consideration of alternatives; and

(iii) the selection of a specific location.

(2) ESTABLISHMENT OF FAIR MARKET VALUE.—The fair market value of land incorporated into a project and credited under paragraph (1) shall be established in the manner determined by the Secretary, except that—

(A) the fair market value shall not include any increase or decrease in the value of donated property caused by the project; and

(B) the fair market value of donated land shall be established as of the earlier of—

(i) the date on which the donation becomes effective; or

(ii) the date on which equitable title to the land vests in the State.

(3) LIMITATION ON APPLICABILITY.—This subsection shall not apply to donations made by an agency of the Federal Government.

(4) LIMITATION ON AMOUNT OF CREDIT.—The credit received by a State pursuant to this subsection may not exceed the State's matching share for the project.

(c) CREDIT FOR DONATIONS OF FUNDS, MATERIALS, OR SERVICES.—Nothing in this title or any other law shall prevent a person from offering to donate funds, materials, or services, or a local government from offering to donate funds, materials, or services performed by local government employees, in connection with a project eligible for assistance under this title. In the case of such a project with respect to which the Federal Government and the State share in paying the cost, any donated funds, or the fair market value of any donated materials or services, that are accepted and incorporated into the project by the State transportation department shall be credited against the State share.

(d) PROCEDURES.—A gift or donation in accordance with subsection (a) may be made at any time during the development of a project. Any document executed as part of such donation prior to the approval of an environmental document prepared pursuant to the National Environmental Policy Act of 1969 (42 U.S.C. 4321 et seq.) shall clearly indicate that—

(1) all alternatives to a proposed alignment will be studied and considered pursuant to such Act;

(2) acquisition of property under this section shall not influence the environmental assessment of a project including the decision relative to the need to construct the project or the selection of a specific location; and

(3) any property acquired by gift or donation shall be revested in the grantor or successors in interest if such property is not required for the alignment chosen after public hearings, if required, and completion of the environmental document.

(Added Pub. L. 93–87, title I, §145(a), Aug. 13, 1973, 87 Stat. 273; amended Pub. L. 93–643, §112, Jan. 4, 1975, 88 Stat. 2285; Pub. L. 100–17, title I, §146(a), Apr. 2, 1987, 101 Stat. 179; Pub. L. 104–59, title III, §322, Nov. 28, 1995, 109 Stat. 591; Pub. L. 105–178, title I, §§1212(a)(2)(A)(i), 1301(b)–(d)(1), June 9, 1998, 112 Stat. 193, 225, 226; Pub. L. 109–59, title I, §1902, Aug. 10, 2005, 119 Stat. 1464; Pub. L. 117–58, div. A, title I, §11525(q), Nov. 15, 2021, 135 Stat. 608.)

§324. PROHIBITION OF DISCRIMINATION ON THE BASIS OF SEX

No person shall on the ground of sex be excluded from participation in, be denied the benefits of, or be subjected to discrimination under any program or activity receiving Federal assistance under this title or carried on under this title. This provision will be enforced through agency provisions and rules similar to those already established, with respect to racial and other discrimination, under title VI of the Civil Rights Act of 1964. However, this remedy is not exclusive and will not prejudice or cut off any other legal remedies available to a discriminatee.

(Added Pub. L. 93–87, title I, §162(a), Aug. 13, 1973, 87 Stat. 280.)

[§325. REPEALED. PUB. L. 117–58, DIV. A, TITLE I, §11525(R), NOV. 15, 2021, 135 STAT. 608]

Section, added Pub. L. 109–59, title VI, §6003(a), Aug. 10, 2005, 119 Stat. 1865, related to State assumption of responsibilities for certain programs and projects.

A prior section 325, added Pub. L. 102–240, title VI, §6003[(a)], Dec. 18, 1991, 105 Stat. 2168, related to international highway transportation outreach program, prior to repeal by Pub. L. 105–178, title V, §5119(b), June 9, 1998, 112 Stat. 452.

§326. STATE ASSUMPTION OF RESPONSIBILITY FOR CATEGORICAL EXCLUSIONS

(a) CATEGORICAL EXCLUSION DETERMINATIONS.—

(1) IN GENERAL.—The Secretary may assign, and a State may assume, responsibility for determining whether certain designated activities are included within classes of action identified in regulation by the Secretary that are categorically

excluded from requirements for environmental assessments or environmental impact statements pursuant to regulations promulgated by the Council on Environmental Quality under part 1500 of title 40, Code of Federal Regulations (as in effect on October 1, 2003).

(2) SCOPE OF AUTHORITY.—A determination described in paragraph (1) shall be made by a State in accordance with criteria established by the Secretary and only for types of activities specifically designated by the Secretary.

(3) CRITERIA.—The criteria under paragraph (2) shall include provisions for public availability of information consistent with section 552 of title 5 and the National Environmental Policy Act of 1969 (42 U.S.C. 4321 et seq.).

(4) PRESERVATION OF FLEXIBILITY.—The Secretary shall not require a State, as a condition of assuming responsibility under this section, to forego project delivery methods that are otherwise permissible for highway projects.

(b) OTHER APPLICABLE FEDERAL LAWS.—

(1) IN GENERAL.—If a State assumes responsibility under subsection (a), the Secretary may also assign and the State may assume all or part of the responsibilities of the Secretary for environmental review, consultation, or other related actions required under any Federal law applicable to activities that are classified by the Secretary as categorical exclusions, with the exception of government-to-government consultation with Indian tribes, subject to the same procedural and substantive requirements as would be required if that responsibility were carried out by the Secretary.

(2) SOLE RESPONSIBILITY.—A State that assumes responsibility under paragraph (1) with respect to a Federal law shall be solely responsible and solely liable for complying with and carrying out that law, and the Secretary shall have no such responsibility or liability.

(c) MEMORANDA OF UNDERSTANDING.—

(1) IN GENERAL.—The Secretary and the State, after providing public notice and opportunity for comment, shall enter into a memorandum of understanding setting forth the responsibilities to be assigned under this section and the terms and conditions under which the assignments are made, including establishment of the circumstances under which the Secretary would reassume responsibility for categorical exclusion determinations.

(2) ASSISTANCE TO STATES.—On request of a Governor of a State, the Secretary shall provide to the State technical assistance, training, or other support relating to—

(A) assuming responsibility under subsection (a);

(B) developing a memorandum of understanding under this subsection; or

(C) addressing a responsibility in need of corrective action under subsection (d)(1)(B).

(3) TERM.—A memorandum of understanding—

(A) except as provided under subparagraph (C), shall have a term of not more than 3 years;

(B) shall be renewable; and

(C) shall have a term of 5 years, in the case of a State that has assumed the responsibility for categorical exclusions under this section for not fewer than 10 years.

(4) ACCEPTANCE OF JURISDICTION.—In a memorandum of understanding, the State shall consent to accept the jurisdiction of the Federal courts for the compliance, discharge, and enforcement of any responsibility of the Secretary that the State assumes.

(5) MONITORING.—The Secretary shall—

(A) monitor compliance by the State with the memorandum of understanding and the provision by the State of financial resources to carry out the memorandum of understanding; and

(B) take into account the performance by the State when considering renewal of the memorandum of understanding.

(d) TERMINATION.—

(1) TERMINATION BY SECRETARY.—The Secretary may terminate the participation of any State in the program if

(A) the Secretary determines that the State is not adequately carrying out the responsibilities assigned to the State;

(B) the Secretary provides to the State—

(i) a notification of the determination of noncompliance;

(ii) a period of not less than 120 days to take such corrective action as the Secretary determines to be necessary to comply with the applicable agreement; and

(iii) on request of the Governor of the State, a detailed description of each responsibility in need of corrective action regarding an inadequacy identified under subparagraph (A); and

(C) the State, after the notification and period described in clauses (i) and (ii) of subparagraph (B), fails to take satisfactory corrective action, as determined by the Secretary.

(2) TERMINATION BY THE STATE.—The State may terminate the participation of the State in the program at any time by providing to the Secretary a notice not later than the date that is 90 days before the date of termination, and subject to such terms and conditions as the Secretary may provide.

(e) STATE AGENCY DEEMED TO BE FEDERAL AGENCY.—A State agency that is assigned a responsibility under a memorandum of understanding shall be deemed to be a Federal agency for the purposes of the Federal law under which the responsibility is exercised.

(f) LEGAL FEES.—A State assuming the responsibilities of the Secretary under this section for a specific project may use funds apportioned to the State under section 104(b)(2) for attorney's fees directly attributable to eligible activities associated with the project.

(Added Pub. L. 109–59, title VI, §6004(a), Aug. 10, 2005, 119 Stat. 1867; amended Pub. L. 112–141, div. A, title I, §1312, July 6, 2012, 126 Stat. 545; Pub. L. 114–94, div. A, title I, §1307, Dec. 4, 2015, 129 Stat. 1390; Pub. L. 117–58, div. A, title I, §11314, Nov. 15, 2021, 135 Stat. 540.)

§327. SURFACE TRANSPORTATION PROJECT DELIVERY PROGRAM

(a) ESTABLISHMENT.—

(1) IN GENERAL.—The Secretary shall carry out a surface transportation project delivery program (referred to in this section as the "program").

(2) ASSUMPTION OF RESPONSIBILITY.—

(A) IN GENERAL.—Subject to the other provisions of this section, with the written agreement of the Secretary and a State, which may be in the form of a memorandum of understanding, the Secretary may assign, and the State may assume, the responsibilities of the Secretary with respect to one or more highway projects within the State under the National Environmental Policy Act of 1969 (42 U.S.C. 4321 et seq.).

(B) ADDITIONAL RESPONSIBILITY.—If a State assumes responsibility under subparagraph (A)—

(i) the Secretary may assign to the State, and the State may assume, all or part of the responsibilities of the Secretary for environmental review, consultation, or other action required under any Federal environmental law pertaining to the review or approval of a specific project;

(ii) at the request of the State, the Secretary may also assign to the State, and the State may assume, the responsibilities of the Secretary with respect to 1 or more railroad, public transportation, or multimodal projects within the State under the National Environmental Policy Act of 1969 (42 U.S.C. 4321 et seq.);

(iii) in a State that has assumed the responsibilities of the Secretary under clause (ii), a recipient of assistance under chapter 53 of title 49 may request that the Secretary maintain the responsibilities of the Secretary with respect to 1 or more public transportation projects within the State under the National Environmental Policy Act of 1969 (42 U.S.C. 4321 et seq.); but

(iv) the Secretary may not assign—

(I) any responsibility imposed on the Secretary by section 134 or 135 or section 5303 or 5304 of title 49; or

(II) responsibility for any conformity determination required under section 176 of the Clean Air Act (42 U.S.C. 7506).

(C) PROCEDURAL AND SUBSTANTIVE REQUIREMENTS.—A State shall assume responsibility under this section subject to the same procedural and substantive requirements as would apply if that responsibility were carried out by the Secretary.

(D) FEDERAL RESPONSIBILITY.—Any responsibility of the Secretary not explicitly assumed by the State by written agreement under this section shall remain the responsibility of the Secretary.

(E) NO EFFECT ON AUTHORITY.—Nothing in this section preempts or interferes with any power, jurisdiction, responsibility, or authority of an agency, other than the Department of Transportation, under applicable law (including regulations) with respect to a project.

(F) PRESERVATION OF FLEXIBILITY.—The Secretary may not require a State, as a condition of participation in the program, to forego project delivery methods that are otherwise permissible for projects.

(G) LEGAL FEES.—A State assuming the responsibilities of the Secretary under this section for a specific project may use funds apportioned to the State under section 104(b)(2) for attorneys' fees directly attributable to eligible activities associated with the project, including the payment of fees awarded under section 2412 of title 28.

(b) STATE PARTICIPATION.—

(1) PARTICIPATING STATES.—All States are eligible to participate in the program.

(2) APPLICATION.—Not later than 270 days after the date on which amendments to this section by the MAP-21 take effect, the Secretary shall amend, as appropriate, regulations that establish requirements relating to information required to be contained in any application of a State to participate in the program, including, at a minimum—

(A) the projects or classes of projects for which the State anticipates exercising the authority that may be granted under the program;

(B) verification of the financial resources necessary to carry out the authority that may be granted under the program; and

(C) evidence of the notice and solicitation of public comment by the State relating to participation of the State in the program, including copies of comments received from that solicitation.

(3) PUBLIC NOTICE.—

(A) IN GENERAL.—Each State that submits an application under this subsection shall give notice of the intent of the State to participate in the program not later than 30 days before the date of submission of the application.

(B) METHOD OF NOTICE AND SOLICITATION.—The State shall provide notice and solicit public comment under this paragraph by publishing the complete application of the State in accordance with the appropriate public notice law of the State.

(4) SELECTION CRITERIA.—The Secretary may approve the application of a State under this section only if—

(A) the regulatory requirements under paragraph (2) have been met;

(B) the Secretary determines that the State has the capability, including financial and personnel, to assume the responsibility; and

(C) the head of the State agency having primary jurisdiction over highway matters enters into a written agreement with the Secretary described in subsection (c).

(5) OTHER FEDERAL AGENCY VIEWS.—If a State applies to assume a responsibility of the Secretary that would have required the Secretary to consult with another Federal agency, the Secretary shall solicit the views of the Federal agency before approving the application.

(c) WRITTEN AGREEMENT.—A written agreement under this section shall—

(1) be executed by the Governor or the top-ranking transportation official in the State who is charged with responsibility for highway construction;

(2) be in such form as the Secretary may prescribe;

(3) provide that the State—

(A) agrees to assume all or part of the responsibilities of the Secretary described in subsection (a);

(B) expressly consents, on behalf of the State, to accept the jurisdiction of the Federal courts for the compliance, discharge, and enforcement of any responsibility of the Secretary assumed by the State;

(C) certifies that State laws (including regulations) are in effect that—

(i) authorize the State to take the actions necessary to carry out the responsibilities being assumed; and

(ii) are comparable to section 552 of title 5, including providing that any decision regarding the public availability of a document under those State laws is reviewable by a court of competent jurisdiction; and

(D) agrees to maintain the financial resources necessary to carry out the responsibilities being assumed;

(4) require the State to provide to the Secretary any information the Secretary reasonably considers necessary to ensure that the State is adequately carrying out the responsibilities assigned to the State;

(5) except as provided under paragraph (7), have a term of not more than 5 years;

(6) be renewable; and

(7) for any State that has participated in a program under this section (or under a predecessor program) for at least 10 years, have a term of 10 years.

(d) JURISDICTION.—

(1) IN GENERAL.—The United States district courts shall have exclusive jurisdiction over any civil action against a State for failure to carry out any responsibility of the State under this section.

(2) LEGAL STANDARDS AND REQUIREMENTS.—A civil action under paragraph (1) shall be governed by the legal standards and requirements that would apply in such a civil action against the Secretary had the Secretary taken the actions in question.

(3) INTERVENTION.—The Secretary shall have the right to intervene in any action described in paragraph (1).

(e) EFFECT OF ASSUMPTION OF RESPONSIBILITY.—A State that assumes responsibility under subsection (a)(2) shall be solely responsible and solely liable for carrying out, in lieu of and without further approval of the Secretary, the responsibilities assumed under subsection (a)(2), until the program is terminated as provided in subsection (j).

(f) LIMITATIONS ON AGREEMENTS.—Nothing in this section permits a State to assume any rulemaking authority of the Secretary under any Federal law.

(g) AUDITS.—

(1) IN GENERAL.—To ensure compliance by a State with any agreement of the State under subsection (c) (including compliance by the State with all Federal laws for which responsibility is assumed under subsection (a)(2)), for each State participating in the program under this section, the Secretary shall—

(A) not later than 180 days after the date of execution of the agreement, meet with the State to review implementation of the agreement and discuss plans for the first annual audit;

(B) conduct annual audits during each of the first 4 years of State participation;

(C) in the case of an agreement period of greater than 5 years pursuant to subsection (c)(7), conduct an audit covering the first 5 years of the agreement period; and

(D) ensure that the time period for completing an audit, from initiation to completion (including public comment and responses to those comments), does not exceed 180 days.

(2) PUBLIC AVAILABILITY AND COMMENT.—

(A) IN GENERAL.—An audit conducted under paragraph (1) shall be provided to the public for comment.

(B) RESPONSE.—Not later than 60 days after the date on which the period for public comment ends, the Secretary shall respond to public comments received under subparagraph (A).

(3) AUDIT TEAM.—

(A) IN GENERAL.—An audit conducted under paragraph (1) shall be carried out by an audit team determined by the Secretary, in consultation with the State, in accordance with subparagraph (B).

(B) CONSULTATION.—Consultation with the State under subparagraph (A) shall include a reasonable opportunity for the State to review and provide comments on the proposed members of the audit team.

(h) MONITORING.—After the fourth year of the participation of a State in the program, the Secretary shall monitor compliance by the State with the written agreement, including the provision by the State of financial resources to carry out the written agreement.

(i) REPORT TO CONGRESS.—The Secretary shall submit to Congress an annual report that describes the administration of the program.

(j) TERMINATION.—

(1) TERMINATION BY SECRETARY.—The Secretary may terminate the participation of any State in the program if—

(A) the Secretary determines that the State is not adequately carrying out the responsibilities assigned to the State;

(B) the Secretary provides to the State—

(i) a notification of the determination of noncompliance;

(ii) a period of not less than 120 days to take such corrective action as the Secretary determines to be necessary to comply with the applicable agreement; and

(iii) on request of the Governor of the State, a detailed description of each responsibility in need of corrective action regarding an inadequacy identified under subparagraph (A); and

(C) the State, after the notification and period provided under subparagraph (B), fails to take satisfactory corrective action, as determined by the Secretary.

(2) TERMINATION BY THE STATE.—The State may terminate the participation of the State in the program at any time by providing to the Secretary a notice by not later than the date that is 90 days before the date of termination, and subject to such terms and conditions as the Secretary may provide.

(k) CAPACITY BUILDING.—The Secretary, in cooperation with representatives of State officials, may carry out education, training, peer-exchange, and other initiatives as appropriate—

(1) to assist States in developing the capacity to participate in the assignment program under this section; and

(2) to promote information sharing and collaboration among States that are participating in the assignment program under this section.

(l) RELATIONSHIP TO LOCALLY ADMINISTERED PROJECTS.—A State granted authority under this section may, as appropriate and at the request of a local government—

(1) exercise such authority on behalf of the local government for a locally administered project; or

(2) provide guidance and training on consolidating and minimizing the documentation and environmental analyses necessary for sponsors of a locally administered project to comply with the National Environmental Policy Act of 1969 (42 U.S.C. 4321 et seq.) and any comparable requirements under State law.

(m) AGENCY DEEMED TO BE FEDERAL AGENCY.—A State agency that is assigned a responsibility under an agreement under this section shall be deemed to be an agency for the purposes of section 2412 of title 28.

(Added Pub. L. 109–59, title VI, §6005(a), Aug. 10, 2005, 119 Stat. 1868; amended Pub. L. 111–322, title II, §2203(c), Dec. 22, 2010, 124 Stat. 3526; Pub. L. 112–140, title I, §101(e)(1), June 29, 2012, 126 Stat. 392; Pub. L. 112–141, div. A, title I, §1313(a)–(h), July 6, 2012, 126 Stat. 545–547; Pub. L. 114–94, div. A, title I, §§1308, 1446(d)(3), Dec. 4, 2015, 129 Stat. 1390, 1438; Pub. L. 117–58, div. A, title I, §11313, Nov. 15, 2021, 135 Stat. 539.)

§328. ELIGIBILITY FOR ENVIRONMENTAL RESTORATION AND POLLUTION ABATEMENT

(a) IN GENERAL.—Subject to subsection (b), environmental restoration and pollution abatement to minimize or mitigate the impacts of any transportation project funded under this title (including retrofitting and construction of stormwater treatment systems to meet Federal and State requirements under sections 401 and 402 of the Federal Water Pollution Control Act (33 U.S.C. 1341; 1342)) may be carried out to address water pollution or environmental degradation caused wholly or partially by a transportation facility.

(b) MAXIMUM EXPENDITURE.—In a case in which a transportation facility is undergoing reconstruction, rehabilitation, resurfacing, or restoration, the expenditure of funds under this section for environmental restoration or pollution abatement described in subsection (a) shall not exceed 20 percent of the total cost of the reconstruction, rehabilitation, resurfacing, or restoration of the facility.

(Added Pub. L. 109–59, title VI, §6006(b), Aug. 10, 2005, 119 Stat. 1872.)

§329. ELIGIBILITY FOR CONTROL OF NOXIOUS WEEDS AND AQUATIC NOXIOUS WEEDS AND ESTABLISHMENT OF NATIVE SPECIES

(a) IN GENERAL.—In accordance with all applicable Federal law (including regulations), funds made available to carry out this section may be used for the following activities if such activities are related to transportation projects funded under this title:

(1) Establishment of plants selected by State and local transportation authorities to perform one or more of the following functions: abatement of stormwater runoff, stabilization of soil, provision of habitat, forage, and migratory way stations for Monarch butterflies, other native pollinators, and honey bees, and aesthetic enhancement.

(2) Management of plants which impair or impede the establishment, maintenance, or safe use of a transportation system.

(b) INCLUDED ACTIVITIES.—The establishment and management under subsection (a)(1) and (a)(2) may include—

(1) right-of-way surveys to determine management requirements to control Federal

or State noxious weeds as defined in the Plant Protection Act (7 U.S.C. 7701 et seq.) or State law, and brush or tree species, whether native or nonnative, that may be considered by State or local transportation authorities to be a threat with respect to the safety or maintenance of transportation systems;

(2) establishment of plants, whether native or nonnative with a preference for native to the maximum extent possible, for the purposes defined in subsection (a)(1);

(3) control or elimination of plants as defined in subsection (a)(2);

(4) elimination of plants to create fuel breaks for the prevention and control of wildfires; and

(5) training.

(c) CONTRIBUTIONS.—

(1) IN GENERAL.—Subject to paragraph (2), an activity described in subsection (a) may be carried out concurrently with, in advance of, or following the construction of a project funded under this title.

(2) CONDITION FOR ACTIVITIES CONDUCTED IN ADVANCE OF PROJECT CONSTRUCTION.—An activity described in subsection (a) may be carried out in advance of construction of a project only if the activity is carried out in accordance with all applicable requirements of Federal law (including regulations) and State transportation planning processes.

(Added Pub. L. 109–59, title VI, §6006(b), Aug. 10, 2005, 119 Stat. 1872; amended Pub. L. 114–94, div. A, title I, §1415(b), Dec. 4, 2015, 129 Stat. 1421.)

§330. PROGRAM FOR ELIMINATING DUPLICATION OF ENVIRONMENTAL REVIEWS

(a) ESTABLISHMENT.—

(1) IN GENERAL.—The Secretary shall establish a pilot program to authorize States that have assumed responsibilities of the Secretary under section 327 and are approved to participate in the program under this section to conduct environmental reviews and make approvals for projects under State environmental laws and regulations instead of the National Environmental Policy Act of 1969 (42 U.S.C. 4321 et seq.), consistent with the requirements of this section.

(2) PARTICIPATING STATES.—The Secretary may select not more than 2 States to participate in the program.

(3) ALTERNATIVE ENVIRONMENTAL REVIEW AND APPROVAL PROCEDURES DEFINED.—In this section, the term "alternative environmental review and approval procedures" means—

(A) substitution of 1 or more State environmental laws for—

(i) the National Environmental Policy Act of 1969 (42 U.S.C. 4321 et seq.);

(ii) any provisions of section 139 establishing procedures for the implementation of the National Environmental Policy Act of 1969 (42 U.S.C. 4321 et seq.) that are under the authority of the Secretary, as the Secretary, in consultation with the State, considers appropriate; and

(iii) related regulations and Executive orders; and

(B) substitution of 1 or more State environmental regulations for—

(i) the National Environmental Policy Act of 1969 (42 U.S.C. 4321 et seq.);

(ii) any provisions of section 139 establishing procedures for the implementation of the National Environmental Policy Act of 1969 (42 U.S.C.

4321 et seq.) that are under the authority of the Secretary, as the Secretary, in consultation with the State, considers appropriate; and

(iii) related regulations and Executive orders.

(b) APPLICATION.—To be eligible to participate in the program, a State shall submit to the Secretary an application containing such information as the Secretary may require, including—

(1) a full and complete description of the proposed alternative environmental review and approval procedures of the State, including—

(A) the procedures the State uses to engage the public and consider alternatives to the proposed action; and

(B) the extent to which the State considers environmental consequences or impacts on resources potentially impacted by the proposed action (such as air, water, or species);

(2) each Federal requirement described in subsection (a)(3) that the State is seeking to substitute;

(3) each State law or regulation that the State intends to substitute for such Federal requirement;

(4) an explanation of the basis for concluding that the State law or regulation is at least as stringent as the Federal requirement described in subsection (a)(3);

(5) a description of the projects or classes of projects for which the State anticipates exercising the authority that may be granted under the program;

(6) verification that the State has the financial resources necessary to carry out the authority that may be granted under the program;

(7) evidence of having sought, received, and addressed comments on the proposed application from the public; and

(8) any such additional information as the Secretary, or, with respect to section (d)(1)(A), the Secretary in consultation with the Chair, may require.

(c) REVIEW OF APPLICATION.—In accordance with subsection (d), the Secretary shall—

(1) review and accept public comments on an application submitted under subsection (b);

(2) approve or disapprove the application not later than 120 days after the date of receipt of an application that the Secretary determines is complete; and

(3) transmit to the State notice of the approval or disapproval, together with a statement of the reasons for the approval or disapproval.

(d) APPROVAL OF APPLICATION.—

(1) IN GENERAL.—The Secretary shall approve an application submitted under subsection (b) only if—

(A) the Secretary, with the concurrence of the Chair and after considering any public comments received pursuant to subsection (c), determines that the laws and regulations of the State described in the application are at least as stringent as the Federal requirements described in subsection (a)(3);

(B) the Secretary, after considering any public comments received pursuant to subsection (c), determines that the State has the capacity, including financial and personnel, to assume the responsibility;

(C) the State has executed an agreement with the Secretary in accordance with section 327; and

(D) the State has executed an agreement with the Secretary under this section that—

(i) has been executed by the Governor or the top-ranking transportation official in the State who is charged with responsibility for highway construction;

(ii) is in such form as the Secretary may prescribe;

(iii) provides that the State—

(I) agrees to assume the responsibilities, as identified by the Secretary, under this section;

(II) expressly consents, on behalf of the State, to accept the jurisdiction of the Federal courts under subsection (e)(1) for the compliance, discharge, and enforcement of any responsibility under this section;

(III) certifies that State laws (including regulations) are in effect that—

(aa) authorize the State to take the actions necessary to carry out the responsibilities being assumed; and

(bb) are comparable to section 552 of title 5, including providing that any decision regarding the public availability of a document under those State laws is reviewable by a court of competent jurisdiction; and

(IV) agrees to maintain the financial resources necessary to carry out the responsibilities being assumed;

(iv) requires the State to provide to the Secretary any information the Secretary reasonably considers necessary to ensure that the State is adequately carrying out the responsibilities assigned to the State;

(v) has a term of not more than 5 years; and

(vi) is renewable.

(2) EXCLUSION.—The National Environmental Policy Act of 1969 (42 U.S.C. 4321 et seq.) shall not apply to a decision by the Secretary to approve or disapprove an application submitted under this section.

(e) JUDICIAL REVIEW.—

(1) IN GENERAL.—The United States district courts shall have exclusive jurisdiction over any civil action against a State relating to the failure of the State—

(A) to meet the requirements of this section; or

(B) to follow the alternative environmental review and approval procedures approved pursuant to this section.

(2) LIMITATION ON REVIEW.—

(A) IN GENERAL.—Notwithstanding any other provision of law, a claim seeking judicial review of a permit, license, or approval issued by a State under this section shall be barred unless the claim is filed not later than 150 days as set forth in section 139(l) after the date of publication in the Federal Register by the Secretary of a notice that the permit, license, or approval is final pursuant to the law under which the action is taken.

(B) DEADLINES.—

(i) NOTIFICATION.—The State shall notify the Secretary of the final action of the State not later than 10 days after the final action is taken.

(ii) PUBLICATION.—The Secretary shall publish the notice of final action in the Federal Register not later than 30 days after the date of receipt of the notice under clause (i).

(C) SAVINGS PROVISION.—Nothing in this subsection creates a right to judicial review or places any limit on filing a claim that a person has violated the terms of a permit, license, or approval.

(3) NEW INFORMATION.—

(A) IN GENERAL.—A State shall consider new information received after the close of a comment period if the information satisfies the requirements for a supplemental environmental impact statement under section 771.130 of title 23, Code of Federal Regulations (or successor regulations).

(B) TREATMENT OF FINAL AGENCY ACTION.—

(i) IN GENERAL.—The final agency action that follows preparation of a supplemental environmental impact statement, if required, shall be considered a separate final agency action, and the deadline for filing a claim for judicial review of the action shall be 150 days as set forth in section 139(l) after the date of publication in the Federal Register by the Secretary of a notice announcing such action.

(ii) DEADLINES.—

(I) NOTIFICATION.—The State shall notify the Secretary of the final action of the State not later than 10 days after the final action is taken.

(II) PUBLICATION.—The Secretary shall publish the notice of final action in the Federal Register not later than 30 days after the date of receipt of the notice under subclause (I).

(f) ELECTION.—A State participating in the programs under this section and section 327, at the discretion of the State, may elect to apply the National Environmental Policy Act of 1969 (42 U.S.C. 4321 et seq.) instead of the alternative environmental review and approval procedures of the State.

(g) ADOPTION OR INCORPORATION BY REFERENCE OF DOCUMENTS.—To the maximum extent practicable and consistent with Federal law, other Federal agencies with authority over a project subject to this section shall adopt or incorporate by reference documents produced by a participating State under this section to satisfy the requirements of the National Environmental Policy Act of 1969 (42 U.S.C. 4321 et seq.).

(h) RELATIONSHIP TO LOCALLY ADMINISTERED PROJECTS.—

(1) IN GENERAL.—A State with an approved program under this section, at the request of a local government, may exercise authority under that program on behalf of up to 25 local governments for locally administered projects.

(2) SCOPE.—For up to 25 local governments selected by a State with an approved program under this section, the State shall be responsible for ensuring that any environmental review, consultation, or other action required under the National Environmental Policy Act of 1969 (42 U.S.C. 4321 et seq.) or the State program, or both, meets the requirements of such Act or program.

(i) REVIEW AND TERMINATION.—

(1) IN GENERAL.—A State program approved under this section shall at all times be in accordance with the requirements of this section.

(2) REVIEW.—The Secretary shall review each State program approved under this section not less than once every 5 years.

(3) PUBLIC NOTICE AND COMMENT.—In conducting the review process under paragraph (2), the Secretary shall provide notice and an opportunity for public comment.

(4) WITHDRAWAL OF APPROVAL.—If the Secretary, in consultation with the Chair, determines at any time that a State is not administering a State program approved under this section in accordance with the requirements of this section, the Secretary shall so notify the State, and if appropriate corrective action is not taken within a reasonable time, not to exceed 90 days, the Secretary shall withdraw approval of the State program.

(5) EXTENSIONS AND TERMINATIONS.—At the conclusion of the review process under paragraph (2), the Secretary may extend for an additional 5-year period or terminate the authority of a State under this section to substitute the laws and regulations of the State for the National Environmental Policy Act of 1969 (42 U.S.C. 4321 et seq.).

(j) REPORT TO CONGRESS.—Not later than 2 years after the date of enactment of this section, and annually thereafter, the Secretary shall submit to the Committee on Transportation and Infrastructure of the House of Representatives and the Committee on Environment and Public Works of the Senate a report that describes the administration of the program, including—

(1) the number of States participating in the program;

(2) the number and types of projects for which each State participating in the program has used alternative environmental review and approval procedures;

(3) a description and assessment of whether implementation of the program has resulted in more efficient review of projects; and

(4) any recommendations for modifications to the program.

(k) SUNSET.—The program shall terminate 12 years after the date of enactment of this section.

(l) DEFINITIONS.—In this section, the following definitions apply:

(1) CHAIR.—The term "Chair" means the Chair of the Council on Environmental Quality.

(2) MULTIMODAL PROJECT.—The term "multimodal project" has the meaning given that term in section 139(a).

(3) PROGRAM.—The term "program" means the pilot program established under this section.

(4) PROJECT.—The term "project" means—

(A) a project requiring approval under this title, chapter 53 of subtitle III of title 49, or subtitle V of title 49; and

(B) a multimodal project.

(Added Pub. L. 114–94, div. A, title I, §1309(b), Dec. 4, 2015, 129 Stat. 1392; amended Pub. L. 115–254, div. B, title V, §578, Oct. 5, 2018, 132 Stat. 3394.)

§331. EVALUATION OF PROJECTS WITHIN AN OPERATIONAL RIGHT-OF-WAY

(a) DEFINITIONS.—

(1) ELIGIBLE PROJECT OR ACTIVITY.—

(A) IN GENERAL.—In this section, the term "eligible project or activity" means a project or activity within an existing operational right-of-way (as defined in section 771.117(c)(22) of title 23, Code of Federal Regulations (or successor regulations))—

    (i)(I) eligible for assistance under this title; or

    (II) administered as if made available under this title;

    (ii) that is—

        (I) a preventive maintenance, preservation, or highway safety improvement project (as defined in section 148(a)); or

        (II) a new turn lane that the State advises in writing to the Secretary would assist public safety; and

    (iii) that—

        (I) is classified as a categorical exclusion under section 771.117 of title 23, Code of Federal Regulations (or successor regulations); or

        (II) if the project or activity does not receive assistance described in clause (i) would be considered a categorical exclusion if the project or activity received assistance described in clause (i).

(B) EXCLUSION.—The term "eligible project or activity" does not include a project to create a new travel lane.

(2) PRELIMINARY EVALUATION.—The term "preliminary evaluation", with respect to an application described in subsection (b)(1), means an evaluation that is customary or practicable for the relevant agency to complete within a 45-day period for similar applications.

(3) RELEVANT AGENCY.—The term "relevant agency" means a Federal agency, other than the Federal Highway Administration, with responsibility for review of an application from a State for a permit, approval, or jurisdictional determination for an eligible project or activity.

(b) ACTION REQUIRED.—

(1) IN GENERAL.—Subject to paragraph (2), not later than 45 days after the date of receipt of an application by a State for a permit, approval, or jurisdictional determination for an eligible project or activity, the head of the relevant agency shall—

    (A) make at least a preliminary evaluation of the application; and

    (B) notify the State of the results of the preliminary evaluation under subparagraph (A).

(2) EXTENSION.—The head of the relevant agency may extend the review period under paragraph (1) by not more than 30 days if the head of the relevant agency provides to the State written notice that includes an explanation of the need for the extension.

(3) FAILURE TO ACT.—If the head of the relevant agency fails to meet a deadline under paragraph (1) or (2), as applicable, the head of the relevant agency shall—

    (A) not later than 30 days after the date of the missed deadline, submit to the State, the Committee on Environment and Public Works of the Senate, and the Committee on Transportation and Infrastructure of the House of Representatives a report that describes why the deadline was missed; and

(B) not later than 14 days after the date on which a report is submitted under subparagraph (A), make publicly available, including on the internet, a copy of that report.

(Added Pub. L. 117–58, div. A, title I, §11309(a), Nov. 15, 2021, 135 Stat. 535.)

§332. POLLINATOR-FRIENDLY PRACTICES ON ROADSIDES AND HIGHWAY RIGHTS-OF-WAY

(a) IN GENERAL.—The Secretary shall establish a program to provide grants to eligible entities to carry out activities to benefit pollinators on roadsides and highway rights-of-way, including the planting and seeding of native, locally-appropriate grasses and wildflowers, including milkweed.

(b) ELIGIBLE ENTITIES.—An entity eligible to receive a grant under this section is—
(1) a State department of transportation;
(2) an Indian tribe; or
(3) a Federal land management agency.

(c) APPLICATION.—To be eligible to receive a grant under this section, an eligible entity shall submit to the Secretary an application at such time, in such manner, and containing such information as the Secretary may require, including a pollinator-friendly practices plan described in subsection (d).

(d) POLLINATOR-FRIENDLY PRACTICES PLAN.—
(1) IN GENERAL.—An eligible entity shall include in the application under subsection (c) a plan that describes the pollinator-friendly practices that the eligible entity has implemented or plans to implement, including—
(A) practices relating to mowing strategies that promote early successional vegetation and limit disturbance during periods of highest use by target pollinator species on roadsides and highway rights-of-way, such as—
(i) reducing the mowing swath outside of the State-designated safety zone;
(ii) increasing the mowing height;
(iii) reducing the mowing frequency;
(iv) refraining from mowing monarch and other pollinator habitat during periods in which monarchs or other pollinators are present;
(v) use of a flushing bar and cutting at reduced speeds to reduce pollinator deaths due to mowing; or
(vi) reducing raking along roadsides and highway rights-of-way;
(B) implementation of an integrated vegetation management plan that includes approaches such as mechanical tree and brush removal, targeted and judicious use of herbicides, and mowing, to address weed issues on roadsides and highway rights-of-way;
(C) planting or seeding of native, locally-appropriate grasses and wildflowers, including milkweed, on roadsides and highway rights-of-way to enhance pollinator habitat, including larval host plants;
(D) removing nonnative grasses from planting and seeding mixes, except for use as nurse or cover crops;
(E) obtaining expert training or assistance on pollinator-friendly practices, including—
(i) native plant identification;

(ii) establishment and management of locally-appropriate native plants that benefit pollinators;

(iii) land management practices that benefit pollinators; and

(iv) pollinator-focused integrated vegetation management; or

(F) any other pollinator-friendly practices the Secretary determines to be appropriate.

(2) COORDINATION.—In developing a plan under paragraph (1), an eligible entity that is a State department of transportation or a Federal land management agency shall coordinate with applicable State agencies, including State agencies with jurisdiction over agriculture and fish and wildlife.

(3) CONSULTATION.—In developing a plan under paragraph (1)—

(A) an eligible entity that is a State department of transportation or a Federal land management agency shall consult with affected or interested Indian tribes; and

(B) any eligible entity may consult with nonprofit organizations, institutions of higher education, metropolitan planning organizations, and any other relevant entities.

(e) AWARD OF GRANTS.—

(1) IN GENERAL.—The Secretary shall provide a grant to each eligible entity that submits an application under subsection (c), including a plan under subsection (d), that the Secretary determines to be satisfactory.

(2) AMOUNT OF GRANTS.—The amount of a grant under this section—

(A) shall be based on the number of pollinator-friendly practices the eligible entity has implemented or plans to implement; and

(B) shall not exceed $150,000.

(f) USE OF FUNDS.—An eligible entity that receives a grant under this section shall use the funds for the implementation, improvement, or further development of the plan under subsection (d).

(g) FEDERAL SHARE.—The Federal share of the cost of an activity carried out with a grant under this section shall be 100 percent.

(h) BEST PRACTICES.—The Secretary shall develop and make available to eligible entities best practices for, and a priority ranking of, pollinator-friendly practices on roadsides and highway rights-of-way.

(i) TECHNICAL ASSISTANCE.—On request of an eligible entity that receives a grant under this section, the Secretary shall provide technical assistance with the implementation, improvement, or further development of a plan under subsection (d).

(j) ADMINISTRATIVE COSTS.—For each fiscal year, the Secretary may use not more than 2 percent of the amounts made available to carry out this section for the administrative costs of carrying out this section.

(k) REPORT.—Not later than 1 year after the date on which the first grant is provided under this section, the Secretary shall submit to the Committee on Environment and Public Works of the Senate and the Committee on Transportation and Infrastructure of the House of Representatives a report on the implementation of the program under this section.

(l) AUTHORIZATION OF APPROPRIATIONS.—

(1) IN GENERAL.—There is authorized to be appropriated to carry out this section

$2,000,000 for each of fiscal years 2022 through 2026.

(2) AVAILABILITY.—Amounts made available under this section shall remain available for a period of 3 years after the last day of the fiscal year for which the funds are authorized.

(Added Pub. L. 117–58, div. A, title I, § 11528(a), Nov. 15, 2021, 135 Stat. 610.)

CHAPTER 4
HIGHWAY SAFETY

CHAPTER 4—HIGHWAY SAFETY

§401. AUTHORITY OF THE SECRETARY

The Secretary is authorized and directed to assist and cooperate with other Federal departments and agencies, State and local governments, private industry, and other interested parties, to increase highway safety. For the purposes of this chapter, the term "State" means any one of the fifty States, the District of Columbia, Puerto Rico, the Virgin Islands, Guam, American Samoa, and the Commonwealth of the Northern Mariana Islands.

(Added Pub. L. 89–564, title I, §101, Sept. 9, 1966, 80 Stat. 731; amended Pub. L. 93–87, title II, §218, Aug. 13, 1973, 87 Stat. 290; Pub. L. 98–363, §3(b), July 17, 1984, 98 Stat. 436; Pub. L. 100–17, title I, §133(b)(19), Apr. 2, 1987, 101 Stat. 172.)

§402. HIGHWAY SAFETY PROGRAMS

(a) PROGRAM REQUIRED.—

(1) IN GENERAL.—Each State shall have in effect a highway safety program that—
(i) is designed to reduce—
(I) traffic crashes; and
(II) deaths, injuries, and property damage resulting from those crashes;
(ii) includes—
(I) an approved, current, triennial highway safety plan in accordance with subsection (k); and
(II) an approved grant application under subsection (l) for the fiscal year;
(iii) demonstrates compliance with the applicable administrative requirements of subsection (b)(1); and
(iv) is approved by the Secretary.

(2) UNIFORM GUIDELINES.—Programs required under paragraph (1) shall comply with uniform guidelines, promulgated by the Secretary and expressed in terms of performance criteria, that—
(A) include programs—
(i) to reduce injuries and deaths resulting from motor vehicles being driven in excess of posted speed limits;
(ii) to encourage the proper use of safety belts by occupants of motor vehicles;

(iii) to encourage more widespread and proper use of child restraints, with an emphasis on underserved populations;

(iv) to reduce injuries and deaths resulting from persons driving motor vehicles while impaired by alcohol or a controlled substance;

(v) to prevent crashes and reduce injuries and deaths resulting from crashes involving motor vehicles and motorcycles;

(vi) to reduce injuries and deaths resulting from crashes involving school buses;

(vii) to reduce crashes resulting from unsafe driving behavior (including aggressive or fatigued driving and distracted driving arising from the use of electronic devices in vehicles);

(viii) to improve law enforcement services in motor vehicle crash prevention, traffic supervision, and post-crash procedures;

(ix) to increase driver awareness of commercial motor vehicles to prevent crashes and reduce injuries and fatalities;

(x) to reduce crashes caused by driver misuse or misunderstanding of new vehicle technology;

(xi) to increase vehicle recall awareness;

(xii) to provide to the public information relating to the risks of child heatstroke death when left unattended in a motor vehicle after the motor is deactivated by the operator;

(xiii) to reduce injuries and deaths resulting from the failure by drivers of motor vehicles to move to another traffic lane or reduce the speed of the vehicle when law enforcement, fire service, emergency medical services, or other emergency or first responder vehicles are stopped or parked on or next to a roadway with emergency lights activated; and

(xiv) to prevent crashes, injuries, and deaths caused by unsecured vehicle loads;

(B) improve driver performance, including—

(i) driver education;

(ii) driver testing to determine proficiency to operate motor vehicles; and

(iii) driver examinations (physical, mental, and driver licensing);

(C) improve pedestrian performance and bicycle safety;

(D) include provisions for—

(i) an effective record system of crashes (including resulting injuries and deaths);

(ii) crash investigations to determine the probable causes of crashes, injuries, and deaths;

(iii) vehicle registration, operation, and inspection; and

(iv) emergency services; and

(E) to the extent determined appropriate by the Secretary, are applicable to federally administered areas where a Federal department or agency controls the highways or supervises traffic operations.

(3) ADDITIONAL CONSIDERATIONS.—A State that has legalized medicinal or recreational marijuana shall take into consideration implementing programs in

addition to the programs described in paragraph (2)(A)—

(A) to educate drivers regarding the risks associated with marijuana-impaired driving; and

(B) to reduce injuries and deaths resulting from individuals driving motor vehicles while impaired by marijuana.

(b) ADMINISTRATION OF STATE PROGRAMS.—

(1) ADMINISTRATIVE REQUIREMENTS.—The Secretary shall not approve a State highway safety program under this section which does not—

(A) provide that the Governor of the State shall be responsible for the administration of the program through a State highway safety agency which shall have adequate powers and be suitably equipped and organized to carry out, to the satisfaction of the Secretary, such program;

(B) provide for a comprehensive, data-driven traffic safety program that results from meaningful public participation and engagement from affected communities, particularly those most significantly impacted by traffic crashes resulting in injuries and fatalities;

(C) except as provided in paragraph (2), provide that at least 40 percent of all Federal funds apportioned under this section to the State for any fiscal year will be expended by the political subdivisions of the State, including Indian tribal governments, in carrying out local highway safety programs;

(D) provide adequate and reasonable access for the safe and convenient movement of individuals, including those with disabilities and those in wheelchairs, across curbs constructed or replaced on or after July 1, 1976, at all pedestrian crosswalks throughout the State;

(E) as part of a comprehensive program, support—

(i) data-driven traffic safety enforcement programs that foster effective community collaboration to increase public safety; and

(ii) data collection and analysis to ensure transparency, identify disparities in traffic enforcement, and inform traffic enforcement policies, procedures, and activities; and

(F) provide satisfactory assurances that the State will implement activities in support of national highway safety goals to reduce motor vehicle related fatalities that also reflect the primary data-related crash factors within a State as identified by the State highway safety planning process, including—

(i) national, high-visibility law enforcement mobilizations coordinated by the Secretary;

(ii) sustained enforcement of statutes addressing impaired driving, occupant protection, and driving in excess of posted speed limits;

(iii) an annual statewide safety belt use survey in accordance with criteria established by the Secretary for the measurement of State safety belt use rates to ensure that the measurements are accurate and representative;

(iv) development of statewide data systems to provide timely and effective data analysis to support allocation of highway safety resources;

(v) ensuring that the State will coordinate its highway safety plan, data collection, and information systems with the State strategic highway safety plan (as defined in section 148(a)); and

(vi) unless the State highway safety program is developed by American Samoa, Guam, the Commonwealth of the Northern Mariana Islands, or the United States Virgin Islands, participation in the Fatality Analysis Reporting System.

(2) WAIVER.—The Secretary may waive the requirement of paragraph (1)(C), in whole or in part, for a fiscal year for any State whenever the Secretary determines that there is an insufficient number of local highway safety programs to justify the expenditure in the State of such percentage of Federal funds during the fiscal year.

(c) USE OF FUNDS.—

(1) USE FOR STATE ACTIVITIES.—

(A) IN GENERAL.—The funds authorized to be appropriated to carry out this section shall be used to aid the States to conduct the highway safety programs approved in accordance with subsection (a), including development and implementation of manpower training programs, and of demonstration programs that the Secretary determines will contribute directly to the reduction of crashes, and deaths and injuries resulting therefrom.

(B) NEIGHBORING STATES.—A State, acting in cooperation with any neighboring State, may use funds provided under this section for a highway safety program that may confer a benefit on the neighboring State.

(2) APPORTIONMENT TO STATES.—

(A) DEFINITION OF PUBLIC ROAD.—In this paragraph, the term "public road" means any road that is—

(i) subject to the jurisdiction of, and maintained by, a public authority; and

(ii) held open to public travel.

(B) APPORTIONMENT.—

(i) IN GENERAL.—Except for the amounts identified in section 403(f) and the amounts subject to subparagraph (C), of the funds made available under this section—

(I) 75 percent shall be apportioned to each State based on the ratio that, as determined by the most recent decennial census—

(aa) the population of the State; bears to

(bb) the total population of all States; and

(II) 25 percent shall be apportioned to each State based on the ratio that, subject to clause (ii)—

(aa) the public road mileage in each State; bears to

(bb) the total public road mileage in all States.

(ii) CALCULATION.—For purposes of clause (i)(II), public road mileage shall be—

(I) determined as of the end of the calendar year preceding the year during which the funds are apportioned;

(II) certified by the Governor of the State; and

(III) subject to approval by the Secretary.

(C) MINIMUM APPORTIONMENTS.—The annual apportionment under this section to—

(i) each State shall be not less than ¾ of 1 percent of the total apportionment;

(ii) the Secretary of the Interior shall be not less than 2 percent of the total apportionment; and

(iii) the United States Virgin Islands, Guam, American Samoa, and the Commonwealth of the Northern Mariana Islands shall be not less than ¼ of 1 percent of the total apportionment.

(D) PENALTY.—

(i) IN GENERAL.—The funds apportioned under this section to a State that does not have approved or in effect a highway safety program described in subsection (a)(1) shall be reduced by an amount equal to not less than 20 percent of the amount that would otherwise be apportioned to the State under this section, until the date on which the Secretary, as applicable—

(I) approves such a highway safety program; or

(II) determines that the State is implementing such a program.

(ii) FACTOR FOR CONSIDERATION.—In determining the amount of the reduction in funds apportioned to a State under this subparagraph, the Secretary shall take into consideration the gravity of the failure by the State to secure approval, or to implement, a highway safety program described in subsection (a)(1).

(E) LIMITATIONS.—

(i) IN GENERAL.—A highway safety program approved by the Secretary shall not include any requirement that a State shall implement such a program by adopting or enforcing any law, rule, or regulation based on a guideline promulgated by the Secretary under this section requiring any motorcycle operator aged 18 years or older, or a motorcycle passenger aged 18 years or older, to wear a safety helmet when operating or riding a motorcycle on the streets and highways of that State.

(ii) EFFECT OF GUIDELINES.—Nothing in this section requires a State highway safety program to require compliance with every uniform guideline, or with every element of every uniform guideline, in every State.

(3) REAPPORTIONMENT.—

(A) IN GENERAL.—The Secretary shall promptly apportion to a State any funds withheld from the State under paragraph (2)(D) if the Secretary makes an approval or determination, as applicable, described in that paragraph by not later than July 31 of the fiscal year for which the funds were withheld.

(B) CONTINUING STATE FAILURE.—If the Secretary determines that a State fails to correct a failure to have approved or in effect a highway safety program described in subsection (a)(1) by the date described in subparagraph (A), the Secretary shall reapportion the funds withheld from that State under paragraph (2)(D) for the fiscal year to the other States in accordance with the formula described in paragraph (2)(B) by not later than the last day of the fiscal year.

(4) AUTOMATED TRAFFIC ENFORCEMENT SYSTEMS.—

(A) AUTOMATED TRAFFIC ENFORCEMENT SYSTEM DEFINED.—In this paragraph, the term "automated traffic enforcement system" means any camera which captures an image of a vehicle for the purposes only of red light and speed enforcement, and does not include hand held radar and other devices operated by law enforcement officers to make an on-the-scene traffic stop, issue a traffic citation, or other enforcement action at the time of the violation.

(B) PROHIBITION.—A State may not expend funds apportioned to that State under this section to carry out a program to purchase, operate, or maintain an automated traffic enforcement system.

(C) SPECIAL RULE FOR SCHOOL AND WORK ZONES.—Notwithstanding subparagraph (B), a State may expend funds apportioned to the State under this section to carry out a program to purchase, operate, or maintain an automated traffic enforcement system in a work zone or school zone.

(D) AUTOMATED TRAFFIC ENFORCEMENT SYSTEM GUIDELINES.—An automated traffic enforcement system installed pursuant to subparagraph (C) shall comply with such guidelines applicable to speed enforcement camera systems and red light camera systems as are established by the Secretary.

(d) All provisions of chapter 1 of this title that are applicable to National Highway System highway funds other than provisions relating to the apportionment formula and provisions limiting the expenditure of such funds to the Federal-aid systems, shall apply to the highway safety funds authorized to be appropriated to carry out this section, except as determined by the Secretary to be inconsistent with this section, and except that the aggregate of all expenditures made during any fiscal year by a State and its political subdivisions (exclusive of Federal funds) for carrying out the State highway safety program (other than planning and administration) shall be available for the purpose of crediting such State during such fiscal year for the non-Federal share of the cost of any project under this section (other than one for planning or administration) without regard to whether such expenditures were actually made in connection with such project and except that, in the case of a local highway safety program carried out by an Indian tribe, if the Secretary is satisfied that an Indian tribe does not have sufficient funds available to meet the non-Federal share of the cost of such program, he may increase the Federal share of the cost thereof payable under this Act to the extent necessary. In applying such provisions of chapter 1 in carrying out this section the term "State transportation department" as used in such provisions shall mean the Governor of a State for the purposes of this section.

(e) Uniform guidelines promulgated by the Secretary to carry out this section shall be developed in cooperation with the States, their political subdivisions, appropriate Federal departments and agencies, and such other public and private organizations as the Secretary deems appropriate.

(f) The Secretary may make arrangements with other Federal departments and agencies for assistance in the preparation of uniform guidelines for the highway safety programs contemplated by subsection (a) and in the administration of such programs. Such departments and agencies are directed to cooperate in such preparation and administration, on a reimbursable basis.

(g) RESTRICTION.—Nothing in this section may be construed to authorize the appropriation or expenditure of funds for highway construction, maintenance, or design (other than design of safety features of highways to be incorporated into guidelines).

(h) APPLICATION IN INDIAN COUNTRY.—

(1) USE OF TERMS.—For the purpose of application of this section in Indian country,

the terms "State" and "Governor of a State" include the Secretary of the Interior and the term "political subdivision of a State" includes an Indian tribe.

(2) EXPENDITURES FOR LOCAL HIGHWAY PROGRAMS.—Notwithstanding subsection (b)(1)(C), 95 percent of the funds apportioned to the Secretary of the Interior under this section shall be expended by Indian tribes to carry out highway safety programs within their jurisdictions.

(3) ACCESS FOR INDIVIDUALS WITH DISABILITIES.—The requirements of subsection (b)(1)(D) shall be applicable to Indian tribes, except to those tribes with respect to which the Secretary determines that application of such provisions would not be practicable.

(4) INDIAN COUNTRY DEFINED.—In this subsection, the term "Indian country" means—

(A) all land within the limits of any Indian reservation under the jurisdiction of the United States, notwithstanding the issuance of any patent and including rights-of-way running through the reservation;

(B) all dependent Indian communities within the borders of the United States, whether within the original or subsequently acquired territory thereof and whether within or without the limits of a State; and

(C) all Indian allotments, the Indian titles to which have not been extinguished, including rights-of-way running through such allotments.

(i) RULEMAKING PROCEEDING.—The Secretary may periodically conduct a rulemaking process to identify highway safety programs that are highly effective in reducing motor vehicle crashes, injuries, and deaths. Any such rulemaking shall take into account the major role of the States in implementing such programs. When a rule promulgated in accordance with this section takes effect, States shall consider these highly effective programs when developing their highway safety programs.

(j) LAW ENFORCEMENT VEHICULAR PURSUIT TRAINING.—A State shall actively encourage all relevant law enforcement agencies in such State to follow the guidelines established for vehicular pursuits issued by the International Association of Chiefs of Police that are in effect on the date of enactment of this subsection or as revised and in effect after such date as determined by the Secretary.

(k) TRIENNIAL HIGHWAY SAFETY PLAN.—

(1) IN GENERAL.—For fiscal year 2024, and not less frequently than once every 3 fiscal years thereafter, the Secretary shall require each State, as a condition of the approval of the State's highway safety program for the 3 fiscal years covered by the plan, to develop and submit to the Secretary for approval a triennial highway safety plan that complies with the requirements under this subsection.

(2) TIMING.—Each State shall submit to the Secretary a triennial highway safety plan by not later than July 1 of the fiscal year preceding the first fiscal year covered by the plan.

(3) ELECTRONIC SUBMISSION.—The Secretary, in coordination with the Governors Highway Safety Association, shall develop procedures to allow States to submit triennial highway safety plans under this subsection, including any attachments to the plans, in electronic form.

(4) CONTENTS.—Each State triennial highway safety plan submitted under

paragraph (1) shall include, with respect to the 3 fiscal years covered by the plan, based on the information available on the date of submission under paragraph (2)—

(A) performance measures required by the Secretary or otherwise necessary to support additional State safety goals, including—

(i) documentation of current safety levels for each performance measure;

(ii) quantifiable performance targets that demonstrate constant or improved performance for each performance measure; and

(iii) a justification for each performance target, that explains why each target is appropriate and evidence-based;

(B) a countermeasure strategy for programming funds under this section for projects that will allow the State to meet the performance targets described in subparagraph (A), including a description—

(i) that demonstrates the link between the effectiveness of each proposed countermeasure strategy and those performance targets; and

(ii) of the manner in which each countermeasure strategy is informed by uniform guidelines issued by the Secretary;

(C) data and data analysis supporting the effectiveness of proposed countermeasures;

(D) a description of any Federal funds that the State plans to use, in addition to funds apportioned to the State under this section, to carry out the strategy described in subparagraph (B); and

(E) a report on the State's success in meeting State safety goals and performance targets set forth in the most recently submitted highway safety plan.

(5) PERFORMANCE MEASURES.—The Secretary shall develop minimum performance measures under paragraph (4)(A) in consultation with the Governors Highway Safety Association.

(6) REVIEW OF TRIENNIAL HIGHWAY SAFETY PLANS.—

(A) IN GENERAL.—Except as provided in subparagraph (B), the Secretary shall review and approve or disapprove a triennial highway safety plan of a State by not later than 60 days after the date on which the plan is received by the Secretary.

(B) ADDITIONAL INFORMATION.—

(i) IN GENERAL.—The Secretary may request a State to submit to the Secretary such additional information as the Secretary determines to be necessary for review of the triennial highway safety plan of the State.

(ii) EXTENSION OF DEADLINE.—On providing to a State a request for additional information under clause (i), the Secretary may extend the deadline to approve or disapprove the triennial highway safety plan of the State under subparagraph (A) for not more than an additional 90 days, as the Secretary determines to be necessary to accommodate that request, subject to clause (iii).

(iii) TIMING.—Any additional information requested under clause (i) shall be submitted to the Secretary by not later than 7 business days after the date of receipt by the State of the request.

(C) APPROVALS AND DISAPPROVALS.—

(i) APPROVALS.—The Secretary shall approve a State's triennial highway safety plan if the Secretary determines that—

(I) the plan and the performance targets contained in the plan are evidence-based and supported by data; and

(II) the plan, once implemented, will allow the State to meet the State's performance targets.

(ii) DISAPPROVALS.—The Secretary shall disapprove a State's triennial highway safety plan if the Secretary determines that—

(I) the plan and the performance targets contained in the plan are not evidence-based or supported by data; or

(II) the plan does not provide for programming of funding in a manner sufficient to allow the State to meet the State's performance targets.

(D) ACTIONS UPON DISAPPROVAL.—If the Secretary disapproves a State's triennial highway safety plan, the Secretary shall—

(i) inform the State of the reasons for such disapproval; and

(ii) require the State to resubmit the plan with any modifications that the Secretary determines to be necessary.

(E) REVIEW OF RESUBMITTED PLANS.—If the Secretary requires a State to resubmit a triennial highway safety plan, with modifications, the Secretary shall review and approve or disapprove the modified plan not later than 30 days after the date on which the Secretary receives such plan.

(F) PUBLIC NOTICE.—A State shall make the State's triennial highway safety plan, and decisions of the Secretary concerning approval or disapproval of a revised plan, available to the public.

(l) ANNUAL GRANT APPLICATION AND REPORTING REQUIREMENTS.—

(1) ANNUAL GRANT APPLICATION.—

(A) IN GENERAL.—To be eligible to receive grant funds under this chapter for a fiscal year, each State shall submit to the Secretary an annual grant application that, as determined by the Secretary—

(i) demonstrates alignment with the approved triennial highway safety plan of the State; and

(ii) complies with the requirements under this subsection.

(B) TIMING.—The deadline for submission of annual grant applications under this paragraph shall be determined by the Secretary in accordance with section 406(d)(2).

(C) CONTENTS.—An annual grant application under this paragraph shall include, at a minimum—

(i) such updates, as necessary, to any analysis included in the triennial highway safety plan of the State;

(ii) an identification of each project and subrecipient to be funded by the State using the grants during the upcoming grant year, subject to the condition that the State shall separately submit, on a date other than the date of submission of the annual grant application, a description of any projects or subrecipients to be funded, as that information becomes available;

(iii) a description of the means by which the strategy of the State to use grant funds was adjusted and informed by the previous report of the State under paragraph (2); and

(iv) an application for any additional grants available to the State under this chapter.

(D) REVIEW.—The Secretary shall review and approve or disapprove an annual grant application under this paragraph by not later than 60 days after the date of submission of the application.

(2) REPORTING REQUIREMENTS.—Not later than 120 days after the end of each fiscal year for which a grant is provided to a State under this chapter, the State shall submit to the Secretary an annual report that includes—

(A) an assessment of the progress made by the State in achieving the performance targets identified in the triennial highway safety plan of the State, based on the most currently available Fatality Analysis Reporting System data; and

(B)(i) a description of the extent to which progress made in achieving those performance targets is aligned with the triennial highway safety plan of the State; and

(ii) if applicable, any plans of the State to adjust a strategy for programming funds to achieve the performance targets.

(m) TEEN TRAFFIC SAFETY.—

(1) IN GENERAL.—Subject to the requirements of the applicable triennial highway safety plan of the State, as approved by the Secretary under subsection (k), a State may use a portion of the amounts received under this section to implement statewide efforts to improve traffic safety for teen drivers.

(2) USE OF FUNDS.—Statewide efforts under paragraph (1)—

(A) shall include peer-to-peer education and prevention strategies in schools and communities designed to—

(i) increase safety belt use;

(ii) reduce speeding;

(iii) reduce impaired and distracted driving;

(iv) reduce underage drinking; and

(v) reduce other behaviors by teen drivers that lead to injuries and fatalities; and

(B) may include—

(i) working with student-led groups and school advisors to plan and implement teen traffic safety programs;

(ii) providing subgrants to schools throughout the State to support the establishment and expansion of student groups focused on teen traffic safety;

(iii) providing support, training, and technical assistance to establish and expand school and community safety programs for teen drivers;

(iv) creating statewide or regional websites to publicize and circulate information on teen safety programs;

(v) conducting outreach and providing educational resources for parents;

(vi) establishing State or regional advisory councils comprised of teen drivers to provide input and recommendations to the governor and the governor's safety representative on issues related to the safety of teen drivers;

(vii) collaborating with law enforcement;

(viii) establishing partnerships and promoting coordination among community stakeholders, including public, not-for-profit, and for profit entities;

(ix) increase driver awareness of commercial motor vehicles to prevent crashes and reduce injuries and fatalities; and

(x) support for school-based driver's education classes to improve teen knowledge about—

(I) safe driving practices; and

(II) State graduated driving license requirements, including behind-the-wheel training required to meet those requirements.

(n) PUBLIC TRANSPARENCY.—

(1) IN GENERAL.—The Secretary shall publicly release on a Department of Transportation website, by not later than 45 calendar days after the applicable date of availability—

(A) each triennial highway safety plan approved by the Secretary under subsection (k);

(B) each State performance target under subsection (k); and

(C) an evaluation of State achievement of applicable performance targets under subsection (k).

(2) STATE HIGHWAY SAFETY PLAN WEBSITE.—

(A) IN GENERAL.—In carrying out paragraph (1), the Secretary shall establish a public website that is easily accessible, navigable, and searchable for the information required under that paragraph, in order to foster greater transparency in approved State highway safety programs.

(B) CONTENTS.—The website established under subparagraph (A) shall—

(i) include the applicable triennial highway safety plan, and the annual report, of each State submitted to, and approved by, the Secretary under subsection (k); and

(ii) provide a means for the public to search the website for State highway safety program content required under subsection (k), including—

(I) performance measures required by the Secretary;

(II) progress made toward meeting the applicable performance targets during the preceding program year;

(III) program areas and expenditures; and

(IV) a description of any sources of funds, other than funds provided under this section, that the State proposes to use to carry out the triennial highway safety plan of the State.

(o) UNATTENDED PASSENGERS.—

(1) IN GENERAL.—Each State shall use a portion of the amounts received by the State under this section to carry out a program to educate the public regarding the risks of leaving a child or unattended passenger in a vehicle after the vehicle motor is deactivated by the operator.

(2) PROGRAM PLACEMENT.—Nothing in this subsection requires a State to carry out a program described in paragraph (1) through the State transportation or highway safety office.

(Added Pub. L. 89–564, title I, §101, Sept. 9, 1966, 80 Stat. 731; amended Pub. L. 90–495, §13, Aug. 23, 1968, 82 Stat. 822; Pub. L. 91–605, title II, §§202(c), (d), (e), 203(a), Dec. 31, 1970, 84 Stat. 1740,

1741; Pub. L. 93–87, title II, §§207, 215–217, 219, 228, 229, 231, Aug. 13, 1973, 87 Stat. 285, 290, 293, 294; Pub. L. 94–280, title II, §§204, 208(a), 211, 212, May 5, 1976, 90 Stat. 453, 454, 455; Pub. L. 95–599, title II, §207(a), (b)(1), (c), (d), Nov. 6, 1978, 92 Stat. 2731, 2732; Pub. L. 97–35, title XI, §1107(c)–(e), Aug. 13, 1981, 95 Stat. 626; Pub. L. 97–424, title II, §208, Jan. 6, 1983, 96 Stat. 2140; Pub. L. 98–363, §§3(a), 5, July 17, 1984, 98 Stat. 436; Pub. L. 100–17, title I, §133(b)(20), title II, §206, Apr. 2, 1987, 101 Stat. 172, 221; Pub. L. 102–240, title II, §2002, Dec. 18, 1991, 105 Stat. 2070; Pub. L. 104–66, title I, §1121(d), Dec. 21, 1995, 109 Stat. 724; Pub. L. 105–178, title I, §1212(a)(2)(A)(i), title II, §2001(a)–(e), June 9, 1998, 112 Stat. 193, 323, 324; Pub. L. 109–59, title II, §2002(a)–(d), Aug. 10, 2005, 119 Stat. 1521; Pub. L. 110–244, title III, §303(a)–(c)(1), June 6, 2008, 122 Stat. 1619; Pub. L. 112–141, div. C, title I, §31102, July 6, 2012, 126 Stat. 734; Pub. L. 114–94, div. A, title IV, §§4002, 4014(1), Dec. 4, 2015, 129 Stat. 1499, 1513; Pub. L. 115–420, §5(a), Jan. 3, 2019, 132 Stat. 5445; Pub. L. 117–58, div. B, title IV, §§24102(a), 24222(b), Nov. 15, 2021, 135 Stat. 785, 835.)

§403. HIGHWAY SAFETY RESEARCH AND DEVELOPMENT

(a) DEFINED TERM.—In this section, the term "Federal laboratory" includes—

(1) a government-owned, government-operated laboratory; and

(2) a government-owned, contractor-operated laboratory.

(b) GENERAL AUTHORITY.—

(1) RESEARCH AND DEVELOPMENT ACTIVITIES.—The Secretary may conduct research and development activities, including demonstration projects, training, education, and the collection and analysis of highway and motor vehicle safety data and related information needed to carry out this section, with respect to—

(A) all aspects of highway and traffic safety systems and conditions relating to—

(i) vehicle, highway, driver, passenger, motorcyclist, bicyclist, and pedestrian characteristics;

(ii) crash causation and investigations;

(iii) communications; and

(iv) emergency medical services, including the transportation of the injured;

(B) human behavioral factors and their effect on highway and traffic safety, including—

(i) driver education;

(ii) impaired driving; and

(iii) distracted driving;

(C) an evaluation of the effectiveness of countermeasures to increase highway and traffic safety, including occupant protection and alcohol- and drug-impaired driving technologies and initiatives;

(D) the development of technologies to detect drug impaired drivers;

(E) research on, evaluations of, and identification of best practices related to driver education programs (including driver education curricula, instructor training and certification, program administration, and delivery mechanisms) and make recommendations for harmonizing driver education and multistage graduated licensing systems; and

(F) the effect of State laws on any aspects, activities, or programs described in subparagraphs (A) through (E).

(2) COOPERATION, GRANTS, AND CONTRACTS.—The Secretary may carry out this section—

(A) independently;

(B) in cooperation with other Federal departments, agencies, and instrumentalities and Federal laboratories;

(C) by entering into contracts, cooperative agreements, and other transactions with the National Academy of Sciences, any Federal laboratory, State or local agency, authority, association, institution, foreign government (in coordination with the Department of State) or person (as defined in chapter 1 of title 1); or

(D) by making grants to the National Academy of Sciences, any Federal laboratory, State or local agency, authority, association, institution, or person (as defined in chapter 1 of title 1).

(c) COLLABORATIVE RESEARCH AND DEVELOPMENT.—

(1) IN GENERAL.—To encourage innovative solutions to highway safety problems, stimulate voluntary improvements in highway safety, and stimulate the marketing of new highway safety related technology by private industry, the Secretary is authorized to carry out, on a cost-shared basis, collaborative research and development with—

(A) non-Federal entities, including State and local governments, foreign governments, colleges, universities, corporations, partnerships, sole proprietorships, organizations, and trade associations that are incorporated or established under the laws of any State or the United States; and

(B) Federal laboratories.

(2) AGREEMENTS.—In carrying out this subsection, the Secretary may enter into cooperative research and development agreements (as defined in section 12 of the Stevenson-Wydler Technology Innovation Act of 1980 (15 U.S.C. 3710a)) in which the Secretary provides not more than 50 percent of the cost of any research or development project under this subsection.

(3) USE OF TECHNOLOGY.—The research, development, or use of any technology pursuant to an agreement under this subsection, including the terms under which technology may be licensed and the resulting royalties may be distributed, shall be subject to the provisions of the Stevenson-Wydler Technology Innovation Act of 1980 (15 U.S.C. 3701 et seq.).

(d) TITLE TO EQUIPMENT.—In furtherance of the purposes set forth in section 402, the Secretary may vest title to equipment purchased for demonstration projects with funds authorized under this section to State or local agencies on such terms and conditions as the Secretary determines to be appropriate.

(e) PROHIBITION ON CERTAIN DISCLOSURES.—Any report of the National Highway Traffic Safety Administration, or of any officer, employee, or contractor of the National Highway Traffic Safety Administration, relating to any highway traffic crash or the investigation of such crash conducted pursuant to this chapter or chapter 301 of title 49 may only be made available to the public in a manner that does not identify individuals.

(f) COOPERATIVE RESEARCH AND EVALUATION.—

(1) ESTABLISHMENT AND FUNDING.—Notwithstanding the apportionment formula set forth in section 402(c)(2), $3,500,000 of the total amount available for apportionment to the States for highway safety programs under section 402(c) in each fiscal year shall be available for expenditure by the Secretary, acting through the Administrator of the National Highway Traffic Safety Administration, for a

cooperative research and evaluation program to research and evaluate priority highway safety countermeasures.

(2) ADMINISTRATION.—The program established under paragraph (1)—

(A) shall be administered by the Administrator of the National Highway Traffic Safety Administration; and

(B) shall be jointly managed by the Governors Highway Safety Association and the National Highway Traffic Safety Administration.

(g) INTERNATIONAL COOPERATION.—The Administrator of the National Highway Traffic Safety Administration may participate and cooperate in international activities to enhance highway safety.

(h) IN-VEHICLE ALCOHOL DETECTION DEVICE RESEARCH.—

(1) DEFINITIONS.—In this subsection:

(A) ALCOHOL-IMPAIRED DRIVING.—The term "alcohol-impaired driving" means the operation of a motor vehicle (as defined in section 30102(a) of title 49) by an individual whose blood alcohol content is at or above the legal limit.

(B) LEGAL LIMIT.—The term "legal limit" means a blood alcohol concentration of 0.08 percent or greater (as set forth in section 163(a)) or such other percentage limitation as may be established by applicable Federal, State, or local law.

(2) IN GENERAL.—The Administrator of the National Highway Traffic Safety Administration shall carry out a collaborative research effort under chapter 301 of title 49 on in-vehicle technology to prevent alcohol-impaired driving.

(3) FUNDING.—The Secretary shall obligate from funds made available to carry out this section for the period covering fiscal years 2022 through 2025, not more than $45,000,000 to conduct the research described in paragraph (2).

(4) PRIVACY PROTECTION.—The Administrator shall not develop requirements for any device or means of technology to be installed in an automobile intended for retail sale that records a driver's blood alcohol concentration.

(5) REPORTS.—The Administrator shall submit an annual report to the Committee on Commerce, Science, and Transportation of the Senate, the Committee on Transportation and Infrastructure of the House of Representatives, and Committee on Science, Space, and Technology of the House of Representatives that—

(A) describes the progress made in carrying out the collaborative research effort; and

(B) includes an accounting for the use of Federal funds obligated or expended in carrying out that effort.

(i) LIMITATION ON DRUG AND ALCOHOL SURVEY DATA.—The Secretary shall establish procedures and guidelines to ensure that any person participating in a program or activity that collects data on drug or alcohol use by drivers of motor vehicles and is carried out under this section is informed that the program or activity is voluntary.

(j) FEDERAL SHARE.—The Federal share of the cost of any project or activity carried out under this section may be not more than 100 percent.

(k) CHILD SAFETY CAMPAIGN.—

(1) IN GENERAL.—The Secretary shall carry out an education campaign to reduce the incidence of vehicular heatstroke of children left in passenger motor vehicles (as defined in section 30102(a) of title 49).

(2) ADVERTISING.—The Secretary may use, or authorize the use of, funds made available to carry out this section to pay for the development, production, and use of broadcast and print media advertising and Internet-based outreach for the education campaign under paragraph (1).

(3) COORDINATION.—In carrying out the education campaign under paragraph (1), the Secretary shall coordinate with—

(A) interested State and local governments;

(B) private industry; and

(C) other parties, as determined by the Secretary.

(l) DEVELOPMENT OF STATE PROCESSES FOR INFORMING CONSUMERS OF RECALLS.—

(1) DEFINITIONS.—In this subsection:

(A) MOTOR VEHICLE.—The term "motor vehicle" has the meaning given the term in section 30102(a) of title 49.

(B) OPEN RECALL.—The term "open recall" means a motor vehicle recall—

(i) for which a notification by a manufacturer has been provided under section 30119 of title 49; and

(ii) that has not been remedied under section 30120 of that title.

(C) PROGRAM.—The term "program" means the program established under paragraph (2)(A).

(D) REGISTRATION.—The term "registration" means the process for registering a motor vehicle in a State (including registration renewal).

(E) STATE.—The term "State" has the meaning given the term in section 101(a).

(2) GRANTS.—

(A) ESTABLISHMENT OF PROGRAM.—Not later than 2 years after the date of enactment of this subsection, the Secretary shall establish a program under which the Secretary shall provide grants to States for use in developing and implementing State processes for informing each applicable owner and lessee of a motor vehicle of any open recall on the motor vehicle at the time of registration of the motor vehicle in the State, in accordance with this paragraph.

(B) ELIGIBILITY.—To be eligible to receive a grant under the program, a State shall—

(i) submit to the Secretary an application at such time, in such manner, and containing such information as the Secretary may require; and

(ii) agree—

(I) to notify each owner or lessee of a motor vehicle presented for registration in the State of any open recall on that motor vehicle; and

(II) to provide to each owner or lessee of a motor vehicle presented for registration, at no cost—

(aa) the open recall information for the motor vehicle; and

(bb) such other information as the Secretary may require.

(C) FACTORS FOR CONSIDERATION.—In selecting grant recipients under the program, the Secretary shall take into consideration the methodology of a State for—

(i) identifying open recalls on a motor vehicle;

(ii) informing each owner and lessee of a motor vehicle of an open recall; and

(iii) measuring performance in—

(I) informing owners and lessees of open recalls; and

(II) remedying open recalls.

(D) PERFORMANCE PERIOD.—A grant provided under the program shall require a performance period of 2 years.

(E) REPORT.—Not later than 90 days after the date of completion of the performance period under subparagraph (D), each State that receives a grant under the program shall submit to the Secretary a report that contains such information as the Secretary considers to be necessary to evaluate the extent to which open recalls have been remedied in the State.

(F) NO REGULATIONS REQUIRED.—Notwithstanding any other provision of law, the Secretary shall not be required to issue any regulations to carry out the program.

(3) PAPERWORK REDUCTION ACT.—Chapter 35 of title 44 (commonly known as the "Paperwork Reduction Act") shall not apply to information collected under the program.

(4) FUNDING.—

(A) IN GENERAL.—For each of fiscal years 2022 through 2026, the Secretary shall obligate from funds made available to carry out this section $1,500,000 to carry out the program.

(B) REALLOCATION.—To ensure, to the maximum extent practicable, that all amounts described in subparagraph (A) are obligated each fiscal year, the Secretary, before the last day of any fiscal year, may reallocate any of those amounts remaining available to increase the amounts made available to carry out any other activities authorized under this section.

(m) INNOVATIVE HIGHWAY SAFETY COUNTERMEASURES.—

(1) IN GENERAL.—In conducting research under this section, the Secretary shall evaluate the effectiveness of innovative behavioral traffic safety countermeasures, other than traffic enforcement, that are considered promising or likely to be effective for the purpose of enriching revisions to the document entitled "Countermeasures That Work: A Highway Safety Countermeasure Guide for State Highway Safety Offices, Ninth Edition" and numbered DOT HS 812 478 (or any successor document).

(2) TREATMENT.—The research described in paragraph (1) shall be in addition to any other research carried out under this section.

(Added Pub. L. 89–564, title I, §101, Sept. 9, 1966, 80 Stat. 733; amended Pub. L. 93–87, title II, §§208(a), 220–222, 226(a), Aug. 13, 1973, 87 Stat. 286, 291, 292; Pub. L. 102–240, title II, §2003, Dec. 18, 1991, 105 Stat. 2071; Pub. L. 105–178, title II, §2002(a), (b)(1), June 9, 1998, 112 Stat. 325; Pub. L. 109–59, title II, §§2003(a), (b), 2013(e), Aug. 10, 2005, 119 Stat. 1522, 1540; Pub. L. 112–141, div. C, title I, §31103, July 6, 2012, 126 Stat. 739; Pub. L. 113–159, title I, §1101(b), Aug. 8, 2014, 128 Stat. 1843; Pub. L. 114–21, title I, §1101(b), May 29, 2015, 129 Stat. 221; Pub. L. 114–41, title I, §1101(b), July 31, 2015, 129 Stat. 448; Pub. L. 114–73, title I, §1101(b), Oct. 29, 2015, 129 Stat. 571; Pub. L. 114–87, title I, §1101(b), Nov. 20, 2015, 129 Stat. 680; Pub. L. 114–94, div. A, title IV, §§4003, 4014(2), div. B, title XXIV, §24202(b), Dec. 4, 2015, 129 Stat. 1500, 1513, 1712; Pub. L. 116–159, div. B, title I, §1103, Oct. 1, 2020, 134 Stat. 726; Pub. L. 117–58, div. B, title IV, §24103, Nov. 15, 2021, 135 Stat. 792.)

§404. HIGH-VISIBILITY ENFORCEMENT PROGRAM

(a) IN GENERAL.—The Secretary shall establish and administer a program under which not less than 3 campaigns will be carried out in each of fiscal years 2022 through 2026.

(b) PURPOSE.—The purpose of each campaign carried out under this section shall be to achieve outcomes related to not less than 1 of the following objectives:

(1) Reduce alcohol-impaired or drug-impaired operation of motor vehicles.

(2) Increase use of seatbelts by occupants of motor vehicles.

(c) ADVERTISING.—The Secretary may use, or authorize the use of, funds available to carry out this section to pay for the development, production, and use of broadcast and print media advertising and Internet-based outreach in carrying out campaigns under this section. In allocating such funds, consideration shall be given to advertising directed at non-English speaking populations, including those who listen to, read, or watch nontraditional media.

(d) COORDINATION WITH STATES.—The Secretary shall coordinate with States in carrying out the campaigns under this section, including advertising funded under subsection (c), with consideration given to—

(1) relying on States to provide law enforcement resources for the campaigns out of funding made available under sections 402 and 405; and

(2) providing, out of National Highway Traffic Safety Administration resources, most of the means necessary for national advertising and education efforts associated with the campaigns.

(e) USE OF FUNDS.—Funds made available to carry out this section may be used only for activities described in subsection (c).

(f) DEFINITIONS.—In this section, the following definitions apply:

(1) CAMPAIGN.—The term "campaign" means a high-visibility traffic safety law enforcement campaign.

(2) STATE.—The term "State" has the meaning given that term in section 401.

(Added Pub. L. 89–564, title I, §101, Sept. 9, 1966, 80 Stat. 733; amended Pub. L. 90–150, Nov. 24, 1967, 81 Stat. 507; Pub. L. 93–87, title II, §223, Aug. 13, 1973, 87 Stat. 292; Pub. L. 94–280, title II, §209, May 5, 1976, 90 Stat. 455; Pub. L. 109–59, title II, §2019, Aug. 10, 2005, 119 Stat. 1543; Pub. L. 114–94, div. A, title IV, §4004(a), Dec. 4, 2015, 129 Stat. 1500; Pub. L. 117–58, div. B, title IV, §24104, Nov. 15, 2021, 135 Stat. 795.)

§405. NATIONAL PRIORITY SAFETY PROGRAMS

(a) PROGRAM AUTHORITY.—

(1) IN GENERAL.—Subject to the requirements of this section, the Secretary shall—

(A) manage programs to address national priorities for reducing highway deaths and injuries; and

(B) allocate funds for the purpose described in subparagraph (A) in accordance with this subsection.

(2) OCCUPANT PROTECTION.—In each fiscal year, 13 percent of the funds provided under this section shall be allocated among States that adopt and implement effective occupant protection programs to reduce highway deaths and injuries resulting from individuals riding unrestrained or improperly restrained in motor vehicles (as described in subsection (b)).

(3) STATE TRAFFIC SAFETY INFORMATION SYSTEM IMPROVEMENTS.—In each fiscal year, 14.5 percent of the funds provided under this section shall be allocated among

States that meet requirements with respect to State traffic safety information system improvements (as described in subsection (c)).

(4) IMPAIRED DRIVING COUNTERMEASURES.—In each fiscal year, 53 percent of the funds provided under this section shall be allocated among States that meet requirements with respect to impaired driving countermeasures (as described in subsection (d)).

(5) DISTRACTED DRIVING.—In each fiscal year, 8.5 percent of the funds provided under this section shall be allocated among States that adopt and implement effective laws to reduce distracted driving (as described in subsection (e)).

(6) MOTORCYCLIST SAFETY.—In each fiscal year, 1.5 percent of the funds provided under this section shall be allocated among States that implement motorcyclist safety programs (as described in subsection (f)).

(7) NONMOTORIZED SAFETY.—In each fiscal year, 7 percent of the funds provided under this section shall be allocated among States that meet requirements with respect to nonmotorized safety (as described in subsection (g)).

(8) PREVENTING ROADSIDE DEATHS.—In each fiscal year, 1 percent of the funds provided under this section shall be allocated among States that meet requirements with respect to preventing roadside deaths under subsection (h).

(9) DRIVER OFFICER SAFETY EDUCATION.—In each fiscal year, 1.5 percent of the funds provided under this section shall be allocated among States that meet requirements with respect to driver and officer safety education under subsection (i).

(10) TRANSFERS.—Notwithstanding paragraphs (2) through (9), the Secretary shall reallocate, before the last day of any fiscal year, any amounts remaining available to carry out any of the activities described in subsections (b) through (i) to increase the amount made available under section 402, in order to ensure, to the maximum extent possible, that all such amounts are obligated during such fiscal year.

(11) POLITICAL SUBDIVISIONS.—A State may provide the funds awarded under this section to a political subdivision of the State or an Indian tribal government.

(b) OCCUPANT PROTECTION GRANTS.—

(1) GENERAL AUTHORITY.—Subject to the requirements under this subsection, the Secretary shall award grants to States that adopt and implement effective occupant protection programs to reduce highway deaths and injuries resulting from individuals riding unrestrained or improperly restrained in motor vehicles.

(2) FEDERAL SHARE.—The Federal share of the costs of activities funded using amounts from grants awarded under this subsection may not exceed 80 percent for each fiscal year for which a State receives a grant.

(3) ELIGIBILITY.—

(A) HIGH SEAT BELT USE RATE.—A State with an observed seat belt use rate of 90 percent or higher, based on the most recent data from a survey that conforms with national criteria established by the National Highway Traffic Safety Administration, shall be eligible for a grant in a fiscal year if the State—

(i) submits an occupant protection plan during the first fiscal year;

(ii) participates in the Click It or Ticket national mobilization;

(iii) has an active network of child restraint inspection stations; and

(iv) has a plan to recruit, train, and maintain a sufficient number of child passenger safety technicians.

(B) LOWER SEAT BELT USE RATE.—A State with an observed seat belt use rate below 90 percent, based on the most recent data from a survey that conforms with national criteria established by the National Highway Traffic Safety Administration, shall be eligible for a grant in a fiscal year if—

(i) the State meets all of the requirements under clauses (i) through (iv) of subparagraph (A); and

(ii) the Secretary determines that the State meets at least 3 of the following criteria:

(I) The State conducts sustained (on-going and periodic) seat belt enforcement at a defined level of participation during the year.

(II) The State has enacted and enforces a primary enforcement seat belt use law.

(III) The State has implemented countermeasure programs for high-risk populations, such as drivers on rural roadways, unrestrained nighttime drivers, or teenage drivers.

(IV) The State has enacted and enforces occupant protection laws requiring front and rear occupant protection use by all occupants in an age-appropriate restraint.

(V) The State has implemented a comprehensive occupant protection program in which the State has—

(aa) conducted a program assessment;

(bb) developed a statewide strategic plan;

(cc) designated an occupant protection coordinator; and

(dd) established a statewide occupant protection task force.

(VI) The State—

(aa) completed an assessment of its occupant protection program during the 5-year period preceding the grant year; or

(bb) will conduct such an assessment during the first year of the grant.

(4) USE OF GRANT AMOUNTS.—

(A) IN GENERAL.—Grant funds received pursuant to this subsection may be used to—

(i) carry out a program to support high-visibility enforcement mobilizations, including paid media that emphasizes publicity for the program, and law enforcement;

(ii) carry out a program to train occupant protection safety professionals, police officers, fire and emergency medical personnel, educators, and parents concerning all aspects of the use of child restraints and occupant protection;

(iii) carry out a program to educate the public concerning the proper use and installation of child restraints, including related equipment and information systems;

(iv) carry out a program to provide community child passenger safety services, including programs about proper seating positions for children and how to reduce the improper use of child restraints;

(v) implement programs—

(I) to recruit and train nationally certified child passenger safety technicians among police officers, fire and other first responders, emergency medical personnel, and other individuals or organizations serving low-income and underserved populations;

(II) to educate parents and caregivers in low-income and underserved populations regarding the importance of proper use and correct installation of child restraints on every trip in a motor vehicle; and

(III) to purchase and distribute child restraints to low-income and underserved populations; and

(vi) establish and maintain information systems containing data concerning occupant protection, including the collection and administration of child passenger safety and occupant protection surveys.

(B) REQUIREMENTS.—Each State that is eligible to receive funds—

(i) under paragraph (3)(A) shall use—

(I) not more than 90 percent of those funds to carry out a project or activity eligible for funding under section 402; and

(II) not less than 10 percent of those funds to carry out subparagraph (A)(v); and

(ii) under paragraph (3)(B) shall use not less than 10 percent of those funds to carry out the activities described in subparagraph (A)(v).

(5) GRANT AMOUNT.—The allocation of grant funds to a State under this subsection for a fiscal year shall be in proportion to the State's apportionment under section 402 for fiscal year 2009.

(6) DEFINITIONS.—In this subsection:

(A) CHILD RESTRAINT.—The term "child restraint" means any device (including child safety seat, booster seat, harness, and excepting seat belts) that is—

(i) designed for use in a motor vehicle to restrain, seat, or position children who weigh 65 pounds (30 kilograms) or less; and

(ii) certified to the Federal motor vehicle safety standard prescribed by the National Highway Traffic Safety Administration for child restraints.

(B) SEAT BELT.—The term "seat belt" means—

(i) with respect to open-body motor vehicles, including convertibles, an occupant restraint system consisting of a lap belt or a lap belt and a detachable shoulder belt; and

(ii) with respect to other motor vehicles, an occupant restraint system consisting of integrated lap and shoulder belts.

(c) STATE TRAFFIC SAFETY INFORMATION SYSTEM IMPROVEMENTS.—

(1) GENERAL AUTHORITY.—Subject to the requirements under this subsection, the Secretary shall award grants to States to support the development and implementation of effective State programs that—

(A) improve the timeliness, accuracy, completeness, uniformity, integration, and accessibility of the State safety data that is needed to identify priorities for Federal, State, and local highway and traffic safety programs;

(B) evaluate the effectiveness of efforts to make such improvements;

(C) link the State data systems, including traffic records, with other data systems within the State, such as systems that contain medical, roadway, and economic data;

(D) improve the compatibility and interoperability of the data systems of the State with national data systems and data systems of other States, including the National EMS Information System;

(E) enhance the ability of the Secretary to observe and analyze national trends in crash occurrences, rates, outcomes, and circumstances.

(2) FEDERAL SHARE.—The Federal share of the cost of adopting and implementing in a fiscal year a State program described in this subsection may not exceed 80 percent.

(3) ELIGIBILITY.—A State shall not be eligible to receive a grant under this subsection for a fiscal year unless the State—

(A) has certified to the Secretary that the State—

(i) has a functioning traffic records coordinating committee (referred to in this paragraph as "TRCC") that meets at least 3 times each year;

(ii) has designated a TRCC coordinator; and

(iii) has established a State traffic record strategic plan that has been approved by the TRCC and describes specific quantifiable and measurable improvements anticipated in the State's core safety databases, including crash, citation or adjudication, driver, emergency medical services or injury surveillance system, roadway, and vehicle databases; and

(B) has demonstrated quantitative progress in relation to the significant data program attribute of—

(i) accuracy;

(ii) completeness;

(iii) timeliness;

(iv) uniformity;

(v) accessibility; or

(vi) integration of a core highway safety database.

(4) USE OF GRANT AMOUNTS.—A State may use a grant received under this subsection to make data program improvements to core highway safety databases relating to quantifiable, measurable progress in any significant data program attribute described in paragraph (3)(B), including through—

(A) software or applications to identify, collect, and report data to State and local government agencies, and enter data into State core highway safety databases, including crash, citation or adjudication, driver, emergency medical services or injury surveillance system, roadway, and vehicle data;

(B) purchasing equipment to improve a process by which data are identified, collated, and reported to State and local government agencies, including technology for use by law enforcement for near-real time, electronic reporting of crash data;

(C) improving the compatibility and interoperability of the core highway safety databases of the State with national data systems and data systems of other States, including the National EMS Information System;

(D) enhancing the ability of a State and the Secretary to observe and analyze local, State, and national trends in crash occurrences, rates, outcomes, and circumstances;

(E) supporting traffic records improvement training and expenditures for law enforcement, emergency medical, judicial, prosecutorial, and traffic records professionals;

(F) hiring traffic records professionals for the purpose of improving traffic information systems (including a State Fatal Accident Reporting System (FARS) liaison);

(G) adoption of the Model Minimum Uniform Crash Criteria, or providing to the public information regarding why any of those criteria will not be used, if applicable;

(H) supporting reporting criteria relating to emerging topics, including—

(i) impaired driving as a result of drug, alcohol, or polysubstance consumption; and

(ii) advanced technologies present on motor vehicles; and

(I) conducting research relating to State traffic safety information systems, including developing programs to improve core highway safety databases and processes by which data are identified, collected, reported to State and local government agencies, and entered into State core safety databases.

(5) GRANT AMOUNT.—The allocation of grant funds to a State under this subsection for a fiscal year shall be in proportion to the State's apportionment under section 402 for fiscal year 2009.

(6) TECHNICAL ASSISTANCE.—

(A) IN GENERAL.—The Secretary shall provide technical assistance to States, regardless of whether a State receives a grant under this subsection, with respect to improving the timeliness, accuracy, completeness, uniformity, integration, and public accessibility of State safety data that are needed to identify priorities for Federal, State, and local highway and traffic safety programs, including on adoption by a State of the Model Minimum Uniform Crash Criteria.

(B) FUNDS.—The Secretary may use not more than 3 percent of the amounts available under this subsection to carry out subparagraph (A).

(d) IMPAIRED DRIVING COUNTERMEASURES.—

(1) IN GENERAL.—Subject to the requirements under this subsection, the Secretary of Transportation shall award grants to States that adopt and implement—

(A) effective programs to reduce driving under the influence of alcohol, drugs, or the combination of alcohol and drugs; or

(B) alcohol-ignition interlock laws.

(2) FEDERAL SHARE.—The Federal share of the costs of activities funded using amounts from grants under this subsection may not exceed 80 percent in any fiscal year in which the State receives a grant.

(3) ELIGIBILITY.—

(A) LOW-RANGE STATES.—Low-range States shall be eligible for a grant under this subsection.

(B) MID-RANGE STATES.—A mid-range State shall be eligible for a grant under this subsection if—

(i) a statewide impaired driving task force in the State developed a statewide plan during the most recent 3 calendar years to address the problem of impaired driving; or

(ii) the State will convene a statewide impaired driving task force to develop such a plan during the first year of the grant.

(C) HIGH-RANGE STATES.—A high-range State shall be eligible for a grant under this subsection if the State—

(i)(I) conducted an assessment of the State's impaired driving program during the most recent 3 calendar years; or

(II) will conduct such an assessment during the first year of the grant;

(ii) convenes, during the first year of the grant, a statewide impaired driving task force to develop a statewide plan that—

(I) addresses any recommendations from the assessment conducted under clause (i);

(II) includes a detailed plan for spending any grant funds provided under this subsection; and

(III) describes how such spending supports the statewide program; and

(iii)(I) submits the statewide plan to the National Highway Traffic Safety Administration during the first year of the grant for the agency's review and approval;

(II) annually updates the statewide plan in each subsequent year of the grant; and

(III) submits each updated statewide plan for the agency's review and comment.

(4) USE OF GRANT AMOUNTS.—

(A) REQUIRED PROGRAMS.—High-range States shall use grant funds for—

(i) high-visibility enforcement efforts; and

(ii) any of the activities described in subparagraph (B) if—

(I) the activity is described in the statewide plan; and

(II) the Secretary approves the use of funding for such activity.

(B) AUTHORIZED PROGRAMS.—Medium-range and low-range States may use grant funds for—

(i) any of the purposes described in subparagraph (A);

(ii) hiring a full-time or part-time impaired driving coordinator of the State's activities to address the enforcement and adjudication of laws regarding driving while impaired by alcohol, drugs, or the combination of alcohol and drugs;

(iii) court support of impaired driving prevention efforts, including—

(I) hiring criminal justice professionals, including law enforcement officers, prosecutors, traffic safety resource prosecutors, judges, judicial outreach liaisons, and probation officers;

(II) training and education of those professionals to assist the professionals in preventing impaired driving and handling impaired driving cases, including by providing compensation to a law enforcement officer to carry out safety grant activities to replace a law enforcement officer who is receiving drug recognition expert training or participating as an instructor in that drug recognition expert training; and

(III) establishing driving while intoxicated courts;

(iv) alcohol ignition interlock programs;

(v) improving blood alcohol and drug concentration screening and testing, detection of potentially impairing drugs (including through the use of oral fluid as a specimen), and reporting relating to testing and detection;

(vi) paid and earned media in support of high-visibility enforcement efforts, conducting initial and continuing standardized field sobriety training, advanced roadside impaired driving evaluation training, law enforcement phlebotomy training, and drug recognition expert training for law enforcement, and equipment and related expenditures used in connection with impaired driving enforcement in accordance with criteria established by the National Highway Traffic Safety Administration;

(vii) training on the use of alcohol and drug screening and brief intervention;

(viii) training for and implementation of impaired driving assessment programs or other tools designed to increase the probability of identifying the recidivism risk of a person convicted of driving under the influence of alcohol, drugs, or a combination of alcohol and drugs and to determine the most effective mental health or substance abuse treatment or sanction that will reduce such risk;

(ix) developing impaired driving information systems;

(x) costs associated with a 24-7 sobriety program; and

(xi) testing and implementing programs, and purchasing technologies, to better identify, monitor, or treat impaired drivers, including—

(I) oral fluid-screening technologies;

(II) electronic warrant programs;

(III) equipment to increase the scope, quantity, quality, and timeliness of forensic toxicology chemical testing;

(IV) case management software to support the management of impaired driving offenders; and

(V) technology to monitor impaired-driving offenders, and equipment and related expenditures used in connection with impaired-driving enforcement in accordance with criteria established by the National Highway Traffic Safety Administration.

(C) OTHER PROGRAMS.—

(i) LOW-RANGE STATES.—Subject to clause (iii), low-range States may use grant funds for any expenditure designed to reduce impaired driving based on problem identification and may use not more than 50 percent of funds made available under this subsection for any project or activity eligible for funding under section 402.

(ii) MEDIUM-RANGE AND HIGH-RANGE STATES.—Subject to clause (iii), medium-range and high-range States may use funds for any expenditure designed to reduce impaired driving based on problem identification upon approval by the Secretary.

(iii) REPORTING AND IMPAIRED DRIVING MEASURES.—A State may use grant funds for any expenditure relating to—

(I) increasing the timely and accurate reporting to Federal, State, and local databases of—

(aa) crash information, including electronic crash reporting systems that allow accurate real- or near-real-time uploading of crash information; and

(bb) impaired driving criminal justice information; or

(II) researching or evaluating impaired driving countermeasures.

(5) GRANT AMOUNT.—Subject to paragraph (6), the allocation of grant funds to a State under this section for a fiscal year shall be in proportion to the State's apportionment under section 402 for fiscal year 2009.

(6) ADDITIONAL GRANTS.—

(A) GRANTS TO STATES WITH ALCOHOL-IGNITION INTERLOCK LAWS.—The Secretary shall make a separate grant under this subsection to each State that—

(i) adopts, and is enforcing, a mandatory alcohol-ignition interlock law for all individuals convicted of driving under the influence of alcohol or of driving while intoxicated;

(ii) does not allow an individual convicted of driving under the influence of alcohol or of driving while intoxicated to receive any driving privilege or driver's license unless the individual installs on each motor vehicle registered, owned, or leased for operation by the individual an ignition interlock for a period of not less than 180 days; or

(iii) has in effect, and is enforcing—

(I) a State law requiring for any individual who is convicted of, or the driving privilege of whom is revoked or denied for, refusing to submit to a chemical or other appropriate test for the purpose of determining the presence or concentration of any intoxicating substance, a State law requiring a period of not less than 180 days of ignition interlock installation on each motor vehicle to be operated by the individual; and

(II) a compliance-based removal program, under which an individual convicted of driving under the influence of alcohol or of driving while intoxicated shall—

(aa) satisfy a period of not less than 180 days of ignition interlock installation on each motor vehicle to be operated by the individual; and

(bb) have completed a minimum consecutive period of not less than 40 percent of the required period of ignition interlock installation immediately preceding the date of release of the individual, without a confirmed violation.

(B) GRANTS TO STATES WITH 24-7 SOBRIETY PROGRAMS.—The Secretary shall make a separate grant under this subsection to each State that—

(i) adopts and is enforcing a law that requires all individuals convicted of driving under the influence of alcohol or of driving while intoxicated to receive a restriction on driving privileges; and

(ii) provides a 24-7 sobriety program.

(C) USE OF FUNDS.—Grants authorized under subparagraph (A) and subparagraph (B) may be used by recipient States for any eligible activities under this subsection or section 402.

(D) ALLOCATION.—Amounts made available under this paragraph shall be allocated among States described in subparagraph (A) and subparagraph (B) in proportion to the State's apportionment under section 402 for fiscal year 2022.

(E) FUNDING.—

(i) FUNDING FOR GRANTS TO STATES WITH ALCOHOL-IGNITION INTERLOCK LAWS.—Not more than 12 percent of the amounts made available to carry out this subsection in a fiscal year shall be made available by the Secretary for making grants under subparagraph (A).

(ii) FUNDING FOR GRANTS TO STATES WITH 24-7 SOBRIETY PROGRAMS.—Not more than 3 percent of the amounts made available to carry out this subsection in a fiscal year shall be made available by the Secretary for making grants under subparagraph (B).

(F) EXCEPTIONS.—A State alcohol-ignition interlock law under subparagraph (A) may include exceptions for the following circumstances:

(i) The individual is required to operate an employer's motor vehicle in the course and scope of employment and the business entity that owns the vehicle is not owned or controlled by the individual.

(ii) The individual is certified by a medical doctor as being unable to provide a deep lung breath sample for analysis by an ignition interlock device.

(iii) A State-certified ignition interlock provider is not available within 100 miles of the individual's residence.

(7) DEFINITIONS.—In this subsection:

(A) 24-7 SOBRIETY PROGRAM.—The term "24-7 sobriety program" means a State law or program that authorizes a State or local court or an agency with jurisdiction, as a condition of bond, sentence, probation, parole, or work permit, to—

(i) require an individual who was arrested for, plead guilty to, or was convicted of driving under the influence of alcohol or drugs to totally abstain from alcohol or drugs for a period of time; and

(ii) require the individual to be subject to testing for alcohol or drugs—

(I) at least twice per day at a testing location;

(II) by continuous transdermal alcohol monitoring via an electronic monitoring device; or

(III) by an alternate method with the concurrence of the Secretary.

(B) AVERAGE IMPAIRED DRIVING FATALITY RATE.—The term "average impaired driving fatality rate" means the number of fatalities in motor vehicle crashes involving a driver with a blood alcohol concentration of at least 0.08 percent for every 100,000,000 vehicle miles traveled, based on the most recently reported 3 calendar years of final data from the Fatality Analysis Reporting System, as calculated in accordance with regulations prescribed by the Administrator of the National Highway Traffic Safety Administration.

(C) HIGH-RANGE STATE.—The term "high-range State" means a State that has an average impaired driving fatality rate of 0.60 or higher.

(D) LOW-RANGE STATE.—The term "low-range State" means a State that has an average impaired driving fatality rate of 0.30 or lower.

(E) MID-RANGE STATE.—The term "mid-range State" means a State that has an average impaired driving fatality rate that is higher than 0.30 and lower than 0.60.

(e) DISTRACTED DRIVING GRANTS.—

(1) DEFINITIONS.—In this subsection:

(A) DRIVING.—The term "driving"—

(i) means operating a motor vehicle on a public road; and

(ii) does not include operating a motor vehicle when the vehicle has pulled over to the side of, or off, an active roadway and has stopped in a location where it can safely remain stationary.

(B) PERSONAL WIRELESS COMMUNICATIONS DEVICE.—

(i) IN GENERAL.—The term "personal wireless communications device" means—

(I) a device through which personal wireless services (as defined in section 332(c)(7)(C) of the Communications Act of 1934 (47 U.S.C. 332(c)(7)(C))) are transmitted; and

(II) a mobile telephone or other portable electronic communication device with which a user engages in a call or writes, sends, or reads a text message using at least 1 hand.

(ii) EXCLUSION.—The term "personal wireless communications device" does not include a global navigation satellite system receiver used for positioning, emergency notification, or navigation purposes.

(C) PRIMARY OFFENSE.—The term "primary offense" means an offense for which a law enforcement officer may stop a vehicle solely for the purpose of issuing a citation in the absence of evidence of another offense.

(D) PUBLIC ROAD.—The term "public road" has the meaning given such term in section 402(c).

(E) TEXT.—The term "text" means—

(i) to read from, or manually to enter data into, a personal wireless communications device, including for the purpose of SMS texting, emailing, instant messaging, or any other form of electronic data retrieval or electronic data communication; and

(ii) manually to enter, send, or retrieve a text message to communicate with another individual or device.

(F) TEXT MESSAGE.—

(i) IN GENERAL.—The term "text message" means—

(I) a text-based message;

(II) an instant message;

(III) an electronic message; and

(IV) email.

(ii) EXCLUSIONS.—The term "text message" does not include—

(I) an emergency, traffic, or weather alert; or

(II) a message relating to the operation or navigation of a motor vehicle.

(2) GRANT PROGRAM.—The Secretary shall provide a grant under this subsection to any State that includes distracted driving awareness as part of the driver's license examination of the State.

(3) ALLOCATION.—

(A) IN GENERAL.—For each fiscal year, not less than 50 percent of the amounts made available to carry out this subsection shall be allocated to States, based on the proportion that—

(i) the apportionment of the State under section 402 for fiscal year 2009; bears to

(ii) the apportionment of all States under section 402 for that fiscal year.

(B) GRANTS FOR STATES WITH DISTRACTED DRIVING LAWS.—

(i) IN GENERAL.—In addition to the allocations under subparagraph (A), for each fiscal year, not more than 50 percent of the amounts made available to carry out this subsection shall be allocated to States that enact and enforce a law that meets the requirements of paragraph (4), (5), or (6)—

(I) based on the proportion that—

(aa) the apportionment of the State under section 402 for fiscal year 2009; bears to

(bb) the apportionment of all States under section 402 for that fiscal year; and

(II) subject to clauses (ii), (iii), and (iv), as applicable.

(ii) PRIMARY LAWS.—Subject to clause (iv), in the case of a State that enacts and enforces a law that meets the requirements of paragraph (4), (5), or (6) as a primary offense, the allocation to the State under this subparagraph shall be 100 percent of the amount calculated to be allocated to the State under clause (i)(I).

(iii) SECONDARY LAWS.—Subject to clause (iv), in the case of a State that enacts and enforces a law that meets the requirements of paragraph (4), (5), or (6) as a secondary enforcement action, the allocation to the State under this subparagraph shall be an amount equal to 50 percent of the amount calculated to be allocated to the State under clause (i)(I).

(iv) TEXTING WHILE DRIVING.—Notwithstanding clauses (ii) and (iii), the allocation under this subparagraph to a State that enacts and enforces a law that prohibits a driver from viewing a personal wireless communications device (except for purposes of navigation) shall be 25 percent of the amount calculated to be allocated to the State under clause (i)(I).

(4) PROHIBITION ON TEXTING WHILE DRIVING.—A State law meets the requirements of this paragraph if the law—

(A) prohibits a driver from texting through a personal wireless communications device while driving;

(B) establishes a fine for a violation of the law; and

(C) does not provide for an exemption that specifically allows a driver to use a personal wireless communications device for texting while stopped in traffic.

(5) PROHIBITION ON HANDHELD PHONE USE WHILE DRIVING.—A State law meets the requirements of this paragraph if the law—

(A) prohibits a driver from holding a personal wireless communications device while driving;

(B) establishes a fine for a violation of that law; and

(C) does not provide for an exemption that specifically allows a driver to use a personal wireless communications device for texting while stopped in traffic.

(6) PROHIBITION ON YOUTH CELL PHONE USE WHILE DRIVING OR STOPPED IN TRAFFIC.—A State law meets the requirements of this paragraph if the law—

(A) prohibits a driver from using a personal wireless communications device while driving if the driver is—

(i) younger than 18 years of age; or

(ii) in the learner's permit or intermediate license stage;

(B) establishes a fine for a violation of the law; and

(C) does not provide for—

(i) an exemption that specifically allows a driver to use a personal wireless communications device for texting while stopped in traffic; or

(ii) an exemption described in paragraph (7)(E).

(7) PERMITTED EXCEPTIONS.—A law that meets the requirements of paragraph (4), (5), or (6) may provide exceptions for—

(A) a driver who uses a personal wireless communications device during an emergency to contact emergency services to prevent injury to persons or property;

(B) emergency services personnel who use a personal wireless communications device while—

(i) operating an emergency services vehicle; and

(ii) engaged in the performance of their duties as emergency services personnel;

(C) an individual employed as a commercial motor vehicle driver or a school bus driver who uses a personal wireless communications device within the scope of such individual's employment if such use is permitted under the regulations promulgated pursuant to section 31136 of title 49;

(D) a driver who uses a personal wireless communications device for navigation;

(E) except for a law described in paragraph (6), the use of a personal wireless communications device—

(i) in a hands-free manner;

(ii) with a hands-free accessory; or

(iii) with the activation or deactivation of a feature or function of the personal wireless communications device with the motion of a single swipe or tap of the finger of the driver; and

(F) any additional exceptions determined by the Secretary through a rulemaking process.

(8) USE OF GRANT FUNDS.—

(A) IN GENERAL.—Except as provided in subparagraph (B), amounts received by a State under this subsection shall be used—

(i) to educate the public through advertising containing information about the dangers of texting or using a cell phone while driving;

(ii) for traffic signs that notify drivers about the distracted driving law of the State; or

(iii) for law enforcement costs related to the enforcement of the distracted driving law.

(B) FLEXIBILITY.—

(i) Not more than 50 percent of amounts received by a State under this subsection may be used for any eligible project or activity under section 402.

(ii) Not more than 75 percent of amounts received by a State under this subsection may be used for any eligible project or activity under section 402 if the State has conformed its distracted driving data to the most recent Model Minimum Uniform Crash Criteria published by the Secretary.

(9) ALLOCATION TO SUPPORT STATE DISTRACTED DRIVING LAWS.—Of the amounts available under this subsection in a fiscal year for distracted driving grants, the Secretary may expend not more than $5,000,000 for the development and placement of broadcast media to reduce distracted driving of motor vehicles.

(f) MOTORCYCLIST SAFETY.—

(1) GRANTS AUTHORIZED.—Subject to the requirements under this subsection, the Secretary shall award grants to States that adopt and implement effective programs to reduce the number of single- and multi-vehicle crashes involving motorcyclists.

(2) GRANT AMOUNT.—The allocation of grant funds to a State under this subsection for a fiscal year shall be in proportion to the State's apportionment under section 402 for fiscal year 2009, except that the amount of a grant awarded to a State for a fiscal year may not exceed 25 percent of the amount apportioned to the State under such section for fiscal year 2009.

(3) GRANT ELIGIBILITY.—A State becomes eligible for a grant under this subsection by adopting or demonstrating to the satisfaction of the Secretary, at least 2 of the following criteria:

(A) MOTORCYCLE RIDER TRAINING COURSES.—An effective motorcycle rider training course that is offered throughout the State, which—

(i) provides a formal program of instruction in crash avoidance and other safety-oriented operational skills to motorcyclists; and

(ii) may include innovative training opportunities to meet unique regional needs.

(B) MOTORCYCLISTS AWARENESS PROGRAM.—An effective statewide program to enhance motorist awareness of the presence of motorcyclists on or near roadways and safe driving practices that avoid injuries to motorcyclists.

(C) HELMET LAW.—A State law requiring the use of a helmet for each motorcycle rider under the age of 18.

(D) REDUCTION OF FATALITIES AND CRASHES INVOLVING MOTORCYCLES.—A reduction for the preceding calendar year in the number of motorcycle fatalities and the rate of motor vehicle crashes involving motorcycles in the State (expressed as a function of 10,000 motorcycle registrations).

(E) IMPAIRED DRIVING PROGRAM.—Implementation of a statewide program to reduce impaired driving, including specific measures to reduce impaired motorcycle operation.

(F) REDUCTION OF FATALITIES AND CRASHES INVOLVING IMPAIRED MOTORCYCLISTS.—A reduction for the preceding calendar year in the number of fatalities and the rate of reported crashes involving alcohol- or drug-impaired motorcycle operators (expressed as a function of 10,000 motorcycle registrations).

(G) FEES COLLECTED FROM MOTORCYCLISTS.—All fees collected by the State from motorcyclists for the purposes of funding motorcycle training and safety programs will be used for motorcycle training and safety purposes.

(4) ELIGIBLE USES.—

(A) IN GENERAL.—A State may use funds from a grant under this subsection only for motorcyclist safety training and motorcyclist awareness programs, including—

(i) improvements to motorcyclist safety training curricula;

(ii) improvements in program delivery of motorcycle training to both urban and rural areas, including—

(I) procurement or repair of practice motorcycles;

(II) instructional materials;

(III) mobile training units; and

(IV) leasing or purchasing facilities for closed-course motorcycle skill training;

(iii) measures designed to increase the recruitment or retention of motorcyclist safety training instructors; and

(iv) public awareness, public service announcements, and other outreach programs to enhance driver awareness of motorcyclists, including "share-the-road" safety messages.

(B) SUBALLOCATIONS OF FUNDS.—An agency of a State that receives a grant under this subsection may suballocate funds from the grant to a nonprofit organization incorporated in that State to carry out this subsection.

(C) FLEXIBILITY.—Not more than 50 percent of grant funds received by a State under this subsection may be used for any eligible project or activity under section 402 if the State is in the lowest 25 percent of all States for motorcycle deaths per 10,000 motorcycle registrations based on the most recent data that conforms with criteria established by the Secretary.

(5) DEFINITIONS.—In this subsection:

(A) MOTORCYCLIST AWARENESS.—The term "motorcyclist awareness" means individual or collective awareness of—

(i) the presence of motorcycles on or near roadways; and

(ii) safe driving practices that avoid injury to motorcyclists.

(B) MOTORCYCLIST AWARENESS PROGRAM.—The term "motorcyclist awareness program" means an informational or public awareness program designed to enhance motorcyclist awareness that is developed by or in coordination with the designated State authority having jurisdiction over motorcyclist safety issues, which may include the State motorcycle safety administrator or a motorcycle advisory council appointed by the governor of the State.

(C) MOTORCYCLIST SAFETY TRAINING.—The term "motorcyclist safety training" means a formal program of instruction that is approved for use in a State by the designated State authority having jurisdiction over motorcyclist safety issues, which may include the State motorcycle safety administrator or a motorcycle advisory council appointed by the governor of the State.

(D) STATE.—The term "State" has the meaning given such term in section 101(a) of title 23, United States Code.

(6) SHARE-THE-ROAD MODEL LANGUAGE.—Not later than 1 year after the date of enactment of this paragraph, the Secretary shall update and provide to the States

model language, for use in traffic safety education courses, driver's manuals, and other driver training materials, that provides instruction for drivers of motor vehicles on the importance of sharing the road safely with motorcyclists.

(g) NONMOTORIZED SAFETY.—

(1) DEFINITION OF NONMOTORIZED ROAD USER.—In this subsection, the term "nonmotorized road user" means—

(A) a pedestrian;

(B) an individual using a nonmotorized mode of transportation, including a bicycle, a scooter, or a personal conveyance; and

(C) an individual using a low-speed or low-horsepower motorized vehicle, including an electric bicycle, electric scooter, personal mobility assistance device, personal transporter, or all-terrain vehicle.

(2) GENERAL AUTHORITY.—Subject to the requirements under this subsection, the Secretary shall award grants to States for the purpose of decreasing nonmotorized road user fatalities involving a motor vehicle in transit on a trafficway.

(3) FEDERAL SHARE.—The Federal share of the cost of a project carried out by a State using amounts from a grant awarded under this subsection may not exceed 80 percent.

(4) ELIGIBILITY.—A State shall receive a grant under this subsection in a fiscal year if the annual combined nonmotorized road user fatalities in the State exceed 15 percent of the total annual crash fatalities in the State, based on the most recently reported final data from the Fatality Analysis Reporting System.

(5) USE OF GRANT AMOUNTS.—Grant funds received by a State under this subsection may be used for the safety of nonmotorized road users, including—

(A) training of law enforcement officials relating to nonmotorized road user safety, State laws applicable to nonmotorized road user safety, and infrastructure designed to improve nonmotorized road user safety;

(B) carrying out a program to support enforcement mobilizations and campaigns designed to enforce State traffic laws applicable to nonmotorized road user safety;

(C) public education and awareness programs designed to inform motorists and nonmotorized road users regarding—

(i) nonmotorized road user safety, including information relating to nonmotorized mobility and the importance of speed management to the safety of nonmotorized road users;

(ii) the value of the use of nonmotorized road user safety equipment, including lighting, conspicuity equipment, mirrors, helmets, and other protective equipment, and compliance with any State or local laws requiring the use of that equipment;

(iii) State traffic laws applicable to nonmotorized road user safety, including the responsibilities of motorists with respect to nonmotorized road users; and

(iv) infrastructure designed to improve nonmotorized road user safety; and

(D) the collection of data, and the establishment and maintenance of data systems, relating to nonmotorized road user traffic fatalities.

(6) GRANT AMOUNT.—The allocation of grant funds to a State under this subsection for a fiscal year shall be in proportion to the State's apportionment under section 402

for fiscal year 2009.

(h) Preventing Roadside Deaths.—

(1) In general.—The Secretary shall provide grants to States to prevent death and injury from crashes involving motor vehicles striking other vehicles and individuals stopped at the roadside.

(2) Federal share.—The Federal share of the cost of carrying out an activity funded through a grant under this subsection may not exceed 80 percent.

(3) Eligibility.—A State shall receive a grant under this subsection in a fiscal year if the State submits to the Secretary a plan that describes the method by which the State will use grant funds in accordance with paragraph (4).

(4) Use of funds.—Amounts received by a State under this subsection shall be used by the State—

(A) to purchase and deploy digital alert technology that—

(i) is capable of receiving alerts regarding nearby first responders; and

(ii) in the case of a motor vehicle that is used for emergency response activities, is capable of sending alerts to civilian drivers to protect first responders on the scene and en route;

(B) to educate the public regarding the safety of vehicles and individuals stopped at the roadside in the State through public information campaigns for the purpose of reducing roadside deaths and injury;

(C) for law enforcement costs relating to enforcing State laws to protect the safety of vehicles and individuals stopped at the roadside;

(D) for programs to identify, collect, and report to State and local government agencies data relating to crashes involving vehicles and individuals stopped at the roadside; and

(E) to pilot and incentivize measures, including optical visibility measures, to increase the visibility of stopped and disabled vehicles.

(5) Grant amount.—The allocation of grant funds to a State under this subsection for a fiscal year shall be in proportion to the apportionment of that State under section 402 for fiscal year 2022.

(i) Driver and Officer Safety Education.—

(1) Definition of peace officer.—In this subsection, the term "peace officer" includes any individual—

(A) who is an elected, appointed, or employed agent of a government entity;

(B) who has the authority—

(i) to carry firearms; and

(ii) to make warrantless arrests; and

(C) whose duties involve the enforcement of criminal laws of the United States.

(2) Grants.—Subject to the requirements of this subsection, the Secretary shall provide grants to—

(A) States that enact or adopt a law or program described in paragraph (4); and

(B) qualifying States under paragraph (7).

(3) Federal share.—The Federal share of the cost of carrying out an activity funded through a grant under this subsection may not exceed 80 percent.

(4) Description of law or program.—A law or program referred to in paragraph

(2)(A) is a law or program that requires 1 or more of the following:

(A) DRIVER EDUCATION AND DRIVING SAFETY COURSES.—The inclusion, in driver education and driver safety courses provided to individuals by educational and motor vehicle agencies of the State, of instruction and testing relating to law enforcement practices during traffic stops, including information relating to—

(i) the role of law enforcement and the duties and responsibilities of peace officers;

(ii) the legal rights of individuals concerning interactions with peace officers;

(iii) best practices for civilians and peace officers during those interactions;

(iv) the consequences for failure of an individual or officer to comply with the law or program; and

(v) how and where to file a complaint against, or a compliment relating to, a peace officer.

(B) PEACE OFFICER TRAINING PROGRAMS.—Development and implementation of a training program, including instruction and testing materials, for peace officers and reserve law enforcement officers (other than officers who have received training in a civilian course described in subparagraph (A)) with respect to proper interaction with civilians during traffic stops.

(5) USE OF FUNDS.—A State may use a grant provided under this subsection for—

(A) the production of educational materials and training of staff for driver education and driving safety courses and peace officer training described in paragraph (4); and

(B) the implementation of a law or program described in paragraph (4).

(6) GRANT AMOUNT.—The allocation of grant funds to a State under this subsection for a fiscal year shall be in proportion to the apportionment of that State under section 402 for fiscal year 2022.

(7) SPECIAL RULE FOR CERTAIN STATES.—

(A) DEFINITION OF QUALIFYING STATE.—In this paragraph, the term "qualifying State" means a State that—

(i) has received a grant under this subsection for a period of not more than 5 years; and

(ii) as determined by the Secretary—

(I) has not fully enacted or adopted a law or program described in paragraph (4); but

(II)(aa) has taken meaningful steps toward the full implementation of such a law or program; and

(bb) has established a timetable for the implementation of such a law or program.

(B) WITHHOLDING.—The Secretary shall—

(i) withhold 50 percent of the amount that each qualifying State would otherwise receive under this subsection if the qualifying State were a State described in paragraph (2)(A); and

(ii) direct any amounts withheld under clause (i) for distribution among the States that are enforcing and carrying out a law or program described in paragraph (4).

(Added Pub. L. 105–178, title II, §2003(a)(1), June 9, 1998, 112 Stat. 325; amended Pub. L. 109–59, title II, §§2002(e), 2004, Aug. 10, 2005, 119 Stat. 1522, 1524; Pub. L. 111–147, title IV, §421(c)(1), Mar. 18, 2010, 124 Stat. 84; Pub. L. 112–30, title I, §121(c)(1), Sept. 16, 2011, 125 Stat. 347; Pub. L. 112–141, div. C, title I, §31105(a), July 6, 2012, 126 Stat. 741; Pub. L. 114–94, div. A, title IV, §§4005, 4014(3), Dec. 4, 2015, 129 Stat. 1501, 1513; Pub. L. 117–58, div. B, title IV, §24105(a), Nov. 15, 2021, 135 Stat. 795.)

§406. GENERAL REQUIREMENTS FOR FEDERAL ASSISTANCE

(a) DEFINITION OF FUNDED PROJECT.—In this section, the term "funded project" means a project funded, in whole or in part, by a grant provided under section 402 or 405.

(b) REGULATORY AUTHORITY.—Each funded project shall be carried out in accordance with applicable regulations promulgated by the Secretary.

(c) STATE MATCHING REQUIREMENTS.—If a grant provided under this chapter requires any State to share in the cost of a funded project, the aggregate of the expenditures made by the State (including any political subdivision of the State) for highway safety activities during a fiscal year, exclusive of Federal funds, for carrying out the funded project (other than expenditures for planning or administration) shall be credited toward the non-Federal share of the cost of any other funded project (other than planning and administration) during that fiscal year, regardless of whether those expenditures were made in connection with the project.

(d) GRANT APPLICATION AND DEADLINE.—

(1) APPLICATIONS.—To be eligible to receive a grant under this chapter, a State shall submit to the Secretary an application at such time, in such manner, and containing such information as the Secretary may require.

(2) DEADLINE.—The Secretary shall establish a single deadline for the submission of applications under paragraph (1) to enable the provision of grants under this chapter early in each applicable fiscal year beginning after the date of submission.

(e) DISTRIBUTION OF FUNDS TO STATES.—Not later than 60 days after the later of the start of a fiscal year or the date of enactment of any appropriations Act making funds available to carry out this chapter for that fiscal year, the Secretary shall distribute to each State the portion of those funds to which the State is entitled for the applicable fiscal year.

(Added Pub. L. 117–58, div. B, title IV, §24101(d)(1)(B), Nov. 15, 2021, 135 Stat. 784.)

§407. DISCOVERY AND ADMISSION AS EVIDENCE OF CERTAIN REPORTS AND SURVEYS

Notwithstanding any other provision of law, reports, surveys, schedules, lists, or data compiled or collected for the purpose of identifying, evaluating, or planning the safety enhancement of potential accident sites, hazardous roadway conditions, or railway-highway crossings, pursuant to sections 130, 144, and 148 of this title or for the purpose of developing any highway safety construction improvement project which may be implemented utilizing Federal-aid highway funds shall not be subject to discovery or admitted into evidence in a Federal or State court proceeding or considered for other purposes in any action for damages arising from any occurrence at a location mentioned or addressed in such reports, surveys, schedules, lists, or data.

(Added Pub. L. 100–17, title I, §132(a), Apr. 2, 1987, 101 Stat. 170, §409; amended Pub. L. 102–240, title I, §1035(a), Dec. 18, 1991, 105 Stat. 1978; Pub. L. 104–59, title III, §323, Nov. 28, 1995, 109 Stat.

591; Pub. L. 109–59, title I, §1401(a)(3)(C), Aug. 10, 2005, 119 Stat. 1225; renumbered §407, Pub. L. 117–58, div. B, title IV, §24101(d)(1)(A), Nov. 15, 2021, 135 Stat. 784.)

§408. Agency accountability

(a) Triennial State Management Reviews.—

(1) In general.—Except as provided under paragraph (2), the Secretary shall conduct a review of each State highway safety program at least once every 3 years.

(2) Exceptions.—The Secretary may conduct reviews of the highway safety programs of the United States Virgin Islands, Guam, American Samoa, and the Commonwealth of the Northern Mariana Islands as often as the Secretary determines to be appropriate.

(3) Components.—Reviews under this subsection shall include—

(A) a management evaluation of all grant programs funded under this chapter;

(B) an assessment of State data collection and evaluation relating to performance measures established by the Secretary;

(C) a comparison of State efforts under subparagraphs (A) and (B) to best practices and programs that have been evaluated for effectiveness; and

(D) the development of recommendations on how each State could—

(i) improve the management and oversight of its grant activities; and

(ii) provide a management and oversight plan for such grant programs.

(b) Recommendations Before Submission.—In order to provide guidance to State highway safety agencies on matters that should be addressed in the goals and initiatives of the State highway safety program before the program is submitted for review, the Secretary shall provide data-based recommendations to each State at least 90 days before the date on which the program is to be submitted for approval.

(c) State Program Review.—The Secretary shall—

(1) conduct a program improvement review of a highway safety program under this chapter of a State that does not make substantial progress over a 3-year period in meeting its priority program goals; and

(2) provide technical assistance and safety program requirements to be incorporated in the State highway safety program for any goal not achieved.

(d) Regional Harmonization.—The Secretary and the Inspector General of the Department of Transportation shall undertake an administrative review of the practices and procedures of the management reviews and program reviews of State highway safety programs under this chapter conducted by the regional offices of the National Highway Traffic Safety Administration and prepare a written report of best practices and procedures for use by the regional offices in conducting such reviews. The report shall be completed within 180 days after the date of enactment of this section.

(e) Best Practices Guidelines.—

(1) Uniform guidelines.—The Secretary shall issue uniform management review guidelines and program review guidelines based on the report under subsection (d). Each regional office shall use the guidelines in executing its State administrative review duties under this section.

(2) Publication.—The Secretary shall make publicly available on the Web site (or successor electronic facility) of the Administration the following documents upon their completion:

(A) The Secretary's management review guidelines and program review guidelines.

(B) All State highway safety programs submitted under this chapter.

(C) State annual accomplishment reports.

(D) The Administration's Summary Report of findings from Management Reviews and Improvement Plans.

(3) REPORTS TO STATE HIGHWAY SAFETY AGENCIES.—The Secretary may not make publicly available a program, report, or review under paragraph (2) that is directed to a State highway safety agency until after the date on which the program, report, or review is submitted to that agency under this chapter.

(f) TRACKING PROCESS.—The Secretary shall develop a process to identify and mitigate possible systemic issues across States and regional offices by reviewing oversight findings and recommended actions identified in triennial State management reviews

(Added Pub. L. 109–59, title II, §2008(a), Aug. 10, 2005, 119 Stat. 1533, §412; amended Pub. L. 112–141, div. C, title I, §31107, July 6, 2012, 126 Stat. 755; Pub. L. 114–94, div. A, title IV, §4006, Dec. 4, 2015, 129 Stat. 1510; renumbered §408, Pub. L. 117–58, div. B, title IV, §24101(d)(1)(A), Nov. 15, 2021, 135 Stat. 784.)

[§409. RENUMBERED §407]

[§§410, 411. REPEALED. PUB. L. 112–141, DIV. C, TITLE I, §31109(E), (F), JULY 6, 2012, 126 STAT. 757]

Section 410, added Pub. L. 100–690, title IX, §9002(a), Nov. 18, 1988, 102 Stat. 4521; amended Pub. L. 101–516, title III, §336, Nov. 5, 1990, 104 Stat. 2186; Pub. L. 102–240, title II, §2004(a), Dec. 18, 1991, 105 Stat. 2073; Pub. L. 102–388, title VI, §§601–606, Oct. 6, 1992, 106 Stat. 1569, 1570; Pub. L. 104–59, title III, §324, Nov. 28, 1995, 109 Stat. 591; Pub. L. 105–18, title II, §8003, June 12, 1997, 111 Stat. 195; Pub. L. 105–130, §6(b), Dec. 1, 1997, 111 Stat. 2558; Pub. L. 105–178, title II, §2004(a), June 9, 1998, 112 Stat. 328; Pub. L. 108–88, §6(e)(1), Sept. 30, 2003, 117 Stat. 1120; Pub. L. 108–310, §6(e)(1), Sept. 30, 2004, 118 Stat. 1152; Pub. L. 109–59, title II, §2007(a), (b), Aug. 10, 2005, 119 Stat. 1529; Pub. L. 110–244, title III, §303(c)(2), (3), June 6, 2008, 122 Stat. 1619; Pub. L. 111–147, title IV, §421(f)(1), Mar. 18, 2010, 124 Stat. 85; Pub. L. 112–30, title I, §121(f)(1), Sept. 16, 2011, 125 Stat. 347, related to alcohol-impaired driving countermeasures.

Section 411, added Pub. L. 105–178, title II, §2005(a), June 9, 1998, 112 Stat. 332; amended Pub. L. 110–244, title III, §303(c)(4), June 6, 2008, 122 Stat. 1619, related to State highway safety data improvements.

[§412. RENUMBERED §408]

CHAPTER 5
RESEARCH, TECHNOLOGY, AND EDUCATION

CHAPTER 5—RESEARCH, TECHNOLOGY, AND EDUCATION

§501. DEFINITIONS

In this chapter, the following definitions apply:

(1) FEDERAL LABORATORY.—The term "Federal laboratory" includes a Government-owned, Government-operated laboratory and a Government-owned, contractor-operated laboratory.

(2) INCIDENT.—The term "incident" means a crash, natural disaster, workzone activity, special event, or other emergency road user occurrence that adversely affects or impedes the normal flow of traffic.

(3) INNOVATION LIFECYCLE.—The term "innovation lifecycle" means the process of innovating through—

(A) the identification of a need;

(B) the establishment of the scope of research to address that need;

(C) setting an agenda;

(D) carrying out research, development, deployment, and testing of the resulting technology or innovation; and

(E) carrying out an evaluation of the costs and benefits of the resulting technology or innovation.

(4) INTELLIGENT TRANSPORTATION INFRASTRUCTURE.—The term "intelligent transportation infrastructure" means fully integrated public sector intelligent transportation system components, as defined by the Secretary.

(5) INTELLIGENT TRANSPORTATION SYSTEM.—The terms "intelligent transportation system" and "ITS" mean electronics, photonics, communications, or information processing used singly or in combination to improve the efficiency or safety of a surface transportation system.

(6) NATIONAL ARCHITECTURE.—For purposes of this chapter, the term "national architecture" means the common framework for interoperability that defines—
(A) the functions associated with intelligent transportation system user services;
(B) the physical entities or subsystems within which the functions reside;
(C) the data interfaces and information flows between physical subsystems; and
(D) the communications requirements associated with the information flows.

(7) PROJECT.—The term "project" means an undertaking to research, develop, or operationally test intelligent transportation systems or any other undertaking eligible for assistance under this chapter.

(8) SAFETY.—The term "safety" includes highway and traffic safety systems, research, and development relating to vehicle, highway, driver, passenger, bicyclist, and pedestrian characteristics, accident investigations, communications, emergency medical care, and transportation of the injured.

(9) STANDARD.—The term "standard" means a document that—
(A) contains technical specifications or other precise criteria for intelligent transportation systems that are to be used consistently as rules, guidelines, or definitions of characteristics so as to ensure that materials, products, processes, and services are fit for the intended purposes of the materials, products, processes, and services; and
(B) may support the national architecture and promote—
(i) the widespread use and adoption of intelligent transportation system technology as a component of the surface transportation systems of the United States; and
(ii) interoperability among intelligent transportation system technologies implemented throughout the States.

(Added Pub. L. 105–178, title V, §5101(2), June 9, 1998, 112 Stat. 422; amended Pub. L. 112–141, div. E, title II, §52001, July 6, 2012, 126 Stat. 865.)

§502. SURFACE TRANSPORTATION RESEARCH, DEVELOPMENT, AND TECHNOLOGY

(a) BASIC PRINCIPLES GOVERNING RESEARCH AND TECHNOLOGY INVESTMENTS.—
(1) APPLICABILITY.—The research, development, and technology provisions of this section shall apply throughout this chapter.

(2) COVERAGE.—Surface transportation research and technology development shall include all activities within the innovation lifecycle leading to technology development and transfer, as well as the introduction of new and innovative ideas, practices, and approaches, through such mechanisms as field applications, education and training, communications, impact analysis, and technical support.

(3) FEDERAL RESPONSIBILITY.—Funding and conducting surface transportation research and technology transfer activities shall be considered a basic responsibility of the Federal Government when the work—
(A) is of national significance;
(B) delivers a clear public benefit and occurs where private sector investment is less than optimal;
(C) supports a Federal stewardship role in assuring that State and local governments use national resources efficiently;
(D) meets and addresses current or emerging needs;

(E) addresses current gaps in research;

(F) presents the best means to align resources with multiyear plans and priorities;

(G) ensures the coordination of highway research and technology transfer activities, including through activities performed by university transportation centers;

(H) educates transportation professionals; or

(I) presents the best means to support Federal policy goals compared to other policy alternatives.

(4) ROLE.—Consistent with these Federal responsibilities, the Secretary shall—

(A) conduct research;

(B) partner with State highway agencies and other stakeholders as appropriate to facilitate research and technology transfer activities;

(C) communicate the results of ongoing and completed research;

(D) lead efforts to coordinate national emphasis areas of highway research, technology, and innovation deployment;

(E) leverage partnerships with industry, academia, international entities, and State departments of transportation;

(F) lead efforts to reduce unnecessary duplication of effort; and

(G) lead efforts to accelerate innovation delivery.

(5) PROGRAM CONTENT.—A surface transportation research program shall include—

(A) fundamental, long-term highway research;

(B) research aimed at significant highway research gaps and emerging issues with national implications; and

(C) research related to all highway objectives seeking to improve the performance of the transportation system.

(6) STAKEHOLDER INPUT.—Federal surface transportation research and development activities shall address the needs of stakeholders. Stakeholders include States, metropolitan planning organizations, local governments, tribal governments, the private sector, researchers, research sponsors, and other affected parties, including public interest groups.

(7) COMPETITION AND PEER REVIEW.—Except as otherwise provided in this chapter, the Secretary shall award, to the maximum extent practicable, all grants, contracts, and cooperative agreements for research and development under this chapter based on open competition and peer review of proposals.

(8) PERFORMANCE REVIEW AND EVALUATION.—

(A) IN GENERAL.—To the maximum extent practicable, all surface transportation research and development projects shall include a component of performance measurement and evaluation.

(B) PERFORMANCE MEASURES.—Performance measures shall be established during the proposal stage of a research and development project and shall, to the maximum extent possible, be outcome-based.

(C) PROGRAM PLAN.—To the maximum extent practicable, each program pursued under this chapter shall be part of a data-driven, outcome-oriented program plan.

(D) Availability of evaluations.—All evaluations under this paragraph shall be made readily available to the public.

(9) Technological innovation.—The programs and activities carried out under this section shall be consistent with the transportation research and development strategic plan under section 6503 of title 49.

(b) General Authority.—

(1) Research, development, and technology transfer activities.—The Secretary may carry out research, development, and technology transfer activities with respect to—

(A) motor carrier transportation;

(B) all phases of transportation planning and development (including construction, operation, transportation system management and operations, modernization, development, design, maintenance, safety, financing, and traffic conditions); and

(C) the effect of State laws on the activities described in subparagraphs (A) and (B).

(2) Tests and development.—The Secretary may test, develop, or assist in testing and developing any material, invention, patented article, or process.

(3) Cooperation, grants, and contracts.—The Secretary may carry out research, development, and technology transfer activities related to transportation—

(A) independently;

(B) in cooperation with other Federal departments, agencies, and instrumentalities and Federal laboratories; or

(C) by making grants to, or entering into contracts and cooperative agreements with one or more of the following: the National Academy of Sciences, the American Association of State Highway and Transportation Officials, any Federal laboratory, Federal agency, State agency, authority, association, institution, for-profit or nonprofit corporation, organization, foreign country, or any other person.

(4) Technological innovation.—The programs and activities carried out under this section shall be consistent with the transportation research and development strategic plan under section 6503 of title 49.

(5) Funds.—

(A) Special account.—In addition to other funds made available to carry out this chapter, the Secretary shall use such funds as may be deposited by any cooperating organization or person in a special account of the Treasury established for this purpose.

(B) Use of funds.—The Secretary shall use funds made available to carry out this chapter to develop, administer, communicate, and promote the use of products of research, development, and technology transfer programs under this chapter.

(6) Pooled funding.—

(A) Cooperation.—To promote effective utilization of available resources, the Secretary may cooperate with a State and an appropriate agency in funding research, development, and technology transfer activities of mutual interest on a pooled funds basis.

(B) Secretary as agent.—The Secretary may enter into contracts, cooperative agreements, and grants as the agent for all participating parties in carrying out such research, development, or technology transfer activities.

(C) TRANSFER OF AMOUNTS AMONG STATES OR TO FEDERAL HIGHWAY ADMINISTRATION.—The Secretary may, at the request of a State, transfer amounts apportioned or allocated to that State under this chapter to another State or the Federal Highway Administration to fund research, development, and technology transfer activities of mutual interest on a pooled funds basis.

(D) TRANSFER OF OBLIGATION AUTHORITY.—Obligation authority for amounts transferred under this subsection shall be disbursed in the same manner and for the same amount as provided for the project being transferred.

(7) PRIZE COMPETITIONS.—

(A) IN GENERAL.—The Secretary may use up to 1 percent of the funds made available under section 51001 of the Transportation Research and Innovative Technology Act of 2012 to carry out a program to competitively award cash prizes to stimulate innovation in basic and applied research and technology development that has the potential for application to the national transportation system.

(B) TOPICS.—In selecting topics for prize competitions under this paragraph, the Secretary shall—

(i) consult with a wide variety of governmental and nongovernmental representatives; and

(ii) give consideration to prize goals that demonstrate innovative approaches and strategies to improve the safety, efficiency, and sustainability of the national transportation system.

(C) ADVERTISING.—The Secretary shall encourage participation in the prize competitions through advertising efforts.

(D) REQUIREMENTS AND REGISTRATION.—For each prize competition, the Secretary shall publish a notice on a public website that describes—

(i) the subject of the competition;

(ii) the eligibility rules for participation in the competition;

(iii) the amount of the prize; and

(iv) the basis on which a winner will be selected.

(E) ELIGIBILITY.—An individual or entity may not receive a prize under this paragraph unless the individual or entity—

(i) has registered to participate in the competition pursuant to any rules promulgated by the Secretary under this section;

(ii) has complied with all requirements under this paragraph;

(iii)(I) in the case of a private entity, is incorporated in, and maintains a primary place of business in, the United States; or

(II) in the case of an individual, whether participating singly or in a group, is a citizen or permanent resident of the United States;

(iv) is not a Federal entity or Federal employee acting within the scope of his or her employment; and

(v) has not received a grant to perform research on the same issue for which the prize is awarded.

(F) LIABILITY.—

(i) ASSUMPTION OF RISK.—

(I) IN GENERAL.—A registered participant shall agree to assume any and all risks and waive claims against the Federal Government and its related entities, except in the case of willful misconduct, for any injury, death, damage, or loss of property, revenue, or profits, whether direct, indirect, or consequential, arising from participation in a competition, whether such injury, death, damage, or loss arises through negligence or otherwise.

(II) RELATED ENTITY.—In this subparagraph, the term "related entity" means a contractor, subcontractor (at any tier), supplier, user, customer, cooperating party, grantee, investigator, or detailee.

(ii) FINANCIAL RESPONSIBILITY.—A participant shall obtain liability insurance or demonstrate financial responsibility, in amounts determined by the Secretary, for claims by—

(I) a third party for death, bodily injury, or property damage, or loss resulting from an activity carried out in connection with participation in a competition, with the Federal Government named as an additional insured under the registered participant's insurance policy and registered participants agreeing to indemnify the Federal Government against third party claims for damages arising from or related to competition activities; and

(II) the Federal Government for damage or loss to Government property resulting from such an activity.

(G) JUDGES.—

(i) SELECTION.—Subject to clause (iii), for each prize competition, the Secretary, either directly or through an agreement under subparagraph (H), may appoint 1 or more qualified judges to select the winner or winners of the prize competition on the basis of the criteria described in subparagraph (D).

(ii) SELECTION.—Judges for each competition shall include individuals from outside the Federal Government, including the private sector.

(iii) LIMITATIONS.—A judge selected under this subparagraph may not—

(I) have personal or financial interests in, or be an employee, officer, director, or agent of, any entity that is a registered participant in a prize competition under this paragraph; or

(II) have a familial or financial relationship with an individual who is a registered participant.

(H) ADMINISTERING THE COMPETITION.—The Secretary may enter into an agreement with a private, nonprofit entity to administer the prize competition, subject to the provisions of this paragraph.

(I) FUNDING.—

(i) IN GENERAL.—

(I) PRIVATE SECTOR FUNDING.—A cash prize under this paragraph may consist of funds appropriated by the Federal Government and funds provided by the private sector.

(II) GOVERNMENT FUNDING.—The Secretary may accept funds from other Federal agencies, State and local governments, and metropolitan planning organizations for a cash prize under this paragraph.

(III) No special consideration.—The Secretary may not give any special consideration to any private sector entity in return for a donation under this subparagraph.

(ii) Availability of funds.—Notwithstanding any other provision of law, amounts appropriated for prize awards under this paragraph—

(I) shall remain available until expended; and

(II) may not be transferred, reprogrammed, or expended for other purposes until after the expiration of the 10-year period beginning on the last day of the fiscal year for which the funds were originally appropriated.

(iii) Savings provision.—Nothing in this subparagraph may be construed to permit the obligation or payment of funds in violation of the Anti-Deficiency Act (31 U.S.C. 1341).

(iv) Prize announcement.—A prize may not be announced under this paragraph until all the funds needed to pay out the announced amount of the prize have been appropriated by a governmental source or committed to in writing by a private source.

(v) Prize increases.—The Secretary may increase the amount of a prize after the initial announcement of the prize under this paragraph if—

(I) notice of the increase is provided in the same manner as the initial notice of the prize; and

(II) the funds needed to pay out the announced amount of the increase have been appropriated by a governmental source or committed to in writing by a private source.

(vi) Congressional notification.—A prize competition under this paragraph may offer a prize in an amount greater than $1,000,000 only after 30 days have elapsed after written notice has been transmitted to the Committee on Commerce, Science, and Transportation of the Senate and the Committees on Transportation and Infrastructure and Science, Space, and Technology of the House of Representatives.

(vii) Award limit.—A prize competition under this section may not result in the award of more than $25,000 in cash prizes without the approval of the Secretary.

(J) Compliance with existing law.—The Federal Government shall not, by virtue of offering or providing a prize under this paragraph, be responsible for compliance by registered participants in a prize competition with Federal law, including licensing, export control, and non-proliferation laws, and related regulations.

(K) Notice and annual report.—

(i) In general.—Not later than 30 days prior to carrying out an activity under subparagraph (A), the Secretary shall notify the Committees on Transportation and Infrastructure and Science, Space, and Technology of the House of Representatives and the Committees on Environment and Public Works and Commerce, Science, and Transportation of the Senate of the intent to use such authority.

(ii) Reports.—

(I) IN GENERAL.—The Secretary shall submit to the committees described in clause (i) on an annual basis a report on the activities carried out under subparagraph (A) in the preceding fiscal year if the Secretary exercised the authority under subparagraph (A) in that fiscal year.

(II) INFORMATION INCLUDED.—A report under this subparagraph shall include, for each prize competition under subparagraph (A)—

(aa) a description of the proposed goals of the prize competition;

(bb) an analysis of why the use of the authority under subparagraph (A) was the preferable method of achieving the goals described in item (aa) as opposed to other authorities available to the Secretary, such as contracts, grants, and cooperative agreements;

(cc) the total amount of cash prizes awarded for each prize competition, including a description of the amount of private funds contributed to the program, the source of such funds, and the manner in which the amounts of cash prizes awarded and claimed were allocated among the accounts of the Department for recording as obligations and expenditures;

(dd) the methods used for the solicitation and evaluation of submissions under each prize competition, together with an assessment of the effectiveness of such methods and lessons learned for future prize competitions;

(ee) a description of the resources, including personnel and funding, used in the execution of each prize competition together with a detailed description of the activities for which such resources were used and an accounting of how funding for execution was allocated among the accounts of the agency for recording as obligations and expenditures; and

(ff) a description of how each prize competition advanced the mission of the Department.

(c) COLLABORATIVE RESEARCH AND DEVELOPMENT.—

(1) IN GENERAL.—To encourage innovative solutions to surface transportation problems and stimulate the deployment of new technology, the Secretary may carry out, on a cost-shared basis, collaborative research and development with—

(A) non-Federal entities, including State and local governments, foreign governments, colleges and universities, corporations, institutions, partnerships, sole proprietorships, and trade associations that are incorporated or established under the laws of any State; and

(B) Federal laboratories.

(2) COOPERATION, GRANTS, CONTRACTS, AND AGREEMENTS.—Notwithstanding any other provision of law, the Secretary may directly initiate contracts, cooperative research and development agreements (as defined in section 12 of the Stevenson-Wydler Technology Innovation Act of 1980 (15 U.S.C. 3710a)) to fund, and accept funds from, the Transportation Research Board of the National Research Council of the National Academy of Sciences, State departments of transportation, cities, counties, and their agents to conduct joint transportation research and technology efforts.

(3) FEDERAL SHARE.—

(A) IN GENERAL.—The Federal share of the cost of activities carried out under a cooperative research and development agreement entered into under this chapter shall not exceed 80 percent, except that if there is substantial public interest or benefit, the Secretary may approve a greater Federal share.

(B) NON-FEDERAL SHARE.—All costs directly incurred by the non-Federal partners, including personnel, travel, and hardware development costs, shall be credited toward the non-Federal share of the cost of the activities described in subparagraph (A).

(4) USE OF TECHNOLOGY.—The research, development, or use of a technology under a cooperative research and development agreement entered into under this chapter, including the terms under which the technology may be licensed and the resulting royalties may be distributed, shall be subject to the Stevenson-Wydler Technology Innovation Act of 1980 (15 U.S.C. 3701 et seq.).

(5) WAIVER OF ADVERTISING REQUIREMENTS.—Section 6101(b) to (d) of title 41 shall not apply to a contract or agreement entered into under this chapter.

(Added Pub. L. 105–178, title V, §5102, June 9, 1998, 112 Stat. 422; amended Pub. L. 109–59, title V, §§5201(b)–(g), (i)(1), (j)(1), (k), (l), 5202(a)(1), Aug. 10, 2005, 119 Stat. 1781–1785; Pub. L. 110–244, title I, §111(g)(1), June 6, 2008, 122 Stat. 1605; Pub. L. 111–350, §5(e)(2), Jan. 4, 2011, 124 Stat. 3847; Pub. L. 112–141, div. E, title II, §52002(a), July 6, 2012, 126 Stat. 866; Pub. L. 114–94, div. A, title VI, §6019(d)(1)(C), Dec. 4, 2015, 129 Stat. 1581.)

§503. RESEARCH AND TECHNOLOGY DEVELOPMENT AND DEPLOYMENT

(a) IN GENERAL.—The Secretary shall—

(1) carry out research, development, and deployment activities that encompass the entire innovation lifecycle; and

(2) ensure that all research carried out under this section aligns with the transportation research and development strategic plan of the Secretary under section 6503 of title 49.

(b) HIGHWAY RESEARCH AND DEVELOPMENT PROGRAM.—

(1) OBJECTIVES.—In carrying out the highway research and development program, the Secretary, to address current and emerging highway transportation needs, shall—

(A) identify research topics;

(B) coordinate research and development activities;

(C) carry out research, testing, and evaluation activities;

(D) provide technology transfer and technical assistance;

(E) engage with public and private entities to spur advancement of emerging transformative innovations through accelerated market readiness; and

(F) consult frequently with public and private entities on new transportation technologies.

(2) IMPROVING HIGHWAY SAFETY.—

(A) IN GENERAL.—The Secretary shall carry out research and development activities from an integrated perspective to establish and implement systematic measures to improve highway safety.

(B) OBJECTIVES.—In carrying out this paragraph, the Secretary shall carry out research and development activities—

(i) to achieve greater long-term safety gains;

(ii) to reduce the number of fatalities and serious injuries on public roads;

(iii) to fill knowledge gaps that limit the effectiveness of research;

(iv) to support the development and implementation of State strategic highway safety plans;

(v) to advance improvements in, and use of, performance prediction analysis for decisionmaking; and

(vi) to expand technology transfer to partners and stakeholders.

(C) CONTENTS.—Research and technology activities carried out under this paragraph may include—

(i) safety assessments and decisionmaking tools;

(ii) data collection and analysis;

(iii) crash reduction projections;

(iv) low-cost safety countermeasures;

(v) innovative operational improvements and designs of roadway and roadside features;

(vi) evaluation of countermeasure costs and benefits;

(vii) development of tools for projecting impacts of safety countermeasures;

(viii) rural road safety measures;

(ix) safety measures for vulnerable road users, including bicyclists and pedestrians;

(x) safety measures to reduce the number of wildlife-vehicle collisions;

(xi) safety policy studies;

(xii) human factors studies and measures;

(xiii) safety technology deployment;

(xiv) safety workforce professional capacity building initiatives;

(xv) safety program and process improvements; and

(xvi) tools and methods to enhance safety performance, including achievement of statewide safety performance targets.

(3) IMPROVING INFRASTRUCTURE INTEGRITY.—

(A) IN GENERAL.—The Secretary shall carry out and facilitate highway and bridge infrastructure research and development activities—

(i) to maintain infrastructure integrity;

(ii) to meet user needs; and

(iii) to link Federal transportation investments to improvements in system performance.

(B) OBJECTIVES.—In carrying out this paragraph, the Secretary shall carry out research and development activities—

(i) to reduce the number of fatalities attributable to infrastructure design characteristics and work zones;

(ii) to improve the safety and security of highway infrastructure;

(iii) to increase the reliability of lifecycle performance predictions used in infrastructure design, construction, and management;

(iv) to improve the ability of transportation agencies to deliver projects that meet expectations for timeliness, quality, and cost;

(v) to reduce user delay attributable to infrastructure system performance, maintenance, rehabilitation, and construction;

(vi) to improve highway condition and performance through increased use of design, materials, construction, and maintenance innovations;

(vii) to reduce the environmental impacts of highway infrastructure through innovations in design, construction, operation, preservation, and maintenance; and

(viii) to study vulnerabilities of the transportation system to seismic activities and extreme events, including weather, and methods to reduce those vulnerabilities.

(C) CONTENTS.—Research and technology activities carried out under this paragraph may include—

(i) long-term infrastructure performance programs addressing pavements, bridges, tunnels, and other structures;

(ii) short-term and accelerated studies of infrastructure performance;

(iii) research to develop more durable infrastructure materials and systems;

(iv) advanced infrastructure design methods;

(v) accelerated highway and bridge construction;

(vi) performance-based specifications;

(vii) construction and materials quality assurance;

(viii) comprehensive and integrated infrastructure asset management;

(ix) infrastructure safety assurance;

(x) sustainable infrastructure design and construction;

(xi) infrastructure rehabilitation and preservation techniques, including techniques to rehabilitate and preserve historic infrastructure;

(xii) hydraulic, geotechnical, and aerodynamic aspects of infrastructure;

(xiii) improved highway construction technologies and practices;

(xiv) improved tools, technologies, and models for infrastructure management, including assessment and monitoring of infrastructure condition;

(xv) studies to improve flexibility and resiliency of infrastructure systems to withstand extreme weather events and climate variability;

(xvi) studies on the effectiveness of fiber-based additives to improve the durability of surface transportation materials in various geographic regions;

(xvii) studies of infrastructure resilience and other adaptation measures;

(xviii) maintenance of seismic research activities, including research carried out in conjunction with other Federal agencies to study the vulnerability of the transportation system to seismic activity and methods to reduce that vulnerability;

(xix) technology transfer and adoption of permeable, pervious, or porous paving materials, practices, and systems that are designed to minimize environmental impacts, stormwater runoff, and flooding and to treat or remove pollutants by allowing stormwater to infiltrate through the pavement in a manner similar to predevelopment hydrologic conditions; and

(xx) studies on the deployment and revenue potential of the deployment of energy and broadband infrastructure in highway rights-of-way, including potential adverse impacts of the use or nonuse of those rights-of-way.

(D) LIFECYCLE COSTS ANALYSIS STUDY.—

(i) IN GENERAL.—In this subparagraph, the term "lifecycle costs analysis" means a process for evaluating the total economic worth of a usable project segment by analyzing initial costs and discounted future costs, such as maintenance, user, reconstruction, rehabilitation, restoring, and resurfacing costs, over the life of the project segment.

(ii) STUDY.—The Comptroller General shall conduct a study of the best practices for calculating lifecycle costs and benefits for federally funded highway projects, which shall include, at a minimum, a thorough literature review and a survey of current lifecycle cost practices of State departments of transportation.

(iii) CONSULTATION.—In carrying out the study, the Comptroller shall consult with, at a minimum—

(I) the American Association of State Highway and Transportation Officials;

(II) appropriate experts in the field of lifecycle cost analysis; and

(III) appropriate industry experts and research centers.

(E) REPORT.—Not later than 1 year after the date of enactment of the Transportation Research and Innovative Technology Act of 2012, the Comptroller General shall submit to the Committee on Environment and Public Works of the Senate and the Committees on Transportation and Infrastructure and Science, Space, and Technology of the House of Representatives a report on the results of the study which shall include—

(i) a summary of the latest research on lifecycle cost analysis; and

(ii) recommendations on the appropriate—

(I) period of analysis;

(II) design period;

(III) discount rates; and

(IV) use of actual material life and maintenance cost data.

(4) STRENGTHENING TRANSPORTATION PLANNING AND ENVIRONMENTAL DECISIONMAKING.—

(A) IN GENERAL.—The Secretary may carry out research—

(i) to minimize the cost of transportation planning and environmental decisionmaking processes;

(ii) to improve transportation planning and environmental decisionmaking processes; and

(iii) to minimize the potential impact of surface transportation on the environment.

(B) OBJECTIVES.—In carrying out this paragraph the Secretary may carry out research and development activities—

(i) to minimize the cost of highway infrastructure and operations;

(ii) to reduce the potential impact of highway infrastructure and operations on the environment;

(iii) to advance improvements in environmental analyses and processes and context sensitive solutions for transportation decisionmaking;

(iv) to improve construction techniques;

(v) to accelerate construction to reduce congestion and related emissions;

(vi) to reduce the impact of highway runoff on the environment;

(vii) to improve understanding and modeling of the factors that contribute to the demand for transportation; and

(viii) to improve transportation planning decisionmaking and coordination.

(C) CONTENTS.—Research and technology activities carried out under this paragraph may include—

(i) creation of models and tools for evaluating transportation measures and transportation system designs, including the costs and benefits;

(ii) congestion reduction efforts;

(iii) transportation and economic development planning in rural areas and small communities;

(iv) improvement of State, local, and tribal government capabilities relating to surface transportation planning and the environment; and

(v) streamlining of project delivery processes.

(5) REDUCING CONGESTION, IMPROVING HIGHWAY OPERATIONS, AND ENHANCING FREIGHT PRODUCTIVITY.—

(A) IN GENERAL.—The Secretary shall carry out research under this paragraph with the goals of—

(i) addressing congestion problems;

(ii) reducing the costs of congestion;

(iii) improving freight movement;

(iv) increasing productivity; and

(v) improving the economic competitiveness of the United States.

(B) OBJECTIVES.—In carrying out this paragraph, the Secretary shall carry out research and development activities to identify, develop, and assess innovations that have the potential—

(i) to reduce traffic congestion;

(ii) to improve freight movement; and

(iii) to reduce freight-related congestion throughout the transportation network.

(C) CONTENTS.—Research and technology activities carried out under this paragraph may include—

(i) active traffic and demand management;

(ii) acceleration of the implementation of Intelligent Transportation Systems technology;

(iii) advanced transportation concepts and analysis;

(iv) arterial management and traffic signal operation;

(v) congestion pricing;

(vi) corridor management;

(vii) emergency operations;

(viii) research relating to enabling technologies and applications;

(ix) freeway management;

(x) evaluation of enabling technologies;

(xi) impacts of vehicle size and weight on congestion;

(xii) freight operations and technology;

(xiii) operations and freight performance measurement and management;

(xiv) organization and planning for operations;

(xv) planned special events management;

(xvi) real-time transportation information;

(xvii) road weather management;

(xviii) traffic and freight data and analysis tools;

(xix) traffic control devices;

(xx) traffic incident management;

(xxi) work zone management;

(xxii) communication of travel, roadway, and emergency information to persons with disabilities;

(xxiii) research on enhanced mode choice and intermodal connectivity;

(xxiv) techniques for estimating and quantifying public benefits derived from freight transportation projects; and

(xxv) other research areas to identify and address emerging needs related to freight transportation by all modes.

(6) EXPLORATORY ADVANCED RESEARCH.—The Secretary shall carry out research and development activities relating to exploratory advanced research—

(A) to leverage the targeted capabilities of the Turner-Fairbank Highway Research Center to develop technologies and innovations of national importance;

(B) to develop potentially transformational solutions to improve the durability, efficiency, environmental impact, productivity, and safety aspects of highway and intermodal transportation systems; and

(C) to support research on non-market-ready technologies in consultation with public and private entities.

(7) TURNER-FAIRBANK HIGHWAY RESEARCH CENTER.—

(A) IN GENERAL.—The Secretary shall continue to operate in the Federal Highway Administration a Turner-Fairbank Highway Research Center.

(B) USES OF THE CENTER.—The Turner-Fairbank Highway Research Center shall support innovations by leading—

(i) the conduct of highway research and development relating to emerging highway technology;

(ii) the development of understandings, tools, and techniques that provide solutions to complex technical problems through the development of economical and environmentally sensitive designs, efficient and quality-controlled construction practices, and durable materials;

(iii) the development of innovative highway products and practices;

(iv) the conduct of long-term, high-risk research to improve the materials used in highway infrastructure; and

(v) the evaluation of information from accelerated market readiness efforts, including non-market-ready technologies, in consultation with other offices of the Federal Highway Administration, the National Highway Traffic Safety Administration, and other key partners.

(8) INFRASTRUCTURE INVESTMENT NEEDS REPORT.—

(A) IN GENERAL.—Not later than July 31, 2013, and July 31 of every second year thereafter, the Secretary shall submit to the Committee on Transportation and Infrastructure of the House of Representatives and the Committee on Environment and Public Works of the Senate a report that describes estimates of the current conditions and future needs of highways, bridges, and tunnels of the United States, including—

(i) the conditions and performance of the highway network for freight movement;

(ii) intelligent transportation systems;

(iii) resilience needs; and

(iv) the backlog of current highway, bridge, and tunnel needs.

(B) COMPARISONS.—Each report under subparagraph (A) shall include all information necessary to relate and compare the conditions and service measures used in the previous biennial reports to conditions and service measures used in the current report.

(C) INCLUSIONS.—Each report under subparagraph (A) shall provide recommendations to Congress on changes to the highway performance monitoring system that address—

(i) improvements to the quality and standardization of data collection on all functional classifications of Federal-aid highways for accurate system length, lane length, and vehicle-mile of travel; and

(ii) changes to the reporting requirements authorized under section 315, to reflect recommendations under this paragraph for collection, storage, analysis, reporting, and display of data for Federal-aid highways and, to the maximum extent practical, all public roads.

(9) ANALYSIS TOOLS.—The Secretary may develop interactive modeling tools and databases that—

(A) track the full condition of highway assets, including interchanges, and the reconstruction history of those assets;

(B) can be used to assess transportation options;

(C) allow for the monitoring and modeling of network-level traffic flows on highways; and

(D) further Federal and State understanding of the importance of national and regional connectivity and the need for long-distance and interregional passenger and freight travel by highway and other surface transportation modes.

(c) TECHNOLOGY AND INNOVATION DEPLOYMENT PROGRAM.—

(1) IN GENERAL.—The Secretary shall carry out a technology and innovation deployment program relating to all aspects of highway transportation, including planning, financing, operation, structures, use of rights-of-way permissible under applicable law, materials, pavements, environment, construction, and the duration of time between project planning and project delivery, with the goals of—

(A) significantly accelerating the adoption of innovative technologies by the surface transportation community;

(B) providing leadership and incentives to demonstrate and promote state-of-the-art technologies, elevated performance standards, and new business practices in highway construction processes that result in improved safety, faster construction, reduced congestion from construction, and improved quality and user satisfaction;

(C) constructing longer-lasting highways through the use of innovative technologies and practices that lead to faster construction of efficient and safe highways and bridges;

(D) improving highway efficiency, safety, mobility, reliability, service life, environmental protection, and sustainability;

(E) developing and deploying new tools, techniques, and practices to accelerate the adoption of innovation in all aspects of highway transportation; and

(F) disseminating and evaluating information from accelerated market readiness efforts, including non-market-ready technologies, to public and private entities.

(2) IMPLEMENTATION.—

(A) IN GENERAL.—The Secretary shall promote, facilitate, and carry out the program established under paragraph (1) to distribute the products, technologies, tools, methods, or other findings that result from highway research and development activities, including research and development activities carried out under this chapter.

(B) ACCELERATED INNOVATION DEPLOYMENT.—In carrying out the program established under paragraph (1), the Secretary shall—

(i) establish and carry out demonstration programs;

(ii) provide technical assistance, and training to researchers and developers; and

(iii) develop and deploy improved tools and methods to accelerate the adoption of early-stage and proven innovative practices and technologies and, as the Secretary determines to be appropriate, support continued implementation of proven innovative practices and technologies as standard practices.

(C) IMPLEMENTATION OF FUTURE STRATEGIC HIGHWAY RESEARCH PROGRAM FINDINGS AND RESULTS.—

(i) IN GENERAL.—The Secretary, in consultation with the American Association of State Highway and Transportation Officials and the Transportation Research Board of the National Academy of Sciences, shall promote research results and products developed under the future strategic highway research program administered by the Transportation Research Board of the National Academy of Sciences.

(ii) BASIS FOR FINDINGS.—The activities carried out under this subparagraph shall be based on the report submitted to Congress by the Transportation Research Board of the National Academy of Sciences under section 510(e).

(iii) PERSONNEL.—The Secretary may use funds made available to carry out this subsection for administrative costs under this subparagraph.

(D) REPORT.—Not later than 2 years after the date of enactment of this subparagraph and every 2 years thereafter, the Secretary shall submit to the Committee on Environment and Public Works of the Senate and the Committee on Transportation and Infrastructure of the House of Representatives and make publicly available on an internet website a report that describes—

(i) the activities the Secretary has undertaken to carry out the program established under paragraph (1); and

(ii) how and to what extent the Secretary has worked to disseminate non-market-ready technologies to public and private entities.

(3) ACCELERATED IMPLEMENTATION AND DEPLOYMENT OF PAVEMENT TECHNOLOGIES.—

(A) IN GENERAL.—The Secretary shall establish and implement a program under the technology and innovation deployment program to promote, implement, deploy, demonstrate, showcase, support, and document the application of innovative pavement technologies, practices, performance, and benefits.

(B) GOALS.—The goals of the accelerated implementation and deployment of pavement technologies program shall include—

(i) the deployment of new, cost-effective designs, materials, recycled materials, and practices to extend the pavement life and performance and to improve user satisfaction;

(ii) the reduction of initial costs and lifecycle costs of pavements, including the costs of new construction, replacement, maintenance, and rehabilitation;

(iii) the deployment of accelerated construction techniques to increase safety and reduce construction time and traffic disruption and congestion;

(iv) the deployment of engineering design criteria and specifications for new and efficient practices, products, and materials for use in highway pavements;

(v) the deployment of new nondestructive and real-time pavement evaluation technologies and construction techniques; and

(vi) effective technology transfer and information dissemination to accelerate implementation of new technologies and to improve life, performance, cost effectiveness, safety, and user satisfaction.

(C) HIGH-FRICTION SURFACE TREATMENT APPLICATION STUDY.—

(i) DEFINITION OF INSTITUTION.—In this subparagraph, the term "institution" means a private sector entity, public agency, research university or other research institution, or organization representing transportation and technology leaders or other transportation stakeholders that, as determined by the Secretary, is capable of working with State highway agencies, the Federal Highway Administration, and the highway construction industry to develop and evaluate new products, design technologies, and construction methods that quickly lead to pavement improvements.

(ii) STUDY.—The Secretary shall seek to enter into an agreement with an institution to carry out a study on the use of natural and synthetic calcined bauxite as a high-friction surface treatment application on pavement.

(iii) REPORT.—Not later than 18 months after the date of enactment of the Surface Transportation Reauthorization Act of 2021, the Secretary shall submit a report on the results of the study under clause (ii) to—

(I) the Committee on Environment and Public Works of the Senate;

(II) the Committee on Transportation and Infrastructure of the House of Representatives;

(III) the Federal Highway Administration; and

(IV) the American Association of State Highway and Transportation Officials.

(D) FUNDING.—The Secretary shall obligate for each of fiscal years 2022 through 2026 from funds made available to carry out this subsection $12,000,000 to accelerate the deployment and implementation of pavement technology.

(E) PUBLICATION.—

(i) IN GENERAL.—Not less frequently than once every 3 years, the Secretary shall issue and make available to the public on an Internet website a report on the cost and benefits from deployment of new technology and innovations that substantially and directly resulted from the program established under this paragraph.

(ii) INCLUSIONS.—The report under clause (i) may include an analysis of—

(I) Federal, State, and local cost savings;

(II) project delivery time improvements;

(III) reduced fatalities;

(IV) congestion impacts;

(V) pavement monitoring and data collection practices;

(VI) pavement durability and resilience;

(VII) stormwater management;

(VIII) impacts on vehicle efficiency;

(IX) the energy efficiency of the production of paving materials and the ability of paving materials to enhance the environment and promote sustainability; and

(X) integration of renewable energy in pavement designs.

(4) ADVANCED TRANSPORTATION TECHNOLOGIES AND INNOVATIVE MOBILITY DEPLOYMENT.—

(A) IN GENERAL.—The Secretary shall provide grants to eligible entities to deploy, install, and operate advanced transportation technologies to improve safety, mobility, efficiency, system performance, intermodal connectivity, and infrastructure return on investment.

(B) CRITERIA.—The Secretary shall develop criteria for selection of an eligible entity to receive a grant under this paragraph, including how the deployment of technology will—

(i) improve the mobility of people and goods;

(ii) improve the durability and extend the life of transportation infrastructure;

(iii) reduce costs and improve return on investments, including through optimization of existing transportation capacity;

(iv) protect the environment and deliver environmental benefits that alleviate congestion and streamline traffic flow;

(v) measure and improve the operational performance of the applicable transportation network;

(vi) reduce the number and severity of traffic crashes and increase driver, passenger, and pedestrian safety;

(vii) collect, disseminate, and use real-time traffic, work zone, weather, transit, paratransit, parking, and other transportation-related information to improve mobility, reduce congestion, and provide for more efficient, accessible, and integrated transportation and transportation services;

(viii) facilitate account-based payments for transportation access and services and integrate payment systems across modes;

(ix) monitor transportation assets to improve infrastructure management, reduce maintenance costs, prioritize investment decisions, and ensure a state of good repair;

(x) deliver economic benefits by reducing delays, improving system performance, and providing for the efficient and reliable movement of goods and services;

(xi) accelerate the deployment of vehicle-to-vehicle, vehicle-to-infrastructure, vehicle-to-pedestrian, autonomous vehicles, and other technologies; or

(xii) incentivize travelers—

(I) to share trips during periods in which travel demand exceeds system capacity; or

(II) to shift trips to periods in which travel demand does not exceed system capacity.

(C) APPLICATIONS.—

(i) REQUEST.—Each fiscal year for which funding is made available for activities under this paragraph, the Secretary shall request applications in accordance with clause (ii).

(ii) CONTENTS.—An application submitted under this subparagraph shall include the following:

(I) PLAN.—A plan to deploy and provide for the long-term operation and maintenance of advanced transportation and congestion management technologies to improve safety, mobility, efficiency, system performance, and return on investment.

(II) OBJECTIVES.—Quantifiable system performance improvements, such as—

(aa) reducing traffic-related crashes, congestion, and costs;

(bb) optimizing system efficiency;

(cc) improving access to transportation services; and

(dd) facilitating payment for transportation services.

(III) RESULTS.—Quantifiable safety, mobility, and environmental benefit projections such as data-driven estimates of how the project will improve the region's transportation system efficiency and reduce traffic congestion.

(IV) PARTNERSHIPS.—A plan for partnering with the private sector or public agencies, including multimodal and multijurisdictional entities, research institutions, organizations representing transportation and technology leaders, or other transportation stakeholders.

(V) LEVERAGING.—A plan to leverage and optimize existing local and regional advanced transportation technology investments.

(D) GRANT SELECTION.—

(i) GRANT AWARDS.—Each fiscal year for which funding is made available for activities under this paragraph, the Secretary shall award grants to not less than

5 and not more than 10 eligible entities.

(ii) GEOGRAPHIC DIVERSITY.—

(I) IN GENERAL.—Subject to subclause (II), in awarding a grant under this paragraph, the Secretary shall ensure, to the extent practicable, that grant recipients represent diverse geographic areas of the United States, including urban and rural areas.

(II) RURAL SET-ASIDE.—Not less than 20 percent of the amounts made available to carry out this paragraph shall be reserved for projects serving rural areas.

(iii) TECHNOLOGY DIVERSITY.—In awarding a grant under this paragraph, the Secretary shall ensure, to the extent practicable, that grant recipients represent diverse technology solutions.

(E) USE OF GRANT FUNDS.—A grant recipient may use funds awarded under this paragraph to deploy advanced transportation and congestion management technologies, including—

(i) advanced traveler information systems;

(ii) advanced transportation management technologies;

(iii) advanced transportation technologies to improve emergency evacuation and response by Federal, State, and local authorities;

(iv) infrastructure maintenance, monitoring, and condition assessment;

(v) advanced public transportation systems;

(vi) transportation system performance data collection, analysis, and dissemination systems;

(vii) advanced safety systems, including vehicle-to-vehicle and vehicle-to-infrastructure communications, technologies associated with autonomous vehicles, and other collision avoidance technologies, including systems using cellular technology;

(viii) integration of intelligent transportation systems with the Smart Grid and other energy distribution and charging systems;

(ix) integrated corridor management systems;

(x) advanced parking reservation or variable pricing systems;

(xi) electronic pricing, toll collection, and payment systems;

(xii) technology that enhances high occupancy vehicle toll lanes, cordon pricing, or congestion pricing;

(xiii) integration of transportation service payment systems;

(xiv) advanced mobility, access, and on-demand transportation service technologies, such as dynamic ridesharing and other shared-use mobility applications and information systems to support human services for elderly and disabled individuals;

(xv) retrofitting dedicated short-range communications (DSRC) technology deployed as part of an existing pilot program to cellular vehicle-to-everything (C–V2X) technology, subject to the condition that the retrofitted technology operates only within the existing spectrum allocations for connected vehicle systems; or

(xvi) advanced transportation technologies, in accordance with the research areas described in section 6503 of title 49.

(F) REPORT TO SECRETARY.—For each eligible entity that receives a grant under this paragraph, not later than 1 year after the entity receives the grant, and each year thereafter, the entity shall submit a report to the Secretary that describes—

(i) deployment and operational costs of the project compared to the benefits and savings the project provides; and

(ii) how the project has met the original expectations projected in the deployment plan submitted with the application, such as—

(I) data on how the project has helped reduce traffic crashes, congestion, costs, and other benefits of the deployed systems;

(II) data on the effect of measuring and improving transportation system performance through the deployment of advanced technologies;

(III) the effectiveness of providing real-time integrated traffic, transit, and multimodal transportation information to the public to make informed travel decisions; and

(IV) lessons learned and recommendations for future deployment strategies to optimize transportation mobility, efficiency, multimodal system performance, and payment system performance.

(G) REPORT.—Not later than 3 years after the date that the first grant is awarded under this paragraph, and each year thereafter, the Secretary shall make available to the public on an Internet website a report that describes the effectiveness of grant recipients in meeting their projected deployment plans, including data provided under subparagraph (F) on how the program has—

(i) reduced traffic-related fatalities and injuries;

(ii) reduced traffic congestion and improved travel time reliability;

(iii) reduced transportation-related emissions;

(iv) optimized multimodal system performance;

(v) improved access to transportation alternatives;

(vi) improved integration of payment systems;

(vii) provided the public with access to real-time integrated traffic, transit, and multimodal transportation information to make informed travel decisions;

(viii) provided cost savings to transportation agencies, businesses, and the traveling public; or

(ix) provided other benefits to transportation users and the general public.

(H) ADDITIONAL GRANTS.—The Secretary may cease to provide additional grant funds to a recipient of a grant under this paragraph if—

(i) the Secretary determines from such recipient's report that the recipient is not carrying out the requirements of the grant; and

(ii) the Secretary provides written notice 60 days prior to withholding funds to the Committees on Transportation and Infrastructure and Science, Space, and Technology of the House of Representatives and the Committees on Environment and Public Works and Commerce, Science, and Transportation of the Senate.

(I) FUNDING.—

(i) IN GENERAL.—From funds made available to carry out subsection (b), this subsection, and sections 512 through 518, the Secretary shall set aside for grants awarded under subparagraph (D) $60,000,000 for each of fiscal years 2022 through 2026.

(ii) EXPENSES FOR THE SECRETARY.—Of the amounts set aside under clause (i), the Secretary may set aside $2,000,000 each fiscal year for program reporting, evaluation, and administrative costs related to this paragraph.

(J) FEDERAL SHARE.—The Federal share of the cost of a project for which a grant is awarded under this subsection shall not exceed 80 percent of the cost of the project.

(K) GRANT LIMITATION.—The Secretary may not award more than 20 percent of the amount described under subparagraph (I) in a fiscal year to a single grant recipient.

(L) EXPENSES FOR GRANT RECIPIENTS.—A grant recipient under this paragraph may use not more than 5 percent of the funds awarded each fiscal year to carry out planning and reporting requirements.

(M) GRANT FLEXIBILITY.—

(i) IN GENERAL.—If, by August 1 of each fiscal year, the Secretary determines that there are not enough grant applications that meet the requirements described in subparagraph (C) to carry out this section for a fiscal year, the Secretary shall transfer to the programs specified in clause (ii)—

(I) any of the funds reserved for the fiscal year under subparagraph (I) that the Secretary has not yet awarded under this paragraph; and

(II) an amount of obligation limitation equal to the amount of funds that the Secretary transfers under subclause (I).

(ii) PROGRAMS.—The programs referred to in clause (i) are—

(I) the program under subsection (b);

(II) the program under this subsection; and

(III) the programs under sections 512 through 518.

(iii) DISTRIBUTION.—Any transfer of funds and obligation limitation under clause (i) shall be divided among the programs referred to in that clause in the same proportions as the Secretary originally reserved funding from the programs for the fiscal year under subparagraph (I).

(N) DEFINITIONS.—In this paragraph:

(i) ELIGIBLE ENTITY.—The term "eligible entity" means a State or local government, a transit agency, metropolitan planning organization, or other political subdivision of a State or local government or a multijurisdictional group or a consortia of research institutions or academic institutions.

(ii) ADVANCED AND CONGESTION MANAGEMENT TRANSPORTATION TECHNOLOGIES.—The term "advanced transportation and congestion management technologies" means technologies that improve the efficiency, safety, or state of good repair of surface transportation systems, including intelligent transportation systems.

(iii) MULTIJURISDICTIONAL GROUP.—The term "multijurisdictional group" means any combination of State governments, local governments, metropolitan planning agencies, transit agencies, or other political subdivisions of a State for which each member of the group—

(I) has signed a written agreement to implement the advanced transportation technologies deployment initiative across jurisdictional boundaries; and

(II) is an eligible entity under this paragraph.

(5) ACCELERATED IMPLEMENTATION AND DEPLOYMENT OF ADVANCED DIGITAL CONSTRUCTION MANAGEMENT SYSTEMS.—

(A) IN GENERAL.—The Secretary shall establish and implement a program under the technology and innovation deployment program established under paragraph (1) to promote, implement, deploy, demonstrate, showcase, support, and document the application of advanced digital construction management systems, practices, performance, and benefits.

(B) GOALS.—The goals of the accelerated implementation and deployment of advanced digital construction management systems program established under subparagraph (A) shall include—

(i) accelerated State adoption of advanced digital construction management systems applied throughout the construction lifecycle (including through the design and engineering, construction, and operations phases) that—

(I) maximize interoperability with other systems, products, tools, or applications;

(II) boost productivity;

(III) manage complexity;

(IV) reduce project delays and cost overruns; and

(V) enhance safety and quality;

(ii) more timely and productive information-sharing among stakeholders through reduced reliance on paper to manage construction processes and deliverables such as blueprints, design drawings, procurement and supply-chain orders, equipment logs, daily progress reports, and punch lists;

(iii) deployment of digital management systems that enable and leverage the use of digital technologies on construction sites by contractors, such as state-of-the-art automated and connected machinery and optimized routing software that allows construction workers to perform tasks faster, safer, more accurately, and with minimal supervision;

(iv) the development and deployment of best practices for use in digital construction management;

(v) increased technology adoption and deployment by States and units of local government that enables project sponsors—

(I) to integrate the adoption of digital management systems and technologies in contracts; and

(II) to weigh the cost of digitization and technology in setting project budgets;

(vi) technology training and workforce development to build the capabilities of project managers and sponsors that enables States and units of local government—

(I) to better manage projects using advanced construction management technologies; and

(II) to properly measure and reward technology adoption across projects of the State or unit of local government;

(vii) development of guidance to assist States in updating regulations of the State to allow project sponsors and contractors—

(I) to report data relating to the project in digital formats; and

(II) to fully capture the efficiencies and benefits of advanced digital construction management systems and related technologies;

(viii) reduction in the environmental footprint of construction projects using advanced digital construction management systems resulting from elimination of congestion through more efficient projects; and

(ix) enhanced worker and pedestrian safety resulting from increased transparency.

(C) FUNDING.—For each of fiscal years 2022 through 2026, the Secretary shall obligate from funds made available to carry out this subsection $20,000,000 to accelerate the deployment and implementation of advanced digital construction management systems.

(D) PUBLICATION.—

(i) IN GENERAL.—Not less frequently than annually, the Secretary shall issue and make available to the public on a website a report on—

(I) progress made in the implementation of advanced digital management systems by States; and

(II) the costs and benefits of the deployment of new technology and innovations that substantially and directly resulted from the program established under this paragraph.

(ii) INCLUSIONS.—The report under clause (i) may include an analysis of—

(I) Federal, State, and local cost savings;

(II) project delivery time improvements;

(III) congestion impacts; and

(IV) safety improvements for roadway users and construction workers.

(6) CENTER OF EXCELLENCE.—

(A) DEFINITIONS.—In this paragraph:

(i) HIGHLY AUTOMATED VEHICLE.—The term "highly automated vehicle" means a motor vehicle that—

(I) has a taxable gross weight (as defined in section 41.4482(b)–1 of title 26, Code of Federal Regulations (or successor regulations)) of 10,000 pounds or less; and

(II) is equipped with a Level 3, Level 4, or Level 5 automated driving system (as defined in the SAE International Recommended Practice numbered J3016 and dated June 15, 2018 (or a subsequent standard adopted by the Secretary)).

(ii) NEW MOBILITY.—The term "new mobility" includes shared services such as—

(I) docked and dockless bicycles;

(II) docked and dockless electric scooters; and

(III) transportation network companies.

(B) ESTABLISHMENT.—Not later than 1 year after the date of enactment of the Surface Transportation Reauthorization Act of 2021, the Secretary shall establish a Center of Excellence to collect, conduct, and fund research on the impacts of new mobility and highly automated vehicles on land use, urban design, transportation, real estate, equity, and municipal budgets.

(C) REPORT.—Not later than 1 year after the date on which the Center of Excellence is established, the Secretary shall submit a report that describes the results of the research regarding the impacts of new mobility and highly automated vehicles to the Committees on Environment and Public Works and Commerce, Science, and Transportation of the Senate and the Committees on Transportation and Infrastructure and Energy and Commerce of the House of Representatives.

(D) PARTNERSHIPS.—In establishing the Center of Excellence under subparagraph (B), the Secretary shall enter into appropriate partnerships with any institution of higher education (as defined in section 101 of the Higher Education Act of 1965 (20 U.S.C. 1001)) or public or private research entity.

(Added Pub. L. 105–178, title V, §5103, June 9, 1998, 112 Stat. 427; amended Pub. L. 109–59, title V, §§5202(b)(1), (2), 5203(a), (b)(1), (c)(1), (d), Aug. 10, 2005, 119 Stat. 1786–1789; Pub. L. 112–141, div. E, title II, §52003(a), July 6, 2012, 126 Stat. 872; Pub. L. 114–94, div. A, title VI, §§6003, 6004, Dec. 4, 2015, 129 Stat. 1562; Pub. L. 117–58, div. A, title III, §13006(a)–(c), Nov. 15, 2021, 135 Stat. 630–637.)

§504. TRAINING AND EDUCATION

(a) NATIONAL HIGHWAY INSTITUTE.—

(1) IN GENERAL.—The Secretary shall operate in the Federal Highway Administration a National Highway Institute (in this subsection referred to as the "Institute"). The Secretary shall administer, through the Institute, the authority vested in the Secretary by this title or by any other law for the development and conduct of education and training programs relating to highways.

(2) DUTIES OF THE INSTITUTE.—In cooperation with State transportation departments, United States industry, and any national or international entity, the Institute shall develop and administer education and training programs of instruction for—

(A) Federal Highway Administration, State, and local transportation agency employees and the employees of any other applicable Federal agency;

(B) regional, State, and metropolitan planning organizations;

(C) State and local police, public safety, and motor vehicle employees; and

(D) United States citizens and foreign nationals engaged or to be engaged in surface transportation work of interest to the United States.

(3) COURSES.—

(A) IN GENERAL.—The Institute shall—

(i) develop or update existing courses in asset management, including courses that include such components as—

(I) the determination of life-cycle costs;

(II) the valuation of assets;

(III) benefit-to-cost ratio calculations; and

(IV) objective decisionmaking processes for project selection; and

(ii) continually develop courses relating to the application of emerging technologies for—

(I) transportation infrastructure applications and asset management;

(II) intelligent transportation systems;

(III) operations (including security operations);

(IV) the collection and archiving of data;

(V) reducing the amount of time required for the planning and development of transportation projects; and

(VI) the intermodal movement of individuals and freight.

(B) ADDITIONAL COURSES.—In addition to the courses developed under subparagraph (A), the Institute, in consultation with State transportation departments, metropolitan planning organizations, and the American Association of State Highway and Transportation Officials, may develop courses relating to technology, methods, techniques, engineering, construction, safety, maintenance, environmental mitigation and compliance, regulations, management, inspection, and finance.

(C) REVISION OF COURSES OFFERED.—The Institute shall periodically—

(i) review the course inventory of the Institute; and

(ii) revise or cease to offer courses based on course content, applicability, and need.

(4) SET-ASIDE; FEDERAL SHARE.—Not to exceed ½ of 1 percent of the funds apportioned to a State under section 104(b)(2) for the surface transportation block grant program shall be available for expenditure by the State transportation department for the payment of not to exceed 80 percent of the cost of tuition and direct educational expenses (excluding salaries) in connection with the education and training of employees of State and local transportation agencies in accordance with this subsection.

(5) FEDERAL RESPONSIBILITY.—

(A) IN GENERAL.—Except as provided in subparagraph (B), education and training of employees of Federal, State, and local transportation (including highway) agencies authorized under this subsection may be provided—

(i) by the Secretary at no cost to the States and local governments if the Secretary determines that provision at no cost is in the public interest; or

(ii) by the State through grants, cooperative agreements, and contracts with public and private agencies, institutions, individuals, and the Institute.

(B) PAYMENT OF FULL COST BY PRIVATE PERSONS.—Private agencies, international or foreign entities, and individuals shall pay the full cost of any education and training received by them unless the Secretary determines that a lower cost is of critical importance to the public interest.

(6) TRAINING FELLOWSHIPS; COOPERATION.—The Institute may—

(A) engage in training activities authorized under this subsection, including the granting of training fellowships; and

(B) carry out its authority independently or in cooperation with any other branch of the Federal Government or any State agency, authority, association, institution, for-profit or nonprofit corporation, other national or international entity, or other person.

(7) COLLECTION OF FEES.—

(A) GENERAL RULE.—In accordance with this subsection, the Institute may assess and collect fees solely to defray the costs of the Institute in developing or administering education and training programs under this subsection.

(B) LIMITATION.—Fees may be assessed and collected under this subsection only in a manner that may reasonably be expected to result in the collection of fees during any fiscal year in an aggregate amount that does not exceed the aggregate amount of the costs referred to in subparagraph (A) for the fiscal year.

(C) PERSONS SUBJECT TO FEES.—Fees may be assessed and collected under this subsection only with respect to—

(i) persons and entities for whom education or training programs are developed or administered under this subsection; and

(ii) persons and entities to whom education or training is provided under this subsection.

(D) AMOUNT OF FEES.—The fees assessed and collected under this subsection shall be established in a manner that ensures that the liability of any person or entity for a fee is reasonably based on the proportion of the costs referred to in subparagraph (A) that relate to the person or entity.

(E) USE.—All fees collected under this subsection shall be used to defray costs associated with the development or administration of education and training programs authorized under this subsection.

(8) RELATION TO FEES.—The funds made available to carry out this subsection may be combined with or held separate from the fees collected under paragraph (7).

(b) LOCAL TECHNICAL ASSISTANCE PROGRAM.—

(1) AUTHORITY.—The Secretary shall carry out a local technical assistance program that will provide access to surface transportation technology to—

(A) highway and transportation agencies in urbanized and rural areas;

(B) contractors that perform work for the agencies; and

(C) infrastructure security staff.

(2) GRANTS, COOPERATIVE AGREEMENTS, AND CONTRACTS.—The Secretary may make grants and enter into cooperative agreements and contracts to provide education and training, technical assistance, and related support services to—

(A) assist rural, local transportation agencies and tribal governments, and the consultants and construction personnel working for the agencies and governments, to—

(i) develop and expand expertise in road and transportation areas (including pavement, bridge, concrete structures, intermodal connections, safety management systems, intelligent transportation systems, incident response, operations, and traffic safety countermeasures);

(ii) improve roads and bridges;

(iii) enhance—

(I) programs for the movement of passengers and freight; and

(II) intergovernmental transportation planning and project selection; and

(iv) deal effectively with special transportation-related problems by preparing and providing training packages, manuals, guidelines, and technical resource materials;

(B) develop technical assistance for tourism and recreational travel;

(C) identify, package, and deliver transportation technology and traffic safety information to local jurisdictions to assist urban transportation agencies in developing and expanding their ability to deal effectively with transportation-related problems (particularly the promotion of regional cooperation);

(D) operate, in cooperation with State transportation departments and universities—

(i) local technical assistance program centers designated to provide transportation technology transfer services to rural areas and to urbanized areas; and

(ii) local technical assistance program centers designated to provide transportation technical assistance to tribal governments; and

(E) allow local transportation agencies and tribal governments, in cooperation with the private sector, to enhance new technology implementation.

(3) FEDERAL SHARE.—

(A) LOCAL TECHNICAL ASSISTANCE CENTERS.—

(i) IN GENERAL.—Subject to subparagraph (B), the Federal share of the cost of an activity carried out by a local technical assistance center under paragraphs (1) and (2) shall be 50 percent.

(ii) NON-FEDERAL SHARE.—The non-Federal share of the cost of an activity described in clause (i) may consist of amounts provided to a recipient under subsection (e) or section 505, up to 100 percent of the non-Federal share.

(B) TRIBAL TECHNICAL ASSISTANCE CENTERS.—The Federal share of the cost of an activity carried out by a tribal technical assistance center under paragraph (2)(D)(ii) shall be 100 percent.

(c) RESEARCH FELLOWSHIPS.—

(1) GENERAL AUTHORITY.—The Secretary, acting either independently or in cooperation with other Federal departments, agencies, and instrumentalities, may make grants for research fellowships for any purpose for which research is authorized by this chapter.

(2) DWIGHT DAVID EISENHOWER TRANSPORTATION FELLOWSHIP PROGRAM.—

(A) IN GENERAL.—The Secretary shall establish and implement a transportation research fellowship program for the purpose of attracting qualified students to the field of transportation, which program shall be known as the "Dwight David Eisenhower Transportation Fellowship Program".

(B) USE OF AMOUNTS.—Amounts provided to institutions of higher education to carry out this paragraph shall be used to provide direct support of student expenses.

(d) GARRETT A. MORGAN TECHNOLOGY AND TRANSPORTATION EDUCATION PROGRAM.—

(1) IN GENERAL.—The Secretary shall establish the Garrett A. Morgan Technology and Transportation Education Program to improve the preparation of students, particularly women and minorities, in science, technology, engineering, and mathematics through curriculum development and other activities related to

transportation.

(2) AUTHORIZED ACTIVITIES.—The Secretary shall award grants under this subsection on the basis of competitive peer review. Grants awarded under this subsection may be used for enhancing science, technology, engineering, and mathematics at the elementary and secondary school level through such means as—

(A) internships that offer students experience in the transportation field;

(B) programs that allow students to spend time observing scientists and engineers in the transportation field; and

(C) developing relevant curriculum that uses examples and problems related to transportation.

(3) APPLICATION AND REVIEW PROCEDURES.—

(A) IN GENERAL.—An entity described in subparagraph (C) seeking funding under this subsection shall submit an application to the Secretary at such time, in such manner, and containing such information as the Secretary may require. Such application, at a minimum, shall include a description of how the funds will be used to serve the purposes described in paragraph (2).

(B) PRIORITY.—In making awards under this subsection, the Secretary shall give priority to applicants that will encourage the participation of women and minorities.

(C) ELIGIBILITY.—Local educational agencies and State educational agencies, which may enter into a partnership agreement with institutions of higher education, businesses, or other entities, shall be eligible to apply for grants under this subsection.

(4) DEFINITIONS.—In this subsection, the following definitions apply:

(A) INSTITUTION OF HIGHER EDUCATION.—The term "institution of higher education" has the meaning given that term in section 101 of the Higher Education Act of 1965 (20 U.S.C. 1001).

(B) LOCAL EDUCATIONAL AGENCY.—The term "local educational agency" has the meaning given that term in section 8101 of the Elementary and Secondary Education Act of 1965.

(C) STATE EDUCATIONAL AGENCY.—The term "State educational agency" has the meaning given that term in section 8101 of the Elementary and Secondary Education Act of 1965.

(e) SURFACE TRANSPORTATION WORKFORCE DEVELOPMENT, TRAINING, AND EDUCATION.—

(1) FUNDING.—Subject to project approval by the Secretary, a State may obligate funds apportioned to the State under paragraphs (1) through (4) of section 104(b) for surface transportation workforce development, training, and education, including—

(A) tuition and direct educational expenses, excluding salaries, in connection with the education and training of employees of State and local transportation agencies;

(B) employee professional development;

(C) student internships;

(D) pre-apprenticeships, apprenticeships, and career opportunities for on-the-job training;

(E) university, college, community college, or vocational school support;

(F) education activities, including outreach, to develop interest and promote participation in surface transportation careers;

(G) activities associated with workforce training and employment services, such as targeted outreach and partnerships with industry, economic development organizations, workforce development boards, and labor organizations;

(H) activities carried out by the National Highway Institute under subsection (a); and

(I) local technical assistance programs under subsection (b).

(2) FEDERAL SHARE.—The Federal share of the cost of activities carried out in accordance with this subsection shall be 100 percent, except for activities carried out under paragraph (1)(I), for which the Federal share shall be 50 percent.

(3) SURFACE TRANSPORTATION WORKFORCE DEVELOPMENT, TRAINING, AND EDUCATION DEFINED.—In this subsection, the term "surface transportation workforce development, training, and education" means activities associated with surface transportation career awareness, student transportation career preparation, and training and professional development for surface transportation workers, including—

(A) activities for women and minorities;

(B) activities that address current workforce gaps, such as work on construction projects, of State and local transportation agencies;

(C) activities to develop a robust surface transportation workforce with new skills resulting from emerging transportation technologies; and

(D) activities to attract new sources of job-creating investment.

(f) TRANSPORTATION EDUCATION AND TRAINING DEVELOPMENT AND DEPLOYMENT PROGRAM.—

(1) ESTABLISHMENT.—The Secretary shall establish a program to make grants to educational institutions or State departments of transportation, in partnership with industry and relevant Federal departments and agencies—

(A) to develop, test, and review new curricula and education programs to train individuals at all levels of the transportation workforce; or

(B) to implement the new curricula and education programs to provide for hands-on career opportunities to meet current and future needs.

(2) SELECTION OF GRANT RECIPIENTS.—In selecting applications for awards under this subsection, the Secretary may consider—

(A) the degree to which the new curricula or education program meets the specific current or future needs of a segment of the transportation industry, States, or regions;

(B) providing for practical experience and on-the-job training;

(C) proposals oriented toward practitioners in the field rather than the support and growth of the research community;

(D) the degree to which the new curricula or program will provide training in areas other than engineering, such as business administration, economics, information technology, environmental science, and law;

(E) programs or curricula that train professionals for work in the transportation field, such as construction, materials, information technology, environmental science, urban planning, and industrial or emerging technology; and

(F) the commitment of industry or a State's department of transportation to the program.

(3) REPORTING.—The Secretary shall establish minimum reporting requirements for grant recipients under this subsection, which may include, with respect to a program carried out with a grant under this subsection—

(A) the percentage or number of program participants that are employed during the second quarter after exiting the program;

(B) the percentage or number of program participants that are employed during the fourth quarter after exiting the program;

(C) the median earnings of program participants that are employed during the second quarter after exiting the program;

(D) the percentage or number of program participants that obtain a recognized postsecondary credential or a secondary school diploma (or a recognized equivalent) during participation in the program or by not later than 1 year after exiting the program; and

(E) the percentage or number of program participants that, during a program year—

(i) are in an education or training program that leads to a recognized postsecondary credential or employment; and

(ii) are achieving measurable skill gains toward such a credential or employment.

(4) LIMITATIONS.—The amount of a grant under this subsection shall not exceed $300,000 per year. After a recipient has received 3 years of Federal funding under this subsection, Federal funding may equal not more than 75 percent of a grantee's program costs.

(g) FREIGHT CAPACITY BUILDING PROGRAM.—

(1) ESTABLISHMENT.—The Secretary shall establish a freight planning capacity building initiative to support enhancements in freight transportation planning in order to—

(A) better target investments in freight transportation systems to maintain efficiency and productivity; and

(B) strengthen the decisionmaking capacity of State transportation departments and local transportation agencies with respect to freight transportation planning and systems.

(2) AGREEMENTS.—The Secretary shall enter into agreements to support and carry out administrative and management activities relating to the governance of the freight planning capacity initiative.

(3) STAKEHOLDER INVOLVEMENT.—In carrying out this section, the Secretary shall consult with the Association of Metropolitan Planning Organizations, the American Association of State Highway and Transportation Officials, and other freight planning stakeholders, including the other Federal agencies, State transportation departments, local governments, nonprofit entities, academia, and the private sector.

(4) ELIGIBLE ACTIVITIES.—The freight planning capacity building initiative shall

include research, training, and education in the following areas:

(A) The identification and dissemination of best practices in freight transportation.

(B) Providing opportunities for freight transportation staff to engage in peer exchange.

(C) Refinement of data and analysis tools used in conjunction with assessing freight transportation needs.

(D) Technical assistance to State transportation departments and local transportation agencies reorganizing to address freight transportation issues.

(E) Facilitating relationship building between governmental and private entities involved in freight transportation.

(F) Identifying ways to target the capacity of State transportation departments and local transportation agencies to address freight considerations in operations, security, asset management, and environmental stewardship in connection with long-range multimodal transportation planning and project implementation.

(5) FEDERAL SHARE.—The Federal share of the cost of an activity carried out under this section shall be up to 100 percent, and such funds shall remain available until expended.

(6) USE OF FUNDS.—Funds made available for the program established under this subsection may be used for research, program development, information collection and dissemination, and technical assistance. The Secretary may use such funds independently or make grants to and enter into contracts and cooperative agreements with a Federal agency, State agency, local agency, federally recognized Indian tribal government or tribal consortium, authority, association, nonprofit or for-profit corporation, or institution of higher education, to carry out the purposes of this subsection.

(h) CENTERS FOR SURFACE TRANSPORTATION EXCELLENCE.—

(1) IN GENERAL.—The Secretary shall make grants under this section to establish and maintain centers for surface transportation excellence.

(2) GOALS.—The goals of a center referred to in paragraph (1) shall be to promote and support strategic national surface transportation programs and activities relating to the work of State departments of transportation in the areas of environment, surface transportation safety, rural safety, and project finance.

(3) ROLE OF THE CENTERS.—To achieve the goals set forth in paragraph (2), any centers established under paragraph (1) shall provide technical assistance, information sharing of best practices, and training in the use of tools and decisionmaking processes that can assist States in effectively implementing surface transportation programs, projects, and policies.

(4) PROGRAM ADMINISTRATION.—

(A) COMPETITION.—A party entering into a contract, cooperative agreement, or other transaction with the Secretary under this subsection, or receiving a grant to perform research or provide technical assistance under this subsection, shall be selected on a competitive basis.

(B) STRATEGIC PLAN.—The Secretary shall require each center to develop a multiyear strategic plan, that—

(i) is submitted to the Secretary at such time as the Secretary requires; and

(ii) describes—

(I) the activities to be undertaken by the center; and

(II) how the work of the center will be coordinated with the activities of the Federal Highway Administration and the various other research, development, and technology transfer activities authorized under this chapter.

(i) USE OF FUNDS.—The Secretary may use funds made available to carry out this section to carry out activities related to workforce development and technical assistance and training if—

(1) the activities are authorized by another provision of this title; and

(2) the activities are for entities other than employees of the Secretary, such as States, units of local government, Federal land management agencies, and Tribal governments.

(Added Pub. L. 105–178, title V, §5104, June 9, 1998, 112 Stat. 429; amended Pub. L. 109–59, title V, §5204(a)(1), (b), (d)(1), (e), (h)(1), Aug. 10, 2005, 119 Stat. 1790, 1792–1794; Pub. L. 112–141, div. E, title II, §52004, July 6, 2012, 126 Stat. 880; Pub. L. 114–94, div. A, title I, §1109(c)(4), Dec. 4, 2015, 129 Stat. 1343; Pub. L. 114–95, title IX, §9215(vvv), Dec. 10, 2015, 129 Stat. 2191; Pub. L. 117–58, div. A, title I, §11525(s), title III, §13007, Nov. 15, 2021, 135 Stat. 608, 639.)

§505. STATE PLANNING AND RESEARCH

(a) GENERAL RULE.—Two percent of the sums apportioned to a State for fiscal year 1998 and each fiscal year thereafter under paragraphs (1) through (5) of section 104(b) shall be available for expenditure by the State, in consultation with the Secretary, only for the following purposes:

(1) Engineering and economic surveys and investigations.

(2) The planning of future highway programs and local public transportation systems and the planning of the financing of such programs and systems, including metropolitan and statewide planning under sections 134 and 135.

(3) Development and implementation of management systems, plans, and processes under sections 119, 148, 149, and 167.

(4) Studies of the economy, safety, and convenience of surface transportation systems and the desirable regulation and equitable taxation of such systems.

(5) Research, development, and technology transfer activities necessary in connection with the planning, design, construction, management, and maintenance of highway, public transportation, and intermodal transportation systems.

(6) Study, research, and training on the engineering standards and construction materials for transportation systems described in paragraph (5), including the evaluation and accreditation of inspection and testing and the regulation and taxation of their use.

(7) The conduct of activities relating to the planning of real-time monitoring elements.

(b) MINIMUM EXPENDITURES ON RESEARCH, DEVELOPMENT, AND TECHNOLOGY TRANSFER ACTIVITIES.—

(1) IN GENERAL.—Subject to paragraph (2), not less than 25 percent of the funds subject to subsection (a) that are apportioned to a State for a fiscal year shall be expended by the State for research, development, and technology transfer activities

described in subsection (a), relating to highway, public transportation, and intermodal transportation systems.

(2) WAIVERS.—The Secretary may waive the application of paragraph (1) with respect to a State for a fiscal year if the State certifies to the Secretary for the fiscal year that total expenditures by the State for transportation planning under sections 134 and 135 will exceed 75 percent of the funds described in paragraph (1) and the Secretary accepts such certification.

(3) NONAPPLICABILITY OF ASSESSMENT.—Funds expended under paragraph (1) shall not be considered to be part of the extramural budget of the agency for the purpose of section 9 of the Small Business Act (15 U.S.C. 638).

(c) IMPLEMENTATION OF FUTURE STRATEGIC HIGHWAY RESEARCH PROGRAM FINDINGS AND RESULTS.—

(1) FUNDS.—A State shall make available to the Secretary to carry out section 503(c)(2)(C) a percentage of funds subject to subsection (a) that are apportioned to that State, that is agreed to by ¾ of States for each of fiscal years 2013 and 2014.

(2) TREATMENT OF FUNDS.—Funds expended under paragraph (1) shall not be considered to be part of the extramural budget of the agency for the purpose of section 9 of the Small Business Act (15 U.S.C. 638).

(d) FEDERAL SHARE.—The Federal share of the cost of a project carried out using funds subject to subsection (a) shall be 80 percent unless the Secretary determines that the interests of the Federal-aid highway program would be best served by decreasing or eliminating the non-Federal share.

(e) ADMINISTRATION OF SUMS.—Funds subject to subsection (a) shall be combined and administered by the Secretary as a single fund and shall be available for obligation for the period described in section 118(b).

(Added Pub. L. 105–178, title V, §5105, June 9, 1998, 112 Stat. 432; amended Pub. L. 109–59, title V, §5205, Aug. 10, 2005, 119 Stat. 1795; Pub. L. 112–141, div. E, title II, §52005, July 6, 2012, 126 Stat. 882; Pub. L. 114–94, div. A, title I, §1104(e)(6), Dec. 4, 2015, 129 Stat. 1332.)

[§§506, 507. REPEALED. PUB. L. 112–141, DIV. E, TITLE II, §§52006(A), 52007(A), JULY 6, 2012, 126 STAT. 882]

Section 506, added Pub. L. 105–178, title V, §5106, June 9, 1998, 112 Stat. 433; amended Pub. L. 109–59, title V, §5206(a), Aug. 10, 2005, 119 Stat. 1795, related to international highway transportation outreach program.

A prior section 506, added Pub. L. 90–495, §30, Aug. 23, 1968, 82 Stat. 832; amended Pub. L. 91–605, title I, §137, Dec. 31, 1970, 84 Stat. 1735, related to replacement housing, prior to repeal by Pub. L. 91–646, title II, §220(a)(10), Jan. 2, 1971, 84 Stat. 1903.

Section 507, added Pub. L. 105–178, title V, §5107, June 9, 1998, 112 Stat. 434; amended Pub. L. 109–59, title V, §5207(a), Aug. 10, 2005, 119 Stat. 1797, related to surface transportation-environmental cooperative research program.

A prior section 507, added Pub. L. 90–495, §30, Aug. 23, 1968, 82 Stat. 832, related to expenses incidental to transfer of property, prior to repeal by Pub. L. 91–646, title II, §220(a)(10), Jan. 2, 1971, 84 Stat. 1903.

§508. Repealed. Pub. L. 114–94, div. A, title VI, 6019(d)(1)(A), Dec. 4, 2015, 129 Stat. 1581]

CHAPTER 5—RESEARCH, TECHNOLOGY, AND EDUCATION

[§508. Repealed. Pub. L. 114–94, div. A, title VI, §6019(d)(1)(A), Dec. 4, 2015, 129 Stat. 1581]

Section, added Pub. L. 105–178, title V, §5108, June 9, 1998, 112 Stat. 435; amended Pub. L. 109–59, title V, §5208(a), Aug. 10, 2005, 119 Stat. 1798; Pub. L. 112–141, div. E, title II, §52013, July 6, 2012, 126 Stat. 897, related to transportation research and development strategic planning.

A prior section 508, added Pub. L. 90–495, §30, Aug. 23, 1968, 82 Stat. 833, related to highway relocation services, prior to repeal by Pub. L. 91–646, title II, §220(a)(10), Jan. 2, 1971, 84 Stat. 1903.

[§509. Repealed. Pub. L. 112–141, div. E, title II, §52008(a), July 6, 2012, 126 Stat. 882]

Section, added Pub. L. 109–59, title V, §5209(a), Aug. 10, 2005, 119 Stat. 1800, related to national cooperative freight transportation research program.

A prior section 509, added Pub. L. 90–495, §30, Aug. 23, 1968, 82 Stat. 833, related to relocation assistance programs on Federal highway projects, prior to repeal by Pub. L. 91–646, title II, §220(a)(10), Jan. 2, 1971, 84 Stat. 1903.

§510. Future strategic highway research program

(a) Establishment.—The Secretary, in consultation with the American Association of State Highway and Transportation Officials, shall establish and carry out, acting through the National Research Council of the National Academy of Sciences, the future strategic highway research program.

(b) Cooperative Agreements.—The Secretary may make grants to, and enter into cooperative agreements with, the American Association of State Highway and Transportation Officials and the National Academy of Sciences to carry out such activities under this section as the Secretary determines are appropriate.

(c) Program Priorities.—

(1) Program elements.—The program established under this section shall be based on the National Research Council Special Report 260, entitled "Strategic Highway Research: Saving Lives, Reducing Congestion, Improving Quality of Life" and the results of the detailed planning work subsequently carried out in 2002 and 2003 to identify the research areas through National Cooperative Research Program Project 20–58. The research program shall include an analysis of the following:

(A) Renewal of aging highway infrastructure with minimal impact to users of the facilities.

(B) Driving behavior and likely crash causal factors to support improved countermeasures.

(C) Reducing highway congestion due to nonrecurring congestion.

(D) Planning and designing new road capacity to meet mobility, economic, environmental, and community needs.

(2) Dissemination of results.—The research results of the program, expressed in terms of technologies, methodologies, and other appropriate categorizations, shall be disseminated to practicing engineers for their use, as soon as practicable.

(d) Program Administration.—In carrying out the program under this section, the National Research Council shall ensure, to the maximum extent practicable, that—

(1) projects and researchers are selected to conduct research for the program on the basis of merit and open solicitation of proposals and review by panels of appropriate experts;

(2) State department of transportation officials and other stakeholders, as appropriate, are involved in the governance of the program at the overall program level and technical level through the use of expert panels and committees;

(3) the Council acquires a qualified, permanent core staff with the ability and expertise to manage the program and multiyear budget; and

(4) there is no duplication of research effort between the program and any other research effort of the Department.

(e) REPORT ON IMPLEMENTATION OF RESULTS.—

(1) REPORT.—The Transportation Research Board of the National Research Council shall complete a report on the strategies and administrative structure to be used for implementation of the results of the future strategic highway research program.

(2) COMPONENTS.—The report under paragraph (1) shall include with respect to the program—

(A) an identification of the most promising results of research under the program (including the persons most likely to use the results);

(B) a discussion of potential incentives for, impediments to, and methods of, implementing those results;

(C) an estimate of costs of implementation of those results; and

(D) recommendations on methods by which implementation of those results should be conducted, coordinated, and supported in future years, including a discussion of the administrative structure and organization best suited to carry out those recommendations.

(3) CONSULTATION.—In developing the report, the Transportation Research Board shall consult with a wide variety of stakeholders, including—

(A) the Federal Highway Administration;

(B) the National Highway Traffic Safety Administration; and

(C) the American Association of State Highway and Transportation Officials.

(4) SUBMISSION.—Not later than February 1, 2009, the report shall be submitted to the Committee on Environment and Public Works of the Senate and the Committee on Transportation and Infrastructure of the House of Representatives.

(f) FUNDING.—

(1) FEDERAL SHARE.—The Federal share of the cost of an activity carried out using amounts made available under a grant or cooperative agreement under this section shall be 100 percent, and such funds shall remain available until expended.

(2) ADVANCE PAYMENTS.—The Secretary may make advance payments as necessary to carry out the program under this section.

(g) LIMITATION OF REMEDIES.—

(1) SAME REMEDY AS IF UNITED STATES.—The remedy against the United States provided by sections 1346(b) and 2672 of title 28 for injury, loss of property, personal injury, or death shall apply to any claim against the National Academy of Sciences for money damages for injury, loss of property, personal injury, or death caused by

any negligent or wrongful act or omission by employees and individuals described in paragraph (3) arising from activities conducted under or in connection with this section. Any such claim shall be subject to the limitations and exceptions which would be applicable to such claim if such claim were against the United States. With respect to any such claim, the Secretary shall be treated as the head of the appropriate Federal agency for purposes of sections 2672 and 2675 of title 28.

(2) EXCLUSIVENESS OF REMEDY.—The remedy referred to in paragraph (1) shall be exclusive of any other civil action or proceeding for the purpose of determining liability arising from any such act or omission without regard to when the act or omission occurred.

(3) TREATMENT.—Employees of the National Academy of Sciences and other individuals appointed by the president of the National Academy of Sciences and acting on its behalf in connection with activities carried out under this section shall be treated as if they are employees of the Federal Government under section 2671 of title 28 for purposes of a civil action or proceeding with respect to a claim described in paragraph (1). The civil action or proceeding shall proceed in the same manner as any proceeding under chapter 171 of title 28 or action against the United States filed pursuant to section 1346(b) of title 28 and shall be subject to the limitations and exceptions applicable to such a proceeding or action.

(4) SOURCES OF PAYMENTS.—Payment of any award, compromise, or settlement of a civil action or proceeding with respect to a claim described in paragraph (1) shall be paid first out of insurance maintained by the National Academy of Sciences, second from funds made available to carry out this section, and then from sums made available under section 1304 of title 31. For purposes of such section, such an award, compromise, or settlement shall be deemed to be a judgment, award, or settlement payable under section 2414 or 2672 of title 28. The Secretary may establish a reserve of funds to carry out this section for making payments under this paragraph.

(h) IMPLEMENTATION.—Notwithstanding any other provision of this section, the Secretary may use funds made available to carry out this section for implementation of research products related to the future strategic highway research program, including development, demonstration, evaluation, and technology transfer activities.

(Added Pub. L. 109–59, title V, §5210(a), Aug. 10, 2005, 119 Stat. 1801; amended Pub. L. 111–322, title II, §2203(d), Dec. 22, 2010, 124 Stat. 3526.)

§511. MULTISTATE CORRIDOR OPERATIONS AND MANAGEMENT

(a) IN GENERAL.—The Secretary shall encourage multistate cooperative agreements, coalitions, or other arrangements to promote regional cooperation, planning, and shared project implementation for programs and projects to improve transportation system management and operations.

(b) INTERSTATE ROUTE 95 CORRIDOR COALITION TRANSPORTATION SYSTEMS MANAGEMENT AND OPERATIONS.—The Secretary shall make grants under this subsection to States to continue intelligent transportation system management and operations in the Interstate Route 95 corridor coalition region initiated under the Intermodal Surface Transportation Efficiency Act of 1991 (Public Law 102–240).

(Added Pub. L. 109–59, title V, §5211(a), Aug. 10, 2005, 119 Stat. 1804.)

§512. NATIONAL ITS PROGRAM PLAN

(a) IN GENERAL.—

(1) UPDATES.—Not later than 1 year after the date of enactment of the SAFETEA–LU, the Secretary, in consultation with interested stakeholders (including State transportation departments) shall develop a 5-year National Intelligent Transportation System (in this section referred to as "ITS") program plan.

(2) SCOPE.—The National ITS program plan shall—

(A) specify the goals, objectives, and milestones for the research and deployment of intelligent transportation systems in the contexts of—

(i) major metropolitan areas;

(ii) smaller metropolitan and rural areas; and

(iii) commercial vehicle operations;

(B) specify the manner in which specific programs and projects will achieve the goals, objectives, and milestones referred to in subparagraph (A), including consideration of a 5-year timeframe for the goals and objectives;

(C) identify activities that provide for the dynamic development, testing, and necessary revision of standards and protocols to promote and ensure interoperability in the implementation of intelligent transportation system technologies, including actions taken to establish standards; and

(D) establish a cooperative process with State and local governments for—

(i) determining desired surface transportation system performance levels; and

(ii) developing plans for accelerating the incorporation of specific intelligent transportation system capabilities into surface transportation systems.

(b) REPORTING.—The National ITS program plan shall be submitted and biennially updated.

(Added Pub. L. 109–59, title V, §5301(a), Aug. 10, 2005, 119 Stat. 1804; amended Pub. L. 114–94, div. A, title VI, §6019(d)(1)(D), Dec. 4, 2015, 129 Stat. 1581.)

§513. USE OF FUNDS FOR ITS ACTIVITIES

(a) DEFINITIONS.—In this section, the following definitions apply:

(1) ELIGIBLE ENTITY.—The term "eligible entity" means a State or local government, tribal government, transit agency, public toll authority, metropolitan planning organization, other political subdivision of a State or local government, or a multistate or multijurisdictional group applying through a single lead applicant.

(2) MULTIJURISDICTIONAL GROUP.—The term "multijurisdictional group" means a combination of State governments, local governments, metropolitan planning agencies, transit agencies, or other political subdivisions of a State that—

(A) have signed a written agreement to implement an activity that meets the grant criteria under this section; and

(B) is comprised of at least 2 members, each of whom is an eligible entity.

(b) PURPOSE.—The purpose of this section is to develop, administer, communicate, and promote the use of products of research, technology, and technology transfer programs.

(c) ITS ADOPTION.—

(1) INNOVATIVE TECHNOLOGIES AND STRATEGIES.—The Secretary shall encourage

the deployment of ITS technologies that will improve the performance of the National Highway System in such areas as traffic operations, emergency response, incident management, surface transportation network management, freight management, traffic flow information, and congestion management by accelerating the adoption of innovative technologies through the use of—

(A) demonstration programs;

(B) grant funding;

(C) incentives to eligible entities; and

(D) other tools, strategies, or methods that will result in the deployment of innovative ITS technologies.

(2) Comprehensive plan.—To carry out this section, the Secretary shall develop a detailed and comprehensive plan that addresses the manner in which incentives may be adopted, as appropriate, through the existing deployment activities carried out by surface transportation modal administrations.

(Added Pub. L. 109–59, title V, §5302(a), Aug. 10, 2005, 119 Stat. 1805; amended Pub. L. 112–141, div. E, title III, §53001, July 6, 2012, 126 Stat. 897.)

§514. Goals and purposes

(a) Goals.—The goals of the intelligent transportation system program include—

(1) enhancement of surface transportation efficiency and facilitation of intermodalism and international trade to enable existing facilities to meet a significant portion of future transportation needs, including public access to employment, goods, and services and to reduce regulatory, financial, and other transaction costs to public agencies and system users;

(2) achievement of national transportation safety goals, including enhancement of safe operation of motor vehicles and nonmotorized vehicles and improved emergency response to collisions, with particular emphasis on decreasing the number and severity of collisions;

(3) protection and enhancement of the natural environment and communities affected by surface transportation, with particular emphasis on assisting State and local governments to achieve national environmental goals;

(4) accommodation of the needs of all users of surface transportation systems, including operators of commercial motor vehicles, passenger motor vehicles, motorcycles, bicycles, and pedestrians (including individuals with disabilities);

(5) enhancement of national defense mobility and improvement of the ability of the United States to respond to security-related or other manmade emergencies and natural disasters; and

(6) enhancement of the national freight system and support to national freight policy goals.

(b) Purposes.—The Secretary shall implement activities under the intelligent transportation system program, at a minimum—

(1) to expedite, in both metropolitan and rural areas, deployment and integration of intelligent transportation systems for consumers of passenger and freight transportation;

(2) to ensure that Federal, State, and local transportation officials have adequate knowledge of intelligent transportation systems for consideration in the transportation

planning process;

(3) to improve regional cooperation and operations planning for effective intelligent transportation system deployment;

(4) to promote the innovative use of private resources in support of intelligent transportation system development;

(5) to facilitate, in cooperation with the motor vehicle industry, the introduction of vehicle-based safety enhancing systems;

(6) to support the application of intelligent transportation systems that increase the safety and efficiency of commercial motor vehicle operations;

(7) to develop a workforce capable of developing, operating, and maintaining intelligent transportation systems;

(8) to provide continuing support for operations and maintenance of intelligent transportation systems;

(9) to ensure a systems approach that includes cooperation among vehicles, infrastructure, and users; and

(10) to assist in the development of cybersecurity research in cooperation with relevant modal administrations of the Department of Transportation and other Federal agencies to help prevent hacking, spoofing, and disruption of connected and automated transportation vehicles.

(Added Pub. L. 112–141, div. E, title III, §53002(a), July 6, 2012, 126 Stat. 898; amended Pub. L. 114–94, div. A, title VI, §§6005, 6006, Dec. 4, 2015, 129 Stat. 1567.)

§515. GENERAL AUTHORITIES AND REQUIREMENTS

(a) SCOPE.—Subject to the provisions of sections 512 through 518, the Secretary shall conduct an ongoing intelligent transportation system program—

(1) to research, develop, and operationally test intelligent transportation systems; and

(2) to provide technical assistance in the nationwide application of those systems as a component of the surface transportation systems of the United States.

(b) POLICY.—Intelligent transportation system research projects and operational tests funded pursuant to sections 512 through 518 shall encourage and not displace public-private partnerships or private sector investment in those tests and projects.

(c) COOPERATION WITH GOVERNMENTAL, PRIVATE, AND EDUCATIONAL ENTITIES.—The Secretary shall carry out the intelligent transportation system program in cooperation with State and local governments and other public entities, the private sector firms of the United States, the Federal laboratories, and institutions of higher education, including historically Black colleges and universities and other minority institutions of higher education.

(d) CONSULTATION WITH FEDERAL OFFICIALS.—In carrying out the intelligent transportation system program, the Secretary shall consult with the heads of other Federal agencies, as appropriate.

(e) TECHNICAL ASSISTANCE, TRAINING, AND INFORMATION.—The Secretary may provide technical assistance, training, and information to State and local governments seeking to implement, operate, maintain, or evaluate intelligent transportation system technologies and services.

(f) TRANSPORTATION PLANNING.—The Secretary may provide funding to support adequate consideration of transportation systems management and operations, including intelligent transportation systems, within metropolitan and statewide transportation planning processes.

(g) INFORMATION CLEARINGHOUSE.—

(1) IN GENERAL.—The Secretary shall—

(A) maintain a repository for technical and safety data collected as a result of federally sponsored projects carried out under sections 512 through 518; and

(B) make, on request, that information (except for proprietary information and data) readily available to all users of the repository at an appropriate cost.

(2) AGREEMENT.—

(A) IN GENERAL.—The Secretary may enter into an agreement with a third party for the maintenance of the repository for technical and safety data under paragraph (1)(A).

(B) FEDERAL FINANCIAL ASSISTANCE.—If the Secretary enters into an agreement with an entity for the maintenance of the repository, the entity shall be eligible for Federal financial assistance under this section.

(3) AVAILABILITY OF INFORMATION.—Information in the repository shall not be subject to sections 552 and 555 of title 5, United States Code.

(h) ADVISORY COMMITTEE.—

(1) IN GENERAL.—The Secretary shall establish an Advisory Committee (referred to in this subsection as the "Advisory Committee") to advise the Secretary on carrying out sections 512 through 518.

(2) MEMBERSHIP.—The Advisory Committee shall have no more than 25 members, be balanced between metropolitan and rural interests, and include, at a minimum—

(A) a representative from a State highway department;

(B) a representative from a local highway department who is not from a metropolitan planning organization;

(C) a representative from a State, local, or regional transit agency;

(D) a representative from a State, local, or regional wildlife, land use, or resource management agency;

(E) a representative from a metropolitan planning organization;

(F) a representative of a national transit association;

(G) a representative of a national, State, or local transportation agency or association;

(H) a private sector user of intelligent transportation system technologies;

(I) a private sector developer of intelligent transportation system technologies, which may include emerging vehicle technologies;

(J) an academic researcher with expertise in computer science or another information science field related to intelligent transportation systems, and who is not an expert on transportation issues;

(K) an academic researcher who is a civil engineer;

(L) an academic researcher who is a social scientist with expertise in transportation issues;

(M) an academic researcher who is a biological or ecological scientist with expertise in transportation issues;

(N) a representative from a nonprofit group representing the intelligent transportation system industry;

(O) a representative from a public interest group concerned with safety;

(P) a representative of a labor organization;

(Q) a representative of a mobility-providing entity;

(R) an expert in traffic management;

(S) a representative from a public interest group concerned with the impact of the transportation system on land use and residential patterns;

(T) a representative from a public interest group concerned with the impact of the transportation system on terrestrial and aquatic species and the habitat of those species; and

(U) members with expertise in planning, safety, telecommunications, and operations;

(V) an expert in cybersecurity; and

(W) an automobile manufacturer.

(3) TERM.—

(A) IN GENERAL.—The term of a member of the Advisory Committee shall be 3 years.

(B) RENEWAL.—On expiration of the term of a member of the Advisory Committee, the member—

(i) may be reappointed; or

(ii) if the member is not reappointed under clause (i), may serve until a new member is appointed.

(4) MEETINGS.—The Advisory Committee—

(A) shall convene not less frequently than twice each year; and

(B) may convene with the use of remote video conference technology.

(5) DUTIES.—The Advisory Committee shall, at a minimum, perform the following duties:

(A) Provide input into the development of the intelligent transportation system aspects of the strategic plan under section 6503 of title 49.

(B) Review, at least annually, areas of intelligent transportation systems programs and research being considered for funding by the Department, to determine—

(i) whether these activities are likely to advance either the state-of-the-practice or state-of-the-art in intelligent transportation systems;

(ii) whether the intelligent transportation system technologies are likely to be deployed by users, and if not, to determine the barriers to deployment; and

(iii) the appropriate roles for government and the private sector in investing in the programs, research, and technologies being considered.

(6) REPORT.—Not later than May 1 of each year, the Secretary shall make available to the public on a Department of Transportation website a report that includes—

(A) all recommendations made by the Advisory Committee during the preceding calendar year;

(B) an explanation of the manner in which the Secretary has implemented those recommendations; and

(C) for recommendations not implemented, the reasons for rejecting the recommendations.

(7) APPLICABILITY OF CHAPTER 10 OF TITLE 5, UNITED STATES CODE.—The Advisory Committee shall be subject to chapter 10 of title 5, United States Code.

(i) REPORTING.—

(1) GUIDELINES AND REQUIREMENTS.—

(A) IN GENERAL.—The Secretary shall issue guidelines and requirements for the reporting and evaluation of operational tests and deployment projects carried out under sections 512 through 518.

(B) OBJECTIVITY AND INDEPENDENCE.—The guidelines and requirements issued under subparagraph (A) shall include provisions to ensure the objectivity and independence of the reporting entity so as to avoid any real or apparent conflict of interest or potential influence on the outcome by parties to any such test or deployment project or by any other formal evaluation carried out under sections 512 through 518.

(C) FUNDING.—The guidelines and requirements issued under subparagraph (A) shall establish reporting funding levels based on the size and scope of each test or project that ensure adequate reporting of the results of the test or project.

(2) SPECIAL RULE.—Any survey, questionnaire, or interview that the Secretary considers necessary to carry out the reporting of any test, deployment project, or program assessment activity under sections 512 through 518 shall not be subject to chapter 35 of title 44, United States Code.

(Added Pub. L. 112–141, div. E, title III, §53003(a), July 6, 2012, 126 Stat. 899; amended Pub. L. 114–94, div. A, title I, §1446(a)(14), title VI, §6007, Dec. 4, 2015, 129 Stat. 1438, 1567; Pub. L. 117–58, div. A, title III, §13008(a), div. B, title V, §25001, Nov. 15, 2021, 135 Stat. 641, 836; Pub. L. 117–286, §4(a)(178), Dec. 27, 2022, 136 Stat. 4325.)

§516. RESEARCH AND DEVELOPMENT

(a) IN GENERAL.—The Secretary shall carry out a comprehensive program of intelligent transportation system research and development, and operational tests of intelligent vehicles, intelligent infrastructure systems, and other similar activities that are necessary to carry out this chapter.

(b) PRIORITY AREAS.—Under the program, the Secretary shall give higher priority to funding projects that—

(1) enhance mobility and productivity through improved traffic management, incident management, transit management, freight management, road weather management, toll collection, traveler information, or highway operations systems and remote sensing products;

(2) use interdisciplinary approaches to develop traffic management strategies and tools to address multiple impacts of congestion concurrently;

(3) address traffic management, incident management, transit management, toll collection traveler information, or highway operations systems;

(4) incorporate research on the potential impact of environmental, weather, and natural conditions on intelligent transportation systems, including the effects of cold climates;

(5) enhance intermodal use of intelligent transportation systems for diverse groups,

including for emergency and health-related services;

(6) enhance safety through improved crash avoidance and protection, crash and other notification, commercial motor vehicle operations, and infrastructure-based or cooperative safety systems, including animal detection systems to reduce the number of wildlife-vehicle collisions; or

(7) facilitate the integration of intelligent infrastructure, vehicle, and control technologies.

(c) FEDERAL SHARE.—The Federal share payable on account of any project or activity carried out under subsection (a) shall not exceed 80 percent.

(Added Pub. L. 112–141, div. E, title III, §53004(a), July 6, 2012, 126 Stat. 902; amended Pub. L. 117–58, div. A, title III, §13008(b), Nov. 15, 2021, 135 Stat. 641.)

§517. NATIONAL ARCHITECTURE AND STANDARDS

(a) IN GENERAL.—

(1) DEVELOPMENT, IMPLEMENTATION, AND MAINTENANCE.—In accordance with section 12(d) of the National Technology Transfer and Advancement Act of 1995 (15 U.S.C. 272 note; 110 Stat. 783; 115 Stat. 1241), the Secretary shall develop and maintain a national ITS architecture and supporting ITS standards and protocols to promote the use of systems engineering methods in the widespread deployment and evaluation of intelligent transportation systems as a component of the surface transportation systems of the United States.

(2) INTEROPERABILITY AND EFFICIENCY.—To the maximum extent practicable, the national ITS architecture and supporting ITS standards and protocols shall promote interoperability among, and efficiency of, intelligent transportation systems and technologies implemented throughout the United States.

(3) USE OF STANDARDS DEVELOPMENT ORGANIZATIONS.—In carrying out this section, the Secretary shall support the development and maintenance of standards and protocols using the services of such standards development organizations as the Secretary determines to be necessary and whose memberships include representatives of the surface transportation and intelligent transportation systems industries.

(b) STANDARDS FOR NATIONAL POLICY IMPLEMENTATION.—If the Secretary finds that a standard is necessary for implementation of a nationwide policy relating to user fee collection or other capability requiring nationwide uniformity, the Secretary, after consultation with stakeholders, may establish and require the use of that standard.

(c) PROVISIONAL STANDARDS.—

(1) IN GENERAL.—If the Secretary finds that the development or balloting of an intelligent transportation system standard jeopardizes the timely achievement of the objectives described in subsection (a), the Secretary may establish a provisional standard, after consultation with affected parties, using, to the maximum extent practicable, the work product of appropriate standards development organizations.

(2) PERIOD OF EFFECTIVENESS.—A provisional standard established under paragraph (1) shall be published in the Federal Register and remain in effect until the appropriate standards development organization adopts and publishes a standard.

(d) CONFORMITY WITH NATIONAL ARCHITECTURE.—

(1) In general.—Except as provided in paragraph (2), the Secretary shall ensure that intelligent transportation system projects carried out using amounts made available

from the Highway Trust Fund, including amounts made available to deploy intelligent transportation systems, conform to the appropriate regional ITS architecture, applicable standards, and protocols developed under subsection (a) or (c).

(2) DISCRETION OF THE SECRETARY.—The Secretary, at the discretion of the Secretary, may offer an exemption from paragraph (1) for projects designed to achieve specific research objectives outlined in the national intelligent transportation system program plan or the surface transportation research and development strategic plan developed under section 508.[1]

(Added Pub. L. 112–141, div. E, title III, §53005(a), July 6, 2012, 126 Stat. 902; amended Pub. L. 114–94, div. A, title VI, §6008, Dec. 4, 2015, 129 Stat. 1567.)

[1] *See References in Text note below.*

§518. VEHICLE-TO-VEHICLE AND VEHICLE-TO-INFRASTRUCTURE COMMUNICATIONS SYSTEMS DEPLOYMENT

(a) IN GENERAL.—Not later than July 6, 2016, the Secretary shall make available to the public on a Department of Transportation website a report that—

(1) assesses the status of dedicated short-range communications technology and applications developed through research and development;

(2) analyzes the known and potential gaps in short-range communications technology and applications;

(3) defines a recommended implementation path for dedicated short-range communications technology and applications that—

(A) is based on the assessment described in paragraph (1); and

(B) takes into account the analysis described in paragraph (2);

(4) includes guidance on the relationship of the proposed deployment of dedicated short-range communications to the National ITS Architecture and ITS Standards; and

(5) ensures competition by not preferencing the use of any particular frequency for vehicle to infrastructure operations.

(b) REPORT REVIEW.—The Secretary shall enter into agreements with the National Research Council and an independent third party with subject matter expertise for the review of the report described in subsection (a).

(Added Pub. L. 112–141, div. E, title III, §53006(a), July 6, 2012, 126 Stat. 904; amended Pub. L. 114–94, div. A, title VI, §6009, Dec. 4, 2015, 129 Stat. 1567.)

§519. INFRASTRUCTURE DEVELOPMENT

Funds made available to carry out this chapter for operational tests of intelligent transportation systems—

(1) shall be used primarily for the development of intelligent transportation system infrastructure, equipment, and systems; and

(2) to the maximum extent practicable, shall not be used for the construction of physical surface transportation infrastructure unless the construction is incidental and critically necessary to the implementation of an intelligent transportation system project.

(Added Pub. L. 114–94, div. A, title VI, §6010(a), Dec. 4, 2015, 129 Stat. 1567.)

§520. Transportation Resilience and Adaptation Centers of Excellence

(a) Definition of Center of Excellence.—In this section, the term "Center of Excellence" means a Center of Excellence for Resilience and Adaptation designated under subsection (b).

(b) Designation.—The Secretary shall designate 10 regional Centers of Excellence for Resilience and Adaptation and 1 national Center of Excellence for Resilience and Adaptation, which shall serve as a coordinator for the regional Centers, to receive grants to advance research and development that improves the resilience of regions of the United States to natural disasters and extreme weather by promoting the resilience of surface transportation infrastructure and infrastructure dependent on surface transportation.

(c) Eligibility.—An entity eligible to be designated as a Center of Excellence is—

(1) an institution of higher education (as defined in section 102 of the Higher Education Act of 1965 (20 U.S.C. 1002)); or

(2) a consortium of nonprofit organizations led by an institution of higher education.

(d) Application.—To be eligible to be designated as a Center of Excellence, an eligible entity shall submit to the Secretary an application at such time, in such manner, and containing such information as the Secretary may require, including a proposal that includes a description of the activities to be carried out with a grant under this section.

(e) Selection.—

(1) Regional centers of excellence.—The Secretary shall designate 1 regional Center of Excellence in each of the 10 Federal regions that comprise the Standard Federal Regions established by the Office of Management and Budget in the document entitled "Standard Federal Regions" and dated April 1974 (circular A–105).

(2) National center of excellence.—The Secretary shall designate 1 national Center of Excellence to coordinate the activities of all 10 regional Centers of Excellence to minimize duplication and promote coordination and dissemination of research among the Centers.

(3) Criteria.—In selecting eligible entities to designate as a Center of Excellence, the Secretary shall consider—

(A) the past experience and performance of the eligible entity in carrying out activities described in subsection (g);

(B) the merits of the proposal of an eligible entity and the extent to which the proposal would—

(i) advance the state of practice in resilience planning and identify innovative resilience solutions for transportation assets and systems;

(ii) support activities carried out under the PROTECT program under section 176;

(iii) support and build on work being carried out by another Federal agency relating to resilience;

(iv) inform transportation decisionmaking at all levels of government;

(v) engage local, regional, Tribal, State, and national stakeholders, including, if applicable, stakeholders representing transportation, transit, urban, and land use planning, natural resources, environmental protection, hazard mitigation, and emergency management; and

(vi) engage community groups and other stakeholders that will be affected by transportation decisions, including underserved, economically disadvantaged, rural, and predominantly minority communities; and

(C) the local, regional, Tribal, State, and national impacts of the proposal of the eligible entity.

(f) GRANTS.—Subject to the availability of appropriations, the Secretary shall provide to each Center of Excellence a grant of not less than $5,000,000 for each of fiscal years 2022 through 2031 to carry out the activities described in subsection (g).

(g) ACTIVITIES.—In carrying out this section, the Secretary shall ensure that a Center of Excellence uses the funds from a grant under subsection (f) to promote resilient transportation infrastructure, including through—

(1) supporting climate vulnerability assessments informed by climate change science, including national climate assessments produced by the United States Global Change Research Program under section 106 of the Global Change Research Act of 1990 (15 U.S.C. 2936), relevant feasibility analyses of resilient transportation improvements, and transportation resilience planning;

(2) development of new design, operations, and maintenance standards for transportation infrastructure that can inform Federal and State decisionmaking;

(3) research and development of new materials and technologies that could be integrated into existing and new transportation infrastructure;

(4) development, refinement, and piloting of new and emerging resilience improvements and strategies, including natural infrastructure approaches and relocation;

(5) development of and investment in new approaches for facilitating meaningful engagement in transportation decisionmaking by local, Tribal, regional, or national stakeholders and communities;

(6) technical capacity building to facilitate the ability of local, regional, Tribal, State, and national stakeholders—

(A) to assess the vulnerability of transportation infrastructure assets and systems;

(B) to develop community response strategies;

(C) to meaningfully engage with community stakeholders; and

(D) to develop strategies and improvements for enhancing transportation infrastructure resilience under current conditions and a range of potential future conditions;

(7) workforce development and training;

(8) development and dissemination of data, tools, techniques, assessments, and information that informs Federal, State, Tribal, and local government decisionmaking, policies, planning, and investments;

(9) education and outreach regarding transportation infrastructure resilience; and

(10) technology transfer and commercialization.

(h) FEDERAL SHARE.—The Federal share of the cost of an activity under this section, including the costs of establishing and operating a Center of Excellence, shall be 50 percent.

(Added Pub. L. 117–58, div. A, title III, §13009(a), Nov. 15, 2021, 135 Stat. 642.)

CHAPTER 6
INFRASTRUCTURE FINANCE

CHAPTER 6—INFRASTRUCTURE FINANCE

§601. GENERALLY APPLICABLE PROVISIONS

(a) DEFINITIONS.—The following definitions apply to sections 601 through 609:

(1) CONTINGENT COMMITMENT.—The term "contingent commitment" means a commitment to obligate an amount from future available budget authority that is—

(A) contingent on those funds being made available in law at a future date; and

(B) not an obligation of the Federal Government.

(2) ELIGIBLE PROJECT COSTS.—The term "eligible project costs" means amounts substantially all of which are paid by, or for the account of, an obligor in connection with a project, including the cost of—

(A) development phase activities, including planning, feasibility analysis, revenue forecasting, environmental review, permitting, preliminary engineering and design work, and other preconstruction activities;

(B) construction, reconstruction, rehabilitation, replacement, and acquisition of real property (including land relating to the project and improvements to land), environmental mitigation, construction contingencies, and acquisition of equipment;

(C) capitalized interest necessary to meet market requirements, reasonably required reserve funds, capital issuance expenses, and other carrying costs during construction; and

(D) capitalizing a rural projects fund.

(3) FEDERAL CREDIT INSTRUMENT.—The term "Federal credit instrument" means a secured loan, loan guarantee, or line of credit authorized to be made available under the TIFIA program with respect to a project.

(4) INVESTMENT-GRADE RATING.—The term "investment-grade rating" means a rating of BBB minus, Baa3, bbb minus, BBB (low), or higher assigned by a rating agency to project obligations.

(5) LENDER.—The term "lender" means any non-Federal qualified institutional buyer (as defined in section 230.144A(a) of title 17, Code of Federal Regulations (or any successor regulation), known as Rule 144A(a) of the Securities and Exchange Commission and issued under the Securities Act of 1933 (15 U.S.C. 77a et seq.)), including—

(A) a qualified retirement plan (as defined in section 4974(c) of the Internal

Revenue Code of 1986) that is a qualified institutional buyer; and

(B) a governmental plan (as defined in section 414(d) of the Internal Revenue Code of 1986) that is a qualified institutional buyer.

(6) LETTER OF INTEREST.—The term "letter of interest" means a letter submitted by a potential applicant prior to an application for credit assistance in a format prescribed by the Secretary on the website of the TIFIA program that—

(A) describes the project and the location, purpose, and cost of the project;

(B) outlines the proposed financial plan, including the requested credit assistance and the proposed obligor;

(C) provides a status of environmental review; and

(D) provides information regarding satisfaction of other eligibility requirements of the TIFIA program.

(7) LINE OF CREDIT.—The term "line of credit" means an agreement entered into by the Secretary with an obligor under section 604 to provide a direct loan at a future date upon the occurrence of certain events.

(8) LIMITED BUYDOWN.—The term "limited buydown" means, subject to the conditions described in section 603(b)(4)(C), a buydown of the interest rate by the obligor if the interest rate has increased between—

(A)(i) the date on which a project application acceptable to the Secretary is submitted; or

(ii) the date on which the Secretary entered into a master credit agreement; and

(B) the date on which the Secretary executes the Federal credit instrument.

(9) LOAN GUARANTEE.—The term "loan guarantee" means any guarantee or other pledge by the Secretary to pay all or part of the principal of and interest on a loan or other debt obligation issued by an obligor and funded by a lender.

(10) MASTER CREDIT AGREEMENT.—The term "master credit agreement" means a conditional agreement to extend credit assistance for a program of related projects secured by a common security pledge covered under section 602(b)(2)(A) or for a single project covered under section 602(b)(2)(B) that does not provide for a current obligation of Federal funds, and that would—

(A) make contingent commitments of 1 or more secured loans or other Federal credit instruments at future dates, subject to—

(i) the availability of future funds being made available to carry out the TIFIA program; and

(ii) the satisfaction of all of the conditions for the provision of credit assistance under the TIFIA program, including section 603(b)(1);

(B) establish the maximum amounts and general terms and conditions of the secured loans or other Federal credit instruments;

(C) identify the 1 or more dedicated non-Federal revenue sources that will secure the repayment of the secured loans or secured Federal credit instruments;

(D) provide for the obligation of funds for the secured loans or secured Federal credit instruments after all requirements have been met for the projects subject to the master credit agreement, including—

(i) completion of an environmental impact statement or similar analysis required under the National Environmental Policy Act of 1969 (42 U.S.C. 4321 et seq.);

(ii) receiving an investment grade rating from a rating agency;

(iii) compliance with such other requirements as are specified under the TIFIA program, including sections 602(c) and 603(b)(1); and

(iv) the availability of funds to carry out the TIFIA program; and

(E) require that contingent commitments result in a financial close and obligation of credit assistance not later than 5 years after the date of entry into the master credit agreement, or release of the commitment, unless otherwise extended by the Secretary.

(11) OBLIGOR.—The term "obligor" means a party that—

(A) is primarily liable for payment of the principal of or interest on a Federal credit instrument; and

(B) may be a corporation, partnership, joint venture, trust, or governmental entity, agency, or instrumentality.

(12) PROJECT.—The term "project" means—

(A) any surface transportation project eligible for Federal assistance under this title or chapter 53 of title 49;

(B) a project for an international bridge or tunnel for which an international entity authorized under Federal or State law is responsible;

(C) a project for intercity passenger bus or rail facilities and vehicles, including facilities and vehicles owned by the National Railroad Passenger Corporation and components of magnetic levitation transportation systems;

(D) a project that—

(i) is a project—

(I) for a public freight rail facility or a private facility providing public benefit for highway users by way of direct freight interchange between highway and rail carriers;

(II) for an intermodal freight transfer facility;

(III) for a means of access to a facility described in subclause (I) or (II);

(IV) for a service improvement for a facility described in subclause (I) or (II) (including a capital investment for an intelligent transportation system); or

(V) that comprises a series of projects described in subclauses (I) through (IV) with the common objective of improving the flow of goods;

(ii) may involve the combining of private and public sector funds, including investment of public funds in private sector facility improvements;

(iii) if located within the boundaries of a port terminal, includes only such surface transportation infrastructure modifications as are necessary to facilitate direct intermodal interchange, transfer, and access into and out of the port; and

(iv) is composed of related highway, surface transportation, transit, rail, or intermodal capital improvement projects eligible for assistance under this section in order to meet the eligible project cost threshold under section 602, by grouping related projects together for that purpose, subject to the condition that the credit assistance for the projects is secured by a common pledge;

(E) a project to improve or construct public infrastructure—

(i) that—

(I) is located within walking distance of, and accessible to, a fixed guideway transit facility, passenger rail station, intercity bus station, or intermodal facility, including a transportation, public utility, or capital project described in section 5302(4)(G)(v) [1] of title 49, and related infrastructure; or

(II) is a project for economic development, including commercial and residential development, and related infrastructure and activities—

(aa) that incorporates private investment;

(bb) that is physically or functionally related to a passenger rail station or multimodal station that includes rail service;

(cc) for which the project sponsor has a high probability of commencing the contracting process for construction by not later than 90 days after the date on which credit assistance under the TIFIA program is provided for the project; and

(dd) that has a high probability of reducing the need for financial assistance under any other Federal program for the relevant passenger rail station or service by increasing ridership, tenant lease payments, or other activities that generate revenue exceeding costs; and

(ii) for which, by not later than September 30, 2026, the Secretary has—

(I) received a letter of interest; and

(II) determined that the project is eligible for assistance;

(F) the capitalization of a rural projects fund;

(G) an eligible airport-related project (as defined in section 40117(a) of title 49) for which, not later than September 30, 2025, the Secretary has—

(i) received a letter of interest; and

(ii) determined that the project is eligible for assistance; and

(H) a project for the acquisition of plant and wildlife habitat pursuant to a conservation plan that—

(i) has been approved by the Secretary of the Interior pursuant to section 10 of the Endangered Species Act of 1973 (16 U.S.C. 1539); and

(ii) in the judgment of the Secretary, would mitigate the environmental impacts of transportation infrastructure projects otherwise eligible for assistance under this title.

(13) PROJECT OBLIGATION.—The term "project obligation" means any note, bond, debenture, or other debt obligation issued by an obligor in connection with the financing of a project, other than a Federal credit instrument.

(14) RATING AGENCY.—The term "rating agency" means a credit rating agency registered with the Securities and Exchange Commission as a nationally recognized statistical rating organization (as that term is defined in section 3(a) of the Securities Exchange Act of 1934 (15 U.S.C. 78c(a))).

(15) RURAL INFRASTRUCTURE PROJECT.—The term "rural infrastructure project" means a surface transportation infrastructure project located in an area that is outside of an urbanized area with a population greater than 150,000 individuals, as determined by the Bureau of the Census.

(16) RURAL PROJECTS FUND.—The term "rural projects fund" means a fund—

(A) established by a State infrastructure bank in accordance with section 610(d)(4);

(B) capitalized with the proceeds of a secured loan made to the bank in accordance with sections 602 and 603; and

(C) for the purpose of making loans to sponsors of rural infrastructure projects in accordance with section 610.

(17) SECURED LOAN.—The term "secured loan" means a direct loan or other debt obligation issued by an obligor and funded by the Secretary in connection with the financing of a project under section 603.

(18) STATE.—The term "State" has the meaning given the term in section 101.

(19) STATE INFRASTRUCTURE BANK.—The term "State infrastructure bank" means an infrastructure bank established under section 610.

(20) SUBSIDY AMOUNT.—The term "subsidy amount" means the amount of budget authority sufficient to cover the estimated long-term cost to the Federal Government of a Federal credit instrument—

(A) calculated on a net present value basis; and

(B) excluding administrative costs and any incidental effects on governmental receipts or outlays in accordance with the Federal Credit Reform Act of 1990 (2 U.S.C. 661 et seq.).

(21) SUBSTANTIAL COMPLETION.—The term "substantial completion" means—

(A) the opening of a project to vehicular or passenger traffic; or

(B) a comparable event, as determined by the Secretary and specified in the credit agreement.

(22) TIFIA PROGRAM.—The term "TIFIA program" means the transportation infrastructure finance and innovation program of the Department established under sections 602 through 609.

(b) TREATMENT OF CHAPTER.—For purposes of this title, this chapter shall be treated as being part of chapter 1.

(Added Pub. L. 105–178, title I, §1503(a), June 9, 1998, 112 Stat. 241, §181; renumbered §601 and amended Pub. L. 109–59, title I, §§1601(a), 1602(b)(1), (5), (d), Aug. 10, 2005, 119 Stat. 1239, 1246, 1247; Pub. L. 109–291, §4(b)(6), Sept. 29, 2006, 120 Stat. 1338; Pub. L. 110–244, title I, §101(r), June 6, 2008, 122 Stat. 1577; Pub. L. 112–141, div. A, title II, §2002, July 6, 2012, 126 Stat. 607; Pub. L. 114–94, div. A, title II, §2001(a), Dec. 4, 2015, 129 Stat. 1439; Pub. L. 117–58, div. A, title II, §12001(a), div. C, §30001(b)(1), Nov. 15, 2021, 135 Stat. 617, 890.)

¹ So in original. Probably should be "section 5302(4)(G)(vi)".

¹ So in original. Probably should be "section 5302(4)(G)(vi)".

§602. DETERMINATION OF ELIGIBILITY AND PROJECT SELECTION

(a) ELIGIBILITY.—

(1) IN GENERAL.—A project shall be eligible to receive credit assistance under the TIFIA program if—

(A) the entity proposing to carry out the project submits a letter of interest prior to submission of a formal application for the project; and

(B) the project meets the criteria described in this subsection.

(2) CREDITWORTHINESS.—

(A) IN GENERAL.—To be eligible for assistance under the TIFIA program, a project shall satisfy applicable creditworthiness standards, which, at a minimum, shall include—

(i) a rate covenant, if applicable;

(ii) adequate coverage requirements to ensure repayment;

(iii) an investment grade rating from at least 2 rating agencies on debt senior to the Federal credit instrument; and

(iv) an investment-grade rating from at least 2 rating agencies on the Federal credit instrument, subject to the condition that, with respect to clause (iii), if the total amount of the senior debt and the Federal credit instrument is less than $150,000,000, 1 rating agency opinion for each of the senior debt and Federal credit instrument shall be sufficient.

(B) SENIOR DEBT.—Notwithstanding subparagraph (A), in a case in which the Federal credit instrument is senior debt, the Federal credit instrument shall be required to receive an investment grade rating from at least 2 rating agencies, unless the total amount of other senior debt and the Federal credit instrument is less than $150,000,000, in which case 1 rating agency opinion shall be sufficient.

(3) INCLUSION IN TRANSPORTATION PLANS AND PROGRAMS.—A project shall satisfy the applicable planning and programming requirements of sections 134 and 135 at such time as an agreement to make available a Federal credit instrument is entered into under the TIFIA program.

(4) APPLICATION.—A State, local government, public authority, public-private partnership, or any other legal entity undertaking the project and authorized by the Secretary shall submit a project application that is acceptable to the Secretary.

(5) ELIGIBLE PROJECT COST PARAMETERS.—

(A) IN GENERAL.—Except as provided in subparagraph (B), a project under the TIFIA program shall have eligible project costs that are reasonably anticipated to equal or exceed the lesser of—

(i) $50,000,000; and

(ii) 33 1/3 percent of the amount of Federal highway funds apportioned for the most recently completed fiscal year to the State in which the project is located.

(B) EXCEPTIONS.—

(i) INTELLIGENT TRANSPORTATION SYSTEMS.—In the case of a project principally involving the installation of an intelligent transportation system, eligible project costs shall be reasonably anticipated to equal or exceed $15,000,000.

(ii) TRANSIT-ORIENTED DEVELOPMENT PROJECTS.—In the case of a project described in section 601(a)(12)(E), eligible project costs shall be reasonably anticipated to equal or exceed $10,000,000.

(iii) RURAL PROJECTS.—In the case of a rural infrastructure project or a project capitalizing a rural projects fund, eligible project costs shall be reasonably anticipated to equal or exceed $10,000,000, but not to exceed $100,000,000.

(iv) LOCAL INFRASTRUCTURE PROJECTS.—Eligible project costs shall be reasonably anticipated to equal or exceed $10,000,000 in the case of a project or program of projects—

(I) in which the applicant is a local government, public authority, or instrumentality of local government;

(II) located on a facility owned by a local government; or

(III) for which the Secretary determines that a local government is substantially involved in the development of the project.

(6) DEDICATED REVENUE SOURCES.—The applicable Federal credit instrument shall be repayable, in whole or in part, from—

(A) tolls;

(B) user fees;

(C) payments owing to the obligor under a public-private partnership; or

(D) other dedicated revenue sources that also secure or fund the project obligations.

(7) PUBLIC SPONSORSHIP OF PRIVATE ENTITIES.—In the case of a project that is undertaken by an entity that is not a State or local government or an agency or instrumentality of a State or local government, the project that the entity is undertaking shall be publicly sponsored as provided in paragraph (3).

(8) APPLICATIONS WHERE OBLIGOR WILL BE IDENTIFIED LATER.—A State, local government, agency or instrumentality of a State or local government, or public authority may submit to the Secretary an application under paragraph (4), under which a private party to a public-private partnership will be—

(A) the obligor; and

(B) identified later through completion of a procurement and selection of the private party.

(9) BENEFICIAL EFFECTS.—The Secretary shall determine that financial assistance for the project under the TIFIA program will—

(A) foster, if appropriate, partnerships that attract public and private investment for the project;

(B) enable the project to proceed at an earlier date than the project would otherwise be able to proceed or reduce the lifecycle costs (including debt service costs) of the project; and

(C) reduce the contribution of Federal grant assistance for the project.

(10) PROJECT READINESS.—

(A) IN GENERAL.—Except as provided in subparagraph (B), to be eligible for assistance under the TIFIA program, the applicant shall demonstrate a reasonable expectation that the contracting process for construction of the project can commence by no later than 90 days after the date on which a Federal credit instrument is obligated for the project under the TIFIA program.

(B) RURAL PROJECTS FUND.—In the case of a project capitalizing a rural projects fund, the State infrastructure bank shall demonstrate, not later than 2 years after the date on which a secured loan is obligated for the project under the TIFIA program, that the bank has executed a loan agreement with a borrower for a rural infrastructure project in accordance with section 610. After the demonstration is made, the bank may draw upon the secured loan. At the end of the 2-year period, to the extent the bank has not used the loan commitment, the Secretary may extend the term of the loan or withdraw the loan commitment.

(11) PUBLIC-PRIVATE PARTNERSHIPS.—In the case of a project to be carried out

through a public-private partnership, the public partner shall have—

    (A) conducted a value for money analysis or similar comparative analysis; and

    (B) determined the appropriateness of the public-private partnership agreement.

(b) SELECTION AMONG ELIGIBLE PROJECTS.—

    (1) ESTABLISHMENT.—The Secretary shall establish a rolling application process under which projects that are eligible to receive credit assistance under subsection (a) shall receive credit assistance on terms acceptable to the Secretary, if adequate funds are available to cover the subsidy costs associated with the Federal credit instrument.

    (2) MASTER CREDIT AGREEMENTS.—

        (A) PROGRAM OF RELATED PROJECTS.—The Secretary may enter into a master credit agreement for a program of related projects secured by a common security pledge on terms acceptable to the Secretary.

        (B) ADEQUATE FUNDING NOT AVAILABLE.—If the Secretary fully obligates funding to eligible projects for a fiscal year and adequate funding is not available to fund a credit instrument, a project sponsor of an eligible project may elect to enter into a master credit agreement and wait to execute a credit instrument until the fiscal year for which additional funds are available to receive credit assistance.

    (3) PRELIMINARY RATING OPINION LETTER.—The Secretary shall require each project applicant to provide a preliminary rating opinion letter from at least 1 rating agency—

        (A) indicating that the senior obligations of the project, which may be the Federal credit instrument, have the potential to achieve an investment-grade rating; and

        (B) including a preliminary rating opinion on the Federal credit instrument.

(c) FEDERAL REQUIREMENTS.—

    (1) IN GENERAL.—In addition to the requirements of this title for highway projects, the requirements of chapter 53 of title 49 for transit projects, the requirements of section 5333(a) of title 49 for rail projects, and the requirements of sections 47112(b) and 50101 of title 49 for airport-related projects, the following provisions of law shall apply to funds made available under the TIFIA program and projects assisted with those funds:

        (A) Title VI of the Civil Rights Act of 1964 (42 U.S.C. 2000d et seq.).

        (B) The National Environmental Policy Act of 1969 (42 U.S.C. 4321 et seq.).

        (C) The Uniform Relocation Assistance and Real Property Acquisition Policies Act of 1970 (42 U.S.C. 4601 et seq.).

    (2) NEPA.—No funding shall be obligated for a project that has not received an environmental categorical exclusion, a finding of no significant impact, or a record of decision under the National Environmental Policy Act of 1969 (42 U.S.C. 4321 et seq.).

    (3) PAYMENT AND PERFORMANCE SECURITY.—

        (A) IN GENERAL.—The Secretary shall ensure that the design and construction of a project carried out with assistance under the TIFIA program shall have appropriate payment and performance security, regardless of whether the obligor is a State, local government, agency or instrumentality of a State or local government, public authority, or private party.

(B) WRITTEN DETERMINATION.—If payment and performance security is required to be furnished by applicable State or local statute or regulation, the Secretary may accept such payment and performance security requirements applicable to the obligor if the Federal interest with respect to Federal funds and other project risk related to design and construction is adequately protected.

(C) NO DETERMINATION OR APPLICABLE REQUIREMENTS.—If there are no payment and performance security requirements applicable to the obligor, the security under section 3131(b) of title 40 or an equivalent State or local requirement, as determined by the Secretary, shall be required.

(d) APPLICATION PROCESSING PROCEDURES.—

(1) PROCESSING TIMELINES.—Except in the case of an application described in subsection (a)(8) and to the maximum extent practicable, the Secretary shall provide an applicant with a specific estimate of the timeline for the approval or disapproval of the application of the applicant, which, to the maximum extent practicable, the Secretary shall endeavor to complete by not later than 150 days after the date on which the applicant submits a letter of interest to the Secretary.

(2) NOTICE OF COMPLETE APPLICATION.—Not later than 30 days after the date of receipt of an application under this section, the Secretary shall provide to the applicant a written notice to inform the applicant whether—

(A) the application is complete; or

(B) additional information or materials are needed to complete the application.

(3) APPROVAL OR DENIAL OF APPLICATION.—Not later than 60 days after the date of issuance of the written notice under paragraph (2), the Secretary shall provide to the applicant a written notice informing the applicant whether the Secretary has approved or disapproved the application.

(e) DEVELOPMENT PHASE ACTIVITIES.—Any credit instrument secured under the TIFIA program may be used to finance up to 100 percent of the cost of development phase activities as described in section 601(a)(2)(A).

(Added Pub. L. 105–178, title I, §1503(a), June 9, 1998, 112 Stat. 243, §182; renumbered §602 and amended Pub. L. 109–59, title I, §§1601(b), (c), 1602(b)(2), (5), (d), Aug. 10, 2005, 119 Stat. 1240, 1247; Pub. L. 112–141, div. A, title II, §2002, July 6, 2012, 126 Stat. 611; Pub. L. 114–94, div. A, title II, §2001(b), Dec. 4, 2015, 129 Stat. 1440; Pub. L. 117–58, div. A, title I, §11508(d)(3), title II, §§12001(b)–(d), (g), 12002(a), Nov. 15, 2021, 135 Stat. 588, 618, 619, 622.)

§603. SECURED LOANS

(a) IN GENERAL.—

(1) AGREEMENTS.—Subject to paragraphs (2) and (3), the Secretary may enter into agreements with 1 or more obligors to make secured loans, the proceeds of which shall be used—

(A) to finance eligible project costs of any project selected under section 602;

(B) to refinance interim construction financing of eligible project costs of any project selected under section 602;

(C) to refinance existing Federal credit instruments for rural infrastructure projects; or

(D) to refinance long-term project obligations or Federal credit instruments, if the refinancing provides additional funding capacity for the completion, enhancement, or expansion of any project that—

(i) is selected under section 602; or

(ii) otherwise meets the requirements of section 602.

(2) LIMITATION ON REFINANCING OF INTERIM CONSTRUCTION FINANCING.—A loan under paragraph (1) shall not refinance interim construction financing under paragraph (1)(B)—

(A) if the maturity of such interim construction financing is later than 1 year after the substantial completion of the project; and

(B) later than 1 year after the date of substantial completion of the project.

(3) RISK ASSESSMENT.—Before entering into an agreement under this subsection, the Secretary, in consultation with the Director of the Office of Management and Budget, shall determine an appropriate capital reserve subsidy amount for each secured loan, taking into account each rating letter provided by an agency under section 602(b)(3)(B).

(b) TERMS AND LIMITATIONS.—

(1) IN GENERAL.—A secured loan under this section with respect to a project shall be on such terms and conditions and contain such covenants, representations, warranties, and requirements (including requirements for audits) as the Secretary determines to be appropriate.

(2) MAXIMUM AMOUNT.—

(A) IN GENERAL.—Except as provided in subparagraph (B), the amount of a secured loan under this section shall not exceed the lesser of 49 percent of the reasonably anticipated eligible project costs or if the secured loan does not receive an investment grade rating, the amount of the senior project obligations.

(B) RURAL PROJECTS FUND.—In the case of a project capitalizing a rural projects fund, the maximum amount of a secured loan made to a State infrastructure bank shall be determined in accordance with section 602(a)(5)(B)(iii).

(3) PAYMENT.—A secured loan under this section—

(A) shall—

(i) be payable, in whole or in part, from—

(I) tolls;

(II) user fees;

(III) payments owing to the obligor under a public-private partnership;

(IV) other dedicated revenue sources that also secure the senior project obligations; or

(V) in the case of a secured loan for a project capitalizing a rural projects fund, any other dedicated revenue sources available to a State infrastructure bank, including repayments from loans made by the bank for rural infrastructure projects; and

(ii) include a rate covenant, coverage requirement, or similar security feature supporting the project obligations; and

(B) may have a lien on revenues described in subparagraph (A), subject to any lien securing project obligations.

(4) INTEREST RATE.—

(A) IN GENERAL.—Except as provided in subparagraphs (B) and (C), the interest rate on a secured loan under this section shall be not less than the yield on United States Treasury securities of a similar maturity to the maturity of the secured loan on the date of execution of the loan agreement.

(B) RURAL INFRASTRUCTURE PROJECTS.—

(i) IN GENERAL.—The interest rate of a loan offered to a rural infrastructure project or a rural projects fund under the TIFIA program shall be at ½ of the Treasury Rate in effect on the date of execution of the loan agreement.

(ii) APPLICATION.—The rate described in clause (i) shall only apply to any portion of a loan the subsidy cost of which is funded by amounts set aside for rural infrastructure projects and rural project funds under section 608(a)(3)(A).

(C) LIMITED BUYDOWNS.—The interest rate of a secured loan under this section may not be lowered by more than the lower of—

(i) 1½ percentage points (150 basis points); or

(ii) the amount of the increase in the interest rate.

(5) MATURITY DATE.—

(A) IN GENERAL.—Except as provided in subparagraphs (B) and (C), the final maturity date of the secured loan shall be the lesser of—

(i) 35 years after the date of substantial completion of the project; and

(ii) if the useful life of the capital asset being financed is of a lesser period, the useful life of the asset.

(B) RURAL PROJECTS FUND.—In the case of a project capitalizing a rural projects fund, the final maturity date of the secured loan shall not exceed 35 years after the date on which the secured loan is obligated.

(C) LONG LIVED ASSETS.—In the case of a capital asset with an estimated life of more than 50 years, the final maturity date of the secured loan shall be the lesser of—

(i) 75 years after the date of substantial completion of the project; or

(ii) 75 percent of the estimated useful life of the capital asset.

(6) NONSUBORDINATION.—

(A) IN GENERAL.—Except as provided in subparagraph (B), the secured loan shall not be subordinated to the claims of any holder of project obligations in the event of bankruptcy, insolvency, or liquidation of the obligor.

(B) PREEXISTING INDENTURE.—

(i) IN GENERAL.—The Secretary shall waive the requirement under subparagraph (A) for a public agency borrower that is financing ongoing capital programs and has outstanding senior bonds under a preexisting indenture, if—

(I) the secured loan is rated in the A category or higher;

(II) the secured loan is secured and payable from pledged revenues not affected by project performance, such as a tax-backed revenue pledge or a system-backed pledge of project revenues; and

(III) the TIFIA program share of eligible project costs is 33 percent or less.

(ii) LIMITATION.—If the Secretary waives the nonsubordination requirement under this subparagraph—

(I) the maximum credit subsidy to be paid by the Federal Government shall be not more than 10 percent of the principal amount of the secured loan; and

(II) the obligor shall be responsible for paying the remainder of the subsidy cost, if any.

(7) FEES.—The Secretary may establish fees at a level sufficient to cover all or a portion of the costs to the Federal Government of making a secured loan under this section.

(8) NON-FEDERAL SHARE.—The proceeds of a secured loan under the TIFIA program may be used for any non-Federal share of project costs required under this title or chapter 53 of title 49, if the loan is repayable from non-Federal funds.

(9) MAXIMUM FEDERAL INVOLVEMENT.—

(A) IN GENERAL.—The total Federal assistance provided for a project receiving a loan under the TIFIA program shall not exceed 80 percent of the total project cost.

(B) RURAL PROJECTS FUND.—A project capitalizing a rural projects fund shall satisfy subparagraph (A) through compliance with the Federal share requirement described in section 610(e)(3)(B).

(c) REPAYMENT.—

(1) SCHEDULE.—The Secretary shall establish a repayment schedule for each secured loan under this section based on—

(A) the projected cash flow from project revenues and other repayment sources; and

(B) the useful life of the project.

(2) COMMENCEMENT.—Scheduled loan repayments of principal or interest on a secured loan under this section shall commence not later than 5 years after the date of substantial completion of the project.

(3) DEFERRED PAYMENTS.—

(A) IN GENERAL.—If, at any time after the date of substantial completion of the project, the project is unable to generate sufficient revenues to pay the scheduled loan repayments of principal and interest on the secured loan, the Secretary may, subject to subparagraph (C), allow the obligor to add unpaid principal and interest to the outstanding balance of the secured loan.

(B) INTEREST.—Any payment deferred under subparagraph (A) shall—

(i) continue to accrue interest in accordance with subsection (b)(4) until fully repaid; and

(ii) be scheduled to be amortized over the remaining term of the loan.

(C) CRITERIA.—

(i) IN GENERAL.—Any payment deferral under subparagraph (A) shall be contingent on the project meeting criteria established by the Secretary.

(ii) REPAYMENT STANDARDS.—The criteria established pursuant to clause (i) shall include standards for reasonable assurance of repayment.

(4) PREPAYMENT.—

(A) USE OF EXCESS REVENUES.—

(i) IN GENERAL.—Except as provided in clause (ii), any excess revenues that remain after satisfying scheduled debt service requirements on the project obligations and secured loan and all deposit requirements under the terms of any trust agreement, bond resolution, or similar agreement securing project obligations may be applied annually to prepay the secured loan without penalty.

(ii) CERTAIN APPLICANTS.—In the case of a secured loan or other secured Federal credit instrument provided after the date of enactment of the Surface Transportation Reauthorization Act of 2021, if the obligor is a governmental entity, agency, or instrumentality, the obligor shall not be required to prepay the secured loan or other secured Federal credit instrument with any excess revenues described in clause (i) if the obligor enters into an agreement to use those excess revenues only for purposes authorized under this title or title 49.

(B) USE OF PROCEEDS OF REFINANCING.—The secured loan may be prepaid at any time without penalty from the proceeds of refinancing from non-Federal funding sources.

(d) SALE OF SECURED LOANS.—

(1) IN GENERAL.—Subject to paragraph (2), as soon as practicable after substantial completion of a project and after notifying the obligor, the Secretary may sell to another entity or reoffer into the capital markets a secured loan for the project if the Secretary determines that the sale or reoffering can be made on favorable terms.

(2) CONSENT OF OBLIGOR.—In making a sale or reoffering under paragraph (1), the Secretary may not change the original terms and conditions of the secured loan without the written consent of the obligor.

(e) LOAN GUARANTEES.—

(1) IN GENERAL.—The Secretary may provide a loan guarantee to a lender in lieu of making a secured loan under this section if the Secretary determines that the budgetary cost of the loan guarantee is substantially the same as that of a secured loan.

(2) TERMS.—The terms of a loan guarantee under paragraph (1) shall be consistent with the terms required under this section for a secured loan, except that the rate on the guaranteed loan and any prepayment features shall be negotiated between the obligor and the lender, with the consent of the Secretary.

(f) STREAMLINED APPLICATION PROCESS.—

(1) IN GENERAL.—Not later than 180 days after the date of enactment of the FAST Act, the Secretary shall make available an expedited application process or processes available at the request of entities seeking secured loans under the TIFIA program that use a set or sets of conventional terms established pursuant to this section.

(2) TERMS.—In establishing the streamlined application process required by this subsection, the Secretary may include terms commonly included in prior credit agreements and allow for an expedited application period, including—

(A) the secured loan is in an amount of not greater than $100,000,000;

(B) the secured loan is secured and payable from pledged revenues not affected by project performance, such as a tax-backed revenue pledge, tax increment financing, or a system-backed pledge of project revenues; and

(C) repayment of the loan commences not later than 5 years after disbursement.

(3) ADDITIONAL TERMS FOR EXPEDITED DECISIONS.—

(A) IN GENERAL.—Not later than 120 days after the date of enactment of this paragraph, the Secretary shall implement an expedited decision timeline for public agency borrowers seeking secured loans that meet—

(i) the terms under paragraph (2); and

(ii) the additional criteria described in subparagraph (B).

(B) ADDITIONAL CRITERIA.—The additional criteria referred to in subparagraph (A)(ii) are the following:

(i) The secured loan is made on terms and conditions that substantially conform to the conventional terms and conditions established by the National Surface Transportation Innovative Finance Bureau.

(ii) The secured loan is rated in the A category or higher.

(iii) The TIFIA program share of eligible project costs is 33 percent or less.

(iv) The applicant demonstrates a reasonable expectation that the contracting process for the project can commence by not later than 90 days after the date on which a Federal credit instrument is obligated for the project under the TIFIA program.

(v) The project has received a categorical exclusion, a finding of no significant impact, or a record of decision under the National Environmental Policy Act of 1969 (42 U.S.C. 4321 et seq.).

(C) WRITTEN NOTICE.—The Secretary shall provide to an applicant seeking a secured loan under the expedited decision process under this paragraph a written notice informing the applicant whether the Secretary has approved or disapproved the application by not later than 180 days after the date on which the Secretary submits to the applicant a letter indicating that the National Surface Transportation Innovative Finance Bureau has commenced the creditworthiness review of the project.

(Added Pub. L. 105–178, title I, §1503(a), June 9, 1998, 112 Stat. 245, §183; renumbered §603 and amended Pub. L. 109–59, title I, §§1601(d), 1602(b)(3), (5), (d), Aug. 10, 2005, 119 Stat. 1240, 1247; Pub. L. 112–141, div. A, title II, §2002, July 6, 2012, 126 Stat. 614; Pub. L. 114–94, div. A, title II, §2001(c), Dec. 4, 2015, 129 Stat. 1442; Pub. L. 117–58, div. A, title II, §12001(e), (f), (h), Nov. 15, 2021, 135 Stat. 619.)

§604. LINES OF CREDIT

(a) IN GENERAL.—

(1) AGREEMENTS.—Subject to paragraphs (2) through (4), the Secretary may enter into agreements to make available to 1 or more obligors lines of credit in the form of direct loans to be made by the Secretary at future dates on the occurrence of certain events for any project selected under section 602.

(2) USE OF PROCEEDS.—The proceeds of a line of credit made available under this section shall be available to pay debt service on project obligations issued to finance eligible project costs, extraordinary repair and replacement costs, operation and maintenance expenses, and costs associated with unexpected Federal or State environmental restrictions.

(3) RISK ASSESSMENT.—Before entering into an agreement under this subsection, the Secretary, in consultation with the Director of the Office of Management and Budget and each rating agency providing a preliminary rating opinion letter under section 602(b)(3), shall determine an appropriate capital reserve subsidy amount for each line of credit, taking into account the rating opinion letter.

(4) INVESTMENT-GRADE RATING REQUIREMENT.—The funding of a line of credit under this section shall be contingent on the senior obligations of the project receiving

an investment-grade rating from 2 rating agencies.

(b) TERMS AND LIMITATIONS.—

(1) IN GENERAL.—A line of credit under this section with respect to a project shall be on such terms and conditions and contain such covenants, representations, warranties, and requirements (including requirements for audits) as the Secretary determines to be appropriate.

(2) MAXIMUM AMOUNTS.—The total amount of a line of credit under this section shall not exceed 33 percent of the reasonably anticipated eligible project costs.

(3) DRAWS.—Any draw on a line of credit under this section shall—

(A) represent a direct loan; and

(B) be made only if net revenues from the project (including capitalized interest, but not including reasonably required financing reserves) are insufficient to pay the costs specified in subsection (a)(2).

(4) INTEREST RATE.—Except as provided in subparagraphs (B) and (C) of section 603(b)(4), the interest rate on a direct loan resulting from a draw on the line of credit shall be not less than the yield on 30-year United States Treasury securities, as of the date of execution of the line of credit agreement.

(5) SECURITY.—A line of credit issued under this section—

(A) shall—

(i) be payable, in whole or in part, from—

(I) tolls;

(II) user fees;

(III) payments owing to the obligor under a public-private partnership; or

(IV) other dedicated revenue sources that also secure the senior project obligations; and

(ii) include a rate covenant, coverage requirement, or similar security feature supporting the project obligations; and

(B) may have a lien on revenues described in subparagraph (A), subject to any lien securing project obligations.

(6) PERIOD OF AVAILABILITY.—The full amount of a line of credit under this section, to the extent not drawn upon, shall be available during the 10-year period beginning on the date of substantial completion of the project.

(7) RIGHTS OF THIRD-PARTY CREDITORS.—

(A) AGAINST FEDERAL GOVERNMENT.—A third-party creditor of the obligor shall not have any right against the Federal Government with respect to any draw on a line of credit under this section.

(B) ASSIGNMENT.—An obligor may assign a line of credit under this section to—

(i) 1 or more lenders; or

(ii) a trustee on the behalf of such a lender.

(8) NONSUBORDINATION.—

(A) IN GENERAL.—Except as provided in subparagraph (B), a direct loan under this section shall not be subordinated to the claims of any holder of project obligations in the event of bankruptcy, insolvency, or liquidation of the obligor.

(B) PRE-EXISTING INDENTURE.—

(i) IN GENERAL.—The Secretary shall waive the requirement of subparagraph

(A) for a public agency borrower that is financing ongoing capital programs and has outstanding senior bonds under a preexisting indenture, if—

(I) the line of credit is rated in the A category or higher;

(II) the TIFIA program loan resulting from a draw on the line of credit is payable from pledged revenues not affected by project performance, such as a tax-backed revenue pledge or a system-backed pledge of project revenues; and

(III) the TIFIA program share of eligible project costs is 33 percent or less.

(ii) LIMITATION.—If the Secretary waives the nonsubordination requirement under this subparagraph—

(I) the maximum credit subsidy to be paid by the Federal Government shall be not more than 10 percent of the principal amount of the secured loan; and

(II) the obligor shall be responsible for paying the remainder of the subsidy cost.

(9) FEES.—The Secretary may establish fees at a level sufficient to cover all or a portion of the costs to the Federal Government of providing a line of credit under this section.

(10) RELATIONSHIP TO OTHER CREDIT INSTRUMENTS.—A project that receives a line of credit under this section also shall not receive a secured loan or loan guarantee under section 603 in an amount that, combined with the amount of the line of credit, exceeds 49 percent of eligible project costs.

(c) REPAYMENT.—

(1) TERMS AND CONDITIONS.—The Secretary shall establish repayment terms and conditions for each direct loan under this section based on—

(A) the projected cash flow from project revenues and other repayment sources; and

(B) the useful life of the asset being financed.

(2) TIMING.—All repayments of principal or interest on a direct loan under this section shall be scheduled—

(A) to commence not later than 5 years after the end of the period of availability specified in subsection (b)(6); and

(B) to conclude, with full repayment of principal and interest, by the date that is 25 years after the end of the period of availability specified in subsection (b)(6).

(Added Pub. L. 105–178, title I, §1503(a), June 9, 1998, 112 Stat. 247, §184; renumbered §604 and amended Pub. L. 109–59, title I, §§1601(e), 1602(b)(4), (d), Aug. 10, 2005, 119 Stat. 1241, 1247; Pub. L. 112–141, div. A, title II, §2002, July 6, 2012, 126 Stat. 617.)

§605. PROGRAM ADMINISTRATION

(a) REQUIREMENT.—The Secretary shall establish a uniform system to service the Federal credit instruments made available under the TIFIA program.

(b) FEES.—The Secretary may collect and spend fees, contingent on authority being provided in appropriations Acts, at a level that is sufficient to cover—

(1) the costs of services of expert firms retained pursuant to subsection (d); and

(2) all or a portion of the costs to the Federal Government of servicing the Federal credit instruments.

(c) SERVICER.—

(1) In general.—The Secretary may appoint a financial entity to assist the Secretary in servicing the Federal credit instruments.

(2) Duties.—A servicer appointed under paragraph (1) shall act as the agent for the Secretary.

(3) Fee.—A servicer appointed under paragraph (1) shall receive a servicing fee, subject to approval by the Secretary.

(d) Assistance From Expert Firms.—The Secretary may retain the services of expert firms, including counsel, in the field of municipal and project finance to assist in the underwriting and servicing of Federal credit instruments.

(e) Expedited Processing.—The Secretary shall implement procedures and measures to economize the time and cost involved in obtaining approval and the issuance of credit assistance under the TIFIA program.

(f) Assistance to Small Projects.—

(1) Reservation of funds.—Of the funds made available to carry out the TIFIA program for each fiscal year, and after the set aside under section 608(a)(6), not less than $2,000,000 shall be made available for the Secretary to use in lieu of fees collected under subsection (b) for projects under the TIFIA program having eligible project costs that are reasonably anticipated not to equal or exceed $75,000,000.

(2) Release of funds.—Any funds not used under paragraph (1) in a fiscal year shall be made available on October 1 of the following fiscal year to provide credit assistance to any project under the TIFIA program.

(Added Pub. L. 105–178, title I, §1503(a), June 9, 1998, 112 Stat. 249, §185; renumbered §605 and amended Pub. L. 109–59, title I, §§1601(f), 1602(b)(5), (d), Aug. 10, 2005, 119 Stat. 1241, 1247; Pub. L. 112–141, div. A, title II, §2002, July 6, 2012, 126 Stat. 619; Pub. L. 114–94, div. A, title II, §2001(d), Dec. 4, 2015, 129 Stat. 1443; Pub. L. 117–58, div. A, title II, §12001(i)(2), Nov. 15, 2021, 135 Stat. 621.)

§606. State and local permits

The provision of credit assistance under the TIFIA program with respect to a project shall not—

(1) relieve any recipient of the assistance of any obligation to obtain any required State or local permit or approval with respect to the project;

(2) limit the right of any unit of State or local government to approve or regulate any rate of return on private equity invested in the project; or

(3) otherwise supersede any State or local law (including any regulation) applicable to the construction or operation of the project.

(Added Pub. L. 105–178, title I, §1503(a), June 9, 1998, 112 Stat. 249, §186; renumbered §606 and amended Pub. L. 109–59, title I, §1602(b)(5), (d), Aug. 10, 2005, 119 Stat. 1247; Pub. L. 112–141, div. A, title II, §2002, July 6, 2012, 126 Stat. 620; Pub. L. 114–94, div. A, title II, §2001(e), Dec. 4, 2015, 129 Stat. 1444.)

§607. Regulations

The Secretary may promulgate such regulations as the Secretary determines to be appropriate to carry out the TIFIA program.

(Added Pub. L. 105–178, title I, §1503(a), June 9, 1998, 112 Stat. 249, §187; renumbered §607 and amended Pub. L. 109–59, title I, §1602(b)(5), (d), Aug. 10, 2005, 119 Stat. 1247; Pub. L. 112–141, div. A, title II, §2002, July 6, 2012, 126 Stat. 620; Pub. L. 114–94, div. A, title II, §2001(f), Dec. 4, 2015, 129 Stat. 1444.)

§608. FUNDING

(a) FUNDING.—

(1) SPENDING AND BORROWING AUTHORITY.—Spending and borrowing authority for a fiscal year to enter into Federal credit instruments shall be promptly apportioned to the Secretary on a fiscal-year basis.

(2) REESTIMATES.—If the subsidy cost of a Federal credit instrument is reestimated, the cost increase or decrease of the reestimate shall be borne by, or benefit, the general fund of the Treasury, consistent with section 504(f) of the Congressional Budget Act of 1974 (2 U.S.C. 661c(f)).

(3) RURAL SET-ASIDE.—

(A) IN GENERAL.—Of the total amount of funds made available to carry out the TIFIA program for each fiscal year, not more than 10 percent shall be set aside for rural infrastructure projects or rural projects funds.

(B) REOBLIGATION.—Any amounts set aside under subparagraph (A) that remain unobligated by June 1 of the fiscal year for which the amounts were set aside shall be available for obligation by the Secretary on projects other than rural infrastructure projects or rural projects funds.

(4) LIMITATION FOR CERTAIN PROJECTS.—

(A) TRANSIT-ORIENTED DEVELOPMENT PROJECTS.—For each fiscal year, the Secretary may use to carry out projects described in section 601(a)(12)(E) not more than 15 percent of the amounts made available to carry out the TIFIA program for that fiscal year.

(B) AIRPORT-RELATED PROJECTS.—The Secretary may use to carry out projects described in section 601(a)(12)(G)—

(i) for each fiscal year, not more than 15 percent of the amounts made available to carry out the TIFIA program under the Surface Transportation Reauthorization Act of 2021 for that fiscal year; and

(ii) for the period of fiscal years 2022 through 2026, not more than 15 percent of the unobligated carryover balances (as of October 1, 2021).

(5) AVAILABILITY.—Amounts made available to carry out the TIFIA program shall remain available until expended.

(6) ADMINISTRATIVE COSTS.—Of the amounts made available to carry out the TIFIA program, the Secretary may use not more than $10,000,000 for each of fiscal years 2022 through 2026 for the administration of the TIFIA program.

(b) CONTRACT AUTHORITY.—

(1) IN GENERAL.—Notwithstanding any other provision of law, execution of a term sheet by the Secretary of a Federal credit instrument that uses amounts made available under the TIFIA program shall impose on the United States a contractual obligation to fund the Federal credit investment.

(2) AVAILABILITY.—Amounts made available to carry out the TIFIA program for a fiscal year shall be available for obligation on October 1 of the fiscal year.

(Added and amended Pub. L. 105–178, title I, §1503(a), (c), June 9, 1998, 112 Stat. 249, §188; Pub. L. 105–206, title IX, §9007(a), July 22, 1998, 112 Stat. 849; Pub. L. 108–88, §5(a)(10), Sept. 30, 2003, 117 Stat. 1115; Pub. L. 108–202, §5(a)(10), Feb. 29, 2004, 118 Stat. 481; Pub. L. 108–224, §4(a)(10), Apr. 30, 2004, 118 Stat. 629; Pub. L. 108–263, §4(a)(10), June 30, 2004, 118 Stat. 700; Pub. L. 108–280,

§4(a)(10), July 30, 2004, 118 Stat. 879; Pub. L. 108–310, §5(a)(10), Sept. 30, 2004, 118 Stat. 1149; Pub. L. 109–14, §4(a)(10), May 31, 2005, 119 Stat. 327; Pub. L. 109–20, §4(a)(10), July 1, 2005, 119 Stat. 348; Pub. L. 109–35, §4(a)(10), July 20, 2005, 119 Stat. 381; Pub. L. 109–37, §4(a)(10), July 22, 2005, 119 Stat. 396; Pub. L. 109–40, §4(a)(10), July 28, 2005, 119 Stat. 413; renumbered §608 and amended Pub. L. 109–59, title I, §§1601(g), 1602(b)(5), (d), Aug. 10, 2005, 119 Stat. 1242, 1247; Pub. L. 112–141, div. A, title II, §2002, July 6, 2012, 126 Stat. 620; Pub. L. 114–94, div. A, title II, §2001(g), Dec. 4, 2015, 129 Stat. 1444; Pub. L. 117–58, div. A, title II, §12001(i)(1), Nov. 15, 2021, 135 Stat. 620.)

§609. REPORTS TO CONGRESS

(a) IN GENERAL.—On June 1, 2012, and every 2 years thereafter, the Secretary shall submit to Congress a report summarizing the financial performance of the projects that are receiving, or have received, assistance under the TIFIA program, including a recommendation as to whether the objectives of the TIFIA program are best served by—

(1) continuing the program under the authority of the Secretary;

(2) establishing a Federal corporation or federally sponsored enterprise to administer the program; or

(3) phasing out the program and relying on the capital markets to fund the types of infrastructure investments assisted by the TIFIA program without Federal participation.

(b) APPLICATION PROCESS REPORT.—

(1) IN GENERAL.—Not later than December 1, 2012, and annually thereafter, the Secretary shall submit to the Committee on Transportation and Infrastructure of the House of Representatives and the Committee on Environment and Public Works of the Senate a report that includes a list of all of the letters of interest and applications received from project sponsors for assistance under the TIFIA program during the preceding fiscal year.

(2) INCLUSIONS.—

(A) IN GENERAL.—Each report under paragraph (1) shall include, at a minimum, a description of, with respect to each letter of interest and application included in the report—

(i) the date on which the letter of interest or application was received;

(ii) the date on which a notification was provided to the project sponsor regarding whether the application was complete or incomplete;

(iii) the date on which a revised and completed application was submitted (if applicable);

(iv) the date on which a notification was provided to the project sponsor regarding whether the project was approved or disapproved; and

(v) if the project was not approved, the reason for the disapproval.

(B) CORRESPONDENCE.—Each report under paragraph (1) shall include copies of any correspondence provided to the project sponsor in accordance with section 602(d).

(c) STATUS REPORTS.—

(1) IN GENERAL.—The Secretary shall publish on the website for the TIFIA program—

(A) on a monthly basis, a current status report on all submitted letters of interest and applications received for assistance under the TIFIA program; and

(B) on a quarterly basis, a current status report on all approved applications for assistance under the TIFIA program.

(2) INCLUSIONS.—Each monthly and quarterly status report under paragraph (1) shall include, at a minimum, with respect to each project included in the status report—

(A) the name of the party submitting the letter of interest or application;

(B) the name of the project;

(C) the date on which the letter of interest or application was received;

(D) the estimated project eligible costs;

(E) the type of credit assistance sought; and

(F) the anticipated fiscal year and quarter for closing of the credit assistance.

(Added Pub. L. 105–178, title I, §1503(a), June 9, 1998, 112 Stat. 250, §189; renumbered §609 and amended Pub. L. 109–59, title I, §§1601(h), 1602(d), Aug. 10, 2005, 119 Stat. 1242, 1247; Pub. L. 112–141, div. A, title II, §2002, July 6, 2012, 126 Stat. 621; Pub. L. 114–94, div. A, title II, §2001(h), Dec. 4, 2015, 129 Stat. 1444; Pub. L. 117–58, div. A, title II, §12001(j), Nov. 15, 2021, 135 Stat. 621.)

§610. STATE INFRASTRUCTURE BANK PROGRAM

(a) DEFINITIONS.—In this section, the following definitions apply:

(1) CAPITAL PROJECT.—The term "capital project" has the meaning such term has under section 5302 of title 49.

(2) OTHER FORMS OF CREDIT ASSISTANCE.—The term "other forms of credit assistance" includes any use of funds in an infrastructure bank—

(A) to provide credit enhancements;

(B) to serve as a capital reserve for bond or debt instrument financing;

(C) to subsidize interest rates;

(D) to insure or guarantee letters of credit and credit instruments against credit risk of loss;

(E) to finance purchase and lease agreements with respect to transit projects;

(F) to provide bond or debt financing instrument security; and

(G) to provide other forms of debt financing and methods of leveraging funds that are approved by the Secretary and that relate to the project with respect to which such assistance is being provided.

(3) STATE.—The term "State" has the meaning such term has under section 401.

(4) CAPITALIZATION.—The term "capitalization" means the process used for depositing funds as initial capital into a State infrastructure bank to establish the infrastructure bank.

(5) COOPERATIVE AGREEMENT.—The term "cooperative agreement" means written consent between a State and the Secretary which sets forth the manner in which the infrastructure bank established by the State in accordance with this section will be administered.

(6) LOAN.—The term "loan" means any form of direct financial assistance from a State infrastructure bank that is required to be repaid over a period of time and that is provided to a project sponsor for all or part of the costs of the project.

(7) GUARANTEE.—The term "guarantee" means a contract entered into by a State infrastructure bank in which the bank agrees to take responsibility for all or a portion of a project sponsor's financial obligations for a project under specified conditions.

(8) INITIAL ASSISTANCE.—The term "initial assistance" means the first round of

funds that are loaned or used for credit enhancement by a State infrastructure bank for projects eligible for assistance under this section.

(9) LEVERAGE.—The term "leverage" means a financial structure used to increase funds in a State infrastructure bank through the issuance of debt instruments.

(10) LEVERAGED.—The term "leveraged", as used with respect to a State infrastructure bank, means that the bank has total potential liabilities that exceed the capital of the bank.

(11) RURAL INFRASTRUCTURE PROJECT.—The term "rural infrastructure project" has the meaning given the term in section 601.

(12) RURAL PROJECTS FUND.—The term "rural projects fund" has the meaning given the term in section 601.

(b) COOPERATIVE AGREEMENTS.—Subject to the provisions of this section, the Secretary may enter into cooperative agreements with States for the establishment of State infrastructure banks for making loans and providing other forms of credit assistance to public and private entities carrying out or proposing to carry out projects eligible for assistance under this section.

(c) INTERSTATE COMPACTS.—

(1) IN GENERAL.—Congress grants consent to two or more of the States, entering into a cooperative agreement under subsection (a) with the Secretary for the establishment by such States of a multistate infrastructure bank in accordance with this section, to enter into an interstate compact establishing such bank in accordance with this section.

(2) RESERVATION OF RIGHTS.—The right to alter, amend, or repeal interstate compacts entered into under this subsection is expressly reserved.

(d) FUNDING.—

(1) HIGHWAY ACCOUNT.—Subject to subsection (j), the Secretary may permit a State entering into a cooperative agreement under this section to establish a State infrastructure bank to deposit into the highway account of the bank not to exceed—

(A) 10 percent of the funds apportioned to the State for each of fiscal years 2022 through 2026 under each of paragraphs (1), (2), and (5) of section 104(b); and

(B) 10 percent of the funds allocated to the State for each of such fiscal years.

(2) TRANSIT ACCOUNT.—Subject to subsection (j), the Secretary may permit a State entering into a cooperative agreement under this section to establish a State infrastructure bank, and any other recipient of Federal assistance under section 5307, 5309, or 5311 of title 49, to deposit into the transit account of the bank not to exceed 10 percent of the funds made available to the State or other recipient in each of fiscal years 2022 through 2026 for capital projects under each of such sections.

(3) RAIL ACCOUNT.—Subject to subsection (j), the Secretary may permit a State entering into a cooperative agreement under this section to establish a State infrastructure bank, and any other recipient of Federal assistance under subtitle V of title 49, to deposit into the rail account of the bank funds made available to the State or other recipient in each of fiscal years 2022 through 2026 for capital projects under such subtitle.

(4) RURAL PROJECTS FUND.—Subject to subsection (j), the Secretary may permit a State entering into a cooperative agreement under this section to establish a State

infrastructure bank to deposit into the rural projects fund of the bank the proceeds of a secured loan made to the bank in accordance with sections 602 and 603.

(5) CAPITAL GRANTS.—

(A) HIGHWAY ACCOUNT.—Federal funds deposited into a highway account of a State infrastructure bank under paragraph (1) shall constitute for purposes of this section a capitalization grant for the highway account of the bank.

(B) TRANSIT ACCOUNT.—Federal funds deposited into a transit account of a State infrastructure bank under paragraph (2) shall constitute for purposes of this section a capitalization grant for the transit account of the bank.

(C) RAIL ACCOUNT.—Federal funds deposited into a rail account of a State infrastructure bank under paragraph 3 shall constitute for purposes of this section a capitalization grant for the rail account of the bank.

(6) SPECIAL RULE FOR URBANIZED AREAS OF OVER 200,000.—Funds in a State infrastructure bank that are attributed to urbanized areas of a State with urbanized populations of over 200,000 under section 133(d)(1)(A)(i) may be used to provide assistance with respect to a project only if the metropolitan planning organization designated for such area concurs, in writing, with the provision of such assistance.

(7) DISCONTINUANCE OF FUNDING.—If the Secretary determines that a State is not implementing the State's infrastructure bank in accordance with a cooperative agreement entered into under subsection (b), the Secretary may prohibit the State from contributing additional Federal funds to the bank.

(e) FORMS OF ASSISTANCE FROM STATE INFRASTRUCTURE BANKS.—

(1) IN GENERAL.—A State infrastructure bank established under this section may—

(A) with funds deposited into the highway account, transit account, or rail account of the bank, make loans or provide other forms of credit assistance to a public or private entity to carry out a project eligible for assistance under this section; and

(B) with funds deposited into the rural projects fund, make loans to a public or private entity to carry out a rural infrastructure project.

(2) SUBORDINATION OF LOAN.—The amount of a loan or other form of credit assistance provided for a project described in paragraph (1) may be subordinated to any other debt financing for the project.

(3) MAXIMUM AMOUNT OF ASSISTANCE.—A State infrastructure bank established under this section may—

(A) with funds deposited into the highway account, transit account, or rail account of the bank, make loans or provide other forms of credit assistance to a public or private entity in an amount up to 100 percent of the cost of carrying out a project eligible for assistance under this section; and

(B) with funds deposited into the rural projects fund, make loans to a public or private entity in an amount not to exceed 80 percent of the cost of carrying out a rural infrastructure project.

(4) INITIAL ASSISTANCE.—Initial assistance provided with respect to a project from Federal funds deposited into a State infrastructure bank under this section may not be made in the form of a grant.

(f) ELIGIBLE PROJECTS.—Subject to subsection (e), funds in an infrastructure bank established under this section may be used only to provide assistance for projects eligible for assistance under this title and capital projects defined in section 5302 of title 49, and any other projects relating to surface transportation that the Secretary determines to be appropriate.

(g) INFRASTRUCTURE BANK REQUIREMENTS.—In order to establish an infrastructure bank under this section, the State establishing the bank shall—

(1) deposit in cash, at a minimum, into the highway account, the transit account, and the rail account of the bank from non-Federal sources an amount equal to 25 percent of the amount of each capitalization grant made to the State and deposited into such account; except that, if the deposit is into the highway account of the bank and the State has a non-Federal share under section 120(b) that is less than 25 percent, the percentage to be deposited from non-Federal sources shall be the lower percentage of such grant;

(2) ensure that the bank maintains on a continuing basis an investment grade rating on its debt, or has a sufficient level of bond or debt financing instrument insurance, to maintain the viability of the bank;

(3) ensure that investment income derived from funds deposited to an account of the bank are—

(A) credited to the account;

(B) available for use in providing loans and other forms of credit assistance to projects eligible for assistance from the account; and

(C) invested in United States Treasury securities, bank deposits, or such other financing instruments as the Secretary may approve to earn interest to enhance the leveraging of projects assisted by the bank;

(4) ensure that any loan from the bank will bear interest at or below market interest rates, as determined by the State, to make the project that is the subject of the loan feasible, except that any loan funded from the rural projects fund of the bank shall bear interest at or below the interest rate charged for the TIFIA loan provided to the bank under section 603;

(5) ensure that repayment of any loan from the bank will commence not later than 5 years after the project has been completed or, in the case of a highway project, the facility has opened to traffic, whichever is later;

(6) ensure that the term for repaying any loan will not exceed 30 years after the date of the first payment on the loan; and

(7) require the bank to make an annual report to the Secretary on its status no later than September 30 of each year and such other reports as the Secretary may require under guidelines issued to carry out this section.

(h) APPLICABILITY OF FEDERAL LAW.—

(1) IN GENERAL.—The requirements of this title and title 49 that would otherwise apply to funds made available under this title or such title and projects assisted with those funds shall apply to—

(A) funds made available under this title or such title and contributed to an infrastructure bank established under this section, including the non-Federal contribution required under subsection (g); and

(B) projects assisted by the bank through the use of the funds, except to the extent that the Secretary determines that any requirement of such title (other than sections 113 and 114 of this title and section 5333 of title 49) is not consistent with the objectives of this section.

(2) REPAYMENTS.—The requirements of this title and title 49 shall apply to repayments from non-Federal sources to an infrastructure bank from projects assisted by the bank. Such a repayment shall be considered to be Federal funds.

(i) UNITED STATES NOT OBLIGATED.—The deposit of Federal funds into an infrastructure bank established under this section shall not be construed as a commitment, guarantee, or obligation on the part of the United States to any third party, nor shall any third party have any right against the United States for payment solely by virtue of the contribution. Any security or debt-financing instrument issued by the infrastructure bank shall expressly state that the security or instrument does not constitute a commitment, guarantee, or obligation of the United States.

(j) MANAGEMENT OF FEDERAL FUNDS.—Sections 3335 and 6503 of title 31 shall not apply to funds deposited into an infrastructure bank under this section.

(k) PROGRAM ADMINISTRATION.—For each of fiscal years 2022 through 2026, a State may expend not to exceed 2 percent of the Federal funds contributed to an infrastructure bank established by the State under this section to pay the reasonable costs of administering the bank.

(Added Pub. L. 109–59, title I, §1602(a), Aug. 10, 2005, 119 Stat. 1243, §190; renumbered §610, Pub. L. 109–59, title I, §1602(d), Aug. 10, 2005, 119 Stat. 1247, as amended Pub. L. 110–244, title I, §101(f), June 6, 2008, 122 Stat. 1574; Pub. L. 112–141, div. A, title I, §1519(c)(11), formerly §1519(c)(12), July 6, 2012, 126 Stat. 577, renumbered §1519(c)(11), Pub. L. 114–94, div. A, title I, §1446(d)(5)(B), Dec. 4, 2015, 129 Stat. 1438; Pub. L. 114–94, div. A, title II, §2001(i), Dec. 4, 2015, 129 Stat. 1444; Pub. L. 117–58, div. A, title II, §12001(k), Nov. 15, 2021, 135 Stat. 621.)

§611. ASSET CONCESSIONS AND INNOVATIVE FINANCE ASSISTANCE

(a) DEFINITIONS.—In this section:

(1) APPROVED INFRASTRUCTURE ASSET.—The term "approved infrastructure asset" means—

(A) a project (as defined in section 601(a)); and

(B) a group of projects (as defined in section 601(a)) considered together in a single asset concession or long-term lease to a concessionaire by 1 or more eligible entities.

(2) ASSET CONCESSION.—The term "asset concession" means a contract between an eligible entity and a concessionaire—

(A) under which—

(i) the eligible entity agrees to enter into a concession agreement or long-term lease with the concessionaire relating to an approved infrastructure asset owned, controlled, or maintained by the eligible entity;

(ii) as consideration for the agreement or lease described in clause (i), the concessionaire agrees—

(I) to provide to the eligible entity 1 or more asset concession payments; and

(II) to maintain or exceed the condition, performance, and service level of the approved infrastructure asset, as compared to that condition, performance, and service level on the date of execution of the agreement or lease; and

(iii) the eligible entity and the concessionaire agree that the costs for a fiscal year of the agreement or lease, and any project carried out under the agreement or lease, shall not be shifted to any taxpayer the annual household income of whom is less than $400,000 per year, including through taxes, user fees, tolls, or any other measure, for use of an approved infrastructure asset; and

(B) the terms of which do not include any noncompete or exclusivity restriction (or any other, similar restriction) on the approval of another project.

(3) ASSET CONCESSION PAYMENT.—The term "asset concession payment" means a payment that—

(A) is made by a concessionaire to an eligible entity for fair market value that is determined as part of the asset concession; and

(B) may be—

(i) a payment made at the financial close of an asset concession; or

(ii) a series of payments scheduled to be made for—

(I) a fixed period; or

(II) the term of an asset concession.

(4) CONCESSIONAIRE.—The term "concessionaire" means a private individual or a private or publicly chartered corporation or entity that enters into an asset concession with an eligible entity.

(5) ELIGIBLE ENTITY.—

(A) IN GENERAL.—The term "eligible entity" means an entity described in subparagraph (B) that—

(i) owns, controls, or maintains an approved infrastructure asset; and

(ii) has the legal authority to enter into a contract to transfer ownership, maintenance, operations, revenues, or other benefits and responsibilities for an approved infrastructure asset.

(B) ENTITIES DESCRIBED.—An entity referred to in subparagraph (A) is any of the following:

(i) A State.

(ii) A Tribal government.

(iii) A unit of local government.

(iv) An agency or instrumentality of a State, Tribal government, or unit of local government.

(v) A special purpose district or public authority.

(b) ESTABLISHMENT.—The Secretary shall establish a program to facilitate access to expert services for, and to provide grants to, eligible entities to enhance the technical capacity of eligible entities to facilitate and evaluate public-private partnerships in which the private sector partner could assume a greater role in project planning, development, financing, construction, maintenance, and operation, including by assisting eligible entities in entering into asset concessions.

(c) APPLICATIONS.—To be eligible to receive a grant under this section, an eligible entity shall submit to the Secretary an application at such time, in such manner, and containing such information as the Secretary may require.

(d) ELIGIBLE ACTIVITIES.—

(1) TECHNICAL ASSISTANCE GRANTS.—An eligible entity may use amounts made available from a grant under this section for technical assistance to build the organizational capacity of the eligible entity to develop, review, or enter into an asset concession, including for—

(A) identifying appropriate assets or projects for asset concessions;

(B) soliciting and negotiating asset concessions, including hiring staff in public agencies;

(C) conducting a value-for-money analysis, or a comparable analysis, to evaluate the comparative benefits of asset concessions and public debt or other procurement methods;

(D) evaluating options for the structure and use of asset concession payments;

(E) evaluating and publicly presenting the risks and benefits of all contract provisions for the purpose of transparency and accountability;

(F) identifying best practices to protect the public interest and priorities;

(G) identifying best practices for managing transportation demand and mobility along a corridor, including through provisions of the asset concession, to facilitate transportation demand management strategies along the corridor that is subject to the asset concession; and

(H) integrating and coordinating pricing, data, and fare collection with other regional operators that exist or may be developed.

(2) EXPERT SERVICES.—An eligible entity seeking to leverage public and private funding in connection with the development of an early-stage approved infrastructure asset, including in the development of alternative approaches to project delivery or procurement, may use amounts made available from a grant under this section to retain the services of an expert firm to provide to the eligible entity direct project level assistance, which services may include—

(A) project planning, feasibility studies, revenue forecasting, economic assessments and cost-benefit analyses, public benefit studies, value-for-money analyses, business case development, lifecycle cost analyses, risk assessment, financing and funding options analyses, procurement alternatives analyses, statutory and regulatory framework analyses and other pre-procurement and pre-construction activities;

(B) financial and legal planning (including the identification of statutory authorization, funding, and financing options);

(C) early assessment of permitting, environmental review, and regulatory processes and costs; and

(D) assistance with entering into an asset concession.

(e) DISTRIBUTION.—

(1) MAXIMUM AMOUNT.—

(A) TECHNICAL ASSISTANCE GRANTS.—The maximum amount of a technical assistance grant under subsection (d)(1) shall be $2,000,000.

(B) EXPERT SERVICES.—The maximum amount of the value of expert services retained by an eligible entity under subsection (d)(2) shall be $2,000,000.

(2) COST SHARING.—

(A) IN GENERAL.—Except as provided in subparagraph (B), the Federal share of the cost of an activity carried out under this section may be up to 100 percent.

(B) CERTAIN PROJECTS.—If the amount of the grant provided to an eligible entity under this section is more than $1,000,000, the Federal share of the cost of an activity carried out using grant amounts in excess of $1,000,000 shall be 50 percent.

(3) STATEWIDE MAXIMUM.—The aggregate amount made available under this section to eligible entities within a State shall not exceed, on a cumulative basis for all eligible entities within the State during any 3-year period, $4,000,000.

(f) REQUIREMENTS.—

(1) IN GENERAL.—The Secretary shall ensure that, as a condition of receiving a grant under this section, for any asset concession for which the grant provides direct assistance—

(A) the asset concession shall not prohibit, discourage, or make it more difficult for an eligible entity to construct new infrastructure, to provide or expand transportation services, or to manage associated infrastructure in publicly beneficial ways, along a transportation corridor or in the proximity of a transportation facility that was a part of the asset concession;

(B) the eligible entity shall have adopted binding rules to publish all major business terms of the proposed asset concession not later than the date that is 30 days before entering into the asset concession, to enable public review, including a certification of public interest based on the results of an assessment under subparagraph (D);

(C) the asset concession shall not result in displacement, job loss, or wage reduction for the existing workforce of the eligible entity or other public entities;

(D) the eligible entity or the concessionaire shall carry out a value-for-money analysis, or similar assessment, to compare the aggregate costs and benefits to the eligible entity of the asset concession against alternative options to determine whether the asset concession generates additional public benefits and serves the public interest;

(E) the full amount of any asset concession payment received by the eligible entity under the asset concession, less any amount paid for transaction costs relating to the asset concession, shall be used to pay infrastructure costs of the eligible entity; and

(F) the terms of the asset concession shall not result in any increase in costs under the asset concession being shifted to taxpayers the annual household income of whom is less than $400,000 per year, including through taxes, user fees, tolls, or any other measure, for use of an approved infrastructure asset.

(2) AUDIT.—Not later than 3 years after the date on which an eligible entity enters into an asset concession as a result of a grant under this section—

(A) the eligible entity shall hire an independent auditor to evaluate the performance of the concessionaire based on the requirements described in paragraph (1); and

(B) the independent auditor shall submit to the eligible entity, and make publicly available, a report describing the results of the audit under subparagraph (A).

(3) TREATMENT.—Unless otherwise provided under paragraph (1), the Secretary

shall not, as a condition of receiving a grant under this section, prohibit or otherwise prevent an eligible entity from entering into, or receiving any asset concession payment under, an asset concession for an approved infrastructure asset owned, controlled, or maintained by the eligible entity.

(4) APPLICABILITY OF FEDERAL LAWS.—Nothing in this section exempts a concessionaire or an eligible entity from a compliance obligation with respect to any applicable Federal or State law that would otherwise apply to the concessionaire, the eligible entity, or an approved infrastructure asset.

(g) FUNDING.—

(1) IN GENERAL.—On October 1, 2021, and on each October 1 thereafter through October 1, 2025, out of any funds in the Treasury not otherwise appropriated, the Secretary of the Treasury shall transfer to the Secretary to carry out this section $20,000,000, to remain available until expended.

(2) RECEIPT AND ACCEPTANCE.—The Secretary shall be entitled to receive, shall accept, and shall use to carry out this section the funds transferred under paragraph (1), without further appropriation.

(Added Pub. L. 117–58, div. G, title X, §71001(a)(1), Nov. 15, 2021, 135 Stat. 1316.)

Selected Provisions of

Subtitle III of Title 23 U.S.C. — Highways

TITLE 49—TRANSPORTATION

This title was enacted by Pub. L. 95–473, §1, Oct. 17, 1978, 92 Stat. 1337; Pub. L. 97–449, §1, Jan. 12, 1983, 96 Stat. 2413; Pub. L. 103–272, July 5, 1994, 108 Stat. 745

* * * * * * *

SUBTITLE III—GENERAL AND INTERMODAL PROGRAMS

* * * * * * *

CHAPTER 53—PUBLIC TRANSPORTATION

[1] *Section repealed by Pub. L. 112–141 without corresponding amendment of chapter analysis.*

§5301. POLICIES AND PURPOSES

(a) DECLARATION OF POLICY.—It is in the interest of the United States, including the economic interest of the United States, to foster the development and revitalization of public transportation systems with the cooperation of both public transportation companies and private companies engaged in public transportation.

(b) GENERAL PURPOSES.—The purposes of this chapter are to—

(1) provide funding to support public transportation;

(2) improve the development and delivery of capital projects;

(3) establish standards for the state of good repair of public transportation infrastructure and vehicles;

(4) promote continuing, cooperative, and comprehensive planning that improves the performance of the transportation network;

(5) establish a technical assistance program to assist recipients under this chapter to more effectively and efficiently provide public transportation service;

(6) continue Federal support for public transportation providers to deliver high quality service to all users, including individuals with disabilities, seniors, and individuals who depend on public transportation;

(7) support research, development, demonstration, and deployment projects dedicated to assisting in the delivery of efficient and effective public transportation service; and

(8) promote the development of the public transportation workforce.

(Pub. L. 103–272, §1(d), July 5, 1994, 108 Stat. 785; Pub. L. 109–59, title III, §§3002(b)(4), 3003, Aug. 10, 2005, 119 Stat. 1545; Pub. L. 112–141, div. B, §20003, July 6, 2012, 126 Stat. 622.)

§5302. DEFINITIONS

Except as otherwise specifically provided, in this chapter the following definitions apply:

(1) ASSAULT ON A TRANSIT WORKER.—The term "assault on a transit worker" means a circumstance in which an individual knowingly, without lawful authority or

permission, and with intent to endanger the safety of any individual, or with a reckless disregard for the safety of human life, interferes with, disables, or incapacitates a transit worker while the transit worker is performing the duties of the transit worker.

(2) ASSOCIATED TRANSIT IMPROVEMENT.—The term "associated transit improvement" means, with respect to any project or an area to be served by a project, projects that are designed to enhance public transportation service or use and that are physically or functionally related to transit facilities. Eligible projects are—

(A) historic preservation, rehabilitation, and operation of historic public transportation buildings, structures, and facilities (including historic bus and railroad facilities) intended for use in public transportation service;

(B) bus shelters;

(C) functional landscaping and streetscaping, including benches, trash receptacles, and street lights;

(D) pedestrian access and walkways;

(E) bicycle access, including bicycle storage shelters and parking facilities and the installation of equipment for transporting bicycles on public transportation vehicles;

(F) signage; or

(G) enhanced access for persons with disabilities to public transportation.

(3) BUS RAPID TRANSIT SYSTEM.—The term "bus rapid transit system" means a bus transit system—

(A) in which the majority of each line operates in a separated right-of-way dedicated for public transportation use during peak periods; and

(B) that includes features that emulate the services provided by rail fixed guideway public transportation systems, including—

(i) defined stations;

(ii) traffic signal priority for public transportation vehicles;

(iii) short headway bidirectional services for a substantial part of weekdays and weekend days; and

(iv) any other features the Secretary may determine are necessary to produce high-quality public transportation services that emulate the services provided by rail fixed guideway public transportation systems.

(4) CAPITAL PROJECT.—The term "capital project" means a project for—

(A) acquiring, constructing, supervising, or inspecting equipment or a facility for use in public transportation, expenses incidental to the acquisition or construction (including designing, engineering, location surveying, mapping, and acquiring rights-of-way), payments for the capital portions of rail trackage rights agreements, transit-related intelligent transportation systems, relocation assistance, acquiring replacement housing sites, and acquiring, constructing, relocating, and rehabilitating replacement housing;

(B) rehabilitating a bus;

(C) remanufacturing a bus;

(D) overhauling rail rolling stock;

(E) preventive maintenance;

(F) leasing equipment or a facility for use in public transportation;

(G) a joint development improvement that—

(i) enhances economic development or incorporates private investment, such as commercial and residential development;

(ii)(I) enhances the effectiveness of public transportation and is related physically or functionally to public transportation; or

(II) establishes new or enhanced coordination between public transportation and other transportation;

(iii) provides a fair share of revenue that will be used for public transportation;

(iv) provides that if equipment to fuel privately owned zero-emission passenger vehicles is installed, the recipient of assistance under this chapter shall collect fees from users of the equipment in order to recover the costs of construction, maintenance, and operation of the equipment;

(v) provides that a person making an agreement to occupy space in a facility constructed under this paragraph shall pay a fair share of the costs of the facility through rental payments and other means; and

(vi) may include—

(I) property acquisition;

(II) demolition of existing structures;

(III) site preparation;

(IV) utilities;

(V) building foundations;

(VI) walkways;

(VII) pedestrian and bicycle access to a public transportation facility;

(VIII) construction, renovation, and improvement of intercity bus and intercity rail stations and terminals;

(IX) renovation and improvement of historic transportation facilities;

(X) open space;

(XI) safety and security equipment and facilities (including lighting, surveillance, and related intelligent transportation system applications);

(XII) facilities that incorporate community services such as daycare or health care;

(XIII) a capital project for, and improving, equipment or a facility for an intermodal transfer facility or transportation mall;

(XIV) construction of space for commercial uses; and

(XV) technology to fuel a zero-emission vehicle;

(H) the introduction of new technology, through innovative and improved products, into public transportation;

(I) the provision of nonfixed route paratransit transportation services in accordance with section 223 of the Americans with Disabilities Act of 1990 (42 U.S.C. 12143), but only for grant recipients that are in compliance with applicable requirements of that Act, including both fixed route and demand responsive service, and only for amounts—

(i) not to exceed 10 percent of such recipient's annual formula apportionment under sections 5307 and 5311; or

(ii) not to exceed 20 percent of such recipient's annual formula apportionment under sections 5307 and 5311, if, consistent with guidance issued by the Secretary, the recipient demonstrates that the recipient meets at least 2 of the following requirements:

(I) Provides an active fixed route travel training program that is available for riders with disabilities.

(II) Provides that all fixed route and paratransit operators participate in a passenger safety, disability awareness, and sensitivity training class on at least a biennial basis.

(III) Has memoranda of understanding in place with employers and the American Job Center to increase access to employment opportunities for people with disabilities.

(J) establishing a debt service reserve, made up of deposits with a bondholder's trustee, to ensure the timely payment of principal and interest on bonds issued by a grant recipient to finance an eligible project under this chapter;

(K) mobility management—

(i) consisting of short-range planning and management activities and projects for improving coordination among public transportation and other transportation service providers carried out by a recipient or subrecipient through an agreement entered into with a person, including a governmental entity, under this chapter (other than section 5309); but

(ii) excluding operating public transportation services;

(L) associated capital maintenance, including—

(i) equipment, tires, tubes, and material, each costing at least .5 percent of the current fair market value of rolling stock comparable to the rolling stock for which the equipment, tires, tubes, and material are to be used; and

(ii) reconstruction of equipment and material, each of which after reconstruction will have a fair market value of at least .5 percent of the current fair market value of rolling stock comparable to the rolling stock for which the equipment and material will be used;

(M) associated transit improvements; or

(N) technological changes or innovations to modify low or no emission vehicles (as defined in section 5339(c)) or facilities.

(5) DESIGNATED RECIPIENT.—The term "designated recipient" means—

(A) an entity designated, in accordance with the planning process under sections 5303 and 5304, by the Governor of a State, responsible local officials, and publicly owned operators of public transportation, to receive and apportion amounts under section 5336 to urbanized areas of 200,000 or more in population; or

(B) a State or regional authority, if the authority is responsible under the laws of a State for a capital project and for financing and directly providing public transportation.

(6) DISABILITY.—The term "disability" has the same meaning as in section 3(1) of the Americans with Disabilities Act of 1990 (42 U.S.C. 12102).

(7) EMERGENCY REGULATION.—The term "emergency regulation" means a regulation—

(A) that is effective temporarily before the expiration of the otherwise specified periods of time for public notice and comment under section 5334(c); and

(B) prescribed by the Secretary as the result of a finding that a delay in the effective date of the regulation—

(i) would injure seriously an important public interest;

(ii) would frustrate substantially legislative policy and intent; or

(iii) would damage seriously a person or class without serving an important public interest.

(8) FIXED GUIDEWAY.—The term "fixed guideway" means a public transportation facility—

(A) using and occupying a separate right-of-way for the exclusive use of public transportation;

(B) using rail;

(C) using a fixed catenary system;

(D) for a passenger ferry system; or

(E) for a bus rapid transit system.

(9) GOVERNOR.—The term "Governor"—

(A) means the Governor of a State, the mayor of the District of Columbia, and the chief executive officer of a territory of the United States; and

(B) includes the designee of the Governor.

(10) JOB ACCESS AND REVERSE COMMUTE PROJECT.—

(A) IN GENERAL.—The term "job access and reverse commute project" means a transportation project to finance planning, capital, and operating costs that support the development and maintenance of transportation services designed to transport welfare recipients and eligible low-income individuals to and from jobs and activities related to their employment, including transportation projects that facilitate the provision of public transportation services from urbanized areas and rural areas to suburban employment locations.

(B) DEFINITIONS.—In this paragraph:

(i) ELIGIBLE LOW-INCOME INDIVIDUAL.—The term "eligible low-income individual" means an individual whose family income is at or below 150 percent of the poverty line (as that term is defined in section 673(2) of the Community Service Block Grant Act (42 U.S.C. 9902(2)), including any revision required by that section) for a family of the size involved.

(ii) WELFARE RECIPIENT.—The term "welfare recipient" means an individual who has received assistance under a State or tribal program funded under part A of title IV of the Social Security Act (42 U.S.C. 601 et seq.) at any time during the 3-year period before the date on which the applicant applies for a grant under section 5307 or 5311.

(11) LOCAL GOVERNMENTAL AUTHORITY.—The term "local governmental authority" includes—

(A) a political subdivision of a State;

(B) an authority of at least 1 State or political subdivision of a State;

(C) an Indian tribe; and

(D) a public corporation, board, or commission established under the laws of a State.

(12) LOW-INCOME INDIVIDUAL.—The term "low-income individual" means an individual whose family income is at or below 150 percent of the poverty line, as that term is defined in section 673(2) of the Community Services Block Grant Act (42 U.S.C. 9902(2)), including any revision required by that section, for a family of the size involved.

(13) NET PROJECT COST.—The term "net project cost" means the part of a project that reasonably cannot be financed from revenues.

(14) NEW BUS MODEL.—The term "new bus model" means a bus model (including a model using alternative fuel)—

(A) that has not been used in public transportation in the United States before the date of production of the model; or

(B) used in public transportation in the United States, but being produced with a major change in configuration or components.

(15) PUBLIC TRANSPORTATION.—The term "public transportation"—

(A) means regular, continuing shared-ride surface transportation services that are open to the general public or open to a segment of the general public defined by age, disability, or low income; and

(B) does not include—

(i) intercity passenger rail transportation provided by the entity described in chapter 243 (or a successor to such entity);

(ii) intercity bus service;

(iii) charter bus service;

(iv) school bus service;

(v) sightseeing service;

(vi) courtesy shuttle service for patrons of one or more specific establishments; or

(vii) intra-terminal or intra-facility shuttle services.

(16) REGULATION.—The term "regulation" means any part of a statement of general or particular applicability of the Secretary designed to carry out, interpret, or prescribe law or policy in carrying out this chapter.

(17) RURAL AREA.—The term "rural area" means an area encompassing a population of less than 50,000 people that has not been designated in the most recent decennial census as an "urbanized area" by the Secretary of Commerce.

(18) SECRETARY.—The term "Secretary" means the Secretary of Transportation.

(19) SENIOR.—The term "senior" means an individual who is 65 years of age or older.

(20) STATE.—The term "State" means a State of the United States, the District of Columbia, Puerto Rico, the Northern Mariana Islands, Guam, American Samoa, and the Virgin Islands.

(21) STATE OF GOOD REPAIR.—The term "state of good repair" has the meaning given that term by the Secretary, by rule, under section 5326(b).

(22) TRANSIT.—The term "transit" means public transportation.

(23) URBAN AREA.—The term "urban area" means an area that includes a municipality or other built-up place that the Secretary, after considering local patterns and trends of urban growth, decides is appropriate for a local public transportation

system to serve individuals in the locality.

(24) URBANIZED AREA.—The term "urbanized area" means an area encompassing a population of not less than 50,000 people that has been defined and designated in the most recent decennial census as an "urbanized area" by the Secretary of Commerce.

(25) VALUE CAPTURE.—The term "value capture" means recovering the increased property value to property located near public transportation resulting from investments in public transportation.

(Pub. L. 103–272, §1(d), July 5, 1994, 108 Stat. 786; Pub. L. 103–331, title III, §335A, Sept. 30, 1994, 108 Stat. 2495; Pub. L. 104–50, title III, §333(a), Nov. 15, 1995, 109 Stat. 457; Pub. L. 104–287, §6(c), Oct. 11, 1996, 110 Stat. 3398; Pub. L. 105–102, §3(a), Nov. 20, 1997, 111 Stat. 2214; Pub. L. 105–178, title III, §3003, June 9, 1998, 112 Stat. 338; Pub. L. 105–206, title IX, §9009(a), July 22, 1998, 112 Stat. 852; Pub. L. 109–59, title III, §§3002(b)(4), 3004, Aug. 10, 2005, 119 Stat. 1545; Pub. L. 110–244, title II, §201(a), June 6, 2008, 122 Stat. 1609; Pub. L. 112–141, div. B, §20004, July 6, 2012, 126 Stat. 623; Pub. L. 114–94, div. A, title III, §3002, Dec. 4, 2015, 129 Stat. 1446; Pub. L. 117–58, div. C, §30001(a), Nov. 15, 2021, 135 Stat. 889.)

§5303. METROPOLITAN TRANSPORTATION PLANNING

(a) POLICY.—It is in the national interest—

(1) to encourage and promote the safe and efficient management, operation, and development of resilient surface transportation systems that will serve the mobility needs of people and freight and foster economic growth and development within and between States and urbanized areas and better connect housing and employment, while minimizing transportation-related fuel consumption and air pollution through metropolitan and statewide transportation planning processes identified in this chapter; and

(2) to encourage the continued improvement and evolution of the metropolitan and statewide transportation planning processes by metropolitan planning organizations, State departments of transportation, and public transit operators as guided by the planning factors identified in subsection (h) and section 5304(d).

(b) DEFINITIONS.—In this section and section 5304, the following definitions apply:

(1) METROPOLITAN PLANNING AREA.—The term "metropolitan planning area" means the geographic area determined by agreement between the metropolitan planning organization for the area and the Governor under subsection (e).

(2) METROPOLITAN PLANNING ORGANIZATION.—The term "metropolitan planning organization" means the policy board of an organization established as a result of the designation process under subsection (d).

(3) NONMETROPOLITAN AREA.—The term "nonmetropolitan area" means a geographic area outside designated metropolitan planning areas.

(4) NONMETROPOLITAN LOCAL OFFICIAL.—The term "nonmetropolitan local official" means elected and appointed officials of general purpose local government in a nonmetropolitan area with responsibility for transportation.

(5) REGIONAL TRANSPORTATION PLANNING ORGANIZATION.—The term "regional transportation planning organization" means a policy board of an organization established as the result of a designation under section 5304(l).

(6) TIP.—The term "TIP" means a transportation improvement program developed by a metropolitan planning organization under subsection (j).

(7) URBANIZED AREA.—The term "urbanized area" means a geographic area with a

population of 50,000 or more, as determined by the Bureau of the Census.

(c) GENERAL REQUIREMENTS.—

(1) DEVELOPMENT OF LONG-RANGE PLANS AND TIPS.—To accomplish the objectives in subsection (a), metropolitan planning organizations designated under subsection (d), in cooperation with the State and public transportation operators, shall develop long-range transportation plans and transportation improvement programs through a performance-driven, outcome-based approach to planning for metropolitan areas of the State.

(2) CONTENTS.—The plans and TIPs for each metropolitan area shall provide for the development and integrated management and operation of transportation systems and facilities (including accessible pedestrian walkways, bicycle transportation facilities, and intermodal facilities that support intercity transportation, including intercity buses and intercity bus facilities and commuter vanpool providers) that will function as an intermodal transportation system for the metropolitan planning area and as an integral part of an intermodal transportation system for the State and the United States.

(3) PROCESS OF DEVELOPMENT.—The process for developing the plans and TIPs shall provide for consideration of all modes of transportation and shall be continuing, cooperative, and comprehensive to the degree appropriate, based on the complexity of the transportation problems to be addressed.

(d) DESIGNATION OF METROPOLITAN PLANNING ORGANIZATIONS.—

(1) IN GENERAL.—To carry out the transportation planning process required by this section, a metropolitan planning organization shall be designated for each urbanized area with a population of more than 50,000 individuals—

(A) by agreement between the Governor and units of general purpose local government that together represent at least 75 percent of the affected population (including the largest incorporated city (based on population) as determined by the Bureau of the Census); or

(B) in accordance with procedures established by applicable State or local law.

(2) STRUCTURE.—Not later than 2 years after the date of enactment of the Federal Public Transportation Act of 2012, each metropolitan planning organization that serves an area designated as a transportation management area shall consist of—

(A) local elected officials;

(B) officials of public agencies that administer or operate major modes of transportation in the metropolitan area, including representation by providers of public transportation; and

(C) appropriate State officials.

(3) REPRESENTATION.—

(A) IN GENERAL.—Designation or selection of officials or representatives under paragraph (2) shall be determined by the metropolitan planning organization according to the bylaws or enabling statute of the organization.

(B) PUBLIC TRANSPORTATION REPRESENTATIVE.—Subject to the bylaws or enabling statute of the metropolitan planning organization, a representative of a provider of public transportation may also serve as a representative of a local municipality.

(C) Powers of certain officials.—An official described in paragraph (2)(B) shall have responsibilities, actions, duties, voting rights, and any other authority commensurate with other officials described in paragraph (2).

(D) Considerations.—In designating officials or representatives under paragraph (2) for the first time, subject to the bylaws or enabling statute of the metropolitan planning organization, the metropolitan planning organization shall consider the equitable and proportional representation of the population of the metropolitan planning area.

(4) Limitation on statutory construction.—Nothing in this subsection shall be construed to interfere with the authority, under any State law in effect on December 18, 1991, of a public agency with multimodal transportation responsibilities—

(A) to develop the plans and TIPs for adoption by a metropolitan planning organization; and

(B) to develop long-range capital plans, coordinate transit services and projects, and carry out other activities pursuant to State law.

(5) Continuing designation.—A designation of a metropolitan planning organization under this subsection or any other provision of law shall remain in effect until the metropolitan planning organization is redesignated under paragraph (6).

(6) Redesignation procedures.—

(A) In general.—A metropolitan planning organization may be redesignated by agreement between the Governor and units of general purpose local government that together represent at least 75 percent of the existing planning area population (including the largest incorporated city (based on population) as determined by the Bureau of the Census) as appropriate to carry out this section.

(B) Restructuring.—A metropolitan planning organization may be restructured to meet the requirements of paragraph (2) without undertaking a redesignation.

(7) Designation of more than 1 metropolitan planning organization.—More than 1 metropolitan planning organization may be designated within an existing urbanized area (as defined by the Bureau of the Census) only if the Governor and the existing metropolitan planning organization determine that the size and complexity of the area make designation of more than 1 metropolitan planning organization for the area appropriate.

(e) Metropolitan Planning Area Boundaries.—

(1) In general.—For the purposes of this section, the boundaries of a metropolitan planning area shall be determined by agreement between the metropolitan planning organization and the Governor.

(2) Included area.—Each metropolitan planning area—

(A) shall encompass at least the existing urbanized area and the contiguous area expected to become urbanized within a 20-year forecast period for the transportation plan; and

(B) may encompass the entire metropolitan statistical area or consolidated metropolitan statistical area, as defined by the Bureau of the Census.

(3) Identification of new urbanized areas within existing planning area boundaries.—The designation by the Bureau of the Census of new urbanized areas

within an existing metropolitan planning area shall not require the redesignation of the existing metropolitan planning organization.

(4) EXISTING METROPOLITAN PLANNING AREAS IN NONATTAINMENT.—

(A) IN GENERAL.—Notwithstanding paragraph (2), except as provided in subparagraph (B), in the case of an urbanized area designated as a nonattainment area for ozone or carbon monoxide under the Clean Air Act (42 U.S.C. 7401 et seq.) as of the date of enactment of the SAFETEA–LU, the boundaries of the metropolitan planning area in existence as of such date of enactment shall be retained.

(B) EXCEPTION.—The boundaries described in subparagraph (A) may be adjusted by agreement of the Governor and affected metropolitan planning organizations in the manner described in subsection (d)(6).

(5) NEW METROPOLITAN PLANNING AREAS IN NONATTAINMENT.—In the case of an urbanized area designated after the date of enactment of the SAFETEA–LU, as a nonattainment area for ozone or carbon monoxide, the boundaries of the metropolitan planning area—

(A) shall be established in the manner described in subsection (d)(1);

(B) shall encompass the areas described in paragraph (2)(A);

(C) may encompass the areas described in paragraph (2)(B); and

(D) may address any nonattainment area identified under the Clean Air Act (42 U.S.C. 7401 et seq.) for ozone or carbon monoxide.

(f) COORDINATION IN MULTISTATE AREAS.—

(1) IN GENERAL.—The Secretary shall encourage each Governor with responsibility for a portion of a multistate metropolitan area and the appropriate metropolitan planning organizations to provide coordinated transportation planning for the entire metropolitan area.

(2) INTERSTATE COMPACTS.—The consent of Congress is granted to any 2 or more States—

(A) to enter into agreements or compacts, not in conflict with any law of the United States, for cooperative efforts and mutual assistance in support of activities authorized under this section as the activities pertain to interstate areas and localities within the States; and

(B) to establish such agencies, joint or otherwise, as the States may determine desirable for making the agreements and compacts effective.

(3) RESERVATION OF RIGHTS.—The right to alter, amend, or repeal interstate compacts entered into under this subsection is expressly reserved.

(g) MPO CONSULTATION IN PLAN AND TIP COORDINATION.—

(1) NONATTAINMENT AREAS.—If more than 1 metropolitan planning organization has authority within an urbanized area (as defined by the Bureau of the Census) or an area which is designated as a nonattainment area for ozone or carbon monoxide under the Clean Air Act (42 U.S.C. 7401 et seq.), each metropolitan planning organization shall consult with the other metropolitan planning organizations designated for such area and the State in the coordination of plans and TIPs required by this section.

(2) TRANSPORTATION IMPROVEMENTS LOCATED IN MULTIPLE MPOS.—If a transportation improvement, funded under this chapter or title 23, is located within

the boundaries of more than 1 metropolitan planning area, the metropolitan planning organizations shall coordinate plans and TIPs regarding the transportation improvement.

(3) RELATIONSHIP WITH OTHER PLANNING OFFICIALS.—

(A) IN GENERAL.—The Secretary shall encourage each metropolitan planning organization to consult with officials responsible for other types of planning activities that are affected by transportation in the area (including State and local planned growth, economic development, housing, tourism, natural disaster risk reduction, environmental protection, airport operations, and freight movements) or to coordinate its planning process, to the maximum extent practicable, with such planning activities.

(B) REQUIREMENTS.—Under the metropolitan planning process, transportation plans and TIPs shall be developed with due consideration of other related planning activities within the metropolitan area, and the process shall provide for the design and delivery of transportation services within the metropolitan area that are provided by—

(i) recipients of assistance under this chapter;

(ii) governmental agencies and nonprofit organizations (including representatives of the agencies and organizations) that receive Federal assistance from a source other than the Department of Transportation to provide nonemergency transportation services; and

(iii) recipients of assistance under section 204 of title 23.

(4) COORDINATION BETWEEN MPOS.—If more than 1 metropolitan planning organization is designated within an urbanized area (as defined by the Bureau of the Census) under subsection (d)(7), the metropolitan planning organizations designated within the area shall ensure, to the maximum extent practicable, the consistency of any data used in the planning process, including information used in forecasting travel demand.

(5) SAVINGS CLAUSE.—Nothing in this subsection requires metropolitan planning organizations designated within a single urbanized area to jointly develop planning documents, including a unified long-range transportation plan or unified TIP.

(h) SCOPE OF PLANNING PROCESS.—

(1) IN GENERAL.—The metropolitan planning process for a metropolitan planning area under this section shall provide for consideration of projects and strategies that will—

(A) support the economic vitality of the metropolitan area, especially by enabling global competitiveness, productivity, and efficiency;

(B) increase the safety of the transportation system for motorized and nonmotorized users;

(C) increase the security of the transportation system for motorized and nonmotorized users;

(D) increase the accessibility and mobility of people and for freight;

(E) protect and enhance the environment, promote energy conservation, improve the quality of life, and promote consistency between transportation improvements and State and local planned growth, housing, and economic development patterns;

(F) enhance the integration and connectivity of the transportation system, across and between modes, for people and freight;

(G) promote efficient system management and operation;

(H) emphasize the preservation of the existing transportation system; and

(I) improve the resiliency and reliability of the transportation system.

(2) PERFORMANCE-BASED APPROACH.—

(A) IN GENERAL.—The metropolitan transportation planning process shall provide for the establishment and use of a performance-based approach to transportation decisionmaking to support the national goals described in section 150(b) of title 23 and the general purposes described in section 5301.

(B) PERFORMANCE TARGETS.—

(i) SURFACE TRANSPORTATION PERFORMANCE TARGETS.—

(I) IN GENERAL.—Each metropolitan planning organization shall establish performance targets that address the performance measures described in section 150(c) of title 23, where applicable, to use in tracking progress towards attainment of critical outcomes for the region of the metropolitan planning organization.

(II) COORDINATION.—Selection of performance targets by a metropolitan planning organization shall be coordinated with the relevant State to ensure consistency, to the maximum extent practicable.

(ii) PUBLIC TRANSPORTATION PERFORMANCE TARGETS.—Selection of performance targets by a metropolitan planning organization shall be coordinated, to the maximum extent practicable, with providers of public transportation to ensure consistency with sections 5326(c) and 5329(d).

(C) TIMING.—Each metropolitan planning organization shall establish the performance targets under subparagraph (B) not later than 180 days after the date on which the relevant State or provider of public transportation establishes the performance targets.

(D) INTEGRATION OF OTHER PERFORMANCE-BASED PLANS.—A metropolitan planning organization shall integrate in the metropolitan transportation planning process, directly or by reference, the goals, objectives, performance measures, and targets described in other State transportation plans and transportation processes, as well as any plans developed by recipients of assistance under this chapter, required as part of a performance-based program.

(3) FAILURE TO CONSIDER FACTORS.—The failure to consider any factor specified in paragraphs (1) and (2) shall not be reviewable by any court under this chapter, title 23, subchapter II of chapter 5 of title 5, or chapter 7 of title 5 in any matter affecting a transportation plan, a TIP, a project or strategy, or the certification of a planning process.

(i) DEVELOPMENT OF TRANSPORTATION PLAN.—

(1) REQUIREMENTS.—

(A) IN GENERAL.—Each metropolitan planning organization shall prepare and update a transportation plan for its metropolitan planning area in accordance with the requirements of this subsection.

(B) FREQUENCY.—

(i) IN GENERAL.—The metropolitan planning organization shall prepare and update such plan every 4 years (or more frequently, if the metropolitan planning organization elects to update more frequently) in the case of each of the following:

(I) Any area designated as nonattainment, as defined in section 107(d) of the Clean Air Act (42 U.S.C. 7407(d)).

(II) Any area that was nonattainment and subsequently designated to attainment in accordance with section 107(d)(3) of that Act (42 U.S.C. 7407(d)(3)) and that is subject to a maintenance plan under section 175A of that Act (42 U.S.C. 7505a).

(ii) OTHER AREAS.—In the case of any other area required to have a transportation plan in accordance with the requirements of this subsection, the metropolitan planning organization shall prepare and update such plan every 5 years unless the metropolitan planning organization elects to update more frequently.

(2) TRANSPORTATION PLAN.—A transportation plan under this section shall be in a form that the Secretary determines to be appropriate and shall contain, at a minimum, the following:

(A) IDENTIFICATION OF TRANSPORTATION FACILITIES.—

(i) IN GENERAL.—An identification of transportation facilities (including major roadways, public transportation facilities, intercity bus facilities, multimodal and intermodal facilities, nonmotorized transportation facilities, and intermodal connectors) that should function as an integrated metropolitan transportation system, giving emphasis to those facilities that serve important national and regional transportation functions.

(ii) FACTORS.—In formulating the transportation plan, the metropolitan planning organization shall consider factors described in subsection (h) as the factors relate to a 20-year forecast period.

(B) PERFORMANCE MEASURES AND TARGETS.—A description of the performance measures and performance targets used in assessing the performance of the transportation system in accordance with subsection (h)(2).

(C) SYSTEM PERFORMANCE REPORT.—A system performance report and subsequent updates evaluating the condition and performance of the transportation system with respect to the performance targets described in subsection (h)(2), including—

(i) progress achieved by the metropolitan planning organization in meeting the performance targets in comparison with system performance recorded in previous reports; and

(ii) for metropolitan planning organizations that voluntarily elect to develop multiple scenarios, an analysis of how the preferred scenario has improved the conditions and performance of the transportation system and how changes in local policies and investments have impacted the costs necessary to achieve the identified performance targets.

(D) MITIGATION ACTIVITIES.—

(i) IN GENERAL.—A long-range transportation plan shall include a discussion of types of potential environmental mitigation activities and potential areas to carry out these activities, including activities that may have the greatest potential to restore and maintain the environmental functions affected by the plan.

(ii) CONSULTATION.—The discussion shall be developed in consultation with Federal, State, and tribal wildlife, land management, and regulatory agencies.

(E) FINANCIAL PLAN.—

(i) IN GENERAL.—A financial plan that—

(I) demonstrates how the adopted transportation plan can be implemented;

(II) indicates resources from public and private sources that are reasonably expected to be made available to carry out the plan; and

(III) recommends any additional financing strategies for needed projects and programs.

(ii) INCLUSIONS.—The financial plan may include, for illustrative purposes, additional projects that would be included in the adopted transportation plan if reasonable additional resources beyond those identified in the financial plan were available.

(iii) COOPERATIVE DEVELOPMENT.—For the purpose of developing the transportation plan, the metropolitan planning organization, transit operator, and State shall cooperatively develop estimates of funds that will be available to support plan implementation.

(F) OPERATIONAL AND MANAGEMENT STRATEGIES.—Operational and management strategies to improve the performance of existing transportation facilities to relieve vehicular congestion and maximize the safety and mobility of people and goods.

(G) CAPITAL INVESTMENT AND OTHER STRATEGIES.—Capital investment and other strategies to preserve the existing and projected future metropolitan transportation infrastructure, provide for multimodal capacity increases based on regional priorities and needs, and reduce the vulnerability of the existing transportation infrastructure to natural disasters.

(H) TRANSPORTATION AND TRANSIT ENHANCEMENT ACTIVITIES.—Proposed transportation and transit enhancement activities, including consideration of the role that intercity buses may play in reducing congestion, pollution, and energy consumption in a cost-effective manner and strategies and investments that preserve and enhance intercity bus systems, including systems that are privately owned and operated.

(3) COORDINATION WITH CLEAN AIR ACT AGENCIES.—In metropolitan areas that are in nonattainment for ozone or carbon monoxide under the Clean Air Act (42 U.S.C. 7401 et seq.), the metropolitan planning organization shall coordinate the development of a transportation plan with the process for development of the transportation control measures of the State implementation plan required by that Act.

(4) OPTIONAL SCENARIO DEVELOPMENT.—

(A) IN GENERAL.—A metropolitan planning organization may, while fitting the needs and complexity of its community, voluntarily elect to develop multiple scenarios for consideration as part of the development of the metropolitan transportation plan, in accordance with subparagraph (B).

(B) RECOMMENDED COMPONENTS.—A metropolitan planning organization that chooses to develop multiple scenarios under subparagraph (A) shall be encouraged to consider—

(i) potential regional investment strategies for the planning horizon;

(ii) assumed distribution of population and employment;

(iii) assumed distribution of population and housing;

(iv) a scenario that, to the maximum extent practicable, maintains baseline conditions for the performance measures identified in subsection (h)(2);

(v) a scenario that improves the baseline conditions for as many of the performance measures identified in subsection (h)(2) as possible;

(vi) revenue constrained scenarios based on the total revenues expected to be available over the forecast period of the plan; and

(vii) estimated costs and potential revenues available to support each scenario.

(C) METRICS.—In addition to the performance measures identified in section 150(c) of title 23, metropolitan planning organizations may evaluate scenarios developed under this paragraph using locally-developed measures.

(5) CONSULTATION.—

(A) IN GENERAL.—In each metropolitan area, the metropolitan planning organization shall consult, as appropriate, with State and local agencies responsible for land use management, natural resources, environmental protection, conservation, and historic preservation concerning the development of a long-range transportation plan.

(B) ISSUES.—The consultation shall involve, as appropriate—

(i) comparison of transportation plans with State conservation plans or maps, if available; or

(ii) comparison of transportation plans to inventories of natural or historic resources, if available.

(6) PARTICIPATION BY INTERESTED PARTIES.—

(A) IN GENERAL.—Each metropolitan planning organization shall provide citizens, affected public agencies, representatives of public transportation employees, public ports, freight shippers, providers of freight transportation services, private providers of transportation (including intercity bus operators, employer-based commuting programs, such as a carpool program, vanpool program, transit benefit program, parking cash-out program, shuttle program, or telework program), representatives of users of public transportation, representatives of users of pedestrian walkways and bicycle transportation facilities, representatives of the disabled, affordable housing organizations, and other interested parties with a reasonable opportunity to comment on the transportation plan.

(B) CONTENTS OF PARTICIPATION PLAN.—A participation plan—

(i) shall be developed in consultation with all interested parties; and

(ii) shall provide that all interested parties have reasonable opportunities to comment on the contents of the transportation plan.

(C) METHODS.—In carrying out subparagraph (A), the metropolitan planning organization shall, to the maximum extent practicable—

(i) hold any public meetings at convenient and accessible locations and times;

(ii) employ visualization techniques to describe plans; and

(iii) make public information available in electronically accessible format and means, such as the World Wide Web, as appropriate to afford reasonable opportunity for consideration of public information under subparagraph (A).

(D) USE OF TECHNOLOGY.—A metropolitan planning organization may use social media and other web-based tools—

(i) to further encourage public participation; and

(ii) to solicit public feedback during the transportation planning process.

(7) PUBLICATION.—A transportation plan involving Federal participation shall be published or otherwise made readily available by the metropolitan planning organization for public review, including (to the maximum extent practicable) in electronically accessible formats and means, such as the World Wide Web, approved by the metropolitan planning organization and submitted for information purposes to the Governor at such times and in such manner as the Secretary shall establish.

(8) SELECTION OF PROJECTS FROM ILLUSTRATIVE LIST.—Notwithstanding paragraph (2)(E), a State or metropolitan planning organization shall not be required to select any project from the illustrative list of additional projects included in the financial plan under paragraph (2)(E).

(j) METROPOLITAN TIP.—

(1) DEVELOPMENT.—

(A) IN GENERAL.—In cooperation with the State and any affected public transportation operator, the metropolitan planning organization designated for a metropolitan area shall develop a TIP for the metropolitan planning area that—

(i) contains projects consistent with the current metropolitan transportation plan;

(ii) reflects the investment priorities established in the current metropolitan transportation plan; and

(iii) once implemented, is designed to make progress toward achieving the performance targets established under subsection (h)(2).

(B) OPPORTUNITY FOR COMMENT.—In developing the TIP, the metropolitan planning organization, in cooperation with the State and any affected public transportation operator, shall provide an opportunity for participation by interested parties in the development of the program, in accordance with subsection (i)(5).

(C) FUNDING ESTIMATES.—For the purpose of developing the TIP, the metropolitan planning organization, public transportation agency, and State shall cooperatively develop estimates of funds that are reasonably expected to be available to support program implementation.

(D) UPDATING AND APPROVAL.—The TIP shall be—

(i) updated at least once every 4 years; and

(ii) approved by the metropolitan planning organization and the Governor.

(2) CONTENTS.—

(A) PRIORITY LIST.—The TIP shall include a priority list of proposed Federally supported projects and strategies to be carried out within each 4-year period after the initial adoption of the TIP.

(B) FINANCIAL PLAN.—The TIP shall include a financial plan that—

(i) demonstrates how the TIP can be implemented;

(ii) indicates resources from public and private sources that are reasonably expected to be available to carry out the program;

(iii) identifies innovative financing techniques to finance projects, programs, and strategies; and

(iv) may include, for illustrative purposes, additional projects that would be included in the approved TIP if reasonable additional resources beyond those identified in the financial plan were available.

(C) DESCRIPTIONS.—Each project in the TIP shall include sufficient descriptive material (such as type of work, termini, length, and other similar factors) to identify the project or phase of the project.

(D) PERFORMANCE TARGET ACHIEVEMENT.—The transportation improvement program shall include, to the maximum extent practicable, a description of the anticipated effect of the transportation improvement program toward achieving the performance targets established in the metropolitan transportation plan, linking investment priorities to those performance targets.

(3) INCLUDED PROJECTS.—

(A) PROJECTS UNDER THIS CHAPTER AND TITLE 23.—A TIP developed under this subsection for a metropolitan area shall include the projects within the area that are proposed for funding under this chapter and chapter 1 of title 23.

(B) PROJECTS UNDER CHAPTER 2 OF TITLE 23.—

(i) REGIONALLY SIGNIFICANT PROJECTS.—Regionally significant projects proposed for funding under chapter 2 of title 23 shall be identified individually in the transportation improvement program.

(ii) OTHER PROJECTS.—Projects proposed for funding under chapter 2 of title 23 that are not determined to be regionally significant shall be grouped in 1 line item or identified individually in the transportation improvement program.

(C) CONSISTENCY WITH LONG-RANGE TRANSPORTATION PLAN.—Each project shall be consistent with the long-range transportation plan developed under subsection (i) for the area.

(D) REQUIREMENT OF ANTICIPATED FULL FUNDING.—The program shall include a project, or an identified phase of a project, only if full funding can reasonably be anticipated to be available for the project or the identified phase within the time period contemplated for completion of the project or the identified phase.

(4) NOTICE AND COMMENT.—Before approving a TIP, a metropolitan planning organization, in cooperation with the State and any affected public transportation operator, shall provide an opportunity for participation by interested parties in the development of the program, in accordance with subsection (i)(5).

(5) SELECTION OF PROJECTS.—

(A) IN GENERAL.—Except as otherwise provided in subsection (k)(4) and in addition to the TIP development required under paragraph (1), the selection of Federally funded projects in metropolitan areas shall be carried out, from the approved TIP—

(i) by—

(I) in the case of projects under title 23, the State; and

(II) in the case of projects under this chapter, the designated recipients of public transportation funding; and

(ii) in cooperation with the metropolitan planning organization.

(B) MODIFICATIONS TO PROJECT PRIORITY.—Notwithstanding any other provision of law, action by the Secretary shall not be required to advance a project included in the approved TIP in place of another project in the program.

(6) SELECTION OF PROJECTS FROM ILLUSTRATIVE LIST.—

(A) NO REQUIRED SELECTION.—Notwithstanding paragraph (2)(B)(iv), a State or metropolitan planning organization shall not be required to select any project from the illustrative list of additional projects included in the financial plan under paragraph (2)(B)(iv).

(B) REQUIRED ACTION BY THE SECRETARY.—Action by the Secretary shall be required for a State or metropolitan planning organization to select any project from the illustrative list of additional projects included in the financial plan under paragraph (2)(B)(iv) for inclusion in an approved TIP.

(7) PUBLICATION.—

(A) PUBLICATION OF TIPS.—A TIP involving Federal participation shall be published or otherwise made readily available by the metropolitan planning organization for public review.

(B) PUBLICATION OF ANNUAL LISTINGS OF PROJECTS.—

(i) IN GENERAL.—An annual listing of projects, including investments in pedestrian walkways and bicycle transportation facilities, for which Federal funds have been obligated in the preceding year shall be published or otherwise made available by the cooperative effort of the State, transit operator, and metropolitan planning organization for public review.

(ii) REQUIREMENT.—The listing shall be consistent with the categories identified in the TIP.

(k) TRANSPORTATION MANAGEMENT AREAS.—

(1) IDENTIFICATION AND DESIGNATION.—

(A) REQUIRED IDENTIFICATION.—The Secretary shall identify as a transportation management area each urbanized area (as defined by the Bureau of the Census) with a population of over 200,000 individuals.

(B) DESIGNATIONS ON REQUEST.—The Secretary shall designate any additional area as a transportation management area on the request of the Governor and the metropolitan planning organization designated for the area.

(2) TRANSPORTATION PLANS.—In a transportation management area, transportation plans shall be based on a continuing and comprehensive transportation planning process carried out by the metropolitan planning organization in cooperation with the State and public transportation operators.

(3) CONGESTION MANAGEMENT PROCESS.—

(A) IN GENERAL.—Within a metropolitan planning area serving a transportation management area, the transportation planning process under this section shall address congestion management through a process that provides for effective management and operation, based on a cooperatively developed and implemented metropolitan-wide strategy, of new and existing transportation facilities eligible for funding under this chapter and title 23 through the use of travel demand reduction (including intercity bus operators, employer-based commuting programs, such as a carpool program, vanpool program, transit benefit program, parking cash-out program, shuttle program, or telework program), job access projects, and operational management strategies.

(B) SCHEDULE.—The Secretary shall establish an appropriate phase-in schedule for compliance with the requirements of this section but no sooner than 1 year after the identification of a transportation management area.

(C) CONGESTION MANAGEMENT PLAN.—A metropolitan planning organization serving a transportation management area may develop a plan that includes projects and strategies that will be considered in the TIP of such metropolitan planning organization. Such plan shall—

(i) develop regional goals to reduce vehicle miles traveled during peak commuting hours and improve transportation connections between areas with high job concentration and areas with high concentrations of low-income households;

(ii) identify existing public transportation services, employer-based commuter programs, and other existing transportation services that support access to jobs in the region; and

(iii) identify proposed projects and programs to reduce congestion and increase job access opportunities.

(D) PARTICIPATION.—In developing the plan under subparagraph (C), a metropolitan planning organization shall consult with employers, private and non-profit providers of public transportation, transportation management organizations, and organizations that provide job access reverse commute projects or job-related services to low-income individuals.

(4) HOUSING COORDINATION PROCESS.—

(A) IN GENERAL.—Within a metropolitan planning area serving a transportation management area, the transportation planning process under this section may address the integration of housing, transportation, and economic development strategies through a process that provides for effective integration, based on a cooperatively developed and implemented strategy, of new and existing transportation facilities eligible for funding under this chapter and title 23.

(B) COORDINATION IN INTEGRATED PLANNING PROCESS.—In carrying out the process described in subparagraph (A), a metropolitan planning organization may—

(i) consult with—

(I) State and local entities responsible for land use, economic development, housing, management of road networks, or public transportation; and

(II) other appropriate public or private entities; and

(ii) coordinate, to the extent practicable, with applicable State and local entities to align the goals of the process with the goals of any comprehensive housing affordability strategies established within the metropolitan planning area pursuant to section 105 of the Cranston-Gonzalez National Affordable Housing Act (42 U.S.C. 12705) and plans developed under section 5A of the

United States Housing Act of 1937 (42 U.S.C. 1437c–1).

(C) HOUSING COORDINATION PLAN.—

(i) IN GENERAL.—A metropolitan planning organization serving a transportation management area may develop a housing coordination plan that includes projects and strategies that may be considered in the metropolitan transportation plan of the metropolitan planning organization.

(ii) CONTENTS.—A plan described in clause (i) may—

(I) develop regional goals for the integration of housing, transportation, and economic development strategies to—

(aa) better connect housing and employment while mitigating commuting times;

(bb) align transportation improvements with housing needs, such as housing supply shortages, and proposed housing development;

(cc) align planning for housing and transportation to address needs in relationship to household incomes within the metropolitan planning area;

(dd) expand housing and economic development within the catchment areas of existing transportation facilities and public transportation services when appropriate, including higher-density development, as locally determined;

(ee) manage effects of growth of vehicle miles traveled experienced in the metropolitan planning area related to housing development and economic development;

(ff) increase share of households with sufficient and affordable access to the transportation networks of the metropolitan planning area;

(II) identify the location of existing and planned housing and employment, and transportation options that connect housing and employment; and

(III) include a comparison of transportation plans to land use management plans, including zoning plans, that may affect road use, public transportation ridership and housing development.

(5) SELECTION OF PROJECTS.—

(A) IN GENERAL.—All Federally funded projects carried out within the boundaries of a metropolitan planning area serving a transportation management area under title 23 (excluding projects carried out on the National Highway System) or under this chapter shall be selected for implementation from the approved TIP by the metropolitan planning organization designated for the area in consultation with the State and any affected public transportation operator.

(B) NATIONAL HIGHWAY SYSTEM PROJECTS.—Projects carried out within the boundaries of a metropolitan planning area serving a transportation management area on the National Highway System shall be selected for implementation from the approved TIP by the State in cooperation with the metropolitan planning organization designated for the area.

(6) CERTIFICATION.—

(A) IN GENERAL.—The Secretary shall—

(i) ensure that the metropolitan planning process of a metropolitan planning organization serving a transportation management area is being carried out in accordance with applicable provisions of Federal law; and

(ii) subject to subparagraph (B), certify, not less often than once every 4 years, that the requirements of this paragraph are met with respect to the metropolitan planning process.

(B) REQUIREMENTS FOR CERTIFICATION.—The Secretary may make the certification under subparagraph (A) if—

(i) the transportation planning process complies with the requirements of this section and other applicable requirements of Federal law; and

(ii) there is a TIP for the metropolitan planning area that has been approved by the metropolitan planning organization and the Governor.

(C) EFFECT OF FAILURE TO CERTIFY.—

(i) WITHHOLDING OF PROJECT FUNDS.—If a metropolitan planning process of a metropolitan planning organization serving a transportation management area is not certified, the Secretary may withhold up to 20 percent of the funds attributable to the metropolitan planning area of the metropolitan planning organization for projects funded under this chapter and title 23.

(ii) RESTORATION OF WITHHELD FUNDS.—The withheld funds shall be restored to the metropolitan planning area at such time as the metropolitan planning process is certified by the Secretary.

(D) REVIEW OF CERTIFICATION.—In making certification determinations under this paragraph, the Secretary shall provide for public involvement appropriate to the metropolitan area under review.

(l) REPORT ON PERFORMANCE-BASED PLANNING PROCESSES.—

(1) IN GENERAL.—The Secretary shall submit to Congress a report on the effectiveness of the performance-based planning processes of metropolitan planning organizations under this section, taking into consideration the requirements of this subsection.

(2) REPORT.—Not later than 5 years after the date of enactment of the Federal Public Transportation Act of 2012, the Secretary shall submit to Congress a report evaluating—

(A) the overall effectiveness of performance-based planning as a tool for guiding transportation investments;

(B) the effectiveness of the performance-based planning process of each metropolitan planning organization under this section;

(C) the extent to which metropolitan planning organizations have achieved, or are currently making substantial progress toward achieving, the performance targets specified under this section and whether metropolitan planning organizations are developing meaningful performance targets; and

(D) the technical capacity of metropolitan planning organizations that operate within a metropolitan planning area with a population of 200,000 or less and their ability to carry out the requirements of this section.

(3) PUBLICATION.—The report under paragraph (2) shall be published or otherwise made available in electronically accessible formats and means, including on the Internet.

(m) ABBREVIATED PLANS FOR CERTAIN AREAS.—

(1) IN GENERAL.—Subject to paragraph (2), in the case of a metropolitan area not designated as a transportation management area under this section, the Secretary may provide for the development of an abbreviated transportation plan and TIP for the metropolitan planning area that the Secretary determines is appropriate to achieve the purposes of this section, taking into account the complexity of transportation problems in the area.

(2) NONATTAINMENT AREAS.—The Secretary may not permit abbreviated plans or TIPs for a metropolitan area that is in nonattainment for ozone or carbon monoxide under the Clean Air Act (42 U.S.C. 7401 et seq.).

(n) ADDITIONAL REQUIREMENTS FOR CERTAIN NONATTAINMENT AREAS.—

(1) IN GENERAL.—Notwithstanding any other provisions of this chapter or title 23, for transportation management areas classified as nonattainment for ozone or carbon monoxide pursuant to the Clean Air Act (42 U.S.C. 7401 et seq.), Federal funds may not be advanced in such area for any highway project that will result in a significant increase in the carrying capacity for single-occupant vehicles unless the project is addressed through a congestion management process.

(2) APPLICABILITY.—This subsection applies to a nonattainment area within the metropolitan planning area boundaries determined under subsection (e).

(o) LIMITATION ON STATUTORY CONSTRUCTION.—Nothing in this section shall be construed to confer on a metropolitan planning organization the authority to impose legal requirements on any transportation facility, provider, or project not eligible under this chapter or title 23.

(p) FUNDING.—Funds apportioned under section 104(b)(6) of title 23 or section 5305(g) shall be available to carry out this section.

(q) CONTINUATION OF CURRENT REVIEW PRACTICE.—Since plans and TIPs described in this section are subject to a reasonable opportunity for public comment, since individual projects included in plans and TIPs are subject to review under the National Environmental Policy Act of 1969 (42 U.S.C. 4321 et seq.), and since decisions by the Secretary concerning plans and TIPs described in this section have not been reviewed under that Act as of January 1, 1997, any decision by the Secretary concerning a plan or TIP described in this section shall not be considered to be a Federal action subject to review under that Act.

(r) BI-STATE METROPOLITAN PLANNING ORGANIZATION.—

(1) DEFINITION OF BI-STATE MPO REGION.—In this subsection, the term "Bi-State Metropolitan Planning Organization" has the meaning given the term "region" in subsection (a) of Article II of the Lake Tahoe Regional Planning Compact (Public Law 96–551; 94 Stat. 3234).

(2) TREATMENT.—For the purpose of this title, the Bi-State Metropolitan Planning Organization shall be treated as—

(A) a metropolitan planning organization;

(B) a transportation management area under subsection (k); and

(C) an urbanized area, which is comprised of a population of 145,000 and 25 square miles of land area and 25 square miles of land area [1] in the State of California and a population of 65,000 and 12 square miles of land area and 12 square miles of land area [1] in the State of Nevada.

(Pub. L. 103–272, §1(d), July 5, 1994, 108 Stat. 788; Pub. L. 104–287, §5(10), Oct. 11, 1996, 110 Stat. 3389; Pub. L. 105–102, §2(4), Nov. 20, 1997, 111 Stat. 2204; Pub. L. 105–178, title III, §§3004, 3029(b)(1)–(3), June 9, 1998, 112 Stat. 341, 372; Pub. L. 105–206, title IX, §9009(b), July 22, 1998, 112 Stat. 852; Pub. L. 109–59, title III, §3005(a), Aug. 10, 2005, 119 Stat. 1547; Pub. L. 110–244, title II, §201(b), June 6, 2008, 122 Stat. 1609; Pub. L. 112–141, div. B, §20005(a), July 6, 2012, 126 Stat. 628; Pub. L. 114–94, div. A, title III, §3003(a), Dec. 4, 2015, 129 Stat. 1447; Pub. L. 114–322, title III, §3603(f)(3), Dec. 16, 2016, 130 Stat. 1789; Pub. L. 115–31, div. K, title I, §192, May 5, 2017, 131 Stat. 756; Pub. L. 117–58, div. C, §30002, Nov. 15, 2021, 135 Stat. 890.)

¹ So in original.

§5304. STATEWIDE AND NONMETROPOLITAN TRANSPORTATION PLANNING

(a) GENERAL REQUIREMENTS.—

(1) DEVELOPMENT OF PLANS AND PROGRAMS.—Subject to section 5303, to accomplish the objectives stated in section 5303(a), each State shall develop a statewide transportation plan and a statewide transportation improvement program for all areas of the State.

(2) CONTENTS.—The statewide transportation plan and the transportation improvement program developed for each State shall provide for the development and integrated management and operation of transportation systems and facilities (including accessible pedestrian walkways, bicycle transportation facilities, and intermodal facilities that support intercity transportation, including intercity buses and intercity bus facilities and commuter vanpool providers) that will function as an intermodal transportation system for the State and an integral part of an intermodal transportation system for the United States.

(3) PROCESS OF DEVELOPMENT.—The process for developing the statewide plan and the transportation improvement program shall provide for consideration of all modes of transportation and the policies stated in section 5303(a) and shall be continuing, cooperative, and comprehensive to the degree appropriate, based on the complexity of the transportation problems to be addressed.

(b) COORDINATION WITH METROPOLITAN PLANNING; STATE IMPLEMENTATION PLAN.—A State shall—

(1) coordinate planning carried out under this section with the transportation planning activities carried out under section 5303 for metropolitan areas of the State and with statewide trade and economic development planning activities and related multistate planning efforts; and

(2) develop the transportation portion of the State implementation plan as required by the Clean Air Act (42 U.S.C. 7401 et seq.).

(c) INTERSTATE AGREEMENTS.—

(1) IN GENERAL.—Two or more States may enter into agreements or compacts, not in conflict with any law of the United States, for cooperative efforts and mutual assistance in support of activities authorized under this section related to interstate areas and localities in the States and establishing authorities the States consider desirable for making the agreements and compacts effective.

(2) RESERVATION OF RIGHTS.—The right to alter, amend, or repeal interstate compacts entered into under this subsection is expressly reserved.

(d) SCOPE OF PLANNING PROCESS.—

(1) IN GENERAL.—Each State shall carry out a statewide transportation planning process that provides for consideration and implementation of projects, strategies, and services that will—

(A) support the economic vitality of the United States, the States, nonmetropolitan areas, and metropolitan areas, especially by enabling global competitiveness, productivity, and efficiency;

(B) increase the safety of the transportation system for motorized and nonmotorized users;

(C) increase the security of the transportation system for motorized and nonmotorized users;

(D) increase the accessibility and mobility of people and freight;

(E) protect and enhance the environment, promote energy conservation, improve the quality of life, and promote consistency between transportation improvements and State and local planned growth and economic development patterns;

(F) enhance the integration and connectivity of the transportation system, across and between modes throughout the State, for people and freight;

(G) promote efficient system management and operation;

(H) emphasize the preservation of the existing transportation system; and

(I) improve the resiliency and reliability of the transportation system.

(2) PERFORMANCE-BASED APPROACH.—

(A) IN GENERAL.—The statewide transportation planning process shall provide for the establishment and use of a performance-based approach to transportation decisionmaking to support the national goals described in section 150(b) of title 23 and the general purposes described in section 5301.

(B) PERFORMANCE TARGETS.—

(i) SURFACE TRANSPORTATION PERFORMANCE TARGETS.—

(I) IN GENERAL.—Each State shall establish performance targets that address the performance measures described in section 150(c) of title 23, where applicable, to use in tracking progress towards attainment of critical outcomes for the State.

(II) COORDINATION.—Selection of performance targets by a State shall be coordinated with the relevant metropolitan planning organizations to ensure consistency, to the maximum extent practicable.

(ii) PUBLIC TRANSPORTATION PERFORMANCE TARGETS.—In areas with a population of fewer than 200,000 individuals, as calculated according to the most recent decennial census, and not represented by a metropolitan planning organization, selection of performance targets by a State shall be coordinated, to the maximum extent practicable, with providers of public transportation to ensure consistency with sections 5326(c) and 5329(d).

(C) INTEGRATION OF OTHER PERFORMANCE-BASED PLANS.—A State shall integrate into the statewide transportation planning process, directly or by reference, the goals, objectives, performance measures, and targets described in this paragraph, in other State transportation plans and transportation processes, as well as any plans developed pursuant to title 23 by providers of public transportation in areas with a population of fewer than 200,000 individuals, as calculated according to the most recent decennial census, and not represented by a metropolitan planning organization, required as part of a performance-based program.

(D) USE OF PERFORMANCE MEASURES AND TARGETS.—The performance measures and targets established under this paragraph shall be considered by a State when developing policies, programs, and investment priorities reflected in the statewide transportation plan and statewide transportation improvement program.

(3) FAILURE TO CONSIDER FACTORS.—The failure to take into consideration the factors specified in paragraphs (1) and (2) shall not be subject to review by any court under this chapter, title 23, subchapter II of chapter 5 of title 5, or chapter 7 of title 5 in any matter affecting a statewide transportation plan, a statewide transportation improvement program, a project or strategy, or the certification of a planning process.

(e) ADDITIONAL REQUIREMENTS.—In carrying out planning under this section, each State shall, at a minimum—

(1) with respect to nonmetropolitan areas, cooperate with affected local officials with responsibility for transportation or, if applicable, through regional transportation planning organizations described in subsection (l);

(2) consider the concerns of Indian tribal governments and Federal land management agencies that have jurisdiction over land within the boundaries of the State; and

(3) consider coordination of transportation plans, the transportation improvement program, and planning activities with related planning activities being carried out outside of metropolitan planning areas and between States.

(f) LONG-RANGE STATEWIDE TRANSPORTATION PLAN.—

(1) DEVELOPMENT.—Each State shall develop a long-range statewide transportation plan, with a minimum 20-year forecast period for all areas of the State, that provides for the development and implementation of the intermodal transportation system of the State.

(2) CONSULTATION WITH GOVERNMENTS.—

(A) METROPOLITAN AREAS.—The statewide transportation plan shall be developed for each metropolitan area in the State in cooperation with the metropolitan planning organization designated for the metropolitan area under section 5303.

(B) NONMETROPOLITAN AREAS.—

(i) IN GENERAL.—With respect to nonmetropolitan areas, the statewide transportation plan shall be developed in cooperation with affected nonmetropolitan officials with responsibility for transportation or, if applicable, through regional transportation planning organizations described in subsection (l).

(ii) ROLE OF SECRETARY.—The Secretary shall not review or approve the consultation process in each State.

(C) INDIAN TRIBAL AREAS.—With respect to each area of the State under the jurisdiction of an Indian tribal government, the statewide transportation plan shall be developed in consultation with the tribal government and the Secretary of the Interior.

(D) CONSULTATION, COMPARISON, AND CONSIDERATION.—

(i) IN GENERAL.—The long-range transportation plan shall be developed, as appropriate, in consultation with State, tribal, and local agencies responsible for land use management, natural resources, environmental protection, conservation, and historic preservation.

(ii) COMPARISON AND CONSIDERATION.—Consultation under clause (i) shall involve comparison of transportation plans to State and tribal conservation plans or maps, if available, and comparison of transportation plans to inventories of natural or historic resources, if available.

(3) PARTICIPATION BY INTERESTED PARTIES.—

(A) IN GENERAL.—In developing the statewide transportation plan, the State shall provide to—

(i) nonmetropolitan local elected officials, or, if applicable, through regional transportation planning organizations described in subsection (l), an opportunity to participate in accordance with subparagraph (B)(i); and

(ii) citizens, affected public agencies, representatives of public transportation employees, public ports, freight shippers, private providers of transportation (including intercity bus operators, employer-based commuting programs, such as a carpool program, vanpool program, transit benefit program, parking cash-out program, shuttle program, or telework program), representatives of users of public transportation, representatives of users of pedestrian walkways and bicycle transportation facilities, representatives of the disabled, providers of freight transportation services, and other interested parties a reasonable opportunity to comment on the proposed plan.

(B) METHODS.—In carrying out subparagraph (A), the State shall, to the maximum extent practicable—

(i) develop and document a consultative process to carry out subparagraph (A)(i) that is separate and discrete from the public involvement process developed under clause (ii);

(ii) hold any public meetings at convenient and accessible locations and times;

(iii) employ visualization techniques to describe plans; and

(iv) make public information available in electronically accessible format and means, such as the World Wide Web, as appropriate to afford reasonable opportunity for consideration of public information under subparagraph (A).

(C) USE OF TECHNOLOGY.—A State may use social media and other web-based tools—

(i) to further encourage public participation; and

(ii) to solicit public feedback during the transportation planning process.

(4) MITIGATION ACTIVITIES.—

(A) IN GENERAL.—A long-range transportation plan shall include a discussion of potential environmental mitigation activities and potential areas to carry out these activities, including activities that may have the greatest potential to restore and maintain the environmental functions affected by the plan.

(B) CONSULTATION.—The discussion shall be developed in consultation with Federal, State, and tribal wildlife, land management, and regulatory agencies.

(5) FINANCIAL PLAN.—The statewide transportation plan may include—

(A) a financial plan that—

(i) demonstrates how the adopted statewide transportation plan can be implemented;

(ii) indicates resources from public and private sources that are reasonably expected to be made available to carry out the plan; and

(iii) recommends any additional financing strategies for needed projects and programs; and

(B) for illustrative purposes, additional projects that would be included in the adopted statewide transportation plan if reasonable additional resources beyond those identified in the financial plan were available.

(6) SELECTION OF PROJECTS FROM ILLUSTRATIVE LIST.—A State shall not be required to select any project from the illustrative list of additional projects included in the financial plan described in paragraph (5).

(7) PERFORMANCE-BASED APPROACH.—The statewide transportation plan should include—

(A) a description of the performance measures and performance targets used in assessing the performance of the transportation system in accordance with subsection (d)(2); and

(B) a system performance report and subsequent updates evaluating the condition and performance of the transportation system with respect to the performance targets described in subsection (d)(2), including progress achieved by the metropolitan planning organization in meeting the performance targets in comparison with system performance recorded in previous reports;

(8) EXISTING SYSTEM.—The statewide transportation plan should include capital, operations and management strategies, investments, procedures, and other measures to ensure the preservation and most efficient use of the existing transportation system.

(9) PUBLICATION OF LONG-RANGE TRANSPORTATION PLANS.—Each long-range transportation plan prepared by a State shall be published or otherwise made available, including (to the maximum extent practicable) in electronically accessible formats and means, such as the World Wide Web.

(g) STATEWIDE TRANSPORTATION IMPROVEMENT PROGRAM.—

(1) DEVELOPMENT.—

(A) IN GENERAL.—Each State shall develop a statewide transportation improvement program for all areas of the State.

(B) DURATION AND UPDATING OF PROGRAM.—Each program developed under subparagraph (A) shall cover a period of 4 years and shall be updated every 4 years or more frequently if the Governor of the State elects to update more frequently.

(2) CONSULTATION WITH GOVERNMENTS.—

(A) METROPOLITAN AREAS.—With respect to each metropolitan area in the State, the program shall be developed in cooperation with the metropolitan planning organization designated for the metropolitan area under section 5303.

(B) NONMETROPOLITAN AREAS.—

(i) IN GENERAL.—With respect to each nonmetropolitan area in the State, the program shall be developed in cooperation with affected nonmetropolitan local officials with responsibility for transportation or, if applicable, through regional transportation planning organizations described in subsection (l).

(ii) ROLE OF SECRETARY.—The Secretary shall not review or approve the specific consultation process in the State.

(C) INDIAN TRIBAL AREAS.—With respect to each area of the State under the jurisdiction of an Indian tribal government, the program shall be developed in consultation with the tribal government and the Secretary of the Interior.

(3) PARTICIPATION BY INTERESTED PARTIES.—In developing the program, the State shall provide citizens, affected public agencies, representatives of public transportation employees, freight shippers, private providers of transportation, providers of freight transportation services, representatives of users of public transportation, representatives of users of pedestrian walkways and bicycle transportation facilities, representatives of the disabled, and other interested parties with a reasonable opportunity to comment on the proposed program.

(4) PERFORMANCE TARGET ACHIEVEMENT.—A statewide transportation improvement program shall include, to the maximum extent practicable, a discussion of the anticipated effect of the statewide transportation improvement program toward achieving the performance targets established in the statewide transportation plan, linking investment priorities to those performance targets.

(5) INCLUDED PROJECTS.—

(A) IN GENERAL.—A transportation improvement program developed under this subsection for a State shall include Federally supported surface transportation expenditures within the boundaries of the State.

(B) LISTING OF PROJECTS.—

(i) IN GENERAL.—An annual listing of projects for which funds have been obligated for the preceding year in each metropolitan planning area shall be published or otherwise made available by the cooperative effort of the State, transit operator, and the metropolitan planning organization for public review.

(ii) FUNDING CATEGORIES.—The listing described in clause (i) shall be consistent with the funding categories identified in each metropolitan transportation improvement program.

(C) PROJECTS UNDER CHAPTER 2.—

(i) REGIONALLY SIGNIFICANT PROJECTS.—Regionally significant projects proposed for funding under chapter 2 of title 23 shall be identified individually in the transportation improvement program.

(ii) OTHER PROJECTS.—Projects proposed for funding under chapter 2 of title 23 that are not determined to be regionally significant shall be grouped in 1 line item or identified individually in the transportation improvement program.

(D) CONSISTENCY WITH STATEWIDE TRANSPORTATION PLAN.—Each project shall be—

(i) consistent with the statewide transportation plan developed under this section for the State;

(ii) identical to the project or phase of the project as described in an approved metropolitan transportation plan; and

(iii) in conformance with the applicable State air quality implementation plan developed under the Clean Air Act (42 U.S.C. 7401 et seq.), if the project is carried out in an area designated as a nonattainment area for ozone, particulate matter, or carbon monoxide under part D of title I of that Act (42 U.S.C. 7501 et seq.).

(E) REQUIREMENT OF ANTICIPATED FULL FUNDING.—The transportation improvement program shall include a project, or an identified phase of a project, only if full funding can reasonably be anticipated to be available for the project within the time period contemplated for completion of the project.

(F) FINANCIAL PLAN.—

(i) IN GENERAL.—The transportation improvement program may include a financial plan that demonstrates how the approved transportation improvement program can be implemented, indicates resources from public and private sources that are reasonably expected to be made available to carry out the transportation improvement program, and recommends any additional financing strategies for needed projects and programs.

(ii) ADDITIONAL PROJECTS.—The financial plan may include, for illustrative purposes, additional projects that would be included in the adopted transportation plan if reasonable additional resources beyond those identified in the financial plan were available.

(G) SELECTION OF PROJECTS FROM ILLUSTRATIVE LIST.—

(i) NO REQUIRED SELECTION.—Notwithstanding subparagraph (F), a State shall not be required to select any project from the illustrative list of additional projects included in the financial plan under subparagraph (F).

(ii) REQUIRED ACTION BY THE SECRETARY.—Action by the Secretary shall be required for a State to select any project from the illustrative list of additional projects included in the financial plan under subparagraph (F) for inclusion in an approved transportation improvement program.

(H) PRIORITIES.—The transportation improvement program shall reflect the priorities for programming and expenditures of funds, including transportation enhancement activities, required by this chapter and title 23.

(6) PROJECT SELECTION FOR AREAS OF LESS THAN 50,000 POPULATION.—

(A) IN GENERAL.—Projects carried out in areas with populations of less than 50,000 individuals shall be selected, from the approved transportation improvement program (excluding projects carried out on the National Highway System and projects carried out under the bridge program or the Interstate maintenance program under title 23 or under sections 5310 and 5311 of this chapter), by the State in cooperation with the affected nonmetropolitan local officials with responsibility for transportation or, if applicable, through regional transportation planning organizations described in subsection (l).

(B) OTHER PROJECTS.—Projects carried out in areas with populations of less than 50,000 individuals on the National Highway System or under the bridge program or the Interstate maintenance program under title 23 or under sections 5310 and 5311 of this chapter shall be selected, from the approved statewide transportation improvement program, by the State in consultation with the affected nonmetropolitan local officials with responsibility for transportation.

(7) TRANSPORTATION IMPROVEMENT PROGRAM APPROVAL.—Every 4 years, a

transportation improvement program developed under this subsection shall be reviewed and approved by the Secretary if based on a current planning finding.

(8) PLANNING FINDING.—A finding shall be made by the Secretary at least every 4 years that the transportation planning process through which statewide transportation plans and programs are developed is consistent with this section and section 5303.

(9) MODIFICATIONS TO PROJECT PRIORITY.—Notwithstanding any other provision of law, action by the Secretary shall not be required to advance a project included in the approved transportation improvement program in place of another project in the program.

(h) PERFORMANCE-BASED PLANNING PROCESSES EVALUATION.—

(1) IN GENERAL.—The Secretary shall establish criteria to evaluate the effectiveness of the performance-based planning processes of States, taking into consideration the following:

(A) The extent to which the State is making progress toward achieving, the performance targets described in subsection (d)(2), taking into account whether the State developed appropriate performance targets.

(B) The extent to which the State has made transportation investments that are efficient and cost-effective.

(C) The extent to which the State—

(i) has developed an investment process that relies on public input and awareness to ensure that investments are transparent and accountable; and

(ii) provides reports allowing the public to access the information being collected in a format that allows the public to meaningfully assess the performance of the State.

(2) REPORT.—

(A) IN GENERAL.—Not later than 5 years after the date of enactment of the Federal Public Transportation Act of 2012, the Secretary shall submit to Congress a report evaluating—

(i) the overall effectiveness of performance-based planning as a tool for guiding transportation investments; and

(ii) the effectiveness of the performance-based planning process of each State.

(B) PUBLICATION.—The report under subparagraph (A) shall be published or otherwise made available in electronically accessible formats and means, including on the Internet.

(i) TREATMENT OF CERTAIN STATE LAWS AS CONGESTION MANAGEMENT PROCESSES.—For purposes of this section and section 5303, and sections 134 and 135 of title 23, State laws, rules, or regulations pertaining to congestion management systems or programs may constitute the congestion management process under this section and section 5303, and sections 134 and 135 of title 23, if the Secretary finds that the State laws, rules, or regulations are consistent with, and fulfill the intent of, the purposes of this section and section 5303, and sections 134 and 135 of title 23, as appropriate.

(j) CONTINUATION OF CURRENT REVIEW PRACTICE.—Since the statewide transportation plan and the transportation improvement program described in this section are subject to a reasonable opportunity for public comment, since individual projects included in the statewide transportation plans and the transportation improvement program are subject to review under the National Environmental Policy Act of 1969 (42 U.S.C. 4321 et seq.), and since decisions by the Secretary concerning statewide transportation plans or the transportation improvement program described in this section have not been reviewed under that Act as of January 1, 1997, any decision by the Secretary concerning a metropolitan or statewide transportation plan or the transportation improvement program described in this section shall not be considered to be a Federal action subject to review under the National Environmental Policy Act of 1969 (42 U.S.C. 4321 et seq.).

(k) SCHEDULE FOR IMPLEMENTATION.—The Secretary shall issue guidance on a schedule for implementation of the changes made by this section, taking into consideration the established planning update cycle for States. The Secretary shall not require a State to deviate from its established planning update cycle to implement changes made by this section. States shall reflect changes made to their transportation plan or transportation improvement program updates not later than 2 years after the date of issuance of guidance by the Secretary under this subsection.

(l) DESIGNATION OF REGIONAL TRANSPORTATION PLANNING ORGANIZATIONS.—

(1) IN GENERAL.—To carry out the transportation planning process required by this section, a State may establish and designate regional transportation planning organizations to enhance the planning, coordination, and implementation of statewide strategic long-range transportation plans and transportation improvement programs, with an emphasis on addressing the needs of nonmetropolitan areas of the State.

(2) STRUCTURE.—A regional transportation planning organization shall be established as a multijurisdictional organization of nonmetropolitan local officials or their designees who volunteer for such organization and representatives of local transportation systems who volunteer for such organization.

(3) REQUIREMENTS.—A regional transportation planning organization shall establish, at a minimum—

(A) a policy committee, the majority of which shall consist of nonmetropolitan local officials, or their designees, and, as appropriate, additional representatives from the State, private business, transportation service providers, economic development practitioners, and the public in the region; and

(B) a fiscal and administrative agent, such as an existing regional planning and development organization, to provide professional planning, management, and administrative support.

(4) DUTIES.—The duties of a regional transportation planning organization shall include—

(A) developing and maintaining, in cooperation with the State, regional long-range multimodal transportation plans;

(B) developing a regional transportation improvement program for consideration by the State;

(C) fostering the coordination of local planning, land use, and economic development plans with State, regional, and local transportation plans and programs;

(D) providing technical assistance to local officials;

(E) participating in national, multistate, and State policy and planning development processes to ensure the regional and local input of nonmetropolitan areas;

(F) providing a forum for public participation in the statewide and regional transportation planning processes;

(G) considering and sharing plans and programs with neighboring regional transportation planning organizations, metropolitan planning organizations, and, where appropriate, tribal organizations; and

(H) conducting other duties, as necessary, to support and enhance the statewide planning process under subsection (d).

(5) STATES WITHOUT REGIONAL TRANSPORTATION PLANNING ORGANIZATIONS.—If a State chooses not to establish or designate a regional transportation planning organization, the State shall consult with affected nonmetropolitan local officials to determine projects that may be of regional significance.

(Pub. L. 103–272, §1(d), July 5, 1994, 108 Stat. 793; Pub. L. 105–178, title III, §3005, June 9, 1998, 112 Stat. 345; Pub. L. 105–206, title IX, §9009(c)(2), July 22, 1998, 112 Stat. 854; Pub. L. 109–59, title III, §3006(a), Aug. 10, 2005, 119 Stat. 1559; Pub. L. 112–141, div. B, §20006, July 6, 2012, 126 Stat. 643; Pub. L. 114–94, div. A, title III, §3003(b), Dec. 4, 2015, 129 Stat. 1449; Pub. L. 117–58, div. C, §30003, Nov. 15, 2021, 135 Stat. 893.)

§5305. PLANNING PROGRAMS

(a) STATE DEFINED.—In this section, the term "State" means a State of the United States, the District of Columbia, and Puerto Rico.

(b) GENERAL AUTHORITY.—

(1) GRANTS AND AGREEMENTS.—Under criteria established by the Secretary, the Secretary may award grants to States, authorities of the States, metropolitan planning organizations, and local governmental authorities, and make agreements with other departments, agencies, or instrumentalities of the Government to—

(A) develop transportation plans and programs;

(B) plan, engineer, design, and evaluate a public transportation project; and

(C) conduct technical studies relating to public transportation.

(2) ELIGIBLE ACTIVITIES.—Activities eligible under paragraph (1) include the following:

(A) Studies related to management, planning, operations, capital requirements, and economic feasibility.

(B) Evaluating previously financed projects.

(C) Peer reviews and exchanges of technical data, information, assistance, and related activities in support of planning and environmental analyses among metropolitan planning organizations and other transportation planners.

(D) Other similar and related activities preliminary to and in preparation for constructing, acquiring, or improving the operation of facilities and equipment.

(c) PURPOSE.—To the extent practicable, the Secretary shall ensure that amounts appropriated or made available under section 5338 to carry out this section and sections 5303, 5304, and 5306 are used to support balanced and comprehensive transportation planning that considers the relationships among land use and all transportation modes, without regard to the programmatic source of the planning amounts.

(d) METROPOLITAN PLANNING PROGRAM.—

(1) APPORTIONMENT TO STATES.—

(A) IN GENERAL.—The Secretary shall apportion 80 percent of the amounts made available under subsection (g)(1) among the States to carry out sections 5303 and 5306 in the ratio that—

(i) the population of urbanized areas in each State, as shown by the latest available decennial census of population; bears to

(ii) the total population of urbanized areas in all States, as shown by that census.

(B) MINIMUM APPORTIONMENT.—Notwithstanding subparagraph (A), a State may not receive less than 0.5 percent of the amount apportioned under this paragraph.

(2) ALLOCATION TO MPO'S.—Amounts apportioned to a State under paragraph (1) shall be made available, not later than 30 days after the date of apportionment, to metropolitan planning organizations in the State designated under this section under a formula that—

(A) considers population of urbanized areas;

(B) provides an appropriate distribution for urbanized areas to carry out the cooperative processes described in this section;

(C) the State develops in cooperation with the metropolitan planning organizations; and

(D) the Secretary approves.

(3) SUPPLEMENTAL AMOUNTS.—

(A) IN GENERAL.—The Secretary shall apportion 20 percent of the amounts made available under subsection (g)(1) among the States to supplement allocations made under paragraph (1) for metropolitan planning organizations.

(B) FORMULA.—The Secretary shall apportion amounts referred to in subparagraph (A) under a formula that reflects the additional cost of carrying out planning, programming, and project selection responsibilities under sections 5303 and 5306 in certain urbanized areas.

(e) STATE PLANNING AND RESEARCH PROGRAM.—

(1) APPORTIONMENT TO STATES.—

(A) IN GENERAL.—The Secretary shall apportion the amounts made available under subsection (g)(2) among the States for grants and contracts to carry out this section and sections 5304 and 5306 in the ratio that—

(i) the population of urbanized areas in each State, as shown by the latest available decennial census; bears to

(ii) the population of urbanized areas in all States, as shown by that census.

(B) MINIMUM APPORTIONMENT.—Notwithstanding subparagraph (A), a State may not receive less than 0.5 percent of the amount apportioned under this paragraph.

(2) SUPPLEMENTAL AMOUNTS.—A State, as the State considers appropriate, may authorize part of the amount made available under this subsection to be used to supplement amounts made available under subsection (d).

(f) GOVERNMENT SHARE OF COSTS.—

(1) IN GENERAL.—Except as provided in paragraph (2), the Government share of

the cost of an activity funded using amounts made available under this section may not exceed 80 percent of the cost of the activity unless the Secretary determines that it is in the interests of the Government—

(A) not to require a State or local match; or

(B) to allow a Government share greater than 80 percent.

(2) CERTAIN ACTIVITIES.—

(A) IN GENERAL.—The Government share of the cost of an activity funded using amounts made available under this section shall be not less than 90 percent for an activity that assists parts of an urbanized area or rural area with lower population density or lower average income levels compared to—

(i) the applicable urbanized area;

(ii) the applicable rural area;

(iii) an adjoining urbanized area; or

(iv) an adjoining rural area.

(B) REPORT.—A State or metropolitan planning organization that carries out an activity described in subparagraph (A) with an increased Government share described in that subparagraph shall report to the Secretary, in a form as determined by the Secretary, how the increased Government share for transportation planning activities benefits commuting and other essential travel in parts of the applicable urbanized area or rural area described in subparagraph (A) with lower population density or lower average income levels.

(g) ALLOCATION OF FUNDS.—Of the funds made available by or appropriated to carry out this section under section 5338(a)(2)(A) for a fiscal year—

(1) 82.72 percent shall be available for the metropolitan planning program under subsection (d); and

(2) 17.28 percent shall be available to carry out subsection (e).

(h) AVAILABILITY OF FUNDS.—Funds apportioned under this section to a State that have not been obligated in the 3-year period beginning after the last day of the fiscal year for which the funds are authorized shall be reapportioned among the States.

(Pub. L. 103–272, §1(d), July 5, 1994, 108 Stat. 794; Pub. L. 105–178, title III, §3006, June 9, 1998, 112 Stat. 346; Pub. L. 105–206, title IX, §9009(d), July 22, 1998, 112 Stat. 854; Pub. L. 109–59, title III, §3007(a), Aug. 10, 2005, 119 Stat. 1566; Pub. L. 111–147, title IV, §431, Mar. 18, 2010, 124 Stat. 88; Pub. L. 111–322, title II, §2301, Dec. 22, 2010, 124 Stat. 3526; Pub. L. 112–5, title III, §301, Mar. 4, 2011, 125 Stat. 18; Pub. L. 112–30, title I, §131, Sept. 16, 2011, 125 Stat. 350; Pub. L. 112–102, title III, §301, Mar. 30, 2012, 126 Stat. 275; Pub. L. 112–140, title III, §301, June 29, 2012, 126 Stat. 396; Pub. L. 112–141, div. B, §20030(a), div. G, title III, §113001, July 6, 2012, 126 Stat. 730, 983; Pub. L. 117–58, div. C, §30004, Nov. 15, 2021, 135 Stat. 893.)

§5306. PRIVATE ENTERPRISE PARTICIPATION IN METROPOLITAN PLANNING AND TRANSPORTATION IMPROVEMENT PROGRAMS AND RELATIONSHIP TO OTHER LIMITATIONS

(a) PRIVATE ENTERPRISE PARTICIPATION.—A plan or program required by section 5303, 5304, or 5305 of this title shall encourage to the maximum extent feasible, as determined by local policies, criteria, and decisionmaking, the participation of private enterprise. If equipment or a facility already being used in an urban area is to be acquired under this chapter, the program shall provide that it be improved so that it will better serve the transportation needs of the area.

(b) RELATIONSHIP TO OTHER LIMITATIONS.—Sections 5303–5305 of this title do not authorize—

(1) a metropolitan planning organization to impose a legal requirement on a transportation facility, provider, or project not eligible under this chapter or title 23; and

(2) intervention in the management of a transportation authority.

(Pub. L. 103–272, §1(d), July 5, 1994, 108 Stat. 795; Pub. L. 109–59, title III, §3008, Aug. 10, 2005, 119 Stat. 1568.)

§5307. URBANIZED AREA FORMULA GRANTS

(a) GENERAL AUTHORITY.—

(1) GRANTS.—The Secretary may make grants under this section for—

(A) capital projects;

(B) planning;

(C) job access and reverse commute projects; and

(D) operating costs of equipment and facilities for use in public transportation in an urbanized area with a population of fewer than 200,000 individuals, as determined by the Bureau of the Census.

(2) The Secretary may make grants under this section to finance the operating cost of equipment and facilities for use in public transportation, excluding rail fixed guideway, in an urbanized area with a population of not fewer than 200,000 individuals, as determined by the Bureau of the Census—

(A) for public transportation systems that—

(i) operate 75 or fewer buses in fixed route service or demand response service, excluding ADA complementary paratransit service, during peak service hours, in an amount not to exceed 75 percent of the share of the apportionment which is attributable to such systems within the urbanized area, as measured by vehicle revenue hours; or

(ii) operate a minimum of 76 buses and a maximum of 100 buses in fixed route service or demand response service, excluding ADA complementary paratransit service, during peak service hours, in an amount not to exceed 50 percent of the share of the apportionment which is attributable to such systems within the urbanized area, as measured by vehicle revenue hours; or

(B) subject to paragraph (3), for public transportation systems that—

(i) operate 75 or fewer buses in fixed route service or demand response service, excluding ADA complementary paratransit service, during peak service hours, in an amount not to exceed 75 percent of the share of the apportionment allocated to such systems within the urbanized area, as determined by the local planning process and included in the designated recipient's final program of projects prepared under subsection (b); or

(ii) operate a minimum of 76 buses and a maximum of 100 buses in fixed route service or demand response service, excluding ADA complementary paratransit service during peak service hours, in an amount not to exceed 50 percent of the share of the apportionment allocated to such systems within the urbanized area, as determined by the local planning process and included in the designated recipient's final program of projects prepared under subsection (b).

(3) The amount available to a public transportation system under subparagraph (B) of paragraph (2) shall be not more than 10 percent greater than the amount that would otherwise be available to the system under subparagraph (A) of that paragraph.

(b) PROGRAM OF PROJECTS.—Each recipient of a grant shall—

(1) make available to the public information on amounts available to the recipient under this section;

(2) develop, in consultation with interested parties, including private transportation providers, a proposed program of projects for activities to be financed;

(3) publish a proposed program of projects in a way that affected individuals, private transportation providers, and local elected officials have the opportunity to examine the proposed program and submit comments on the proposed program and the performance of the recipient;

(4) provide an opportunity for a public hearing in which to obtain the views of individuals on the proposed program of projects;

(5) ensure that the proposed program of projects provides for the coordination of public transportation services assisted under section 5336 of this title with transportation services assisted from other United States Government sources;

(6) consider comments and views received, especially those of private transportation providers, in preparing the final program of projects; and

(7) make the final program of projects available to the public.

(c) GRANT RECIPIENT REQUIREMENTS.—A recipient may receive a grant in a fiscal year only if—

(1) the recipient, within the time the Secretary prescribes, submits a final program of projects prepared under subsection (b) of this section and a certification for that fiscal year that the recipient (including a person receiving amounts from a Governor under this section)—

(A) has or will have the legal, financial, and technical capacity to carry out the program, including safety and security aspects of the program;

(B) has or will have satisfactory continuing control over the use of equipment and facilities;

(C) will maintain equipment and facilities in accordance with the recipient's transit asset management plan;

(D) will ensure that, during non-peak hours for transportation using or involving a facility or equipment of a project financed under this section, a fare that is not more than 50 percent of the peak hour fare will be charged for any—

(i) senior;

(ii) individual who, because of illness, injury, age, congenital malfunction, or other incapacity or temporary or permanent disability (including an individual who is a wheelchair user or has semiambulatory capability), cannot use a public transportation service or a public transportation facility effectively without special facilities, planning, or design; and

(iii) individual presenting a Medicare card issued to that individual under title II or XVIII of the Social Security Act (42 U.S.C. 401 et seq. and 1395 et seq.);

(E) in carrying out a procurement under this section, will comply with sections 5323 and 5325;

(F) has complied with subsection (b) of this section;

(G) has available and will provide the required amounts as provided by subsection (d) of this section;

(H) will comply with sections 5303 and 5304;

(I) has a locally developed process to solicit and consider public comment before raising a fare or carrying out a major reduction of transportation;

(J)(i) will expend for each fiscal year for public transportation security projects, including increased lighting in or adjacent to a public transportation system (including bus stops, subway stations, parking lots, and garages), increased camera surveillance of an area in or adjacent to that system, providing an emergency telephone line to contact law enforcement or security personnel in an area in or adjacent to that system, and any other project intended to increase the security and safety of an existing or planned public transportation system, at least 1 percent of the amount the recipient receives for each fiscal year under section 5336 of this title; or

(ii) has decided that the expenditure for security projects is not necessary;

(K) in the case of a recipient for an urbanized area with a population of not fewer than 200,000 individuals, as determined by the Bureau of the Census, will submit an annual report listing projects carried out in the preceding fiscal year under this section for associated transit improvements as defined in section 5302; and

(L) will comply with section 5329(d); and

(2) the Secretary accepts the certification.

(d) GOVERNMENT SHARE OF COSTS.—

(1) CAPITAL PROJECTS.—A grant for a capital project under this section shall be for 80 percent of the net project cost of the project. The recipient may provide additional local matching amounts.

(2) OPERATING EXPENSES.—A grant for operating expenses under this section may not exceed 50 percent of the net project cost of the project.

(3) REMAINING COSTS.—Subject to paragraph (4), the remainder of the net project costs shall be provided—

(A) in cash from non-Government sources other than revenues from providing public transportation services;

(B) from revenues from the sale of advertising and concessions;

(C) from an undistributed cash surplus, a replacement or depreciation cash fund or reserve, or new capital;

(D) from amounts appropriated or otherwise made available to a department or agency of the Government (other than the Department of Transportation) that are eligible to be expended for transportation; and

(E) from amounts received under a service agreement with a State or local social service agency or private social service organization.

(4) USE OF CERTAIN FUNDS.—For purposes of subparagraphs (D) and (E) of paragraph (3), the prohibitions on the use of funds for matching requirements under section 403(a)(5)(C)(vii) of the Social Security Act (42 U.S.C. 603(a)(5)(C)(vii)) shall not apply to Federal or State funds to be used for transportation purposes.

(e) UNDERTAKING PROJECTS IN ADVANCE.—

(1) PAYMENT.—The Secretary may pay the Government share of the net project cost to a State or local governmental authority that carries out any part of a project eligible under subparagraph (A) or (B) of subsection (a)(1) without the aid of amounts of the Government and according to all applicable procedures and requirements if—

(A) the recipient applies for the payment;

(B) the Secretary approves the payment; and

(C) before carrying out any part of the project, the Secretary approves the plans and specifications for the part in the same way as for other projects under this section.

(2) APPROVAL OF APPLICATION.—The Secretary may approve an application under paragraph (1) of this subsection only if an authorization for this section is in effect for the fiscal year to which the application applies. The Secretary may not approve an application if the payment will be more than—

(A) the recipient's expected apportionment under section 5336 of this title if the total amount authorized to be appropriated for the fiscal year to carry out this section is appropriated; less

(B) the maximum amount of the apportionment that may be made available for projects for operating expenses under this section.

(3) FINANCING COSTS.—

(A) IN GENERAL.—The cost of carrying out part of a project includes the amount of interest earned and payable on bonds issued by the recipient to the extent proceeds of the bonds are expended in carrying out the part.

(B) LIMITATION ON THE AMOUNT OF INTEREST.—The amount of interest allowed under this paragraph may not be more than the most favorable financing terms reasonably available for the project at the time of borrowing.

(C) CERTIFICATION.—The applicant shall certify, in a manner satisfactory to the Secretary, that the applicant has shown reasonable diligence in seeking the most favorable financing terms.

(f) REVIEWS, AUDITS, AND EVALUATIONS.—

(1) ANNUAL REVIEW.—

(A) IN GENERAL.—At least annually, the Secretary shall carry out, or require a recipient to have carried out independently, reviews and audits the Secretary considers appropriate to establish whether the recipient has carried out—

(i) the activities proposed under subsection (c) of this section in a timely and effective way and can continue to do so; and

(ii) those activities and its certifications and has used amounts of the Government in the way required by law.

(B) AUDITING PROCEDURES.—An audit of the use of amounts of the Government shall comply with the auditing procedures of the Comptroller General.

(2) TRIENNIAL REVIEW.—At least once every 3 years, the Secretary shall review and evaluate completely the performance of a recipient in carrying out the recipient's program, specifically referring to compliance with statutory and administrative requirements and the extent to which actual program activities are consistent with the activities proposed under subsection (c) of this section and the planning process required under sections 5303, 5304, and 5305 of this title. To the extent practicable,

the Secretary shall coordinate such reviews with any related State or local reviews.

(3) ACTIONS RESULTING FROM REVIEW, AUDIT, OR EVALUATION.—The Secretary may take appropriate action consistent with a review, audit, and evaluation under this subsection, including making an appropriate adjustment in the amount of a grant or withdrawing the grant.

(g) TREATMENT.—For purposes of this section, the United States Virgin Islands shall be treated as an urbanized area, as defined in section 5302.

(h) PASSENGER FERRY GRANTS.—

(1) IN GENERAL.—The Secretary may make grants under this subsection to recipients for passenger ferry projects that are eligible for a grant under subsection (a).

(2) GRANT REQUIREMENTS.—Except as otherwise provided in this subsection, a grant under this subsection shall be subject to the same terms and conditions as a grant under subsection (a).

(3) COMPETITIVE PROCESS.—The Secretary shall solicit grant applications and make grants for eligible projects on a competitive basis.

(Pub. L. 103–272, §1(d), July 5, 1994, 108 Stat. 795; Pub. L. 103–429, §6(7), Oct. 31, 1994, 108 Stat. 4378; Pub. L. 104–287, §5(11), Oct. 11, 1996, 110 Stat. 3389; Pub. L. 105–178, title III, §3007(a)(1), (b)–(h), June 9, 1998, 112 Stat. 347, 348; Pub. L. 105–206, title IX, §9009(e), July 22, 1998, 112 Stat. 855; Pub. L. 107–232, §1, Oct. 1, 2002, 116 Stat. 1478; Pub. L. 108–88, §8(n), Sept. 30, 2003, 117 Stat. 1125; Pub. L. 108–202, §9(n), Feb. 29, 2004, 118 Stat. 488; Pub. L. 108–224, §7(n), Apr. 30, 2004, 118 Stat. 636; Pub. L. 108–263, §7(n), June 30, 2004, 118 Stat. 708; Pub. L. 108–280, §7(n), July 30, 2004, 118 Stat. 885; Pub. L. 108–310, §8(n), Sept. 30, 2004, 118 Stat. 1158; Pub. L. 109–14, §7(m), May 31, 2005, 119 Stat. 333; Pub. L. 109–20, §7(m), July 1, 2005, 119 Stat. 355; Pub. L. 109–35, §7(m), July 20, 2005, 119 Stat. 389; Pub. L. 109–37, §7(m), July 22, 2005, 119 Stat. 404; Pub. L. 109–40, §7(m), July 28, 2005, 119 Stat. 420; Pub. L. 109–59, title III, §§3002(b)(4), 3009(a)–(h), Aug. 10, 2005, 119 Stat. 1545, 1568–1571; Pub. L. 110–244, title II, §201(c), June 6, 2008, 122 Stat. 1609; Pub. L. 111–147, title IV, §432, Mar. 18, 2010, 124 Stat. 88; Pub. L. 111–322, title II, §2302, Dec. 22, 2010, 124 Stat. 3526; Pub. L. 112–5, title III, §302, Mar. 4, 2011, 125 Stat. 18; Pub. L. 112–30, title I, §132, Sept. 16, 2011, 125 Stat. 350; Pub. L. 112–102, title III, §302, Mar. 30, 2012, 126 Stat. 275; Pub. L. 112–140, title III, §302, June 29, 2012, 126 Stat. 396; Pub. L. 112–141, div. B, §20007, div. G, title III, §113002, July 6, 2012, 126 Stat. 652, 983; Pub. L. 114–94, div. A, title III, §3004, Dec. 4, 2015, 129 Stat. 1450; Pub. L. 115–31, div. K, title I, §165, May 5, 2017, 131 Stat. 749.)

[§5308. REPEALED. PUB. L. 112–141, DIV. B, §20002(A), JULY 6, 2012, 126 STAT. 622]

Section, Pub. L. 103–272, §1(d), July 5, 1994, 108 Stat. 800; Pub. L. 105–178, title III, §3008(a), (c), June 9, 1998, 112 Stat. 348; Pub. L. 105–206, title IX, §9009(f), July 22, 1998, 112 Stat. 855; Pub. L. 109–59, title III, §3010(a), Aug. 10, 2005, 119 Stat. 1572, related to a grant program for clean fuel buses.

§5309. FIXED GUIDEWAY CAPITAL INVESTMENT GRANTS

(a) DEFINITIONS.—In this section, the following definitions shall apply:

(1) APPLICANT.—The term "applicant" means a State or local governmental authority that applies for a grant under this section.

(2) CORE CAPACITY IMPROVEMENT PROJECT.—The term "core capacity improvement project" means a substantial corridor-based capital investment in an existing fixed guideway system that increases the capacity of a corridor by not less than 10 percent. The term does not include project elements designed to maintain a state of good repair

of the existing fixed guideway system.

(3) CORRIDOR-BASED BUS RAPID TRANSIT PROJECT.—The term "corridor-based bus rapid transit project" means a small start project utilizing buses in which the project represents a substantial investment in a defined corridor as demonstrated by features that emulate the services provided by rail fixed guideway public transportation systems, including defined stations; traffic signal priority for public transportation vehicles; short headway bidirectional services for a substantial part of weekdays; and any other features the Secretary may determine support a long-term corridor investment, but the majority of which does not operate in a separated right-of-way dedicated for public transportation use during peak periods.

(4) FIXED GUIDEWAY BUS RAPID TRANSIT PROJECT.—The term "fixed guideway bus rapid transit project" means a bus capital project—

(A) in which the majority of the project operates in a separated right-of-way dedicated for public transportation use during peak periods;

(B) that represents a substantial investment in a single route in a defined corridor or subarea; and

(C) that includes features that emulate the services provided by rail fixed guideway public transportation systems, including—

(i) defined stations;

(ii) traffic signal priority for public transportation vehicles;

(iii) short headway bidirectional services for a substantial part of weekdays and weekend days; and

(iv) any other features the Secretary may determine are necessary to produce high-quality public transportation services that emulate the services provided by rail fixed guideway public transportation systems.

(5) NEW FIXED GUIDEWAY CAPITAL PROJECT.—The term "new fixed guideway capital project" means—

(A) a new fixed guideway project that is a minimum operable segment or extension to an existing fixed guideway system; or

(B) a fixed guideway bus rapid transit project that is a minimum operable segment or an extension to an existing bus rapid transit system.

(6) SMALL START PROJECT.—The term "small start project" means a new fixed guideway capital project or corridor-based bus rapid transit project for which—

(A) the Federal assistance provided or to be provided under this section is less than $150,000,000; and

(B) the total estimated net capital cost is less than $400,000,000.

(b) GENERAL AUTHORITY.—The Secretary may make grants under this section to State and local governmental authorities to assist in financing—

(1) new fixed guideway capital projects or small start projects, including the acquisition of real property, the initial acquisition of rolling stock for the system, the acquisition of rights-of-way, and relocation, for fixed guideway corridor development for projects in the advanced stages of project development or engineering; and

(2) core capacity improvement projects, including the acquisition of real property, the acquisition of rights-of-way, double tracking, signalization improvements, electrification, expanding system platforms, acquisition of rolling stock associated

with corridor improvements increasing capacity, construction of infill stations, and such other capacity improvement projects as the Secretary determines are appropriate to increase the capacity of an existing fixed guideway system corridor by at least 10 percent. Core capacity improvement projects do not include elements to improve general station facilities or parking, or acquisition of rolling stock alone.

(c) GRANT REQUIREMENTS.—

(1) IN GENERAL.—The Secretary may make a grant under this section for new fixed guideway capital projects, small start projects, or core capacity improvement projects, if the Secretary determines that—

(A) the project is part of an approved transportation plan required under sections 5303 and 5304;

(B) the applicant has, or will have—

(i) the legal, financial, and technical capacity to carry out the project, including the safety and security aspects of the project;

(ii) satisfactory continuing control over the use of the equipment or facilities; and

(iii) the technical and financial capacity to maintain new and existing equipment and facilities; and

(C) the applicant has made progress toward meeting the performance targets in section 5326(c)(2).

(2) CERTIFICATION.—An applicant that has submitted the certifications required under subparagraphs (A), (B), (C), and (H) of section 5307(c)(1) shall be deemed to have provided sufficient information upon which the Secretary may make the determinations required under this subsection.

(3) TECHNICAL CAPACITY.—The Secretary shall use an expedited technical capacity review process for applicants that have recently and successfully completed at least 1 new fixed guideway capital project, or core capacity improvement project, if—

(A) the applicant achieved budget, cost, and ridership outcomes for the project that are consistent with or better than projections; and

(B) the applicant demonstrates that the applicant continues to have the staff expertise and other resources necessary to implement a new project.

(4) RECIPIENT REQUIREMENTS.—A recipient of a grant awarded under this section shall be subject to all terms, conditions, requirements, and provisions that the Secretary determines to be necessary or appropriate for purposes of this section.

(d) NEW FIXED GUIDEWAY GRANTS.—

(1) PROJECT DEVELOPMENT PHASE.—

(A) ENTRANCE INTO PROJECT DEVELOPMENT PHASE.—A new fixed guideway capital project shall enter into the project development phase when—

(i) the applicant—

(I) submits a letter to the Secretary describing the project and requesting entry into the project development phase; and

(II) initiates activities required to be carried out under the National Environmental Policy Act of 1969 (42 U.S.C. 4321 et seq.) with respect to the project; and

(ii) the Secretary—

(I) responds in writing to the applicant within 45 days whether the information provided is sufficient to enter into the project development phase, including, when necessary, a detailed description of any information deemed insufficient; and

(II) provides concurrent notice to the Committee on Banking, Housing, and Urban Affairs of the Senate and the Committee on Transportation and Infrastructure of the House of Representatives of whether the new fixed guideway capital project is entering the project development phase.

(B) ACTIVITIES DURING PROJECT DEVELOPMENT PHASE.—Concurrent with the analysis required to be made under the National Environmental Policy Act of 1969 (42 U.S.C. 4321 et seq.), each applicant shall develop sufficient information to enable the Secretary to make findings of project justification and local financial commitment under this subsection.

(C) COMPLETION OF PROJECT DEVELOPMENT ACTIVITIES REQUIRED.—

(i) IN GENERAL.—Not later than 2 years after the date on which a project enters into the project development phase, the applicant shall complete the activities required to obtain a project rating under subsection (g)(2) and submit completed documentation to the Secretary.

(ii) EXTENSION OF TIME.—Upon the request of an applicant, the Secretary may extend the time period under clause (i), if the applicant submits to the Secretary—

(I) a reasonable plan for completing the activities required under this paragraph; and

(II) an estimated time period within which the applicant will complete such activities.

(2) ENGINEERING PHASE.—

(A) IN GENERAL.—A new fixed guideway capital project may advance to the engineering phase upon completion of activities required under the National Environmental Policy Act of 1969 (42 U.S.C. 4321 et seq.), as demonstrated by a record of decision with respect to the project, a finding that the project has no significant impact, or a determination that the project is categorically excluded, only if the Secretary determines that the project—

(i) is selected as the locally preferred alternative at the completion of the process required under the National Environmental Policy Act of 1969 (42 U.S.C. 4321 et seq.);

(ii) is adopted into the metropolitan transportation plan required under section 5303;

(iii) is justified based on a comprehensive review of the project's mobility improvements, the project's environmental benefits, congestion relief associated with the project, economic development effects associated with the project, policies and land use patterns of the project that support public transportation, and the project's cost-effectiveness as measured by cost per rider; and

(iv) is supported by an acceptable degree of local financial commitment (including evidence of stable and dependable financing sources), as required under subsection (f).

(B) DETERMINATION THAT PROJECT IS JUSTIFIED.—In making a determination under subparagraph (A)(iii), the Secretary shall evaluate, analyze, and consider—

(i) the reliability of the forecasting methods used to estimate costs and utilization made by the recipient and the contractors to the recipient; and

(ii) population density and current public transportation ridership in the transportation corridor.

(e) CORE CAPACITY IMPROVEMENT PROJECTS.—

(1) PROJECT DEVELOPMENT PHASE.—

(A) ENTRANCE INTO PROJECT DEVELOPMENT PHASE.—A core capacity improvement project shall be deemed to have entered into the project development phase if—

(i) the applicant—

(I) submits a letter to the Secretary describing the project and requesting entry into the project development phase; and

(II) initiates activities required to be carried out under the National Environmental Policy Act of 1969 (42 U.S.C. 4321 et seq.) with respect to the project; and

(ii) the Secretary—

(I) responds in writing to the applicant within 45 days whether the information provided is sufficient to enter into the project development phase, including when necessary a detailed description of any information deemed insufficient; and

(II) provides concurrent notice to the Committee on Banking, Housing, and Urban Affairs of the Senate and the Committee on Transportation and Infrastructure of the House of Representatives of whether the core capacity improvement project is entering the project development phase.

(B) ACTIVITIES DURING PROJECT DEVELOPMENT PHASE.—Concurrent with the analysis required to be made under the National Environmental Policy Act of 1969 (42 U.S.C. 4321 et seq.), each applicant shall develop sufficient information to enable the Secretary to make findings of project justification and local financial commitment under this subsection.

(C) COMPLETION OF PROJECT DEVELOPMENT ACTIVITIES REQUIRED.—

(i) IN GENERAL.—Not later than 2 years after the date on which a project enters into the project development phase, the applicant shall complete the activities required to obtain a project rating under subsection (g)(2) and submit completed documentation to the Secretary.

(ii) EXTENSION OF TIME.—Upon the request of an applicant, the Secretary may extend the time period under clause (i), if the applicant submits to the Secretary—

(I) a reasonable plan for completing the activities required under this paragraph; and

(II) an estimated time period within which the applicant will complete such activities.

(2) ENGINEERING PHASE.—

(A) IN GENERAL.—A core capacity improvement project may advance into the engineering phase upon completion of activities required under the National Environmental Policy Act of 1969 (42 U.S.C. 4321 et seq.), as demonstrated by a record of decision with respect to the project, a finding that the project has no significant impact, or a determination that the project is categorically excluded, only if the Secretary determines that the project—

(i) is selected as the locally preferred alternative at the completion of the process required under the National Environmental Policy Act of 1969;

(ii) is adopted into the metropolitan transportation plan required under section 5303;

(iii) is in a corridor that is—

(I) at or over capacity; or

(II) projected to be at or over capacity within the next 10 years, without regard to any temporary measures employed by the applicant expected to increase short-term capacity within the next 10 years;

(iv) is justified based on a comprehensive review of the project's mobility improvements, the project's environmental benefits, congestion relief associated with the project, economic development effects associated with the project, the capacity needs of the corridor, and the project's cost-effectiveness as measured by cost per rider; and

(v) is supported by an acceptable degree of local financial commitment (including evidence of stable and dependable financing sources), as required under subsection (f).

(B) DETERMINATION THAT PROJECT IS JUSTIFIED.—In making a determination under subparagraph (A)(iv), the Secretary shall evaluate, analyze, and consider—

(i) the reliability of the forecasting methods used to estimate costs and utilization made by the recipient and the contractors to the recipient;

(ii) whether the project will increase capacity at least 10 percent in a corridor;

(iii) whether the project will improve interconnectivity among existing systems; and

(iv) whether the project will improve environmental outcomes.

(f) FINANCING SOURCES.—

(1) REQUIREMENTS.—In determining whether a project is supported by an acceptable degree of local financial commitment and shows evidence of stable and dependable financing sources for purposes of subsection (d)(2)(A)(v) or (e)(2)(A)(v), the Secretary shall require that—

(A) the proposed project plan provides for the availability of contingency amounts that the Secretary determines to be reasonable to cover unanticipated cost increases or funding shortfalls;

(B) each proposed local source of capital and operating financing is stable, reliable, and available within the proposed project timetable; and

(C) local resources are available to recapitalize, maintain, and operate the overall existing and proposed public transportation system, including essential feeder bus and other services necessary to achieve the projected ridership levels without requiring a reduction in existing public transportation services or level of service to operate the project.

(2) CONSIDERATIONS.—In assessing the stability, reliability, and availability of proposed sources of local financing for purposes of subsection (d)(2)(A)(v) or (e)(2)(A)(v), the Secretary shall consider—

(A) the reliability of the forecasting methods used to estimate costs and revenues made by the recipient and the contractors to the recipient;

(B) existing grant commitments;

(C) the degree to which financing sources are dedicated to the proposed purposes;

(D) any debt obligation that exists, or is proposed by the recipient, for the proposed project or other public transportation purpose;

(E) the extent to which the project has a local financial commitment that exceeds the required non-Government share of the cost of the project; and

(F) private contributions to the project, including cost-effective project delivery, management or transfer of project risks, expedited project schedule, financial partnering, and other public-private partnership strategies.

(g) PROJECT ADVANCEMENT AND RATINGS.—

(1) PROJECT ADVANCEMENT.—A new fixed guideway capital project or core capacity improvement project proposed to be carried out using a grant under this section may not advance from the project development phase to the engineering phase, or from the engineering phase to the construction phase, unless the Secretary determines that—

(A) the project meets the applicable requirements under this section; and

(B) there is a reasonable likelihood that the project will continue to meet the requirements under this section.

(2) RATINGS.—

(A) OVERALL RATING.—In making a determination under paragraph (1), the Secretary shall evaluate and rate a project as a whole on a 5-point scale (high, medium-high, medium, medium-low, or low) based on—

(i) in the case of a new fixed guideway capital project, the project justification criteria under subsection (d)(2)(A)(iii), and the degree of local financial commitment; and

(ii) in the case of a core capacity improvement project, the capacity needs of the corridor, the project justification criteria under subsection (e)(2)(A)(iv), and the degree of local financial commitment.

(B) INDIVIDUAL RATINGS FOR EACH CRITERION.—In rating a project under this paragraph, the Secretary shall—

(i) provide, in addition to the overall project rating under subparagraph (A), individual ratings for each of the criteria established under subsection (d)(2)(A)(iii) or (e)(2)(A)(iv), as applicable; and

(ii) give comparable, but not necessarily equal, numerical weight to each of the criteria established under subsections (d)(2)(A)(iii) or (e)(2)(A)(iv), as applicable, in calculating the overall project rating under clause (i).

(C) MEDIUM RATING NOT REQUIRED.—The Secretary shall not require that any single project justification criterion meet or exceed a "medium" rating in order to advance the project from one phase to another.

(3) WARRANTS.—The Secretary shall, to the maximum extent practicable, develop and use special warrants for making a project justification determination under subsection (d)(2) or (e)(2), as applicable, for a project proposed to be funded using a grant under this section, if—

(A) the share of the cost of the project to be provided under this section does not exceed 50 percent of the total cost of the project;

(B) the applicant requests the use of the warrants;

(C) the applicant certifies that its existing public transportation system is in a state of good repair; and

(D) the applicant meets any other requirements that the Secretary considers appropriate to carry out this subsection.

(4) LETTERS OF INTENT AND EARLY SYSTEMS WORK AGREEMENTS.—In order to expedite a project under this subsection, the Secretary shall, to the maximum extent practicable, issue letters of intent and enter into early systems work agreements upon issuance of a record of decision for projects that receive an overall project rating of medium or better.

(5) POLICY GUIDANCE.—The Secretary shall issue policy guidance regarding the review and evaluation process and criteria—

(A) not later than 180 days after the date of enactment of the Federal Public Transportation Act of 2012; and

(B) each time the Secretary makes significant changes to the process and criteria, but not less frequently than once every 2 years.

(6) RULES.—Not later than 1 year after the date of enactment of the Federal Public Transportation Act of 2012, the Secretary shall issue rules establishing an evaluation and rating process for—

(A) new fixed guideway capital projects that is based on the results of project justification, policies and land use patterns that promote public transportation, and local financial commitment, as required under this subsection; and

(B) core capacity improvement projects that is based on the results of the capacity needs of the corridor, project justification, and local financial commitment.

(7) PROJECT RE-ENTRY.—In carrying out ratings and evaluations under this subsection, the Secretary shall provide full and fair consideration to projects that seek an updated rating after a period of inactivity following an earlier rating and evaluation.

(8) APPLICABILITY.—This subsection shall not apply to a project for which the Secretary issued a letter of intent, entered into a full funding grant agreement, or entered into a project construction agreement before the date of enactment of the Federal Public Transportation Act of 2012.

(h) SMALL START PROJECTS.—

(1) IN GENERAL.—A small start project shall be subject to the requirements of this subsection.

(2) PROJECT DEVELOPMENT PHASE.—

(A) ENTRANCE INTO PROJECT DEVELOPMENT PHASE.—A new small starts project shall enter into the project development phase when—

(i) the applicant—

(I) submits a letter to the Secretary describing the project and requesting entry into the project development phase; and

(II) initiates activities required to be carried out under the National Environmental Policy Act of 1969 (42 U.S.C. 4321 et seq.) with respect to the project; and

(ii) the Secretary—

(I) responds in writing to the applicant within 45 days whether the information provided is sufficient to enter into the project development phase, including, when necessary, a detailed description of any information deemed insufficient; and

(II) provides concurrent notice to the Committee on Banking, Housing, and Urban Affairs of the Senate and the Committee on Transportation and Infrastructure of the House of Representatives of whether the small starts project is entering the project development phase.

(B) ACTIVITIES DURING PROJECT DEVELOPMENT PHASE.—Concurrent with the analysis required to be made under the National Environmental Policy Act of 1969 (42 U.S.C. 4321 et seq.), each applicant shall develop sufficient information to enable the Secretary to make findings of project justification, policies and land use patterns that promote public transportation, and local financial commitment under this subsection.

(3) SELECTION CRITERIA.—The Secretary may provide Federal assistance for a small start project under this subsection only if the Secretary determines that the project—

(A) has been adopted as the locally preferred alternative as part of the metropolitan transportation plan required under section 5303;

(B) is based on the results of an analysis of the benefits of the project as set forth in paragraph (4); and

(C) is supported by an acceptable degree of local financial commitment.

(4) EVALUATION OF BENEFITS AND FEDERAL INVESTMENT.—In making a determination for a small start project under paragraph (3)(B), the Secretary shall analyze, evaluate, and consider the following evaluation criteria for the project (as compared to a no-action alternative): mobility improvements, environmental benefits, congestion relief, economic development effects associated with the project, policies and land use patterns that support public transportation and cost-effectiveness as measured by cost per rider.

(5) EVALUATION OF LOCAL FINANCIAL COMMITMENT.—For purposes of paragraph (3)(C), the Secretary shall require that each proposed local source of capital and operating financing is stable, reliable, and available within the proposed project timetable.

(6) RATINGS.—

(A) IN GENERAL.—In carrying out paragraphs (4) and (5) for a small start project, the Secretary shall evaluate and rate the project on a 5-point scale (high, medium-high, medium, medium-low, or low) based on an evaluation of the benefits of the project as compared to the Federal assistance to be provided and the degree of local financial commitment, as required under this subsection. In rating the projects, the Secretary shall provide, in addition to the overall project rating, individual ratings for each of the criteria established by this subsection and shall give comparable, but not necessarily equal, numerical weight to the benefits that the project will bring to the community in calculating the overall project rating.

(B) OPTIONAL EARLY RATING.—At the request of the project sponsor, the Secretary shall evaluate and rate the project in accordance with paragraphs (4) and (5) and subparagraph (A) of this paragraph upon completion of the analysis required under the National Environmental Policy Act of 1969 (42 U.S.C. 4321 et seq.).

(7) GRANTS AND EXPEDITED GRANT AGREEMENTS.—

(A) IN GENERAL.—The Secretary, to the maximum extent practicable, shall provide Federal assistance under this subsection in a single grant. If the Secretary cannot provide such a single grant, the Secretary may execute an expedited grant agreement in order to include a commitment on the part of the Secretary to provide funding for the project in future fiscal years.

(B) TERMS OF EXPEDITED GRANT AGREEMENTS.—In executing an expedited grant agreement under this subsection, the Secretary may include in the agreement terms similar to those established under subsection (k)(2).

(C) NOTICE OF PROPOSED GRANTS AND EXPEDITED GRANT AGREEMENTS.—At least 10 days before making a grant award or entering into a grant agreement for a project under this subsection, the Secretary shall notify, in writing, the Committee on Transportation and Infrastructure and the Committee on Appropriations of the House of Representatives and the Committee on Banking, Housing, and Urban Affairs and the Committee on Appropriations of the Senate of the proposed grant or expedited grant agreement, as well as the evaluations and ratings for the project.

(i) PROGRAMS OF INTERRELATED PROJECTS.—

(1) FUTURE BUNDLING.—

(A) DEFINITION.—In this paragraph, the term "future bundling request" means a letter described in subparagraph (B) that requests future funding for additional projects.

(B) REQUEST.—When an applicant submits a letter to the Secretary requesting entry of a project into the project development phase under subsection (d)(1)(A)(i)(I), (e)(1)(A)(i)(I), or (h)(2)(A)(i)(I), the applicant may include a description of other projects for consideration for future funding under this section. An applicant shall include in the request the amount of funding requested under this section for each additional project and the estimated capital cost of each project.

(C) READINESS.—Other projects included in the request shall be ready to enter the project development phase under subsection (d)(1)(A), (e)(1)(A), or (h)(2)(A), within 5 years of the initial project submitted as part of the request.

(D) PLANNING.—Projects in the future bundling request shall be included in the metropolitan transportation plan in accordance with section 5303(i).

(E) PROJECT SPONSOR.—The applicant that submits a future bundling request shall be the project sponsor for each project included in the request.

(F) PROGRAM AND PROJECT SHARE.—A future bundling request submitted under this paragraph shall include a proposed share of each of the request's projects that is consistent with the requirements of subsections (k)(2)(C)(ii) or (h)(7), as applicable.

(G) BENEFITS.—The bundling of projects under this subsection—

(i) shall enhance, or increase the capacity of—

(I) the total transportation system of the applicant; or

(II) the transportation system of the region the applicant serves (which, in the case of a State whose request addresses a single region, means that region); and

(ii) shall—

(I) streamline procurements for the applicant; or

(II) enable time or cost savings for the projects.

(H) EVALUATION.—Each project submitted for consideration for funding in a future bundling request shall be subject to the applicable evaluation criteria under this section for the project type, including demonstrating the availability of local resources to recapitalize, maintain, and operate the overall existing and proposed public transportation system pursuant to subsection (f)(1)(C).

(I) LETTER OF INTENT.—

(i) IN GENERAL.—Upon entering into a grant agreement for the initial project for which an applicant submits a future bundling request, the Secretary may issue a letter of intent to the applicant that announces an intention to obligate, for 1 or more additional projects included in the request, an amount from future available budget authority specified in law that is not more than the amount stipulated as the financial participation of the Secretary in the additional project or projects in the future bundling. Such letter may include a condition that the project or projects must meet the evaluation criteria in this subsection before a grant agreement can be executed.

(ii) AMOUNT.—The amount that the Secretary announces an intention to obligate for an additional project in the future bundling request through a letter of intent issued under clause (i) shall be sufficient to complete at least an operable segment of the project.

(iii) TREATMENT.—The issuance of a letter of intent under clause (i) shall not be deemed to be an obligation under sections 1108(c), 1501, and 1502(a) of title 31 or an administrative commitment.

(2) IMMEDIATE BUNDLING.—

(A) DEFINITION.—In this paragraph, the term "immediate bundling request" means a letter described in subparagraph (B) that requests immediate funding for multiple projects.

(B) REQUEST.—An applicant may submit a letter to the Secretary requesting entry of multiple projects into the project development phase under subsection (d)(1)(A)(i)(I), (e)(1)(A)(i)(I), or (h)(2)(A)(i)(I), for consideration for funding under this section. An applicant shall include in the request the amount of funding requested under this section for each additional project and the estimated capital cost of each project.

(C) READINESS.—Projects included in the request must be ready to enter the project development phase under subsection (d)(1)(A), (e)(1)(A), or (h)(2)(A) at the same time.

(D) PLANNING.—Projects in the bundle shall be included in the metropolitan transportation plan in accordance with section 5303(i).

(E) PROJECT SPONSOR.—The applicant that submits an immediate bundling request shall be the project sponsor for each project included in the request.

(F) PROGRAM AND PROJECT SHARE.—An immediate bundling request submitted under this subsection shall include a proposed share of each of the request's projects that is consistent with the requirements of subsections (k)(2)(C)(ii) or (h)(7), as applicable.

(G) BENEFITS.—The bundling of projects under this subsection—

(i) shall enhance, or increase the capacity of—

(I) the total transportation system of the applicant; or

(II) the transportation system of the region the applicant serves (which, in the case of a State whose request addresses a single region, means that region); and

(ii) shall—

(I) streamline procurements for the applicant; or

(II) enable time or cost savings for the projects.

(H) EVALUATION.—A project submitted for consideration for immediate funding in an immediate bundling request shall be subject to the applicable evaluation criteria under this section for the project type, including demonstrating the availability of local resources to recapitalize, maintain, and operate the overall existing and proposed public transportation system pursuant to subsection (f)(1)(C).

(I) LETTER OF INTENT OR SINGLE GRANT AGREEMENT.—

(i) IN GENERAL.—Upon entering into a grant agreement for the initial project for which an applicant submits a request, the Secretary may issue a letter of intent or single, combined grant agreement to the applicant.

(ii) LETTER OF INTENT.—

(I) IN GENERAL.—A letter of intent announces an intention to obligate, for 1 or more additional projects included in the request, an amount from future available budget authority specified in law that is not more than the amount stipulated as the financial participation of the Secretary in the additional project or projects. Such letter may include a condition that the project or projects must meet the evaluation criteria in this subsection before a grant agreement can be executed.

(II) AMOUNT.—The amount that the Secretary announces an intention to obligate for an additional project in a letter of intent issued under clause (i) shall be sufficient to complete at least an operable segment of the project.

(III) TREATMENT.—The issuance of a letter of intent under clause (i) shall not be deemed to be an obligation under sections 1108(c), 1501, and 1502(a) of title 31 or an administrative commitment.

(3) EVALUATION CRITERIA.—When the Secretary issues rules or policy guidance under this section, the Secretary may request comment from the public regarding

potential changes to the evaluation criteria for project justification and local financial commitment under subsections (d), (e), (f), and (h) for the purposes of streamlining the evaluation process for projects included in a future bundling request or an immediate bundling request, including changes to enable simultaneous evaluation of multiple projects under 1 or more evaluation criteria. Notwithstanding paragraphs (1)(H) and (2)(H), such criteria may be utilized for projects included in a future bundling request or an immediate bundling request under this subsection upon promulgation of the applicable rule or policy guidance.

(4) GRANT AGREEMENTS.—

(A) NEW START AND CORE CAPACITY IMPROVEMENT PROJECTS.—A new start project or core capacity improvement project in an immediate bundling request or future bundling request shall be carried out through a full funding grant agreement or expedited grant agreement pursuant to subsection (k)(2).

(B) SMALL START.—A small start project shall be carried out through a grant agreement pursuant to subsection (h)(7).

(C) REQUIREMENT.—A combined grant agreement described in paragraph (2)(I)(i) shall—

(i) include only projects in an immediate future bundling request that are ready to receive a grant agreement under this section,

(ii) be carried out through a full funding grant agreement or expedited grant agreement pursuant to subsection (k)(2) for the included projects, if a project seeking assistance under the combined grant agreement is a new start project or core capacity improvement project; and

(iii) be carried out through a grant agreement pursuant to subsection (h)(7) for the included projects, if the projects seeking assistance under the combined grant agreement consist entirely of small start projects.

(D) SAVINGS PROVISION.—The use of a combined grant agreement shall not waive or amend applicable evaluation criteria under this section for projects included in the combined grant agreement.

(j) PREVIOUSLY ISSUED LETTER OF INTENT OR FULL FUNDING GRANT AGREEMENT.—Subsections (d) and (e) shall not apply to projects for which the Secretary has issued a letter of intent, approved entry into final design, entered into a full funding grant agreement, or entered into a project construction grant agreement before the date of enactment of the Federal Public Transportation Act of 2012.

(k) LETTERS OF INTENT, FULL FUNDING GRANT AGREEMENTS, AND EARLY SYSTEMS WORK AGREEMENTS.—

(1) LETTERS OF INTENT.—

(A) AMOUNTS INTENDED TO BE OBLIGATED.—The Secretary may issue a letter of intent to an applicant announcing an intention to obligate, for a new fixed guideway capital project or core capacity improvement project, an amount from future available budget authority specified in law that is not more than the amount stipulated as the financial participation of the Secretary in the project. When a letter is issued for a capital project under this section, the amount shall be sufficient to complete at least an operable segment.

(B) TREATMENT.—The issuance of a letter under subparagraph (A) is deemed not to be an obligation under sections 1108(c), 1501, and 1502(a) of title 31 or an administrative commitment.

(2) FULL FUNDING GRANT AGREEMENTS.—

(A) IN GENERAL.—A new fixed guideway capital project or core capacity improvement project shall be carried out through a full funding grant agreement.

(B) CRITERIA.—The Secretary shall enter into a full funding grant agreement, based on the evaluations and ratings required under subsection (d), (e), or (i), as applicable, with each grantee receiving assistance for a new fixed guideway capital project or core capacity improvement project that has been rated as high, medium-high, or medium, in accordance with subsection (g)(2)(A) or (i)(3)(B), as applicable.

(C) TERMS.—A full funding grant agreement shall—

(i) establish the terms of participation by the Government in a new fixed guideway capital project or core capacity improvement project;

(ii) establish the maximum amount of Federal financial assistance for the project;

(iii) include the period of time for completing the project, even if that period extends beyond the period of an authorization; and

(iv) make timely and efficient management of the project easier according to the law of the United States.

(D) SPECIAL FINANCIAL RULES.—

(i) IN GENERAL.—A full funding grant agreement under this paragraph obligates an amount of available budget authority specified in law and may include a commitment, contingent on amounts to be specified in law in advance for commitments under this paragraph, to obligate an additional amount from future available budget authority specified in law.

(ii) STATEMENT OF CONTINGENT COMMITMENT.—The agreement shall state that the contingent commitment is not an obligation of the Government.

(iii) INTEREST AND OTHER FINANCING COSTS.—Interest and other financing costs of efficiently carrying out a part of the project within a reasonable time are a cost of carrying out the project under a full funding grant agreement, except that eligible costs may not be more than the cost of the most favorable financing terms reasonably available for the project at the time of borrowing. The applicant shall certify, in a way satisfactory to the Secretary, that the applicant has shown reasonable diligence in seeking the most favorable financing terms.

(iv) COMPLETION OF OPERABLE SEGMENT.—The amount stipulated in an agreement under this paragraph for a new fixed guideway capital project shall be sufficient to complete at least an operable segment.

(E) INFORMATION COLLECTION AND ANALYSIS PLAN.—

(i) SUBMISSION OF PLAN.—Applicants seeking a full funding grant agreement under this paragraph shall submit a complete plan for the collection and analysis of information to identify the impacts of the new fixed guideway capital project or core capacity improvement project and the accuracy of the forecasts prepared during the development of the project. Preparation of this plan shall be included in the full funding grant agreement as an eligible activity.

(ii) CONTENTS OF PLAN.—The plan submitted under clause (i) shall provide for—

(I) collection of data on the current public transportation system regarding public transportation service levels and ridership patterns, including origins and destinations, access modes, trip purposes, and rider characteristics;

(II) documentation of the predicted scope, service levels, capital costs, operating costs, and ridership of the project;

(III) collection of data on the public transportation system 2 years after the opening of a new fixed guideway capital project or core capacity improvement project, including analogous information on public transportation service levels and ridership patterns and information on the as-built scope, capital, and financing costs of the project; and

(IV) analysis of the consistency of predicted project characteristics with actual outcomes.

(F) COLLECTION OF DATA ON CURRENT SYSTEM.—To be eligible for a full funding grant agreement under this paragraph, recipients shall have collected data on the current system, according to the plan required under subparagraph (E)(ii), before the beginning of construction of the proposed new fixed guideway capital project or core capacity improvement project. Collection of this data shall be included in the full funding grant agreement as an eligible activity.

(3) EARLY SYSTEMS WORK AGREEMENTS.—

(A) CONDITIONS.—The Secretary may enter into an early systems work agreement with an applicant if a record of decision under the National Environmental Policy Act of 1969 (42 U.S.C. 4321 et seq.) has been issued on the project and the Secretary finds there is reason to believe—

(i) a full funding grant agreement for the project will be made; and

(ii) the terms of the work agreement will promote ultimate completion of the project more rapidly and at less cost.

(B) CONTENTS.—

(i) IN GENERAL.—An early systems work agreement under this paragraph obligates budget authority available under this chapter and title 23 and shall provide for reimbursement of preliminary costs of carrying out the project, including land acquisition, timely procurement of system elements for which specifications are decided, and other activities the Secretary decides are appropriate to make efficient, long-term project management easier.

(ii) CONTINGENT COMMITMENT.—An early systems work agreement may include a commitment, contingent on amounts to be specified in law in advance for commitments under this paragraph, to obligate an additional amount from future available budget authority specified in law.

(iii) PERIOD COVERED.—An early systems work agreement under this paragraph shall cover the period of time the Secretary considers appropriate. The period may extend beyond the period of current authorization.

(iv) INTEREST AND OTHER FINANCING COSTS.—Interest and other financing costs of efficiently carrying out the early systems work agreement within a reasonable time are a cost of carrying out the agreement, except that eligible costs may not be more than the cost of the most favorable financing terms reasonably available for the project at the time of borrowing. The applicant shall certify, in a way satisfactory to the Secretary, that the applicant has shown reasonable diligence in seeking the most favorable financing terms.

(v) FAILURE TO CARRY OUT PROJECT.—If an applicant does not carry out the project for reasons within the control of the applicant, the applicant shall repay all Federal grant funds awarded for the project from all Federal funding sources, for all project activities, facilities, and equipment, plus reasonable interest and penalty charges allowable by law or established by the Secretary in the early systems work agreement.

(vi) CREDITING OF FUNDS RECEIVED.—Any funds received by the Government under this paragraph, other than interest and penalty charges, shall be credited to the appropriation account from which the funds were originally derived.

(4) LIMITATION ON AMOUNTS.—

(A) IN GENERAL.—The Secretary may enter into full funding grant agreements under this subsection for new fixed guideway capital projects and core capacity improvement projects that contain contingent commitments to incur obligations in such amounts as the Secretary determines are appropriate.

(B) APPROPRIATION REQUIRED.—An obligation may be made under this subsection only when amounts are appropriated for the obligation.

(5) NOTIFICATION TO CONGRESS.—Not later than 15 days before issuing a letter of intent, entering into a full funding grant agreement, or entering into an early systems work agreement under this section, the Secretary shall notify, in writing, the Committee on Banking, Housing, and Urban Affairs and the Committee on Appropriations of the Senate and the Committee on Transportation and Infrastructure and the Committee on Appropriations of the House of Representatives of the proposed letter or agreement. The Secretary shall include with the notification a copy of the proposed letter or agreement as well as the evaluations and ratings for the project.

(l) GOVERNMENT SHARE OF NET CAPITAL PROJECT COST.—

(1) IN GENERAL.—

(A) ESTIMATION OF NET CAPITAL PROJECT COST.—Based on engineering studies, studies of economic feasibility, and information on the expected use of equipment or facilities, the Secretary shall estimate the net capital project cost.

(B) GRANTS.—

(i) GRANT FOR NEW FIXED GUIDEWAY CAPITAL PROJECT.—A grant for a new fixed guideway capital project shall not exceed 80 percent of the net capital project cost.

(ii) FULL FUNDING GRANT AGREEMENT FOR NEW FIXED GUIDEWAY CAPITAL PROJECT.—A full funding grant agreement for a new fixed guideway capital project shall not include a share of more than 60 percent from the funds made available under this section.

(iii) GRANT FOR CORE CAPACITY IMPROVEMENT PROJECT.—A grant for a core capacity improvement project shall not exceed 80 percent of the net capital project cost of the incremental cost to increase the capacity in the corridor.

(iv) GRANT FOR SMALL START PROJECT.—A grant for a small start project shall not exceed 80 percent of the net capital project costs.

(2) ADJUSTMENT FOR COMPLETION UNDER BUDGET.—The Secretary may adjust the final net capital project cost of a new fixed guideway capital project or core capacity improvement project evaluated under subsection (d), (e), or (i) to include the cost of eligible activities not included in the originally defined project if the Secretary determines that the originally defined project has been completed at a cost that is significantly below the original estimate.

(3) MAXIMUM GOVERNMENT SHARE.—The Secretary may provide a higher grant percentage than requested by the grant recipient if—

(A) the Secretary determines that the net capital project cost of the project is not more than 10 percent higher than the net capital project cost estimated at the time the project was approved for advancement into the engineering phase; and

(B) the ridership estimated for the project is not less than 90 percent of the ridership estimated for the project at the time the project was approved for advancement into the engineering phase.

(4) REMAINING COSTS.—The remainder of the net capital project costs shall be provided—

(A) in cash from non-Government sources;

(B) from revenues from the sale of advertising and concessions; or

(C) from an undistributed cash surplus, a replacement or depreciation cash fund or reserve, or new capital.

(5) LIMITATION ON STATUTORY CONSTRUCTION.—Nothing in this section shall be construed as authorizing the Secretary to require a non-Federal financial commitment for a project that is more than 20 percent of the net capital project cost.

(6) SPECIAL RULE FOR ROLLING STOCK COSTS.—In addition to amounts allowed pursuant to paragraph (1), a planned extension to a fixed guideway system may include the cost of rolling stock previously purchased if the applicant satisfies the Secretary that only amounts other than amounts provided by the Government were used and that the purchase was made for use on the extension. A refund or reduction of the remainder may be made only if a refund of a proportional amount of the grant of the Government is made at the same time.

(7) LIMITATION ON APPLICABILITY.—This subsection shall not apply to projects for which the Secretary entered into a full funding grant agreement before the date of enactment of the Federal Public Transportation Act of 2012.

(8) SPECIAL RULE FOR FIXED GUIDEWAY BUS RAPID TRANSIT PROJECTS.—For up to three fixed-guideway bus rapid transit projects each fiscal year the Secretary shall—

(A) establish a Government share of at least 80 percent; and

(B) not lower the project's rating for degree of local financial commitment for purposes of subsections (d)(2)(A)(v) or (h)(3)(C) as a result of the Government share specified in this paragraph.

(m) UNDERTAKING PROJECTS IN ADVANCE.—

(1) IN GENERAL.—The Secretary may pay the Government share of the net capital project cost to a State or local governmental authority that carries out any part of a project described in this section without the aid of amounts of the Government and

according to all applicable procedures and requirements if—

(A) the State or local governmental authority applies for the payment;

(B) the Secretary approves the payment; and

(C) before the State or local governmental authority carries out the part of the project, the Secretary approves the plans and specifications for the part in the same way as other projects under this section.

(2) FINANCING COSTS.—

(A) IN GENERAL.—The cost of carrying out part of a project includes the amount of interest earned and payable on bonds issued by the State or local governmental authority to the extent proceeds of the bonds are expended in carrying out the part.

(B) LIMITATION ON AMOUNT OF INTEREST.—The amount of interest under this paragraph may not be more than the most favorable interest terms reasonably available for the project at the time of borrowing.

(C) CERTIFICATION.—The applicant shall certify, in a manner satisfactory to the Secretary, that the applicant has shown reasonable diligence in seeking the most favorable financing terms.

(n) AVAILABILITY OF AMOUNTS.—

(1) IN GENERAL.—An amount made available or appropriated for a new fixed guideway capital project or core capacity improvement project shall remain available to that project for 4 fiscal years, including the fiscal year in which the amount is made available or appropriated. Any amounts that are unobligated to the project at the end of the 4-fiscal-year period may be used by the Secretary for any purpose under this section.

(2) USE OF DEOBLIGATED AMOUNTS.—An amount available under this section that is deobligated may be used for any purpose under this section.

(o) REPORTS ON NEW FIXED GUIDEWAY AND CORE CAPACITY IMPROVEMENT PROJECTS.—

(1) ANNUAL REPORT ON FUNDING RECOMMENDATIONS.—Not later than the first Monday in February of each year, the Secretary shall submit to the Committee on Banking, Housing, and Urban Affairs and the Committee on Appropriations of the Senate and the Committee on Transportation and Infrastructure and the Committee on Appropriations of the House of Representatives a report that includes—

(A) a proposal of allocations of amounts to be available to finance grants for projects under this section among applicants for these amounts;

(B) evaluations and ratings, as required under subsections (d), (e), and (i), for each such project that is in project development, engineering, or has received a full funding grant agreement; and

(C) recommendations of such projects for funding based on the evaluations and ratings and on existing commitments and anticipated funding levels for the next 3 fiscal years based on information currently available to the Secretary.

(2) BIENNIAL GAO REVIEW.—The Comptroller General of the United States shall—

(A) conduct a biennial review that—

(i) assesses—

(I) the processes and procedures for evaluating, rating, and recommending all new fixed guideway capital projects and core capacity improvement projects for grant agreements under this section and section 3005(b) of the Federal Public Transportation Act of 2015 (49 U.S.C. 5309 note; Public Law 114–94); and

(II) the Secretary's implementation of such processes and procedures;

(ii) includes, with respect to projects that entered into revenue service since the previous biennial review—

(I) a description and analysis of the impacts of the projects on public transportation services and public transportation ridership;

(II) a description and analysis of the consistency of predicted and actual benefits and costs of the innovative project development and delivery methods of, or innovative financing for, the projects; and

(III) an identification of the reasons for any differences between predicted and actual outcomes for the projects; and

(iii) in conducting the review under clause (ii), incorporates information from the plans submitted by applicants under subsection (k)(2)(E)(i); and

(B) report to Congress on the results of such review by May 31 of the applicable year.

(p) SPECIAL RULE.—For the purposes of calculating the cost effectiveness of a project described in subsection (d) or (e), the Secretary shall not reduce or eliminate the capital costs of art and non-functional landscaping elements from the annualized capital cost calculation.

(q) JOINT PUBLIC TRANSPORTATION AND INTERCITY PASSENGER RAIL PROJECTS.—

(1) IN GENERAL.—The Secretary may make grants for new fixed guideway capital projects and core capacity improvement projects that provide both public transportation and intercity passenger rail service.

(2) ELIGIBLE COSTS.—Eligible costs for a project under this subsection shall be limited to the net capital costs of the public transportation costs attributable to the project based on projected use of the new segment or expanded capacity of the project corridor, not including project elements designed to achieve or maintain a state of good repair, as determined by the Secretary under paragraph (4).

(3) PROJECT JUSTIFICATION AND LOCAL FINANCIAL COMMITMENT.—A project under this subsection shall be evaluated for project justification and local financial commitment under subsections (d), (e), (f), and (h), as applicable to the project, based on—

(A) the net capital costs of the public transportation costs attributable to the project as determined under paragraph (4); and

(B) the share of funds dedicated to the project from sources other than this section included in the unified finance plan for the project.

(4) CALCULATION OF NET CAPITAL PROJECT COST.—The Secretary shall estimate the net capital costs of a project under this subsection based on—

(A) engineering studies;

(B) studies of economic feasibility;

(C) the expected use of equipment or facilities; and

(D) the public transportation costs attributable to the project.

(5) GOVERNMENT SHARE OF NET CAPITAL PROJECT COST.—

(A) GOVERNMENT SHARE.—The Government share shall not exceed 80 percent of the net capital cost attributable to the public transportation costs of a project under this subsection as determined under paragraph (4).

(B) NON-GOVERNMENT SHARE.—The remainder of the net capital cost attributable to the public transportation costs of a project under this subsection shall be provided from an undistributed cash surplus, a replacement or depreciation cash fund or reserve, or new capital.

(r) CAPITAL INVESTMENT GRANT DASHBOARD.—

(1) IN GENERAL.—The Secretary shall make publicly available in an easily identifiable location on the website of the Department of Transportation a dashboard containing the following information for each project seeking a grant agreement under this section:

(A) Project name.

(B) Project sponsor.

(C) City or urbanized area and State in which the project will be located.

(D) Project type.

(E) Project mode.

(F) Project length and number of stops, including length of exclusive bus rapid transit lanes, if applicable.

(G) Anticipated total project cost.

(H) Anticipated share of project costs to be sought under this section.

(I) Date of compliance with the National Environmental Policy Act of 1969 (42 U.S.C. 4321 et seq.).

(J) Date on which the project entered the project development phase.

(K) Date on which the project entered the engineering phase, if applicable.

(L) Date on which a Letter of No Prejudice was requested, and date on which a Letter of No Prejudice was issued or denied, if applicable.

(M) Date of the applicant's most recent project ratings, including date of request for updated ratings, if applicable.

(N) Status of the project sponsor in securing non-Federal matching funds.

(O) Date on which a project grant agreement is anticipated to be executed.

(2) UPDATES.—The Secretary shall update the information provided under paragraph (1) not less frequently than monthly.

(3) PROJECT PROFILES.—The Secretary shall continue to make profiles for projects that have applied for or are receiving assistance under this section publicly available in an easily identifiable location on the website of the Department of Transportation, in the same manner as the Secretary did as of the day before the date of enactment of this subsection.

(Pub. L. 103–272, §1(d), July 5, 1994, 108 Stat. 800; Pub. L. 104–287, §5(9), (12), Oct. 11, 1996, 110 Stat. 3389; Pub. L. 102–240, title III, §3049(a), as added Pub. L. 105–130, §8, Dec. 1, 1997, 111 Stat. 2559; Pub. L. 105–178, title III, §3009(a), (c)–(h)(1), (3)(D), (i)–(k), June 9, 1998, 112 Stat. 352–357; Pub. L. 105–206, title IX, §9009(g), (h)(3), July 22, 1998, 112 Stat. 855, 856; Pub. L. 106–69, title III, §347, Oct. 9, 1999, 113 Stat. 1024; Pub. L. 106–346, §101(a) [title III, §380], Oct. 23, 2000, 114 Stat. 1356, 1356A–42; Pub. L. 106–554, §1(a)(4) [div. A, §1101], Dec. 21, 2000, 114 Stat. 2763, 2763A–201; Pub. L. 108–88, §8(a), Sept. 30, 2003, 117 Stat. 1121; Pub. L. 108–202, §9(a), Feb. 29, 2004, 118 Stat. 484; Pub. L. 108–224, §7(a), Apr. 30, 2004, 118 Stat. 632; Pub. L. 108–263, §7(a), June 30, 2004, 118

Stat. 704; Pub. L. 108–271, §8(b), July 7, 2004, 118 Stat. 814; Pub. L. 108–280, §7(a), July 30, 2004, 118 Stat. 882; Pub. L. 108–310, §8(a), Sept. 30, 2004, 118 Stat. 1154; Pub. L. 109–14, §7(a), May 31, 2005, 119 Stat. 330; Pub. L. 109–20, §7(a), July 1, 2005, 119 Stat. 352; Pub. L. 109–35, §7(a), July 20, 2005, 119 Stat. 386; Pub. L. 109–37, §7(a), July 22, 2005, 119 Stat. 401; Pub. L. 109–40, §7(a), July 28, 2005, 119 Stat. 417; Pub. L. 109–59, title III, §3011(a), Aug. 10, 2005, 119 Stat. 1573; Pub. L. 110–244, title II, §201(d), June 6, 2008, 122 Stat. 1610; Pub. L. 111–147, title IV, §433, Mar. 18, 2010, 124 Stat. 88; Pub. L. 111–322, title II, §2303, Dec. 22, 2010, 124 Stat. 3527; Pub. L. 112–5, title III, §303, Mar. 4, 2011, 125 Stat. 18; Pub. L. 112–30, title I, §133, Sept. 16, 2011, 125 Stat. 350; Pub. L. 112–102, title III, §303, Mar. 30, 2012, 126 Stat. 275; Pub. L. 112–140, title III, §303, June 29, 2012, 126 Stat. 396; Pub. L. 112–141, div. B, §20008(a), div. G, title III, §113003, July 6, 2012, 126 Stat. 656, 984; Pub. L. 114–94, div. A, title III, §3005(a), Dec. 4, 2015, 129 Stat. 1450; Pub. L. 117–58, div. C, §30005(a), Nov. 15, 2021, 135 Stat. 894.)

§5310. Formula grants for the enhanced mobility of seniors and individuals with disabilities

(a) Definitions.—In this section, the following definitions shall apply:

(1) Recipient.—The term "recipient" means—

(A) a designated recipient or a State that receives a grant under this section directly; or

(B) a State or local governmental entity that operates a public transportation service.

(2) Subrecipient.—The term "subrecipient" means a State or local governmental authority, a private nonprofit organization, or an operator of public transportation that receives a grant under this section indirectly through a recipient.

(b) General Authority.—

(1) Grants.—The Secretary may make grants under this section to recipients for—

(A) public transportation projects planned, designed, and carried out to meet the special needs of seniors and individuals with disabilities when public transportation is insufficient, inappropriate, or unavailable;

(B) public transportation projects that exceed the requirements of the Americans with Disabilities Act of 1990 (42 U.S.C. 12101 et seq.);

(C) public transportation projects that improve access to fixed route service and decrease reliance by individuals with disabilities on complementary paratransit; and

(D) alternatives to public transportation that assist seniors and individuals with disabilities with transportation.

(2) Limitations for capital projects.—

(A) Amount available.—The amount available for capital projects under paragraph (1)(A) shall be not less than 55 percent of the funds apportioned to the recipient under this section.

(B) Allocation to subrecipients.—A recipient of a grant under paragraph (1)(A) may allocate the amounts provided under the grant to—

(i) a private nonprofit organization; or

(ii) a State or local governmental authority that—

(I) is approved by a State to coordinate services for seniors and individuals with disabilities; or

(II) certifies that there are no private nonprofit organizations readily available in the area to provide the services described in paragraph (1)(A).

(3) ADMINISTRATIVE EXPENSES.—A recipient may use not more than 10 percent of the amounts apportioned to the recipient under this section to administer, plan, and provide technical assistance for a project funded under this section.

(4) ELIGIBLE CAPITAL EXPENSES.—The acquisition of public transportation services is an eligible capital expense under this section.

(5) COORDINATION.—

(A) DEPARTMENT OF TRANSPORTATION.—To the maximum extent feasible, the Secretary shall coordinate activities under this section with related activities under other Federal departments and agencies.

(B) OTHER FEDERAL AGENCIES AND NONPROFIT ORGANIZATIONS.—A State or local governmental authority or nonprofit organization that receives assistance from Government sources (other than the Department of Transportation) for nonemergency transportation services shall—

(i) participate and coordinate with recipients of assistance under this chapter in the design and delivery of transportation services; and

(ii) participate in the planning for the transportation services described in clause (i).

(6) PROGRAM OF PROJECTS.—

(A) IN GENERAL.—Amounts made available to carry out this section may be used for transportation projects to assist in providing transportation services for seniors and individuals with disabilities, if such transportation projects are included in a program of projects.

(B) SUBMISSION.—A recipient shall annually submit a program of projects to the Secretary.

(C) ASSURANCE.—The program of projects submitted under subparagraph (B) shall contain an assurance that the program provides for the maximum feasible coordination of transportation services assisted under this section with transportation services assisted by other Government sources.

(7) MEAL DELIVERY FOR HOMEBOUND INDIVIDUALS.—A public transportation service provider that receives assistance under this section or section 5311(c) may coordinate and assist in regularly providing meal delivery service for homebound individuals, if the delivery service does not conflict with providing public transportation service or reduce service to public transportation passengers.

(c) APPORTIONMENT AND TRANSFERS.—

(1) FORMULA.—The Secretary shall apportion amounts made available to carry out this section as follows:

(A) LARGE URBANIZED AREAS.—Sixty percent of the funds shall be apportioned among designated recipients for urbanized areas with a population of 200,000 or more individuals, as determined by the Bureau of the Census, in the ratio that—

(i) the number of seniors and individuals with disabilities in each such urbanized area; bears to

(ii) the number of seniors and individuals with disabilities in all such urbanized areas.

(B) SMALL URBANIZED AREAS.—Twenty percent of the funds shall be apportioned among the States in the ratio that—

(i) the number of seniors and individuals with disabilities in urbanized areas with a population of fewer than 200,000 individuals, as determined by the Bureau of the Census, in each State; bears to

(ii) the number of seniors and individuals with disabilities in urbanized areas with a population of fewer than 200,000 individuals, as determined by the Bureau of the Census, in all States.

(C) RURAL AREAS.—Twenty percent of the funds shall be apportioned among the States in the ratio that—

(i) the number of seniors and individuals with disabilities in rural areas in each State; bears to

(ii) the number of seniors and individuals with disabilities in rural areas in all States.

(2) AREAS SERVED BY PROJECTS.—

(A) IN GENERAL.—Except as provided in subparagraph (B)—

(i) funds apportioned under paragraph (1)(A) shall be used for projects serving urbanized areas with a population of 200,000 or more individuals, as determined by the Bureau of the Census;

(ii) funds apportioned under paragraph (1)(B) shall be used for projects serving urbanized areas with a population of fewer than 200,000 individuals, as determined by the Bureau of the Census; and

(iii) funds apportioned under paragraph (1)(C) shall be used for projects serving rural areas.

(B) EXCEPTIONS.—A State may use funds apportioned to the State under subparagraph (B) or (C) of paragraph (1)—

(i) for a project serving an area other than an area specified in subparagraph (A)(ii) or (A)(iii), as the case may be, if the Governor of the State certifies that all of the objectives of this section are being met in the area specified in subparagraph (A)(ii) or (A)(iii); or

(ii) for a project anywhere in the State, if the State has established a statewide program for meeting the objectives of this section.

(C) LIMITED TO ELIGIBLE PROJECTS.—Any funds transferred pursuant to subparagraph (B) shall be made available only for eligible projects selected under this section.

(D) CONSULTATION.—A recipient may transfer an amount under subparagraph (B) only after consulting with responsible local officials, publicly owned operators of public transportation, and nonprofit providers in the area for which the amount was originally apportioned.

(d) GOVERNMENT SHARE OF COSTS.—

(1) CAPITAL PROJECTS.—A grant for a capital project under this section shall be in an amount equal to 80 percent of the net capital costs of the project, as determined by the Secretary.

(2) OPERATING ASSISTANCE.—A grant made under this section for operating assistance may not exceed an amount equal to 50 percent of the net operating costs of the project, as determined by the Secretary.

(3) REMAINDER OF NET COSTS.—The remainder of the net costs of a project carried out under this section—

(A) may be provided from an undistributed cash surplus, a replacement or depreciation cash fund or reserve, a service agreement with a State or local social service agency or a private social service organization, or new capital; and

(B) may be derived from amounts appropriated or otherwise made available—

(i) to a department or agency of the Government (other than the Department of Transportation) that are eligible to be expended for transportation; or

(ii) to carry out the Federal lands highways program under section 204 [1] of title 23.

(4) USE OF CERTAIN FUNDS.—For purposes of paragraph (3)(B)(i), the prohibition under section 403(a)(5)(C)(vii) of the Social Security Act (42 U.S.C. 603(a)(5)(C)(vii)) on the use of grant funds for matching requirements shall not apply to Federal or State funds to be used for transportation purposes.

(e) GRANT REQUIREMENTS.—

(1) IN GENERAL.—A grant under this section shall be subject to the same requirements as a grant under section 5307, to the extent the Secretary determines appropriate.

(2) CERTIFICATION REQUIREMENTS.—

(A) PROJECT SELECTION AND PLAN DEVELOPMENT.—Before receiving a grant under this section, each recipient shall certify that—

(i) the projects selected by the recipient are included in a locally developed, coordinated public transit-human services transportation plan;

(ii) the plan described in clause (i) was developed and approved through a process that included participation by seniors, individuals with disabilities, representatives of public, private, and nonprofit transportation and human services providers, and other members of the public; and

(iii) to the maximum extent feasible, the services funded under this section will be coordinated with transportation services assisted by other Federal departments and agencies, including any transportation activities carried out by a recipient of a grant from the Department of Health and Human Services.

(B) ALLOCATIONS TO SUBRECIPIENTS.—If a recipient allocates funds received under this section to subrecipients, the recipient shall certify that the funds are allocated on a fair and equitable basis.

(f) COMPETITIVE PROCESS FOR GRANTS TO SUBRECIPIENTS.—

(1) AREAWIDE SOLICITATIONS.—A recipient of funds apportioned under subsection (c)(1)(A) may conduct, in cooperation with the appropriate metropolitan planning organization, an areawide solicitation for applications for grants under this section.

(2) STATEWIDE SOLICITATIONS.—A recipient of funds apportioned under subparagraph (B) or (C) of subsection (c)(1) may conduct a statewide solicitation for applications for grants under this section.

(3) APPLICATION.—If the recipient elects to engage in a competitive process, a recipient or subrecipient seeking to receive a grant from funds apportioned under subsection (c) shall submit to the recipient making the election an application in such form and in accordance with such requirements as the recipient making the election

shall establish.

(g) TRANSFERS OF FACILITIES AND EQUIPMENT.—A recipient may transfer a facility or equipment acquired using a grant under this section to any other recipient eligible to receive assistance under this chapter, if—

(1) the recipient in possession of the facility or equipment consents to the transfer; and

(2) the facility or equipment will continue to be used as required under this section.

(h) PERFORMANCE MEASURES.—

(1) IN GENERAL.—Not later than 1 year after the date of enactment of the Federal Public Transportation Act of 2012, the Secretary shall submit a report to the Committee on Banking, Housing, and Urban Affairs of the Senate and the Committee on Transportation and Infrastructure of the House of Representatives making recommendations on the establishment of performance measures for grants under this section. Such report shall be developed in consultation with national nonprofit organizations that provide technical assistance and advocacy on issues related to transportation services for seniors and individuals with disabilities.

(2) MEASURES.—The performance measures to be considered in the report under paragraph (1) shall require the collection of quantitative and qualitative information, as available, concerning—

(A) modifications to the geographic coverage of transportation service, the quality of transportation service, or service times that increase the availability of transportation services for seniors and individuals with disabilities;

(B) ridership;

(C) accessibility improvements; and

(D) other measures, as the Secretary determines is appropriate.

(i) BEST PRACTICES.—The Secretary shall collect from, review, and disseminate to public transportation agencies—

(1) innovative practices;

(2) program models;

(3) new service delivery options;

(4) findings from activities under subsection (h); and

(5) transit cooperative research program reports.

(Pub. L. 103–272, §1(d), July 5, 1994, 108 Stat. 807; Pub. L. 105–178, title III, §3013(a), June 9, 1998, 112 Stat. 359; Pub. L. 109–59, title III, §§3002(b)(2), 3012(a), Aug. 10, 2005, 119 Stat. 1544, 1589; Pub. L. 112–141, div. B, §20009, July 6, 2012, 126 Stat. 675; Pub. L. 114–94, div. A, title III, §3006(a), Dec. 4, 2015, 129 Stat. 1462.)

[1] *See References in Text note below.*

§5311. FORMULA GRANTS FOR RURAL AREAS

(a) DEFINITIONS.—As used in this section, the following definitions shall apply:

(1) RECIPIENT.—The term "recipient" means a State or Indian tribe that receives a Federal transit program grant directly from the Government.

(2) SUBRECIPIENT.—The term "subrecipient" means a State or local governmental authority, a nonprofit organization, or an operator of public transportation or intercity bus service that receives Federal transit program grant funds indirectly through a

recipient.

(b) GENERAL AUTHORITY.—

(1) GRANTS AUTHORIZED.—Except as provided by paragraph (2), the Secretary may award grants under this section to recipients located in rural areas for—

(A) planning, provided that a grant under this section for planning activities shall be in addition to funding awarded to a State under section 5305 for planning activities that are directed specifically at the needs of rural areas in the State;

(B) public transportation capital projects;

(C) operating costs of equipment and facilities for use in public transportation;

(D) job access and reverse commute projects; and

(E) the acquisition of public transportation services, including service agreements with private providers of public transportation service.

(2) STATE PROGRAM.—

(A) IN GENERAL.—A project eligible for a grant under this section shall be included in a State program for public transportation service projects, including agreements with private providers of public transportation service.

(B) SUBMISSION TO SECRETARY.—Each State shall submit to the Secretary annually the program described in subparagraph (A).

(C) APPROVAL.—The Secretary may not approve the program unless the Secretary determines that—

(i) the program provides a fair distribution of amounts in the State, including Indian reservations; and

(ii) the program provides the maximum feasible coordination of public transportation service assisted under this section with transportation service assisted by other Federal sources.

(3) RURAL TRANSPORTATION ASSISTANCE PROGRAM.—

(A) IN GENERAL.—The Secretary shall carry out a rural transportation assistance program in rural areas.

(B) GRANTS AND CONTRACTS.—In carrying out this paragraph, the Secretary may use not more than 2 percent of the amount made available under section 5338(a)(2)(F) to make grants and contracts for transportation research, technical assistance, training, and related support services in rural areas.

(C) PROJECTS OF A NATIONAL SCOPE.—Not more than 15 percent of the amounts available under subparagraph (B) may be used by the Secretary to carry out competitively selected projects of a national scope, with the remaining balance provided to the States.

(4) DATA COLLECTION.—Each recipient under this section shall submit an annual report to the Secretary containing information on capital investment, operations, and service provided with funds received under this section, including—

(A) total annual revenue;

(B) sources of revenue;

(C) total annual operating costs;

(D) total annual capital costs;

(E) fleet size and type, and related facilities;

(F) vehicle revenue miles; and

(G) ridership.

(c) APPORTIONMENTS.—

(1) IN GENERAL.—Of the amounts made available or appropriated for each fiscal year pursuant to section 5338(a)(2)(F) to carry out this section—

(A) an amount equal to 5 percent shall be available to carry out paragraph (2); and

(B) 3 percent shall be available to carry out paragraph (3).

(2) PUBLIC TRANSPORTATION ON INDIAN RESERVATIONS.—For each fiscal year, the amounts made available under paragraph (1)(A) shall be apportioned for grants to Indian tribes for any purpose eligible under this section, under such terms and conditions as may be established by the Secretary, of which—

(A) 20 percent shall be distributed by the Secretary on a competitive basis; and

(B) 80 percent shall be apportioned as formula grants as provided in subsection (j).

(3) APPALACHIAN DEVELOPMENT PUBLIC TRANSPORTATION ASSISTANCE PROGRAM.—

(A) DEFINITIONS.—In this paragraph—

(i) the term "Appalachian region" has the same meaning as in section 14102 of title 40; and

(ii) the term "eligible recipient" means a State that participates in a program established under subtitle IV of title 40.

(B) IN GENERAL.—The Secretary shall carry out a public transportation assistance program in the Appalachian region.

(C) APPORTIONMENT.—Of amounts made available or appropriated for each fiscal year under section 5338(a)(2)(F) to carry out this paragraph, the Secretary shall apportion funds to eligible recipients for any purpose eligible under this section, based on the guidelines established under section 9.5(b) of the Appalachian Regional Commission Code.

(D) SPECIAL RULE.—An eligible recipient may use amounts that cannot be used for operating expenses under this paragraph for a highway project if—

(i) that use is approved, in writing, by the eligible recipient after appropriate notice and an opportunity for comment and appeal are provided to affected public transportation providers; and

(ii) the eligible recipient, in approving the use of amounts under this subparagraph, determines that the local transit needs are being addressed.

(4) REMAINING AMOUNTS.—

(A) IN GENERAL.—The amounts made available or appropriated for each fiscal year pursuant to section 5338(a)(2)(F) that are not apportioned under paragraph (1) or (2) shall be apportioned in accordance with this paragraph.

(B) APPORTIONMENT BASED ON LAND AREA AND POPULATION IN NONURBANIZED AREAS.—

(i) IN GENERAL.—83.15 percent of the amount described in subparagraph (A) shall be apportioned to the States in accordance with this subparagraph.

(ii) LAND AREA.—

(I) IN GENERAL.—Subject to subclause (II), each State shall receive an amount that is equal to 20 percent of the amount apportioned under clause (i), multiplied by the ratio of the land area in rural areas in that State and divided by the land area in all rural areas in the United States, as shown by the most recent decennial census of population.

(II) MAXIMUM APPORTIONMENT.—No State shall receive more than 5 percent of the amount apportioned under subclause (I).

(iii) POPULATION.—Each State shall receive an amount equal to 80 percent of the amount apportioned under clause (i), multiplied by the ratio of the population of rural areas in that State and divided by the population of all rural areas in the United States, as shown by the most recent decennial census of population.

(C) APPORTIONMENT BASED ON LAND AREA, VEHICLE REVENUE MILES, AND LOW-INCOME INDIVIDUALS IN NONURBANIZED AREAS.—

(i) IN GENERAL.—16.85 percent of the amount described in subparagraph (A) shall be apportioned to the States in accordance with this subparagraph.

(ii) LAND AREA.—Subject to clause (v), each State shall receive an amount that is equal to 29.68 percent of the amount apportioned under clause (i), multiplied by the ratio of the land area in rural areas in that State and divided by the land area in all rural areas in the United States, as shown by the most recent decennial census of population.

(iii) VEHICLE REVENUE MILES.—Subject to clause (v), each State shall receive an amount that is equal to 29.68 percent of the amount apportioned under clause (i), multiplied by the ratio of vehicle revenue miles in rural areas in that State and divided by the vehicle revenue miles in all rural areas in the United States, as determined by national transit database reporting.

(iv) LOW-INCOME INDIVIDUALS.—Each State shall receive an amount that is equal to 40.64 percent of the amount apportioned under clause (i), multiplied by the ratio of low-income individuals in rural areas in that State and divided by the number of low-income individuals in all rural areas in the United States, as shown by the Bureau of the Census.

(v) MAXIMUM APPORTIONMENT.—No State shall receive—

(I) more than 5 percent of the amount apportioned under clause (ii); or

(II) more than 5 percent of the amount apportioned under clause (iii).

(d) USE FOR LOCAL TRANSPORTATION SERVICE.—A State may use an amount apportioned under this section for a project included in a program under subsection (b) of this section and eligible for assistance under this chapter if the project will provide local transportation service, as defined by the Secretary of Transportation, in a rural area.

(e) USE FOR ADMINISTRATION, PLANNING, AND TECHNICAL ASSISTANCE.—The Secretary may allow a State to use not more than 10 percent of the amount apportioned under this section to administer this section and provide technical assistance to a subrecipient, including project planning, program and management development, coordination of public transportation programs, and research the State considers appropriate to promote effective delivery of public transportation to a rural area.

(f) INTERCITY BUS TRANSPORTATION.—

(1) IN GENERAL.—A State shall expend at least 15 percent of the amount made available in each fiscal year to carry out a program to develop and support intercity

bus transportation. Eligible activities under the program include—

(A) planning and marketing for intercity bus transportation;

(B) capital grants for intercity bus facilities;

(C) joint-use facilities;

(D) operating grants through purchase-of-service agreements, user-side subsidies, and demonstration projects; and

(E) coordinating rural connections between small public transportation operations and intercity bus carriers.

(2) CERTIFICATION.—A State does not have to comply with paragraph (1) of this subsection in a fiscal year in which the Governor of the State certifies to the Secretary, after consultation with affected intercity bus service providers, that the intercity bus service needs of the State are being met adequately.

(g) GOVERNMENT SHARE OF COSTS.—

(1) CAPITAL PROJECTS.—

(A) IN GENERAL.—Except as provided by subparagraph (B), a grant awarded under this section for a capital project or project administrative expenses shall be for 80 percent of the net costs of the project, as determined by the Secretary.

(B) EXCEPTION.—A State described in section 120(b) of title 23 shall receive a Government share of the net costs in accordance with the formula under that section.

(2) OPERATING ASSISTANCE.—

(A) IN GENERAL.—Except as provided by subparagraph (B), a grant made under this section for operating assistance may not exceed 50 percent of the net operating costs of the project, as determined by the Secretary.

(B) EXCEPTION.—A State described in section 120(b) of title 23 shall receive a Government share of the net operating costs equal to 62.5 percent of the Government share provided for under paragraph (1)(B).

(3) REMAINDER.—The remainder of net project costs—

(A) may be provided in cash from non-Government sources;

(B) may be provided from revenues from the sale of advertising and concessions;

(C) may be provided from an undistributed cash surplus, a replacement or depreciation cash fund or reserve, a service agreement with a State or local social service agency or a private social service organization, or new capital;

(D) may be derived from amounts appropriated or otherwise made available to a department or agency of the Government (other than the Department of Transportation) that are eligible to be expended for transportation;

(E) notwithstanding subparagraph (B), may be derived from amounts made available to carry out the Federal lands highway program established by section 204 [1] of title 23; and

(F) in the case of an intercity bus project that includes both feeder service and an unsubsidized segment of intercity bus service to which the feeder service connects, may be derived from the costs of a private operator for the unsubsidized segment of intercity bus service, including all operating and capital costs of such service whether or not offset by revenue from such service, as an in-kind match for the operating costs of connecting rural intercity bus feeder service funded under subsection (f), if the private operator agrees in writing to the use of the costs of the private operator for the unsubsidized segment of intercity bus service as an in-kind match.

(4) USE OF CERTAIN FUNDS.—For purposes of paragraph (3)(B), the prohibitions on the use of funds for matching requirements under section 403(a)(5)(C)(vii) of the Social Security Act (42 U.S.C. 603(a)(5)(C)(vii)) shall not apply to Federal or State funds to be used for transportation purposes.

(5) LIMITATION ON OPERATING ASSISTANCE.—A State carrying out a program of operating assistance under this section may not limit the level or extent of use of the Government grant for the payment of operating expenses.

(h) TRANSFER OF FACILITIES AND EQUIPMENT.—With the consent of the recipient currently having a facility or equipment acquired with assistance under this section, a State may transfer the facility or equipment to any recipient eligible to receive assistance under this chapter if the facility or equipment will continue to be used as required under this section.

(i) RELATIONSHIP TO OTHER LAWS.—

(1) IN GENERAL.—Section 5333(b) applies to this section if the Secretary of Labor utilizes a special warranty that provides a fair and equitable arrangement to protect the interests of employees.

(2) RULE OF CONSTRUCTION.—This subsection does not affect or discharge a responsibility of the Secretary of Transportation under a law of the United States.

(j) FORMULA GRANTS FOR PUBLIC TRANSPORTATION ON INDIAN RESERVATIONS.—

(1) APPORTIONMENT.—

(A) IN GENERAL.—Of the amounts described in subsection (c)(2)(B)—

(i) 50 percent of the total amount shall be apportioned so that each Indian tribe providing public transportation service shall receive an amount equal to the total amount apportioned under this clause multiplied by the ratio of the number of vehicle revenue miles provided by an Indian tribe divided by the total number of vehicle revenue miles provided by all Indian tribes, as reported to the Secretary;

(ii) 25 percent of the total amount shall be apportioned equally among each Indian tribe providing at least 200,000 vehicle revenue miles of public transportation service annually, as reported to the Secretary; and

(iii) 25 percent of the total amount shall be apportioned among each Indian tribe providing public transportation on tribal lands (American Indian Areas, Alaska Native Areas, and Hawaiian Home Lands, as defined by the Bureau of the Census) on which more than 1,000 low-income individuals reside (as determined by the Bureau of the Census) so that each Indian tribe shall receive an amount equal to the total amount apportioned under this clause multiplied by the ratio of the number of low-income individuals residing on an Indian tribe's lands divided by the total number of low-income individuals on tribal lands on which more than 1,000 low-income individuals reside.

(B) LIMITATION.—No recipient shall receive more than $300,000 of the amounts apportioned under subparagraph (A)(iii) in a fiscal year.

(C) REMAINING AMOUNTS.—Of the amounts made available under subparagraph (A)(iii), any amounts not apportioned under that subparagraph shall be allocated among Indian tribes receiving less than $300,000 in a fiscal year according to the formula specified in that clause.

(D) LOW-INCOME INDIVIDUALS.—For purposes of subparagraph (A)(iii), the term "low-income individual" means an individual whose family income is at or below 100 percent of the poverty line, as that term is defined in section 673(2) of the Community Services Block Grant Act (42 U.S.C. 9902(2)), including any revision required by that section, for a family of the size involved.

(E) ALLOCATION BETWEEN MULTIPLE INDIAN TRIBES.—If more than 1 Indian tribe provides public transportation service on tribal lands in a single Tribal Statistical Area, and the Indian tribes do not determine how to allocate the funds apportioned under clause (iii) of subparagraph (A) between the Indian tribes, the Secretary shall allocate the funds so that each Indian tribe shall receive an amount equal to the total amount apportioned under such clause (iii) multiplied by the ratio of the number of annual unlinked passenger trips provided by each Indian tribe, as reported to the National Transit Database, to the total unlinked passenger trips provided by all Indian tribes in the Tribal Statistical Area.

(2) NON-TRIBAL SERVICE PROVIDERS.—A recipient that is an Indian tribe may use funds apportioned under this subsection to finance public transportation services provided by a non-tribal provider of public transportation that connects residents of tribal lands with surrounding communities, improves access to employment or healthcare, or otherwise addresses the mobility needs of tribal members.

(Pub. L. 103–272, §1(d), July 5, 1994, 108 Stat. 809; Pub. L. 105–178, title III, §3014(a), June 9, 1998, 112 Stat. 359; Pub. L. 109–59, title III, §§3002(b)(4), 3013(a)–(h), Aug. 10, 2005, 119 Stat. 1545, 1593–1596; Pub. L. 110–244, title II, §201(e), June 6, 2008, 122 Stat. 1610; Pub. L. 111–147, title IV, §434, Mar. 18, 2010, 124 Stat. 89; Pub. L. 111–322, title II, §2304, Dec. 22, 2010, 124 Stat. 3527; Pub. L. 112–5, title III, §304, Mar. 4, 2011, 125 Stat. 19; Pub. L. 112–30, title I, §134, Sept. 16, 2011, 125 Stat. 351; Pub. L. 112–102, title III, §304, Mar. 30, 2012, 126 Stat. 277; Pub. L. 112–140, title III, §304, June 29, 2012, 126 Stat. 398; Pub. L. 112–141, div. B, §20010, div. G, title III, §113004, July 6, 2012, 126 Stat. 680, 985; Pub. L. 113–159, title I, §1201, Aug. 8, 2014, 128 Stat. 1845; Pub. L. 114–21, title I, §1201, May 29, 2015, 129 Stat. 222; Pub. L. 114–41, title I, §1201, July 31, 2015, 129 Stat. 450; Pub. L. 114–73, title I, §1201, Oct. 29, 2015, 129 Stat. 572; Pub. L. 114–87, title I, §1201, Nov. 20, 2015, 129 Stat. 681; Pub. L. 114–94, div. A, title III, §3007, Dec. 4, 2015, 129 Stat. 1464; Pub. L. 117–58, div. C, §30006, Nov. 15, 2021, 135 Stat. 900.)

[1] *See References in Text note below.*

§5312. PUBLIC TRANSPORTATION INNOVATION

(a) IN GENERAL.—The Secretary shall provide assistance for projects and activities to advance innovative public transportation research and development in accordance with the requirements of this section.

(b) RESEARCH, DEVELOPMENT, DEMONSTRATION, AND DEPLOYMENT PROJECTS.—

(1) IN GENERAL.—The Secretary may make grants and enter into contracts, cooperative agreements, and other agreements for research, development, demonstration, and deployment projects, and evaluation of research and technology of national significance to public transportation, that the Secretary determines will improve public transportation.

(2) AGREEMENTS.—In order to carry out paragraph (1), the Secretary may make

grants to and enter into contracts, cooperative agreements, and other agreements with—

(A) departments, agencies, and instrumentalities of the Government, including Federal laboratories;

(B) State and local governmental entities;

(C) providers of public transportation;

(D) private or non-profit organizations;

(E) institutions of higher education; and

(F) technical and community colleges.

(3) APPLICATION.—

(A) IN GENERAL.—To receive a grant, contract, cooperative agreement, or other agreement under this section, an entity described in paragraph (2) shall submit an application to the Secretary.

(B) FORM AND CONTENTS.—An application under subparagraph (A) shall be in such form and contain such information as the Secretary may require, including—

(i) a statement of purpose detailing the need being addressed;

(ii) the short- and long-term goals of the project, including opportunities for future innovation and development, the potential for deployment, and benefits to riders and public transportation; and

(iii) the short- and long-term funding requirements to complete the project and any future objectives of the project.

(4) ACCELERATED IMPLEMENTATION AND DEPLOYMENT OF ADVANCED DIGITAL CONSTRUCTION MANAGEMENT SYSTEMS.—

(A) IN GENERAL.—The Secretary shall establish and implement a program under this subsection to promote, implement, deploy, demonstrate, showcase, support, and document the application of advanced digital construction management systems, practices, performance, and benefits.

(B) GOALS.—The goals of the accelerated implementation and deployment of advanced digital construction management systems program established under subparagraph (A) shall include—

(i) accelerated adoption of advanced digital systems applied throughout the lifecycle of transportation infrastructure (including through the planning, design and engineering, construction, operations, and maintenance phases) that—

(I) maximize interoperability with other systems, products, tools, or applications;

(II) boost productivity;

(III) manage complexity;

(IV) reduce project delays and cost overruns;

(V) enhance safety and quality; and

(VI) reduce total costs for the entire lifecycle of transportation infrastructure assets;

(ii) more timely and productive information-sharing among stakeholders through reduced reliance on paper to manage construction processes and deliverables such as blueprints, design drawings, procurement and supply-chain orders, equipment logs, daily progress reports, and punch lists;

(iii) deployment of digital management systems that enable and leverage the use of digital technologies on construction sites by contractors, such as state-of-the-art automated and connected machinery and optimized routing software that allows construction workers to perform tasks faster, safer, more accurately, and with minimal supervision;

(iv) the development and deployment of best practices for use in digital construction management;

(v) increased technology adoption and deployment by States, local governmental authorities, and designated recipients that enables project sponsors—

(I) to integrate the adoption of digital management systems and technologies in contracts; and

(II) to weigh the cost of digitization and technology in setting project budgets;

(vi) technology training and workforce development to build the capabilities of project managers and sponsors that enables States, local governmental authorities, or designated recipients—

(I) to better manage projects using advanced construction management technologies; and

(II) to properly measure and reward technology adoption across projects;

(vii) development of guidance to assist States, local governmental authorities, and designated recipients in updating regulations to allow project sponsors and contractors—

(I) to report data relating to the project in digital formats; and

(II) to fully capture the efficiencies and benefits of advanced digital construction management systems and related technologies;

(viii) reduction in the environmental footprint of construction projects using advanced digital construction management systems resulting from elimination of congestion through more efficient projects; and

(ix) enhanced worker and pedestrian safety resulting from increased transparency.

(C) PUBLICATION.—The reporting requirements for the accelerated implementation and deployment of advanced digital construction management systems program established under section 503(c)(5) of title 23 shall include data and analysis collected under this section.

(c) RESEARCH.—

(1) IN GENERAL.—The Secretary may make a grant to or enter into a contract, cooperative agreement, or other agreement under this section with an entity described in subsection (b)(2) to carry out a public transportation research project that has as its ultimate goal the development and deployment of new and innovative ideas, practices, and approaches.

(2) PROJECT ELIGIBILITY.—A public transportation research project that receives assistance under paragraph (1) shall focus on—

(A) providing more effective and efficient public transportation service, including services to—

(i) seniors;

(ii) individuals with disabilities; and

(iii) low-income individuals;

(B) mobility management and improvements and travel management systems;

(C) data and communication system advancements;

(D) system capacity, including—

(i) train control;

(ii) capacity improvements; and

(iii) performance management;

(E) capital and operating efficiencies;

(F) planning and forecasting modeling and simulation;

(G) advanced vehicle design;

(H) advancements in vehicle technology;

(I) asset maintenance and repair systems advancement;

(J) construction and project management;

(K) alternative fuels;

(L) the environment and energy efficiency;

(M) safety improvements; or

(N) any other area that the Secretary determines is important to advance the interests of public transportation.

(d) INNOVATION AND DEVELOPMENT.—

(1) IN GENERAL.—The Secretary may make a grant to or enter into a contract, cooperative agreement, or other agreement under this section with an entity described in subsection (b)(2) to carry out a public transportation innovation and development project that seeks to improve public transportation systems nationwide in order to provide more efficient and effective delivery of public transportation services, including through technology and technological capacity improvements.

(2) PROJECT ELIGIBILITY.—A public transportation innovation and development project that receives assistance under paragraph (1) shall focus on—

(A) the development of public transportation research projects that received assistance under subsection (c) that the Secretary determines were successful;

(B) planning and forecasting modeling and simulation;

(C) capital and operating efficiencies;

(D) advanced vehicle design;

(E) advancements in vehicle technology;

(F) the environment and energy efficiency;

(G) system capacity, including train control and capacity improvements; or

(H) any other area that the Secretary determines is important to advance the interests of public transportation.

(e) DEMONSTRATION, DEPLOYMENT, AND EVALUATION.—

(1) IN GENERAL.—The Secretary may, under terms and conditions that the Secretary prescribes, make a grant to or enter into a contract, cooperative agreement, or other agreement with an entity described in paragraph (2) to promote the early deployment and demonstration of innovation in public transportation that has broad applicability.

(2) PARTICIPANTS.—An entity described in this paragraph is—

(A) an entity described in subsection (b)(2); or

(B) a consortium of entities described in subsection (b)(2), including a provider of public transportation, that will share the costs, risks, and rewards of early deployment and demonstration of innovation.

(3) PROJECT ELIGIBILITY.—A demonstration, deployment, or evaluation project that receives assistance under paragraph (1) shall seek to build on successful research, innovation, and development efforts to facilitate—

(A) the deployment of research and technology development resulting from private efforts or Federally funded efforts;

(B) the implementation of research and technology development to advance the interests of public transportation; or

(C) the deployment of low or no emission vehicles, zero emission vehicles, or associated advanced technology.

(4) EVALUATION.—Not later than 2 years after the date on which a project receives assistance under paragraph (1), the Secretary shall conduct a comprehensive evaluation of the success or failure of the projects funded under this subsection and any plan for broad-based implementation of the innovation promoted by successful projects.

(5) PROHIBITION.—The Secretary may not make grants under this subsection for the demonstration, deployment, or evaluation of a vehicle that is in revenue service unless the Secretary determines that the project makes significant technological advancements in the vehicle.

(6) DEFINITIONS.—In this subsection—

(A) the term "direct carbon emissions" means the quantity of direct greenhouse gas emissions from a vehicle, as determined by the Administrator of the Environmental Protection Agency;

(B) the term "low or no emission vehicle" means—

(i) a passenger vehicle used to provide public transportation that the Secretary determines sufficiently reduces energy consumption or harmful emissions, including direct carbon emissions, when compared to a comparable standard vehicle; or

(ii) a zero emission vehicle used to provide public transportation; and

(C) the term "zero emission vehicle" means a low or no emission vehicle that produces no carbon or particulate matter.

(f) ANNUAL REPORT ON RESEARCH.—

(1) IN GENERAL.—Not later than the first Monday in February of each year, the Secretary shall make available to the public on the Web site of the Department of Transportation, a report that includes—

(A) a description of each project that received assistance under this section during the preceding fiscal year;

(B) an evaluation of each project described in paragraph (1), including any evaluation conducted under subsection (e)(4) for the preceding fiscal year; and

(C) a strategic research roadmap proposal for allocations of amounts for assistance under this section for the current and subsequent fiscal year, including anticipated work areas, proposed demonstrations and strategic partnership opportunities;

(2) UPDATES.—Not less than every 3 months, the Secretary shall update on the Web site of the Department of Transportation the information described in paragraph (1)(C) to reflect any changes to the Secretary's plans to make assistance available under this section.

(3) LONG-TERM RESEARCH PLANS.—The Secretary is encouraged to develop long-term research plans and shall identify in the annual report under paragraph (1) and in updates under paragraph (2) allocations of amounts for assistance and notices of funding opportunities to execute long-term strategic research roadmap plans.

(g) GOVERNMENT SHARE OF COSTS.—

(1) IN GENERAL.—The Government share of the cost of a project carried out under this section shall not exceed 80 percent, except that if there is substantial public interest or benefit, the Secretary may approve a greater Federal share.

(2) NON-GOVERNMENT SHARE.—The non-Government share of the cost of a project carried out under this section may be derived from in-kind contributions.

(3) FINANCIAL BENEFIT.—If the Secretary determines that there would be a clear and direct financial benefit to an entity under a grant, contract, cooperative agreement, or other agreement under this section, the Secretary shall establish a Government share of the costs of the project to be carried out under the grant, contract, cooperative agreement, or other agreement that is consistent with the benefit.

(h) LOW OR NO EMISSION VEHICLE COMPONENT ASSESSMENT.—

(1) DEFINITIONS.—In this subsection—

(A) the term "covered institution of higher education" means an institution of higher education with which the Secretary enters into a contract or cooperative agreement, or to which the Secretary makes a grant, under paragraph (2)(B) to operate a facility selected under paragraph (2)(A);

(B) the terms "direct carbon emissions" and "low or no emission vehicle" have the meanings given those terms in subsection (e)(6);

(C) the term "institution of higher education" has the meaning given the term in section 102 of the Higher Education Act of 1965 (20 U.S.C. 1002); and

(D) the term "low or no emission vehicle component" means an item that is separately installed in and removable from a low or no emission vehicle.

(2) ASSESSING LOW OR NO EMISSION VEHICLE COMPONENTS.—

(A) IN GENERAL.—The Secretary shall competitively select at least 1 facility—

(i) to conduct testing, evaluation, and analysis of low or no emission vehicle components intended for use in low or no emission vehicles; and

(ii) to conduct directed technology research.

(B) TESTING, EVALUATION, AND ANALYSIS.—

(i) IN GENERAL.—The Secretary shall enter into a contract or cooperative agreement with, or make a grant to, at least 1 institution of higher education to operate and maintain a facility to conduct testing, evaluation, and analysis of low or no emission vehicle components, and new and emerging technology components, intended for use in low or no emission vehicles.

(ii) REQUIREMENTS.—An institution of higher education described in clause (i) shall have—

(I) capacity to carry out transportation-related advanced component and vehicle evaluation;

(II) laboratories capable of testing and evaluation; and

(III) direct access to or a partnership with a testing facility capable of emulating real-world circumstances in order to test low or no emission vehicle components installed on the intended vehicle.

(C) FEES.—A covered institution of higher education shall establish and collect fees, which shall be approved by the Secretary, for the assessment of low or no emission vehicle components at the applicable facility selected under subparagraph (A).

(D) AVAILABILITY OF AMOUNTS TO PAY FOR ASSESSMENT.—The Secretary shall enter into a contract or cooperative agreement with, or make a grant to an institution of higher education under which—

(i) the Secretary shall pay 50 percent of the cost of assessing a low or no emission vehicle component at the applicable facility selected under subparagraph (A) from amounts made available to carry out this section; and

(ii) the remaining 50 percent of such cost shall be paid from amounts recovered through the fees established and collected pursuant to subparagraph (C).

(E) VOLUNTARY TESTING.—A manufacturer of a low or no emission vehicle component is not required to assess the low or no emission vehicle component at a facility selected under subparagraph (A).

(F) COMPLIANCE WITH SECTION 5318.—Notwithstanding whether a low or no emission vehicle component is assessed at a facility selected under subparagraph (A), each new bus model shall comply with the requirements under section 5318.

(G) SEPARATE FACILITY.—A facility selected under subparagraph (A) shall be separate and distinct from the facility operated and maintained under section 5318.

(H) CAPITAL EQUIPMENT AND DIRECTED RESEARCH.—A facility operated and maintained under subparagraph (A) may use funds made available under this subsection for—

(i) acquisition of equipment and capital projects related to testing low or no emission vehicle components; or

(ii) research related to advanced vehicle technologies that provides advancements to the entire public transportation industry.

(I) COST SHARE.—The cost share for activities described in subparagraph (H) shall be subject to the terms in subsection (g).

(3) LOW OR NO EMISSION VEHICLE COMPONENT PERFORMANCE REPORTS.—Not later than 2 years after the date of enactment of the Federal Public Transportation Act of 2015, and annually thereafter, the Secretary shall issue a report on low or no emission vehicle component assessments conducted at each facility selected under paragraph (2)(A), which shall include information related to the maintainability, reliability, performance, structural integrity, efficiency, and noise of those low or no emission vehicle components, as applicable.

(4) PUBLIC AVAILABILITY OF ASSESSMENTS.—Each assessment conducted at a facility

[§5313. Repealed. Pub. L. 114–94, div. A, title III, §3030(b), Dec. 4, 2015, 129 Stat. 1496]

CHAPTER 53—PUBLIC TRANSPORTATION

selected under paragraph (2)(A) shall be made publicly available, including to affected industries.

(5) RULE OF CONSTRUCTION.—Nothing in this subsection shall be construed to require—

(A) a low or no emission vehicle component to be tested at a facility selected under paragraph (2)(A); or

(B) the development or disclosure of a privately funded component assessment.

(i) TRANSIT COOPERATIVE RESEARCH PROGRAM.—

(1) IN GENERAL.—The amounts made available under section 5338(a)(2)(G)(ii) are available for a public transportation cooperative research program.

(2) INDEPENDENT GOVERNING BOARD.—

(A) ESTABLISHMENT.—The Secretary shall establish an independent governing board for the program under this subsection.

(B) RECOMMENDATIONS.—The board shall recommend public transportation research, development, and technology transfer activities the Secretary considers appropriate.

(3) FEDERAL ASSISTANCE.—The Secretary may make grants to, and enter into cooperative agreements with, the National Academy of Sciences to carry out activities under this subsection that the Secretary considers appropriate.

(4) GOVERNMENT SHARE OF COSTS.—If there would be a clear and direct financial benefit to an entity under a grant or contract financed under this subsection, the Secretary shall establish a Government share consistent with that benefit.

(5) LIMITATION ON APPLICABILITY.—Subsections (f) and (g) shall not apply to activities carried out under this subsection.

(Pub. L. 103–272, §1(d), July 5, 1994, 108 Stat. 811; Pub. L. 105–178, title III, §3015(a), June 9, 1998, 112 Stat. 359; Pub. L. 109–59, title III, §§3002(b)(4), 3014(a)–(e)(1), Aug. 10, 2005, 119 Stat. 1545, 1596, 1597; Pub. L. 110–244, title II, §201(f), June 6, 2008, 122 Stat. 1610; Pub. L. 112–141, div. B, §20011, July 6, 2012, 126 Stat. 686; Pub. L. 114–94, div. A, title III, §3008(a), (b), Dec. 4, 2015, 129 Stat. 1465, 1468; Pub. L. 117–58, div. C, §30007(a), (c), Nov. 15, 2021, 135 Stat. 900, 902.)

[§5313. REPEALED. PUB. L. 114–94, DIV. A, TITLE III, §3030(B), DEC. 4, 2015, 129 STAT. 1496]

Section, Pub. L. 103–272, §1(d), July 5, 1994, 108 Stat. 812; Pub. L. 105–178, title III, §3029(b)(4), (5), June 9, 1998, 112 Stat. 372; Pub. L. 109–59, title III, §§3002(b)(4), 3015(a), (b)(1), Aug. 10, 2005, 119 Stat. 1545, 1597; Pub. L. 112–141, div. B, §20030(b), July 6, 2012, 126 Stat. 730, related to transit cooperative research program.

§5314. TECHNICAL ASSISTANCE AND WORKFORCE DEVELOPMENT

(a) TECHNICAL ASSISTANCE AND STANDARDS.—

(1) TECHNICAL ASSISTANCE AND STANDARDS DEVELOPMENT.—

(A) IN GENERAL.—The Secretary may make grants and enter into contracts, cooperative agreements, and other agreements (including agreements with departments, agencies, and instrumentalities of the Government) to carry out activities that the Secretary determines will assist recipients of assistance under this chapter to—

(i) more effectively and efficiently provide public transportation service;

(ii) administer funds received under this chapter in compliance with Federal law; and

(iii) improve public transportation.

(B) ELIGIBLE ACTIVITIES.—The activities carried out under subparagraph (A) may include—

(i) technical assistance; and

(ii) the development of voluntary and consensus-based standards and best practices by the public transportation industry, including standards and best practices for safety, fare collection, intelligent transportation systems, accessibility, procurement, security, asset management to maintain a state of good repair, operations, maintenance, vehicle propulsion, communications, and vehicle electronics.

(2) TECHNICAL ASSISTANCE.—The Secretary, through a competitive bid process, may enter into contracts, cooperative agreements, and other agreements with national nonprofit organizations that have the appropriate demonstrated capacity to provide public-transportation-related technical assistance under this subsection. The Secretary may enter into such contracts, cooperative agreements, and other agreements to assist providers of public transportation to—

(A) comply with the Americans with Disabilities Act of 1990 (42 U.S.C. 12101 et seq.) through technical assistance, demonstration programs, research, public education, and other activities related to complying with such Act;

(B) comply with human services transportation coordination requirements and to enhance the coordination of Federal resources for human services transportation with those of the Department of Transportation through technical assistance, training, and support services related to complying with such requirements;

(C) meet the transportation needs of elderly individuals;

(D) increase transit ridership in coordination with metropolitan planning organizations and other entities through development around public transportation stations through technical assistance and the development of tools, guidance, and analysis related to market-based development around transit stations;

(E) address transportation equity with regard to the effect that transportation planning, investment, and operations have for low-income and minority individuals;

(F) facilitate best practices to promote bus driver safety;

(G) meet the requirements of sections 5323(j) and 5323(m);

(H) assist with the development and deployment of low or no emission vehicles (as defined in section 5339(c)(1)) or low or no emission vehicle components (as defined in section 5312(h)(1)); and

(I) any other technical assistance activity that the Secretary determines is necessary to advance the interests of public transportation.

(3) ANNUAL REPORT ON TECHNICAL ASSISTANCE.—Not later than the first Monday in February of each year, the Secretary shall submit to the Committee on Banking, Housing, and Urban Affairs and the Committee on Appropriations of the Senate and the Committee on Transportation and Infrastructure, the Committee on Science, Space, and Technology, and the Committee on Appropriations of the House of

Representatives a report that includes—

(A) a description of each project that received assistance under this subsection during the preceding fiscal year;

(B) an evaluation of the activities carried out by each organization that received assistance under this subsection during the preceding fiscal year;

(C) a proposal for allocations of amounts for assistance under this subsection for the subsequent fiscal year; and

(D) measurable outcomes and impacts of the programs funded under subsections (b) and (c).

(4) GOVERNMENT SHARE OF COSTS.—

(A) IN GENERAL.—The Government share of the cost of an activity carried out using a grant under this subsection may not exceed 80 percent.

(B) NON-GOVERNMENT SHARE.—The non-Government share of the cost of an activity carried out using a grant under this subsection may be derived from in-kind contributions.

(b) HUMAN RESOURCES AND TRAINING.—

(1) IN GENERAL.—The Secretary may undertake, or make grants and contracts for, programs that address human resource needs as they apply to public transportation activities. A program may include—

(A) an employment training program;

(B) an outreach program to increase employment for veterans, females, individuals with a disability, minorities (including American Indians or Alaska Natives, Asian, Black or African Americans, native Hawaiians or other Pacific Islanders, and Hispanics) in public transportation activities;

(C) research on public transportation personnel and training needs;

(D) training and assistance for veteran and minority business opportunities; and

(E) consensus-based national training standards and certifications in partnership with industry stakeholders.

(2) INNOVATIVE PUBLIC TRANSPORTATION FRONTLINE WORKFORCE DEVELOPMENT PROGRAM.—

(A) IN GENERAL.—The Secretary shall establish a competitive grant program to assist the development of innovative activities eligible for assistance under paragraph (1).

(B) ELIGIBLE PROGRAMS.—A program eligible for assistance under paragraph (1) shall—

(i) develop apprenticeships, on-the-job training, and instructional training for public transportation maintenance and operations occupations;

(ii) build local, regional, and statewide public transportation training partnerships with local public transportation operators, labor union organizations, workforce development boards, and State workforce agencies to identify and address workforce skill gaps;

(iii) improve safety, security, and emergency preparedness in local public transportation systems through improved safety culture and workforce communication with first responders and the riding public; and

(iv) address current or projected workforce shortages by developing partnerships with high schools, community colleges, and other community organizations.

(C) SELECTION OF RECIPIENTS.—To the maximum extent feasible, the Secretary shall select recipients that—

(i) are geographically diverse;

(ii) address the workforce and human resources needs of large public transportation providers;

(iii) address the workforce and human resources needs of small public transportation providers;

(iv) address the workforce and human resources needs of urban public transportation providers;

(v) address the workforce and human resources needs of rural public transportation providers;

(vi) advance training related to maintenance of low or no emission vehicles and facilities used in public transportation;

(vii) target areas with high rates of unemployment;

(viii) advance opportunities for minorities, women, veterans, individuals with disabilities, low-income populations, and other underserved populations; and

(ix) address in-demand industry sector or occupation, as such term is defined in section 3 of the Workforce Innovation and Opportunity Act (29 U.S.C. 3102).

(D) PROGRAM OUTCOMES.—A recipient of assistance under this subsection shall demonstrate outcomes for any program that includes skills training, on-the-job training, and work-based learning, including—

(i) the impact on reducing public transportation workforce shortages in the area served;

(ii) the diversity of training participants;

(iii) the number of participants obtaining certifications or credentials required for specific types of employment;

(iv) employment outcomes, including job placement, job retention, and wages, using performance metrics established in consultation with the Secretary and the Secretary of Labor and consistent with metrics used by programs under the Workforce Innovation and Opportunity Act (29 U.S.C. 3101 et seq.); and

(v) to the extent practical, evidence that the program did not preclude workers who are participating in skills training, on-the-job training, and work-based learning from being referred to, or hired on, projects funded under this chapter without regard to the length of time of their participation in the program.

(E) REPORT TO CONGRESS.—The Secretary shall make publicly available a report on the Frontline Workforce Development Program for each fiscal year, not later than December 31 of the calendar year in which that fiscal year ends. The report shall include a detailed description of activities carried out under this paragraph, an evaluation of the program, and policy recommendations to improve program effectiveness.

(3) GOVERNMENT'S SHARE OF COSTS.—The Government share of the cost of a project carried out using a grant under paragraph (1) or (2) shall be 50 percent.

(4) AVAILABILITY OF AMOUNTS.—Not more than 0.5 percent of amounts made

available to a recipient under sections 5307, 5337, and 5339 is available for expenditures by the recipient, with the approval of the Secretary, to pay not more than 80 percent of the cost of eligible activities under this subsection.

(c) NATIONAL TRANSIT INSTITUTE.—

(1) ESTABLISHMENT.—The Secretary shall establish a national transit institute and award grants to a public 4-year degree-granting institution of higher education, as defined in section 101(a) of the Higher Education Act of 1965 (20 U.S.C. 1001(a)), in order to carry out the duties of the institute.

(2) DUTIES.—

(A) IN GENERAL.—In cooperation with the Federal Transit Administration, State transportation departments, public transportation authorities, and national and international entities, the institute established under paragraph (1) shall develop and conduct training and educational programs for Federal, State, and local transportation employees, United States citizens, and foreign nationals engaged or to be engaged in Government-aid public transportation work.

(B) TRAINING AND EDUCATIONAL PROGRAMS.—The training and educational programs developed under subparagraph (A) may include courses in recent developments, techniques, and procedures related to—

(i) intermodal and public transportation planning;

(ii) management;

(iii) environmental factors;

(iv) acquisition and joint use rights-of-way;

(v) engineering and architectural design;

(vi) procurement strategies for public transportation systems;

(vii) turnkey approaches to delivering public transportation systems;

(viii) new technologies;

(ix) emission reduction technologies;

(x) ways to make public transportation accessible to individuals with disabilities;

(xi) construction, construction management, insurance, and risk management;

(xii) maintenance;

(xiii) contract administration;

(xiv) inspection;

(xv) innovative finance;

(xvi) workplace safety; and

(xvii) public transportation security.

(3) PROVISION FOR EDUCATION AND TRAINING.—Education and training of Government, State, and local transportation employees under this subsection shall be provided—

(A) by the Secretary at no cost to the States and local governments for subjects that are a Government program responsibility; or

(B) when the education and training are paid under paragraph (4), by the State, with the approval of the Secretary, through grants and contracts with public and private agencies, other institutions, individuals, and the institute.

(4) AVAILABILITY OF AMOUNTS.—

(A) IN GENERAL.—Not more than 0.5 percent of amounts made available to a recipient under sections 5307, 5337, and 5339 is available for expenditures by the recipient, with the approval of the Secretary, to pay not more than 80 percent of the cost of eligible activities under this subsection.

(B) EXISTING PROGRAMS.—A recipient may use amounts made available under subparagraph (A) to carry out existing local education and training programs for public transportation employees supported by the Secretary, the Department of Labor, or the Department of Education.

(Pub. L. 103–272, §1(d), July 5, 1994, 108 Stat. 812; Pub. L. 105–178, title III, §§3016, 3029(b)(6), June 9, 1998, 112 Stat. 361, 372; Pub. L. 109–59, title III, §§3002(b)(4), 3016(a), (b), Aug. 10, 2005, 119 Stat. 1545, 1598, 1599; Pub. L. 110–244, title II, §201(g), June 6, 2008, 122 Stat. 1610; Pub. L. 112–141, div. B, §20012, July 6, 2012, 126 Stat. 690; Pub. L. 114–94, div. A, title III, §3009(a), Dec. 4, 2015, 129 Stat. 1469.)

§5315. PRIVATE SECTOR PARTICIPATION

(a) GENERAL PURPOSES.—In the interest of fulfilling the general purposes of this chapter under section 5301(b), the Secretary shall—

(1) better coordinate public and private sector-provided public transportation services;

(2) promote more effective utilization of private sector expertise, financing, and operational capacity to deliver costly and complex new fixed guideway capital projects; and

(3) promote transparency and public understanding of public-private partnerships affecting public transportation.

(b) ACTIONS TO PROMOTE BETTER COORDINATION BETWEEN PUBLIC AND PRIVATE SECTOR PROVIDERS OF PUBLIC TRANSPORTATION.—The Secretary shall—

(1) provide technical assistance to recipients of Federal transit grant assistance, at the request of a recipient, on practices and methods to best utilize private providers of public transportation; and

(2) educate recipients of Federal transit grant assistance on laws and regulations under this chapter that impact private providers of public transportation.

(c) ACTIONS TO PROVIDE TECHNICAL ASSISTANCE FOR ALTERNATIVE PROJECT DELIVERY METHODS.—Upon request by a sponsor of a new fixed guideway capital project, the Secretary shall—

(1) identify best practices for public-private partnerships models in the United States and in other countries;

(2) develop standard public-private partnership transaction model contracts; and

(3) perform financial assessments that include the calculation of public and private benefits of a proposed public-private partnership transaction.

(d) RULE OF CONSTRUCTION.—Nothing in this section shall be construed to alter—

(1) the eligibilities, requirements, or priorities for assistance provided under this chapter; or

(2) the requirements of section 5306(a).

(Pub. L. 103–272, §1(d), July 5, 1994, 108 Stat. 813; Pub. L. 104–287, §5(13), Oct. 11, 1996, 110 Stat. 3390; Pub. L. 105–178, title III, §3017(a), June 9, 1998, 112 Stat. 361; Pub. L. 105–206, title IX, §9009(l), July 22, 1998, 112 Stat. 857; Pub. L. 109–59, title III, §3017, Aug. 10, 2005, 119 Stat.

1600; Pub. L. 112–141, div. B, §20013(a), July 6, 2012, 126 Stat. 692; Pub. L. 114–94, div. A, title III, §3010(a), Dec. 4, 2015, 129 Stat. 1474.)

[§§5316, 5317. REPEALED. PUB. L. 112–141, DIV. B, §20002(A), JULY 6, 2012, 126 STAT. 622]

Section 5316, added Pub. L. 109–59, title III, §3018(a), Aug. 10, 2005, 119 Stat. 1601, related to job access and reverse commute formula grants.

A prior section 5316, Pub. L. 103–272, §1(d), July 5, 1994, 108 Stat. 814; Pub. L. 104–59, title III, §338(c)(5), Nov. 28, 1995, 109 Stat. 605, related to university research institutes, prior to repeal by Pub. L. 105–178, title V, §5110(c), June 9, 1998, 112 Stat. 444.

Section 5317, added Pub. L. 109–59, title III, §3019(a), Aug. 10, 2005, 119 Stat. 1605, related to the New Freedom grant program to assist individuals with disabilities with public transportation.

A prior section 5317, Pub. L. 103–272, §1(d), July 5, 1994, 108 Stat. 815; Pub. L. 104–287, §5(14), Oct. 11, 1996, 110 Stat. 3390; Pub. L. 105–178, title III, §3029(b)(7), June 9, 1998, 112 Stat. 372, related to transportation centers, prior to repeal by Pub. L. 105–178, title V, §5110(c), June 9, 1998, 112 Stat. 444.

§5318. BUS TESTING FACILITY

(a) FACILITY.—The Secretary shall maintain one facility for testing a new bus model for maintainability, reliability, safety, performance (including braking performance), structural integrity, fuel economy, emissions, and noise.

(b) OPERATION AND MAINTENANCE.—The Secretary shall enter into a contract or cooperative agreement with, or make a grant to, a qualified person or organization to operate and maintain the facility. The contract, cooperative agreement, or grant may provide for the testing of rail cars and other public transportation vehicles at the facility.

(c) FEES.—The person operating and maintaining the facility shall establish and collect fees for the testing of vehicles at the facility. The Secretary must approve the fees.

(d) AVAILABILITY OF AMOUNTS TO PAY FOR TESTING.—The Secretary shall enter into a contract or cooperative agreement with, or make a grant to, the operator of the facility under which the Secretary shall pay 80 percent of the cost of testing a vehicle at the facility from amounts available to carry out this section. The entity having the vehicle tested shall pay 20 percent of the cost.

(e) ACQUIRING NEW BUS MODELS.—

(1) IN GENERAL.—Amounts appropriated or otherwise made available under this chapter may be obligated or expended to acquire a new bus model only if—

(A) a bus of that model has been tested at a facility authorized under subsection (a); and

(B) the bus tested under subparagraph (A) met—

(i) performance standards for maintainability, reliability, performance (including braking performance), structural integrity, fuel economy, emissions, and noise, as established by the Secretary by rule; and

(ii) the minimum safety performance standards established by the Secretary pursuant to section 5329(b).

[§5319. Repealed. Pub. L. 114–94, div. A, title III, §3030(c), Dec. 4, 2015, 129 Stat. 1497]

CHAPTER 53—PUBLIC TRANSPORTATION

(2) BUS TEST "PASS/FAIL" STANDARD.—Not later than 2 years after the date of enactment of the Federal Public Transportation Act of 2012, the Secretary shall issue a final rule under subparagraph (B)(i). The final rule issued under paragraph [1] (B)(i) shall include a bus model scoring system that results in a weighted, aggregate score that uses the testing categories under subsection (a) and considers the relative importance of each such testing category. The final rule issued under subparagraph (B)(i) shall establish a "pass/fail" standard that uses the aggregate score described in the preceding sentence. Amounts appropriated or otherwise made available under this chapter may be obligated or expended to acquire a new bus model only if the new bus model has received a passing aggregate test score. The Secretary shall work with the bus testing facility, bus manufacturers, and transit agencies to develop the bus model scoring system under this paragraph. A passing aggregate test score under the rule issued under subparagraph (B)(i) indicates only that amounts appropriated or made available under this chapter may be obligated or expended to acquire a new bus model and shall not be interpreted as a warranty or guarantee that the new bus model will meet a purchaser's specific requirements.

(f) CAPITAL EQUIPMENT.—A facility operated and maintained under this section may use funds made available under this section for the acquisition of equipment and capital projects related to testing new bus models.

(Pub. L. 103–272, §1(d), July 5, 1994, 108 Stat. 817; Pub. L. 103–429, §6(8), Oct. 31, 1994, 108 Stat. 4378; Pub. L. 105–178, title III, §§3018, 3029(b)(8), June 9, 1998, 112 Stat. 361, 372; Pub. L. 109–59, title III, §§3002(b)(4), 3020, Aug. 10, 2005, 119 Stat. 1545, 1608; Pub. L. 112–141, div. B, §20014, July 6, 2012, 126 Stat. 694; Pub. L. 117–58, div. C, §30008, Nov. 15, 2021, 135 Stat. 903.)

[1] So in original. Probably should be "subparagraph".

[§5319. REPEALED. PUB. L. 114–94, DIV. A, TITLE III, §3030(C), DEC. 4, 2015, 129 STAT. 1497]

Section, Pub. L. 103–272, §1(d), July 5, 1994, 108 Stat. 818; Pub. L. 105–178, title III, §3019, June 9, 1998, 112 Stat. 362; Pub. L. 109–59, title III, §3002(b)(4), Aug. 10, 2005, 119 Stat. 1545; Pub. L. 110–244, title II, §201(h), June 6, 2008, 122 Stat. 1610; Pub. L. 112–141, div. B, §20030(c), July 6, 2012, 126 Stat. 730, made certain bicycle facilities eligible for assistance under sections 5307, 5309, and 5311 of this title.

[§5320. REPEALED. PUB. L. 112–141, DIV. B, §20002(A), JULY 6, 2012, 126 STAT. 622]

Section, added Pub. L. 109–59, title III, §3021(a), Aug. 10, 2005, 119 Stat. 1608; amended Pub. L. 110–244, title II, §201(i), June 6, 2008, 122 Stat. 1610, related to alternative transportation in parks and public lands.

A prior section 5320, Pub. L. 103–272, §1(d), July 5, 1994, 108 Stat. 818; Pub. L. 103–429, §6(9), Oct. 31, 1994, 108 Stat. 4379; Pub. L. 105–178, title III, §3009(h)(3)(A), June 9, 1998, 112 Stat. 356; Pub. L. 105–206, title IX, §9009(h)(1), July 22, 1998, 112 Stat. 856, related to construction of a suspended light rail system technology pilot project, prior to repeal by Pub. L. 109–59, title III, §3021(a), Aug. 10, 2005, 119 Stat. 1608.

§5321. Crime prevention and security

The Secretary of Transportation may make capital grants from amounts available under section 5338 of this title to public transportation systems for crime prevention and security. This chapter does not prevent the financing of a project under this section when a local governmental authority other than the grant applicant has law enforcement responsibilities.

(Pub. L. 103–272, §1(d), July 5, 1994, 108 Stat. 820; Pub. L. 109–59, title III, §3002(b)(4), Aug. 10, 2005, 119 Stat. 1545.)

[§5322. Repealed. Pub. L. 114–94, div. A, title III, §3030(d), Dec. 4, 2015, 129 Stat. 1497]

Section, Pub. L. 103–272, §1(d), July 5, 1994, 108 Stat. 820; Pub. L. 109–59, title III, §§3002(b)(4), 3022, Aug. 10, 2005, 119 Stat. 1545, 1614; Pub. L. 112–141, div. B, §20015, July 6, 2012, 126 Stat. 695, provided for programs that address human resource needs in public transportation activities.

§5323. General provisions

(a) Interests in Property.—

(1) In general.—Financial assistance provided under this chapter to a State or a local governmental authority may be used to acquire an interest in, or to buy property of, a private company engaged in public transportation, for a capital project for property acquired from a private company engaged in public transportation after July 9, 1964, or to operate a public transportation facility or equipment in competition with, or in addition to, transportation service provided by an existing public transportation company, only if—

(A) the Secretary determines that such financial assistance is essential to a program of projects required under sections 5303, 5304, and 5306;

(B) the Secretary determines that the program provides for the participation of private companies engaged in public transportation to the maximum extent feasible; and

(C) just compensation under State or local law will be paid to the company for its franchise or property.

(2) Limitation.—A governmental authority may not use financial assistance of the United States Government to acquire land, equipment, or a facility used in public transportation from another governmental authority in the same geographic area.

(b) Relocation and Real Property Requirements.—The Uniform Relocation Assistance and Real Property Acquisition Policies Act of 1970 (42 U.S.C. 4601 et seq.) shall apply to financial assistance for capital projects under this chapter.

(c) Consideration of Economic, Social, and Environmental Interests.—

(1) Cooperation and consultation.—The Secretary shall cooperate and consult with the Secretary of the Interior and the Administrator of the Environmental Protection Agency on each project that may have a substantial impact on the environment.

(2) Compliance with nepa.—The National Environmental Policy Act of 1969 (42 U.S.C. 4321 et seq.) shall apply to financial assistance for capital projects under this chapter.

(d) CONDITION ON CHARTER BUS TRANSPORTATION SERVICE.—

(1) AGREEMENTS.—Financial assistance under this chapter may be used to buy or operate a bus only if the applicant, governmental authority, or publicly owned operator that receives the assistance agrees that, except as provided in the agreement, the governmental authority or an operator of public transportation for the governmental authority will not provide charter bus transportation service outside the urban area in which it provides regularly scheduled public transportation service. An agreement shall provide for a fair arrangement the Secretary of Transportation considers appropriate to ensure that the assistance will not enable a governmental authority or an operator for a governmental authority to foreclose a private operator from providing intercity charter bus service if the private operator can provide the service.

(2) VIOLATIONS.—

(A) INVESTIGATIONS.—On receiving a complaint about a violation of the agreement required under paragraph (1), the Secretary shall investigate and decide whether a violation has occurred.

(B) ENFORCEMENT OF AGREEMENTS.—If the Secretary decides that a violation has occurred, the Secretary shall correct the violation under terms of the agreement.

(C) ADDITIONAL REMEDIES.—In addition to any remedy specified in the agreement, the Secretary shall bar a recipient or an operator from receiving Federal transit assistance in an amount the Secretary considers appropriate if the Secretary finds a pattern of violations of the agreement.

(e) BOND PROCEEDS ELIGIBLE FOR LOCAL SHARE.—

(1) USE AS LOCAL MATCHING FUNDS.—Notwithstanding any other provision of law, a recipient of assistance under section 5307, 5309, or 5337 may use the proceeds from the issuance of revenue bonds as part of the local matching funds for a capital project.

(2) MAINTENANCE OF EFFORT.—The Secretary shall approve of the use of the proceeds from the issuance of revenue bonds for the remainder of the net project cost only if the Secretary finds that the aggregate amount of financial support for public transportation in the urbanized area provided by the State and affected local governmental authorities during the next 3 fiscal years, as programmed in the State transportation improvement program under section 5304, is not less than the aggregate amount provided by the State and affected local governmental authorities in the urbanized area during the preceding 3 fiscal years.

(3) DEBT SERVICE RESERVE.—The Secretary may reimburse an eligible recipient for deposits of bond proceeds in a debt service reserve that the recipient establishes pursuant to section 5302(4)(J) from amounts made available to the recipient under section 5309.

(f) SCHOOLBUS TRANSPORTATION.—

(1) AGREEMENTS.—Financial assistance under this chapter may be used for a capital project, or to operate public transportation equipment or a public transportation facility, only if the applicant agrees not to provide schoolbus transportation that exclusively transports students and school personnel in competition with a private schoolbus operator. This subsection does not apply—

(A) to an applicant that operates a school system in the area to be served and a separate and exclusive schoolbus program for the school system; and

(B) unless a private schoolbus operator can provide adequate transportation that complies with applicable safety standards at reasonable rates.

(2) VIOLATIONS.—If the Secretary finds that an applicant, governmental authority, or publicly owned operator has violated the agreement required under paragraph (1), the Secretary shall bar a recipient or an operator from receiving Federal transit assistance in an amount the Secretary considers appropriate.

(g) BUYING BUSES UNDER OTHER LAWS.—Subsections (d) and (f) of this section apply to financial assistance to buy a bus under sections 133 and 142 of title 23.

(h) GRANT AND LOAN PROHIBITIONS.—A grant or loan may not be used to—

(1) pay ordinary governmental or nonproject operating expenses;

(2) pay incremental costs of incorporating art or non-functional landscaping into facilities, including the costs of an artist on the design team; or

(3) support a procurement that uses an exclusionary or discriminatory specification.

(i) GOVERNMENT SHARE OF COSTS FOR CERTAIN PROJECTS.—

(1) ACQUIRING VEHICLES AND VEHICLE-RELATED EQUIPMENT OR FACILITIES.—

(A) VEHICLES.—A grant for a project to be assisted under this chapter that involves acquiring vehicles for purposes of complying with or maintaining compliance with the Americans with Disabilities Act of 1990 (42 U.S.C. 12101 et seq.) or the Clean Air Act is for 85 percent of the net project cost.

(B) VEHICLE-RELATED EQUIPMENT OR FACILITIES.—A grant for a project to be assisted under this chapter that involves acquiring vehicle-related equipment or facilities required by the Americans with Disabilities Act of 1990 (42 U.S.C. 12101 et seq.) or vehicle-related equipment or facilities (including clean fuel or alternative fuel vehicle-related equipment or facilities) for purposes of complying with or maintaining compliance with the Clean Air Act, is for 90 percent of the net project cost of such equipment or facilities attributable to compliance with those Acts. The Secretary shall have discretion to determine, through practicable administrative procedures, the costs of such equipment or facilities attributable to compliance with those Acts.

(2) COSTS INCURRED BY PROVIDERS OF PUBLIC TRANSPORTATION BY VANPOOL.—

(A) LOCAL MATCHING SHARE.—The local matching share provided by a recipient of assistance for a capital project under this chapter may include any amounts expended by a provider of public transportation by vanpool for the acquisition of rolling stock to be used by such provider in the recipient's service area, excluding any amounts the provider may have received in Federal, State, or local government assistance for such acquisition.

(B) USE OF REVENUES.—A private provider of public transportation by vanpool may use revenues it receives in the provision of public transportation service in the service area of a recipient of assistance under this chapter that are in excess of the provider's operating costs for the purpose of acquiring rolling stock, if the private provider enters into a legally binding agreement with the recipient that requires the provider to use the rolling stock in the recipient's service area.

(C) DEFINITIONS.—In this paragraph, the following definitions apply:

(i) PRIVATE PROVIDER OF PUBLIC TRANSPORTATION BY VANPOOL.—The term "private provider of public transportation by vanpool" means a private entity providing vanpool services in the service area of a recipient of assistance under this chapter using a commuter highway vehicle or vanpool vehicle.

(ii) COMMUTER HIGHWAY VEHICLE; VANPOOL VEHICLE.—The term "commuter highway vehicle or vanpool vehicle" means any vehicle—

(I) the seating capacity of which is at least 6 adults (not including the driver); and

(II) at least 80 percent of the mileage use of which can be reasonably expected to be for the purposes of transporting commuters in connection with travel between their residences and their place of employment.

(j) BUY AMERICA.—

(1) IN GENERAL.—The Secretary may obligate an amount that may be appropriated to carry out this chapter for a project only if the steel, iron, and manufactured goods used in the project are produced in the United States.

(2) WAIVER.—The Secretary may waive paragraph (1) of this subsection if the Secretary finds that—

(A) applying paragraph (1) would be inconsistent with the public interest;

(B) the steel, iron, and goods produced in the United States are not produced in a sufficient and reasonably available amount or are not of a satisfactory quality;

(C) when procuring rolling stock (including train control, communication, traction power equipment, and rolling stock prototypes) under this chapter—

(i) the cost of components and subcomponents produced in the United States—

(I) for fiscal years 2016 and 2017, is more than 60 percent of the cost of all components of the rolling stock;

(II) for fiscal years 2018 and 2019, is more than 65 percent of the cost of all components of the rolling stock; and

(III) for fiscal year 2020 and each fiscal year thereafter, is more than 70 percent of the cost of all components of the rolling stock; and

(ii) final assembly of the rolling stock has occurred in the United States; or

(D) including domestic material will increase the cost of the overall project by more than 25 percent.

(3) WRITTEN WAIVER DETERMINATION AND ANNUAL REPORT.—

(A) WRITTEN DETERMINATION.—Before issuing a waiver under paragraph (2), the Secretary shall—

(i) publish in the Federal Register and make publicly available in an easily identifiable location on the website of the Department of Transportation a detailed written explanation of the waiver determination; and

(ii) provide the public with a reasonable period of time for notice and comment.

(B) ANNUAL REPORT.—Not later than 1 year after the date of enactment of the Federal Public Transportation Act of 2012, and annually thereafter, the Secretary shall submit to the Committee on Banking, Housing, and Urban Affairs of the Senate and the Committee on Transportation and Infrastructure of the House of Representatives a report listing any waiver issued under paragraph (2) during the preceding year.

(4) LABOR COSTS FOR FINAL ASSEMBLY.—In this subsection, labor costs involved in final assembly are not included in calculating the cost of components.

(5) ROLLING STOCK FRAMES OR CAR SHELLS.—In carrying out paragraph (2)(C) in the case of a rolling stock procurement receiving assistance under this chapter in which the average cost of a rolling stock vehicle in the procurement is more than $300,000, if rolling stock frames or car shells are not produced in the United States, the Secretary shall include in the calculation of the domestic content of the rolling stock the cost of steel or iron that is produced in the United States and used in the rolling stock frames or car shells.

(6) CERTIFICATION OF DOMESTIC SUPPLY AND DISCLOSURE.—

(A) CERTIFICATION OF DOMESTIC SUPPLY.—If the Secretary denies an application for a waiver under paragraph (2), the Secretary shall provide to the applicant a written certification that—

(i) the steel, iron, or manufactured goods, as applicable, (referred to in this subparagraph as the "item") is produced in the United States in a sufficient and reasonably available amount;

(ii) the item produced in the United States is of a satisfactory quality; and

(iii) includes a list of known manufacturers in the United States from which the item can be obtained.

(B) DISCLOSURE.—The Secretary shall disclose the waiver denial and the written certification to the public in an easily identifiable location on the website of the Department of Transportation.

(7) WAIVER PROHIBITED.—The Secretary may not make a waiver under paragraph (2) of this subsection for goods produced in a foreign country if the Secretary, in consultation with the United States Trade Representative, decides that the government of that foreign country—

(A) has an agreement with the United States Government under which the Secretary has waived the requirement of this subsection; and

(B) has violated the agreement by discriminating against goods to which this subsection applies that are produced in the United States and to which the agreement applies.

(8) PENALTY FOR MISLABELING AND MISREPRESENTATION.—A person is ineligible under subpart 9.4 of the Federal Acquisition Regulation, or any successor thereto, to receive a contract or subcontract made with amounts authorized under the Federal Public Transportation Act of 2015 if a court or department, agency, or instrumentality of the Government decides the person intentionally—

(A) affixed a "Made in America" label, or a label with an inscription having the same meaning, to goods sold in or shipped to the United States that are used in a project to which this subsection applies but not produced in the United States; or

(B) represented that goods described in subparagraph (A) of this paragraph were produced in the United States.

(9) STATE REQUIREMENTS.—The Secretary may not impose any limitation on assistance provided under this chapter that restricts a State from imposing more stringent requirements than this subsection on the use of articles, materials, and

supplies mined, produced, or manufactured in foreign countries in projects carried out with that assistance or restricts a recipient of that assistance from complying with those State-imposed requirements.

(10) OPPORTUNITY TO CORRECT INADVERTENT ERROR.—The Secretary may allow a manufacturer or supplier of steel, iron, or manufactured goods to correct after bid opening any certification of noncompliance or failure to properly complete the certification (but not including failure to sign the certification) under this subsection if such manufacturer or supplier attests under penalty of perjury that such manufacturer or supplier submitted an incorrect certification as a result of an inadvertent or clerical error. The burden of establishing inadvertent or clerical error is on the manufacturer or supplier.

(11) ADMINISTRATIVE REVIEW.—A party adversely affected by an agency action under this subsection shall have the right to seek review under section 702 of title 5.

(12) STEEL AND IRON.—For purposes of this subsection, steel and iron meeting the requirements of section 661.5(b) of title 49, Code of Federal Regulations may be considered produced in the United States.

(13) DEFINITION OF SMALL PURCHASE.—For purposes of determining whether a purchase qualifies for a general public interest waiver under paragraph (2)(A) of this subsection, including under any regulation promulgated under that paragraph, the term "small purchase" means a purchase of not more than $150,000.

(k) PARTICIPATION OF GOVERNMENTAL AGENCIES IN DESIGN AND DELIVERY OF TRANSPORTATION SERVICES.—Governmental agencies and nonprofit organizations that receive assistance from Government sources (other than the Department of Transportation) for nonemergency transportation services shall—

(1) participate and coordinate with recipients of assistance under this chapter in the design and delivery of transportation services; and

(2) be included in the planning for those services.

(l) RELATIONSHIP TO OTHER LAWS.—

(1) FRAUD AND FALSE STATEMENTS.—Section 1001 of title 18 applies to a certificate, submission, or statement provided under this chapter. The Secretary may terminate financial assistance under this chapter and seek reimbursement directly, or by offsetting amounts, available under this chapter if the Secretary determines that a recipient of such financial assistance has made a false or fraudulent statement or related act in connection with a Federal public transportation program.

(2) POLITICAL ACTIVITIES OF NONSUPERVISORY EMPLOYEES.—The provision of assistance under this chapter shall not be construed to require the application of chapter 15 of title 5 to any nonsupervisory employee of a public transportation system (or any other agency or entity performing related functions) to whom such chapter does not otherwise apply.

(m) PREAWARD AND POSTDELIVERY REVIEW OF ROLLING STOCK PURCHASES.—The Secretary shall prescribe regulations requiring a preaward and postdelivery review of a grant under this chapter to buy rolling stock to ensure compliance with Government motor vehicle safety requirements, subsection (j) of this section, and bid specifications requirements of grant recipients under this chapter. Under this subsection, independent inspections and review are required, and a manufacturer certification is not sufficient.

Rolling stock procurements of 20 vehicles or fewer made for the purpose of serving rural areas and urbanized areas with populations of 200,000 or fewer shall be subject to the same requirements as established for procurements of 10 or fewer buses under the post-delivery purchaser's requirements certification process under section 663.37(c) of title 49, Code of Federal Regulations.

(n) SUBMISSION OF CERTIFICATIONS.—A certification required under this chapter and any additional certification or assurance required by law or regulation to be submitted to the Secretary may be consolidated into a single document to be submitted annually as part of a grant application under this chapter. The Secretary shall publish annually a list of all certifications required under this chapter with the publication required under section 5336(d)(2).

(o) GRANT REQUIREMENTS.—The grant requirements under sections 5307, 5309, and 5337 apply to any project under this chapter that receives any assistance or other financing under chapter 6 (other than section 609) of title 23.

(p) ALTERNATIVE FUELING FACILITIES.—A recipient of assistance under this chapter may allow the incidental use of federally funded alternative fueling facilities and equipment by nontransit public entities and private entities if—

(1) the incidental use does not interfere with the recipient's public transportation operations;

(2) all costs related to the incidental use are fully recaptured by the recipient from the nontransit public entity or private entity;

(3) the recipient uses revenues received from the incidental use in excess of costs for planning, capital, and operating expenses that are incurred in providing public transportation; and

(4) private entities pay all applicable excise taxes on fuel.

(q) CORRIDOR PRESERVATION.—

(1) IN GENERAL.—The Secretary may assist a recipient in acquiring right-of-way before the completion of the environmental reviews for any project that may use the right-of-way if the acquisition is otherwise permitted under Federal law.

(2) ENVIRONMENTAL REVIEWS.—Right-of-way acquired under this subsection may not be developed in anticipation of the project until all required environmental reviews for the project have been completed.

(r) REASONABLE ACCESS TO PUBLIC TRANSPORTATION FACILITIES.—A recipient of assistance under this chapter may not deny reasonable access for a private intercity or charter transportation operator to federally funded public transportation facilities, including intermodal facilities, park and ride lots, and bus-only highway lanes. In determining reasonable access, capacity requirements of the recipient of assistance and the extent to which access would be detrimental to existing public transportation services must be considered.

(s) VALUE CAPTURE REVENUE ELIGIBLE FOR LOCAL SHARE.—Notwithstanding any other provision of law, a recipient of assistance under this chapter may use the revenue generated from value capture financing mechanisms as local matching funds for capital projects and operating costs eligible under this chapter.

(t) SPECIAL CONDITION ON CHARTER BUS TRANSPORTATION SERVICE.—If, in a fiscal year, the Secretary is prohibited by law from enforcing regulations related to charter bus service under part 604 of title 49, Code of Federal Regulations, for any transit agency that during fiscal year 2008 was both initially granted a 60-day period to come into compliance with such part 604, and then was subsequently granted an exception from such part—

(1) the transit agency shall be precluded from receiving its allocation of urbanized area formula grant funds for such fiscal year; and

(2) any amounts withheld pursuant to paragraph (1) shall be added to the amount that the Secretary may apportion under section 5336 in the following fiscal year.

(u) LIMITATION ON CERTAIN ROLLING STOCK PROCUREMENTS.—

(1) IN GENERAL.—Except as provided in paragraph (5), financial assistance made available under this chapter shall not be used in awarding a contract or subcontract to an entity on or after the date of enactment of this subsection for the procurement of rolling stock for use in public transportation if the manufacturer of the rolling stock—

(A) is incorporated in or has manufacturing facilities in the United States; and

(B) is owned or controlled by, is a subsidiary of, or is otherwise related legally or financially to a corporation based in a country that—

(i) is identified as a nonmarket economy country (as defined in section 771(18) of the Tariff Act of 1930 (19 U.S.C. 1677(18))) as of the date of enactment of this subsection;

(ii) was identified by the United States Trade Representative in the most recent report required by section 182 of the Trade Act of 1974 (19 U.S.C. 2242) as a foreign country included on the priority watch list defined in subsection (g)(3) of that section; and

(iii) is subject to monitoring by the Trade Representative under section 306 of the Trade Act of 1974 (19 U.S.C. 2416).

(2) EXCEPTION.—For purposes of paragraph (1), the term "otherwise related legally or financially" does not include—

(A) a minority relationship or investment; or

(B) relationship with or investment in a subsidiary, joint venture, or other entity based in a country described in paragraph (1)(B) that does not export rolling stock or components of rolling stock for use in the United States.

(3) INTERNATIONAL AGREEMENTS.—This subsection shall be applied in a manner consistent with the obligations of the United States under international agreements.

(4) CERTIFICATION FOR RAIL ROLLING STOCK.—

(A) IN GENERAL.—Except as provided in paragraph (5), as a condition of financial assistance made available in a fiscal year under section 5337, a recipient that operates rail fixed guideway service shall certify in that fiscal year that the recipient will not award any contract or subcontract for the procurement of rail rolling stock for use in public transportation with a rail rolling stock manufacturer described in paragraph (1).

(B) SEPARATE CERTIFICATION.—The certification required under this paragraph shall be in addition to any certification the Secretary establishes to ensure compliance with the requirements of paragraph (1).

(5) SPECIAL RULES.—

(A) PARTIES TO EXECUTED CONTRACTS.—This subsection, including the certification requirement under paragraph (4), shall not apply to the award of any contract or subcontract made by a public transportation agency with a rail rolling stock manufacturer described in paragraph (1) if the manufacturer and the public transportation agency have executed a contract for rail rolling stock before the date of enactment of this subsection.

(B) ROLLING STOCK.—Except as provided in subparagraph (C) and for a contract or subcontract that is not described in subparagraph (A), this subsection, including the certification requirement under paragraph (4), shall not apply to the award of a contract or subcontract made by a public transportation agency with any rolling stock manufacturer for the 2-year period beginning on or after the date of enactment of this subsection.

(C) EXCEPTION.—Subparagraph (B) shall not apply to the award of a contract or subcontract made by the Washington Metropolitan Area Transit Authority.

(v) CYBERSECURITY CERTIFICATION FOR RAIL ROLLING STOCK AND OPERATIONS.—

(1) CERTIFICATION.—As a condition of financial assistance made available under this chapter, a recipient that operates a rail fixed guideway public transportation system shall certify that the recipient has established a process to develop, maintain, and execute a written plan for identifying and reducing cybersecurity risks.

(2) COMPLIANCE.—For the process required under paragraph (1), a recipient of assistance under this chapter shall—

(A) utilize the approach described by the voluntary standards and best practices developed under section 2(c)(15) of the National Institute of Standards and Technology Act (15 U.S.C. 272(c)(15)), as applicable;

(B) identify hardware and software that the recipient determines should undergo third-party testing and analysis to mitigate cybersecurity risks, such as hardware or software for rail rolling stock under proposed procurements; and

(C) utilize the approach described in any voluntary standards and best practices for rail fixed guideway public transportation systems developed under the authority of the Secretary of Homeland Security, as applicable.

(3) LIMITATIONS ON STATUTORY CONSTRUCTION.—Nothing in this subsection shall be construed to interfere with the authority of—

(A) the Secretary of Homeland Security to publish or ensure compliance with requirements or standards concerning cybersecurity for rail fixed guideway public transportation systems; or

(B) the Secretary of Transportation under section 5329 to address cybersecurity issues as those issues relate to the safety of rail fixed guideway public transportation systems.

(Pub. L. 103–272, §1(d), July 5, 1994, 108 Stat. 821; Pub. L. 103–429, §6(10), Oct. 31, 1994, 108 Stat. 4379; Pub. L. 104–287, §5(15), Oct. 11, 1996, 110 Stat. 3390; Pub. L. 105–178, title III, §3020, June 9, 1998, 112 Stat. 362; Pub. L. 109–59, title III, §§3002(b)(4), 3023(a)–(i)(3), (j)–(m), Aug. 10, 2005, 119 Stat. 1545, 1615–1619; Pub. L. 110–244, title II, §201(j), June 6, 2008, 122 Stat. 1611; Pub. L. 112–141, div. B, §20016, July 6, 2012, 126 Stat. 697; Pub. L. 114–94, div. A, title III, §3011, Dec. 4, 2015, 129 Stat. 1474; Pub. L. 116–92, div. F, title LXXVI, §7613, Dec. 20, 2019, 133 Stat. 2314; Pub. L. 117–58, div. C, §§30001(b)(2), 30010, Nov. 15, 2021, 135 Stat. 890, 904.)

§5324. PUBLIC TRANSPORTATION EMERGENCY RELIEF PROGRAM

(a) DEFINITION.—In this section the following definitions shall apply:

(1) ELIGIBLE OPERATING COSTS.—The term "eligible operating costs" means costs relating to—

(A) evacuation services;

(B) rescue operations;

(C) temporary public transportation service; or

(D) reestablishing, expanding, or relocating public transportation route service before, during, or after an emergency.

(2) EMERGENCY.—The term "emergency" means a natural disaster affecting a wide area (such as a flood, hurricane, tidal wave, earthquake, severe storm, or landslide) or a catastrophic failure from any external cause, as a result of which—

(A) the Governor of a State has declared an emergency and the Secretary has concurred; or

(B) the President has declared a major disaster under section 401 of the Robert T. Stafford Disaster Relief and Emergency Assistance Act (42 U.S.C. 5170).

(b) GENERAL AUTHORITY.—The Secretary may make grants and enter into contracts and other agreements (including agreements with departments, agencies, and instrumentalities of the Government) for—

(1) capital projects to protect, repair, reconstruct, or replace equipment and facilities of a public transportation system operating in the United States or on an Indian reservation that the Secretary determines is in danger of suffering serious damage, or has suffered serious damage, as a result of an emergency; and

(2) eligible operating costs of public transportation equipment and facilities in an area directly affected by an emergency during—

(A) the 1-year period beginning on the date of a declaration described in subsection (a)(2); or

(B) if the Secretary determines there is a compelling need, the 2-year period beginning on the date of a declaration described in subsection (a)(2).

(c) COORDINATION OF EMERGENCY FUNDS.—

(1) USE OF FUNDS.—Funds appropriated to carry out this section shall be in addition to any other funds available under this chapter.

(2) NO EFFECT ON OTHER GOVERNMENT ACTIVITY.—The provision of funds under this section shall not affect the ability of any other agency of the Government, including the Federal Emergency Management Agency, or a State agency, a local governmental entity, organization, or person, to provide any other funds otherwise authorized by law.

(3) NOTIFICATION.—The Secretary shall notify the Secretary of Homeland Security of the purpose and amount of any grant made or contract or other agreement entered into under this section.

(d) GRANT REQUIREMENTS.—A grant awarded under this section or under section 5307 or 5311 that is made to address an emergency defined under subsection (a)(2) shall be—

(1) subject to the terms and conditions the Secretary determines are necessary; and

(2) made only for expenses that are not reimbursed under the Robert T. Stafford

Disaster Relief and Emergency Assistance Act (42 U.S.C. 5121 et seq.).

(e) GOVERNMENT SHARE OF COSTS.—

(1) CAPITAL PROJECTS AND OPERATING ASSISTANCE.—A grant, contract, or other agreement for a capital project or eligible operating costs under this section shall be, at the option of the recipient, for not more than 80 percent of the net project cost, as determined by the Secretary.

(2) NON-FEDERAL SHARE.—The remainder of the net project cost may be provided from an undistributed cash surplus, a replacement or depreciation cash fund or reserve, or new capital.

(3) WAIVER.—The Secretary may waive, in whole or part, the non-Federal share required under—

(A) paragraph (2); or

(B) section 5307 or 5311, in the case of a grant made available under section 5307 or 5311, respectively, to address an emergency.

(f) INSURANCE.—Before receiving a grant under this section following an emergency, an applicant shall—

(1) submit to the Secretary documentation demonstrating proof of insurance required under Federal law for all structures related to the grant application; and

(2) certify to the Secretary that the applicant has insurance required under State law for all structures related to the grant application.

(Pub. L. 103–272, §1(d), July 5, 1994, 108 Stat. 824; Pub. L. 109–59, title III, §3024(a), Aug. 10, 2005, 119 Stat. 1619; Pub. L. 112–141, div. B, §20017(a), July 6, 2012, 126 Stat. 703; Pub. L. 117–58, div. C, §30011, Nov. 15, 2021, 135 Stat. 904.)

§5325. CONTRACT REQUIREMENTS

(a) COMPETITION.—Recipients of assistance under this chapter shall conduct all procurement transactions in a manner that provides full and open competition as determined by the Secretary.

(b) ARCHITECTURAL, ENGINEERING, AND DESIGN CONTRACTS.—

(1) PROCEDURES FOR AWARDING CONTRACT.—A contract or requirement for program management, architectural engineering, construction management, a feasibility study, and preliminary engineering, design, architectural, engineering, surveying, mapping, or related services for a project for which Federal assistance is provided under this chapter shall be awarded in the same way as a contract for architectural and engineering services is negotiated under chapter 11 of title 40 or an equivalent qualifications-based requirement of a State adopted before August 10, 2005.

(2) ADDITIONAL REQUIREMENTS.—When awarding a contract described in paragraph (1), recipients of assistance under this chapter shall comply with the following requirements:

(A) PERFORMANCE OF AUDITS.—Any contract or subcontract awarded under this chapter shall be performed and audited in compliance with cost principles contained in part 31 of the Federal Acquisition Regulation, or any successor thereto.

(B) INDIRECT COST RATES.—A recipient of funds under a contract or subcontract awarded under this chapter shall accept indirect cost rates established in accordance with the Federal Acquisition Regulation for 1-year applicable accounting periods by a cognizant Federal or State government agency, if such rates are not currently under dispute.

    (C) APPLICATION OF RATES.—After a firm's indirect cost rates are accepted under subparagraph (B), the recipient of the funds shall apply such rates for the purposes of contract estimation, negotiation, administration, reporting, and contract payment, and shall not be limited by administrative or de facto ceilings.

    (D) PRENOTIFICATION; CONFIDENTIALITY OF DATA.—A recipient requesting or using the cost and rate data described in subparagraph (C) shall notify any affected firm before such request or use. Such data shall be confidential and shall not be accessible or provided by the group of agencies sharing cost data under this subparagraph, except by written permission of the audited firm. If prohibited by law, such cost and rate data shall not be disclosed under any circumstances.

  (c) EFFICIENT PROCUREMENT.—A recipient may award a procurement contract under this chapter to other than the lowest bidder if the award furthers an objective consistent with the purposes of this chapter, including improved long-term operating efficiency and lower long-term costs.

  (d) DESIGN-BUILD PROJECTS.—

    (1) TERM DEFINED.—In this subsection, the term "design-build project"—

    (A) means a project under which a recipient enters into a contract with a seller, firm, or consortium of firms to design and build a public transportation system, or an operable segment of such system, that meets specific performance criteria; and

    (B) may include an option to finance, or operate for a period of time, the system or segment or any combination of designing, building, operating, or maintaining such system or segment.

    (2) FINANCIAL ASSISTANCE FOR CAPITAL COSTS.—Federal financial assistance under this chapter may be provided for the capital costs of a design-build project after the recipient complies with Government requirements.

  (e) MULTIYEAR ROLLING STOCK.—

    (1) CONTRACTS.—A recipient procuring rolling stock with Government financial assistance under this chapter may make a multiyear contract to buy the rolling stock and replacement parts under which the recipient has an option to buy additional rolling stock or replacement parts for—

    (A) not more than 5 years after the date of the original contract for bus procurements; and

    (B) not more than 7 years after the date of the original contract for rail procurements, provided that such option does not allow for significant changes or alterations to the rolling stock.

    (2) COOPERATION AMONG RECIPIENTS.—The Secretary shall allow recipients to act on a cooperative basis to procure rolling stock in compliance with this subsection and other Government procurement requirements.

  (f) ACQUIRING ROLLING STOCK.—A recipient of financial assistance under this chapter may enter into a contract to expend that assistance to acquire rolling stock—

    (1) based on—

    (A) initial capital costs; or

(B) performance, standardization, life cycle costs, and other factors; or

(2) with a party selected through a competitive procurement process.

(g) EXAMINATION OF RECORDS.—Upon request, the Secretary and the Comptroller General, or any of their representatives, shall have access to and the right to examine and inspect all records, documents, and papers, including contracts, related to a project for which a grant is made under this chapter.

(h) GRANT PROHIBITION.—A grant awarded under this chapter or the Federal Public Transportation Act of 2015 may not be used to support a procurement that uses an exclusionary or discriminatory specification.

(i) BUS DEALER REQUIREMENTS.—No State law requiring buses to be purchased through in-State dealers shall apply to vehicles purchased with a grant under this chapter.

(j) AWARDS TO RESPONSIBLE CONTRACTORS.—

(1) IN GENERAL.—Federal financial assistance under this chapter may be provided for contracts only if a recipient awards such contracts to responsible contractors possessing the ability to successfully perform under the terms and conditions of a proposed procurement.

(2) CRITERIA.—Before making an award to a contractor under paragraph (1), a recipient shall consider—

(A) the integrity of the contractor;

(B) the contractor's compliance with public policy;

(C) the contractor's past performance; and

(D) the contractor's financial and technical resources.

(k) VETERANS EMPLOYMENT.—Recipients and subrecipients of Federal financial assistance under this chapter shall ensure that contractors working on a capital project funded using such assistance give a hiring preference, to the extent practicable, to veterans (as defined in section 2108 of title 5) who have the requisite skills and abilities to perform the construction work required under the contract. This subsection shall not be understood, construed or enforced in any manner that would require an employer to give a preference to any veteran over any equally qualified applicant who is a member of any racial or ethnic minority, female, an individual with a disability, or a former employee.

(Pub. L. 103–272, §1(d), July 5, 1994, 108 Stat. 825; Pub. L. 104–287, §5(16), Oct. 11, 1996, 110 Stat. 3390; Pub. L. 105–178, title III, §3022, June 9, 1998, 112 Stat. 363; Pub. L. 105–206, title IX, §9009(n), July 22, 1998, 112 Stat. 857; Pub. L. 107–217, §3(n)(2), Aug. 21, 2002, 116 Stat. 1302; Pub. L. 109–59, title III, §3025(a), Aug. 10, 2005, 119 Stat. 1620; Pub. L. 110–244, title II, §201(k), June 6, 2008, 122 Stat. 1611; Pub. L. 112–141, div. B, §§20018, 20030(d), July 6, 2012, 126 Stat. 706, 730; Pub. L. 114–94, div. A, title III, §3030(e), Dec. 4, 2015, 129 Stat. 1497.)

§5326. TRANSIT ASSET MANAGEMENT

(a) DEFINITIONS.—In this section the following definitions shall apply:

(1) CAPITAL ASSET.—The term "capital asset" includes equipment, rolling stock, infrastructure, and facilities for use in public transportation and owned or leased by a recipient or subrecipient of Federal financial assistance under this chapter.

(2) TRANSIT ASSET MANAGEMENT PLAN.—The term "transit asset management plan" means a plan developed by a recipient of funding under this chapter that—

(A) includes, at a minimum, capital asset inventories and condition assessments, decision support tools, and investment prioritization; and

(B) the recipient certifies complies with the rule issued under this section.

(3) TRANSIT ASSET MANAGEMENT SYSTEM.—The term "transit asset management system" means a strategic and systematic process of operating, maintaining, and improving public transportation capital assets effectively throughout the life cycle of such assets.

(b) TRANSIT ASSET MANAGEMENT SYSTEM.—The Secretary shall establish and implement a national transit asset management system, which shall include—

(1) a definition of the term "state of good repair" that includes objective standards for measuring the condition of capital assets of recipients, including equipment, rolling stock, infrastructure, and facilities;

(2) a requirement that recipients and subrecipients of Federal financial assistance under this chapter develop a transit asset management plan;

(3) a requirement that each designated recipient of Federal financial assistance under this chapter report on the condition of the system of the recipient and provide a description of any change in condition since the last report;

(4) an analytical process or decision support tool for use by public transportation systems that—

(A) allows for the estimation of capital investment needs of such systems over time; and

(B) assists with asset investment prioritization by such systems; and

(5) technical assistance to recipients of Federal financial assistance under this chapter.

(c) PERFORMANCE MEASURES AND TARGETS.—

(1) IN GENERAL.—Not later than 1 year after the date of enactment of the Federal Public Transportation Act of 2012, the Secretary shall issue a final rule to establish performance measures based on the state of good repair standards established under subsection (b)(1).

(2) TARGETS.—Not later than 3 months after the date on which the Secretary issues a final rule under paragraph (1), and each fiscal year thereafter, each recipient of Federal financial assistance under this chapter shall establish performance targets in relation to the performance measures established by the Secretary.

(3) REPORTS.—Each designated recipient of Federal financial assistance under this chapter shall submit to the Secretary an annual report that describes—

(A) the progress of the recipient during the fiscal year to which the report relates toward meeting the performance targets established under paragraph (2) for that fiscal year; and

(B) the performance targets established by the recipient for the subsequent fiscal year.

(d) RULEMAKING.—Not later than 1 year after the date of enactment of the Federal Public Transportation Act of 2012, the Secretary shall issue a final rule to implement the transit asset management system described in subsection (b).

(Added Pub. L. 112–141, div. B, §20019, July 6, 2012, 126 Stat. 707.)

§5327. PROJECT MANAGEMENT OVERSIGHT

(a) PROJECT MANAGEMENT PLAN REQUIREMENTS.—To receive Federal financial assistance for a major capital project for public transportation under this chapter or any other provision of Federal law, a recipient must prepare a project management plan approved by the Secretary and carry out the project in accordance with the project management plan. The plan shall provide for—

(1) adequate recipient staff organization with well-defined reporting relationships, statements of functional responsibilities, job descriptions, and job qualifications;

(2) a budget covering the project management organization, appropriate consultants, property acquisition, utility relocation, systems demonstration staff, audits, and miscellaneous payments the recipient may be prepared to justify;

(3) a construction schedule for the project;

(4) a document control procedure and recordkeeping system;

(5) a change order procedure that includes a documented, systematic approach to the handling of construction change orders;

(6) organizational structures, management skills, and staffing levels required throughout the construction phase;

(7) quality control and quality assurance functions, procedures, and responsibilities for construction, system installation, and integration of system components;

(8) material testing policies and procedures;

(9) internal plan implementation and reporting requirements;

(10) criteria and procedures to be used for testing the operational system or its major components;

(11) periodic updates of the plan, especially related to project budget and project schedule, financing, ridership estimates, and the status of local efforts to enhance ridership where ridership estimates partly depend on the success of those efforts;

(12) the recipient's commitment to submit a project budget and project schedule to the Secretary quarterly; and

(13) safety and security management.

(b) PLAN APPROVAL.—(1) The Secretary shall approve a plan not later than 60 days after it is submitted. If the approval cannot be completed within 60 days, the Secretary shall notify the recipient, explain the reasons for the delay, and estimate the additional time that will be required.

(2) The Secretary shall inform the recipient of the reasons when a plan is disapproved.

(c) ACCESS TO SITES AND RECORDS.—Each recipient of Federal financial assistance for public transportation under this chapter or any other provision of Federal law shall provide the Secretary and a contractor the Secretary chooses under section 5338(f) [1] with access to the construction sites and records of the recipient when reasonably necessary.

(d) REGULATIONS.—The Secretary shall prescribe regulations necessary to carry out this section. The regulations shall include—

(1) a definition of "major capital project" for section 5338(f) [1] that excludes a project to acquire rolling stock or to maintain or rehabilitate a vehicle;

(2) a requirement that oversight—

(A) begin during the project development phase of a project, unless the Secretary finds it more appropriate to begin the oversight during another phase of the project, to maximize the transportation benefits and cost savings associated with project management oversight; and

(B) be limited to quarterly reviews of compliance by the recipient with the project management plan approved under subsection (b) unless the Secretary finds that the recipient requires more frequent oversight because the recipient has failed to meet the requirements of such plan and the project may be at risk of going over budget or becoming behind schedule; and

(3) a process for recipients that the Secretary has found require more frequent oversight to return to quarterly reviews for purposes of paragraph (2)(B).

(Pub. L. 103–272, §1(d), July 5, 1994, 108 Stat. 826; Pub. L. 103–429, §6(12), Oct. 31, 1994, 108 Stat. 4379; Pub. L. 104–287, §5(17), Oct. 11, 1996, 110 Stat. 3390; Pub. L. 105–178, title III, §3024, June 9, 1998, 112 Stat. 364; Pub. L. 109–59, title III, §3026, Aug. 10, 2005, 119 Stat. 1622; Pub. L. 112–141, div. B, §20020, July 6, 2012, 126 Stat. 708; Pub. L. 114–94, div. A, title III, §3012, Dec. 4, 2015, 129 Stat. 1475.)

¹ See References in Text note below.

[§5328. REPEALED. PUB. L. 112–141, DIV. B, §20002(A), JULY 6, 2012, 126 STAT. 622]

Section, Pub. L. 103–272, §1(d), July 5, 1994, 108 Stat. 828; Pub. L. 104–205, title III, §336, Sept. 30, 1996, 110 Stat. 2974; Pub. L. 104–287, §5(9), Oct. 11, 1996, 110 Stat. 3389; Pub. L. 105–178, title III, §3009(h)(2), (3)(B), (C), June 9, 1998, 112 Stat. 356; Pub. L. 105–206, title IX, §9009(h)(2), (3), July 22, 1998, 112 Stat. 856; Pub. L. 109–59, title III, §3027, Aug. 10, 2005, 119 Stat. 1623, related to project review and advancement by the Secretary.

§5329. PUBLIC TRANSPORTATION SAFETY PROGRAM

(a) DEFINITION.—In this section, the term "recipient" means a State or local governmental authority, or any other operator of a public transportation system, that receives financial assistance under this chapter.

(b) NATIONAL PUBLIC TRANSPORTATION SAFETY PLAN.—

(1) IN GENERAL.—The Secretary shall create and implement a national public transportation safety plan to improve the safety of all public transportation systems that receive funding under this chapter.

(2) CONTENTS OF PLAN.—The national public transportation safety plan under paragraph (1) shall include—

(A) safety performance criteria for all modes of public transportation, or, in the case of a recipient receiving assistance under section 5307 that is serving an urbanized area with a population of 200,000 or more, safety performance measures, including measures related to the risk reduction program under subsection (d)(1)(I), for all modes of public transportation;

(B) the definition of the term "state of good repair" established under section 5326(b);

(C) minimum safety performance standards for public transportation vehicles used in revenue operations that—

(i) do not apply to rolling stock otherwise regulated by the Secretary or any other Federal agency; and

(ii) to the extent practicable, take into consideration—

(I) relevant recommendations of the National Transportation Safety Board;

(II) recommendations of, and best practices standards developed by, the public transportation industry; and

(III) innovations in driver assistance technologies and driver protection infrastructure, where appropriate, and a reduction in visibility impairments that contribute to pedestrian fatalities;

(D) in consultation with the Secretary of Health and Human Services, precautionary and reactive actions required to ensure public and personnel safety and health during an emergency (as defined in section 5324(a));

(E) minimum safety standards to ensure the safe operation of public transportation systems that—

(i) are not related to performance standards for public transportation vehicles developed under subparagraph (C); and

(ii) to the extent practicable, take into consideration—

(I) relevant recommendations of the National Transportation Safety Board;

(II) best practices standards developed by the public transportation industry;

(III) any minimum safety standards or performance criteria being implemented across the public transportation industry;

(IV) relevant recommendations from the report under section 3020 of the Federal Public Transportation Act of 2015; and

(V) any additional information that the Secretary determines necessary and appropriate;

(F) a public transportation safety certification training program, as described in subsection (c); and

(G) consideration, where appropriate, of performance-based and risk-based methodologies.

(3) PLAN UPDATES.—The Secretary shall update the national public transportation safety plan under paragraph (1) as necessary with respect to recipients receiving assistance under section 5307 that serve an urbanized area with a population of 200,000 or more.

(c) PUBLIC TRANSPORTATION SAFETY CERTIFICATION TRAINING PROGRAM.—The Secretary shall establish a public transportation safety certification training program for Federal and State employees, or other designated personnel, who conduct safety audits and examinations of public transportation systems and employees of public transportation agencies directly responsible for safety oversight.

(d) PUBLIC TRANSPORTATION AGENCY SAFETY PLAN.—

(1) IN GENERAL.—Each recipient or State, as described in paragraph (3), shall certify that the recipient or State has established a comprehensive agency safety plan that includes, at a minimum—

(A) a requirement that the board of directors (or equivalent entity) of the recipient approve, or, in the case of a recipient receiving assistance under section

5307 that is serving an urbanized area with a population of 200,000 or more, the safety committee of the entity established under paragraph (5), followed by the board of directors (or equivalent entity) of the recipient approve, the agency safety plan and any updates to the agency safety plan;

(B) for each recipient serving an urbanized area with a population of fewer than 200,000, a requirement that the agency safety plan be developed in cooperation with frontline employee representatives;

(C) methods for identifying and evaluating safety risks throughout all elements of the public transportation system of the recipient;

(D) strategies to minimize the exposure of the public, personnel, and property to hazards and unsafe conditions, and consistent with guidelines of the Centers for Disease Control and Prevention or a State health authority, minimize exposure to infectious diseases;

(E) a process and timeline for conducting an annual review and update of the safety plan of the recipient;

(F) performance targets based on—

(i) the safety performance criteria and state of good repair standards established under subparagraphs (A) and (B), respectively, of subsection (b)(2); or

(ii) in the case of a recipient receiving assistance under section 5307 that is serving an urbanized area with a population of 200,000 or more, safety performance measures established under the national public transportation safety plan, as described in subsection (b)(2)(A);

(G) assignment of an adequately trained safety officer who reports directly to the general manager, president, or equivalent officer of the recipient;

(H) a comprehensive staff training program for—

(i) the operations personnel and personnel directly responsible for safety of the recipient that includes—

(I) the completion of a safety training program; and

(II) continuing safety education and training; or

(ii) in the case of a recipient receiving assistance under section 5307 that is serving an urbanized area with a population of 200,000 or more, the operations and maintenance personnel and personnel directly responsible for safety of the recipient that includes—

(I) the completion of a safety training program;

(II) continuing safety education and training; and

(III) de-escalation training; and

(I) in the case of a recipient receiving assistance under section 5307 that is serving an urbanized area with a population of 200,000 or more, a risk reduction program for transit operations to improve safety by reducing the number and rates of accidents, injuries, and assaults on transit workers based on data submitted to the national transit database under section 5335, including—

(i) a reduction of vehicular and pedestrian accidents involving buses that includes measures to reduce visibility impairments for bus operators that contribute to accidents, including retrofits to buses in revenue service and specifications for future procurements that reduce visibility impairments; and

(ii) the mitigation of assaults on transit workers, including the deployment of assault mitigation infrastructure and technology on buses, including barriers to restrict the unwanted entry of individuals and objects into the workstations of bus operators when a risk analysis performed by the safety committee of the recipient established under paragraph (5) determines that such barriers or other measures would reduce assaults on transit workers and injuries to transit workers.

(2) INTERIM AGENCY SAFETY PLAN.—A system safety plan developed pursuant to part 659 of title 49, Code of Federal Regulations, as in effect on the date of enactment of the Federal Public Transportation Act of 2012, shall remain in effect until such time as this subsection takes effect.

(3) PUBLIC TRANSPORTATION AGENCY SAFETY PLAN DRAFTING AND CERTIFICATION,—

(A) SECTION 5311.—For a recipient receiving assistance under section 5311, a State safety plan may be drafted and certified by the recipient or a State.

(B) SECTION 5307.—Not later than 120 days after the date of enactment of the Federal Public Transportation Act of 2012, the Secretary shall issue a rule designating recipients of assistance under section 5307 that are small public transportation providers or systems that may have their State safety plans drafted or certified by a State.

(4) RISK REDUCTION PERFORMANCE TARGETS.—

(A) IN GENERAL.—The safety committee of a recipient receiving assistance under section 5307 that is serving an urbanized area with a population of 200,000 or more established under paragraph (5) shall establish performance targets for the risk reduction program required under paragraph (1)(I) using a 3-year rolling average of the data submitted by the recipient to the national transit database under section 5335.

(B) SAFETY SET ASIDE.—A recipient receiving assistance under section 5307 that is serving an urbanized area with a population of 200,000 or more shall allocate not less than 0.75 percent of those funds to safety-related projects eligible under section 5307.

(C) FAILURE TO MEET PERFORMANCE TARGETS.—A recipient receiving assistance under section 5307 that is serving an urbanized area with a population of 200,000 or more that does not meet the performance targets established under subparagraph (A) shall allocate the amount made available in subparagraph (B) in the following fiscal year to projects described in subparagraph (D).

(D) ELIGIBLE PROJECTS.—Funds set aside under subparagraph (C) shall be used for projects that are reasonably likely to assist the recipient in meeting the performance targets established in subparagraph (A), including modifications to rolling stock and de-escalation training.

(5) SAFETY COMMITTEE.—

(A) IN GENERAL.—For purposes of this subsection, the safety committee of a recipient shall—

(i) be convened by a joint labor-management process;

(ii) consist of an equal number of—

(I) frontline employee representatives, selected by a labor organization representing the plurality of the frontline workforce employed by the recipient or, if applicable, a contractor to the recipient, to the extent frontline employees are represented by labor organizations; and

(II) management representatives; and

(iii) have, at a minimum, responsibility for—

(I) identifying and recommending risk-based mitigations or strategies necessary to reduce the likelihood and severity of consequences identified through the agency's safety risk assessment;

(II) identifying mitigations or strategies that may be ineffective, inappropriate, or were not implemented as intended; and

(III) identifying safety deficiencies for purposes of continuous improvement.

(B) APPLICABILITY.—This paragraph applies only to a recipient receiving assistance under section 5307 that is serving an urbanized area with a population of 200,000 or more.

(e) STATE SAFETY OVERSIGHT PROGRAM.—

(1) APPLICABILITY.—This subsection applies only to eligible States.

(2) DEFINITION.—In this subsection, the term "eligible State" means a State that has—

(A) a rail fixed guideway public transportation system within the jurisdiction of the State that is not subject to regulation by the Federal Railroad Administration; or

(B) a rail fixed guideway public transportation system in the engineering or construction phase of development within the jurisdiction of the State that will not be subject to regulation by the Federal Railroad Administration.

(3) IN GENERAL.—In order to obligate funds apportioned under section 5338 to carry out this chapter, effective 3 years after the date on which a final rule under this subsection becomes effective, an eligible State shall have in effect a State safety oversight program approved by the Secretary under which the State—

(A) assumes responsibility for overseeing rail fixed guideway public transportation safety;

(B) adopts and enforces Federal and relevant State laws on rail fixed guideway public transportation safety;

(C) establishes a State safety oversight agency;

(D) determines, in consultation with the Secretary, an appropriate staffing level for the State safety oversight agency that is commensurate with the number, size, and complexity of the rail fixed guideway public transportation systems in the eligible State;

(E) requires that employees and other designated personnel of the eligible State safety oversight agency who are responsible for rail fixed guideway public transportation safety oversight are qualified to perform such functions through appropriate training, including successful completion of the public transportation safety certification training program established under subsection (c); and

(F) prohibits any public transportation agency from providing funds to the State safety oversight agency or an entity designated by the eligible State as the State safety oversight agency under paragraph (4).

(4) STATE SAFETY OVERSIGHT AGENCY.—

(A) IN GENERAL.—Each State safety oversight program shall establish a State safety oversight agency that—

(i) is financially and legally independent from any public transportation entity that the State safety oversight agency oversees;

(ii) does not directly provide public transportation services in an area with a rail fixed guideway public transportation system subject to the requirements of this section;

(iii) does not employ any individual who is also responsible for the administration of rail fixed guideway public transportation programs subject to the requirements of this section;

(iv) has the authority to review, approve, oversee, and enforce the implementation by the rail fixed guideway public transportation agency of the public transportation agency safety plan required under subsection (d);

(v) has investigative, inspection, and enforcement authority with respect to the safety of rail fixed guideway public transportation systems of the eligible State;

(vi) audits, at least once triennially, the compliance of the rail fixed guideway public transportation systems in the eligible State subject to this subsection with the public transportation agency safety plan required under subsection (d); and

(vii) provides, at least once annually, a status report on the safety of the rail fixed guideway public transportation systems the State safety oversight agency oversees to—

(I) the Federal Transit Administration;

(II) the Governor of the eligible State; and

(III) the board of directors, or equivalent entity, of any rail fixed guideway public transportation system that the State safety oversight agency oversees.

(B) WAIVER.—At the request of an eligible State, the Secretary may waive clauses (i) and (iii) of subparagraph (A) for eligible States with 1 or more rail fixed guideway systems in revenue operations, design, or construction, that—

(i) have fewer than 1,000,000 combined actual and projected rail fixed guideway revenue miles per year; or

(ii) provide fewer than 10,000,000 combined actual and projected unlinked passenger trips per year.

(5) PROGRAMS FOR MULTI-STATE RAIL FIXED GUIDEWAY PUBLIC TRANSPORTATION SYSTEMS.—An eligible State that has within the jurisdiction of the eligible State a rail fixed guideway public transportation system that operates in more than 1 eligible State shall—

(A) jointly with all other eligible States in which the rail fixed guideway public transportation system operates, ensure uniform safety standards and enforcement procedures that shall be in compliance with this section, and establish and implement a State safety oversight program approved by the Secretary; or

(B) jointly with all other eligible States in which the rail fixed guideway public transportation system operates, designate an entity having characteristics consistent with the characteristics described in paragraph (3) to carry out the State safety oversight program approved by the Secretary.

(6) GRANTS.—

(A) IN GENERAL.—The Secretary shall make grants to eligible States to develop or carry out State safety oversight programs under this subsection. Grant funds may be used for program operational and administrative expenses, including employee training activities.

(B) APPORTIONMENT.—

(i) FORMULA.—The amount made available for State safety oversight under section 5336(h) shall be apportioned among eligible States under a formula to be established by the Secretary. Such formula shall take into account fixed guideway vehicle revenue miles, fixed guideway route miles, and fixed guideway vehicle passenger miles attributable to all rail fixed guideway systems not subject to regulation by the Federal Railroad Administration within each eligible State.

(ii) ADMINISTRATIVE REQUIREMENTS.—Grant funds apportioned to States under this paragraph shall be subject to uniform administrative requirements for grants and cooperative agreements to State and local governments under part 18 of title 49, Code of Federal Regulations, and shall be subject to the requirements of this chapter as the Secretary determines appropriate.

(C) GOVERNMENT SHARE.—

(i) IN GENERAL.—The Government share of the reasonable cost of a State safety oversight program developed or carried out using a grant under this paragraph shall be 80 percent.

(ii) IN-KIND CONTRIBUTIONS.—Any calculation of the non-Government share of a State safety oversight program shall include in-kind contributions by an eligible State.

(iii) NON-GOVERNMENT SHARE.—The non-Government share of the cost of a State safety oversight program developed or carried out using a grant under this paragraph may not be met by—

(I) any Federal funds;

(II) any funds received from a public transportation agency; or

(III) any revenues earned by a public transportation agency.

(iv) SAFETY TRAINING PROGRAM.—Recipients of funds made available to carry out sections 5307 and 5311 may use not more than 0.5 percent of their formula funds to pay not more than 80 percent of the cost of participation in the public transportation safety certification training program established under subsection (c), by an employee of a State safety oversight agency or a recipient who is directly responsible for safety oversight.

(7) CERTIFICATION PROCESS.—

(A) IN GENERAL.—Not later than 1 year after the date of enactment of the Federal Public Transportation Act of 2012, the Secretary shall determine whether or not each State safety oversight program meets the requirements of this subsection and the State safety oversight program is adequate to promote the purposes of this section.

(B) ISSUANCE OF CERTIFICATIONS AND DENIALS.—The Secretary shall issue a certification to each eligible State that the Secretary determines under subparagraph (A) adequately meets the requirements of this subsection, and shall issue a denial of certification to each eligible State that the Secretary determines under subparagraph (A) does not adequately meet the requirements of this subsection.

(C) DISAPPROVAL.—If the Secretary determines that a State safety oversight program does not meet the requirements of this subsection and denies certification, the Secretary shall transmit to the eligible State a written explanation and allow the eligible State to modify and resubmit the State safety oversight program for approval.

(D) FAILURE TO CORRECT.—If the Secretary determines that a modification by an eligible State of the State safety oversight program is not sufficient to certify the program, the Secretary—

(i) shall notify the Governor of the eligible State of such denial of certification and failure to adequately modify the program, and shall request that the Governor take all possible actions to correct deficiencies in the program to ensure the certification of the program; and

(ii) may—

(I) withhold funds available under paragraph (6) in an amount determined by the Secretary;

(II) withhold not more than 5 percent of the amount required to be appropriated for use in a State or urbanized area in the State under section 5307 of this title, until the State safety oversight program has been certified; or

(III) require fixed guideway public transportation systems under such State safety oversight program to provide up to 100 percent of Federal assistance made available under this chapter only for safety-related improvements on such systems, until the State safety oversight program has been certified.

(8) FEDERAL SAFETY MANAGEMENT.—

(A) IN GENERAL.—If the Secretary determines that a State safety oversight program is not being carried out in accordance with this section, has become inadequate to ensure the enforcement of Federal safety regulation, or is incapable of providing adequate safety oversight consistent with the prevention of substantial risk of death, or personal injury, the Secretary shall administer the State safety oversight program until the eligible State develops a State safety oversight program certified by the Secretary in accordance with this subsection.

(B) TEMPORARY FEDERAL OVERSIGHT.—In making a determination under subparagraph (A), the Secretary shall—

(i) transmit to the eligible State and affected recipient or recipients, a written explanation of the determination or subsequent finding, including any intention to withhold funding under this section, the amount of funds proposed to be withheld, and if applicable, a formal notice of a withdrawal of State safety oversight program approval; and

(ii) require the State to submit a State safety oversight program or modification for certification by the Secretary that meets the requirements of this subsection.

(C) FAILURE TO CORRECT.—If the Secretary determines in accordance with subparagraph (A), that a State safety oversight program or modification required pursuant to subparagraph (B)(ii), submitted by a State is not sufficient, the Secretary may—

(i) withhold funds available under paragraph (6) in an amount determined by the Secretary;

(ii) beginning 1 year after the date of the determination, withhold not more than 5 percent of the amount required to be appropriated for use in a State or an urbanized area in the State under section 5307, until the State safety oversight program or modification has been certified; and

(iii) use any other authorities authorized under this chapter considered necessary and appropriate.

(D) ADMINISTRATIVE AND OVERSIGHT ACTIVITIES.—To carry out administrative and oversight activities authorized by this paragraph, the Secretary may use grant funds apportioned to an eligible State, under paragraph (6), to develop or carry out a State safety oversight program.

(9) EVALUATION OF PROGRAM AND ANNUAL REPORT.—The Secretary shall continually evaluate the implementation of a State safety oversight program by a State safety oversight agency, and shall submit on or before July 1 of each year to the Committee on Banking, Housing, and Urban Affairs of the Senate and the Committee on Transportation and Infrastructure of the House of Representatives a report on—

(A) the amount of funds apportioned to each eligible State; and

(B) the certification status of each State safety oversight program, including what steps a State program that has been denied certification must take in order to be certified.

(10) FEDERAL OVERSIGHT.—The Secretary shall—

(A) oversee the implementation of each State safety oversight program under this subsection;

(B) audit the operations of each State safety oversight agency at least once triennially; and

(C) issue rules to carry out this subsection.

(11) EFFECTIVENESS OF ENFORCEMENT AUTHORITIES AND PRACTICES.—The Secretary shall develop and disseminate to State safety oversight agencies the process and methodology that the Secretary will use to monitor the effectiveness of the enforcement authorities and practices of State safety oversight agencies.

(f) AUTHORITY OF SECRETARY.—In carrying out this section, the Secretary may—

(1) conduct inspections, investigations, audits, examinations, and testing of the equipment, facilities, rolling stock, and operations of the public transportation system of a recipient;

(2) make reports and issue directives with respect to the safety of the public transportation system of a recipient or the public transportation industry generally;

(3) in conjunction with an accident investigation or an investigation into a pattern or practice of conduct that negatively affects public safety, issue a subpoena to, and

take the deposition of, any employee of a recipient or a State safety oversight agency, if—

(A) before the issuance of the subpoena, the Secretary requests a determination by the Attorney General of the United States as to whether the subpoena will interfere with an ongoing criminal investigation; and

(B) the Attorney General—

(i) determines that the subpoena will not interfere with an ongoing criminal investigation; or

(ii) fails to make a determination under clause (i) before the date that is 30 days after the date on which the Secretary makes a request under subparagraph (A);

(4) require the production of documents by, and prescribe recordkeeping and reporting requirements for, a recipient or a State safety oversight agency;

(5) investigate public transportation accidents and incidents and provide guidance to recipients regarding prevention of accidents and incidents;

(6) at reasonable times and in a reasonable manner, enter and inspect equipment, facilities, rolling stock, operations, and relevant records of the public transportation system of a recipient; and

(7) issue rules to carry out this section.

(g) ENFORCEMENT ACTIONS.—

(1) TYPES OF ENFORCEMENT ACTIONS.—The Secretary may take enforcement action against a recipient that does not comply with Federal law with respect to the safety of the public transportation system, including—

(A) issuing directives;

(B) requiring more frequent oversight of the recipient by a State safety oversight agency or the Secretary;

(C) imposing more frequent reporting requirements;

(D) requiring that any Federal financial assistance provided under this chapter be spent on correcting safety deficiencies identified by the Secretary or the State safety oversight agency before such funds are spent on other projects; and

(E) withholding not more than 25 percent of financial assistance under section 5307.

(2) USE OR WITHHOLDING OF FUNDS.—

(A) IN GENERAL.—The Secretary may require the use of funds or withhold funds in accordance with paragraph (1)(D) or (1)(E) only if the Secretary finds that a recipient is engaged in a pattern or practice of serious safety violations or has otherwise refused to comply with Federal law relating to the safety of the public transportation system.

(B) NOTICE.—Before withholding funds from a recipient, the Secretary shall provide to the recipient—

(i) written notice of a violation and the amount proposed to be withheld; and

(ii) a reasonable period of time within which the recipient may address the violation or propose and initiate an alternative means of compliance that the Secretary determines is acceptable.

(h) RESTRICTIONS AND PROHIBITIONS.—

(1) RESTRICTIONS AND PROHIBITIONS.—The Secretary shall issue restrictions and prohibitions by whatever means are determined necessary and appropriate, without regard to section 5334(c), if, through testing, inspection, investigation, audit, or research carried out under this chapter, the Secretary determines that an unsafe condition or practice, or a combination of unsafe conditions and practices, exist such that there is a substantial risk of death or personal injury.

(2) NOTICE.—The notice of restriction or prohibition shall describe the condition or practice, the subsequent risk and the standards and procedures required to address the restriction or prohibition.

(3) CONTINUED AUTHORITY.—Nothing in this subsection shall be construed as limiting the Secretary's authority to maintain a restriction or prohibition for as long as is necessary to ensure that the risk has been substantially addressed.

(i) CONSULTATION BY THE SECRETARY OF HOMELAND SECURITY.—The Secretary of Homeland Security shall consult with the Secretary of Transportation before the Secretary of Homeland Security issues a rule or order that the Secretary of Transportation determines affects the safety of public transportation design, construction, or operations.

(j) ACTIONS UNDER STATE LAW.—

(1) RULE OF CONSTRUCTION.—Nothing in this section shall be construed to preempt an action under State law seeking damages for personal injury, death, or property damage alleging that a party has failed to comply with—

(A) a Federal standard of care established by a regulation or order issued by the Secretary under this section; or

(B) its own program, rule, or standard that it created pursuant to a rule or order issued by the Secretary.

(2) EFFECTIVE DATE.—This subsection shall apply to any cause of action under State law arising from an event or activity occurring on or after the date of enactment of the Federal Public Transportation Act of 2012.

(3) JURISDICTION.—Nothing in this section shall be construed to create a cause of action under Federal law on behalf of an injured party or confer Federal question jurisdiction for a State law cause of action.

(k) INSPECTIONS.—

(1) INSPECTION ACCESS.—

(A) IN GENERAL.—A State safety oversight program shall provide the State safety oversight agency established by the program with the authority and capability to enter the facilities of each rail fixed guideway public transportation system that the State safety oversight agency oversees to inspect infrastructure, equipment, records, personnel, and data, including the data that the rail fixed guideway public transportation agency collects when identifying and evaluating safety risks.

(B) POLICIES AND PROCEDURES.—A State safety oversight agency, in consultation with each rail fixed guideway public transportation agency that the State safety oversight agency oversees, shall establish policies and procedures regarding the access of the State safety oversight agency to conduct inspections of the rail fixed guideway public transportation system, including access for inspections that occur without advance notice to the rail fixed guideway public transportation agency.

(2) DATA COLLECTION.—

(A) IN GENERAL.—A rail fixed guideway public transportation agency shall provide the applicable State safety oversight agency with the data that the rail fixed guideway public transportation agency collects when identifying and evaluating safety risks, in accordance with subparagraph (B).

(B) POLICIES AND PROCEDURES.—A State safety oversight agency, in consultation with each rail fixed guideway public transportation agency that the State safety oversight agency oversees, shall establish policies and procedures for collecting data described in subparagraph (A) from a rail fixed guideway public transportation agency, including with respect to frequency of collection, that is commensurate with the size and complexity of the rail fixed guideway public transportation system.

(3) INCORPORATION.—Policies and procedures established under this subsection shall be incorporated into—

(A) the State safety oversight program standard adopted by a State safety oversight agency under section 674.27 of title 49, Code of Federal Regulations (or any successor regulation); and

(B) the public transportation agency safety plan established by a rail fixed guideway public transportation agency under subsection (d).

(4) ASSESSMENT BY SECRETARY.—In assessing the capability of a State safety oversight agency to conduct inspections as required under paragraph (1), the Secretary shall ensure that—

(A) the inspection practices of the State safety oversight agency are commensurate with the number, size, and complexity of the rail fixed guideway public transportation systems that the State safety oversight agency oversees;

(B) the inspection program of the State safety oversight agency is risk-based; and

(C) the State safety oversight agency has sufficient resources to conduct the inspections.

(5) SPECIAL DIRECTIVE.—The Secretary shall issue a special directive to each State safety oversight agency on the development and implementation of risk-based inspection programs under this subsection.

(6) ENFORCEMENT.—The Secretary may use any authority under this section, including any enforcement action authorized under subsection (g), to ensure the compliance of a State safety oversight agency or State safety oversight program with this subsection.

(Pub. L. 103–272, §1(d), July 5, 1994, 108 Stat. 830; Pub. L. 109–59, title III, §3028(a), Aug. 10, 2005, 119 Stat. 1624; Pub. L. 112–141, div. B, §20021(a), July 6, 2012, 126 Stat. 709; Pub. L. 114–94, div. A, title III, §3013, Dec. 4, 2015, 129 Stat. 1476; Pub. L. 117–58, div. C, §30012(a), Nov. 15, 2021, 135 Stat. 904.)

[§5330. REPEALED. PUB. L. 112–141, DIV. B, §20030(E), JULY 6, 2012, 126 STAT. 731]

Section, Pub. L. 103–272, §1(d), July 5, 1994, 108 Stat. 831; Pub. L. 109–59, title III, §§3002(b)(4), 3029(a), Aug. 10, 2005, 119 Stat. 1545, 1625, related to State safety oversight of certain rail fixed guideway public transportation systems.

§5331. ALCOHOL AND CONTROLLED SUBSTANCES TESTING

(a) DEFINITIONS.—In this section—

(1) "controlled substance" means any substance under section 102 of the Comprehensive Drug Abuse Prevention and Control Act of 1970 (21 U.S.C. 802) whose use the Secretary decides has a risk to transportation safety.

(2) "person" includes any entity organized or existing under the laws of the United States, a State, territory, or possession of the United States, or a foreign country.

(3) "public transportation" means any form of public transportation, except a form the Secretary decides is covered adequately, for employee alcohol and controlled substances testing purposes, under section 20140 or 31306 of this title or section 2303a, 7101(i), or 7302(e) of title 46. The Secretary may also decide that a form of public transportation is covered adequately, for employee alcohol and controlled substances testing purposes, under the alcohol and controlled substance statutes or regulations of an agency within the Department of Transportation or the Coast Guard.

(b) TESTING PROGRAM FOR PUBLIC TRANSPORTATION EMPLOYEES.—(1)(A) In the interest of public transportation safety, the Secretary shall prescribe regulations that establish a program requiring public transportation operations that receive financial assistance under section 5307, 5309, or 5311 of this title to conduct preemployment, reasonable suspicion, random, and post-accident testing of public transportation employees responsible for safety-sensitive functions (as decided by the Secretary) for the use of a controlled substance in violation of law or a United States Government regulation, and to conduct reasonable suspicion, random, and post-accident testing of such employees for the use of alcohol in violation of law or a United States Government regulation. The regulations shall permit such operations to conduct preemployment testing of such employees for the use of alcohol.

(B) When the Secretary considers it appropriate in the interest of safety, the Secretary may prescribe regulations for conducting periodic recurring testing of public transportation employees responsible for safety-sensitive functions (as decided by the Secretary) for the use of alcohol or a controlled substance in violation of law or a Government regulation.

(2) In prescribing regulations under this subsection, the Secretary—

(A) shall require that post-accident testing of such a public transportation employee be conducted when loss of human life occurs in an accident involving public transportation; and

(B) may require that post-accident testing of such a public transportation employee be conducted when bodily injury or significant property damage occurs in any other serious accident involving public transportation.

(c) DISQUALIFICATIONS FOR USE.—(1) When the Secretary considers it appropriate, the Secretary shall require disqualification for an established period of time or dismissal of any employee referred to in subsection (b)(1) of this section who is found—

(A) to have used or been impaired by alcohol when on duty; or

(B) to have used a controlled substance, whether or not on duty, except as allowed for medical purposes by law or regulation.

(2) This section does not supersede any penalty applicable to a public transportation

employee under another law.

(d) TESTING AND LABORATORY REQUIREMENTS.—In carrying out subsection (b) of this section, the Secretary shall develop requirements that shall—

(1) promote, to the maximum extent practicable, individual privacy in the collection of specimens;

(2) for laboratories and testing procedures for controlled substances, incorporate the Department of Health and Human Services scientific and technical guidelines dated April 11, 1988, and any amendments to those guidelines, including mandatory guidelines establishing—

(A) comprehensive standards for every aspect of laboratory controlled substances testing and laboratory procedures to be applied in carrying out this section, including standards requiring the use of the best available technology to ensure the complete reliability and accuracy of controlled substances tests and strict procedures governing the chain of custody of specimens collected for controlled substances testing;

(B) the minimum list of controlled substances for which individuals may be tested; and

(C) appropriate standards and procedures for periodic review of laboratories and criteria for certification and revocation of certification of laboratories to perform controlled substances testing in carrying out this section;

(3) require that a laboratory involved in controlled substances testing under this section have the capability and facility, at the laboratory, of performing screening and confirmation tests;

(4) provide that all tests indicating the use of alcohol or a controlled substance in violation of law or a Government regulation be confirmed by a scientifically recognized method of testing capable of providing quantitative information about alcohol or a controlled substance;

(5) provide that each specimen be subdivided, secured, and labeled in the presence of the tested individual and that a part of the specimen be retained in a secure manner to prevent the possibility of tampering, so that if the individual's confirmation test results are positive the individual has an opportunity to have the retained part tested by a 2d confirmation test done independently at another certified laboratory if the individual requests the 2d confirmation test not later than 3 days after being advised of the results of the first confirmation test;

(6) ensure appropriate safeguards for testing to detect and quantify alcohol in breath and body fluid samples, including urine and blood, through the development of regulations that may be necessary and in consultation with the Secretary of Health and Human Services;

(7) provide for the confidentiality of test results and medical information (except information about alcohol or a controlled substance) of employees, except that this clause does not prevent the use of test results for the orderly imposition of appropriate sanctions under this section; and

(8) ensure that employees are selected for tests by nondiscriminatory and impartial methods, so that no employee is harassed by being treated differently from other employees in similar circumstances.

(e) REHABILITATION.—The Secretary shall prescribe regulations establishing requirements for rehabilitation programs that provide for the identification and opportunity for treatment of any public transportation employee referred to in subsection (b)(1) of this section who is found to have used alcohol or a controlled substance in violation of law or a Government regulation. The Secretary shall decide on the circumstances under which employees shall be required to participate in a program. This subsection does not prevent a public transportation operation from establishing a program under this section in cooperation with another public transportation operation.

(f) RELATIONSHIP TO OTHER LAWS, REGULATIONS, STANDARDS, AND ORDERS.—(1) A State or local government may not prescribe, issue, or continue in effect a law, regulation, standard, or order that is inconsistent with regulations prescribed under this section. However, a regulation prescribed under this section does not preempt a State criminal law that imposes sanctions for reckless conduct leading to loss of life, injury, or damage to property.

(2) In prescribing regulations under this section, the Secretary—

(A) shall establish only requirements that are consistent with international obligations of the United States; and

(B) shall consider applicable laws and regulations of foreign countries.

(g) CONDITIONS ON FEDERAL ASSISTANCE.—

(1) INELIGIBILITY FOR ASSISTANCE.—A person that receives funds under this chapter is not eligible for financial assistance under section 5307, 5309, or 5311 of this title if the person is required, under regulations the Secretary prescribes under this section, to establish a program of alcohol and controlled substances testing and does not establish the program in accordance with this section.

(2) ADDITIONAL REMEDIES.—If the Secretary determines that a person that receives funds under this chapter is not in compliance with regulations prescribed under this section, the Secretary may bar the person from receiving Federal transit assistance in an amount the Secretary considers appropriate.

(Pub. L. 103–272, §1(d), July 5, 1994, 108 Stat. 832; Pub. L. 103–429, §6(13), Oct. 31, 1994, 108 Stat. 4379; Pub. L. 104–59, title III, §342(a), Nov. 28, 1995, 109 Stat. 608; Pub. L. 109–59, title III, §§3002(b)(3), (4), 3030, Aug. 10, 2005, 119 Stat. 1545, 1625; Pub. L. 112–141, div. B, §§20022, 20030(f), July 6, 2012, 126 Stat. 717, 731.)

§5332. NONDISCRIMINATION

(a) DEFINITION.—In this section, "person" includes a governmental authority, political subdivision, authority, legal representative, trust, unincorporated organization, trustee, trustee in bankruptcy, and receiver.

(b) PROHIBITIONS.—A person may not be excluded from participating in, denied a benefit of, or discriminated against under, a project, program, or activity receiving financial assistance under this chapter because of race, color, religion, national origin, sex, disability, or age.

(c) COMPLIANCE.—(1) The Secretary shall take affirmative action to ensure compliance with subsection (b) of this section.

(2) When the Secretary decides that a person receiving financial assistance under this chapter is not complying with subsection (b) of this section, a civil rights law of the United States, or a regulation or order under that law, the Secretary shall notify the

person of the decision and require action be taken to ensure compliance with subsection (b).

(d) AUTHORITY OF SECRETARY FOR NONCOMPLIANCE.—If a person does not comply with subsection (b) of this section within a reasonable time after receiving notice, the Secretary shall—

(1) direct that no further financial assistance of the United States Government under this chapter be provided to the person;

(2) refer the matter to the Attorney General with a recommendation that a civil action be brought;

(3) proceed under title VI of the Civil Rights Act of 1964 (42 U.S.C. 2000d et seq.); or

(4) take any other action provided by law.

(e) CIVIL ACTIONS BY ATTORNEY GENERAL.—The Attorney General may bring a civil action for appropriate relief when—

(1) a matter is referred to the Attorney General under subsection (d)(2) of this section; or

(2) the Attorney General believes a person is engaged in a pattern or practice in violation of this section.

(f) APPLICATION AND RELATIONSHIP TO OTHER LAWS.—This section applies to an employment or business opportunity and is in addition to title VI of the Civil Rights Act of 1964 (42 U.S.C. 2000d et seq.).

(Pub. L. 103–272, §1(d), July 5, 1994, 108 Stat. 834; Pub. L. 112–141, div. B, §§20023(a), 20030(g), July 6, 2012, 126 Stat. 717, 731.)

§5333. LABOR STANDARDS

(a) PREVAILING WAGES REQUIREMENT.—The Secretary of Transportation shall ensure that laborers and mechanics employed by contractors and subcontractors in construction work financed with a grant or loan under this chapter be paid wages not less than those prevailing on similar construction in the locality, as determined by the Secretary of Labor under sections 3141 through 3144, 3146, and 3147 of title 40. The Secretary of Transportation may approve a grant or loan only after being assured that required labor standards will be maintained on the construction work. For a labor standard under this subsection, the Secretary of Labor has the same duties and powers stated in Reorganization Plan No. 14 of 1950 (eff. May 24, 1950, 64 Stat. 1267) and section 3145 of title 40.

(b) EMPLOYEE PROTECTIVE ARRANGEMENTS.—(1) As a condition of financial assistance under sections 5307–5312, 5316,[1] 5318, 5323(a)(1), 5323(b), 5323(d), 5328,[1] 5337, and 5338(b) of this title, the interests of employees affected by the assistance shall be protected under arrangements the Secretary of Labor concludes are fair and equitable. The agreement granting the assistance under sections 5307–5312, 5316,[1] 5318, 5323(a)(1), 5323(b), 5323(d), 5328,[1] 5337, and 5338(b) shall specify the arrangements.

(2) Arrangements under this subsection shall include provisions that may be necessary for—

(A) the preservation of rights, privileges, and benefits (including continuation of pension rights and benefits) under existing collective bargaining agreements or otherwise;

(B) the continuation of collective bargaining rights;

(C) the protection of individual employees against a worsening of their positions related to employment;

(D) assurances of employment to employees of acquired public transportation systems;

(E) assurances of priority of reemployment of employees whose employment is ended or who are laid off; and

(F) paid training or retraining programs.

(3) Arrangements under this subsection shall provide benefits at least equal to benefits established under section 11326 of this title.

(4) Fair and equitable arrangements to protect the interests of employees utilized by the Secretary of Labor for assistance to purchase like-kind equipment or facilities, and grant amendments which do not materially revise or amend existing assistance agreements, shall be certified without referral.

(5) When the Secretary is called upon to issue fair and equitable determinations involving assurances of employment when one private transit bus service contractor replaces another through competitive bidding, such decisions shall be based on the principles set forth in the Department of Labor's decision of September 21, 1994, as clarified by the supplemental ruling of November 7, 1994, with respect to grant NV–90–X021. This paragraph shall not serve as a basis for objections under section 215.3(d) of title 29, Code of Federal Regulations.

(Pub. L. 103–272, §1(d), July 5, 1994, 108 Stat. 835; Pub. L. 104–88, title III, §308(e), Dec. 29, 1995, 109 Stat. 947; Pub. L. 105–178, title III, §3029(b)(9), June 9, 1998, 112 Stat. 372; Pub. L. 107–217, §3(n)(3), Aug. 21, 2002, 116 Stat. 1302; Pub. L. 109–59, title III, §§3002(b)(4), 3031, Aug. 10, 2005, 119 Stat. 1545, 1625; Pub. L. 112–141, div. B, §20030(h), July 6, 2012, 126 Stat. 731.)

[1] See References in Text note below.

§5334. ADMINISTRATIVE PROVISIONS

(a) GENERAL AUTHORITY.—In carrying out this chapter, the Secretary of Transportation may—

(1) prescribe terms for a project that receives Federal financial assistance under this chapter (except terms the Secretary of Labor prescribes under section 5333(b) of this title);

(2) sue and be sued;

(3) foreclose on property or bring a civil action to protect or enforce a right conferred on the Secretary of Transportation by law or agreement;

(4) buy property related to a loan under this chapter;

(5) agree to pay an annual amount in place of a State or local tax on real property acquired or owned under this chapter;

(6) sell, exchange, or lease property, a security, or an obligation;

(7) obtain loss insurance for property and assets the Secretary of Transportation holds;

(8) consent to a modification in an agreement under this chapter;

(9) include in an agreement or instrument under this chapter a covenant or term the Secretary of Transportation considers necessary to carry out this chapter;

(10) collect fees to cover the costs of training or conferences, including costs of promotional materials, sponsored by the Federal Transit Administration to promote public transportation and credit amounts collected to the appropriation concerned; and

(11) issue regulations as necessary to carry out the purposes of this chapter.

(b) PROHIBITIONS AGAINST REGULATING OPERATIONS AND CHARGES.—

(1) IN GENERAL.—Except for purposes of national defense or in the event of a national or regional emergency, or for purposes of establishing and enforcing a program to improve the safety of public transportation systems in the United States as described in section 5329, the Secretary may not regulate the operation, routes, or schedules of a public transportation system for which a grant is made under this chapter. The Secretary may not regulate the rates, fares, tolls, rentals, or other charges prescribed by any provider of public transportation.

(2) LIMITATION ON STATUTORY CONSTRUCTION.—Nothing in this subsection shall be construed to prevent the Secretary from requiring a recipient of funds under this chapter to comply with the terms and conditions of its Federal assistance agreement.

(c) PROCEDURES FOR PRESCRIBING REGULATIONS.—(1) The Secretary shall prepare an agenda listing all areas in which the Secretary intends to propose regulations governing activities under this chapter within the following 12 months. The Secretary shall publish the proposed agenda in the Federal Register as part of the Secretary's semiannual regulatory agenda that lists regulatory activities of the Federal Transit Administration. The Secretary shall submit the agenda to the Committee on Banking, Housing, and Urban Affairs and the Committee on Appropriations of the Senate and the Committee on Transportation and Infrastructure and the Committee on Appropriations of the House of Representatives on the day the agenda is published.

(2) Except for emergency regulations, the Secretary shall give interested parties at least 60 days to participate in a regulatory proceeding under this chapter by submitting written information, views, or arguments, with or without an oral presentation, except when the Secretary for good cause finds that public notice and comment are unnecessary because of the routine nature or insignificant impact of the regulation or that an emergency regulation should be issued. The Secretary may extend the 60-day period if the Secretary decides the period is insufficient to allow diligent individuals to prepare comments or that other circumstances justify an extension.

(3) An emergency regulation ends 120 days after it is issued.

(4) The Secretary shall comply with this subsection when proposing or carrying out a regulation governing an activity under this chapter, except for a routine matter or a matter with no significant impact.

(d) BUDGET PROGRAM AND SET OF ACCOUNTS.—The Secretary shall—

(1) submit each year a budget program as provided in section 9103 of title 31; and

(2) maintain a set of accounts for audit under chapter 35 of title 31.

(e) DEPOSITORY AND AVAILABILITY OF AMOUNTS.—The Secretary shall deposit amounts made available to the Secretary under this chapter in a checking account in the Treasury. Receipts, assets, and amounts obtained or held by the Secretary to carry out this chapter are available for administrative expenses to carry out this chapter.

(f) BINDING EFFECT OF FINANCIAL TRANSACTION.—A financial transaction of the Secretary under this chapter and a related voucher are binding on all officers and employees of the United States Government.

(g) DEALING WITH ACQUIRED PROPERTY.—Notwithstanding another law related to the Government acquiring, using, or disposing of real property, the Secretary may deal with property acquired under paragraph (3) or (4) of subsection (a) in any way. However, this subsection does not—

(1) deprive a State or political subdivision of a State of jurisdiction of the property; or

(2) impair the civil rights, under the laws of a State or political subdivision of a State, of an inhabitant of the property.

(h) TRANSFER OF ASSETS NO LONGER NEEDED.—

(1) IN GENERAL.—If a recipient of assistance under this chapter decides an asset acquired under this chapter at least in part with that assistance is no longer needed for the purpose for which such asset was acquired, the Secretary may authorize the recipient to transfer such asset to—

(A) a local governmental authority to be used for a public purpose with no further obligation to the Government if the Secretary decides—

(i) the asset will remain in public use for at least 5 years after the date the asset is transferred;

(ii) there is no purpose eligible for assistance under this chapter for which the asset should be used;

(iii) the overall benefit of allowing the transfer is greater than the interest of the Government in liquidation and return of the financial interest of the Government in the asset, after considering fair market value and other factors; and

(iv) through an appropriate screening or survey process, that there is no interest in acquiring the asset for Government use if the asset is a facility or land; or

(B) a local governmental authority, nonprofit organization, or other third party entity to be used for the purpose of transit-oriented development with no further obligation to the Government if the Secretary decides—

(i) the asset is a necessary component of a proposed transit-oriented development project;

(ii) the transit-oriented development project will increase transit ridership;

(iii) at least 40 percent of the housing units offered in the transit-oriented development, including housing units owned by nongovernmental entities, are legally binding affordability restricted to tenants with incomes at or below 60 percent of the area median income and owners with incomes at or below 60 percent [1] the area median income, which shall include at least 20 percent of such housing units offered restricted to tenants with incomes at or below 30 percent of the area median income and owners with incomes at or below 30 percent the area median income;

(iv) the asset will remain in use as described in this section for at least 30 years after the date the asset is transferred; and

(v) with respect to a transfer to a third party entity—

(I) a local government authority or nonprofit organization is unable to receive the property;

(II) the overall benefit of allowing the transfer is greater than the interest of the Government in liquidation and return of the financial interest of the Government in the asset, after considering fair market value and other factors; and

(III) the third party has demonstrated a satisfactory history of construction or operating an affordable housing development.

(2) A decision under paragraph (1) must be in writing and include the reason for the decision.

(3) This subsection is in addition to any other law related to using and disposing of a facility or equipment under an assistance agreement.

(4) PROCEEDS FROM THE SALE OF TRANSIT ASSETS.—

(A) IN GENERAL.—When real property, equipment, or supplies acquired with assistance under this chapter are no longer needed for public transportation purposes as determined under the applicable assistance agreement, the Secretary may authorize the sale, transfer, or lease of the assets under conditions determined by the Secretary and subject to the requirements of this subsection.

(B) REIMBURSEMENT.—

(i) FAIR MARKET VALUE OF LESS THAN $5,000.—With respect to rolling stock and equipment with a unit fair market value of $5,000 or less per unit and unused supplies with a total aggregate fair market value of $5,000 or less that was purchased using Federal financial assistance under this chapter, the rolling stock, equipment, and supplies may be retained, sold, or otherwise disposed of at the end of the service life of the rolling stock, equipment, or supplies without any obligation to reimburse the Federal Transit Administration.

(ii) FAIR MARKET VALUE OF MORE THAN $5,000.—

(I) IN GENERAL.—With respect to rolling stock and equipment with a unit fair market value of more than $5,000 per unit and unused supplies with a total aggregate fair market value of more than $5,000 that was purchased using Federal financial assistance under this chapter, the rolling stock, equipment, and supplies may be retained or sold at the end of the service life of the rolling stock, equipment, or supplies.

(II) REIMBURSEMENT REQUIRED.—If rolling stock, equipment, or supplies described in subclause (I) is sold, of the proceeds from the sale—

(aa) the recipient shall retain an amount equal to the sum of—

(AA) $5,000; and

(BB) of the remaining proceeds, a percentage of the amount equal to the non-Federal share expended by the recipient in making the original purchase; and

(bb) any amounts remaining after application of item (aa) shall be returned to the Federal Transit Administration.

(iii) ROLLING STOCK AND EQUIPMENT RETAINED.—Rolling stock, equipment, or supplies described in clause (i) or (ii) that is retained by a recipient under those clauses may be used by the recipient for other public transportation projects or programs with no obligation to reimburse the Federal Transit Administration, and no approval of the Secretary to retain that rolling stock, equipment, or supplies is required.

(C) USE.—The net income from asset sales, uses, or leases (including lease renewals) under this subsection shall be used by the recipient to reduce the gross project cost of other capital projects carried out under this chapter.

(D) RELATIONSHIP TO OTHER AUTHORITY.—The authority of the Secretary under this subsection is in addition to existing authorities controlling allocation or use of recipient income otherwise permissible in law or regulation in effect prior to the date of enactment of this paragraph.

(i) TRANSFER OF AMOUNTS AND NON-GOVERNMENT SHARE.—(1) Amounts made available for a public transportation project under title 23 may be transferred to and administered by the Secretary under this chapter. Amounts made available for a highway project under this chapter shall be transferred to and administered by the Secretary under title 23.

(2) The provisions of title 23 related to the non-Government share apply to amounts under title 23 used for public transportation projects. The provisions of this chapter related to the non-Government share apply to amounts under this chapter used for highway projects.

(j) NOTIFICATION OF PENDING DISCRETIONARY GRANTS.—Not less than 3 full business days before announcement of award by the Secretary of any discretionary grant, letter of intent, or full funding grant agreement totaling $1,000,000 or more, the Secretary shall notify the Committee on Banking, Housing, and Urban Affairs and the Committee on Appropriations of the Senate and the Committee on Transportation and Infrastructure and the Committee on Appropriations of the House of Representatives.

(k) AGENCY STATEMENTS.—

(1) IN GENERAL.—The Administrator of the Federal Transit Administration shall follow applicable rulemaking procedures under section 553 of title 5 before the Federal Transit Administration issues a statement that imposes a binding obligation on recipients of Federal assistance under this chapter.

(2) BINDING OBLIGATION DEFINED.—In this subsection, the term "binding obligation" means a substantive policy statement, rule, or guidance document issued by the Federal Transit Administration that grants rights, imposes obligations, produces significant effects on private interests, or effects a significant change in existing policy.

(Pub. L. 103–272, §1(d), July 5, 1994, 108 Stat. 836; Pub. L. 104–287, §5(9), Oct. 11, 1996, 110 Stat. 3389; Pub. L. 104–316, title I, §127(a), Oct. 19, 1996, 110 Stat. 3840; Pub. L. 105–178, title III, §§3023(c), 3025(a), (b)(1), (c), June 9, 1998, 112 Stat. 364, 365; Pub. L. 109–59, title III, §§3002(b)(4), 3032, Aug. 10, 2005, 119 Stat. 1545, 1626; Pub. L. 111–350, §5(o)(3), Jan. 4, 2011, 124 Stat. 3853; Pub. L. 112–141, div. B, §§20024, 20030(i), July 6, 2012, 126 Stat. 718, 731; Pub. L. 117–58, div. C, §30013, Nov. 15, 2021, 135 Stat. 909; Pub. L. 117–81, div. F, title LXVI, §6609, Dec. 27, 2021, 135 Stat. 2446.)

¹ So in original. Probably should be followed by "of".

§5335. NATIONAL TRANSIT DATABASE

(a) NATIONAL TRANSIT DATABASE.—To help meet the needs of individual public transportation systems, the United States Government, State and local governments, and the public for information on which to base public transportation service planning, the Secretary shall maintain a reporting system, using uniform categories to accumulate public transportation financial, operating, geographic service area coverage, and asset condition information and using a uniform system of accounts. The reporting and uniform systems shall contain appropriate information to help any level of government make a public sector investment decision. The Secretary may request and receive appropriate information from any source.

(b) REPORTING AND UNIFORM SYSTEMS.—The Secretary may award a grant under section 5307 or 5311 only if the applicant, and any person that will receive benefits directly from the grant, are subject to the reporting and uniform systems.

(c) DATA REQUIRED TO BE REPORTED.—Each recipient of a grant under this chapter shall report to the Secretary, for inclusion in the national transit database under this section—

(1) any information relating to a transit asset inventory or condition assessment conducted by the recipient;

(2) any data on assaults on transit workers of the recipients; and

(3) any data on fatalities that result from an impact with a bus.

(Pub. L. 103–272, §1(d), July 5, 1994, 108 Stat. 838; Pub. L. 104–287, §5(9), (18), Oct. 11, 1996, 110 Stat. 3389, 3390; Pub. L. 104–316, title I, §127(b), Oct. 19, 1996, 110 Stat. 3840; Pub. L. 105–178, title III, §3026, June 9, 1998, 112 Stat. 365; Pub. L. 109–59, title III, §§3002(b)(4), 3033(a), Aug. 10, 2005, 119 Stat. 1545, 1627; Pub. L. 112–141, div. B, §§20025(a), 20030(j), July 6, 2012, 126 Stat. 718, 731; Pub. L. 117–58, div. C, §30014, Nov. 15, 2021, 135 Stat. 910.)

§5336. APPORTIONMENT OF APPROPRIATIONS FOR FORMULA GRANTS

(a) BASED ON URBANIZED AREA POPULATION.—Of the amount apportioned under subsection (h)(5) to carry out section 5307—

(1) 9.32 percent shall be apportioned each fiscal year only in urbanized areas with a population of less than 200,000 so that each of those areas is entitled to receive an amount equal to—

(A) 50 percent of the total amount apportioned multiplied by a ratio equal to the population of the area divided by the total population of all urbanized areas with populations of less than 200,000 as shown in the most recent decennial census; and

(B) 50 percent of the total amount apportioned multiplied by a ratio for the area based on population weighted by a factor, established by the Secretary, of the number of inhabitants in each square mile; and

(2) 90.68 percent shall be apportioned each fiscal year only in urbanized areas with populations of at least 200,000 as provided in subsections (b) and (c) of this section.

(b) BASED ON FIXED GUIDEWAY VEHICLE REVENUE MILES, DIRECTIONAL ROUTE MILES, AND PASSENGER MILES.—(1) In this subsection, "fixed guideway vehicle revenue miles" and "fixed guideway directional route miles" include passenger ferry operations directly or under contract by the designated recipient.

(2) Of the amount apportioned under subsection (a)(2) of this section, 33.29 percent shall be apportioned as follows:

(A) 95.61 percent of the total amount apportioned under this subsection shall be apportioned so that each urbanized area with a population of at least 200,000 is entitled to receive an amount equal to—

(i) 60 percent of the 95.61 percent apportioned under this subparagraph multiplied by a ratio equal to the number of fixed guideway vehicle revenue miles attributable to the area, as established by the Secretary, divided by the total number of all fixed guideway vehicle revenue miles attributable to all areas; and

(ii) 40 percent of the 95.61 percent apportioned under this subparagraph multiplied by a ratio equal to the number of fixed guideway directional route miles attributable to the area, established by the Secretary, divided by the total number of all fixed guideway directional route miles attributable to all areas.

An urbanized area with a population of at least 750,000 in which commuter rail transportation is provided shall receive at least .75 percent of the total amount apportioned under this subparagraph.

(B) 4.39 percent of the total amount apportioned under this subsection shall be apportioned so that each urbanized area with a population of at least 200,000 is entitled to receive an amount equal to—

(i) the number of fixed guideway vehicle passenger miles traveled multiplied by the number of fixed guideway vehicle passenger miles traveled for each dollar of operating cost in an area; divided by

(ii) the total number of fixed guideway vehicle passenger miles traveled multiplied by the total number of fixed guideway vehicle passenger miles traveled for each dollar of operating cost in all areas.

An urbanized area with a population of at least 750,000 in which commuter rail transportation is provided shall receive at least .75 percent of the total amount apportioned under this subparagraph.

(C) Under subparagraph (A) of this paragraph, fixed guideway vehicle revenue or directional route miles, and passengers served on those miles, in an urbanized area with a population of less than 200,000, where the miles and passengers served otherwise would be attributable to an urbanized area with a population of at least 1,000,000 in an adjacent State, are attributable to the governmental authority in the State in which the urbanized area with a population of less than 200,000 is located. The authority is deemed an urbanized area with a population of at least 200,000 if the authority makes a contract for the service.

(D) A recipient's apportionment under subparagraph (A)(i) of this paragraph may not be reduced if the recipient, after satisfying the Secretary that energy or operating efficiencies would be achieved, reduces vehicle revenue miles but provides the same frequency of revenue service to the same number of riders.

(E) For purposes of subparagraph (A) and section 5337(c)(3), the Secretary shall deem to be attributable to an urbanized area not less than 27 percent of the fixed guideway vehicle revenue miles or fixed guideway directional route miles in the public transportation system of a recipient that are located outside the urbanized area for which the recipient receives funds, in addition to the fixed guideway vehicle revenue miles or fixed guideway directional route miles of the recipient that are located inside the urbanized area.

(c) BASED ON BUS VEHICLE REVENUE MILES AND PASSENGER MILES.—Of the amount apportioned under subsection (a)(2) of this section, 66.71 percent shall be apportioned as follows:

(1) 90.8 percent of the total amount apportioned under this subsection shall be apportioned as follows:

(A) 73.39 percent of the 90.8 percent apportioned under this paragraph shall be apportioned so that each urbanized area with a population of at least 1,000,000 is entitled to receive an amount equal to—

(i) 50 percent of the 73.39 percent apportioned under this subparagraph multiplied by a ratio equal to the total bus vehicle revenue miles operated in or directly serving the urbanized area divided by the total bus vehicle revenue miles attributable to all areas;

(ii) 25 percent of the 73.39 percent apportioned under this subparagraph multiplied by a ratio equal to the population of the area divided by the total population of all areas, as shown in the most recent decennial census; and

(iii) 25 percent of the 73.39 percent apportioned under this subparagraph multiplied by a ratio for the area based on population weighted by a factor, established by the Secretary, of the number of inhabitants in each square mile.

(B) 26.61 percent of the 90.8 percent apportioned under this paragraph shall be apportioned so that each urbanized area with a population of at least 200,000 but not more than 999,999 is entitled to receive an amount equal to—

(i) 50 percent of the 26.61 percent apportioned under this subparagraph multiplied by a ratio equal to the total bus vehicle revenue miles operated in or directly serving the urbanized area divided by the total bus vehicle revenue miles attributable to all areas;

(ii) 25 percent of the 26.61 percent apportioned under this subparagraph multiplied by a ratio equal to the population of the area divided by the total population of all areas, as shown by the most recent decennial census; and

(iii) 25 percent of the 26.61 percent apportioned under this subparagraph multiplied by a ratio for the area based on population weighted by a factor, established by the Secretary, of the number of inhabitants in each square mile.

(2) 9.2 percent of the total amount apportioned under this subsection shall be apportioned so that each urbanized area with a population of at least 200,000 is entitled to receive an amount equal to—

(A) the number of bus passenger miles traveled multiplied by the number of bus passenger miles traveled for each dollar of operating cost in an area; divided by

(B) the total number of bus passenger miles traveled multiplied by the total number of bus passenger miles traveled for each dollar of operating cost in all areas.

(d) DATE OF APPORTIONMENT.—The Secretary shall—

(1) apportion amounts appropriated under section 5338(a)(2)(C) of this title to carry out section 5307 of this title not later than the 10th day after the date the amounts are appropriated or October 1 of the fiscal year for which the amounts are appropriated, whichever is later; and

(2) publish apportionments of the amounts, including amounts attributable to each

urbanized area with a population of more than 50,000 and amounts attributable to each State of a multistate urbanized area, on the apportionment date.

(e) AMOUNTS NOT APPORTIONED TO DESIGNATED RECIPIENTS.—The Governor of a State may expend in an urbanized area with a population of less than 200,000 an amount apportioned under this section that is not apportioned to a designated recipient.

(f) TRANSFERS OF APPORTIONMENTS.—(1) The Governor of a State may transfer any part of the State's apportionment under subsection (a)(1) of this section to supplement amounts apportioned to the State under section 5311(c)(3).[1] The Governor may make a transfer only after consulting with responsible local officials and publicly owned operators of public transportation in each area for which the amount originally was apportioned under this section.

(2) The Governor of a State may transfer any part of the State's apportionment under section 5311(c)(3)[1] to supplement amounts apportioned to the State under subsection (a)(1) of this section.

(3) The Governor of a State may use throughout the State amounts of a State's apportionment remaining available for obligation at the beginning of the 90-day period before the period of the availability of the amounts expires.

(4) A designated recipient for an urbanized area with a population of at least 200,000 may transfer a part of its apportionment under this section to the Governor of a State. The Governor shall distribute the transferred amounts to urbanized areas under this section.

(5) Capital and operating assistance limitations applicable to the original apportionment apply to amounts transferred under this subsection.

(g) PERIOD OF AVAILABILITY TO RECIPIENTS.—An amount apportioned under this section may be obligated by the recipient for 5 years after the fiscal year in which the amount is apportioned. Not later than 30 days after the end of the 5-year period, an amount that is not obligated at the end of that period shall be added to the amount that may be apportioned under this section in the next fiscal year.

(h) APPORTIONMENTS.—Of the amounts made available for each fiscal year under section 5338(a)(2)(C)—

(1) $30,000,000 shall be set aside each fiscal year to carry out section 5307(h);

(2) 3.07 percent shall be apportioned to urbanized areas in accordance with subsection (j);

(3) of amounts not apportioned under paragraphs (1) and (2), 3 percent shall be apportioned to urbanized areas with populations of less than 200,000 in accordance with subsection (i);

(4) 0.75 percent shall be apportioned to eligible States for State safety oversight program grants in accordance with section 5329(e)(6); and

(5) any amount not apportioned under paragraphs (1), (2), (3), and (4) shall be apportioned to urbanized areas in accordance with subsections (a) through (c).

(i) SMALL TRANSIT INTENSIVE CITIES FORMULA.—

(1) DEFINITIONS.—In this subsection, the following definitions apply:

(A) ELIGIBLE AREA.—The term "eligible area" means an urbanized area with a population of less than 200,000 that meets or exceeds in one or more performance categories the industry average for all urbanized areas with a population of at least

200,000 but not more than 999,999, as determined by the Secretary in accordance with subsection (c)(2).

(B) PERFORMANCE CATEGORY.—The term "performance category" means each of the following:

(i) Passenger miles traveled per vehicle revenue mile.

(ii) Passenger miles traveled per vehicle revenue hour.

(iii) Vehicle revenue miles per capita.

(iv) Vehicle revenue hours per capita.

(v) Passenger miles traveled per capita.

(vi) Passengers per capita.

(2) APPORTIONMENT.—

(A) APPORTIONMENT FORMULA.—The amount to be apportioned under subsection (h)(3) shall be apportioned among eligible areas in the ratio that—

(i) the number of performance categories for which each eligible area meets or exceeds the industry average in urbanized areas with a population of at least 200,000 but not more than 999,999; bears to

(ii) the aggregate number of performance categories for which all eligible areas meet or exceed the industry average in urbanized areas with a population of at least 200,000 but not more than 999,999.

(B) DATA USED IN FORMULA.—The Secretary shall calculate apportionments under this subsection for a fiscal year using data from the national transit database used to calculate apportionments for that fiscal year under this section.

(j) APPORTIONMENT FORMULA.—The amounts apportioned under subsection (h)(2) shall be apportioned among urbanized areas as follows:

(1) 75 percent of the funds shall be apportioned among designated recipients for urbanized areas with a population of 200,000 or more in the ratio that—

(A) the number of eligible low-income individuals in each such urbanized area; bears to

(B) the number of eligible low-income individuals in all such urbanized areas.

(2) 25 percent of the funds shall be apportioned among designated recipients for urbanized areas with a population of less than 200,000 in the ratio that—

(A) the number of eligible low-income individuals in each such urbanized area; bears to

(B) the number of eligible low-income individuals in all such urbanized areas.

(Pub. L. 103–272, §1(d), July 5, 1994, 108 Stat. 840; Pub. L. 104–287, §5(19), Oct. 11, 1996, 110 Stat. 3390; Pub. L. 105–178, title III, §§3027(a), (b), 3029(b)(10), (11), June 9, 1998, 112 Stat. 366, 373; Pub. L. 109–59, title III, §§3002(b)(4), 3034, Aug. 10, 2005, 119 Stat. 1545, 1627; Pub. L. 110–244, title II, §201(l), June 6, 2008, 122 Stat. 1611; Pub. L. 112–141, div. B, §20026, July 6, 2012, 126 Stat. 719; Pub. L. 113–159, title I, §1202, Aug. 8, 2014, 128 Stat. 1845; Pub. L. 114–21, title I, §1202, May 29, 2015, 129 Stat. 223; Pub. L. 114–41, title I, §1202, July 31, 2015, 129 Stat. 450; Pub. L. 114–73, title I, §1202, Oct. 29, 2015, 129 Stat. 573; Pub. L. 114–87, title I, §1202, Nov. 20, 2015, 129 Stat. 682; Pub. L. 114–94, div. A, title III, §3014, Dec. 4, 2015, 129 Stat. 1478; Pub. L. 117–58, div. C, §§30001(b)(3), 30015(a), (b)(1), Nov. 15, 2021, 135 Stat. 890, 910.)

[1] *See References in Text note below.*

§5337. STATE OF GOOD REPAIR GRANTS

(a) DEFINITIONS.—In this section, the following definitions shall apply:

(1) FIXED GUIDEWAY.—The term "fixed guideway" means a public transportation facility—

(A) using and occupying a separate right-of-way for the exclusive use of public transportation;

(B) using rail;

(C) using a fixed catenary system;

(D) for a passenger ferry system; or

(E) for a bus rapid transit system.

(2) STATE.—The term "State" means the 50 States, the District of Columbia, and Puerto Rico.

(3) STATE OF GOOD REPAIR.—The term "state of good repair" has the meaning given that term by the Secretary, by rule, under section 5326(b).

(4) TRANSIT ASSET MANAGEMENT PLAN.—The term "transit asset management plan" means a plan developed by a recipient of funding under this chapter that—

(A) includes, at a minimum, capital asset inventories and condition assessments, decision support tools, and investment prioritization; and

(B) the recipient certifies that the recipient complies with the rule issued under section 5326(d).

(b) GENERAL AUTHORITY.—

(1) ELIGIBLE PROJECTS.—The Secretary may make grants under this section to assist State and local governmental authorities in financing capital projects to maintain public transportation systems in a state of good repair, including projects to replace and rehabilitate—

(A) rolling stock;

(B) track;

(C) line equipment and structures;

(D) signals and communications;

(E) power equipment and substations;

(F) passenger stations and terminals;

(G) security equipment and systems;

(H) maintenance facilities and equipment;

(I) operational support equipment, including computer hardware and software;

(J) development and implementation of a transit asset management plan; and

(K) other replacement and rehabilitation projects the Secretary determines appropriate.

(2) INCLUSION IN PLAN.—A recipient shall include a project carried out under paragraph (1) in the transit asset management plan of the recipient upon completion of the plan.

(c) HIGH INTENSITY FIXED GUIDEWAY STATE OF GOOD REPAIR FORMULA.—

(1) IN GENERAL.—Of the amount authorized or made available under section 5338(a)(2)(K),[1] 97.15 percent shall be apportioned to recipients in accordance with this subsection.

(2) AREA SHARE.—

(A) IN GENERAL.—50 percent of the amount described in paragraph (1) shall be apportioned for fixed guideway systems in accordance with this paragraph.

(B) SHARE.—A recipient shall receive an amount equal to the amount described in subparagraph (A), multiplied by the amount the recipient would have received under this section, as in effect for fiscal year 2011, if the amount had been calculated in accordance with the provisions of section 5336(b)(1) and using the definition of the term "fixed guideway" under subsection (a) of this section, as such sections are in effect on the day after the date of enactment of the Federal Public Transportation Act of 2012, and divided by the total amount apportioned for all areas under this section for fiscal year 2011.

(C) RECIPIENT.—For purposes of this paragraph, the term "recipient" means an entity that received funding under this section, as in effect for fiscal year 2011.

(3) VEHICLE REVENUE MILES AND DIRECTIONAL ROUTE MILES.—

(A) IN GENERAL. 50 percent of the amount described in paragraph (1) shall be apportioned to recipients in accordance with this paragraph.

(B) VEHICLE REVENUE MILES.—A recipient in an urbanized area shall receive an amount equal to 60 percent of the amount described in subparagraph (A), multiplied by the number of fixed guideway vehicle revenue miles attributable to the urbanized area, as established by the Secretary, divided by the total number of all fixed guideway vehicle revenue miles attributable to all urbanized areas.

(C) DIRECTIONAL ROUTE MILES.—A recipient in an urbanized area shall receive an amount equal to 40 percent of the amount described in subparagraph (A), multiplied by the number of fixed guideway directional route miles attributable to the urbanized area, as established by the Secretary, divided by the total number of all fixed guideway directional route miles attributable to all urbanized areas.

(4) LIMITATION.—

(A) IN GENERAL.—Except as provided in subparagraph (B), the share of the total amount apportioned under this subsection that is apportioned to an area under this subsection shall not decrease by more than 0.25 percentage points compared to the share apportioned to the area under this subsection in the previous fiscal year.

(B) SPECIAL RULE FOR FISCAL YEAR 2013.—In fiscal year 2013, the share of the total amount apportioned under this subsection that is apportioned to an area under this subsection shall not decrease by more than 0.25 percentage points compared to the share that would have been apportioned to the area under this section, as in effect for fiscal year 2011, if the share had been calculated using the definition of the term "fixed guideway" under subsection (a) of this section, as in effect on the day after the date of enactment of the Federal Public Transportation Act of 2012.

(5) USE OF FUNDS.—Amounts made available under this subsection shall be available for the exclusive use of fixed guideway projects.

(6) RECEIVING APPORTIONMENT.—

(A) IN GENERAL.—Except as provided in subparagraph (B), for an area with a fixed guideway system, the amounts provided under this subsection shall be apportioned to the designated recipient for the urbanized area in which the system operates.

(B) EXCEPTION.—An area described in the amendment made by section 3028(a) of the Transportation Equity Act for the 21st Century (Public Law 105–178; 112 Stat. 366) shall receive an individual apportionment under this subsection.

(7) APPORTIONMENT REQUIREMENTS.—For purposes of determining the number of fixed guideway vehicle revenue miles or fixed guideway directional route miles attributable to an urbanized area for a fiscal year under this subsection, only segments of fixed guideway systems placed in revenue service not later than 7 years before the first day of the fiscal year shall be deemed to be attributable to an urbanized area.

(d) HIGH INTENSITY MOTORBUS STATE OF GOOD REPAIR.—

(1) DEFINITION.—For purposes of this subsection, the term "high intensity motorbus" means public transportation that is provided on a facility with access for other high-occupancy vehicles.

(2) APPORTIONMENT.—Of the amount authorized or made available under section 5338(a)(2)(K),[1] 2.85 percent shall be apportioned to urbanized areas for high intensity motorbus vehicle state of good repair in accordance with this subsection.

(3) VEHICLE REVENUE MILES AND DIRECTIONAL ROUTE MILES.—

(A) IN GENERAL.—The amount described in paragraph (2) shall be apportioned to each area in accordance with this paragraph.

(B) VEHICLE REVENUE MILES.—Each area shall receive an amount equal to 60 percent of the amount described in subparagraph (A), multiplied by the number of high intensity motorbus vehicle revenue miles attributable to the area, as established by the Secretary, divided by the total number of all high intensity motorbus vehicle revenue miles attributable to all areas.

(C) DIRECTIONAL ROUTE MILES.—Each area shall receive an amount equal to 40 percent of the amount described in subparagraph (A), multiplied by the number of high intensity motorbus directional route miles attributable to the area, as established by the Secretary, divided by the total number of all high intensity motorbus directional route miles attributable to all areas.

(4) APPORTIONMENT REQUIREMENTS.—For purposes of determining the number of high intensity motorbus vehicle revenue miles or high intensity motorbus directional route miles attributable to an urbanized area for a fiscal year under this subsection, only segments of high intensity motorbus systems placed in revenue service not later than 7 years before the first day of the fiscal year shall be deemed to be attributable to an urbanized area.

(5) USE OF FUNDS.—Amounts apportioned under this subsection may be used for any project that is an eligible project under subsection (b)(1).

(e) GOVERNMENT SHARE OF COSTS.—

(1) CAPITAL PROJECTS.—A grant for a capital project under this section shall be for 80 percent of the net project cost of the project. The recipient may provide additional local matching amounts.

(2) REMAINING COSTS.—The remainder of the net project cost shall be provided—

(A) in cash from non-Government sources;

(B) from revenues derived from the sale of advertising and concessions; or

(C) from an undistributed cash surplus, a replacement or depreciation cash fund or reserve, or new capital.

(f) COMPETITIVE GRANTS FOR RAIL VEHICLE REPLACEMENT.—

(1) IN GENERAL.—The Secretary may make grants under this subsection to assist State and local governmental authorities in financing capital projects for the replacement of rail rolling stock.

(2) GRANT REQUIREMENTS.—Except as otherwise provided in this subsection, a grant under this subsection shall be subject to the same terms and conditions as a grant under subsection (b).

(3) COMPETITIVE PROCESS.—The Secretary shall solicit grant applications and make not more than 3 new awards to eligible projects under this subsection on a competitive basis each fiscal year.

(4) CONSIDERATION.—In awarding grants under this subsection, the Secretary shall consider—

(A) the size of the rail system of the applicant;

(B) the amount of funds available to the applicant under this subsection;

(C) the age and condition of the rail rolling stock of the applicant that has exceeded or will exceed the useful service life of the rail rolling stock in the 5-year period following the grant; and

(D) whether the applicant has identified replacement of the rail vehicles as a priority in the investment prioritization portion of the transit asset management plan of the recipient pursuant to part 625 of title 49, Code of Federal Regulations (or successor regulations).

(5) MAXIMUM SHARE OF COMPETITIVE GRANT ASSISTANCE.—The amount of grant assistance provided by the Secretary under this subsection, as a share of eligible project costs, shall be not more than 50 percent.

(6) GOVERNMENT SHARE OF COST.—The Government share of the cost of an eligible project carried out under this subsection shall not exceed 80 percent.

(7) MULTI-YEAR GRANT AGREEMENTS.—

(A) IN GENERAL.—An eligible project for which a grant is provided under this subsection may be carried out through a multi-year grant agreement in accordance with this paragraph.

(B) REQUIREMENTS.—A multi-year grant agreement under this paragraph shall—

(i) establish the terms of participation by the Federal Government in the project; and

(ii) establish the maximum amount of Federal financial assistance for the project that may be provided through grant payments to be provided in not more than 3 consecutive fiscal years.

(C) FINANCIAL RULES.—A multi-year grant agreement under this paragraph—

(i) shall obligate an amount of available budget authority specified in law; and

(ii) may include a commitment, contingent on amounts to be specified in law in advance for commitments under this paragraph, to obligate an additional amount from future available budget authority specified in law.

(D) STATEMENT OF CONTINGENT COMMITMENT.—A multi-year agreement under this paragraph shall state that the contingent commitment is not an obligation of the Federal Government.

(Pub. L. 103–272, §1(d), July 5, 1994, 108 Stat. 844; Pub. L. 103–429, §6(14), Oct. 31, 1994, 108 Stat. 4379; Pub. L. 102–240, title III, §3049(b), as added Pub. L. 105–130, §8, Dec. 1, 1997, 111 Stat. 2559;

Pub. L. 105–178, title III, §§3028, 3029(b)(12), June 9, 1998, 112 Stat. 366, 373; Pub. L. 105–206, title IX, §9009(p), July 22, 1998, 112 Stat. 858; Pub. L. 108–88, §8(b)(2), Sept. 30, 2003, 117 Stat. 1121; Pub. L. 109–59, title III, §3035(a), Aug. 10, 2005, 119 Stat. 1629; Pub. L. 110–244, title II, §201(m), June 6, 2008, 122 Stat. 1611; Pub. L. 111–147, title IV, §435, Mar. 18, 2010, 124 Stat. 89; Pub. L. 111–322, title II, §2305, Dec. 22, 2010, 124 Stat. 3528; Pub. L. 112–5, title III, §305, Mar. 4, 2011, 125 Stat. 19; Pub. L. 112–30, title I, §135, Sept. 16, 2011, 125 Stat. 352; Pub. L. 112–102, title III, §305, Mar. 30, 2012, 126 Stat. 277; Pub. L. 112–140, title III, §305, June 29, 2012, 126 Stat. 398; Pub. L. 112–141, div. B, §20027, div. G, title III, §113005, July 6, 2012, 126 Stat. 723, 985; Pub. L. 114–94, div. A, title III, §3015, Dec. 4, 2015, 129 Stat. 1478; Pub. L. 117–58, div. C, §30016, Nov. 15, 2021, 135 Stat. 911.)

[1] *See References in Text note below.*

§5338. AUTHORIZATIONS

(a) GRANTS.—

(1) IN GENERAL.—There shall be available from the Mass Transit Account of the Highway Trust Fund to carry out sections 5305, 5307, 5310, 5311, 5312, 5314, 5318, 5335, 5337, 5339, and 5340, section 20005(b) of the Federal Public Transportation Act of 2012 (49 U.S.C. 5303 note; Public Law 112–141), and section 3006(b) of the Federal Public Transportation Act of 2015 (49 U.S.C. 5310 note; Public Law 114–94)—

(A) $13,355,000,000 for fiscal year 2022;

(B) $13,634,000,000 for fiscal year 2023;

(C) $13,990,000,000 for fiscal year 2024;

(D) $14,279,000,000 for fiscal year 2025; and

(E) $14,642,000,000 for fiscal year 2026.

(2) ALLOCATION OF FUNDS.—Of the amounts made available under paragraph (1)—

(A) $184,647,343 for fiscal year 2022, $188,504,820 for fiscal year 2023, $193,426,906 for fiscal year 2024, $197,422,644 for fiscal year 2025, and $202,441,512 for fiscal year 2026 shall be available to carry out section 5305;

(B) $13,157,184 for fiscal year 2022, $13,432,051 for fiscal year 2023, $13,782,778 for fiscal year 2024, $14,067,497 for fiscal year 2025, and $14,425,121 for fiscal year 2026 shall be available to carry out section 20005(b) of the Federal Public Transportation Act of 2012 (49 U.S.C. 5303 note; Public Law 112–141);

(C) $6,408,288,249 for fiscal year 2022, $6,542,164,133 for fiscal year 2023, $6,712,987,840 for fiscal year 2024, $6,851,662,142 for fiscal year 2025, and $7,025,844,743 for fiscal year 2026 shall be allocated in accordance with section 5336 to provide financial assistance for urbanized areas under section 5307;

(D) $371,247,094 for fiscal year 2022, $379,002,836 for fiscal year 2023, $388,899,052 for fiscal year 2024, $396,932,778 for fiscal year 2025, and $407,023,583 for fiscal year 2026 shall be available to provide financial assistance for services for the enhanced mobility of seniors and individuals with disabilities under section 5310;

(E) $4,605,014 for fiscal year 2022, $4,701,218 for fiscal year 2023, $4,823,972 for fiscal year 2024, $4,923,624 for fiscal year 2025, and $5,048,792 for fiscal year 2026 shall be available for the pilot program for innovative coordinated access and mobility under section 3006(b) of the Federal Public Transportation Act of 2015

(49 U.S.C. 5310 note; Public Law 114–94);

(F) $875,289,555 for fiscal year 2022, $893,575,275 for fiscal year 2023, $916,907,591 for fiscal year 2024, $935,848,712 for fiscal year 2025, and $959,639,810 for fiscal year 2026 shall be available to provide financial assistance for rural areas under section 5311;

(G) $36,840,115 for fiscal year 2022, $37,609,743 for fiscal year 2023, $38,591,779 for fiscal year 2024, $39,388,993 for fiscal year 2025, and $40,390,337 for fiscal year 2026 shall be available to carry out section 5312, of which—

(i) $5,000,000 for fiscal year 2022, $5,104,455 for fiscal year 2023, $5,237,739 for fiscal year 2024, $5,345,938 for fiscal year 2025, and $5,481,842 for fiscal year 2026 shall be available to carry out section 5312(h); and

(ii) $6,578,592 for fiscal year 2022, $6,716,026 for fiscal year 2023, $6,891,389 for fiscal year 2024, $7,033,749 for fiscal year 2025, and $7,212,560 for fiscal year 2026 shall be available to carry out section 5312(i);

(H) $11,841,465 for fiscal year 2022, $12,088,846 for fiscal year 2023, $12,404,500 for fiscal year 2024, $12,660,748 for fiscal year 2025, and $12,982,608 for fiscal year 2026 shall be available to carry out section 5314, of which $6,578,592 for fiscal year 2022, $6,716,026 for fiscal year 2023, $6,891,389 for fiscal year 2024, $7,033,749 for fiscal year 2025, and $7,212,560 for fiscal year 2026 shall be available for the national transit institute under section 5314(c);

(I) $5,000,000 for fiscal year 2022, $5,104,455 for fiscal year 2023, $5,237,739 for fiscal year 2024, $5,345,938 for fiscal year 2025, and $5,481,842 for fiscal year 2026 shall be available for bus testing under section 5318;

(J) $131,000,000 for fiscal year 2022, $134,930,000 for fiscal year 2023, $138,977,900 for fiscal year 2024, $143,147,237 for fiscal year 2025, and $147,441,654 for fiscal year 2026 shall be available to carry out section 5334;

(K) $5,262,874 for fiscal year 2022, $5,372,820 for fiscal year 2023, $5,513,111 for fiscal year 2024, $5,626,999 for fiscal year 2025, and $5,770,048 for fiscal year 2026 shall be available to carry out section 5335;

(L) $3,515,528,226 for fiscal year 2022, $3,587,778,037 for fiscal year 2023, $3,680,934,484 for fiscal year 2024, $3,755,675,417 for fiscal year 2025, and $3,850,496,668 for fiscal year 2026 shall be available to carry out section 5337, of which $300,000,000 for each of fiscal years 2022 through 2026 shall be available to carry out section 5337(f);

(M) $603,992,657 for fiscal year 2022, $616,610,699 for fiscal year 2023, $632,711,140 for fiscal year 2024, $645,781,441 for fiscal year 2025, and $662,198,464 for fiscal year 2026 shall be available for the bus and buses facilities program under section 5339(a);

(N) $447,257,433 for fiscal year 2022, $456,601,111 for fiscal year 2023, $468,523,511 for fiscal year 2024, $478,202,088 for fiscal year 2025, and $490,358,916 for fiscal year 2026 shall be available for buses and bus facilities competitive grants under section 5339(b) and no or low emission grants under section 5339(c), of which $71,561,189 for fiscal year 2022, $73,056,178 for fiscal year 2023, $74,963,762 for fiscal year 2024, $76,512,334 for fiscal year 2025, and

$78,457,427 for fiscal year 2026 shall be available to carry out section 5339(c); and

(O) $741,042,792 for fiscal year 2022, $756,523,956 for fiscal year 2023, $776,277,698 for fiscal year 2024, $792,313,742 for fiscal year 2025, and $812,455,901 for fiscal year 2026, to carry out section 5340 to provide financial assistance for urbanized areas under section 5307 and rural areas under section 5311, of which—

(i) $392,752,680 for fiscal year 2022, $400,957,696 for fiscal year 2023, $411,427,180 for fiscal year 2024, $419,926,283 for fiscal year 2025, and $430,601,628 for fiscal year 2026 shall be for growing States under section 5340(c); and

(ii) $348,290,112 for fiscal year 2022, $355,566,259 for fiscal year 2023, $364,850,518 for fiscal year 2024, $372,387,459 for fiscal year 2025, and $381,854,274 for fiscal year 2026 shall be for high density States under section 5340(d).

(b) CAPITAL INVESTMENT GRANTS.—There are authorized to be appropriated to carry out section 5309 of this title and section 3005(b) of the Federal Public Transportation Act of 2015 (49 U.S.C. 5309 note; Public Law 114–94), $3,000,000,000 for each of fiscal years 2022 through 2026.

(c) OVERSIGHT.—

(1) IN GENERAL.—Of the amounts made available to carry out this chapter for a fiscal year, the Secretary may use not more than the following amounts for the activities described in paragraph (2):

(A) 0.5 percent of amounts made available to carry out section 5305.

(B) 0.75 percent of amounts made available to carry out section 5307.

(C) 1 percent of amounts made available to carry out section 5309.

(D) 1 percent of amounts made available to carry out section 601 of the Passenger Rail Investment and Improvement Act of 2008 (Public Law 110–432; 126 Stat. 4968).[1]

(E) 0.5 percent of amounts made available to carry out section 5310.

(F) 0.5 percent of amounts made available to carry out section 5311.

(G) 1 percent of amounts made available to carry out section 5337, of which not less than 0.25 percent of amounts made available for this subparagraph shall be available to carry out section 5329.

(H) 0.75 percent of amounts made available to carry out section 5339.

(2) ACTIVITIES.—The activities described in this paragraph are as follows:

(A) Activities to oversee the construction of a major capital project.

(B) Activities to review and audit the safety and security, procurement, management, and financial compliance of a recipient or subrecipient of funds under this chapter.

(C) Activities to provide technical assistance generally, and to provide technical assistance to correct deficiencies identified in compliance reviews and audits carried out under this section.

(D) Activities to carry out section 5334.

(3) GOVERNMENT SHARE OF COSTS.—The Government shall pay the entire cost of

carrying out a contract under this subsection.

(4) AVAILABILITY OF CERTAIN FUNDS.—Funds made available under paragraph (1)(C) shall be made available to the Secretary before allocating the funds appropriated to carry out any project under a full funding grant agreement.

(d) GRANTS AS CONTRACTUAL OBLIGATIONS.—

(1) GRANTS FINANCED FROM HIGHWAY TRUST FUND.—A grant or contract that is approved by the Secretary and financed with amounts made available from the Mass Transit Account of the Highway Trust Fund pursuant to this section is a contractual obligation of the Government to pay the Government share of the cost of the project.

(2) GRANTS FINANCED FROM GENERAL FUND.—A grant or contract that is approved by the Secretary and financed with amounts appropriated in advance from the General Fund of the Treasury pursuant to this section is a contractual obligation of the Government to pay the Government share of the cost of the project only to the extent that amounts are appropriated for such purpose by an Act of Congress.

(e) AVAILABILITY OF AMOUNTS.—Amounts made available by or appropriated under this section shall remain available until expended.

(Pub. L. 103–272, §1(d), July 5, 1994, 108 Stat. 845; Pub. L. 104–287, §5(20), Oct. 11, 1996, 110 Stat. 3390; Pub. L. 102–240, §3049(c), as added Pub. L. 105–130, §8, Dec. 1, 1997, 111 Stat. 2559; Pub. L. 105–178, title III, §3029(a), (c), June 9, 1998, 112 Stat. 368; Pub. L. 105–206, title IX, §9009(q), July 22, 1998, 112 Stat. 858; Pub. L. 108–88, §8(c), (e)–(g), (i), (k), Sept. 30, 2003, 117 Stat. 1121–1124; Pub. L. 108–202, §9(c), (e)–(g), (i), (k), Feb. 29, 2004, 118 Stat. 485–487; Pub. L. 108–224, §7(c), (e)–(g), (i), (k), Apr. 30, 2004, 118 Stat. 633–636; Pub. L. 108–263, §7(c), (e)–(g), (i), (k), June 30, 2004, 118 Stat. 704–707; Pub. L. 108–280, §7(c), (e)–(g), (i), (k), July 30, 2004, 118 Stat. 882–884; Pub. L. 108–310, §8(c), (e)–(g), (i), (k), Sept. 30, 2004, 118 Stat. 1154–1157; Pub. L. 109–14, §7(b), (d)–(f), (h), (j), May 31, 2005, 119 Stat. 331–333; Pub. L. 109–20, §7(b), (d)–(f), (h), (j), July 1, 2005, 119 Stat. 353–355; Pub. L. 109–35, §7(b), (d)–(f), (h), (j), July 20, 2005, 119 Stat. 386–388; Pub. L. 109–37, §7(b), (d)–(f), (h), (j), July 22, 2005, 119 Stat. 401–403; Pub. L. 109–40, §7(b), (d)–(f), (h), (j), July 28, 2005, 119 Stat. 417–419; Pub. L. 109–42, §5(a), July 30, 2005, 119 Stat. 436; Pub. L. 109–59, title III, §3036, Aug. 10, 2005, 119 Stat. 1629; Pub. L. 110–244, title II, §201(n), June 6, 2008, 122 Stat. 1611; Pub. L. 111–147, title IV, §436, Mar. 18, 2010, 124 Stat. 90; Pub. L. 111–322, title II, §2306, Dec. 22, 2010, 124 Stat. 3528; Pub. L. 112–5, title III, §306, Mar. 4, 2011, 125 Stat. 19; Pub. L. 112–30, title I, §136, Sept. 16, 2011, 125 Stat. 352; Pub. L. 112–102, title III, §306, Mar. 30, 2012, 126 Stat. 278; Pub. L. 112–140, title III, §306, June 29, 2012, 126 Stat. 398; Pub. L. 112–141, div. B, §20028, div. G, title III, §113006, July 6, 2012, 126 Stat. 726, 985; Pub. L. 113–159, title I, §1203, Aug. 8, 2014, 128 Stat. 1845; Pub. L. 114–21, title I, §1203, May 29, 2015, 129 Stat. 223; Pub. L. 114–41, title I, §1203, July 31, 2015, 129 Stat. 450; Pub. L. 114–73, title I, §1203, Oct. 29, 2015, 129 Stat. 573; Pub. L. 114–87, title I, §1203, Nov. 20, 2015, 129 Stat. 682; Pub. L. 114–94, div. A, title III, §3016, Dec. 4, 2015, 129 Stat. 1479; Pub. L. 117–58, div. C, §30017, Nov. 15, 2021, 135 Stat. 912.)

[1] So in original. Should be "122 Stat. 4968)." See References in Text note below.

§5339. GRANTS FOR BUSES AND BUS FACILITIES

(a) FORMULA GRANTS.—

(1) DEFINITIONS.—In this subsection—

(A) the term "low or no emission vehicle" has the meaning given that term in subsection (c)(1);

(B) the term "State" means a State of the United States; and

(C) the term "territory" means the District of Columbia, Puerto Rico, the Northern Mariana Islands, Guam, American Samoa, and the United States Virgin

Islands.

(2) GENERAL AUTHORITY.—The Secretary may make grants under this subsection to assist eligible recipients described in paragraph (4)(A) in financing capital projects—

(A) to replace, rehabilitate, and purchase buses and related equipment, including technological changes or innovations to modify low or no emission vehicles or facilities; and

(B) to construct bus-related facilities.

(3) GRANT REQUIREMENTS.—The requirements of—

(A) section 5307 shall apply to recipients of grants made in urbanized areas under this subsection; and

(B) section 5311 shall apply to recipients of grants made in rural areas under this subsection.

(4) ELIGIBLE RECIPIENTS.—

(A) RECIPIENTS.—Eligible recipients under this subsection are—

(i) designated recipients that allocate funds to fixed route bus operators; or

(ii) State or local governmental entities that operate fixed route bus service.

(B) SUBRECIPIENTS.—A recipient that receives a grant under this subsection may allocate amounts of the grant to subrecipients that are public agencies or private nonprofit organizations engaged in public transportation.

(5) DISTRIBUTION OF GRANT FUNDS.—Funds allocated under section 5338(a)(2)(L) [1] shall be distributed as follows:

(A) NATIONAL DISTRIBUTION.—$206,000,000 each fiscal year shall be allocated to all States and territories, with each State receiving $4,000,000 for each such fiscal year and each territory receiving $1,000,000 for each such fiscal year.

(B) DISTRIBUTION USING POPULATION AND SERVICE FACTORS.—The remainder of the funds not otherwise distributed under subparagraph (A) shall be allocated pursuant to the formula set forth in section 5336 other than subsection (b).

(6) TRANSFERS OF APPORTIONMENTS.—

(A) TRANSFER FLEXIBILITY FOR NATIONAL DISTRIBUTION FUNDS.—The Governor of a State may transfer any part of the State's apportionment under paragraph (5)(A) to supplement amounts apportioned to the State under section 5311(c) or amounts apportioned to urbanized areas under subsections (a) and (c) of section 5336.

(B) TRANSFER FLEXIBILITY FOR POPULATION AND SERVICE FACTORS FUNDS.—The Governor of a State may expend in an urbanized area with a population of less than 200,000 any amounts apportioned under paragraph (5)(B) that are not allocated to designated recipients in urbanized areas with a population of 200,000 or more.

(7) GOVERNMENT SHARE OF COSTS.—

(A) CAPITAL PROJECTS.—A grant for a capital project under this subsection shall be for 80 percent of the net capital costs of the project. A recipient of a grant under this subsection may provide additional local matching amounts.

(B) REMAINING COSTS.—The remainder of the net project cost shall be provided—

(i) in cash from non-Government sources other than revenues from providing public transportation services;

(ii) from revenues derived from the sale of advertising and concessions;

(iii) from an undistributed cash surplus, a replacement or depreciation cash fund or reserve, or new capital;

(iv) from amounts received under a service agreement with a State or local social service agency or private social service organization; or

(v) from revenues generated from value capture financing mechanisms.

(8) PERIOD OF AVAILABILITY TO RECIPIENTS.—Amounts made available under this subsection may be obligated by a recipient for 3 fiscal years after the fiscal year in which the amount is apportioned. Not later than 30 days after the end of the 3-fiscal-year period described in the preceding sentence, any amount that is not obligated on the last day of such period shall be added to the amount that may be apportioned under this subsection in the next fiscal year.

(9) PILOT PROGRAM FOR COST-EFFECTIVE CAPITAL INVESTMENT.—

(A) IN GENERAL.—For each of fiscal years 2016 through 2020, the Secretary shall carry out a pilot program under which an eligible recipient (as described in paragraph (4)) in an urbanized area with population of not less than 200,000 and not more than 999,999 may elect to participate in a State pool in accordance with this paragraph.

(B) PURPOSE OF STATE POOLS.—The purpose of a State pool shall be to allow for transfers of formula grant funds made available under this subsection among the designated recipients participating in the State pool in a manner that supports the transit asset management plans of the designated recipients under section 5326.

(C) REQUESTS FOR PARTICIPATION.—A State, and eligible recipients in the State described in subparagraph (A), may submit to the Secretary a request for participation in the program under procedures to be established by the Secretary. An eligible recipient for a multistate area may participate in only 1 State pool.

(D) ALLOCATIONS TO PARTICIPATING STATES.—For each fiscal year, the Secretary shall allocate to each State participating in the program the total amount of funds that otherwise would be allocated to the urbanized areas of the eligible recipients participating in the State's pool for that fiscal year pursuant to the formulas referred to in paragraph (5).

(E) ALLOCATIONS TO ELIGIBLE RECIPIENTS IN STATE POOLS.—A State shall distribute the amount that is allocated to the State for a fiscal year under subparagraph (D) among the eligible recipients participating in the State's pool in a manner that supports the transit asset management plans of the recipients under section 5326.

(F) ALLOCATION PLANS.—A State participating in the program shall develop an allocation plan for the period of fiscal years 2016 through 2020 to ensure that an eligible recipient participating in the State's pool receives under the program an amount of funds that equals the amount of funds that would have otherwise been available to the eligible recipient for that period pursuant to the formulas referred to in paragraph (5).

(G) GRANTS.—The Secretary shall make grants under this subsection for a fiscal year to an eligible recipient participating in a State pool following notification by the State of the allocation amount determined under subparagraph (E).

(10) MAXIMIZING USE OF FUNDS.—

(A) IN GENERAL.—Eligible recipients and subrecipients under this subsection should, to the extent practicable, seek to utilize the procurement tools authorized under section 3019 of the FAST Act (49 U.S.C. 5325 note; Public Law 114–94).

(B) WRITTEN EXPLANATION.—If an eligible recipient or subrecipient under this subsection purchases less than 5 buses through a standalone procurement, the eligible recipient or subrecipient shall provide to the Secretary a written explanation regarding why the tools authorized under section 3019 of the FAST Act (49 U.S.C. 5325 note; Public Law 114–94) were not utilized.

(b) BUSES AND BUS FACILITIES COMPETITIVE GRANTS.—

(1) IN GENERAL.—The Secretary may make grants under this subsection to eligible recipients (as described in subsection (a)(4)) to assist in the financing of buses and bus facilities capital projects, including—

(A) replacing, rehabilitating, purchasing, or leasing buses or related equipment; and

(B) rehabilitating, purchasing, constructing, or leasing bus-related facilities.

(2) GRANT CONSIDERATIONS.—In making grants under this subsection, the Secretary shall consider the age and condition of buses, bus fleets, related equipment, and bus-related facilities.

(3) STATEWIDE APPLICATIONS.—A State may submit a statewide application on behalf of a public agency or private nonprofit organization engaged in public transportation in rural areas or other areas for which the State allocates funds. The submission of a statewide application shall not preclude the submission and consideration of any application under this subsection from other eligible recipients (as described in subsection (a)(4)) in an urbanized area in a State.

(4) REQUIREMENTS FOR THE SECRETARY.—The Secretary shall—

(A) disclose all metrics and evaluation procedures to be used in considering grant applications under this subsection upon issuance of the notice of funding availability in the Federal Register; and

(B) publish a summary of final scores for selected projects, metrics, and other evaluations used in awarding grants under this subsection in the Federal Register.

(5) RURAL PROJECTS.—

(A) IN GENERAL.—Subject to subparagraph (B), not less than 15 percent of the amounts made available under this subsection in a fiscal year shall be distributed to projects in rural areas.

(B) UNUTILIZED AMOUNTS.—The Secretary may use less than 15 percent of the amounts made available under this subsection in a fiscal year for the projects described in subparagraph (A) if the Secretary cannot meet the requirement of that subparagraph due to insufficient eligible applications.

(6) GRANT REQUIREMENTS.—

(A) IN GENERAL.—A grant under this subsection shall be subject to the requirements of—

(i) section 5307 for eligible recipients of grants made in urbanized areas; and

(ii) section 5311 for eligible recipients of grants made in rural areas.

(B) GOVERNMENT SHARE OF COSTS.—The Government share of the cost of an eligible project carried out under this subsection shall not exceed 80 percent.

(7) AVAILABILITY OF FUNDS.—Any amounts made available to carry out this subsection—

(A) shall remain available for 3 fiscal years after the fiscal year for which the amount is made available; and

(B) that remain unobligated at the end of the period described in subparagraph (A) shall be added to the amount made available to an eligible project in the following fiscal year.

(8) LIMITATION.—Of the amounts made available under this subsection, not more than 10 percent may be awarded to a single grantee.

(9) COMPETITIVE PROCESS.—The Secretary shall—

(A) not later than 30 days after the date on which amounts are made available for obligation under this subsection for a full fiscal year, solicit grant applications for eligible projects on a competitive basis; and

(B) award a grant under this subsection based on the solicitation under subparagraph (A) not later than the earlier of—

(i) 75 days after the date on which the solicitation expires; or

(ii) the end of the fiscal year in which the Secretary solicited the grant applications.

(10) CONTINUED USE OF PARTNERSHIPS.—

(A) IN GENERAL.—An eligible recipient of a grant under this subsection may submit an application in partnership with other entities, including a transit vehicle manufacturer that intends to participate in the implementation of a project under this subsection and subsection (c).

(B) COMPETITIVE PROCUREMENT.—Projects awarded with partnerships under this subsection shall be considered to satisfy the requirement for a competitive procurement under section 5325.

(11) MAXIMIZING USE OF FUNDS.—

(A) IN GENERAL.—Eligible recipients under this subsection should, to the extent practicable, seek to utilize the procurement tools authorized under section 3019 of the FAST Act (49 U.S.C. 5325 note; Public Law 114–94).

(B) WRITTEN EXPLANATION.—If an eligible recipient under this subsection purchases less than 5 buses through a standalone procurement, the eligible recipient shall provide to the Secretary a written explanation regarding why the tools authorized under section 3019 of the FAST Act (49 U.S.C. 5325 note; Public Law 114–94) were not utilized.

(c) LOW OR NO EMISSION GRANTS.—

(1) DEFINITIONS.—In this subsection—

(A) the term "direct carbon emissions" means the quantity of direct greenhouse gas emissions from a vehicle, as determined by the Administrator of the Environmental Protection Agency;

(B) the term "eligible project" means a project or program of projects in an eligible area for—

(i) acquiring low or no emission vehicles;

(ii) leasing low or no emission vehicles;

(iii) acquiring low or no emission vehicles with a leased power source;

(iv) constructing facilities and related equipment for low or no emission vehicles;

(v) leasing facilities and related equipment for low or no emission vehicles;

(vi) constructing new public transportation facilities to accommodate low or no emission vehicles; or

(vii) rehabilitating or improving existing public transportation facilities to accommodate low or no emission vehicles;

(C) the term "leased power source" means a removable power source, as defined in subsection (c)(3) of section 3019 of the Federal Public Transportation Act of 2015 that is made available through a capital lease under such section;

(D) the term "low or no emission bus" means a bus that is a low or no emission vehicle;

(E) the term "low or no emission vehicle" means—

(i) a passenger vehicle used to provide public transportation that the Secretary determines sufficiently reduces energy consumption or harmful emissions, including direct carbon emissions, when compared to a comparable standard vehicle; or

(ii) a zero emission vehicle used to provide public transportation;

(F) the term "recipient" means a designated recipient, a local governmental authority, or a State that receives a grant under this subsection for an eligible project; and

(G) the term "zero emission vehicle" means a low or no emission vehicle that produces no carbon or particulate matter.

(2) GENERAL AUTHORITY.—The Secretary may make grants to recipients to finance eligible projects under this subsection.

(3) GRANT REQUIREMENTS.—

(A) IN GENERAL.—A grant under this subsection shall be subject to—

(i) with respect to eligible recipients in urbanized areas, section 5307; and

(ii) with respect to eligible recipients in rural areas, section 5311.

(B) GOVERNMENT SHARE OF COSTS FOR CERTAIN PROJECTS.—Section 5323(i) applies to eligible projects carried out under this subsection, unless the recipient requests a lower grant percentage.

(C) COMBINATION OF FUNDING SOURCES.—

(i) COMBINATION PERMITTED.—An eligible project carried out under this subsection may receive funding under section 5307 or any other provision of law.

(ii) GOVERNMENT SHARE.—Nothing in this subparagraph shall be construed to alter the Government share required under paragraph (7), section 5307, or any other provision of law.

(D) FLEET TRANSITION PLAN.—In awarding grants under this subsection or under subsection (b) for projects related to zero emission vehicles, the Secretary shall require the applicant to submit a zero emission transition plan, which, at a minimum—

(i) demonstrates a long-term fleet management plan with a strategy for how the applicant intends to use the current application and future acquisitions;

(ii) addresses the availability of current and future resources to meet costs;

(iii) considers policy and legislation impacting technologies;

(iv) includes an evaluation of existing and future facilities and their relationship to the technology transition;

(v) describes the partnership of the applicant with the utility or alternative fuel provider of the applicant; and

(vi) examines the impact of the transition on the applicant's current workforce by identifying skill gaps, training needs, and retraining needs of the existing workers of the applicant to operate and maintain zero emission vehicles and related infrastructure and avoids the displacement of the existing workforce.

(4) COMPETITIVE PROCESS.—The Secretary shall—

(A) not later than 30 days after the date on which amounts are made available for obligation under this subsection for a full fiscal year, solicit grant applications for eligible projects on a competitive basis; and

(B) award a grant under this subsection based on the solicitation under subparagraph (A) not later than the earlier of—

(i) 75 days after the date on which the solicitation expires; or

(ii) the end of the fiscal year in which the Secretary solicited the grant applications.

(5) CONSIDERATION.—In awarding grants under this subsection, the Secretary—

(A) shall consider eligible projects relating to the acquisition or leasing of low or no emission buses or bus facilities that make greater reductions in energy consumption and harmful emissions, including direct carbon emissions, than comparable standard buses or other low or no emission buses; and

(B) shall, for no less than 25 percent of the funds made available to carry out this subsection, only consider eligible projects related to the acquisition of low or no emission buses or bus facilities other than zero emission vehicles and related facilities.

(6) AVAILABILITY OF FUNDS.—Any amounts made available to carry out this subsection—

(A) shall remain available to an eligible project for 3 fiscal years after the fiscal year for which the amount is made available; and

(B) that remain unobligated at the end of the period described in subparagraph (A) shall be added to the amount made available to an eligible project in the following fiscal year.

(7) GOVERNMENT SHARE OF COSTS.—

(A) IN GENERAL.—The Federal share of the cost of an eligible project carried out under this subsection shall not exceed 80 percent.

(B) NON-FEDERAL SHARE.—The non-Federal share of the cost of an eligible project carried out under this subsection may be derived from in-kind contributions.

(8) CONTINUED USE OF PARTNERSHIPS.—

(A) IN GENERAL.—A recipient of a grant under this subsection may submit an application in partnership with other entities, including a transit vehicle manufacturer, that intends to participate in the implementation of an eligible project under this subsection.

(B) Competitive procurement.—Eligible projects awarded with partnerships under this subsection shall be considered to satisfy the requirement for a competitive procurement under section 5325.

(d) Workforce Development Training Activities.—5 percent of grants related to zero emissions vehicles (as defined in subsection (c)(1)) or related infrastructure under subsection (b) or (c) shall be used by recipients to fund workforce development training, as described in section 5314(b)(2) (including registered apprenticeships and other labor-management training programs) under the recipient's plan to address the impact of the transition to zero emission vehicles on the applicant's current workforce under subsection (c)(3)(D), unless the recipient certifies a smaller percentage is necessary to carry out that plan.

(Added Pub. L. 108–7, div. I, title III, §356, Feb. 20, 2003, 117 Stat. 421; amended Pub. L. 109–59, title III, §3037(a), Aug. 10, 2005, 119 Stat. 1635; Pub. L. 112–141, div. B, §20029(a), July 6, 2012, 126 Stat. 729; Pub. L. 113–159, title I, §1204, Aug. 8, 2014, 128 Stat. 1847; Pub. L. 114–21, title I, §1204, May 29, 2015, 129 Stat. 225; Pub. L. 114–41, title I, §1204, July 31, 2015, 129 Stat. 452; Pub. L. 114–73, title I, §1204, Oct. 29, 2015, 129 Stat. 575; Pub. L. 114–87, title I, §1204, Nov. 20, 2015, 129 Stat. 684; Pub. L. 114–94, div. A, title III, §3017(a), Dec. 4, 2015, 129 Stat. 1482; Pub. L. 117–58, div. C, §30018, Nov. 15, 2021, 135 Stat. 915.)

[1] See References in Text note below.

§5340. Apportionments based on growing States and high density States formula factors

(a) Definition.—In this section, the term "State" shall mean each of the 50 States of the United States.

(b) Allocation.—The Secretary shall apportion the amounts made available under section 5338(b)(2)(N) [1] in accordance with subsection (c) and subsection (d).

(c) Growing State Apportionments.—

(1) Apportionment among states.—The amounts apportioned under subsection (b)(1) shall provide each State with an amount equal to the total amount apportioned multiplied by a ratio equal to the population of that State forecast for the year that is 15 years after the most recent decennial census, divided by the total population of all States forecast for the year that is 15 years after the most recent decennial census. Such forecast shall be based on the population trend for each State between the most recent decennial census and the most recent estimate of population made by the Secretary of Commerce.

(2) Apportionments between urbanized areas and other than urbanized areas in each state.—

(A) In general.—The Secretary shall apportion amounts to each State under paragraph (1) so that urbanized areas in that State receive an amount equal to the amount apportioned to that State multiplied by a ratio equal to the sum of the forecast population of all urbanized areas in that State divided by the total forecast population of that State. In making the apportionment under this subparagraph, the Secretary shall utilize any available forecasts made by the State. If no forecasts are available, the Secretary shall utilize data on urbanized areas and total population from the most recent decennial census.

(B) REMAINING AMOUNTS.—Amounts remaining for each State after apportionment under subparagraph (A) shall be apportioned to that State and added to the amount made available for grants under section 5311.

(3) APPORTIONMENTS AMONG URBANIZED AREAS IN EACH STATE.—The Secretary shall apportion amounts made available to urbanized areas in each State under paragraph (2)(A) so that each urbanized area receives an amount equal to the amount apportioned under paragraph (2)(A) multiplied by a ratio equal to the population of each urbanized area divided by the sum of populations of all urbanized areas in the State. Amounts apportioned to each urbanized area shall be added to amounts apportioned to that urbanized area under section 5336, and made available for grants under section 5307.

(d) HIGH DENSITY STATE APPORTIONMENTS.—Amounts to be apportioned under subsection (b)(2) shall be apportioned as follows:

(1) ELIGIBLE STATES.—The Secretary shall designate as eligible for an apportionment under this subsection all States with a population density in excess of 370 persons per square mile.

(2) STATE URBANIZED LAND FACTOR.—For each State qualifying for an apportionment under paragraph (1), the Secretary shall calculate an amount equal to—

(A) the total land area of the State (in square miles); multiplied by

(B) 370; multiplied by

(C)(i) the population of the State in urbanized areas; divided by

(ii) the total population of the State.

(3) STATE APPORTIONMENT FACTOR.—For each State qualifying for an apportionment under paragraph (1), the Secretary shall calculate an amount equal to the difference between the total population of the State less the amount calculated in paragraph (2).

(4) STATE APPORTIONMENT.—Each State qualifying for an apportionment under paragraph (1) shall receive an amount equal to the amount to be apportioned under this subsection multiplied by the amount calculated for the State under paragraph (3) divided by the sum of the amounts calculated under paragraph (3) for all States qualifying for an apportionment under paragraph (1).

(5) APPORTIONMENTS AMONG URBANIZED AREAS IN EACH STATE.—The Secretary shall apportion amounts made available to each State under paragraph (4) so that each urbanized area receives an amount equal to the amount apportioned under paragraph (4) multiplied by a ratio equal to the population of each urbanized area divided by the sum of populations of all urbanized areas in the State. Amounts apportioned to each urbanized area shall be added to amounts apportioned to that urbanized area under section 5336, and made available for grants under section 5307.

(Added Pub. L. 109–59, title III, §3038(a), Aug. 10, 2005, 119 Stat. 1636; amended Pub. L. 114–94, div. A, title III, §3030(f), Dec. 4, 2015, 129 Stat. 1497.)

[1] So in original. Probably should have been "section 5338(a)(2)(N)" in original.

* * * * * * *

§13908. Registration and other reforms

References in Text

Section 14504, referred to in subsec. (a)(1), was repealed by Pub. L. 109–59, title IV, §4305(a), Aug. 10, 2005, 119 Stat. 1764; Pub. L. 110–53, title XV, §1537(a), Aug. 3, 2007, 121 Stat. 467, effective Jan. 1, 2008.

The effective date of this section, referred to in subsec. (c), probably means the date of enactment of Pub. L. 109–59, which amended this section generally and was approved Aug. 10, 2005.

Regulations

Pub. L. 110–53, title XV, §1537(b), Aug. 3, 2007, 121 Stat. 467, provided that: "Not later than October 1, 2007, the Federal Motor Carrier Safety Administration shall issue final regulations to establish the Unified Carrier Registration System, as required by section 13908 of title 49, United States Code, and set fees for the unified carrier registration agreement for calendar year 2007 or subsequent calendar years to be charged to motor carriers, motor private carriers, and freight forwarders under such agreement, as required by 14504a of title 49, United States Code."

SELECTED PROVISIONS OF
TITLE 26 U.S.C. — INTERNAL REVENUE CODE

TITLE 26—INTERNAL REVENUE CODE

(Aug. 16, 1954, ch. 736, 68A Stat. 3; Pub. L. 99–514, §2, Oct. 22, 1986, 100 Stat. 2095.)

* * * * * * *

Subtitle A—Income Taxes

* * * * * * *

CHAPTER 1—NORMAL TAXES AND SURTAXES

* * * * * * *

Subchapter B—Computation of Taxable Income

* * * * * * *

PART III—ITEMS SPECIFICALLY EXCLUDED FROM GROSS INCOME

* * * * * * *

§132. Certain fringe benefits

(A) Exclusion from gross income

Gross income shall not include any fringe benefit which qualifies as a—
(1) no-additional-cost service,
(2) qualified employee discount,
(3) working condition fringe,
(4) de minimis fringe,
(5) qualified transportation fringe,
(6) qualified moving expense reimbursement,
(7) qualified retirement planning services, or
(8) qualified military base realignment and closure fringe.

(B) No-additional-cost service defined

* * * * * * *

(F) QUALIFIED TRANSPORTATION FRINGE

(1) IN GENERAL

For purposes of this section, the term "qualified transportation fringe" means any of the following provided by an employer to an employee:

(A) Transportation in a commuter highway vehicle if such transportation is in connection with travel between the employee's residence and place of employment.

(B) Any transit pass.

(C) Qualified parking.

(D) Any qualified bicycle commuting reimbursement.

(2) LIMITATION ON EXCLUSION

The amount of the fringe benefits which are provided by an employer to any employee and which may be excluded from gross income under subsection (a)(5) shall not exceed—

(A) $175 per month in the case of the aggregate of the benefits described in subparagraphs (A) and (B) of paragraph (1),

(B) $175 per month in the case of qualified parking, and

(C) the applicable annual limitation in the case of any qualified bicycle commuting reimbursement.

(3) CASH REIMBURSEMENTS

For purposes of this subsection, the term "qualified transportation fringe" includes a cash reimbursement by an employer to an employee for a benefit described in paragraph (1). The preceding sentence shall apply to a cash reimbursement for any transit pass only if a voucher or similar item which may be exchanged only for a transit pass is not readily available for direct distribution by the employer to the employee.

(4) NO CONSTRUCTIVE RECEIPT

No amount shall be included in the gross income of an employee solely because the employee may choose between any qualified transportation fringe (other than a qualified bicycle commuting reimbursement) and compensation which would otherwise be includible in gross income of such employee.

(5) DEFINITIONS

For purposes of this subsection—

(A) TRANSIT PASS

The term "transit pass" means any pass, token, farecard, voucher, or similar item entitling a person to transportation (or transportation at a reduced price) if such transportation is—

(i) on mass transit facilities (whether or not publicly owned), or

(ii) provided by any person in the business of transporting persons for compensation or hire if such transportation is provided in a vehicle meeting the requirements of subparagraph (B)(i).

(B) Commuter highway vehicle

The term "commuter highway vehicle" means any highway vehicle—
(i) the seating capacity of which is at least 6 adults (not including the driver), and
(ii) at least 80 percent of the mileage use of which can reasonably be expected to be—
(I) for purposes of transporting employees in connection with travel between their residences and their place of employment, and
(II) on trips during which the number of employees transported for such purposes is at least ½ of the adult seating capacity of such vehicle (not including the driver).

(C) Qualified parking

The term "qualified parking" means parking provided to an employee on or near the business premises of the employer or on or near a location from which the employee commutes to work by transportation described in subparagraph (A), in a commuter highway vehicle, or by carpool. Such term shall not include any parking on or near property used by the employee for residential purposes.

(D) Transportation provided by employer

Transportation referred to in paragraph (1)(A) shall be considered to be provided by an employer if such transportation is furnished in a commuter highway vehicle operated by or for the employer.

(E) Employee

For purposes of this subsection, the term "employee" does not include an individual who is an employee within the meaning of section 401(c)(1).

(F) Definitions related to bicycle commuting reimbursement

(I) Qualified bicycle commuting reimbursement

The term "qualified bicycle commuting reimbursement" means, with respect to any calendar year, any employer reimbursement during the 15-month period beginning with the first day of such calendar year for reasonable expenses incurred by the employee during such calendar year for the purchase of a bicycle and bicycle improvements, repair, and storage, if such bicycle is regularly used for travel between the employee's residence and place of employment.

(II) Applicable annual limitation

The term "applicable annual limitation" means, with respect to any employee for any calendar year, the product of $20 multiplied by the number of qualified bicycle commuting months during such year.

(III) Qualified bicycle commuting month

The term "qualified bicycle commuting month" means, with respect to any employee, any month during which such employee—
(I) regularly uses the bicycle for a substantial portion of the travel between

the employee's residence and place of employment, and

(II) does not receive any benefit described in subparagraph (A), (B), or (C) of paragraph (1).

(6) INFLATION ADJUSTMENT

(A) IN GENERAL

In the case of any taxable year beginning in a calendar year after 1999, the dollar amounts contained in subparagraphs (A) and (B) of paragraph (2) shall be increased by an amount equal to—

(i) such dollar amount, multiplied by

(ii) the cost-of-living adjustment determined under section 1(f)(3) for the calendar year in which the taxable year begins, by substituting "calendar year 1998" for "calendar year 2016" in subparagraph (A)(ii) thereof.

(B) ROUNDING

If any increase determined under subparagraph (A) is not a multiple of $5, such increase shall be rounded to the next lowest multiple of $5.

(7) COORDINATION WITH OTHER PROVISIONS

For purposes of this section, the terms "working condition fringe" and "de minimis fringe" shall not include any qualified transportation fringe (determined without regard to paragraph (2)).

* * * * * * *

(Added Pub. L. 98–369, div. A, title V, §531(a)(1), July 18, 1984, 98 Stat. 877; amended Pub. L. 99–272, title XIII, §13207(a)(1), (b)(1), Apr. 7, 1986, 100 Stat. 319; Pub. L. 99–514, title XI, §§1114(b)(5), 1151(e)(2)(A), (g)(5), title XVIII, §§1853(a), 1899A(5), Oct. 22, 1986, 100 Stat. 2451, 2506, 2507, 2870, 2958; Pub. L. 100–647, title I, §1011B(a)(31)(B), title VI, §6066(a), Nov. 10, 1988, 102 Stat. 3488, 3702; Pub. L. 101–140, title II, §203(a)(1), (2), Nov. 8, 1989, 103 Stat. 830; Pub. L. 101–239, title VII, §§7101(b), 7841(d)(7), (19), Dec. 19, 1989, 103 Stat. 2304, 2428, 2429; Pub. L. 102–486, title XIX, §1911(a)–(c), Oct. 24, 1992, 106 Stat. 3012–3014; Pub. L. 103–66, title XIII, §§13101(b), 13201(b)(3)(F), 13213(d)(1), (2), (3)(B), (C), Aug. 10, 1993, 107 Stat. 420, 459, 474; Pub. L. 105–34, title IX, §970(a), title X, §1072(a), Aug. 5, 1997, 111 Stat. 897, 948; Pub. L. 105–178, title IX, §9010(a)(1), (b)(1), (2), (c)(1), (2), June 9, 1998, 112 Stat. 507, 508; Pub. L. 107–16, title VI, §665(a), (b), June 7, 2001, 115 Stat. 143; Pub. L. 108–121, title I, §103(a), (b), Nov. 11, 2003, 117 Stat. 1337; Pub. L. 108–311, title II, §207(13), Oct. 4, 2004, 118 Stat. 1177; Pub. L. 110–343, div. B, title II, §211(a)–(d), Oct. 3, 2008, 122 Stat. 3840, 3841; Pub. L. 111–5, div. B, title I, §1151(a), Feb. 17, 2009, 123 Stat. 333; Pub. L. 111–92, §14(a), Nov. 6, 2009, 123 Stat. 2995; Pub. L. 111–312, title VII, §727(a), Dec. 17, 2010, 124 Stat. 3317; Pub. L. 112–240, title II, §203(a), Jan. 2, 2013, 126 Stat. 2323; Pub. L. 113–295, div. A, title I, §103(a), Dec. 19, 2014, 128 Stat. 4013; Pub. L. 114–113, div. Q, title I, §105(a), Dec. 18, 2015, 129 Stat. 3046; Pub. L. 115–97, title I, §§11002(d)(5), 11047(a), 11048(a), Dec. 22, 2017, 131 Stat. 2061, 2088; Pub. L. 115–141, div. U, title I, §101(b), title IV, §401(a)(38), Mar. 23, 2018, 132 Stat. 1160, 1186.)

* * * * * * *

PART IV—TAX EXEMPTION REQUIREMENTS FOR STATE AND LOCAL BONDS

* * * * * * *

SUBPART A—PRIVATE ACTIVITY BONDS

* * * * * * *

* * * * * * *

§141. PRIVATE ACTIVITY BOND; QUALIFIED BOND

(A) PRIVATE ACTIVITY BOND

For purposes of this title, the term "private activity bond" means any bond issued as part of an issue—
(1) which meets—
(A) the private business use test of paragraph (1) of subsection (b), and
(B) the private security or payment test of paragraph (2) of subsection (b), or
(2) which meets the private loan financing test of subsection (c).

(B) PRIVATE BUSINESS TESTS

(1) PRIVATE BUSINESS USE TEST

Except as otherwise provided in this subsection, an issue meets the test of this paragraph if more than 10 percent of the proceeds of the issue are to be used for any private business use.

(2) PRIVATE SECURITY OR PAYMENT TEST

Except as otherwise provided in this subsection, an issue meets the test of this paragraph if the payment of the principal of, or the interest on, more than 10 percent of the proceeds of such issue is (under the terms of such issue or any underlying arrangement) directly or indirectly—
(A) secured by any interest in—
(i) property used or to be used for a private business use, or
(ii) payments in respect of such property, or
(B) to be derived from payments (whether or not to the issuer) in respect of property, or borrowed money, used or to be used for a private business use.

(3) 5 PERCENT TEST FOR PRIVATE BUSINESS USE NOT RELATED OR DISPROPORTIONATE TO
GOVERNMENT USE FINANCED BY THE ISSUE

(A) IN GENERAL

An issue shall be treated as meeting the tests of paragraphs (1) and (2) if such tests would be met if such paragraphs were applied—

(i) by substituting "5 percent" for "10 percent" each place it appears, and

(ii) by taking into account only—

(I) the proceeds of the issue which are to be used for any private business use which is not related to any government use of such proceeds,

(II) the disproportionate related business use proceeds of the issue, and

(III) payments, property, and borrowed money with respect to any use of proceeds described in subclause (I) or (II).

(B) DISPROPORTIONATE RELATED BUSINESS USE PROCEEDS

For purposes of subparagraph (A), the disproportionate related business use proceeds of an issue is an amount equal to the aggregate of the excesses (determined under the following sentence) for each private business use of the proceeds of an issue which is related to a government use of such proceeds. The excess determined under this sentence is the excess of—

(i) the proceeds of the issue which are to be used for the private business use, over

(ii) the proceeds of the issue which are to be used for the government use to which such private business use relates.

(4) LOWER LIMITATION FOR CERTAIN OUTPUT FACILITIES

An issue 5 percent or more of the proceeds of which are to be used with respect to any output facility (other than a facility for the furnishing of water) shall be treated as meeting the tests of paragraphs (1) and (2) if the nonqualified amount with respect to such issue exceeds the excess of—

(A) $15,000,000, over

(B) the aggregate nonqualified amounts with respect to all prior tax-exempt issues 5 percent or more of the proceeds of which are or will be used with respect to such facility (or any other facility which is part of the same project).

There shall not be taken into account under subparagraph (B) any bond which is not outstanding at the time of the later issue or which is to be redeemed (other than in an advance refunding) from the net proceeds of the later issue.

(5) COORDINATION WITH VOLUME CAP WHERE NONQUALIFIED AMOUNT EXCEEDS
$15,000,000

If the nonqualified amount with respect to an issue—

(A) exceeds $15,000,000, but

(B) does not exceed the amount which would cause a bond which is part of such issue to be treated as a private activity bond without regard to this paragraph,

such bond shall nonetheless be treated as a private activity bond unless the issuer allocates a portion of its volume cap under section 146 to such issue in an amount equal to the excess of such nonqualified amount over $15,000,000.

(6) PRIVATE BUSINESS USE DEFINED

(A) IN GENERAL

For purposes of this subsection, the term "private business use" means use (directly or indirectly) in a trade or business carried on by any person other than a governmental unit. For purposes of the preceding sentence, use as a member of the general public shall not be taken into account.

(B) CLARIFICATION OF TRADE OR BUSINESS

For purposes of the 1st sentence of subparagraph (A), any activity carried on by a person other than a natural person shall be treated as a trade or business.

(C) CLARIFICATION RELATING TO QUALIFIED CARBON DIOXIDE CAPTURE FACILITIES

For purposes of this subsection, the sale of carbon dioxide produced by a qualified carbon dioxide capture facility (as defined in section 142(o)) which is owned by a governmental unit shall not constitute private business use.

(7) GOVERNMENT USE

The term "government use" means any use other than a private business use.

(8) NONQUALIFIED AMOUNT

For purposes of this subsection, the term "nonqualified amount" means, with respect to an issue, the lesser of—

(A) the proceeds of such issue which are to be used for any private business use, or

(B) the proceeds of such issue with respect to which there are payments (or property or borrowed money) described in paragraph (2).

(9) EXCEPTION FOR QUALIFIED 501(C)(3) BONDS

There shall not be taken into account under this subsection or subsection (c) the portion of the proceeds of an issue which (if issued as a separate issue) would be treated as a qualified 501(c)(3) bond if the issuer elects to treat such portion as a qualified 501(c)(3) bond.

(C) PRIVATE LOAN FINANCING TEST

(1) IN GENERAL

An issue meets the test of this subsection if the amount of the proceeds of the issue which are to be used (directly or indirectly) to make or finance loans (other than loans described in paragraph (2)) to persons other than governmental units exceeds the lesser of—

(A) 5 percent of such proceeds, or

(B) $5,000,000.

(2) EXCEPTION FOR TAX ASSESSMENT, ETC., LOANS

For purposes of paragraph (1), a loan is described in this paragraph if such loan—

(A) enables the borrower to finance any governmental tax or assessment of general application for a specific essential governmental function,

(B) is a nonpurpose investment (within the meaning of section 148(f)(6)(A)), or

(C) is a qualified natural gas supply contract (as defined in section 148(b)(4)).

(D) CERTAIN ISSUES USED TO ACQUIRE NONGOVERNMENTAL OUTPUT PROPERTY TREATED AS PRIVATE ACTIVITY BONDS

(1) IN GENERAL

For purposes of this title, the term "private activity bond" includes any bond issued as part of an issue if the amount of the proceeds of the issue which are to be used (directly or indirectly) for the acquisition by a governmental unit of nongovernmental output property exceeds the lesser of—

(A) 5 percent of such proceeds, or

(B) $5,000,000.

(2) NONGOVERNMENTAL OUTPUT PROPERTY

Except as otherwise provided in this subsection, for purposes of paragraph (1), the term "nongovernmental output property" means any property (or interest therein) which before such acquisition was used (or held for use) by a person other than a governmental unit in connection with an output facility (within the meaning of subsection (b)(4)) (other than a facility for the furnishing of water). For purposes of the preceding sentence, use (or the holding for use) before October 14, 1987, shall not be taken into account.

(3) EXCEPTION FOR PROPERTY ACQUIRED TO PROVIDE OUTPUT TO CERTAIN AREAS

For purposes of paragraph (1)—

(A) IN GENERAL

The term "nongovernmental output property" shall not include any property which is to be used in connection with an output facility 95 percent or more of the output of which will be consumed in—

(i) a qualified service area of the governmental unit acquiring the property, or

(ii) a qualified annexed area of such unit.

(B) DEFINITIONS

For purposes of subparagraph (A)—

(I) QUALIFIED SERVICE AREA

The term "qualified service area" means, with respect to the governmental unit acquiring the property, any area throughout which such unit provided (at all times during the 10-year period ending on the date such property is acquired by such unit) output of the same type as the output to be provided by such property. For purposes of the preceding sentence, the period before October 14, 1987, shall not be taken into account.

(II) QUALIFIED ANNEXED AREA

The term "qualified annexed area" means, with respect to the governmental unit acquiring the property, any area if—

(I) such area is contiguous to, and annexed for general governmental purposes into, a qualified service area of such unit,

(II) output from such property is made available to all members of the general public in the annexed area, and

(III) the annexed area is not greater than 10 percent of such qualified service area.

(C) LIMITATION ON SIZE OF ANNEXED AREA NOT TO APPLY WHERE OUTPUT CAPACITY DOES NOT INCREASE BY MORE THAN 10 PERCENT

Subclause (III) of subparagraph (B)(ii) shall not apply to an annexation of an area by a governmental unit if the output capacity of the property acquired in connection with the annexation, when added to the output capacity of all other property which is not treated as nongovernmental output property by reason of subparagraph (A)(ii) with respect to such annexed area, does not exceed 10 percent of the output capacity of the property providing output of the same type to the qualified service area into which it is annexed.

(D) RULES FOR DETERMINING RELATIVE SIZE, ETC.

For purposes of subparagraphs (B)(ii) and (C)—

(i) The size of any qualified service area and the output capacity of property serving such area shall be determined as the close of the calendar year preceding the calendar year in which the acquisition of nongovernmental output property or the annexation occurs.

(ii) A qualified annexed area shall be treated as part of the qualified service area into which it is annexed for purposes of determining whether any other area annexed in a later year is a qualified annexed area.

(4) EXCEPTION FOR PROPERTY CONVERTED TO NONOUTPUT USE

For purposes of paragraph (1)—

(A) IN GENERAL

The term "nongovernmental output property" shall not include any property which is to be converted to a use not in connection with an output facility.

(B) EXCEPTION

Subparagraph (A) shall not apply to any property which is part of the output function of a nuclear power facility.

(5) SPECIAL RULES

In the case of a bond which is a private activity bond solely by reason of this subsection—

(A) subsections (c) and (d) of section 147 (relating to limitations on acquisition of land and existing property) shall not apply, and

(B) paragraph (8) of section 142(a) shall be applied as if it did not contain "local".

(6) TREATMENT OF JOINT ACTION AGENCIES

With respect to nongovernmental output property acquired by a joint action agency the members of which are governmental units, this subsection shall be applied at the member level by treating each member as acquiring its proportionate share of such property.

(7) EXCEPTION FOR QUALIFIED ELECTRIC AND NATURAL GAS SUPPLY CONTRACTS

The term "nongovernmental output property" shall not include any contract for the prepayment of electricity or natural gas which is not investment property under section 148(b)(2).

(E) QUALIFIED BOND

For purposes of this part, the term "qualified bond" means any private activity bond if—

(1) IN GENERAL

Such bond is—

(A) an exempt facility bond,

(B) a qualified mortgage bond,

(C) a qualified veterans' mortgage bond,

(D) a qualified small issue bond,

(E) a qualified student loan bond,

(F) a qualified redevelopment bond, or

(G) a qualified 501(c)(3) bond.

(2) VOLUME CAP

Such bond is issued as part of an issue which meets the applicable requirements of section 146, and [1]

(3) OTHER REQUIREMENTS

Such bond meets the applicable requirements of each subsection of section 147.

(Added Pub. L. 99–514, title XIII, §1301(b), Oct. 22, 1986, 100 Stat. 2603; amended Pub. L. 100–203, title X, §10631(a), Dec. 22, 1987, 101 Stat. 1330–453; Pub. L. 100–647, title I, §1013(a)(38), Nov. 10, 1988, 102 Stat. 3544; Pub. L. 109–58, title XIII, §1327(b), (c), Aug. 8, 2005, 119 Stat. 1019; Pub. L. 117–58, div. H, title IV, §80402(d), Nov. 15, 2021, 135 Stat. 1334.)

[1] *So in original. Probably should end with a period after "146".*

§142. EXEMPT FACILITY BOND

(A) GENERAL RULE

For purposes of this part, the term "exempt facility bond" means any bond issued as part of an issue 95 percent or more of the net proceeds of which are to be used to provide—

(1) airports,

(2) docks and wharves,

(3) mass commuting facilities,

(4) facilities for the furnishing of water,
(5) sewage facilities,
(6) solid waste disposal facilities,
(7) qualified residential rental projects,
(8) facilities for the local furnishing of electric energy or gas,
(9) local district heating or cooling facilities,
(10) qualified hazardous waste facilities,
(11) high-speed intercity rail facilities,
(12) environmental enhancements of hydroelectric generating facilities,
(13) qualified public educational facilities,
(14) qualified green building and sustainable design projects,
(15) qualified highway or surface freight transfer facilities,
(16) qualified broadband projects, or
(17) qualified carbon dioxide capture facilities.

(B) SPECIAL EXEMPT FACILITY BOND RULES

For purposes of subsection (a)—

(1) CERTAIN FACILITIES MUST BE GOVERNMENTALLY OWNED

(A) IN GENERAL

A facility shall be treated as described in paragraph (1), (2), (3), or (12) of subsection (a) only if all of the property to be financed by the net proceeds of the issue is to be owned by a governmental unit.

(B) SAFE HARBOR FOR LEASES AND MANAGEMENT CONTRACTS

For purposes of subparagraph (A), property leased by a governmental unit shall be treated as owned by such governmental unit if—
(i) the lessee makes an irrevocable election (binding on the lessee and all successors in interest under the lease) not to claim depreciation or an investment credit with respect to such property,
(ii) the lease term (as defined in section 168(i)(3)) is not more than 80 percent of the reasonably expected economic life of the property (as determined under section 147(b)), and
(iii) the lessee has no option to purchase the property other than at fair market value (as of the time such option is exercised).
Rules similar to the rules of the preceding sentence shall apply to management contracts and similar types of operating agreements.

(2) LIMITATION ON OFFICE SPACE

An office shall not be treated as described in a paragraph of subsection (a) unless—
(A) the office is located on the premises of a facility described in such a paragraph, and
(B) not more than a de minimis amount of the functions to be performed at such office is not directly related to the day-to-day operations at such facility.

(C) AIRPORTS, DOCKS AND WHARVES, MASS COMMUTING FACILITIES AND HIGH-SPEED INTERCITY RAIL FACILITIES

For purposes of subsection (a)—

(1) STORAGE AND TRAINING FACILITIES

Storage or training facilities directly related to a facility described in paragraph (1), (2), (3) or (11) of subsection (a) shall be treated as described in the paragraph in which such facility is described.

(2) EXCEPTION FOR CERTAIN PRIVATE FACILITIES

Property shall not be treated as described in paragraph (1), (2), (3) or (11) of subsection (a) if such property is described in any of the following subparagraphs and is to be used for any private business use (as defined in section 141(b)(6)).

(A) Any lodging facility.

(B) Any retail facility (including food and beverage facilities) in excess of a size necessary to serve passengers and employees at the exempt facility.

(C) Any retail facility (other than parking) for passengers or the general public located outside the exempt facility terminal.

(D) Any office building for individuals who are not employees of a governmental unit or of the operating authority for the exempt facility.

(E) Any industrial park or manufacturing facility.

(D) QUALIFIED RESIDENTIAL RENTAL PROJECT

For purposes of this section—

(1) IN GENERAL

The term "qualified residential rental project" means any project for residential rental property if, at all times during the qualified project period, such project meets the requirements of subparagraph (A) or (B), whichever is elected by the issuer at the time of the issuance of the issue with respect to such project:

(A) 20–50 TEST

The project meets the requirements of this subparagraph if 20 percent or more of the residential units in such project are occupied by individuals whose income is 50 percent or less of area median gross income.

(B) 40–60 TEST

The project meets the requirements of this subparagraph if 40 percent or more of the residential units in such project are occupied by individuals whose income is 60 percent or less of area median gross income.

For purposes of this paragraph, any property shall not be treated as failing to be residential rental property merely because part of the building in which such property is located is used for purposes other than residential rental purposes.

(2) DEFINITIONS AND SPECIAL RULES

For purposes of this subsection—

(A) QUALIFIED PROJECT PERIOD

The term "qualified project period" means the period beginning on the 1st day on which 10 percent of the residential units in the project are occupied and ending on the latest of—

(i) the date which is 15 years after the date on which 50 percent of the residential units in the project are occupied,

(ii) the 1st day on which no tax-exempt private activity bond issued with respect to the project is outstanding, or

(iii) the date on which any assistance provided with respect to the project under section 8 of the United States Housing Act of 1937 terminates.

(B) INCOME OF INDIVIDUALS; AREA MEDIAN GROSS INCOME

(I) IN GENERAL

The income of individuals and area median gross income shall be determined by the Secretary in a manner consistent with determinations of lower income families and area median gross income under section 8 of the United States Housing Act of 1937 (or, if such program is terminated, under such program as in effect immediately before such termination). Determinations under the preceding sentence shall include adjustments for family size. Subsections (g) and (h) of section 7872 shall not apply in determining the income of individuals under this subparagraph.

(II) SPECIAL RULE RELATING TO BASIC HOUSING ALLOWANCES

For purposes of determining income under this subparagraph, payments under section 403 of title 37, United States Code, as a basic pay allowance for housing shall be disregarded with respect to any qualified building.

(III) QUALIFIED BUILDING

For purposes of clause (ii), the term "qualified building" means any building located—

(I) in any county in which is located a qualified military installation to which the number of members of the Armed Forces of the United States assigned to units based out of such qualified military installation, as of June 1, 2008, has increased by not less than 20 percent, as compared to such number on December 31, 2005, or

(II) in any county adjacent to a county described in subclause (I).

(IV) QUALIFIED MILITARY INSTALLATION

For purposes of clause (iii), the term "qualified military installation" means any military installation or facility the number of members of the Armed Forces of the United States assigned to which, as of June 1, 2008, is not less than 1,000.

(C) STUDENTS

Rules similar to the rules of section 42(i)(3)(D) shall apply for purposes of this subsection.

(D) Single-room occupancy units

A unit shall not fail to be treated as a residential unit merely because such unit is a single-room occupancy unit (within the meaning of section 42).

(E) Hold harmless for reductions in area median gross income

(i) In general

Any determination of area median gross income under subparagraph (B) with respect to any project for any calendar year after 2008 shall not be less than the area median gross income determined under such subparagraph with respect to such project for the calendar year preceding the calendar year for which such determination is made.

(ii) Special rule for certain census changes

In the case of a HUD hold harmless impacted project, the area median gross income with respect to such project for any calendar year after 2008 (hereafter in this clause referred to as the current calendar year) shall be the greater of the amount determined without regard to this clause or the sum of—

(I) the area median gross income determined under the HUD hold harmless policy with respect to such project for calendar year 2008, plus

(II) any increase in the area median gross income determined under subparagraph (B) (determined without regard to the HUD hold harmless policy and this subparagraph) with respect to such project for the current calendar year over the area median gross income (as so determined) with respect to such project for calendar year 2008.

(iii) HUD hold harmless policy

The term "HUD hold harmless policy" means the regulations under which a policy similar to the rules of clause (i) applied to prevent a change in the method of determining area median gross income from resulting in a reduction in the area median gross income determined with respect to certain projects in calendar years 2007 and 2008.

(iv) HUD hold harmless impacted project

The term "HUD hold harmless impacted project" means any project with respect to which area median gross income was determined under subparagraph (B) for calendar year 2007 or 2008 if such determination would have been less but for the HUD hold harmless policy.

(3) Current income determinations

For purposes of this subsection—

(A) In general

The determination of whether the income of a resident of a unit in a project exceeds the applicable income limit shall be made at least annually on the basis of the current income of the resident. The preceding sentence shall not apply with respect to any project for any year if during such year no residential unit in the project is occupied by a new resident whose income exceeds the applicable income limit.

(B) CONTINUING RESIDENT'S INCOME MAY INCREASE ABOVE THE APPLICABLE LIMIT

If the income of a resident of a unit in a project did not exceed the applicable income limit upon commencement of such resident's occupancy of such unit (or as of any prior determination under subparagraph (A)), the income of such resident shall be treated as continuing to not exceed the applicable income limit. The preceding sentence shall cease to apply to any resident whose income as of the most recent determination under subparagraph (A) exceeds 140 percent of the applicable income limit if after such determination, but before the next determination, any residential unit of comparable or smaller size in the same project is occupied by a new resident whose income exceeds the applicable income llmlt.

(C) EXCEPTION FOR PROJECTS WITH RESPECT TO WHICH AFFORDABLE HOUSING CREDIT IS ALLOWED

In the case of a project with respect to which credit is allowed under section 42, the second sentence of subparagraph (B) shall be applied by substituting "building (within the meaning of section 42)" for "project".

(4) SPECIAL RULE IN CASE OF DEEP RENT SKEWING

(A) IN GENERAL

In the case of any project described in subparagraph (B), the 2d sentence of subparagraph (B) of paragraph (3) shall be applied by substituting—
(i) "170 percent" for "140 percent", and
(ii) "any low-income unit in the same project is occupied by a new resident whose income exceeds 40 percent of area median gross income" for "any residential unit of comparable or smaller size in the same project is occupied by a new resident whose income exceeds the applicable income limit".

(B) DEEP RENT SKEWED PROJECT

A project is described in this subparagraph if the owner of the project elects to have this paragraph apply and, at all times during the qualified project period, such project meets the requirements of clauses (i), (ii), and (iii):
(i) The project meets the requirements of this clause if 15 percent or more of the low-income units in the project are occupied by individuals whose income is 40 percent or less of area median gross income.
(ii) The project meets the requirements of this clause if the gross rent with respect to each low-income unit in the project does not exceed 30 percent of the applicable income limit which applies to individuals occupying the unit.
(iii) The project meets the requirements of this clause if the gross rent with respect to each low-income unit in the project does not exceed ½ of the average gross rent with respect to units of comparable size which are not occupied by individuals who meet the applicable income limit.

(C) Definitions applicable to subparagraph (B)

For purposes of subparagraph (B)—

(i) Low-income unit

The term "low-income unit" means any unit which is required to be occupied by individuals who meet the applicable income limit.

(ii) Gross rent

The term "gross rent" includes—

(I) any payment under section 8 of the United States Housing Act of 1937, and

(II) any utility allowance determined by the Secretary after taking into account such determinations under such section 8.

(5) Applicable income limit

For purposes of paragraphs (3) and (4), the term "applicable income limit" means—

(A) the limitation under subparagraph (A) or (B) of paragraph (1) which applies to the project, or

(B) in the case of a unit to which paragraph (4)(B)(i) applies, the limitation which applies to such unit.

(6) Special rule for certain high cost housing area

In the case of a project located in a city having 5 boroughs and a population in excess of 5,000,000, subparagraph (B) of paragraph (1) shall be applied by substituting "25 percent" for "40 percent".

(7) Certification to Secretary

The operator of any project with respect to which an election was made under this subsection shall submit to the Secretary (at such time and in such manner as the Secretary shall prescribe) an annual certification as to whether such project continues to meet the requirements of this subsection. Any failure to comply with the provisions of the preceding sentence shall not affect the tax-exempt status of any bond but shall subject the operator to penalty, as provided in section 6652(j).

(e) Facilities for the furnishing of water

For purposes of subsection (a)(4), the term "facilities for the furnishing of water" means any facility for the furnishing of water if—

(1) the water is or will be made available to members of the general public (including electric utility, industrial, agricultural, or commercial users), and

(2) either the facility is operated by a governmental unit or the rates for the furnishing or sale of the water have been established or approved by a State or political subdivision thereof, by an agency or instrumentality of the United States, or by a public service or public utility commission or other similar body of any State or political subdivision thereof.

(f) Local furnishing of electric energy or gas

For purposes of subsection (a)(8)—

(1) In general

The local furnishing of electric energy or gas from a facility shall only include furnishing solely within the area consisting of—

(A) a city and 1 contiguous county, or

(B) 2 contiguous counties.

(2) Treatment of certain electric energy transmitted outside local area

(A) In general

A facility shall not be treated as failing to meet the local furnishing requirement of subsection (a)(8) by reason of electricity transmitted pursuant to an order of the Federal Energy Regulatory Commission under section 211 or 213 of the Federal Power Act (as in effect on the date of the enactment of this paragraph) if the portion of the cost of the facility financed with tax-exempt bonds is not greater than the portion of the cost of the facility which is allocable to the local furnishing of electric energy (determined without regard to this paragraph).

(B) Special rule for existing facilities

In the case of a facility financed with bonds issued before the date of an order referred to in subparagraph (A) which would (but for this subparagraph) cease to be tax-exempt by reason of subparagraph (A), such bonds shall not cease to be tax-exempt bonds (and section 150(b)(4) shall not apply) if, to the extent necessary to comply with subparagraph (A)—

(i) an escrow to pay principal of, premium (if any), and interest on the bonds is established within a reasonable period after the date such order becomes final, and

(ii) bonds are redeemed not later than the earliest date on which such bonds may be redeemed.

(3) Termination of future financing

For purposes of this section, no bond may be issued as part of an issue described in subsection (a)(8) with respect to a facility for the local furnishing of electric energy or gas on or after the date of the enactment of this paragraph unless—

(A) the facility will—

(i) be used by a person who is engaged in the local furnishing of that energy source on January 1, 1997, and

(ii) be used to provide service within the area served by such person on January 1, 1997 (or within a county or city any portion of which is within such area), or

(B) the facility will be used by a successor in interest to such person for the same use and within the same service area as described in subparagraph (A).

(4) Election to terminate tax-exempt bond financing by certain furnishers

(A) In general

In the case of a facility financed with bonds issued before the date of the enactment of this paragraph which would cease to be tax-exempt by reason of the failure to meet the local furnishing requirement of subsection (a)(8) as a result of a service area expansion, such bonds shall not cease to be tax-exempt bonds (and section 150(b)(4) shall not apply) if the person engaged in such local furnishing by such facility makes an election described in subparagraph (B).

(B) ELECTION

An election is described in this subparagraph if it is an election made in such manner as the Secretary prescribes, and such person (or its predecessor in interest) agrees that—

(i) such election is made with respect to all facilities for the local furnishing of electric energy or gas, or both, by such person,

(ii) no bond exempt from tax under section 103 and described in subsection (a)(8) may be issued on or after the date of the enactment of this paragraph with respect to all such facilities of such person,

(iii) any expansion of the service area—

(I) is not financed with the proceeds of any exempt facility bond described in subsection (a)(8), and

(II) is not treated as a nonqualifying use under the rules of paragraph (2), and

(iv) all outstanding bonds used to finance the facilities for such person are redeemed not later than 6 months after the later of—

(I) the earliest date on which such bonds may be redeemed, or

(II) the date of the election.

(C) RELATED PERSONS

For purposes of this paragraph, the term "person" includes a group of related persons (within the meaning of section 144(a)(3)) which includes such person.

(G) LOCAL DISTRICT HEATING OR COOLING FACILITY

(1) IN GENERAL

For purposes of subsection (a)(9), the term "local district heating or cooling facility" means property used as an integral part of a local district heating or cooling system.

(2) LOCAL DISTRICT HEATING OR COOLING SYSTEM

(A) IN GENERAL

For purposes of paragraph (1), the term "local district heating or cooling system" means any local system consisting of a pipeline or network (which may be connected to a heating or cooling source) providing hot water, chilled water, or steam to 2 or more users for—

(i) residential, commercial, or industrial heating or cooling, or

(ii) process steam.

(B) LOCAL SYSTEM

For purposes of this paragraph, a local system includes facilities furnishing heating and cooling to an area consisting of a city and 1 contiguous county.

(H) QUALIFIED HAZARDOUS WASTE FACILITIES

For purposes of subsection (a)(10), the term "qualified hazardous waste facility" means any facility for the disposal of hazardous waste by incineration or entombment but only if—

(1) the facility is subject to final permit requirements under subtitle C of title II of the Solid Waste Disposal Act (as in effect on the date of the enactment of the Tax Reform Act of 1986), and

(2) the portion of such facility which is to be provided by the issue does not exceed the portion of the facility which is to be used by persons other than—

(A) the owner or operator of such facility, and

(B) any related person (within the meaning of section 144(a)(3)) to such owner or operator.

(I) HIGH-SPEED INTERCITY RAIL FACILITIES

(1) IN GENERAL

For purposes of subsection (a)(11), the term "high-speed intercity rail facilities" means any facility (not including rolling stock) for the fixed guideway rail transportation of passengers and their baggage between metropolitan statistical areas (within the meaning of section 143(k)(2)(B)) using vehicles that are reasonably expected to be capable of attaining a maximum speed in excess of 150 miles per hour between scheduled stops, but only if such facility will be made available to members of the general public as passengers.

(2) ELECTION BY NONGOVERNMENTAL OWNERS

A facility shall be treated as described in subsection (a)(11) only if any owner of such facility which is not a governmental unit irrevocably elects not to claim—

(A) any deduction under section 167 or 168, and

(B) any credit under this subtitle,

with respect to the property to be financed by the net proceeds of the issue.

(3) USE OF PROCEEDS

A bond issued as part of an issue described in subsection (a)(11) shall not be considered an exempt facility bond unless any proceeds not used within a 3-year period of the date of the issuance of such bond are used (not later than 6 months after the close of such period) to redeem bonds which are part of such issue.

(J) ENVIRONMENTAL ENHANCEMENTS OF HYDROELECTRIC GENERATING FACILITIES

(1) IN GENERAL

For purposes of subsection (a)(12), the term "environmental enhancements of hydroelectric generating facilities" means property—

(A) the use of which is related to a federally licensed hydroelectric generating facility owned and operated by a governmental unit, and

(B) which—

(i) protects or promotes fisheries or other wildlife resources, including any fish by-pass facility, fish hatchery, or fisheries enhancement facility, or

(ii) is a recreational facility or other improvement required by the terms and conditions of any Federal licensing permit for the operation of such generating facility.

(2) USE OF PROCEEDS

A bond issued as part of an issue described in subsection (a)(12) shall not be considered an exempt facility bond unless at least 80 percent of the net proceeds of the issue of which it is a part are used to finance property described in paragraph (1)(B)(i).

(K) QUALIFIED PUBLIC EDUCATIONAL FACILITIES

(1) IN GENERAL

For purposes of subsection (a)(13), the term "qualified public educational facility" means any school facility which is—

(A) part of a public elementary school or a public secondary school, and

(B) owned by a private, for-profit corporation pursuant to a public-private partnership agreement with a State or local educational agency described in paragraph (2).

(2) PUBLIC-PRIVATE PARTNERSHIP AGREEMENT DESCRIBED

A public-private partnership agreement is described in this paragraph if it is an agreement—

(A) under which the corporation agrees—

(i) to do 1 or more of the following: construct, rehabilitate, refurbish, or equip a school facility, and

(ii) at the end of the term of the agreement, to transfer the school facility to such agency for no additional consideration, and

(B) the term of which does not exceed the term of the issue to be used to provide the school facility.

(3) SCHOOL FACILITY

For purposes of this subsection, the term "school facility" means—

(A) any school building,

(B) any functionally related and subordinate facility and land with respect to such building, including any stadium or other facility primarily used for school events, and

(C) any property, to which section 168 applies (or would apply but for section 179), for use in a facility described in subparagraph (A) or (B).

(4) PUBLIC SCHOOLS

For purposes of this subsection, the terms "elementary school" and "secondary school" have the meanings given such terms by section 14101 of the Elementary and Secondary Education Act of 1965 (20 U.S.C. 8801), as in effect on the date of the enactment of this subsection.

(5) ANNUAL AGGREGATE FACE AMOUNT OF TAX-EXEMPT FINANCING

(A) IN GENERAL

An issue shall not be treated as an issue described in subsection (a)(13) if the aggregate face amount of bonds issued by the State pursuant thereto (when added to the aggregate face amount of bonds previously so issued during the calendar year) exceeds an amount equal to the greater of—
  (i) $10 multiplied by the State population, or
  (ii) $5,000,000.

(B) ALLOCATION RULES

(I) IN GENERAL

Except as otherwise provided in this subparagraph, the State may allocate the amount described in subparagraph (A) for any calendar year in such manner as the State determines appropriate.

(II) RULES FOR CARRYFORWARD OF UNUSED LIMITATION

A State may elect to carry forward an unused limitation for any calendar year for 3 calendar years following the calendar year in which the unused limitation arose under rules similar to the rules of section 146(f), except that the only purpose for which the carryforward may be elected is the issuance of exempt facility bonds described in subsection (a)(13).

(L) QUALIFIED GREEN BUILDING AND SUSTAINABLE DESIGN PROJECTS

(1) IN GENERAL

For purposes of subsection (a)(14), the term "qualified green building and sustainable design project" means any project which is designated by the Secretary, after consultation with the Administrator of the Environmental Protection Agency, as a qualified green building and sustainable design project and which meets the requirements of clauses (i), (ii), (iii), and (iv) of paragraph (4)(A).

(2) DESIGNATIONS

(A) IN GENERAL

Within 60 days after the end of the application period described in paragraph (3)(A), the Secretary, after consultation with the Administrator of the Environmental Protection Agency, shall designate qualified green building and sustainable design projects. At least one of the projects designated shall be located in, or within a 10-mile radius of, an empowerment zone as designated pursuant to section 1391, and at least one of the projects designated shall be located in a rural State. No more than one project shall be designated in a State. A project shall not be designated if such project includes a stadium or arena for professional sports exhibitions or games.

(B) MINIMUM CONSERVATION AND TECHNOLOGY INNOVATION OBJECTIVES

The Secretary, after consultation with the Administrator of the Environmental

Protection Agency, shall ensure that, in the aggregate, the projects designated shall—

(i) reduce electric consumption by more than 150 megawatts annually as compared to conventional generation,

(ii) reduce daily sulfur dioxide emissions by at least 10 tons compared to coal generation power,

(iii) expand by 75 percent the domestic solar photovoltaic market in the United States (measured in megawatts) as compared to the expansion of that market from 2001 to 2002, and

(iv) use at least 25 megawatts of fuel cell energy generation.

(3) Limited designations

A project may not be designated under this subsection unless—

(A) the project is nominated by a State or local government within 180 days of the enactment of this subsection, and

(B) such State or local government provides written assurances that the project will satisfy the eligibility criteria described in paragraph (4).

(4) Application

(A) In general

A project may not be designated under this subsection unless the application for such designation includes a project proposal which describes the energy efficiency, renewable energy, and sustainable design features of the project and demonstrates that the project satisfies the following eligibility criteria:

(i) Green building and sustainable design

At least 75 percent of the square footage of commercial buildings which are part of the project is registered for United States Green Building Council's LEED certification and is reasonably expected (at the time of the designation) to receive such certification. For purposes of determining LEED certification as required under this clause, points shall be credited by using the following:

(I) For wood products, certification under the Sustainable Forestry Initiative Program and the American Tree Farm System.

(II) For renewable wood products, as credited for recycled content otherwise provided under LEED certification.

(III) For composite wood products, certification under standards established by the American National Standards Institute, or such other voluntary standards as published in the Federal Register by the Administrator of the Environmental Protection Agency.

(ii) Brownfield redevelopment

The project includes a brownfield site as defined by section 101(39) of the Comprehensive Environmental Response, Compensation, and Liability Act of 1980 (42 U.S.C. 9601), including a site described in subparagraph (D)(ii)(II)(aa) thereof.

(III) STATE AND LOCAL SUPPORT

The project receives specific State or local government resources which will support the project in an amount equal to at least $5,000,000. For purposes of the preceding sentence, the term "resources" includes tax abatement benefits and contributions in kind.

(IV) SIZE

The project includes at least one of the following:
(I) At least 1,000,000 square feet of building.
(II) At least 20 acres.

(V) USE OF TAX BENEFIT

The project proposal includes a description of the net benefit of the tax-exempt financing provided under this subsection which will be allocated for financing of one or more of the following:
(I) The purchase, construction, integration, or other use of energy efficiency, renewable energy, and sustainable design features of the project.
(II) Compliance with certification standards cited under clause (i).
(III) The purchase, remediation, and foundation construction and preparation of the brownfields site.

(VI) PROHIBITED FACILITIES

An issue shall not be treated as an issue described in subsection (a)(14) if any proceeds of such issue are used to provide any facility the principal business of which is the sale of food or alcoholic beverages for consumption on the premises.

(VII) EMPLOYMENT

The project is projected to provide permanent employment of at least 1,500 full time equivalents (150 full time equivalents in rural States) when completed and construction employment of at least 1,000 full time equivalents (100 full time equivalents in rural States).

The application shall include an independent analysis which describes the project's economic impact, including the amount of projected employment.

(B) PROJECT DESCRIPTION

Each application described in subparagraph (A) shall contain for each project a description of—
(i) the amount of electric consumption reduced as compared to conventional construction,
(ii) the amount of sulfur dioxide daily emissions reduced compared to coal generation,
(iii) the amount of the gross installed capacity of the project's solar photovoltaic capacity measured in megawatts, and
(iv) the amount, in megawatts, of the project's fuel cell energy generation.

(5) Certification of use of tax benefit

No later than 30 days after the completion of the project, each project must certify to the Secretary that the net benefit of the tax-exempt financing was used for the purposes described in paragraph (4).

(6) Definitions

For purposes of this subsection—

(A) Rural State

The term "rural State" means any State which has—

(i) a population of less than 4,500,000 according to the 2000 census,

(ii) a population density of less than 150 people per square mile according to the 2000 census, and

(iii) increased in population by less than half the rate of the national increase between the 1990 and 2000 censuses.

(B) Local government

The term "local government" has the meaning given such term by section 1393(a)(5).

(C) Net benefit of tax-exempt financing

The term "net benefit of tax-exempt financing" means the present value of the interest savings (determined by a calculation established by the Secretary) which result from the tax-exempt status of the bonds.

(7) Aggregate face amount of tax-exempt financing

(A) In general

An issue shall not be treated as an issue described in subsection (a)(14) if the aggregate face amount of bonds issued by the State or local government pursuant thereto for a project (when added to the aggregate face amount of bonds previously so issued for such project) exceeds an amount designated by the Secretary as part of the designation.

(B) Limitation on amount of bonds

The Secretary may not allocate authority to issue qualified green building and sustainable design project bonds in an aggregate face amount exceeding $2,000,000,000.

(8) Termination

Subsection (a)(14) shall not apply with respect to any bond issued after September 30, 2012.

(9) Treatment of current refunding bonds

Paragraphs (7)(B) and (8) shall not apply to any bond (or series of bonds) issued to refund a bond issued under subsection (a)(14) before October 1, 2012, if—

(A) the average maturity date of the issue of which the refunding bond is a part is not later than the average maturity date of the bonds to be refunded by such issue, (B) the amount of the refunding bond does not exceed the outstanding amount of the refunded bond, and

(C) the net proceeds of the refunding bond are used to redeem the refunded bond not later than 90 days after the date of the issuance of the refunding bond.

For purposes of subparagraph (A), average maturity shall be determined in accordance with section 147(b)(2)(A).

(M) QUALIFIED HIGHWAY OR SURFACE FREIGHT TRANSFER FACILITIES

(1) IN GENERAL

For purposes of subsection (a)(15), the term "qualified highway or surface freight transfer facilities" means—

(A) any surface transportation project which receives Federal assistance under title 23, United States Code (as in effect on the date of the enactment of this subsection),

(B) any project for an international bridge or tunnel for which an international entity authorized under Federal or State law is responsible and which receives Federal assistance under title 23, United States Code (as so in effect), or

(C) any facility for the transfer of freight from truck to rail or rail to truck (including any temporary storage facilities directly related to such transfers) which receives Federal assistance under either title 23 or title 49, United States Code (as so in effect).

(2) NATIONAL LIMITATION ON AMOUNT OF TAX-EXEMPT FINANCING FOR FACILITIES

(A) NATIONAL LIMITATION

The aggregate amount allocated by the Secretary of Transportation under subparagraph (C) shall not exceed $30,000,000,000.

(B) ENFORCEMENT OF NATIONAL LIMITATION

An issue shall not be treated as an issue described in subsection (a)(15) if the aggregate face amount of bonds issued pursuant to such issue for any qualified highway or surface freight transfer facility (when added to the aggregate face amount of bonds previously so issued for such facility) exceeds the amount allocated to such facility under subparagraph (C).

(C) ALLOCATION BY SECRETARY OF TRANSPORTATION

The Secretary of Transportation shall allocate the amount described in subparagraph (A) among qualified highway or surface freight transfer facilities in such manner as the Secretary determines appropriate.

(3) EXPENDITURE OF PROCEEDS

An issue shall not be treated as an issue described in subsection (a)(15) unless at least 95 percent of the net proceeds of the issue is expended for qualified highway or surface freight transfer facilities within the 5-year period beginning on the date of issuance. If at least 95 percent of such net proceeds is not expended within such

5-year period, an issue shall be treated as continuing to meet the requirements of this paragraph if the issuer uses all unspent proceeds of the issue to redeem bonds of the issue within 90 days after the end of such 5-year period. The Secretary, at the request of the issuer, may extend such 5-year period if the issuer establishes that any failure to meet such period is due to circumstances beyond the control of the issuer.

(4) EXCEPTION FOR CURRENT REFUNDING BONDS

Paragraph (2) shall not apply to any bond (or series of bonds) issued to refund a bond issued under subsection (a)(15) if—

(A) the average maturity date of the issue of which the refunding bond is a part is not later than the average maturity date of the bonds to be refunded by such issue,

(B) the amount of the refunding bond does not exceed the outstanding amount of the refunded bond, and

(C) the refunded bond is redeemed not later than 90 days after the date of the issuance of the refunding bond.

For purposes of subparagraph (A), average maturity shall be determined in accordance with section 147(b)(2)(A).

* * * * * * *

(Added Pub. L. 99–514, title XIII, §1301(b), Oct. 22, 1986, 100 Stat. 2606; amended Pub. L. 100–647, title I, §1013(a)(1), (39), title VI, §6180(a)–(b)(2), Nov. 10, 1988, 102 Stat. 3537, 3544, 3727, 3728; Pub. L. 101–239, title VII, §§7108(e)(3), (n)(1), 7816(s)(1), Dec. 19, 1989, 103 Stat. 2313, 2318, 2423; Pub. L. 102–486, title XIX, §§1919(a), 1921(a), (b)(1), (2), Oct. 24, 1992, 106 Stat. 3025, 3027, 3028; Pub. L. 104–188, title I, §§1608(a), 1704(j)(7), Aug. 20, 1996, 110 Stat. 1840, 1882; Pub. L. 105–206, title VI, §6023(5), July 22, 1998, 112 Stat. 825; Pub. L. 107–16, title IV, §422(a), (b), June 7, 2001, 115 Stat. 65; Pub. L. 108–357, title VII, §701(a), (b), Oct. 22, 2004, 118 Stat. 1536; Pub. L. 109–59, title XI, §11143(a), (b), Aug. 10, 2005, 119 Stat. 1963; Pub. L. 109–222, title II, §209(b)(2), May 17, 2006, 120 Stat. 352; Pub. L. 110–289, div. C, title I, §§3005(a), 3008(a)–(c), 3009(a), 3010(a), July 30, 2008, 122 Stat. 2885–2888; Pub. L. 110–343, div. B, title III, §307(a), (b), Oct. 3, 2008, 122 Stat. 3849; Pub. L. 111–5, div. B, title I, §1504(a), Feb. 17, 2009, 123 Stat. 355; Pub. L. 115–141, div. U, title IV, §401(a)(47), Mar. 23, 2018, 132 Stat. 1186; Pub. L. 117–58, div. H, title IV, §§80401(a), (b), 80402(a), (b), 80403(a), Nov. 15, 2021, 135 Stat. 1330, 1331, 1335; Pub. L. 117–169, title I, §13104(a)(2)(B), Aug. 16, 2022, 136 Stat. 1925.)

* * * * * * *

fHigh itempath:/260/Subtitle A/CHAPTER 1/Subchapter B/PART IV/Subpart A/Sec. 146 -->

§146. VOLUME CAP

(A) GENERAL RULE

A private activity bond issued as part of an issue meets the requirements of this section if the aggregate face amount of the private activity bonds issued pursuant to such issue, when added to the aggregate face amount of tax-exempt private activity bonds previously issued by the issuing authority during the calendar year, does not exceed such authority's volume cap for such calendar year.

(B) VOLUME CAP FOR STATE AGENCIES

For purposes of this section—

(1) In general

The volume cap for any agency of the State authorized to issue tax-exempt private activity bonds for any calendar year shall be 50 percent of the State ceiling for such calendar year.

(2) Special rule where State has more than 1 agency

If more than 1 agency of the State is authorized to issue tax-exempt private activity bonds, all such agencies shall be treated as a single agency.

(c) Volume cap for other issuers

For purposes of this section—

(1) In general

The volume cap for any issuing authority (other than a State agency) for any calendar year shall be an amount which bears the same ratio to 50 percent of the State ceiling for such calendar year as—

(A) the population of the jurisdiction of such issuing authority, bears to

(B) the population of the entire State.

(2) Overlapping jurisdictions

For purposes of paragraph (1)(A), if an area is within the jurisdiction of 2 or more governmental units, such area shall be treated as only within the jurisdiction of the unit having jurisdiction over the smallest geographical area unless such unit agrees to surrender all or part of such jurisdiction for such calendar year to the unit with overlapping jurisdiction which has the next smallest geographical area.

(d) State ceiling

For purposes of this section—

(1) In general

The State ceiling applicable to any State for any calendar year shall be the greater of—

(A) an amount equal to $75 ($62.50 in the case of calendar year 2001) multiplied by the State population, or

(B) $225,000,000 ($187,500,000 in the case of calendar year 2001).

(2) Cost-of-living adjustment

In the case of a calendar year after 2002, each of the dollar amounts contained in paragraph (1) shall be increased by an amount equal to—

(A) such dollar amount, multiplied by

(B) the cost-of-living adjustment determined under section 1(f)(3) for such calendar year by substituting "calendar year 2001" for "calendar year 2016" in subparagraph (A)(ii) thereof.

If any increase determined under the preceding sentence is not a multiple of $5 ($5,000 in the case of the dollar amount in paragraph (1)(B)), such increase shall be rounded to the nearest multiple thereof.

(3) SPECIAL RULE FOR STATES WITH CONSTITUTIONAL HOME RULE CITIES

For purposes of this section—

(A) IN GENERAL

The volume cap for any constitutional home rule city for any calendar year shall be determined under paragraph (1) of subsection (c) by substituting "100 percent" for "50 percent".

(B) COORDINATION WITH OTHER ALLOCATIONS

In the case of any State which contains 1 or more constitutional home rule cities, for purposes of applying subsections (b) and (c) with respect to issuing authorities in such State other than constitutional home rule cities, the State ceiling for any calendar year shall be reduced by the aggregate volume caps determined for such year for all constitutional home rule cities in such State.

(C) CONSTITUTIONAL HOME RULE CITY

For purposes of this section, the term "constitutional home rule city" means, with respect to any calendar year, any political subdivision of a State which, under a State constitution which was adopted in 1970 and effective on July 1, 1971, had home rule powers on the 1st day of the calendar year.

(4) SPECIAL RULE FOR POSSESSIONS WITH POPULATIONS OF LESS THAN THE POPULATION OF THE LEAST POPULOUS STATE

(A) IN GENERAL

If the population of any possession of the United States for any calendar year is less than the population of the least populous State (other than a possession) for such calendar year, the limitation under paragraph (1)(A) shall not be less than the amount determined under subparagraph (B) for such calendar year.

(B) LIMITATION

The limitation determined under this subparagraph, with respect to a possession, for any calendar year is an amount equal to the product of—
(i) the fraction—
(I) the numerator of which is the amount applicable under paragraph (1)(B) for such calendar year, and
(II) the denominator of which is the State population of the least populous State (other than a possession) for such calendar year, and
(ii) the population of such possession for such calendar year.

(5) INCREASE AND SET ASIDE FOR HOUSING BONDS FOR 2008

(A) INCREASE FOR 2008

In the case of calendar year 2008, the State ceiling for each State shall be increased by an amount equal to $11,000,000,000 multiplied by a fraction—
(i) the numerator of which is the State ceiling applicable to the State for calendar year 2008, determined without regard to this paragraph, and

(ii) the denominator of which is the sum of the State ceilings determined under clause (i) for all States.

(B) Set aside

(I) In general

Any amount of the State ceiling for any State which is attributable to an increase under this paragraph shall be allocated solely for one or more qualified housing issues.

(II) Qualified housing issue

For purposes of this paragraph, the term "qualified housing issue" means—
(I) an issue described in section 142(a)(7) (relating to qualified residential rental projects), or
(II) a qualified mortgage issue (determined by substituting "12-month period" for "42-month period" each place it appears in section 143(a)(2)(D)(i)).

(E) State may provide for different allocation

For purposes of this section—

(1) In general

Except as provided in paragraph (3), a State may, by law provide a different formula for allocating the State ceiling among the governmental units (or other authorities) in such State having authority to issue tax-exempt private activity bonds.

(2) Interim authority for Governor

(A) In general

Except as otherwise provided in paragraph (3), the Governor of any State may proclaim a different formula for allocating the State ceiling among the governmental units (or other authorities) in such State having authority to issue private activity bonds.

(B) Termination of authority

The authority provided in subparagraph (A) shall not apply to bonds issued after the earlier of—
(i) the last day of the 1st calendar year after 1986 during which the legislature of the State met in regular session, or
(ii) the effective date of any State legislation with respect to the allocation of the State ceiling.

(3) State may not alter allocation to constitutional home rule cities

Except as otherwise provided in a State constitutional amendment (or law changing the home rule provision adopted in the manner provided by the State constitution), the authority provided in this subsection shall not apply to that portion of the State ceiling which is allocated to any constitutional home rule city in the State unless such city agrees to such different allocation.

(F) Elective carryforward of unused limitation for specified purpose

(1) In general

If—

(A) an issuing authority's volume cap for any calendar year after 1985, exceeds

(B) the aggregate amount of tax-exempt private activity bonds issued during such calendar year by such authority,

such authority may elect to treat all (or any portion) of such excess as a carryforward for 1 or more carryforward purposes.

(2) Election must identify purpose

In any election under paragraph (1), the issuing authority shall—

(A) identify the purpose for which the carryforward is elected, and

(B) specify the portion of the excess described in paragraph (1) which is to be a carryforward for each such purpose.

(3) Use of carryforward

(A) In general

If any issuing authority elects a carryforward under paragraph (1) with respect to any carryforward purpose, any private activity bonds issued by such authority with respect to such purpose during the 3 calendar years following the calendar year in which the carryforward arose shall not be taken into account under subsection (a) to the extent the amount of such bonds does not exceed the amount of the carryforward elected for such purpose.

(B) Order in which carryforward used

Carryforwards elected with respect to any purpose shall be used in the order of the calendar years in which they arose.

(4) Election

Any election under this paragraph (and any identification or specification contained therein), once made, shall be irrevocable.

(5) Carryforward purpose

The term "carryforward purpose" means—

(A) the purpose of issuing exempt facility bonds described in 1 of the paragraphs of section 142(a),

(B) the purpose of issuing qualified mortgage bonds or mortgage credit certificates,

(C) the purpose of issuing qualified student loan bonds, and

(D) the purpose of issuing qualified redevelopment bonds.

(6) Special rules for increased volume cap under subsection (d)(5)

No amount which is attributable to the increase under subsection (d)(5) may be used—

(A) for any issue other than a qualified housing issue (as defined in subsection (d)(5)), or

(B) to issue any bond after calendar year 2010.

(G) EXCEPTION FOR CERTAIN BONDS

Only for purposes of this section, the term "private activity bond" shall not include—

(1) any qualified veterans' mortgage bond,

(2) any qualified 501(c)(3) bond,

(3) any exempt facility bond issued as part of an issue described in paragraph (1), (2), (12), (13), (14), or (15) of section 142(a),

(4) 75 percent of any exempt facility bond issued as part of an issue described in paragraph (11) of section 142(a) (relating to high-speed intercity rail facilities),

(5) 75 percent of any exempt facility bond issued as part of an issue described in paragraph (16) of section 142(a) (relating to qualified broadband projects), and

(6) 75 percent of any exempt facility bond issued as part of an issue described in paragraph (17) of section 142(a) (relating to qualified carbon dioxide capture facilities).

Paragraphs (4) and (5) shall be applied without regard to "75 percent of" if all of the property to be financed by the net proceeds of the issue is to be owned by a governmental unit (within the meaning of section 142(b)(1)).

(H) EXCEPTION FOR GOVERNMENT-OWNED SOLID WASTE DISPOSAL FACILITIES

(1) IN GENERAL

Only for purposes of this section, the term "private activity bond" shall not include any exempt facility bond described in section 142(a)(6) which is issued as part of an issue if all of the property to be financed by the net proceeds of such issue is to be owned by a governmental unit.

(2) SAFE HARBOR FOR DETERMINATION OF GOVERNMENT OWNERSHIP

In determining ownership for purposes of paragraph (1), section 142(b)(1)(B) shall apply, except that a lease term shall be treated as satisfying clause (ii) thereof if it is not more than 20 years.

(I) TREATMENT OF REFUNDING ISSUES

For purposes of the volume cap imposed by this section—

(1) IN GENERAL

The term "private activity bond" shall not include any bond which is issued to refund another bond to the extent that the amount of such bond does not exceed the outstanding amount of the refunded bond.

(2) SPECIAL RULES FOR STUDENT LOAN BONDS

In the case of any qualified student loan bond, paragraph (1) shall apply only if the maturity date of the refunding bond is not later than the later of—

(A) the average maturity date of the qualified student loan bonds to be refunded by the issue of which the refunding bond is a part, or

(B) the date 17 years after the date on which the refunded bond was issued (or in the case of a series of refundings, the date on which the original bond was issued).

(3) SPECIAL RULES FOR QUALIFIED MORTGAGE BONDS

In the case of any qualified mortgage bond, paragraph (1) shall apply only if the maturity date of the refunding bond is not later than the later of—

(A) the average maturity date of the qualified mortgage bonds to be refunded by the issue of which the refunding bond is a part, or

(B) the date 32 years after the date on which the refunded bond was issued (or in the case of a series of refundings, the date on which the original bond was issued).

(4) AVERAGE MATURITY

For purposes of paragraphs (2) and (3), average maturity shall be determined in accordance with section 147(b)(2)(A).

(5) EXCEPTION FOR ADVANCE REFUNDING

This subsection shall not apply to any bond issued to advance refund another bond.

(6) TREATMENT OF CERTAIN RESIDENTIAL RENTAL PROJECT BONDS AS REFUNDING
BONDS IRRESPECTIVE OF OBLIGOR

(A) IN GENERAL

If, during the 6-month period beginning on the date of a repayment of a loan financed by an issue 95 percent or more of the net proceeds of which are used to provide projects described in section 142(d), such repayment is used to provide a new loan for any project so described, any bond which is issued to refinance such issue shall be treated as a refunding issue to the extent the principal amount of such refunding issue does not exceed the principal amount of the bonds refunded.

(B) LIMITATIONS

Subparagraph (A) shall apply to only one refunding of the original issue and only if—

(i) the refunding issue is issued not later than 4 years after the date on which the original issue was issued,

(ii) the latest maturity date of any bond of the refunding issue is not later than 34 years after the date on which the refunded bond was issued, and

(iii) the refunding issue is approved in accordance with section 147(f) before the issuance of the refunding issue.

(J) POPULATION

For purposes of this section, determinations of the population of any State (or issuing authority) shall be made with respect to any calendar year on the basis of the most recent census estimate of the resident population of such State (or issuing authority) released by the Bureau of Census before the beginning of such calendar year.

(K) FACILITY MUST BE LOCATED WITHIN STATE

(1) IN GENERAL

Except as provided in paragraphs (2) and (3), no portion of the State ceiling applicable to any State for any calendar year may be used with respect to financing for a facility located outside such State.

(2) EXCEPTION FOR CERTAIN FACILITIES WHERE STATE WILL GET PROPORTIONATE SHARE
OF BENEFITS

Paragraph (1) shall not apply to any exempt facility bond described in paragraph
(4), (5), (6), or (10) of section 142(a) if the issuer establishes that the State's share
of the use of the facility (or its output) will equal or exceed the State's share of the
private activity bonds issued to finance the facility.

(3) TREATMENT OF GOVERNMENTAL BONDS TO WHICH VOLUME CAP ALLOCATED

Paragraph (1) shall not apply to any bond to which volume cap is allocated under
section 141(b)(5)—

(A) for an output facility, or

(B) for a facility of a type described in paragraph (4), (5), (6), or (10) of section
142(a),

if the issuer establishes that the State's share of the private business use (as defined by
section 141(b)(6)) of the facility will equal or exceed the State's share of the volume
cap allocated with respect to bonds issued to finance the facility.

(L) ISSUER OF QUALIFIED SCHOLARSHIP FUNDING BONDS

In the case of a qualified scholarship funding bond, such bond shall be treated for
purposes of this section as issued by a State or local issuing authority (whichever is
appropriate).

(M) TREATMENT OF AMOUNTS ALLOCATED TO PRIVATE ACTIVITY PORTION OF GOVERNMENT
USE BONDS

(1) IN GENERAL

The volume cap of an issuer shall be reduced by the amount allocated by the issuer
to an issue under section 141(b)(5).

(2) ADVANCE REFUNDINGS

Except as otherwise provided by the Secretary, any advance refunding of any part
of an issue to which an amount was allocated under section 141(b)(5) (or would have
been allocated if such section applied to such issue) shall be taken into account under
this section to the extent of the amount of the volume cap which was (or would have
been) so allocated.

(N) REDUCTION FOR MORTGAGE CREDIT CERTIFICATES, ETC.

The volume cap of any issuing authority for any calendar year shall be reduced by the
sum of—

(1) the amount of qualified mortgage bonds which such authority elects not to issue
under section 25(c)(2)(A)(ii) during such year, plus

(2) the amount of any reduction in such ceiling under section 25(f) applicable to
such authority for such year.

(Added Pub. L. 99–514, title XIII, §1301(b), Oct. 22, 1986, 100 Stat. 2630; amended Pub. L. 100–203,
title X, §10631(b), Dec. 22, 1987, 101 Stat. 1330–455; Pub. L. 100–647, title I, §1013(a)(9), (10), (28),
(40), title VI, §6180(b)(3), Nov. 10, 1988, 102 Stat. 3538, 3543, 3544, 3728; Pub. L. 101–239, title VII,
§7816(s)(2), Dec. 19, 1989, 103 Stat. 2423; Pub. L. 102–486, title XIX, §1921(b)(3), Oct. 24, 1992, 106
Stat. 3028; Pub. L. 103–66, title XIII, §13121(a), Aug. 10, 1993, 107 Stat. 432; Pub. L. 105–277, div. J,

title II, §2021(a), Oct. 21, 1998, 112 Stat. 2681–903; Pub. L. 106–554, §1(a)(7) [title I, §161(a)], Dec. 21, 2000, 114 Stat. 2763, 2763A–624; Pub. L. 107–16, title IV, §422(c), June 7, 2001, 115 Stat. 66; Pub. L. 108–357, title VII, §701(c), Oct. 22, 2004, 118 Stat. 1539; Pub. L. 109–59, title XI, §11143(c), Aug. 10, 2005, 119 Stat. 1965; Pub. L. 110–289, div. C, title I, §§3007(a), 3021(a), July 30, 2008, 122 Stat. 2886, 2892; Pub. L. 115–97, title I, §11002(d)(1)(O), Dec. 22, 2017, 131 Stat. 2060; Pub. L. 117–58, div. H, title IV, §§80401(c), 80402(c), Nov. 15, 2021, 135 Stat. 1331, 1334.)

* * * * * * *

Subtitle D—Miscellaneous Excise Taxes

* * * * * * *

CHAPTER 31—RETAIL EXCISE TAXES

Subchapter B—Special Fuels

Sec.
4041.   Imposition of tax.
4042.   Tax on fuel used in commercial transportation on inland waterways.

* * * * * * *

§4041. Imposition of tax

(a) Diesel fuel and special motor fuels

(1) Tax on diesel fuel and kerosene in certain cases

(A) In general

There is hereby imposed a tax on any liquid other than gasoline (as defined in section 4083)—

(i) sold by any person to an owner, lessee, or other operator of a diesel-powered highway vehicle or a diesel-powered train for use as a fuel in such vehicle or train, or

(ii) used by any person as a fuel in a diesel-powered highway vehicle or a diesel-powered train unless there was a taxable sale of such fuel under clause (i).

(B) Exemption for previously taxed fuel

No tax shall be imposed by this paragraph on the sale or use of any liquid if tax was imposed on such liquid under section 4081 (other than such tax at the Leaking Underground Storage Tank Trust Fund financing rate) and the tax thereon was not credited or refunded.

(C) Rate of tax

(i) In general

Except as otherwise provided in this subparagraph, the rate of the tax imposed by this paragraph shall be the rate of tax specified in section 4081(a)(2)(A) on diesel fuel which is in effect at the time of such sale or use.

(ii) Rate of tax on trains

In the case of any sale for use, or use, of diesel fuel in a train, the rate of tax imposed by this paragraph shall be—

(I) 3.3 cents per gallon after December 31, 2004, and before July 1, 2005,

(II) 2.3 cents per gallon after June 30, 2005, and before January 1, 2007, and

(III) 0 after December 31, 2006.

(III) RATE OF TAX ON CERTAIN BUSES

(I) IN GENERAL

Except as provided in subclause (II), in the case of fuel sold for use or used in a use described in section 6427(b)(1) (after the application of section 6427(b)(3)), the rate of tax imposed by this paragraph shall be 7.3 cents per gallon (4.3 cents per gallon after September 30, 2028).

(II) SCHOOL BUS AND INTRACITY TRANSPORTATION

No tax shall be imposed by this paragraph on any sale for use, or use, described in subparagraph (B) or (C) of section 6427(b)(2).

(2) ALTERNATIVE FUELS

(A) IN GENERAL

There is hereby imposed a tax on any liquid (other than gas oil, fuel oil, or any product taxable under section 4081 (other than such tax at the Leaking Underground Storage Tank Trust Fund financing rate))—

(i) sold by any person to an owner, lessee, or other operator of a motor vehicle or motorboat for use as a fuel in such motor vehicle or motorboat, or

(ii) used by any person as a fuel in a motor vehicle or motorboat unless there was a taxable sale of such liquid under clause (i).

(B) RATE OF TAX

The rate of the tax imposed by this paragraph shall be—

(i) except as otherwise provided in this subparagraph, the rate of tax specified in section 4081(a)(2)(A)(i) which is in effect at the time of such sale or use,

(ii) in the case of liquefied petroleum gas, 18.3 cents per energy equivalent of a gallon of gasoline,

(iii) in the case of any liquid fuel (other than ethanol and methanol) derived from coal (including peat) and liquid hydrocarbons derived from biomass (as defined in section 45K(c)(3)), 24.3 cents per gallon, and

(iv) in the case of liquefied natural gas, 24.3 cents per energy equivalent of a gallon of diesel.

(C) ENERGY EQUIVALENT OF A GALLON OF GASOLINE

For purposes of this paragraph, the term "energy equivalent of a gallon of gasoline" means, with respect to a liquefied petroleum gas fuel, the amount of such fuel having a Btu content of 115,400 (lower heating value). For purposes of the preceding sentence, a Btu content of 115,400 (lower heating value) is equal to 5.75 pounds of liquefied petroleum gas.

(D) ENERGY EQUIVALENT OF A GALLON OF DIESEL

For purposes of this paragraph, the term "energy equivalent of a gallon of diesel" means, with respect to a liquefied natural gas fuel, the amount of such fuel having a Btu content of 128,700 (lower heating value). For purposes of the preceding sentence, a Btu content of 128,700 (lower heating value) is equal to 6.06 pounds of liquefied natural gas.

(3) COMPRESSED NATURAL GAS

(A) IN GENERAL

There is hereby imposed a tax on compressed natural gas—
(i) sold by any person to an owner, lessee, or other operator of a motor vehicle or motorboat for use as a fuel in such motor vehicle or motorboat, or
(ii) used by any person as a fuel in a motor vehicle or motorboat unless there was a taxable sale of such gas under clause (i).
The rate of the tax imposed by this paragraph shall be 18.3 cents per energy equivalent of a gallon of gasoline.

(B) BUS USES

No tax shall be imposed by this paragraph on any sale for use, or use, described in subparagraph (B) or (C) of section 6427(b)(2) (relating to school bus and intracity transportation).

(C) ADMINISTRATIVE PROVISIONS

For purposes of applying this title with respect to the taxes imposed by this subsection, references to any liquid subject to tax under this subsection shall be treated as including references to compressed natural gas subject to tax under this paragraph, and references to gallons shall be treated as including references to energy equivalent of a gallon of gasoline with respect to such gas.

(D) ENERGY EQUIVALENT OF A GALLON OF GASOLINE

For purposes of this paragraph, the term "energy equivalent of a gallon of gasoline" means 5.66 pounds of compressed natural gas.

(B) EXEMPTION FOR OFF-HIGHWAY BUSINESS USE; REDUCTION IN TAX FOR QUALIFIED METHANOL AND ETHANOL FUEL

(1) EXEMPTION FOR OFF-HIGHWAY BUSINESS USE

(A) IN GENERAL

No tax shall be imposed by subsection (a) on liquids sold for use or used in an off-highway business use.

(B) TAX WHERE OTHER USE

If a liquid on which no tax was imposed by reason of subparagraph (A) is used otherwise than in an off-highway business use, a tax shall be imposed by paragraph (1)(B), (2)(B), or (3)(A)(ii) of subsection (a) (whichever is appropriate) and by the corresponding provision of subsection (d)(1) (if any).

(C) OFF-HIGHWAY BUSINESS USE DEFINED

For purposes of this subsection, the term "off-highway business use" has the meaning given to such term by section 6421(e)(2); except that such term shall not, for purposes of subsection (a)(1), include use in a diesel-powered train.

(2) QUALIFIED METHANOL AND ETHANOL FUEL

(A) IN GENERAL

In the case of any qualified methanol or ethanol fuel—

(i) the rate applicable under subsection (a)(2) shall be the applicable blender rate per gallon less than the otherwise applicable rate (6 cents per gallon in the case of a mixture none of the alcohol in which consists of ethanol), and

(ii) subsection (d)(1) shall be applied by substituting "0.05 cent" for "0.1 cent" with respect to the sales and uses to which clause (i) applies.

(B) QUALIFIED METHANOL AND ETHANOL FUEL PRODUCED FROM COAL

The term "qualified methanol or ethanol fuel" means any liquid at least 85 percent of which consists of methanol, ethanol, or other alcohol produced from coal (including peat).

(C) APPLICABLE BLENDER RATE

For purposes of subparagraph (A)(i), the applicable blender rate is—

(i) except as provided in clause (ii), 5.4 cents, and

(ii) for sales or uses during calendar years 2001 through 2008, 1/10 of the blender amount applicable under section 40(h)(2) for the calendar year in which the sale or use occurs.

(D) TERMINATION

On and after January 1, 2009, subparagraph (A) shall not apply.

(c) CERTAIN LIQUIDS USED AS A FUEL IN AVIATION

(1) IN GENERAL

There is hereby imposed a tax upon any liquid for use as a fuel other than aviation gasoline—

(A) sold by any person to an owner, lessee, or other operator of an aircraft for use in such aircraft, or

(B) used by any person in an aircraft unless there was a taxable sale of such fuel under subparagraph (A).

(2) EXEMPTION FOR PREVIOUSLY TAXED FUEL

No tax shall be imposed by this subsection on the sale or use of any liquid for use as a fuel other than aviation gasoline if tax was imposed on such liquid under section 4081 (other than such tax at the Leaking Underground Storage Tank Trust Fund financing rate) and the tax thereon was not credited or refunded.

(3) RATE OF TAX

The rate of tax imposed by this subsection shall be 21.8 cents per gallon (4.3 cents per gallon with respect to any sale or use for commercial aviation).

(D) Additional taxes to fund Leaking Underground Storage Tank Trust Fund

(1) Tax on sales and uses subject to tax under subsection (a)

In addition to the taxes imposed by subsection (a), there is hereby imposed a tax of 0.1 cent a gallon on the sale or use of any liquid (other than liquefied petroleum gas and other than liquefied natural gas) if tax is imposed by subsection (a)(1) or (2) on such sale or use. No tax shall be imposed under the preceding sentence on the sale or use of any liquid if tax was imposed with respect to such liquid under section 4081 at the Leaking Underground Storage Tank Trust Fund financing rate.

(2) Liquids used in aviation

In addition to the taxes imposed by subsection (c), there is hereby imposed a tax of 0.1 cent a gallon on any liquid (other than gasoline (as defined in section 4083))—

(A) sold by any person to an owner, lessee, or other operator of an aircraft for use as a fuel in such aircraft, or

(B) used by any person as a fuel in an aircraft unless there was a taxable sale of such liquid under subparagraph (A).

No tax shall be imposed by this paragraph on the sale or use of any liquid if there was a taxable sale of such liquid under section 4081.

(3) Diesel fuel used in trains

In the case of any sale for use or use after December 31, 2006, there is hereby imposed a tax of 0.1 cent per gallon on any liquid other than gasoline (as defined in section 4083)—

(A) sold by any person to an owner, lessee, or other operator of a diesel-powered train for use as a fuel in such train, or

(B) used by any person as a fuel in a diesel-powered train unless there was a taxable sale of such fuel under subparagraph (A).

No tax shall be imposed by this paragraph on the sale or use of any liquid if tax was imposed on such liquid under section 4081.

(4) Termination

The taxes imposed by this subsection shall not apply during any period during which the Leaking Underground Storage Tank Trust Fund financing rate under section 4081 does not apply.

(5) Nonapplication of exemptions other than for exports

For purposes of this section, the tax imposed under this subsection shall be determined without regard to subsections (b)(1)(A), (f), (g), (h), and (l). The preceding sentence shall not apply with respect to subsection (g)(3) and so much of subsection (g)(1) as relates to vessels (within the meaning of section 4221(d)(3)) employed in foreign trade or trade between the United States and any of its possessions.

[(E) REPEALED. PUB. L. 108–357, TITLE VIII, §853(D)(2)(C), OCT. 22, 2004, 118 STAT. 1613]

(F) EXEMPTION FOR FARM USE

(1) EXEMPTION

Under regulations prescribed by the Secretary, no tax shall be imposed under this section on any liquid sold for use or used on a farm for farming purposes.

(2) USE ON A FARM FOR FARMING PURPOSES

For purposes of paragraph (1) of this subsection, use on a farm for farming purposes shall be determined in accordance with paragraphs (1), (2), and (3) of section 6420(c).

(G) OTHER EXEMPTIONS

Under regulations prescribed by the Secretary, no tax shall be imposed under this section—

(1) on any liquid sold for use or used as supplies for vessels or aircraft (within the meaning of section 4221(d)(3));

(2) with respect to the sale of any liquid for the exclusive use of any State, any political subdivision of a State, or the District of Columbia, or with respect to the use by any of the foregoing of any liquid as a fuel;

(3) upon the sale of any liquid for export, or for shipment to a possession of the United States, and in due course so exported or shipped;

(4) with respect to the sale of any liquid to a nonprofit educational organization for its exclusive use, or with respect to the use by a nonprofit educational organization of any liquid as a fuel; and

(5) with respect to the sale of any liquid to a qualified blood collector organization (as defined in section 7701(a)(49)) for such organization's exclusive use in the collection, storage, or transportation of blood.

For purposes of paragraph (4), the term "nonprofit educational organization" means an educational organization described in section 170(b)(1)(A)(ii) which is exempt from income tax under section 501(a). The term also includes a school operated as an activity of an organization described in section 501(c)(3) which is exempt from income tax under section 501(a), if such school normally maintains a regular faculty and curriculum and normally has a regularly enrolled body of pupils or students in attendance at the place where its educational activities are regularly carried on.

(H) EXEMPTION FOR USE BY CERTAIN AIRCRAFT MUSEUMS

(1) EXEMPTION

Under regulations prescribed by the Secretary, no tax shall be imposed under this section on any liquid sold for use or used by an aircraft museum in an aircraft or vehicle owned by such museum and used exclusively for purposes set forth in paragraph (2)(C).

(2) DEFINITION OF AIRCRAFT MUSEUM

For purposes of this subsection, the term "aircraft museum" means an organization—

(A) described in section 501(c)(3) which is exempt from income tax under section 501(a),

(B) operated as a museum under charter by a State or the District of Columbia, and

(C) operated exclusively for the procurement, care, and exhibition of aircraft of the type used for combat or transport in World War II.

[(I) REPEALED. PUB. L. 108–357, TITLE VIII, §853(D)(2)(D), OCT. 22, 2004, 118 STAT. 1613]

(J) SALES BY UNITED STATES, ETC.

The taxes imposed by this section shall apply with respect to liquids sold at retail by the United States, or by any agency or instrumentality of the United States, unless sales by such agency or instrumentality are by statute specifically exempted from such taxes.

[(K) REPEALED. PUB. L. 108–357, TITLE III, §301(C)(6), OCT. 22, 2004, 118 STAT. 1461]

(L) EXEMPTION FOR CERTAIN USES

No tax shall be imposed under this section on any liquid sold for use in, or used in, a helicopter or a fixed-wing aircraft for purposes of providing transportation with respect to which the requirements of subsection (f) or (g) of section 4261 are met.

(M) CERTAIN ALCOHOL FUELS

(1) IN GENERAL

In the case of the sale or use of any partially exempt methanol or ethanol fuel the rate of the tax imposed by subsection (a)(2) shall be—

(A) after September 30, 1997, and before October 1, 2028—

(i) in the case of fuel none of the alcohol in which consists of ethanol, 9.15 cents per gallon, and

(ii) in any other case, 11.3 cents per gallon, and

(B) after September 30, 2028—

(i) in the case of fuel none of the alcohol in which consists of ethanol, 2.15 cents per gallon, and

(ii) in any other case, 4.3 cents per gallon.

(2) PARTIALLY EXEMPT METHANOL OR ETHANOL FUEL

The term "partially exempt methanol or ethanol fuel" means any liquid at least 85 percent of which consists of methanol, ethanol, or other alcohol produced from natural gas.

(Aug. 16, 1954, ch. 736, 68A Stat. 478; Mar. 30, 1955, ch. 18, §3(a)(1), 69 Stat. 14; Mar. 29, 1956, ch. 115, §3(a)(1), 70 Stat. 66; Apr. 2, 1956, ch. 160, §2(a)(1), 70 Stat. 89; June 29, 1956, ch. 462, title II, §202, 70 Stat. 387; Pub. L. 85–859, title I, §119(b)(1), Sept. 2, 1958, 72 Stat. 1286; Pub. L. 86–342, title II, §201(b), Sept. 21, 1959, 73 Stat. 613; Pub. L. 87–61, title II, §201(a), (c), (d), June 29, 1961, 75 Stat. 123, 124; Pub. L. 89–44, title VIII, §802(a)(2), June 21, 1965, 79 Stat. 159; Pub. L. 91–258, title II, §202, May 21, 1970, 84 Stat. 237; Pub. L. 91–605, title III, §303(a)(1), (2), Dec. 31, 1970, 84 Stat. 1743; Pub. L. 94–280, title III, §303(a)(1), (2), May 5, 1976, 90 Stat. 456; Pub. L. 94–455, title XIX, §§1904(a)(1)(B), (C), 1906(b)(13)(A), Oct. 4, 1976, 90 Stat. 1810, 1811, 1834; Pub. L. 94–530,

§1(a), Oct. 17, 1976, 90 Stat. 2487; Pub. L. 95–599, title V, §502(a)(1), (b), Nov. 6, 1978, 92 Stat. 2756, 2757; Pub. L. 95–600, title VII, §703(l)(1), (2), Nov. 6, 1978, 92 Stat. 2942; Pub. L. 95–618, title II, §§221(b)(1), 222(a)(2), 233(a)(3)(B), Nov. 9, 1978, 92 Stat. 3185, 3187, 3191; Pub. L. 96–223, title II, §232(a)(2), Apr. 2, 1980, 94 Stat. 273; Pub. L. 96–298, §1(a), July 1, 1980, 94 Stat. 829; Pub. L. 97–248, title II, §279(a), (b)(1), Sept. 3, 1982, 96 Stat. 563; Pub. L. 97–424, title V, §§511(a)(2), (b)(1), (c)(2), (d)(2), (g)(1), 516(a)(1), (b)(1), Jan. 6, 1983, 96 Stat. 2169–2171, 2173, 2182, 2183; Pub. L. 98–369, div. A, title IX, §§911(a), 912(a), 913(a), title X, §1018(a), July 18, 1984, 98 Stat. 1005, 1007, 1008, 1021; Pub. L. 99–499, title V, §521(a)(2), (d)(1)–(3), Oct. 17, 1986, 100 Stat. 1776, 1779; Pub. L. 99–514, title IV, §422(a)(1), (2), title XVII, §1702(a), title XVIII, §1878(c)(1), Oct. 22, 1986, 100 Stat. 2229, 2773, 2903; Pub. L. 100–17, title V, §502(a)(1), (b)(1)–(3), (c)(1), Apr. 2, 1987, 101 Stat. 256, 257; Pub. L. 100–203, title X, §10502(b), Dec. 22, 1987, 101 Stat. 1330–441; Pub. L. 100–223, title IV, §§402(b), 404(b), 405(b)(3), Dec. 30, 1987, 101 Stat. 1532, 1533, 1535; Pub. L. 100–647, title I, §1017(c)(3), (4), title II, §2001(d)(2), (3)(A)–(D), Nov. 10, 1988, 102 Stat. 3576, 3595; Pub. L. 101–508, title XI, §§11211(a)(4), (b)(3), (6)(C)–(E)(i), (F), (d)(1), (2), (e)(1), (2), 11213(b)(2)(A), (B), (d)(2)(B), (e)(3), Nov. 5, 1990, 104 Stat. 1388–423, 1388–425 to 1388–427, 1388–433, 1388–436; Pub. L. 102–240, title VIII, §8002(b)(1), (2), Dec. 18, 1991, 105 Stat. 2203; Pub. L. 103–66, title XIII, §§13163(a)(2), 13241(b)(2)(A), (B)(iii), (c), (e), (f)(1), (2), 13242(d)(3)–(13), Aug. 10, 1993, 107 Stat. 453, 510, 511, 522–524; Pub. L. 104–188, title I, §§1208, 1609(a)(3), (g)(3), (4)(A), Aug. 20, 1996, 110 Stat. 1776, 1841–1843; Pub. L. 105–2, §2(a)(3), Feb. 28, 1997, 111 Stat. 4; Pub. L. 105–34, title IX, §§902(b)(1), (2), 907(a), (b), title X, §§1031(a)(3), 1032(e)(1), (2), title XIV, §1435(b), title XVI, §1601(f)(4)(A), (B), Aug. 5, 1997, 111 Stat. 873, 875, 929, 935, 1053, 1090; Pub. L. 105–178, title IX, §§9002(a)(1)(A)–(C), 9003(a)(1)(A), (B), (b)(2)(A), 9006(a), June 9, 1998, 112 Stat. 499, 501, 502, 506; Pub. L. 105–206, title VI, §6010(g)(1), July 22, 1998, 112 Stat. 814; Pub. L. 108–357, title II, §241(a)(1), (2)(A), title III, §301(c)(5), (6), title VIII, §853(a)(6), (d)(2)(A)–(E), Oct. 22, 2004, 118 Stat. 1437, 1461, 1611–1613; Pub. L. 109–58, title XIII, §1362(b)(2), Aug. 8, 2005, 119 Stat. 1059; Pub. L. 109–59, title XI, §§11101(a)(1)(A)–(C), 11113(a), 11151(e)(2), 11161(b)(1), (3)(A), Aug. 10, 2005, 119 Stat. 1943, 1946, 1969–1971; Pub. L. 109–280, title XII, §1207(a), Aug. 17, 2006, 120 Stat. 1070; Pub. L. 109–432, div. A, title II, §208, Dec. 20, 2006, 120 Stat. 2946; Pub. L. 110–172, §6(d)(1)(A), (2)(A), (3), Dec. 29, 2007, 121 Stat. 2480, 2481; Pub. L. 112–30, title I, §142(a)(1)(A), (B), (2)(A), Sept. 16, 2011, 125 Stat. 355, 356; Pub. L. 112–102, title IV, §402(a)(1)(A), (B), (2)(A), Mar. 30, 2012, 126 Stat. 281, 282; Pub. L. 112–140, title IV, §402(a)(1)(A), (B), (2)(A), June 29, 2012, 126 Stat. 402; Pub. L. 112–141, div. D, title I, §40102(a)(1)(A), (B), (2)(A), July 6, 2012, 126 Stat. 844; Pub. L. 114–41, title II, §2008(a)–(c), July 31, 2015, 129 Stat. 459, 460; Pub. L. 114–94, div. C, title XXXI, §31102(a)(1)(A), (B), (2)(A), Dec. 4, 2015, 129 Stat. 1727; Pub. L. 117–58, div. H, title I, §80102(a)(1)(A), (B), (2)(A), Nov. 15, 2021, 135 Stat. 1327.)

* * * * * * *

Subchapter C—Heavy Trucks and Trailers

Sec.
4051. Imposition of tax on heavy trucks and trailers sold at retail.
4052. Definitions and special rules.
4053. Exemptions.

§4051. IMPOSITION OF TAX ON HEAVY TRUCKS AND TRAILERS SOLD AT RETAIL

(A) IMPOSITION OF TAX

(1) IN GENERAL

There is hereby imposed on the first retail sale of the following articles (including in each case parts or accessories sold on or in connection therewith or with the sale thereof) a tax of 12 percent of the amount for which the article is so sold:

(A) Automobile truck chassis.

(B) Automobile truck bodies.

(C) Truck trailer and semitrailer chassis.

(D) Truck trailer and semitrailer bodies.

(E) Tractors of the kind chiefly used for highway transportation in combination with a trailer or semitrailer.

(2) EXCLUSION FOR TRUCKS WEIGHING 33,000 POUNDS OR LESS

The tax imposed by paragraph (1) shall not apply to automobile truck chassis and automobile truck bodies, suitable for use with a vehicle which has a gross vehicle weight of 33,000 pounds or less (as determined under regulations prescribed by the Secretary).

(3) EXCLUSION FOR TRAILERS WEIGHING 26,000 POUNDS OR LESS

The tax imposed by paragraph (1) shall not apply to truck trailer and semitrailer chassis and bodies, suitable for use with a trailer or semitrailer which has a gross vehicle weight of 26,000 pounds or less (as determined under regulations prescribed by the Secretary).

(4) EXCLUSION FOR TRACTORS WEIGHING 19,500 POUNDS OR LESS

The tax imposed by paragraph (1) shall not apply to tractors of the kind chiefly used for highway transportation in combination with a trailer or semitrailer if—

(A) such tractor has a gross vehicle weight of 19,500 pounds or less (as determined by the Secretary), and

(B) such tractor, in combination with a trailer or semitrailer, has a gross combined weight of 33,000 pounds or less (as determined by the Secretary).

(5) SALE OF TRUCKS, ETC., TREATED AS SALE OF CHASSIS AND BODY

For purposes of this subsection, a sale of an automobile truck or truck trailer or semitrailer shall be considered to be a sale of a chassis and of a body described in paragraph (1).

(B) SEPARATE PURCHASE OF TRUCK OR TRAILER AND PARTS AND ACCESSORIES THEREFOR

Under regulations prescribed by the Secretary—

(1) IN GENERAL

If—

(A) the owner, lessee, or operator of any vehicle which contains an article taxable under subsection (a) installs (or causes to be installed) any part or accessory on such vehicle, and

(B) such installation is not later than the date 6 months after the date such vehicle (as it contains such article) was first placed in service,

then there is hereby imposed on such installation a tax equal to 12 percent of the price of such part or accessory and its installation.

(2) EXCEPTIONS

Paragraph (1) shall not apply if—

(A) the part or accessory installed is a replacement part or accessory, or

(B) the aggregate price of the parts and accessories (and their installation) described in paragraph (1) with respect to any vehicle does not exceed $1,000 (or such other amount or amounts as the Secretary may by regulations prescribe).

(3) INSTALLERS SECONDARILY LIABLE FOR TAX

The owners of the trade or business installing the parts or accessories shall be secondarily liable for the tax imposed by paragraph (1).

(C) TERMINATION

On and after October 1, 2028, the taxes imposed by this section shall not apply.

(D) CREDIT AGAINST TAX FOR TIRE TAX

If—

(1) tires are sold on or in connection with the sale of any article, and

(2) tax is imposed by this subchapter on the sale of such tires,

there shall be allowed as a credit against the tax imposed by this subchapter an amount equal to the tax (if any) imposed by section 4071 on such tires.

(Added Pub. L. 97–424, title V, §512(b)(1), Jan. 6, 1983, 96 Stat. 2174; amended Pub. L. 98–369, div. A, title VII, §734(g), title IX, §921, July 18, 1984, 98 Stat. 980, 1009; Pub. L. 99–514, title XVIII, §§1877(c), 1899A(47), Oct. 22, 1986, 100 Stat. 2902, 2961; Pub. L. 100–17, title V, §502(a)(2), Apr. 2, 1987, 101 Stat. 256; Pub. L. 101–508, title XI, §11211(c)(1), Nov. 5, 1990, 104 Stat. 1388–426; Pub. L. 102–240, title VIII, §8002(a)(1), Dec. 18, 1991, 105 Stat. 2203; Pub. L. 105–34, title XIV, §§1401(a), 1402(a), 1432(a), Aug. 5, 1997, 111 Stat. 1045, 1046, 1050; Pub. L. 105–178, title IX, §9002(a)(1)(D), June 9, 1998, 112 Stat. 499; Pub. L. 109–59, title XI, §§11101(a)(1)(D), 11112(a), Aug. 10, 2005, 119 Stat. 1943, 1946; Pub. L. 112–30, title I, §142(a)(2)(B), Sept. 16, 2011, 125 Stat. 356; Pub. L. 112–102, title IV, §402(a)(2)(B), Mar. 30, 2012, 126 Stat. 282; Pub. L. 112–140, title IV, §402(a)(2)(B), June 29, 2012, 126 Stat. 402; Pub. L. 112–141, div. D, title I, §40102(a)(2)(B), July 6, 2012, 126 Stat. 844; Pub. L. 114–94, div. C, title XXXI, §31102(a)(2)(B), Dec. 4, 2015, 129 Stat. 1727; Pub. L. 115–141, div. U, title IV, §401(a)(219), Mar. 23, 2018, 132 Stat. 1194; Pub. L. 117–58, div. H, title I, §80102(a)(2)(B), Nov. 15, 2021, 135 Stat. 1327.)

§4052. DEFINITIONS AND SPECIAL RULES

(A) FIRST RETAIL SALE

For purposes of this subchapter—

(1) IN GENERAL

The term "first retail sale" means the first sale, for a purpose other than for resale or leasing in a long-term lease, after production, manufacture, or importation.

(2) LEASES CONSIDERED AS SALES

Rules similar to the rules of section 4217 shall apply.

(3) USE TREATED AS SALE

(A) IN GENERAL

If any person uses an article taxable under section 4051 before the first retail sale of such article, then such person shall be liable for tax under section 4051 in the same manner as if such article were sold at retail by him.

(B) EXEMPTION FOR USE IN FURTHER MANUFACTURE

Subparagraph (A) shall not apply to use of an article as material in the manufacture or production of, or as a component part of, another article to be manufactured or produced by him.

(C) COMPUTATION OF TAX

In the case of any person made liable for tax by subparagraph (A), the tax shall be computed on the price at which similar articles are sold at retail in the ordinary course of trade, as determined by the Secretary.

(B) DETERMINATION OF PRICE

(1) IN GENERAL

In determining price for purposes of this subchapter—

(A) there shall be included any charge incident to placing the article in condition ready for use,

(B) there shall be excluded—

(i) the amount of the tax imposed by this subchapter,

(ii) if stated as a separate charge, the amount of any retail sales tax imposed by any State or political subdivision thereof or the District of Columbia, whether the liability for such tax is imposed on the vendor or vendee, and

(iii) the value of any component of such article if—

(I) such component is furnished by the first user of such article, and

(II) such component has been used before such furnishing, and

(C) the price shall be determined without regard to any trade-in.

(2) SALES NOT AT ARM'S LENGTH

In the case of any article sold (otherwise than through an arm's-length transaction) at less than the fair market price, the tax under this subchapter shall be computed on the price for which similar articles are sold at retail in the ordinary course of trade, as determined by the Secretary.

(3) LONG-TERM LEASE

(A) IN GENERAL

In the case of any long-term lease of an article which is treated as the first retail sale of such article, the tax under this subchapter shall be computed on a price equal to—

(i) the sum of—

(I) the price (determined under this subchapter but without regard to paragraph (4)) at which such article was sold to the lessor, and

(II) the cost of any parts and accessories installed by the lessor on such article before the first use by the lessee or leased in connection with such long-term lease, plus

(ii) an amount equal to the presumed markup percentage of the sum described in clause (i).

(B) Presumed markup percentage

For purposes of subparagraph (A), the term "presumed markup percentage" means the average markup percentage of retailers of articles of the type involved, as determined by the Secretary.

(C) Exceptions under regulations

To the extent provided in regulations prescribed by the Secretary, subparagraph (A) shall not apply to specified types of leases where its application is not necessary to carry out the purposes of this subsection.

(4) Special rule where tax paid by manufacturer, producer, or importer

(A) In general

In any case where the manufacturer, producer, or importer of any article (or a related person) is liable for tax imposed by this subchapter with respect to such article, the tax under this subchapter shall be computed on a price equal to the sum of—

(i) the price which would (but for this paragraph) be determined under this subchapter, plus

(ii) the product of the price referred to in clause (i) and the presumed markup percentage determined under paragraph (3)(B).

(B) Related person

For purposes of this paragraph—

(I) In general

Except as provided in clause (ii), the term "related person" means any person who is a member of the same controlled group (within the meaning of section 5061(e)(3)) as the manufacturer, producer, or importer.

(II) Exception for retail establishment

To the extent provided in regulations prescribed by the Secretary, a person shall not be treated as a related person with respect to the sale of any article if such article is sold through a permanent retail establishment in the normal course of the trade or business of being a retailer.

(c) Certain combinations not treated as manufacture

(1) In general

For purposes of this subchapter (other than subsection (a)(3)(B)), a person shall not be treated as engaged in the manufacture of any article by reason of merely combining such article with any item listed in paragraph (2).

(2) Items

The items listed in this paragraph are any coupling device (including any fifth wheel), wrecker crane, loading and unloading equipment (including any crane, hoist, winch, or power liftgate), aerial ladder or tower, snow and ice control equipment, earthmoving, excavation and construction equipment, spreader, sleeper cab, cab shield, or wood or metal floor.

(D) CERTAIN OTHER RULES MADE APPLICABLE

Under regulations prescribed by the Secretary, rules similar to the rules of subsections (c) and (d) of section 4216 (relating to partial payments) shall apply for purposes of this subchapter.

(E) LONG-TERM LEASE

For purposes of this section, the term "long-term lease" means any lease with a term of 1 year or more. In determining a lease term for purposes of the preceding sentence, the rules of section 168(i)(3)(A) shall apply.

(F) CERTAIN REPAIRS AND MODIFICATIONS NOT TREATED AS MANUFACTURE

(1) IN GENERAL

An article described in section 4051(a)(1) shall not be treated as manufactured or produced solely by reason of repairs or modifications to the article (including any modification which changes the transportation function of the article or restores a wrecked article to a functional condition) if the cost of such repairs and modifications does not exceed 75 percent of the retail price of a comparable new article.

(2) EXCEPTION

Paragraph (1) shall not apply if the article (as repaired or modified) would, if new, be taxable under section 4051 and the article when new was not taxable under such section or the corresponding provision of prior law.

(G) REGULATIONS

The Secretary shall prescribe regulations which permit, in lieu of any other certification, persons who are purchasing articles taxable under this subchapter for resale or leasing in a long-term lease to execute a statement (made under penalties of perjury) on the sale invoice that such sale is for resale. The Secretary shall not impose any registration requirement as a condition of using such procedure.

(Added Pub. L. 97–424, title V, §512(b)(1), Jan. 6, 1983, 96 Stat. 2175; amended Pub. L. 98–369, div. A, title VII, §§731, 735(b)(2), July 18, 1984, 98 Stat. 976, 981; Pub. L. 100–17, title V, §§505(a)–(c), 506(a), Apr. 2, 1987, 101 Stat. 258, 259; Pub. L. 100–647, title VI, §6111(a), Nov. 10, 1988, 102 Stat. 3713; Pub. L. 105–34, title XIV, §§1402(b), 1434(a), (b), Aug. 5, 1997, 111 Stat. 1046, 1052; Pub. L. 105–206, title VI, §6014(c), July 22, 1998, 112 Stat. 820.)

§4053. EXEMPTIONS

No tax shall be imposed by section 4051 on any of the following articles:

(1) CAMPER COACHES BODIES FOR SELF-PROPELLED MOBILE HOMES

Any article designed—

(A) to be mounted or placed on automobile trucks, automobile truck chassis, or automobile chassis, and

(B) to be used primarily as living quarters or camping accommodations.

(2) FEED, SEED, AND FERTILIZER EQUIPMENT

Any body primarily designed—

(A) to process or prepare seed, feed, or fertilizer for use on farms,

(B) to haul feed, seed, or fertilizer to and on farms,

(C) to spread feed, seed, or fertilizer on farms,

(D) to load or unload feed, seed, or fertilizer on farms, or

(E) for any combination of the foregoing.

(3) HOUSE TRAILERS

Any house trailer.

(4) AMBULANCES, HEARSES, ETC.

Any ambulance, hearse, or combination ambulance-hearse.

(5) CONCRETE MIXERS

Any article designed—

(A) to be placed or mounted on an automobile truck chassis or truck trailer or semitrailer chassis, and

(B) to be used to process or prepare concrete.

(6) TRASH CONTAINERS, ETC.

Any box, container, receptacle, bin or other similar article—

(A) which is designed to be used as a trash container and is not designed for the transportation of freight other than trash, and

(B) which is not designed to be permanently mounted on or permanently affixed to an automobile truck chassis or body.

(7) RAIL TRAILERS AND RAIL VANS

Any chassis or body of a trailer or semitrailer which is designed for use both as a highway vehicle and a railroad car. For purposes of the preceding sentence, piggy-back trailer or semitrailer shall not be treated as designed for use as a railroad car.

(8) MOBILE MACHINERY

Any vehicle which consists of a chassis—

(A) to which there has been permanently mounted (by welding, bolting, riveting, or other means) machinery or equipment to perform a construction, manufacturing, processing, farming, mining, drilling, timbering, or similar operation if the operation of the machinery or equipment is unrelated to transportation on or off the public highways,

(B) which has been specially designed to serve only as a mobile carriage and mount (and a power source, where applicable) for the particular machinery or equipment involved, whether or not such machinery or equipment is in operation, and

(C) which, by reason of such special design, could not, without substantial structural modification, be used as a component of a vehicle designed to perform a function of transporting any load other than that particular machinery or equipment or similar machinery or equipment requiring such a specially designed chassis.

(9) IDLING REDUCTION DEVICE

Any device or system of devices which—

(A) is designed to provide to a vehicle those services (such as heat, air conditioning, or electricity) that would otherwise require the operation of the main drive engine while the vehicle is temporarily parked or remains stationary using one or more devices affixed to a tractor, and

(B) is determined by the Administrator of the Environmental Protection Agency, in consultation with the Secretary of Energy and the Secretary of Transportation, to reduce idling of such vehicle at a motor vehicle rest stop or other location where such vehicles are temporarily parked or remain stationary.

(10) ADVANCED INSULATION

Any insulation that has an R value of not less than R35 per inch.

(Added Pub. L. 97–424, title V, §512(b)(1), Jan. 6, 1983, 96 Stat. 2176; amended Pub. L. 98–369, div. A, title VII, §735(b)(1), July 18, 1984, 98 Stat. 981; Pub. L. 108–357, title VIII, §851(a)(1), Oct. 22, 2004, 118 Stat. 1607; Pub. L. 110–343, div. B, title II, §206(a), Oct. 3, 2008, 122 Stat. 3839.)

CHAPTER 32—MANUFACTURERS EXCISE TAXES

* * * * * * *

Subchapter A—Automotive and Related Items

* * * * * * *

PART II—TIRES

§4071. IMPOSITION OF TAX

(A) IMPOSITION AND RATE OF TAX

There is hereby imposed on taxable tires sold by the manufacturer, producer, or importer thereof a tax at the rate of 9.45 cents (4.725 cents in the case of a biasply tire or super single tire) for each 10 pounds so much of the maximum rated load capacity thereof as exceeds 3,500 pounds.

(B) SPECIAL RULE FOR MANUFACTURERS WHO SELL AT RETAIL

Under regulations prescribed by the Secretary, if the manufacturer, producer, or importer of any tire delivers such tire to a retail store or retail outlet of such manufacturer, producer, or importer, he shall be liable for tax under subsection (a) in respect of such tire in the same manner as if it had been sold at the time it was delivered to such retail store or outlet. This subsection shall not apply to an article in respect to which tax has been imposed by subsection (a). Subsection (a) shall not apply to an article in respect of which tax has been imposed by this subsection.

(C) TIRES ON IMPORTED ARTICLES

For the purposes of subsection (a), if an article imported into the United States is equipped with tires—

(1) the importer of the article shall be treated as the importer of the tires with which such article is equipped, and

(2) the sale of the article by the importer thereof shall be treated as the sale of the tires with which such article is equipped.

This subsection shall not apply with respect to the sale of an automobile bus chassis or an automobile bus body.

(D) TERMINATION

On and after October 1, 2028, the taxes imposed by subsection (a) shall not apply.

(Aug. 16, 1954, ch. 736, 68A Stat. 482; June 29, 1956, ch. 462, title II, §204(a), 70 Stat. 388; Pub. L. 86–440, §1(a), Apr. 22, 1960, 74 Stat. 80; Pub. L. 87–61, title II, §202, June 29, 1961, 75 Stat. 124; Pub. L. 89–523, §1(a), Aug. 1, 1966, 80 Stat. 331; Pub. L. 91–605, title III, §303(a)(5), Dec. 31, 1970, 84 Stat. 1744; Pub. L. 92–178, title IV, §401(f), Dec. 10, 1971, 85 Stat. 533; Pub. L. 94–280, title III, §303(a)(5), May 5, 1976, 90 Stat. 456; Pub. L. 94–455, title XIX, §1906(b)(13)(A), Oct. 4, 1976, 90 Stat. 1834; Pub.

L. 95–599, title V, §502(a)(4), Nov. 6, 1978, 92 Stat. 2756; Pub. L. 96–222, title I, §108(c)(2)(C), Apr. 1, 1980, 94 Stat. 227; Pub. L. 96–596, §4(a)(1), Dec. 24, 1980, 94 Stat. 3475; Pub. L. 96–598, §1(d), Dec. 24, 1980, 94 Stat. 3486; Pub. L. 97–424, title V, §§514(a), 516(a)(2), Jan. 6, 1983, 96 Stat. 2181, 2182; Pub. L. 98–369, div. A, title VII, §735(c)(2), July 18, 1984, 98 Stat. 982; Pub. L. 100–17, title V, §502(a)(3), Apr. 2, 1987, 101 Stat. 256; Pub. L. 101–508, title XI, §11211(c)(2), Nov. 5, 1990, 104 Stat. 1388–426; Pub. L. 102–240, title VIII, §8002(a)(2), Dec. 18, 1991, 105 Stat. 2203; Pub. L. 105–178, title IX, §9002(a)(1)(E), June 9, 1998, 112 Stat. 499; Pub. L. 108–357, title VIII, §869(a), (d)(1), Oct. 22, 2004, 118 Stat. 1623; Pub. L. 109–59, title XI, §11101(a)(1)(E), Aug. 10, 2005, 119 Stat. 1943; Pub. L. 112–30, title I, §142(a)(2)(C), Sept. 16, 2011, 125 Stat. 356; Pub. L. 112–102, title IV, §402(a)(2)(C), Mar. 30, 2012, 126 Stat. 282; Pub. L. 112–140, title IV, §402(a)(2)(C), June 29, 2012, 126 Stat. 402; Pub. L. 112–141, div. D, title I, §40102(a)(2)(C), July 6, 2012, 126 Stat. 844; Pub. L. 114–94, div. C, title XXXI, §31102(a)(2)(C), Dec. 4, 2015, 129 Stat. 1727; Pub. L. 117–58, div. H, title I, §80102(a)(2)(C), Nov. 15, 2021, 135 Stat. 1327.)

§4072. DEFINITIONS

(A) TAXABLE TIRE

For purposes of this chapter, the term "taxable tire" means any tire of the type used on highway vehicles if wholly or in part made of rubber and if marked pursuant to Federal regulations for highway use.

(B) RUBBER

For purposes of this chapter, the term "rubber" includes synthetic and substitute rubber.

(C) TIRES OF THE TYPE USED ON HIGHWAY VEHICLES

For purposes of this part, the term "tires of the type used on highway vehicles" means tires of the type used on—
  (1) motor vehicles which are highway vehicles, or
  (2) vehicles of the type used in connection with motor vehicles which are highway vehicles.

Such term shall not include tires of a type used exclusively on vehicles described in section 4053(8).

(D) BIASPLY

For purposes of this part, the term "biasply tire" means a pneumatic tire on which the ply cords that extend to the beads are laid at alternate angles substantially less than 90 degrees to the centerline of the tread.

(E) SUPER SINGLE TIRE

For purposes of this part, the term "super single tire" means a single tire greater than 13 inches in cross section width designed to replace 2 tires in a dual fitment. Such term shall not include any tire designed for steering.

(Aug. 16, 1954, ch. 736, 68A Stat. 482; June 29, 1956, ch. 462, title II, §204(b), 70 Stat. 389; Pub. L. 98–369, div. A, title VII, §735(c)(3), July 18, 1984, 98 Stat. 982; Pub. L. 108–357, title VIII, §§851(c)(1), 869(b), Oct. 22, 2004, 118 Stat. 1608, 1623; Pub. L. 109–58, title XIII, §1364(a), Aug. 8, 2005, 119 Stat. 1060.)

§4073. EXEMPTIONS

The tax imposed by section 4071 shall not apply to tires sold for the exclusive use of the Department of Defense or the Coast Guard.

(Aug. 16, 1954, ch. 736, 68A Stat. 482; June 29, 1956, ch. 462, title II, §204(c), 70 Stat. 389; Pub. L. 94–455, title XIX, §1906(b)(13)(A), Oct. 4, 1976, 90 Stat. 1834; Pub. L. 98–369, div. A, title VII, §735(c)(4), July 18, 1984, 98 Stat. 982; Pub. L. 108–357, title VIII, §869(c), Oct. 22, 2004, 118 Stat. 1623.)

PART III—PETROLEUM PRODUCTS

* * * * * * *

Subpart A—Motor and Aviation Fuels

Sec.

§4081. Imposition of tax

(a) Tax imposed

(1) Tax on removal, entry, or sale

(A) In general

There is hereby imposed a tax at the rate specified in paragraph (2) on—

(i) the removal of a taxable fuel from any refinery,

(ii) the removal of a taxable fuel from any terminal,

(iii) the entry into the United States of any taxable fuel for consumption, use, or warehousing, and

(iv) the sale of a taxable fuel to any person who is not registered under section 4101 unless there was a prior taxable removal or entry of such fuel under clause (i), (ii), or (iii).

(B) Exemption for bulk transfers to registered terminals or refineries

(I) In general

The tax imposed by this paragraph shall not apply to any removal or entry of a taxable fuel transferred in bulk by pipeline or vessel to a terminal or refinery if the person removing or entering the taxable fuel, the operator of such pipeline or vessel (except as provided in clause (ii)), and the operator of such terminal or refinery are registered under section 4101.

(II) Nonapplication of registration to vessel operators entering by deep-draft vessel

For purposes of clause (i), a vessel operator is not required to be registered with respect to the entry of a taxable fuel transferred in bulk by a vessel described in section 4042(c)(1).

(2) RATES OF TAX

(A) IN GENERAL

The rate of the tax imposed by this section is—

(i) in the case of gasoline other than aviation gasoline, 18.3 cents per gallon,

(ii) in the case of aviation gasoline, 19.3 cents per gallon, and

(iii) in the case of diesel fuel or kerosene, 24.3 cents per gallon.

(B) LEAKING UNDERGROUND STORAGE TANK TRUST FUND TAX

The rates of tax specified in subparagraph (A) shall each be increased by 0.1 cent per gallon. The increase in tax under this subparagraph shall in this title be referred to as the Leaking Underground Storage Tank Trust Fund financing rate.

(C) TAXES IMPOSED ON FUEL USED IN AVIATION

In the case of kerosene which is removed from any refinery or terminal directly into the fuel tank of an aircraft for use in aviation, the rate of tax under subparagraph (A)(iii) shall be—

(i) in the case of use for commercial aviation by a person registered for such use under section 4101, 4.3 cents per gallon, and

(ii) in the case of use for aviation not described in clause (i), 21.8 cents per gallon.

(D) DIESEL-WATER FUEL EMULSION

In the case of diesel-water fuel emulsion at least 14 percent of which is water and with respect to which the emulsion additive is registered by a United States manufacturer with the Environmental Protection Agency pursuant to section 211 of the Clean Air Act (as in effect on March 31, 2003), subparagraph (A)(iii) shall be applied by substituting "19.7 cents" for "24.3 cents". The preceding sentence shall not apply to the removal, sale, or use of diesel-water fuel emulsion unless the person so removing, selling, or using such fuel is registered under section 4101.

(3) CERTAIN REFUELER TRUCKS, TANKERS, AND TANK WAGONS TREATED AS TERMINAL

(A) IN GENERAL

For purposes of paragraph (2)(C), a refueler truck, tanker, or tank wagon shall be treated as part of a terminal if—

(i) such terminal is located within an airport,

(ii) any kerosene which is loaded in such truck, tanker, or wagon at such terminal is for delivery only into aircraft at the airport in which such terminal is located,

(iii) such truck, tanker, or wagon meets the requirements of subparagraph (B) with respect to such terminal, and

(iv) except in the case of exigent circumstances identified by the Secretary in regulations, no vehicle registered for highway use is loaded with kerosene at such terminal.

(B) Requirements

A refueler truck, tanker, or tank wagon meets the requirements of this subparagraph with respect to a terminal if such truck, tanker, or wagon—

(i) has storage tanks, hose, and coupling equipment designed and used for the purposes of fueling aircraft,

(ii) is not registered for highway use, and

(iii) is operated by—

(I) the terminal operator of such terminal, or

(II) a person that makes a daily accounting to such terminal operator of each delivery of fuel from such truck, tanker, or wagon.

(C) Reporting

The Secretary shall require under section 4101(d) reporting by such terminal operator of—

(i) any information obtained under subparagraph (B)(iii)(II), and

(ii) any similar information maintained by such terminal operator with respect to deliveries of fuel made by trucks, tankers, or wagons operated by such terminal operator.

(D) Applicable rate

For purposes of paragraph (2)(C), in the case of any kerosene treated as removed from a terminal by reason of this paragraph—

(i) the rate of tax specified in paragraph (2)(C)(i) in the case of use described in such paragraph shall apply if such terminal is located within a secured area of an airport, and

(ii) the rate of tax specified in paragraph (2)(C)(ii) shall apply in all other cases.

(4) Liability for tax on kerosene used in commercial aviation

For purposes of paragraph (2)(C)(i), the person who uses the fuel for commercial aviation shall pay the tax imposed under such paragraph. For purposes of the preceding sentence, fuel shall be treated as used when such fuel is removed into the fuel tank.

(B) Treatment of removal or subsequent sale by blender

(1) In general

There is hereby imposed a tax at the rate determined under subsection (a) on taxable fuel removed or sold by the blender thereof.

(2) Credit for tax previously paid

If—

(A) tax is imposed on the removal or sale of a taxable fuel by reason of paragraph (1), and

(B) the blender establishes the amount of the tax paid with respect to such fuel by reason of subsection (a),

the amount of the tax so paid shall be allowed as a credit against the tax imposed by reason of paragraph (1).

(c) Later Separation of Fuel from Diesel-Water Fuel Emulsion

If any person separates the taxable fuel from a diesel-water fuel emulsion on which tax was imposed under subsection (a) at a rate determined under subsection (a)(2)(D) (or with respect to which a credit or payment was allowed or made by reason of section 6427), such person shall be treated as the refiner of such taxable fuel. The amount of tax imposed on any removal of such fuel by such person shall be reduced by the amount of tax imposed (and not credited or refunded) on any prior removal or entry of such fuel.

(d) Termination

(1) In general

The rates of tax specified in clauses (i) and (iii) of subsection (a)(2)(A) shall be 4.3 cents per gallon after September 30, 2028.

(2) Aviation fuels

The rates of tax specified in subsection (a)(2)(A)(ii) and (a)(2)(C)(ii) shall be 4.3 cents per gallon—

(A) after December 31, 1996, and before the date which is 7 days after the date of the enactment of the Airport and Airway Trust Fund Tax Reinstatement Act of 1997, and

(B) after September 30, 2028.

(3) Leaking Underground Storage Tank Trust Fund financing rate

The Leaking Underground Storage Tank Trust Fund financing rate under subsection (a)(2) shall apply after September 30, 1997, and before October 1, 2028.

(e) Refunds in certain cases

Under regulations prescribed by the Secretary, if any person who paid the tax imposed by this section with respect to any taxable fuel establishes to the satisfaction of the Secretary that a prior tax was paid (and not credited or refunded) with respect to such taxable fuel, then an amount equal to the tax paid by such person shall be allowed as a refund (without interest) to such person in the same manner as if it were an overpayment of tax imposed by this section.

(Aug. 16, 1954, ch. 736, 68A Stat. 483; Mar. 30, 1955, ch. 18, §3(a)(3), 69 Stat. 14; Mar. 29, 1956, ch. 115, §3(a)(3), 70 Stat. 66; June 29, 1956, ch. 462, title II, §205, 70 Stat. 389; Pub. L. 86–342, title II, §201(a), Sept. 21, 1959, 73 Stat. 613; Pub. L. 87–61, title II, §201(b)–(d), June 29, 1961, 75 Stat. 123, 124; Pub. L. 91–605, title III, §303(a)(6), Dec. 31, 1970, 84 Stat. 1744; Pub. L. 94–280, title III, §303(a)(6), May 5, 1976, 90 Stat. 456; Pub. L. 95–599, title V, §502(a)(5), Nov. 6, 1978, 92 Stat. 2756; Pub. L. 95–618, title II, §221(a)(1), Nov. 9, 1978, 92 Stat. 3185; Pub. L. 96–223, title II, §232(a)(1), (b)(3)(A), (d)(3), Apr. 2, 1980, 94 Stat. 273, 276, 277; Pub. L. 97–424, title V, §§511(a)(1), (d)(1), 516(a)(3), Jan. 6, 1983, 96 Stat. 2169, 2171, 2182; Pub. L. 98–369, div. A, title VII, §732(a)(1), (2), title IX, §912(b), (f), July 18, 1984, 98 Stat. 976, 977, 1007; Pub. L. 99–499, title V, §521(a)(1), Oct. 17, 1986, 100 Stat. 1774; Pub. L. 99–514, title XVII, §1703(a), Oct. 22, 1986, 100 Stat. 2774; Pub. L. 100–17, title V, §502(a)(4), (c)(2), Apr. 2, 1987, 101 Stat. 256, 257; Pub. L. 100–203, title X, §10502(d)(2), Dec. 22, 1987, 101 Stat. 1330–444; Pub. L. 100–647, title I, §1017(c)(1), (14), title II, §2001(d)(5), title VI, §6104(a), Nov. 10, 1988, 102 Stat. 3575, 3577, 3595, 3711; Pub. L. 101–508, title XI, §§11211(a)(1)–(3), (5)(A)–(C), (c)(3), (e)(3), 11212(a), (d)(1), (e)(2), 11215(a), Nov. 5, 1990, 104

Stat. 1388–423, 1388–424, 1388–426, 1388–427, 1388–430, 1388–432, 1388–436; Pub. L. 102–240, title VIII, §8002(a)(3), Dec. 18, 1991, 105 Stat. 2203; Pub. L. 102–486, title XIX, §1920(a), (b), Oct. 24, 1992, 106 Stat. 3026; Pub. L. 103–66, title XIII, §§13241(a), 13242(a), Aug. 10, 1993, 107 Stat. 510, 514; Pub. L. 104–188, title I, §1609(a)(2), (g)(1), (2), (4)(B), Aug. 20, 1996, 110 Stat. 1841–1843; Pub. L. 105–2, §2(a)(2), Feb. 28, 1997, 111 Stat. 4; Pub. L. 105–34, title X, §§1031(a)(2), 1032(b), 1033, Aug. 5, 1997, 111 Stat. 929, 933, 937; Pub. L. 105–178, title IX, §§9002(a)(1)(F), 9003(a)(1)(C), (b)(2)(B), (C), June 9, 1998, 112 Stat. 499, 502, 503; Pub. L. 108–357, title III, §301(c)(7), title VIII, §§853(a)(1)–(3)(A), (4), 860(a), Oct. 22, 2004, 118 Stat. 1461, 1609–1611, 1618; Pub. L. 109–6, §1(a), Mar. 31, 2005, 119 Stat. 20; Pub. L. 109–58, title XIII, §§1343(a), (b)(2), 1362(a), Aug. 8, 2005, 119 Stat. 1051, 1052, 1059; Pub. L. 109–59, title XI, §§11101(a)(1)(F), 11151(b)(1), (2), 11161(a)(1)–(4)(D), 11166(b)(1), Aug. 10, 2005, 119 Stat. 1944, 1968–1970, 1976; Pub. L. 110–161, div. K, title I, §116(a), Dec. 26, 2007, 121 Stat. 2381; Pub. L. 110–190, §2(a), Feb. 28, 2008, 122 Stat. 643; Pub. L. 110–253, §2(a), June 30, 2008, 122 Stat. 2417; Pub. L. 110–330, §2(a), Sept. 30, 2008, 122 Stat. 3717; Pub. L. 111–12, §2(a), Mar. 30, 2009, 123 Stat. 1457; Pub. L. 111–69, §2(a), Oct. 1, 2009, 123 Stat. 2054; Pub. L. 111–116, §2(a), Dec. 16, 2009, 123 Stat. 3031; Pub. L. 111–153, §2(a), Mar. 31, 2010, 124 Stat. 1084; Pub. L. 111–161, §2(a), Apr. 30, 2010, 124 Stat. 1126; Pub. L. 111–197, §2(a), July 2, 2010, 124 Stat. 1353; Pub. L. 111–216, title I, §101(a), Aug. 1, 2010, 124 Stat. 2349; Pub. L. 111–249, §2(a), Sept. 30, 2010, 124 Stat. 2627; Pub. L. 111–329, §2(a), Dec. 22, 2010, 124 Stat. 3566; Pub. L. 112–7, §2(a), Mar. 31, 2011, 125 Stat. 31; Pub. L. 112–16, §2(a), May 31, 2011, 125 Stat. 218; Pub. L. 112–21, §2(a), June 29, 2011, 125 Stat. 233; Pub. L. 112–27, §2(a), Aug. 5, 2011, 125 Stat. 270; Pub. L. 112–30, title I, §142(a)(1)(C), (2)(D), title II, §202(a), Sept. 16, 2011, 125 Stat. 356, 357; Pub. L. 112–91, §2(a), Jan. 31, 2012, 126 Stat. 3; Pub. L. 112–95, title XI, §1101(a), Feb. 14, 2012, 126 Stat. 148; Pub. L. 112–102, title IV, §402(a)(1)(C), (2)(D), Mar. 30, 2012, 126 Stat. 282; Pub. L. 112–140, title IV, §402(a)(1)(C), (2)(D), June 29, 2012, 126 Stat. 402; Pub. L. 112–141, div. D, title I, §40102(a)(1)(C), (2)(D), July 6, 2012, 126 Stat. 844; Pub. L. 114–55, title II, §202(a), Sept. 30, 2015, 129 Stat. 525; Pub. L. 114–94, div. C, title XXXI, §31102(a)(1)(C), (2)(D), Dec. 4, 2015, 129 Stat. 1727; Pub. L. 114–141, title II, §202(a), Mar. 30, 2016, 130 Stat. 324; Pub. L. 114–190, title I, §1202(a), July 15, 2016, 130 Stat. 619; Pub. L. 115–63, title II, §202(a), Sept. 29, 2017, 131 Stat. 1171; Pub. L. 115–141, div. M, title I, §202(a), Mar. 23, 2018, 132 Stat. 1048; Pub. L. 115–254, div. B, title VIII, §802(a), Oct. 5, 2018, 132 Stat. 3428; Pub. L. 117–58, div. H, title I, §80102(a)(1)(C), (2)(D), Nov. 15, 2021, 135 Stat. 1327; Pub. L. 118–15, div. B, title II, §2212(a), Sept. 30, 2023, 137 Stat. 85; Pub. L. 118–34, title II, §202(a), Dec. 26, 2023, 137 Stat. 1115; Pub. L. 118–41, title II, §202(a), Mar. 8, 2024, 138 Stat. 23; Pub. L. 118–63, title XIII, §1302(a), May 16, 2024, 138 Stat. 1433.)

§4082. EXEMPTIONS FOR DIESEL FUEL AND KEROSENE

(A) IN GENERAL

The tax imposed by section 4081 shall not apply to diesel fuel and kerosene—

(1) which the Secretary determines is destined for a nontaxable use,

(2) which is indelibly dyed by mechanical injection in accordance with regulations which the Secretary shall prescribe, and

(3) which meets such marking requirements (if any) as may be prescribed by the Secretary in regulations.

Such regulations shall allow an individual choice of dye color approved by the Secretary or chosen from any list of approved dye colors that the Secretary may publish.

(B) NONTAXABLE USE

For purposes of this section, the term "nontaxable use" means—

(1) any use which is exempt from the tax imposed by section 4041(a)(1) other than by reason of a prior imposition of tax,

(2) any use in a train, and

(3) any use described in section 4041(a)(1)(C)(iii)(II).

The term "nontaxable use" does not include the use of kerosene in an aircraft and such term shall not include any use described in section 6421(e)(2)(C).

(C) EXCEPTION TO DYEING REQUIREMENTS

Paragraph (2) of subsection (a) shall not apply with respect to any diesel fuel and kerosene—

(1) removed, entered, or sold in a State for ultimate sale or use in an area of such State during the period such area is exempted from the fuel dyeing requirements under subsection (i) of section 211 of the Clean Air Act (as in effect on the date of the enactment of this subsection) by the Administrator of the Environmental Protection Agency under paragraph (4) of such subsection (i) (as so in effect), and

(2) the use of which is certified pursuant to regulations issued by the Secretary.

(D) ADDITIONAL EXCEPTIONS TO DYEING REQUIREMENTS FOR KEROSENE

(1) USE FOR NON-FUEL FEEDSTOCK PURPOSES

Subsection (a)(2) shall not apply to kerosene—

(A) received by pipeline or vessel for use by the person receiving the kerosene in the manufacture or production of any substance (other than gasoline, diesel fuel, or special fuels referred to in section 4041), or

(B) to the extent provided in regulations, removed or entered—

(i) for such a use by the person removing or entering the kerosene, or

(ii) for resale by such person for such a use by the purchaser,

but only if the person receiving, removing, or entering the kerosene and such purchaser (if any) are registered under section 4101 with respect to the tax imposed by section 4081.

(2) WHOLESALE DISTRIBUTORS

To the extent provided in regulations, subsection (a)(2) shall not apply to kerosene received by a wholesale distributor of kerosene if such distributor—

(A) is registered under section 4101 with respect to the tax imposed by section 4081 on kerosene, and

(B) sells kerosene exclusively to ultimate vendors described in section 6427(l)(5)(B) with respect to kerosene.

(E) KEROSENE REMOVED INTO AN AIRCRAFT

In the case of kerosene (other than kerosene with respect to which tax is imposed under section 4043) which is exempt from the tax imposed by section 4041(c) (other than by reason of a prior imposition of tax) and which is removed from any refinery or terminal directly into the fuel tank of an aircraft—

(1) the rate of tax under section 4081(a)(2)(A)(iii) shall be zero, and

(2) if such aircraft is employed in foreign trade or trade between the United States and any of its possessions, the increase in such rate under section 4081(a)(2)(B) shall be zero.

For purposes of this subsection, any removal described in section 4081(a)(3)(A) shall be treated as a removal from a terminal but only if such terminal is located within a secure area of an airport.

(F) EXCEPTION FOR LEAKING UNDERGROUND STORAGE TANK TRUST FUND FINANCING RATE

(1) IN GENERAL

Subsection (a) shall not apply to the tax imposed under section 4081 at the Leaking Underground Storage Tank Trust Fund financing rate.

(2) EXCEPTION FOR EXPORT, ETC.

Paragraph (1) shall not apply with respect to any fuel if the Secretary determines that such fuel is destined for export or for use by the purchaser as supplies for vessels (within the meaning of section 4221(d)(3)) employed in foreign trade or trade between the United States and any of its possessions.

(G) REGULATIONS

The Secretary shall prescribe such regulations as may be necessary to carry out this section, including regulations requiring the conspicuous labeling of retail diesel fuel and kerosene pumps and other delivery facilities to assure that persons are aware of which fuel is available only for nontaxable uses.

(H) CROSS REFERENCE

For tax on train and certain bus uses of fuel purchased tax-free, see subsections (a)(1) and (d)(3) of section 4041.

(Aug. 16, 1954, ch. 736, 68A Stat. 483; Pub. L. 86–342, title II, §201(e)(1), (2), Sept. 21, 1959, 73 Stat. 615; Pub. L. 89–44, title VIII, §802(a)(1), (b)(1), June 21, 1965, 79 Stat. 159; Pub. L. 91–258, title II, §205(c)(6), May 21, 1970, 84 Stat. 242; Pub. L. 98–369, div. A, title VII, §§733(a), 734(c)(1), July 18, 1984, 98 Stat. 977, 979; Pub. L. 99–514, title XVII, §1703(a), Oct. 22, 1986, 100 Stat. 2775; Pub. L. 103–66, title XIII, §13242(a), Aug. 10, 1993, 107 Stat. 517; Pub. L. 104–188, title I, §1801(a), Aug. 20, 1996, 110 Stat. 1891; Pub. L. 105–34, title X, §1032(c)(1), (2), (e)(3)(A), Aug. 5, 1997, 111 Stat. 933, 935; Pub. L. 105–206, title VI, §6010(h)(3), (4), July 22, 1998, 112 Stat. 815; Pub. L. 108–357, title II, §241(a)(2)(B), title VIII, §§851(d)(2), 853(a)(5), 854(a), 857(a), Oct. 22, 2004, 118 Stat. 1438, 1608, 1611, 1615, 1617; Pub. L. 109–58, title XIII, §1362(b)(1), Aug. 8, 2005, 119 Stat. 1059; Pub. L. 109–59, title XI, §11161(a)(4)(A), (E), (b)(3)(C), Aug. 10, 2005, 119 Stat. 1970, 1971; Pub. L. 109–432, div. A, title IV, §420(b)(2), Dec. 20, 2006, 120 Stat. 2969; Pub. L. 110–172, §§6(d)(2)(B), (C), 11(a)(28), Dec. 29, 2007, 121 Stat. 2480, 2481, 2487; Pub. L. 112–95, title XI, §1103(a)(2), Feb. 14, 2012, 126 Stat. 150.)

§4083. DEFINITIONS; SPECIAL RULE; ADMINISTRATIVE AUTHORITY

(A) TAXABLE FUEL

For purposes of this subpart—

(1) IN GENERAL

The term "taxable fuel" means—
(A) gasoline,
(B) diesel fuel, and
(C) kerosene.

(2) GASOLINE

The term "gasoline"—
(A) includes any gasoline blend, other than qualified methanol or ethanol fuel

(as defined in section 4041(b)(2)(B)), partially exempt methanol or ethanol fuel (as defined in section 4041(m)(2)), or a denatured alcohol, and

(B) includes, to the extent prescribed in regulations—

(i) any gasoline blend stock, and

(ii) any product commonly used as an additive in gasoline (other than alcohol).

For purposes of subparagraph (B)(i), the term "gasoline blend stock" means any petroleum product component of gasoline.

(3) DIESEL FUEL

(A) IN GENERAL

The term "diesel fuel" means—

(i) any liquid (other than gasoline) which is suitable for use as a fuel in a diesel-powered highway vehicle, or a diesel-powered train,

(ii) transmix, and

(iii) diesel fuel blend stocks identified by the Secretary.

(B) TRANSMIX

For purposes of subparagraph (A), the term "transmix" means a byproduct of refined products pipeline operations created by the mixing of different specification products during pipeline transportation.

(B) COMMERCIAL AVIATION

For purposes of this subpart, the term "commercial aviation" means any use of an aircraft in a business of transporting persons or property for compensation or hire by air, unless properly allocable to any transportation exempt from the taxes imposed by sections 4261 and 4271 by reason of section 4281 or 4282 or by reason of subsection (h) or (i) of section 4261. Such term shall not include the use of any aircraft before October 1, 2028, if tax is imposed under section 4043 with respect to the fuel consumed in such use or if no tax is imposed on such use under section 4043 by reason of subsection (c)(5) thereof.

(C) CERTAIN USES DEFINED AS REMOVAL

If any person uses taxable fuel (other than in the production of taxable fuels or special fuels referred to in section 4041), such use shall for the purposes of this chapter be considered a removal.

(D) ADMINISTRATIVE AUTHORITY

(1) IN GENERAL

In addition to the authority otherwise granted by this title, the Secretary may in administering compliance with this subpart, section 4041, and penalties and other administrative provisions related thereto—

(A) enter any place at which taxable fuel is produced or is stored (or may be stored) for purposes of—

(i) examining the equipment used to determine the amount or composition of such fuel and the equipment used to store such fuel,

(ii) taking and removing samples of such fuel, and

(iii) inspecting any books and records and any shipping papers pertaining to such fuel, and

(B) detain, for the purposes referred in subparagraph (A), any container which contains or may contain any taxable fuel.

(2) INSPECTION SITES

The Secretary may establish inspection sites for purposes of carrying out the Secretary's authority under paragraph (1)(B).

(3) PENALTY FOR REFUSAL OF ENTRY

(A) FORFEITURE

The penalty provided by section 7342 shall apply to any refusal to admit entry or other refusal to permit an action by the Secretary authorized by paragraph (1), except that section 7342 shall be applied by substituting "$1,000" for "$500" for each such refusal.

(B) ASSESSABLE PENALTY

For additional assessable penalty for the refusal to admit entry or other refusal to permit an action by the Secretary authorized by paragraph (1), see section 6717.

(Aug. 16, 1954, ch. 736, 68A Stat. 483; Pub. L. 94–455, title XIX, §1906(b)(13)(A), Oct. 4, 1976, 90 Stat. 1834; Pub. L. 99–514, title XVII, §1703(a), Oct. 22, 1986, 100 Stat. 2776; Pub. L. 103–66, title XIII, §13242(a), Aug. 10, 1993, 107 Stat. 517; Pub. L. 105–34, title IX, §902(b)(3), title X, §1032(a), (e)(4), Aug. 5, 1997, 111 Stat. 873, 933, 935; Pub. L. 105–206, title VI, §6010(h)(1), July 22, 1998, 112 Stat. 815; Pub. L. 108–357, title III, §301(c)(8), title VIII, §§853(b), 858(a), 859(b)(1), 870(a), Oct. 22, 2004, 118 Stat. 1461, 1611, 1617, 1618, 1623; Pub. L. 109–59, title XI, §11123(b), Aug. 10, 2005, 119 Stat. 1952; Pub. L. 112–95, title XI, §1103(b), Feb. 14, 2012, 126 Stat. 151; Pub. L. 114–55, title II, §202(c)(1), Sept. 30, 2015, 129 Stat. 525; Pub. L. 114–141, title II, §202(c)(1), Mar. 30, 2016, 130 Stat. 324; Pub. L. 114–190, title I, §1202(c)(1), July 15, 2016, 130 Stat. 619; Pub. L. 115–63, title II, §202(c)(1), Sept. 29, 2017, 131 Stat. 1171; Pub. L. 115–141, div. M, title I, §202(c)(1), Mar. 23, 2018, 132 Stat. 1048; Pub. L. 115–254, div. B, title VIII, §802(c)(2), Oct. 5, 2018, 132 Stat. 3429; Pub. L. 118–15, div. B, title II, §2212(c)(2), Sept. 30, 2023, 137 Stat. 85; Pub. L. 118–34, title II, §202(c)(2), Dec. 26, 2023, 137 Stat. 1116; Pub. L. 118–41, title II, §202(c)(2), Mar. 8, 2024, 138 Stat. 24; Pub. L. 118–63, title XIII, §1302(c)(2), May 16, 2024, 138 Stat. 1433.)

§4084. CROSS REFERENCES

(1) For provisions to relieve farmers from excise tax in the case of gasoline used on the farm for farming purposes, see section 6420.

(2) For provisions to relieve purchasers of gasoline from excise tax in the case of gasoline used for certain nonhighway purposes, used by local transit systems, or sold for certain exempt purposes, see section 6421.

(3) For provisions to relieve purchasers from excise tax in the case of taxable fuel not used for taxable purposes, see section 6427.

(Added Pub. L. 103–66, title XIII, §13242(a), Aug. 10, 1993, 107 Stat. 518.)

* * * * * * *

CHAPTER 36—CERTAIN OTHER EXCISE TAXES

* * * * * * *

Subchapter D—Tax on Use of Certain Vehicles

§4481. IMPOSITION OF TAX

(A) IMPOSITION OF TAX

A tax is hereby imposed on the use of any highway motor vehicle which (together with the semitrailers and trailers customarily used in connection with highway motor vehicles of the same type as such highway motor vehicle) has a taxable gross weight of at least 55,000 pounds at the rate specified in the following table:

Taxable gross weight:	Rate of tax:
At least 55,000 pounds, but not over 75,000 pounds	$100 per year plus $22 for each 1,000 pounds (or fr
Over 75,000 pounds	

(B) BY WHOM PAID

The tax imposed by this section shall be paid by the person in whose name the highway motor vehicle is, or is required to be, registered under the law of the State or contiguous foreign country in which such vehicle is, or is required to be, registered, or, in case the highway motor vehicle is owned by the United States, by the agency or instrumentality of the United States operating such vehicle.

(C) PRORATION OF TAX

(1) WHERE FIRST USE OCCURS AFTER FIRST MONTH

If in any taxable period the first use of the highway motor vehicle is after the first month in such period, the tax shall be reckoned proportionately from the first day of the month in which such use occurs to and including the last day in such taxable period.

(2) WHERE VEHICLE SOLD, DESTROYED, OR STOLEN

(A) IN GENERAL

If in any taxable period a highway motor vehicle is sold, destroyed, or stolen before the first day of the last month in such period and not subsequently used during such taxable period, the tax shall be reckoned proportionately from the first day of the month in such period in which the first use of such highway motor vehicle occurs to and including the last day of the month in which such highway motor vehicle was sold, destroyed, or stolen.

(B) DESTROYED

For purposes of subparagraph (A), a highway motor vehicle is destroyed if such vehicle is damaged by reason of an accident or other casualty to such an extent that it is not economic to rebuild.

(D) ONE TAX LIABILITY PER PERIOD

To the extent that the tax imposed by this section is paid with respect to any highway motor vehicle for any taxable period, no further tax shall be imposed by this section for such taxable period with respect to such vehicle.

(E) ELECTRONIC FILING

Any taxpayer who files a return under this section with respect to 25 or more vehicles for any taxable period shall file such return electronically.

(F) PERIOD TAX IN EFFECT

The tax imposed by this section shall apply only to use before October 1, 2029.

(Added June 29, 1956, ch. 462, title II, §206(a), 70 Stat. 390; amended Pub. L. 87–61, title II, §203(a), (b)(1), (2)(A), (B), June 29, 1961, 75 Stat. 124; Pub. L. 91–605, title III, §303(a)(7), (8), Dec. 31, 1970, 84 Stat. 1744; Pub. L. 94–280, title III, §303(a)(7), (8), May 5, 1976, 90 Stat. 456; Pub. L. 95–599, title V, §502(a)(6), (7), Nov. 6, 1978, 92 Stat. 2756; Pub. L. 97–424, title V, §§513(a), (d), 516(a)(4), Jan. 6, 1983, 96 Stat. 2177, 2179, 2182; Pub. L. 98–369, div. A, title VII, §734(f), title IX, §901(a), July 18, 1984, 98 Stat. 980, 1003; Pub. L. 100–17, title V, §§502(a)(5), 507(a), Apr. 2, 1987, 101 Stat. 256, 260; Pub. L. 101–508, title XI, §11211(c)(5), Nov. 5, 1990, 104 Stat. 1388–426; Pub. L. 102–240, title VIII, §8002(a)(5), Dec. 18, 1991, 105 Stat. 2203; Pub. L. 104–188, title I, §1704(t)(57), Aug. 20, 1996, 110 Stat. 1890; Pub. L. 105–178, title IX, §9002(a)(1)(G), June 9, 1998, 112 Stat. 499; Pub. L. 108–357, title VIII, §867(a), (c), Oct. 22, 2004, 118 Stat. 1622; Pub. L. 109–14, §9(c)(1), May 31, 2005, 119 Stat. 336; Pub. L. 109–59, title XI, §11101(a)(2)(A), Aug. 10, 2005, 119 Stat. 1944; Pub. L. 112–30, title I, §142(b)(1), Sept. 16, 2011, 125 Stat. 356; Pub. L. 112–102, title IV, §402(b)(1), Mar. 30, 2012, 126 Stat. 282; Pub. L. 112–141, div. D, title I, §40102(b)(1)(A), July 6, 2012, 126 Stat. 844; Pub. L. 114–94, div. C, title XXXI, §31102(b)(1), Dec. 4, 2015, 129 Stat. 1727; Pub. L. 115–141, div. U, title IV, §401(b)(43), Mar. 23, 2018, 132 Stat. 1204; Pub. L. 117–58, div. H, title I, §80102(b)(1), Nov. 15, 2021, 135 Stat. 1327.)

§4482. DEFINITIONS

(A) HIGHWAY MOTOR VEHICLE

For purposes of this subchapter, the term "highway motor vehicle" means any motor vehicle which is a highway vehicle.

(B) TAXABLE GROSS WEIGHT

For purposes of this subchapter, the term "taxable gross weight", when used with respect to any highway motor vehicle, means the sum of—

(1) the actual unloaded weight of—
(A) such highway motor vehicle fully equipped for service, and
(B) the semitrailers and trailers (fully equipped for service) customarily used in connection with highway motor vehicles of the same type as such highway motor

vehicle, and

(2) the weight of the maximum load customarily carried on highway motor vehicles of the same type as such highway motor vehicle and on the semitrailers and trailers referred to in paragraph (1)(B).

Taxable gross weight shall be determined under regulations prescribed by the Secretary (which regulations may include formulas or other methods for determining the taxable gross weight of vehicles by classes, specifications, or otherwise).

(C) OTHER DEFINITIONS AND SPECIAL RULE

For purposes of this subchapter—

(1) STATE

The term "State" means a State and the District of Columbia.

(2) YEAR

The term "year" means the one-year period beginning on July 1.

(3) USE

The term "use" means use in the United States on the public highways.

(4) TAXABLE PERIOD

The term "taxable period" means any year beginning before July 1, 2029, and the period which begins on July 1, 2029, and ends at the close of September 30, 2029.

(5) CUSTOMARY USE

A semitrailer or trailer shall be treated as customarily used in connection with a highway motor vehicle if such vehicle is equipped to tow such semitrailer or trailer.

(D) SPECIAL RULE FOR TAXABLE PERIOD IN WHICH TERMINATION DATE OCCURS

In the case of the taxable period which ends on September 30, 2029, the amount of the tax imposed by section 4481 with respect to any highway motor vehicle shall be determined by reducing each dollar amount in the table contained in section 4481(a) by 75 percent.

(Added June 29, 1956, ch. 462, title II, §206(a), 70 Stat. 390; amended Pub. L. 87–61, title II, §203(b)(2)(C), June 29, 1961, 75 Stat. 125; Pub. L. 91–605, title III, §303(a)(9), Dec. 31, 1970, 84 Stat. 1744; Pub. L. 94–280, title III, §303(a)(9), May 5, 1976, 90 Stat. 456; Pub. L. 94–455, title XIX, §§1904(c), 1906(b)(13)(A), Oct. 4, 1976, 90 Stat. 1818, 1834; Pub. L. 95–599, title V, §502(a)(8), Nov. 6, 1978, 92 Stat. 2756; Pub. L. 97–424, title V, §§513(c), (e), 516(a)(4), Jan. 6, 1983, 96 Stat. 2179, 2182; Pub. L. 100–17, title V, §502(a)(5), Apr. 2, 1987, 101 Stat. 256; Pub. L. 101–508, title XI, §11211(c)(5), Nov. 5, 1990, 104 Stat. 1388–426; Pub. L. 102–240, title VIII, §8002(a)(5), Dec. 18, 1991, 105 Stat. 2203; Pub. L. 105–178, title IX, §9002(a)(1)(H), (I), June 9, 1998, 112 Stat. 499; Pub. L. 109–14, §9(c)(2), (3), May 31, 2005, 119 Stat. 336; Pub. L. 109–59, title XI, §11101(a)(2)(B), (C), Aug. 10, 2005, 119 Stat. 1944; Pub. L. 112–30, title I, §142(b)(2), Sept. 16, 2011, 125 Stat. 356; Pub. L. 112–102, title IV, §402(b)(2), Mar. 30, 2012, 126 Stat. 282; Pub. L. 112–140, title IV, §402(e), June 29, 2012, 126 Stat. 403; Pub. L. 112–141, div. D, title I, §40102(b)(1)(B), (2)(A), July 6, 2012, 126 Stat. 845; Pub. L. 114–94, div. C, title XXXI, §31102(b)(2), Dec. 4, 2015, 129 Stat. 1727; Pub. L. 117–58, div. H, title I, §80102(b)(2), Nov. 15, 2021, 135 Stat. 1327.)

§4483. EXEMPTIONS

(A) STATE AND LOCAL GOVERNMENTAL EXEMPTION

Under regulations prescribed by the Secretary, no tax shall be imposed by section 4481 on the use of any highway motor vehicle by any State or any political subdivision of a State.

(B) EXEMPTION FOR UNITED STATES

The Secretary of the Treasury may authorize exemption from the tax imposed by section 4481 as to the use by the United States of any particular highway motor vehicle, or class of highway motor vehicles, if he determines that the imposition of such tax with respect to such use will cause substantial burden or expense which can be avoided by granting tax exemption and that full benefit of such exemption, if granted, will accrue to the United States.

(C) CERTAIN TRANSIT-TYPE BUSES

Under regulations prescribed by the Secretary, no tax shall be imposed by section 4481 on the use of any bus which is of the transit type (rather than of the intercity type) by a person who, for the last 3 months of the preceding year (or for such other period as the Secretary may by regulations prescribe for purposes of this subsection), met the 60-percent passenger fare revenue test set forth in section 6421(b)(2) (as in effect on the day before the date of the enactment of the Energy Tax Act of 1978) as applied to the period prescribed for purposes of this subsection.

(D) EXEMPTION FOR TRUCKS USED FOR LESS THAN 5,000 MILES ON PUBLIC HIGHWAYS

(1) SUSPENSION OF TAX

(A) IN GENERAL

If—

(i) it is reasonable to expect that the use of any highway motor vehicle on public highways during any taxable period will be less than 5,000 miles, and

(ii) the owner of such vehicle furnishes such information as the Secretary may by forms or regulations require with respect to the expected use of such vehicle, then the collection of the tax imposed by section 4481 with respect to the use of such vehicle shall be suspended during the taxable period.

(B) SUSPENSION CEASES TO APPLY WHERE USE EXCEEDS 5,000 MILES

Subparagraph (A) shall cease to apply with respect to any highway motor vehicle whenever the use of such vehicle on public highways during the taxable period exceeds 5,000 miles.

(2) EXEMPTION

If—

(A) the collection of the tax imposed by section 4481 with respect to any highway motor vehicle is suspended under paragraph (1),

(B) such vehicle is not used during the taxable period on public highways for more than 5,000 miles, and

(C) except as otherwise provided in regulations, the owner of such vehicle furnishes such information as the Secretary may require with respect to the use of such vehicle during the taxable period,

then no tax shall be imposed by section 4481 on the use of such vehicle for the taxable period.

(3) REFUND WHERE TAX PAID AND VEHICLE NOT USED FOR MORE THAN 5,000 MILES

If—

(A) the tax imposed by section 4481 is paid with respect to any highway motor vehicle for any taxable period, and

(B) the requirements of subparagraphs (B) and (C) of paragraph (2) are met with respect to such taxable period,

the amount of such tax shall be credited or refunded (without interest) to the person who paid such tax.

(4) RELIEF FROM LIABILITY FOR TAX UNDER CERTAIN CIRCUMSTANCES WHERE TRUCK IS TRANSFERRED

Under regulations prescribed by the Secretary, the owner of a highway motor vehicle with respect to which the collection of the tax imposed by section 4481 is suspended under paragraph (1) shall not be liable for the tax imposed by section 4481 (and the new owner shall be liable for such tax) with respect to such vehicle if—

(A) such vehicle is transferred to a new owner,

(B) such suspension is in effect at the time of such transfer, and

(C) the old owner furnishes such information as the Secretary by forms and regulations requires with respect to the transfer of such vehicle.

(5) 7,500-MILES EXEMPTION FOR AGRICULTURAL VEHICLES

(A) IN GENERAL

In the case of an agricultural vehicle, paragraphs (1) and (2) shall be applied by substituting "7,500" for "5,000" each place it appears.

(B) DEFINITIONS

For purposes of this paragraph—

(I) AGRICULTURAL VEHICLE

The term "agricultural vehicle" means any highway motor vehicle—

(I) used primarily for farming purposes, and

(II) registered (under the laws of the State in which such vehicle is required to be registered) as a highway motor vehicle used for farming purposes.

(II) FARMING PURPOSES

The term "farming purposes" means the transporting of any farm commodity to or from a farm or the use directly in agricultural production.

(III) FARM COMMODITY

The term "farm commodity" means any agricultural or horticultural commodity, feed, seed, fertilizer, livestock, bees, poultry, fur-bearing animals, or wildlife.

(6) OWNER DEFINED

For purposes of this subsection, the term "owner" means, with respect to any highway motor vehicle, the person described in section 4481(b).

(E) REDUCTION IN TAX FOR TRUCKS USED IN LOGGING

The tax imposed by section 4481 shall be reduced by 25 percent with respect to any highway motor vehicle if—

(1) the exclusive use of such vehicle during any taxable period is the transportation, to and from a point located on a forested site, of products harvested from such forested site, and

(2) such vehicle is registered (under the laws of the State in which such vehicle is required to be registered) as a highway motor vehicle used in the transportation of harvested forest products.

[(F) REPEALED. PUB. L. 108–357, TITLE VIII, §867(D), OCT. 22, 2004, 118 STAT. 1622]

(G) EXEMPTION FOR MOBILE MACHINERY

No tax shall be imposed by section 4481 on the use of any vehicle described in section 4053(8).

(H) EXEMPTION FOR VEHICLES USED IN BLOOD COLLECTION

(1) IN GENERAL

No tax shall be imposed by section 4481 on the use of any qualified blood collector vehicle by a qualified blood collector organization.

(2) QUALIFIED BLOOD COLLECTOR VEHICLE

For purposes of this subsection, the term "qualified blood collector vehicle" means a vehicle at least 80 percent of the use of which during the prior taxable period was by a qualified blood collector organization in the collection, storage, or transportation of blood.

(3) SPECIAL RULE FOR VEHICLES FIRST PLACED IN SERVICE IN A TAXABLE PERIOD

In the case of a vehicle first placed in service in a taxable period, a vehicle shall be treated as a qualified blood collector vehicle for such taxable period if such qualified blood collector organization certifies to the Secretary that the organization reasonably expects at least 80 percent of the use of such vehicle by the organization during such taxable period will be in the collection, storage, or transportation of blood.

(4) QUALIFIED BLOOD COLLECTOR ORGANIZATION

The term "qualified blood collector organization" has the meaning given such term by section 7701(a)(49).

(I) TERMINATION OF EXEMPTIONS

Subsections (a) and (c) shall not apply on and after October 1, 2029.

(Added June 29, 1956, ch. 462, title II, §206(a), 70 Stat. 391; amended Pub. L. 94–455, title XIX,

§1906(b)(13)(A), (B), Oct. 4, 1976, 90 Stat. 1834; Pub. L. 95–618, title II, §233(a)(3)(C), Nov. 9, 1978, 92 Stat. 3191; Pub. L. 97–424, title V, §§513(b), 516(b)(3), Jan. 6, 1983, 96 Stat. 2177, 2183; Pub. L. 98–369, div. A, title IX, §§902(a), 903(a), July 18, 1984, 98 Stat. 1004; Pub. L. 100–17, title V, §§502(b)(5), 507(b), Apr. 2, 1987, 101 Stat. 257, 260; Pub. L. 101–508, title XI, §11211(d)(4), Nov. 5, 1990, 104 Stat. 1388–427; Pub. L. 102–240, title VIII, §8002(b)(4), Dec. 18, 1991, 105 Stat. 2203; Pub. L. 105–178, title IX, §9002(b)(2), June 9, 1998, 112 Stat. 500; Pub. L. 108–357, title VIII, §§851(b)(1), 867(d), Oct. 22, 2004, 118 Stat. 1607, 1622; Pub. L. 109–14, §9(c)(4), May 31, 2005, 119 Stat. 336; Pub. L. 109–59, title XI, §11101(b)(2), Aug. 10, 2005, 119 Stat. 1944; Pub. L. 109–280, title XII, §1207(d), Aug. 17, 2006, 120 Stat. 1070; Pub. L. 112–30, title I, §142(d), Sept. 16, 2011, 125 Stat. 356; Pub. L. 112–102, title IV, §402(d), Mar. 30, 2012, 126 Stat. 282; Pub. L. 112–140, title IV, §402(c), June 29, 2012, 126 Stat. 403; Pub. L. 112–141, div. D, title I, §40102(d)(2), July 6, 2012, 126 Stat. 845; Pub. L. 114–94, div. C, title XXXI, §31102(d)(2), Dec. 4, 2015, 129 Stat. 1727; Pub. L. 117–58, div. H, title I, §80102(d)(2), Nov. 15, 2021, 135 Stat. 1328.)

§4484. CROSS REFERENCES

(1) For penalties and administrative provisions applicable to this subchapter, see subtitle F.

(2) For exemption for uses by Indian tribal governments (or their subdivisions), see section 7871.

(Added June 29, 1956, ch. 462, title II, §206(a), 70 Stat. 391; amended Pub. L. 97–473, title II, §202(b)(10), Jan. 14, 1983, 96 Stat. 2610.)

* * * * * * *

Subtitle I—Trust Fund Code

§9500. SHORT TITLE

This subtitle may be cited as the "Trust Fund Code of 1981".

(Added Pub. L. 97–119, title I, §103(a), Dec. 29, 1981, 95 Stat. 1636.)

CHAPTER 98—TRUST FUND CODE

Subchapter A—Establishment of Trust Funds

Sec.

* * * * * * *

§9503. HIGHWAY TRUST FUND

(A) CREATION OF TRUST FUND

There is established in the Treasury of the United States a trust fund to be known as the "Highway Trust Fund", consisting of such amounts as may be appropriated or credited to the Highway Trust Fund as provided in this section or section 9602(b).

(B) TRANSFER TO HIGHWAY TRUST FUND OF AMOUNTS EQUIVALENT TO CERTAIN TAXES AND PENALTIES

(1) CERTAIN TAXES

There are hereby appropriated to the Highway Trust Fund amounts equivalent to the taxes received in the Treasury before October 1, 2028, under the following provisions—

(A) section 4041 (relating to taxes on diesel fuels and special motor fuels),

(B) section 4051 (relating to retail tax on heavy trucks and trailers),

(C) section 4071 (relating to tax on tires),

(D) section 4081 (relating to tax on gasoline, diesel fuel, and kerosene), and

(E) section 4481 (relating to tax on use of certain vehicles).

For purposes of this paragraph, taxes received under sections 4041 and 4081 shall be determined without reduction for credits under section 6426 and taxes received under section 4081 shall be determined without regard to tax receipts attributable to the rate specified in section 4081(a)(2)(C).

(2) Liabilities incurred before October 1, 2028

There are hereby appropriated to the Highway Trust Fund amounts equivalent to the taxes which are received in the Treasury after September 30, 2028, and before July 1, 2029, and which are attributable to liability for tax incurred before October 1, 2028, under the provisions described in paragraph (1).

[(3) Repealed. Pub. L. 109–59, title XI, §11161(c)(2)(C), Aug. 10, 2005, 119 Stat. 1972]

(4) Certain taxes not transferred to Highway Trust Fund

For purposes of paragraphs (1) and (2), there shall not be taken into account the taxes imposed by—

(A) section 4041(d),

(B) section 4081 to the extent attributable to the rate specified in section 4081(a)(2)(B),

(C) section 4041 or 4081 to the extent attributable to fuel used in a train, or

(D) in the case of gasoline and special motor fuels used as described in paragraph (3)(D) or (4)(B) of subsection (c), section 4041 or 4081 with respect to so much of the rate of tax as exceeds—

(i) 11.5 cents per gallon with respect to taxes imposed before October 1, 2001,

(ii) 13 cents per gallon with respect to taxes imposed after September 30, 2001, and before October 1, 2003, and

(iii) 13.5 cents per gallon with respect to taxes imposed after September 30, 2003, and before October 1, 2005.

(5) Certain penalties

(A) In general

There are hereby appropriated to the Highway Trust Fund amounts equivalent to the penalties paid under sections 6715, 6715A, 6717, 6718, 6719, 6720A, 6725, 7232, and 7272 (but only with regard to penalties under such section related to failure to register under section 4101).

(B) Penalties related to motor vehicle safety

(i) In general

There are hereby appropriated to the Highway Trust Fund amounts equivalent to covered motor vehicle safety penalty collections.

(ii) Covered motor vehicle safety penalty collections

For purposes of this subparagraph, the term "covered motor vehicle safety penalty collections" means any amount collected in connection with a civil penalty under section 30165 of title 49, United States Code, reduced by any award authorized by the Secretary of Transportation to be paid to any person in connection with information provided by such person related to a violation of chapter 301 of such title which is a predicate to such civil penalty.

(6) LIMITATION ON TRANSFERS TO HIGHWAY TRUST FUND

(A) IN GENERAL

Except as provided in subparagraph (B), no amount may be appropriated to the Highway Trust Fund on and after the date of any expenditure from the Highway Trust Fund which is not permitted by this section. The determination of whether an expenditure is so permitted shall be made without regard to—

(i) any provision of law which is not contained or referenced in this title or in a revenue Act, and

(ii) whether such provision of law is a subsequently enacted provision or directly or indirectly seeks to waive the application of this paragraph.

(B) EXCEPTION FOR PRIOR OBLIGATIONS

Subparagraph (A) shall not apply to any expenditure to liquidate any contract entered into (or for any amount otherwise obligated) before October 1, 2026, in accordance with the provisions of this section.

(C) EXPENDITURES FROM HIGHWAY TRUST FUND

(1) FEDERAL-AID HIGHWAY PROGRAM

Except as provided in subsection (e), amounts in the Highway Trust Fund shall be available, as provided by appropriation Acts, for making expenditures before October 1, 2026, to meet those obligations of the United States heretofore or hereafter incurred which are authorized to be paid out of the Highway Trust Fund under the Infrastructure Investment and Jobs Act or any other provision of law which was referred to in this paragraph before the date of the enactment of such Act (as such Act and provisions of law are in effect on the date of the enactment of such Act).

(2) FLOOR STOCKS REFUNDS

The Secretary shall pay from time to time from the Highway Trust Fund into the general fund of the Treasury amounts equivalent to the floor stocks refunds made before July 1, 2029, under section 6412(a). The amounts payable from the Highway Trust Fund under the preceding sentence shall be determined by taking into account only the portion of the taxes which are deposited into the Highway Trust Fund.

(3) TRANSFERS FROM THE TRUST FUND FOR MOTORBOAT FUEL TAXES

(A) TRANSFER TO LAND AND WATER CONSERVATION FUND

(I) IN GENERAL

The Secretary shall pay from time to time from the Highway Trust Fund into the land and water conservation fund provided for in chapter 2003 of title 54 amounts (as determined by the Secretary) equivalent to the motorboat fuel taxes received on or after October 1, 2005, and before October 1, 2028.

(II) LIMITATION

The aggregate amount transferred under this subparagraph during any fiscal year shall not exceed $1,000,000.

(B) Excess funds transferred to Sport Fish Restoration and Boating Trust Fund

Any amounts in the Highway Trust Fund—

(i) which are attributable to motorboat fuel taxes, and

(ii) which are not transferred from the Highway Trust Fund under subparagraph (A),

shall be transferred by the Secretary from the Highway Trust Fund into the Sport Fish Restoration and Boating Trust Fund.

(C) Motorboat fuel taxes

For purposes of this paragraph, the term "motorboat fuel taxes" means the taxes under section 4041(a)(2) with respect to special motor fuels used as fuel in motorboats and under section 4081 with respect to gasoline used as fuel in motorboats, but only to the extent such taxes are deposited into the Highway Trust Fund.

(D) Determination

The amount of payments made under this paragraph after October 1, 1986 shall be determined by the Secretary in accordance with the methodology described in the Treasury Department's Report to Congress of June 1986 entitled "Gasoline Excise Tax Revenues Attributable to Fuel Used in Recreational Motorboats."

(4) Transfers from the Trust Fund for small-engine fuel taxes

(A) In general

The Secretary shall pay from time to time from the Highway Trust Fund into the Sport Fish Restoration and Boating Trust Fund amounts (as determined by him) equivalent to the small-engine fuel taxes received on or after December 1, 1990, and before October 1, 2028.

(B) Small-engine fuel taxes

For purposes of this paragraph, the term "small-engine fuel taxes" means the taxes under section 4081 with respect to gasoline used as a fuel in the nonbusiness use of small-engine outdoor power equipment, but only to the extent such taxes are deposited into the Highway Trust Fund.

(5) Transfers from the Trust Fund for certain aviation fuel taxes

The Secretary shall pay at least monthly from the Highway Trust Fund into the Airport and Airway Trust Fund amounts (as determined by the Secretary) equivalent to the taxes received on or after October 1, 2005, under section 4081 with respect to so much of the rate of tax as does not exceed—

(A) 4.3 cents per gallon of kerosene subject to section 6427(l)(4)(A) with respect to which a payment has been made by the Secretary under section 6427(l), and

(B) 21.8 cents per gallon of kerosene subject to section 6427(l)(4)(B) with respect to which a payment has been made by the Secretary under section 6427(l). Transfers under the preceding sentence shall be made on the basis of estimates by the Secretary, and proper adjustments shall be made in the amounts subsequently transferred to the extent prior estimates were in excess of or less than the amounts required to be transferred. Any amount allowed as a credit under section 34 by reason of paragraph (4) of section 6427(l) shall be treated for purposes of subparagraphs (A) and (B) as a payment made by the Secretary under such paragraph.

(D) ADJUSTMENTS OF APPORTIONMENTS

(1) ESTIMATES OF UNFUNDED HIGHWAY AUTHORIZATIONS AND NET HIGHWAY RECEIPTS

The Secretary of the Treasury, not less frequently than once in each calendar quarter, after consultation with the Secretary of Transportation, shall estimate—

(A) the amount which would (but for this subsection) be the unfunded highway authorizations at the close of the next fiscal year, and

(B) the net highway receipts for the 48-month period beginning at the close of such fiscal year.

(2) PROCEDURE WHERE THERE IS EXCESS UNFUNDED HIGHWAY AUTHORIZATIONS

If the Secretary of the Treasury determines for any fiscal year that the amount described in paragraph (1)(A) exceeds the amount described in paragraph (1)(B)—

(A) he shall so advise the Secretary of Transportation, and

(B) he shall further advise the Secretary of Transportation as to the amount of such excess.

(3) ADJUSTMENT OF APPORTIONMENTS WHERE UNFUNDED AUTHORIZATIONS EXCEED 4 YEARS' RECEIPTS

(A) DETERMINATION OF PERCENTAGE

If, before any apportionment to the States is made, in the most recent estimate made by the Secretary of the Treasury there is an excess referred to in paragraph (2)(B), the Secretary of Transportation shall determine the percentage which—

(i) the excess referred to in paragraph (2)(B), is of

(ii) the amount authorized to be appropriated from the Trust Fund for the fiscal year for apportionment to the States.

If, but for this sentence, the most recent estimate would be one which was made on a date which will be more than 3 months before the date of the apportionment, the Secretary of the Treasury shall make a new estimate under paragraph (1) for the appropriate fiscal year.

(B) ADJUSTMENT OF APPORTIONMENTS

If the Secretary of Transportation determines a percentage under subparagraph (A) for purposes of any apportionment, notwithstanding any other provision of law, the Secretary of Transportation shall apportion to the States (in lieu of the amount which, but for the provisions of this subsection, would be so apportioned) the amount obtained by reducing the amount authorized to be so apportioned by such percentage.

(4) APPORTIONMENT OF AMOUNTS PREVIOUSLY WITHHELD FROM APPORTIONMENT

If, after funds have been withheld from apportionment under paragraph (3)(B), the

Secretary of the Treasury determines that the amount described in paragraph (1)(A) does not exceed the amount described in paragraph (1)(B) or that the excess described in paragraph (1)(B) is less than the amount previously determined, he shall so advise the Secretary of Transportation. The Secretary of Transportation shall apportion to the States such portion of the funds so withheld from apportionment as the Secretary of the Treasury has advised him may be so apportioned without causing the amount described in paragraph (1)(A) to exceed the amount described in paragraph (1)(B). Any funds apportioned pursuant to the preceding sentence shall remain available for the period for which they would be available if such apportionment took effect with the fiscal year in which they are apportioned pursuant to the preceding sentence.

(5) DEFINITIONS

For purposes of this subsection—

(A) UNFUNDED HIGHWAY AUTHORIZATIONS

The term "unfunded highway authorizations" means, at any time, the excess (if any) of—

(i) the total potential unpaid commitments at such time as a result of the apportionment to the States of the amounts authorized to be appropriated from the Highway Trust Fund, over

(ii) the amount available in the Highway Trust Fund at such time to defray such commitments (after all other unpaid commitments at such time which are payable from the Highway Trust Fund have been defrayed).

(B) NET HIGHWAY RECEIPTS

The term "net highway receipts" means, with respect to any period, the excess of—

(i) the receipts (including interest) of the Highway Trust Fund during such period, over

(ii) the amounts to be transferred during such period from such Fund under subsection (c) (other than paragraph (1) thereof).

(6) MEASUREMENT OF NET HIGHWAY RECEIPTS

For purposes of making any estimate under paragraph (1) of net highway receipts for periods ending after the date specified in subsection (b)(1), the Secretary shall treat—

(A) each expiring provision of subsection (b) which is related to appropriations or transfers to the Highway Trust Fund to have been extended through the end of the 48-month period referred to in paragraph (1)(B), and

(B) with respect to each tax imposed under the sections referred to in subsection (b)(1), the rate of such tax during the 48-month period referred to in paragraph (1)(B) to be the same as the rate of such tax as in effect on the date of such estimate.

(7) REPORTS

Any estimate under paragraph (1) and any determination under paragraph (2) shall be reported by the Secretary of the Treasury to the Committee on Ways and

Means of the House of Representatives, the Committee on Finance of the Senate, the Committees on the Budget of both Houses, the Committee on Public Works and Transportation of the House of Representatives, and the Committee on Environment and Public Works of the Senate.

(E) ESTABLISHMENT OF MASS TRANSIT ACCOUNT

(1) CREATION OF ACCOUNT

There is established in the Highway Trust Fund a separate account to be known as the "Mass Transit Account" consisting of such amounts as may be transferred or credited to the Mass Transit Account as provided in this section or section 9602(b).

(2) TRANSFERS TO MASS TRANSIT ACCOUNT

The Secretary of the Treasury shall transfer to the Mass Transit Account the mass transit portion of the amounts appropriated to the Highway Trust Fund under subsection (b) which are attributable to taxes under sections 4041 and 4081 imposed after March 31, 1983. For purposes of the preceding sentence, the term "mass transit portion" means, for any fuel with respect to which tax was imposed under section 4041 or 4081 and otherwise deposited into the Highway Trust Fund, the amount determined at the rate of—

(A) except as otherwise provided in this sentence, 2.86 cents per gallon,

(B) 1.43 cents per gallon in the case of any partially exempt methanol or ethanol fuel (as defined in section 4041(m)) none of the alcohol in which consists of ethanol,

(C) 1.86 cents per energy equivalent of a gallon of diesel (as defined in section 4041(a)(2)(D)) in the case of liquefied natural gas,

(D) 2.13 cents per energy equivalent of a gallon of gasoline (as defined in section 4041(a)(2)(C)) in the case of liquefied petroleum gas, and

(E) 9.71 cents per MCF (determined at standard temperature and pressure) in the case of compressed natural gas.

(3) EXPENDITURES FROM ACCOUNT

Amounts in the Mass Transit Account shall be available, as provided by appropriation Acts, for making capital or capital related expenditures (including capital expenditures for new projects) before October 1, 2026, in accordance with the Infrastructure Investment and Jobs Act or any other provision of law which was referred to in this paragraph before the date of the enactment of such Act (as such Act and provisions of law are in effect on the date of the enactment of such Act).

(4) LIMITATION

Rules similar to the rules of subsection (d) shall apply to the Mass Transit Account.

(5) PORTION OF CERTAIN TRANSFERS TO BE MADE FROM ACCOUNT

(A) IN GENERAL

Transfers under paragraphs (2) and (3) of subsection (c) shall be borne by the Highway Account and the Mass Transit Account in proportion to the respective revenues transferred under this section to the Highway Account (after the application of paragraph (2)) and the Mass Transit Account.

(B) Highway Account

For purposes of subparagraph (A), the term "Highway Account" means the portion of the Highway Trust Fund which is not the Mass Transit Account.

(F) Determination of Trust Fund balances after September 30, 1998

(1) In general

For purposes of determining the balances of the Highway Trust Fund and the Mass Transit Account after September 30, 1998, the opening balance of the Highway Trust Fund (other than the Mass Transit Account) on October 1, 1998, shall be $8,000,000,000. The Secretary shall cancel obligations held by the Highway Trust Fund to reflect the reduction in the balance under this paragraph.

(2) Restoration of foregone interest

Out of money in the Treasury not otherwise appropriated, there is hereby appropriated—

(A) $14,700,000,000 to the Highway Account (as defined in subsection (e)(5)(B)) in the Highway Trust Fund; and

(B) $4,800,000,000 to the Mass Transit Account in the Highway Trust Fund.

(3) Increase in Fund balance

There is hereby transferred to the Highway Account (as defined in subsection (e)(5)(B)) in the Highway Trust Fund amounts appropriated from the Leaking Underground Storage Tank Trust Fund under section 9508(c)(2).

(4) Additional appropriations to Trust Fund

Out of money in the Treasury not otherwise appropriated, there is hereby appropriated to—

(A) the Highway Account (as defined in subsection (e)(5)(B)) in the Highway Trust Fund—

(i) for fiscal year 2013, $6,200,000,000, and

(ii) for fiscal year 2014, $10,400,000,000, and

(B) the Mass Transit Account in the Highway Trust Fund, for fiscal year 2014, $2,200,000,000.

(5) Additional sums

Out of money in the Treasury not otherwise appropriated, there is hereby appropriated—

(A) $7,765,000,000 to the Highway Account (as defined in subsection (e)(5)(B)) in the Highway Trust Fund; and

(B) $2,000,000,000 to the Mass Transit Account in the Highway Trust Fund.

(6) Additional increase in Fund balance

There is hereby transferred to the Highway Account (as defined in subsection (e)(5)(B)) in the Highway Trust Fund amounts appropriated from the Leaking

Underground Storage Tank Trust Fund under section 9508(c)(3).

(7) ADDITIONAL SUMS

Out of money in the Treasury not otherwise appropriated, there is hereby appropriated—

(A) $6,068,000,000 to the Highway Account (as defined in subsection (e)(5)(B)) in the Highway Trust Fund; and

(B) $2,000,000,000 to the Mass Transit Account in the Highway Trust Fund.

(8) FURTHER TRANSFERS TO TRUST FUND

Out of money in the Treasury not otherwise appropriated, there is hereby appropriated—

(A) $51,900,000,000 to the Highway Account (as defined in subsection (e)(5)(B)) in the Highway Trust Fund; and

(B) $18,100,000,000 to the Mass Transit Account in the Highway Trust Fund.

(9) ADDITIONAL INCREASE IN FUND BALANCE

There is hereby transferred to the Highway Account (as defined in subsection (e)(5)(B)) in the Highway Trust Fund amounts appropriated from the Leaking Underground Storage Tank Trust Fund under section 9508(c)(4).

(10) FURTHER TRANSFERS TO TRUST FUND

Out of money in the Treasury not otherwise appropriated, there is hereby appropriated—

(A) $10,400,000,000 to the Highway Account (as defined in subsection (e)(5)(B)) in the Highway Trust Fund; and

(B) $3,200,000,000 to the Mass Transit Account in the Highway Trust Fund.

(11) FURTHER TRANSFERS TO TRUST FUND

Out of money in the Treasury not otherwise appropriated, there is hereby appropriated—

(A) $90,000,000,000 to the Highway Account (as defined in subsection (e)(5)(B)) in the Highway Trust Fund; and

(B) $28,000,000,000 to the Mass Transit Account in the Highway Trust Fund.

(12) TREATMENT OF AMOUNTS

Any amount appropriated or transferred under this subsection to the Highway Trust Fund shall remain available without fiscal year limitation.

(Added Pub. L. 97–424, title V, §531(a), Jan. 6, 1983, 96 Stat. 2187; amended Pub. L. 98–369, div. A, title IV, §474(r)(43), title IX, §911(d)(1), title X, §1016(b), July 18, 1984, 98 Stat. 847, 1006, 1020; Pub. L. 99–499, title V, §521(b)(1), Oct. 17, 1986, 100 Stat. 1777; Pub. L. 99–640, §7(a), Nov. 10, 1986, 100 Stat. 3547; Pub. L. 100–17, title V, §§503(a), (b), 504, Apr. 2, 1987, 101 Stat. 257, 258; Pub. L. 100–203, title X, §10502(d)(13)–(15), Dec. 22, 1987, 101 Stat. 1330–444, 1330–445; Pub. L. 100–448, §6(a)(1), (3), Sept. 28, 1988, 102 Stat. 1839; Pub. L. 101–239, title VII, §7822(b)(6), Dec. 19, 1989, 103 Stat. 2425; Pub. L. 101–508, title XI, §11211(a)(5)(D)–(F), (b)(6)(H), (g)(1), (h)(1), (i)(1), Nov. 5, 1990, 104 Stat. 1388–424, 1388–426, 1388–427; Pub. L. 102–240, title VIII, §§8002(d)(1), (2)(A), (e), (f), 8003(b), Dec. 18, 1991, 105 Stat. 2204, 2205; Pub. L. 103–66, title XIII, §§13242(d)(34)–(41), 13244(a), Aug. 10, 1993, 107 Stat. 527, 529; Pub. L. 103–429, §4, Oct. 31, 1994, 108 Stat. 4378; Pub. L.

105–34, title IX, §901(a)–(d), title X, §1032(e)(13), (14), title XVI, §1601(f)(2), Aug. 5, 1997, 111 Stat. 871, 872, 935, 1090; Pub. L. 105–102, §1, Nov. 20, 1997, 111 Stat. 2204; Pub. L. 105–130, §9(a), Dec. 1, 1997, 111 Stat. 2560; Pub. L. 105–178, title IX, §§9002(c)(1), (2)(A), (3)–(e)(1), (f), 9004(a)(1), (b)(1), (c), (d), 9005(a), 9011(b)(1), (2), June 9, 1998, 112 Stat. 500, 501, 503, 504, 508; Pub. L. 105–206, title IX, §9015(a), July 22, 1998, 112 Stat. 867; Pub. L. 105–225, §7(a), Aug. 12, 1998, 112 Stat. 1511; Pub. L. 105–277, div. A, title IV, §4006(b)(1), Oct. 21, 1998, 112 Stat. 2681–912; Pub. L. 105–354, §2(c)(2), Nov. 3, 1998, 112 Stat. 3244; Pub. L. 106–554, §1(a)(7) [title III, §318(e)(1)], Dec. 21, 2000, 114 Stat. 2763, 2763A–645; Pub. L. 108–88, §12(a), Sept. 30, 2003, 117 Stat. 1128; Pub. L. 108–202, §12(a), Feb. 29, 2004, 118 Stat. 491; Pub. L. 108–224, §10(a), Apr. 30, 2004, 118 Stat. 638; Pub. L. 108–263, §10(a), June 30, 2004, 118 Stat. 710; Pub. L. 108–280, §10(a)(1)–(3), July 30, 2004, 118 Stat. 887; Pub. L. 108–310, §13(a)(1)–(3), (c), Sept. 30, 2004, 118 Stat. 1163, 1164; Pub. L. 108–357, title III, §301(c)(11)–(13), title VIII, §868(a), (b), Oct. 22, 2004, 118 Stat. 1462, 1463, 1622; Pub. L. 109–14, §9(a), May 31, 2005, 119 Stat. 335; Pub. L. 109–20, §9(a), July 1, 2005, 119 Stat. 357; Pub. L. 109–35, §9(a), July 20, 2005, 119 Stat. 390; Pub. L. 109–37, §9(a), July 22, 2005, 119 Stat. 405; Pub. L. 109–40, §9(a), July 28, 2005, 119 Stat. 421; Pub. L. 109–42, §7(a), (d)(1), July 30, 2005, 119 Stat. 436, 438; Pub. L. 109–59, title XI, §§11101(c)(1), (2)(A), (d)(1), 11102(a), (b), 11115(a), 11161(c)(1), (2)(C), 11167(b), Aug. 10, 2005, 119 Stat. 1944, 1945, 1949, 1972, 1977; Pub. L. 109–432, div. A, title IV, §420(b)(6), Dec. 20, 2006, 120 Stat. 2969; Pub. L. 110–172, §11(a)(44), Dec. 29, 2007, 121 Stat. 2488; Pub. L. 110–244, title I, §121(c), June 6, 2008, 122 Stat. 1608; Pub. L. 110–318, §1(a), (b), Sept. 15, 2008, 122 Stat. 3532; Pub. L. 111–46, §1, Aug. 7, 2009, 123 Stat. 1970; Pub. L. 111–68, div. B, §159(a)(2), (b)(2), Oct. 1, 2009, 123 Stat. 2052; Pub. L. 111–88, div. B, §103, Oct. 30, 2009, 123 Stat. 2972; Pub. L. 111–147, title IV, §§441(a), (b), 442(a), (b), 443(a), 444(a), (b)(2)–(4), 445(a), Mar. 18, 2010, 124 Stat. 93, 94; Pub. L. 111–322, title II, §2401(a), Dec. 22, 2010, 124 Stat. 3531; Pub. L. 112–5, title IV, §401(a), Mar. 4, 2011, 125 Stat. 22; Pub. L. 112–30, title I, §§141(a), 142(e)(1), (2)(A), Sept. 16, 2011, 125 Stat. 355, 356; Pub. L. 112–102, title IV, §§401(a), 402(e)(1), (2)(A), Mar. 30, 2012, 126 Stat. 281, 282; Pub. L. 112–140, title IV, §§401(a), 402(d)(1), (2)(A), June 29, 2012, 126 Stat. 402, 403; Pub. L. 112–141, div. D, title I, §§40101(a), 40102(e)(1), (2)(A), title II, §§40201(b), 40251, July 6, 2012, 126 Stat. 844–846, 864; Pub. L. 113–159, title II, §§2001(a), 2002(a), Aug. 8, 2014, 128 Stat. 1848; Pub. L. 113–287, §5(h), Dec. 19, 2014, 128 Stat. 3269; Pub. L. 113–295, div. A, title II, §217(a), Dec. 19, 2014, 128 Stat. 4035; Pub. L. 114–21, title II, §2001(a), May 29, 2015, 129 Stat. 226; Pub. L. 114–41, title II, §§2001(a), 2002, July 31, 2015, 129 Stat. 453, 454; Pub. L. 114–73, title II, §2001(a), Oct. 29, 2015, 129 Stat. 582; Pub. L. 114–87, title II, §2001(a), Nov. 20, 2015, 129 Stat. 685; Pub. L. 114–94, div. C, title XXXI, §§31101(a), 31102(e)(1), (2)(A), 31201, 31202(a), Dec. 4, 2015, 129 Stat. 1726–1728; Pub. L. 115–141, div. U, title I, §104(b), title IV, §401(a)(341), Mar. 23, 2018, 132 Stat. 1170, 1200; Pub. L. 116–159, div. B, title II, §§1201, 1204, Oct. 1, 2020, 134 Stat. 727, 728; Pub. L. 117–44, title II, §201(a), Oct. 2, 2021, 135 Stat. 386; Pub. L. 117–52, §4(a), Oct. 31, 2021, 135 Stat. 409; Pub. L. 117–58, div. H, title I, §§80101(a), 80102(e)(1), (2)(A), 80103, Nov. 15, 2021, 135 Stat. 1327, 1328.)

§9504. Sport Fish Restoration and Boating Trust Fund

(a) Creation of Trust Fund

There is hereby established in the Treasury of the United States a trust fund to be known as the "Sport Fish Restoration and Boating Trust Fund". Such Trust Fund shall consist of such amounts as may be appropriated, credited, or paid to it as provided in this section, section 9503(c)(3), section 9503(c)(4), or section 9602(b).

(b) Sport Fish Restoration and Boating Trust Fund

(1) Transfer of certain taxes to Trust Fund

There is hereby appropriated to the Sport Fish Restoration and Boating Trust Fund amounts equivalent to the following amounts received in the Treasury on or after October 1, 1984—

(A) the taxes imposed by section 4161(a) (relating to sport fishing equipment), and

(B) the import duties imposed on fishing tackle under heading 9507 of the Harmonized Tariff Schedule of the United States (19 U.S.C. 1202) and on yachts and pleasure craft under chapter 89 of the Harmonized Tariff Schedule of the United States.

(2) EXPENDITURES FROM TRUST FUND

Amounts in the Sport Fish Restoration and Boating Trust Fund shall be available, as provided by appropriation Acts, for making expenditures—

(A) to carry out the purposes of the Dingell-Johnson Sport Fish Restoration Act (as in effect on the date of the enactment of the Infrastructure Investment and Jobs Act),

(B) to carry out the purposes of section 7404(d) of the Transportation Equity Act for the 21st Century (as in effect on the date of the enactment of the Infrastructure Investment and Jobs Act), and

(C) to carry out the purposes of the Coastal Wetlands Planning, Protection and Restoration Act (as in effect on the date of the enactment of the Infrastructure Investment and Jobs Act).

Amounts transferred to such account under section 9503(c)(4) may be used only for making expenditures described in subparagraph (C) of this paragraph.

(C) EXPENDITURES FROM BOAT SAFETY ACCOUNT

Amounts remaining in the Boat Safety Account on October 1, 2005, and amounts thereafter credited to the Account under section 9602(b), shall be available, without further appropriation, for making expenditures before October 1, 2010, to carry out the purposes of section 15 [1] of the Dingell-Johnson Sport Fish Restoration Act (as in effect on the date of the enactment of the Safe, Accountable, Flexible, Efficient Transportation Equity Act: A Legacy for Users). For purposes of section 9602, the Boat Safety Account shall be treated as a Trust Fund established by this subchapter.

(D) LIMITATION ON TRANSFERS TO TRUST FUND

(1) IN GENERAL

Except as provided in paragraph (2), no amount may be appropriated or paid to the Sport Fish Restoration and Boating Trust Fund on and after the date of any expenditure from such Trust Fund which is not permitted by this section. The determination of whether an expenditure is so permitted shall be made without regard to—

(A) any provision of law which is not contained or referenced in this title or in a revenue Act, and

(B) whether such provision of law is a subsequently enacted provision or directly or indirectly seeks to waive the application of this subsection.

(2) EXCEPTION FOR PRIOR OBLIGATIONS

Paragraph (1) shall not apply to any expenditure to liquidate any contract entered into (or for any amount otherwise obligated) before October 1, 2026, in accordance with the provisions of this section.

(E) CROSS REFERENCE

For provision transferring motorboat fuels taxes to Sport Fish Restoration and Boating Trust Fund, see section 9503(c)(3).

(Added Pub. L. 98–369, div. A, title X, §1016(a), July 18, 1984, 98 Stat. 1019; amended Pub. L. 100–418, title I, §1214(p)(2), Aug. 23, 1988, 102 Stat. 1159; Pub. L. 100–448, §6(a)(2), (c)(3), Sept. 28, 1988, 102 Stat. 1839, 1841; Pub. L. 101–508, title XI, §11211(i)(2), (3), Nov. 5, 1990, 104 Stat. 1388–428; Pub. L. 102–240, title VIII, §8002(d)(2)(C), (i), Dec. 18, 1991, 105 Stat. 2204, 2205; Pub. L. 105–130, §9(b), Dec. 1, 1997, 111 Stat. 2561; Pub. L. 105–178, title IX, §9005(b)–(d), (f), June 9, 1998, 112 Stat. 505; Pub. L. 105–206, title IX, §9015(b), July 22, 1998, 112 Stat. 867; Pub. L. 106–408, title I, §126, Nov. 1, 2000, 114 Stat. 1775; Pub. L. 108–88, §12(b), Sept. 30, 2003, 117 Stat. 1129; Pub. L. 108–202, §12(b), Feb. 29, 2004, 118 Stat. 491; Pub. L. 108–224, §10(b), Apr. 30, 2004, 118 Stat. 639; Pub. L. 108–263, §10(b), June 30, 2004, 118 Stat. 710; Pub. L. 108–280, §10(b), July 30, 2004, 118 Stat. 888; Pub. L. 108–310, §13(b), Sept. 30, 2004, 118 Stat. 1163; Pub. L. 109–14, §9(b), May 31, 2005, 119 Stat. 335; Pub. L. 109–20, §9(b), July 1, 2005, 119 Stat. 357; Pub. L. 109–35, §9(b), July 20, 2005, 119 Stat. 391; Pub. L. 109–37, §9(b), July 22, 2005, 119 Stat. 406; Pub. L. 109–40, §9(b), July 28, 2005, 119 Stat. 422; Pub. L. 109–42, §7(b), (d)(2), (3), July 30, 2005, 119 Stat. 437, 438; Pub. L. 109–59, title XI, §§11101(d)(2), 11115(b)(1)–(2)(D), (c), 11151(c), (e)(1), Aug. 10, 2005, 119 Stat. 1945, 1949, 1950, 1968, 1969; Pub. L. 109–74, title III, §301(a), Sept. 29, 2005, 119 Stat. 2032; Pub. L. 109–304, §16(c)(2), Oct. 6, 2006, 120 Stat. 1706; Pub. L. 110–181, div. C, title XXXV, §3529(c)(1), Jan. 28, 2008, 122 Stat. 603; Pub. L. 111–68, div. B, §161(a), Oct. 1, 2009, 123 Stat. 2052; Pub. L. 111–88, div. B, §103, Oct. 30, 2009, 123 Stat. 2972; Pub. L. 111–147, title IV, §§444(b)(5)–(7), 445(b), Mar. 18, 2010, 124 Stat. 94, 95; Pub. L. 111–322, title IV, §2401(b), Dec. 22, 2010, 124 Stat. 3531; Pub. L. 112–5, title IV, §401(b), Mar. 4, 2011, 125 Stat. 22; Pub. L. 112–30, title I, §141(b), Sept. 16, 2011, 125 Stat. 355; Pub. L. 112–102, title IV, §401(b), Mar. 30, 2012, 126 Stat. 281; Pub. L. 112–140, title IV, §401(b), June 29, 2012, 126 Stat. 402; Pub. L. 112–141, div. D, title I, §40101(b), July 6, 2012, 126 Stat. 844; Pub. L. 113–159, title II, §2001(b), Aug. 8, 2014, 128 Stat. 1848; Pub. L. 114–21, title II, §2001(b), May 29, 2015, 129 Stat. 226; Pub. L. 114–41, title II, §2001(b), July 31, 2015, 129 Stat. 454; Pub. L. 114–73, title II, §2001(b), Oct. 29, 2015, 129 Stat. 582; Pub. L. 114–87, title II, §2001(b), Nov. 20, 2015, 129 Stat. 685; Pub. L. 114–94, div. C, title XXXI, §31101(b), Dec. 4, 2015, 129 Stat. 1727; Pub. L. 116–159, div. B, title II, §1202, Oct. 1, 2020, 134 Stat. 727; Pub. L. 117–44, title II, §201(b), Oct. 2, 2021, 135 Stat. 386; Pub. L. 117–52, §4(b), Oct. 31, 2021, 135 Stat. 409; Pub. L. 117–58, div. H, title I, §80101(b), Nov. 15, 2021, 135 Stat. 1327.)

* * * * * * *

§9505. HARBOR MAINTENANCE TRUST FUND

(A) CREATION OF TRUST FUND

There is hereby established in the Treasury of the United States a trust fund to be known as the "Harbor Maintenance Trust Fund", consisting of such amounts as may be—

(1) appropriated to the Harbor Maintenance Trust Fund as provided in this section,

(2) transferred to the Harbor Maintenance Trust Fund by the Great Lakes St. Lawrence Seaway Development Corporation pursuant to section 13(a) of the Act of May 13, 1954, or

(3) credited to the Harbor Maintenance Trust Fund as provided in section 9602(b).

(B) TRANSFER TO HARBOR MAINTENANCE TRUST FUND OF AMOUNTS EQUIVALENT TO CERTAIN TAXES

There are hereby appropriated to the Harbor Maintenance Trust Fund amounts equivalent to the taxes received in the Treasury under section 4461 (relating to harbor maintenance tax).

(C) EXPENDITURES FROM HARBOR MAINTENANCE TRUST FUND

Amounts in the Harbor Maintenance Trust Fund shall be available, as provided by appropriation Acts, for making expenditures—

(1) to carry out section 210 of the Water Resources Development Act of 1986,

(2) for payments of rebates of tolls or charges pursuant to section 13(b) of the Act of May 13, 1954 (as in effect on April 1, 1987), and

(3) for the payment of all expenses of administration incurred by the Department of the Treasury, the Army Corps of Engineers, and the Department of Commerce related to the administration of subchapter A of chapter 36 (relating to harbor maintenance tax), but not in excess of $5,000,000 for any fiscal year.

(Added Pub. L. 99–662, title XIV, §1403(a), Nov. 17, 1986, 100 Stat. 4269; amended Pub. L. 103–182, title VI, §683(a), Dec. 8, 1993, 107 Stat. 2218; Pub. L. 104–303, title VI, §601, Oct. 12, 1996, 110 Stat. 3792; Pub. L. 113–121, title II, §2102(c), June 10, 2014, 128 Stat. 1278; Pub. L. 116–260, div. AA, title V, §512(c)(3), Dec. 27, 2020, 134 Stat. 2756.)

§9506. INLAND WATERWAYS TRUST FUND

(A) CREATION OF TRUST FUND

There is hereby established in the Treasury of the United States a trust fund to be known as the "Inland Waterways Trust Fund", consisting of such amounts as may be appropriated or credited to such Trust Fund as provided in this section or section 9602(b).

(B) TRANSFER TO TRUST FUND OF AMOUNTS EQUIVALENT TO CERTAIN TAXES

There are hereby appropriated to the Inland Waterways Trust Fund amounts equivalent to the taxes received in the Treasury under section 4042 (relating to tax on fuel used in commercial transportation on inland waterways). The preceding sentence shall apply only to so much of such taxes as are attributable to the Inland Waterways Trust Fund financing rate under section 4042(b).

(C) EXPENDITURES FROM TRUST FUND

(1) IN GENERAL

Except as provided in paragraph (2), amounts in the Inland Waterways Trust Fund shall be available, as provided by appropriation Acts, for making construction and rehabilitation expenditures for navigation on the inland and coastal waterways of the United States described in section 206 of the Inland Waterways Revenue Act of 1978, as in effect on the date of the enactment of this section.

(2) EXCEPTION FOR CERTAIN PROJECTS

Not more than ½ of the cost of any construction to which section 102(a) of the Water Resources Development Act of 1986 applies (as in effect on the date of the enactment of this section) may be paid from the Inland Waterways Trust Fund.

(Added Pub. L. 99–662, title XIV, §1405(a), Nov. 17, 1986, 100 Stat. 4271; amended Pub. L. 99–499, title V, §521(b)(3), Oct. 17, 1986, 100 Stat. 1778; Pub. L. 100–647, title I, §1018(u)(18), Nov. 10, 1988, 102 Stat. 3591.)

§9507. Hazardous Substance Superfund

(A) Creation of Trust Fund

There is established in the Treasury of the United States a trust fund to be known as the "Hazardous Substance Superfund" (hereinafter in this section referred to as the "Superfund"), consisting of such amounts as may be—

(1) appropriated to the Superfund as provided in this section,

(2) appropriated to the Superfund pursuant to section 517(b) of the Superfund Revenue Act of 1986, or

(3) credited to the Superfund as provided in section 9602(b).

(B) Transfers to Superfund

There are hereby appropriated to the Superfund amounts equivalent to—

(1) the taxes received in the Treasury under section 4611, 4661, or 4671 (relating to environmental taxes),

(2) amounts recovered on behalf of the Superfund under the Comprehensive Environmental Response, Compensation, and Liability Act of 1980 (hereinafter in this section referred to as "CERCLA"),

(3) all moneys recovered or collected under section 311(b)(6)(B) of the Clean Water Act,[1]

(4) penalties assessed under title I of CERCLA, and

(5) punitive damages under section 107(c)(3) of CERCLA.

In the case of the tax imposed by section 4611, paragraph (1) shall apply only to so much of such tax as is attributable to the Hazardous Substance Superfund financing rate under section 4611(c).

(C) Expenditures from Superfund

(1) In general

Amounts in the Superfund shall be available, as provided in appropriation Acts, only for purposes of making expenditures—

(A) to carry out the purposes of—

(i) paragraphs (1), (2), (5), and (6) of section 111(a) of CERCLA as in effect on the date of the enactment of the Superfund Amendments and Reauthorization Act of 1986,

(ii) section 111(c) of CERCLA (as so in effect), other than paragraphs (1) and (2) thereof, and

(iii) section 111(m) of CERCLA (as so in effect), or

(B) hereafter authorized by a law which does not authorize the expenditure out of the Superfund for a general purpose not covered by subparagraph (A) (as so in effect).

(2) Exception for certain transfers, etc., of hazardous substances

No amount in the Superfund or derived from the Superfund shall be available or used for the transfer or disposal of hazardous waste carried out pursuant to a cooperative agreement between the Administrator of the Environmental Protection Agency and a State if the following conditions apply—

(A) the transfer or disposal, if made on December 13, 1985, would not comply with a State or local requirement,

(B) the transfer is to a facility for which a final permit under section 3005(a) of the Solid Waste Disposal Act was issued after January 1, 1983, and before November 1, 1984, and

(C) the transfer is from a facility identified as the McColl Site in Fullerton, California.

(D) AUTHORITY TO BORROW

(1) IN GENERAL

There are authorized to be appropriated to the Superfund, as repayable advances, such sums as may be necessary to carry out the purposes of the Superfund.

(2) LIMITATION ON AGGREGATE ADVANCES

The maximum aggregate amount of repayable advances to the Superfund which is outstanding at any one time shall not exceed an amount equal to the amount which the Secretary estimates will be equal to the sum of the amounts appropriated to the Superfund under subsection (b)(1) during the following 24 months.

(3) REPAYMENT OF ADVANCES

(A) IN GENERAL

Advances made to the Superfund shall be repaid, and interest on such advances shall be paid, to the general fund of the Treasury when the Secretary determines that moneys are available for such purposes in the Superfund.

(B) FINAL REPAYMENT

No advance shall be made to the Superfund after December 31, 2032, and all advances to such Fund shall be repaid on or before such date.

(C) RATE OF INTEREST

Interest on advances made to the Superfund shall be at a rate determined by the Secretary of the Treasury (as of the close of the calendar month preceding the month in which the advance is made) to be equal to the current average market yield on outstanding marketable obligations of the United States with remaining periods to maturity comparable to the anticipated period during which the advance will be outstanding and shall be compounded annually.

(E) LIABILITY OF UNITED STATES LIMITED TO AMOUNT IN TRUST FUND

(1) GENERAL RULE

Any claim filed against the Superfund may be paid only out of the Superfund.

(2) COORDINATION WITH OTHER PROVISIONS

Nothing in CERCLA or the Superfund Amendments and Reauthorization Act of 1986 (or in any amendment made by either of such Acts) shall authorize the payment by the United States Government of any amount with respect to any such claim out of any source other than the Superfund.

(3) Order in which unpaid claims are to be paid

If at any time the Superfund has insufficient funds to pay all of the claims payable out of the Superfund at such time, such claims shall, to the extent permitted under paragraph (1), be paid in full in the order in which they were finally determined.

(Added Pub. L. 99–499, title V, §517(a), Oct. 17, 1986, 100 Stat. 1772; amended Pub. L. 99–509, title VIII, §8032(c)(4), Oct. 21, 1986, 100 Stat. 1959; Pub. L. 101–508, title XI, §11231(c), Nov. 5, 1990, 104 Stat. 1388–445; Pub. L. 113–295, div. A, title II, §221(a)(12)(L), Dec. 19, 2014, 128 Stat. 4039; Pub. L. 117–169, title I, §13601(b), Aug. 16, 2022, 136 Stat. 1982.)

[1] *See References in Text note below.*

* * * * * * *

§9508. Leaking Underground Storage Tank Trust Fund

(a) Creation of Trust Fund

There is established in the Treasury of the United States a trust fund to be known as the "Leaking Underground Storage Tank Trust Fund", consisting of such amounts as may be appropriated or credited to such Trust Fund as provided in this section or section 9602(b).

(b) Transfers to Trust Fund

There are hereby appropriated to the Leaking Underground Storage Tank Trust Fund amounts equivalent to—

(1) taxes received in the Treasury under section 4041(d) (relating to additional taxes on motor fuels),

(2) taxes received in the Treasury under section 4081 (relating to tax on gasoline, diesel fuel, and kerosene) to the extent attributable to the Leaking Underground Storage Tank Trust Fund financing rate under such section,

(3) taxes received in the Treasury under section 4042 (relating to tax on fuel used in commercial transportation on inland waterways) to the extent attributable to the Leaking Underground Storage Tank Trust Fund financing rate under such section, and

(4) amounts received in the Treasury and collected under section 9003(h)(6) of the Solid Waste Disposal Act.

For purposes of this subsection, there shall not be taken into account the taxes imposed by sections 4041 and 4081 on diesel fuel sold for use or used as fuel in a diesel-powered boat.

(c) Expenditures

(1) In general

Except as provided in paragraphs (2), (3), and (4), amounts in the Leaking Underground Storage Tank Trust Fund shall be available, as provided in appropriation Acts, only for purposes of making expenditures to carry out sections 9003(h), 9003(i), 9003(j), 9004(f), 9005(c), 9010, 9011, 9012, and 9013 of the Solid Waste Disposal Act as in effect on the date of the enactment of Public Law 109–168.

(2) TRANSFER TO HIGHWAY TRUST FUND

Out of amounts in the Leaking Underground Storage Tank Trust Fund there is hereby appropriated $2,400,000,000 to be transferred under section 9503(f)(3) to the Highway Account (as defined in section 9503(e)(5)(B)) in the Highway Trust Fund.

(3) ADDITIONAL TRANSFER TO HIGHWAY TRUST FUND

Out of amounts in the Leaking Underground Storage Tank Trust Fund there is hereby appropriated $1,000,000,000 to be transferred under section 9503(f)(6) to the Highway Account (as defined in section 9503(e)(5)(B)) in the Highway Trust Fund.

(4) ADDITIONAL TRANSFER TO HIGHWAY TRUST FUND

Out of amounts in the Leaking Underground Storage Tank Trust Fund there is hereby appropriated—

(A) on the date of the enactment of the FAST Act, $100,000,000,

(B) on October 1, 2016, $100,000,000, and

(C) on October 1, 2017, $100,000,000,

to be transferred under section 9503(f)(9) to the Highway Account (as defined in section 9503(e)(5)(B)) in the Highway Trust Fund.

(D) LIABILITY OF THE UNITED STATES LIMITED TO AMOUNT IN TRUST FUND

(1) GENERAL RULE

Any claim filed against the Leaking Underground Storage Tank Trust Fund may be paid only out of such Trust Fund.

(2) COORDINATION WITH OTHER PROVISIONS

Nothing in the Comprehensive Environmental Response, Compensation, and Liability Act of 1980 or the Superfund Amendments and Reauthorization Act of 1986 (or in any amendment made by either of such Acts) shall authorize the payment by the United States Government of any amount with respect to any such claim out of any source other than the Leaking Underground Storage Tank Trust Fund.

(3) ORDER IN WHICH UNPAID CLAIMS ARE TO BE PAID

If at any time the Leaking Underground Storage Tank Trust Fund has insufficient funds to pay all of the claims out of such Trust Fund at such time, such claims shall, to the extent permitted under paragraph (1), be paid in full in the order in which they were finally determined.

(E) LIMITATION ON TRANSFERS TO LEAKING UNDERGROUND STORAGE TANK TRUST FUND

(1) IN GENERAL

Except as provided in paragraph (2), no amount may be appropriated to the Leaking Underground Storage Tank Trust Fund on and after the date of any expenditure from the Leaking Underground Storage Tank Trust Fund which is not permitted by this section. The determination of whether an expenditure is so permitted shall be made without regard to—

(A) any provision of law which is not contained or referenced in this title or in a revenue Act, and

(B) whether such provision of law is a subsequently enacted provision or directly or indirectly seeks to waive the application of this paragraph.

(2) EXCEPTION FOR PRIOR OBLIGATIONS

Paragraph (1) shall not apply to any expenditure to liquidate any contract entered into (or for any amount otherwise obligated) before October 1, 2026, in accordance with the provisions of this section.

(Added Pub. L. 99–499, title V, §522(a), Oct. 17, 1986, 100 Stat. 1780; amended Pub. L. 100–203, title X, §10502(d)(16), (17), Dec. 22, 1987, 101 Stat. 1330–445; Pub. L. 101–239, title VII, §7822(b)(7), Dec. 19, 1989, 103 Stat. 2425; Pub. L. 103–66, title XIII, §§13163(c), 13242(d)(42), Aug. 10, 1993, 107 Stat. 454, 528; Pub. L. 105–34, title X, §1032(e)(13), Aug. 5, 1997, 111 Stat. 935; Pub. L. 108–357, title VIII, §853(d)(2)(P), (Q), Oct. 22, 2004, 118 Stat. 1614; Pub. L. 109–58, title XIII, §1362(c), Aug. 8, 2005, 119 Stat. 1059; Pub. L. 109–59, title XI, §11147(a), Aug. 10, 2005, 119 Stat. 1967; Pub. L. 109–432, div. A, title II, §210(a), Dec. 20, 2006, 120 Stat. 2947; Pub. L. 109–433, §1(a), Dec. 20, 2006, 120 Stat. 3196; Pub. L. 112–30, title I, §141(c), Sept. 16, 2011, 125 Stat. 355; Pub. L. 112–102, title IV, §401(c), Mar. 30, 2012, 126 Stat. 281; Pub. L. 112–140, title IV, §401(c), June 29, 2012, 126 Stat. 402; Pub. L. 112–141, div. D, title I, §40101(c), title II, §40201(a), July 6, 2012, 126 Stat. 844, 846; Pub. L. 113–159, title II, §§2001(c), 2002(b), Aug. 8, 2014, 128 Stat. 1848; Pub. L. 114–21, title II, §2001(c), May 29, 2015, 129 Stat. 226; Pub. L. 114–41, title II, §2001(c), July 31, 2015, 129 Stat. 454; Pub. L. 114–73, title II, §2001(c), Oct. 29, 2015, 129 Stat. 583; Pub. L. 114–87, title II, §2001(c), Nov. 20, 2015, 129 Stat. 685; Pub. L. 114–94, div. C, title XXXI, §§31101(c), 31203, Dec. 4, 2015, 129 Stat. 1727, 1729; Pub. L. 115–141, div. U, title IV, §401(a)(342), Mar. 23, 2018, 132 Stat. 1200; Pub. L. 116–159, div. B, title II, §1203, Oct. 1, 2020, 134 Stat. 727; Pub. L. 117–44, title II, §201(c), Oct. 2, 2021, 135 Stat. 386; Pub. L. 117–52, §4(c), Oct. 31, 2021, 135 Stat. 410; Pub. L. 117–58, div. H, title I, §80101(c), Nov. 15, 2021, 135 Stat. 1327.)

* * * * * * *

Subchapter B—General Provisions

§9601. TRANSFER OF AMOUNTS

The amounts appropriated by any section of subchapter A to any Trust Fund established by such subchapter shall be transferred at least monthly from the general fund of the Treasury to such Trust Fund on the basis of estimates made by the Secretary of the Treasury of the amounts referred to in such section. Proper adjustments shall be made in the amounts subsequently transferred to the extent prior estimates were in excess of or less than the amounts required to be transferred.

(Added Pub. L. 97–119, title I, §103(a), Dec. 29, 1981, 95 Stat. 1638.)

§9602. MANAGEMENT OF TRUST FUNDS

(A) REPORT

It shall be the duty of the Secretary of the Treasury to hold each Trust Fund established by subchapter A, and (after consultation with any other trustees of the Trust Fund) to report to the Congress each year on the financial condition and the results of the operations of each such Trust Fund during the preceding fiscal year and on its expected condition and operations during the next 5 fiscal years. Such report shall be printed as a

House document of the session of the Congress to which the report is made.

(B) INVESTMENT

(1) IN GENERAL

It shall be the duty of the Secretary of the Treasury to invest such portion of any Trust Fund established by subchapter A as is not, in his judgment, required to meet current withdrawals. Such investments may be made only in interest-bearing obligations of the United States. For such purpose, such obligations may be acquired—
(A) on original issue at the issue price, or
(B) by purchase of outstanding obligations at the market price.

(2) SALE OF OBLIGATIONS

Any obligation acquired by a Trust Fund established by subchapter A may be sold by the Secretary of the Treasury at the market price.

(3) INTEREST ON CERTAIN PROCEEDS

The interest on, and the proceeds from the sale or redemption of, any obligations held in a Trust Fund established by subchapter A shall be credited to and form a part of the Trust Fund.

(Added Pub. L. 97–119, title I, §103(a), Dec. 29, 1981, 95 Stat. 1638.)

* * * * * * *

★

SELECTED PROVISIONS OF

TITLE 40 U.S.C. — PUBLIC BUILDINGS, PROPERTY, AND WORKS

TITLE 40—PUBLIC BUILDINGS, PROPERTY, AND WORKS

This title was enacted by Pub. L. 107–217, §1, Aug. 21, 2002, 116 Stat. 1062

* * * * * * *

SUBTITLE IV—APPALACHIAN REGIONAL DEVELOPMENT

* * * * * * *

CHAPTER 145—SPECIAL APPALACHIAN PROGRAMS

SUBCHAPTER I—PROGRAMS

SUBCHAPTER II—ADMINISTRATIVE

[1] *So in original. Probably should be followed by a period.*

SUBCHAPTER I—PROGRAMS

§14501. Appalachian development highway system

(a) PURPOSE.—To provide a highway system which, in conjunction with the Interstate System and other Federal-aid highways in the Appalachian region, will open up an area with a developmental potential where commerce and communication have been inhibited by lack of adequate access, the Secretary of Transportation may assist in the construction of an Appalachian development highway system and local access roads serving the Appalachian region. Construction on the development highway system shall not be more than three thousand and ninety miles. There shall not be more than 1,400 miles of local access roads that serve specific recreational, residential, educational, commercial, industrial, or similar facilities or facilitate a school consolidation program.

(b) COMMISSION DESIGNATIONS.—

(1) WHAT IS TO BE DESIGNATED.—The Appalachian Regional Commission shall transmit to the Secretary its designations of—

(A) the general corridor location and termini of the development highways;

(B) local access roads to be constructed;

(C) priorities for the construction of segments of the development highways; and

(D) other criteria for the program authorized by this section.

(2) STATE TRANSPORTATION DEPARTMENT RECOMMENDATION REQUIRED.—Before a state member participates in or votes on designations, the member must obtain the recommendations of the state transportation department of the State which the member represents.

(c) ADDITION TO FEDERAL-AID PRIMARY SYSTEM.—When completed, each development highway not already on the Federal-aid primary system shall be added to the system.

(d) USE OF SPECIFIC MATERIALS AND PRODUCTS.—

(1) INDIGENOUS MATERIALS AND PRODUCTS.—In the construction of highways and roads authorized under this section, a State may give special preference to the use of materials and products indigenous to the Appalachian region.

(2) COAL DERIVATIVES.—For research and development in the use of coal and coal products in highway construction and maintenance, the Secretary may require each participating State, to the maximum extent possible, to use coal derivatives in the construction of not more than 10 percent of the roads authorized under this subtitle.

(e) FEDERAL SHARE.—Federal assistance to any construction project under this section shall not be more than 80 percent of the cost of the project.

(f) CONSTRUCTION WITHOUT FEDERAL AMOUNTS.—

(1) PAYMENT OF FEDERAL SHARE.—When a participating State constructs a segment of a development highway without the aid of federal amounts and the construction is in accordance with all procedures and requirements applicable to the construction of segments of Appalachian development highways with those amounts, except for procedures and requirements that limit a State to the construction of projects for which federal amounts have previously been appropriated, the Secretary, on application by the State and with the approval of the Commission, may pay to the State the federal share, which shall not be more than 80 percent of the cost of the construction of the segment, from any amounts appropriated and allocated to the State

to carry out this section.

(2) No COMMITMENT OR OBLIGATION.—This subsection does not commit or obligate the Federal Government to provide amounts for segments of development highways constructed under this subsection.

(g) APPLICATION OF TITLE 23.—

(1) SECTIONS 106(a) AND 118.—Sections 106(a) and 118 of title 23 apply to the development highway system and the local access roads.

(2) CONSTRUCTION AND MAINTENANCE.—States are required to maintain each development highway and local access road as provided for Federal-aid highways in title 23. All other provisions of title 23 that are applicable to the construction and maintenance of Federal-aid primary and secondary highways and which the Secretary decides are not inconsistent with this subtitle shall apply to the system and roads, respectively.

(Pub. L. 107–217, Aug. 21, 2002, 116 Stat. 1265; Pub. L. 108–199, div. F, title I, §123(a), Jan. 23, 2004, 118 Stat. 296.)

§14502. DEMONSTRATION HEALTH PROJECTS

(a) PURPOSE.—To demonstrate the value of adequate health facilities and services to the economic development of the Appalachian region, the Secretary of Health and Human Services may make grants for the planning, construction, equipment, and operation of multi-county demonstration health, nutrition, and child care projects, including hospitals, regional health diagnostic and treatment centers, and other facilities and services necessary for the purposes of this section.

(b) PLANNING GRANTS.—

(1) AUTHORITY TO PROVIDE AMOUNTS AND MAKE GRANTS.—The Secretary may provide amounts to the Appalachian Regional Commission for the support of its Health Advisory Committee and may make grants for expenses of planning necessary for the development and operation of demonstration health projects for the region.

(2) LIMITATION ON AVAILABLE AMOUNTS.—The amount of a grant under this section for planning shall not be more than 75 percent of expenses.

(3) SOURCES OF ASSISTANCE.—The federal contribution may be provided entirely from amounts authorized under this section or in combination with amounts provided under other federal or federal grant programs.

(4) FEDERAL SHARE.—Notwithstanding any provision of law limiting the federal share in those other programs, amounts appropriated to carry out this section may be used to increase the federal share to the maximum percentage cost of a grant authorized by this subsection.

(c) CONSTRUCTION AND EQUIPMENT GRANTS.—

(1) ADDITIONAL USES FOR CONSTRUCTION GRANTS.—Grants under this section for construction may also be used for—

(A) the acquisition of privately owned facilities—

(i) not operated for profit; or

(ii) previously operated for profit if the Commission finds that health services would not otherwise be provided in the area served by the facility if the acquisition is not made; and

(B) initial equipment.

(2) STANDARDS FOR MAKING GRANTS.—Grants under this section for construction shall be made in accordance with section 14523 of this title and shall not be incompatible with the applicable provisions of title VI of the Public Health Service Act (42 U.S.C. 291 et seq.), the Developmental Disabilities Assistance and Bill of Rights Act of 2000 (42 U.S.C. 15001 et seq.), and other laws authorizing grants for the construction of health-related facilities, without regard to any provisions in those laws relating to appropriation authorization ceilings or to allotments among the States.

(3) LIMITATION ON AVAILABLE AMOUNTS.—A grant for the construction or equipment of any component of a demonstration health project shall not be more than 80 percent of the cost.

(4) SOURCES OF ASSISTANCE.—The federal contribution may be provided entirely from amounts authorized under this section or in combination with amounts provided under other federal grant programs for the construction or equipment of health-related facilities.

(5) FEDERAL SHARE.—Notwithstanding any provision of law limiting the federal share in those other programs, amounts authorized under this section may be used to increase federal grants for component facilities of a demonstration health project to a maximum of 80 percent of the cost of the facilities.

(d) OPERATION GRANTS.—

(1) STANDARDS FOR MAKING GRANTS.—A grant for the operation of a demonstration health project shall not be made—

(A) unless the facility is publicly owned, or owned by a public or private nonprofit organization, and is not operated for profit;

(B) after five years following the commencement of the initial grant for operation of the project, except that child development demonstrations assisted under this section during fiscal year 1979 may be approved under section 14322 of this title for continued support beyond that period, on request of the State, if the Commission finds that no federal, state, or local amounts are available to continue the project; and

(C) unless the Secretary of Health and Human Services is satisfied that the operation of the project will be conducted under efficient management practices designed to obviate operating deficits.

(2) LIMITATION ON AVAILABLE AMOUNTS.—Grants under this section for the operation (including initial operating amounts and operating deficits, which include the cost of attracting, training, and retaining qualified personnel) of a demonstration health project, whether or not constructed with amounts authorized to be appropriated by this section, may be made for up to—

(A) 50 percent of the cost of that operation;

(B) in the case of a project to be carried out in a county for which a distressed county designation is in effect under section 14526, 80 percent of the cost of that operation; or

(C) in the case of a project to be carried out for a county for which an at-risk county designation is in effect under section 14526, 70 percent of the cost of that operation.

(3) SOURCES OF ASSISTANCE.—The federal contribution may be provided entirely from amounts appropriated to carry out this section or in combination with amounts provided under other federal grant programs for the operation of health related facilities and the provision of health and child development services, including parts A and B of title IV and title XX of the Social Security Act (42 U.S.C. 601 et seq., 620 et seq., 1397 et seq.).

(4) FEDERAL SHARE.—Notwithstanding any provision of law limiting the federal share in those other programs, amounts appropriated to carry out this section may be used to increase federal grants for operating components of a demonstration health project to the maximum percentage cost of a grant authorized by this subsection.

(5) STATE DEEMED TO MEET REQUIREMENT OF PROVIDING ASSISTANCE OR SERVICES ON STATEWIDE BASIS.—Notwithstanding any provision of the Social Security Act (42 U.S.C. 301 et seq.) requiring assistance or services on a statewide basis, a State providing assistance or services under a federal grant program described in paragraph (2) in any area of the region approved by the Commission is deemed to be meeting that requirement.

(e) GRANT SOURCES AND USE OF GRANTS IN COMPUTING ALLOTMENTS.—Grants under this section—

(1) shall be made only out of amounts specifically appropriated for the purpose of carrying out this subtitle; and

(2) shall not be taken into account in computing allotments among the States under any other law.

(f) MAXIMUM COMMISSION CONTRIBUTION.—

(1) IN GENERAL.—Subject to paragraphs (2) and (3), the Commission may contribute not more than 50 percent of any project cost eligible for financial assistance under this section from amounts appropriated to carry out this subtitle.

(2) DISTRESSED COUNTIES.—The maximum Commission contribution for a project to be carried out in a county for which a distressed county designation is in effect under section 14526 of this title may be increased to the lesser of—

(A) 80 percent; or

(B) the maximum federal contribution percentage authorized by this section.

(3) AT-RISK COUNTIES.—The maximum Commission contribution for a project to be carried out in a county for which an at-risk county designation is in effect under section 14526 may be increased to the lesser of—

(A) 70 percent; or

(B) the maximum Federal contribution percentage authorized by this section.

(g) EMPHASIS ON OCCUPATIONAL DISEASES FROM COAL MINING.—To provide for the further development of the Appalachian region's human resources, grants under this section shall give special emphasis to programs and research for the early detection, diagnosis, and treatment of occupational diseases arising from coal mining, such as black lung.

(Pub. L. 107–217, Aug. 21, 2002, 116 Stat. 1266; Pub. L. 110–371, §2(b), Oct. 8, 2008, 122 Stat. 4038.)

§14503. ASSISTANCE FOR PROPOSED LOW- AND MIDDLE-INCOME HOUSING PROJECTS

(a) APPALACHIAN HOUSING FUND.—

(1) ESTABLISHMENT.—There is an Appalachian Housing Fund.

(2) SOURCE AND USE OF AMOUNTS IN FUND.—Amounts allocated to the Secretary of Housing and Urban Development for the purposes of this section shall be deposited in the Fund. The Secretary shall use the Fund as a revolving fund to carry out those purposes. Amounts in the Fund not needed for current operation may be invested in bonds or other obligations the Federal Government guarantees as to principal and interest. General expenses of administration of this section may be charged to the Fund.

(b) PURPOSE.—To encourage and facilitate the construction or rehabilitation of housing to meet the needs of low- and moderate-income families and individuals, the Secretary may make grants and loans from the Fund, under terms and conditions the Secretary may prescribe. The grants and loans may be made to nonprofit, limited dividend, or cooperative organizations and public bodies and are for planning and obtaining federally insured mortgage financing or other financial assistance for housing construction or rehabilitation projects for low- and moderate-income families and individuals, in any area of the Appalachian region the Appalachian Regional Commission establishes, under—

(1) section 221 of the National Housing Act (12 U.S.C. 1715l);

(2) section 8 of the United States Housing Act of 1937 (42 U.S.C. 1437f);

(3) section 515 of the Housing Act of 1949 (42 U.S.C. 1485); or

(4) any other law of similar purpose administered by the Secretary or any other department, agency, or instrumentality of the Federal Government or a state government.

(c) PROVIDING AMOUNTS TO STATES FOR GRANTS AND LOANS.—The Secretary or the Commission may provide amounts to the States for making grants and loans to nonprofit, limited dividend, or cooperative organizations and public bodies for the purposes for which the Secretary may provide amounts under this section.

(d) LOANS.—

(1) LIMITATION ON AVAILABLE AMOUNTS.—A loan under subsection (b) for the cost of planning and obtaining financing (including the cost of preliminary surveys and analyses of market needs, preliminary site engineering and architectural fees, site options, application and mortgage commitment fees, legal fees, and construction loan fees and discounts) of a project described in that subsection may be made for up to—

(A) 50 percent of that cost;

(B) in the case of a project to be carried out in a county for which a distressed county designation is in effect under section 14526, 80 percent of that cost; or

(C) in the case of a project to be carried out for a county for which an at-risk county designation is in effect under section 14526, 70 percent of that cost.

(2) INTEREST.—A loan shall be made without interest, except that a loan made to an organization established for profit shall bear interest at the prevailing market rate authorized for an insured or guaranteed loan for that type of project.

(3) PAYMENT.—The Secretary shall require payment of a loan made under this section, under terms and conditions the Secretary may require, no later than on completion of the project. Except for a loan to an organization established for profit, the Secretary may cancel any part of a loan made under this section on determining

that a permanent loan to finance the project cannot be obtained in an amount adequate for repayment of a loan made under this section.

(e) GRANTS.—

(1) IN GENERAL.—A grant under this section for expenses incidental to planning and obtaining financing for a project under this section that the Secretary considers to be unrecoverable from the proceeds of a permanent loan made to finance the project shall—

(A) not be made to an organization established for profit; and

(B) except as provided in paragraph (2), not exceed—

(i) 50 percent of those expenses;

(ii) in the case of a project to be carried out in a county for which a distressed county designation is in effect under section 14526, 80 percent of those expenses; or

(iii) in the case of a project to be carried out in a county for which an at-risk county designation is in effect under section 14526, 70 percent of those expenses.

(2) SITE DEVELOPMENT COSTS AND OFFSITE IMPROVEMENTS.—The Secretary may make grants and commitments for grants, and may advance amounts under terms and conditions the Secretary may require, to nonprofit, limited dividend, or cooperative organizations and public bodies for reasonable site development costs and necessary offsite improvements, such as sewer and water line extensions, when the grant, commitment, or advance is essential to the economic feasibility of a housing construction or rehabilitation project for low- and moderate-income families and individuals which otherwise meets the requirements for assistance under this section. A grant under this paragraph for—

(A) the construction of housing shall not be more than 10 percent of the cost of the project; and

(B) the rehabilitation of housing shall not be more than 10 percent of the reasonable value of the rehabilitation housing, as determined by the Secretary.

(f) INFORMATION, ADVICE, AND TECHNICAL ASSISTANCE.—The Secretary or the Commission may provide, or contract with public or private organizations to provide, information, advice, and technical assistance with respect to the construction, rehabilitation, and operation by nonprofit organizations of housing for low- or moderate- income families in areas of the region the Commission establishes.

(g) APPLICATION OF CERTAIN PROVISIONS.—Programs and projects assisted under this section are subject to the provisions cited in section 14701 of this title to the extent provided in the laws authorizing assistance for low- and moderate-income housing.

(Pub. L. 107–217, Aug. 21, 2002, 116 Stat. 1268; Pub. L. 110–371, §2(c), Oct. 8, 2008, 122 Stat. 4038.)

§14504. TELECOMMUNICATIONS AND TECHNOLOGY INITIATIVE

(a) PROJECTS TO BE ASSISTED.—The Appalachian Regional Commission may provide technical assistance, make grants, enter into contracts, or otherwise provide amounts to persons or entities in the region for projects—

(1) to increase affordable access to advanced telecommunications, entrepreneurship, and management technologies or applications in the region;

(2) to provide education and training in the use of telecommunications and technology;

(3) to develop programs to increase the readiness of industry groups and businesses in the region to engage in electronic commerce; or

(4) to support entrepreneurial opportunities for businesses in the information technology sector.

(b) LIMITATION ON AVAILABLE AMOUNTS.—Of the cost of any activity eligible for a grant under this section, not more than—

(1) 50 percent may be provided from amounts appropriated to carry out this section;

(2) in the case of a project to be carried out in a county for which a distressed county designation is in effect under section 14526, 80 percent may be provided from amounts appropriated to carry out this section; or

(3) in the case of a project to be carried out in a county for which an at-risk county designation is in effect under section 14526, 70 percent may be provided from amounts appropriated to carry out this section.

(c) SOURCES OF ASSISTANCE.—Assistance under this section may be provided entirely from amounts made available to carry out this section, in combination with amounts made available under other federal programs, or from any other source.

(d) FEDERAL SHARE.—Notwithstanding any provision of law limiting the federal share under any other federal program, amounts made available to carry out this section may be used to increase that federal share, as the Commission decides is appropriate.

(Pub. L. 107–217, Aug. 21, 2002, 116 Stat. 1270; Pub. L. 110–371, §2(d), Oct. 8, 2008, 122 Stat. 4039.)

§14505. ENTREPRENEURSHIP INITIATIVE

(a) BUSINESS INCUBATOR SERVICE.—In this section, the term "business incubator service" means a professional or technical service necessary for the initiation and initial sustainment of the operations of a newly established business, including a service such as—

(1) a legal service, including aid in preparing a corporate charter, partnership agreement, or basic contract;

(2) a service in support of the protection of intellectual property through a patent, a trademark, or any other means;

(3) a service in support of the acquisition and use of advanced technology, including the use of Internet services and Web-based services; and

(4) consultation on strategic planning, marketing, or advertising.

(b) PROJECTS TO BE ASSISTED.—The Appalachian Regional Commission may provide technical assistance, make grants, enter into contracts, or otherwise provide amounts to persons or entities in the region for projects—

(1) to support the advancement of, and provide, entrepreneurial training and education for youths, students, and businesspersons;

(2) to improve access to debt and equity capital by such means as facilitating the establishment of development venture capital funds;

(3) to aid communities in identifying, developing, and implementing development strategies for various sectors of the economy;

(4) to develop a working network of business incubators; and

(5) to support entities that provide business incubator services.

(c) LIMITATION ON AVAILABLE AMOUNTS.—Of the cost of any activity eligible for a grant under this section, not more than—

(1) 50 percent may be provided from amounts appropriated to carry out this section;

(2) in the case of a project to be carried out in a county for which a distressed county designation is in effect under section 14526, 80 percent may be provided from amounts appropriated to carry out this section; or

(3) in the case of a project to be carried out in a county for which an at-risk county designation is in effect under section 14526, 70 percent may be provided from amounts appropriated to carry out this section.

(d) SOURCES OF ASSISTANCE.—Assistance under this section may be provided entirely from amounts made available to carry out this section, in combination with amounts made available under other federal programs, or from any other source.

(e) FEDERAL SHARE.—Notwithstanding any provision of law limiting the federal share under any other federal program, amounts made available to carry out this section may be used to increase that federal share, as the Commission decides is appropriate.

(Pub. L. 107–217, Aug. 21, 2002, 116 Stat. 1271; Pub. L. 110–371, §2(e), Oct. 8, 2008, 122 Stat. 4039.)

§14506. REGIONAL SKILLS PARTNERSHIPS

(a) ELIGIBLE ENTITY.—In this section, the term "eligible entity" means a consortium that—

(1) is established to serve one or more industries in a specified geographic area; and

(2) consists of representatives of—

(A) businesses (or a nonprofit organization that represents businesses);

(B) labor organizations;

(C) State and local governments; or

(D) educational institutions.

(b) PROJECTS TO BE ASSISTED.—The Appalachian Regional Commission may provide technical assistance, make grants, enter into contracts, or otherwise provide amounts to eligible entities in the region for projects to improve the job skills of workers for a specified industry, including projects for—

(1) the assessment of training and job skill needs for the industry;

(2) the development of curricula and training methods, including, in appropriate cases, electronic learning or technology-based training;

(3) the identification of training providers;

(4) the development of partnerships between the industry and educational institutions, including community colleges;

(5) the development of apprenticeship programs;

(6) the development of training programs for workers, including dislocated workers; and

(7) the development of training plans for businesses.

(c) ADMINISTRATIVE COSTS.—An eligible entity may use not more than 10 percent of amounts made available to the eligible entity under subsection (b) to pay administrative costs associated with the projects described in subsection (b).

(d) LIMITATION ON AVAILABLE AMOUNTS.—Of the cost of any activity eligible for a grant under this section, not more than—

(1) 50 percent may be provided from amounts appropriated to carry out this section;

(2) in the case of a project to be carried out in a county for which a distressed county designation is in effect under section 14526, 80 percent may be provided from amounts appropriated to carry out this section; or

(3) in the case of a project to be carried out in a county for which an at-risk county designation is in effect under section 14526, 70 percent may be provided from amounts appropriated to carry out this section.

(e) SOURCES OF ASSISTANCE.—Assistance under this section may be provided entirely from amounts made available to carry out this section, in combination with amounts made available under other federal programs, or from any other source.

(f) FEDERAL SHARE.—Notwithstanding any provision of law limiting the federal share under any other federal program, amounts made available to carry out this section may be used to increase that Federal share, as the Commission decides is appropriate.

(Pub. L. 107–217, Aug. 21, 2002, 116 Stat. 1271; Pub. L. 110–371, §2(f), Oct. 8, 2008, 122 Stat. 4039.)

§14507. SUPPLEMENTS TO FEDERAL GRANT PROGRAMS

(a) DEFINITION.—

(1) FEDERAL GRANT PROGRAMS.—In this section, the term "federal grant programs"—

(A) means any federal grant program that provides assistance for the acquisition or development of land, the construction or equipment of facilities, or other community or economic development or economic adjustment activities, including a federal grant program authorized by—

(i) the Consolidated Farm and Rural Development Act (7 U.S.C. 1921 et seq.);

(ii) chapter 2003 of title 54;

(iii) the Watershed Protection and Flood Prevention Act (16 U.S.C. 1001 et seq.);

(iv) the Carl D. Perkins Career and Technical Education Act of 2006 (20 U.S.C. 2301 et seq.);

(v) the Federal Water Pollution Control Act (33 U.S.C. 1251 et seq.) (known as the Clean Water Act);

(vi) title VI of the Public Health Services Act (42 U.S.C. 291 et seq.);

(vii) sections 201 and 209 of the Public Works and Economic Development Act of 1965 (42 U.S.C. 3141, 3149);

(viii) title I of the Housing and Community Development Act of 1974 (42 U.S.C. 5301 et seq.); and

(ix) part IV of title III of the Communications Act of 1934 (47 U.S.C. 390 et seq.); but

(B) does not include—

(i) the program for the construction of the development highway system authorized by section 14501 of this title or any other program relating to highway or road construction authorized by title 23; or

(ii) any other program to the extent that financial assistance other than a grant is authorized.

(2) CERTAIN SEWAGE TREATMENT WORKS DEEMED CONSTRUCTED WITH FEDERAL GRANT ASSISTANCE.—For the purpose of this section, any sewage treatment works constructed pursuant to title II of the Federal Water Pollution Control Act (33 U.S.C. 1281 et seq.) (known as the Clean Water Act) without federal grant assistance under that title is deemed to be constructed with that assistance.

(b) PURPOSE.—To enable the people, States, and local communities of the Appalachian region, including local development districts, to take maximum advantage of federal grant programs for which they are eligible but for which, because of their economic situation, they cannot supply the required matching share, or for which there are insufficient amounts available under the federal law authorizing the programs to meet pressing needs of the region, the Federal Cochairman may use amounts made available to carry out this section—

(1) for any part of the basic federal contribution to projects or activities under the federal grant programs authorized by federal laws; and

(2) to increase the federal contribution to projects and activities under the programs above the fixed maximum part of the cost of the projects or activities otherwise authorized by the applicable law.

(c) CERTIFICATION REQUIRED.—For a program, project, or activity for which any part of the basic federal contribution to the project or activity under a federal grant program is proposed to be made under subsection (b), the contribution shall not be made until the responsible federal official administering the federal law authorizing the contribution certifies that the program, project, or activity meets the applicable requirements of the federal law and could be approved for federal contribution under that law if amounts were available under the law for the program, project, or activity.

(d) LIMITATIONS IN OTHER LAWS INAPPLICABLE.—Amounts provided pursuant to this subtitle are available without regard to any limitations on areas eligible for assistance or authorizations for appropriation in any other law.

(e) ACCEPTANCE OF CERTAIN MATERIAL.—For a supplemental grant for a project or activity under a federal grant program, the Federal Cochairman shall accept any finding, report, certification, or documentation required to be submitted to the head of the department, agency, or instrumentality of the Federal Government responsible for the administration of the program.

(f) FEDERAL SHARE.—The federal portion of the cost of a project or activity shall not—

(1) be increased to more than the percentages the Commission establishes; nor

(2) be more than 80 percent of the cost.

(g) MAXIMUM COMMISSION CONTRIBUTION.—

(1) IN GENERAL.—Subject to paragraphs (2) and (3), the Commission may contribute not more than 50 percent of a project or activity cost eligible for financial assistance under this section from amounts appropriated to carry out this subtitle.

(2) DISTRESSED COUNTIES.—The maximum Commission contribution for a project

or activity to be carried out in a county for which a distressed county designation is in effect under section 14526 of this title may be increased to 80 percent.

(3) At-risk counties.—The maximum Commission contribution for a project to be carried out in a county for which an at-risk county designation is in effect under section 14526 may be increased to 70 percent.

(Pub. L. 107–217, Aug. 21, 2002, 116 Stat. 1272; Pub. L. 109–270, §2(j), Aug. 12, 2006, 120 Stat. 748; Pub. L. 110–371, §2(g), Oct. 8, 2008, 122 Stat. 4040; Pub. L. 113–287, §5(j)(7), Dec. 19, 2014, 128 Stat. 3269.)

§14508. Economic and energy development initiative

(a) Projects To Be Assisted.—The Appalachian Regional Commission may provide technical assistance, make grants, enter into contracts, or otherwise provide amounts to persons or entities in the Appalachian region for projects and activities—

(1) to promote energy efficiency in the Appalachian region to enhance the economic competitiveness of the Appalachian region;

(2) to increase the use of renewable energy resources, particularly biomass, in the Appalachian region to produce alternative transportation fuels, electricity, and heat; and

(3) to support the development of regional, conventional energy resources to produce electricity and heat through advanced technologies that achieve a substantial reduction in emissions, including greenhouse gases, over the current baseline.

(b) Limitation on Available Amounts.—Of the cost of any activity eligible for a grant under this section, not more than—

(1) 50 percent may be provided from amounts appropriated to carry out this section;

(2) in the case of a project to be carried out in a county for which a distressed county designation is in effect under section 14526, 80 percent may be provided from amounts appropriated to carry out this section; or

(3) in the case of a project to be carried out in a county for which an at-risk county designation is in effect under section 14526, 70 percent may be provided from amounts appropriated to carry out this section.

(c) Sources of Assistance.—Subject to subsection (b), grants provided under this section may be provided from amounts made available to carry out this section in combination with amounts made available under other Federal programs or from any other source.

(d) Federal Share.—Notwithstanding any provision of law limiting the Federal share under any other Federal program, amounts made available to carry out this section may be used to increase that Federal share, as the Commission decides is appropriate.

(Added Pub. L. 110–371, §3(a), Oct. 8, 2008, 122 Stat. 4040.)

§14509. High-speed broadband deployment initiative

(a) In General.—The Appalachian Regional Commission may provide technical assistance, make grants, enter into contracts, or otherwise provide amounts to individuals or entities in the Appalachian region for projects and activities to increase affordable access to broadband networks throughout the Appalachian region.

(b) Eligible Projects and Activities.—A project or activity eligible to be carried out under this section is a project or activity—

(1) to conduct research, analysis, and training to increase broadband adoption efforts in the Appalachian region; or

(2) for the construction and deployment of broadband service-related infrastructure in the Appalachian region.

(c) LIMITATION ON AVAILABLE AMOUNTS.—Of the cost of any activity eligible for a grant under this section—

(1) not more than 50 percent may be provided from amounts appropriated to carry out this section; and

(2) notwithstanding paragraph (1)—

(A) in the case of a project to be carried out in a county for which a distressed county designation is in effect under section 14526, not more than 80 percent may be provided from amounts appropriated to carry out this section; and

(B) in the case of a project to be carried out in a county for which an at-risk designation is in effect under section 14526, not more than 70 percent may be provided from amounts appropriated to carry out this section.

(d) SOURCES OF ASSISTANCE.—Subject to subsection (c), a grant provided under this section may be provided from amounts made available to carry out this section in combination with amounts made available—

(1) under any other Federal program; or

(2) from any other source.

(e) FEDERAL SHARE.—Notwithstanding any provision of law limiting the Federal share under any other Federal program, amounts made available to carry out this section may be used to increase that Federal share, as the Appalachian Regional Commission determines to be appropriate.

(f) REQUEST FOR DATA.—Before making a grant for a project or activity described in subsection (b)(2), the Appalachian Regional Commission shall request from the Federal Communications Commission, the National Telecommunications and Information Administration, the Economic Development Administration, and the Department of Agriculture data on—

(1) the level and extent of broadband service that exists in the area proposed to be served by the broadband service-related infrastructure; and

(2) the level and extent of broadband service that will be deployed in the area proposed to be served by the broadband service-related infrastructure pursuant to another Federal program.

(g) REQUIREMENT.—For each fiscal year, not less than 65 percent of the amounts made available to carry out this section shall be used for grants for projects and activities described in subsection (b)(2).

(Added Pub. L. 114–94, div. A, title I, §1436(a)(1), Dec. 4, 2015, 129 Stat. 1430; amended Pub. L. 117–58, div. A, title I, §11506(d), Nov. 15, 2021, 135 Stat. 584.)

§14510. DRUG ABUSE MITIGATION INITIATIVE

(a) IN GENERAL.—The Appalachian Regional Commission may provide technical assistance to, make grants to, enter into contracts with, or otherwise provide amounts to individuals or entities in the Appalachian region for projects and activities to address drug abuse, including opioid abuse, in the region, including projects and activities—

(1) to facilitate the sharing of best practices among States, counties, and other experts in the region with respect to reducing such abuse;

(2) to initiate or expand programs designed to eliminate or reduce the harm to the workforce and economic growth of the region that results from such abuse;

(3) to attract and retain relevant health care services, businesses, and workers; and

(4) to develop relevant infrastructure, including broadband infrastructure that supports the use of telemedicine.

(b) LIMITATION ON AVAILABLE AMOUNTS.—Of the cost of any activity eligible for a grant under this section—

(1) not more than 50 percent may be provided from amounts appropriated to carry out this section; and

(2) notwithstanding paragraph (1)—

(A) in the case of a project to be carried out in a county for which a distressed county designation is in effect under section 14526, not more than 80 percent may be provided from amounts appropriated to carry out this section; and

(B) in the case of a project to be carried out in a county for which an at-risk designation is in effect under section 14526, not more than 70 percent may be provided from amounts appropriated to carry out this section.

(c) SOURCES OF ASSISTANCE.—Subject to subsection (b), a grant provided under this section may be provided from amounts made available to carry out this section in combination with amounts made available—

(1) under any other Federal program (subject to the availability of subsequent appropriations); or

(2) from any other source.

(d) FEDERAL SHARE.—Notwithstanding any provision of law limiting the Federal share under any other Federal program, amounts made available to carry out this section may be used to increase that Federal share, as the Appalachian Regional Commission determines to be appropriate.

(Added Pub. L. 115–271, title VIII, §8062(a), Oct. 24, 2018, 132 Stat. 4094.)

§14511. APPALACHIAN REGIONAL ENERGY HUB INITIATIVE

(a) IN GENERAL.—The Appalachian Regional Commission may provide technical assistance to, make grants to, enter into contracts with, or otherwise provide amounts to individuals or entities in the Appalachian region for projects and activities—

(1) to conduct research and analysis regarding the economic impact of an ethane storage hub in the Appalachian region that supports a more-effective energy market performance due to the scale of the project, such as a project with the capacity to store and distribute more than 100,000 barrels per day of hydrocarbon feedstock with a minimum gross heating value of 1,700 Btu per standard cubic foot;

(2) with the potential to significantly contribute to the economic resilience of the area in which the project is located; and

(3) that will help establish a regional energy hub in the Appalachian region for natural gas and natural gas liquids, including hydrogen produced from the steam methane reforming of natural gas feedstocks.

(b) LIMITATION ON AVAILABLE AMOUNTS.—Of the cost of any project or activity eligible for a grant under this section—

(1) except as provided in paragraphs (2) and (3), not more than 50 percent may be provided from amounts made available to carry out this section;

(2) in the case of a project or activity to be carried out in a county for which a distressed county designation is in effect under section 14526, not more than 80 percent may be provided from amounts made available to carry out this section; and

(3) in the case of a project or activity to be carried out in a county for which an at-risk county designation is in effect under section 14526, not more than 70 percent may be provided from amounts made available to carry out this section.

(c) SOURCES OF ASSISTANCE.—Subject to subsection (b), a grant provided under this section may be provided from amounts made available to carry out this section, in combination with amounts made available—

(1) under any other Federal program; or

(2) from any other source.

(d) FEDERAL SHARE.—Notwithstanding any provision of law limiting the Federal share under any other Federal program, amounts made available to carry out this section may be used to increase that Federal share, as the Appalachian Regional Commission determines to be appropriate.

(Added Pub. L. 117–58, div. A, title I, §11506(e)(1), Nov. 15, 2021, 135 Stat. 585.)

SUBCHAPTER II—ADMINISTRATIVE

§14521. REQUIRED LEVEL OF EXPENDITURE

A State or political subdivision of a State is not eligible to receive benefits under this subtitle unless the aggregate expenditure of state amounts, except expenditures for participation in the Dwight D. Eisenhower System of Interstate and Defense Highways and local and federal amounts, for the benefit of the area within the State located in the Appalachian region is maintained at a level which does not fall below the average level of those expenditures for the State's last two full fiscal years prior to March 9, 1965. In computing the level, a State's past expenditure for participation in the Dwight D. Eisenhower System of Interstate and Defense Highways and expenditures of local and federal amounts shall not be included. The Commission shall recommend to the President a lesser requirement when it finds that a substantial population decrease in that part of a State which lies within the region would not justify a state expenditure equal to the average level of the last two years or when it finds that a State's average level of expenditure in an individual program has been disproportionate to the present need for that part of the State.

(Pub. L. 107–217, Aug. 21, 2002, 116 Stat. 1274.)

§14522. CONSENT OF STATES

This subtitle does not require a State to engage in or accept a program under this subtitle without its consent.

(Pub. L. 107–217, Aug. 21, 2002, 116 Stat. 1274.)

§14523. PROGRAM IMPLEMENTATION

(a) REQUIREMENTS.—A program or project authorized under this chapter shall not be implemented until—

(1) the responsible federal official has decided that applications and plans relating to the program or project are not incompatible with the provisions and objectives of federal laws that the official administers that are not inconsistent with this subtitle; and

(2) the Appalachian Regional Commission has approved the program or project and has determined that it—

(A) meets the applicable criteria under section 14524 of this title and the requirements of the development planning process under section 14525 of this title; and

(B) will contribute to the development of the Appalachian region.

(b) DECISION IS CONTROLLING.—A decision under subsection (a)(2) is controlling and shall be accepted by the federal agencies.

(Pub. L. 107–217, Aug. 21, 2002, 116 Stat. 1274.)

§14524. PROGRAM DEVELOPMENT CRITERIA

(a) FACTORS TO BE CONSIDERED.—In considering programs and projects to be given assistance under this subtitle, and in establishing a priority ranking of the requests for assistance presented to the Appalachian Regional Commission, the Commission shall follow procedures that will ensure consideration of—

(1) the relationship of the project or class of projects to overall regional development, including its location in a severely and persistently distressed county or area;

(2) the population and area to be served by the project or class of projects, including the per capita market income and the unemployment rates in the area;

(3) the relative financial resources available to the State or political subdivisions or instrumentalities of the State that seek to undertake the project;

(4) the importance of the project or class of projects in relation to other projects or classes of projects that may be in competition for the same amounts;

(5) the prospects that the project for which assistance is sought will improve, on a continuing rather than a temporary basis, the opportunities for employment, the average level of income, or the economic and social development of the area served by the project; and

(6) the extent to which the project design provides for detailed outcome measurements by which grant expenditures may be evaluated.

(b) LIMITATION ON USE.—Financial assistance made available under this subtitle shall not be used to assist establishments relocating from one area to another.

(c) DETERMINATION REQUIRED BEFORE AMOUNTS MAY BE PROVIDED.—Amounts may be provided for programs and projects in a State under this subtitle only if the Commission determines that the level of federal and state financial assistance under other laws for the same type of programs or projects in that part of the State within the Appalachian region will not be diminished in order to substitute amounts authorized by this subtitle.

(d) MINIMUM AMOUNT OF ASSISTANCE TO DISTRESSED COUNTIES AND AREAS.—For each fiscal year, not less than 50 percent of the amount of grant expenditures the

Commission approves shall support activities or projects that benefit severely and persistently distressed counties and areas.

(Pub. L. 107–217, Aug. 21, 2002, 116 Stat. 1275.)

§14525. STATE DEVELOPMENT PLANNING PROCESS

(a) STATE DEVELOPMENT PLAN.—Pursuant to policies the Appalachian Regional Commission establishes, each state member shall submit a development plan for the area of the State within the Appalachian region. The plan shall—

(1) be submitted according to a schedule the Commission prescribes;

(2) reflect the goals, objectives, and priorities identified in the regional development plan and in any subregional development plan that may be approved for the subregion of which the State is a part;

(3) describe the state organization and continuous process for Appalachian development planning, including—

(A) the procedures established by the State for the participation of local development districts in the process;

(B) how the process is related to overall statewide planning and budgeting processes; and

(C) the method of coordinating planning and projects in the region under this subtitle, the Public Works and Economic Development Act of 1965 (42 U.S.C. 3121 et seq.), and other federal, state, and local programs;

(4) set forth the goals, objectives, and priorities of the State for the region, as established by the Governor, and identify the needs on which the goals, objectives, and priorities are based; and

(5) describe the development strategies for achieving the goals, objectives, and priorities, including funding sources, and recommendations for specific projects to receive assistance under this subtitle.

(b) AREAWIDE ACTION PROGRAMS.—The Commission shall encourage the preparation and execution of areawide action programs that specify interrelated projects and schedules of actions, the necessary agency funding, and other commitments to implement the programs. The programs shall make appropriate use of existing plans affecting the area.

(c) LOCAL DEVELOPMENT DISTRICTS.—Local development districts certified by the State as described in section 14102(a)(2) of this title provide the linkage between state and substate planning and development. The districts shall assist the States in the coordination of areawide programs and projects and may prepare and adopt areawide plans or action programs. In carrying out the development planning process, including the selection of programs and projects for assistance, States shall consult with local development districts, local units of government, and citizen groups and shall consider the goals, objectives, priorities, and recommendations of those bodies.

(d) FEDERAL RESPONSIBILITIES.—To the maximum extent practicable, federal departments, agencies, and instrumentalities undertaking or providing financial assistance for programs or projects in the region shall—

(1) take into account the policies, goals, and objectives the Commission and its member States establish pursuant to this subtitle;

(2) recognize Appalachian state development strategies approved by the Commission as satisfying requirements for overall economic development planning under the programs or projects; and

(3) accept the boundaries and organization of any local development district certified under this subtitle that the Governor may designate as the areawide agency required under any of those programs undertaken or assisted by those federal departments, agencies, and instrumentalities.

(Pub. L. 107–217, Aug. 21, 2002, 116 Stat. 1275.)

§14526. DISTRESSED, AT-RISK, AND ECONOMICALLY STRONG COUNTIES

(a) DESIGNATIONS.—

(1) IN GENERAL.—The Appalachian Regional Commission, in accordance with criteria the Commission may establish, each year shall—

(A) designate as "distressed counties" those counties in the Appalachian region that are the most severely and persistently distressed;

(B) designate as "at-risk counties" those counties in the Appalachian region that are most at risk of becoming economically distressed; and

(C) designate two categories of economically strong counties, consisting of—

(i) "competitive counties", which shall be those counties in the region that are approaching economic parity with the rest of the United States; and

(ii) "attainment counties", which shall be those counties in the region that have attained or exceeded economic parity with the rest of the United States.

(2) ANNUAL REVIEW OF DESIGNATIONS.—The Commission shall—

(A) conduct an annual review of each designation of a county under paragraph (1) to determine if the county still meets the criteria for the designation; and

(B) renew the designation for another one-year period only if the county still meets the criteria.

(b) DISTRESSED COUNTIES.—In program and project development and implementation and in the allocation of appropriations made available to carry out this subtitle, the Commission shall give special consideration to the needs of counties for which a distressed county designation is in effect under this section.

(c) ECONOMICALLY STRONG COUNTIES.—

(1) COMPETITIVE COUNTIES.—Except as provided in paragraphs (3) and (4), assistance under this subtitle for a project that is carried out in a county for which a competitive county designation is in effect under this section shall not be more than 30 percent of the project cost.

(2) ATTAINMENT COUNTIES.—Except as provided in paragraphs (3) and (4), amounts may not be provided under this subtitle for a project that is carried out in a county for which an attainment county designation is in effect under this section.

(3) EXCEPTIONS.—Paragraphs (1) and (2) do not apply to—

(A) a project on the Appalachian development highway system authorized by section 14501 of this title;

(B) a local development district administrative project assisted under section 14321(a)(1)(A) of this title; or

(C) a multicounty project that is carried out in at least two counties designated under this section if—

(i) at least one of the participating counties is designated as a distressed county under this section; and

(ii) the project will be of substantial direct benefit to at least one distressed county.

(4) WAIVER.—

(A) IN GENERAL.—The Commission may waive the requirements of paragraphs (1) and (2) for a project when the recipient of assistance for the project shows the existence of any of the following:

(i) a significant pocket of distress in the part of the county in which the project is carried out.

(ii) a significant potential benefit from the project in at least one area of the region outside the designated county.

(B) REPORTS TO CONGRESS.—The Commission shall submit to the Committee on Environment and Public Works of the Senate and the Committee on Transportation and Infrastructure of the House of Representatives an annual report describing each waiver granted under subparagraph (A) during the period covered by the report.

(Pub. L. 107–217, Aug. 21, 2002, 116 Stat. 1277; Pub. L. 110–371, §4(a), Oct. 8, 2008, 122 Stat. 4041.)

★

www.ingramcontent.com/pod-product-compliance
Lightning Source LLC
Chambersburg PA
CBHW061543120626
46550CB00004B/1348